ΠΕΤΡΟΥϹΙΠΙϹΤΟΝΗΛ
ΠΕΤΡΟϹΑΠΟϹΤΟΛΟϹΙΥ ΧΡΥϹΕΛ
ΚΤΟΙϹΠΑΡΕΠΕΙΔΙΑΜΟΥ ΔΙΑϹΤ
ΡΑϹΠΟΝΤΟΥΓΑΛΑ ϹΙΑϹΚΑΠΠΑΔΟ
ΚΙΑϹΑϹΕΙΑϹΤΑΙΒΙΘΥΝΙΑϹ ΔΕ ΚΑΤΑ
ΓΝΩϹΙΝΘΥ ΠΟ ΕΝΑΓΙΑ
ϹΜΩΤΗϹ ΕΙϹΥΠΑΚΟΗΝ ΚΑΙΡΑΝ
ΤΙϹΜΟΝΑΙΜΑΤΟϹΙΥ ΟΥ ΧΑΡΕΙ
ϹΥΜΙΝΚΑΙ ΕΙΡΗΝΗ ΠΛΗΘΥΝΘΕΙΗ
ΕΥΛΟΓΗΤΟϹΟΘϹ ΚΑΙΠΑΤΟΥ
ΗΜΩΝ ΙΥ ΧΡΥ ΟΚΑΤΑΠΟΛΥΕΛΕ
ΟϹΑΥΤΟΥΑΝΑ ΓΕΝΝΗϹΑϹΕΙϹ
ΕΛΠΙΔΑ ΔΙΑΑΝΑϹΤΑϹΕ
ΩϹ ΧΡΥ ΕΚΝΕΚΡΩΝ ΕΙϹΚΛΗΡΟ
ΝΟΜΙΑΝΑΦΘΑΡΤΟΝΚΑΙΑΜΙΑ
ΝΤΟΝΤΕΤΗΡΗΜΕΝ

**Hermeneia
—A Critical
and Historical
Commentary
on the Bible**

1 Peter

A Commentary on First Peter

by Paul J. Achtemeier

Edited by Eldon Jay Epp

Fortress Press

Minneapolis

1 Peter
A Commentary on First Peter

Cover and interior design: Kenneth Hiebert
Production management by Publisher's WorkGroup
Typesetting by Polebridge Press

Library of Congress Cataloging-in-Publication Data

Achtemeier, Paul J.
    1 Peter / by Paul J. Achtemeier : edited by Eldon
Jay Epp.
       p.   cm. — (Hermeneia—a critical and
historical commentary on the Bible)
    Includes bibliographical references and indexes.
    ISBN 0-8006-6030-7 (alk. paper)
    1. Bible. N.T. Peter, 1st—Criticism,
interpretation, etc.
    I. Epp, Eldon Jay. II. Title. III. Series.
BS2795.2.A24 1996   95-19564
                                 CIP

Manufactured in the U.S.A.   AF 1–6030

00 99 98 97 96   1 2 3 4 5 6 7 8 9 10

FOR

RACHEL, SARAH, AND JOSHUA
MICHAEL AND ROBERT
AND THEIR PARENTS

Paul J. Achtemeier is the Herbert Worth and Annie H. Jackson Professor of Biblical Interpretation at Union Theological Seminary, Richmond, Virginia. Born in Lincoln, Nebraska, he received his theological education at Union Theological Seminary, New York, and has done additional study at Princeton Theological Seminary, the University of Heidelberg, and the University of Basel. He has taught New Testament at Elmhurst College, his alma mater, at Lancaster Theological Seminary, and, since 1973, at Union Theological Seminary in Virginia. He has been a visiting professor at several seminaries and universities in North America and Europe, and has received a number of honors, including five appointments as Staley Foundation Distinguished Scholar.

Active in learned societies, he has served as Executive Secretary and as President of the Society of Biblical Literature, and is the first Protestant scholar to have been elected President of the Catholic Biblical Society of America. He is also an elected member of the American Theological Society and the international Studiorum Novi Testamenti Societas.

Professor Achtemeier has contributed to several major aspects of New Testament scholarship in his thirteen books and numerous scholarly articles as well as his editing of scholarly journals and reference books. He is General Editor of *Harper's Bible Dictionary*, new edition (1985), and Consulting Editor for *Harper's Bible Commentary* (1985–88). Among his Fortress Press books are *The Quest for Unity in the New Testament Church* (1987) and *Mark*, second edition, Proclamation Commentaries (1986).

Contents

The name *Hermeneia*, Greek ἑρμηνεία, has been chosen as the title of the commentary series to which this volume belongs. The word *Hermeneia* has a rich background in the history of biblical interpretation as a term used in the ancient Greek-speaking world for the detailed, systematic exposition of a scriptural work. It is hoped that the series, like its name, will carry forward this old and venerable tradition. A second, entirely practical reason for selecting the name lies in the desire to avoid a long descriptive title and its inevitable acronym, or worse, an unpronounceable abbreviation.

The series is designed to be a critical and historical commentary to the Bible without arbitrary limits in size or scope. It will utilize the full range of philological and historical tools, including textual criticism (often slighted in modern commentaries), the methods of the history of tradition (including genre and prosodic analysis), and the history of religion.

Hermeneia is designed for the serious student of the Bible. It will make full use of ancient Semitic and classical languages; at the same time, English translations of all comparative materials—Greek, Latin, Canaanite, or Akkadian—will be supplied alongside the citation of the source in its original language. Insofar as possible, the aim is to provide the student or scholar with full critical discussion of each problem of interpretation and with the primary data upon which the discussion is based.

Hermeneia is designed to be international and interconfessional in the selection of authors; its editorial boards were formed with this end in view. Occasionally the series will offer translations of distinguished commentaries which originally appeared in languages other than English. Published volumes of the series will be revised continually, and eventually, new commentaries will replace older works in order to preserve the currency of the series. Commentaries are also being assigned for important literary works in the categories of apocryphal and pseudepigraphical works relating to the Old and New Testaments, including some of Essene or Gnostic authorship.

The editors of *Hermeneia* impose no systematic-theological perspective upon the series (directly, or indirectly by selection of authors). It is expected that authors will struggle to lay bare the ancient meaning of a biblical work or pericope. In this way the text's human relevance should become transparent, as is always the case in competent historical discourse. However, the series eschews for itself homiletical translation of the Bible.

The editors are heavily indebted to Fortress Press for its energy and courage in taking up an expensive, long-term project, the rewards of which will accrue chiefly to the field of biblical scholarship.

The editor responsible for this volume is Eldon Jay Epp of Case Western Reserve University.

Frank Moore Cross   *Helmut Koester*
For the Old Testament   For the New Testament
Editorial Board   Editorial Board

Although one of the shorter epistles in the New Testament, the First Epistle of Peter has more than its share of conundrums associated with it. In dispute are author, readers, time of writing, situation in the Roman Empire vis-à-vis the Christian faith when it was composed, and the overall structure of the argument, to mention but a few. Also notorious are the difficulties connected with understanding such passages as 3:18–22 or 4:1–6, the former long recognized as one of the more opaque paragraphs in the New Testament. Yet the letter is written with style and verve, and contains within its short compass a wealth of theological insight. It is the task of this commentary to provide an encounter with this letter, to indicate the material necessary to reach informed decisions about the problems one confronts in reading it, and to furnish a substantial review of the solutions proposed by other scholars.

In the Introduction, relevant data—linguistic, social, economic, political, religious —will be examined for the light they shed on the culture out of which, and for which, this letter was written. That is necessary since the communities from which and for which 1 Peter was written did not exist in a vacuum; they existed within a society that exerted a number of pressures upon them, and it is necessary to be aware of them if we are to gain more than a superficial understanding of the intention of this letter. It is to that end, and not the desire to verify or falsify some modern social theory, that these data will be examined. If in the course of such an examination, some long-held theories are shown to be based more on supposition than on evidence, that will need to be noted, but it is not the purpose for which these introductory paragraphs are written. Rather, their intention is to introduce to the reader the situation faced by the original writer and his readers, and in that way facilitate a useful encounter with this biblical text.

Because 1 Peter is not only a piece of literature, but also a piece of literature invested by the Christian community with canonical status, such literary questions as authorship and date of composition, type and integrity of the letter, and the status of its intended readers have been invested not only with literary but also with religious value. That can influence the kind of results that are found allowable, and may put limits on the range of inquiry about such matters, with the result that conclusions are reached that are cherished more on religious grounds than on grounds of literary or historical probability. If in the course of our investigation of literary and historical questions, some long-held theories in this area are also shown to be based more upon supposition or upon religious preference than upon evidence, that too will need to be noted. But again, that is not the intent of these investigations. Rather, their intent is here also to encourage a useful encounter with this biblical text by achieving clarity on what kind of literature we confront, and therefore what we may, and what we may not, reasonably expect to find in it. Only when we know as much as we can about the literary dimensions of this letter, and the environment which shaped it and into which it was sent, will it prove fruitful to undertake a detailed investigation of its content in order to determine the theological message it intends to convey.

In the body of the commentary, the discussion is divided into three categories: translation, analysis, and comment. The translation seeks to convey some of the broader nuances of the Greek text, and the notes provide insight into the more important textual variations available to us. The text-critical notations have followed the system of identification of texts employed in the Nestle-Aland *Novum Testamentum Graece*. The analysis considers among others such elements as structure of the passage, its possible sources, and its import, whether the passage represents a major division of the letter (e.g., *prooemium*, 1:3–12, body opening, 1:13—2:10) or a smaller unit within one of those major divisions (e.g., 1:3–5, 2:1–3, 3:1–7). In addition to the analyses of the passages, there are extended comments on the individual verses, covering elements ranging from grammar to theological intent. The reader may thus find a convenient summary of the points to be discussed in the analysis, or may, if that seems useful, turn immediately to the verse(s) in question.

For the most part, discussion with other scholars who have written on 1 Peter, along with other notations of evidence called upon in the discussion of the text, are relegated to the footnotes and the various excursus, so that the reader is not constantly interrupted by names, book titles, and a recitation of the opinions of others. Those who desire to pursue in more detail such arguments and evidence will find ample opportunity in those notes, but I have sought to provide a commentary whose narrative flows more smoothly than is sometimes the case in so detailed a commentary as this one.

Because the commentary represents an encounter with the text of 1 Peter as it appears in the New Testament, I have sought to avoid the expedient of blaming ill-understood or partially relevant portions drawn from earlier traditions to explain the obscure portions of the letter. There is of course no question that the author of 1 Peter is drawing on earlier religious traditions, Jewish as well as Christian. Yet from whatever source, the material thus derived was in the author's view relevant to the discussion at hand, and since that material, however derived, now constitutes part of the letter itself, it must be dealt with as a part of the text that does in fact confront us.

It has not been my intent to prove wrong all who preceded me with commentaries on 1 Peter, nor have I sought as a matter of principle to occupy the safer middle ground between extreme scholarly opinions. I have avoided neither the conventional nor, on occasion, the more radical suggestions when in my estimate they best explain the available evidence. I have not deliberately striven for novelty, but when a novel approach seemed best, I have followed it, always seeking to be guided by the total situation of the letter as I have understood it.

The references to classical literature, Greek and Latin, generally conform to the texts to be found in the Loeb Classical Library (LCL), published by Harvard University Press, or to the identifications found in Luci Berkowitz and Karl A. Squitier, *Thesaurus Linguae Graecae: Canon of Greek Authors and Works* (3d ed.; New York/Oxford: Oxford University Press, 1990). The latter are the forms used in the *Thesaurus Linguae Graecae* (*TLG*) computer-available text (CD Rom #D). References to inscriptions and papyri conform to the system used by the Packard Humanities Institute (PHI) in their computer-available text (Demonstration CD Rom #6); references to Latin literature to the material in the same format also issued by the PHI (CD Rom #5.3). When none of those sources contained the literature, references are to Migne, *Patrologia Latina* (*PL*) or Graeca (*PG*). Unless otherwise indicated, all translations are my own. In the case of modern languages other than English, where the nuance of the language is helpful for understanding the author's point, I have included the original text along with the translation; where such nuances are not at issue, I have simply provided the translation. In part for the sake of convenience, in part because of customs that have evolved among commentators on 1 Peter, there are one or two instances where the organization of the verses in the body of the commentary differs from that of the outline furnished at the end of the Introduction. Where that is the case, a new rubric has been set over the groups of verses that differ in the body of the commentary, a rubric that more closely describes the content of that unit. Finally, I may note that because I had already completed most of my research by the time the English translation of Leonhard Goppelt's commentary appeared, I have cited the German version in the footnotes. I have provided the equivalent pages in the English translation (ET) for the Introduction, since the material there can be difficult to locate, but have not done so for the other chapters. There one can verify my citations in the English version simply by turning to the pages where Goppelt comments on the verse in question.

It would be futile to attempt to list all those who have assisted me in the preparation of this volume. I must, however, single out some. I owe a debt of gratitude to Union Theological Seminary, not only for leaves granted to pursue this project and support of a more general kind but also for providing me with an IBYCUS computer system, without which I could not have written this book. Members of Union's library staff have also rendered invaluable help, principally Martha Aycock, a reference librarian without peer in my experience; with her retirement, her able successor Patsy Verreault has carried on the noble tradition. Robin Schreiber also gave me able assistance in the organizing of collected reference materials. Among the many friends and fellow scholars to whom I am indebted, let me single out but four: John H. Elliott, with whom I have discussed, and from whom I have learned much about, 1 Peter; Harry Attridge, who trod this path before me, and who has lent moral support by his interest and his words of encouragement; Prof. Jack Kingsbury and Prof. Peter Lampe, colleagues who were always ready to discuss problems and offer helpful suggestions whenever I approached them. I must, however, lay exclusive claim to any defects in this work. I must also thank the many students of Union Seminary, past and present, whose encouragement and interest have often spurred on my lagging spirits. To my wife Betty I owe more than I can express, but her loving heart, her willingness to listen, and her intelligent questions and comments throughout this, and many other, projects have made my scholarly life possible. Finally, to the ones to whom the volume is dedicated, grandchildren in every sense of the word, go my fond affections and my sincere conviction that the same Lord who sustained the Christians to whom this letter was originally addressed will continue to sustain the five of them, their parents, and all others who in the future continue to confess Jesus Christ as their living Lord.

Richmond, Virginia   *Paul J. Achtemeier*
January 1996

Reference Codes

1. Abbreviations

Aesop
  Fab. synt.   *Fabulae syntipae philosophi*
AJBI   Annual of the Japanese Biblical
                        Institute
AnBib   Analecta biblica
Anton.   *Antonianum*
Ap. Const.   *Apostolic Constitutions*
Apoc. Pet.   *Apocalypse of Peter*
Apuleius
  Metam.   *Metamorphoses* (= The Golden
                        Ass)
Aristotle
  Pol.   *Politica*
  Rhet.   *Rhetorica*
Asc. Isa.   *Ascension of Isaiah*
As. Mos.   *Assumption of Moses*
ASNU   Acta seminarii neotestamentici
                        upsaliensis
AsSeign   *Assemblées du Seigneur*
Athanasius
  Ad Ant. ducem   *Questiones ad Antiochum ducem*
  Ep. Epic.   *Epistula ad Epictetus*
  Morb. et val.   *De morbo et valetudine*
AThANT   Abhandlungen zu Theologie des
                        Alten und Neuen Testaments
ATR   *Anglican Theological Review*
Augustine
  Ep. Euod.   *Epistula ad Euodium*
AusBR   *Australian Biblical Review*
b.   Babylonian Talmud
2 Bar.   *Syriac Apocalypse of Baruch*
3 Bar.   *Greek Apocalypse of Baruch*
Barn.   *Epistle of Barnabas*
BBB   Bonner biblische Beiträge
BBE   Beiträge zur biblischen Exegese
BDF   F. Blass, A. Debrunner, and R.
                        W. Funk, *A Greek Grammar of the
                        New Testament and Other Early
                        Christian Literature*
BeO   *Bibbia e oriente*
BEThL   Bibliotheca ephemeridum theo-
                        logicarum lovaniensium
BFCTh   Beiträge zur Förderung
                        christlicher Theologie
Bib   *Biblica*
BibLeb   *Bibel und Leben*
BibOr   Biblica et orientalia
BK   *Bibel und Kirche*
BLit   *Bibel und Liturgie*
BNTC   Black's New Testament Com-
                        mentaries
BSac   *Bibliotheca Sacra*
BT   *The Bible Translator*
BTB   *Biblical Theology Bulletin*

BVC   *Bible et vie chrétienne*
BZ   *Biblische Zeitschrift*
BZNW   Beihefte zur *ZNW*
CBQ   *Catholic Biblical Quarterly*
John Chrysostom
  De paen.   *De paenitentia*
  Int. in Dan.   *Interpretatio in Danielem pro-
                        phetam*
Cicero
  Ad Her.   *Rhetorica ad Herennium* (author
                        not certain)
  De off.   *De officiis*
  Tusc. disp.   *Tusculanae disputationes*
1 Clem.   *The First Epistle of Clement*
2 Clem.   *The Second Epistle of Clement*
Clement of Alexandria
  Adum. Petr.   *Adumbrationes in epistula Petri
                        prima catholica* (Frag. 24)
  Paed.   *Paedagogus*
  Quis div. salv.   *Quis dives salvetur*
  Strom.   *Stromata*
ConNT   Coniectanea Neotestamentica
Corp. Herm.   *Corpus Hermeticum*
CQR   *Church Quarterly Review*
CTM   *Concordia Theological Monthly*
Cyprian
  De hab. virg.   *De habitu virginum*
  De cath. eccl.   *De ecclesiae catholicae unitate*
Cyril of Jerusalem
  Catech.   *Catechesis mystagogica*
  Procatech.   *Procatechesis*
DB   *Dictionnaire de la Bible*
Did.   *Didache*
Dio Cassius
  Hist. Rom.   *Historia Romae*
Dio Chrysostom
  Ep.   *Epistulae*
  Or.   *Orationes*
Diodorus Siculus
  Bib. hist.   *Bibliotheca historica*
Diogn.   *Epistle of Diognetus*
Dionysius of Halicarnassus
  Ant. Rom.   *Antiquitates Romanae*
  Dem. dic.   *De Demosthenis dictione*
ed(s).   editor(s)
EKKNT   Evangelisch-Katholischer
                        Kommentar zum Neuen
                        Testament
1 Enoch   *Ethiopic Enoch*
2 Enoch   *Slavonic Enoch*
3 Enoch   *Hebrew Enoch*
Ep. Arist.   *Epistle of Aristeas*
Epictetus
  Diss.   *Dissertationes*
  Enchir.   *Enchiridion*

Epiphanius		*Vit.*	*Vita*
Anc.	*Ancoratus*	*JSNT*	*Journal for the Study of the New Testament*
Pan.	*Panarion (= Adversus haereses)*		
EstBib	*Estudios Bíblicos*	*JSNTSup*	Journal for the Study of the New Testament Supplement Series
EstTeol	*Estudios teológicos*		
EThL	*Ephemerides theologicae lovanienses*		
EThR	*Etudes théologiques et religieuses*	*JSS*	*Journal of Semitic Studies*
Eusebius		*JTS*	*Journal of Theological Studies*
Hist. eccl.	*Historia ecclesiastica*	*Jub.*	*Jubilees*
EvQ	*Evangelical Quarterly*	Justin	Justin Martyr
ExpT	*Expository Times*	*1 Apol.*	*First Apology*
FRLANT	Forschungen zur Religion und Literatur des Alten und Neuen Testaments	*Dial.*	*Dialogue with Trypho*
		Juvenal	
		Sat.	*Satires*
GCS	Griechische christliche Schrift-steller	*KD*	*Kerygma und Dogma*
		KEK	Kritisch-exegetischer Kommentar über das Neue Testament
Gos. Thom.	*Gospel of Thomas*		
Greg	*Gregorianum*		
Hermas	*The Shepherd of Hermas*	LCL	Loeb Classical Library
Man.	*Mandate*	LD	Lectio Divina
Sim.	*Similitude*	LEC	Library of Early Christianity
Vis.	*Vision*	Longus	
Herodotus		*Daphn.*	*Daphnis et Chloe*
Hist.	*Historiae*	*LQ*	*Lutheran Quarterly*
Hippolytus		LSJ	Liddell-Scott-Jones, *Greek-English Lexicon*
Ap. Trad.	*Apostolic Traditions*		
Hist. Alex.	*Historia Alexandri Magni*	Lucian of Samosata	
HNT	Handbuch zum Neuen Testament	*Alex.*	*Alexander*
		Conviv.	*Convivium*
HNTC	Harper's New Testament Commentary	*Dial. mar.*	*Dialogi Marini*
		Imag.	*Imagines*
HThKNT	Herders theologischer Kommentar zum Neuen Testament	*Pergr. mort.*	*De Peregrini morte*
		LXX	Septuagint
HTR	*Harvard Theological Review*	Marcus Aurelius	
ICC	International Critical Commentary	*Med.*	*Meditationes*
		Martial	
Iamblichos		*Epig.*	*Epigrammata*
De vit. Pyth.	*De vita Pythagorica*	*Mart. Pol.*	*Martyrdom of Polycarp*
Ignatius		MNTC	Moffatt New Testament Commentary
Eph.	*Letter to the Ephesians*		
Magn.	*Letter to the Magnesians*	MS(S).	manuscript(s)
Phld.	*Letter to the Philadelphians*	MT	Masoretic Text
Pol.	*Letter to Polycarp*	*NEB*	*New English Bible*
Rom.	*Letter to the Romans*	*NedThT*	*Nederlands theologisch tijdschrift*
Smyrn.	*Letter to the Smyrnaeans*	*Neot*	*Neotestamentica*
Trall.	*Letter to the Trallians*	NF	Neue Folge
Int	*Interpretation*	*NovT*	*Novum Testamentum*
Irenaeus		NovTSup	Novum Testamentum, Supplements
Adv. haer.	*Adversus haereses*		
JBL	*Journal of Biblical Literature*	*NRSV*	*New Revised Standard Version*
Jerome		*NRTh*	*La nouvelle revue théologique*
Ep.	*Epistulae*	n.s.	new series
JETS	*Journal of the Evangelical Theological Society*	NT	New Testament
		NTAbh	Neutestamentliche Abhandlungen
Jos. Asen.	*Joseph and Asenath*		
Josephus		*NTS*	*New Testament Studies*
Ant.	*Antiquities of the Jews*	*Odes Sol.*	*Odes of Solomon*
Ap.	*Contra Apionem*	Origen	
Bell.	*Bellum Judaicum*	*Con. Cels.*	*Contra Celsum*

Com. Joan.	*Commentarii in evangelium Joannis*		*Pan.*	*Panegyricus*
Com. Matt.	*Commentarium in evangelium Matthaei*		Plutarch	
			Mor.	*Moralia*
Com. Rom.	*Comentarii in epistulam ad Romanos*		*con. pr.*	*Coniugalia praecepta*
			Exil.	*De exilio*
Frag. i ad Cor.	*Fragmenta ex commentariis in epistulam i ad Corinthios*		*Lat. viv.*	*De latenter vivendo*
			Quaest. conv.	*Queastiones convivalium*
Frag. Joan.	*Fragmenta in evangelium Joannis*		*Vit.*	*Vitae parallelae*
Frag. Luc.	*Fragmenta in Lucam*		*Lucull.*	*Lucullus*
Hom. Lev.	*Homiliae in Leviticum*		Polybius	
In Jer.	*In Jeremiam*		*Hist.*	*Historiae*
Orosius			Polycarp	
Hist.	*Historiarum adversum paganos libri septem*		*Phil.*	*Letter to the Philippians*
			Ps. Sol.	*Psalms of Solomon*
OT	Old Testament		*PSTJ*	*Perkins (School of Theology) Journal*
Ovid			PTMS	Pittsburgh (Princeton) Theological Monograph Series
Amor.	*Amores*			
Fas.	*Fasti*		PW	Pauly-Wissowa, *Real-encyclopädie der classischen Altertumswissen- schaft*
Metam.	*Metamorphoses*			
par.	parallel(s)			
para.	paragraph(s)		QL	Qumran Literature
Petronius			CD	Cairo (Genizah Text of the) *Damascus (Document)*
Satyr.	*Satyricon*			
PG	J.-P. Migne, *Patrologiae Cursus Completus,* series graeca (162 vols.; Paris: Migne, 1844–55)		1QapGen	*Genesis Apocryphon* from Qumran Cave 1
			1QH	*Thanksgiving Hymns* from Qumran Cave 1
Philo			1QM	*War Scroll* from Qumran Cave 1
Abr.	*De Abrahamo*		1QpHab	*Pesher on Habakkuk* from Qumran Cave 1
Agric.	*De agricultura*			
Conf. ling.	*De confusione linguarum*		1QS	*Rule of the Community (Manual of Discipline)*
Decal.	*De decalogo*			
Deus imm.	*Quod Deus sit immutabilis*		1QSa	Appendix A to 1QS
Ebr.	*De ebrietate*		1QSb	Appendix B to 1QS
Fug.	*De fuga et inventione*		1Q27	*Book of Mysteries / Triumph of Righteousness* from Qumran Cave 1
Gig.	*De gigantibus*			
Hyp.	*Hypothetica or Apologia pro Judaeis*			
Jos.	*De Josepho*		4QFlor	*Florilegium* from Qumran Cave 4
Leg. all.	*Legum allegoriae*		4QpIsa	*Pesher on Isaiah* from Qumran Cave 4
Leg. Gaj.	*Legatio ad Gajum*			
Migr. Abr.	*De migratione Abrahami*		4QpNah	*Pesher on Nahum* from Qumran Cave 4
Mut. nom.	*De mutationum nominum*			
Op. mun.	*De opificio mundi*		4QTestim	*Testimonia* from Qumran Cave 4
Praem. poen.	*De praemiis et poenis*		11QMelch	*Melchizedek* from Qumran Cave 11
Rer. div. her.	*Quis rerum divinarum heres sit*			
Sobr.	*De sobrietate*			
Som.	*De somniis*		Quintilian	
Spec. leg.	*De specialibus legibus*		*Inst.*	*Institutio oratoria*
Virt.	*De virtutibus*		RAC	*Reallexikon für Antike und Christentum*
Vit. Mos.	*De vita Mosis*			
Philostratus	Flavius Philostratus		RB	*Revue biblique*
Her.	*Heroicus*		RechSR	*Recherches de science religieuse*
Vit. Ap.	*Vita Apollonii*		ResQ	*Restoration Quarterly*
PL	J.-P. Migne, *Patrologiae Cursus Completus,* series latina (217 vols.; Paris: Migne, 1857–66)		RevExp	*Review and Expositor*
			RevQ	*Revue de Qumran*
			RevScRel	*Revue des sciences religieuses*
Pliny	Pliny the Elder		RevThom	*Revue thomiste*
Hist. nat.	*Historia naturalis*		RGG	*Religion in Geschichte und Gegenwart*
Pliny	Pliny the Younger			
Ep.	*Epistulae*			

RHPhR	*Revue d'histoire et de philosophie religieuses*	*Cultu fem.*	*De cultu feminarum*
RivB	*Rivista biblica*	*Orat.*	*De oratione*
RSV	Revised Standard Version	*Scorp.*	*Scorpiace*
RThL	*Revue théologique de Louvain*	*T. Abr.*	*Testament of Abraham*
RV	Revised Version	*T. 12 Patr.*	*Testaments of the Twelve Patriarchs*
Sallustius		*T. Benj.*	*Testament of Benjamin*
De deis	*De deis et mundo*	*T. Dan*	*Testament of Dan*
SB	Sources bibliques	*T. Iss.*	*Testament of Issachar*
SBFLA	*Studii biblici franciscani liber annuus*	*T. Jos.*	*Testament of Joseph*
		T. Jud.	*Testament of Judah*
SBLDS	SBL Dissertation Series	*T. Levi*	*Testament of Levi*
SBLSBS	SBL Sources for Biblical Study	*T. Naph.*	*Testament of Naphtali*
SBS	Stuttgarter Bibelstudien	*T. Reub.*	*Testament of Reuben*
ScEs	*Science et esprit*	*T. Sim.*	*Testament of Simeon*
SEÅ	*Svensk exegetisk årsbok*	*T. Zeb.*	*Testament of Zebulon*
Seneca *Contr.*	Seneca the Elder *Controversiae*	*ThBei*	*Theologische Beiträge*
Seneca	Seneca the Younger	*ThGl*	*Theologie und Glaube*
Apocol.	*Apocolocyntosis*	*ThLZ*	*Theologische Literaturzeitung*
Benef.	*De beneficiis*	*ThStK*	*Theologische Studien und Kritiken*
Clem.	*De clementia*	*ThWNT*	G. Kittel and G. Friedrich, eds.,
Const.	*De constantia*		*Theologisches Wörterbuch zum*
Ep.	*Epistulae morales*		*Neuen Testament*
Ad Helv.	*De consolatione ad Helviam*	*ThZ*	*Theologische Zeitschrift*
Ad Marc.	*De consolatione ad Marciam*	TLG	Thesaurus Linguae Graecae
Oed.	*Oedipus*		(CD Rom Disc #D)
Prov.	*De providentia*	*TS*	*Theological Studies*
Ques. nat.	*Questiones naturales*	*TThZ*	*Trierer theologische Zeitschrift*
Vit. beat.	*De vita beata*	TU	Texte und Untersuchungen zur
Sib. Or.	*Sibylline Oracles*		Geschichte der altchristlichen
SJT	*Scottish Journal of Theology*		Literatur
Sophocles		*TynBul*	*Tyndale Bulletin*
Oed. Col.	*Oedipus Coloneus*	v(v).	verse(s)
StEv	*Studia Evangelica* I–III (= TU 73 [1959], 87 [1964], 88 [1964])	*VD*	*Verbum Domini*
		Virgil	
Strabo		*Aen.*	*Aeneid*
Geog.	*Geographica*	*VSpir*	*Vie spirituelle*
Str-B	[H. Strack and] P. Billerbeck, *Kommentar zum Neuen Testament aus Talmud und Midrasch*	WA	M. Luther, Kritische Gesamt-ausgabe (= "Weimar" edition)
		WTJ	*Westminster Theological Journal*
StTh	*Studia Theologica*	WUNT	Wissenschaftliche
Suetonius			Untersuchungen zum Neuen
Vit.	*Vitae Caesarum*		Testament
Tacitus		Xenophon	
Agric.	*Agricola*	*Apol.*	*Apologia Socratis*
Ann.	*Annales*	*Mem.*	*Memorabilia*
Frag.	*Fragments*	*Oecon.*	*Oeconomicus*
Ger.	*Germania*	*ZMR*	*Zeitschrift für Missionskunde und Religionswissenschaft*
Hist.	*Historiae*		
Tertullian		*ZNW*	*Zeitschrift für die neutestamentliche Wissenschaft*
Ad nat.	*Ad nationes*		
Ad ux.	*Ad uxores*	*ZSTh*	*Zeitschrift für systematische Theologie*
Adv. Marc.	*Adversus Marcionem*		
Apol.	*Apologia*	*ZWTh*	*Zeitschrift für wissenschaftliche Theologie*
Bapt.	*De baptismo*		

2. Short Titles of Commentaries, Studies, and Articles Often Cited

Achtemeier, "New-born Babes"
Paul J. Achtemeier, "New-born Babes and Living Stones: Literal and Figurative in 1 Peter," in M. P. Horgan and P. J. Kobelski, eds., *To Touch the Text: Biblical and Related Studies in Honor of Joseph H. Fitzmyer* (New York: Crossroad/Continuum, 1988) 207–36.

Achtemeier, *"Omne verbum sonat"*
Paul J. Achtemeier, *"Omne verbum sonat*: The New Testament and the Oral Environment of Late Western Antiquity," *JBL* 109 (1990) 3–27.

Agnew, "Translation"
Francis H. Agnew, C.M., "1 Peter 1:2—An Alternative Translation," *CBQ* 45 (1983) 68–73.

Aland and Aland, *Text*
Kurt Aland and Barbara Aland, *The Text of the New Testament* (2nd ed.; trans. Erroll F. Rhodes; Grand Rapids: Eerdmans, 1987).

Andresen, "Formular"
Carl Andresen, "Zum Formular frühchristlicher Gemeindebriefe," *ZNW* 56 (1965) 233–59.

Arichea, "God or Christ?"
Daniel C. Arichea, Jr., "God or Christ? A Study of Implicit Information," *BT* 28 (1977) 412–18.

Arichea and Nida, *Translator's Handbook*
Daniel C. Arichea and Eugene A. Nida, *A Translator's Handbook on the First Letter from Peter* (Helps for Translators; New York: United Bible Societies, 1980).

Aune, *Literary Environment*
David E. Aune, *The New Testament in Its Literary Environment* (LEC 8; ed. W. A. Meeks; Philadelphia: Westminster, 1987).

Badian, *Foreign Clientelae*
E. Badian, *Foreign Clientelae (264–70 B.C.)* (Oxford: Clarendon, 1958).

Balch, "Early Christian Criticism"
David L. Balch, "Early Christian Criticism of Patriarchal Authority: I Peter 2:11—3:12," *Union Seminary Quarterly Review* 39 (1984) 161–73.

Balch, "Hellenization/Acculturation"
David L. Balch, "Hellenization/Acculturation in 1 Peter," in Talbert, *Perspectives*, 79–102.

Balch, "Household Codes"
David L. Balch, "Household Codes," in D. E. Aune, ed., *Greco-Roman Literature and the New Testament: Selected Forms and Genres* (SBLSBS 21; Atlanta: Scholars Press, 1988) 25–50.

Balch, *Wives*
David L. Balch, *Let Wives Be Submissive: The Domestic Code in 1 Peter* (SBLMS 26; Chico: Scholars Press, 1981).

Bammel, "Commands"
Ernst Bammel, "The Commands in I Peter II.17," *NTS* 11 (1964/65) 279–81.

Banks, "Who Are the Spirits in Prison?"
William L. Banks, "Who Are the Spirits in Prison?" *Eternity Magazine* 16 (1966) 23–26.

Barnett, *Literary Influence*
Albert E. Barnett, *Paul Becomes a Literary Influence* (Chicago: University of Chicago Press, 1941).

Barr, "Submission Ethic"
Allan Barr, "Submission Ethic in the First Epistle of Peter," *Hartford Quarterly* 2 (1962) 27–33.

Barr, "בארץ ‎ ‎μόλις"
James Barr, "בארץ ‎ ‎μόλις: Prov. xi. 31, I Pet. iv. 18," *JSS* 20 (1975) 149–64.

Barth, "1 Petrus 1, 3–9"
Gerhard Barth, "1 Petrus 1, 3–9 Exegese, Meditation und Predigt," *EstTeol* 6 (1966) 148–60.

Bauckham, "James, 1 and 2 Peter, Jude"
Richard Bauckham, "James, 1 and 2 Peter, Jude," in D. A. Carson and H. G. M. Williamson, eds., *It Is Written: Scripture Citing Scripture: Essays in Honour of Barnabas Lindars, SS* (Cambridge: Cambridge University Press, 1988) 303–17.

Bauer
Johannes Baptist Bauer, *Der erste Petrusbrief* (Die Welt der Bibel. Kleinkommentare zur Heiligen Schrift; Düsseldorf: Patmos, 1971).

Bauer, "Aut maleficus"
Johannes Baptist Bauer, "Aut maleficus aut alieni speculator (1 Petr 4,15)," *BZ*, NF 22 (1978) 109–15.

Bauer, "Könige und Priester"
Johannes Baptist Bauer, "Könige und Priester, ein heiliges Volk (Ex 19,6)," *BZ*, NF 2 (1958) 283–86.

Bauer, "Verfolgung"
Johannes Baptist Bauer, "Der erste Petrusbrief und die Verfolgung unter Domitian," in R. Schnackenburg et al., eds., *Die Kirche des Anfangs: Für Heinz Schürmann* (Freiburg: Herder, 1978) 513–27.

Beare
Francis Wright Beare, *The First Epistle of Peter: The Greek Text with Introduction and Notes* (3d ed.; Oxford: Blackwell, 1970).

Beare, "Some Remarks"
Francis Wright Beare, "Some Remarks on the Text of I Peter in the Bodmer Papyrus (P[72])," *StEv* III, part II: *The New Testament Message* (TU 88; ed. F. L. Cross; Berlin: Akademie-Verlag, 1964) 263–65.

Beare, "Teaching"
Francis Wright Beare, "The Teaching of First Peter," *ATR* 27 (1945) 284–96.

Beare, "Text"
Francis Wright Beare, "The Text of 1 Peter in Papyrus 72," *JBL* 80 (1961) 253–60.

Bengel, *Gnomon*
Johann Albrecht Bengel, *Gnomon Novi Testamenti* (4th ed.; Tübingen: J. H. P. Schramm, 1742).

Bennetch, "Exegetical Studies"
John Henry Bennetch, "Exegetical Studies in 1 Peter," *BSac* 101 (1944) 193–98.

Berger, "Apostelbrief"
Klaus Berger, "Apostelbrief und apostolische Rede: Zum Formular frühchristlicher Briefe," *ZNW* 65 (1974) 190–231.

Best
Ernest Best, *1 Peter* (New Century Bible; London: Oliphants, 1971; reprinted Grand Rapids: Eerdmans, 1982).

Best, "I Peter II 4–10"
Ernest Best, "I Peter II 4–10—A Reconsideration," *NovT* 11 (1969) 270–93.

Best, "I Peter and the Gospel"
Ernest Best, "I Peter and the Gospel Tradition," *NTS* 16 (1970) 95–113.

Bieder, "Reicke"
Werner Bieder, "Bo Reicke, The Disobedient Spirits and Christian Baptism" (review), *ThZ* 2 (1946) 456–62.

Bieder, *Grund und Kraft*
Werner Bieder, *Grund und Kraft der Mission nach dem 1. Petrusbrief* (Theologische Studien 29; Zurich: Evangelischer Verlag, 1950).

Bieder, *Höllenfahrt Jesu*
Werner Bieder, *Die Vorstellung von der Höllenfahrt Jesu Christi* (AThANT 19; Zurich: Zwingli, 1949).

Bigg
Charles A. Bigg, *Critical and Exegetical Commentary on the Epistles of St. Peter and St. Jude* (ICC; New York: Scribner's, 1901).

Bishop, "*Oligoi* in 1 Pet. 3:20"
Eric F. F. Bishop, "*Oligoi* in 1 Pet. 3:20," *CBQ* 13 (1951) 44–45.

Blazen, "Suffering and Cessation"
Ivan T. Blazen, "Suffering and Cessation from Sin according to 1 Peter 4:1," *Andrews University Seminary Studies* 21 (1983) 27–50.

Blendinger, "Kirche als Fremdlingschaft"
Christian Blendinger, "Kirche als Fremdlingschaft," *Communio Viatorum* 10 (1967) 123–34.

Blinzler, "IEPATEYMA"
Josef Blinzler, "IEPATEYMA: Zur Exegesis von 1 Petr 2,5 u. 9," in *Episcopus, Studien über das Bischofsamt; Festschrift Kardinal Michael von Faulhaber* (Regensburg: Gregorius, 1949) 49–65.

Boismard, "Liturgie" [1]
Marie-Emile Boismard, "Une liturgie baptismale dans la *Prima Petri*," *RB* 63 (1956) 182–208.

Boismard, "Liturgie" [2]
Marie-Emile Boismard, "Une liturgie baptismale dans la *Prima Petri*," *RB* 64 (1957) 161–83.

Boismard, *Quatre Hymnes*
Marie-Emile Boismard, *Quatre Hymnes baptismales dans la Première Epître de Pierre* (Paris: Cerf, 1961).

Borchert, "Conduct of Christians"
Gerald L. Borchert, "The Conduct of Christians in the Face of the 'Fiery Ordeal,'" *RevExp* 74 (1982) 451–62.

Bornemann, "Taufrede"
W. Bornemann, "Der erste Petrusbrief—eine Taufrede des Silvanus," *ZNW* 19 (1919/20) 143–65.

Bovon, "Foi chrétienne"
François Bovon, "Foi chrétienne et religion populaire dans la première Epître de Pierre," *EThR* 53 (1978) 25–41.

Brandt, "Wandel"
Wilhelm Brandt, "Wandel als Zeugnis nach dem 1. Petrusbrief," in W. Foerster, ed., *Verbum Dei manet in aeternum* (Festschrift O. Schmitz; Witten: Luther-Verlag, 1953) 10–25.

Brockington, "Septuagintal Background"
L. H. Brockington, "The Septuagintal Background to the New Testament Use of δόξα," in D. E. Nineham, ed., *Studies in the Gospels: Essays in Memory of R. H. Lightfoot* (Oxford: Blackwell, 1957) 1–8.

Brooks, "1 Peter 3:21"
O. S. Brooks, "1 Peter 3:21—The Clue to the Literary Structure of the Epistle," *NovT* 16 (1974) 290–305.

Brown and Meier, *Antioch and Rome*
Raymond E. Brown and John P. Meier, *Antioch and Rome* (New York: Paulist, 1983).

Brown et al., *Peter*
Raymond E. Brown, Karl P. Donfried, and John Reumann, eds., *Peter in the New Testament* (Minneapolis: Augsburg, 1973).

Brox
Norbert Brox, *Der erste Petrusbrief* (EKKNT; Zurich: Benziger, 1979).

Brox, *Falsche Verfasserangaben*
Norbert Brox, *Falsche Verfasserangaben: Zur Erklärung der frühchristlichen Pseudepigraphia* (SBS 79; Stuttgart: Katholisches Bibelwerk, 1975).

Brox, "Literarischen Tradition"
Norbert Brox, "Der erste Petrusbrief in der literarischen Tradition des Urchristentums," *Kairos,* NF 20 (1978) 182–92.

Brox, "Pseudepigraphischen Rahmung"
Norbert Brox, "Zur pseudepigraphischen Rahmung des ersten Petrusbriefes," *BZ,* NF 19 (1975) 78–96.

Brox, "Sara zum Beispiel"
Norbert Brox, "'Sara zum Beispiel . . .' Israel im 1. Petrusbrief," in P.-G. Müller and W. Stegner, eds., *Kontinuität und Einheit; Für Franz Mussner* (Freiburg: Herder, 1981) 484–93.

Brox, "Situation und Sprache"
Norbert Brox, "Situation und Sprache der Minderheit im ersten Petrusbrief," *Kairos,* NF 19 (1977) 1–13.

Brox, "Tendenz"
Norbert Brox, "Tendenz und Pseudepigraphie im ersten Petrusbrief," *Kairos,* NF 20 (1978) 110–20.

Bultmann, "Bekenntnis- und Liedfragmente"
  Rudolph Bultmann, "Bekenntnis- und Lied-
  fragmente im ersten Petrusbrief," ConNT in
  Honorem Antonii Fridrichsen (Lund: C. W. K.
  Gloerup, 1947) 11 (1947) 1–14.
Calloud, "Ce que parler"
  Jean Calloud, "Ce que parler veut dire (1 P 1,10–
  12)," in Perrot, Etudes, 175–206.
Calvin
  John Calvin, Commentaries on the Catholic Epistles
  (trans. J. Owen; Grand Rapids: Eerdmans, 1948).
Carmignac, "La théologie"
  Jean Carmignac, "La théologie de la souffrance
  dans les Hymnes de Qumrân," RevQ 3/11 (1961)
  365–86.
Carrez, "L'esclavage"
  Maurice Carrez, "L'esclavage dans la première
  épître de Pierre," in Perrot, Etudes, 207–17.
Carrington, "Saint Peter's Epistle"
  Philip Carrington, "Saint Peter's Epistle," in S. E.
  Johnson, ed., The Joy of Study: Papers on New
  Testament and Related Subjects Presented to Honor
  Frederick Clifton Grant (New York: Macmillan,
  1951) 57–63.
Chase, "Peter"
  F. H. Chase, "Peter, First Epistle," Dictionary of the
  Bible (ed. J. Hastings; Edinburgh: Clark, 1900)
  3.779–96.
Chevallier, "Comment lire"
  Max-Alain Chevallier, "Comment lire aujourd'hui
  la première épître de Pierre," in Perrot, Etudes,
  129–52.
Chevallier, "Condition"
  Max-Alain Chevallier, "Condition et vocation des
  Chrétiens en diaspora: Remarques exégétiques sur
  la 1re Epître de Pierre," RevScRel 48 (1974) 387–
  400.
Chevallier, "I Pierre 1/1 à 2/10"
  Max-Alain Chevallier, "I Pierre 1/1 à 2/10:
  Structure littéraire et conséquences exégétiques,"
  RHPhR 51 (1971) 129–42.
Combrini, "Structure"
  H. J. B. Combrini, "The Structure of I Peter,"
  Neot 9 (1980) 34–63.
Cook, "I Peter iii.20"
  David Cook, "I Peter iii.20: An Unnecessary
  Problem," JTS, n.s. 31 (1980) 72–78.
Coppens, "Le sacerdoce royal"
  Joseph Coppens, "Le sacerdoce royal des fidèles:
  un commentaire de I Petr. II, 4–10," in Au Service
  de la Parole de Dieu: Mélanges . . . à . . . André-Marie
  Charue (Gembloux: Duculot, 1969) 61–75.
Cothenet, "La Première Epître de Pierre"
  Edouard Cothenet, "La Première Epître de
  Pierre, L'Epître de Jacques," in J. Delorme, ed., Le
  ministère et les ministères selon le Nouveau Testament
  (Parole de Dieu; Paris: Seuil, 1974) 138–54.
Cothenet, "Le réalisme"
  Edouard Cothenet, "Le réalisme de l'espérance

chrétienne selon I Pierre," NTS 27 (1981) 564–
  72.
Cothenet, "Les orientations"
  Edouard Cothenet, "Les orientations actuelles de
  l'exégèse de la première lettre de Pierre," in
  Perrot, Etudes, 13–42.
Coutts, "Ephesians"
  J. Coutts, "Ephesians I.3–14 and I Peter I.3–13,"
  NTS 3 (1956/57) 115–27.
Cranfield
  C. E. B. Cranfield, I and II Peter and Jude: Intro-
  duction and Commentary (Torch Bible Com-
  mentaries; London: SCM, 1960).
Cranfield, "Interpretation"
  C. E. B. Cranfield, "The Interpretation of I Peter
  iii.19 and iv.6," ExpT 69 (1958) 369–72.
Cross, Paschal Liturgy
  Frank L. Cross, 1 Peter: A Paschal Liturgy (London:
  Mowbray, 1954).
Cullmann, Earliest Christian Confessions
  Oscar Cullmann, The Earliest Christian Confessions
  (trans. J. K. S. Reid; London: Lutterworth, 1949).
Cullmann, Peter
  Oscar Cullmann, Peter: Disciple, Apostle, Martyr
  (trans. F. V. Filson; 2d ed.; Philadelphia: West-
  minster, 1962).
Dalmer, "Zu 1. Petri 1,18.19"
  Johannes Dalmer, "Zu 1. Petri 1,18.19," BFCTh
  2/6 (1898/99) 75–87.
Dalton, Christ's Proclamation
  William Joseph Dalton, Christ's Proclamation to the
  Spirits: A Study of 1 Peter 3:18—4:6 (AnBib 23;
  Rome: Pontifical Biblical Institute, 1965).
Dalton, Christ's Proclamation (2d ed.)
  William Joseph Dalton, Christ's Proclamation to the
  Spirits; A Study of 1 Peter 3:18—4:6 (2d ed.; AnBib
  23; Rome: Pontifical Biblical Institute, 1989).
Dalton, "Interpretation"
  William Joseph Dalton, "The Interpretation of 1
  Peter 3,19 and 4,6: Light from 2 Peter," Bib 60
  (1979) 547–55.
Dalton, "Interpretation and Tradition"
  William Joseph Dalton, "Interpretation and
  Tradition: An Example from 1 Peter," Greg 49
  (1968) 11–37.
Dalton, "So That Your Faith"
  William Joseph Dalton, "'So That Your Faith May
  Also Be Your Hope in God' (I Peter 1:21)," in R.
  Banks, ed., Reconciliation and Hope: New Testament
  Essays on Atonement and Eschatology Presented to L. L.
  Morris on His 60th Birthday (Exeter: Paternoster;
  Grand Rapids: Eerdmans, 1974) 262–74.
Daniel, "Anti-Semitism"
  Jerry L. Daniel, "Anti-Semitism in the Hellenistic-
  Roman Period," JBL 98 (1979) 45–65.
Danker, "I Peter 1:23—2:17"
  Frederick W. Danker, "I Peter 1:23—2:17—A
  Consolatory Pericope," ZNW 58 (1967) 93–102.

Daube, "κερδαίνω"
    David Daube, "κερδαίνω as a Missionary Term," *HTR* 40 (1947) 109–20.

Daube, "Participle"
    David Daube, "Participle and Imperative in I Peter," appended note in Selwyn, 467–88.

Dautzenberg, "σωτηρία ψυχῶν"
    P. Gerhard Dautzenberg, "σωτηρία ψυχῶν (1 Pt. 1:9)," *BZ* 8 (1964) 262–76.

Davids
    Peter H. Davids, *The First Epistle of Peter* (New International Commentary on the New Testament; Grand Rapids: Eerdmans, 1990).

Davies, "Primitive Christology in I Peter"
    Paul E. Davies, "Primitive Christology in I Peter," in E. H. Barth and R. E. Cocroft, eds., *Festschrift to Honor F. Wilbur Gingrich* (Leiden: Brill, 1972) 115–22.

Déaut, "Le Targum de Gen. 22,8"
    Robert le Déaut, "Le Targum de Gen. 22,8 et 1 Pt. 1, 20," *RechSR* 49 (1961) 103–6.

Delling, "Der Bezug"
    Gerhard Delling, "Der Bezug der christlichen Existenz auf das Heilshandeln Gottes nach dem ersten Petrusbrief," in H. D. Betz and L. Schottroff, eds., *Neues Testament und christliche Existenz: Festschrift für Herbert Braun zum 70. Geburtstag* (Tübingen: Mohr [Siebeck], 1973) 95–113.

Deterding, "Exodus Motifs"
    Paul E. Deterding, "Exodus Motifs in First Peter," *Concordia Journal* 7 (1981) 58–65.

Dibelius, "Petrusbriefe"
    Martin Dibelius, "Petrusbriefe," *RGG* (ed. H. Gunkel et al.; 2d ed.; Tübingen: Mohr [Siebeck], 1930) 4.1113–15.

Dickey, "Conditions"
    S. Dickey, "Some Economic and Social Conditions of Asia Minor Affecting the Expansion of Christianity," in S. J. Case, ed., *Studies in Early Christianity* (New York: Century, 1928) 393–416.

Duplacy and Amphoux, "A propos de l'histoire du texte"
    Jean Duplacy and Christian-Bernard Amphoux, "A propos de l'histoire du texte de la première épître de Pierre," in Perrot, *Etudes*, 155–73.

Elliott, *Elect*
    John Hall Elliott, *The Elect and the Holy: An Exegetical Examination of 1 Peter 2:4–10 and the Phrase βασίλειον ἱεράτευμα* (NovTSup 12; Leiden: Brill, 1966).

Elliott, "1 Peter"
    John Hall Elliott, "1 Peter, Its Situation and Strategy: A Discussion with David Balch," in Talbert, *Perspectives*, 61–78.

Elliott, *Home*
    John Hall Elliott, *A Home for the Homeless: A Sociological Exegesis of 1 Peter, Its Situation and Strategy* (Philadelphia: Fortress, 1981).

Elliott, "Ministry"
    John Hall Elliott, "Ministry and Church Order in the NT: A Traditio-Historical Analysis (1 Pt 5, 1–5 & plls.)," *CBQ* 32 (1970) 367–91.

Elliott, "Patronage and Clientism"
    John Hall Elliott, "Patronage and Clientism in Early Christian Society," *Forum* 3 (1987) 39–48.

Elliott, "Peter, Silvanus and Mark"
    John Hall Elliott, "Peter, Silvanus and Mark in 1 Peter and Acts," in W. Haubeck and M. Bachmann, eds., *Wort in der Zeit: Neutestamentlichen Studien: Festgabe für Karl Heinrich Rengstorf zum 75. Geburtstag* (Leiden: Brill, 1980) 250–67.

Elliott, "Rehabilitation"
    John Hall Elliott, "The Rehabilitation of an Exegetical Step-Child: 1 Peter in Recent Research," in Talbert, *Perspectives*, 3–16. Reprinted from *JBL* 95 (1976) 243–54.

Erbes, "Was bedeutet"
    K. Erbes, "Was bedeutet ἀλλοτριοεπίσκοπος 1 Pt 4,15?" *ZNW* 19 (1919/20) 39–44.

Feinberg, "1 Peter 3:18–20"
    John S. Feinberg, "1 Peter 3:18–20, Ancient Mythology, and the Intermediate State," *WTJ* 48 (1986) 303–36.

Ferris, "Comparison"
    T. E. S. Ferris, "A Comparison of I. Peter and Hebrews," *CQR* 111 (1930) 123–27.

Ferris, "Epistle of James"
    T. E. S. Ferris, "The Epistle of James in Relation to 1 Peter," *CQR* 128 (1939) 303–8.

Feuillet, "Sacrifices"
    A. Feuillet, "Les 'sacrifices spirituels' du sacerdoce royal des baptisés (I P 2,5) et leur préparation dans l'Ancien Testament," *NRTh* 94 (1974) 704–28.

Filson, "Partakers"
    Floyd V. Filson, "Partakers with Christ: Suffering in First Peter," *Int* 9 (1955) 400–412.

Fink, "Use and Significance"
    Paul R. Fink, "The Use and Significance of en hōi in I Peter," *Grace Journal* 8/2 (1967) 33–39.

Fitzmyer, "First Peter"
    Joseph A. Fitzmyer, S.J., "The First Epistle of Peter," in R. E. Brown, J. A. Fitzmyer, and R. E. Murphy, eds., *The Jerome Biblical Commentary* (Englewood Cliffs, N.J.: Prentice-Hall, 1968) 362–68.

Flusser, "Dead Sea Sect"
    David Flusser, "The Dead Sea Sect and Pre-Pauline Christianity," in C. Rabin and Y. Yadin, eds., *Aspects of the Dead Sea Scrolls* (Scripta hierosolymitana 4; Jerusalem: Magnes, 1958) 215–66.

Foster, *Literary Relations*
    Ora Delmar Foster, *The Literary Relations of the "First Epistle of Peter"* (Transactions of the Connecticut Academy of Arts and Sciences 17; New Haven: Yale University Press, 1913) 363–538.

France, "Exegesis in Practice"
R. T. France, "Exegesis in Practice: Two Samples," in I. H. Marshall, ed., *New Testament Interpretation: Essays on Principles and Methods* (Grand Rapids: Eerdmans, 1977) 252–81.

Francis, "'Like Newborn Babes'"
J. Francis, "'Like Newborn Babes'—The Image of the Child in 1 Peter 2:2–3," in E. A. Livingstone, ed., *Studia Biblica 1978* (JSNTSup 3; Sheffield: JSOT Press, 1980) 3.111–17.

Fransen, "Une homélie"
Irénée Fransen, "Une homélie chrétienne: La première Épître de Pierre," *BVC* 31 (1960) 28–38.

Frings, "Zu I Petr 3,19 und 4,6"
Jos. Frings, "Zu I Petr 3,19 und 4,6," *BZ* 17 (1926) 75–88.

Furnish, "Elect Sojourners"
Victor Paul Furnish, "Elect Sojourners in Christ: An Approach to the Theology of I Peter," *PSTJ* 28 (1975) 1–11.

Gagé, *Classes*
Jean Gagé, *Les Classes Sociales dans l'Empire Romain* (Paris: Payot, 1964).

Galot, "La descente du Christ"
Jean Galot, "La descente du Christ aux enfers," *NRTh* 83 (1961) 471–91.

Gangel, "Pictures"
Kenneth O. Gangel, "Pictures of the Church in I Peter," *Grace Journal* 10 (1969) 29–35.

Gerhardsson, *Memory and Manuscript*
Birger Gerhardsson, *Memory and Manuscript* ASNU 22; (Lund: Gleerup, 1961).

Goldstein, "Kirche"
Horst Goldstein, "Die Kirche als Schar derer, die ihrem leidenden Herrn mit dem Ziel der Gottesgemeinschaft nachfolgen: Zum Gemeinverständnis von 1 Petr 2,21–25 und 3,18–22," *BibLeb* 15 (1974) 38–54.

Goldstein, "Paränese"
Horst Goldstein, "Die politischen Paränese in 1 Petr und Röm 13," *BibLeb* 14 (1973) 88–104.

Goldstein, *Paulinische Gemeinde*
Horst Goldstein, *Paulinische Gemeinde im Ersten Petrusbrief* (SBS 80; Stuttgart: Katholisches Bibelwerk, 1975).

Golebiewski, "L'Epître (1 P 5,6–11)"
R. P. E. Golebiewski, "L'Epître (1 P 5,6–11): Dieu nous console dans l'épreuve," *AsSeign* 57 (1965) 17–23.

Goodspeed, "Some Greek Notes"
Edgar J. Goodspeed, "Some Greek Notes: IV: Enoch in I Peter 3:19," *JBL* 73 (1954) 91–92.

Goppelt
Leonhard Goppelt, *Der Erste Petrusbrief* (KEK; ed. F. Hahn; Göttingen: Vandenhoeck & Ruprecht, 1978). ET by John E. Alsup, *A Commentary on 1 Peter* (Grand Rapids: Eerdmans, 1993).

Goppelt, *Christentum*
Leonhard Goppelt, *Christentum und Judentum im ersten und zweiten Jahrhundert* (BFCTh 2/55; Gütersloh: Bertelsmann, 1954).

Goppelt, "Der Staat"
Leonhard Goppelt, "Der Staat in der Sicht des Neuen Testaments," in H. Dombois and E. Wilkens, eds., *Macht und Recht: Beiträge zur lutherischen Staatslehre der Gegenwart* (Berlin: Lutherisches Verlagshaus, 1956) 9–21.

Goppelt, "Jesus"
Leonhard Goppelt, "Jesus und die 'Haustafel'-Tradition," in P. Hoffmann, ed. *Orientierung an Jesus: zur Theologie der Synoptiker; Für Joseph Schmid* (Freiburg: Herder, 1973) 93–106.

Goppelt, "Mission ou Révolution?"
Leonhard Goppelt, "Mission ou Révolution? La responsabilité du chrétien dans la société d'après la Première Epître de Pierre" (trans. A. Greiner), *Positions luthériennes* 194 (1969) 202–16.

Goppelt, "Prinzipien"
Leonhard Goppelt, "Prinzipien neutestamentlicher Sozialethik nach dem I Petrusbrief," in H. Baltensweiler and B. Reicke, eds., *Neues Testament und Geschichte; Historisches Geschehen und Deutung in Neuen Testament: Oscar Cullmann zum 70. Geburtstag* (Tübingen: Mohr [Siebeck], 1972) 285–96.

Gourbillon, "La Première Epître"
J. G. Gourbillon, "La Première Epître de Pierre," *Evangile* 50 (1963) 5–91.

Greeven, "Propheten"
Heinrich Greeven, "Propheten, Lehrer, Vorsteher bei Paulus," *ZNW* 44 (1952–53) 1–43.

Grosheide, "Kol. 3:1–4; 1 Petr. 1:3–5"
F. W. Grosheide, "Kol. 3:1–4; 1 Petr. 1:3–5; 1 Joh. 3:1–2," *Gereformeerd Theologisch Tijdschrift* 54 (1954) 139–47.

Grudem
Wayne A. Grudem, *The First Epistle of Peter: An Introduction and Commentary* (Tyndale New Testament Commentaries 17; Grand Rapids: Eerdmans, 1988).

Grundmann, "Die ΝΗΠΙΟΙ"
Walter Grundmann, "Die ΝΗΠΙΟΙ in der urchristlichen Paränese," *NTS* 5 (1959) 188–205.

Grunewald
W. Grunewald, with K. Januck, eds., *Das Neue Testament auf Papyrus*, vol. 1: *Die Katholischen Briefe* (Arbeiten zur Neutestamentlichen Textforschung 6; Berlin: de Gruyter, 1986).

Gschwind, *Die Niederfahrt*
Karl Gschwind, *Die Niederfahrt Christi in die Unterwelt* (NTAbh 2.3–5; Münster: Aschendorff, 1911).

Gundry, "Further *Verba*"
Robert H. Gundry, "Further *Verba* on *Verba Christi* in First Peter," *Bib* 55 (1974) 211–32.

Gundry, "*Verba Christi*"
Robert H. Gundry, "*Verba Christi* in I Peter: Their Implications Concerning the Authorship of I Peter and the Authenticity of the Gospel Tradi-

tion," *NTS* 13 (1967) 336–50.

Halas, "Sens dynamique"
Stanislas Halas, SCJ, "Sens dynamique de l'expression λαὸς εἰς περιποίησιν en 1 P 2,9," *Bib* 65 (1984) 254–58.

Hall, "For to This"
Randy Hall, "For to This You Have Been Called: The Cross and Suffering in 1 Peter," *ResQ* 19 (1976) 137–47.

Hall, "Paschal Baptism"
S. G. Hall, "Paschal Baptism," *StEv* 6 (TU 112; ed. E. A. Livingstone; Berlin: Akademie-Verlag, 1973) 239–51.

Hanson, "Salvation Proclaimed"
Anthony Hanson, "Salvation Proclaimed: I: 1 Peter 3:18–22," *ExpT* 93 (1981/82) 100–112.

Hardy, *Christianity*
Ernest George Hardy, *Christianity and the Roman Government* (London: Allen and Unwin, 1925).

Harrington, "Church"
Daniel J. Harrington, "The Church as Minority Group," in *God's People in Christ: New Testament Perspectives on the Church and Judaism* (Philadelphia: Fortress, 1980) 81–94.

Harris, "Emendation"
J. Rendel Harris, "An Emendation to 1 Peter 1.13," *ExpT* 41 (1929/30) 43.

Harris, "Further Note"
J. Rendel Harris, "A Further Note on the Use of Enoch in 1 Peter," *Expositor*, series 6, 4 (1901) 346–49.

Harris, "History"
J. Rendel Harris, "The History of a Conjectural Emendation," *Expositor*, series 6, 6 (1902) 378–90.

Harris, "Religious Meaning"
J. Rendel Harris, "The Religious Meaning of 1 Peter V.5," *Expositor*, series 8, 18 (1919) 131–39.

Harrison, "Exegetical Studies" [97]
Everett Falconer Harrison, "Exegetical Studies in 1 Peter," *BSac* 97 (1940) 200–209, 325–34, 448–55.

Harrison, "Exegetical Studies" [98]
Everett Falconer Harrison, "Exegetical Studies in 1 Peter," *BSac* 98 (1941) 459–68.

Hart
J. H. A. Hart, *The First Epistle General of Peter* (Expositor's Greek Testament; 5 vols.; ed. W. R. Nicoll; reprinted Grand Rapids: Eerdmans, 1974) 5.3–80.

Haselhurst, "Mark, My Son"
R. S. T. Haselhurst, "'Mark, My Son,'" *Theology* 13 (1926) 34–36.

Havelock, "Oral Composition"
Eric A. Havelock, "Oral Composition in the Oedipus Tyrannus of Sophocles," *New Literary History* 16 (1984) 175–97.

Hemer, "Address"
C. J. Hemer, "The Address of 1 Peter," *ExpT* 89 (1977/78) 239–43.

Hengel, *Judentum*
Martin Hengel, *Judentum und Hellenismus* (WUNT 10; Tübingen: Mohr [Siebeck], 1969).

Herrmann et al., "Genossenschaft"
P. Herrmann (84–99), J. H. Waszink (99–117), and K. Colpe (117–42), "Genossenschaft," *RAC* 10 (1978) 83–155.

Hiebert, "Example"
D. Edmond Hiebert, "Following Christ's Example: An Exposition of 1 Peter 2:21–25," *BSac* 139 (1982) 32–45.

Hiebert, "Living"
D. Edmond Hiebert, "Living in the Light of Christ's Return: An Exposition of 1 Peter 4:7–11," *BSac* 139 (1982) 243–54.

Hiebert, "Peter's Thanksgiving"
D. Edmond Hiebert, "Peter's Thanksgiving for Our Salvation," *Studia Missionalia* 29 (1980) 85–103.

Hill, "On Suffering and Baptism"
D. Hill, "On Suffering and Baptism in 1 Peter," *NovT* 18 (1976) 181–89.

Hillyer
Norman Hillyer, *1 and 2 Peter, Jude* (New International Biblical Commentary; Peabody, Mass.: Hendrickson, 1992).

Hillyer, "First Peter"
Norman Hillyer, "First Peter and the Feast of Tabernacles," *TynBul* 21 (1970) 39–70.

Hillyer, "'Rock-Stone' Imagery"
Norman Hillyer, "'Rock-Stone' Imagery in I Peter," *TynBul* 22 (1971) 58–81.

Hillyer, "Servant"
Norman Hillyer, "The Servant of God," *EvQ* 41 (1969) 143–60.

Hillyer, "Spiritual Milk"
N. Hillyer, "Spiritual Milk . . . Spiritual House," *TynBul* 20 (1969) 126.

Holmer and de Boor
Uwe Holmer and Werner de Boor, *Die Briefe des Petrus und der Brief des Judas* (Wuppertal: Brockhaus, 1978).

Holtz, "Dalton"
Traugott Holtz, "Dalton, William Joseph, S.J., Prof.: Christ's Proclamation to the Spirits. A Study of 1 Peter 3:18—4:6," (review) *ThLZ* 92 (1967) 359–60.

Hort
Fenton John Anthony Hort, *The First Epistle of St. Peter: I.1—II.17: The Greek Text with Introductory Lecture, Commentary, and Additional Notes* (London: Macmillan, 1898).

Hunzinger, "Babylon als Deckname"
Claus-Hunno Hunzinger, "Babylon als Deckname für Rom und die Datierung des 1. Petrusbriefes," in H. Graf Reventlow, ed., *Gottes Wort und Gottes Land: Hans-Wilhelm Hertzberg zum 70. Geburtstag* (Göttingen: Vandenhoeck & Ruprecht, 1965) 67–77.

Hunzinger, "Zur Struktur"
Claus-Hunno Hunzinger, "Zur Struktur der Christus-Hymnen in Phil 2 und 1. Petr 3," in E. Lohse, with C. Burchard and B. Schaller, eds., *Der Ruf Jesu und die Antwort der Gemeinde: Exegetische Untersuchungen: Joachim Jeremias zum 70. Geburtstag* (Göttingen: Vandenhoeck & Ruprecht, 1970) 142–56.

Hutton, "Ruling"
John A. Hutton, "A Ruling from 'First Peter,'" *Expositor*, series 8, 23 (1922) 420–27.

Jeremias, "Zwischen Karfreitag und Ostern"
Joachim Jeremias, "Zwischen Karfreitag und Ostern: Descensus und Ascensus in der Karfreitagstheologie des Neuen Testamentes," *ZNW* 42 (1949) 194–201.

Johnson, "Fire"
Dennis E. Johnson, "Fire in God's House: Imagery from Malachi 3 in Peter's Theology of Suffering (1 Pet 4:12–19)," *JETS* 29 (1986) 285–94.

Johnson, "Will of God"
George Johnson, "The Will of God: V: In I Peter and I John," *ExpT* 72 (1960/61) 237–40.

Johnson, "Asia Minor"
Sherman E. Johnson, "Asia Minor and Early Christianity," in J. Neusner, ed., *Christianity, Judaism, and Other Greco-Roman Cults: Studies for Morton Smith at Sixty, Part Two: Early Christianity* (4 vols.; Leiden: Brill, 1975) 2.77–145.

Johnson, "Early Christianity"
Sherman E. Johnson, "Early Christianity in Asia Minor," *JBL* 77 (1958) 1–17.

Johnson, "Preaching"
Sherman E. Johnson, "The Preaching to the Dead," *JBL* 79 (1960) 48–51.

Johnson, "Unresolved Questions"
Sherman E. Johnson, "Unresolved Questions about Early Christianity in Asia Minor," in D. E. Aune, ed., *Studies in New Testament and Early Christian Literature: Essays in Honor of Allen P. Wikgren* (NovTSup 33; Leiden: Brill, 1972) 181–93.

Jones, "Christian Behavior"
Russell Bradley Jones, "Christian Behavior under Fire (First Epistle of Peter)," *RevExp* 46 (1949) 56–66.

Jonsen, "Moral Theology"
A. R. Jonsen, "The Moral Theology of the First Epistle of St. Peter," *Sciences ecclésiastiques* 16 (1964) 93–105.

Judge, *Social Pattern*
E. A. Judge, *The Social Pattern of the Christian Groups in the First Century* (London: Tyndale, 1960).

Kamlah, "ὑποτάσσεσθαι"
Ehrhard Kamlah, "ὑποτάσσεσθαι in den neutestamentlichen 'Haustafeln,'" in O. Böcher and K. Haacker, eds., *Verborum Veritas: Festschrift für Gustar Stählin zum 70. Geburtstag* (Wuppertal: Brockhaus, 1970) 237–43.

Kelly
J. N. D. Kelly, *A Commentary on the Epistles of Peter and of Jude* (BNTC; London: Black; HNTC; New York: Harper & Row, 1969).

Kendall, "Function"
David W. Kendall, "The Literary and Theological Function of 1 Peter 1:3–12," in Talbert, *Perspectives*, 103–20.

Kennedy, *Classical Rhetoric*
George A. Kennedy, *Classical Rhetoric and Its Christian and Secular Tradition from Ancient to Modern Times* (Chapel Hill: University of North Carolina Press, 1980).

Kennedy, *NT Interpretation*
George A. Kennedy, *New Testament Interpretation through Rhetorical Criticism* (Chapel Hill: University of North Carolina Press, 1984).

Ketter
Peter Ketter, *Hebräerbrief, Jakobusbrief, Petrusbriefe, Judasbrief* (Herders Bibelkommentar; Freiburg: Herder, 1950).

Ketter, "Das allgemeine Priestertum: II"
Peter Ketter, "Das allgemeine Priestertum: II. Das allgemeine Priestertum der Gläubigen nach dem ersten Petrusbrief," *TThZ* 56 (1947) 43–51.

Kiley, "Like Sara"
Mark Kiley, "Like Sara: The Tale of Terror Behind 1 Peter 3:6," *JBL* 106 (1987) 689–92.

Kirk, "Endurance in Suffering"
Gorden E. Kirk, "Endurance in Suffering in I Peter," *BSac* 138 (1981) 46–56.

Kline, "Ethics"
Leslie Kline, "Ethics for the End Time: An Exegesis of I Peter 4:7–11," *ResQ* 7 (1963) 113–23.

Knibb, *Qumran*
Michael A. Knibb, *The Qumran Community* (Cambridge Commentaries on Writings of the Jewish and Christian World, 200 BC to AD 200; Cambridge: Cambridge University Press, 1987).

Knopf
Rudolph Knopf, *Die Briefe Petri und Judä* (KEK 7th ed.; Göttingen: Vandenhoeck & Ruprecht, 1912).

Knox, "Pliny and I Peter"
John Knox, "Pliny and I Peter: A Note on I Pet 4:14–16 and 3:15," *JBL* 72 (1953) 187–89.

Krafft, "Christologie"
Eva Krafft, "Christologie und Anthropologie im 1. Petrusbrief," *EvTh* 10 (1950/51) 120–26.

Krodel
Gerhard Krodel, *The First Letter of Peter* (Proclamation Commentaries: The New Testament Witness for Preaching; Philadelphia: Fortress, 1977).

Kuhn, "New Light"
Karl Georg Kuhn, "New Light on Temptation, Sin, and Flesh in the New Testament," in K.

Stendahl, ed., *The Scrolls and the New Testament* (New York: Harper and Brothers, 1957) 94–113.

Kühschelm, "Lebendige Hoffnung"
Roman Kühschelm, "'Lebendige Hoffnung' (1 Petr 1,3–12)," *BLit* 56 (1983) 202–6.

Kümmel, *Introduction*
Werner Georg Kümmel, *Introduction to the New Testament* (trans. H. C. Kee; Nashville: Abingdon, 1975).

Lampe, "Das Spiel"
Peter Lampe, "Das Spiel mit dem Petrusnamen— Matt. xvi.18," *NTS* 25 (1978/79) 227–45.

Lampe and Luz, "Nachpaulinisches Christentum"
Peter Lampe and Ulrich Luz, "Nachpaulinisches Christentum und pagane Gesellschaft," in J. Becker, ed., *Die Anfänge des Christentums* (Stuttgart: Kohlhammer, 1987) 185–216.

LaVerdiere, "Covenant Theology"
Eugene A. LaVerdiere, "Covenant Theology in 1 Peter 1:1—2:10," *Bible Today* 42 (1969) 2909–16.

LaVerdiere, "Grammatical Ambiguity"
Eugene A LaVerdiere, "A Grammatical Ambiguity in 1 Pet. 2:12," *CBQ* 36 (1974) 89–94.

Lea, "How Peter Learned the OT"
Thomas Lea, "How Peter Learned the Old Testament," *Southwestern Journal of Theology* 22 (1980) 96–102.

Leaney
A. R. C. Leaney, *The Letters of Peter and Jude* (Cambridge Bible Commentary; Cambridge: University Press, 1967).

Leaney, "Passover"
A. R. C. Leaney, "I Peter and the Passover: An Interpretation," *NTS* 10 (1964) 238–51.

Lecomte, "Aimer la vie"
Pierre Lecomte, "Aimer la vie: I Pierre 3/10 (Psaume 34/13)," *EThR* 56 (1981) 288–93.

Lepelley, "Le contexte"
Claude Lepelley, "Le contexte historique de la première lettre de Pierre," in Perrot, *Etudes,* 43–64.

Lewis and Reinhold, "Conflict of Religions"
N. Lewis and M. Reinhold, eds., "The Conflict of Religions and the Triumph of Christianity," in *Roman Civilization: Sourcebook II: The Empire* (New York: Harper & Row, 1966) 552–610.

Lippert, "Leben"
Peter Lippert, "Leben als Zeugnis," *Studia Moralia* 3 (1965) 226–68.

Lohse, "Parenesis"
Eduard Lohse, "Parenesis and Kerygma in 1 Peter" (trans. John Steely), in Talbert, *Perspectives,* 37–60. ET of "Paränese und Kerygma im 1. Petrusbrief," *ZNW* 45 (1954) 68–89.

Love, "First Epistle"
Julian Price Love, "The First Epistle of Peter," *Int* 8 (1954) 63–87.

Lührmann, "Neutestamentliche Haustafeln"
Dieter Lührmann, "Neutestamentliche Haustafeln und antike Ökonomie," *NTS* 27 (1980) 83–97.

Luther
Martin Luther, *D. Martin Luthers Epistel-Auslegung* (ed. H. Günther and E. Volk; Göttingen: Vandenhoeck & Ruprecht, 1983).

Lutz, *Musonius Rufus*
Cora E. Lutz, *Musonius Rufus, "The Roman Socrates"* (Yale Classical Studies 10; New Haven: Yale University Press, 1947).

Magie, *Roman Rule*
David Magie, *Roman Rule in Asia Minor to the End of the Third Century after Christ* (2 vols.; Princeton: Princeton University Press, 1950; reprinted New York: Arno, 1988]).

Malherbe, *Ancient Epistolary Theorists*
Abraham J. Malherbe, *Ancient Epistolary Theorists* (SBLSBS 19; Atlanta: Scholars Press, 1988).

Malherbe, *Moral Exhortation*
Abraham J. Malherbe, *Moral Exhortation: A Greco-Roman Sourcebook* (LEC 4; Philadelphia: Westminster, 1986).

Manley, "Babylon on the Nile"
G. T. Manley, "Babylon on the Nile," *EvQ* 16 (1944) 138–46.

Manns, "'La maison'"
Frederic Manns, "'La maison où réside l'Esprit.' 1 P 2,5 et son arrière-plan juif," *SBFLA* 34 (1984) 207–24.

Manns, "Sara"
Frederic Manns, "Sara, modèle de la femme obéissante: Etude de l'arrière-plan juif de 1 Pierre 3,5–6," *BeO* 26 (1984) 65–73.

Manson, "Grace in the NT"
William Manson, "Grace in the New Testament," in W. T. Whitly, ed., *The Doctrine of Grace* (New York: Macmillan, 1931) 33–60.

Margot
Jean-Claude Margot, *Les Epîtres de Pierre* (Geneva: Labor et Fides, 1960).

Marshall, "Holy House"
John S. Marshall, "'An Holy House, an Holy Priesthood' (I Peter ii.5)," *ATR* 28 (1946) 227–28.

Martin, "Composition"
Ralph P. Martin, "The Composition of I Peter in Recent Study," *Vox Evangelica* 1 (1962) 29–42.

Martin, *Metaphor*
Troy W. Martin, *Metaphor and Composition in 1 Peter* (SBLDS 131; Atlanta: Scholars Press, 1992).

Martin, "Present Indicative"
Troy W. Martin, "The Present Indicative in the Eschatological Statements of 1 Peter 1:6, 8," *JBL* 111 (1992) 307–12.

Marxsen, "Der Mitälteste"
Willi Marxsen, "Der Mitälteste und Zeuge der Leiden Christi," in C. Andresen and G. Klein, eds., *Theologia Crucis—Signum Crucis; Festschrift für Erich Dinkler zum 70. Geburtstag* (Tübingen: Mohr [Siebeck] 1979) 377–93.

May, "Die Zeit ist da"
Gerhard May, "Die Zeit ist da, dass das Gericht angänge am Hause Gottes," in Franklin Clark Fry, ed., *Geschichtswirklichkeit und Glaubensbewährung* (*Festschrift* Fr. Miller; Stuttgart: Evangelisches Verlagswerk, 1967) 41–49.

McCabe, "What Is the Church?"
Herbert McCabe, "What Is the Church?—VIII," *Life of the Spirit* 18 (1963) 162–74.

McCaughey, "Re-Reading"
J. D. McCaughey, "On Re-Reading 1 Peter," *AusBR* 31 (1983) 33–44.

McCaughey, "Three 'Persecution Documents'"
J. D. McCaughey, "Three 'Persecution Documents' of the New Testament," *AusBR* 17 (1969) 27–40.

Meade, *Pseudonymity and Canon*
David G. Meade, *Pseudonymity and Canon: An Investigation into the Relationship of Authorship and Authority in Jewish and Earliest Christian Tradition* (WUNT 39; Tübingen: Mohr [Siebeck], 1986; Grand Rapids: Eerdmans, 1987).

Meecham, "First Epistle"
H. G. Meecham, "The First Epistle of St. Peter," *ExpT* 48 (1936/37) 22–24.

Meecham, "Note"
H. G. Meecham, "A Note on 1 Peter ii.12," *ExpT* 75 (1953/54) 93.

Meeks, *Moral World*
Wayne A. Meeks, *The Moral World of the First Christians* (LEC 6; Philadelphia: Westminster, 1986).

Michaels
J. Ramsey Michaels, *1 Peter* (Word Biblical Commentary 49; Waco: Word, 1988).

Michaels, "Eschatology"
J. Ramsey Michaels, "Eschatology in I Peter iii.17," *NTS* 13 (1967) 394–400.

Michl, "Die Presbyter"
Johann Michl, "Die Presbyter des ersten Petrusbriefes," in H. Fleckenstein, ed., *Ortskirche, Weltkirche: Festgabe für Julius Kardinal Döpfner* (Würzburg: Echter, 1973) 48–62.

Millauer, *Leiden*
Helmut Millauer, *Leiden als Gnade: Eine Traditionsgeschichtliche Untersuchung zur Leidenstheologie des ersten Petrusbriefes* (Europäische Hochschulschriften, 23/56; Bern: Herbert Lang, 1976).

Miller, "Deliverance and Destiny"
Donald G. Miller, "Deliverance and Destiny: Salvation in First Peter," *Int* 9 (1955) 413–25.

Minear, "House of Living Stones"
Paul S. Minear, "The House of Living Stones: A Study of 1 Peter 2:4–12," *Ecumenical Review* 34 (1982) 238–48.

Mitton, "Relationship"
C. L. Mitton, "The Relationship between I Peter and Ephesians," *JTS*, n.s. 1 (1950) 67–73.

Moffatt
James Moffatt, *The General Epistles: James, Peter, and Jude* (MNTC; Garden City, N.Y.: Doubleday, Doran, 1928).

Morris, "1 Peter iii.19"
W. D. Morris, "1 Peter iii.19," *ExpT* 38 (1926/27) 470.

Moule, "Nature"
Charles F. D. Moule, "The Nature and Purpose of I Peter," *NTS* 3 (1956) 1–11.

Moule, "Sanctuary"
Charles F. D. Moule, "Sanctuary and Sacrifice in the Church of the New Testament," *JTS*, n.s. 1 (1950) 29–41.

Moule, "Some Reflections"
Charles F. D. Moule, "Some Reflections on the 'Stone' Testimonia in Relation to the Name Peter," *NTS* 2 (1955/56) 56–59.

Moulton and Milligan, *Vocabulary*
J. H. Moulton and G. Milligan, *The Vocabulary of the Greek Testament* (London: Hodder and Stoughton, 1914; reprinted Grand Rapids: Eerdmans, 1949).

Nauck, "Freude"
Wolfgang Nauck, "Freude im Leiden: Zum Problem einer urchristlichen Verfolgungstradition," *ZNW* 46 (1955) 68–80.

Nauck, "Probleme"
Wolfgang Nauck, "Probleme des frühchristlichen Amtsverständnisses," *ZNW* 48 (1957) 200–220.

Neugebauer, "Zur Deutung"
F. Neugebauer, "Zur Deutung und Bedeutung des 1. Petrusbriefes," *NTS* 26 (1980) 61–86.

Omanson, "Suffering"
Roger Omanson, "Suffering for Righteousness' Sake (1 Pet 3:13—4:11)," *RevExp* 79 (1982) 439–50.

Osborne, "Guide Lines"
Thomas P. Osborne, "Guide Lines for Christian Suffering: A Source-Critical and Theological Study of 1 Peter 2,21–25," *Bib* 64 (1983) 381–408.

Osborne, "L'utilisation"
T. P. Osborne, "L'utilisation des citations de l'Ancien Testament dans la première épître de Pierre," *RThL* 12 (1981) 64–77.

Patterson, "Roles in Marriage"
Dorothy Patterson, "Roles in Marriage: A Study in Submission: 1 Peter 3:1–7," *Theological Educator* 13 (1982) 70–79.

Percy, *Probleme*
Ernst Percy, *Die Probleme der Kolosser- und Epheserbriefe* (Skrifter utgivvne av Kungl. Humanistika Vetenskapssamfundet i Lund 39; Acta Reg. Societatis Humaniorum Litterarum Lundensis; Lund: Gleerup, 1946).

Perdelwitz, *Mysterienreligion*
E. Richard Perdelwitz, *Die Mysterienreligion und das*

Problem des 1. Petrusbriefes (Religionsversuche und Vorarbeiten 11/3; Giessen: Töpelmann, 1911).

Perrot, "La descente aux enfers"
C. Perrot, "La descente aux enfers et la predication aux morts," in Perrot, Etudes, 231–46.

Perrot, Etudes
C. Perrot, ed., Etudes sur la Première Lettre de Pierre (LD 102; Paris: Cerf, 1980).

Philipps, Kirche
Karl Philipps, Kirche in der Gesellschaft nach dem 1. Petrusbrief (Gütersloh: Gütersloher Verlagshaus-Gerd Mohn, 1971).

Piper, "Hope"
John Piper, "Hope as the Motivation of Love: I Peter 3:9–12," NTS 26 (1980) 212–31.

Premerstein, "Clientes"
A. von Premerstein, "Clientes," PW 7.23–55.

Prete, "L'espressione"
Benedetto Prete, "L'espressione hē en Babylōni syneklektē di 1 Pt. 5,13," Vetera Christianorum 21 (1984) 335–52.

Price, Rituals and Power
S. R. F. Price, Rituals and Power: The Roman Imperial Cult in Asia Minor (Cambridge: Cambridge University Press, 1984).

Quinn, "Notes"
Jerome D. Quinn, "Notes on the Text of the P[72] 1 Pt 2,3; 5,14; and 5,9," CBQ 27 (1965) 241–49.

Radermacher, "Der erste Petrusbrief"
Ludwig Radermacher, "Der erste Petrusbrief und Silvanus; mit einem Nachwort in eigener Sache," ZNW 25 (1926) 287–99.

Refoulé, "Bible"
François Refoulé, "Bible et éthique sociale: Lire aujourd'hui 1 Pierre," Le Supplément 131 (1979) 457–82.

Reicke
Bo Reicke, The Epistles of James, Peter and Jude (Anchor Bible 37; Garden City: Doubleday, 1964).

Reicke, "Gnosis"
Bo Reicke, "Die Gnosis der Männer nach I. Ptr. 3:7," in W. Eltester, ed., Neutestamentliche Studien für Rudolph Bultmann zu seinem 70. Geburtstag (ZNW Beihefte 21; Berlin: Töpelmann, 1954) 296–304.

Reicke, Spirits
Bo Reicke, The Disobedient Spirits and Christian Baptism (ASNU 13; Copenhagen: Munksgaard, 1946).

Reynolds, "Zero Tense"
Stephen M. Reynolds, "The Zero Tense in Greek: A Critical Note," WTJ 32 (1969) 68–72.

Richard, "Christology"
Earl Richard, "The Functional Christology of 1 Peter," in Talbert, Perspectives, 121–40.

Richards, "I Pet. iii 21"
G. C. Richards, "I Pet.' iii 21," JTS 32 (1931) 77.

Robinson, Redating
John A. T. Robinson, Redating the New Testament (Philadelphia: Westminster, 1976).

Russell, "Eschatology"
Ronald Russell, "Eschatology and Ethics in 1 Peter," EvQ 47 (1975) 78–84.

Sander, "ΠΨΡΩΣΙΣ and the First Epistle of Peter"
Emilie T. Sander, "ΠΨΡΩΣΙΣ and the First Epistle of Peter 4:12" (précis), HTR 60 (1967) 501.

Sandevoir, "Un Royaume de Prêtres?"
Pierre Sandevoir, "Un Royaume de Prêtres?" in Perrot, Etudes, 219–29.

Schaefer, "Paroikoi"
Hans Schaefer, "Paroikoi," PW Halbband 36.18.4, 1695–1707.

Scharlemann, "Descant"
Martin H. Scharlemann, "An Apostolic Descant (An Exegetical Study of 1 Peter 1:3–12)," Concordia Journal 2 (1976) 9–17.

Scharlemann, "Exodus Ethics"
Martin H. Scharlemann, "Exodus Ethics: Part One—I Peter 1:13–16," Concordia Journal 2 (1976) 165–70.

Scharlemann, "'He descended'"
Martin H. Scharlemann, "'He descended into Hell': An Interpretation of 1 Peter 3:18–20," CTM 27 (1956) 81–94.

Scharlemann, "Why the Kuriou"
Martin H. Scharlemann, "Why the Kuriou in 1 Peter 1:25?" CTM 30 (1959) 352–56.

Schattenmann, "Apocalypse"
Johannes Schattenmann, "The Little Apocalypse of the Synoptics and the First Epistle of Peter," Theology Today 11 (1954) 193–98.

Schelkle
Karl Hermann Schelkle, Die Petrusbriefe, der Judasbrief (3d ed.; HThKNT; Freiburg: Herder, 1970).

Schelkle, "Leiden"
Karl Hermann Schelkle, "Das Leiden des Gottesknechtes als Form christlichen Lebens (nach dem ersten Petrusbrief)," BK 16 (1961) 14–16.

Schiwy
Günther Schiwy, Die Katholischen Briefe (Der Christ in der Welt. Eine Enzyklopädie, Reihe VI; Das Buch der Bücher 12; Stein am Rhein: Christiana, 1973).

Schlier, "Adhortatio"
Heinrich Schlier, "Eine Adhortatio aus Rom: Die Botschaft des Ersten Petrusbriefes," in idem, ed., Strukturen christlicher Existenz: Beiträge zur Erneuerung des geistlichen Lebens: Festgabe P. Friedrich Wulf (Würzburg: Echter, 1968) 59–80.

Schlier, "γάλα"
Heinrich Schlier, "γαλά," ThWNT 1.644–45.

Schlosser, "Ancien Testament"
Jacques Schlosser, "Ancien Testament et

Christologie dans la Prima Petri," in Perrot, *Etudes*, 65–96.

Schlosser, "I Pierre 3,5b–6"
Jacques Schlosser, "I Pierre 3,5b–6," *Bib* 64 (1983) 409–10.

Scholer, "Women's Adornment"
David Scholer, "Women's Adornment," *Daughters of Sarah* 6 (1980) 3–6.

Schroeder, "Once you were no people"
David Schroeder, "Once you were no people . . . ," in Harry Huebner, ed., *The Church as Theological Community: Essays in Honour of David Schroeder* (Winnipeg: CMBC Publications, 1990) 37–65.

Schröger, "Lasst euch auferbauen"
Friedrich Schröger, "'Lasst euch auferbauen zu einem geisterfüllten Haus' (1 Ptr 2,4.5): Eine Überlegung zu dem Verhältnis von Ratio und Pneuma," in W. Friedberger and F. Schnider, eds., *Theologie, Gemeinde, Seelsorger* (Munich: Kösel, 1979) 138–45.

Schröger, "Verfassung"
Friedrich Schröger, "Die Verfassung der Gemeinde des ersten Petrusbriefes," in J. Hainz, ed., *Kirche im Werden: Studien zum Thema Amt und Gemeinde im Neuen Testament* (Munich: Schöningh, 1976) 239–52.

Schückler, "Wandel im Glauben"
Georg Schückler, "Wandel im Glauben als missionarisches Zeugnis," *ZMR* 51 (1967) 289–99.

Schüssler Fiorenza, "Cultic Language in Qumran"
Elisabeth Schüssler Fiorenza, "Cultic Language in Qumran and in the NT," *CBQ* 38 (1976) 159–77.

Schutter, *Hermeneutic*
William L. Schutter, *Hermeneutic and Composition in I Peter* (WUNT 2/30; Tübingen: Mohr [Siebeck], 1989).

Schwank, "Diabolus"
P. Benedikt Schwank, "Diabolus tamquam leo rugiens," *Erbe und Auftrag* 38 (1962) 15–20.

Schwank, "L'Epître (1 P 3,8–15)"
P. Benedikt Schwank, "L'Epître (1 P 3,8–15)," *AsSeign* 59 (1966) 16–32.

Schwank, "Wie Freie"
P. Benedikt Schwank, "Wie Freie—aber als Sklaven Gottes (1 Petr 2,16)," *Erbe und Auftrag* 36 (1960) 5–12.

Schwank et al.
Benedikt Schwank, Alois Stöger, and Wilhelm Thüsing, *The Epistles of St. Peter, St. John and St. Jude* (New Testament for Spiritual Reading 11; London: Sheed and Ward, 1969).

Schweizer
Eduard Schweizer, *Der Erste Petrusbrief* (3d ed.; Zürcher Bibelkommentare; Zurich: Theologischer Verlag, 1972).

Schweizer, "1. Petrus 4,6"
Eduard Schweizer, "1. Petrus 4,6 . . . ," *ThZ* 8 (1952) 152–54.

Selwyn
Ernest Gordon Selwyn, *The First Epistle of St. Peter* (2d ed.; London: Macmillan, 1955).

Selwyn, "Eschatology"
Ernest Gordon Selwyn, "Eschatology in I Peter," in W. D. Davies and D. Daube, eds., *The Background of the New Testament and Its Eschatology* (Festschrift C. H. Dodd; Cambridge: University Press, 1956) 394–401.

Selwyn, "Persecutions"
Ernest Gordon Selwyn, "The Persecutions in I Peter," *Bulletin of the Studiorum Novi Testamenti Societas* 1 (1950) 39–50.

Selwyn, "Problem"
Ernest Gordon Selwyn, "The Problem of the Authorship of I Peter," *ExpT* 59 (1947/48) 256–58.

Senior
Donald Senior, *1 and 2 Peter* (NT Message 20; Wilmington: Glazier, 1980).

Senior, "Conduct"
Donald Senior, "The Conduct of Christians in the World (2:11—3:12)," *RevExp* 79 (1982) 427–38.

Seufert, "Das Abhängigkeitsverhältnis"
W. Seufert, "Das Abhängigkeitsverhältnis des I. Petrusbriefs vom Römerbrief," *ZWTh* 16 (1874) 360–88.

Shimada, "Formula"
Kazuhito Shimada, "The Christological Creedal Formula in I Peter 3:18–22—Reconsidered," *AJBI* 5 (1979) 154–76.

Shimada, *Formulary Material*
Kazuhito Shimada, *The Formulary Material in First Peter* (Ann Arbor: Xerox University Microfilms, 1966).

Sieffert, "Die Heilsbedeutung"
E. L. Sieffert, "Die Heilsbedeutung des Leidens und Sterbens Christi nach dem ersten Briefe des Petrus," *Jahrbücher für deutsche Theologie* 20 (1875) 371–440.

Sleeper, "Political Responsibility"
C. Freeman Sleeper, "Political Responsibility According to I Peter," *NovT* 10 (1968) 270–86.

Smith, *Petrine Controversies*
Terence V. Smith, *Petrine Controversies in Early Christianity* (WUNT 2/15; Tübingen: Mohr [Siebeck], 1985).

Smothers, "Letter"
Edgar R. Smothers, "A Letter from Babylon," *Classical Journal* 22 (1926) 202–9.

Snodgrass, "I Peter II.1–10"
Klyne R. Snodgrass, "I Peter II.1–10: Its Formation and Literary Affinities," *NTS* 24 (1977) 97–106.

Sordi, *Christians*
Marta Sordi, *The Christians and the Roman Empire* (trans. A. Bedini; Norman: University of Oklahoma Press, 1986).

Souček, "Das Gegenüber"
  J. B. Souček, "Das Gegenüber von Gemeinde und Welt nach dem ersten Petrusbrief," *Communio Viatorum* 3 (1960) 5–13.
Spicq
  Ceslas Spicq, *Les Epîtres de Saint Pierre* (SB; Paris: Librairie Lecoffre, 1966).
Spicq, "La Iᵃ Petri"
  Ceslas Spicq, "La Iᵃ Petri et le témoignage évangélique de saint Pierre," *StTh* 20 (1966) 37–61.
Spicq, "L'Epître (1 P 4,7–11)
  Ceslas Spicq, "L'Epître (1 P 4,7–11)," *AsSeign* 50 (1966) 15–29.
Spicq, "Place"
  Ceslas Spicq, "La place ou le rôle des jeunes dans certaines communautés néotestamentaires," *RB* 76 (1969) 508–27.
Spörri, *Gemeindegedanke*
  Theophil Spörri, *Der Gemeindegedanke im ersten Petrusbrief* (Neutestamentliche Forschung 2/2; Gütersloh: Bertelsmann, 1925).
Steuer, "1 Petr 3,17—4,6"
  A. Steuer, "1 Petr 3,17—4,6," *ThGl* 30 (1938) 675–78.
Steuernagel, "Exiled Community"
  Valdir R. Steuernagel, "An Exiled Community as a Missionary Community: A Study Based on 1 Peter 2:9, 10," *Evangelical Review of Theology* 10 (1986) 8–18.
Strobel, "Leiden"
  August Strobel, "Macht Leiden von Sünde frei? Zur Problematik von 1. Petr. 4,1f.," *ThZ* 19 (1963) 412–25.
Strugnell, "Notes"
  John Strugnell, "Notes on 1QS 1,17–18; 8,3–4 and 1QM 17,8–9," *CBQ* 29 (1967) 580–82.
Stuhlmueller, "Baptism"
  Carroll Stuhlmueller, "Baptism: New Life through the Blood of Jesus, *Worship* 39 (1965) 207–17.
Sylva, "Studies"
  Dennis Sylva, "1 Peter Studies: The State of the Discipline," *BTB* 10 (1980) 155–63.
Synge, "1 Peter 3:18–21"
  F. C. Synge, "1 Peter 3:18–21," *ExpT* 82 (1970/71) 311.
Talbert, *Learning Through Suffering*
  Charles H. Talbert, "The Educational Value of Suffering in 1 Peter," in idem, *Learning Through Suffering: The Educational Value of Suffering in the New Testament and in Its Milieu* (Zacchaeus Studies: New Testament; Collegeville, Minn.: Liturgical Press, 1991) 42–57.
Talbert, "Once Again"
  Charles H. Talbert, "Once Again: The Plan of 1 Peter," in Talbert, *Perspectives,* 141–51.
Talbert, *Perspectives*
  Charles H. Talbert, ed., *Perspectives on 1 Peter*

(NABPR Special Series 9; Macon, Ga.: Mercer University Press, 1986).
Tarrech, "Le milieu"
  Armand Puig Tarrech, "Le milieu de la Première Epître de Pierre," *Revista Catalana de Teología* 5 (1980) 95–129, 331–402.
Teichert "1. Ptr. 2,13"
  Horst Teichert, "1. Ptr. 2,13—eine crux interpretum?" *ThLZ* 74 (1949) 303–4.
Tenney, "Parallels"
  Merrill C. Tenney, "Some Possible Parallels between 1 Peter and John," in R. N. Longenecker and M. C. Tenney, eds., *New Dimensions in New Testament Study* (Grand Rapids: Zondervan, 1974) 370–77.
Thiede, "Babylone"
  C. P. Thiede, "Babylone, der andere Ort: Anmerkungen zu 1 Petr 5,13 und Apg 12,17," *Bib* 67 (1986) 532–38.
Thompson, "Submissive"
  James W. Thompson, "'Be Submissive to Your Masters': A Study of I Peter 2:18–25," *ResQ* 9 (1966) 66–78.
Thornton, "Liturgy"
  T. C. G. Thornton, "I Peter: A Paschal Liturgy?" *JTS,* n.s. 12 (1961) 14–26.
Thraede, "Frau"
  K. Thraede, "Frau," *RAC* 8 (1972) 197–269.
Thurston, "Interpreting First Peter"
  Robert W. Thurston, "Interpreting First Peter," *JETS* 17 (1974) 171–82.
du Toit, "Significance"
  A. B. du Toit, "The Significance of Discourse Analysis for New Testament Interpretation and Translation: Introductory Remarks with Special Reference to I Peter 1:3–13," *Neot* 8 (1974) 54–79.
Tripp, "Eperōtēma"
  David H. Tripp, "Eperōtēma (I Peter 3²¹): A Liturgist's Note," *ExpT* 92 (1980/81) 267–70.
van Unnik, "Christianity"
  W. C. van Unnik, "Christianity According to I Peter," *ExpT* 68 (1956/57) 79–83.
van Unnik, "Classical Parallel"
  W. C. van Unnik, "A Classical Parallel to I Peter II 14 and 20," in idem, *Sparsa Collecta* 2.106–10.
van Unnik, "Die Rücksicht"
  W. C. van Unnik, "Die Rücksicht auf die Reaktion der Nicht-Christen in der altchristlichen Paränese," in idem, *Sparsa Collecta* 2.307–22.
van Unnik, "Paganism"
  W. C. van Unnik, "The Critique of Paganism in I Peter 1:28," in E. E. Ellis and M. Wilcox; eds., *Neotestamentica et Semitica: Studies in Honour of Matthew Black* (Edinburgh: Clark, 1969) 129–42.
van Unnik, "Redemption"
  W. C. van Unnik, "The Redemption in 1 Peter I 18–19 and the Problem of the First Epistle of Peter," in idem, *Sparsa Collecta* 2.3–82.

van Unnik, *Sparsa Collecta*

W. C. van Unnik, *Sparsa Collecta* (2 vols.; NovTSup 29, 30; Leiden: Brill, 1973, 1980).

van Unnik, "Teaching"

W. C. van Unnik, "The Teaching of Good Works in 1 Peter," in idem, *Sparsa Collecta* 2.83–105.

Vanhoye, "L'Epître (I P 2,1–10)"

Albert Vanhoye, S.J. "L'Epître (I P 2,1–10): La maison spirituelle," *AsSeign* 43 (1964) 16–29.

Vanhoye, "1 Pierre"

Albert Vanhoye, S.J., "1 Pierre au carrefour des théologies du nouveau Testament," in Perrot, *Etudes*, 97–128.

de Villiers, "Joy"

J. L. de Villiers, "Joy in Suffering in I Peter," *Neot* 9 (1975; 2d ed. 1980) 64–86.

Vogels, *Christi Abstieg*

Heinz-Jürgen Vogels, *Christi Abstieg ins Totenreich und das Läuterung an den Toten* (Freiburger Theologische Studien 102; Freiburg: Herder, 1976).

Völter, "Bemerkungen"

D. Völter, "Bemerkungen zu I. Pt 3 und 4," *ZNW* 9 (1908) 74–77.

Wand

J. W. C. Wand, *The General Epistles of St. Peter and St. Jude* (Westminster Commentaries; London: Methuen, 1934).

Wand, "Lessons"

J. W. C. Wand, "The Lessons of First Peter: A Survey of Recent Interpretation," *Int* 9 (1955) 387–99.

Wells, "Images"

Paul Wells, "Les images bibliques de l'Église dans I Pierre 2, 9–10," *Etudes Evangéliques* 33 (1973) 20–25, 53–65.

Wheelan, "Priesthood"

Joseph B. Wheelan, "The Priesthood of the Laity," *Doctrine and Life* 15 (1965) 539–46.

White, "Ancient Greek Letters"

John L. White, "Ancient Greek Letters," in D. E. Aune, ed., *Greco-Roman Literature and the New Testament: Selected Forms and Genres* (SBLSBS 21; Atlanta: Scholars Press, 1988) 85–106.

Wifstrand, "Stylistic Problems"

Albert Wifstrand, "Stylistic Problems in the Epistles of James and Peter," *StTh* 1 (1948) 170–82.

Wilder, *Rhetoric*

Amos Wilder, *Early Christian Rhetoric: The Language of the Gospel* (London: SCM, 1964).

Windisch

Hans Windisch, *Die Katholischen Briefe* (3d ed.; rev. and ed. H. Preisker; HNT; Tübingen: Mohr [Siebeck], 1951).

Wolff, "Christ und Welt"

Christian Wolff, "Christ und Welt im 1. Petrusbrief," *ThLZ* 100 (1975) 334–42.

Yates, "Message"

Thomas Yates, "The Message of the Epistles: The First Epistle of Peter," *ExpT* 45 (1933/34) 391–93.

The English translation of 1 Peter was provided by the author; it reflects his exegetical decisions. Other biblical texts are usually from the *Revised Standard Version.* Quotations from the Latin and Greek authors follow the texts of the Loeb Classical Library or other standard editions; the translations, except where noted, are the author's.

The endpapers of this volume reproduce the first leaf of 1 Peter, containing 1:1–4, from Papyrus Bodmer VIII (P[72]). This codex, from around the turn of the fourth century, contains the entirety of 1 Peter (and also 2 Peter and Jude) and is the oldest manuscript of these NT writings. The original codex, which came to light in the mid-1950s and was held in the Bibliotheca Bodmeriana in Cologny/ Geneva, Switzerland, contained several other Jewish and Christian writings; the portion with 1–2 Peter was relocated to the Vatican Library and is reproduced by permission.

I. Authorship

The very first words of this letter, "Peter, apostle of Jesus Christ," pose a problem for many modern interpreters. To be sure, for centuries, and in some quarters still, the identification of the author as Simon Peter of Galilee has been accepted at face value and the letter understood as coming from the mind, if not the pen, of the apostle himself. Arguments to support such a judgment point to the early and continued identification of the author as Peter,[1] or to the use of the first person singular, which is taken to reflect Peter as the author,[2] or to the faith and personality of Peter reflected in the content of the letter,[3] or to the perception that the objections to Petrine authorship are simply "unpersuasive."[4]

For many other contemporary scholars, however, authorship constitutes one of the major literary problems of this epistle.[5] Its solution involves a consideration of many different kinds of evidence, all of which are interdependent, so that discussion of authorship may seem complicated to the point of distraction. Yet the nature of the letter, its destination, and its content impose such complication on any attempt to resolve the problem.[6]

Among the first things that will strike the reader of this letter is the quality of its Greek, and the fact that its structure often reveals a certain facility in rhetoric, an anomaly for one who in another context is identified as "unlettered" (Acts 4:13). The overwhelming dependence on the Greek version of the OT is also found surprising for the historical Peter. The solution that finds in Silvanus the source of the actual language is a familiar one, but poses its own problems.

Another element often noted is the apparent lack of references to events in the life of Jesus, references that would be appropriate for one who had accompanied him during his ministry. Such a connection is often sought in similarities between what Peter says in his speeches in Acts and the content of this epistle. In a similar vein, the

---

1   See F. H. Chase, "Peter, First Epistle," *Dictionary of the Bible* (ed. J. Hastings; Edinburgh: Clark, 1900) 3.781; Everett Falconer Harrison, "Exegetical Studies in 1 Peter," *BSac* 97 (1940) 201.

2   See, e.g., Ernest Gordon Selwyn, *The First Epistle of St. Peter* (2d ed.; London: Macmillan, 1955) 28, who cites 2:11; 5:1, 12; he also finds an eyewitness reflected in 1:3, 7, 8, 9, 10–12; 2:20–25; 3:15; 5:1, 2.

3   See Ceslas Spicq, "La Iᵃ Petri et le témoignage évangélique de saint Pierre," *StTh* 20 (1966) 39: "Toute l'Epître reflète la foi de Pierre" "the entire epistle reflects the faith of Peter"; the content reflects "de cette spontanéité et de cette ardeur" "that spontaneity and that zeal" which characterized Peter's temperament (52).

4   So Wayne A. Grudem, *The First Epistle of Peter: An Introduction and Commentary* (Tyndale New Testament Commentaries; Grand Rapids: Eerdmans, 1988) 33; Uwe Holmer and Werner de Boor, *Die Briefe des Petrus und der Brief des Judas* (Wuppertal: Brockhaus, 1978) 18; see also Peter Ketter, *Hebräerbrief, Jakobusbrief, Petrusbriefe, Judasbrief* (Herders Bibelkommentar; Freiburg: Herder, 1950) 191, who identifies it as "the first encyclical of the first pope." Edouard Cothenet lists a number of recent authors who support (and others who deny) Petrine authorship ("Les orientations actuelles de l'exégèse de la première lettre de Pierre," in C. Perrot, ed., *Etudes sur la Première Lettre de Pierre* [LD 102; Paris: Cerf, 1980] 37). For a sophisticated discussion of Simon Peter as author, see J. H. A. Hart, *The First Epistle General of Peter* (ed. W. R. Nicoll; 5 vols.; Expositor's

Greek Testament; reprinted Grand Rapids: Eerdmans, 1974) 5.9–17.

5   Authorship has been such a dominant concern of modern scholarship that, as Norbert Brox notes, 1 Peter is typically evaluated more on the basis of its authorship than its contents ("Situation und Sprache der Minderheit im ersten Petrusbrief," *Kairos*, NF 19 [1977] 1). E. G. Selwyn's judgment that Petrine authorship lends a coherence to its argument otherwise lost is an example ("The Problem of the Authorship of I Peter," *ExpT* 59 [1947/48] 256).

6   For a convenient summary of the points that argue against Petrine authorship, see Grudem, 25; Francis Wright Beare, *The First Epistle of Peter: The Greek Text with Introduction and Notes* (3d ed.; Oxford: Blackwell, 1970) 44; Karl Hermann Schelkle, *Die Petrusbriefe, der Judasbrief* (3d ed.; ThKNT; Freiburg: Herder, 1970) 13; William L. Schutter, *Hermeneutic and Composition in I Peter* (WUNT 2/30; Tübingen: Mohr [Siebeck], 1989) 5–6. For a summary of views on all introductory matters, see Werner Georg Kümmel, *Introduction to the New Testament* (trans. H. C. Kee; Nashville: Abingdon, 1975) 416–24.

strongly Pauline flavor of the letter, in both its language and its contents, and the evident use made of other early Christian traditions seem unexpected from one who would surely have had his own understanding and expression of the Christian faith based on his experiences with both the earthly and the risen Jesus.

The situation presumed by the letter, both the external pressures on the readers reflected in the references to persecutions and the internal structures of ecclesiastical organization the author seems to presume, also has a bearing on authorship since, as many have argued, that situation in Asia Minor reflects a time later than one could assume Peter had lived.

Rejection of the claim to authorship by Peter means one must see the letter as pseudonymous. Such pseudonymity has often either been judged in terms of modern literary sensibilities and seen as something totally reprehensible and hence impossible for an honorable person, or simply been assumed to be a normal ancient practice and thus seen as posing no problem and hence warranting no further investigation. The decision for pseudonymity brings with it the question of why the name Peter would be chosen for a letter so transparently Pauline in its conception, and that problem also merits discussion.

Until all such elements, and more, are clarified, we will not be in a position to make a measured judgment on the probable authorship of the letter. We must therefore now turn to a detailed discussion of these problems, paying attention to the arguments of those who question, as well as those who defend, Petrine authorship.[7]

A. Language

The kind of Greek in which the epistle is written is often cited as a reason for rejecting authorship by Simon Peter.

1. Types of Greek

Three kinds of style are found in the first century: Asianism, Atticism, and Koine.[8] Asianism, named for a style used by orators who came mostly from Asia Minor, was self-consciously ornate, "artificial and undisciplined."[9] Atticism, the language of grammarians and rhetoricians, sought to imitate Greek literary prose of the fifth and fourth centuries BCE.[10] Koine was the common language spoken in the Mediterranean basin in late antiquity (the Hellenistic period).[11]

Although the language of the NT has been identified with the everyday language of street and marketplace, that is not the case with the language of 1 Peter.[12] While there is a simplicity and directness to it, it shows the longer periods and balanced style of a prose not unacquainted with rhetorical structures.[13] The language can be compared favorably with that of the letters of Paul,[14] and belongs stylistically with the best prose of the NT.[15] The quality of its Greek ought nevertheless not be exaggerated.[16]

7 However carefully or exhaustively that is done, it remains the case that conclusions will, as David G. Meade noted, "inevitably be based more on surmise than on hard evidence in either direction" (*Pseudonymity and Canon: An Investigation into the Relationship of Authorship and Authority in Jewish and Earliest Christian Tradition* [WUNT 39; Tübingen: Mohr (Siebeck), 1986] 166). That does not relieve us of the necessity of the attempt, however.

8 George A. Kennedy, *New Testament Interpretation through Rhetorical Criticism* (Chapel Hill: University of North Carolina Press, 1984) 32. Quintilian (*Inst.* 4.8.11) names the three kinds of style: the Grand ("smooth and ornate arrangement of impressive words"), the Middle ("words of a lower, . . . not lowest and most colloquial, class"), and Simple ("most current idiom of standard speech"). 1 Peter would fit the "Middle."

9 George A. Kennedy, *Classical Rhetoric and Its Christian and Secular Tradition from Ancient to Modern Times* (Chapel Hill: University of North Carolina Press, 1980) 86. Kennedy (*NT Interpretation*, 32)

identifies Melito of Sardis as a Christian example. Petronius (*Satyr.* 5) parodies this style as a "flatulent and formless flow of words . . . a modern immigrant from Asia to Athens."

10 The Greek of the second-century apologists falls in this category; Kennedy (*NT Interpretation*, 32) thinks Luke and Paul "could have written Attic Greek if they had wished to."

11 The language of the Gospels of Mark, Matthew, and John would perhaps fall here; see Kennedy, *NT Interpretation*, 32.

12 Norbert Brox holds the language and style of 1 Peter to be "überdurchschnittlich" "above average" (*Der Erste Petrusbrief* [EKKNT; Zurich: Benziger, 1979] 45).

13 Schelkle, 13: "Er vermag auch einige rhetorische Kunstmittel zu verwenden" "he was able to use some rhetorical artistry"; cf. also Chase, "Peter," 782; Ludwig Radermacher, "Der erste Petrusbrief und Silvanus; mit einem Nachwort in eigener Sache," *ZNW* 25 (1926) 288. Armand Puig Tarrech mentions the use "d'un rhétorique élémentaire" "of an

2. Language of 1 Peter

a. Care of Composition. Individual characteristics of the author's style show that the letter has been composed with care. Written in a direct if somewhat studied style,[17] the prose is marked by such characteristics as the frequent use of comparison (1:7, 13; 2:2, 16, 25; 3:4–5; 5:8),[18] often introduced by the particle ὡς (1:19; 2:2, 5, 25; 3:7; 5:8);[19] series of words with similar sounds (1:4, 19; 3:18);[20] the accumulation of synonyms (1:8, 10; 2:25; 3:4);[21] the use of anaphora to introduce parallel phrases (4:11) or to organize a passage (ὑποτάσσειν, 2:13—3:1);[22] the use of antithetic (2:14; 3:18; 4:6) and synthetic (2:22–23; 4:11; 5:2–3) parallelism;[23] coordinate parallel expressions, first negative, then positive, underlining the same idea (1:14–15, 18–21, 23; 2:16; 5:2–3);[24] rhythmic structure (1:3–12);[25] the frequent use of the imperative (typical of NT style as compared to the diatribe);[26] the frequent use of conjunctive participles (e.g., 1:8, 9, 11, 23) and relative clauses,[27] which can lead to long periods (e.g., 1:17–21).[28] 1 Peter, along with Luke, is also unique in the NT in the use of εἰ with the optative (3:14, 17);[29] conversely the author does not

---

elementary rhetoric"; somewhat speculatively, he thinks it accords with "la psychologie de la population rurale" "the psychology of the rural population" ("Le milieu de la Première Epître de Pierre," *Revista Catalana de Teología* 5 [1980] 401). Albert Wifstrand notes that the language of 1 Peter is not the language of "everyday chatter" ("Stylistic Problems in the Epistles of James and Peter," *StTh* 1 [1948] 180; cf. also 174–76, 182).

14 Schutter (*Hermeneutic*, 5) finds it to rival that of Paul; Martin Dibelius calls it "verhältnismässig gepflegte(s) Griechisch" "relatively polished Greek" and finds it "etwas gewählter . . . als die Sprache des Paulus" "somewhat superior to the language of Paul" ("Petrusbriefe," *RGG*, [ed. H. Gunkel et al.; 2d ed.; Tübingen: Mohr, 1930] 4.1114). H. G. Meecham notes 1 Pet 3:3 as an example of balanced clauses "more carefully wrought out than is customary with Paul" ("The First Epistle of St. Peter," *ExpT* 48 [1936/37] 22).

15 See, e.g., Charles Bigg, *A Critical and Exegetical Commentary on the Epistles of St. Peter and St. Jude* (ICC; New York: Scribner's, 1901) 4; Eduard Schweizer, *Der Erste Petrusbrief* (3d ed.; Zürcher Bibelkommentare; Zurich: Theologischer Verlag, 1972) 9; Beare, 44.

16 J. N. D. Kelly concedes the use of "a limited range of rhetorical conventions" but decries "the extravagant eulogies" 1 Peter has received; he characterizes the style as "unimaginative, monotonous and at times clumsy" (*A Commentary on the Epistles of Peter and of Jude* [BNTC; London: Black; HNTC; New York: Harper & Row, 1969] 31). Cf. also Radermacher, "Der erste Petrusbrief," 288; Wifstrand, "Stylistic Problems," 175.

17 Ceslas Spicq, *Les Epîtres de Saint Pierre* (SB; Paris: Librairie Lecoffre, 1966) 13; Selwyn, 25; Meecham, "First Epistle," 22; but cf. Chase, "Peter," 782.

18 Schelkle, 13; Radermacher, "Der erste Petrusbrief," 289.

19 Radermacher ("Der erste Petrusbrief," 288); but he notes nevertheless the general absence in 1 Peter of particles and prepositions (289).

20 Schelkle, 13. The attempt by Philip Carrington to demonstrate that series of triads are characteristic of 1 Peter is somewhat forced and on the whole unconvincing ("Saint Peter's Epistle," in S. E. Johnson, ed., *The Joy of Study: Papers on New Testament and Related Subjects Presented to Honor Frederick Clifton Grant* [New York: Macmillan, 1951] 62).

21 Irénée Fransen, "Une homélie chrétienne: La première Epître de Pierre," *BVC* 31 (1960) 29.

22 Radermacher, "Der erste Petrusbrief," 288; Schelkle, 13.

23 Leonhard Goppelt, *Der Erste Petrusbrief* (KEK; Göttingen: Vandenhoeck & Ruprecht, 1978) 46 (ET 25). Radermacher ("Der erste Petrusbrief," 288) notes the presence of parisosis and homoioteleuton: 2:14, 23; 3:18; 4:6; 5:2.

24 Fransen, "Une homélie," 29.

25 Fransen, "Une homélie," 29.

26 Wifstrand ("Stylistic Problems," 174) notes it is used more than twice as frequently in 1 Peter as in Epictetus.

27 Radermacher, "Der erste Petrusbrief," 289. Wifstrand ("Stylistic Problems," 176) notes that they are used three times more frequently in 1 Peter than in Epictetus.

28 Wifstrand ("Stylistic Problems", 181) observes that "in that respect, but not in others, we can place the language . . . at the side of that of Philo."

29 Meecham, "First Epistle," 22.

use the common particle ἄν.[30]

b. Semiticisms. The Greek is not notable for the presence of Semiticisms;[31] there are fewer than appear in Paul,[32] and such as are present are more likely derived from the language of the LXX than from a direct dependence of the author on Hebrew thought-forms.[33] The presence in 1 Peter of participles that bear the force of imperatives, often assumed, is less assured than might appear. Such a use was unknown in classical Greek and is highly questionable even in later Hellenistic Greek. D. Daube has argued that such presence is likely to be due to Hebraic use, since in rabbinic Hebrew they refer to habitual action rather than seeking to impart individual commands,[34] a characteristic of those places in 1 Peter that have the strongest claim on such use. Daube finds such a use of participles in 1 Peter limited to 2:18; 3:1,[35] 7–9; and 4:7–10.[36] If in fact present, such a use would more likely be due to 1 Peter's use of common Christian tradition rather than to any direct dependence on Hebrew literature, since there is no evidence in those verses that the author is translating from the Hebrew.[37]

c. Vocabulary. The vocabulary is distinctly Christian, with additional influence from the LXX.[38] There are some sixty-two hapax legomena for the NT; thirty-nine of them appear also in some Greek version of the OT,[39] and others have been identified as "classical" in origin.[40] Aside from a fondness for verbs compounded with ἀνα-,[41] the vocabulary is not unique or unusual in the NT.

d. Rhetorical Elements. The type of Greek found in 1 Peter reveals that whether or not the author was born a Greek,[42] he had enjoyed some level of formal education; if not an "advanced" education in rhetoric or philosophy, at least a "middle" education that would have included, along with geometry, arithmetic, and music, a reading of such classical authors as Homer.[43] While one may surely presume some facility in Greek even among Palestinian fishermen in the first century who lacked formal educa-

---

30 It occurs some 167 times in the NT; see also note 42.
31 Radermacher, "Der erste Petrusbrief," 290; Wifstrand, "Stylistic Problems," 176. Bigg (3) also notes the absence of Latinisms.
32 Goppelt, 45 (ET 24).
33 Wifstrand ("Stylistic Problems," 182), who in addition mentions as illustrations such instances as the frequent use of καρδία ("heart"), phrases such as τέκνα ὑπακοῆς ("children of obedience," 1:14) and πεπορευμένους ἐν ἀσελγείαις, ἐπιθυμίαις ("having proceeded in licentiousness, passions," 4:3), and the abundance of abstract nouns such as one also finds in the Wisdom of Solomon (177, 180).
34 In Selwyn, 467–88. On their use in the Dead Sea literature, see Eduard Lohse, "Parenesis and Kerygma in 1 Peter" (trans. John Steely), in C. H. Talbert, ed., *Perspectives on First Peter* (NAPBR Special Series 9; Macon, Ga.: Mercer University Press, 1986) 46; Goppelt, 45 n. 60 (ET 24, n. 63).
35 Cothenet ("Les orientations," 31) provides some correlative evidence for these instances by noting that the verb ὑποτάσσειν used in these two places is not used in the moral discourse of the Stoics and hence could not derive from them.
36 He finds doubtful such use in 1:14 (although see Lohse, "Parenesis," 46) and in 2:12.
37 Their use is, however, not so common as is often asserted; see below, "Excursus: Imperative Use of Participles in 1 Peter."
38 On the vocabulary generally, see Albert Vanhoye, S.J., "1 Pierre au carrefour des théologies du nouveau Testament," in C. Perrot, ed., *Etudes sur la*

Première Lettre de Pierre (LD 102; Paris: Cerf, 1980) 105–7; on the LXX, see Chase, "Peter," 781.
39 Bigg, 2–3.
40 Chase ("Peter," 782) lists eleven words and two phrases, although even here some also appear in the LXX.
41 Ἀναγεννάω ("begotten anew"), 1:3, 22; ἀναζώννμμι ("gird up"), 1:13; ἀναστρέφω ("behave"), 1:17; ἀναφέρω ("offer up"), 2:5, 24; ἀναπαύω ("rest"), 4:14 (see Meecham, "First Epistle," 22). ἀναστροφή ("behavior") is used in 1:15, 18; 2:12; 3:1, 2, 16, but its use may be due to the hortatory nature of the content.
42 Bigg (5) cites the absence of the particle ἄν to be sufficient evidence of itself to show "the writer was not a Greek"; cf. Ketter, 193.
43 See Peter Lampe and Ulrich Luz ("Nachpaulinisches Christentum und pagane Gesellschaft," in J. Becker, ed., *Die Anfänge des Christentums* [Stuttgart: Kohlhammer, 1987] 188): that the author "bis zum 17. Lebensjahr die Grammatikerschule absolvierte, erklärt die vorhandenen Elemente hinreichend" "the elements in the letter are explained sufficiently if [the author] completed grammar school at age 17." See also Wifstrand ("Stylistic Problems," 178), who also cites the use of "the optative in a hypothetic clause" and "the participle of the future tense" as evidence of the author's elevation beyond acquaintance "with careless ordinary spoken Greek" (177). While women normally did not enjoy such an education, some in fact did. I will refer to the author as masculine since the letter is attributed to Peter, without prejudice to

tion,[44] the kind of Greek found in this epistle was probably beyond such a person, and hence the language was in all likelihood not given its present form by Simon Peter.[45]

The extent to which a specific rhetorical form was employed by the author of 1 Peter is more difficult to determine than is the presence of individual rhetorical devices. It is not a question of whether the author employed "rhetoric"; to the extent that rhetoric is "that quality in discourse by which a speaker or writer seeks to accomplish his [or her] purposes,"[46] every piece of writing employs rhetoric. What is at issue is whether or not the author of 1 Peter consciously shaped this letter in terms of formal Hellenistic rhetoric.[47]

Hellenistic rhetoricians, following Aristotle, divided oratory into three types, which they considered exhaustive: deliberative, forensic, and epideictic. Of these, the deliberative dealt with future events about which a decision needed to be made, and involved exhortation; the forensic dealt with accusation and defense relative to past events, and sought justice; the epideictic dealt with praise or blame of a person living in the present, and involved honor or dishonor.[48] The basic structure included exordium, narration, demonstration, and conclusion, with various elaborations and subdivisions.[49]

While it may be difficult, or even inadvisable, to try to classify such an NT document as 1 Peter within one of these categories,[50] since epistles may treat a variety of subjects and hence display parts colored now by one form, now by another, one can seek to find those places where our letter reflects one of the three classes, and look at the letter as a whole as an expression of one of them.

While there are passages in 1 Peter that imply a judicial tone, with the implication being a denial of the accusations leveled against Christians (3:15–16; 4:15–16; cf. 4:4), the letter itself is not cast as a formal defense of Christians and/or their beliefs in light of charges that have been brought against them.

Similarly, while the arrangement of 1 Peter reflects epideictic structure, in which there appears between exordium (1:3–13) and epilogue (5:6–11) "an orderly sequence of amplified topics dealing with . . . the qualities of the concept under consideration,"[51] and while the discussion clearly implies the desire to strengthen the recipients' adherence to Christian values,[52] the language does not show the fondness for ornament, nor does the author betray the desire to be admired, elements that characterized the epideictic style.[53]

Again, while the arrangement of 1 Peter as a whole does not betray very clearly the proposition and proof that in the deliberative structure follow the exordium, a significant part of the discussion does follow that form,

---

the possibility that an educated Christian woman could have written it.

44 Brox, 44; cf. Kelly, 31. To assume university education to account for fluency in more than one language is rendered nugatory by peasants in Alsace-Lorraine or lumberjacks in Canada who speak more than one language fluently; on this point see also F. Neugebauer, "Zur Deutung und Bedeutung des 1. Petrusbriefes," *NTS* 26 (1980) 72.

45 That Peter wrote it is "unthinkable" (Goppelt, 67); "doubtful" (Cothenet, "Les orientations," 37); "a feat plainly beyond the powers of a Galilean fisherman" (Beare, 47); cf. Meade, *Pseudonymity and Canon,* 166; Bigg, 5.

46 Kennedy, *NT Interpretation,* 3. Quintilian (*Inst.* 3.5.2) lists as the aims of rhetoric the need to "instruct, move, and charm" one's audience.

47 Such formal rhetoric concentrated primarily on oratory, yet as Kennedy (*NT Interpretation,* 86) notes, the "close formal connection between the oration and the epistle" implies that the rhetorical conventions could also apply to the letter.

48 *Rhet.* 1.3 (1358a-b); see also Cicero *Ad Her.* 1.2.2; Quintilian *Inst.* 3.4.15.

49 So Kennedy, *Classical Rhetoric,* 112; see 92–95 for a summary of Cicero's views.

50 For an approach to NT literature in terms of formal rhetoric, see Kennedy, *Classical Rhetoric*; see also his caveat, 32–33.

51 Kennedy, *NT Interpretation,* 24.

52 Kennedy, *NT Interpretation,* 74; cf. Reginald H. Fuller, "Classics and the Gospels: The Seminar," in Wm. O. Walker, ed., *The Relationships among the Gospels: An Interdisciplinary Dialogue* (San Antonio: Trinity University Press, 1978) 185.

53 Kennedy, *NT Interpretation,* 75. He does not specifically address the status of 1 Peter.

with the proposition that Christians maintain good conduct among nonbelievers (2:11–13) followed by the proof divided into a series of headings under which the discussion is pursued: subordination of all to governmental authorities (2:13–17), of slaves to masters (2:18–25), of wives to husbands (3:1–7), of each to all (3:8–12),[54] a discussion that includes the sort of historical examples (Christ, 2:21–25; Sarah, 3:6) highly prized in deliberative rhetoric.[55] The basic thrust of 1 Peter—exhortations to a course of action—is also typical of deliberative oratory,[56] as is the kind of direct, straightforward language that typifies this letter.[57] While great weight is not placed on the authority of the author, nor is there great appeal to emotions, both typical in deliberative rhetoric,[58] both are surely implied: the apostolic authority of Peter stands behind the letter (1:1; cf. 5:1), and emotional appeal, direct here and there (2:11; 4:12), is implied throughout by the tone of the exhortations.

The letter, therefore, beginning with a carefully crafted exordium whose purpose was to win the attention of the audience,[59] followed by a series of topical discussions and concluding with a peroration, shows elements of judicial and epideictic structures, but seems to reflect most closely the deliberative rhetoric of its Hellenistic age.[60] Whether or not the author set out deliberately to craft a letter that included such elements of formal Hellenistic rhetoric is difficult to say,[61] although it would be equally difficult to deny him all acquaintance with formal rhetoric in light of the shape of the letter itself.

While one may not absolutely rule out such a command of Greek on the part of Simon Peter of Galilee, it is nevertheless rather difficult to imagine someone like the Peter described in the Gospels as having possessed such knowledge and skills, whether or not they imply some degree of formal schooling in rhetoric.

e. Author's Acquaintance with Greek. The intimate acquaintance of our author with the Greek language is shown by the text of the OT which the author quotes and to which he alludes frequently: it is the LXX rather than the MT.[62] Direct quotation is limited to two instances (γέγραπται, 1:16; ἐν γραφῇ, 2:6), and there the text is rather clearly the LXX (1:16 from Lev 19:2; 2:6 from Isa 40:6–8, though with modifications); additional clear examples of quotation would include Isa 40:6–8 at 1:24–25 and Ps 33:13–17 (MT Ps 34) at 3:10–12, in both instances with modifications.[63] In addition to quotations,

54 For the overall structure, see Kennedy, *NT Interpretation,* 24.

55 Quintilian *Inst.* 3.8.36; Abraham J. Malherbe, *Moral Exhortation: A Greco-Roman Sourcebook* (LEC 4; Philadelphia: Westminster, 1986) 511–12.

56 Quintilian *Inst.* 3.8.22–23; cf. Cicero *Ad Her.* 3.1 (2); Kennedy, *NT Interpretation,* 146.

57 Quintilian *Inst.* 3.8.62, 65.

58 Quintilian *Inst.* 3.8.12–13. Quintilian discusses in this section, without naming them, the three types of proof first enunciated by Aristotle: ethos, the authority of the author; pathos, the emotional reaction of the audience; and logos, the facts of the argument (cf. Kennedy, *NT Interpretation,* 14). In these terms one could say that the ethos of 1 Peter is the authority of the apostle Peter, the logos is the suffering and triumph of Jesus open to those who follow him, and the pathos is the appeal not to abandon the faith in the face of suffering lest one lose the promised glory.

59 On the importance of the exordium, see Cicero *Ad Her.* 1.7.11; Quintilian *Inst.* 4.1.33–34. 1 Pet 1:3–12 even conforms to the "law" that the exordium consist of no more than four sentences (Quintilian *Inst.* 4.1.62; Quintilian thinks those who propound it "laughable" [*ridendi*]).

60 Since 1 Peter shares with deliberative oratory the intention to move to action (*Ad Her.* 3.2), and since, as Kennedy (*Classical Rhetoric,* 74) notes, "much of Christian rhetoric is deliberative," it should not be surprising that 1 Peter should have closest affinity to this type (see also Kennedy, *NT Interpretation,* 146).

61 Schutter (*Hermeneutic,* 5) thinks the author shows skill in formal rhetoric. For other discussions of the rhetorical skill of the author that do not employ the formal rhetorical criteria discussed in Cicero and Quintilian, see in addition to Schutter, Charles H. Talbert, "Once Again: The Plan of 1 Peter," in Talbert, *Perspectives,* 141–51.

62 This point has been made frequently: T. P. Osborne, "L'utilisation des citations de l'Ancien Testament dans la première épître de Pierre," *RThL* 12 (1981) 73; Chase, "Peter," 781; Fransen, "Une homélie," 29; J. Ramsey Michaels, *1 Peter* (Word Biblical Commentary 49; Waco: Word, 1988) xl. Sometimes it is made in exaggerated form (e.g., Ernest Best, *1 Peter* [New Century Bible; London: Oliphants, 1971; reprinted Grand Rapids: Eerdmans, 1982] 29: Peter "always" follows LXX, "never" MT), sometimes with more zeal than accuracy (e.g., Cothenet, "Les orientations," 28, who bases such an assertion on "la citation d'Ex 19.5 [*sic*] en 1 P 2,5 [*sic*].9"). Contrariwise, Neugebauer ("Zur Deutung," 81) claims that although the author used the LXX in references to

allusions to the OT that contain LXX language occur in such places as 2:3, 7, 9–10, 22–25; 3:14; 4:14; 5:8, indicating that the author was saturated with the language of the Greek Bible.[64] The absence of influence of the language of the Hebrew Bible or the Targumim on the one hand, and the clear influence of the LXX on the other, show that the author was at home in Greek rather than Semitic culture, and such is likely not to have been the case with Simon Peter.[65]

Some have attempted to preserve direct Petrine authorship by arguing for his possession of the kind of linguistic skills reflected in the letter. The adjective ἀγράμματος applied to Peter (Acts 4:13) can mean no more than deficient in formal rabbinic training;[66] and his business (export of fish), which very likely involved

contact with foreigners, along with his brother, who bore a Greek name, points to the possibility of a knowledge of Greek.[67] It has also been argued that Peter, aware of the imperative for mission, would have prepared himself for that by improving his ability in the lingua franca of his world,[68] an opportunity open even to slaves.[69]

f. Role of Silvanus. Far more common is the attempt to preserve authenticity by appealing to Silvanus to account for the superior diction of the letter.[70] The basis for this theory is the phrase διὰ Σιλουανοῦ in 1 Pet 5:12, which is taken to mean that Silvanus was the one who did the actual writing.[71] This Silvanus is identified with the Silas described in Acts as a member of the Jerusalem community who with Judas as its representatives, along with Paul and Barnabas, carried the apostolic letter to

---

Proverbs in 4:18 and 5:5, he used the MT or Targum in 1 Pet 2:17; 3:6; 4:8. Such a judgment is questionable, however, in light of the fact that 2:17 and 3:6 are allusions rather than quotations, and in both instances (Prov 24:21 in 2:17 and Prov 3:25 in 3:6) the LXX and MT agree against 1 Peter. Moreover, 1 Pet 4:8 comes from neither the LXX nor the MT, but is closer to Jas 5:20, perhaps indicating it came from a Christian source (cf. Chase, "Peter," 781). Detailed analyses of the OT texts to which reference is made in 1 Peter will be found in the comments on the appropriate verses.

63 Chase ("Peter," 781) accounts for these variations by asserting that the author quotes from memory or is influenced by their use in other NT writings. On this latter point see also Osborne ("L'utilisation," 73), who notes the possibility that such passages were drawn from liturgical or catechetical texts.

64 Schelkle (13) argues that such florilegium-like passages as 2:1–10 or 2:22–25 could only result from "regular use of the Greek Bible." Wifstrand ("Stylistic Problems," 176) sees such Semitisms as appear in 1 Peter as due to this saturation in the LXX rather than to any direct knowledge of Hebrew.

65 Again, a point frequently made: Schutter, *Hermeneutic*, 5; Beare, 47; Goppelt, 67 (ET 50). Osborne ("L'utilisation," 73) suggests such dependence on the Greek Bible may indicate the author was "himself a pagan converted to Christianity."

66 E.g., Grudem (26), who points (31) to Joseph Conrad as an example of one who became an accomplished writer in a foreign language without benefit of formal training. Seneca (*Benef.* 5.13.3) defines *inlitteratum* not as totally ignorant but as untutored in higher learning ("non ex toto rudem, sed ad litteras altiores non perductum").

67 Spicq (22) argues that since the Zebedees had boats and servants, and were involved in the export of fish, which required even the servants to know Greek, Peter can hardly have had less knowledge of Greek than that required of the Zebedees' servants; Philip, who also came from Bethsaida, shows the prevalence of Greek names there. Thus the fact that they will have conversed in Greek as did the other natives of Bethsaida means that "le pseudo-ignorance du Grec par Pierre ne devrait plus figurer dans les discussions sur l'authenticité de la 1. Pt" "the pseudo-ignorance of Greek on the part of Peter ought no longer figure in discussions about the authenticity of 1 Peter." One need hardly point out the speculative nature of such an argument.

68 Chase ("Peter," 787) mentions otherwise unspecified "opportunities which certainly were within his reach" for such linguistic improvement.

69 Grudem (29 n. 3) cites Josephus *Ant.* 20.263 (*sic*; correctly 20.264) to support this point. Josephus is explaining why fluency in Greek is not highly prized by his fellow Jews: in their opinion it is common to freemen, and even slaves can achieve it; hence it confers no distinction.

70 Representative of those for whom authenticity is preserved whether the letter was written by Peter or by Silvanus as amanuensis is J. L. de Villiers, "Joy in Suffering in I Peter," *Neot* 9 (1975; 2d ed. 1980) 64.

71 For example, Kelly, 214; James Moffatt, *The General Epistles: James, Peter, and Jude* (MNTC; Garden City, N.Y.: Doubleday, Doran, 1928) 86. Best (177) notes the ambiguity of the preposition διά (it could also mean "carried by"), a possibility on occasion, I think wrongly, denied; e.g., Kelly, 215. For a complete discussion of the significance of this διά in this phrase, see below and the discussion at 5:12.

Antioch.[72] Later accompanying Paul on his mission,[73] Silvanus was also the cosender of 1 and 2 Thessalonians, the similarity of which to 1 Peter is used to confirm Silvanus as author of the latter.[74] To account for the actual language of 1 Peter, however, Silvanus must be credited with more than simply taking down verbatim what Peter said; room must be given for Silvanus to have fashioned the letter himself, either because Peter dictated in Aramaic and Silvanus put it into Greek,[75] or because Peter simply laid down the guidelines that Silvanus then fleshed out into the present letter.[76]

Silvanus, it is asserted, spoke Greek and was steeped in Greek culture,[77] and thus possessed the rhetorical and linguistic skills reflected in 1 Peter, for whose form and for much of whose content he was largely responsible.[78] The final verses are then ascribed to Peter's own hand, in accordance with ancient custom, thus confirming the letter's authenticity.[79]

Such a solution is not without its own problems, aside from the speculation necessarily involved. It is by no means certain that the phrase διὰ Σιλουανοῦ can mean "written by"; in fact it probably cannot.[80] In a sense, the

---

72 Acts 15:22, 27; he was a "prophet," 15:32. As examples of a reconstruction of the career of Silvanus, based on Acts 15:1—17:15; 18:5; 2 Cor 1:19; 1 Thess 1:1; 2 Thess 1:1, see Selwyn, 9–17; W. Bornemann, "Der erste Petrusbrief—eine Taufrede des Silvanus," *ZNW* 19 (1919/20) 160–61. The latter postulates in addition a possible sojourn for Silvanus in Asia Minor, perhaps as a presbyter (see 5:1) in a congregation there, and concludes that he was "hochbegabter . . . Mann," "trefflicher Redner," with "eine reiche Lebenserfahrung, Menschenkenntnis . . . und ein gewandte Beherrschung der griechischen Sprache" "highly gifted . . . man, an effective orator, [with] an extensive experience of life, knowledge of human nature and of the world . . . and a polished mastery of the Greek language." By contrast, A. R. C. Leaney concludes that one to whom the unknown author of 1 Peter referred was "a real Silvanus, but one otherwise unknown to us," thus eliminating such speculation about him (*The Letters of Peter and Jude* [Cambridge Bible Commentary; Cambridge: University Press, 1967] 72).

73 Acts 15:40; he took the place of Barnabas, who had left Paul (15:39). On the nature of this dispute, reflected in Gal 2:13, see Paul J. Achtemeier, *The Quest for Unity in the New Testament Church* (Philadelphia: Fortress, 1987) 16–17.

74 Selwyn, 14–17; Julian Price Love, "The First Epistle of Peter," *Int* 8 (1954) 66.

75 E.g., Bigg, 6.

76 This is a widespread solution; e.g., Joseph A. Fitzmyer ("The First Epistle of Peter," in R. E. Brown, J. A. Fitzmyer and R. E. Murphy, eds., *Jerome Biblical Commentary* Englewood Cliffs, N.J.: Prentice-Hall, 1968] 362): substance from Peter, words from Silvanus; Schweizer (12): Silvanus as the author who writes at the command of Peter; C. E. B. Cranfield (*I and II Peter and Jude: Introduction and Commentary* [Torch Bible Commentaries; London: SCM, 1960]

16): Silvanus was "much more than a mere amanuensis"; Selwyn (11): Silvanus contributed to "the substance no less than to the language"; Goppelt (37, ET 14): Silvanus is the one who actually wrote the letter.

77 E.g., Moffatt, 169–70; Cranfield, 14. Martin Hengel includes Silas/Silvanus among Jerusalem Jews who spoke Greek as their mother tongue (*Judentum und Hellenismus* [WUNT 1; Tübingen: Mohr (Siebeck), 1969] 193–94). Norbert Brox correctly observes that that is no more than a supposition ("Tendenz und Pseudepigraphie im ersten Petrusbrief," *Kairos,* NF 20 [1978] 110 n. 7).

78 E.g., Cranfield, 14; Selwyn, "Problem," 256. Radermacher ("Der erste Petrusbrief," 293) is even able to conclude "dass die Schreibkunst sein Beruf war" "that his profession was that of scribe."

79 E.g., Kelly, 214; Jean-Claude Margot, *Les Epîtres de Pierre* (Geneva: Labor et Fides, 1960) 89. J. W. C. Wand judges it "probably" by Peter (*The General Epistles of St. Peter and St. Jude* [Westminster Commentaries; London: Methuen, 1934] 128); Bigg (195) judges it "possibly" by him.

80 The phrase is at best ambiguous and may simply refer to the one who carried the letter; so Best, 58, 177; Goppelt, 34; Wand, 128. Cf. Rom 16:22, where a scribe is designated and διά is not used, with Ignatius *Rom.* 10.1; *Phld.* 11.2; *Smyrn.* 12.1; *Pol.* 14.1, where διά is used to name the one who delivers the letter; see also Goppelt, 347 (ET 369). For a full discussion of this problem, see the comments on 5:12 below.

more room one gives to Silvanus's own literary creativity in solving the problem of the language of the letter, the less one is able to ascribe it in any meaningful way to Peter.[81] The alleged similarity of 1 Peter to 1 and 2 Thessalonians has been challenged,[82] and the question raised why, if Silvanus had such a hand in the creation of 1 Peter, he would not have been named cosender, as he was in the two Pauline letters.[83] To attribute the language and to greater or lesser degree the content of 1 Peter to Silvanus, about whom even less is known than about Peter, seems in fact little more than a "device of desperation" to save some kind of authenticity for the letter.[84]

B. Reflections of the Life and Teaching of Jesus of Nazareth

1. Personal Reminiscences

An argument often cited against the authenticity of 1 Peter is the lack of personal reminiscences from the life of Jesus, something one would surely expect in a letter

from one who had accompanied him from Galilean ministry to resurrection.[85] In defense of Petrine authorship, a variety of indications have been cited that are held to represent such reminiscences. For example, the alternation of first and second person in 1:3–9 is claimed to show that while the readers have not seen Jesus (v. 6), the author (by implication) has (v. 3).[86] Again, the reference to "witness" in 5:1 is taken to mean Peter is calling himself an eyewitness to the passion of Jesus, a witness reflected supremely in 2:22–25.[87] The difficulty with finding assurances of the report of an eyewitness there is that these verses are patently drawn from Isaiah 53, and hence may owe more to the author's demonstrable reliance on the OT,[88] and even to a notion of the fulfillment of the OT prophecy by Jesus,[89] than to the reminiscences of an eyewitness.[90]

81 Best (57) notes it is impossible to tell which parts came from Peter, which from Silvanus; see also Schutter, *Hermeneutic,* 6. Brox ("Tendenz," 111) observes that the more credit one gives to Silvanus for language and form, the less meaningful it is to attribute it to Peter. One also loses any Petrine authenticity to be derived from reminiscences of the gospel tradition if Silvanus is responsible for the letter; see Ernest Best, "I Peter and the Gospel Tradition," *NTS* 16 (1970) 95.

82 Best (57) thinks the extent of such affinities "is doubtful"; Goppelt (68 n. 133, ET 50 n. 135) judges that the attempt to establish such similarities "fails"; see also Spicq, 178.

83 Beare, 209; Chase, "Peter," 790; Best, 57. Goppelt (68, ET 51) wonders how one who was Paul's coworker could send a letter to Asia Minor with no mention of his former mentor; for such reference to Paul, see *1 Clem.* 47:1–3; Ignatius *Eph.* 12.2; *Rom.* 4.3; Polycarp *Phil.* 3.2; 9.1; 2 Pet 3:15.

84 The phrase is from Beare, 209. Cranfield (14) sums up the case well: "It is true that there is no evidence that Silvanus was capable of writing elegant Greek; but at least there is in his case no particular reason for thinking that he was not." On so fragile a foundation rests the argument for Silvanus as secretary!

85 The uncertain state of the evidence allows some to find such references (e.g., Robert H. Gundry, *"Verba Christi* in I Peter: Their Implications Concerning the Authorship of I Peter and the Authenticity of the Gospel Tradition," *NTS* 13 [1967] 348), others to

deny their existence (e.g., Brox, 45). Even if present, such reminiscences remain ambiguous, however, since in 2 Peter (e.g., 2:16–18) they are widely recognized as a device to lend authenticity to a pseudonymous letter.

86 Neugebauer, "Zur Deutung," 69. Chase ("Peter," 787) relates the verse to John 21:15–16. Selwyn (28) argues that the verses in the first person come from Peter, not Silvanus.

87 Chase ("Peter," 787) finds reflected in 2:23 "what St. Peter saw as he lingered in the high priest's vestibule"; Neugebauer ("Zur Deutung," 70) sees in 2:22–23 an account of Jesus' behavior at his trial that is the opposite of the behavior of Peter as recorded in the Gospels, evidence Peter himself must have written it. See also Gundry, *"Verba Christi,"* 347; Spicq, "La Iª Petri," 39; D. Edmond Hiebert, "Following Christ's Example: An Exposition of 1 Peter 2:21–25," *BSac* 139 (1982) 35.

88 So Beare, 44. For a careful analysis of the OT as source for the language and thought of 1 Peter, see Schutter, *Hermeneutic,* 35–43.

89 So, e.g., Karl-Hermann Schelkle, "Das Leiden des Gottesknechtes als Form christlichen Lebens (nach dem ersten Petrusbrief)," *BK* 16 (1961) 15, although he argues this within the context of Petrine authorship.

90 Carrington ("Saint Peter's Epistle," 60) seeks to save authenticity by finding in the references to Isaiah 53 Peter's familiarity with the liturgical associations of that passage, which would have intruded themselves on his mind as he described Jesus' passion; in a

Such "witness" of Peter is not limited to Jesus' passion, however. 1 Pet 5:5 is found to reflect Jesus' binding a towel about himself in John 13:4,[91] as the comparable allusions to rebirth in 1 Peter and the dominical sayings in John 3 are said to reflect the close association of Peter and John as disciples of Jesus.[92] Again, 1 Pet 1:3 is held to reflect the catastrophe that befell Peter on the night of Jesus' arrest and the future he regained at Easter,[93] and the sequence of events rehearsed in 1 Pet 3:21–22 to reflect an eyewitness at Pentecost (Acts 2:32–35).[94] Such reflections are evanescent at best, and tend to be persuasive principally for those committed on prior grounds to Petrine authorship.

2. Sayings of Jesus

Again, reflections of sayings of Jesus also found in the Gospels are adduced as evidence that the author of 1 Peter was the apostle who had heard Jesus himself speak those words.[95] The difficulty resides in differentiating between those words of Jesus reflected in 1 Peter that the author could have gotten from the early Christian traditions, or from the Gospels themselves, and those that the author must necessarily have derived from concourse with the historical Jesus.[96] A relatively large number of reflections of the words of Jesus have been identified in 1 Peter,[97] but only a handful have any persuasive power. Among the clearest are a reflection of Jesus' beatitude in Matt 5:10 in the reference in 1 Pet 3:14 (cf. also 4:14) to the blessedness of the righteous who suffer,[98] and a reflection of Matt 5:11–12 in the assumption in 1 Pet 2:12b that the believer's good works

---

similar vein Spicq ("La I[a] Petri," 44–45 n. 18) sees this as the way apostolic Christology was developed, namely, by associating experience with the OT witness. Similarly also Hiebert, "Example," 37.

91 Merrill C. Tenney admits there is no linguistic connection between 1 Peter's ἐγκομβώσασθε ("clothe yourselves," from ἐγκόμβωμα, the slave's apron) and John's λέντιον ("towel") ("Some Possible Parallels between 1 Peter and John," in R. N. Longenecker and M. C. Tenney, eds., *New Dimensions in New Testament Study* [Grand Rapids: Zondervan, 1974] 376).

92 Robert H. Gundry finds such agreements "too subtle to have been contrived" ("Further *Verba* on *Verba Christi* in First Peter," *Bib* 55 [1974] 219); others might find in them evidence that the author of 1 Peter was acquainted with the Gospel of John. Tenney ("Parallels," 377) notes as a possibility a common tradition on which the authors of 1 Peter and John drew, but rejects it in favor of personal shared experiences of John of Zebedee and Simon Peter.

93 Neugebauer, "Zur Deutung," 70.

94 Spicq ("La I[a] Petri," 54) finds a reprise of the events in 1 Pet 1:12b. Selwyn (28) finds additional witness to events in Jesus' life in 1:3, 7, 9, 10–12, 3:15; 5:2.

95 For a consideration of the words of Jesus in 1 Peter and John, see Tenney, "Parallels"; for the Synoptics, see Best, "I Peter and the Gospel"; Gundry, "*Verba Christi*"; and idem, "Further *Verba*," an exchange in which Best has much the better of it. If Gundry demonstrates anything, it is that 1 Peter is dependent on the present shape of the Jesus tradition as preserved in the canonical Gospels.

96 For the fragility of an attempt to make such a differentiation, see Spicq, "La I[a] Petri," who in

finding reflections of words of Jesus heard by Simon Peter must assume a historicity for the Gospel accounts that they are unlikely to contain, as must Gundry, "*Verba Christi*"; cf. esp. 350. For a further critique, see Norbert Brox, "Der erste Petrusbrief in der literarischen Tradition des Urchristentums," *Kairos*, NF 20 (1978) 188.

97 The following parallels, with varying degrees of similarity, have been identified: 1 Pet 1:3, 23/John 3:3; 1 Pet 1:4/Luke 12:23; Matt 5:5; 6:20; 25:34; 1 Pet 1:6/Matt 5:12; 1 Pet 1:8/John 20:29; 1 Pet 1:10/Luke 10:24; 1 Pet 1:11/Luke 24:26, 44; 1 Pet 1:13/Luke 12:35; 21:34; 1 Pet 1:17/Matt 6:9; Luke 11:2; 1 Pet 1:19/John 1:29, 36; 1 Pet 1:22/John 13:34–35; 15:12; 1 Pet 2:2/Matt 18:2–3; 19:14; Luke 18:17; 1 Pet 2:4/Matt 11:28; 1 Pet 2:5/Matt 16:18; 1 Pet 2:7/Matt 21:42; 1 Pet 2:9/John 8:12; 12:46; 1 Pet 2:12/Matt 5:16; 1 Pet 2:13, 17/Matt 22:21; 1 Pet 2:19–20/Luke 6:32–35; 1 Pet 2:21/Matt 10:38; 1 Pet 2:23/Luke 23:46; 1 Pet 2:25/Matt 9:36; Luke 15:4; John 10:11, 14, 16; 1 Pet 3:9/Luke 6:27–28; 1 Pet 3:13/Luke 10:19; 21:18; 1 Pet 3:14/Matt 5:10; 10:26–28; 1 Pet 3:16/Luke 6:28; 1 Pet 4:7/Matt 24:42; 25:13; 26:41; Luke 12:27; 21:34; 1 Pet 4:14/Matt 5:11–12; 1 Pet 4:19/Matt 6:25–27; 1 Pet 5:1/Luke 24:47; Matt 19:28; Luke 22:28–30; 1 Pet 5:2, 4/John 21:16, 17; 1 Pet 5:3/Matt 20:25–26; 1 Pet 5:6/Matt 23:12; 1 Pet 5:8–9/Mark 14:38; 1 Pet 5:3–5/Luke 22:25–30; Mark 10:42–45. Cf. Brox, "Literarischen Tradition," 188; Chase, "Peter," 787–88.

98 Cf. Randy Hall, "For to This You Have Been Called: The Cross and Suffering in I Peter," *ResQ* 19 (1976) 145; Gundry, "*Verba Christi*," 342. Best (39) assumes here "an obvious reference to a more original form of the beatitude" than that found in Matt 5:10.

bring glory to God.[99] The thought of a preserved inheritance in 1 Pet 1:4 may reflect Jesus' saying in Matt 25:34,[100] and the reference to prophetic searching in 1 Pet 1:11 may be an echo of Luke 24:26–27,[101] but none of them compels one to posit a personal relationship between the author of 1 Peter and Jesus to account for their existence. Some supposed reflections are simply unpersuasive: the use of two words for "joy" in 1 Pet 1:6, 8 (ἀγαλλιάω) and 4:13 (χαίρω) hardly compels one to recognize derivation from Matt 5:12, where both are present, to account for them,[102] nor is it likely that the proverb quoted in 1 Pet 4:8 (love covers a multitude of sins) is best accounted for as having come from Simon Peter's recollection of Jesus' statement about the necessity of multiple forgiveness (Matt 18:21–22),[103] or that

the references to prayer and sobriety in light of the impending eschaton in 1 Pet 4:7 derive from Jesus' sayings on similar themes in Luke 21:31, 34, and 36.[104]

Most telling against such an argument is that time after time, those who find such reflections depend on the present Greek text of the Gospels to display similarities,[105] something unlikely if Simon Peter were remembering sayings of Jesus almost surely delivered in Aramaic, and making his own translations.[106] Reflec-

---

99 Best ("I Peter and the Gospel," 109–10) identifies this as the "clearest parallel" in 1 Peter, based on the use here of καλ- as in Matthew, instead of 1 Peter's more common αγαθ-.

100 E.g., Brox, "Literarischen Tradition," 188. Chase ("Peter," 787) also cites as (I think less likely) parallels Matt 5:5 (!) and 6:20.

101 That Peter was not present at that point in Luke's narrative belies Gundry's contention ("Verba Christi," 345; cf. also 350) that all such reflections represent Gospel contexts where Peter was present. Sometimes the contexts Gundry finds are simply based on hypothesis: "perhaps" the disciple who remarked on the beauty of the temple was Peter (in a context of eschatological warnings Mark 13:1/1 Pet 1:13; 4:7; 5:8–9); "we can be sure" Peter was "especially incensed" by the request of James and John for seats of glory (Mark 10:41/1 Pet 5:3–5). Spicq ("La Iᵃ Petri," 55) finds a broader parallel between 1 Pet 1:10–12 and Matt 13:17; Luke 10:23–24.

102 That is the only reason I can infer for Chase ("Peter," 787) to see these as parallels. Equally general and unpersuasive is the attempt by Spicq ("La Iᵃ Petri," 43) to derive 1 Peter's emphasis on putting faith into action (2:15; 3:1–2, 13) from the concluding parable of the Sermon on the Mount (Matt 7:21–27).

103 Neugebauer, "Zur Deutung," 82. On the same level Gundry ("Verba Christi," 347) finds an allusion in 1 Pet 4:19 to Jesus' last word from the cross (Luke 23:46), since the "scene of the crucifixion had left an indelible impression on the author's mind." Yet more fanciful is the proposed derivation of 1 Pet 2:3–10 with its "association of rock-Tabernacles" (sic) from Simon Peter's experience on the Mount of Transfiguration that occurred at the time of the Feast of Tabernacles (Norman Hillyer, "First Peter and the

Feast of Tabernacles," TynBul 21 [1970] 62), or the derivation of 1 Pet 5:8 from Simon Peter's concern with Judas's betrayal (Acts 1:15–20) after Satan had entered into him (John 13:27; Tenney, "Parallels," 376).

104 Gundry, "Verba Christi," 343. In a similar vein, the use of γρηγορέω ("be awake") in 1 Pet 5:8 is hardly a compelling reference to Mark 13:35 par. Matt 24:42 (Johannes Schattenmann, "The Little Apocalypse of the Synoptics and the First Epistle of Peter," Theology Today 11 [1954] 194; cf. Gundry, "Verba Christi," 344), since that same word is used frequently not only in the other Synoptics, but also in the Pauline literature, in Hebrews, and in Revelation. Such an idea associated with Jesus' return had apparently long since passed into general Christian tradition.

105 Paradigmatic is Gundry's derivation ("Verba Christi," 347) of 1 Pet 1:21–22; 3:8; 4:8; 5:3–5 from the "Upper Room" by noting the same sequence of the Greek prepositions εἰς and διά in those passages and in John 14:1, 6. Similarly Spicq ("La Iᵃ Petri," 43) finds 1 Pet 3:1–4 to be an application of the beatitude in Matt 5:5 because of the common presence of the root πραε-. If such examples demonstrate anything, it is the dependence of the author of 1 Peter on the canonical Gospel texts, not the necessary recollections by Simon Peter of words he heard from Jesus of Nazareth.

106 Best, "I Peter and the Gospel," 95. To assume otherwise is to assume either that Jesus spoke in Greek which was taken down stenographically by the Gospel authors and identically recalled by Simon Peter, or that both Peter and the Gospels arrived independently of one another at virtually identical translations of Jesus' Aramaic sayings. The activity of

tions of "special M" as well as materials in the other Gospels[107] make it more likely that the author of 1 Peter stood in the mainstream of Christian tradition that produced not only the Gospels but the other writings of the NT as well.[108] Supposed reflections of the logia of Jesus thus constitute no compelling demonstration that Simon Peter is the author of this epistle.[109]

C. Thought-World of 1 Peter

Knowledge of the sources upon which the author of 1 Peter drew and the background such sources represent have been called upon to aid in determining who the author can, and cannot, have been.

1. Old Testament

The only source identified by quotation formulae in the epistle is the OT. The formulae appear in 1:16 (διότι γέγραπται ["wherefore it is written"], Lev 19:2) and 2:6–8 (διότι περιέχει ἐν γραφῇ ["wherefore it stands in Scripture"], Isa 28:16; Ps 118:22; Isa 8:14); also to be included, since the quotations are exact, are 1:24–25a

(διότι ["wherefore"], Isa 40:6–8) and 3:10–12 (γάρ ["for"], Ps 34:13–17).[110] In addition to such explicit citations, 1 Peter abounds in OT language in the form of phrases, allusions, and imagery, to the extent that it is difficult to be precise in every instance about what OT passage may be in mind.[111] All three types of OT literature are represented (Torah, Prophets, Writings), with a preference for Isaiah, Psalms, and Proverbs,[112] and they are as often combined[113] or placed in a kind of florilegium[114] as they are quoted in extenso.[115] Such is the abundance of references to and motifs from the OT that virtually all of the imagery of 1 Peter is drawn from its writings.[116] Yet the material so drawn is used far more often as illustration than as proof, attesting to the fact that while the traditions contained in the sacred writings of Israel informed the thought of the author of this epistle, they did not furnish the fundamental basis for his convictions.[117] Presence of such traditions delivers decisive evidence neither for nor against author-

Silvanus, invoked in other contexts, is totally omitted here.

107 On the relationship of 1 Peter to special M, see Best, "I Peter and the Gospel," 109–10; to Q, see Michaels, xli; to Matthew, Cothenet, "Les orientations," 29–30; to Luke, Bigg, 23; J. G. Gourbillon, "La Première Epître de Pierre," *Evangile* 50 (1963) 5–91 passim; Gundry, "Further *Verba*," 225 et passim; to John, Cothenet, "Les orientations," 30; Tenney, "Parallels," passim.

108 So also Brox, 45; Goppelt, 70 (ET 52–53); Best, "I Peter and the Gospel," 96, 111–12.

109 Cf. Meade, *Pseudonymity and Canon,* 174; such evidence is most convincing to those who on other grounds assume Simon Peter to be the author.

110 Schutter (*Hermeneutic,* 37) suggests three further explicit quotations in 4:8 (ὅτι ["because"], Prov 10:12), 4:18 (καί ["and"], Prov 11:31), and 5:5b (ὅτι Prov 3:34). Osborne ("L'utilisation," 66) agrees with one exception: he classes 4:8 as an allusion rather than a citation.

111 See Ernest Best, "I Peter II 4–10—A Reconsideration," *NovT* 11 (1969) 274–75. Schutter (*Hermeneutic,* 35–43) and Osborne ("L'utilisation," esp. 65–66) discuss such use, but do not agree on number (Osborne [65] finds thirty-one; Schutter [43] finds forty-one) or type of citations. For discussion of specific uses of the OT see the commentary on the individual verses below.

112 Osborne ("L'utilisation," 66) finds thirteen references to Isaiah, six to the Psalms, five to Proverbs, and one each to Exodus, Leviticus, Deuteronomy,

Jeremiah, and Hosea. He speculates (73) that such distribution may show diminished value placed on the Pentateuch, and more on Prophets and Psalms in primitive Christianity.

113 E.g., Isa 28:16 and Ps 118:22 in 2:4; Isa 43:20–21; Exod 19:6; 23:22; and Hos 1:6, 9 in 2:9–10; cf. also Osborne, "L'utilisation," 74.

114 E.g., the numerous texts combined in 2:3–10; cf. Schutter, *Hermeneutic,* 43. 1 Pet 2:21–25 reads almost like a midrash on Isaiah 53, as 2:4–8 is almost a *pesher* on the stone imagery found in various texts.

115 E.g., Ps 34:13–17 in 3:10–12. Bornemann ("Taufrede," see 148–51) argued, not entirely persuasively, that 1 Pet 1:3–5:11 is best understood as "eine Rede, bzw. Ansprache im Anschluss an Psalm 34" "a speech or address in connection with Psalm 34." For a recent thorough and detailed critique of that view, see Schutter, *Hermeneutic,* 44–49.

116 So Chase, "Peter," 782. For a list of motifs (e.g., flood, patriarchs, exodus, covenant ceremony, temple) see Jacques Schlosser, "Ancien Testament et Christologie dans la Prima Petri," in Perrot, *Etudes,* 66. Schlosser also notes (67) that relative to its size, 1 Peter probably has more material drawn from the OT than any other NT writing; so also Schutter, *Hermeneutic,* 3.

117 So thoroughly has the author appropriated the language and motifs of the OT for the understanding of the Christian faith that Israel as an entity, along with its law, has disappeared as a theological problem for him. The Scriptures of Israel furnish

ship by Simon Peter, since the NT as a whole is saturated with OT traditions.

2. Qumran

Along with the evidence that the author of 1 Peter used material from Jewish Scriptures, there is some evidence that he may also have drawn on material which originated at Qumran.[118] In addition to a general agreement between the thought-world of Qumran and the early Christianity in which 1 Peter shared, seen in terms of such general ideas as election, baptism, spiritual temple, the fulfillment of prophecy, the eschatological punishment of the unrighteous and deliverance of the chosen,[119] there are more specific points of similarity. The notion, for example, that adherents of the group necessarily live as strangers and exiles in present society, or that the adherent has been given a new life by God,[120] shows such similarity of self-understanding. The similarity of ways of using Scripture—the catena of verses, or the florilegium—may also point to such similarity.[121] This evidence has led some to posit a stream of theological thought from the Qumran community to early Christianity, a stream in which 1 Peter then naturally shared.[122] The outcome of that stream, however, is

markedly different in Qumran and in 1 Peter at least with respect to one's involvement in the society in relation to which one is an alien and an exile: in Qumran it resulted in virtual total withdrawal from that society, a result quite alien to 1 Peter's assumption that Christians continue to live in that society and where possible conform to those laws and customs that do not compromise their commitment to Christ.[123] If such thought could influence the apostle Paul, as Flusser claims, there is no reason the presence of such thought in 1 Peter should be any more probative of apostolic authorship than it is decisive against authorship by Simon Peter.

3. Mystery Religions

A further possible source of influence on 1 Peter has been found in the doctrines and practices of the mystery religions. Proposed in most detail by E. R. Perdelwitz,[124] it has found some positive echoes from time to time,[125] but on the whole, because of the later development of

---

illustrations for, but do not prove, the validity of the Christian faith.

118 Related materials are confined for the most part to the first two chapters of 1 Peter. For comments on the relationship of specific verses to possible Qumran materials, see the comments on the individual verses below.

119 For general themes, see David Flusser, "The Dead Sea Sect and Pre-Pauline Christianity," in C. Rabin and Y. Yadin, eds., *Aspects of the Dead Sea Scrolls* (Scripta hierosolymitana 4; Jerusalem: Magnes, 1958) 264; for prophetic fulfillment, see Schutter, *Hermeneutic*, 117; for a discussion of divine punishment, see Jean Carmignac, "La théologie de la souffrance dans les Hymnes de Qumrân," *RevQ* 3/11 (1961) 371–73. Carmignac draws no comparisons with Christianity, but the similarities are obvious from his presentation.

120 Leonhard Goppelt compares 1 Pet 1:3—2:10 with the general tenor of the Qumran writings, and 1:3 with 1 QH 3:19–21 ("Prinzipien neutestamentlicher Sozialethik nach dem I Petrusbrief," in H. Baltensweiler and B. Reicke, eds., *Neues Testament und Geschichte: Historisches Geschehen und Deutung im Neuen Testament: Oscar Cullmann zum 70. Geburtstag* [Tübingen: Mohr (Siebeck), 1972] 286).

121 Schutter (*Hermeneutic*, 87) finds such similarities

between catenae in 1 Pet 2:6–8 and 4QTestim; and between florilegia in 1 Pet 2:3–10 and 4QFlor; 11QMelch.

122 Flusser ("Dead Sea Sect," 265) argues that with respect to the general themes common to the two movements, "the whole body of ideas . . . could have come into Christianity only from the Qumran Sect"; he further (216–17) identifies this stream with Bultmann's "*Kerygma* of the Hellenistic Community," and finds its influence in both Paul's letters and the Gospel of John.

123 Goppelt ("Prinzipien," esp. 287) makes this point well.

124 E. Richard Perdelwitz proposed such a relationship to solve the literary problem of disunity between 1 Pet 1:3—4:11 and the remainder of the letter, and laid special emphasis on the relationship between the Taurobolium and baptism (*Die Mysterienreligion und das Problem des 1. Petrusbriefes* [Religionsversuche und Vorarbeite 11/3; Giessen: Töpelmann, 1911]). For a negative evaluation of Perdelwitz, see Selwyn, 305–11. Possible mystery religion influence at specific points in 1 Peter will be discussed in the comments on individual verses.

125 Beare (37), for example, while disclaiming any possibility of such specific influences as that of the Taurobolium on 1 Peter's discussion of baptism, nevertheless says it is "impossible to escape" more

such religions relative to primitive Christianity and the paucity of information concerning their practices and beliefs,[126] this source of influence, decidedly negative toward authorship by Simon Peter, has not found wide acceptance.

4. Acts

Similarities in thought and expression between 1 Peter and the speeches of Peter in Acts have been adduced to demonstrate the Petrine authorship of the epistle. Some have appealed to similarities in vocabulary[127] or in the use of the phrase παῖς θεοῦ ("servant of God") to identify Jesus,[128] while others have noted, more general similarities such as the propensity of both epistle and speeches to appeal to Scripture[129] or to the universal applicability of salvation announced in both,[130] or to the prominence of other broad agreements in language or thought.[131]

The difficulty with such an attempt lies in the fact that many of the general similarities, such as an emphasis on baptism or on resurrection, also characterize the rest of the NT.[132] Further difficulty is provided by the fact that many of the characteristics of the Petrine speeches in Acts are also characteristic of the Pauline speeches,[133] thus limiting if not eliminating their viability in showing Simon Peter as the person behind both speeches and the epistle. The conclusion that the "common ground" between them lies in the "mind of St. Peter"[134] is thus shown to rest on highly questionable evidence, and cannot serve to demonstrate legitimate Petrine authorship of 1 Peter.

---

general traces of mystery terminology; see also his "Teaching of First Peter," *ATR* 27 (1945) 286. More representative of recent thought is the discussion of Selwyn, 305–11; see also Cranfield (16), who finds such traces "highly problematic" and doubts whether any such terms occurring in 1 Peter "cannot equally well be traced to others sources."

126 For a sober analysis of the possibility of such influence, see Martin P. Nilsson, *Geschichte der griechischen Religion* (2d ed.; 2 vols.; Munich: Beck'sche, 1961), esp. "Die griechischen Mysterien-kulte," 2.345–72; and "Die Religionen und die Mysterien der fremden Götter," 2.622–701.

127 Spicq ("La Iª Petri," 60), for example, notes the following words as demonstrating such a similarity: προσωπολήμπτης ("partiality"), Acts 10:34; 1 Pet 1:17 (but in the form ἀπροσωπολήμπτης ["impartiality"]; the form found in Acts 10:34, it is also used by Paul in Rom 2:11, and appears in Eph 6:9; cf. also Col 3:25); ἀγνοία ("ignorance"), Acts 3:17; 1 Pet 1:14 (it is also used in Acts 17:30, a speech by Paul, and in Eph 4:18); ἀπειλέω ("to threaten"), Acts 4:17; 1 Pet 2:23 (it is spoken in Acts not by Peter but by the Jews; as a noun see Acts 9:1, a speech of Paul; cf. also Eph 6:9); νεώτεροι ("young [men]"), Acts 5:6; 1 Pet 5:5 (it is not spoken by Peter in Acts 5; cf. 1 Tim 5:1, 2, 11, 14; 2 Tim 2:22; Titus 2:6); πρόγνωσις ("foreknowledge"), Acts 2:23; 1 Pet 1:2 (for the verbal form, see Rom 8:29; 11:12); ἀργύριον, χρυσίον ("silver, gold"), Acts 3:6; 1 Pet 1:18 (the phrase appears also in Acts 20:33 in a speech by Paul; for the idea, cf. also 1 Cor 6:20). Wand (27) cites as a "striking similarity" between Acts and 1 Peter the use of the word ξύλον ("wood") for Jesus' cross (Acts 5:30; 10:39; 1 Pet 2:24; it is also used by Paul, however, Acts 13:29; Gal 3:13). Spicq ("La Iª Petri," 55) notes that in Peter's first speech in Acts, he cites Ps 110 (2:24), a passage also used in 1 Pet 3:22, yet the phrase about sitting at God's right hand appears in other epistles as well (e.g., Rom 8:34; Col 3:1; Eph 1:20; Heb 10:12). Such vocabulary has therefore little probative value in this matter.

128 The phrase appears only in Acts, in each instance either spoken by Peter (Acts 3:13, 26) or used when he was present (Acts 4:27, 30; cf. O. Cullmann, *Peter, Disciple, Apostle, Martyr* [trans. F. V. Filson; 2d ed.; Philadelphia: Westminster, 1962] 68). Spicq ("La Iª Petri," 53) links the four passages in Acts to the references in 1 Peter to Isaiah 53 (1:19 = 53:7; 2:22 = 53:9; 3:18 = 53:10–11; 2:25 = 53:6), thus establishing a connection between Acts and 1 Peter, albeit a rather roundabout one.

129 E.g., Gourbillon, "La première Epître," 10. A quick glance at the remaining speeches in Acts and the other epistles in the NT shows that is hardly a unique characteristic of Acts' speeches and 1 Peter.

130 So Kazuhito Shimada (*The Formulary Material in First Peter* [Ann Arbor: Xerox University Microfilms, 1966] 228) and Spicq ("La Iª Petri," 59–60); both base such universal applicability on the idea of God's impartiality (Acts 2:39; 10:34; 1 Pet 1:17). Again, such universal applicability is hardly unique to Peter's speeches in Acts and 1 Peter; cf. Rom 1:16; 2:6–10; 10:12–13; Titus 2:11.

131 See "Excursus: Conceptual Similarities between Acts and 1 Peter."

132 See the discussion in nn. 127–131 above.

133 Meade, *Pseudonymity and Canon*, 174; Best, 53. Best ("I Peter and the Gospel," 98) also notes that in one instance at least, a passage in 1 Peter (5:2–4) is closer to a Pauline than to a Petrine speech in Acts (20:28). For further arguments, see Terence V. Smith, *Petrine Controversies in Early Christianity* (WUNT 2/15; Tübingen: Mohr [Siebeck], 1985) 151.

Excursus: Conceptual Similarities between Acts and 1 Peter

J. P. Love[135] has sought to add weight to the argument that 1 Peter truly was written by the apostle by listing a series of conceptual similarities between Acts and 1 Peter. A close examination, however, shows the passages from Acts have at least as great a similarity, sometimes a greater similarity, to other passages in Acts or in other NT material unrelated to Peter.

In the following list, the passage from Acts is given first, then the passage from 1 Peter.

2:14–20 and 1:10–12: the outpouring of the Spirit (but cf. Rom 5:5; Titus 3:5–6)

2:31 and 3:18: Jesus' resurrection (but cf. Acts 13:37, a speech of Paul that is closer to Peter's speech than either is to 1 Peter)

2:32–36 and 1:21; 3:22: resurrection and ascension (but cf. Phil 2:9–11)

2:38 and 3:21: purpose of baptism (but Acts mentions forgiveness and the Holy Spirit, both omitted in 1 Peter)

3:17 and 1:14: on ignorance (little relationship of context; cf. also 1 Cor 2:8)

3:20 and 1:7, 13; 4:13: return of Christ (again, hardly unique to these two NT writings)

3:23 and 2:8: rejection of unbelievers (Acts 3:23 refers to prediction of Moses; 1 Pet 2:8 is closer to Rom 9:33 than to Acts; cf. also Rom 12:8–9)

3:26; 10:43 and 2:7, 10: forgiveness of sins (cf. Acts 13:38–39, a speech of Paul, closer to Peter's speech in Acts than either is to 1 Peter)

3:18 and 1:20: need for Christ's suffering (cf. Acts 26:22–23, closer to Peter's speech than either is to 1 Peter).[136]

The attempt must therefore be judged to lack probative force.

5. Pauline Letters

If agreements with Acts have been used to argue for the authenticity of 1 Peter, agreements with the Pauline epistles, particularly Romans and Ephesians,[137] have been used to argue against such authenticity.[138] Such agreements, interpreted to mean literary dependence, at one point enjoyed the status of consensus,[139] but in recent years those agreements have undergone reevaluation, and the consensus of an earlier period no longer pertains.[140]

a. Romans. Dependence on Romans has often been cited as being virtually without serious question,[141] although specific passages on which scholars call to demonstrate such dependence vary widely,[142] and the evidence

134 The phrase is from Selwyn, 36. Spicq (23) and Wand (28) also support such a view. Ora Delmar Foster (*The Literary Relations of the "First Epistle of Peter"* [Transactions of the Connecticut Academy of the Arts and Sciences; New Haven: Yale University Press, 1913] 508) attributes such similarities as exist to Luke's possible borrowing from 1 Peter.

135 "First Epistle," 67, drawing on Selwyn, 33–36.

136 Although he cites further "similarities," they are so vague as to be meaningless.

137 E.g., Foster, *Literary Relations,* 376, 473 (see also B. W. Bacon's introduction in the same volume, 368); Beare, "Teaching," 286; Brox, 40; and the discussion in Lohse, "Parenesis," 40.

138 The proposal that Paul depended on 1 Peter because 1 Peter was written earlier than the Pauline epistles, argued by Bernhard Weiss (*Der Petrinische Lehrbegriff* [Berlin: Schultze, 1855], esp. 406–25), failed to gain many adherents. For a critical discussion of Weiss, see W. Seufert, "Das Abhängigkeitsverhältnis des I. Petrusbriefs vom Römerbrief," *ZNW* 16 (1874) 360–88. Attempts to save authenticity by arguing that

Simon Peter knew of Romans from reading it (Foster, *Literary Relations,* 473), or from his contacts with Paul in Rome, or that he had read some of the Pauline letters (e.g., Bigg, 15) lack probative force.

139 Foster (*Literary Relations,* 474 et passim) saw it supported by "the overwhelming weight of scholarship"; cf. Albert E. Barnett, *Paul Becomes a Literary Influence* (Chicago: University of Chicago Press, 1941) 52; Beare, 28. Seufert ("Das Abhängigkeitsverhältnis," passim) illustrates, rather than demonstrates, an assumed dependence.

140 E.g., John H. Elliott, "The Rehabilitation of an Exegetical Step-Child: 1 Peter in Recent Research," in Talbert, *Perspectives,* 7–8; Schutter, *Hermeneutic,* 34.

141 Chase ("Peter," 788): "There is no doubt" of such an acquaintance; Schweizer (64): Romans is "presupposed in its entirety"; Seufert ("Das Abhängigkeitsverhältnis," 388): the dependence "may be assumed to be proved" (cf. also 360).

142 They range from Brox ("Literarischen Tradition," 183) who finds five parallels, to Barnett (*Literary*

adduced to show such dependence is at times questionable at best.[143]

Of those passages where dependence is located, the following deserve the most careful attention:

1 Peter	Romans
1:14	12:2
2:6–8	9:32–33
2:13–17	13:1–7
3:8–9	12:16–17
4:10–11	12:6

In addition, the following may be listed:

1 Peter	Romans
1:22	12:9
2:5	12:1
2:10	9:25
3:11	12:18[144]

It is interesting to note that the passages from Romans are limited to chaps. 9, 12, and 13, with the material in chap. 9 limited to quotation of similar passages from the OT, and the material in chap. 13 limited to the passage on Christian responsibility to the state.[145] The remainder deal with single words (a form of συσχηματίζομαι in 1:14/12:2, of χάρισμα in 4:10–11/12:6, of θυσία in 2:5/12:1, ἀνυπόκριτος and the stem ἀγαπ- in 1:22/12:9, and a form of the stem εἰρην- in 3:11/12:18), and a recollection of a saying of Jesus (3:9/12:17).[146] In each instance the context is one of general exhortation to Christian virtues, things most likely to be contained in general traditional, if not catechetical, materials. On the whole, then, the only literal agreements deal with OT quotations,[147] with the result that literary influence of Romans on 1 Peter is hardly indicated.[148] More likely is a common sharing of Christian traditions.[149]

b. Ephesians. The dependence of 1 Peter on Ephesians has also been argued,[150] often in the form of direct literary dependence,[151] although as in the case of Romans, the passages cited as evidence vary widely.[152] Those cited most frequently include the following:

Influence) who finds twenty-four, to Foster (Literary Relations, 440) who identifies sixty.

143 This is particularly true of Seufert ("Das Abhängigkeitsverhältnis"), who finds evidence of dependence of 1 Pet 4:11 on Rom 12:6–7 precisely in the absence in 1 Peter of the key Pauline idea of σῶμα χριστοῦ and the key word πίστις (364); or the dependence of 1 Pet 2:13 on Rom 13:1 because Paul's key word ἐξουσία is deliberately avoided in 1 Peter (368). Such argumenta e silentio, of which there are many more examples, allow one to "prove" virtually anything.

144 These are drawn from Brox, "Literarischen Tradition," 183; and from W. Sandy and A. C. Headlam, A Critical and Exegetical Commentary on the Epistle to the Romans (13th ed.; ICC; New York: Scribner's, 1911) lxxiv–lxxv. Goppelt (49, ET 28) adds 1 Pet 4:1/Rom 6:7 and 4:13; 5:1/8:17; the former is somewhat similar in thought (suffering/death covers/frees from sin) but not in vocabulary, while the latter is a commonplace of Christian thought (suffering with Christ now means glory with him later), again expressed with quite different language.

145 For closer analysis of similarities and differences, see the comments on the individual verses.

146 Many of the parallels identified by Foster (Literary Relations) are similarly tenuous, and depend on a single word, or a general similarity of thought.

147 So Goppelt, 49 (ET 28–29).

148 See the careful analysis by Kazuhito Shimada, "Is 1 Peter Dependent on Romans?" AJBI 19 (1993) 87–

137, which results in a negative judgment about dependence; so also, e.g., Hans Windisch, Die Katholischen Briefe (3d ed. rev. Herbert Preisker; HNT; Tübingen: Mohr [Siebeck], 1951) 61.

149 So Cothenet, "Les orientations," 34; Bigg, 20; N. Hillyer, "'Rock-Stone' Imagery in I Peter," TynBul 22 (1971) 60–61.

150 E.g., Chase ("Peter," 789): 1 Peter's familiarity with Ephesians is "beyond doubt."

151 Foster (Literary Relations, 479–80, quoting B. W. Bacon): literary dependence of 1 Peter on Ephesians is "one of the most solid results of criticism"; Barnett (Literary Influence, 54): literary relationship is "a matter of practical certainty"; cf. also C. L. Mitton, "The Relationship between I Peter and Ephesians," JTS, n.s. 1 (1950) 67, 73. For a critique of Mitton's work, see Kazuhito Shimada, "Is 1 Peter Dependent on Ephesians? A Critique of C. L. Mitton," AJBI 17 (1991) 77–106.

152 Foster (Literary Relations, 454) lists forty-five passages that show parallels; Barnett (Literary Influence, 51) finds twenty-three; Goppelt (49, ET 28) lists seven; Brox ("Literarischen Tradition," 183) lists six.

1 Peter	Ephesians
1:3	1:3
1:3–5	1:18
1:10–12	3:5
1:14	2:2–3
2:4–6	2:20–22
3:22	1:20–22[153]

In addition, the following may be considered:

1 Peter	Ephesians
1:1	1:1
1:26	3:11 (1:4)
5:8	6:11[154]

These parallels, with one exception, occur in the first half of each epistle. Agreements are of various types. In some instances they consist of a similar word or words, although the context is not always the same. Thus 1 Pet 1:1 and Eph 1:1 agree in using ἀπόστολος ("apostle") and Ἰησοῦς Χριστός ("Jesus Christ," though not in the same order), but in a common epistolary formula;[155] 1 Pet 1:3–5 and Eph 1:18–19 agree in forms of ἐλπίς, κληρο-νομία, and δύναμις ("hope," "inheritance," "power") but the words are used in different ways;[156] both 1 Pet 1:10–12 and Eph 3:5 use ἀπεκαλύφθη ("revealed") but in a quite different context (1 Peter: salvation revealed then to prophets; Ephesians: union of Jews and Gentiles in Christ not known in past revealed now to apostles and prophets);[157] 1 Pet 1:14 and Eph 2:2–3 agree in

ἐπιθυμία, τέκνα ("desires," "children") but little more; 1 Pet 1:20 and Eph 1:4 have in common the phrase πρὸ καταβολῆς κόσμου ("before the foundation of the world"), but in 1 Peter it refers to God foreknowing Christ, while in Ephesians it refers to God choosing us in Christ; 1 Pet 5:8 and Eph 6:11 agree only in using the common NT word διάβολος ("devil") at the end of their respective discussions.[158] In other instances where the agreements are more impressive, they center around the use of OT passages common in early Christianity: 1 Pet 2:4–6/Eph 2:20–22 = Isa 28:16, although some of the key words differ;[159] 1 Pet 3:22/Eph 1:20–22 = Ps 110:1;[160] or in passages that are rather obviously liturgical: 1 Pet 1:3a/Eph 1:3a, although similarity ceases at the conclusion of the doxological formula (compare here also 1 Pet 3:22/Eph 1:20–22); or in passages that are paranetic in intent: 1 Pet 2:1/Eph 4:25, 31 or 1 Pet 3:1/Eph 5:22, although again the similarities may derive as easily from common Christian tradition as from literary dependence.[161]

Despite efforts to find direct literary dependence of the author of 1 Peter on Ephesians, the nature of the similarities is such that where they do not depend on obviously common Christian materials,[162] the parallels are not of sufficiently compelling nature as to demand a necessary literary dependence. The two letters move in different theological spheres, so that linguistic parallels

---

153 These are listed as a group in Brox, "Literarischen Tradition," 183, and discussed by most others who concern themselves with this problem, e.g., Barnett, *Literary Influence*; Ernst Percy, *Die Probleme der Kolosser- und Epheserbriefe* (Skrifter utgivne av Kungl. Humanistika Vetenskapssamfundet i Lund 39; Lund: Gleerup, 1946); Foster, *Literary Relations*.

154 These are also included by Barnett (*Literary Influence*, 52), Foster (*Literary Relations*, 447), and Percy (*Probleme*, 440), respectively. Such a list is not exhaustive, obviously, but represents those that have the greatest claim to attention.

155 Barnett (*Literary Influence*, 52) suggests the author of 1 Peter drew the idea of a general epistle from Ephesians.

156 Barnett (*Literary Influence*, 54) takes phrases from 1 Pet 1:3–13 and Eph 1:3–20, and despite the fact that the vocabulary is quite different, finds a "literary relationship" to be "a matter of practical certainty." Percy (*Probleme*, 437) finds 1 Peter to be the earlier form but finds it impossible to draw any compelling conclusion ("zwingender Schluss").

157 Despite these differences, Percy (*Probleme*, 436) thinks this is the closest example of direct dependence of 1 Peter on Ephesians; cf. also Leaney, 20; Mitton, "Relationship," 70.

158 Percy (*Probleme*, 440) is reluctant, in view of the differing contexts, to draw any conclusion of dependence from this use of διάβολος.

159 Percy (*Probleme*, 438) thinks 1 Peter may be prior, but is unwilling to affirm that Ephesians derives from 1 Peter because the idea expressed was widely held in the early church. Mitton ("Relationship," 71) finds 1 Peter dependent on Ephesians.

160 Foster (*Literary Relations*, 446) finds Zahn's observation justified that in this instance: "Peter and Silvanus had Ephesians before them." Mitton ("Relationship," 71) argues that 1 Peter "reflects acquaintance" with Ephesians; Percy (*Probleme*, 439) thinks both drew from common Christian tradition.

161 So, e.g., Goppelt, 49 (ET 29).

162 In addition to those cited above, see Goppelt (49, ET 29), who finds the similarities due to common use of common early Christian traditions and thus finds no

are more apparent than real.[163]

c. Other Pauline Letters. Attempts to establish literary dependence on other letters of the Pauline corpus have been made, but the evidence is less compelling than that for Romans or Ephesians,[164] and it remains unpersuasive.

Evidence other than the literary relationship of passages in 1 Peter to passages in Pauline letters have been noted, however. They are formal, linguistic, and theological.

Formally, the letter reflects the structure of the Pauline letters, from the bipartite formula that identifies sender and receivers to the division of the body of the letter into three parts to the final conclusion and greetings.[165] While kerygma and paranesis are not separated into larger blocks as they are in Romans or Galatians,[166] that is not an unalterable characteristic of Pauline letters (e.g., the Corinthian correspondence, or Philippians). Whether or not such similarity means that the author of 1 Peter is deliberately imitating Paul,[167] or that by the time 1 Peter was written that form had become normal for such correspondence, having passed into the broader tradition from its use by Paul, is difficult to determine.

Linguistically, typically Pauline words and phrases appear in 1 Peter, such as ἐν Χριστῷ (3:16; 5:10, 14), ἀποκάλυψις (1:7, 13; 4:13), διακονέω (1:12; 4:10) in

connection with χαρίσματα (4:10),[168] and the letter as a whole is informed by a theology in which God's initiative for human salvation takes the form of the passion and resurrection of Jesus, participation in which saves from sin and creates new life for those who accept it in trust.[169] Yet despite such undeniable similarities, there exist with them significant differences both in vocabulary and content. A number of key Pauline words are missing, such as σάρξ, ἐκκλησία, θλίψις, and "old" and "new Adam."[170] The atonement in 1 Peter is expounded in terms of the suffering servant drawn from Isaiah, a concept absent in Paul, and uses as the key phrase πάσχω in place of the typically Pauline σταυρός, σταυρόω.[171]

Theologically, many key Pauline concepts are absent from 1 Peter, such as the church as body of Christ, the work of the Holy Spirit, the idea of righteousness by faith apart from the law, and above all the tension between Israel and the church, indeed the whole dialectic of the relationship between Israel as chosen people and the Christian community as chosen.[172]

While the relationship of 1 Peter to the Pauline way of theological reflection cannot be denied,[173] how much of the "Pauline" flavor of 1 Peter is the result of a common use of early liturgical or confessional material[174] is difficult to say with precision. Similarly, whether the author of 1 Peter was aware of the Pauline letters, or had read them, or whether the "Pauline" material in 1 Peter

reason to think of literary dependence; cf. also Percy, *Probleme*, 440.

163 Horst Goldstein, *Paulinische Gemeinde im Ersten Petrusbrief* (SB 80; Stuttgart: Katholisches Bibelwerk, 1975) 79–80; Cothenet, "Les orientations," 34–35. Cf. Bigg (17), who for that reason finds difficulty in detecting the "subtle affinities" between the two epistles that others find.

164 Foster (*Literary Relations*) finds evidence of "probable" dependence on Galatians (414) and 1 Corinthians (418), but no others. Claims for dependence on 1 and 2 Thessalonians would be persuasive for those who think Silvanus had a hand in drafting 1 Peter, since his name appears at the head of those two Pauline letters, but such similarities are (remarkably) absent.

165 For a careful comparison, see Schutter, *Hermeneutic*, 24–27, who notes similarities in the opening formula (1:1–2), the blessing/prayer (1:3–12), the tripartite division of the body of the letter (1:13–2:10; 2:11–4:11; 4:12–5:11), and the conclusion (5:12–14). See also Brox, 50.

166 Neugebauer ("Zur Deutung," 71), in noting this, gives the impression that it is more characteristic of Paul than is actually the case.

167 Both Schutter (*Hermeneutic*, 24) and Brox (50) note that 1 Peter follows this form more closely than the Deutero-Pauline letters. Enough differences do exist in form, however, to allow Schutter (26) to conclude, I think correctly, that 1 Peter is not a slavish copy of the Pauline form, but represents a thorough appropriation of it, used with considerable literary skill.

168 Goppelt (50, ET 30) notes they are used in a way represented in Paul's theology; cf. also Goldstein, *Paulinische Gemeinde*, 61. Lohse ("Parenesis," 53 n. 87) finds a similar appropriation in *1 Clement*.

169 Schelkle, 5; Goldstein, *Paulinische Gemeinde*, 50–54.

170 Brox, 49.

171 Martin H. Scharlemann, "Why the *Kuriou* in 1 Peter 1:25?" *CTM* 30 (1959) 93; Goppelt, 50 (ET 30).

172 On such differences, see Meade, *Pseudonymity and Canon*, 170; Brox, 46–51; Cothenet, "Les orientations," 35; Goldstein, *Paulinische Gemeinde*, 109;

had already passed into common tradition by the time 1 Peter was written is equally difficult to demonstrate.[175]

However that question be resolved, it is apparent that while there are some developments of Pauline ideas in 1 Peter,[176] along with certain Pauline turns of phrase,[177] 1 Peter is not a deliberate attempt to theologize in the Pauline mode, or to defend Paulinism as a way of carrying on theological reflection.[178] Rather, it appears that the language is more Pauline than the actual content;[179] as a result, the notion of the dependence of 1 Peter on Pauline theology, to say nothing of literary

dependence on the Pauline corpus, seems often to have been exaggerated.[180] The differences on the whole seem more significant for the theology of 1 Peter than the similarities,[181] with the result that the notion of 1 Peter belonging to the Pauline "school," or deliberately cast in the Pauline mode, is wide of the mark.[182]

6. Other New Testament Writings

In addition to similarities to Pauline literature, similarities have been found between 1 Peter and several other NT books. The most significant are James, Hebrews, and the Johannine literature.

François Bovon, "Foi chrétienne et religion populaire dans la première Epître de Pierre," *EThR* 53 (1978) 30; Neugebauer, "Zur Deutung," 71. For further discussion, see the comments on the individual verses.

173 Goldstein, *Paulinische Gemeinde*, esp. 56, 62, 104; Willi Marxsen, "Der Mitälteste und Zeuge der Leiden Christi," in C. Andersen and G. Klein, eds., *Theologia Crucis—Signum Crucis, Festschrift für E. Dinkler* (Tübingen: Mohr [Siebeck] 1979) 392; William Manson, "Grace in the New Testament," in W. T. Whitly, ed., *The Doctrine of Grace* (New York: Macmillan, 1931) 56; Norbert Brox, "Zur pseudepigraphischen Rahmung des ersten Petrusbriefes," *BZ*, NF 19 (1975) 95. Schweizer (12) denies that any enmity between Peter and Paul could have made such a situation impossible.

174 Selwyn (384) and Carrington ("Saint Peter's Epistle," 58) were important in launching this view; cf. also Goldstein, *Paulinische Gemeinde*, 105; Elliott, "Rehabilitation," 8; Cranfield, 14; Hillyer, "'Rock-Stone' Imagery," 61. This point is made particularly in relation to the similarities of 1 Peter with Ephesians: Percy, *Probleme*, 434; Raymond E. Brown, Karl P. Donfried, and John Reumann, eds., *Peter in the New Testament* (Minneapolis: Augsburg, 1973) 152; Wand, 20; Mitton, "Relationship," 68; Ronald Russell, "Eschatology and Ethics in 1 Peter," *EvQ* 47 (1975) 81. Such traditional material is now commonly regarded as oral rather than written in form; see, e.g., Schutter, *Hermeneutic*, 33–34.

175 Michaels, xliii; Bovon, "Foi chrétienne," 29; Dennis Sylva, "1 Peter Studies: The State of the Discipline," *BTB* 10 (1980) 162.

176 Such developments often move in such different directions that even the term *development* must be used with care; cf. baptism, which "saves" and is primarily related to Christ's resurrection (so Goldstein, *Paulinische Gemeinde*, 62; Michaels, lxii); the church more as building than as body, yet understood differently than in the Pastorals (so Goldstein, *Paulinische Gemeinde*, 55, 101, 111); the

relation to Christ, but more in terms of imitation than participation (so Bovon, "Foi chrétienne," 30).

177 In addition to n. 166 above, cf. Helmut Millauer, *Leiden als Gnade: Eine Traditionsgeschichtliche Untersuchung zur Leidenstheologie des ersten Petrusbriefes* (Europäische Hochschulschriften 23/56; Bern: Herbert Lang, 1976) 187, 191.

178 Brox (47): "(1 Pet) hat nichts von Programmcharakter an sich" "[1 Peter] has nothing about it of a programmatic character" in regard to Pauline theology; Brox ("Tendenz," 118) also fails to find any dependence on Pauline theology in 1 Peter.

179 The phrase is from Brox, 50.

180 So Spicq, 16–17 n. 5; see Daube ("Appended Note," in Selwyn, 488), who argues against literary dependence by questioning why 1 Peter, with its good Greek, would have taken Pauline imperatives and turned them into participles (cf., e.g., Rom 12:2 with 1 Pet 1:14).

181 Cothenet, "Les orientations," 35. The following are cited as examples: (1) the difference in treatment of Israel as a theological problem (Norbert Brox, "'Sara zum Beispiel . . .' Israel im 1. Petrusbrief," in P.-G. Müller and W. Stegner, eds., *Kontinuität und Einheit: Für Franz Mussner* [Freiburg: Herder, 1981] 486–87; Frederic Manns, "Sara, modèle de la femme obéissante: Etude de l'arrière-plan juif de 1 Pierre 3,5–6," *BeO* 26 [1984] 65–66; Bovon, "Foi chrétienne," 32–33); (2) the difference in the view of the church, i.e., building under way, not body (Goldstein, *Paulinische Gemeinde*, 109); (3) the relationship of Christian to state (Brox, 49). These matters will be discussed in detail in the comments on individual verses below.

182 Goppelt, 50 (ET 30); Brox, "Situation und Sprache," 2; cf. Goldstein, *Paulinische Gemeinde*, 106–7.

a. James. The following passages have been identified as showing a relationship between 1 Peter and James:

1 Peter	James
1:1	1:1
1:6–7	1:2–3
1:23—2:2	1:10–11, 18–22
4:8	5:20
5:5–9	4:6–10[183]

Of these, one is restricted to one word (διασπόρα ["diaspora"], 1 Pet 1:1/Jas 1:1), and another to a quotation from an OT passage (1 Pet 4:8/Jas 5:20 = Prov 10:12). The remaining three passages show greater parallels. 1 Pet 1:6–7/Jas 1:2–3 refer to joy (different words) because of πειρασμοῖς ποικίλοις (["various trials"] but in different order) that are related to the δοκίμιον ὑμῶν τῆς πίστεως ("character of your faith"), although the understanding of the last phrase is different (James: temptations allow present δοκίμιον to bring about endurance; 1 Peter: temptations come so that resulting δοκίμιον may lead to praise, glory, and honor at Christ's return). Both 1 Pet 1:24–25a and Jas 1:10–11, 18–22 refer to Isa 40:6–7 (1 Peter in quotation, James in paraphrase), both advise putting off (ἀποθέμενοι) vices (including forms of πᾶσα κακία ["every evil"]) and turning to (God's) word instead, this latter in quite different language, however, and for different purposes (James: the fate of the rich man, then advice to his readers, with unrelated material in between these two points; 1 Peter: the fate of the Christian in unified discourse). 1 Pet 5:5–9 and Jas 4:6–10 begin by quoting Prov 3:34 (LXX), advise resisting the διάβολος ("devil") and being humble (ταπεινώθητε)

before God, who exalts (ὑψως-) those who do; nevertheless, these points are made in varying order and interspersed with further unrelated commands. In these passages, the presence of similar words used to make somewhat different points in differing contexts makes dependence difficult to determine[184]—does Peter depend on James?[185] James on Peter?[186]—and is probably best understood as independent use of common traditions.[187]

b. Hebrews. Among the parallels between 1 Peter and Hebrews, the following are often cited:

1 Peter	Hebrews
1:2; 2:11	11:13
1:2	12:24
2:25, (5:4)	13:20
3:9	12:17
3:18	9:28
4:14	13:13[188]

In those cases where there is a similarity of language, it is most often restricted to one word (παρεπιδήμος ["exile"], 1 Pet 1:2, 2:11/Heb 11:13; ποιμήν ["shepherd"], 1 Pet 2:25 [God]/Heb 13:20 [Jesus]; ἅπαξ ["once for all"], 1 Pet 3:18/Heb 9:28) or one root (ὀνειδιδ-, 1 Pet 4:14/Heb 13:13); in the two instances where there is more than one word, they either stand in grammatically different relationship to one another (ῥαντισμὸν αἵματος ["sprinkling of blood"], 1 Pet 1:2; αἵματι ῥαντισμοῦ ["of sprinkling with blood"], Heb 12:24), or they are used in a radically different context (1 Pet 3:9, εὐλογίαν κληρονομήσητε: believers to return good for evil *in order to inherit blessing*; Heb 12:17, κληρονομῆσαι τὴν εὐλογίαν:

---

183 For lists of similarities, see Chase, "Peter," 788; Foster, *Literary Relations,* 508; Goppelt, 51 (ET 31); Brox, "Literarischen Tradition," 186; Bigg, 23; Spicq, 16–17 n. 5; Marie-Emile Boismard, "Une liturgie baptismale dans la *Prima Petri,*" *RB* 64 (1957) 173. The variety of parallels suggested shows the precariousness of the attempt.

184 Meecham ("First Epistle," 22) thinks any literary dependence is doubtful; by contrast, Bigg (23) has "little doubt" of "positive literary connexion."

185 Chase ("Peter," 788) thinks Peter studied James "soon after it was written"; cf. also the authorities cited by Foster, *Literary Relations,* 517.

186 Wand (25) is "fairly certain" that the author of James knew 1 Peter; see also Foster, *Literary Relations,* 377, 517–18; T. E. S. Ferris, "The Epistle of James in Relation to 1 Peter," *CQR* 128 (1939) 303.

187 This seems to be a growing consensus: Michaels, xliv; Goppelt, 51 (ET 31); Brox, "Literarischen Tradition," 186. Gospel authors used traditions in the same way; see Matt 18:12–14 and Luke 15:4–7 for an example of a similar story used for different purposes in different contexts.

188 Lists of parallels differ widely, from forty-nine located by Foster (*Literary Relations,* 491) to the handful noted by Goppelt (52, ET 31) or Brox ("Literarischen Tradition," 185). The absence of significant linguistic parallels makes the task difficult.

Esau unable *to inherit his blessing*). Such tenuous parallels have led to widely different conclusions: Hebrews depends on 1 Peter,[189] 1 Peter depends on Hebrews,[190] both depend on Paul.[191] The most likely solution appears to be that two authors, whose works were unknown to each other, have addressed a similar situation of persecution and in doing so have used similar commonplaces of early Christian theology.[192]

c. John. The most common parallels cited between 1 Peter and the Gospel of John[193] are the following:

1 Peter	John
1:8	20:29
5:2	21:16
5:5	13:4; 21:7[194]

Such similarities of language as exist (1 Pet 1:8, forms of ὁράω, πιστεύω ["to see, to believe"]; 5:2, forms of ποιμαίνω ["tend"]) are so general as to allow of no proof of literary dependence. Again, the idea of humility in 5:5 is such a commonplace in Christian teaching, drawn often from the example of Jesus, that no literary relationship is necessary to explain the similarity.[195] Rather than literary dependence, one would better speak of a similar spiritual atmosphere, one dealing with the rebirth of

Christians through Christ crucified and risen, whose glorious fate they will ultimately share at his return if they prove faithful.[196] Such a spiritual atmosphere is finally the Christian tradition writ large, the likely source of similarities here.[197]

d. Synoptic Gospels. Relationships between 1 Peter and the Synoptic Gospels have been proposed,[198] particularly between 1 Peter and the Gospel of Mark because of the traditional association of Mark with Peter (see 1 Pet 5:13),[199] but no evidence of literary dependence has been adduced. The closest linguistic parallels are with the material special to Matthew,[200] but again they are not extensive enough to demonstrate literary dependence.[201]

e. Common Christian Tradition. More likely is the suggestion that the many reflections of both NT and OT in 1 Peter show the author to be anchored in common early Christian tradition,[202] individual elements of which were then reworked to apply to the particular situation being

---

189 E.g., T. E. S. Ferris, "A Comparison of I. Peter and Hebrews," *CQR* 111 (1930) 123.
190 E.g., Foster, *Literary Relations*, 377.
191 Foster (*Literary Relations*, 491) finds such dependence "certain."
192 So Brox, "Literarischen Tradition," 185; Goppelt, 52 (ET 31); cf. also Selwyn, 464.
193 For putative relationships between 1 Peter and 1 John, see Foster, *Literary Relations*, 522. I would agree with Goppelt (51, ET 30) in seeing no relationship between them.
194 Lists of relationships range from the twenty-three found by Foster (*Literary Relations*, 532) to ten suggested by Meecham ("First Epistle," 23) to two proposed by Cothenet ("Les orientations," 30); see also Tenney, "Parallels."
195 Foster (*Literary Relations*, 533) concludes that the Johannine literature "depends directly upon" 1 Peter. Others explain the similarity as due to the similarity of the lives of the disciples Peter and John, e.g., Tenney ("Parallels" 376–77) or Spicq ("La Iᵃ Petri" 39 n. 9). Such an explanation rests on assumptions about Johannine authorship not everyone will make.
196 George Johnson sees such a similar, general view shared by 1 John ("The Will of God: V: In I Peter and I John," *ExpT* 72 [1960/61] 238).
197 The references in 1 Peter and John to sheep and shepherd also belong to general Christian tradition, drawn in the first instance from the OT.
198 See the discussion of 1 Peter and Jesus' sayings above.
199 The proposal that both 1 Peter and Mark reflect the same interpretation of Jesus' death (e.g., Best, 60; Love, "First Epistle," 66), even if true, would say nothing about literary dependence. The same is true of the fanciful proposal that the key to 1 Peter is to see it as a commentary on Mark 13 (Schattenmann, "Apocalypse," esp. 196).
200 Suggested by Best, "I Peter and the Gospel," 109–10; cf. esp. 1 Pet 2:12b/Matt 5:16b.
201 Foster (*Literary Relations*) finds no evidence for literary relationship either with Matthew (500) or Luke (502).
202 Bovon, "Foi chrétienne," 27; Marie-Emile Boismard, "Une liturgie baptismale dans la *Prima Petri*," *RB* 63 (1956) 201; Leonhard Goppelt, "Jesus und die 'Haustafel'-Tradition," in P. Hoffmann, ed., *Orientierung an Jesus: Für Joseph Schmid* (Freiburg: Herder, 1973) 100. Such traditions are often taken to be oral rather than written: Schutter, *Hermeneutic*, 35; Wolfgang Nauck, "Freude im Leiden: Zum Problem einer urchristlichen Verfolgungstradition," *ZNW* 46 (1955) 73; John Piper, "Hope as the Motivation of Love: I Peter 3:9–12," *NTS* 26 (1980)

addressed.[203] That such tradition consisted in a number of commonplaces which expressed the theological insights and liturgical and catechetical practices of the early Christian communities is all but certain, and such commonplaces can be identified in 1 Peter.[204] Among them are:

1. liturgical traditions, particularly found in hymnic or confessional form, e.g., 1:18–21; 2:21–25; 3:18–22;[205]

2. catechetical topoi, commonly used in the early church for the instruction of converts, e.g., 1:18–21; 3:18–22;[206]

3. hortatory traditions, supported by sayings of Jesus, often taking the form in 1 Peter of finding in Christ, particularly his suffering, the pattern for Christian life, e.g., 2:21–25;[207]

4. persecution traditions, linked to Jewish martyrological traditions that developed in Maccabean times, e.g., 1:6; 4:1.[208]

The precision with which such individual traditions can be isolated in 1 Peter is limited, since they must be reconstructed from their present contexts[209] primarily on the basis of content rather than form,[210] and can be

---

218–19; although Lohse ("Parenesis," 42) suggests it may occasionally have assumed written form. Hillyer ("First Peter," 52) finds evidence that such traditions were held "more tenaciously" in Asia Minor than elsewhere, and cites Papias (see Eusebius *HE* 3.39.4, 11) and Polycarp (see Irenaeus *Adv. haer.* 3.3–4) as evidence.

203 François Refoulé, "Bible et éthique sociale: Lire aujourd'hui 1 Pierre," *Le Supplément* 131 (1979) 466; Millauer, *Leiden*, 186–87; Goldstein, *Paulinische Gemeinde*, 11.

204 Most developed in Selwyn, 363–466, although his conclusions are strongly influenced by his (I think questionable) conviction that Simon Peter and Silvanus wrote 1 Peter, and that Silvanus's hand is to be seen in 1 and 2 Thessalonians and some other underlying documents of tradition used in 1 Peter. Selwyn's ability to differentiate minutely between various traditions is also questionable. His formulations have nevertheless been influential.

205 So, e.g., Günther Schiwy, *Die Katholischen Briefe* (Der Christ in der Welt: Eine Enzyklopädie, Reihe VI; Das Buch der Bücher 12; Stein am Rhein: Christiana, 1973) 40; Lohse, "Parenesis," 59; Cothenet, "Les orientations," 24; Schelkle, "Leiden," 14. Michaels (xliii) finds the case weakest for the second; Schelkle (111) identifies the first and third as "christological symbols," the second as a hymn. M.-E. Boismard (*Quatre Hymnes baptismales dans la Première Épître de Pierre* [Paris: Cerf, 1961] 133–163) finds a fourth in 5:5–9. On Rudolph Bultmann's attempt ("Bekenntnis- und Liedfragmente im ersten Petrusbrief," *ConNT* 11 [1947] 1–14) to reconstruct a hymn from 1:20 and 3:18–22, see Horst Goldstein, "Die Kirche als Schar derer, die ihren leidenden Herrn mit dem Ziel der Gottesgemeinschaft nachfolgen: Zum Gemeinverständnis von 1 Petr 2,21–25 und 3,18–22," *BibLeb* 15 (1974) 38–40; Ralph P. Martin, "Composition in Recent Study," *Vox Evangelica* 1 (1962) 29–42. For more on these hymns, see the discussion below of 1 Peter as baptismal homily, and

the comments on the individual verses.

206 Such a catechism was first proposed by Alfred Seeberg, *Der Catechismus der Urchristenheit* (1903; reprinted Munich: Kaiser, 1966); finding the pattern in 1 Cor 15:3–4, he located elements of the formula in 1 Pet 3:18–22; 4:5 as well as 1:18–21 and 1:11. The idea of such a catechism was developed by Philip Carrington (*Primitive Christian Catechism* [Cambridge: University Press, 1940]) and Selwyn (369–400; his *Formgeschichte* is based more on vocabulary, e.g., forms of ἀπέχεσθαι, ἀποτέθημι ["abstain, put away"], the phrase "children of light," than on formal criteria). For a discussion of these attempts, see Shimada, *Formulary Material*, 54–55; Vanhoye, "1 Pierre," 108–9. Lohse ("Parenesis," 55) judges the attempt to disengage such fixed catechetical schema "a highly questionable undertaking."

207 Schutter (*Hermeneutic*, 61) finds the "prevalence of imperatival participles and adjectives" evidence of a "pre-existing collection" of such traditions; on the relationship of such language to Jewish hortatory traditions, see Daube, "Participle and Imperative in 1 Peter," in Selwyn, esp. 484–88. On its connection to words of Jesus, see Goppelt, "Jesus," 100; Neugebauer, "Zur Deutung," 75; to Jesus' suffering, see Schelkle, "Leiden," 16; Millauer, *Leiden*, 186.

208 Spicq, 16; Nauck, "Freude," passim but esp. 72; on the relation to Jewish traditions, 76. For a discussion of these proposals, see de Villiers, "Joy," 69. Neugebauer ("Zur Deutung," 76) traces this tradition to Jesus' own view of suffering (77); cf. also Millauer, *Leiden*, 186.

209 This is particularly true of the "hymns." Earl Richard thinks there is little hope of reconstructing the originals ("The Functional Christology of 1 Peter," in Talbert, *Perspectives*, 129); cf. also Goldstein, "Kirche," 40.

210 So, e.g., Cothenet, "Les orientations," 24; see also n. 206 above.

compared only with other Christian traditions similarly derived from other NT documents. Their identification thus remains theoretically highly probable, but concretely something less than precise.

Whatever the specific shape of individual traditions may have been, however, the themes common to other writings of the NT found in 1 Peter[211] are best explained on the basis of their common dependence on a linguistically stabilized tradition[212] that by this time represents a fusion of Pauline and Synoptic elements.[213] Owing more to the OT and to its adaptation by other Jewish communities, perhaps especially Qumran,[214] than to secular Hellenistic religious thought, the tradition itself took its origin, as did that of the Synoptics, in the Palestinian church, a tradition then enriched and adapted by the gentile churches of the Mediterranean world of late antiquity.[215] 1 Peter is thus linked to the other NT writings by their common dependence on that tradition, rather than on some sort of literary dependence within that literature.[216]

If, then, evidence in 1 Peter of reminiscences of Jesus of Nazareth cannot be used to demonstrate authorship by Simon Peter, literary dependence on other NT writings cannot be used to demonstrate the letter's pseudonymity. On such evidence, authorship remains unresolved.

D. Historical Situation of 1 Peter

It is evident that the author of 1 Peter knows that the readers suffer the disfavor of, indeed persecution by, those who do not share the Christian faith. If the historical locus of such attitudes to Christianity can be

fixed with some precision, it will be possible to determine whether Simon Peter could or could not have been the author. The later the time of such conditions, the less likely such authorship will be.

Perspective on the situation reflected in the letter, therefore, can be gained by an investigation of Roman policies and attitudes toward non-Roman religions, toward volunteer groups (collegia) in general, and toward the imperial cult. Attention must then be turned to the kind of persecution reflected in 1 Peter, namely, whether it was due to official Roman policy, and if so when it occurred, or whether it was of a more unofficial nature. After such investigations have been completed, some conclusions regarding authorship can be drawn.

1. Roman Policy

Much speculation on when official persecutions of the Christian community occurred is based on erroneous notions of the general Roman attitude to non-Roman religions, and how religions became "legal" or were declared "illegal." A careful examination of Roman policy will show that much of that speculation, and its terminology, owes more to historical imagination than historical fact.

A further caveat is necessary at the outset of this kind of investigation. It is this: the person investigating the way Roman policy worked itself out, particularly in the provinces like those located in Asia Minor, must be careful to avoid the assumption that once a policy was enunciated, or a practice followed, whether in Rome or some province, that thenceforth that policy was always and everywhere and equally applied throughout the

211 Goppelt (54, ET 34) lists as such themes Jesus as shepherd (2:25; 5:2, 4), Jesus' death as ransom (1:18–19), the call to be awake, sober (5:8), the identification of the passion of Jesus and his followers as πάσχειν ("to suffer," 2:19–21, 23), calling on God as Father (2:17).
212 The phrase ("sprachlich verfestigte Traditionen") is from Brox, "Literarischen Tradition," 182; cf. also Best, 31, 36; Spicq, 15.
213 Sherman E. Johnson cites as further examples the Pastoral Epistles and Polycarp ("Asia Minor and Early Christianity," in J. Neusner, ed., *Christianity, Judaism, and Other Greco-Roman Cults: Studies for Morton Smith at Sixty: Part Two: Early Christianity* [4 vols.; Leiden: Brill, 1975] 2.117). The themes cited in n. 210 above also demonstrate such fusion.
214 See esp. Flusser, "Dead Sea Sect," 264–65, for a

summary of Qumran beliefs, a summary that also reads much like a summary of 1 Peter, e.g., "The company of the Elect is a kind of spiritual temple; this company is constituted by a new covenant with God; this covenant is eschatological." Cf. also Goppelt ("Prinzipien," 286–87), who points out, however, that whereas Qumran withdrew from society, 1 Peter assumes continued existence of the community in its midst.
215 Goppelt, 54, 56 (ET 35, 36). Beare (57) suggests that such adaptation accounts for any Hellenistic flavor, rather than a "borrow(ing) from . . . contemporary Hellenistic modes of religious thought."
216 I agree with Brox ("Literarischen Tradition," 190) when he calls attempts to find literary dependencies fruitless ("überholte erfolglose Versuche").

Roman Empire. That is simply not the case. To be sure, broad lines of policy were followed, but even with regard to such policies, applications varied. Yet even here caution is advisable. Not only did different emperors follow different policies, but different regions saw differing applications of the policies being pursued at any given time. One must take care, therefore, not to draw hasty conclusions on the basis of overly broad generalizations.

a. Roman Policies on Non-Roman Religions. Fundamentally, the policy of the Roman Empire toward the practice of non-Roman religions by non-Roman peoples was one of tolerance.[217] Foreign religious customs, like any other foreign customs, were permitted to those for whom such practices were ancestral, provided such practices did not pose a threat to Roman hegemony.[218] Roman religion, as ancestral to the Roman people, was not expected to be practiced by non-Romans; indeed, policies for Roman religion valid in Rome were not to be exported to other peoples or imposed on their religious practices.[219] In a similar vein, the practice by Romans of foreign religious rites was not encouraged, even though such rites were tolerated when practiced by non-Romans.[220] That does not mean Romans did not participate in such rites, and so long as no overt danger to Roman stability was perceived, such participation was also tolerated.[221] When instability threatened, however, such rites could be and were suppressed.[222] Within those broad rubrics, Roman policy functioned with respect to Jews and Christians.

Roman attitudes toward Jews and their religious customs and practices ranged from protection to annoyance to outright suppression. Under Julius Caesar, Jews were granted certain privileges relating to the practice of their religion, privileges that succeeding emperors reaffirmed.[223] Coupled with such policy, however, was an abiding distaste for Jewish religious practices,[224] a distaste that was frequently translated into official policy.

---

217 Dionysius of Halicarnassus (*Ant. Rom.* 2.19.3) notes that foreigners in Rome are "under great obligation to worship their ancestral gods according to the rules that apply"; similarly Celsus (Origen *Con. Cels.* 5.35). Suetonius (*Vit.* 2.93) mentions Augustus's tolerance of ancient religious rites of other people; Augustus commended his grandson Gaius for not offering prayers in Jerusalem as he passed through, something evidently inappropriate for a Roman. Even human sacrifice, normally proscribed (see following note), went unpunished, if in the future forbidden, when shown to conform to ancestral custom (Plutarch *Mor., The Roman Questions* 283, 83). See also N. Lewis and M. Reinhold, eds., "The Conflict of Religions and the Triumph of Christianity," in *Roman Civilization: Sourcebook II: The Empire* [New York: Harper & Row, 1966) 573; Lampe and Luz, "Nachpaulinisches Christentum," 197; Hart, 21.

218 Cf. Marta Sordi, *The Christians and the Roman Empire* (trans. Bedini; Norman: University of Oklahoma Press, 1986) 167; Ernest George Hardy, *Christianity and the Roman Government* (London: Allen and Unwin, 1925) 28; Josephus, quoting the emperor Claudius (*Ant.* 20.1.2 [§ 13]). An exception was religions that prescribed human sacrifice, e.g., the Druids; so Suetonius *Vit.* 5.25.5; cf. Hardy (*Christianity,* 14) for further references. Since Roman power was ascribed to Roman gods (see Horace *Odes* 3.6.1–8), religious duty by its citizens was primarily directed to the safety of the state (Hardy, *Christianity,* 3). Despite that, "piety" could be quite lackadaisical: cf. Dio Chrysostom *Or.* 31.10, 15.

219 For example, Trajan writes to Pliny that Roman laws of consecration do not apply to foreign cities (Pliny *Ep.* 10.50).

220 Hardy, *Christianity,* 27. For this policy in the Roman army, see G. R. Watson, *The Roman Soldier* (Ithaca: Cornell University Press, 1969) 128; Jerry L. Daniel, "Anti-Semitism in the Hellenistic-Roman Period," *JBL* 98 (1979) 63. Plutarch (*Mor., Superstition* 166B) thinks participation by Romans in non-Roman religion disgraces their ancestral gods; when individual foreign rites were introduced, they were first purged of all "foreign nonsense" (τερθρεία μύθικη; see also Dionysius of Halicarnassus *Ant. Rom.* 2.19.3). On occasion such religions were banned, e.g., under Tiberius (so Suetonius *Vit.* 3.36.1); that was not always the case, however (see Suetonius *Vit.* 7.8.3).

221 A famous example is the exoneration of Pomponia Graecina, a senator's wife, who was a devotee of a "foreign superstition" (*superstitio externa*), but who went unpunished (Tacitus *Ann.* 13.32; cf. Sordi, *Christians,* 26–27, who wrongly identifies the accusation as *superstitio illicita*). The emperor Otho was apparently a devotee of Isis (Suetonius *Vit.* 7.12.2).

222 The suppression of the sect of Bacchus in Rome in 186 BCE is a classic example; see Livy *Ab Urbe condita* 39.8–19; cf. Hardy, *Christianity,* ix; P. Herrmann, J. H. Waszink, and K. Colpe, "Genossenschaft," *RAC* 10 (1978) 110.

223 From Julius Caesar through Claudius, Caligula alone appears to have ignored them; see Hardy, *Christianity,* 18–23. Even after the fall of Jerusalem in 70,

Tiberius, for example, at one point forbade the practice of Jewish and Egyptian rites, and banished large numbers of those who practiced them.[225] Claudius forbade mass meetings by Jews,[226] and feared their proselytizing practices would foment trouble where they lived in large numbers.[227] After the Jewish war, Vespasian and then Titus levied a tax specifically on Jews,[228] but even then continued certain privileges that had previously been granted to them.

While we must examine Roman attitudes and practices toward Christians in more detail below, it is useful to note that the distaste inspired by Jewish exclusivity was transferred to Christians,[229] who suffered the additional disadvantage of not being able to plead ancestral custom for their religious practices. Despite that fact, the basic Roman tolerance for foreign religious rites could also be applied to the Christian faith.[230]

b. Roman Policies on Collegia. In addition to Roman attitudes toward non-Roman religions, Roman attitudes toward organized groups (collegia) also played a role. Because the Romans had not developed the idea of a legal corporate "person," the collegia played many of the roles assumed in modern society by corporations.[231]

Given a variety of names—*collegium, corpus, universitas, sodalitas, sodalicium, societas,* and where the purposes were primarily political, *hetaeria*[232]—such groups were associations of individuals formed to promote some common interest, whether commercial, religious, social, cultural (artists, musicians), sport, age (youth, elderly), or even neighborhood or geographic origin.[233] Often organized under the sponsorship of a prominent citizen of the area and with a god or gods named as tutelary deities, the members held monthly meetings, often accompanied by a meal, were expected to pay regular dues, and elected a variety of officers to maintain order and pursue the common interests of the members.[234] The varied interests served by these groups meant that they existed in large numbers,[235] and that they were subject to official scrutiny, ordinarily both at the time they were organized and during their continuing existence.[236] Although some types of collegia were

---

some privileges continued; see below.

224 Among other things Jews were thought to be atheists (Daniel, "Anti-Semitism," 61; Sordi, *Christians,* 46), to worship clouds (Juvenal *Sat.* 14.96–97), to have "base and abominable" customs (Tacitus *Hist.* 5.5), and to be snobbish and exclusive (Goppelt, 59 [ET 40], citing Philostratus *Vit. Ap.* 5.33; Tacitus *Hist.* 5.5; see also Daniel, "Anti-Semitism," 51, 58–59). For a collection of such obloquies, see Daniel, "Anti-Semitism," 57.

225 Tacitus *Ann.* 2.85; Suetonius *Vit.* 3.36. They had been expelled as early as 139 BCE; so Hardy, *Christianity,* 15.

226 Dio Cassius *Hist. Rom.* 60.6.6 (they were too numerous to expel, but he forbade their meeting together); cf. Sordi, *Christians,* 26. Suetonius (*Vit.* 5.25.4) claimed they were in fact expelled; cf. Acts 18:2.

227 Cf. the riots in Alexandria between Jews and non-Jews during his reign; see Sordi, *Christians,* 26.

228 The *fiscus Iudaicus* of one drachma; see Sordi, *Christians,* 47–48. It was continued under Domitian (Suetonius *Vit.* 8.12.2).

229 See Hardy, *Christianity,* 28; Goppelt, 59 (ET 40); Celsus, cited by Origen *Con. Cels.* 35.148.43; Best, 37. The accusation was often of witchcraft and magic (Hardy, *Christianity,* 53).

230 As the case of Pomponia Graecina showed: a family council found her innocent (Tacitus *Ann.* 13.32; see also n. 221 above). Trajan's unwillingness to lay down general rules regarding punishment of Christians also shows that such tolerance continued: "neque enim in universum aliquid quod quasi certam formam habeat constitui potest" ("one cannot lay down a specific rule which would have universal application"; Pliny *Ep.* 10.97).

231 For a good discussion of this point, see Herrmann et al., "Genossenschaft."

232 Herrmann et al., "Genossenschaft," 91, 100.

233 Sordi, *Christians,* 182–83; Hardy, *Christianity,* 129; Herrmann et al., "Genossenschaft," 95–96; David Magie, *Roman Rule in Asia Minor to the End of the Third Century after Christ* (2 vols., Princeton: Princeton University Press, 1950; reprinted New York: Arno, 1988) 1.584, 598.

234 For the bylaws of such a collegium, see Lewis and Reinhold, "Conflict of Religions," 273–75; cf. also Herrmann et al., "Genossenschaft," 96; Sordi, *Christians,* 182; Jean Gagé, *Les Classes Sociales dans l'Empire Romain* (Paris: Payot, 1964) 308.

235 Hardy, *Christianity,* 131.

236 For a variety of terms indicating official permission granted to such a group, see Hardy, *Christianity,* 129; cf. also 130–31. One term never encountered is the

officially recognized[237]—the most common types were professional and religious (burial) societies[238]—inscriptional evidence shows only a small minority in fact had official permission to exist.[239]

The proliferation of such organizations apart from official sanctions presented a constant problem to the governing authorities. Steps were taken as early the second century BCE to control them; such steps were repeated in the next century,[240] and then regularly, beginning with Julius Caesar, who banned all groups save those who could claim origins in antiquity.[241] At one time or another Augustus,[242] Claudius,[243] Nero,[244] and Trajan[245] also attempted to exercise some degree of control over them. The long discussion between Pliny and the emperor Trajan about the early Christian church in Asia Minor probably has more to do with Trajan's fear of collegia than his concern about religion.[246] It was fear of secret organizations pursuing political interests (*hetaeriae*) that exercised these emperors and that caused Trajan to ban even a fire company in Niocomedia.[247] It is on the face of it more likely, therefore, that the earliest confrontations of Christian groups with Roman officials were due to the fact that those Christian groups looked to them more like *hetaeriae* than like anything they recognized as "religion."[248]

c. Roman Policies on the Imperial Cult. In a strict sense, one cannot speak of an official Roman policy on the cult of the emperor prior to the third century, when Decius coupled a kind of political loyalty oath to the imperial cult.[249] For the period about which we are concerned—

---

fictional *collegium licitum* or *illicitum* (Selwyn, 52); it is absent from secular Latin literature, although Tertullian (*Apol.* 38.1) uses the terms *(inter) licitas factiones* and *(de) inlicitis factionibus*. Equally fictional are the terms *religio licita* (Selwyn, 51) or *religio illicita*, both absent from secular Latin literature, although again, the former term appears in Tertullian (*Apol.* 21.1), where he describes Judaism as "religionis, certe licitae," apparently coining the term.

237 Gagé, *Classes*, 310; Sordi, *Christians*, 183.

238 Gagé, *Classes*, 309–11. On professional collegia, see Herrmann et al., "Genossenschaft," 108–9; on burial societies (*collegium funeraticum*), Herrmann, 102–3; Gagé, 308.

239 Hardy, *Christianity*, 131.

240 The measures taken against the followers of Bacchus in Rome in 186 BCE fall under this type of action; the senate banned all collegia in 64 BCE, a ban removed in 58 BCE. The major fear was that they would pursue political objectives (i.e., become a *hetaeria*: Herrmann et al., "Genossenschaft," 92, 112). For that reason they were permanently banned within the army (ibid., 111).

241 "Praeter antiquitus constituta" ("except those constituted in antiquity"; Suetonius *Vit.* 1.42.3); cf. Herrmann et al., "Genossenschaft," 110. The Jews were specifically exempted from this ban; see Hardy, *Christianity*, 18–19, and the sources mentioned there.

242 The lex Julia de collegiis (Herrmann et al., "Genossenschaft," 111); it again excepted "collegia . . . antiqua et legitima" ("ancient and legal groups"; Suetonius *Vit.* 2.32.2), including the Jews; cf. Hardy, *Christianity*, 128–29, 134. From the passage in Suetonius, and from Josephus (*Ant.* 14.10.8 [215]), Magie (*Roman Rule*, 2.1458 n. 20) infers that those permitted to exist had "obtained licenses from the Senate," although there is no mention of the senate,

or any procedure of licensing, in either text.

243 τὰς ἑταιρείας: Dio Cassius *Hist. Rom.* 60.6.6; they had apparently been permitted under Gaius Caligula.

244 Because of fights at a gladiatorial game, Nero banned assembly by, and all collegia of, the Pompeians for ten years (Tacitus *Ann.* 14.17).

245 Trajan permitted collegia in Asia Minor only if ancient precedent permitted, as, for example, at Amisus (Pliny *Ep.* 10.92, 93); cf. Magie, *Roman Rule*, 1.602.

246 What Pliny required of Christians was to determine political, not religious, loyalty, thus assuring no hostile political intent, i.e., no *hetaeria*. Pliny allowed Christians their morning assembly, but not the evening meetings, which included meals, and hence looked too much like such a collegium. Cf. Sordi, *Christians*, 60–61.

247 Pliny *Ep.* 10.33, 34; Trajan feared any such group would eventually become a *hetaeria*.

248 Christians lacked such characteristic marks of religion as a temple, a priesthood, ancestral deities, and ancient cultic rites. The varied ethnic and geographical origins of Christians would have added further confusion. See also the perceptive discussion in Claude Lepelley, "Le contexte historique de la première lettre de Pierre," in Perrot, *Etudes*, 50, 58–59.

249 See Lewis and Reinhold, "Conflict of Religions," 596, for the text of a certificate verifying such participation in the imperial cult.

mid-first to early second century—the practice of according divine honors to the emperor varied with what individual emperors would permit (or, far less frequently, require), and participation in the cult was more important in the provinces, particularly those in Asia Minor, than it was in Rome. While there had been some movement on the part of, and on behalf of, Julius Caesar to obtain divine honors for him,[250] the movement took on greater impetus with the accession of Augustus and the stability he brought to a people torn by years of civil strife.[251] While the general policy of Augustus was to forbid veneration of himself as divine,[252] he did permit some temples to be built.[253] Tiberius,[254] Claudius,[255] and Trajan[256] continued the policy of discouraging such activity, and even Gaius Caligula, who later fostered notions of his divinity,[257] began his rule by forbidding such ideas.[258] Domitian, who demanded he be addressed in terms of divinity (*dominus et deus noster*),[259] was unable to establish such reverence beyond his own death.[260] At the end of our period, Tacitus could claim that it continued to be the policy in Rome than an emperor was revered only after his death.[261]

In the provinces, however, particularly Asia Minor,[262] it was another matter. All of the emperors mentioned above had divine honors paid to them.[263] Two forces were at work in this activity. On the one hand, for Rome it provided a convenient way to allow various cities to show their loyalty to the empire, since the attitude to such a cult reflected the attitude to Rome.[264] For the provinces, on the other hand, it was a way to allow them to fit the political reality of their subjugation to Rome into the context of their ancient Greek culture, a culture that had provided a framework for subjugation in the form of cultic reverence for the gods. The imperial cult thus served the purpose of allowing the leading families of the various cities to maintain cultural continuity in the face of a radically altered political situation.[265] The cult flourished, therefore, not as an attempt to flatter an

---

250 That he claimed too much for himself, see Suetonius *Vit.* 1.76.1; after his death, a memorial to him was a locus for sacrifices (*Vit.* 1.85).

251 S. R. F. Price argues that the imperial cult was a way of objectifying and institutionalizing Augustus's charismatic authority (*Rituals and Power: The Roman Imperial Cult in Asia Minor* [Cambridge: Cambridge University Press, 1984] 58–59).

252 He refused to be called "dominus" even by his children and grandchildren (Suetonius *Vit.* 2.53), and he forbade anyone to accord him divine honors or to offer him sacrifices (Dio Cassius *Hist. Rom.* 60.4). His son Germanicus similarly forbade such honors (Lewis and Reinhold, "Conflict of Religions," 562–63).

253 He permitted a temple to himself in Spain (Tacitus *Ann.* 1.78) and in Asia (*Ann.* 4.37; cf. Magie, *Roman Rule,* 1.469). After his death signs of his divinity appeared (Dio Cassius *Hist. Rom.* 56.46.1–2; cf. Ovid *Fas.* 3.421–28). For divine honors in Galatia, cf. Magie, *Roman Rule,* 1.465.

254 Although he permitted such temples in Asia, he refused them in Spain and spurned divine honors directed to himself (Tacitus *Ann.* 4.37–38).

255 Dio Cassius *Hist. Rom.* 60.5.4; see Claudius's letter to Alexandrian Jews, lines 48–50 (for the text, see John L. White, *Light from Ancient Letters* [Philadelphia: Fortress, 1986] 133–36). There was apparently a temple to him in Britain (Seneca *Apocol.* 8).

256 Pliny *Ep.* 10.9; cf. 10.82; Martial *Epig.* 10.72.

257 Suetonius *Vit.* 4.22; Tacitus *Hist.* 5.9; Dio Cassius *Hist. Rom.* 59.4.4; 28.1; Philo *Leg. Gaj.* 198, 353.

258 So Magie, *Roman Rule,* 1.511.

259 Martial *Epig.* 5.8; 9.66; Suetonius *Vit.* 8.13.2; Dio Chrysostom *Or.* 45.1; cf. Quintilian *Inst.,* 4 Preface 5.

260 Cf. Martial *Ep.* 10.72; Pliny *Ep.* 8.14.

261 *Ann.* 15.74; cf. Price, *Rituals and Power,* 75. The Romans also distinguished between a god (*deus*) and a divine emperor (*divus*; Price, 220). It was a distinction the Greeks did not make, and hence reverence of the emperor as "god" developed more readily in Greek-speaking provinces.

262 Hardy, *Christianity,* 72; Magie, *Roman Rule,* 1.470, 481, 502; Price, *Rituals and Power,* 130, 198. For a chart of chronological distribution of imperial temples and sanctuaries in Asia Minor, see Price, 59.

263 Temples to Vespasian and Titus also existed in Asia Minor; see Magie, *Roman Rule,* 1.572; Price, *Rituals and Power,* 179.

264 For example, the charge of neglecting the cult of Augustus in Cyzicus in Phrygia was immediately coupled with the charge of abusing Roman citizens (Tacitus *Ann.* 4.36; cf. 4.37).

265 This thesis is argued persuasively by Price, *Rituals and Power,* passim.

individual emperor;[266] temples regularly combined honors to a given emperor with honors to Rome as such,[267] and the cult tended not to last long after that emperor's death.[268] Rather, the cult flourished as a way to maintain cultural stability and control in a situation of political subjugation.

Such cultic reverence for the emperor and for Rome thus permeated the entire culture of the Greek cities of Asia Minor,[269] precisely because it provided a way for these cities to relate themselves to the center of the Roman Empire—the emperor—in terms of their own central values, this is, in terms of the gods.[270] As a result, a challenge to the emperor cult in those provinces was not only a challenge to Roman rule, it was a challenge to the social fabric itself, and constituted a threat to unravel the cultural continuity such cultic activity provided. Pressure to conform therefore would be greater from the local indigenous authorities than from the Roman overlords, and it would be pressure for social conformity much more than for conformity to specific religious or political beliefs.[271] That fact must be taken into account when determining the kind of persecution reflected in 1 Peter,[272] and hence its date and possible authorship.[273]

2. Persecutions

The evidence in the NT makes clear that the primitive church understood itself as having undergone persecution of some form or another from its very inception. Sayings of Jesus in the Gospels point to the suffering such rejection entails,[274] a rejection then reflected in the remaining literature of the NT.[275] Such persecution and the suffering that resulted are also reflected in 1 Peter. The question is thus not whether such persecutions were occurring when this letter was written,[276] but rather what kind of persecutions are therein reflected, and what caused such rejection of the Christians by their contemporary society.

While some of the references to suffering in 1 Peter are of a rather general nature (e.g., 1:6; 4:12, 19; 5:9, 12), others give a more specific indication of the reason: Christians have their faith challenged (3:15), they are abused for their Christian behavior (3:16; 4:4; cf. 3:14) and suffer because they bear the name "Christian" (4:14, 16). In addition, a number of the exhortations contain in themselves clues about the reasons Christians experienced opposition. Foremost is perhaps the charge that the Christians were generally guilty of immoral or

---

266 Price, *Rituals and Power*, 71.

267 Gagé, *Classes*, 77; Augustus's first monument, on Samos, was to the god Augustus and to the goddess Roma (Magie, *Roman Rule*, 1.469); according to Suetonius (*Vit.* 2.52), Augustus accepted temples only if they were also dedicated to Rome. For similar phenomena in other areas, see also Magie, *Roman Rule*, 1.447, 459, 471, 501; Tacitus *Ann.* 4.15.

268 Price, *Rituals and Power*, 61; later in the second and early third centuries, emperor cults died out (58).

269 It was a matter not only of "public ceremonial" but also of "private associations" (i.e., collegia); Price, *Rituals and Power*, 118.

270 I owe this insight to Price, *Rituals and Power*, 206, 225.

271 "The (imperial) cult . . . enhanced the dominance of local elites over the populace, of cities over other cities, and of Greek over indigenous cultures. That is, the cult was a major part of the web of power that formed the fabric of society" (Price, *Rituals and Power*, 248).

272 Jewish monotheism and Jewish and Christian rejection of idolatry made such a conflict inevitable; cf. Daniel, "Anti-Semitism," 60; Price, *Rituals and Power*, 221.

273 For the evidence that at the time of the writing of 1 Peter, pressure to take part in the imperial cult was in

fact exerted upon Christians, see the comments on 2:13–17 below. The existence of such pressure is of little help in determining the date and hence possible authorship, however, since participation in the cult of the emperor was so pervasive for so long a period precisely in the provinces in Asia Minor. Evidence in the letter of its possible existence does not guarantee a date later than the death of Simon Peter any more than absence of such evidence guarantees a date prior to his death.

274 E.g., Matt 5:10–11; Mark 13:11–13; Luke 12:51–53; John 15:18–20.

275 For a sampling of such passages, see C. F. D. Moule, "The Nature and Purpose of I Peter," *NTS* 3 (1956) 9–10; cf. also Ernest Gordon Selwyn, "The Persecutions in I Peter," *Bulletin of the Studiorum Novi Testamenti Societas* 1 (1950) 43; Goppelt, 60 (ET 41).

276 The attempt by F. L. Cross (*1 Peter: A Paschal Liturgy* [London: Mowbray, 1954]) to deny persecution in 1 Peter by relating the verb πάσχειν ("to suffer") to πάσχα ("Passover" = eucharist), and thus to the Christian's incorporation into Christ who suffered, has not found wide acceptance. Against the notion that the optative cases in 3:14, 17 mean suffering was only potential, not actual (so, e.g., J. R. Michaels, "Eschatology in I Peter iii.17," *NTS* 13 [1967] 396), see the comments on those verses below.

scurrilous behavior. It is such a charge that is evidently countered by the exhortations in our letter to live blameless lives that will give the lie to such charges (2:15; cf. 3:9, 13, 16).[277] Again, the accusation of disloyalty to governing powers surely underlies the exhortations to civil obedience (2:13–17).[278] More generally, underlying all such accusations is the perceived aloofness and strangeness of the Christian lifestyle,[279] a perception that resulted in general rejection (e.g., Tacitus's *odium humani generis* ["hatred of the human race"]).[280]

None of that, however, indicates the source or origin of the persecution reflected in 1 Peter: whether it was general and the result of official accusations and legal condemnation or whether it was more localized and the result of popular contempt. Each of those possibilities must be examined.

a. General Persecution. In addition to the general impression given in the letter that being identified as a Christian was sufficient to warrant persecution (e.g., 4:14, 16),[281]

support for the argument that the suffering undergone by the readers of 1 Peter was due to official persecution is drawn principally from two references. In 3:15 the admonition to be ready to give an apologia for one's Christian hope can be understood to refer to official court proceedings resulting from the accusation that one is a Christian.[282] More generally, the reference to universal suffering by Christians in 5:9 can be taken to imply empirewide legal persecution of the faith.[283] Scholars have traditionally attempted to locate such official persecution of the church particularly in the reigns of Nero, Domitian, and Trajan.[284] Each of those periods must be examined for evidence of the existence within it of a general, official persecution of the Christian community.[285]

1) Nero (54–68). Although the emperor Claudius (41–54) expelled Jews from Rome "impulsore Chresto" ("at the instigation of Chrestus"),[286] there is no evidence he

---

277 There may have been some illegal behavior on the part of Christians for which they were then justly condemned (2:16; 4:15), although this may also reflect no more than the kind of accusations made by others (so Lampe and Luz, "Nachpaulinisches Christentum," 200).

278 While charges of political disloyalty and immoral behavior were leveled against Christians until the fourth century, there is no identifiable trace in 1 Peter of two common later accusations: cannibalism and incest (cf. Justin *1 Apol.* 26; Tertullian *Apol.* 2.5; 7.1; 8.2–4, 7–9; Minucius Felix *Octavius* 9.5–7); nor is there any trace of fear on the part of non-Christians of economic loss (as in Acts 16:19; 19:24–27).

279 Goppelt (60) identifies it accurately as "das grund-sätzliche Anderssein der Christen" "the fundamental otherness of the Christians."

280 *Ann.* 15.44; cf. Suetonius *Vit.* 6.16.3; Pliny *Ep.* 10.96.

281 Selwyn ("Persecutions," 43–44) questions whether such references can be used to argue for official persecution.

282 So, e.g., Lepelley, "Le contexte," 48–49. See also the comments on 3:15 below.

283 So, e.g., Hall, "For to This," 138. Gourbillon ("La Première Epître de Pierre," 18) calls the persecution "d'une certaine manière, officielle" "in a certain way, official"; cf. also Goppelt, 60 (ET 41). Brox (27) and Lepelley ("Le contexte," 46) would limit the extent to Christians in Asia Minor. Selwyn ("Persecutions," 43) quotes with approval Mommsen's claim that persecution of Christians in the first century was "a

standing matter." David L. Balch ("Early Christian Criticism of Patriarchal Authority: I Peter 2:11—3:12," *Union Seminary Quarterly Review* 39 [1984] 162) argues for official persecution on the basis of official Roman opposition to "foreign religions which criticize Roman social and religious values," but his evidence (Polybius *Hist.* 6.2.9–10; Dionysius of Halicarnassus *Ant. Rom.* 2.3.5) is somewhat forced and his conclusion overstated.

284 For example, Brox, 24; Richard, "Christology," 126.

285 There is no reliable evidence of official opposition to Christians prior to Nero. Orosius supposed Suetonius's report of Claudius's exile of Jews (cf. *Vit.* 5.25.4) from Rome had to do with Christians as well (*Chrestos = Christos*), something Sordi (*Christians,* 24–25) thinks unlikely to be the case. On the other hand, Sordi (17–19) argues for the authenticity of Tertullian's report (*Apol.* 5.2) that Tiberius proposed to the Roman Senate the recognition of Christ's divinity, and maintains that the resulting *Senatus consultum* which refused Tiberius's proposal constituted thereafter the legal basis for later persecution of Christians by Nero and Domitian. Since there is no other record of such a *Senatus consultum,* its authenticity has not been widely recognized; cf., e.g., Johannes B. Bauer, "Der erste Petrusbrief und die Verfolgung unter Domitian," in R. Schnackenburg et al., eds., *Die Kirche des Anfangs: Für Heinz Schürmann* (Freiburg: Herder, 1978) 514–16.

286 So Suetonius *Vit.* 5.25.4. On the common confusion of *Chrestus* for *Christus,* see Tertullian *Apol.* 3.

engaged in any persecution of Christians as Christians. The first evidence of such specific persecution comes from the reign of Nero.[287] Although Tacitus accounts for the persecution in terms of Nero's need to find a scapegoat for the fire in Rome in 64 CE that he was accused of setting,[288] Suetonius omits mention of the fire as the reason, affirming instead that Christians were persecuted as people who held a "new and nefarious superstition."[289] The motivation in this instance is not so important as the extent of the persecution: did it extend beyond the bounds of the city of Rome? While some have argued that must have been the case,[290] there is no clear evidence for such an inference in either Suetonius or Tacitus, and while Nero's action will certainly have given credence to a negative view of Christians,[291] no empire-wide persecution appears to have resulted from his actions.[292] It seems most probable that Nero's persecution remained a local event, confined to the city of Rome,[293] and did not have the result of making Chris-

tianity itself a crime from that point on.[294] In that event, it is unlikely that the persecutions in Asia Minor, reflected in 1 Peter, were undertaken as official actions of the Roman government stemming from Nero's execution of Christians in Rome.

2) Vespasian (69–79). The successful elimination of the Jewish revolt and the destruction of Jerusalem under the Flavian emperors Vespasian and Titus led the former at least to seek to prevent further uprisings by eliminating descendants of David,[295] but there is no evidence for any systematic persecution of Christians.[296] The generally tolerant rule of Vespasian, acknowledged by Roman and Christian alike,[297] seems to have carried over to his attitude toward Christians as well.[298] There is no evidence for any kind of official persecution of Christians during his reign.[299]

3) Domitian (81–96). Although this last of the Flavian emperors had shown himself earlier to be the debauched son of the emperor Vespasian,[300] the beginning of

---

287   So, e.g., Tertullian *Apol.* 5.3; cf. *Ad nat.* 1.7; Eusebius *Hist. eccl.* 4.26.9; Goppelt, 61 (ET 43); Sordi, *Christians*, 30.

288   Tacitus *Ann.* 15.44.

289   *Genus hominum superstitionis novae ac maleficae* (*Vit.* 6.16). Whether such identification of Christians means they had already been persecuted earlier (so Sordi, *Christians*, 31) or reflects Suetonius's (later) evaluation of them is difficult to determine; the latter is rendered somewhat more likely by the fact that Tacitus, who does blame the persecution on the fire, nevertheless also identifies Christians as holding a "destructive superstition" (*exitiabilis superstitio*), and says they were "despised for their vices" (*per flagitia invisos*) and their "hatred of the human race" (*odio humani generis; Ann.* 15.44), thus sharing Suetonius's view of the new sect.

290   Orosius (*Hist.* 7.7.10), writing in the fifth century, affirms an empirewide persecution, but his views are for the most part not taken seriously. Yet cf. Sordi, *Christians*, 30–31; see also Beare, 15; Hart, 27.

291   So Lampe and Luz, "Nachpaulinisches Christentum," 197. Cf. Goppelt (62, ET 43): such an effect would make local persecutions more likely throughout the empire.

292   Brox (27) argues that the sources make such a notion "phantastisch"; cf. also Wand, 14; Johnson, "Will of God," 237; de Villiers, "Joy," 68.

293   Tertullian's language also clearly implies a persecution limited to Rome (*Apol.* 5.3; 21.25); see also Lampe and Luz, "Nachpaulinisches Christentum," 197.

294   So Best, 41. The wide influence of Christians in Bithynia reported by Pliny (*Ep.* 10.96) over a half-century later indicates that being a Christian had not been considered illegal in that area.

295   So Eusebius *Hist. eccl.* 3.12. Tacitus (*Frag.* 2) reports that Titus was in favor of destroying the temple in Jerusalem so that the religion of the Jews and the Christians would be more fully destroyed, but there is no record that such destruction of either religion became imperial policy under Titus as emperor.

296   The suggestion of William M. Ramsay (*The Church in the Roman Empire Before A.D. 170* [5th ed.; London: Hodder and Stoughton, 1897], e.g., 280–81) that sometime between 75 and 80 CE Roman policy was fixed that ordered Christians persecuted *propter nomen ipsum* ("for the name alone") has not won wide acceptance (cf. Hardy, *Christianity*, 61; Bigg, 30) since it is based largely on evidence from 1 Peter.

297   Tacitus acclaims his *moderatio* (*Hist.* 4.42); Eusebius notes he planned no evil against Christians (*Hist. eccl.* 3.17); cf. also Sordi, *Christians*, 43.

298   Eusebius quotes Tertullian to that effect (*Hist. eccl.* 5.5.7). Hegesippus's account, quoted in Eusebius (*Hist. eccl.* 3.19.1–7), of Domitian's questioning and release of two Christians during a persecution of Davidic descendants appears from internal evidence rather to have occurred under Vespasian; on this point see Sordi, *Christians*, 35–43.

299   Hardy (*Christianity*, 60–62) is surely correct in pointing out that the elimination of the Jews as a political entity would have exposed Christians to Roman attention as a group that had "no national

Domitian's rule was marked by vigor and intelligence,[301] particularly in his administration of the provinces.[302] Later in his reign, however, he showed himself a cruel persecutor,[303] who put many persons, particularly of the nobility, to death,[304] confiscated their estates,[305] persecuted and banished philosophers—particularly Stoics—from Rome,[306] and earned the almost universal condemnation of his contemporaries,[307] a condemnation usually expressed only after his death, however. It is clear from the outset, therefore, that persecution of Christians by Domitian would have been quite in character for him, and while it could have been intentional, it could as easily have been part of the general expression of his misanthropy.

While some have argued that Domitian did not persecute Christians,[308] or that he ended it shortly after he had begun to do so,[309] there is ample evidence that Christians did in fact fall victim to Domitian's lethal wrath.[310] This included many of the nobility, even some within Domitian's own household,[311] who at this time were apparently turning in increasing numbers to Christianity.[312] Part of the problem, for Christians as well as others, lay in Domitian's desire to be addressed as a divinity (a favorite title was *deus et dominus noster* ["our god and lord"]),[313] an excess which Christians would clearly resist[314] but for which he was condemned by non-Christians as well.[315]

That is not to say, however, that the persecution of Christians became official policy throughout the empire.[316] Rather, it appears that such persecution

claim to toleration," but that does not appear to have translated into official negative policy during Vespasian's rule.

300 Tacitus *Hist.* 4.2; because of that Vespasian turned the armies in Judea over to Titus rather than to Domitian (4.51).

301 Suetonius *Vit.* 8.8.1–4. The fulsome praise of the *Sibylline Oracles* (12.126–30), Martial (*Epig.* 4.1, 2; 5.1; 6.4; 7.5; 8.36), and Quintilian (*Inst.* 4, Preface 5) is probably based more on political expediency than sincerity; for sentiments of some contemporaries after Domitian's death, see n. 307 below.

302 Suetonius *Vit.* 8.8.2; cf. Magie, *Roman Rule*, 1.577.

303 Suetonius *Vit.* 8.10.1; Tacitus *Agric.* 44–45; cf. Sordi, *Christians*, 29; Goppelt, 62 (ET 44).

304 Suetonius *Vit.* 8.3.2; 10.2–3; 11–12; Tacitus *Ann.* 6.29; *Agric.* 3, 44; Eusebius *Hist. eccl.* 3.17; cf. Hardy, *Christianity*, 66; Bauer, "Verfolgung," 522; Sordi, *Christians*, 53.

305 Suetonius *Vit.* 8.12.1–2; see also Pliny *Pan.* 43.3 (cf. 50.5–6), who refers in addition to enforced bequests to Domitian.

306 Suetonius *Vit.* 8.10.3; Pliny *Ep.* 3.11; cf. Sherman E. Johnson, "Unresolved Questions about Early Christianity in Asia Minor," in D. E. Aune, ed., *Studies in New Testament and Early Christian Literature: Essays in Honor of Allen P. Wikgren* (NovTSup 33; Leiden: Brill, 1972) 193; Sordi, *Christians*, 47, 55.

307 Martial *Epig.* 10.72; 12.6, 15; cf. an epigram of uncertain position (Martial *Epig.*; LCL 2.516–17); *Sib. Or.* 4.40; Pliny *Ep.* 8.14; *Pan.* 48.3; 49.2, where he is accused of "odio hominum"; 90.5; Tacitus *Agric.* 39, 43; Dio Chrysostom *Or.* 45.1.

308 For a negative evaluation of this view, see Wand, 14; Sordi, *Christians*, 42–44; Bauer, "Verfolgung," 523.

309 Tertullian *Apol.* 5.4. This is probably due to a confusion with the cessation of hostilities enforced by Domitian's successor, Nerva; cf. Sordi, *Christians*, 42.

310 Eusebius *Hist. eccl.* 3.18.4–19.1, 4.26.9; *1 Clem.* 1.1; cf. Sordi, *Christians*, 42, 45, 50; Hardy, *Christianity*, 66; Selwyn, "Persecutions," 46.

311 Sordi (*Christians*, 43) argues that there were Christians among the family of Vespasian's brother, Flavius Sabinus. Domitian's niece, Flavia Domitilla, was almost certainly a Christian, and was exiled for it (Hardy, *Christianity*, 67); Domitian's cousin Flavius Clemens and his wife, also named Domitilla, were exiled for the same reason (Bauer, "Verfolgung," 524). For a justification of seeing the two Domitillas as separate persons, see Sordi, *Christians*, 44–45, 49. For a thorough review of the evidence, and an argument that there was only one Domitilla, a niece of Domitian and wife of Flavius Clemens, see Peter Lampe, *Die Stadtrömischen Christen in den ersten beiden Jahrhunderten* (Tübingen: Mohr [Siebeck], 1987) 166–71.

312 Cf. Sordi, *Christians*, 44–53, for a discussion of sources and their interpretation.

313 Suetonius (*Vit.* 8.13.2) says it became custom to address him with that title; cf. also Dio Chrysostom *Or.* 45.1 (καὶ δεσπότην καὶ θεόν ["both lord and god"]); Martial *Epig.* 5.8; 8.2; 9.66.

314 The emperor cult that the title implies probably existed in parts of Asia Minor (cf. Sordi, *Christians*, 53; Lampe and Luz, "Nachpaulinisches Christentum," 147). It is, I think, incorrect to assert that 1 Peter has no trace of divine honors required to be paid to the emperor (e.g., Goppelt, 63, ET 45); see the comments on 2:13–17 below.

315 E.g., Martial *Epig.* 10.72; Pliny *Pan.* 2.3–4 (I owe this latter reference to Bauer, "Verfolgung," 522).

316 It extended at least to Asia Minor (Goppelt, 63, ET 45) and perhaps throughout the empire (Sordi, *Christians*, 53); but see de Villiers, "Joy," 68.

remained spasmodic,[317] and lacked the kind of organization that would allow it to be labeled "official persecution." Rather, the persecution of Christians by Domitian, however extensive it may have been, appears to have been the result of his larger policy of suppressing all opposition, real or imagined, to his rule and his self-imputed divinity.[318] Such persecution could fit the situation presumed in 1 Peter, but so late a date would virtually preclude Simon Peter as author.

Domitian's immediate successor, Nerva (96–98), brought an end to Domitian's excesses, including the persecution of Christians, and recalled those who had been banished, again including Christians.[319] His rule was short-lived however, and he was succeeded after two years by Trajan.

4) Trajan (97–117). The primary source for our knowledge of the persecution of Christians during the reign of Trajan derives from the correspondence he had on that subject with his legate Pliny the Younger,[320] whom he had sent to Bithynia to bring order into the fiscal and administrative chaos that had developed there.[321] Some people had been denounced to Pliny as Christians, he had conducted some trials, and had written to the emperor for confirmation of what he had done and for instruction on how to proceed.

A careful look at Pliny's letter reveals the following situation: Pliny, because he had not attended trials of Christians, was ignorant of any rules of procedure, for example, whether recantation allows pardon, or whether being a Christian in itself (*nomen ipsum*), apart from other crimes, is punishable.[322] The implication is that while he knew such trials had taken place, and that certain crimes were associated with the name "Christian," he was not aware of a general policy by which to govern his actions toward them.[323] Trajan in his response confirmed such a lack of general policy; he said it was not possible to lay down any general rule to cover the treatment of Christians.

In the interim, Pliny had followed a practice whereby a thrice-repeated confession of being a Christian under questioning brought death,[324] but more for obstinacy and inflexible stubbornness (*pertinaciam . . . et inflexibilem obstinationem*) than anything else. Those who repeated after Pliny an appeal to the gods, adored and sacrificed to Trajan's image, and cursed Christ, were released. Trajan again confirmed such a policy toward unrepentant Christians, and agreed that recantation was to lead to pardon.

Finally, Pliny had ascertained that Christians were politically and morally harmless;[325] their danger lay in their adherence to a perverse and immoderate superstition (*superstitionem pravam, immodicam*) whose contagion had caused large numbers of people to abandon normal participation in temple worship and sacred festivals. Trajan in his response said while confessed Christians were to be punished,[326] no anonymous accusations were to be credited, and no search was to be instituted for them, that is, no general persecution was to be undertaken.[327]

Several points are clear: (1) Trials of Christians had taken place, and certain crimes were associated with the movement; thus there was general mistrust of Christians.

---

317 So Bauer, "Verfolgung," 524; Hardy, *Christianity,* 66.

318 Cf. Lampe and Luz, "Nachpaulinisches Christentum," 198; Goppelt, 62 (ET 44).

319 Nerva also forbade bringing accusations of atheism or of following Jewish customs, the former of which surely also applied to Christians. See Sordi (*Christians,* 58), who suggests Nerva may have been under pro-Christian influence.

320 Pliny's letter is *Ep.* 10.96; Trajan's reply is 10.97.

321 Pliny's letters give ample evidence of such disorder; cf. also Hardy, *Christianity,* 79–80.

322 See the discussion in Sordi, *Christians,* 60–63; his conclusion (63) that there was a special law forbidding Christians to exist is countered by Pliny's questions to Trajan, which make it evident that Pliny at least was unaware of such a law.

323 So also Lampe and Luz, "Nachpaulinisches Christentum," 197; Lepelley, "Le contexte," 49 n. 10; Michaels, lxvi.

324 Hardy (*Christianity,* 82) argues that this shows profession of Christianity as such was illegal; Best (41) and de Villiers ("Joy," 68) argue that it shows it was not.

325 Pliny reports that they took no illegal oaths, and that even their evening meetings with meals had been abandoned after he forbade all *hetaeriae* ("political groups"). See Hardy (*Christianity,* 143), who suggests this may have been the occasion for separating the eucharistic celebration from the "agape" meal.

326 Trajan does not make clear if this is because of their stubbornness and superstition, or because Christians would not take part in normal religious activities.

327 Sordi (*Christians,* 64) infers from this that Trajan was "convinced of the political harmlessness of

(2) There was no general Roman policy regarding Christians, and Trajan was unwilling to establish one.[328] (3) The persecution Pliny undertook was localized, and Trajan forbade any effort to broaden it by seeking out and punishing Christians.[329]

While Pliny appears to condemn Christians for religious rather than political reasons,[330] the political threat embodied in any kind of association cannot lie far beneath the surface,[331] and the recantation was at least as much a matter of political loyalty (fealty to the emperor) as it was of right religion (curse Christ, invoke the gods); in fact, in the mind-set of late antiquity, the two were inextricably intertwined.[332]

If one can speak here of an official persecution, therefore, one must also speak of it as localized and limited, and one can speak neither of a general policy of persecuting Christians prior to this time, nor of such a policy instituted by Trajan and in effect thereafter. Finally, it is apparent that if the situation underlying 1 Peter reflects the situation described by Pliny, it was written too late for the author to have been Simon Peter. *5) Conclusions.* From the evidence available, it is clear that there was no official empirewide persecution against the Christian religion or its adherents in the latter decades of the first century or the opening decades of the second.[333] While Nero's persecution of the Christians was certainly "official" to the extent that the emperor ordered it, it was local, affecting only the Christians in Rome.[334] Domitian clearly put a number of Christians to death, some of whom were members of his household, but the reason was more a suspicion of disloyalty (they would not participate in official functions) than persecution of a "religion." His general cruelty to other members of the ruling classes who were not Christians shows his "persecutions" reflected more his general attitude than a specific singling out of Christians.[335] Pliny's queries show that he was unaware of any general policy with respect to Christians,[336] and Trajan's answer makes clear his unwillingness to establish one,[337] or to authorize a search for Christians, a procedure normally followed in the case of recognized enemies of the state.[338] One cannot therefore use such a supposed official, empirewide persecution in any attempt to determine the authorship of 1 Peter, based on the possible date of this letter.[339]

Christians."

328 So Bigg, 32; Michaels, lxvi.

329 So de Villiers, "Joy," 68; Best, 41. It was widely known, however; Tertullian (*Apol.* 2), for example, has a very accurate knowledge of this correspondence.

330 So Sordi, *Christians,* 62.

331 Trajan himself mentioned such a danger when he forbade the formation of fire companies (Pliny *Ep.* 10.34). Johnson ("Asia Minor," 96) points in addition to the latent hostility to Rome in Anatolia that could emerge in any popular movement.

332 Cf. Sordi, *Christians,* 57. Tertullian (*Apol.* 38) also attributes official opposition to groups to a desire to keep the state from being divided into parties.

333 E.g., Schutter, *Hermeneutic,* 13–14, and the further evidence cited there. In fact, the first systematic persecution of Christians in the Roman Empire occurred under the emperor Decius in 249–251 CE; see Lewis and Reinhold, "Conflict of Religions," 596–97, for the text of certificates of loyalty he required.

334 That this local persecution established Christianity as a "superstitio illicita" or as a "religio illicita" (phrases never occurring in secular Latin literature from the first two centuries), as argued by Schutter (*Hermeneutic,* 35), is open to doubt.

335 Lampe and Luz ("Nachpaulinisches Christentum," 198) find no persecution of Christians organized by Domitian; Christians were rather the "gleichsam ungewollte Opfer des politischen Programms" of Domitian ("as it were unintended victims of the political program"). For a similar judgment, see Duane Warden, "Imperial Persecution and the Dating of 1 Peter and Revelation," *JETS* 34 (1991) 203–12.

336 Lampe and Luz ("Nachpaulinisches Christentum," 197) speak of "Pliny's helpless question addressed to Caesar"; it is difficult to see how Sordi (*Christians,* 63) can find in Pliny's letter evidence of a "special law" that forbade the Christian faith.

337 Hardy (*Christianity,* 89) finds "groundless" the argument that Trajan's answer was "the first legal authorization of persecution as the virtual proscription of Christianity."

338 Hardy (*Christianity,* 88) points out that those accused as "*latrones, sacrilegi, plagiarii* ['thieves, temple robbers, kidnappers'], etc.," were, as "active enemies of society," subject to such searching out by officials.

339 See, e.g., Brox, "Situation und Sprache," 4.

b. Local Persecution. It remains clear, however, that our author was aware that Christians were suffering, and that such suffering was widespread.[340] In all likelihood, general anti-Christian feelings among the local populaces more than rescripts from the Roman emperors[341] motivated the persecutions visited upon the Christians in general, and upon the recipients of 1 Peter in particular.[342] Christians thus suffered the fate of any group in the empire that isolated itself from society and refused to conform to normal expectations.[343] Such harassment could be widespread, could break out at any time, and could result from either official or unofficial actions. Such types of persecution must be investigated, to see what light they shed on the authorship of 1 Peter.

1) Official Local Persecutions. In the absence of official policy initiated from Rome, whether Christians were to be persecuted would depend more on the situation in a given locality than on any official judicial policy,[344] and would often be a matter of police administration rather than the law courts.[345] The result was that persecution of Christians was spasmodic, varying in extent and intensity from time to time and from region to region.[346]

The principal legal basis of such persecution appears to have been the procedure of *coercitio* that local authorities had at their disposal, and that allowed them, at their own discretion, to decree and enforce policies intended to maintain public order.[347] Unlike the procedures mandated by the imperial courts (*ordo iudiciorum publicorum*), the *coercitio* could but was not obligated to follow normal judicial norms in adjudicating conflicts and breaches of civil peace.[348] Allowing the Roman magistrate the broadest latitude in all respects, from gathering evidence to decreeing punishment,[349] *coercitio* was the type of judicial action most often employed by provincial magistrates, and is the form most often used in the first decades of the existence of the Christian community to visit official punishment on those who were members of it.[350]

2) Unofficial Local Persecutions. In addition to pressure initiated by legal authorities, Christians faced what was perhaps an even graver threat from the attitudes of the general populace.[351] Accused of a general hatred for people because of their unwillingness to participate in the general religio-cultural activities, including festivals, held regularly in the cities of Asia Minor as they were throughout the Roman Empire,[352] Christians were

340 E.g., 1 Pet 5:9.

341 Cf. Donald Senior, *1 and 2 Peter* (*NT Message* 20; Wilmington: Glazier, 1980) 3; Selwyn, "Persecutions," 44; Sordi, *Christians*, 198; Hardy, *Christianity*, 77.

342 The absence in 1 Peter of technical terms for official persecution (διωγμός, κατηγορία, θλίψις) supports such an inference; cf. Kelly, 10; Spicq, 18.

343 Lampe and Luz ("Nachpaulinisches Christentum," 201) identify such self-isolation from society as the origin of the accusation of "odium humani generis" ("hatred for the human race") that made life dangerous for Christians during this period; see also Brox, "Situation und Sprache," 12. Other groups similarly treated included Jews and Stoic philosophers (Sordi, *Christians*, 33.)

344 That an organization was officially "illegal" did not mean it would always and everywhere be resolutely put down. Unless there was some provocation, even technically illegal societies tended to be tolerated (cf. Hardy, *Christianity*, 135; Herrmann et al., "Genossenschaft," 112). The same will have held true for Christians.

345 This is currently the generally accepted view; e.g., Selwyn, 55; Hardy, *Christianity*, 62–63; John H. Elliott, "1 Peter, Its Situation and Strategy: A Discussion with David Balch," in Talbert, *Perspectives*,

62; Lampe and Luz, "Nachpaulinisches Christentum," 199; Kelly, 10.

346 E.g., Kelly, 29; Selwyn, 237, citing Mommsen. The sporadic nature can be seen in the case of Ignatius, bishop of Antioch, sentenced to death in Rome; before he even arrived at Rome, the persecution had ceased in Antioch (*Phld.* 10.1; *Pol.* 7.1); cf. Lampe and Luz, "Nachpaulinisches Christentum," 198.

347 For detailed discussion of *coercitio*, see Karl Johannes Neumann, "Coercitio," PW 1. Reihe, 4.1.201–4.

348 See ibid., 203, lines 60–68.

349 Punishment ranged from the death penalty to being sold into slavery to imprisonment to various forms of forfeiture of goods. For a detailed description of the punishments, see Theodor Mommsen, *Römisches Staatsrecht* (3d ed.; Leipzig: Hirzel, 1887) 1.149–61.

350 So Neumann, PW 1. Reihe, 4.1.203–4; see Kelly, 28; Schutter, *Hermeneutic*, 14. It was clearly exercised by Pliny, whose description of his procedure makes that clear (*Ep.* 10.96; cf. Bauer, "Verfolgung," 514–15). Evidence of its application has been found in Acts 16:19–24 (cf. Sordi, *Christians*, 201–2), and it could be reflected in 1 Pet 3:15 (ἀπολογία, λόγον αἰτεῖν; cf. Brox, 29).

351 So Lampe and Luz, "Nachpaulinisches Christentum," 200; Hall, "For to This," 138–39; Floyd V. Filson, "Partakers with Christ: Suffering in First Peter," *Int* 9

accused of offending the gods by such behavior and thus bringing divine disfavor upon the communities in which they lived,[353] to say nothing of the negative effect on economic conditions brought about by their attitudes.[354] As a result, Christians were regularly accused of antisocial acts,[355] even criminal behavior,[356] and were frequently harassed because of the association of such crimes with the name "Christian" itself.[357]

It is this kind of situation that seems reflected in 1 Peter. While Christians do in fact suffer (1:6; 3:14; 4:1, 12, 16, 19; 5:10), and while this suffering is widespread (5:9), it is sporadic (1:6; 5:10—"a little while") and takes the form more of being reviled (3:9, 16; 4:14) than of martyrdom. The recipients of the letter hold aloof from normal societal intercourse (4:3–4) and are called to account for it (3:15), undergoing the general accusation of being malefactors (2:12) and perhaps of being disloyal to Rome (implied in 2:13–17). Being identified as a Christian is enough to cause such harassment (4:16; cf. 4:14), but there is no indication such harassment necessarily brings lethal consequences, and there is some hope that recognizably good behavior can mitigate ill treatment (2:15; 3:13). The suffering therefore seems to be due more to social pressure with occasional intervention by officials than to any wide-ranging judicial attempt to locate and root out all Christian communities.

c. Conclusions. Some conclusions can now be drawn about the persecutions faced by the readers of 1 Peter, conclusions that have a direct bearing on the question of authorship. In the absence of any empirewide "official" persecution of Christians, it is apparent that such persecution cannot underlie 1 Peter, and therefore the situation in the letter cannot be identified with any of the three supposed "official" persecutions of Christians attributed respectively to Nero, Domitian, or Trajan.[358] Because of the sporadic nature of such persecutions, further, the possibility of identifying 1 Peter with any specific persecution of which we have records recedes to the point of invisibility.[359] Finally, because the practice of the emperor cult in Asia Minor was due more to the zeal of local elites than to the emperors themselves, the presence (or absence) in our letter of possible references to pressure to participate in such a cult cannot be used to argue for (or against) some kind of official, empirewide persecution of the Christians for their failure to participate willingly in it.

Rather, the persecutions faced by the readers of 1 Peter were in the nature of the case due more to unofficial harassment than to official policy,[360] more

---

(1955) 402; Spicq, 19; Donald Senior, "The Conduct of Christians in the World (2:11—3:12)," *RevExp* 79 (1982) 427; Margot, 10. This state of affairs continued even to the time of Hadrian (see Sordi, *Christians,* 194).

352 Lepelley, "Le contexte," 49; Schutter, *Hermeneutic,* 11; Lampe and Luz, "Nachpaulinisches Christentum," 201; Brox, 30; Schelkle, 8; such a situation is clearly mirrored in 1 Pet 4:2–4.

353 Sordi, *Christians,* 5, 203; Talbert, "Once Again," 145. This situation is also reflected in Acts 16:19–24; Apuleius *Metam.* 14; and Tertullian *Apol.* 10. The twin charges of treason and sacrilege show that religious and civil offenses were regarded as one and the same.

354 Hardy, *Christianity,* 35. The situation is also reflected in Acts 19:24–27, where economic distortion is coupled with sacrilege; cf. also Sordi, *Christians,* 202.

355 Suetonius *Vit.* 6.16.2; cf. also Tertullian *Apol.* 2; Minucius Felix *Octavius* 8–12. Although these are later writers, such associations are already reflected in 1 Pet 2:20b; 3:14, as they are in the ἕνεκεν ἐμοῦ

("because of me") of Matt 5:11; 10:18. Cf. also Schelkle, 9.

356 Neugebauer ("Zur Deutung," 62) argues that the advice in 1 Pet 2:19–20; 3:14, 17; 4:15–16, 19, not to become lawbreakers may well indicate the kind of accusations leveled at Christians.

357 Suffering "for the name" is attested sufficiently in the NT (e.g., Mark 13:13; Luke 21:12; Acts 5:41; 9:16; cf. Matt 5:11–12 ["for me"]) to indicate it did not first come into existence at the time of Trajan (cf. Kelly, 29; Selwyn, "Problem," 258; Brox, 30). Such suffering could result from private harassment as well as public prosecution (so Dibelius, "Petrusbriefe," 1113; Moule, "Nature," 8; Sylva, "Studies," 161).

358 Best, 39; Cothenet, "Le réalisme de l'espérance chrétienne selon 1 Pierre," *NTS* 27 (1981) 567; Goppelt, 62 (ET 44); Selwyn, "Problem," 257; Willem C. van Unnik, "Christianity According to I Peter," *ExpT* 68 (1956/57) 80; Fitzmyer, "First Peter," 363.

359 Cf. Best, 42; Cothenet, "Les orientations," 21.

360 So Moule, "Nature," 8; Hall, "For to This," 139;

local than regional,[361] and more at the initiation of the general populace as the result of a reaction against the lifestyle of the Christians[362] than at the initiation of Roman officials because of some general policy of seeking out and punishing Christians.[363] That does not rule out the possibility that persecutions occurred over large areas of the empire; they surely did, but they were spasmodic and broke out at different times in different places, the result of the flare-up of local hatreds rather than because Roman officials were engaged in the regular discharge of official policy.[364]

As a result, we cannot fix a specific date to the persecutions reflected in 1 Peter, and such references to persecution are therefore of no value in seeking to determine whether Simon Peter could still have been alive when they occurred, and hence could have been the author of this letter.[365]

E. Content of 1 Peter

The content of 1 Peter has often been consulted for any characteristics that would help resolve the problem of its authorship. Among those elements most often discussed in this connection are ecclesiology and church order, Christology, and ethical admonitions.

1. Ecclesiology and Church Order

Although the word ἐκκλησία is absent from the text of our letter,[366] it is clear from the letter's contents that the Christian community is of central importance. The understanding of the community is closely connected to its Christology: the church draws its nature from its suffering and risen Lord.[367] This close connection is also shown in the way the author interprets Scripture: Christ as the rejected stone reflects the church's fate,[368] and the community is described in terms drawn from the OT.[369]

There is some debate on the extent to which this ecclesiology builds on insights from the apostle Paul. The emphasis on the church as body of priests is a unique development from the notion of church as building[370] or body, and, it can be argued, shows an understanding of

Lampe and Luz, "Nachpaulinisches Christentum," 200–201. While Willem C. van Unnik ("The Teaching of Good Works in 1 Peter," in idem, *Sparsa Collecta* [2 vols., NovTSup 29, 30; Leiden: Brill, 1980] 2.95) recognizes that the suffering mentioned in 1 Peter is not necessarily due to state intervention, his argument that because such sufferings are shared by the whole brotherhood, they cannot be local, is to miss the point that *local* persecutions occurred sporadically *throughout* the empire, since Christians showed the same self-isolation wherever a church was established. Because 1 Pet 2:13–17 has a favorable attitude to Roman authorities, van Unnik argues that the sufferings experienced by the readers of 1 Peter were inflicted by Jews, not Romans ("The Redemption in 1 Peter I 18–19 and the Problem of the First Epistle of Peter," in idem, *Sparsa Collecta* 2.79; but cf. John A. T. Robinson, *Redating the New Testament* [Philadelphia: Westminster, 1976] 152). That such an inference may not be drawn from 2:13–17 will be shown in the comments on those verses below.

361 Peter Lippert, "Leben als Zeugnis," *Studia Moralia* 3 (1965) 236; Moule, "Sanctuary and Sacrifice in the Church of the New Testament," *JTS*, n.s. 1 (1950) 41; Brox, "Situation und Sprache," 6; de Villiers, "Joy," 67.

362 This view is currently widely accepted; cf. Richard, "Christology," 127, 204; Brox, 29, 31; Price, *Rituals and Power*, 123–24; Karl Philipps, *Kirche in der Gesellschaft nach dem 1. Petrusbrief* (Gütersloh: Gütersloher Verlagshaus-Gerd Mohn, 1971) 28; Hardy, *Christianity*, 34; Meade, *Pseudonymity and*

Canon, 164; Holmer and de Boor, 94. The Jews confronted similar hostility because of their lifestyle (Tacitus *Hist.* 5.5; cf. Daniel, "Anti-Semitism," 61).

363 Pliny's opening paragraph to Trajan makes clear that even at that later date, he knows of no such official policy (*Ep.* 10.96).

364 For a similar judgment, see Lampe and Luz, "Nachpaulinisches Christentum," 200.

365 So, e.g., Meade, *Pseudonymity and Canon*, 164. This can be argued either way; it could be used to argue for authorship by Simon Peter, as de Villiers ("Joy," 67) points out.

366 Cothenet ("Les orientations," 42) finds its absence "surprising" but thinks it may be accidental in so short a letter.

367 On the suffering Christ, see Goldstein, "Kirche," 38; on the risen Christ, see Goldstein, *Paulinische Gemeinde*, 50, 58. See also Theophil Spörri, *Der Gemeindegedanke im ersten Petrusbrief* (Gütersloh: Bertelsmann, 1925) 259.

368 Brox, "Situation und Sprache," 8.

369 Noteworthy in this respect is 1 Pet 2:4–10.

370 Goldstein (*Paulinische Gemeinde*, 111) sees the notion of a building in process of being built as a development of Pauline ecclesiology (e.g., 1 Cor 3:9–11), with the movement from building to corporate priesthood an original addition.

the church more developed than that of Paul or of the letter to the Ephesians.[371]

The nature of the church order represented in 1 Peter has also been called upon to argue for its composition at a time after Simon Peter would have lived. On the one hand, the notion of Christ as chief shepherd and bishop, with the implication of underlings exercising such oversight, the danger of elders "lording it over" the people under their charge,[372] and the warning not to assume church leadership for material gain, implying a paid leadership, could, taken together, point to a more advanced, and hence later, stage of church order.[373] On the other hand, the lack of explicit orders of ministry, such as one finds in the pastorals (bishop, elder, deacon), and the limitation of the foundation of the church to Christ, excluding mention of prophets and apostles, as in Ephesians,[374] would point in the opposite direction.[375]

2. Christology

While it is clear in 1 Peter that God is the ruler over all things, who through divine foreknowledge and power is absolute lord of creation,[376] it is equally clear that that lordship is exercised exclusively through Christ,[377] who occupies a position superior to that of all other powers.[378] The letter is therefore predicated on Christology.

The emphasis on the suffering of Jesus as a prelude to his exaltation forms the core of that Christology,[379] and it is expressed in terms derived from the course of his career: suffering, death, resurrection, ascension, and exaltation, a career to which he was destined from the very beginning.[380] Since the christological statements in the letter are not thematic but rather are adduced to support the ethical admonitions about which the author is primarily concerned, there is no explicit discussion of Christology. Further, a number of christological affirmations seem derived from fragments of hymns and/or confessions.[381] It is therefore difficult to determine what kind of Christology the author espoused, and consequently difficult to determine whether it is "primitive" or "advanced."

If, for example, the Christology of 1 Peter has close affinity to that of the Epistle to the Hebrews—Jesus, whose career centered on his suffering and subsequent exaltation (2:9–10) and who bore our sins (9:28), became in that way the pioneer and perfecter of faith (12:2) and the forerunner of salvation for those who obey him (5:9; 6:20)[382]—such affinity would point to a later Christology. If, alternatively the Christology lacks any clear notion of preexistence,[383] it could be identified as being rather primitive, and hence representing an earlier and less developed theological stage in the life of the church.

Taken by itself, therefore, the Christology of 1 Peter offers ambiguous evidence for the attempt to determine whether it belongs to a time in the theological develop-

---

371 So Goldstein, *Paulinische Gemeinde*, 75.

372 E.g., Moule, "Nature," 2.

373 Senior (xiii) sees this, along with other elements, arguing "against Petrine authorship."

374 Neugebauer ("Zur Deutung," 72) makes this point.

375 E.g., Spörri, *Gemeindegedanke*, 258. For further discussion on this point, see the comments on 5:1–5 below.

376 Goldstein, *Paulinische Gemeinde*, 27; cf. Richard, "Christology," 130.

377 Philipps (*Kirche*, 18) calls it the leitmotif of the letter.

378 Philipps (*Kirche*, 19) emphasizes this point.

379 Although some see the significance of Christ's suffering in terms of moral example (e.g., E. L. Sieffert, "Die Heilsbedeutung des Leidens und Sterbens Christi nach dem ersten Briefe des Petrus," *Jahrbücher für deutsche Theologie* 20 [1875] 430, 432; Eva Krafft, "Christologie und Anthropologie im 1. Petrusbrief," *EvTh* 10 [1950/51] 122–23), it is better understood as an atoning act (so, e.g., Schelkle, 112; Norman Hillyer, "The Servant of God," *EvQ* 41 [1969] 159).

380 Wand (23) finds six "moments in the life of Christ" that make up the Christology: preexistence, suffering, descent into hell, resurrection, ascension, and appearance as final judge. Richard ("Christology," 130) finds similar elements in the hymnic material (i.e., 1:20; 3:18–22) that he thinks 1 Peter has incorporated. Krafft ("Christologie," 122) puts emphasis on Christ being elect by God for his destiny.

381 So, e.g., David L. Balch, "Hellenization/Acculturation in 1 Peter," in Talbert, *Perspectives*, 100; see also n. 380 above.

382 So Michaels, lxxiii.

383 While some have presumed it (e.g., Wand, 23), others have argued it is a matter of Christ being destined and manifested rather than preexistent and incarnated (e.g., Richard, "Christology," 131; Krafft, "Christologie," 121).

ment of the church contemporary with, or subsequent to, the lifetime of Simon Peter.

3. Ethical Admonitions

While the basic ethical imperative of 1 Peter is expressed as being holy because the God who saved them is holy,[384] such holiness is shown in Christ, and again, principally in his behavior during his passion, which is then the model for Christian existence.[385] Thus the Christian is to find the norm for correct behavior in Christ, perhaps in his command to love as well as in his behavior under persecution, and is to follow it because of Christ.[386]

The imperative for action is found in the new eschatological reality represented by the risen and glorified Christ.[387] The saving grace brought to reality in that divine act results in a distinctive way of life[388] in which God's plan for the whole of the world begins to take place: in the Christians' actions the divine plan and indeed the divine presence are manifested.[389] Salvation is thus to be a constituent element of the community (rather than of the believing individual) in which this future assumes present reality.[390] Much of the admonitory material is intended to maintain the salvific integrity of that community in the face of hostile pressure against it.

Equally important, the ethical stance of the Christian in 1 Peter is not withdrawal from society; it is a nuanced participation in society, limited to those events which do not compromise the basic commitment to Christ as exclusive Lord.[391] Thus Christians share with the best elements of their society what they take to be good,[392] and their behavior will correlatively be recognized as good by those same social elements. Christian ethics means therefore both to follow the good and to resist the bad in the social environment.[393] The call is thus not to reform the social order but to exhibit true goodness within it,[394] in the conviction that such behavior will then be recognized as positive rather than as threatening to the best of pagan values.

Such an ethical stance assumes that Christian communities are well enough known that they have attracted the attention of pagan authorities, and that the future of those communities lies in their ability to exist within a sporadically hostile environment. Such a situation could have existed virtually from the outset of the Christian mission to non-Jewish areas,[395] but the ethos of the letter seems to reflect rather a later than an earlier attempt to come to terms with the social environment within which the Christian community necessarily had to live. It thus points to a time and to a situation that make it less likely that Simon Peter was the author.

4. Conclusion

The content of 1 Peter is at best ambiguous about the time at which and the situation for which the letter was

---

384 So also Russell, "Eschatology," 83.

385 E.g., Goldstein, *Paulinische Gemeinde,* 28.

386 Lippert, "Zeugnis," 260; Lohse, "Parenesis," 56; Neugebauer ("Zur Deutung," 80, 83) also emphasizes the love command.

387 Cf. John H. Elliott, *The Elect and the Holy: An Exegetical Examination of 1 Peter 2:4–10 and the Phrase* βασίλειον ἱεράτευμα (NovTSup 12; Leiden: Brill, 1966) 84. As van Unnik ("Teaching," 104) points out, there is nevertheless no indication of an "interim ethic" in 1 Peter.

388 David W. Kendall calls attention to this connection ("The Literary and Theological Function of 1 Peter 1:3–12," in Talbert, *Perspectives,* 110).

389 So A. R. Jonsen, "The Moral Theology of the First Epistle of St. Peter," *Sciences ecclésiastiques* 16 (1964) 104; Brox, "Situation und Sprache," 9.

390 Refoulé ("Bible," 481) emphasizes that salvation is not an individual matter; see also Donald G. Miller, "Deliverance and Destiny: Salvation in First Peter," *Int* 9 (1955) 424.

391 This is a special emphasis of Goppelt, "Prinzipien,"

288–89; see also Philipps, *Kirche,* 34; Cothenet, "Le réalisme," 571.

392 So, e.g., Talbert, "Once Again," 148; van Unnik, "Teaching," 102–3. See Malherbe, *Moral Exhortation,* 32, for Musonius Rufus's exposition (Fragment 16) of what Zeus bids one to do.

393 Cf. Malherbe, *Moral Exhortation,* 14; Goppelt, "Prinzipien," 290; Lippert, "Zeugnis," 261; van Unnik, "Teaching," 102.

394 So Beare, "Teaching," 291. The use of the word ἀγαθοποιεῖν ("to do [the] good") in 1 Peter to describe Christian behavior points in this same direction (e.g., 2:14–15, 20). Interestingly, it is a word that does not appear in the Pauline literature in the NT.

395 Van Unnik ("Teaching," 105) notes that the problem of "good works" cannot be relegated to "the second generation" of Christians.

written, and is therefore of no decisive value for determining its authorship.

F. Further Considerations for Determining Authorship

Some further considerations have been adduced in the attempt to determine the authorship of 1 Peter. For example, had 1 Peter been written by the apostle from Rome,[396] it would have been late in his career, and at a time when Paul was also imprisoned in Rome. Absence from the letter of any reference to Paul,[397] especially at 5:13 where it would have been most appropriate, would argue against Simon Peter as its author.[398]

Again, the area to which the epistle is addressed is an area more often associated with Paul than with Peter,[399] and the assumption that Peter had authority in Asia Minor is more likely to have arisen at a later time when such authority began to coalesce around this apostle. Yet of the five areas mentioned, only Asia and Galatia have any direct connection with Paul's missionary efforts; the other parts of Asia Minor that Acts reports Paul visited lie to the south of the area addressed in the letter.

A further item adduced is the complete lack of tension evidenced in the letter between Christians and Jews. Israel is never mentioned, it plays no role vis-à-vis the church, and its history and nomenclature are dissolved into descriptions of the Christian community.[400] While this lack of tension can hardly be decisive in indicating a period either within, or later than, the lifetime of Simon Peter, since there was no time within the first two centuries when such tension between Christian and Jewish communities was generally absent, either in Asia Minor or elsewhere in the Roman Empire, such lack of

discussion of that relationship would in fact seem strange on the part of one specifically charged with a mission to the Jews (cf. Gal 2:7).

Finally, while there is no mention of 1 Peter in the early Canon Muratori, that absence is as likely to be due to the corrupt nature of its manuscript as it is to any doubt by its compiler(s) that the letter was of apostolic origin. For that reason, that absence is of highly limited significance for the question of authorship.[401]

On the whole, then, these further considerations tend more to cast doubt on, rather than deliver support for, the authorship of this epistle by Simon Peter.

G. 1 Peter as Pseudonymous

Absence of clarity about the authorship of 1 Peter by Simon Peter has led to the suggestion that the letter is pseudonymous. Yet the very practice of pseudonymity, and hence the possibility of early Christians having practiced it, has often been challenged by those wishing to affirm authorship by Simon Peter. If such a practice was in fact morally repugnant to the culture in which 1 Peter arose, or would have been to the Christian community, doubt would be cast on whether pseudonymity was possible, and thus strength would be added to the case for Simon Peter as author.

1. Practice of Pseudonymity in the New Testament Environment

While it is inadvisable to apply modern moral sensitivity in deciding what would have been acceptable to the early Christian communities in the matter of pseudonymity,[402]

---

396 This is quite probably the meaning of "Babylon" in 5:13; see the discussion below on "Origin of 1 Peter," and the comments on 5:13.

397 Best (49) finds a comparable situation in Paul's mention of Peter when the former wrote to the Corinthian Christians, although there Peter was invoked because of controversy (e.g., 1 Cor 1:12; 3:4, 22; 9:5). Goldstein (*Paulinische Gemeinde*, 118) thinks 1 Pet 1:1 or 1:12 (*sic*) would have provided opportunity to mention Paul.

398 Harrison ("Exegetical Studies" [97], 203) attempts to meet this objection by arguing that Paul had earlier been released from prison, and was now "in the far west" (i.e., Spain), as he had proposed in Rom 15:28. Such an attempt remains unconvincing.

399 Brox, "Pseudepigraphischen Rahmung," 80, 96.

400 As often noted, 1 Peter differs greatly on this point

from the Pauline letters. See Brox, 49; Manns, "Sara," 65–66.

401 So, e.g., Harrison, "Exegetical Studies" [97], 201. If, as A. C. Sundberg, Jr., argued, Canon Muratori belonged to the fourth rather than to the second century, any bearing it might have on the authorship of 1 Peter would disappear ("Canon Muratori: A Fourth Century List," *HTR* 66 [1973] 1–41).

402 So also Norbert Brox, *Falsche Verfasserangaben: Zur Erklärung der frühchristlichen Pseudepigraphia* (SBS 79; Stuttgart: Katholisches Bibelwerk, 1975) 60; this work is most helpful in the matter of pseudonymity. Although Eric A. Havelock ("Oral Composition in the Oedipus Tyrannus of Sophocles," *New Literary History* 16 [1984]) 185–86) argues that it was the shift from verbal to written culture that fostered the notion of ownership and hence authorship of a

neither can such practices be routinely affirmed as a harmless convention.[403] Falsification of authorship was in fact not routinely regarded as harmless; the *Gospel of Peter* was rejected as a falsification,[404] as was the *Acts of Paul* when the true author became known.[405] In both cases, however, one must note that it was the content more than any moral repugnance at pseudonymity which prompted the rejection.[406] Writings whose content was above suspicion tended to be accepted, even when doubts about authorship existed.[407]

A variety of motives can be ascertained for assigning a writing to someone other than its actual author. Modesty in not seeking personal fame could be such a motive,[408] as could the less laudable desire of persons of no reputation to gain attention for their writings.[409] More widely attested, however, was the notion that students who in their writings enunciated a master's teachings were obliged to attribute that writing not to themselves, but to the one who originated such doctrine.[410] Thus the author of *Ad Herennium* (Cicero?) warned against the impudence of seeking to extract, from the labor of others, praise for one's own name;[411] rabbis held that handing on a tradition in the teacher's rather than the

tradent's name clarified the authority of those words;[412] students of the Pythagorean school routinely attributed their writings to its founder;[413] and Tertullian enunciated the principle that what disciples publish should be regarded as their master's work.[414] In these terms, apostolic pseudepigraphers who understood themselves as standing in the tradition of a given apostle,[415] and who sought to actualize that authoritative tradition for a later situation,[416] would find it natural to assign such work to that apostle.

The routine inclusion in NT pseudepigraphic writings of personal information about the reputed author as part of the fictive process,[417] however, may point to a motive beyond that of respect for the apostolic originator of the traditions enunciated. That motive can be termed the "therapeutic lie," a concept whose existence is widely attested in the Greco-Roman world. Plato had already tolerated such a notion,[418] the physician's lie to the patient for the latter's good embodied it,[419] and an orator was permitted leeway with the truth if it enabled him the better to make his point.[420] The notion that what is done for salvation stands outside the normal category of "lie" is also widely attested in the church

---

writing, a shift not yet complete in the NT world (on this whole question see P. J. Achtemeier, "*Omne Verbum Sonat*: The New Testament and the Oral Environment of Late Western Antiquity," *JBL* 109 [1990] 3–27), there was nonetheless already some centuries earlier, as William Chase Greene has pointed out, an "almost fierce concern to assert the personal authorship and ownership of compositions," and that concern existed in an environment where borrowing from the works of others occurred freely and with no disapproval ("The Spoken and the Written Word," *Harvard Studies in Classical Philology* 60 [1951] 34–36).

403 Brox (*Falsche Verfasserangaben*, 13–14) makes this point persuasively (cf. also 65, 71–77).

404 By Bishop Serapion because of its docetic Christology (Eusebius *Hist. eccl.* 6.12).

405 The author, a presbyter who wrote it out of "respect for Paul," was removed from office as a result. See Tertullian (*Bapt.* 17), who makes clear it contained false teachings. For a discussion of these two writings, see Brox, *Falsche Verfasserangaben* 79, 126–27.

406 With Goppelt (69, ET 52), who points out that it is the content and not the "author" that is decisive.

407 Brox, *Falsche Verfasserangaben*, 65, 79, 126. Such insight renders nugatory the observation that a later letter could not be attributed to Simon Peter, since

the readers would have known that by that time, he was dead; so, e.g., Selwyn, "Persecutions," 48.

408 See Brox, *Falsche Verfasserangaben*, 107–9.

409 See the comment by a Neoplatonic commentator on Aristotle named David (cited in Brox, *Falsche Verfasserangaben* 54).

410 See the discussion in Brox, *Falsche Verfasserangaben*, 72–74.

411 *Ad Her.* 4.3.5.

412 See Birger Gerhardsson, *Memory and Manuscript* (ASNU 22; Lund: Gleerup, 1961) 131, esp. n. 1.

413 So Iamblichos *De vit. Pyth.* 29.158.6–11; 31.198.9–11.

414 *Adv. Marc.* 4.5.

415 Amos Wilder, *Early Christian Rhetoric: The Language of the Gospel* (London: SCM, 1964) 41; Brox, *Falsche Verfasserangaben*, 113.

416 Meade, *Pseudonymity and Canon*, 42, 177–79 (see also 43–71); Brox, *Falsche Verfasserangaben*, 113.

417 Such material may be drawn from tradition (e.g., Mark in 1 Pet 5:13; cf. Acts 12:12), but it is included to further the fictive process, not simply to convey information, as Brox ("Pseudepigraphischen Rahmung," 85, 90–91) correctly notes; cf. also Brox, *Falsche Verfasserangaben*, 61.

418 He limited it to physicians and rulers: *Republic* 389b-c (I was pointed to this material by Brox, *Falsche*

fathers:[421] Chrysostom celebrated Rahab's lie for the good of the Israelites,[422] Jerome thought Christ's assuming the appearance of sinful flesh was a legitimate deception,[423] and Origen celebrated instances of God's salvific deception in dealing with sinful humanity.[424] Such a concept of "salvific deception" was nevertheless held within the larger context of a morality that stood against dishonesty, lies, and deception.

If such a notion of the "therapeutic lie," found in the early church fathers, can be projected back into the mentality of Christians at the time the NT writings were being composed—and given its prevalence in the secular environment of that time such a projection is not unlikely—then one can understand how an author would attribute apostolic authorship to sound doctrine. Indeed, to fail to do that if it would make the writing more effective would itself be wrong.[425]

Thus these two elements—the notion of a student's duty to the master, and the legitimacy of the "therapeutic lie" for the greater good—combine to provide the framework within which pseudonymity would be practiced, within which it would be tolerated in writings of sound character and condemned in writings that did not promote such salvific ends. The notion of 1 Peter as pseudonymous thus does not lie beyond the pale of early Christian morality, and has, indeed, much to recommend it.

2. Why Peter?

Establishing pseudonymity as a possible practice for authors of NT writings, thus making it possible for 1 Peter to be pseudonymous, raises the question of why this letter should be attributed to Peter. Lack of compelling reasons for such pseudonymous attribution would make the claim that 1 Peter is pseudonymous seem to be that much less likely.

Nothing in the letter itself would immediately identify it with Peter;[426] if the first word were not there, one would be much more likely to attribute it to Paul.[427] That fact has been used to affirm its (pseudonymous) purpose: for example, to show there was no disagreement between Peter and Paul,[428] or to strengthen with Peter's name and the authority of Jerusalem a Pauline theology that was in danger of being lost.[429]

More likely, however, is the argument that attribution to Peter is intended to strengthen its claim to be "apostolic." Written at a time when what was old was revered over what was new, and when all valid doctrine was assumed to have been present from the apostolic beginnings of the church,[430] the assignment of the letter to Peter would reflect the desire to relate its content to that apostolic beginning.[431] Thus, since all apostles agreed from the beginning,[432] the assignment to Peter would have been intended to designate its contents as

Verfasserangaben, 84–85).

419 E.g., Clement of Alexandria *Strom.* 7.9.53.2 (I was pointed to this reference by Brox, *Falsche Verfasserangaben*, 87; cf. also 100–101).

420 "Ementiri in historiis" ("to fabricate in narratives"); so Cicero *Brutus* 11.42 (cf. Brox, *Falsche Verfasserangaben*, 71, from whom I got this reference).

421 On this point, see Brox, *Falsche Verfasserangaben*, 85 et passim.

422 *De paen.* 49.331; in the same passage he terms her the "image of the church" (εἰκὼν τῆς ἐκκλησίας; 49.330–31). For further discussion, see Brox, *Falsche Verfasserangaben*, 90–92.

423 So Brox, *Falsche Verfasserangaben*, 93.

424 *In Jer.* 19.15; regarding monogamy: 20.4; cf. *Con. Cels.* 4.19. For further discussion, see Brox, *Falsche Verfasserangaben*, 88–97.

425 Brox (*Falsche Verfasserangaben*, 99) also draws this conclusion (cf. also 95).

426 Cf. the oft-quoted remark of A. Jülicher that if "Petros" were not in the first verse, no one would think of attributing it to him (*Einleitung in das Neue*

Testament [6th ed.; Tübingen: Mohr (Siebeck), 1906] 178).

427 Cf. Brox, *Falsche Verfasserangaben*, 17; idem, "Pseudepigraphischen Rahmung," 78–79; Bornemann, "Taufrede," 145. The suggestion of K. M. Fischer (*Tendenz und Absicht des Epheserbriefes* [FRLANT 111; Göttingen: Vandenhoeck & Ruprecht, 1973] 15 n. 3) that a copyist substituted Πέτρος for an original Παῦλος has been rightly rejected (e.g., Cothenet, "Les orientations," 34; Marxsen, "Der Mitälteste," 379 n. 13).

428 So F. C. Baur (cited in Brox, "Tendenz," 116); cf. Beare, 49.

429 So Brox, "Tendenz," 116, citing W. Trilling ("Zum Petrusamt im NT: Traditionsgeschichtliche Überlegungen anhand von Matthaeus, 1 Petrus und Johannes," *ThQ* 151 [1971] 123–26).

430 Brox (*Falsche Verfasserangaben*, 37, 52–53, 64–65, 106, 118–19) sees the importance of this point.

431 Rightly Brox, "Tendenz," 120.

432 Brox ("Tendenz," 119; *Falsche Verfasserangaben*, 78, 115) emphasizes this point.

apostolic, rather than specifically Petrine.[433] Nevertheless, even the desire primarily to identify the content of the letter as apostolic would in itself suggest the name of Peter. Peter's role in NT traditions—he was the first to see the risen Lord;[434] he played a leading role in the Gospel narratives;[435] he was commanded by Jesus to comfort his brother disciples;[436] he stumbled, recovered, and ultimately suffered martyrdom, thus representing a comfort for people caught in persecution;[437] he was recognized by Paul as a significant figure in the early church[438]—together with the association of Peter with a Roman church that enjoyed increasing prestige in the early Christian world[439] and as a result the growing identification of Peter with apostolic authority,[440] all that would contribute toward making Peter a logical candidate for pseudonymous authorship of an expression of apostolic faith.

Such attribution, given the understanding of pseudonymity described above, would best be explained if the letter were the product of a Petrine group who looked to Peter as their teacher. Such groups or schools were known in both secular and Christian circles,[441] and the existence of a Petrine group may well be reflected in the NT evidence cited above.[442] If that evidence does point to the existence of such a school,[443] 1 Peter may be understood as having emerged from that group,[444] written by one or more tradents of the Petrine tradition who was located in Rome[445] and who intended the letter to embody the kerygma and social outlook that were associated with the apostle Peter.[446]

H. Conclusions

Evidence to solve definitively the question of the authorship of 1 Peter remains unavailable. While language and style along with absence of reminiscences of Jesus' life argue against authorship by Simon Peter, lack of definitive evidence of dependence on Pauline letters or other NT literature weakens the argument against such authorship. Examination of Roman policy toward groups

433 So Cothenet, "Les orientations," 37; Brox, "Pseud-epigraphischen Rahmung," 92–93.

434 1 Cor 15:3; Luke 24:34; see Acts 10:41; John 20:6 (Peter is first to enter the empty tomb); Mark 16:7 (Peter is singled out in regard to seeing the risen Christ in Galilee). See the discussion of this point in Goppelt, 31 (ET 7).

435 He is the first disciple called (Mark 1:16; Luke 5:8, 10); one of the inner group (Mark 9:2; 13:3); the first human to confess Jesus as the Christ (Mark 8:29); he is named the foundation of church (Matt 16:18) and charged with feeding Christ's sheep/lambs (John 21:15–24).

436 Luke 22:31–32; that command alone would make probable the emergence of some account of Simon Peter doing just that.

437 So Schutter, *Hermeneutic*, 6–7; Smith, *Petrine Controversies*, 155–56; see also John H. Elliott, "Peter, Silvanus and Mark in 1 Peter and Acts," in W. Haubeck and M. Bachmann, eds., *Wort in der Zeit: Neutestamentliche Studien; Festgabe für Karl Heinrich Rengstorf* (Leiden: Brill, 1980) 259.

438 1 Cor 1:12; 9:5; Gal 1:18–19; 2:8–9, 11.

439 This is a widely held point: e.g., Leaney, 10; Michaels, lxvi-lxvii; Philipps, *Kirche*, 16; Brox, "Tendenz," 115; Schiwy, 33; Elliott, "Peter, Silvanus and Mark," 264.

440 So Brox, "Tendenz," 119; cf. Brown et al., *Peter*, 162–68.

441 See Cothenet, "Les orientations," 39.

442 So Elliott, "Rehabilitation," 9; idem, "Peter, Silvanus and Mark," 256. Meade (*Pseudonymity and Canon*,

164) notes the existence of a "Peter Party" already at the time of the writing of 1 Cor 1:12 (cf. also William G. Doty, *Letters in Primitive Christianity* [Guides to Biblical Scholarship; Philadelphia: Fortress, 1979] 177).

443 Not all agree there was such a group; its existence has been called into question by Brox ("Tendenz," 114–15; *Falsche Verfasserangaben*, 111; "Situation und Sprache," 3) largely on the basis of the absence of any identifiable "Petrine" theology in Acts and the letters assigned to him. See also Meade, *Pseudonymity and Canon*, 174; Best, 60.

444 So, e.g., Best, 63; John H. Elliott, *A Home for the Homeless: A Sociological Exegesis of 1 Peter, Its Situation and Strategy* (Philadelphia: Fortress, 1981) 273; Tarrech, "Le milieu," 98; Goppelt, 69 (ET 52).

445 In addition to n. 439 above, see also Elliott, "Peter, Silvanus and Mark," 253.

446 So, e.g., Elliott, "Peter, Silvanus and Mark," 257; Goppelt, 69 (ET 52). In the judgment of Brox ("Literarischen Tradition," 187), however, the existence of such traditions, based on the NT data in Acts and the Petrine correspondence, can be maintained only by employing "viel Phantasie" "a good deal of fantasy" to reach "unhaltbare Ergeb-nisse" "indefensible conclusions."

shows that the common notion that 1 Peter reflects some official Roman policy of opposition toward those communities is without foundation, and hence of less help in determining authorship than has often been assumed. The content of the letter is such as again to deliver at best only ambiguous evidence about its authorship.

Examination of the outlook on, and practice of, pseudonymity in the NT world has revealed it to be a possible solution to the question of authorship. Although 1 Peter does not demonstrate some traits usually associated with pseudonymity—it defends no particular doctrine or church order against attack,[447] it lacks the kind of references often included to make authorship credible[448]—their absence does not render it impossible.

Pseudonymity does presume some author, however, and a number of suggestions have been proposed, in addition to its authorship by Silvanus:[449] they range from an otherwise unknown Peter associated with two equally unknown persons named Silvanus and Mark,[450] to an unknown, second generation disciple of Peter.[451] In fact, the evidence available allows us to do little more than engage in such speculations.[452]

In sum, although authorship by Simon Peter continues

to have its defenders,[453] the evidence adduced for that position is weak enough and the evidence against it strong enough to make it apposite to reject that as a possibility and to assume pseudonymity. Yet the very absence of identifiably Petrine elements in the letter argues strongly for some internal association with the apostle Peter; otherwise, it is difficult to imagine why the letter would have been ascribed to him.[454] While no definitive conclusion can be reached, therefore,[455] the best working hypothesis is anonymous authorship of a pseudonymous letter[456] that, in its intent to be apostolic, drew on traditions historically associated with Simon Peter. Beyond that, the author remains unknown to us.

II. Date
Two kinds of evidence can be called upon to resolve the problem of the date of a piece of literature like 1 Peter; they are data external to the letter itself, by which the existence of the letter can be demonstrated, and data internal to the letter, by means of which the letter can then be correlated to datable external events.

447 So Chase, "Peter," 785–86; the conclusion is favorably cited in Robinson, *Redating,* 164.

448 E.g., such elements as 2 Pet 1:1, 13–15, 17–18; 3:1. See the discussion of this point in Brox, "Tendenz," 113–14.

449 Brox ("Pseudepigraphischen Rahmung," 84) notes that inclusion of the actual author's name (i.e., Silvanus) in a pseudepigraphic writing, thus imperiling the purpose of the letter, lies in the realm of the improbable.

450 Perdelwitz, *Mysterienreligion,* 105; the suggestion has remained deservedly ignored.

451 For a list of suggested authors for 1 Peter, see Brox, "Tendenz," 110.

452 Even such claims as those of Schutter (*Hermeneutic*) that, given the "peculiarly Jewish hermeneutical tradition" evident in 1 Peter (109), the author was therefore very likely "a Jew by birth and education" (84) does little to pinpoint the identity of the author.

453 While few would call the letter with Steuer ("1 Petr 3,17—4,6," 678) the first encyclical of the first pope, W. J. Dalton does find authorship by Simon Peter a good "working hypothesis" ("'So That Your Faith May Also Be Your Hope in God' [1 Peter 1:21]," in R. Banks, ed., *Reconciliation and Hope: New Testament Essays on Atonement and Eschatology Presented to L. L. Morris on His 60th Birthday* [Exeter: Paternoster;

Grand Rapids: Eerdmans, 1974] 262–66). See also Bornemann, "Taufrede," 163; de Villiers, "Joy," 64–65; Norman Hillyer, *1 and 2 Peter, Jude* (New International Biblical Commentary, Peabody, Mass.: Hendrickson, 1992) 9.

454 So also Philipps (*Kirche,* 16), although he suggests, as I would not, that this may point to Simon Peter, through Silvanus, as having personal responsibility for the letter.

455 So also Schelkle (15), who observes that with respect to authorship critical studies have not been able to clarify the question in any convincing fashion.

456 Pseudonymity has wide support; cf., e.g., Beare, 48; Best, 49; Kelly, 32; Leaney, 5; Gerhard Krodel, *The First Letter of Peter* (Proclamation Commentaries: The New Testament Witness for Preaching; Philadelphia: Fortress, 1977) 58; Schutter, *Hermeneutic,* 7; R. E. Brown and John P. Meier, *Antioch and Rome* (New York: Paulist, 1983) 130; Meade, *Pseudonymity and Canon,* 172.

A. External Attestation

The clearest and most reliable external attestation to the existence, and hence the date, of 1 Peter consists in the description or citation of identifiable passages from the letter by name. A second type of external attestation, less reliable because more open to differing interpretations, consists in references to phrases, or unique words, in 1 Peter, but without any reference to 1 Peter itself or to the fact that the material is being cited from another source.

External attestation of the first type can be readily identified in literature datable toward the end of the second century. Tertullian, for example, names the author and cites as well as quotes identifiable passages,[457] while Clement of Alexandria similarly identifies the author ("Peter") and quotes extensive portions of 1 Peter.[458] Somewhat earlier, and for the first time, Irenaeus cites 1 Peter by name as a letter.[459] By the late second century, therefore, 1 Peter was widely known and regarded as important, as the citations indicate.[460]

As one moves to the earlier literature, certainty of citation begins to lessen, principally because the letter is not specifically identified as the source of certain citations. For example, claims of citation in Justin Martyr[461] or the *Epistle of Barnabas*[462] betray on closer examination nothing more than probability; similar words are used, but the contexts differ and the material appears clearly to belong to common Christian tradition.

In the case of the letter of Polycarp to the Philippians, we have the general affirmation by Eusebius (*Hist. eccl.* 4.19.9) that Polycarp did quote 1 Peter, but Eusebius gives no specific passages from either of the letters, and the frequent affirmation that such quotation occurs, often with passages cited,[463] proves less convincing when those passages are examined in detail. Of the numerous passages that have been cited as demonstrating that 1 Peter was known to and used by Polycarp, a number have only one or two words in common,[464] or have similar language but in the midst of a combination of traditional elements and in a different context.[465]

Three passages, however, do merit serious consideration as evidence of Polycarp's knowledge of 1 Peter. Of them, two show the clearest evidence: *Phil.* 1.3 shares with 1 Pet 1:8 similar language and an unusual use of the word δεδοξασμένη ("glorified"),[466] while *Phil.* 8.1 shares with 1 Pet 2:24 and 2:22 a number of similar phrases

---

457 In *Scorp.* 12 he cites 1 Pet 2:20–21 with emendation, 1 Pet 4:12–16 verbatim; in *Scorp.* 14 he attributes and describes 1 Pet 2:13. In a more general way, in *Orat.* 20 he attributes and describes 1 Pet 3:1–6.

458 *Paed.* 1.6.44 (by name) = 1 Pet 2:1–3; 3.11.74 (by name) = 1 Pet 2:18; 3.12.85 (by name) = 1 Pet 1:17b–19, 4:3; *Strom.* 3.11.75 (by name) = 1 Pet 2:11–12a, 15–16 (as one quotation, with minor variations); 3.18.110 (by name) = 1 Pet 1:21a–22b, 14–16 (in that order, as one quote, with minor variations); 4.7.46 (by name) = 1 Pet 3:14–17 (minor variations); 4.7.47 (by name) = 1 Pet 4:12–14 (minor variations); 4.20.129 (by name) = 1 Pet 1:6–9 (minor variations); *Excerpta ex Theodoto* 1.12.2 (by name) = 1:12 (εἰς ἃ and παρακῦψαι).

459 Cited by name and letter: *Adv. haer.* 4.9.2 = 1 Pet 1:8 (*Petrus ait in epistula sua* ["Peter said in his letter"]); by name: *Adv. haer.* 4.16.5 = 1 Pet 2:16; 5.7.2 = 1 Pet 1:8.

460 If Canon Muratori is a second-century document (but see Sundberg, *HTR* 66 [1973] 1–41), absence of mention of 1 Peter may mean the compiler did not know of it (e.g., Brox, 40), or its absence may be due either to the carelessness of a translator or scribe, or to the mutilation of the original document. See Chase, "Peter," 780; Bigg, 14; Michaels, xxxiii–xxxiv; Schutter, *Hermeneutic*, 7; Schelkle, 16.

461 E.g., *Dial.* 116 = 1 Pet 2:9; 138 = 1 Pet 3:18–21; 116 = 1 Pet 4:12; 119 = 1 Pet 2:10; 35, 110 = 1 Pet 1:19; 114 = 1 Pet 2:6. In every case similarities are limited to a single word or to a general description. Only in *Dial.* 138 = 1 Pet 3:18–21 is there greater similarity; it could imply acquaintance but hardly demonstrates literary dependence on 1 Peter, as Foster (*Literary Relations*, 383) thinks probable.

462 The closest similarities either quote the same OT passages (e.g., *Barn.* 6.2 = 1 Pet 2:6; *Barn.* 6.6 = 1 Pet 2:7b) or place similar words or phrases in different contexts (e.g., *Barn.* 5.5 = 1 Pet 1:20). The most likely source of such similarities is common Christian tradition; it is surely not necessary to conclude with Foster (*Literary Relations,* 387) that the author of *Barnabas* "knew and used" 1 Peter.

463 E.g., Goppelt, 53 (ET 32–33); Brox, 39; Michaels, xxxii; Best, 43–44; Beare, 28; Moule, "Nature," 1.

464 1 Pet 1:2, *Phil.* opening: πληθυνθείη; 1 Pet 2:11, *Phil.* opening: παροικ-; 1 Pet 2:21, *Phil.* 8.2: ὑπογραμμόν; 1 Pet 2:11, *Phil.* 5.3: ἐπιθυμι- . . . στρατευ-; 1 Pet 4:7, *Phil.* 7.2: νηφ- . . . -ευχας; 1 Pet 2:11–12, *Phil.* 10.2: *ex bonis operibus*; 1 Pet 2:13, *Phil.* 12.3: *pro reg-*.

465 1 Pet 3:9, *Phil.* 2.2: μὴ ἀποδιδόντες κακὸν ἀντὶ κακοῦ ἢ λοιδορίαν ἀντὶ λοιδορίας, in the midst of a catalog of vices.

466 1 Pet 1:8: ὃν οὐκ ἰδόντες ἀγαπᾶτε . . . πιστεύοντες . . .

that, despite altered word order (1 Pet 2:24) and the common quotation of LXX Isa 53:9 (1 Pet 2:22, but with identical substitution of ἁμαρτίας for ἀνομίαν),[467] appear to have their source in 1 Peter. In the third instance, *Phil.* 2.1 shares with 1 Pet 1:13, 21 similar language,[468] but the phrases are scattered in 1 Peter, and they occur in the midst of many other traditional elements in Polycarp, and for that reason remain less convincing as evidence of direct dependence. While the material in these three passages could be due to common use of Christian traditions, the extent of the similarities makes it probable that Polycarp was acquainted with 1 Peter.

In the case of *1 Clement*, a variety of passages are often cited as showing evidence of acquaintance with, if not dependence on, 1 Peter. To a large extent, however, the similarities are limited to a word or two,[469] and, although many are limited to 1 Peter and *1 Clement*, they nevertheless probably tell us more about Christian tradition in Rome in the late first century than they do about any literary dependence. Discussions of common topics[470] lack common vocabulary and even common exposition, and passages that do display more than a word or two in common[471] also appear to be due to a reliance on Christian tradition. In none of these instances is there the same degree of probability of a relationship between the two epistles as there was in the case of Polycarp.[472] *1 Clement* does not therefore offer clear and unambiguous evidence of acquaintance with, or use of, 1 Peter.[473]

The same is likely the case with other examples of supposed linkage, for example, the *Didache*, the *Shepherd of Hermas*, and the *Epistle to Diognetus*. In each case, the more probable explanation of such similarities as they display is mutual dependence on *loci communes* of common tradition.[474] One may include in this category the reference in 2 Pet 3:1 to an earlier letter. Its value depends on the certainty of that reference to what we know as 1 Peter,[475] and, granted such a reference, on the date of 2 Peter; Irenaeus, for example, seems not to have known of 2 Peter's existence in the late second century.[476]

More surprising, perhaps, is the absence of any clear reference to 1 Peter in the letters of Ignatius of Antioch, since Ignatius traveled through parts of Asia Minor that were apparently included in the addressees of 1 Peter. Had 1 Peter been written earlier and circulated to those

---

χαρᾷ ἀνεκλαλήτῳ καὶ δεδοξασμένη; *Phil.* 1.3: εἰς ὃν οὐκ ἰδόντες πιστεύετε χαρᾷ ἀνεκλαλήτῳ καὶ δεδοξασμένη.

467 1 Pet 2:22: ὃς ἁμαρτίαν οὐκ ἐποίησεν, οὐδὲ εὑρέθη δόλος ἐν τῷ στόματι αὐτοῦ; 1 Pet 2:24: ὃς τὰς ἁμαρτίας ἡμῶν ἀνήνεγκεν ἐν τῷ σώματι αὐτοῦ ἐπὶ τὸ ξύλον; *Phil.* 8.1: ὃς ἀνήνεγκεν ἡμῶν τὰς ἁμαρτίας τῷ ἰδίῳ σώματι ἐπὶ τὸ ξύλον, ὃς ἁμαρτίαν οὐκ ἐποίησεν, οὐδὲ εὑρέθη δόλος ἐν τῷ στόματι αὐτοῦ.

468 The phrases διὸ ἀναζωσάμενοι τὰς ὀσφύας . . . τὸν ἐγείραντα . . . ἐκ νεκρῶν καὶ δόντα αὐτῷ δόξαν.

469 See the discussion in Foster, *Literary Relations*, 399–411; Lohse, "Parenesis," 53–54, esp. n. 90.

470 Noah: 1 Pet 3:20, *1 Clem.* 7.6; 9.3–4; wives: 1 Pet 3:1–6; *1 Clem.* 21.7; elders: 1 Pet 5:5, *1 Clem.* 57.1.

471 1 Pet 1:2, *1 Clem.* opening: χάρις ὑμῖν καὶ εἰρήνη . . . πληθυνθείη; 1 Pet 4:8, *1 Clem.* 49.5: ἀγάπη καλύπτει πλῆθος ἁμαρτιῶν; 1 Pet 3:10–12 and *1 Clem.* 22.2–6 quote Psalm 34, but *1 Clement* quotes more verses and is more faithful to the LXX text.

472 So also Michaels, xxxiii; Bigg, 8. For a contrary view, see Foster, *Literary Relations*, 411.

473 Goppelt, 52 (ET 31–32); Brox, 39; Rudolph Knopf, *Die Briefe Petri und Judä* (KEK 7; Göttingen: Vandenhoeck & Ruprecht, 1912) 10. *1 Clement* does mention the martyr deaths of both Peter (5.4) and Paul (5.5–7), and Paul's letter to the church in Corinth (47.1–3), which, since Peter was known there (e.g., 1 Cor

1:12; 9:5), could make the absence of any clear reference to 1 Peter surprising. Yet *1 Clement*, writing to Corinth, did have more occasion to mention Paul's letter to that church than to mention 1 Peter, which had no connection with it.

474 Wand (9–10) finds that all three betray a knowledge of 1 Peter; Foster (*Literary Relations*, 391) thinks *Hermas* dependent on 1 Peter. Yet while *Did.* 1.4 (ἀπέχου τῶν σαρκικῶν . . . ἐπιθυμιῶν) has similar vocabulary to 1 Pet 2:11, as does *Diogn.* 9.2 (δίκαιον ὑπὲρ τῶν ἀδίκων) to 1 Pet 3:18, there is nothing in the context or the wording to make dependence necessary. It is more likely that both represent common Christian tradition. The reference in *Hermas Vis.* 4.3.4 to trial by fire is too common a figure (cf. Sir 2:5; Prov 17:3; Job 22:10) to demand derivation exclusively from 1 Pet 1:6, and to attribute the discussion of stones in *Hermas Vis.* 3.2 to 1 Pet 3:4–5 borders on the fanciful.

475 Given the plethora of works attributed to Peter (*Gospel, Acts, Kerygma*), there is no certainty in this matter; cf. Sylva, "Studies," 157.

476 In citing 1 Peter, Irenaeus (*Adv. haer.* 4.9.1) says "et Petrus ait *in epistula sua*" ("and Peter said *in his epistle*"; emphasis added), implying that he knew only one letter attributed to Peter.

addressees, it is difficult to see why Ignatius would not have referred to it as he did to Paul's letters (ad *Eph.* 12).[477]

The conclusion to be drawn from this is that demonstrable literary dependence on 1 Peter is to be found in the latter part of the second century in the writings of Irenaeus, Clement of Alexandria, and Tertullian. It is possible that it was known somewhat earlier by Polycarp, although not used so extensively as is often argued. It is less likely that it is reflected in *1 Clement,* the *Epistle of Barnabas,* or other early Christian literature. Here such "resemblances" as appear seem due more to mutual dependence on common early Christian tradition. The terminus ad quem delivered by external attestation would therefore be sometime in the early decades of the second century, since prior to that there is no unambiguous evidence that 1 Peter was known.

B. Internal Evidence

The content of 1 Peter has not yielded unambiguous evidence for its date, partly because of the nature of the evidence, partly because of the subjective elements that must be brought to bear on that evidence in the attempt to determine its time. While the discussions of suffering in 1 Peter, for example, assume it to be widespread, thus implying contact among widely separated churches and hence pointing to a somewhat later period,[478] the suffering itself seems due more to a generally negative

cultural evaluation of Christianity than to a specific period of official persecution.[479] Such references are for that reason less useful for precise dating, since, as is clear from Acts and the letters of Paul, such negative evaluation attended the Christian mission from its beginnings.

Again, the attempt to determine the time during which 1 Peter was written by appeals to the church order it implies, or the various doctrinal positions it reflects, runs a twofold danger. The first is the assumption that doctrine and church order advanced uniformly across the face of the Mediterranean basin, so that a position represented in one church or one area at a given time must necessarily also represent the stage reached by all churches in all areas at the same time.[480] The second is the degree of subjective judgment necessary to decide whether such doctrinal positions or church order represents an "earlier" or a "later" development.[481]

A similarly questionable attempt to determine the time of composition is based on the argument that 1 Peter's confidence in Roman justice (3:13) or the appeal to honor the emperor (2:13–17) could not have been included once intense persecution broke out[482] or the imperial cult became widespread.[483] At that point, it is argued, Rome became the Antichrist, and it was seen to be in league with Satan, as in the Apocalypse of John.[484] Yet the argument that there is no trace of the emperor cult in 1 Peter becomes less than convincing when one

---

477 So also J. D. McCaughey, "Three 'Persecution Documents' of the New Testament," *AusBR* 17 (1969) 39; Beare, 34; Foster (*Literary Relations,* 398) finds similarity of ideas but no literary relationship.

478 Brox, "Situation und Sprache," 10.

479 This conclusion is now widely accepted; e.g., David L. Balch, *Let Wives Be Submissive: The Domestic Code in 1 Peter* (SBLMS 26; Chico: Scholars Press, 1981) 136; Millauer, *Leiden,* 60; Brox, 32; de Villiers, "Joy," 68. Tacitus's description (*Hist.* 1.2) of this period as "abundant in misfortunes" (*opimum casibus*) means the unsettled conditions reflected in 1 Peter could have occurred any time during the later first and early second centuries.

480 For such an assumption in regard to the parousia, see Johann Michl, "Die Presbyter des ersten Petrusbriefes," in H. Fleckenstein, ed., *Ortskirche, Weltkirche: Festgabe für Julius Kardinal Döpfner* (Würzburg: Echter, 1973) 50; in regard to the Christian attitude toward Judaism, see Tarrech, "Le milieu," 99; Max-Allain Chevallier, "Comment lire aujourd'hui la première épître de Pierre," in Perrot, *Etudes,* 139; in

regard to church order, see Goppelt, 64–65 (ET 46–47).

481 The same evidence has been judged to point both to an earlier date (Kelly, 30; Selwyn, 75; Meade, *Pseudonymity and Canon,* 170; Schweizer, 11; Schutter, *Hermeneutic,* 4; Cothenet, "Les orientations," 38, 40) and to a later one (Brown and Meier, *Antioch and Rome,* 138–39; Margot, 17; Best, 45, 48).

482 E.g., Grudem, 36; Selwyn, "Persecutions," 49; Michaels, lxiii; Meade, *Pseudonymity and Canon,* 164.

483 E.g., Robinson, *Redating,* 155; Hall, "For to This," 139–40 n. 4; Bo Reicke, *The Epistles of James, Peter and Jude* (Anchor Bible 37; Garden City: Doubleday, 1964) 72; Goppelt, 63 (ET 43); Millauer, *Leiden,* 190. That veneration of deified Roman emperors was practiced in the cities of Asia at least from the time of Nero, perhaps even from the time of Claudius, see Magie, *Roman Rule,* 1.544.

484 Balch, *Wives,* 138; Millauer, *Leiden,* 191; Robinson, *Redating,* 153; Neugebauer, "Zur Deutung," 64; Cothenet, "Les orientations," 20.

examines carefully the language of 2:13–17,[485] and the larger argument about persecution fails in face of convincing evidence that long after severe persecutions had in fact broken out, Christians persisted in expressing their loyalty to the emperor and in praying for the continued existence of the Roman state.[486]

It is the difficulty attendant upon identifying and interpreting internal evidence as it bears on this problem that underlies the lack of unanimity in assigning a precise date for the composition of 1 Peter. The following survey of representative suggestions for a date illustrates that point, and illustrates why there is no more than limited probability to any suggested solution.

1. Prior to 70 CE

Evidence for an early date, often associated with affirmation of authorship by Simon Peter, centers around the Neronian persecution,[487] echoes of which are found in the hatred (4:4) and arrest (4:16) of Christians, the "fiery ordeal" (4:12) that surprised them, and the general air of foreboding that permeates the letter.[488] For those for whom such evidence is persuasive, the question is whether to date the letter just prior to (or during)[489] or immediately subsequent to[490] those persecutions. The

problem with this data is that Nero's persecutions were limited to Rome, and the letter is addressed to the Asia subcontinent; if the references are to Nero's hostility, the letter would reflect the situation of the author rather than the readers, a strange situation at best.[491]

Other evidence for an early date is found in (1) a supposed literary dependence of Ephesians, James, and other Pauline letters on 1 Peter,[492] thus necessitating an early date for 1 Peter; or (2) on an absence of mention of Paul, implying he was not yet, or no longer, present in Rome.[493] The literary evidence cited is less than convincing, however,[494] as are arguments from silence about mention of Paul.[495]

2. Subsequent to 70 CE

Many who argue for a date subsequent to 70 CE call attention to the use of "Babylon" as a cipher for Rome (5:13), and affirm that since this use is not found until after the fall of Jerusalem, 1 Peter must be dated accordingly.[496] If, however, such an identification had already appeared in Daniel, this argument loses its persuasive power.[497] Again, one can note that Israel is not a theological problem for 1 Peter as it clearly was for

---

485 This is especially the case when it is compared with the language of Rom 13:1–7; see Philipps, *Kirche,* 54; and the comments on 1 Pet 2:13–17 below. J. B. Bauer finds possible reference to veneration of the emperor in 1 Pet 5:8–9 (*Der erste Petrusbrief* [Die Welt der Bible; Kleinkommentare zur Heiligen Schrift; Düsseldorf: Patmos, 1971] 61).

486 E.g., *1 Clem.* 61.1–2; the Scillitan Martyrs (quoted in Lewis and Reinhold, "Conflict of Religions," 593–94); Tertullian *Apol.* 30.1, 4; 32.1, 3; 33.1–2; cf. Sordi, *Christians,* 176.

487 The tradition that Peter died during the Neronian persecution is attested at least since the second half of the second century (cf. Goppelt, 35–36, ET 13); that tradition is important for those affirming authorship by Simon Peter.

488 E.g., Cranfield, 17; Robinson, *Redating,* 157; Meade, *Pseudonymity and Canon,* 172. Selwyn (57) attributes the feeling of being exiles and aliens to the martyrdom of James in 62.

489 E.g., Love, "First Epistle," 68; Ketter, 198; Reicke, 71; Fitzmyer, "First Peter," 362; Bigg, 87; Cranfield, 17; Selwyn, 57; Schiwy, 33.

490 E.g., Robert W. Thurston, "Interpreting First Peter," *JETS* 17 (1974) 177; Robinson, *Redating,* 161; Jonsen, "Moral Theology," 94; Meade, *Pseudonymity and Canon,* 172.

491 E.g., Robinson, *Redating,* 157. Beare (30), however, argues that the situation presumed in the letter and the situation in Rome under Nero were quite different.

492 For this position, see Ferris, "Comparison," 127.

493 E.g., Grudem, 36; that it was subsequent to Paul's acquittal, see Chase, "Peter," 791.

494 See the discussion of this point under "Authorship: Thought-World of 1 Peter."

495 The additional argument of van Unnik ("Redemption," 70 et passim) for an early date, namely, that the language of 1:18–19 refers to proselyte sacrifices in the temple and thus must presume its existence (i.e., pre-70), remains unconvincing. The author of Hebrews could write much about such sacrifice long after the temple had been destroyed.

496 Claus-Junno Hunzinger, "Babylon als Deckname für Rom und die Datierung des 1. Petrusbriefes," in H. Graf Reventlow, ed., *Gottes Wort und Gottes Land: Hans-Wilhelm Hertzberg zum 70. Geburtstag* (Göttingen: Vandenhoeck & Ruprecht, 1965) 76–77; Meade, *Pseudonymity and Canon,* 165; Best, 179; Michaels, lxiii; Bauer, "Verfolgung," 518.

497 So Meade, *Pseudonymity and Canon,* 165.

Paul, and can argue that since Israel ceased to be a theological problem with the fall of Jerusalem in 70 CE, 1 Peter must be dated after that event. Evidence in later NT literature, however, such as Matthew, Luke-Acts, and the Gospel and Revelation of John, indicates that relations with the Jews continued to pose a problem for Christians, thus diminishing the power of this argument in determining any date for this letter, whether early or late.

The presence of Christianity in Asia Minor (1 Pet 1:1) does point to a later rather than an earlier date,[498] as does the lack of clear reference to 1 Peter in *1 Clement* and the letters of Ignatius. While some have attempted to locate the date of composition in the decade of the 70s,[499] lack of clear evidence concerning the nature of the persecutions, the relationship of Christians to Roman officials, the kind of church order prevalent in the period, and the relationship of 1 Peter with other early Christian literature during that decade makes such precision difficult.[500]

3. During the Period 80–100 CE

Evidence for placing the composition of 1 Peter in this period tends to center around conditions under the reign of Domitian. While a general persecution of Christians under Domitian, often cited to account for the accusations against them (4:14, 16) and the resulting alienation (2:11; 4:4) and suffering (1:6; 3:17; 4:1, 12–13, 19:

5:9),[501] is unlikely to have occurred,[502] there is evidence that Christianity had penetrated into the royal family itself,[503] thus indicating that the broad geographic spread of the church and the suffering of its members, indicated in 1 Peter (1:1; 5:9), reflect a condition in existence at this time.

A further argument for a date during this period is based on a statement of Pliny that some of those who had been accused as Christians had in fact renounced their faith some twenty-five years earlier.[504] That renunciation, which would thus have occurred sometime around 85–90, could well have resulted from the kind of crisis reflected in 1 Peter, and to which it was directed.[505] While there is no indication in Pliny that this earlier defection was due to persecution or involved large numbers of people, neither can such conditions be ruled out, and it remains an interesting suggestion.

Again, the absence of unambiguous reference to 1 Peter in *1 Clement* and Ignatius's letters would comport with a date for 1 Peter in this period, although more toward its end than its beginning. Finally, if, as we saw, one cannot argue the priority of 1 Peter from the Apocalypse of John on the basis of their differing attitudes toward the Roman Empire and its ruler, the suffering that both works reflect in the same general geographic area could argue for dating both to this period of time.[506]

---

498 Cf. Goppelt, 29, 64 (ET 5–6, 47).

499 Millauer, *Leiden*, 195; Ramsay, *The Church in the Roman Empire*, 282. The attempt of Goppelt (65, ET 47) to date 1 Peter on the basis of the close correspondence of 1 Pet 4:10–11 with Acts 6:2–4 and 1 Pet 5:2a with Acts 20:28 remains, in the absence of convincing linguistic similarity and in light of the general nature of the material, unpersuasive.

500 Many scholars therefore prefer to assign 1 Peter to a wider time span: 65–90 (E. A. Judge, *The Social Pattern of the Christian Groups in the First Century* [London: Tyndale, 1960] 138); 70–95 (Brox, "Situation und Sprache," 4) or 70–100 (Brox, 41); 73–92 (Elliott, 87); 80–111 (Krodel, 59).

501 Friedrich Schröger, "Die Verfassung der Gemeinde des ersten Petrusbriefes," in J. Hainz, ed., *Kirche im Werden* (Munich: Schöningh, 1976) 248; Selwyn, "Persecutions," 47; Bauer, 12; Hart, 18; Margot, 10, 21, 26.

502 Domitian's cruelty was general (cf. Tacitus *Agric.* 3; Pliny *Ep.* 8.14); the persecution of Christians was incidental to broader political concerns; see the

discussion under "Authorship: Persecutions."

503 See n. 310 above.

504 "Alii ab indice nominati esse se Christianus dixerunt et mox negaverunt; fuisse quidem, sed desiisse . . . non nemo etiam ante viginti quinque" ("Others accused first said they were Christians, and then they denied it; they had been but had ceased . . . a few even twenty-five years ago"; Pliny *Ep.* 10.96 para. 3).

505 Foster, *Literary Relations*, 378; Bauer, 11; Beare, 32; Moule ("Nature," 9) identifies the period as "twenty years."

506 One cannot discount such an association on the assumption that all Christians had a consistent attitude on all issues, nor can one assume a consistent attitude toward Christians either by all officials or by the general populace wherever they lived. Attitudes varied from place to place and time to time, persecutions were sporadic, and the imperial cult did not enjoy identical observance in all cities even in Asia Minor. See Goldstein, *Paulinische Gemeinde*, 108, and the discussion above, "Authorship: Persecutions."

4. Subsequent to 100 CE

While some other evidence has been cited as a basis for proposing a date for 1 Peter at this time,[507] such a proposal is based most persuasively on similarities that are detected between the conditions reflected in 1 Peter and the description Pliny gives in his letter to Trajan concerning his conduct in the investigation and punishment of Christians. There is Pliny's confusion about whether Christians are to be persecuted simply because they bear the name "Christian," or whether additional crimes need to be proved. Had the name itself been cause for persecution at some earlier time, it is difficult to imagine why Pliny would have been perplexed on this question.[508] If one may nevertheless interpret Pliny's report of putting some Christians to death for their beliefs as being done simply because they were Christians,[509] then the situation reflected in 1 Pet 4:14, 16 will have occurred for the first time in the early years of the second century. Further, Pliny's description of Christians' innocent activity—they were obligated by their faith to perform no wicked deeds, no fraud, theft, adultery, or lies, no refusal to return entrusted money[510] —sounds enough like the admonitions in 1 Pet 4:15 to make it possible to see here some congruence.[511] Finally, 1 Peter's advice to its readers to be ready to defend their beliefs but in a gentle and respectful way (3:15) can be construed as formulated in response to Pliny's statement that he executed Christians because of their "contumacy and inflexible obstinacy."[512] Taken together, that evidence has seemed to some scholars compelling indication of a date about the time of Pliny's letter.[513]

Yet it is also the case that 1 Peter does not in fact reflect a situation where Christians are in mortal danger because of their faith. To be sure, they suffer, but there is no direct reference to martyrdom (cf. Rev 2:13; 6:9–11; 17:6; 20:4) or even to its possibility (cf. Heb 12:4).[514] On that basis, the similarities between Pliny's reported executions and the advice in 1 Pet 3:15 seem less likely to be directly related,[515] and 4:14–16 can as easily reflect local persecutions and social opprobrium as it can the situation described by Pliny. Finally, a date as late as the first decade of the second century makes the silence of Ignatius about any letter of Peter all the more remarkable.[516]

5. Conclusions

Lack of precise information about the external situation reflected in 1 Peter makes any attempt to establish an exact date difficult. If, as we have argued, it is a pseudonymous document, a date in the 60s is quite unlikely, a point also argued by its assumption of the spread of Christianity to northern Asia Minor. Lack of clear reference to the letter until late in the first century or early in the second confirms such an observation. On the other hand, lack of direct reference to martyrdom would place it prior to Pliny's lethal persecution in Bithynia around 112–114 CE. Again, the situation presumed in 1 Peter could easily reflect the conditions that led eventually to the denunciation of Christians that created the problem about which Pliny seeks advice: suspicion and even hatred of Christians as outsiders who refused participation in normal social activities, an attitude exacerbated by the general unease associated with the

---

507 Because of the general situation: Lepelley, "Le contexte," 62; Anthony Hanson, "Salvation Proclaimed: I: 1 Peter 3:18–22," *ExpT* 93 (1981/82) 101; because the readers were devotees of some mystery cult, probably that of Cybele: Perdelwitz, *Mysterienreligion,* 96. For the Tübingen school, it was written to reconcile Petrine and Pauline Christianity: cf. Smith, *Petrine Controversies,* 152.

508 Pliny (*Ep.* 10.96 para. 1) says he is unaware of any precedents because he has never been present at such a trial and hence he must seek Trajan's counsel; cf. Beare, "Teaching," 285.

509 Pliny *Ep.* 10.96 para. 2.

510 Pliny *Ep.* 10.96 para. 2.

511 Cf. Bauer, "Verfolgung," 519–20.

512 "pertinaciam certe et inflexibilem obstinationem debere puniri" ("surely stubbornness and inflexible

obstinacy deserved to be punished"; *Ep.* 10.96 para. 2); John Knox, "Pliny and I Peter: A Note on I Pet 4:14–16 and 3:15," *JBL* 72 (1953) 188; Bauer, "Verfolgung," 518.

513 Beare, 14, 33; cf. "Teaching," 284–85; Leaney, 10. For a more cautious approach to this evidence, see Brox, 28–29.

514 Christian Blendinger, "Kirche als Fremdlingschaft," *Communio Viatorum* 10 (1967) 125; Filson, "Partakers," 404; Lepelley, "Le contexte," 47.

515 For reservations about such a date, see Robinson, *Redating,* 154; Best, 41; J. B. Souček, "Das Gegenüber von Gemeinde und Welt nach dem ersten Petrusbrief," *Communio Viatorum* 3 (1960) 9–10.

516 See n. 477 above.

final years of Domitian's rule. Pliny's reference in about 110 CE to the defection of some Christians twenty-five years earlier, would point to a date sometime between 80 and 100 CE, most likely in the earlier years of that range.

III. Readers

Formidable problems face one in the attempt to determine the situation and status of the original readers of 1 Peter. The addressees were scattered over a wide geographic area, at least the entire northern half of Asia Minor,[517] with the result that the situation and status of those in one part of the area may have been quite different from those in another part.[518] What prevails in the large and prosperous cities of western Asia, for example, may not be the situation in the rural areas of northern Galatia. Further, it lies in the nature of a letter intended for so wide an area that the readers will be addressed in as broad terms as possible, so that at least some parts of the letter will be relevant to each of the different groups of its readers. That will pertain both to descriptions of the status of Christians in relation to the society around them as well as to their interrelationships within the Christian community. Precise data on any specific group of readers will therefore necessarily be limited if not absent from the letter, since it must appeal to as many of its diverse readers as possible.

Further, the data contained in the letter from which one may infer something about its readers' situation are quite ambiguous, and it is therefore difficult to interpret the data the letter does present. The difficulty in determining the extent to which the author employed metaphor in the description of the situation of the Christian in the world is but one complicating factor. The widely differing conclusions that have been reached about the racial origin of the readers, as well as about their social and economic status, both presently and prior to their becoming Christians, attest to the ambiguity inherent in the data.

A. Racial Origin

The ambiguity of the data in 1 Peter surfaces with the question of the racial origin of the readers, namely, whether they were of Jewish or gentile extraction. The letter contains direct quotations from the OT (e.g., 1:24; 2:6; 3:10–12) and abounds in allusions to it, in phrases (e.g., 1:16; 2:3, 7, 8, 9–10, 22, 24; 3:14; 4:18; 5:5), characters (Sarah and Abraham, 3:6; Noah, 3:20), and in references that evoke Jewish history (e.g., dispersion, 1:1; exiles and aliens, 2:11; Babylon, 5:13).[519] Such identification of the readers with events and figures from Jewish history,[520] and the readers' apparent familiarity with the OT, have led scholars from earliest times to the conclusion that the readers were Christians of Jewish origin,[521] an inference supported by Paul's statement in Gal 2:7 that Peter's mission was to the Jews.[522] Absence

---

517 If as seems likely the names in 1 Pet 1:1 reflect Roman province names, the area is Asia Minor north and west of the Taurus Mountains; so, e.g., Kelly (3), who notes the four provinces formed "a recognized geographical entity" (Strabo *Geog.* 2.5.31; Dio Cassius *Hist. Rom.* 71.23). See also Beare, 38; F. J. A. Hort, *The First Epistle of St. Peter: I.1—II.17: The Greek Text with Introductory Lecture, Commentary, and Additional Notes* (London: Macmillan, 1898) 17. That it was meant for the whole of Asia Minor, see Elliott, *Home*, 27. For further discussion, see comments on 1:1 below.

518 Best (13), who also cautions "we do not know how well author and readers were acquainted" (14). See also Brox, 26; Michaels, xlv; Schelkle, 3.

519 For a comprehensive discussion of the various ways 1 Peter uses the OT, see Schutter, *Hermeneutic*, 35–43.

520 Such phrases must be meant literally (not metaphorically) for this position to be valid; see van Unnik, "Redemption," 71.

521 E.g., Eusebius *Hist. eccl.* 3.4; quoting Origen, 3.1; most of the Greek fathers: Selwyn 42; John Calvin,

Commentaries on the Catholic Epistles (trans. J. Owen; Grand Rapids: Eerdmans, 1948) 25; Thomas Yates, "The Message of the Epistles: The First Epistle of Peter," *ExpT* 45 (1933/34) 391; Bernhard Weiss, *Der Petrinische Lehrbegriff* (Berlin: Schultze, 1855) 144–59. Cothenet ("Les orientations," 19) speaks of the readers coming from a "milieu synagogal." See Brox (25 n. 34) for the names of other more modern commentators who hold this view. Tarrech ("Le milieu," 369) and Schutter (*Hermeneutic,* 81) call attention to the readers' apparent familiarity with the OT, without specifically identifying them as Jewish in origin, however.

522 E.g., Calvin, 25.

in the letter of any reference to tension with Christians of Jewish origin, as one regularly finds in Acts and the Pauline epistles, for example, could also argue for a Jewish origin of the readers. In order to account for the prevalence of Gentiles in the areas addressed by the letter,[523] some have posited converted "God-fearers," formerly associated with Judaism, as the group from which, in large measure, the readers of this letter were drawn.[524]

Yet references also abound in 1 Peter that clearly assume a gentile origin for its readers. References to the unholy state of their preconversion life (e.g., 1:14, 18; 2:10, 25; 4:3–4; cf. 3:6) are, in the view of many commentators both ancient[525] and modern,[526] decisive in indicating a gentile background for its readers. Again, the surprise evoked by religious persecution that is reflected in the letter (e.g., 4:12; cf. 1:6; 5:6–9) would be less likely in Christians of Jewish origin, since religious persecution bulked so large in their history.[527] Furthermore, the familiarity with the OT presumed in the readers is as likely to be the result of instruction both before and after their conversion as it is of their racial origin. The OT was, after all, the Bible of those early

communities.[528] Within the overall thought-world of the letter, moreover, the identification of the readers with the history of Israel is best understood in terms of a metaphorical use of that material in relation to the Christian faith, whereby the Christian community has assumed the mantle of chosen people formerly worn by Israel.[529]

Perhaps the most careful conclusion is to posit a mixture of both gentile and Jewish readers,[530] although some evidence, especially 1:14; 4:3–4, points rather clearly to a vast preponderance of readers who, prior to their conversion, took part in the social and religious observances of the Greco-Roman world.[531] Such Jews as were found among the addressees of 1 Peter were, it appears, a decided minority.

B. Social and Economic Status

A major source of information about the status of the readers in relation to the Greco-Roman society surrounding them is represented by the "household code"[532] contained in 1 Pet 2:18—3:7.[533] Knowledge of the origin of such codes and their function in the Greco-Roman world of this period is helpful in evaluating such

---

523 This is not to say there were no Jews there. On the spread of Jews throughout the Mediterranean world, and esp. Asia Minor, see Josephus *Bell.* 2.398; *Ant.* 14.110–18 (quoting other ancient writers as well); Philo *Leg. Gaj.* 281–82.

524 Van Unnik ("Redemption," esp. 30–32, 75–77) strongly argues this point. Cothenet ("Les orientations," 19) says Acts indicates that many early Christians came from this group.

525 Most western fathers held this view (see Selwyn, 42), as did Luther (*D. Martin Luthers Epistel-Auslegung* [ed. H. Günther and E. Volk; Göttingen: Vandenhoeck & Ruprecht, 1983] 184).

526 E.g., Best, 19; Schelkle, 2, 45 n. 3; Windisch, 50; Hart, 4; Holmer and de Boor, 14; Fitzmyer, "First Peter," 362; Love, "First Peter," 68; Peter H. Davids, *The First Epistle of Peter* (New International Commentary on the New Testament; Grand Rapids: Eerdmans, 1990) 8–9; Brox, 25; Schutter, *Hermeneutic,* 10; Hall, "For to This," 138; Richard, "Christology," 123.

527 Cf. Hall, "For to This," 138.

528 On this basis I do not agree that familiarity with the OT would eliminate gentile converts, as, e.g., Wand (32), Selwyn (42), and Lippert ("Zeugnis," 234) argue. Tarrech ("Le milieu," 377) notes, for example, that in 1 Pet 3:6 the Christian women have

become (ἐγενήθητε) daughters of Sarah. One may also note Paul's use of the OT in his letters to the very gentile Corinthian Christians, indicating they were familiar with it as their Scripture.

529 Beare, 74; see also Paul J. Achtemeier, "New-born Babes and Living Stones: Literal and Figurative in 1 Peter," in M. P. Horgan and P. J. Kobelski, eds., *To Touch the Text: Biblical and Related Studies in Honor of Joseph A. Fitzmyer* (New York: Crossroad/Continuum, 1988) 207–36, as well as the discussion "Theological Shape of 1 Peter: Controlling Metaphor" below.

530 That the readers included some Jews, but within a gentile majority, see, e.g., Grudem, 38; Chase, "Peter," 783; Spicq, 13; Elliott, *Home,* 65; Kelly, 4.

531 For further discussion of these verses, see the comments below.

532 This term, a translation of the German *Haustafel,* points both to the origin and to the function of such lists of duties in the world contemporary to 1 Peter, and is therefore preferable to the more general term "social codes."

533 While 2:13–17 and 3:8–12 may belong to this section of exhortation in 1 Peter, they do not belong to the household code proper. For further discussion, see the comments on those texts below.

information about the readers as these verses may contain.

1. Household Codes

General formulations of moral exhortation on how one ought to conduct oneself in relation to other human beings are found in politically as well as philosophically oriented literature from the Greco-Roman world. There has been some debate on the kind of formulations that represent the direct antecedents of the household codes, and therefore the purpose they are intended to serve.

a. Origin. The earlier consensus that household codes of the type found in the NT and other early Christian literature[534] derived from Stoic catalogs of individual duty[535] is being replaced by an emerging consensus that their origin is rather to be found in the categories derived from household regulations (οἰκονομία) that go back at least to the time of Aristotle.[536] Characterized by a mutuality of relationships absent from Stoic tables of duties,[537] such household codes represent the basic social and economic modes of existence in the ancient world, rather than simply one example among many such modes.[538] Based on the premise that men are most rational, women least rational, children prerational (or immature), and slaves irrational, such codes portrayed the orders of authority and submission for each of the classes.[539] This ordering was then adopted as the prevailing political ideology and was applied within Roman culture as well as by the Romans to conquered peoples.[540] As a result, a challenge to these categories of authority and submission at any level would ultimately be seen as a challenge to the Roman political order and its basic ideology.

It is hardly surprising that such codes, with their emphasis on interrelationships, an emphasis reflected in sayings of Jesus himself,[541] were adopted by Christians from earliest times.[542] The use of such codes was a mixed blessing, however. To be sure, they formed a link with non-Christian culture, but at the same time the equality among people of all classes implied in the Christian faith (e.g., Gal 3:28–29) meant that such codes as they were formulated within the Christian communities presumed a kind of mutual submission to one another (e.g., Eph 5:21)[543] that was at odds with the hierarchy of submissions which formed the very fabric of Greco-Roman culture. Such interrelationships therefore between men, women, children, and slaves would be

---

534 Eph 5:22—6:9; Col 3:18—4:1; 1 Tim 2:8–15; 5:3–8; 6:1–2; Titus 2:1–10. In addition, see the lists of virtues that include some items also normally included in household codes, e.g., *Did.* 4.9–11; *Barn.* 19.5–7; *1 Clem.* 1.3; 21.6–9; Polycarp *Phil.* 4.2—6.2 (I owe this list to Schelkle, 96); cf. also Lampe and Luz, "Nachpaulinisches Christentum," 190.

535 For a good summary of this view and its origin in the work of Martin Dibelius and Karl Weidinger, see Dieter Lührmann, "Neutestamentliche Haustafeln und antike Ökonomie," *NTS* 27 (1980) 83–97, esp. 83–88; Elliott, *Home,* 208–20. It is still maintained, e.g., Spicq, 96 (citing Diogenes Laertius 7.84, 107–10; Cicero *De off.* 1.3.8–9); see also Goppelt ("Jesus," 96), who proposed Christian modification of Stoic codes on the basis of OT apodictic divine law. The notion that the Christian codes derive from Hellenistic Judaism (from such material as Philo *Decal.* 165–67; *Hyp.* 7.14; *Spec. leg.* 2.226–27; Josephus *Ap.* 2.190–219; Pseudo-Phocylides *Maxims* 175–227; cf. Michaels, 122) has not been widely accepted. See Goppelt, "Jesus," 95, who denies such correspondence.

536 Decisive for this view is the work of Balch, *Wives* (see esp. chap. 3); in "Household Codes" (in D. E. Aune, ed., *Greco-Roman Literature and the New Testament: Selected Forms and Genres* [SBLSBS 21; Atlanta: Scholars Press, 1988] 26) Balch cites Aristotle *Pol.* I 1253b1–14, as a key text. See also Lührmann, "Neutestamentliche Haustafeln"; Elliott, *Home,* 208–20.

537 E.g., Epictetus *Diss.* 2.14.8, 17.31; 3.2.4; cf. Schelkle, 96–97.

538 So Lührmann, "Neutestamentliche Haustafeln," 87.

539 See Balch, "Household Codes," 41–42, quoting Arius Didymus; cf. also idem, *Wives,* 35–36, 42.

540 See Senior, "Conduct," 431–32; Balch, "Household Codes," 43; cf. idem, *Wives,* 52.

541 Goppelt, "Jesus," 104; cf. idem, "Prinzipien," 290.

542 Lührmann, "Neutestamentliche Haustafeln," 93, 96; thus the early Christian communities, like Israel before them, organized themselves not as a religious organization ("Kultverein") but with a specific legal structure (94). The argument that the household codes in the NT are a Christian creation has received little support; see Elliott, *Home,* 136–39.

543 Such mutuality of duties was absent in Greco-Roman household codes; in them duties moved only in one direction, i.e., they were owed by inferior to superior. See Lührmann, "Neutestamentliche Haustafeln," 84.

points of particular sensitivity in the Christian communities' relationship to their cultural environment, and in the evaluation by that environment concerning the acceptability of the Christian communities and their way of life.[544] That sensitivity is reflected in the household codes of 1 Peter, and in the way their intentions have been evaluated by modern scholars.

b. Purpose. The Christian communities existing within the larger context of Greco-Roman culture faced a twofold danger: loss of internal cohesion resulting in the disintegration of the group, and the rise of external suspicion on the part of non-Christians that could lead to hostility and active oppression.[545] There were two opposing ways Christians could react to this situation, given their powerlessness to change the structures of external society.[546] They could either withdraw as far as possible from all contact with external society, forming as it were a Christian ghetto,[547] or they could adapt themselves to prevailing cultures to the extent that they no longer presented an offense. In the former case, the community would abdicate its missionary role as witness to the gospel; in the latter case, it would lose its central values.

That the intention of 1 Peter in general, and the household codes in particular, is to urge the acculturation of the church to Hellenistic social values has been vigorously argued by David Balch.[548] Assuming that Greco-Roman society suspected and criticized foreign religions, impressed with the evidences of the disharmony caused by Christians within Hellenistic households as that is implied in the house-code advice to slaves and wives, and assuming the code continues to 3:8, with its further call for harmony, Balch infers that the message of 1 Peter to churches of Asia Minor is that, for their survival, they needed to be less emphatic about Christian values that caused such disharmony and more willing to accommodate themselves to the Hellenistic cultural values embodied in the household codes.[549] Balch has a negative evaluation of such advice, seeing it "in tension both with the Mosaic covenant (e.g. Exod. 21:1–6; Deut. 15:12–18) and with the Jesus tradition itself (e.g. Mark 10:15, 28–30)."[550]

To be sure, one finds in 1 Peter emphasis on the need to give non-Christians a clear view of what values the Christian community does affirm (e.g., 2:12; 3:15b–16), and Christian values that are also prized in Hellenistic culture are emphasized.[551] Yet there is also in 1 Peter a strong warning to the Christian recipients against participation in, and hence accommodation to, Hellenistic culture (e.g., 1:14–16; 4:3–4); they are to be as exiles and aliens in relation to it (2:11; cf. 1:1) and thus can expect to be reviled and persecuted (1:6; 3:14, 17; 4:1, 12, 14, 16) precisely as Christians, that is, for their Christian values. Accommodation is thus hardly the intention of the letter or the household codes;[552] rather it is to warn against such accommodation, even if that means suffering.[553]

---

544 Cf. Areius Didymus *Politics* 151.9–12: "Seditions in cities occur either rationally or emotionally. They occur rationally whenever those with equal rights are compelled to be unequal, or *when those who are unequal have equality*" (emphasis added; the quotation is from Balch, "Household Codes," 43).

545 See Elliott, "1 Peter," 69; Talbert, "Once Again," 146.

546 See Lepelley, "Le contexte," 64. Refoulé ("Bible," 477) compares the situation to that once faced by Christian communities in Iron Curtain countries, and to that currently faced in Muslim countries (479).

547 That this alternative was not adopted, see Senior, 7; cf. Neugebauer, "Zur Deutung," 74–75.

548 E.g., *Wives*, 93 et passim.

549 Cf. Balch, *Wives*, 108–9.

550 Balch, "Household Codes," 32.

551 Max-Allain Chevallier points to the use of ἀγαθοποιεῖν (2:14, 15, 20; 3:6, 11, 17; 4:19; cf. 3:13, 16) as an example ("Condition et vocation des chrétiens en diaspora: Remarques exégétiques sur la 1ʳᵉ Epître de Pierre," *RevScRel* 48 [1974] 397). Senior (7) finds a more positive attitude to culture in 1 Peter than in any other NT writing; see also Neugebauer, "Zur Deutung," 74–75.

552 So correctly Elliott, "1 Peter," 72–73; see also Souček, "Das Gegenüber," 8–9; Leonhard Goppelt, "Der Staat in der Sicht des Neuen Testaments," in H. Dombois and E. Wilkens, eds., *Macht und Recht: Beiträge zur lutherischen Staatslehre der Gegenwart* (Berlin: Lutherisches Verlagshaus, 1956) 16.

553 So Philipps, *Kirche*, 27; Schweizer, 109; Kendall, "Function," 119. Lührmann ("Neutestamentliche Haustafeln," 86, 95) argues that the use of the

The household code therefore presented to the Christian community a way of reacting to both internal and external threats that would sacrifice neither missionary role nor central values. On the one hand, to the extent that the household code could be shaped to express Christian values,[554] it could become the focus for internal cohesion through its expression of the mutual interrelationships envisioned by the Christian community.[555] On the other hand, because it also reflected values highly prized by the potentially hostile external culture,[556] the adoption of the household code was capable of reducing tension with Roman society by identifying shared values.[557] Adherence to those values in the Christian's social conduct would thus be a way of avoiding discredit being brought upon the Christian community.[558]

The household code in 1 Peter reflects both the adaptation of that social tradition to Christian values[559] and its adaptation to a particular situation.[560] It is this latter adaptation that is of interest to those seeking to determine the social makeup and status of the readers of 1 Peter. Does this adaptation allow us to draw inferences about the kind of readers to whom the letter was addressed? The answer to that question depends on the purpose for which the household code was formulated by the author of 1 Peter. If the code was formulated to address the major groups that constituted the Christian community in Asia Minor, it will provide rich data for determining the social status of that community. If, however, the code was formulated for reasons other than reflecting the major groups of people to whom the letter

was addressed, then those singled out in the household code will provide no clue to the social makeup of those communities. In fact, much in both 1 Peter and in the code argues for seeing their purpose in terms of the relationship of the readers to Greco-Roman culture and its ruling ideologies, and hence reflects a purpose that would cause the author to choose elements from the household code for purposes other than their reflection of the status of the recipients. That conclusion is based on the following reflections.

A major clue to the purpose of the household codes in 1 Peter is the exhortation with which they begin (2:13). It is subordination, an act that frames the material in the codes (2:15, 16, 19, 20, 3:4; cf. 5:5a) and that, as the first set of instructions (2:13–17) and the conclusion of all the instructions (3:8–12; cf. 5:5b) indicate, is appropriate for all Christians. A further clue is provided with the address to slaves. That address, common in other NT household codes (e.g., Eph 6:5–8; Col 3:22), is broadened when the suffering of Christ is cited as an example for their conduct (1 Pet 2:21–25), because that example is later cited as relevant to all Christians (3:17; 4:1; cf. 4:14, 16). Slaves thus seem representative of all Christians who play a subordinate role in their culture. The address to wives, also common in such codes (Eph 5:22–24; Col 3:18), is here given expanded treatment (1 Pet 3:1–6) with a similar emphasis on subordination, in contrast to the far shorter treatment accorded to husbands, who do not play so subordinate a role in Greco-Roman society. In both instances, the groups chosen, slaves and wives, provide instances of those at the mercy of others who can inflict

household codes implied latent political claims by the church from the beginning and hence represented a denial of the ideology of unity used to justify Roman hegemony; see also Balch, "Household Codes," 26.

554 Philipps (*Kirche*, 53) argues correctly that they could.

555 So Elliott, "1 Peter," 70.

556 See Lührmann ("Neutestamentliche Haustafeln," 94), who also notes that this represented a conservative Roman view of relationships that had already been superseded in practice; cf. also Balch, "Hellenization/Acculturation," 99.

557 Reicke, 73; cf. also Balch, *Wives*, 81–82, 94.

558 This is a widely accepted view; see, e.g., Refoulé, "Bible," 478; Lepelley, "Le contexte," 60–61; Schröger, "Verfassung," 246; Lampe and Luz, "Nachpaulinisches Christentum," 214; Balch, *Wives*, 105.

559 Balch, "Early Christian Criticism," 166; Philipps, *Kirche*, 24–25. Stephen Motyer argues that the household codes were "transformed" in NT usage, but he has little to say about 1 Peter specifically ("The Relationship between Paul's Gospel of 'All One in Christ Jesus' (Galatians 3:28) and the Household Codes," *Vox Evangelica* 19 [1989] 42–43).

560 E.g., Radermacher ("Der erste Petrusbrief," 290), who notes the reversal of the usual order in 1 Peter. Michaels (122) notes its lack of symmetry and its focus on relationships with those outside the Christian community.

punishment on them, arbitrarily if they so desire.

In that light, it appears that the intention behind the formulation of the household code in 1 Peter is not so much to take a position relative to secular society, whether positive or negative,[561] as it is to present examples of the way Christians are to live vis-à-vis their world. That is, because Christians follow values radically transformed under the lordship of Christ,[562] they are as open to contemptuous social treatment as slaves, or as wives who go counter to family tradition. Yet despite such treatment, they are still to maintain conduct appropriate to their Christian values.[563] The household code thus presents examples of groups who, like all Christians, are vulnerable to the dominant forces of secular society but who nevertheless are to maintain appropriate Christian conduct.

Given such an intention for the household codes, one can hardly infer from their emphasis in 1 Peter on slaves and women that those groups made up the majority of the recipients of the letter, or that absence of reference to masters meant there were none present in the Christian communities addressed.[564] That is not to say there were no slaves or women among the intended readers, or that many women in the Christian communities were not married to unbelieving husbands;[565] it is simply to say that the author emphasized these two groups as illustrative of the kind of treatment Christians could expect from a hostile world, and the kind of response Christians were to give to the negative treatment they received.[566] If, then, the household codes cannot provide information about the makeup of the communities addressed in this letter, other evidence must be found to determine the social and economic class of the recipients.

2. Social and Economic Status of the Intended Readers

The general social status of Christians in Asia Minor has long been a matter of debate.[567] Partly because of the perceived attraction of a Christian message (ultimate loyalty to Christ as a lord superior to Caesar) that relativized the importance of the political structures of the Roman world for those excluded from, and hence alienated by, those structures; partly because of a perceived glorification within early Christian traditions of the socially and economically depressed, a glorification that such classes would find attractive (evident, for example, in the Gospel of Luke); partly because of a kind of ideological romanticizing of the powerless in some strands of twentieth-century theology, early Christians have been understood to have come from the lower classes of society, attracted to Christianity because it promised a way out of their oppression and submerged status.[568] Evidence for that in 1 Peter is found in extended advice to slaves with no corresponding advice to masters,[569] and in the identification of Christians as "exiles and aliens" taken as a description of their political

---

561 Philipps (*Kirche,* 52, 54) notes that because in the Christian view secular society was transitory, the Christian community neither supported nor opposed it as such.

562 Philipps, *Kirche,* 26, 28, 53; cf. Senior, 3; Ketter, 197; Schelkle, 66–67.

563 Cf. Souček, "Das Gegenüber," 8; Elliott, *Home,* 201–7; Achtemeier, "New-born Babes," 229–31. This is probably why the codes lack the symmetry of those in Ephesians and Colossians, and why the usual order is reversed. For further discussion, see the comments on 2:18—3:7 below.

564 For such conclusions, see, e.g., Krodel, 75; Love, "First Epistle," 77; Best, "The Haustafel in Ephesians (Eph 5.22—6.9)," *Irish Biblical Studies* 16 (1994) 148.

565 Cf. Lampe and Luz, "Nachpaulinisches Christentum," 188; de Villiers, "Joy," 76.

566 On the legal status of slaves, see Balch, *Wives,* passim; for examples of unjust suffering by slaves, see Tacitus *Ann.* 13.32; Petronius *Satyr.* 57; Seneca *On Mercy* 1.18.1; 1.26.1; *Ep.* 47.11. For a summary of the legal status of women, see Lampe and Luz, "Nach-

paulinisches Christentum," 191.

567 For a general discussion of the situation, see Magie, *Roman Rule,* 1; Lepelley, "Le contexte"; S. Dickey, "Some Economic and Social Conditions of Asia Minor Affecting the Expansion of Christianity," in S. J. Case, ed., *Studies in Early Christianity* (New York: Century, 1928) 393–416.

568 So, e.g., Reicke, 73; Cothenet, "Le réalisme," 569; Tarrech, "Le milieu," 402; Wand, 8; Beare, "Teaching," 295; Lepelley, "Le contexte," 50; Perdelwitz, *Mysterienreligion,* 21.

569 E.g., Krodel, 75; Love, "First Epistle," 77; Sylva, "Studies," 158; Filson, "Partakers," 408; Reicke, 73; but see Schutter, *Hermeneutic,* 11 n. 48.

status prior to their conversion.[570] The recipients of 1 Peter have therefore been identified as coming from the lowest social classes in Asia Minor, from the politically and culturally dispossessed, perhaps even from the rural, rather than the more sophisticated urban, population.[571]

While there is a certain ideological coherence to such a view of the recipients of 1 Peter, it ignores evidence contained in the letter and in other sources. The following points are relevant:

a. Slaves. As we saw above, the attention paid to slaves in 1 Pet 2:18–25 does not necessarily point to a preponderance of them among the readers. Two other points need to be taken into account. The first is that the word used to describe slaves is the more specific οἰκέται rather than the more general δοῦλοι, pointing to slaves of a higher and more cultured ranking.[572] The second point is that the cultural level of slaves in the world of 1 Peter was higher than has often been recognized by modern writers; to be a slave did not necessarily mean lack of culture.[573]

b. Aliens and Exiles. These terms, appearing in 1:1 (παρεπίδημος) and 2:11 (παρεπίδημος with πάροικος), designate politically those who are presently not residing in their homeland, but whether they refer to the preconversion political status of the readers remains conjectural.[574] The fact that the phrase in 2:11 is introduced with ὡς, a particle regularly used in 1 Peter to identify a metaphorical word or phrase, points rather to a metaphorical than a literal intention of the two concepts,[575] and the situation presumed in such verses as 4:3–4 indicates rather a reduction of social acceptance than a failure to increase it as a result of becoming Christian. It is therefore unlikely that one can deduce anything about the prior political status of the readers by the use of these terms in 1 Peter.

c. People of Means. While advice about the conduct of persons in the civil arena (1 Pet 2:13–17) or references to former participation in cultural events (4:3) may or may not imply some wealthy individuals, such people are surely not precluded by those references.[576] Again, although the presence in the household code of advice to women married to unbelievers probably does not allow us to infer that most of the intended readers would be women, the kind of advice included (e.g., 3:3) appears to point to women who commanded a certain amount of wealth.[577] It is therefore most likely that the readers

570 So Elliott, *Home*, 23, 29, 42, 49; Tarrech, "Le milieu," 107–8, 112, 395; Valdir R. Steuernagel, "An Exiled Community as a Missionary Community: A Study Based on 1 Peter 2:9, 10," *Evangelical Review of Theology* 10 (1986) 12. Yet as Elliott (*Home*, 83) implies, the shock at their rejection by former friends, as implied in 4:3–4, would be greater if they had previously been part of that society, rather than socially marginal prior to their conversion. The temptation to become acceptable through "social conformity or assimilation" (84) was not open to them if they had been unacceptable to that society originally!

571 See Elliott (*Home*, 62–63) for a discussion of the rather tenuous evidence in 1 Peter on which this view of rural population is based; cf. also Tarrech, "Le milieu," 96–97, 103, 128, 396. Warnings such as those contained in 1 Pet 4:15 could be construed as attempts to restrain Christians from criminal practices, perhaps because they had been guilty of them before.

572 For the problem this presents to those who maintain a rural setting for the addressees, see Tarrech, "Le milieu," 120–21, 396.

573 So, e.g., Ketter, 239. Slaves were frequently highly cultured: Nero's physician was a slave (Suetonius *Vit.* 6.2.3); Pliny's reader, Encolpius, was a slave (*Ep.* 8.1),

as was Julius Caesar's secretary (Plutarch *Vit., Caesar* 17.3). For a discussion of literacy among slaves in this period, see William V. Harris, *Ancient Literacy* (Cambridge: Harvard University Press, 1989) 255–59.

574 As Senior ("Conduct," 428) points out. The combination used in 1 Pet 2:11 (πάροικος καὶ παρεπίδημος, "alien and exile") occurs nowhere in secular Greek. It is used only in LXX (Gen 23:4; Ps 38:13) and here in 1 Peter; in later literature it appears only in references to one of those three passages. For additional discussion, see the comments on 2:11 below.

575 E.g., 2:2: ὡς ἀρτιγέννητα βρέφη ("as newborn babies"); 2:5: ὡς λίθοι ζῶντες ("as living stones"); cf. also Senior, "Conduct," 428. For further discussion, see the comments under "Controlling Metaphor" below.

576 Asia Minor enjoyed unparalleled prosperity in this period (Magie, *Roman Rule*, 1.582) and was the home of such wealthy cities as Pergamum, Ephesus, and Smyrna (585). Bithynia, despite chronic shortages of grain (cf. Dio Chrysostom *Or.* 46.8) against which Domitian took measures (he ordered the reduction of vineyards to allow more grain to be cultivated; Magie, 580), persistent social unrest (cf. Dio Chrysostom *Or.* 38.22, 45; 48; Pliny *Ep.* 10.17A, 32;

represent people from mixed economic and social backgrounds.[578]

d. Diversity of Background. In Pliny's letter to Trajan seeking advice about, and possible confirmation of, the treatment he has meted out to confessed Christians encountered in Bithynia, Pliny describes those brought before him as coming from both sexes and from the most diverse backgrounds in regard to social and political status and to age.[579] Absent here is any hint that Christians tended to come predominantly from a particular social or economic group. While this situation probably postdates 1 Peter by twenty years or so, one may derive some inferences about the composition of the Christian communities when the letter was addressed to them.

It would appear therefore from both internal and external evidence that the Christian communities to which 1 Peter was addressed were made up of people from the most varied of social and economic levels,[580] that while the preponderance of them lived in cities[581] the movement was already spreading to nonurban areas,[582] and that therefore any attempt to limit the readers to one social or economic class does not conform to the actual situation of great diversity among them. The best conjecture is that the intended readers of this epistle represented the broad spectrum of people living in northern Asia Minor.[583]

3. Internal Status of the Christian Community

There is no obvious indication in 1 Peter that the communities addressed are threatened by internal disorder or potential schism.[584] Neither unacceptable Christian teachers nor tensions resulting from the Jewish roots of the Christian faith appear on the horizon of the readers, as judged from this letter. While some have found evidence pointing to numbers of recent converts within these churches, for example, putative references to baptism[585] or to the way they conducted themselves prior to their conversion,[586] such evidence is neither extensive nor compelling, and can equally be explained as Christian commonplaces one might expect in a general letter such as this.

That there was some danger that people might accept positions of leadership within the community because of the financial stipend may be inferred from 1 Pet 5:2. As communities grew in size, paid administrators seem to have been common, and the temptation to assume the position for the emolument may well have too frequently accompanied this administrative step, but it was not unique to the churches of Asia Minor (cf. 1 Tim 3:3, 8). Again, warning to church leaders against authoritarian tactics (1 Pet 5:3), and to others against attitudes of hypocrisy, envy, and slander (1:22; 2:1; 3:8–9),[587] may well be present simply because that sort of thing tended

Magie, 600), and civic disputes (cf. Pliny *Ep.* 10.37, 39; Magie, 581, 599), enjoyed similar prosperity (Magie, 588). Some people of means apparently did become Christians in these areas, as Pliny noted (see n. 579 below).

577 E.g., Lampe and Luz, "Nachpaulinisches Christentum," 187; Sylva, "Studies," 158. The objection of Tarrech ("Le milieu," 124 n. 100) to this inference is labored and unconvincing.

578 In addition to the following, see Selwyn, 49; Best, 17.

579 *Ep.* 10.96: He describes them as "Multi enim omnis aetatis, omnis ordinis, utriusque sexus" ("many of every age, every rank, and both sexes"), reports he has tortured two female slaves ("ancillis") who were "ministrae," that some guilty of death he could not so punish since they were Roman citizens ("civis Romani"), and that this "superstition" is not confined to the cities, but has also spread to the villages and to rural areas ("vicos etiam atque agros . . . pervagata est").

580 See the excellent summary of evidence in Lampe and Luz, "Nachpaulinisches Christentum," 187–88. It

was also at this time that Domitilla, a member of Domitian's family, had been exiled because of her Christian faith (Eusebius *Hist. eccl.* 3.18.4).

581 Since the time of Paul, Christianity had been preponderantly an urban phenomenon; cf. Reicke, 72; Lampe and Luz, "Nachpaulinisches Christentum," 188; Wayne A. Meeks, *The First Urban Christians* (New Haven: Yale University Press, 1983) esp. 9–50.

582 Pliny notes that Christianity was not confined to cities but had also spread to villages and rural areas; see n. 579 above.

583 That would be further argument for the metaphorical intention of such terms as παρεπίδημος ("exile"), πάροικος ("alien"), and even οἰκέται ("household slave"), which otherwise would point to specific social or economic classes.

584 So, e.g., Brox, 34.

585 E.g., van Unnik, "Teaching," 91.

586 E.g., Kelly, 5.

587 E.g., Tarrech, "Le milieu," 384, 398.

to be present where the church had experienced considerable growth. That such warnings constituted routine types of advice, representing Christian commonplaces, does not reduce the likelihood that they were used in this letter because of the author's awareness of the situation in some at least of the churches in the area to which the letter is addressed. In the nature of the case, however, the letter will be cast in the broadest terms, making any attempt to locate specific internal problems or threats rather difficult.

That is likely also to be true about the suffering of the readers; they, like Christians everywhere, are threatened with suffering, a suffering that brings with it the temptation to abjure the faith. Their need to hold fast to their beneficial present that promises a greater future was then also shared by Christians worldwide, as the author implies (5:9). To find more specific references to individual Christian communities in this letter is probably ruled out by the author's need to address the many and diverse Christian communities located in Asia Minor.[588]

IV. Literary Shape of 1 Peter

Questions about the literary shape of 1 Peter concern (A) its unity as a piece of literature, (B) the type of letter it represents, and (C) the place where it originated.

A. Literary Unity of 1 Peter

Questions about the unity of 1 Peter have been raised on the basis of evidence that can be understood to point to a composite origin, and a variety of theories have been proposed to account for the present shape of the letter.

1. Evidence for 1 Peter as Composite

What appears to be a break in the letter occurs between 4:11 and 4:12. 4:11 ends with a doxology and an "Amen," which culminates what could be concluding remarks in 4:7–10, while 4:12 calls attention to a potentially surprising negative turn of events.[589] Examination of the two parts of the letter revealed apparent differences in the references to suffering—prior to 4:11 they can be seen as potential (1:6; 3:13, 14, 17), whereas in 4:12 (as in 4:19) they seem to be present[590]—as well as differences in style,[591] in literary form,[592] and in content.[593] The letter appeared therefore to have consisted originally of two separate parts.[594] The discerned absence of a coherent train of thought carried out within the letter, or even of a sustained argument represented within it,[595] further contributed to the impression that the letter was not originally a unity.

Furthermore, multiple allusions to baptism[596] have been found scattered throughout the first half of the letter. In addition to the use of the word itself (3:21) and references to new birth (1:3, 23), allusions to early baptismal ritual were found in references to milk (2:2, in early ritual combined with honey),[597] light (2:9), the baptismal formula (1:23–25), the role of the celebrant (2:25), and the putting off of ornamentation (3:3).[598] Even the point at which baptism was administered was then identified: either between 1:21 and 1:22,[599] or subsequent to 3:21.[600] On that basis, it was concluded that 1 Peter was a composite document that had to do with baptism[601] and that had been adapted to its present

---

588 E.g., the inference that because 1 Pet 4:3 suggests activities typical of the celebrations of "industrial guilds or associations of traders" many members came from them (Elliott, *Home*, 70), or that the religious terminology in the letter implies that its readers were once adherents of some mystery cult, most likely that of Cybele (Perdelwitz, *Mysterienreligion*, 95). The data are far too general to allow such inferences.

589 E.g., Moule, "Nature," 2; Fitzmyer, "First Peter," 363, among many others.

590 E.g., Perdelwitz, *Mysterienreligion*, 12.

591 For a summary, see Sylva, "Studies," 160.

592 So Marxsen ("Der Mitälteste," 382), who argues that 1:3—4:11 show none of the characteristics of a letter found in 4:12–5:11.

593 E.g., Perdelwitz (*Mysterienreligion*), who finds much

repetition in the two parts (13), opposing points of view in 1:8 and 4:12 (14), unnecessary separation of the household code in 2:18—3:7 and 5:1–5 (15), and the δι' ὀλίγων ("briefly") of 5:12 to be more appropriate if limited to 1:1–2, 4:12—5:14 (18); cf. also Beare, 7.

594 E.g., Schröger, "Verfassung," 240–41; A. R. C. Leaney, "I Peter and the Passover: An Interpretation," *NTS* 10 (1964) 240; Perdelwitz, *Mysterienreligion*, 16.

595 E.g., Dibelius, "Petrusbriefe," 1113; Goppelt, 37–38 (ET 15–16).

596 E.g., Boismard, "Liturgie" [1], 182: 1 Peter "contains many allusions to baptism"; cf. also Fransen, "Une homélie," 30; Bornemann, "Taufrede," 156–57.

597 So, e.g., O. S. Brooks ("1 Peter 3:21—The Clue to the Literary Structure of the Epistle," *NovT* 16

letter form with the addition of 1:1–2 and 5:12–14.[602]

2. Origin of 1 Peter as a Composite Letter

The evidence of 1 Peter as a composite piece of literature, along with the references to baptism, led to the suggestion that an original baptismal homily to newly baptized Christians, consisting in 1:3—4:11, with its anticipated suffering (1:6; 3:13–14, 17) and its emphasis on the "now" of the ritual (1:3, 6, 8, 12; 2:2, 10, 25; 3:21), had been joined to a brief word of comfort (5:12), consisting of 1:1–2; 4:12—5:14, and sent to communities in Asia Minor then undergoing persecution (4:12). First suggested by Richard Perdelwitz,[603] this solution proved immensely popular and was adopted and modified by many others writing on 1 Peter.[604]

A second solution found in 1 Peter the more or less complete text of a baptismal liturgy, in which the various participants could be identified on the basis of their style of speech and the content of their message. Given its most detailed treatment by Herbert Preisker,[605] this

solution was also adopted by other scholars,[606] some of whom sought confirmation in similar material contained in other NT letters.[607] Perhaps the most significant variation was that of F. L. Cross. On the basis of (a) the frequent appearance in 1 Peter of the word for "suffering" ($\pi\acute{\alpha}\sigma\chi\omega$) and the close relation between that word and the word for "Passover" ($\pi\acute{\alpha}\sigma\chi\alpha$), which was taken into Christian vocabulary as the word for "Easter," and (b) the strange juxtaposition in the letter of the ideas of "joy" and "suffering," Cross argued that 1 Peter is based on a play on those words, with the references to suffering pointing not to actual suffering but to the mystical suffering of the Christian united with Christ. Such an

---

[1974] 298), who cites *Apostolic Tradition* 23.2.

598 See Fransen, "Une homélie," 30; Elliott, *Elect*, 207.

599 So, e.g., Windisch (156), who argues that 1:3–21 have imperatives and future tenses whereas 1:22–23 have past tenses.

600 So Bornemann ("Taufrede," 154), based on the present $\sigma\acute{\omega}\zeta\epsilon\iota$ ("saves") and what he sees as a clear parallel in Titus 3:5.

601 E.g., Moule, "Nature," 4: "who, indeed, could deny it?"

602 First suggested by A. Harnack, *Die Chronologie der altchristlichen Litteratur bis Eusebius* (2 vols.; Leipzig: J. C. Hinrichs, 1897–1904) I, 451–65 (I owe this reference to Bornemann, "Taufrede," 143). See also Brox, 19 n. 7; Bornemann, "Taufrede," 158.

603 *Mysterienreligion*.

604 As a sermon to baptisands, see Brooks, "1 Peter 3:21," 305; van Unnik, "Christianity," 79; Beare, 6, 25–26; Love, "First Epistle," 73; Cranfield, 13; Perdelwitz, *Mysterienreligion*, 24; Martin, "Composition," 36; Scharlemann, "Why the *Kuriou*," 355. That it is based on Psalm 34, see Bornemann, "Taufrede," 147; that it is perhaps a reworking of the author's own notes, see Richard, "Christology," 125.

605 Preisker (Windisch, 157–60) found the following elements, isolated on the basis of differences in style and vocabulary, which constituted a baptismal liturgy of the Christian community in Rome: "Gebetspsalm" "prayer psalm," 1:3–12; "belehrende Rede" "didactic speech," 1:13–21 (baptism occurs between 1:21 and 1:22); "Taufvotum" "baptismal vow," 1:22–25; "dreistrophiges Festlied" "festival hymn in three

strophes," 2:1–10 (delivered by a "Pneumatiker" "spirit-filled person," with vv. 6–8 a later insertion into the hymn); "Paranese" "exhortation" (delivered by another "Prediger" "preacher"), 2:11—3:12; "Offenbarungsrede" "revelatory speech," 3:13—4:7a; "Christuslied" "Christ hymn," 3:18–19, 22, to which an explanatory vv. 20–21 were added; "briefgemässer Ersatz" "letter-form substitute" for "Schlussgebet" "a closing prayer" 4:7b–11c. This baptismal liturgy was then followed by a shorter "Schlussgottesdienst" "concluding worship" of the entire congregation; it began with "eschatologische Offenbarungsrede" "an eschatological revelatory speech," 4:12–19; followed by "Mahnrede" "an admonitory speech," 5:1–9 (delivered by same person who delivered 2:11—3:12); and concluding with "Segensspruch" "a pronouncement of blessing," 5:10 and "Schlussdoxologie" "a concluding doxology" of the whole community, 5:11. The liturgy was framed with greetings (1:1–2) and conclusions (5:12–14) and sent to the churches of Asia Minor.

606 E.g., Carroll Stuhlmueller, "Baptism: New Life Through the Blood of Jesus," *Worship* 39 (1965) 207–17; Boismard, "Liturgie" [1].

607 E.g., J. Coutts ("Ephesians I.3–14 and I Peter I.3–13," *NTS* 3 [1956/57] 115–27), who found similar liturgical elements in Eph 1:3–14; Fransen ("Une homélie," 31), who found them in Titus, 1 John, and James (so also Boismard, "Liturgie" [1]).

emphasis, he concluded, would be particularly appropriate for an Easter baptismal service.[608]

A third solution proposed that rather than adapted homilies or liturgies, 1 Peter consisted originally of two letters, perhaps written at different times and subsequently joined,[609] perhaps written by the same author,[610] perhaps even at the same time, with each of the two intended for a different circumstance, the appropriate one to be determined by the person who delivered them.[611] Subsequently joined, the composite nature of 1 Peter is thus accounted for.

3. Recent Evaluation of Evidence and Proposals

Both the interpretation of the evidence cited to justify theories of composite origin and, as a result, the theories themselves have in recent decades undergone reconsideration.

a. Evidence of Its Composite Nature. That there is a break in the letter between 4:11 and 4:12 has been seriously challenged. The presence of the doxology does not

indicate the end of a letter; while such doxologies can end an NT letter (e.g., Rom 16:25–27 in some MSS.; Phil 4:20; 1 Pet 5:11; 2 Pet 3:18), they also appear frequently within its body when there is a reference to God (e.g., Rom 1:25; 9:5; 11:36; Gal 1:5; Eph 3:21; 1 Tim 1:17; Rev 1:6);[612] it is as likely that the latter is the case at 1 Pet 4:11 as the former. Other parallels within the supposed two parts of the letter also argue against such a break.[613] Nor is there a clear difference in the ways suffering is referred to within the letter. Suffering is as present in the earlier part (1:3—4:11) as it is in the later part (4:12—5:11).[614] A closer examination of differences in style between the putative parts has a similar negative result:[615] the letter is a literary unity on the basis both of style and of literary technique.[616] Even the epistolary framing forms a unity with the body of the letter.[617] That baptism is a major theme of the letter is not borne out by the evidence. References to new birth are not necessarily tied to baptism,[618] nor are baptismal

---

608 *I Peter: A Paschal Liturgy* (London: Mowbray, 1954). He found confirmation for his thesis in Melito of Sardis (*Homily on the Passion*) and in works attributed to Hippolytus (*Apostolic Tradition*, a paschal homily wrongly attributed to John Chrysostom, and the final two chapters of the *Epistle to Diognetus*). Leaney ("Passover") attempted to refine the hypothesis.

609 E.g., Michaels, xl; Leaney, "Passover," 242 (perhaps written at the same time); Perdelwitz, *Mysterienreligion*, 26 (perhaps written by the same person at different times).

610 Cf. Moule ("Nature," 2) for a review of those who hold this opinion. Tenney ("Parallels," 371) suggests 4:12—5:14 was a postscript written when news arrived that the expected trial had begun.

611 This is the suggestion of Moule, "Nature," 10.

612 *1 Clement* also has doxologies in the body of the work following mention of God or Jesus: 20.12; 32.4; 38.4; 43.6; 45.7; 50.7; 58.2; 61.3, as well as at the end: 64; 65.2.

613 E.g., Max-Alain Chevallier ("I Pierre 1/1 à 2/10: Structure littéraire et conséquences exégétiques," *RHPR* 51 [1972] 142), who noted specifically the parallels between 2:11 and 4:12 and between 4:11 and 5:11. Cf. Bornemann ("Taufrede," 158), who found no division within 1:3—5:11 even though he argued that the material was only later adapted to letter form. For a careful analysis of the coherence of content and style in the letter as a whole, see Schutter, *Hermeneutic,* "A Generic and Compositional Analysis," esp. 28–32.

614 That the conditional forms in 1:6 and 3:14 do not

necessarily mean suffering is only potential, see Richard, "Christology," 125; Brox, 33; cf. 30, 36; Meade, *Pseudonymity and Canon,* 168. For a denial of any break between 4:11 and 12, cf. William Joseph Dalton, *Christ's Proclamation to the Spirits: A Study of 1 Peter 3:18—4:6* (AnBib 23; Rome: Pontifical Biblical Institute, 1965) 10, 25, 68; Goppelt, 43 (ET 21–22); de Villiers, "Joy," 67; Michaels, xxxvi. For further discussion of the grammar, see the comments on the individual verses below.

615 E.g., Balch, *Wives,* 123; William Joseph Dalton, "Interpretation and Tradition: An Example from 1 Peter," *Greg* 49 (1968) 21–22; Wand, 2; see also n. 613 above.

616 A good summary of such arguments is given by Best, 26–28. See also H. J. B. Combrini, "The Structure of I Peter," *Neot* 9 (1980) 34–63; Beare, 41–42; Chevallier, "I Pierre 1/1 à 2/10," 141; Frederick W. Danker, "I Peter 1:23—2:17—A Consolatory Pericope," *ZNW* 58 (1967) 100 n. 38; Selwyn, 32 n. 2.

617 So, e.g., Chevallier, "1 Pierre 1/1 à 2/10," 138; Balch, *Wives,* 124–25.

618 Blendinger ("Kirche als Fremdlingschaft," 129) notes the surprising absence of any specific reference to baptism in 1:21–25, probably because, as Dalton ("So That Your Faith," 266) points out, the new birth described in those verses is engendered by proclamation, not by baptism.

themes any more prominent here than in other NT letters.[619] Baptism is in fact not a major theme, and allusions to it seem no more than incidental to the discussion of the kind of life Christians must live under adverse conditions.[620]

b. Theories of Its Composite Nature. With such different evaluations of the evidence of the putative composite nature of 1 Peter has come a general dissatisfaction with theories attempting to account for it. The notion that 1 Peter is an adapted baptismal homily has proved unconvincing,[621] as has the notion of the embodiment within it of some sort of baptismal liturgy, whether general or paschal.[622] The evidence for the specific time of the baptismal act has not been persuasive,[623] and the notion, critical for such a theory, that a fixed liturgical sequence existed has largely been dismissed.[624] References to a paschal celebration are if anything more tenuous,[625] and must presume that references to suffering cannot be meant literally.[626] As a result, such theories have been largely abandoned.

Again, with the questioning of a definite break between 4:11 and 4:12, and the further rejection of differences of style and content between the respective parts, has come a general rejection of the notion that 1 Peter represents the combination of two separate letters, whether they be conceived as having been written at the same or at different times.[627]

c. Emerging Consensus. As a result of continuing work on the content and style of 1 Peter, the emerging scholarly consensus is that far from being a composite work, the letter must rather be seen as a literary unity.[628] That is due on the one hand to the fact that advocates of the embodiment of some sort of baptismal homily or liturgy have been unable to find agreement among themselves about either its nature or its extent,[629] and on the other to the fact that there is no compelling internal evidence

619 Danker ("I Peter 1:23—2:17," 101) points to Rom 6:1–4; Gal 3:27; Eph 4:24; Col 2:12; D. Hill ("On Suffering and Baptism in 1 Peter," *NovT* 18 [1976] 181) adds Hebrews 6. See also Kendall, "Function," 118.

620 For a summary of scholars holding this position see Martin, "Composition," 35; see also Souček, "Das Gegenüber," 6; D. Hill, "On Suffering and Baptism," 185, 189; Werner Bieder, *Grund und Kraft der Mission nach dem 1. Petrusbrief* (Theologische Studien 29; Zurich: Evangelischer Verlag, 1950) 26. On the specific relation of that life to suffering, see Brox, 22; Moule, "Nature," 11.

621 So, e.g., Beare, 40; Dalton, *Christ's Proclamation*, 70; Chase, "Peter," 786; Grudem, 41; Schweizer, 10; J. W. C. Wand, "The Lessons of First Peter: A Survey of Recent Interpretation," *Int* 9 (1955) 387–99) 395; J. Francis, "'Like Newborn Babes'—The Image of the Child in 1 Peter 2:2–3," in E. A. Livingstone, ed., *Studia Biblica 1978* (JSNTSup 3; Sheffield: JSuT Press, 1980) 3.111.

622 E.g., Kelly, 15–20; Goppelt, 40 (ET 18); Margot, 12. Best (20–28) questions the usefulness to Christians in Asia of elements of a baptismal liturgy used in Rome; see also Michaels, xxxix; Lohse, "Parenesis," 39–40. The stenographic exactness of the various participants' speeches embodied in 1 Peter presumed by such schemes as Preisker's (see note 605 above) cause them to fall of their own weight.

623 Dalton (*Christ's Proclamation*, 70) correctly denies baptismal immediacy to the temporal particles νῦν and ἄρτι; see also Meade, *Pseudonymity and Canon*,

168; Schelkle, 4 n. 3. Nor do the verb tenses prior and subsequent to 1:21 support this theory since new birth is presumed already to have taken place in 1:3; see also Martin, "Composition," 37.

624 E.g., David H. Tripp, "Eperōtēma (I Peter 3²¹): A Liturgist's Note," *ExpT* 92 (1980/81) 268; Kelly, 19; Schelkle, 5; Brox, 21.

625 For thorough analysis and telling critiques, see S. G. Hall, "Paschal Baptism," *StEv* 6 (TU 112; ed. E. A. Livingstone; Berlin: Akademie-Verlag, 1973) 234–51; and T. C. G. Thornton, "I Peter: A Paschal Liturgy?" *JTS*, n.s. 12 (1961) 14–26; cf. also Kelly, 19; Brox, 20–21; Cothenet, "Les orientations," 23.

626 Hill ("On Suffering and Baptism," 183) makes this point.

627 E.g., Brox, 34; Bauer, 55; Best, 27–28.

628 E.g., Best, 27; Chase, "Peter," 168; Dalton, *Christ's Proclamation*, 68; Michaels, xxxix; Richard, "Christology," 124; Brox, 18, 22. Brox cautions ("Pseudepigraphischen Rahmung," 94) that the ease with which the epistolary verses 1:1–2; 5:12–14 can be separated from the rest of the letter does not justify their removal.

629 So Martin, "Composition," 39.

against the letter's integrity.[630] As a result, the letter is probably best understood as a piece of genuine correspondence[631] that, whatever elements may have gone into its composition,[632] has received in its present form from its final author its point, direction, and meaning, thus forming it into a unified whole.

B. Type of Letter

If, as seems likely, 1 Peter is not an adaptation of some earlier Christian ritual, and if, as also seems likely, it was composed in its present form, there is good reason to see it as a true letter.[633] That impression is confirmed by the fact that it follows rather closely the form of the Pauline letter, with an opening expanded in typically Pauline fashion, (1:1–2),[634] a blessing (1:3–12; while this usually takes the form of a thanksgiving in Paul's letters, a blessing period can be seen in 2 Cor 1:3–7, whose opening language [v. 3] is close to that of 1 Pet 1:3),[635] a body (1:13—5:11; as in Paul, it can be divided into body opening [1:13—2:10], body middle [2:11—4:11], and body closing [4:12—5:11]),[636] and a closing (5:12–14).

The opening verses also make apparent that it is intended for a larger circle of readers than the members of one church or those of the churches in one community.[637] Parallels to such a general, circular letter indicate the form was known at this time.[638] There are for example, a number of Jewish letters written to large areas, dealing with a question or questions common to their readers;[639] the circular letter purported to be sent by Alexander the Great to locations in the eastern Mediterranean basin is evidence that such letters were not unknown in the Greco-Roman world.[640]

Examples of such circular letters are represented by Acts 15:23–29 (sent to Antioch, Syria, Cilicia) and by James (sent to the diaspora),[641] and the remaining Catholic epistles can also be seen as comparable, but more in terms of their content than of their specific addressees.[642] Again, the address of 1 Peter to the "exiles" of the "dispersion" (cf. Jas 1:1)[643] may show its indebtedness to the OT and Jewish circular letters already mentioned,[644] although 1 Peter's address is more likely to reflect theological intent than literary influence.[645]

There is therefore little reason to question the identification of 1 Peter as a circular letter addressed to Christian communities scattered over the northern half of Asia Minor.[646]

---

630 Schutter (*Hermeneutic*, 82) reaches this conclusion on the basis of a careful comparison of 1 Peter with the Pauline letter form.

631 So, e.g., Goppelt, 44 (ET 23); Elliott, "Rehabilitation," 10; Dalton, *Christ's Proclamation*, 70; Brox, 22; Best, 13.

632 That is not to deny the use of traditional materials, pace Spicq (18), who is reacting against the proposals of Selwyn (e.g., 19), which are too firmly wedded to the theory of the baptismal origin of 1 Peter to be convincing. On the use of traditional materials, cf. Kelly, 19.

633 So, e.g., as early as van Unnik, "Christianity," 80; for the contrary view, see, e.g., Bornemann, "Taufrede," 144.

634 For a letter opening in non-Pauline form, see Jas 1:1.

635 Klaus Berger ("Apostelbrief und apostolische Rede: Zum Formular frühchristlicher Briefe," *ZNW* 65 [1974] 219–20) finds the absent thanksgiving implied in these verses.

636 For an astute discussion of this structure, see Schutter, *Hermeneutic*, 24–27.

637 E.g., Michaels, xxxix; Lampe and Luz, "Nachpaulinisches Christentum," 198.

638 Cf. Spicq, 13; David E. Aune, *The New Testament in Its Literary Environment* (LEC 8; ed. W. A. Meeks; Philadelphia: Westminster, 1987) 180; Beare, 45.

639 E.g., Jer 29:4–23 (sent to the exiles in Babylonia); 2 Macc 1:1–9; 1:10—2:18 (sent to Jews in Egypt); *2 Bar.* 78.1—86.2 (sent to exiles); Esth 9:20–32 (sent to "all the Jews" in King Ahasuerus's provinces); see also Acts 9:2; 15:23–29. For further references, see Aune, *Literary Environment*, 180.

640 See *Pseudo-Calisthenes* 2.11.2–3; the letter is addressed to Syria, Cilicia, Cappadocia, Paphlagonia, Arabia, "and the other nations" (τοῖς ἑτέροις ἔθνεσι).

641 Although Rev 1:4 implies a communication to the whole of Asia Minor, the letters themselves are addressed to specific Christian communities, and are thus not a real parallel to a circular letter.

642 Cf. Carl Andresen, "Zum Formular frühchristlicher Gemeindebriefe," *ZNW* 56 (1965) 241, and the works cited there. Such letters tend to transcend local situations altogether, and to give "didactic instruction which transcends time and space" (so John L. White, "Ancient Greek Letters," in D. E. Aune, ed., *Greco-Roman Literature and the New Testament: Selected Forms and Genres* [SBLSBS 21; Atlanta: Scholars Press, 1988] 102; see also Brox, 15).

643 Michaels (xlvii) points to an interesting parallel: on the pattern of the diaspora letter, 1 Peter is from Babylon to scattered "Jews" who are gentile Christians, while James is from Jerusalem to scattered Christians who are Jews.

C. Origin of 1 Peter

The implied point of origin of the letter is "Babylon" (5:13), but whether this can be taken at face value is disputed. On the one hand, some have attempted to identify the originating locus as the ancient city of Babylon situated on the Euphrates River, but contemporary sources indicate little was to be found at the original location other than ruins.[647] A second Babylon existed in the Nile Delta near Old Cairo;[648] it was a military post for a Roman legion. Because of its name, it has been suggested as the locus of origination,[649] but this suggestion has little to commend it other than saving a literal meaning for "Babylon."[650]

On the other hand, many argue for an identification of Babylon with Rome as the origin of this letter.[651] The evidence for such a view consists in the following points:

1. Because Babylon had represented a proud, immoral, world-dominating city to the OT prophets, an identification of Rome with Babylon became common in the late first and early second centuries when Rome's suppression of Jews as well as Christians became widespread.[652] For that reason, identifying Rome with Babylon would have been appropriate for a letter to Christian communities under similar suppression.

2. Some similarities in language between 1 Peter and *1 Clement,* which clearly originated in Rome, point to a Roman origin for 1 Peter.[653]

3. The early identification of Simon Peter with Rome[654] would argue for such an origin.

4. An origin in Rome is probably also intended with the additional reference to Mark.[655]

Acceptance of the identification of Babylon with Rome remained virtually unquestioned until the Reformation, when it was challenged more for ecclesiastical political reasons than any others: such an identification appeared to favor papal claims to succession in Rome of Petrine authority.[656]

644 If Schutter (*Hermeneutic,* 93, 99) is correct that 1:14—2:9 resembles the pattern of a homiletic midrash, it could lend further evidence of such dependence.

645 See, e.g., Brox (43, and the literature cited in n. 133), who suggests it may be a metaphor "for the interpretation of life as exile." On this point, see below, "Controlling Metaphor."

646 Whether such a circular letter presumed multiple copies as suggested by Brox (23) is difficult to determine on the basis of the available evidence.

647 So Diodorus Siculus *Bib. hist.* 2.9.9, writing in the first century BCE: "As for the palaces and the other buildings, time has either entirely effaced them or left them in ruins; and in fact of Babylon itself but a small part is inhabited at this time, and most of the area within its walls is given over to agriculture" (I owe this quotation to Grudem, 33); in 115 CE, Trajan, visiting the site, found "little but ruins" (Dio Cassius *Hist. Rom.* 68.30). According to Josephus (*Ant.* 18.371–79), Jews had already been forced to leave Babylon under Claudius (41–54).

648 This Babylon is mentioned in Strabo (*Geog.* 17.1.30; I owe this reference to Kelly, 218); cf. also G. T. Manley, "Babylon on the Nile," *EvQ* 16 (1944) 138; Josephus *Ant.* 2.315.

649 See, e.g., Manley ("Babylon on the Nile," passim) for the kind of speculation necessary to make such an origin "possible, and perhaps slightly probable" (145).

650 E.g., Schelkle (134), who argues that "Babylon" in 1 Pet 5:13 cannot mean the military post in Egypt mentioned by Strabo and Josephus. For further discussion of Babylon, see the comments on 5:13 below.

651 E.g., Goppelt, 351 (ET 373); Selwyn, 243; Reicke, 134; Spicq, 181; Michaels, 311; Best, 65, 178; Robinson, *Redating,* 160; Brox, "Pseudepigraphischen Rahmung," 95; Kelly, 34; Brown and Meier, *Antioch and Rome,* 130; Ketter, 198. The identification is as early as Clement of Alexandria (so Eusebius *Hist. eccl.* 2.15.2). For those who accept Petrine authorship, the absence of any reference to or greeting from Paul is a problem; see Schweizer, 13. For further literature, see Goppelt, 33.

652 E.g., *2 Bar.* 11.1–2; 67.7; 2 Esdr 3:1–2, 28; *Sib. Or.* 5.143, 159–61; Rev 14:8; 16:19; chaps. 17–18.

653 So, e.g., Brox, "Literarischen Tradition," 187; Goppelt, 66 (ET 48); Beare, 204; Best, "I Peter and the Gospel," 113. Some also cite similarities to Hippolytus's *Apostolic Traditions,* e.g., Elliott, "Rehabilitation," 13.

654 For early traditions that put Peter in Rome, see Schelkle, 12; Edgar R. Smothers, "A Letter from Babylon," *Classical Journal* 22 (1926) 202; Knopf, 13–14.

655 So, e.g., Kelly, 33.

656 So Bigg, 76; cf. Calvin (154) on the identification in 1 Peter of Babylon with Rome: "nor do I see why it was approved by Eusebius and others, except that they were already led astray by that error, that Peter had been at Rome."

The challenge to an origination in Rome in more recent times is based not so much on opposition to Roman ecclesiastical political claims as on other considerations:

1. The difficulties in communication between Rome and such far-flung addressees.[657]

2. The inherent likelihood that the author and the addressees lived in the same general area.[658]

3. The apparent familiarity with it on the part of Polycarp of Smyrna.[659]

4. The absence of reference to it in Canon Muratori.[660]

5. The fact that it seems to have been more widely known at an earlier time in the east than in the west.[661]

Such arguments have been used to posit an origin somewhere in Asia Minor[662] or in Syria.[663] Yet the absence of any identifiable reflection of 1 Peter in the letters of Ignatius indicates the letter was unknown in Antioch near the end of the first century,[664] and there is no association of Peter with either Antioch or Asia Minor to justify calling upon his authority in this pseudonymous epistle. This latter point alone makes an origin outside Rome most questionable.

Rome remains, therefore, the most likely point of origin of 1 Peter,[665] a letter intended as a circular missive seeking to strengthen the faith of Christians undergoing social and religious harassment in the provinces located in northern Asia Minor. As such, it represents what is probably the first attempt by the Roman Christians to express concern for and exercise oversight of the faith and morals of Christian communities in the Mediterranean world.

V. Theological Shape of 1 Peter

The theological riches of the material contained in 1 Peter have regularly been recognized; Martin Luther affirmed that it contained all that it was necessary for a Christian to know.[666] Although some have argued that there is no unified theme to the letter,[667] others have found in a variety of theological themes the principal emphasis of the letter.

A. Theme and Purpose

Suffering, potential and actual, has often been recognized as playing a central role in the letter's discussions, whether as the dominant theme,[668] or as expressed in the form of exhortation to those who suffer that they

---

657 Beare, "Teaching," 296. He later argued for a Roman origin (Beare, 183). For others who held this position see Manley, "Babylon on the Nile," 142. Contrariwise, a strong argument against such difficulties of epistolary transmission is presented by Eldon J. Epp ("New Testament Papyrus Manuscripts and Letter Carrying in Greco-Roman Times," *The Future of Early Christianity: Essays in Honor of Helmut Koester* [ed. B. Pearson; Minneapolis: Fortress, 1991] 35–56, esp. 52–56), who has mounted a well-documented demonstration that letters were in fact transmitted with remarkable celerity in the Hellenistic world.

658 E.g., Hunzinger, "Babylon als Deckname," 77; Marxsen, "Der Mitälteste," 391, and the additional literature cited there; Lampe and Luz, "Nach-paulinisches Christentum," 198; Johnson, "Asia Minor," 93.

659 Cf. Marxsen, "Der Mitälteste," 391 n. 62.

660 Cf. Kelly (33), who identifies the Canon as a Roman document.

661 So Marxsen, "Der Mitälteste," 391 n. 62.

662 Polycarp's familiarity with the letter would make Smyrna a possible point of origin in Asia Minor; cf. Schutter, *Hermeneutic*, 7.

663 E.g., Lampe and Luz, "Nachpaulinisches Christentum," 186. Boismard ("Liturgie" [2], 183 n. 1)

suggested Antioch on the ground that the earliest evidence of the epithet "Christian" that occurs in 1 Pet 4:16 is associated in Acts with Antioch (Acts 11:26; if Luke-Acts originated in Antioch, the argument is by that much strengthened), and the indication of early acceptance of the *descensus ad inferos*, traditionally found in 1 Pet 3:19, in Syria.

664 So also Beare, 204.

665 This is nevertheless far from certain; it depends solely on 5:13 and signals only the intent of the pseudonymous author, not necessarily the actual point of origin. Cf. Brox, "Pseudepigraphischen Rahmung," 95; Bornemann, "Taufrede," 158; Robinson, *Redating*, 150.

666 Luther (236) wrote: "The one who understands this letter has without doubt enough so as not to need more . . . because the apostle did not forget anything in this letter that is necessary for a Christian to know." He also termed it "one of the noblest books in the New Testament" (186).

667 E.g., Bigg, 6; this view was often linked with the argument that the letter was composite, e.g., Beare, 8. For further literature, see Goppelt, 37–39 (ET 15–18).

668 E.g., Meade, *Pseudonymity and Canon*, 170; McCaughey, "Three 'Persecution Documents,'" 40; Millauer, *Leiden*, 187; de Villiers, "Joy," 65; Beare,

remain faithful,[669] or as comfort for those caught up in such adverse circumstances.[670] Such formulations provide insight into the concern of the author of 1 Peter to provide a perspective on Christian life that will enable the community to survive persecution with its faith intact.[671] Another theme often identified as central to the theological shape of the letter, closely related to that of suffering but providing the necessary antidote, is that of hope.[672] Proposed as 1 Peter's counterpart to Pauline faith,[673] hope in this letter points the Christian to a future when the present time of suffering will have been overcome.[674]

Underlying these two themes of suffering and hope is the figure of Christ, who has been recognized as playing a key role in the theological thought of the letter.[675]

Indeed, his passion, death, and subsequent resurrection show the way present suffering is related to future glory,[676] and thus provide Christians with a model for the way they are to live a faithful life in the midst of a hostile society.[677] Little agreement exists on what form such a Christian life is to take. On the one hand, emphasis on the Christian life as exile, with its true locus in heaven,[678] can lead to indifference toward secular culture.[679] On the other hand, 1 Peter has more recently been seen as a call to social responsibility,[680] often specifically in the form of a mission to the unbelievers.[681] Related to this constellation of ideas is the proposal that one finds in 1 Peter a call for assimilation of Christian values and practices to secular society as a way to avoid unnecessary persecution;[682] others have argued con-

41–42; Filson, "Partakers," 410; Goppelt, 41 (ET 19); Hall, "For to This," 137.

669 E.g., Brox, 16; Hall, "For to This," 137; cf. Albert Vanhoye, S.J., "L'Epître (I P 2,1–10): La maison spirituelle," *AsSeign* 43 (1964) 17.

670 E.g., Elliott, "1 Peter," 65; Lohse, "Parenesis," 50.

671 E.g., de Villiers, "Joy," 64; Schelkle, 99; cf. Goldstein, "Kirche," 46.

672 As the theme of the whole letter, see Cothenet, "Le réalisme," 567; Brox, 17; Wand, 18; Love, "First Epistle," 82; C. Freeman Sleeper, "Political Responsibility According to I Peter," *NovT* 10 (1968) 280; Lippert, "Leben," 254; Roman Kühschelm, "'Lebendige Hoffnung' (1Petr 1,3–12)," *BLit* 56 (1983) 206; James W. Thompson, "'Be Submissive to your Masters': A Study of I Peter 2:18–25," *ResQ* 9 (1966) 68; Neugebauer, "Zur Deutung," 73; Beare, "Teaching," 288 (but see Beare, 56: such an idea is "quite false").

673 E.g., Cothenet, "Le réalisme," 564; Selwyn, 110; Neugebauer, "Zur Deutung," 74.

674 So, e.g., Wilhelm Brandt, "Wandel als Zeugnis nach dem 1. Petrusbrief," in W. Foerster, ed., *Verbum Dei manet in aeternum;* (Festschrift O. Schmitz; Witten: Luther-Verlag, 1953) 15.

675 Spörri (*Gemeindegedanke,* 251; cf. 248–49) would limit the significance of Christ for 1 Peter to his death on the cross; cf. Sieffert, "Die Heilsbedeutung," 373. That Christ's resurrection plays the role for Christians that the exodus played for the Jews, see Cothenet, "Le réalisme," 566; cf. also Brooks, "1 Peter 3:21," 296. For the assertion that 1 Peter is theocentric, not christocentric, see Love, "First Epistle," 70.

676 E.g., Gerhard Delling, "Der Bezug der christlichen Existenz auf das Heilshandeln Gottes nach dem

ersten Petrusbrief," in H. D. Betz and L. Schottroff, eds., *Neues Testament und christliche Existenz: Festschrift für Herbert Braun zum 70. Geburtstag* (Tübingen: Mohr [Siebeck], 1973) 112. Michaels (xlviii) finds similarities here with *2 Baruch.*

677 E.g., Kendall, "Function," 116; Richard, "Christology," 135.

678 Cf. Paul E. Deterding, "Exodus Motifs in First Peter," *Concordia Journal* 7 (1981) 61; Bigg, 6; Martin H. Scharlemann, "Exodus Ethics: Part One—I Peter 1:13–16," *Concordia Journal* 2 (1976) 165.

679 E.g., Calvin, 21; Beare, "Teaching," 288.

680 This has been a special emphasis of Goppelt; see, e.g., "Prinzipien," 285, 288 et passim; see also Elliott, *Home,* 49; Goldstein, *Paulinische Gemeinde,* 26; Cothenet, "Les orientations," 41.

681 Steuernagel, "Exiled Community," passim; Goldstein, *Paulinische Gemeinde,* 32, 113; Brandt, "Wandel," 20 et passim; Edouard Cothenet, "La Première Epître de Pierre, L'Epître de Jacques," in J. Delorme, ed., *Le ministère et les ministères selon le Nouveau Testament* (Parole de Dieu; Paris: Seuil, 1974) 152; de Villiers, "Joy," 75; Christian Wolff, "Christ und Welt im 1. Petrusbrief," *ThLZ* 100 (1975) 339; Margot, 17. Elliott ("1 Peter," 67) contrasts it in this respect with the sect at Qumran. For a dissenting voice, see Balch, *Wives,* 133; idem, "Hellenization/Acculturation," 84.

682 See esp. Balch, *Wives,* passim; the conclusion is based primarily on his analysis of the household code in 1 Peter. On that point see Elliott, "1 Peter," 63–64.

vincingly that such a view runs counter to the thrust of the letter.[683]

On a broader scale, there are a variety of proposals for understanding the larger structural intent of this letter. Concern of the author with baptism has been seen as the point of unity of the letter,[684] either as the theological underpinning of the letter as a whole,[685] or with the content of the letter understood as an example of the teaching given to converts at the time of their admission into the church.[686] Again, the need to reinforce a sense of communal identity has been seen as the major intent.[687] A more specific proposal sees the major contrast between life within and outside the Christian community in terms of household residents and resident aliens as the way communal integrity is encouraged.[688] The need to reduce theological tension within the church has also been seen as the broad intent of 1 Peter, specifically that between Peter and Paul, or between Paul and the Jerusalemite traditions.[689] Related to that is the perceived intent of the letter to broaden the influence of the authority of Simon Peter, or of his followers.[690]

B. Theological Coherence

Such a variety of proposals, each with its evidence drawn from the letter itself, indicates the theological richness of its content. Rather than attempting to isolate a single theme or purpose for the letter, a more fruitful approach will be to see the interrelationship of the theological emphases contained within it. That interrelationship can be investigated under three rubrics, each providing perspective on the unified theological conception of 1 Peter. They are the letter's theological logic, its theological structure, and its ruling metaphor.

1. Theological Logic

The theological logic of 1 Peter is grounded in the events of the passion of Jesus Christ: his suffering (2:21) and death, (1:19) and his subsequent resurrection (1:21) and glorification (3:21). The logic thus grounded structures both the new reality and consequently the new behavior of those who follow Christ.

These fundamental events of the career of Jesus that free persons from their sinful past (1:19) are not accidental, but conform to God's plan, which predates creation (1:20) and whose announcement predates their occurrence (1:11). It is the announcement of the new reality constituted by those events, the "gospel" (1:25b), that makes it possible for people to share that new reality. The metaphor for such entry is a "new begetting" and the resultant "new birth" (1:3; 2:2), and it occurs through the agency precisely of the word of the gospel (1:23).[691] Such begetting for, and new birth into, a new reality is expressed in three key concepts—hope, inheritance, salvation—that spell out its consequences. These three concepts, discussed at the beginning of the opening statement (*prooemium*) of the letter (1:3–12), and

683 E.g., Brox, "Situation und Sprache," 6–7; Lampe and Luz, "Nachpaulinisches Christentum," 211; Elliott, "1 Peter," 63–64; cf. Achtemeier, "New-born Babes," 220–22.

684 E.g., Brooks, "1 Peter 3:21," 294–95.

685 E.g., Spicq, 59; A. Feuillet, "Les 'sacrifices spirituels' du sacerdoce royal des baptisés (I P 2,5) et leur préparation dans l'Ancien Testament," *NRTh* 94 (1974) 712.

686 So, e.g., Beare, "Teaching," 287.

687 So Elliott, "1 Peter," 66, 68; cf. Francis, "'Like Newborn Babes,'" 111; Brox, "Situation und Sprache," 6, where it is implied.

688 A special emphasis of Elliott; see, e.g., *Home*, 201, 229; "1 Peter," 63.

689 This was the thesis of F. Ch. Baur, as Meade (*Pseudonymity and Canon*, 168) and Brox ("Situation und Sprache," 1) point out; for further literature, see Vanhoye, "1 Pierre," 101 nn. 8, 9. Vanhoye ("1 Pierre," 115) sees it furnishing the "point de passage" between Peter and James. For a speculative reconstruction of events, see Chase, "Peter," 791–92:

To aid consolidation in churches in Asia Minor, Peter wrote the letter, to be carried by Silvanus, showing unity between himself and Paul. On another tack, Schröger ("Verfassung," passim) suggests it was intended to reduce tensions between the more charismatic church organization of Asia Minor and the less charismatic church organization of Rome.

690 So, e.g., Elliott, "Peter, Silvanus and Mark," 266–67; see also Brox ("Tendenz," 117) and Marxsen ("Der Mitälteste," 387) for further discussion of literature.

691 This is for 1 Peter the origin of the imagery of new birth, not baptism; baptism is simply an analogy for such new birth, and as such cannot be thematic for the letter; cf. Achtemeier, "New-born Babes," 225–26, and the literature cited there.

each introduced in rhetorically parallel structure: εἰς ἐλπίδα ("into a hope," 1:3), εἰς κληρονομίαν ("into an inheritance," 1:4), and εἰς σωτηρίαν ("into a salvation," 1:5b), provide, along with their consequences, the logical coherence of the remainder of the letter.

a. Hope. One of the realities of the new begetting and subsequent new birth brought about by the generative power of God's word is expressed by the phrase ἐλπίς ζῶσαν ("living hope," 1:3), its form indicating on the one hand its origin in the risen and living Christ, and on the other hand its contrast to other hopes that cannot be characterized by their relationship to life.[692] Such new hope brings with it a new set of loyalties that grow out of it and that are hence attuned to its reality. This new set of loyalties is therefore at odds with former loyalties, and it transforms those who hold them from participants (1:14; 4:4) in, to people exiled and alienated from, the society dominated by those former loyalties (1:1, 17; 2:11). The consequence of such alienation is rejection by those who hold the former loyalties, a rejection that expresses itself in suffering being brought upon those who share in the new reality (1:6; 2:18–20; 3:14, 17; 4:12). The conformation of such alienation and suffering to the new reality is demonstrated by the fact that that is precisely the course of events visited upon Christ (2:21–24), on whom the new reality is based (4:1–2).

b. Inheritance. Another of the realities of the new birth brought about by the generative power of God's word is expressed by the term κληρονομία ("inheritance," 1:4), whose locus (τετερημένη ἐν οὐρανοῖς, "kept in heaven") indicates that it stands in contrast to any former inheritance, entered into by one's physical birth. Because birth is always into a specific people, new birth means one is born into a new people, a people who formerly did not exist (2:10) but who now exist through the deliberate decision of God (1:2; 2:9). The language by which this new people is described makes clear that it is understood in terms of Israel as chosen people, and indeed has assumed Israel's role. Language that the OT uses to describe Israel is taken over and applied without remainder to the new people whose existence is grounded, as was Israel's, in God's election.

Since every people has by inheritance its own customs and practices, members of the new people of God will be no different. They too will have, by their new inheritance, customs and practices appropriate to their new reality. Thus ethical admonitions (2:11) follow directly on the description of the new people (2:9–10). Such new customs and practices (2:1–3, 4–5, 12, 13–16; 3:9; 4:8–11) apply not only within the bounds of the Christian community (1:22; 3:8–12) but are also to be practiced outside its confines, that is, practiced in the midst of the societal structures conformed to the old reality (2:12–17; 4:3). In addition to maintaining in that way the integrity of their reality as a new people (3:8; 4:8–11), those practices can also have the effect of winning over those who find offensive the acts of the new people of God (3:14–16).[693]

c. Salvation. The third reality of the new begetting and new birth brought about by the generative power of God's word is expressed by the term σωτηρία ("salvation," 1:5b), which refers primarily to deliverance at the time of the final judgment (1:9), a judgment that will fall on all people (1:17a; 3:17; 4:5), the dead as well as the living (4:6). Since that judgment lies in the future, however close at hand it may be (cf. 1:20), and since the fate of Christians in that judgment will be one of glory (5:10), those who participate in the new reality through their new birth also have a new future, different from the future that awaits those who do not share the new reality (4:17). It is that new and certain future that frees the Christians from present anxiety (5:7; again, following Christ, 2:23c) and allows them to bear present suffering with joy, knowing that such suffering is temporary and soon to end (1:6; 4:13).

For that very reason, Christians can look forward to the future with hope (1:13), knowing that their glorious future that will follow their present suffering is made

---

692 Cothenet ("Le réalisme," 565) notes that while ἐλπίς ("hope") was seen as a virtue by the devotees of the Eleusinian mystery, the Stoics saw it as "une passion déplorable" that fostered dangerous illusions.

693 The references to the common Hellenistic virtue ἀγαθοποιεῖν ("do [the] good"; 2:15, 20; 3:6, 17) are to be understood in this connection, and point to a missionary imperative rather than to a desire to accommodate the Christian faith to secular values. For further discussion, see the comments on the individual verses below.

certain by the similar course of events related to Christ (4:13). It is just such hope, however, that is the first of the three realities which grow out of the new birth. Thus the third reality, salvation, leads again to the first, hope, in that way demonstrating the closure intended by these three consequences of the new birth through God's generative word.

2. Theological Structure

Just as the theological logic of 1 Peter is christocentric in that it grows out of the salvific suffering and glorification of Christ, so that logic is cast in terms of a theological structure that is similarly christocentric, patterned on those same events. That theological structure is shaped by the categories of past, present, and future, used in two sets of parallels. In the one set of parallels, Christ's past and the Christians' present are paralleled, and Christ's present and the Christians' future are similarly paralleled. In the second set of parallels, which grow out of the first, the Christians' past is contrasted with their present, and their present is contrasted with their future. In that way, the events of Christ's passion become the pattern for the temporal structure of the Christians' life and fate.

a. Past, Present, and Future: Christ and the Fate of the Christian. The structure by means of which 1 Peter discusses the career of Jesus Christ is that of his *past,* which was characterized by his rejection (2:4) and unjust suffering (2:21–24; 3:18, 4:1–2) followed by his resurrection (1:21; 3:21b); the *present,* which is characterized by the glory into which he entered subsequent to his resurrection (3:22; cf. 1:11); and the *future,* which will be marked by his return in glory (1:5, 7, 13; 4:5; 5:4).[694] Similarly, the career of the Christians is discussed in terms of their *past,* which was characterized by birth from perishable seed (1:23) into a life of ignorance (1:14), futility (1:18), and profligacy (4:3), a life marked by darkness (2:9) and separation from God (2:10, 23); their *present,* which is characterized by trials (1:5–6), false accusations (2:12), and unjust suffering (3:9, 14) due to

their new birth (1:3–4) and good conduct (2:12; 20b–21a), but also characterized by joy in anticipation of the future (1:6, 8; 4:13);[695] and their *future,* which will bring blessing (3:9, 14), salvation (1:5–6, 9), an imperishable inheritance (1:4), and glory (1:7; 5:1, 4). Thus what characterized Christ's past now characterizes the Christians' present, and what characterizes Christ's present will characterize the Christians' future.

b. Christians' Past, Present; Present, Future. A second set of parallels, based on the first, concerns the contrast between the Christians' past and their present (1:14–15, 18; 1:23; 2:9c, 10; 2:25; 4:3–4) and the Christians' present and their future (1:5–6; 3:9, 14; 4:12–13; 5:10; cf. 5:2–4). These parallels inform the argument of the entire letter. The purpose of the past/present parallelism is to call the readers' attention to how much better is their present as newborn members of the people of God than was their past when they followed their futile ancestral ways (e.g., 1:18; 2:25; 4:3).[696] In its turn, awareness of that contrast in their status is intended to provide the readers with the assurance that the present/future contrast will be as sure and as complete as the past/present contrast has shown itself to be (4:12–13; 5:10).[697] That is why there is such emphasis on the contrast between past and present; it serves to buttress the main intention of the letter, which is to strengthen the readers in the "now" of their suffering and persecution by assuring them that the future of glory will transform their present condition as surely as their present situation represents a transformation from their past (e.g., 3:14).[698] That is the burden of the exposition contained in the letter.

Closely allied to that logic and structure of the exposition contained in the letter is the logic and structure of its exhortations: the Christian readers are urged not to revert to their past ways, lest in doing that they lose not only their new present as members of God's people but also the future glory that is to grow out of their current faithful obedience in suffering (e.g., 1:13–

---

694 So also Beare, 52.

695 For a similar point, see Schlosser, "Ancien Testament," 65; Elliott, *Elect,* 198.

696 So also Perdelwitz, *Mysterienreligion,* 18.

697 On this point, cf. Goldstein, *Paulinische Gemeinde,* 30; Thurston, "Interpreting First Peter," 181; Dalton, "So That Your Faith," 269.

698 Jean Calloud wrongly argues there is no temporal

succession envisaged in the pre- and post-resurrection terminology in 1 Peter ("Ce que parler veut dire [1 P 1,10–12]," in Perrot, *Etudes,* 178). Similarly, a misunderstanding of the force of νῦν ("now") led to the notion that it designated the instant of the baptismal act; see the references in Moule, "Nature," 6.

21).[699] The corollary to that is the need to hold fast to their faith despite the unpleasant present it brings, since that is the only path to the glorious future that awaits God's new people (2:19–20). That is the burden of the exhortation contained in the letter.

Both parallels, therefore, with their contrasts between past/present and present/future, inform and structure the exposition (the "kerygma") and the exhortation (the "paranesis)" of the letter, and give it its unity and its theological impact.

3. Controlling Metaphor[700]

In common with the rest of the NT, 1 Peter draws significantly on the OT for the language and concepts it uses to describe the Christian community. From its almost casual references to Sarah as the model for the Christian wife (3:6) or its use of the word "flock" to designate the local congregation (5:2) to its more massive use of Isaiah 53 to describe the passion of Jesus (2:22, 24–25) or Psalm 34 to describe conduct within the community of faith (3:10–12), 1 Peter relies on the writings of the people of Israel for language to describe the new people of God.[701]

Yet there is more to this use of the OT than simply

seeing in the people of Israel the model for, or the forerunner of, the Christian community as chosen people.[702] In a way virtually unique among Christian canonical writings, 1 Peter has appropriated the language of Israel for the church in such a way that Israel as a totality has become for this letter the controlling metaphor in terms of which its theology is expressed.[703] Unlike Paul, who finds a continuing place for Israel in God's plan of salvation, 1 Peter has no references at all to Israel as an independent entity, either before or after the advent of Christ. Nor is Israel explicitly understood as a forerunner to the more perfect covenant realized through Jesus Christ, as is the case in Hebrews.[704] In 1 Peter, the language and hence the reality of Israel pass without remainder into the language and hence the reality of the new people of God.[705] As a result, that language is more than simply illustrative—it is foundational and constitutive for the Christian community in a way that has not always been recognized by those who have studied this epistle.[706]

The constitutive nature of such language is most evident in 1 Pet 2:9–10. In this thematic description of

699 Cf. Selwyn, 81.

700 On the use of metaphor generally in 1 Peter, see Troy W. Martin, *Metaphor and Composition in 1 Peter* (SBLDS 131; Atlanta: Scholars Press, 1992); J. D. McCaughey, "On Re-Reading 1 Peter," *AusBR* 31 (1983) 40–42; Tarrech, "Le milieu," 393–94; Achtemeier, "New-born Babes," passim. Such use is not the concern here, only the controlling metaphor in terms of which the author of 1 Peter formulates his theology.

701 See Schutter (*Hermeneutic*, 35–43) for a cataloging of the many ways 1 Peter uses the OT.

702 For this view, see, e.g., Best, 46; it is also implied in the attempt by Brown and Meier (*Antioch and Rome*, 133–34) to trace in 1 Peter's OT citations an outline of the history of Israel. Closer to the mark is Brox ("Sara zum Beispiel," 489): the use of the OT is not in the service of a continuity of "Heilsgeschichte."

703 Quite different is the case of *Barn.* 5.2, which sees the language of Isaiah 53 referring partly to Israel, partly to Christians; there is no such implication in 1 Peter.

704 On the absence of all reference to historic Israel, see also Vanhoye, "1 Pierre," 112.

705 In agreement with Brox, "Sara zum Beispiel," 490, 492; see also Tarrech, "Le milieu," 335; Chase, "Peter," 794; Scharlemann, "Exodus Ethics," 165; Kelly, 26. Jonsen ("Moral Theology," 102) wrongly

narrows the scope in limiting the purpose of such appropriation of rhetoric to the idea of a "new Temple"; cf. also Schutter, *Hermeneutic*, 176.

706 More common is the identification of some aspect or aspects of Israelite history as underlying the appropriation of OT language: (a) the exodus: Brooks, "1 Peter 3:21," 297; cf. Deterding, "Exodus Motifs," passim; (b) the exile: Michaels, xlv; Beare, 74; see Elliott, *Home*, 131, 226; (c) election/covenant: Eugene A. LaVerdiere, "Covenant Theology in 1 Peter 1:1—2:10," *Bible Today* 42 (1969) 2914; see Victor Paul Furnish, "Elect Sojourners in Christ: An Approach to the Theology of I Peter," *PSTJ* 28 (1975) 3; (d) exodus, election, restoration: Heinrich Schlier, "Eine Adhortatio aus Rom: Die Botschaft des Ersten Petrusbriefes," in idem, ed., *Strukturen christlicher Existenz: Beiträge zur Erneuerung des geistlichen Lebens: Festgabe P. Friedrich Wulf* (Würzburg: Echter, 1968) 60–61, 68; (e) exodus, suffering servant, scapegoat: Hall, "For to This," 140–41. Because all such elements, and more, are present, it is better to speak of Israel as such as the controlling metaphor.

the Christian community, the author deliberately selects terms that in the OT designated the uniqueness of Israel in its relation to God (γένος ἐκλεκτόν ["elect generation"], Isa 43:20; βασίλειον ἱεράτευμα ["royal priesthood"], Exod 19:6; 23:22; ἔθνος ἅγιον ["holy nation"], Isa 43:21; λαὸς εἰς περιποίησιν ["people for peculiar possession"], Isa 43:21). This practice is continued in 2:10, where a quotation from Hos 2:23 (MT 2:25; see also Hos 1:6, 9; 2:3), used by the prophet to describe the reconstitution of Israel into a renewed people of God, is here applied to the Christian community. The programmatic nature of this description is evident from the fact that these two verses represent the climax of an exposition begun in 2:4 that discusses the nature of the Christian community as grounded in the living Christ. That that exposition in its turn had at its center the "stone testimonies" respectively of Isa 28:16, Ps 117:22, and Isa 8:14 attests further the constitutive nature of the language of Israel for this letter.[707]

Of comparable importance to the theological program is the quotation in 1 Pet 1:16 of God's statement to Israel that defines the nature of that people in terms of the God who has chosen them: "You shall be holy, for I am holy." This phrase, occurring repeatedly in Leviticus (LXX 11:44, 45; 19:2; 20:7, 26), describes as clearly as the phrases from the OT collected in 1 Pet 2:9 what sets Israel apart from all other nations, and hence makes of them the chosen people (see esp. LXX Lev 20:26, where this is made doubly explicit by the use of ἀφορίσας ["set apart"] as well as ἅγιοι ["holy"]). Its use for the Christian community shows again how the terminology of Israel as chosen people has been appropriated for the Christian community. Further, its use not only grounds the ethical admonitions contained in 1 Peter (so 1:17), but also accounts for the priestly and sacrificial terminology in 2:5: only the special people can offer sacrifices acceptable to God.

Remarkable again is that there is no indication that the Christian community has now taken over the character of chosen people from Israel, or that it is a continuation or fulfillment of the destiny of Israel.[708] The language is simply applied without remainder to this new people of God.

In that light, it is not surprising that the letter begins and ends with terms drawn from the life of Israel: in 1:1 the readers are addressed as the chosen people (ἐκλεκτοῖς) who are now exiles in the diaspora.[709] In 5:13 there is the identification of Rome as Babylon, symbol of the power that sent that chosen people into its exile. These two uses of OT symbols form in that way an inclusio for the entire epistle, confirming the programmatic nature of Israel as the controlling metaphor for our author's understanding of the Christian community.

The hermeneutical presupposition for that appropriation of the language of Israel for the Christian community is stated in 1 Pet 1:10–12. Here is the only implication that the Christians church is the heir to, or fulfillment of, Israel as chosen people: that about which the prophets spoke was in fact the grace that was to constitute the church (1:10). That was the case because it was the very spirit of Christ that caused them to search, and speak, as they did (1:11). That in its turn implies that Israel existed as chosen people simply to point forward to the people who would be chosen in Christ (1:12a). Finally, the reference in v. 11 to the content of prophetic utterance, namely, τὰ εἰς χριστὸν παθήματα ("the sufferings [coming] to Christ"), carries the clear implication that for our author the prophetic writings as a whole were by their very nature christocentric, and hence could be read correctly only in that context. Yet the use in 1 Peter not only of the prophetic corpus but of passages from the Torah and the Writings as well carries the further implication that for our author the entire OT was to be read and understood in such a christocentric context. It is that understanding of Israel's Scripture, and hence of Israel itself, that underlies 1 Peter's appropriation for the Christian church of the language of Israel sedimented in the OT. In that way, Israel and

707 That these passages were drawn from Christian tradition (e.g., Rom 9:25) does not detract from their importance here; the choice of such traditions says as much about the viewpoint of the author as would original citations of the OT; so also Furnish, "Elect Sojourners," 2.

708 I do not find evident, as does Cothenet ("Les orientations," 18; cf. also Beare, 76) that 1 Peter sees

the church as part of a plan of God realized "aux phases successives."

709 Cf. Lippert, "Leben," 241. Martin (*Metaphor*, 144) limits the controlling metaphor, I think unnecessarily, to diaspora images.

its history became the means by which the Christian community was to be understood, or, to express it differently, became the controlling metaphor for the understanding of that new community of faith.

Such an understanding of Israel as the controlling metaphor for the Christian community clarifies some points that have been problematic in the history of the interpretation of 1 Peter.

First, it clarifies the fact that despite the terminology employed, the letter was not written to Jewish-Christian readers.[710] The characterization of those outside the Christian community and their behavior with the rubric "gentile" (2:12; 4:3; cf. 1:18) does not point to ethnic Jews as readers, any more than does the address to them as "exiles of the dispersion" (1:1). The characterization is due to the controlling metaphor of Israel for the church, and would be so employed regardless of the ethnic origin of the readers.

Second, it makes possible the proper evaluation of the phrase "exiles and aliens" (παροίκους καὶ παρεπιδήμους), which occurs in 2:11. This phrase occurs in Hellenistic literature, other than in direct reference to this passage in 1 Peter, overwhelmingly only in direct dependence on Genesis 23 or Psalm 28.[711] Such dependence takes the form either of reference to the progenitor of the chosen people, Abraham, as a stranger in the very land God had promised to him (Gen 23:4), or to the psalmist (David,

according to the superscription), who likewise was not at home in the place where he found himself (Ps 39:12 [LXX 38:13]). The phrase is therefore not descriptive of the secular political status of the readers, whether before or after their conversion.[712] Rather, the language is chosen once again under the influence of the controlling metaphor of Israel to describe the status of Christians within the world they inhabit. That is not to deny that their religious status as "exiles and aliens" had social or political ramifications. The suffering they underwent is ample testimony to that fact. It is to affirm, however, that the choice of the terminology grew not from the political vocabulary of the Greco-Roman world but rather from the language of Israel, whose faith and history functioned as the controlling metaphor for the Christian community.[713] The phrase therefore cannot be used to infer anything about the prior political status of those persons who were subsequently converted to the Christian faith and who made up the readers of this epistle.[714]

Third, it clarifies the self-understanding of the Christian community as a group that saw itself not merely as a collection of individuals who shared similar religious convictions but as a new people of God, with all the social and even political implications such a self-understanding implies.[715] The Christian community as new people shared a loyalty to a lord other than to the

---

710 In agreement with Michaels (lii), who correctly sees the metaphorical nature of OT language in 1 Peter.

711 Aside from lexicographers, who use one word in the definition of the other, the two words are used in combination only in Jewish and Christian literature. E.g., Philo uses the phrase as a quotation from Gen 23 (*Conf. ling.* 79; he employs the combination a second time in *Conf. ling.* 76, but not as a phrase); Clement of Alexandria used it twice in the *Stromata*, once as a quotation from Genesis (4.26.165.2), once as a quotation from 1 Peter (3.11.75.1); two of the Cappadocian fathers (Gregory Nazianzus quoted it from LXX Ps 38:13 [*Funebris oratio* 49.3]; Basil [*Homiliae super Psalmos* 29.252]) and Athanasius (*Expositiones in Psalmos* 27.100, 489) also used the phrase, as did John Chrysostom, among others.

712 Contra Elliott, *Home*, 42–43, 47. πάροικος ("alien") would not have been a particularly appropriate word to describe people estranged from their surrounding culture in any case, since there is good evidence that the word described a class of people whose status was recognized by the state, and whose names were

contained in an official register; see Hans Schaefer, "Paroikoi," PW Halbband 36.18.4; 1695–1707, esp. 1698–99.

713 Cf. Cothenet, "La Première Épître de Pierre," 141; Selwyn, 68, 153, 278; Blendinger, "Kirche als Fremdlingschaft," 125.

714 E.g., Talbert ("Once Again," 144): the phrase is figurative language; Chevallier ("Condition," 394): the phrase is true of *all* Christians (emphasis his); Daniel J. Harrington ("The Church as Minority Group," in *God's People in Christ* [Philadelphia: Fortress, 1980] 81): the phrase shows the author "drew upon imagery expressing ancient Israel's sense of peoplehood" to express the Christians' "own consciousness as a community."

715 In agreement with Elliott, *Elect*, 222–23. See also Lührmann ("Neutestamentliche Haustafeln," 86, 95), who argues for the presence of latent political claims in the church's self-understanding from the beginning.

political ruler, and shared a sense of social reality other than that shared by their contemporaries. While they were to live in such a way as to minimize the danger to the community that such "alien" social and political customs inevitably brought with them, when the confrontation came, they were to suffer rather than conform to the secular practices that once had been their own.[716] They were not only a new household, although they were that (e.g., 4:17);[717] they were a new and distinct people, as surely as Israel had been, and the choice of Israel as controlling metaphor makes that fact abundantly clear.

Fourth, it helps clarify the absence of any mention of historical Israel within the letter. Nowhere is there any hint of the source from which the language of the controlling metaphor has been drawn. This is evidently not an instance of anti-Semitism. There is neither the kind of negative invective that characterized the anti-Semitism of the Hellenistic world at this time,[718] nor any hint that the Jews have been rejected by God. If anything, the implication appears to be that Jews and Gentiles alike have now been taken up into the one chosen people.[719] Nor can it be the case that Jews are simply absent from the regions to which the letter is addressed. There were large Jewish populations throughout the Mediterranean world, including the regions in Asia Minor to which this letter is sent.[720] The reason is simply that for the author of 1 Peter, Israel has become the controlling metaphor for the new people of God, and as such its rhetoric has passed without remainder into that of the Christian community.[721]

4. Theological Coherence

The controlling metaphor and the theological structure of 1 Peter are of course related. Together they provide the theological coherence of the letter. Israel understood itself in terms of events from its past that had great impact on how it was to conduct itself in its present life, and both past and present were in their turn impacted and reinterpreted in light of the future that lay before it. The people of Israel faced the constant danger of reverting to customs and practices unacceptable to the God who had called them, or of falling into the practices of those peoples surrounding them that would constitute a denial of the significance of that call. Israel also faced the danger of losing their promised redemptive and more glorious future through activity in the present unacceptable to the God who had promised them that future. Again and again, from their conduct in the wilderness to their policies as a nation, Israel by their actions endangered their promised future. Characteristic therefore of being the chosen people in the OT was the constant reminder of the danger of falling into a kind of behavior that would jeopardize the future they had been promised. When the author of 1 Peter took as his controlling metaphor the history and reality of Israel as the people of God, he took over as well this contrast of past/present and present/future as the structuring elements of his kerygma as well as his paranesis, in that way also providing for the epistle its theological coherence.

Underlying this appropriation of Israel as controlling metaphor and its derivative structuring elements is the author's conviction that it was precisely the fate of Christ that made possible the existence of a new people chosen in and through him, the second element of our epistle's theological coherence. It was the suffering of Christ and his subsequent glory that provided the insight (cf. 1:10–12) that made useful the appropriation of Israel as the metaphor for the way this (new) chosen people (cf. 2:9–10), whose glorious future had also been repeatedly

---

716 Absence of any advice to withdraw from secular society argues against the idea that this self-consciousness came to the church via Qumran, as Goppelt (55, ET 36) suggested.

717 This is the emphasis of Elliott: e.g., *Home*, 21–58, 118–32, 200–237; "1 Peter," 77; "Peter, Silvanus and Mark," 255.

718 E.g., Tacitus *Hist.* 5.4–5; Petronius *Satyr.* 68; Martial *Epig.* 12.57; Plutarch *Mor., Table–Talk* 4.669F, 671C, 689C.

719 So also Love, "First Epistle," 85.

720 So Josephus *Bell.* 2.398; *Ant.* 14.110–18; Philo *Leg.*

Gaj. 245, 281–82.

721 Unnecessarily speculative is the suggestion of Michaels (liv) that absence of mention of Israel is due to a "tacit alliance" between gentile Christians and Jews in common opposition to Rome.

threatened by present apostasy (cf. 3:10–12), was to be understood.[722] If such an insight into the relation between Israel and the Christian community was shared with the Christian community as a whole, and hence not a unique contribution of our epistle, the consistency with which that insight is carried through is unique, and represents our author's contribution to the understanding of "the true grace of God" in which the Christian community stands (5:12).

VI. Structure and Outline

A. Structure

In accordance with ancient letters, and more particularly Christian letters, the epistolary opening (1:1–2) and introductory words, usually cast in the form of prayer or blessing (1:3–12), are followed by the body of the letter (1:13–5:11) and an epistolary closing (5:12–14). That is also the case with 1 Peter, as the parenthetical references indicate.

The body itself, particularly in the Pauline letters, is normally divided into three parts, the body opening, body middle, and body closing, a structure that is also repeated in 1 Peter.[723] The dominance of the imperative in 1:13—2:10, a verb form hitherto not used in the epistle, points to these verses as the beginning of that main body of the letter (body opening). The presence of δίο in 1:13 indicates that the body opening grows directly out of the preceding section (1:3–12), thus pointing to the fact that those opening verses serve here more as the introduction (prooemium) to the letter as a whole than simply as an opening prayer or blessing.[724] The introductory use of ἀγαπητοί ("beloved") at 2:11 and 4:12, coupled with the benediction at the conclusion of 4:11 and in 5:11, marks out those sections as body middle (2:12—4:11) and body closing (4:12—5:11). The greetings, summary, and final benediction mark 5:12–14 as the formal epistolary conclusion.

Such an account of the structure of the letter must remain tentative, given the nature of the discussion contained within it, a discussion that tends to move from topic to topic with no sequential organization, and with frequent repetitions and further developments of ideas already broached.[725] Because this proposal does allow one to see the letter in terms of early Christian epistolary composition, however, and because it is based on linguistic structures rather than impressions of content, it is perhaps the most useful one to follow.

B. Outline

I. 1:1–2 Epistolary Introduction
II. 1:3–12 *Prooemium*
    A. 1:3–5 A New Life and Its Consequences
    B. 1:6–9 Trials in the Present, Salvation in the Future
    C. 1:10–12 Salvation in Christ Revealed to the Prophets
III. 1:13—2:10 Body Opening
    A. 1:13–25 Tasks (and Nature) of the Christian Community
        1. 1:13–21 Lives of hope are holy, actions must conform
            a. 1:13, 14–16 Lives of hope are holy lives
            b. 1:17–21 Act in ways appropriate to your redemption
        2. 1:22–25 Begotten by God's word, you must love one another
            a. 1:22–23 Begotten by God's word, therefore love
            b. 1:24–25 Such begetting is the content of the gospel
    B. 2:1–10 (Tasks and) Nature of the Christian Community
        1. 2:1–3 Desire appropriate things
        2. 2:4–10 You are a chosen people
            a. 2:4–6 You are living stones
            b. 2:7–10 You are the chosen people
IV. 2:11—4:11 Body Middle
    A. 2:11–12 Thwarting False Accusations by Good Behavior
    B. 2:13–3:7 Call to Appropriate Subordination
        1. 2:13–17 All readers to civil authorities
        2. 2:18–25 Household slaves to their masters
            a. 2:18–20 Subordination by right conduct
            b. 2:21–25 Suffering Christ as basis
        3. 3:1–6 Believing wives to their unbelieving husbands
        3:7 Subunit: Believing husbands to show respect for their believing wives
    C. 3:8—4:11 Call to Right Conduct
        1. 3:8–12 Call to all readers to nonretaliation for evil
        2. 3:13–22 Call to all readers to right conduct facing suffering
            a. 3:13–17 Bearing undeserved suffering
            b. 3:18–22 Suffering and triumphant Christ as basis
        3. 4:1–6 Call to all readers to right conduct among unbelievers

---

722 Cf. Paul S. Minear ("The House of Living Stones: A Study of 1 Peter 2:4–12," *Ecumenical Review* 34 [1982] 243): "As the passion story was the story of Zion writ small, the story of Zion was the story of Jesus writ large."

723 For a convenient summary of these points, see Schutter, *Hermeneutic*, 19–32.

724 In the Pauline letters, the opening prayer can also announce themes to be discussed, as in the case of 1 Cor 1:4–9, but the opening period of 1 Peter is much more comprehensive in content than is the case in Paul's letters.

725 See Brox, 73.

4. 4:7–11 Call to all readers to right conduct within the fellowship
V. 4:12—5:11 Body Closing
   A. 4:12–19 Suffering of Christians in Present and Eschatological Context
      1. 4:12–13 Suffering of Christians and joy
      2. 4:14–16 Suffering of Christians as Christians
      3. 4:17–19 Suffering of Christians as prelude to final judgment
   B. 5:1–5 Appropriate Conduct in the Community
      1. 5:1–4 Conduct of elders
      2. 5:5a Conduct of young people
      3. 5:5b Conduct of all
   C. 5:6–11 Appropriate Conduct in Eschatological Suffering
      1. 5:6–7 Toward God
      2. 5:8–9 Toward the devil
      3. 5:10–11 Conclusion
VI. 5:12–14 Epistolary Closing

VII. Text of 1 Peter

The text of 1 Peter is contained in its entirety in one papyrus manuscript,[726] ten uncials, and several hundred minuscules. Parts of its text have been preserved in two additional papyrus manuscripts and five additional uncials.[727] As is the case with other NT writings, the various texts so preserved are of varying quality.

A. Papyrus Manuscripts

The full text of 1 Peter is contained only in P[72] (P. Bodmer VIII), a manuscript of the third/fourth century.[728] While the scribe who copied it was evidently somewhat careless,[729] the underlying text appears to belong to the Alexandrian type, with its readings most often agreeing with Vaticanus as well as Sinaiticus, Ephraemi, and Athous Lavrensis, in addition to the minuscules 1739 and 323.[730]

Partial texts of 1 Peter are contained in P[74] (parts of the first three chapters), a manuscript from the sixth/seventh century[731] of good quality;[732] and in P[81] (2:20—3:1; 3:4–12), a fragment from the fourth/fifth century in a wretched state of preservation, and hence very difficult to read.[733]

B. Uncials

The uncials in which the text of 1 Peter is preserved in its entirety are ℵ, A, B, K, L, P, Ψ, 049, 056, and 0142. In addition partial texts are contained in C (chaps. 2–3, parts of chaps. 1, 4), 048 (parts of chap. 1), 093 (parts of chaps. 2, 3), and 0206 and 0247 (parts of chap. 5 in each).[734] The quality of these texts varies, with ℵ, B, and A ranking high,[735] C, Ψ, and 048 of somewhat lesser quality,[736] and 049, 056, and 0142 representing a text of very low quality.[737]

C. Minuscules

Of the hundreds of minuscules that contain the text of 1 Peter, those which may be noted because of their high quality are 33, from the ninth century; 1241, from the twelfth century, with a much higher quality of text for the Catholic epistles than for the remainder of the NT;

---

726 2 Peter is the only other NT canonical writing to have its full text so preserved.

727 K. Aland and B. Aland, *The Text of the New Testament* (2d ed.; trans. E. F. Rhodes; Grand Rapids: Eerdmans, 1989), charts included in the rear cover of the book.

728 Aland and Aland, *Text,* 100.

729 Certain characteristics of the manuscript's orthography point to an Egyptian whose native language was Coptic; see W. Grunewald, with K. Junack, eds., *Das Neue Testament auf Papyrus,* vol. 1: *Die Katholischen Briefe* (Arbeiten zur neutestamentliche Textforschung 6; Berlin: de Gruyter, 1986) 24; Frank W. Beare, "The Text of 1 Peter in Papyrus 72," *JBL* 80 (1961) 253; Jerome D. Quinn, "Notes on the Text of the P[72] 1 Pt 2,3; 5,14; and 5,9," *CBQ* 27 (1965) 242.

730 Cothenet, "Les orientations," 14; see Frank W. Beare, "Some Remarks on the Text of I Peter in the Bodmer Papyrus (P[72])," *StEv* III, part II: *The New Testament Message* (TU 88; ed. F. L. Cross, Berlin: Akademie-Verlag, 1964) 263; Quinn, "Notes," 241.

For a full description of the papyrus, see Grunewald, 16–25. Also important is Beare, "Text," 254, which includes a catalog of singular readings as well as a comparison of its readings with other known variants.

731 For a full description, see Grunewald, 25–28.

732 Aland and Aland (*Text,* 101) identify it as an Egyptian text, and assign it to their Category I, i.e., "manuscripts of a very special quality."

733 For a full description see Grunewald, 30–31; Aland and Aland (*Text,* 101) assign it to Category II, i.e., "manuscripts of a special quality."

734 Aland and Aland, *Text,* charts included inside rear cover of book.

735 Aland and Aland (*Text,* 107, 109, 159–60) rank them as Category I texts.

736 Aland and Aland (*Text,* 109, 118, 160) place them in Category II.

737 Aland and Aland (*Text,* 118–19; 122, 160–61) put them in Category V, i.e., "purely or predominantly Byzantine."

1243, from the eleventh century, with a text also of higher quality for the Catholic epistles; and 1739.[738] In addition, five minuscules are of lesser but nevertheless considerable value; they are: 2344 (eleventh century); 1735 (eleventh/twelfth century); 1292, 1852 (thirteenth century); and 1409 (fourteenth century).[739]

D. Text Types

Of the various textual traditions that have been identified by text critics over the years, it is clear that the Egyptian (or Alexandrian) type is represented by such uncials as ℵ, B, A, C, P, and Ψ, along with the minuscules 33, 72, 81, 326, 1175, and 1739.[740] The Byzantine (or Koine) tradition is represented by such uncials as K, L, and S, and by the great mass of the minuscules.[741] The absence of the text of 1 Peter from Codex D (Bezae), and the fragmentary nature of its preservation in the Old Latin manuscripts, make it difficult to determine whether the "Western" tradition is represented.[742]

Taking a cue from the work of H. von Soden, Jean Duplacy and Christian-Bernard Amphoux[743] have proposed three categories for the textual traditions represented in the manuscripts of 1 Peter. Group I includes such uncials as L, 049, 156, and 0142, along with a number of minuscules, such as 356, 643, 1022, 2401, 2423, 307, 610, 453, 69, 218, 642, 808; on the periphery of this group belongs the uncial 018, and 025 is identified as an intermediate text between Group I and Group II. In Group II are to be found the uncials ℵ, A, B, C, Ψ, and P[72], along with such minuscules as 5, 623, 1739, 2298, 323. Group III consists primarily of minuscules; among them are 206, 1758, 429, 1831, 1611, 1108, 2138, 1518, 614, 1799, and 2412; peripherally, there could also be included 522, 1852, 383, 2147, 913, 1765, 255, and 378. In addition, two subgroups have been identified; the one contains 206, 429, 1758, 1799, and 1831; the other 614, 1108, 1518, 1611, 2138, and 2412. Group I perhaps originated in Syria, Group II corresponds to the Egyptian or Alexandrian tradition, while Group III may be evidence of a "Western" tradition.[744]

The discovery of P[72] and its evaluation gave a renewed impetus to the study of the textual tradition of 1 Peter, but as is evident from the differing proposals concerning that textual history, the last word has not yet been spoken.

---

738 Aland and Aland (*Text,* 129, 134) rank these four minuscules as Category I texts; Cothenet ("Les orientations," 14) notes that 1739 and 323 often accord in their readings with P[72].

739 Aland and Aland (*Text,* 134–37) rank these as Category II texts.

740 Cf. Goppelt, 72–73 (ET 55–57); Schelkle, 16; Beare, "Some Remarks," 263; Grunewald, 27.

741 Cf. Goppelt, 72 (ET 55); Schelkle, 16.

742 For the argument that it is, see Jean Duplacy and Christian-Bernard Amphoux, "A propos de l'histoire du texte de la première épître de Pierre," in Perrot,

Etudes, 157, 171. Goppelt (72 [ET 56]) suggests possible "Western" influence in minuscule 383.

743 "A propos de l'histoire du texte," 161–62.

744 Duplacy and Amphoux, "A propos de l'histoire du texte," 170–71.

1

Epistolary Introduction

1 Peter, apostle[1] of Jesus Christ, to the elect[2] who are sojourners of the diaspora of Pontus, Galatia, Cappadocia, Asia, and Bithynia,[3] 2/ (elect) in accordance with the purpose of God the Father by means of the sanctification of the Spirit for the purpose of obedience and the sprinkling of the blood of Jesus Christ: my wish is that God may multiply grace and peace for you.

1 Customarily, the second word is translated "an apostle," since there is no definite article, yet that tends to lessen the implied force of this claim. To be sure, Peter is one among at least twelve, but the force of the title is not that he is one of a group, but that what is being written carries apostolic authority.

2 A very few MSS. (אֲ*, sy) insert "and" (καί) between these two substantival adjectives, perhaps to emphasize that both words describe the readers and reduce the impression that "elect" modifies "sojourners."

3 There is some uncertainty in the MSS. about the phrase that names the fourth and fifth areas; some minuscules omit the "and" (καί) between them; B* drops "and Bithynia" ("purely accidental" omission: Spicq, 40); אֲ* and a few others omit "Asia"; some minuscules (e.g., 614, 1243, 1852, 2495) add "and" before Asia as well. None of these readings is significant, and the majority of the texts read as I have translated.

Analysis

These two verses form the epistolary opening of the letter,[4] and are interesting for several reasons. First, the absence of definite articles in this epistolary introduction as a whole is noteworthy. Articles tended to be omitted in formulaic language, and hence were often absent from epistolary introductions;[5] these two verses, however, are longer than the normal ancient letter opening. As presently structured, the language has a solemn, even archaic flavor.[6]

Second, the opening of the letter shares in the kind of expansion on the standard epistolary greeting that also characterized the Pauline letters, and includes the Pauline formula "grace to you and peace" (χάρις ὑμῖν καὶ εἰρήνη).[7] The conclusion from this that the author of 1 Peter is dependent on the Pauline letters,[8] however, seems unwarranted in light of the greater similarity between this introduction and that of Jewish letters. In addition to a reference to readers in the diaspora, or other specific areas,[9] such Jewish letters characteristically used the salutation "may (grace and) peace (be) increase(d) for you,"[10] and cast it in the optative, not the

---

4 This would be the case no matter how the composition of the epistle is envisioned, since, as Furnish ("Elect Sojourners," 2) notes, these verses would have been the last to be added even if 1 Peter were composite in origin, and would thus have had the remainder of the writing in view.

5 See Ludwig Radermacher, *Neutestamentliche Grammatik* (HNT 1; 2d ed.; Tübingen: Mohr [Siebeck], 1925) 113, 114; BDF § 252, 261.

6 So also Goppelt, 78. Shimada (*Formulary Material*, 119) suggested it may be explained in part by "the so-called Apollonius' canon" (nouns in a regimen will all have an article or none will); see his n. 1 for further literature. But see A. T. Robertson (*A Grammar of the Greek New Testament in the Light of Historical Research* [3d ed.; New York: Doran 1919] 756): "The older language and higher poetry are more anarthrous

than Attic prose"; and Berger ("Apostelbrief und apostolische Rede," 197), who notes that this kind of epistolary introduction would have seemed strange and archaic to Hellenistic contemporaries of the late first century.

7 Schelkle (23) argues that since this formula appears in all thirteen Pauline letters, but not prior to Paul, Paul is responsible for its formulation; cf. Shimada, *Formulary Material*, 125.

8 E.g., Beare, 73.

9 Such letters to exiles are already known in the OT (Jer 29:4–23) as well as in later Jewish literature (*2 Bar.* 78.2; 1 Macc 1:1, 10b).

10 E.g., Dan 4:1; 6:26 (LXX Theodotion); 4:37c (LXX), where the word πληθυνθείη is used; cf. also *2 Bar.* 78.3, and the letters of Gamaliel in *b. Sanh.* 11b. For this form in Christian literature, cf. Jude 2; *1*

indicative, which is characteristic of Greek letters.[11] The further absence of characteristic Pauline words found in his epistolary introductions (e.g., ἀγαπητός, κλήτος, ἅγιος, πιστός, ἐκκλησία)[12] leads to the conclusion that the introduction of 1 Peter is closer to Jewish diaspora letters than to those written by Paul.[13]

Third, the opening two verses set the stage for what is to follow in the letter in terms of content and themes. The three prepositional phrases of v. 2 are further expanded in the next few verses, with God's directive activity developed in 1:3–12, the concept of holiness in 1:13–17, and the theme of obedience and Christ's sacrifice in 1:18–25.[14] Again, the theme of exile, announced in the first verse, serves as an introduction to the larger section 1:3—2:10, and with the addition of πάροικοι in 2:11, continues to underlie the discussion of 2:11—4:11.[15]

In a larger sense, the interrelationship of the three words describing of the readers in v. 1 (ἐκλεκτός, παρεπίδημος, διασπορά; "elect, exile, diaspora") reveals the author's underlying convictions about the nature of the Christian community and its relationship to its surrounding world.

Members of the community are such because of the direct intention of God; the process by which their divine election occurs in Christ predates even the creation of the world (1:20). The community thus owes its existence to the direct intention of God. Their status as exiles grows directly out of such election to participation in the divinely willed community. To be exiles in their surroundings as a result of their election is again not a sociological accident; it grows directly out of membership in a community whose members are by definition to exclude themselves from the value systems and mores of that world (4:2–4).

As exiles, they are dispersed throughout the world, as was Israel of old in its diaspora.[16] Thus the Christian community, estranged by its customs and beliefs from its surrounding world, awaits a transformation that will finally end its status as scattered exiles and unite it in a transformed world directly under the will of God (4:17–19; 5:10).

Finally, the language itself, taken from the record of God's dealing with his chosen people Israel, shows the history in light of which the author understands God's intention for the community grounded in God's act in Christ. Describing that community in terms taken directly from the OT records of Israel as the chosen people (2:9–10), the author of 1 Peter makes evident where the community is to look to find the means of interpreting its existence in its own world: to the record of the existence of God's chosen people, which furnishes language and perspective for the self-understanding of the people of Christ (1:10–12).

Thus the understanding of the Christian community as the new people of God, an understanding that dominates the discussion in 1 Peter, is announced in the first words used to describe its members.[17]

Comment

■ 1 The name "Peter" (πέτρος), given to Simon by Jesus,[18] is the translation of the Aramaic כיפא, transliterated into Greek as κηφᾶς.[19] Πέτρος, unknown as a personal name prior to its Christian use for the disciple Simon,[20] supplanted the earlier κηφᾶς in the tradition sedimented in the NT,[21] a tradition also followed here in 1 Peter. The identification of Peter as ἀπόστολος ("apostle"), while it underlines his importance in Christian tradition, points more to the importance of the sender (Christ) than the one sent,[22] and is intended to cloak the message of the epistle in an authority derived from Christ. Since

Clement (introduction); Polycarp *Phil.* (introduction); cf. Michaels, 4; Beare, 74; Andresen, "Formular," 236–37, 241.

11 Cf. Schelkle, 18 n. 1. In the NT, the typical χαίρειν ("greetings") is found in Acts 15:23; 23:26; Jas 1:1.

12 I owe this list to Goppelt, 76.

13 With, e.g., Kelly, 39; Shimada, *Formulary Material*, 131–32.

14 With Bigg, 95.

15 With, e.g., Goppelt, 79; for another analysis of key words present in vv. 1–2, see Chevallier, "1 Pierre 1/1 à 2/10," 132.

16 Although there are echoes in 1 Peter of the exodus and the establishment of the covenant in the wilderness (e.g., 1:16, 19; 2:9; see Boismard, "Liturgie" [2], 181), the major prototype of the Christian community's experience in the world is here furnished by the exile.

17 For further development of the thematic nature of the Christian community as the new people of God in 1 Peter, see Achtemeier, "New-born Babes," 224–31.

18 Matt 16:18; Mark 3:16; Luke 6:14; John 1:42.

19 See John 1:42.

20 Peter Lampe, "Das Spiel mit dem Petrusnamen—

there is little in the letter that can be specifically identified with the events in Peter's career as disciple (contrast 2 Pet 1:14, 16–18), and thus provide the reason for attribution to him, that reason is probably best understood as the author's conviction that the name "Peter" would command a hearing in Asia Minor,[23] despite the fact that Peter himself had not been a missionary to the areas addressed.[24] The source of Peter's authority is identified with the formula Ἰησοῦ Χριστοῦ[25] ("Jesus Christ"),[26] a more common formula in the NT than the Pauline "Christ Jesus."[27]

The readers are identified by the use of three substantives (ἐκλεκτός, παρεπίδημος, διασπορά) that announce important themes in the letter.[28] The identification of the readers as "elect" (ἐκλεκτοῖς) employs a term that in the OT refers to Israel's special status as the people chosen by God.[29] This term, also familiar to the covenanters of Qumran,[30] became a common designation in the NT for Christians.[31] The idea of Christians as elect

receives its fullest treatment in the NT in 1 Pet 1:3—2:10, with the specific term repeated in 2:9, indicating the importance the author ascribes to the OT understanding of the special place Israel occupied in God's economy of salvation as paradigmatic for understanding the new elect community. In 1 Peter, such election is based in Christ, whose election as the foundation for the church is from eternity (1:20; 2:4). Such election eventuates in final salvation (5:10), but as the ethical admonitions throughout the letter make clear, such election puts upon those elected the responsibility to live in accordance with the character of the one who elected them (1:15–16).[32]

The term παρεπίδημος ("exile"), rare in the Bible,[33] is not uncommon in secular Greek, and is widely used among later Christian authors,[34] where it designates one who, willingly or not, dwells in a foreign land. Frequently used as a punishment, exile was regarded as a calamity,[35] but because of the social conditions in the

Matt. xvi.18," NTS 25 (1978/79) 228.

21   Its early use is witnessed by Paul (1 Cor 1:12; 3:22; 9:5; 15:4; Gal 1:18; 2:9, 11, 14; cf. also John 1:42), who also knew the Greek form Πέτρος (Gal 2:7, 8). While "Petros" is the more common name in early noncanonical Christian writings (e.g., Ignatius *Rom.* 4.3; *Smyrn.* 3.2; *Pol.* 1.1; *1 Clem.* 5.4; *2 Clem.* 5.3), the name "Kephas" also appears, but its use there draws on its use in the NT (e.g., Clement of Alexandria *Strom.* 4.15.96; Epiphanius *Pan.* 25.366; 31.266, 267).

22   Cranfield (27) argues that it is closer to the Jewish use of שליח than the Greek use of ἀπόστολος.

23   Schelkle, 18; Goppelt, 76.

24   Preisker (Windisch, 51) notes that 1 Pet 1:12 makes that evident.

25   It is to be construed as a "genitive of origin and relationship" (BDF 162 [7]).

26   The author of this letter also refers to Jesus with the title "Christ" alone, but never with the name "Jesus" alone, perhaps indicating the extent to which the title had already become part of the name.

27   "Jesus Christ" appears in the NT 134 times, "Christ Jesus" 90 times; 84 (of which 5 are textually questionable) of those are in the Pauline letters, the remainder in Acts. In the introductory identification of the author in the Pauline letters, the phrase "Jesus Christ" appears only in Titus 1:1; in every other instance, the formula is "Christ Jesus." On this point see also Schelkle, 18.

28   See also the discussion above in "Analysis."

29   E.g., Deut 4:37; 7:6–8; 10:15; 14:2; Isa 14:1; 41:8–

9; 43:20; 45:4; 51:2; 65:9, 15, 22; Hos 11:1; Ezek 20:5; LXX Pss 88:4; 105:6, 43; 2 Macc 1:25. See also Deterding ("Exodus Motifs," 59), who relates election to the exodus.

30   E.g., 1QS 8.6; 11.16; 1QpHab 10.13; CD 3.21–4.6; 6.4–5. Goppelt (81) finds here the origin of the three substantives in 1 Peter, since CD 3.21—4.6 contains, as does 1 Peter, the notions of election, sojourning, exodus, and exile. These themes are common enough in the OT, however, and are taken over often enough in the NT, to render such a judgment superfluous.

31   For ἐκλεκτός, see Matt 24:24; Mark 13:20; Luke 18:7; Rom 8:33; 16:13; Col 3:12; 1 Tim 5:21; 2 Tim 2:10; Titus 1:1; Rev 17:14; for the similar κλητός, see Rom 1:6, 7; 8:28; 1 Cor 1:2, 24; Jude 1; but see also Matt 22:14, where they are not identical.

32   See the discussions in Chevallier, "Condition," 395; Schelkle, 19; Krafft, "Christologie," 122.

33   In the LXX it occurs only in Gen 23:4; Ps 38:13; in the NT in 1 Pet 1:1; 2:11; Heb 11:13.

34   The adjectival form is not so common as is often asserted, however; e.g., Selwyn (118), quoting Zahn. It is used more frequently in Christian than in secular authors; the opposite is the case with the verb ἐπιδημέω and the noun ἐπιδημία, however, which are used more frequently by secular than by Christian authors. The more common Greek substantives to describe people not living in their native area were ξένος or φυγάς (e.g., Plutarch *Mor., Exil.* 601A; 607A, B).

35   See Plutarch *Mor., Exil.* 599.3; 607.17; Seneca the

Roman Empire in the first century CE, there were large numbers of people living in places other than their native lands.[36] In this verse, however, the word is used metaphorically,[37] and its association with "elect" and "diaspora" indicates that its origin lies in the story of Abraham rather than in the political situation of the first century.[38] Used of Christians, it describes the fact that because of their unwillingness to adopt the mores of their surrounding society,[39] they can expect the disdainful treatment often accorded exiles (e.g., 1 Pet 4:3–4).[40] It refers for that reason less to the notion of Christians disdaining the temporal because of their longing for their eternal, heavenly home,[41] with its implications of withdrawal from secular society, than to the notion that despite such treatment, they must never-

theless continue to practice their faith in the midst of those who abuse them (e.g., 2:12; 3:9, 15b–16; 4:19).[42]

The term διασπορά ("diaspora") is, like ἐκλεκτός (elect), drawn from Jewish tradition.[43] Because of that fact, some commentators have concluded that the letter was addressed to Jewish Christians.[44] The whole tenor of 1 Peter, however, argues for this to be metaphorical, and hence to refer to all Christians,[45] who, like the exiled Jews, lived as strangers in their surrounding culture.[46] It is thus closely linked with παρεπίδημος ("exile"), since both point to Christians as people who share values other than those of the surrounding world,[47] with the implication that, as a result, they will suffer for their nonconformity. Thus these opening words set the pattern for the ethical admonitions that center on the need to live in

Elder Contr. 6.2; cf. Judge, Social Pattern 28.

36 E.g., Seneca (Ep., Ad Helv. 6.4), who remarks that no major city is without a large proportion of people from elsewhere ("nulla non magnam partem peregrinae multitudinis habet"); I owe this reference to Phillip H. de Lacy and Benedict Einarson (Plutarch's Moralia [LCL; Cambridge: Harvard University Press, 1959] 7.514 n. 2).

37 So also Bovon, "Foi chrétienne," 40; Best, 70; Russell, "Eschatology," 79; Thurston, "Interpreting First Peter," 174; on whether it refers to the political status of believers prior to their conversion, see the Introduction § III, "Readers."

38 So also Schelkle, 19; Blendinger, "Kirche als Fremdlingschaft," 126.

39 So also, e.g., Goppelt, 80; Schelkle, 20.

40 When Reicke (76) argues for the implication that the readers are to "compare themselves with the Jews of the dispersion who, in the Greco-Roman cities, were legally treated as resident aliens without the rights of citizenship," he overstates the case, since in fact there were Jews who were also Roman citizens; cf. Josephus Ant. 14.228, 232, 234, 237, 240; Vit. 423 (himself); Ap. 2.41–42.

41 This has long been a popular position; see Boismard, "Liturgie" [2], 181; Beare, 75; Wand, 37; van Unnik, "Christianity," 79; Harrison, "Exegetical Studies" [97], 207; P. Benedikt Schwank, "L'Epître (1 P 3,8–15)," AsSeign 59 (1966) 20.

42 I owe this insight originally to John H. Elliott, both from his published works and from conversations with him. It is also an emphasis of Goppelt; see esp. "Prinzipien," and "Mission ou Révolution? La responsabilité du chrétien dans la société d'après la Première Epître de Pierre" (trans. A. Greiner), Positions lutheriennes 194 (1969) 202–16.

43 The word, rare in secular Greek, appears in the LXX twelve times, in the NT twice (John 7:35; Jas 1:1), and frequently in Christian and Jewish writers. The dispersion of the Jews resulted from the exile and was understood in the OT as punishment, e.g., Deut 28:25; Jer 13:13–14; 34:17–22; see further Michaels, 8; Schelkle, 19.

44 E.g., John Albert Bengel, Gnomon of the New Testament (trans. A. R. Fausset; 5. vols.; Edinburgh: Clark, 1859) 2.727. Kelly (40) notes that was true of the Greek fathers, but not of Jerome or Augustine. That there were Jews in the general area, see Philo Leg. Gaj. 245, 281. See also the Introduction § III, "Readers."

45 So also Bigg, 91; Harrison, "Exegetical Studies" [97], 209; Thurston, "Interpreting First Peter," 171; Richard, "Christology," 123. Gourbillon ("La Première Epître," 42) relates the term to the Hellenists dispersed following the death of Stephen (Acts 8:1, 4; 11:19), although that may be to put too fine a point on it.

46 So, e.g., Michaels, 6; Gerhard May, "Die Zeit ist da, dass das Gericht angänge am Hause Gottes," in Franklin Clark Fry, ed., Geschichtswirklichkeit und Glaubensbewährung (Festschrift Fr. Miller; Stuttgart: Evangelisches Verlagswerk, 1967) 44; that this did not imply withdrawal from contact with that world, see above. Tarrech ("Le milieu," 397) wrongly links such isolation to his notion that the readers lived in a rural rather than an urban situation.

47 So also Senior, 9; Wolff, "Christ und Welt," 334; Schelkle, 19;

a potentially hostile world as true followers of Christ. It also anticipates the argument, developed later in the epistle, that the Christians are the new people of God.[48]

The diaspora is defined by the following references to five areas.[49] While there is no unanimity on whether the areas were intended to be Roman provinces, or why they were put in their present order,[50] it is clear that they embrace the northern half of the peninsula of Asia Minor. Although there is some overlap with the area of Paul's missionary activity (Galatia), they include areas he did not, or was forbidden to, visit (Cappadocia, Asia, and Bithynia).[51] These areas, along with Pontus, are included in the list of places from which people had come who were present in Jerusalem at Pentecost (Acts 2:9), indicating that the Christian mission was carried on there by others, not by Paul.[52] It is likely therefore that 1 Peter is intended not so much to show the agreement between Peter and Paul as to address areas in which Paul did not found churches.[53]

Excursus: Area Addressed in 1:1

The area included in the opening verse of 1 Peter (Pontus, Galatia, Cappadocia, Asia, Bithynia) was part of the Anatolian peninsula, which was very important in the mission of the early church, and appears to have been Christianized very rapidly.[54] The five areas named cover virtually the entire peninsula except for the regions south of the Taurus Mountains, in all some 300,000 square miles.[55] It was not a homogeneous area, either in terms of culture—while in general this area was very Greek in its culture,[56] Asia, Bithynia, and Pontus were more completely Hellenized, Galatia and especially Cappadocia to a lesser extent[57]—or in terms of wealth—while the area as a whole was prosperous, there was great inequality in its distribution of wealth,[58] a general characteristic of the Roman Empire at this time. The area enjoyed for the most part competent administration on the part of the Romans during the time 1 Peter was written,[59]

48 E.g., Wolff, "Christ und Welt," 334; see also n. 18 above.
49 Like διασπορᾶς, their case is the genitive of place; see, e.g., Selwyn, 118.
50 For further discussion of these problems, see "Excursus: Area Addressed in 1:1."
51 According to Acts 16:6–7, the Holy Spirit forbade Paul to preach in either Asia or Bithynia. Although he later reached Ephesus (Asia), Acts is clear he did not found the church there (18:24—19:1; cf. 19:22–41; 21:17–38; see also Eph 1:15); but see 1 Cor 16:8–9, where, in light of Rom 15:20, one would assume he did found the church there. Elliott ("Peter, Silvanus and Mark," 261) notes there is no mention of Paul having been in Cappadocia. Thus the force of the argument of Brown et al. (Peter, 151) that the author of 1 Peter could address churches founded by Paul, since that is what the author of 1 Clement did when he wrote to Corinth, would be limited to Galatia.
52 So, e.g., Brown and Meier, Antioch and Rome, 131–32; Bigg, 73; cf. also Selwyn, 45; Michaels, 9.
53 On this point see also Elliott, "Peter, Silvanus and Mark," 261.
54 On the rapidity, see Dickey, "Conditions," 414–15; Leonhard Goppelt, Christentum und Judentum im ersten und zweiten Jahrhundert (BFCTh 2/55; Gütersloh: Bertelsmann, 1954) 246. While Acts 16:6–7 records that Paul was forbidden to preach in Asia or Bithynia, the reference to people present at Pentecost from this area (Pontus, Cappadocia, Asia) probably reflects early mission activity in that area; so

also Bigg, 72. On the importance of this area for Christianity, see Sherman E. Johnson, "Early Christianity in Asia Minor," JBL (1958) 1; idem, "Unresolved Questions," 181. It is difficult to account for the judgment of Beare (74) that when 1 Peter was written (in his judgment in the time of Pliny's trip to Bithynia and Pontus), except for Asia, "the Christian cause was feeble and its adherents few and far between," especially in light of Pliny's complaint that temples, religious festivals, and meat markets had been all but abandoned because of Christian influence (Ep. 10.96).
55 Michaels, 4.
56 E.g., Lepelley, "Le contexte," 53; see also Johnson, "Unresolved Questions," 182; Goppelt, 29. A highly ornate style of Greek was termed "Asiatic," because of its place of origin; for a description see Quintilian Inst. 12.10.12; cf. Petronius Satyr. 2; see also the Introduction § I.A, "Language."
57 Best, 16.
58 Cranfield, 29. For a discussion of the various kinds of land tenure in Asia Minor, see Dickey, "Conditions," 406–8.
59 Suetonius (Vit. 8.2) claims that because of the oversight exercised by Domitian, at no time were the governors of provinces more honest or just; see also Magie, Roman Rule, 1.578–79.

and was a scene of continuing and extensive road building.[60]

Bithynia lay in the northwestern portion of Asia Minor where it formed the southern shore of the Black Sea. It came under Roman power when its king, Nicomedes IV, bequeathed it to Rome at the time of his death in 74 BCE.[61] In 64 BCE Pompey combined it with the region of Pontus, the former kingdom of Mithradates, and put it under the governor of the province of Bithynia. At that point the "double" province of Bithynia-Pontus came into existence.[62]

Pontus lay to the east of Bithynia, and formed with it a large portion of the southern shore of the Black Sea. Although an area called Pontus had been part of the province of Bithynia-Pontus since 64 BCE, it was extended when in 64 CE, in the reign of Nero, King Polemo II retired and turned his kingdom over to the Romans.[63] At first incorporated into the province of Galatia, it later was joined to the already existing Bithynia-Pontus to enlarge that province eastward.[64] Because of Trajan's desire to correct financial abuses in the provinces, he took control about 110 CE of what had been since the time of Augustus the senatorial province of Pontus-Bithynia, and sent Pliny to set matters in order.[65] It was an area where by that time Christianity had taken a firm and broad hold.[66]

Galatia became a province of the Roman Empire under Augustus in 25 BCE when King Amyntas was killed preserving his territory in the Taurus Mountains, and his sons were prevented from inheriting his domain.[67] As originally constituted, it stretched from the Paphlagonian Mountains in the north to the Taurus Mountains in the south, and contained a variety of peoples and territories.[68] When in 72 CE the provinces were reorganized by Vespasian, Galatia, enlarged by the addition of Polemo and Lesser Armenia, was combined with Cappadocia to form a single administrative unit that covered virtually all of eastern Asia Minor.[69] This area in turn was divided during the rule of Trajan into two provinces, with Galatia comprising roughly the territories to the west and Cappadocia those to the east.[70] It remained one of the less Hellenized provinces, particularly the interior areas. It is the one of two provinces mentioned in 1 Peter in which there is also a report of Pauline travel (the other is Asia).

Cappadocia became a Roman province under Tiberius in 17 CE. The aged king of Cappadocia, Archelaus, was summoned by Tiberius to Rome on charges of treason,[71] and although not convicted, he was detained and died in Rome, whereupon emperor and Senate jointly declared Cappadocia a Roman province under the supervision of the emperor.[72] Combined with Galatia by Vespasian and separated again by Trajan, Cappadocia was, along with Galatia, one of the least Hellenized of the provinces of Asia Minor.[73] Its mention in Acts 2:9 indicates early Christian missionary activity there, although that is all that is known of it.[74]

Asia was the name given to the province formed from the kingdom of Pergamum (Pergamon), which, because of the bequest of its king, Attalus III, passed with his death in 133 BCE into Roman possession.[75] Originally a senatorial province, it came finally under

---

60 Such building is attested under Claudius, Vespasian, Titus, and Domitian; see Magie, *Roman Rule*, 1.570–71, 579. On the other hand, the imperial messenger service inaugurated by Augustus proved a burden on the area, since the various cities were obliged to bear the expense of riders and mounts for this service; see Magie, *Roman Rule*, 1.487.

61 Magie, *Roman Rule*, 1.320; Johannes Weiss, "Asia Minor in the Apostolic Time," *The New Schaff-Herzog Encyclopedia of Religious Knowledge* (ed. S. M. Jackson; New York: Funk and Wagnalls, 1908) 1.316.

62 Magie, *Roman Rule*, 1.369.

63 Suetonius *Vit.* 6.18.

64 See Magie, *Roman Rule*, 1.561.

65 Magie, *Roman Rule*, 1.596–97; *Pliny: Letters* (trans. William Melmoth; rev. W. M. L. Hutchinson; LCL; Cambridge: Harvard University Press, 1940), "Introduction," 1.xiii; Pliny *Ep.* 10.32. Pliny's mission probably also had to do with Trajan's desire to secure the lines of communication for his planned invasion of the Parthian territory to the east; cf. Magie, *Roman Rule*, 1.606–7. On the contentiousness

of the area, especially Bithynia, see, e.g., Dio Chrysostom *Or.* 48.4; they were at odds with their Roman governors, whom they accused of maladministration, e.g., Pliny *Ep.* 4.9; 5.20; 6.13; see also Tacitus *Ann.* 14.47; 16.18–19.

66 C. J. Hemer, "The Address of 1 Peter," *ExpT* 89 (1977/78) 241; Pliny *Ep.* 10.96.

67 Magie, *Roman Rule*, 1.453; Wand, 42.

68 Magie, *Roman Rule*, 1.458.

69 Hemer, "Address," 242; Magie, *Roman Rule*, 1.574.

70 Magie, *Roman Rule*, 1.605.

71 Magie, *Roman Rule*, 1.491; Suetonius (*Vit.* 3.37) says Tiberius lured rulers who had aroused his suspicions to Rome by flattering promises ("per blanditias atque promissa").

72 Magie, *Roman Rule*, 1.495.

73 According to Magie (*Roman Rule*, 1.493), Strabo says that at the time of Augustus only two settlements could be called "cities," both in the western portion of the land. A similar situation is reflected when Suetonius (*Vit.* 8.4) notes that Vespasian was obliged to send additional legions to Cappadocia "because of

the control of the emperor Vespasian as part of his policy of increased control of senatorial provinces.[76] It was one of the most Hellenized,[77] most thickly populated, and wealthiest of the Roman provinces.[78] The province was the scene of a devastating earthquake in 17 CE that destroyed twelve major cities,[79] something that apparently occurred with alarming frequency[80] but it did little to dampen Asia's wealth or culture. If its most famous city was Pergamum,[81] there were a host of other large and wealthy cities, many of which played an important role in the early church.[82] It was apparently an early and important location of Christian missionary activity.[83]

It is difficult to achieve clarity on whether the author intended the five areas named in 1:1 to designate Roman provinces. That the author did not in fact give official names is clear, since by any reckoning of time of writing, Bithynia and Pontus will have constituted a single province.[84] If, however, one wishes to argue that the author *intended* by those names to indicate provinces rather than districts,[85] one will probably have to argue for authorial ignorance in geographical matters.[86] Since such penetration of the author's intention must of necessity remain speculative, it is probably best simply to take the geographic designations as intending to include the part of Asia Minor north of the Taurus Mountains, perhaps deliberately excluding such Pauline missionary areas in Asia Minor as Pamphylia (Acts 13:13), Pisidia (13:14; 14:1), Lycaonia (14:6), Cilicia (15:41), and Phrygia (16:6).[87]

A further difficulty consists in inferring the reason for the order in which the names are given. Perhaps the most common solution is to propose that the names represent the areas in the order in which the bearer of the letter would traverse them,[88] beginning perhaps at the Pontian port of Sinope or Amisus,[89] moving south to Cappadocia, then west to Galatia and Asia, and finally north to Bithynia.[90] This would be only an approximate route, however, since a person moving south from Pontus would first traverse part of Galatia before reaching Cappadocia.[91] Why a messenger from Rome would bypass the nearer Bithynia to land at Pontus involves further speculation: perhaps because the persecution was strongest in Pontus;[92] perhaps as the latest converted they faced most acutely the problem of converting their lives from former beliefs and customs to those of the Christian faith;[93] perhaps the Christians in

incessant incursions by barbarians" ("propter adsiduos barbarorum incursus"), presumably because the population was too sparse to deter them.

74 Hort (17) thus exaggerates only slightly when he says of Cappadocia "we have no primitive Christian record."

75 Preisker (Windisch) 51; Dickey, "Conditions," 396.

76 Magie, *Roman Rule,* 1.568–69.

77 Seneca (*Ep., Ad Helv.* 7.2) refers to a host of Athenians living in Asia.

78 Cranfield, 28. Pliny the Elder (*Hist. nat.* 33.52.148–49) claims luxury was first introduced into Italy with the conquest of Asia, and that Asia's reception as a province hence dealt a serious blow to Roman morals.

79 It was more terrifying because it occurred at night; Tacitus *Ann.* 2.47; cf. Suetonius *Vit.* 3.47.

80 See Seneca *Ep.* 91.9.

81 So Pliny the Elder *Hist. nat.* 5.33.126.

82 A list of them can be found in Rev 2:1—3:22.

83 Paul spent some time there (1 Cor 16:8–9; according to Acts 19:10, two years), although his mission in the province was not altogether successful (2 Cor 1:8). The province is also mentioned in Acts 2:9.

84 Also noted by Fitzmyer, "First Peter," 364.

85 E.g., with no qualification, Spicq, 12, 41; Knopf, 1; as highly probable, Schutter, *Hermeneutic,* 8; Brox, 25; Schiwy, 33; with some hesitancy, Best, 14–15;

86 As does, e.g., Brox, 25–26.

87 With, e.g., Reicke, 77, and against Schelkle, 1, who thinks 1 Peter intended to include all of Asia Minor, since otherwise the Pauline missionary areas to the south would be omitted, something Schelkle thinks unlikely.

88 Sylva, "Studies," 159; Selwyn, 119; both cite the earlier suggestion of Hort, 17; see also Wand, 31; Kelly, 42; Spicq, 41; Goppelt, 28; Hart, 40; Michaels, 9.

89 Sinope, e.g., Hort, 176; Amisus, e.g., Hemer, "Address," 240. Hemer gives a complete summary of geographical possibilities, including a map of possible roads.

90 E.g., Schutter, *Hermeneutic,* 8.

91 So Hemer, "Address," 241.

92 Sylva, "Studies," 159.

93 Goppelt, 29.

Tarrech, "Le milieu," 117–18. To argue, as does Goppelt (27–28), that they represent both districts and provinces is to beg the question.

Pontus conceived of a mission to these areas and asked Peter for guidance.[94]

Another attempt to account for the order which moves roughly from west to east has been to link it to the author's location: the order moves from the area nearest to the area furthest for an author writing in Chaldean Babylon;[95] or conversely, it moves from the area furthest to the area nearest for one writing in Rome.[96] Since undocumentable speculation attends all such attempts to account for the order, the best solution is probably to admit that the reason for the order can no longer be recovered with any degree of certainty.[97]

■ **2** The triad of prepositional phrases with the references to God the Father, the Holy Spirit, and Jesus Christ in this salutation has parallels in NT writings (Matt 28:19; 2 Cor 13:13 [v. 14 in many English versions]; Eph 4:6; Jude 20–21; cf. 1 Cor 12:4–6; 2 Thess 2:13–14), but it is unique among the salutations of the letters found in the NT.[98] This construction, along with the other NT passages, displays the kind of reflections that eventuated in the trinitarian formulations embodied in the Nicene Creed, but it is probably anachronistic to refer here to "trinitarian formulations."[99] The referent of the divine activity described in these three phrases is to be construed as ἐκλεκτοῖς[100] rather than ἀπόστολος, since the apostolicity of Peter is not at issue in this letter, while the reality of divine election for estranged and persecuted

Christians goes to the heart of the problem this epistle is addressing.[101]

In the first of the prepositional phrases (κατὰ πρόγνωσιν θεοῦ πατρός), "foreknowledge" (πρόγνωσιν) refers not simply to God's ability to know what is to occur, but also to the fact that what occurs does so in accordance with (κατά) his plan.[102] The phrase is thus meant to point to the divine initiative in the readers' election as Christians,[103] and to assure them that the ensuing situation of peril is not the result of accident or divine oversight, but is indeed part of God's plan for them.[104] The identification of God as Father (πατρός) points to the Christian understanding of the intimate and loving relationship of God with his people,[105] and adds further assurance that God's plan for them is gracious and redemptive, despite contrary appearances in their life in the world.

If the first phrase gives the plan in accordance with which the readers have become elect sojourners, the second phrase (ἐν ἁγιασμῷ πνεύματος) gives the means by which that election occurred: it is through the setting apart (ἁγιασμῷ—instrumental dative)[106] accomplished by the Spirit (πνεύματος—subjective genitive).[107] Mention of such activity by the Spirit is not unique to 1 Peter (cf. Rom 15:16; 2 Thess 2:13; it can also be attributed to the agency of Christ, as in 1 Cor 1:2), and gives a fuller explanation for the common reference to

---

94   Bigg, 70; cf. Best, 16.

95   Bengel, *Gnomon*, 727, 759.

96   So Tarrech ("Le milieu," 119), who finds the clue in the geographic order mentioned in Acts 2:9–11, which moves counterclockwise beginning with the east.

97   So also Bauer, 14; Schelkle, 1; Reicke, 77.

98   Vanhoye, "1 Pierre," 105; Delling, "Der Bezug," 107; for a comparison of the elements in 2 Thessalonians, 2 Corinthians, and Matthew, see Selwyn, 247–50.

99   So Schelkle, 24. Hort (18) notes correctly that each phrase sets forth "the operation of the Father, the Holy Spirit, and the Son, respectively."

100   With Francis H. Agnew, C.M., "1 Peter 1:2—An Alternative Translation," *CBQ* 45 (1983) 69; Schelkle, 20; Goppelt, 83. There is no warrant in the structure of vv. 1–2 to limit the reference to ἐκλεκτοῖς to individual phrases such as κατὰ . . . πατρός (e.g., Reicke, 77; cf. Bengel, *Gnomon*, 727; Wand, 38) or ἐν πνεύματι . . . (cf. Schweizer, 18).

101   With Michaels, 4; Kelly, 42; see also Harrison,

"Exegetical Studies" [97], 326. The suggestion that the referent includes both ἀπόστολος and ἐκλεκτοῖς (e.g., Selwyn, 119; cf. Hart, 40; Best, 70; Beare, 75–76) is thus unnecessary.

102   So also Cranfield, 31; Schelkle, 20; Spicq, 42; Goppelt, 85; Furnish, "Elect Sojourners," 5.

103   Schelkle, 20; Selwyn, 65.

104   For similar use of "foreknowledge" to identify God's plan, see 1 Pet 1:20; Acts 2:23; Rom 8:29; 11:2.

105   While Greeks could address Zeus as "Father" (e.g., Dio Chrysostom *Or.* 36.35–36; see 1.42; 12.22, 74; Seneca *Ep.* 107.11), the term tended to be thought of in physical terms with Zeus as begetter of the race of humans as well as of the gods (e.g., Dio Chrysostom *Or.* 12.22; 53.12; Seneca, *Hercules Furens* 64–68; so also Schelkle, 21). God is also known as Father in the OT (e.g., 1 Chr 29:10; Isa 63:16; 64:8; Jer 3:19; 31:9; Mal 2:10), but there within the framework of God's covenantal election of Israel, even when the term "beget" is used (as in Deut 32:6, 18). Schelkle (21) notes its absence from the Qumran literature.

106   Beare, 76; Best, 71; Schelkle, 21. Selwyn (199)

Christians as "ones set apart" (ἅγιος, e.g., Acts 9:13; 1 Cor 6:2; 2 Cor 1:1; 13:12; Eph 1:1, 18; 3:18; Phil 1:1; 4:22; Col 1:2; 2 Thess 1:10; Heb 6:10; Jude 3), that is, set apart for God, and thus "pure" or "holy."[108]

The third phrase admits of no easy understanding. The major problems concern the force of the preposition εἰς, the meaning of the phrase ῥαντισμὸν αἵματος ("sprinkling of blood") and its relationship to ὑπακοή (obedience), and the relationship of both to Ἰησοῦ Χριστοῦ ("Jesus Christ").

The significance of the preposition εἰς, if it has here its normal telic force, is to indicate the goal and thus the purpose of God's plan carried out by the Spirit, namely, "obedience" and "sprinkling." In this context, such obedience is probably to be understood in the broad sense in which it is also used by Paul: as the acceptance of the obligations incumbent on those redeemed by Christ, and thus as a virtual substitute for faith.[109]

Standing in parallel to obedience is the phrase ῥαντισμὸν αἵματος ("sprinkling of blood"), also to be construed with the preposition εἰς, and giving the second result of the divine activity. The genitive Ἰησοῦ Χριστοῦ indicates the source of the blood, and gives to the phrase the meaning "the sprinkling of Jesus Christ's blood." The meaning of the phrase is ambiguous, however; to what does it refer? The most obvious inference would be to see it as a reference to Jesus' death on the cross,[110] but even then the meaning of the phrase remains obscure: what can it mean that Christians are elect sojourners according to God's plan carried out by the Spirit for the purpose of obedience and *Christ's sacrifice on the cross*? To

construe the genitive Ἰησοῦ Χριστοῦ as subjective, making Christ the one who sprinkles the blood: "(for the purpose of) the sprinkling of blood by Jesus Christ," helps only marginally unless that genitive could also be construed with ὑπακοήν ("obedience"). If so construed it would refer to Christ's obedience[111] and to his sacrifice on the cross, but that would lead one far afield from the intention of these verses, namely, to show the divine plan and power that enable Christians to become elect.

If, on the other hand, the preposition εἰς could have causative force ("because"), a meaning it can carry, the phrase would provide the reason why Christians can be elect sojourners by divine plan and power: it is because of Jesus' obedience, which led him to his self-sacrifice on the cross.[112] This is an attractive suggestion and would make good sense in the context. The difficulty rests in the fact that in the immediately following verses 3–5, εἰς is used three times with its normally telic force, indicating the likelihood that the author also meant it to have that force in this phrase.

A different resolution of the problem consists in the proposal that the relationship of the genitive Ἰησοῦ Χριστοῦ has objective force with relation to ὑπακοήν— "obedience *to* Jesus Christ"—and possessive force with relation to ῥαντισμὸν αἵματος—"blood *of* Jesus Christ." Yet that demands that the same genitive Ἰησοῦ Χριστοῦ function two different ways in the same sentence, something of a grammatical monstrosity and surely confusing to the reader/listener.[113] A similar solution lies in the suggestion that ὑπακοήν forms a hendiadys with ῥαντισμόν indicating that Christ's blood seals a

---

prefers dative of sphere.

107 The point is not that the human spirit is sanctified, which would require the objective genitive, but that sanctification occurs by means of the divine agent. Similar NT uses confirm the subjective genitive here; so also Hort, 21; Wand, 39; Selwyn, 119, 249; Michaels, 11; Schelkle, 22: "genitivus auctoris." Mention of the Spirit as agent of God's power is rarer in the OT than in the NT, though of course it is present, e.g., 1 Sam 16:13; Isa 11:2.

108 Bigg, 92.

109 E.g., Rom 1:5: ὑπακοὴν πίστεως, "obedience that consists in faith"; 10:16: "not all obeyed the gospel"; see Kelly, 44; Moffatt, 91; Best, 71. Obedience as used here indicates that faith demands appropriate action, not merely mental assent; so also Sieffert, "Die Heilsbedeutung," 377; Hort, 22. The word

ὑπακοή was apparently unknown to secular Greek, and occurred only once in the LXX (2 Sam 22:36). Paul used it some twelve times, 1 Peter three times; it was then used widely by later Christian writers.

110 E.g., Bigg, 93. Less likely is the view of Hall ("For to This," 142) that it means sharing in Christ's suffering, a theme prominent in 1 Peter but unlikely to be the point here.

111 Delling ("Der Bezug," 106) takes it in that sense.

112 This case has been carefully argued by Agnew, "Translation," passim.

113 This solution was adopted by the *RSV* and continued in the *NRSV*; it is admitted as a possibility by Hart (41) but correctly termed "awkward" by Agnew ("Translation," 70). Such a translation presumes the Greek to read εἰς ὑπακοήν Ἰησοῦ Χριστοῦ καὶ ῥαντισμὸν αἵματος αὐτοῦ, thus attributing each

covenant that requires obedience from the people.[114]

The most likely solution is to understand ὑπακοήν as used absolutely, with no relation to the genitive Ἰησοῦ Χριστοῦ. That genitive in turn would then be construed exclusively with ῥαντισμὸν αἵματος,[115] with that whole second phrase understood as identifying a further result of God's plan and power. The phrase would then read "for obedience, and for the sprinkling of the blood of Christ." But in that context, to what does the sprinkling refer?[116] Some have concluded that it refers to Christian baptism,[117] a conclusion further strengthened by the inclusion here of the triadic reference to God used in the baptismal ceremony (e.g., Matt 28:19),[118] with the additional reference in this formulation to action by the Spirit.[119] The reference here to blood rather than to the water used in baptism could perhaps be explained by an understanding of baptism similar to that of Paul, whereby in the baptismal act the person is united with Christ in his death.[120] Identifying baptism as being sprinkled by Christ's blood is not, however, part of Paul's discussion, nor is it a prominent feature in early Christian baptismal rituals, or even in references to the significance of baptism.

A more direct parallel to the sprinkling of blood, however, is found in the OT account of the establishment of the covenant between God and Israel (Exod 24:3–8).[121] In that ceremony, the people pledge their obedience (24:3), after which a sacrifice is made and blood is sprinkled on the altar (24:4–6). After a second pledge to obey God (24:7), the remaining blood is sprinkled on the people (24:8), and the covenant is declared to be in force. Thus the two elements in the ceremony, obedience and sprinkling of blood, reflect the order and content of 1 Pet 1:2,[122] and present a closer parallel than do elements of the Christian baptismal ceremony, where the sprinkling is with water, not blood. When the author refers to Christians as a people of particular possession, a kingdom of priests, and a holy

---

genitival use to a separate word. That is not, however, the way the text reads, and ought to be adopted only if no other possibility exists.

114 Beare, 76–77; the *NEB* apparently followed this suggestion. The covenantal background of the phrase is discussed more fully below.

115 In agreement with van Unnik, "Redemption," 62; Michaels, 11.

116 The somewhat similar phrase in *Barn.* 5.1, if anything more confusing than the phrase here, affirms that the shedding of Christ's blood brought about forgiveness of sin, a point also made in 1 John 1:7. As Beare (77) correctly notes, such ideas of atonement or vicarious suffering are absent here (though hinted at in 1:18–19); but see Kelly, 44.

117 Schiwy, 35. Goppelt (86) finds this the explanation for the combination of sprinkling and obedience, a combination which is otherwise "überraschend" "surprising"; because of a possible influence of 1QS 3.6–8, a description of the Essene initiation ritual, Goppelt suggests that v. 2 reflects a Palestinian-Syrian baptismal catechism (cf. *Did.* 7.1) influenced by the Essenes, which then influenced the liturgy of the Roman community, and is reflected here. However, the association of obedience and sprinkling of blood in the covenant ritual renders such speculation unprofitable. Also unlikely is the attempt of Bieder (*Grund und Kraft*, 15 n. 13) to find in the combination of obedience and sprinkling references respectively to baptism and Eucharist. The suggestion of Perdelwitz (*Mysterienreligion*, 97–98) that the notion of sprinkling derives from the use of the

Taurobolium in the Attis mystery has been rightly rejected (Kelly, 44: "absurdly far-fetched"; van Unnik, "Redemption," 63: "impossible").

118 Selwyn ("Persecutions," 60) finds the theme of baptism announced by that formulation in this verse.

119 Kelly (43) sees baptism as the moment of sanctification mentioned in the phrase ἐν ἁγιασμῷ πνεύματος ("through the sanctification of the Spirit").

120 E.g., Rom 6:3–5, 8, 11; Paul does not mention Christ's shed blood in this discussion, and the imagery seems to imply union with Christ's death (perhaps even entry into his tomb) as the initiate enters the water, rather than that union being effected by being sprinkled with Christ's shed blood.

121 Sieffert ("Die Heilsbedeutung," 379) notes that three ceremonies in the OT required the shedding of blood: covenant (Exod 24), dedication of priests (Lev 8:30), and the purification of lepers (Lev 14:1–7); his observation that the shedding of blood in all three instances means sanctification (381) is more appropriate to this context than his conclusion that because of the reference to Christians as a priesthood in 1 Pet 2:5, 9, the author has in mind priestly consecration (383; so also Cranfield, 32).

122 The second account of obedience and sprinkling in Exod 24:7–8 is most probably the specific reference in the author's mind.

nation in 2:9, he is drawing further on covenantal language (Exod 19:5–6), confirming his acquaintance with, and use of language from, this event.[123]

If, as seems most probable, this is the background of the verse,[124] then its force will be that Christians have become elect[125] sojourners in accordance with God's plan empowered by the sanctifying action[126] of the Spirit to the end that they be the people of a new covenant,[127] which like the covenant with Israel entails obedience and sacrifice, in this case the sacrifice of Christ.

In the final greeting, the word $\chi\acute{\alpha}\rho\iota\varsigma$ ("grace") is probably less a Christian adaptation of the normal Greek salutation $\chi\alpha\acute{\iota}\rho\epsilon\iota\nu$ ("greetings")[128] than it is an adaptation of the normal Jewish epistolary salutation[129] that regularly also included the word $\epsilon\acute{\iota}\rho\acute{\eta}\nu\eta$ ("peace"; Heb. שלום). The two words together include therefore the entire range of divine blessing.[130] The final wish for increase ($\pi\lambda\eta\theta\upsilon\nu\theta\epsilon\acute{\iota}\eta$),[131] unknown in the earlier Pauline letters, became increasingly common in later Christian letters.[132]

---

123 The currency of language reflecting this covenantal ceremony is shown in Heb 9:11–22, where the use of Christ's blood in terms of new covenant ratification is thematic; cf. also 10:22; 12:24. It is probably not necessary to link it to proselyte admission to the covenant in order to see this background, although that admission, which required a blood sacrifice (see van Unnik, "Redemption," 62 et passim), is further indication of the currency of this idea.

124 This is a widely held conclusion: D. C. Arichae, Jr., "God or Christ?" 413; Selwyn, 67, 120; Cranfield, 32; Michaels, 12; Richard, "Christology," 134; Beare, "Teaching," 294; Deterding, "Exodus Motifs," 60; Fransen, "Une homélie," 32; Hort, 24; Wand, 39; Holmer and de Boor, 26. The similarity to 1QS 4.21: "(God) will sprinkle upon him the spirit of truth like waters for purification," cited by Michael A. Knibb (*The Qumran Community* [Cambridge Commentaries on Writings of the Jewish and Christian World 200 BC to AD 200; Cambridge: Cambridge University Press, 1987] 2.101) is remote.

125 "Elect" is itself a covenantal term; cf. Isa 43:20c–21.

126 Again, such sanctification, or setting apart, also belongs to the language of the covenant; see its repeated use in the context of covenantal law giving in Lev 11:44–45; 19:2; 20:7, 26, and its use in 1 Pet 1:16.

127 For van Unnik ("Redemption," 63), the meaning of

the phrase is "admission into the covenant"; see also Kelly, 44.

128 So Berger, "Apostelbrief," 201; but see Hort (23), who suggests that $\chi\acute{\alpha}\rho\iota\varsigma$ "combine(s) the force of the two Hebrew words" חן and חסד. The form $\chi\alpha\acute{\iota}\rho\epsilon\iota\nu$, used in Jas 1:1, occurs frequently in later Christian letters, e.g., the opening of the letters of Ignatius (the sole exception is *Phil.*), *Barn.* 1.1.

129 So also Kelly, 45.

130 $X\acute{\alpha}\rho\iota\varsigma$ is the NT word for God's blessing bestowed through Christ; $\epsilon\acute{\iota}\rho\acute{\eta}\nu\eta$ (Heb. שלום) refers to all the blessings God bestows, as Kelly (45) observes; see also Cranfield, 33.

131 The passive form of the verb "multiply" ($\pi\lambda\eta\theta\upsilon\nu\theta\epsilon\acute{\iota}\eta$) is probably a "reverential passive," a form used among Jews to avoid mentioning God's name, or even the word "God." The form passed into Christian parlance (e.g., Matt 5:4; Luke 6:21; Rom 2:13). On this point, see Arichae, "God or Christ?" 413. In the optative mood, the verb expresses the wish of the author.

132 E.g., 2 Pet 1:2; Jude 2; Polycarp *Phil.* opening; *1 Clem.* opening. This is a further indication of the later date of 1 Peter.

Analysis

Following the epistolary opening, these ten verses provide an introduction to the subject matter of the letter. Cast in the form of a singe if rather complex sentence,[1] these verses divide themselves into three major parts, the second and third with two subparts each, by means of relative clauses introduced with relative pronouns.[2] The major divisions occur at 1:6 and 1:10, each introduced with a preposition and a relative pronoun (1:6, ἐν ᾧ; 1:10, περί ἧς). The sections are further subdivided by means of relative pronouns at 1:8 (ὅν) and 1:12 (οἷς), with the concluding verse containing three relative pronouns (οἷς, ἅ, εἰς ἅ), perhaps as a way of indicating the conclusion of this introduction.[3] Thus the sentence has three major sections: 3–5; 6–9, with two subdivisions, 6–7 and 8–9; and 10–12, with two subdivisions, 10–11 and 12.[4]

A different division into three segments comprising vv. 3–7, 8–9, 10–12,[5] sometimes on the basis of a content

that then reflects respectively Father, Jesus, and Holy Spirit, has also been proposed,[6] but such a division is weakened by the mention of Jesus three times in the first section (vv. 3 [bis], 7) and twice in the third (v. 11), thus indicating that the author did not have such a division of subject matter foremost in his mind as he wrote this material. While such a division based on content thus has less to recommend it, there is little question that the triadic reference to God found in v. 2 is also present here, thus linking the epistolary opening to this first sentence.[7]

The complex nature of this opening sentence has also led to the conclusion that the author is here either using or adapting a previously existing hymn,[8] with the mention of rebirth perhaps even suggesting its origin in a baptismal ritual.[9] The difficulty in identifying length of strophes, or even their number, along with the rather elegant compositional elements that appear in the rest of the text of 1 Peter, would suggest to the contrary that

---

1 Reicke, 79. Despite its complexity, it is "eine kunstvolle Periode" "an artistic period" (Windisch, 52). On that basis, Lohse ("Parenesis," 47) judges it to be "clearly distinguished from the rest of the epistle in style." It would probably be closer to say it is an expansion of the style found in such sentences as 1:17–21; 2:1–5; or 4:3–6.

2 So also Dalton, "So That Your Faith," 267–68.

3 Coutts ("Ephesians," 116–17) notes that the introduction to Ephesians (1:3–14) is divided into three parts by the threefold use of the phrase εἰς ἔπαινον δόξης in vv. 6, 12, and 14; see also Schutter, Hermeneutic, 24 n. 25. Such repeated constructions were helpful in indicating the divisions in ancient texts, which did not yet have visual means to do that, and which were in addition virtually always read aloud, whether by an individual or, in the case of NT literature, more often to a group. Such grammatical and syntactic repetitions thus aided the hearer in understanding how the author meant the text to be understood. For the theoretical basis for such a judgment, and further examples, see Paul J. Achtemeier, "Omne verbum sonat: The New Testament and the Oral Environment of Late Western Antiquity," JBL 109 (1990) 3–27.

4 So also Goppelt, 91; Moffatt, 92; Hart, 41; D. Edmond Hiebert, "Peter's Thanksgiving for Our Salvation," Studia Missionalia 29 (1980) 86; Boismard, "Liturgie" [1], 183. While the ἐις ὅν in v. 8 seems to argue against such a division, its close link to the ὅν that precedes it, and its content that amplifies the first phrase, indicate that its rhetorical position is

secondary to that of the ὅν.

5 E.g., Coutts, "Ephesians," 118–19; Schutter (Hermeneutic, 24 n. 25) arrives at this division on the basis of the "obvious seam at 7/8," but, as noted above, that is a seam more similar to the one at 11/12 than those at 5/6 and 9/10.

6 E.g., Bornemann, "Taufrede," 153; cf. A. B. du Toit, "The Significance of Discourse Analysis for New Testament Interpretation and Translation: Introductory Remarks with Special Reference to I Peter 1:3–13," Neot 8 (1974) 68. The attempt by Coutts ("Ephesians," see esp. 118–19) to justify such a division is prejudiced by his forced comparison with Eph 1:3–14 and his speculative attempts to recover the "original form" of the verses in Ephesians.

7 So also Moffatt, 92. The attempt by Hillyer ("Servant," 154) to find in these verses a "string of parallels" to the Aqedah traditions appears forced and hence unconvincing.

8 Stuhlmueller ("Baptism," 214): "undoubtedly a portion of an early Christian hymn." Preisker (Windisch, 52) proposed five strophes of seven or five lines each; the proposal was reviewed with approval by Martin ("Composition," 31).

9 See, e.g., Philipps (Kirche, 17), who assumes it; Brooks ("1 Peter 3:21," 295) accepts and expands the original proposal by Boismard ("Liturgie" [1]); Bornemann ("Taufrede," 146) thinks it part of a baptismal homily based on Psalm 34. Goppelt (91) argues correctly that even if it were a hymn, its original form is no longer recoverable.

these verses are in fact a composition of the author himself.[10] That the verb ἀναγεννάω in the active sense in v. 3 points to a rebegetting rather than a rebirth, a begetting this time by God's word rather than through human agency (1:23), weakens any putative direct derivation from a baptismal liturgy.[11] That baptism was intimately related to the content of these verses is not to be disputed, but that does not justify finding here direct derivation from a baptismal liturgy.[12]

This section therefore functions as the *prooemium*[13] for the discussion to follow, showing how the triune God has established the church as a community of hope by reason of the resurrection of Jesus, with vv. 3–5 discussing the creation of such a living hope and its consequences for the community that follows him, vv. 6–9 pointing to the present joy despite the testing it must undergo, and vv. 10–12 showing that such activity was reflected in earlier times through the divinely prompted searchings of the prophets.[14] In that way the major themes of the ensuing discussion of the present and future fate of the new people of God are announced in these opening verses.[15]

10 With Gerhard Barth, "1 Petrus 1, 3–9 Exegese, Meditation und Predigt," *EstTeol* 6 (1966) 148.

11 Boismard ("Liturgie" [1], 183–86) thought the similarity to Titus 3:4–7, with its reference to the washing of regeneration, showed these verses also to be from a baptismal liturgy, but it is precisely the absence of reference here to any kind of washing that argues against such an origin. The reference to water in John 3:5, where new birth is also discussed, makes the absence of reference to water or washing here all the more telling.

12 Paul's references to baptism in his discussion in Romans 6 do not necessitate the origin of his language in a baptismal liturgy. The importance of baptism for the early church is enough to explain such references to it.

13 So also Dibelius, "Petrusbriefe," 1113; cf. Berger, "Apostelbrief," 226, 229 n. 187. Quintilian, who prefers the implications of Greek προοίμιον (*prooi-mion*) to the Latin *exordium*, defines its purpose as preparing the hearers to listen more readily (the *captatio benevolentiae*) to the subsequent parts of the plea (*Inst.* 4.1.5.; cf. [Cicero] *De ratione dicendi* [*Ad Her.*] 1.7.1). The author of 1 Peter here probably desires to win a favorable hearing for his subsequent discussion by giving an indication of the substance of it.

14 Similarly Martin H. Scharlemann, "An Apostolic Descant (An Exegetical Study of 1 Peter 1:3–12)," *Concordia Journal* 2 (1976) 10; cf. Brox, 59–60. Du Toit ("Significance," 72) summarizes: "From God you have received a glorious expectation of things to come; rejoice in it in spite of affliction."

15 For a careful analysis of the way these verses serve as an introduction to the subsequent discussion in 1 Peter, see David W. Kendall, "The Introductory Character of 1 Peter 1:3–12" (Ph.D. diss., Union Theological Seminary in Virginia, 1984), passim.

1 A New Life and Its Consequences

3   **Blessed be the God and Father of our Lord Jesus Christ, who in accordance with his great mercy has begotten us anew for a living[1] hope through the resurrection of Jesus Christ from the dead, 4/ for an inheritance imperishable and uncorrupted and unfading kept in heaven for you[2] 5/ who are guarded by God's[3] power through faith, for a salvation ready to be revealed at the last time.**

1   A few MSS. (1505, 1852, 2495, some other minuscules, vg^mss, sy, bo) read ζωῆς in place of ζῶσαν, probably as objective genitive ("hope for life").

2   P[72] appears to substitute ἡμᾶς ("us"; supported by a few Vulgate MSS.), to conform to the same word in v. 3, although that reading is also changed in a few minuscules. The only certainty of person comes with the second person verb in v. 6; the first two pronouns in vv. 3, 4 thus remain questionable, and too much should not be made of the shift from first person in v. 3 to second person in v. 4.

3   P[72] omits θεοῦ, thus changing the meaning from "guarded by God" to "powerfully protected," perhaps to emphasize the power of faith.

Analysis

The first segment of the *prooemium* of 1 Peter consists in vv. 3–5, which describe the divine act of rebegetting, and the consequences that follow the resulting new life.[4] Those consequences are designated by a threefold repetition[5] of the preposition εἰς, in each instance followed by a description of one of the consequences: a hope (v. 3), an inheritance (v. 4), and a salvation (v. 5). Further, what is distinctive about this new status is indicated by adjectives that modify those nouns: *living* hope (v. 3); an *imperishable, uncorrupted, unfading* inheritance (v. 4); a salvation *ready* (to be revealed—v. 5). Again, each εἰς phrase concludes with a divine reason for the new condition: resurrection of Jesus (v. 3); power of God (v. 4); activity of God (v. 5—ἀποκαλυφθῆναι is a reverential passive, and implies that the revelation is accomplished by God). In that way the segment is structured by the easily recognizable repetition of the preposition and its following phrases.[6]

Theologically, the opening blessing of God for what he has done, namely, create a new people, places the new life in implied contrast with the old life with its dead hope, its perishable inheritance, and its unreliable salvation. The blessing thus sets the condition upon which what has preceded, and all that follows, depends: it is precisely as a new people that Christians now find themselves in a new situation characterized both by the threat of losing that blessing should they fall back into the old life, and by the promise of keeping the blessing when they live out the reality of the new life. It is the working out of the interrelationship of those two elements of threat and promise that constitutes the content of what follows in this letter.

Finally, the passage contains references to the beginning of the Christian era (Christ's resurrection), its present continuation (Christians are upheld by God's power), and its future consummation (revealing of God's salvation), concepts that will also play a key role in the

---

4   On the basis of discourse analysis, Combrini ("Structure," 35) finds these verses to constitute a separate colon.

5   This part of 1 Peter is marked by a predilection for groups of three, e.g., three prepositional phrases in 1:2; three alliterative adjectives in v. 4; three phrases beginning with εἰς in vv. 3–5; a triad of nouns in v. 7; even the division of this *prooemium* into three segments; on this point see also du Toit, "Significance," 66.

6   This threefold use of εἰς is also recognized by Beare, 82; Michaels, 19; Stanislas Halas, SCJ, "Sens dyna-

mique de l'expression λαὸς εἰς περιποίησιν en 1 P 2,9," *Bib* 65 (1984) 255; du Toit, "Significance," 64. Bengel (*Gnomon*, 728) correctly terms it "a remarkable anaphora." Not all agree: see Cranfield, 39; Brox, 62–63; Shimada, *Formulary Material*, 147 n. 1.

further development of the author's message.

Excursus: Common Baptismal Liturgy Underlying 1 Peter 1:3–5 and Titus 3:5–7

The content of these verses has led to the suggestion that they were derived from the same kind of baptismal material that underlies Titus 3:5–7.[7] Such a suggestion is based on similarities between the two passages, for example, the phrase κατὰ τὸ αὐτοῦ ἔλεος, the appearance in the same passage of the stem κληρονομ- with ἐλπίδα, the association of ἐλπίδα with a form of ζω-, the appearance of words signifying salvation (ἔσωσεν, σωτῆρος in Titus, σωτηρίαν in 1 Peter), and the similarity in concept of the words παλιγγενεσία in Titus 3:5 and ἀναγεννήσας in 1 Pet 1:3.

Yet such similarities show themselves on further examination to be more apparent than real.[8] The phrase κατὰ τὸ αὐτοῦ ἔλεος, modified in 1 Peter with the addition of πολύ, is associated in Titus with the washing of regeneration and renewal by the pouring out of the Holy Spirit, something quite absent from 1 Peter. Other key elements in Titus—the prominence of the notion of justification, as a noun in 3:5 and a verb in 3:7, and the idea of eternal life (also mentioned in Titus 1:2)—are also absent from 1 Peter. Conversely, such key elements in the argument of 1 Peter as the resurrection of Jesus, the current preservation of the inheritance in heaven, the key role of faith, and the reference to the last times, are absent from Titus. The association of hope and life is also more apparent than real, since in Titus (eternal) life (a noun) is the object of hope, while in 1 Peter hope is itself defined as "living" (an adjectival participle). Again, in Titus both God and Jesus are identified as savior (3:4, 6, respectively), but neither as Lord, while in 1 Peter Jesus is identified as Lord (1:3), but neither God nor Jesus as savior.[9]

Finally, even the putative references to baptism are rather different, since Titus refers to a new birth (παλιγγενεσία) accomplished by lustration (λουτρόν), a concept that clearly reflects baptism, while 1 Peter speaks in terms of a rebegetting (ἀναγεννήσας)[10] accomplished by God's word (1:22) through preaching (1:25), a concept that hardly demands such a reference to baptism.

In sum, virtually all the similarities belong to the central core of Christian conviction and vocabulary, as do the key differences, indicating mutually independent formulations of Christian truth rather than mutual dependence on a common source.

Comment

■ **3** Typical for NT literature, the word with which this verse begins (εὐλογητός) is applied to God.[11] The phrase it introduces appears in identical form in 2 Cor 1:3, where it stands in place of the usual Pauline opening prayer (e.g., Rom 1:8; 1 Cor 1:4; Phil 1:3; 1 Thess 1:2; cf. Col 1:3), and is also reproduced in Eph 1:3. It is not typical enough of Paul to say with confidence the author of 1 Peter must have gotten it from him;[12] it is more likely that it represents an early Christian doxological formula, used by both Paul and the author of 1 Peter.[13] While it was typical in Hellenistic rhetoric that one should begin by invoking the gods, a topos that was carried over into epistolary custom,[14] it is more likely that the formula here was derived from its use in the OT

---

7   This case has been argued most extensively by Boismard, "Liturgie" [1], 63, esp. 183–86. Kelly (46) also finds unmistakable references to baptism in 1 Pet 1:3–5; see also Shimada, *Formulary Material,* 196.

8   See also Shimada, *Formulary Material,* 179.

9   Σωτήρ is a favorite term of Titus, used of Christ in 1:4; 2:13; and 3:6, of God in 1:3; 2:10; and 3:4. It does not appear in 1 Peter. If it was part of the baptismal liturgy, the author of 1 Peter deliberately omitted it.

10   When the author of 1 Peter wants to refer to new birth, as in the reference to newborn babes in 2:2, he uses a different word (ἀρτιγέννητα).

11   While it is applied only to God in the NT (even in the problematic Rom 9:5, the reference is to God), in the LXX it can be applied either to God (e.g., Gen 14:20; 24:27; 1 Sam 25:32; 1 Kings 8:15; Ps 40:14)

or to human beings (e.g., Gen 12:2; 14:19; 26:29; 1 Sam 15:13).

12   Against Beare (82), who sees it as reflecting "the dependence of our writer upon St. Paul."

13   Even though Best (74) thinks the phrase originated with Paul, he sees it passing into the liturgical, epistolary use of the church; so also Kelly, 47; Schelkle, 27 n. 3; cf. Terence Y. Mullins, "Ascription as a Literary Form," NTS 19 (1972/73) 203. Shimada (*Formulary Material,* 150) argues correctly that all the eulogical expressions in the NT (Luke 1:68; Rom 1:25; 9:5; 2 Cor 11:31 in addition to those mentioned) bear a "liturgical-formulary character."

14   See Berger, "Apostelbrief," 224–25, and the examples given below in nn. 15–18.

and the Jewish world,[15] and then adapted by the similarly traditional reference to God as the Father of the Lord Jesus Christ.[16] That the letter begins with such praise to God indicates the theocentric nature of the author's thought, despite the great prominence played in it by the figure of Christ. If one cannot know God except as the Father of Jesus Christ, it is still God who is the one who controls the destiny of the Christians to whom the letter is addressed, as God is the one who determined the destiny of Jesus Christ (e.g., 1:20–21).

It is that God who has also become, through Christ, the "Father" of all Christians though his merciful act of begetting them anew through his Word (1:23, 25). The use of the rare word ἀναγεννάω[17] puts emphasis rather on rebegetting or begetting anew than on being born anew,[18] although of course the subsequent new birth is assumed (e.g., 2:2). Such an emphasis on begetting anew[19] means this phrase has less reference to baptism than has often been asserted.[20] It points rather to the totally new and unique origins of the Christian community,[21] beginning not merely with a new birth but with a new origin altogether.[22] It is by reason of this total newness that Christians are aliens and exiles in the world,[23] and the fact that that situation is due to God's mercy[24] indicates clearly enough that such status is to be seen as a blessing, not a curse, a point those undergoing persecution would need to hear.

The blessing of that new status is then further defined by a threefold goal, of which hope has pride of place. While hope was not a universally recognized virtue in the

---

15 For a detailed examination of this material, including examples from the OT (e.g., Exod 18:10; 1 Kings 25:32), Apocrypha (e.g., Tob 13:1; 1 Macc 4:30), Pseudepigrapha (e.g., *1 Enoch* 22.14; 39.13), Dead Sea Scrolls (e.g., 1QS 11.15; 1QM 13.1; 1QH 5.20), and rabbinic traditions, including the *Shemoneh-Esreh* (esp. the first petition), see Shimada, *Formulary Material*, 141–44; or Furnish, "Elect Sojourners," 6; see also Delling, "Der Bezug," 95; Selwyn, 122. Somewhat forced are the attempts by Jonsen ("Moral Theology," 96) to derive it from the Shema, and by Bornemann ("Taufrede," 147) from Ps 34:2 (part of his equally forced attempt to understand the whole of 1 Peter as a kind of midrash on that psalm).

16 This identification supplants that of God as "God of Israel" (e.g., 1 Sam 25:32; 1 Kings 1:48; 1 Chr 29:10; 2 Chr 6:4; Pss 40:14; 71:18), or as "God of the fathers" (e.g., Neh 7:27; Dan 3:26, 52); so Calvin, 28; see also Goppelt, 92.

17 While the word ἀναγεννάω technically means "beget again" or "rebeget," the translation "beget anew" accurately conveys the totally changed and hence new situation in which the regebotten persons find themselves. The word was apparently unknown prior to its use here (see also Goppelt, 92); it does appear in Josephus *Bell.* 4.484, but in a totally different context. There are some references to divine begetting in the LXX (e.g., Deut 32:18a; Ps 2:7; Prov 8:25), but they are not of a kind to suggest a source for 1 Pet 1:3 (pace Deterding ["Exodus Motifs," 59], who sees Deut 32:18 and the exodus as the source of the Petrine idea), and they do not refer to a "new" begetting.

18 Its use in 1:23 with σπορά (= σπέρμα, "seed") demonstrates this; see also Schelkle, 27; Cranfield, 35.

19 This emphasis itself is enough to render suspect any attempt to derive this language from the concept of rebirth prevalent in mystery religions, as do, e.g., Perdelwitz (*Mysterienreligion*, 42–45), Shimada (*Formulary Material*, 175–76), and Moffatt (93); cf. Bigg, 99. In fact, sources for our information about this aspect of the mystery religions postdate the writing of 1 Peter; the term ἀναγεννάω does not appear in such a context until the fourth century CE (Sallustius *De deis* 4.10.9); the Latin *renatus* ("rebirth") appears in Apuleius *Metam.* 11.21, but is hardly an exact equivalent of the ἀναγεννήσας ("begotten anew") of 1 Pet 1:3.

20 Such assertions range from the certain (e.g., Scharlemann ["Descant," 11]: "an unambiguous reference"; see Leaney, 18) to the probable (e.g., Cranfield, 36) to the less likely (e.g., Schelkle [28], who notes it could also refer to the resurrection of Christ as the moment of our "new birth"; see also his "Exkurs zu 1 Petr 1,3: Die Wiedergeburt," 28–31). Kelly (49) notes that whatever the relationship, the aorist tense of ἀναγεννήσας means the baptism cannot have occurred at 1:21, as some proponents of an underlying baptismal liturgy have suggested.

21 So also Goppelt (92): it rests on God's act, not on human decision or acceptance of some information.

22 This point also renders less likely the suggestion that the author of 1 Peter had in mind the Jewish idea that the proselyte was the equivalent of a newly born child, e.g., *b. Yeb.* 22a, 48b; see Shimada, *Formulary Material*, 168; Schelkle, 20.

23 Wolff ("Christ und Welt," 334) notes that it was in fact one's origin that constituted a person παρεπίδημος (1:1; 2:11) or πάροικος (2:11) in the Hellenistic world.

24 Delling ("Der Bezug," 96) correctly draws the inference from this that the former existence was without merit before God (see Titus 3:5a in the same

Hellenistic world,[25] it assumes here great importance, since it is understood as a true hope rather than merely an assertion in the face of despair (1:21). Such validity for this hope is constituted by its modification with the concept "living,"[26] to be understood in contrast to a dead or vain hope, one that is based on no reality and hence has neither present nor future validity. Christian hope is a living hope rather than a futile hope because it is linked to, and grounded in, the resurrection of Jesus Christ,[27] a linkage unique to this letter.[28]

Thus the result of the new situation in which Christians are placed by God's generative act is a living hope, not merely an empty wish,[29] and thus it functions as the content of the Christian life.[30] That life in turn has a present that is defined by its link to the power of the risen Christ (1:6; 3:22) and a future that is defined by the assurance of Christ's return (1:7) and the blessings that event will bring (4:13, 14; 5:10).[31]

■ 4 Following the logic of new begetting and hence new birth, the second of the results of the new origin is announced to be an inheritance (κληρονομία). Although the content of the inheritance is not defined here, its presence with the other two members of the triad, hope and salvation, points to its divine origin and eschatological nature,[32] a nature reinforced by the fact that by definition an inheritance points to the future.[33] The three adjectives that qualify the inheritance are a further indication of its eschatological nature.[34] As ἄφθαρτος it shares in the very nature of God and in the eschato-

context); cf. Schelkle (27), who calls attention to 1 Pet 2:10.

25 On the one hand, among the anecdotal evidence for a lack of hope is Sophocles (*Oed. Col.* 1225–26), who says best is not to be born, second best is, immediately upon birth, to return whence one has come; an epitaph of one who never married and wished his father had not either (I owe both examples to Scharlemann, "Descant," 11); the Stoic opinion that hope was a vice, not a virtue (see Cothenet, "Le réalisme," 565). On the other hand, Plutarch mentions philosophers called Ἐλπίστικοι who argue for hope as the strongest bond of life, while its absence renders life unendurable (*Mor., Quaest. conv.* 4.4, 668E), and ἀγαθὴ ἐλπίς ("good hope") played an important part in the Eleusinian mystery (Cothenet, "Le réalisme," 565). It is thus difficult to draw broad generalizations on this matter.

26 The use here of a participle (ζῶσαν) rather than the noun (ζωή) argues against seeing life as the object of hope, as does Bauer (16), perhaps following Luther (190). Rather, the participle here describes the character of the hope; see also the following note.

27 Cothenet, "Le réalisme" 565; Filson, "Partakers," 411; Richard, "Christology," 132; Goppelt, 94; Delling, "Der Bezug," 96; Best, 75; cf. Barth, "1 Petrus 1, 3–9," 156, 159. Hiebert ("Peter's Thanksgiving," 89) and Michaels (19) see the reference to "resurrection" being linked not to living hope but to our being begotten by God, but the redundant ἐκ νεκρῶν linked to ἀνάστασις argues against it. The suggestion that the link here between ἀναγεννήσας and δι' ἀναστάσεως Ἰησοῦ Χριστοῦ could be due to an early Christian idea of Jesus' resurrection as the new begetting of the Son by the Father (based on LXX Ps 2:7, reflected in Acts 13:33; Heb 1:5; 5:5) is

28 unlikely in light of 1 Pet 1:20.
Vanhoye ("1 Pierre," 120) emphasizes this point.

29 While κενὴ ἐλπίς ("vain hope," Sir 34:1; Job 7:6; see Windisch, 53) can well serve as the opposite of a living hope, the tenor of the letter (e.g., 1:18; 4:3) points less to a contrast with Judaism than with the hopelessness of pagan religions.

30 Barth, "1 Petrus 1, 3–9," 150, 154; Michaels, 19; Goppelt, 94. As Goppelt (95) points out, in 1 Peter it is "hope" rather than, as in Paul, "faith" that describes the orientation of Christian existence; see esp. 1 Pet 3:15.

31 It thus does not refer primarily to the Christian praxis that grows out of hope, as Kühschelm ("Lebendige Hoffnung," 203) argues, but to the whole content of the Christian faith, of which such praxis constitutes a part.

32 F. W. Grosheide notes the virtual identity of hope, inheritance, and salvation in this context ("Kol. 3:1–4; 1 Petr. 1:3–5; 1 Joh. 3:1–2," *Gereformeerd Theologisch Tijdschrift* 54 [1954] 144).

33 Michaels, 20; Scharlemann, "Descant," 12.

34 Schelkle, 32; Goppelt, 96. Harrison ("Exegetical Studies" [97], 332), quoting Trench, thinks the fact that all three begin with *alpha*-privative words points to the realization that such eschatological reality can be described only through negations. Because such reality transcends normal experience, one can describe only what it is not, not what it is. Perdelwitz (*Mysterienreligion*, 49) proposes that the adjectives are a deliberate contrast to the results of the ritual of the Taurobolium with its (perishable) initiation that had to be renewed after twenty years, its (defiled) bloodstained garment resulting from the sacrifice, and the (fading) crown the initiate wore; he has found few followers.

logical reality he will establish.[35] As ἀμίαντος it shares in the undefiled nature of God himself, and hence of the place of his presence and of the perfect high priest who serves him.[36] As ἀμάραντος it is not subject to the erosion of time as are all human possessions.[37]

On the one hand, given that the author has already used language to describe the Christian community which was normally used to describe Israel, one could readily understand an implied contrast here between such an inheritance and the land that had been the promised inheritance of Israel.[38] The presence of the three descriptive adjectives in the Bible, and in later Jewish literature,[39] when Israel's inheritance subsequent to its loss of the land underwent an eschatological reinterpretation,[40] would reinforce such a background for this verse. The final description of the inheritance as currently preserved "in heaven," that is, by God, and hence not yet present on earth, a concept also used in later Jewish literature, gives further reinforcement.[41]

On the other hand, the notion of an eschatological inheritance currently preserved[42] by God is also found in sayings of Jesus,[43] and the notion of a totally transformed eschatological reality is familiar to Paul.[44] It is therefore possible that the Jewish background of these ideas had already been included in the Christian traditions that form the more immediate background of these verses.[45] Nevertheless, the consistent pattern of our author's use of the language of Israel to describe the Christian community would tend to point to a more direct and intentional use of that language in this verse, the point of which is the total certainty of that inheritance in contrast with any other,[46] including the inheritance of land promised to Israel.[47]

While some have understood the change in this verse from first (ἡμῶν, v. 3) to second person (ὑμᾶς) to point to an abandonment of the liturgical form of the earlier verses,[48] the textual uncertainty of the personal pronouns, as well as the tenuous nature of that proposed

---

35 In Wis 12:1 ἄφθαρτος describes God's πνεῦμα ("spirit"); in 18:4 it describes the light proceeding from the law; in the NT it describes God (Rom 1:23; 1 Tim 1:17), the risen dead (1 Cor 15:52), and the eschatological reward (a crown, 1 Cor 9:25).

36 In 2 Macc 14:36; 15:34 ἀμίαντος describes God's temple; in Wis 3:12 it describes sexual purity (cf. 8:20); in 4:2 it describes virtue's prize; in the NT it refers to Christ as high priest (Heb 7:26), sexual purity (Heb 13:4), and perfect piety (Jas 1:27).

37 In Wis 6:12 ἀμάραντος describes divine wisdom; in the NT it describes the divine reward (a crown; 1 Pet 5:4). It is also used in eschatological contexts in the Christian *Sib. Or.* 8.409–12; *Apoc. Pet.* 15 (Akhmim version; see *New Testament Apocrypha* [ed. Edgar Hennecke; rev. Wilhelm Schneemelcher; trans. and ed. R. McL. Wilson; 2 vols.; Philadelphia: Westminster, 1965] 2.738, 2.681–82, respectively; I owe these references to Michaels, 21).

38 E.g., Gen 12:7; 17:8; Deut 34:4. This view is widely held: Chevallier, "Condition," 391; Grosheide, "Kol. 3:1–4; 1 Petr. 1:3–5," 142; Deterding, "Exodus Motifs," 63; Hort, 36; Cranfield, 38; Selwyn, 124; Best, 76; Beare, 82; Margot, 22. Scharlemann ("Descant," 12) and Cranfield (38) suggest the three adjectives are intended to contrast with the frequent plundering of Israel by Assyrians, Babylonians, and Romans. That the inherited land could be polluted, see Ps 79:1; Isa 24:3–4; Jer 2:7, 23; 3:2.

39 See nn. 35–37 above; all three words occur in Wisdom to describe heavenly realities. Kelly (51) argues that the point is not to contrast the Christians'

inheritance with Israel's promise of land but to show that the inheritance promised the Christians is totally unlike other human possessions.

40 Kelly (50–51) notes that unlike the earlier equation of Israel's promised inheritance with the land (e.g., Deut 15:4; 19:10), postexilic thought tended to identify that inheritance as God himself (e.g., Pss 16:5; 73:25–26; Lam 3:24) or as eternal life (e.g., Dan 12:13; cf. *Ps. Sol.* 14.10; 15.15; 1QS 11.7); see also Schelkle, 31; Cranfield, 39.

41 E.g., *1 Enoch* 11.1; 48:7; 58.5; *2 Bar.* 4.6; *Asc. Isa.* 8.25–26; similar is the idea of a new Jerusalem, to come from heaven where it is now preserved, e.g., *4 Ezra* 7.26; 10.54; *1 Enoch* 90.28–29. On this matter, see Michaels, 21; Kelly, 52; Bigg, 102; Delling, "Der Bezug," 96.

42 That is the force of the perfect participle τετερημένην.

43 Matt 5:12a; 6:19–20; Luke 12:33; see Michaels, 21. Some (e.g., Gundry, "*Verba Christi*," 337; Boismard, "Liturgie" [1], 198) have found here, I think incorrectly, literary dependence on the Gospels.

44 E.g., 1 Cor 15:52–54; on Christian reality hidden in heaven, cf. Col 3:1–3. Cranfield (39) deduces from this that Christ is considered our future and thus our inheritance.

45 See Spicq, 46; Michaels, 20; cf. Kelly, 51.

46 So also Kühschelm, "Lebendige Hoffnung," 203; Beare, 83. As Michaels (21) points out correctly, the passive τετερημένην as well as the noun οὐρανός points to divine activity; it is God who preserves the Christian's inheritance.

47 The attempt by Perdelwitz (*Mysterienreligion*, 49) to

liturgical background, make it difficult to come to that conclusion. The point is that this inheritance is for the benefit (εἰς ὑμᾶς) of the Christian community,[49] whether the author in this instance explicitly includes himself or not.

■ **5a** The divine (θεοῦ) preservation (φρουρουμένους) of Christians (ὑμᾶς) described here is parallel to the description of the divine (ἐν οὐρανοῖς) preservation (τετερημένην) of their inheritance, and adds further certainty to the promise of the new inheritance into which they have been born.[50] The image evoked by the language is that of a position guarded (φρουρέω) by a military sentinel (διὰ πίστεως) as evidence of the military force (δύναμις θεοῦ) he represents.[51] That image lends probability to understanding the verb as passive[52] rather than middle,[53] that is, the Christians are being guarded by God's power,[54] rather than guarding themselves by its use. That divine guarding is now visibly appropriated by the Christians' trust (διὰ πίστεως),[55] which becomes the instrument

whereby the divine protection becomes reality.[56] Such Christian faith is therefore the visible evidence of the unseen reality evoking that trust.

■ **5b** This is the third of the three prepositional phrases (εἰς ἐλπίδα, εἰς κληρονομίαν, εἰς σωτηρίαν) that describe the goal of the Christians' new existence granted by God through the resurrection of Christ. While the word used to describe that goal (σωτηρία) was familiar in secular sources,[57] in this instance the probability favors its derivation from its use in the OT and other Jewish sources,[58] the more so since a few verses later (1:10) it is associated with the biblical prophets. Rather than simply describing the content of the inheritance mentioned in v. 4,[59] or serving as a synonym for "hope" and "inheritance,"[60] salvation describes the ultimate rescue of Christians from their current oppression,[61] and is thus oriented to the future.[62] Its point of reference is not individual salvation, however, but escape from God's eschatological judgment (cf. 4:17),[63] as the phrase ἐν

---

find here a contrast to the garment stained with blood from the Taurobolium that was preserved in the temple until the renewal of the initiation after twenty years is ingenious but hardly convincing. See n. 34 above.

48 So, e.g., Coutts, "Ephesians," 120; Kelly, 52; cf. Brox, 62. But see Moffatt (94): the change is "simply the preacher addressing the people." This would be more convincing if in fact 1 Peter had originated as a baptismal homily.

49 So also Michaels, 22.

50 So also Schelkle, 32; Michaels, 22; Goppelt, 97; Kühschelm, "Lebendige Hoffnung," 203; Schiwy, 37; Barth, "1 Petrus 1, 3–9," 151.

51 Beare, 84; Bigg, 101; Tarrech, "Le milieu," 363. The presence of φρουρέω and πίστις in Gal 3:23 hardly argues for literary dependence, as Barnett (*Literary Influence*, 55) contends. Even dependence on a common source, as suggested by Boismard ("Liturgie" [1], 189–90), seems unlikely, given the total divergence in context.

52 Cf. Best, 77. The parallel passive perfect participle τετερημένην of v. 4 and the passive infinitive ἀποκαλυφθῆναι in this same verse reinforce such an understanding.

53 Against Perdelwitz, *Mysterienreligion*, 51; Brox, 63.

54 I.e., in an instrumental sense, rather than in the sense of the dative of sphere, as Hort (38) implies.

55 While Arichae ("God or Christ?" 414) suggests the implicit object of faith is Jesus Christ, the subject of the sentence in v. 3 is God; it is trust in him, includ-

ing his act of raising Christ from the dead, which seems implied here.

56 So also Hort, 38; cf. P. Gerhard Dautzenberg, "σωτηρία ψυχῶν (1 Pt. 1:9)," *BZ* 8 (1964) 271.

57 So, e.g., Beare, 84. Schelkle (33) points out that σωτήρ ("savior") was a common title for pagan deities, as it was for Hellenistic rulers, but 1 Peter shows no evidence of borrowing from such sources, as it does in the direct quotations from the OT.

58 So, e.g., Kelly, 52; Schelkle, 33. The use of the words σωτήρ and σωτηρία some 340 times in the LXX is sufficient to explain the source of this language in 1 Peter, given our author's predilection for quoting the OT.

59 As Brox (62–63) notes, such a construal would overload the phrase describing inheritance; cf. also Arichae, "God or Christ?" 414.

60 So Schelkle, 32.

61 E.g., Goppelt, 97.

62 With Michaels, 23. Cranfield (40) notes that is the normal orientation throughout the NT.

63 So also Best, 77; Schelkle, 32.

καιρῷ ἐσχάτῳ also indicates.[64] That eschatological
judgment and the ensuing salvation are no longer far off;
rather that salvation is "ready to be revealed" (ἑτοίμην
ἀποκαλυφθῆναι), a theme sounded frequently in this
letter[65] and a theme that adds urgency to its message.

---

64   While that phrase could mean "when things are at
      their worst," the eschatological tenor of 1 Peter
      makes that sense most unlikely here; so also Moffatt,
      95; Michaels, 23; Schelkle, 32; Schiwy, 37; Hort (39)
      wants, wrongly I think, to give it a noneschatological
      sense.

65   So also Best, 77. In 4:5 the same root ἑτοιμ- is used;
      see also 4:7, 17a; 5:10; cf. 1:20; 4:13.

1 Trials in the Present, Salvation in the Future

6 For that reason you rejoice,[1] even though [or, At that time you will rejoice, even if] you are now for a short time necessarily distressed[2] by a variety of[3] trials 7/ so that the proved character[4] of your faith, more precious than gold, which even though it is a perishable substance is tested by fire, may result in praise and glory and honor at the revelation of Jesus Christ, 8/ whom, even though you have not seen,[5] you love; in whom, although you do not now see but (nevertheless) believe, you rejoice[6] with an inexpressible and glory-laden joy, 9/ because you are receiving the culmination of your[7] faith that is your salvation.

1 P[72] reads ἀγαλλιάσαντες, thus eliminating the ἐν ᾧ whose referent is unclear. Latin mss. did tend to read the future form: *exultabitis* (vg, Irenaeus *Adv. haer.* 5.7.2; 4.9.2); *gaudibitis* (Polycarp *Phil.* [Latin] 1:3; see Michaels, 25). Origen's ἀγαλλιάσεσθε (future; *Exhortatio ad martyrium* 39; I owe this reference to de Villiers, "Joy," 71) has no support in any Greek mss.; such changes in tense allowed the ἐν ᾧ of v. 6 to refer to the καιρῷ ἐσχάτῳ of v. 5 (e.g., Kelly, 53). See also the comments on v. 6 below.

2 The grammatically difficult λυπηθέντες is changed by ℵ*, L, and a number of minuscules to λυπηθέντας, agreeing with the implied ὑμᾶς as the object of δέον; a few minuscules change it to λυπηθέναι, again to correct the grammar. The meaning is not significantly affected.

3 P[72] substitutes πολλοῖς ("many").

4 P[72] and a few minuscules substitute the more common δόκιμον for the rare δοκίμιον that appears in most texts.

5 A, P, Ψ, Koine, bo, Cl (Aug) read εἰδότες, which Moffatt (97) regards as the original reading. The meaning would not be altered.

6 OL, vg, Irenaeus, Aug, and some other mss. read the future tense; Kelly (57), correctly: "a prosaic correction springing from a failure to grasp the paradox."

7 The uncertainty of pronominal reference continues when some mss. omit the ὑμῶν, others substitute ἡμῶν; a similar substitution of ἡμῖν for ὑμῖν occurs in v. 12. Neither change has overwhelming textual support.

Analysis

These four verses constitute the second of the three parts (vv. 3–5, 6–9, 10–12) into which this opening period is divided. The gaze is shifted in these verses from the future results of God's merciful act of begetting a new people (hope, inheritance, salvation) to the present results: suffering and testing. Thus the theme touched on in the opening verse—Christians as dispersed exiles—is now put in fuller perspective: It is precisely because they are a new people that they no longer fit in well with the society in which they were once at home (see 1:18; 4:4). Yet it is their resolute holding to the savior whom they have neither seen in the past nor see in the present that will guarantee them participation in the fulfillment of the new life on which they have already embarked. The movement of the verses hinges on the two relative pronouns the author has employed: the present state of alienation, introduced with ἐν ᾧ (v. 6), and the future

state guaranteed by their present holding fast in the face of such alienation, introduced with ὅν (v. 8). In each case, the joy of the Christians is mentioned (vv. 6, 8), and in each instance the future culmination concludes the discussion. While the emphasis is therefore on present and future, both are predicated upon the past appearance of Christ (v. 8). There is contained in these verses therefore a movement from a present (vv. 6–7) determined by God's act of sending Christ in the past (v. 8) to a future that fulfills both past and present (vv. 7b, 9). It is a pattern that is repeated frequently in 1 Peter, and which represents the underlying pattern both of its kerygma and of its paranesis.

Comment

■ **6** The idea of joy in the midst of suffering is not unique to 1 Peter. Not only does it occur elsewhere in the NT (Rom 5:35; Heb 10:32–36; Jas 1:2), perhaps based on sayings understood to come from Jesus (Matt 5:11–12;

Luke 6:22–23),[8] but it is also found reflected in Wis 3:4–6,[9] *2 Bar.* 52.6–7, and *Sib. Or.* 5.269–70, indicating its presence in Jewish thought.[10]

The antecedent of the relative pronoun ᾧ with which the verse begins presents a problem.[11] Grammatically, it could be either masculine or neuter. As a masculine pronoun, its antecedent would be the καιρῷ that immediately precedes it, but grammatically it would also be possible for it to refer either to the θεός or the Χριστοῦ of v. 3,[12] though that is less likely because of the intervening words. If the antecedent is καιρῷ,[13] it will point to a future time (καιρῷ ἐσχάτῳ) when rejoicing will occur. That of course would demand that the ἀγαλλιᾶσθε, though present in tense, be understood as a future.[14] While that cannot be ruled out, it would be preferable to find a meaning that could allow the present tense its normal function.[15] If the relative pronoun be understood as neuter, its antecedent would be the content of the previous verses, finding in that the reason for

rejoicing despite the unfavorable present circumstances.[16] Such an understanding is given support by the fact that the same ἐν ᾧ construction occurs in 1 Pet 4:4. There the ἐν ᾧ is used proleptically, anticipating the ensuing genitive absolute (μὴ συντρεχόντων ὑμῶν) as the cause for offense on the part of unbelievers, and bears the meaning "therefore," or "for that reason."[17] On that basis, it is preferable to find here as well the meaning "for that reason," pointing out that Christians find as the reason for their rejoicing the realities described in the preceding verses.

Because ἀγαλλιᾶσθε[18] is present, its mode could be either imperative[19] ("Therefore, rejoice [despite the unhappy present]"), or indicative[20] ("For that reason you are rejoicing [despite the unhappy present]"). Because the same form occurs in v. 8, where it is more likely indicative than imperative, it is best to see that force here as well. The point is therefore that despite present suffering which would point to a different attitude, that

---

8   The similarity is more likely due to a widespread early Christian tradition (e.g., Barth, "1 Petrus 1, 3–9," 151; Nauck, "Freude," 71; Furnish, "Elect Sojourners," 9) than to direct literary dependence (e.g., Barnett, *Literary Influence*, 55; Boismard, "Liturgie" [2], 167).

9   While the thought pattern is close to that of Wis 3:4–6 (after God disciplines his faithful a little, trying them like gold in a furnace, he will show them kindness), the vocabulary is quite different, with the only common words varying forms of ὀλίγος and δοκιμάζω; even the words for "gold" differ (Wisdom, χρυσός; 1 Peter, χρυσίον).

10 Nauck ("Freude," 78–79) argues that the origin of this tradition is to be located in the Maccabean period.

11 For a convenient summary of the possibilities, see Selwyn, 126; du Toit, "Significance," 68.

12 So, e.g., Hort, 41.

13 So, e.g., Windisch, 53; Bigg, 103; Wand, 46; Michaels, 27.

14 Michaels (27) draws that specific inference; see also Goppelt, 98–99; Moffatt, 96; Beare, 87; Stephen M. Reynolds, "The Zero Tense in Greek: A Critical Note," *WTJ* 32 (1969) 69 et passim; Troy Martin, "The Present Indicative in the Eschatological Statements of 1 Peter 1:6, 8," *JBL* 111 (1992) 311–12.

15 In agreement with Nauck, "Freude," 72; Kühschelm, "Lebendige Hoffnung," 203; Barth, "1 Petrus 1, 3–9," 151; Leaney, 20; Margot, 23; Hiebert, "Peter's

Thanksgiving," 93.

16 So, e.g, Best, 77; Kelly, 53; Schweizer, 24; Beare, 86; Cranfield, 41; de Villiers, "Joy," 71; Barth, "1 Petrus 1, 3–9," 151.

17 In agreement with du Toit, "Significance," 68; Barth, "1 Petrus 1, 3–9," 151; Kühschelm, "Lebendige Hoffnung," 204; Kelly, 53; Schweizer, 24; Selwyn, 126; Paul R. Fink, "The Use and Significance of *en hōi* in I Peter," *Grace Journal* 8 (1967) 35; Nauck, "Freude," 71.

18 The verb ἀγαλλιάω is found only in biblical Greek and in Greek influenced by it (so also Best, 77); the nominal form ἀγαλλίασις is found in *Hist. Alex.*, recensio β 2.22.51 and γ 22.66.

19 E.g., du Toit, "Significance," 70; Combrini, "Structure," 35; Schiwy, 37.

20 E.g., Calvin, 31; de Villiers, "Joy," 72; Brox, 63; Best, 77; Kelly, 53. Schelkle (34 n. 4) thinks it difficult to determine ("kaum zu entscheiden"). Hiebert ("Peter's Thanksgiving," 93) notes that while understanding the verb as imperative goes back at least to Augustine, the context here is "clearly declarative," with the hortatory tone beginning with v. 13; so also Martin, "Present Indicative," 308.

is, mourning or fear, rejoicing remains the appropriate stance for Christians because of the new realities described earlier.[21]

A further difficulty in the verse is presented by the phrase εἰ δέον.[22] The conditional particle εἰ normally expresses a factual rather than a hypothetical condition, and it is probably to be understood in that sense here.[23] As the neuter participle of the impersonal verb δεῖ ("a necessary thing"; see 1 Macc 12:11; 2 Macc 1:18; Sir Prol. 3), one would expect it to be completed by an infinitive, and to have an accusative "subject" (see Sir Prol. 4; Acts 19:36), a correction undertaken by those manuscripts that read λυπηθῆναι and evidently presume ὑμᾶς, or, less obviously, that read λυπηθέντας. Given the nominative form λυπηθέντες, the sentence would construe admirably without the phrase εἰ δέον ("for this reason you rejoice, although you are for a short time distressed by many trials"); its presence adds the note of inevitability to such trials ("since indeed it is a necessary thing"), an inevitability in this context most likely of divine origin[24] (cf. Matt 16:21; Mark 9:11; Luke 4:43; John 3:30; Acts 4:12; Rom 8:26; 1 Cor 15:25; 2 Cor 5:10; 1 Thess 4:1; 1 Tim 3:15; Heb 11:6; 2 Pet 3:11;

Rev 4:1). The accusative ὀλίγον more likely refers to duration of time[25] rather than to the relative unimportance of the suffering;[26] its combination with ἄρτι implies the characteristic contrast in this letter between present suffering and future redemption.[27] The source of the variety of trials[28] remains unstated, although the context would imply a divine source[29] rather than satanic[30] origin, since part of the comfort to be derived from this letter by readers who currently confront persecutions of various sorts comes from the fact that even such unfortunate circumstances are not beyond the control of the benevolent God who in Christ will rescue those who remain steadfast (e.g., 1:18–21; 4:14, 17–20; the warrant is of course Christ himself, e.g., 4:13).[31]

■ 7 The purpose (ἵνα) of the trials mentioned in v. 6 is here stipulated: they are to test and prove the Christians' faith[32] so they may receive approval at Christ's return. The figure of the necessary refining of gold by fire was a common one in the Greco-Roman world, and ranged from the simple observation that fire tests and improves gold[33] to the metaphor that as fire tests gold, misery tests brave men,[34] indeed that God uses afflictions to harden

21 The notion of joy in the midst of suffering is a NT commonplace: Matt 5:11; Luke 6:22–23; Acts 5:41; Rom 5:3–4; 8:18; 2 Cor 4:17; 6:10; 7:4; 8:2; 1 Thess 1:6; Heb 10:32–36. While it is surely true, as Michaels (36–37) and de Villiers ("Joy," 72) argue, that the anticipation of future vindication also prompts Christians to rejoice, what God has already done in and through Christ is sufficient reason for such joy (so also Spicq, 48; Bieder, *Grund und Kraft*, 15; cf. 1 Thess 1:6). Best (7) and Selwyn (127) link the paradox to joy in the midst of the sufferings that are the necessary birth pangs of the new age (the "messianic woes"; see Ezek 38, 39; Hag 2:6–7; Zech 11, 12; *Jub.* 23; *T. Levi* 10; *T. Dan* 5; *2 Bar.* 26–30; 2 Esdr 5:1–12; 6:18–24).

22 So also Bigg, 103.

23 So also Schweizer, 24; Bengel, *Gnomon,* 729; Brox, 64; Michaels, 28. Kelly (53) cites in addition the aorist participle λυπηθέντες as indicating "the actuality of the trials." Selwyn (53, 127) and Hort (41) argue that the force of conditional εἰ δέον is to indicate that the trials were "local and haphazard" and "spasmodic rather than universal." That it indicates a hypothetical condition, see Beare, 86.

24 So also Goppelt, 100; Schelkle, 35; Best, 78; Kelly, 54; de Villiers, "Joy," 73; cf. Brox, 64.

25 E.g., Schelkle, 35.

26 As, e.g., Hort, 40.

27 Cf. Moffatt, 96.

28 Πειρασμός bears the sense of "testing" in the LXX (Selwyn, "Persecutions," 39), as it also does here. Its similarity to Jas 1:2 does not necessarily mean that was its source, as Hort (41) would have it.

29 So also Goppelt, 100; Best, 77. In a similar context, Wis 3:5 attributes such testing directly to God (ὁ θεὸς ἐπείρασεν αὐτούς, "God tested them").

30 So, e.g., Schelkle, 34; Karl G. Kuhn, "New Light on Temptation, Sin, and Flesh in the New Testament," in K. Stendahl, ed., *The Scrolls and the New Testament* (New York: Harper & Brothers, 1957) 96. Nauck ("Freude," 80) finds the clue for such an understanding in 1 Pet 5:8.

31 To find with Gordon E. Kirk ("Endurance in Suffering in I Peter," *BSac* 138 [1981] 53) a reference to grace here based on the description of the trials as ποικίλος, a word also used to describe grace in 4:10, is far-fetched and fanciful.

32 Best (78) and Arichae ("God or Christ?" 415) rightly note that πίστις here has more the connotation of faithfulness than the notion of believing in something.

33 Pliny the Elder (*Hist. nat.* 33.19.59) thought repeated firings improved gold.

34 E.g., Seneca: "ignis aurum probat, miseria fortes viros" ("fire tests gold, affliction [tests] strong men";

men to serve him.[35] The related idea that the purity of a person's trust in God was tested by adversity as precious metal was tested by fire was a commonplace of Jewish thought,[36] and the notion of faith tested by (fiery) adversity appears in the NT as well.[37] The comparison in this verse, with its emphasis on the perishable (ἀπολλυμένου) nature of gold, implies an argument from the lesser to the greater: if perishable, and hence less valuable, gold must be so tested, how much more must faith, which is imperishable and hence of greater value.[38] The emphasis here is not on faith itself so much as on the nature of the faith that results from such trials. It is that tested and proved character (δοκίμιον)[39] of faith which is more precious (πολυτιμότερον)[40] than gold and which brings approval from God at the last judgment.[41] That approval is described in the form of three attributes, praise, glory, and honor, which belong to God himself[42] and which he alone can give.[43] These three words also carry in themselves an eschatological flavor,[44] implying that such results of testing will not be seen until the final judgment,[45] an implication confirmed by the reference to the return of Christ.[46] The thrust of the two verses is therefore that present trials may be greeted with joy, since they are necessary if faith is to have the kind of proved character that God finds acceptable at the final judgment.

■ 8 The relative pronoun ὅν has as its antecedent Jesus Christ, whose future coming is mentioned at the end of v. 7, and whose current absence is discussed in this verse.[47] That contrast, directly related to a central problem for the readers, namely, the discrepancy between their present experience of suffering and their anticipated future glory,[48] takes the form here of the tension between faith and sight, a commonplace in early Christian teaching (e.g., Mark 15:32; John 4:48; 6:30; 20:29; 2 Cor 5:7).[49]

Although the thrust of the verse is clear, the intention of the parallel negatived participial phrases, with their

---

35   Seneca *Prov.* 1.6.

36   E.g., Ps 66:10; Sir 2:5; Prov 17:3; 27:21; Zech 13:9; Mal 3:3; Wis 3:4–6; Jdt 8:25–27; cf. *Hermas Vis.* 4.3, 4.

37   Jas 1:2–3 is particularly close to this verse. The idea appears again in 1 Pet 4:12; cf. also 1 Cor 3:13. Goppelt (101) finds here evidence of an early Christian tradition.

38   So also Cranfield, 42; Reicke, 80; de Villiers, "Joy," 73. Michaels (30) sees the function of this ἵνα clause to be to extol the value in God's sight of such tested faith, and to point to its "ultimate . . . significance."

39   Because δοκίμιον means "test" or "means of testing" rather than "the result of testing," Hort (42) thinks the true reading must be δόκιμον, which means "approved" (as a result of testing); see also Bigg, 103. δοκίμιον is found in the same sense in Jas 1:3, where some minor mss. change it to δόκιμον as do P[72] and a few others here in 1 Peter. But, as Selwyn (129) notes, Deissmann found the words "interchangeable in the papyri of the first three centuries"; see also Beare, 87; Kelly, 54. The same meaning would therefore prevail, whichever word were original.

40   It is better to construe πολυτιμότερον with δοκίμιον, whether in apposition (e.g., Hart, 44) or in an adjectival sense, than to see it as the predicate of εὑρεθῇ (e.g., Selwyn, 130). Not only would the latter construal require the phrase εἰς ἔπαινον . . . τίμην to be regarded as a second predicate (as Kelly [54] recognizes), but it would also render the meaning somewhat banal: "in order that God may recognize the tested character of your faith to be more precious than gold." The preciousness of gold is clearly a secondary factor in the sentence, and serves merely as a metaphor for the way humans (not God!) recognize the value of faith.

41   It is the εἰς phrase that expresses such approval that forms the predicate of the verb εὑρεθῇ; so also, e.g., Michaels, 30; Hart, 44. Tested faithfulness is found (by God) to result in praise, glory, and honor.

42   So, e.g., Goppelt, 102. Even though "praise" (2:14) and "honor" (2:17; 3:7) do not always carry such meaning in 1 Peter, in this eschatological context they surely do; cf. Rom 2:10 in the context of Rom 2:6.

43   See Rom 2:29; 8:17, 30; 1 Cor 4:5; Col 3:4; cf. Best, 78; de Villiers, "Joy," 73. It is also implied by the reverential passive εὑρεθῇ, which assumes God as its subject.

44   Beare (88) correctly points to Rom 2:5–11; 1 Cor 4:3–5.

45   So also Goppelt, 101; cf. Schweizer, 25.

46   Such a reference includes within itself the idea of the final judgment; so also Beare, 88. Whether the genitive Ἰησοῦ Χριστοῦ is subjective ("when Jesus Christ reveals himself"; e.g., Arichae, "God or Christ?" 415) or objective ("at the revelation of Jesus Christ [by God]"; e.g., Hort, 44; Schelkle, 36 n. 1) has no real bearing on the meaning of the sentence.

47   So also Hort, 45; Michaels, 32; Cranfield, 42. The relative pronoun serves as object both of the participle (ἰδόντες) and of the finite verb (ἀγαπᾶτε).

48   Kühschelm, "Lebendige Hoffnung," 204; Brox, 66.

differing form of the negative (οὐκ, μή) and their differing tenses (ἰδόντες, aorist; ὁρῶντες, present) is not.[50] On the one hand, the οὐκ that denies historical fact but is not normally used with a participle,[51] here combined with an aorist participle, could refer to their not having seen the historical Jesus,[52] while the μή, here in its normal use and combined with a present participle, could refer to their current inability to see the risen Christ.[53]

On the other hand, the paralleled second phrase could be intended to reinforce the first.[54] If both participles for seeing can be construed as adversative[55] ("although you do not see, you love; although you do not see but believe, you rejoice"), such an emphasized repetition would be the case. The difficulty for such a construal resides in the εἰς ὅν and the δέ. That the δέ is to be understood as contrasting the two participles rather than linking πιστεύοντες and ἀγαλλιᾶσθε is indicated by a parallel construction in v. 12, where the δέ follows the two words (ἑαυτοῖς, ὑμῖν) it is intended to contrast. Such a contrast ("you do not now see *but* believe") makes it difficult to construe the εἰς ὅν with the πιστεύοντες ("in whom you believe although you do not now see") since that leaves no connection between it and ἀγαλλιᾶσθε.

Construal of εἰς ὅν with ἀγαλλιᾶσθε resolves the difficulty: "in whom, although you do not now see but believe, you rejoice," and is perhaps to be preferred. However one resolves it, the primary parallel is between the verbs "to love and "to rejoice," with the object of the love qualified as one whom they have never seen, the cause for the rejoicing qualified as one whom they trust even though they do not now see him.

The two finite verbs ἀγαπᾶτε[56] and ἀγαλλιᾶσθε are better understood as indicative[57] than imperative,[58] since the author is still describing the situation of his readers; the imperatival implications do not begin until 1:13. Nor is ἀγαλλιᾶσθε here to be given a future sense;[59] their joy is present just as are their love and their faith (ἄρτι!).[60] The description of the joy that characterizes their rejoicing (χαρᾷ), although it has an eschatological dimension,[61] nevertheless is also to be understood here in a present rather than a future sense.[62] The joy is, however, clearly not of human origin: it cannot be expressed in human speech (the literal meaning of ἀνεκλαλήτῳ), and as a joy suffused with glory (δεδοξασμένη), it carries within itself a foretaste of the glorious future (cf. δόξα in v. 7) that awaits those who remain

49 Schutter, *Hermeneutic*, 44; Barth, "1 Petrus 1, 3–9," 152; Cranfield, 42; Beare, 88. Gundry ("*Verba Christi*," 337) tries, I think unsuccessfully, to link it to words of the historical Jesus remembered by Simon Peter. To say with Goppelt (103) that the "not seeing" means the recognition that all Christian experience is ambiguous is to press the words a bit too far.

50 The difficulty is illustrated by the way the words are altered to eliminate all ambiguity in Polycarp *Phil.* 1.3: εἰς ὅν οὐκ ἰδόντες πιστεύετε χαρᾷ ἀνεκλαλήτῳ ("in whom you believe with great joy, even though you do not see [him]").

51 E.g., Stuhlmueller, "Baptism," 208.

52 Cf. Selwyn, 131; Hort, 45; cf. BDF § 430 (3).

53 So Barth, "1 Petrus 1, 3–9," 153; Harrison, "Exegetical Studies" [97], 454. The suggestion that there is an implied contrast between the author who saw and the readers who did not (e.g., Schiwy, 38; Windisch, 53) is rightly rejected by Beare (88), Best (79), Kelly (56), and Michaels (32), among others.

54 E.g., Michaels, 33. The phrase εἰς ὅν is related to both participles (ὁρῶντες, πιστεύοντες) and to the main verb (ἀγαλλιᾶσθε), although the preposition relates it more closely to πιστεύοντες ("trust in") and ἀγαλλιᾶσθε ("rejoice in") than to ὁρῶντες, for which it

55 implies a direct object ("you see *him*").

55 So, e.g., Bigg, 105.

56 The love for Christ expressed by this verb is typical of the NT: John 8:42; 14:21; 21:15–16; 1 Cor 16:22; Eph 6:24; 2 Tim 4:8; cf. Goppelt, 103; Best, 79; Schelkle, 38.

57 E.g., Hiebert, "Peter's Thanksgiving," 96; cf. Stuhlmueller, "Baptism," 208; Spicq, 51.

58 As, e.g., du Toit ("Significance," 70) and Reicke (80) would have it.

59 As, e.g., Moffatt (98), Selwyn (258–59), and Schelkle (37) aver.

60 Bigg (106) rightly points out that the present ἀγαπᾶτε argues against a future sense for ἀγαλλιᾶσθε.

61 See its use in Matt 25:21, 23; John 16:22; Rom 14:17.

62 It characterizes life in the Spirit in Gal 5:22 and is linked to the life of faith in Rom 15:13; 2 Cor 1:24; Phil 1:25; cf. also John 15:11.

faithful to Christ.[63] It is thus a present joy "lit up by the light of eternity,"[64] and allows the Christian to be sure of that future salvation with its attendant glory[65] despite present circumstances that militate against such confidence. It is that confidence the author seeks to reinforce in this verse.

■ **9** Because the present participle κομιζόμενοι depends for its temporal understanding on the tense of the principal verb (in this case ἀγαπᾶτε and ἀγαλλιᾶσθε), it must be understood here as describing a present activity[66] and is probably best understood in a causal sense:[67] you are to love and rejoice because you are obtaining[68] the goal of your faith.[69] That it has a future orientation is nevertheless not to be denied; σωτηρία is here an eschatological term.[70] The sense is that Christians now obtain by faith what they will only fully enter into at the end; the power of the new age is already at work[71] and allows Christians in their present plight nevertheless to experience something of the eschatological joy awaiting them.[72]

The object of κομιζόμενοι is τέλος, used here with πίστις and σωτηρία in a combination unique in the NT.[73] Indicating result rather than purpose,[74] τέλος is further identified by an explanatory apposition (σωτηρίαν ψυχῶν)[75] that makes clear the eschatological nature of that goal.[76] That eschatological context, at home in the Hebrew rather than the Greek tradition,[77] gives to ψυχῶν the sense of the salvation of the entire person rather than simply the rescue of a higher or spiritual part of a person in contrast to the body.[78] Because such Hebrew tradition in which the human being is understood to be a psychosomatic unity[79] is dominant in the NT,[80] redemption (here σωτηρία) is understood in terms of a new creation rather than of the release of the soul from imprisonment in the body.[81] A translation that implies salvation of only part of the person (e.g., "soul") is therefore misleading,[82] since in 1 Peter elsewhere ψυχή is used to mean the whole person.[83] It is better to translate simply "your redemption"[84] or "the rescue of your lives" to capture the Semitic tradition that underlies the use of this phrase here.

This verse serves as a confirmation of v. 7b,[85] and thus concludes the line of thought that has dominated this portion (vv. 6–9) of the *prooemium*: If the present reality is suffering, it will surely result in eschatological redemption. Joy is therefore the appropriate stance however incongruous it may appear in present circumstances.

63 So also Hart, 45; Margot, 24.
64 That felicitous phrase is from Scharlemann, "Descant," 14; see also Barth, "1 Petrus 1, 3–9," 153.
65 The same point is made in Rom 8:31–39.
66 It would have a future sense if that were also true of the main verbs, as, e.g., Goppelt (104) argues; the whole eschatological context of the letter, however, points to a present sense, as I have argued above. See also Dautzenberg, "σωτηρία ψυχῶν," 272: "Der unbedingte, präsentische Zuspruch der eschatologischen σωτηρία ψυχῶν . . ." "the unqualified present promise of the eschatological salvation."
67 With, e.g., Bigg (10), rather than as attendant circumstance, as Hort (47) argues: "receiving withal the end."
68 The verb refers to carrying off a prize, or obtaining a deserved punishment. In the NT it is often used as here with reference to the final judgment, e.g., 2 Cor 5:10; Eph 6:8; Col 3:25; Heb 10:36; 11:39; 1 Pet 5:4; cf. Kelly, 58.
69 In this context πίστις is probably best understood as "faithfulness," rather than "belief."
70 With Bengel, *Gnomon*, 80; it is elsewhere used in this sense with "faith": Acts 16:31; Eph 2:8; Heb 10:39.
71 With Kelly, 58.
72 So also, e.g., Beare, 89; Best, 80.
73 Dautzenberg, "σωτηρία ψυχῶν," 264.
74 So also, e.g., Hort, 47.
75 With Hiebert, "Peter's Thanksgiving," 97.
76 So also Dautzenberg, "σωτηρία ψυχῶν," 264; Brox, 67.
77 See, e.g., Dautzenberg, "σωτηρία ψυχῶν," 276; he finds examples of it also in the Qumran literature (266–67).
78 With Dautzenberg, "σωτηρία ψυχῶν," 274–75; Hort, 48. Michaels (35) calls attention to a comparable use in Mark 8:35 par. For the opposed view, see the discussion in Dautzenberg, "σωτηρία ψυχῶν," 274, and the literature cited there; cf. also Schelkle, 38.
79 A view carried over into the Qumran community; see 1Q27 ("Livre des Mystères") 1.3–4 (I owe this reference to Dautzenberg, "σωτηρία ψυχῶν," 266).
80 For a good discussion of this point, see Dautzenberg, "σωτηρία ψυχῶν," 267, 270, 272–73 et passim.
81 Margot, 24.
82 As Dautzenberg ("σωτηρία ψυχῶν," 275) notes.
83 An emphasis in Dautzenberg, "σωτηρία ψυχῶν," esp. 273, 275.
84 Best (80) points out that ψυχή can be used almost as a personal pronoun, and cites as examples 1 Pet 1:9, 22; 2:25; 4:19. For such a translation, see Dautzenberg ("σωτηρία ψυχῶν," 276): *eure* endgültige Rettung" (italics added; "*your* final rescue" or "salvation").
85 Michaels, 35.

1

Salvation in Christ
Revealed to the Prophets

10 It was about that salvation that the prophets searched and sought who prophesied about the grace which has come to you, **11/** seeking out which or what sort of time the spirit of Christ which was in them was indicating,[1] as it foretold the sufferings coming to Christ and the glories to follow. **12/** To them it was revealed that their service in these matters was not for their benefit but for yours,[2] matters that have now been announced to you by those who, empowered by the Holy Spirit sent down from heaven, preached the gospel to you, matters of which angels would like to catch a glimpse.[3]

1 A number of MSS. (P[72], ℵ, A, B*, C, K, L, P, Ψ, some minuscules) read the imperfect middle ἐδηλοῦτο, derived by combining the imperfect active ἐδήλου with the following neuter article τό. The imperfect active is to be preferred on stylistic grounds, since the structure then represented (τὸ ἐν αὐτοῖς πνεῦμα = article, modifying prepositional phrase, substantive) occurs twice more in this verse (τὰ εἰς χριστὸν παθήματα, τὰς μετὰ ταῦτα δόξας).

2 See the note on v. 4 relative to personal pronouns.

3 The import is that these matters are so important that even angels would be happy simply to catch a glimpse of them.

Analysis

These three verses constitute the last of the three parts (vv. 3–5, 6–9, 10–12) into which the opening section of the letter is divided. These verses now focus directly on the salvation that was mentioned at the end of each of the two earlier sections (vv. 5b, 9), thus serving as both conclusion and climax to this portion of the letter.[4] If the first part had major emphasis on the future results of God's act of begetting believers anew (especially inheritance and salvation), and the second part put emphasis on the present results (suffering, love, and joy), this part lays the emphasis on the past, in which the rudiments of this salvation were discerned, specifically through the intervention of the divine Spirit (πνεῦμα Χριστοῦ, v. 11; πνεῦμα ἅγιον, v. 12).[5] In that way, the readers are comforted by the assurance that their salvation is surely in the hands of God, since it is part of the divine plan that had long ago been set (e.g., 1:20), and that is now at the point of its fulfillment.

Such a periodization of the elements of the discussion that climax in the eschatological deliverance, along with the reference to angelic desires to witness such events (v. 12c), probably reflect the kind of apocalyptic outlook familiar to much of the literature in the NT.[6] While such an apocalyptic outlook is not made thematic, as it is in Revelation, it nevertheless underlies our author's assumption that history is in fact moving to its climax, a climax to be preceded by suffering and culminating in judgment.

Excursus: Apocalyptic and 1 Peter

The form and content of the letter make it appropriate to speak of elements of an apocalyptic eschatology rather than a full-blown apocalyptic system.[7] That an apocalyptic background exists for the eschatology of 1 Peter has often been suggested. Such suggestions are

4 Cf. Schelkle, 38. It does not function, as Michaels (49) suggested, merely "as an appendix"; it represents the climax of the section, as σωτηρία represents the climax of each of the first two sections.

5 Its use here reflects part of the early kerygma, understood to be rooted in Jesus' teaching (e.g., Luke 24:25–26); to find here the reflection of an acquaintance of Simon Peter with the historical Jesus, as does Gundry ("*Verba Christi*," 338), is to go far beyond the evidence.

6 So also Brox, 68; Dautzenberg, "σωτηρία ψυχῶν," 265; cf. Schutter, *Hermeneutic*, 111 n. 83.

7 One must take care not to confuse eschatological references with apocalyptic eschatological elements; it is quite possible to have an eschatology that is not apocalyptic. For example, the statement that one day a salvation will be revealed for those who follow Christ is an eschatological statement, but not necessarily an apocalyptic one. To add that such salvation is kept in heaven until that time would make an apocalyptic background somewhat more likely. The affirmation that the revelation of that salvation will be accompanied by a resurrection from the dead and a transformation of reality from, say,

drawn from the presence of the Greek verb ἀποκαλύπτειν,[8] from the apocalyptic "flavor" of a variety of verses,[9] from the hypothesis that in the liturgy underlying 1 Peter, 3:13—4:7a represent the word of an "Apokalyptiker,"[10] and from the fact that 1 Peter is addressed to Asia Minor, the home of such figures as Papias, Montanus, and Justin Martyr, all of whom are identified as apocalyptic millenarian thinkers.[11] It has even been suggested that the apocalyptic vision of history dominates 1 Peter and gives it its coherence and unity.[12] However, the attempt to find elements of an apocalyptic eschatology in 1 Peter needs more than the discernment of "flavor" or location, or some loose definition that allows apocalyptic to be found virtually anywhere there is an eschatology.

As a point of reference against which apocalyptic elements may be measured, I will use the provisional definition of the genre "apocalypse" proposed by John J. Collins and augmented by Adela Yarbro Collins.[13] The first element in that definition speaks of a narrative framework as part of the apocalyptic genre, something that is patently not the case with 1 Peter. That the letter form can be associated with a clearly apocalyptic work, as it is in the case of the letters to the seven churches in the Apocalypse of John, indicates that the letter is not so unlikely a candidate for apocalyptic elements as might at first glance seem to be the case.[14]

The next element concerns revelation mediated by an otherworldly being, to a recipient who is usually a venerable figure of the past. The material is thus pseudonymous. While there is no direct reference to a supernatural source of the information conveyed in the letter, nor a discussion of how the recipient received it, there is within the letter a reference to a supernatural source of information: it is the "Spirit of

Christ" indwelling the prophets, informing them of the events surrounding Christ's suffering and subsequent glory (1:11). It is also the case that the author of the letter is a venerable figure in the early Christian church, and it is highly likely that the letter is pseudonymous. Again, the location of the author, "Babylon," stands for Rome in some apocalyptic literature of this period.[15] Such material, while reminiscent of apocalyptic writings, is nevertheless hardly of itself compelling evidence for the presence of apocalyptic elements in this epistle.

Apocalyptic elements in 1 Peter can be discerned, however, when it is a question of the disclosure of a transcendent reality both temporal and spatial. While the prophecy discussed in 1 Peter is not *ex eventu* as is the case in clearly apocalyptic works, our author does understand his readers to be living in the time of the fulfillment of the OT (e.g., 1:10–12; 2:9–10), a perspective also found in the Qumran community.[16] Again, that there is an eschatological crisis which may express itself in persecutions is clearly assumed by our author. While the existence of that crisis and the suffering it entails can be expressed in terms that are not necessarily apocalyptic (e.g., 1:6; 4:2, 7a), it is also expressed in a way that makes an apocalyptic framework probable. Thus, for example, the appearance of the word πειρασμός (1:6; 4:12), used in Qumran in connection with the conflict between God and Satan,[17] coupled with the reference to Satan as a lion seeking to devour Christians, another figure for this conflict (5:8b–9),[18] indicates that this crisis and the resulting suffering are seen against the background of an apocalyptic vision of history.[19] That the apocalyptic judgment is anticipated in the suffering of the Christians in 1 Peter[20] points to another element that characterizes apocalyptic, namely, the destruction to come upon the wicked at the final judgment.

corruptible to incorruptible, would allow one to find there an apocalyptic eschatology.

8 So du Toit, "Significance," 66.

9 E.g., Refoulé, "Bible," 464; Paul E. Davies, "Primitive Christology in I Peter," in E. H. Barth and R. E. Cocroft, eds., *Festschrift to Honor F. Wilbur Gingrich* (Leiden: Brill, 1972) 118; Cothenet, "Les orientations," 32.

10 Windisch, 157–60; cf. Martin, "Composition," 37.

11 Dickey, "Conditions," 413–14; Johnson, "Asia Minor," 109.

12 Refoulé, "Bible," 464, 479–80.

13 "Introduction: Towards the Morphology of a Genre," in J. J. Collins, ed., *Apocalypse: The Morphology of a Genre* (Semeia 14; Missoula: Scholars Press, 1979) 9; see also elements characteristic of the genre, 6–8. See the important addition to that definition in Adela

Y. Collins, "Introduction," in A. Y. Collins, ed., *Early Christian Apocalypticism: Genre and Social Setting* (Semeia 36; Atlanta: Scholars Press, 1986) 7.

14 Berger, "Apostelbrief," 308.

15 See Brox, "Pseudepigraphischen Rahmung," 95.

16 Osborne, "L'utilisation," 70. Dautzenberg ("σωτηρία ψυχῶν," 265) compares 1 Pet 2:1–10 with 1QpHab 7.1–6, 8, 14; 8.2; and 2.8–10.

17 Kuhn, "New Light," 108.

18 Kuhn, "New Light," 96, 97; Refoulé, "Bible," 463.

19 Refoulé, "Bible," 463.

20 Cothenet, "Les orientations," 32.

While there are several references to judgment (God judges impartially, 1:17; some destined to such judgment and condemnation, 2:8; day of visitation and hence of vindication for Christians, 2:12; God judges living and dead, 4:5), most important in this regard is 4:17–18, where the notion of judgment on and (implied) destruction of the ungodly is clearly present. The fact that the suffering of the church is understood as the beginning of that judgment probably means that every reference to such suffering is to be understood against the background of the final, universal judgment.[21]

With universal judgment there comes also salvation (σωτηρία ψυχῶν, 1:9), itself a concept with apocalyptic associations.[22] While salvation is on occasion referred to as already present (1:3, 23; 3:21), the large majority of such references are to salvation in the future (1:5, 13; 3:14, 15, 18; 4:13; 5:4, 6, 10). This is due to the close connection of such salvation to the glorious return of Christ,[23] itself an apocalyptic notion.[24] All of that is close to the notion of cosmic transformation that brings personal salvation, often in the form of resurrection, which, as Collins noted, are elements characterizing the genre "apocalypse."

In addition to those elements that function on what Collins identified as the "temporal axis," there are also elements that function on the "spatial axis," some of which are also present in 1 Peter. There is, for example, a heaven where Jesus now is (3:22) and where salvation is currently preserved (1:9); there is also an abode of the dead (4:6). The enigmatic reference to "spirits in prison" (3:19–20) may well reflect not only a supernatural place but also supernatural beings (see also 1:12), another characteristic of the genre of apocalypse. Christ's present rule over them in this context (3:22) represents the reality that will become visible with the transformation of the ages that such a rule implies.

Perhaps most characteristic of 1 Peter are those elements that interpret present, earthly circumstances in light of the supernatural world and the future (e.g., 1:6–7; 4:12–13, 15–18; 5:1–4, 9–10) and seek in that

way to influence both the understanding and the behavior of the readers (e.g., 1:10–17; 4:4–5; perhaps also 2:18–24 and 3:17–18). In fact, the apparent purpose of the letter is precisely to implement those characteristics.

Finally, one must ask whether the larger framework within which these individual apocalyptic elements appear betrays any sort of apocalyptic flavor. Two characteristics point in that direction. The first is the dominance of the contrast between present and future that is found throughout the letter.[25] This contrast is at least a pointer to the kind of cosmic transformation characteristic of apocalyptic thought. Buttressing this contrast is an equally pervasive contrast between present and past.[26] Emphasis on that contrast seeks not only to convince the readers that the contrast between their present and their future will be as dramatic as that between their present and their past, but also to insure that the readers do not forfeit that future by forfeiting present faithfulness to the God who will bring in that glorious future. That means that the temporal axis which functions as a major structuring element in 1 Peter also grounds the paranesis, another characteristic of the apocalyptic genre.

The second characteristic that betrays an apocalyptic flavor is the ruling metaphor 1 Peter employs: that of Christians as chosen people, a people who also had it as their fate to be "exiles and aliens" in this world.[27] In the context of 1 Peter, the readers are most likely to be thought of as temporal rather than spatial exiles and aliens; that is, their true home is not heaven as a locus so much as it is the future age when God's judgment will redeem them from the suffering they now undergo. Taken in conjunction with the temporal axis which structures 1 Peter, that ruling metaphor itself therefore points to the glorious and promised future when God's judgment will usher in the new age of salvation for those who have been faithful to his Son. In that way the ruling metaphor also points to the broad apocalyptic point of view that underlies 1 Peter and that surfaces explicitly in the specific elements discussed above.

21 Brox, "Situation und Sprache," 12; Werner Bieder, *Die Vorstellung von der Höllenfahrt Jesu Christ* (Zurich: Zwingli, 1949) 124.
22 Dautzenberg ("σωτηρία ψυχῶν," 266) referring to 1Q27 1, 3–4; see also 274–75.
23 Dautzenberg, "σωτηρία ψυχῶν," 272.
24 Schlier, "Adhortatio," 62; Michl, "Die Presbyter," 57 n. 50.
25 There are some twenty references to such a contrast. They may be found cataloged in Achtemeier, "New-born Babes," 232–33.
26 This contrast is present in some nineteen passages.

They are cataloged in Achtemeier, "New-born Babes," 234.
27 That this is meant metaphorically is shown by the fact that the combination of the two words occurs in Greek literature only in Gen 23:4, Ps 39:12, and 1 Pet 2:11, or in authors who quote one or another of those passages. It is thus never used to describe a general social status, only that status which characterized Abraham, who as exile and alien is nevertheless the progenitor of the chosen people.

Comment

■ **10** The nature of the salvation referred to at the end of v. 9 is now further clarified as ἡ χάρις εἰς ὑμᾶς, a phrase that must be given some such meaning as "the grace coming to you" or "destined for you" (cf. the phrase in v. 11: τὰ εἰς Χριστὸν παθήματα—"the sufferings coming to" or "destined for Christ").[28] The phrase points to the continuing dynamic of the divine initiative in such salvation, and illumines both the present and the future character of such salvation: its power is already present (in their faith), but not yet fulfilled (e.g., 1:4–5).[29] While that grace surely implies the inclusion of the Gentiles into the community of salvation,[30] it is not here limited in its meaning to that inclusion.[31]

The two verbs describing the activity of the prophets (ἐξεζήτησαν, ἐξεραύνησαν, "they sought," "they searched")[32] have basically the same meaning,[33] and function as a hendiadys[34] to emphasize the persistence and thoroughness of their search.[35] Because the verb ἐραυνᾶν is used in John 5:39 and 7:52 in the phrase "search the Scripture," it has been argued that the same meaning must be found here in the use of ἐξεραυνᾶν, and since it would be truer to speak of NT "prophets" searching Scripture (i.e., the OT) than to speak in that way of OT prophets, that, it is asserted, is the meaning one is to find here.[36] That understanding is then reinforced by the argument that the phrase τὰ εἰς

Χριστὸν παθήματα in v. 11 must be understood to mean not "Christ's" suffering, but rather "Christward" suffering, i.e., the "sufferings of the Christward road," sufferings that Christian prophets had announced to the Christians in Asia.[37]

Yet while (ἐξ)εραυνᾶν can refer to searching Scripture in John, it can also be used in LXX Ps 119:2 (= ἐξεραυνᾶν) to describe seeking the testimonies of the Lord and even seeking out the Lord himself.[38] Further, both the language of v. 11 (προμαρτυρόμενον), which indicates that the prophets in question preceded Christ,[39] and the contrast between the words of the prophets (vv. 10–11) and the proclamation of the gospel (v. 12),[40] point rather to OT than NT prophets.[41]

In fact these words are reminiscent of the NT tradition that the OT[42] is prophetic of Christ (e.g., Matt 13:16–17; Luke 10:23–24; 24:25–27; John 5:39, 45–47; 8:56; Acts 7:52; 8:30–32; 17:2–4)[43] and that as a result what is written there is useful for Christians (explicit in Rom 4:23–24; 15:4; 1 Cor 9:10; 10:11, but implied wherever the OT is cited to support a statement in the Gospels or Epistles).[44] The reference to the OT prophets searching out the grace in which the NT community stands points to the continuity of God's purpose and thus the unity of the divine revelation,[45] which in its turn underlines the certainty of the announced salvation in Christ in the midst of circumstances that contradict

---

28 So also Beare, 91.

29 Goppelt (106) contrasts this aspect of salvation in the NT with the purely future salvation displayed in Jewish apocalyptic, e.g., *4 Ezra* 7.26–33.

30 Moffatt (99) and Hort (49–50) would limit χάρις to that meaning here.

31 In agreement with Best, 81.

32 There is little evidence that the author has in mind LXX Ps 118:2, where in the context of seeking God and searching out things that witness to him the two verbs do occur. To argue that the verbs were "borrowed outright" from 1 Macc 9:26, where ἐραυνᾶν is found instead of ἐξεραυνᾶν and in a wholly different context, as does Beare (90), or even to find a reminiscence of 1 Maccabees, as do Schelkle (39 n. 2), Bigg (107), and Wand (49), seems even less justified.

33 In agreement with Schelkle, 39 n. 2.

34 Less persuasive is the suggestion of Beare (90) that we have here an example of paronomasia.

35 So also Arichae, "God or Christ?" 415.

36 So Selwyn, 134; cf. also 260; Duane Warden, "The

Prophets of 1 Peter 1:10–12," *ResQ* 31 (1989) 12.

37 Selwyn, 263, 265, respectively. Love ("First Epistle," 69) thinks it means both OT and NT prophets.

38 I owe these references to Michaels, 40.

39 Best, 80. The suggestion of Love ("First Epistle," 69) that the word may mean simply "publicly proclaiming" has found little acceptance.

40 Senior, 16.

41 This view is widely held; e.g., Kelly, 59; Schweizer 27; Windisch, 54; Reicke, 80; Hart, 45; Spicq, 55; Wand, 49; Michaels, 41; Beare, 90; Hiebert, "Peter's Thanksgiving," 98.

42 Since there is no indication in the context that the author had any specific prophet in mind, we should probably, as, e.g., Senior (18) suggests, understand "prophets" to mean the whole OT, which in early Christian understanding was predictive of Christ.

43 So, e.g., Calvin, 38; Kelly, 60; Moffatt, 100; Cranfield, 43; Hart, 46.

44 Cf. Best, 80; it is less likely that this tradition originated with 1 Cor 15:4, as Goppelt (106) held, than that what is there recalled also belongs to that

rather than confirm it (cf. v. 6).

■ **11** This verse further defines the activity of the prophets mentioned in v. 10, specifically their act of "searching"[46] (ἐραννῶντες; cf. ἐξηραύνησαν, v. 10). The grammar is not so clear as it might be. The problem lies in determining the object of the verb ἐδήλου. Either the phrase εἰς τίνα ἤ ποῖον καιρόν must serve as object both for the participle ἐραννῶντες and the main verb ἐδήλου,[47] or the phrase τὰ εἰς . . . ταῦτα δόξας must serve as object both of ἐδήλου and προμαρτυρόμενον.[48] While either is possible, the flow of the clause seems better served by the former alternative, with the sense that their searching and the Spirit's making manifest coincide, resulting in the prophetic announcement (προμαρτυρόμενον) of Christ's passion, an announcement also due to the Spirit.[49]

What it was that the Spirit made manifest to the prophetic searching is also grammatically somewhat difficult, since both τίνα and ποῖον can be understood as interrogative adjectives modifying καιρόν ("which or what sort of time"),[50] or τίνα may be understood as an interrogative pronoun used substantively rather than adjectivally, with ποῖον alone as an interrogative adjective ("whom or what sort of time").[51] This latter construal is supported by the fact that in 1 Peter every other use of the interrogative τίς is as a pronoun (3:13; 4:17; 5:8), a use that, along with ποῖον as interrogative adjective, represents general NT practice.[52] A similar construction

in Acts 8:34, where, in a question about prophetic intention, τίς is used substantivally, lends support to seeing such a use here. On the other hand, τίς is also used in the NT as interrogative adjective (e.g., Matt 5:46; Luke 14:31; John 2:18; Acts 10:21; Rom 3:1), and construing both adjectives with καιρόν yields results similar to the double question in Mark 13:4 (πότε, τί, "when," "what"),[53] and is paralleled in sense by the double reference to time in 1 Thess 5:1 (χρόνοι, κρονοῖ, "times," "seasons"), and in Mark 13:32 (ἡμέρας, ὥρας, "day," "hour"). That inquiry into events and times is more frequent in apocalyptic Judaism than inquiry into person and times lends weight to such an understanding.[54] On that basis, a translation such as "which or what manner of time" is perhaps preferable,[55] although certainty in this matter is unattainable.

While some have suggested that the phrase "spirit of Christ" (πνεῦμα Χριστοῦ) refers not to the presence of the preexistent Christ among the prophets (ἐν αὐτοῖς), but rather (a) to the spirit that reveals things about Christ,[56] or (b) to the spirit that later revealed itself in Jesus Christ,[57] or even (c) to the spirit Christ received at his baptism,[58] it is clear from 1:20 that the author knew of

early tradition about the OT.

45 Margot, 25.
46 This is best understood as an adverbial participle of attendant circumstance: "as they searched," or "searching, as they were, . . ."
47 E.g., Hart, 46.
48 E.g., Hort, 51; cf. Michaels, 43. In either case, ἐδήλου is to be understood as transitive, as Hort (50) notes.
49 The prediction derives from the Spirit, not the prophets, since the singular neuter participle (προμαρτυρόμενον) must modify "Spirit," not the plural masculine "prophets." It is tempting to see here an adverbial participle of means: the Spirit made the times clear to the prophets *by pointing beforehand* to Christ's passion, but it may also simply be an adverbial temporal participle: "when."
50 Wand (50): "What, or at least what manner of, time"; cf. Goppelt (107): "wann und unter welchen Umständen" "when and under what circumstances"; cf. *4 Ezra* 4.33, "how long or when."
51 Best (81) and William J. Dalton ("The Interpretation of 1 Peter 3,19 and 4,6: Light from 2 Peter," *Bib* 60

[1979] 549): "What person or time"; Scharlemann ("Descant," 15): "'Who is going to do this?' and, 'What kind of age will it be?'"; cf. Schutter, *Hermeneutic,* 106.
52 G. D. Kilpatrick, "1 Peter 1:11 τίνα ἤ ποῖον καιρόν," *NovT* 28/1 (1986) 91–92.
53 Hiebert, "Peter's Thanksgiving," 99.
54 E.g., Dan 9:2, 23–27; 12:6–13; *4 Ezra* 4.33—5:13; 1QpHab 7.1–8; cf. Best, 81; Michaels, 41; Kelly, 60.
55 This is also the reading suggested by BDF § 298 (2) as a "tautology for emphasis."
56 Margot, 25.
57 Schweizer, 28.
58 Beare, 192.

Christ's preexistence,[59] and that is likely also to be the case here.[60] This phrase points therefore to the continuity between prophets and gospel: both have the same inspirer and ultimately the same content.[61] Underlying such continuity is the unity of the one people of God,[62] a unity that justified the author's appropriation for the Christian community of the history of, and language for, Israel found in the OT.

While the content of such prophetic witness[63] prompted by Christ is the fate of Christ—his suffering and subsequent glories—there is some question whether those phrases about suffering and glory are understood here to concern the fate of Jesus of Nazareth. Three considerations about the meaning of the phrase τὰ εἰς Χριστὸν παθήματα come into play.

1. The meaning of the prepositional phrase εἰς Χριστὸν. It has been argued that since the normal phrase τοῦ Χριστοῦ ("sufferings of Christ") is not present here, the author must mean not Christ's sufferings but the sufferings of those who take Christ as their goal, that is, "the sufferings of the Christward road."[64] Yet the εἰς Χριστὸν is similar to the εἰς ὑμᾶς of v. 10, where it clearly means "the grace that is yours,"[65] and the idea that Christ's destiny was suffering is a commonplace of early Christian tradition.[66]

2. The meaning of τὰ παθήματα. That this is a reference to the idea of the messianic woes associated with the coming of the Messiah found in apocalyptic Judaism has been argued.[67] Yet in this context it seems unlikely that such a general reference would be intended,[68] since in the following verse the sufferings and glory are identified as the content of the gospel.[69]

3. The meaning of Χριστόν. If suffering refers to the messianic woes, then the Messiah need not be Jesus; it can simply be the Messiah of OT prophecy.[70] Again, however, the context argues for seeing it in fact as the Jesus proclaimed in the gospel as Messiah.[71]

The point of the verse therefore is to demonstrate the

---

59   Best, 81. Schelkle (41–42) argues that a similar Christology underlies 1 Cor 10:4; Heb 11:26; and John 12:41; cf. *Barn.* 5.6. Dalton ("Interpretation," 549) finds a similar view of prophecy in 2 Pet 1:21, although there it is the Spirit of God, not Christ.

60   Calvin, 40; Calloud, "Ce que parler," 185; Schlosser, "Ancien Testament," 94–95. But, as Goppelt (107) points out, the Spirit of Christ motivating the prophets is found only here in the NT. The genitive Χριστοῦ, presumed here to be epexegetic ("the Spirit, namely, Christ"), may also be genitive of origin, pointing to the preexistent Christ as its source (so Bigg, 109). The idea that Christ inspired and appeared to the OT prophets is popular in post-NT Christian literature, e.g., *2 Clem.* 17.4; Ignatius *Magn.* 8.2; *Barn.* 5.6; *Hermas, Sim.* 9.12.1–2; Justin *1 Apol.* 31–33; 62.3–4; *Dial.* 56–57; Irenaeus *Adv. haer.* 4.20.4. Cf. Kelly, 61; Schelkle, 41 n. 41.

61   Schlosser, "Ancien Testament," 95; Brox, 70. Bigg (110) and Kelly (61) find here a possible reference to Luke 24:26–27; in any case, that passage surely intends to make the same point.

62   Spörri, *Gemeindegedanke,* 257.

63   While Hort (53) argued that since προμαρτυρόμενον was in the middle voice, it had to mean summoning another (i.e., God) to witness, Beare (92) argues correctly that it can, and here does, also mean "testify beforehand."

64   Selwyn, 136; cf. 263. Stuhlmueller ("Baptism," 209) follows him; few others have.

65   Calloud, "Ce que parler," 187–88 n. 14; Beare, 92. Wand (50) argues that it, like the phrase εἰς ὑμᾶς in

1:10, is a Hebraism, and means "that belong to Christ," a meaning, if not a derivation, agreed to by Best (81), Cranfield (44), Beare (91), Hiebert ("Peter's Thanksgiving," 100), and Coutts ("Ephesians," 119). Michaels (44) argues that when the author of 1 Peter speaks of Christ's suffering from a standpoint in the present, he uses τὰ τοῦ Χριστοῦ παθήματα (4:13; 5:1); here he uses εἰς Χριστόν because he is speaking from a standpoint in the past, an argument that would be more convincing if the evidence were not limited to this one instance.

66   E.g., the pre-Pauline tradition in Phil 2:8; 1 Cor 15:3; cf. Schlier, "Adhortatio," 64; Schelkle, 40. Trypho the Jew admits, in his dialogue with Justin Martyr, that the prophets predicted the Messiah would suffer (*Dial.* 36).

67   E.g., Selwyn, 112; Hillyer, "First Peter," 66; see Schutter, *Hermeneutic,* 107 n. 75 for further literature.

68   So also, e.g., Schutter, *Hermeneutic,* 107.

69   As such, it also includes not only Christ's suffering but also that of his followers; see Calvin, 40; Luther, 197; Beare, 52.

70   E.g., Hort, 54; Windisch, 54.

71   E.g., Hart 46; Michaels, 44; Schiwy, 38.

continuity between prophetic message and Christian gospel, both in terms of its source, namely, the pre-existent Christ, and its content, namely, the passion and death of Christ and his resurrection and glorious return.[72]

■ **12** The readers now learn more of the content (αὐτά; cf. τὰ . . . δόξας) that was made clear (ἀπεκαλύφθη; cf. ἐδήλου) to the prophets (οἷς; cf. προφῆται) by the indwelling Spirit of Christ: their insights were aimed at others than themselves and, by implication, their contemporaries. This is not a new insight; the OT prophets had presentiments that the divine intervention they announced was not intended for their day,[73] and the notion that prophets served not themselves but others became a commonplace in apocalyptic literature[74] and at Qumran.[75] Nor is 1 Peter unique in this respect: the unfulfilled longing of the OT saints is known in the NT,[76] and in a similar vein Paul is convinced the OT writings have value for his Christian contemporaries.[77] The addition in this verse to the tradition that the prophets' service (διακόνουν) benefited Christians is the affirmation that that very insight had also been revealed to them (οὐχ ἑαυτοῖς ὑμῖν δέ)[78] as the reason for their activity. Gram-matically there is some question whether that ministry has as its subject the prophets (implied by οἷς) or their insights (αὐτά).[79] In the former case, it is the prophets whose ministry benefits the Christians;[80] in the latter case, it is those insights themselves that perform such a ministry.[81] A similar construction in 4:10 (cf. also 2 Tim 1:18; *Herm. Sim.* 2.10) argues for the former.

The next clause (ἃ νῦν . . . ἀπ᾽ οὐρανοῦ) tells how those prophetic insights have been of benefit to Christians: they are included in the proclamation of the gospel.[82] The passive ἀνηγγέλη (cf. ἀπεκαλύφθη) probably emphasizes the divine origin of this proclamation,[83] since the announcers themselves are merely given the status of agents or instruments (διά).[84] The reference to the Holy Spirit and its heavenly origin, again described in the passive (ἀποσταλέντι), is probably intended not so much to remind the readers of the descent of the Spirit at Pentecost[85] as to reinforce such divine origin and

---

72 The plural δόξας ("glories") is rare in the NT (elsewhere only at 2 Pet 2:10; Jude 8; it normally occurs in this context in the singular, e.g., Luke 24:26), and may refer here to the successive phases of Christ's glorification, e.g., resurrection, ascension, session at God's right hand, and return in glory; so also Hiebert, "Peter's Thanksgiving," 100; Bigg, 110; Schelkle, 40; Spicq, 56; Wand, 51; cf. Schlosser, "Ancien Testament," 96.

73 E.g., Num 24:17; Deut 18:15; Hab 2:1–3; 2 Esdr 4:51–52 (I owe these references to Kelly, 62).

74 It finds programmatic formulation in *1 Enoch* 1.2; cf. Brox, 70. Moffatt (101) thinks the author of 1 Peter had this verse specifically in mind.

75 1QpHab 7.1–8: God did not tell the prophets when the final time would be, only the Teacher of Righteousness; cf. Schutter, *Hermeneutic,* 111; Goppelt, 108; Dautzenberg, "σωτηρία ψυχῶν," 266–67.

76 E.g., Matt 13:17 and Luke 10:24; Heb 11:13; cf. John 8:56; 12:41.

77 Most clearly in Rom 4:23–24a; 15:4; 1 Cor 9:9–10; see also 1 Cor 10:11. The idea is also reflected in 2 Tim 3:16.

78 Goppelt (107) points out that while the notion was common that prophets spoke for others than themselves, the notion that they spoke for the benefit of the Christian community was not. He suggests the

source for such an idea may lie in Dan 9:2, 22–27; 12:6–13, where Daniel is told that his prophecy is for the end-time community.

79 The pronoun αὐτά has as its antecedent the τὰ . . . παθήματα (probably also the τὰς δόξας) with which v. 11 concludes; the other two relative pronouns (ἅ, εἰς ἅ) have as their antecedent the pronoun αὐτά, and by implication the same phrases from v. 11. See, e.g., Kazuhito Shimada, "A Critical Note on I Peter 1,12," *AJBI* 7 (1981) 147.

80 E.g., Michaels (46), who notes the rarity of such a use.

81 E.g., Shimada, *AJBI* 7 (1981) 147; he is the only scholar of whom I am aware who has proposed this construction.

82 The general phrase used to designate those who evangelized the readers (τῶν εὐαγγελισαμένων ὑμᾶς) indicates that the author of the letter is unaware of any tradition that Peter carried on missionary work in this area; cf. Best, 82.

83 Michaels (47) correctly sees these passives as indicating "divine initiative"; he finds similar divine initiative in Isa 52:7 (see v. 6; the verse is also used in Rom 10:15) and LXX Ps 67:2, both of which also use a form of εὐαγγελίζομαι.

84 So, e.g., Hort, 59.

85 So, e.g., Wand, 52.

initiative.[86] Since the human preachers are identified as the means by which this proclamation occurs, the Holy Spirit ($\pi\nu\epsilon\acute{u}\mu\alpha\tau\iota\ \dot{\alpha}\gamma\acute{\iota}\dot{\omega}$)[87] is probably not to be understood here as the instrument[88] but as the one who empowers that proclamation,[89] although, to be sure, the two ideas are intimately related.[90]

The final clause with its reference to angelic desire ($\dot{\epsilon}\pi\iota\theta\nu\mu o\hat{u}\sigma\iota\nu$)[91] and activity ($\pi\alpha\rho\alpha\kappa\acute{u}\psi\alpha\iota$)[92] poses the riddle of how these $\mathring{\alpha}\gamma\gamma\epsilon\lambda o\iota$ ("angels") are to be understood. While there was a tradition that angelic knowledge about redemption was superior to that of human beings,[93] the thrust of this clause seems rather to reflect an equally widespread tradition of the angels' lack of knowledge[94] and of their resultant inferiority to human beings.[95] Hence they desire merely to glimpse[96] what is now openly proclaimed in the gospel.[97] Whether this further implies an envy on the part of the angels,[98] who can only see but not share in those salvific events, or whether the import is angelic fascination with these divine events now playing themselves out among human beings,[99] is difficult to determine on the basis of the limited evidence presented in the text. What does seem to be implied is that this angelic desire points to the greatness of what Christians now hear announced to them,[100] and further underlines one of the author's main purposes for writing the letter: the readers live in a time firmly under God's control when history is about to reach its climax. They therefore have reason rather to rejoice than to despair.[101]

The import of the verse as a whole serves to reinforce

86   So, e.g., Kelly (63), Spicq (57), neither of whom finds here a reference to Pentecost.

87   As Bigg (111) notes, lack of definite article here does not mean "a holy Spirit" any more than it did in 1:2.

88   Wand (52), to the contrary, does identify it as "instrumental," but finds support in the $\dot{\epsilon}\nu$, which is absent in some early texts.

89   So also Michaels, 47, who identifies it as associative dative, or dative of accompanying circumstances and manner.

90   As Hort (61) observes; he terms it a "true 'dynamic' dative" that expresses "that *in virtue of which*" something exists or occurs.

91   Chevallier ("1 Pierre 1/1 à 2/10," 140) identifies it as a word whose precise meaning is hard to determine; he thinks it was chosen to serve as catchword with the $\dot{\epsilon}\pi\iota\theta\nu\mu\acute{\iota}\alpha\iota\varsigma$ in v. 14.

92   The "things" ($\mathring{\alpha}$) that they desire to glimpse are the $\tau\grave{\alpha}$ ... $\delta\acute{o}\xi\alpha\varsigma$ of v. 11, which function as the antecedent of the other two pronouns ($\alpha\dot{u}\tau\acute{\alpha}$, $\mathring{\alpha}$) in this verse as well.

93   It is reflected in such passages as Dan 7:16; Zech 1:9; *1 Enoch* 1.2; 72.1; 108.5–7; Philo *Fug.* 203; cf. Kelly, 63.

94   It is reflected in such passages as Mark 13:32; Rom 16:25; 1 Cor 2:8; *1 Enoch* 16.3; *2 Enoch* 24.3; Ignatius *Eph.* 19.1; they learn of redemption from the church, Eph 3:10.

95   On angelic inferiority, see 1 Cor 6:3; Heb 1:14; 2:16; as messengers, see Gal 1:8; on their language, see 1 Cor 13:1. That that implies that the angels here being discussed are the "dark spiritual forces that hold sway over the lower realms of being" (so Beare, 94) is unlikely, however; Eph 3:10 is probably a closer analogy than 1 Cor 2:8.

96   The word $\pi\alpha\rho\alpha\kappa\acute{u}\psi\alpha\iota$ probably emphasizes here less the act of "peeping into" (as, e.g., John 20:5) than the looking forth (a use Hart [48] notes it has assumed in LXX Greek) by the angels from heaven (e.g., *1 Enoch* 9.1). Michaels (49) notes correctly that the point is their intense interest in the salvific events, with the implied limitations on their knowledge; more than that our author does not wish to say about angelic beings.

97   Kühschelm, "Lebendige Hoffnung," 205; cf. Reicke, 81. See also n. 44 on 1:7 above.

98   So, e.g., Kühschelm, "Lebendige Hoffnung," 205; Hillyer ("Servant," 147) notes a tradition of angelic envy of humans as a result of the dignity that the Aqedah (sacrifice of Isaac) confers upon humanity, but none of the references cited (n. 35: *Tanḥuma Wayyera* 18; *Soṭa* 6.5; *Gen. Rab.* 56.3) even remotely supports this point.

99   So, e.g., Moffatt, 102; Calvin (43) thought it meant the angelic desire to see the kingdom of Christ, a living image of which is set forth in the gospel; Thomas Aquinas thought it meant that angels, rather than being frustrated at their lack of knowledge, never weary of knowing God's plans (cited in Spicq, 57).

100   So, e.g., Leaney, 22; de Villiers, "Joy," 74; Spicq, "La Iª Petri," 55; Scharlemann, "Descant," 16.

101   So also Goppelt, 108–9. To find with Schweizer (30) that it means that the future glory of the return of Christ is greater than any angelic glory is perhaps to find more than is in the text.

the idea of the unity of the origin and content of the witness of the OT and the Christian gospel: as the Spirit of Christ informed the message of the prophets, the Holy Spirit impels the proclamation of the gospel.[102] That unity centers in Jesus Christ, the announcement of whose appearance (ἃ νῦν ἀνηγγέλη) is the fulfillment of the prophets' message[103] and is itself the beginning of the eschatological fulfillment they foresaw.[104] That that new reality can already shape the lives of those who live within it is the thrust of the ethical admonitions that commence in the next section of the letter.

102 So also Kelly, 62; Schweizer, 29. We are probably not to understand differing origins for the message of prophets (πνεῦμα Χριστοῦ) and evangelists (πνεῦμα ἅγιον) so much as to see the common origin of both in the divine Spirit who underlies both activities. The emphasis in v. 11 on the Spirit of Christ points to that figure as the center of both witnesses, something obvious in the case of the gospel. On this point see also Schelkle, 42; Hiebert, "Peter's Thanksgiving," 102.

103 Hort, 59; Margot, 26; cf. Brox, "Pseudepigraphischen Rahmung," 70.

104 Cf. Goppelt, 109.

Analysis
1. Structure

The pattern that dominates these verses and that gives them a linguistic unity is the aorist imperative with associated nominative plural participles. They are found in v. 13 (ἐλπίσατε with ἀναζωσάμενοι and νήφοντες), vv. 14–16 (γενήθητε with συσχηματιζόμενοι), vv. 16–21 (ἀναστράφητε with εἰδότες), vv. 22–23 (ἀγαπήσατε with ἠγνικότες and ἀναγεγεννημένοι), and 2:1–3 (ἐπιποθήσατε with ἀποθέμενοι). The participle/verb pattern is absent in the OT quotation in vv. 24–25, perhaps indicating a conclusion. That pattern is repeated in 2:4–6 (οἰκο-δομεῖσθε with προσερχόμενοι), but the context indicates the mood of the main verb to be indicative rather than imperative.[1] The pattern is again absent from the final verses (2:7–10), which have no main verb at all, probably in that way signaling the end of the section.

Such a linguistic pattern allows us to divide the passage into sense-segments corresponding to its presence: 1:13, 14–16, 17–21, 22–23 with 24–25 to be included as conclusion, 2:1–3, 4–6 with 7–10 to be included, again as conclusion.[2] Further division of the passage is possible by observing some other linguistic patterns: 1:13 begins with a consequential conjunction and participle (διὸ and ἀναζωσάμενοι) as does 2:1 (ἀποθέμενοι and οὖν), a pattern nowhere else repeated, although the οὖν in 2:7 does introduce the concluding verses, 7–10. On that basis the body opening consists of two major sections, 1:13–25 and 2:1–10.

The individual sections can be further divided on the basis of the sense-segments. Clearest is the second section, with the first major part consisting of 2:1–6 and the second of 7–10 on the basis of the introductory οὖν; they can be further divided into 2:1–3 and 4–6, since each begins with a nominative plural participle, and 7–9

and 10, with each beginning with ὑμεῖς and a conjunction (οὖν v. 7, δέ in v. 9). Less clear is the division of 1:13–25, although vv. 13 and 22 each have two participles associated with the imperative, something nowhere else the case. That would allow a division into two major parts, 1:13–21 and 22–25. Sense-units would then allow a division into three segments in the first part, vv. 13, 14–16, and 17–21, and two in the second, vv. 22–23, and 24–25.[3] The outline would then be as follows:[4]

I. 1:13–25 Part One
    A. 13–21 Lives of hope are holy, and actions must conform
        1. 13, 14–16 Lives of hope are holy lives*
        2. 17–21 Act in ways appropriate to your redemption*
    B. 22–25 Begotten by God's word, you must love one another*
        1. 22–23 Begotten by God's word, therefore love
        2. 24–25 Such begetting is the content of the gospel
II. 2:1–10 Part Two
    A. 1–3 Desire appropriate things*
    B. 4–10 You are a chosen people*
        1. 4–6 You are living stones
        2. 7–10 You are the chosen people

Such a division is confirmed by other linguistic indications. 1:13–21 shows itself a unity when it begins and ends with words for "hope" (1:13, ἐλπίσατε; 1:21, ἐλπίδα).[5] The unity of 1:13–25 is indicated by the fact that words for "sanctification" and "obedience" figure prominently in 1:13–21 and 22–25 (ὑπακοῆς, 1:14, ὑπακοῇ, 1:22; ἅγιος, ἅγιοι, 1:16, ἠγνικότες, 1:22). The unity of the entire section is displayed when the author asserts in 1:14 that wrong desires (ἐπιθυμίαις) are to be abandoned, while in 2:2 he asserts that more appropriate desires are to be fostered (ἐπιποθήσατε); when mention of new begetting/new birth is found near the end of the first major part (1:23, ἀναγεγεννημένοι) and near the beginning of the second (2:2, ἀρτιγέννητα); and when faith is emphasized in both major sections (1:21, πιστούς, πίστιν; 2:7, πιστεύουσιν/ἀπιστοῦσιν).

---

1   In contrast, e.g., to Goppelt (110), who thinks all the main verbs, including οἰκοδομεῖσθε, are imperatival.

2   Some, e.g., LaVerdiere ("Covenant Theology," 2913), would end the passage with 2:6, finding three sections, viz., 1:13–21, 22–25, 2:1–6, based on a scheme of ignorance, obedience, and full revelation, respectively. The weakness of such schemes is lack of linguistic evidence indicating patterns or divisions.

3   See also Chevallier, "1 Pierre 1/1 à 2/10," 134–35; Dalton, "So That Your Faith," 268.

4   Sections marked with an asterisk (*) are treated subsequently as units, in each case representing the

main subunits of the body opening with the exception that subhead "A" of Part One was further subdivided to avoid a unit of excessive length.

5   So also, e.g., Goppelt, 114; Michaels, 52. One needs to note, however, that in 1:21 hope is coordinated with faith, also mentioned at the beginning of the verse. That weakens the *inclusio,* and thus indicates that the major section does not end there.

The close ties between the *prooemium* (1:3–12) and the body opening are indicated by the fact that the body opening begins and ends with the same concept with which the *prooemium* began (1:3, ἐλπίδα; 1:13, ἐλπίσατε; 1:21, ἐλπίδα). It is further signaled by the prominent use in both of the notion of new begetting/new birth (1:3, ἀναγεννήσας; 1:23, ἀναγεγεννημένοι; 2:2, ἀρτιγέννητα),[6] and of the idea of Christian proclamation (1:12, εὐαγγελισαμένων; 1:25, εὐαγγελισθέν).[7]

2. Imagery

There has been some discussion of the dominance in the body opening of imagery drawn from the OT account of the exodus. Among the more prominent images are: the girded loins (1 Pet 1:13; Exod 12:11), the blood of a spotless lamb (1 Pet 1:19; Exod 12:5), and a kingdom of priests, a holy nation (1 Pet 2:9; Exod 19:5–6). Further images include the desires of former times (1 Pet 1:14; cf. Exod 16:3), liberation from pagan servitude (1 Pet 1:18; cf. Exod 15:2–4), and obedience to God (1 Pet 1:13, 22; cf. Exod 15:26; 19:8).[8]

While such imagery is surely present, it would be an exaggeration to say that it dominates the passage. Some of the force of such a dominance depends on the notion of 1 Peter either representing, or heavily influenced by, a baptismal liturgy,[9] a force that lessens with the fading of that notion. Again, while "girded loins" and "spotless lamb" figure in the exodus account, neither is limited in the OT to that narrative.[10] Further, if some of the titles applied to the Christian community in 1 Pet 2:9 are in fact found in the exodus account, equally prominent are materials drawn from Leviticus (1 Pet 1:16), Hosea

(2:10), and, most prominently, Isaiah (1:24, 25; 2:6, 8). It would be more accurate to say the account is dominated by the notion of the Christian community as the chosen people, with a variety of images drawn from the OT to reinforce that point.

3. Theological Import

The succession of imperative verbs in 1:13—2:10 after a similar succession of indicative verbs in 1:3–12 indicates the characteristic alternation between indicative and imperative found in 1 Peter.[11] More significantly, however, it points to the fact that in this letter, as in early Christian proclamation in general, the imperative grows out of the indicative.[12] That is shown here by the consequential conjunction διό ("therefore") with which the passage begins: the announcement of grace includes the necessity to make such grace a reality in the lives of Christians in their present world.[13] The hope that is given to Christians by God's act for them in the resurrection of Christ (1:3) lays upon them the obligation to make such hope a reality in the way they conduct their lives (1:13). The sanctification worked by God's Spirit (1:2) that effected their divine election (1:1) is to be made reality in the way they live (1:16) in the midst of their present world.

Yet the very fact that grace brings with it obligations is itself an expression of grace, since it indicates that God wants Christians involved in the new kind of world he is bringing into being. They are not merely bystanders, passive and acted upon. They are to be active participants, partners in the gracious covenant God established through his Son.[14] Such participation means to

---

6 Cf. also Dalton, "So That Your Faith," 274.
7 Cf. Dalton, "So That Your Faith," 267; Chevallier ("1 Pierre 1/1 à 2/10," 134), who also notes (130) an *inclusio* involving "mercy": 1:3, κατά τὸ πολὺ αὐτοῦ ἔλεος; 2:10, ἠλεημένοι, ἐλεηθέντες.
8 E.g., Goppelt, 113; Cothenet, "Les orientations," 22, citing J. Daniélou; cf. Michaels, 52. The attempt by Hillyer ("First Peter," 60–61) to find the theme for this passage in the succession of events that occur during the Jewish month Tishri (New Year, Atonement, Tabernacles) is ingenious but no more persuasive than his attempt to link 1 Pet 1:3–12 to the traditions of the Aqedah. For further discussion, see the comment on 1:13 below.
9 E.g., Reicke, 83. Boismard ("Liturgie" [1], 195) bases it on the exodus as a "type of Christian baptism."
10 On the sacrifice of spotless lambs, see Num 28–29;

on girding the loins as divine command, Jer 1:17; on that act as metaphor, Isa 11:5; Prov 31:17.
11 Cf. Chevallier, "1 Pierre 1/1 à 2/10," 131.
12 E.g., Brox, 73; Schweizer, 32; Cranfield, 46.
13 E.g., Kelly, 65; Goppelt, 111, although one need not qualify it as he does (again in dependence on the notion of baptismal background) as not so much a general paranetic section (e.g., Rom 12–15) as a baptismal exhortation (Rom 6:11–14). I find that to be a distinction without difference, both in 1 Peter and in the examples he cites from Romans.
14 In agreement with Goppelt, 112.

abandon their sin-laden past (1:18), an abandonment that will signal to all who see them the new reality God is bringing about.[15] While this becomes more explicit in later passages (e.g., 2:12; 3:15b–16), it has its beginning here. It is the grace-empowered conduct of Christians that makes effective their membership in the holy people, that bears witness to the world of God's trans-forming power, and that will enable Christians to withstand God's final judgment. In 1 Peter as in other early Christian proclamation, therefore, the imperative mode belongs as surely as the indicative to the announcement of God's gracious lordship over human beings.

---

15 Even the aorist tense of the imperative verbs points to this transformation; the aorist in the imperative mood implies conduct different from that practiced before, rather than continuing a practice already engaged in, the import of the imperative in the present tense. See BDF § 337 (1).

1

Lives of Hope Are Holy Lives

13 **Therefore you, people whose minds are girded for action, who are sober, must set your hope totally upon the grace that comes to you at the appearance of Jesus Christ. 14/ As obedient children, you must not continue to be people shaped by the desires that were characteristic of your former time of ignorance; 15/ rather, as the One who called you is holy, even you yourselves must become holy in every aspect of your lives, 16/ because Scripture says,[1] "You shall be[2] holy, because I am[3] holy."**

1   An additional ὅτι to introduce the quotation in the Greek, included in B, Ψ, and some minuscules, is omitted in many ancient texts (among them P⁷², ℵ, A, C, P), probably as redundant in light of the introductory διότι γέγραπται.

2   Some minor mss. read γένεσθε, probably in conformity with v. 15, rather than the far more widely attested ἔσεσθε that appears in LXX Lev 11:44, 45; 19:2; 20:7, 26.

3   Some early mss. (ℵ, B, A*) along with the later tradition omit the εἰμί with Lev 19:2; 20:7, 26, while the majority of early mss. retain it with Lev 11:44, 45.

Excursus: Imperatival Use of Participles in 1 Peter

There is a marked tendency in commentators on 1 Peter to assume that the author regularly used participles, in addition to verbs in the imperatival mood, to convey commands.[4] This use, sanctioned by grammarians,[5] is based on some evidence from the papyri presented by James Hope Moulton,[6] who concluded that such use of the participle had become normal in Hellenistic Greek (225). Yet that conclusion has been severely challenged by David Daube in an article[7] too often ignored by commentators on 1 Peter. In that article, Daube examines the evidence presented by Moulton, finds that the seven instances cited by the latter can be reduced to three, or even two, analyzes those instances, and concludes that that evidence "does not show that the participle was a substitute for the imperative in Hellenistic language" (469). If such a use is to be found, therefore, its source will have to be found elsewhere. Daube suggests the source may be found in the tannaitic use of participles (476), from which NT examples would then derive. On the basis of the way participles are used in such literature as the Mishna, Tosephta, and Baraita, Daube proposes that only those participles have imperatival force that express "a duty, positive or negative, with the person or class concerned sometimes named, and sometimes omitted, and other imperatival forms employed in the same context, as on the same level" (484). Applying such a rule, Daube suggests imperatival participles in 1

Peter are limited to 1:14 (which he nevertheless considers doubtful, since συσχηματιζόμενοι may be construed with ἐλπίσατε according to normal grammatical rules); 2:18; 3:1, 7–9 (including imperatival adjectives, which he supposes may also reflect Hebrew participles); and 4:7–10 (also with imperatival adjectives).

At the least, Daube's thesis counsels caution in identifying participles as imperatives, since such usage cannot be said to have been normal practice in Hellenistic Greek. Where participles can be construed in normal ways, the commentator ought not overlook that possibility by jumping immediately to the (erroneous) assumption that its intention is imperatival because that is the way it would normally have been understood by Greek-speaking readers. If, as seems likely, 1 Peter is addressing precisely such readers, caution in identifying this unusual use of the participle is all the more in order.

Analysis

While v. 13 could stand alone because of its structure (i.e., it has both nominative participle and aorist imperative), its close ties to the content of the next three verses make it appropriate to see them as a unity of thought. As the announcement of a new hope set the theme for the *prooemium* (1:3), so the command to make that hope a reality (1:13) begins the discussion here. Such hope, grounded in the sure return of Christ in glory, has as its

---

4   E.g., Beare (97): the writer of 1 Peter is "exceptionally fond of using the participle as an imperative."

5   E.g., BDF 468 (2).

6   *Grammar of New Testament Greek,* vol. 1: *Prolegomena* (Edinburgh: Clark, 1906) 222–24; the next page reference in the text is also to this article.

7   "Appended Note, Participle and Imperative in 1 Peter," Selwyn, 467–88; the ensuing page references

in the text are also to this article.

consequence the abandonment of former practices carried out in ignorance of that reality (1:14; see also 1:18) and the assumption of a life lived in conformity to the God whose grace brought them into that new reality (1:15–16). Thus the call to holiness climaxes the call to hope; it shows both the character and the content of the grace upon which Christians are called to place their hope. If that grace is a future event, it nevertheless also has its effects in the present. The grace-bearing return of Christ already casts its shadow back onto the present. Yet grace is so powerful that even its shadow affects present reality. The content of the present reality of that grace is the content of the imperatives of this section. Given the new reality in hope, Christians must now make that reality present in their own lives.

These verses thus echo the central theme of the letter, expressed again and again in various ways: Christians must behave in accordance with their new reality in Christ, which means living in a way at odds with their former lifestyle. Vv. 14–16 give content to the command in v. 13 to set their hope on eschatological grace, and show why such conduct gives them the status of exiles and aliens within the social and cultural environment in which they lived.[8]

Comment

■ **13** While this verse is imperatival in force, the consecutive conjunction διό ("Therefore") indicates that the command grows directly out of the announcement of the new reality, given by God in Christ, which was described in 1:3–12.[9] The two participles (ἀναζωσάμενοι, νήφοντες) derive imperatival force from their association with the imperative ἐλπίσατε, but their force is less that of a direct command[10] than it is a description of the kind of people who can benefit from such an imperative, namely, those who are ready for disciplined effort.[11] Their respective tenses indicate that girding up (aorist) precedes the hoping, sobriety (present) accompanies it. While this metaphorical use of the phrase "girding the loins" (here lit. "girding the loins of the mind")[12] can recall the exodus event,[13] it may be equally reminiscent of Luke 12:35.[14] Yet the language of Luke, identical to LXX Exod 12:11,[15] differs from that in this verse,[16] surprising if our author wants deliberately to recall the Exodus verse since he is quite capable of reproducing exactly the language of the LXX when he wishes.[17] Perhaps the author here is simply using a common metaphor not intentionally derived from either Exodus or Luke,[18] the point being that one is to get any impediment, like a long garment, out of one's way,[19] and to be sober,[20] so one can do the work required. Drunken people in long garments are not very good at hard labor.[21]

Although it is possible for the adverb τελείως ("completely") to be construed either with "sober"[22] or with

---

8   Margot, 28.
9   See above, "1:13—2:10 Body Opening: 3. Theological Import."
10   See above, "Excursus: Imperatival Use of Participles in 1 Peter."
11   They are most likely to be adverbial participles of attendant circumstance, describing what accompanies the action of the main verb; less likely, though possible: adverbial participles of cause ("because you have girded up your minds and are sober").
12   As Scharlemann ("Exodus Ethics," 166) notes correctly, it refers to "tough thinking"; people ready to live lives counter to those of their contemporaries needed to be aware of what that meant.
13   E.g., Hart, 48; Michaels, 54; Benedikt Schwank, Alois Stöger, and Wilhelm Thüsing, *The Epistles of St. Peter, St. John and St. Jude* (London: Sheed and Ward, 1969) 22; Boismard, "Liturgie" [1], 191; Jonsen, "Moral Theology," 97; Deterding, "Exodus Motifs," 62; cf. Schlier, "Adhortatio," 70. More carefully, Dalton ("So That Your Faith," 270): it is a common figure, but here "probably does recall the Exodus event."
14   E.g., Delling, "Der Bezug," 98; Beare, 96; Bigg, 112; Calvin, 44. Gundry (*Verba Christi*," 339) and Boismard ("Liturgie" [1], 197) see the participle νήφοντες summing up the point of Luke 12:42–46.
15   Περιεζωσμέναι, passive participle construed with ὀσφύας.
16   Ἀναζωσάμενοι, middle participle construed with the subject of ἐλπίσατε.
17   Cf. 1 Pet 1:16 with Lev 19:2.
18   In agreement with Best (84) and Kelly (65–66), who cite 1 Kings 18:46; 2 Kings 4:29; 9:1 (cf. Luke 17:8); they also cite as implying mental attitude Job 38:3; 40:7 (cf. Eph 6:14). See also p. 115 n. 10 above.
19   Schwank et al. 22. As Scharlemann ("Exodus Ethics," 166) notes, the equivalent in modern parlance would be rolling up one's sleeves; it is an act that allows one to get on with a difficult task.
20   Here also with metaphorical connotations; see Best, 85; Kelly, 66; cf. Reicke, 83. It probably does not mean "stay awake"; the metaphor is labor done during the day (e.g., 2 Tim 4:5), not a warning

"hope,"[23] and while both make good sense in this sentence, general practice seems to argue for its use with the latter.[24] The verb itself, in the aorist, implies an undertaking in contrast with prior activity, an implication clearly in line not only with this passage but with the letter as a whole (e.g., 1:18; 2:11; 4:3–4).[25] The phrase ἐπὶ τὴν φερομένην χάριν functions not so much as the object of hope ("hope for the grace")[26] as its ground ("set your hope on the grace").[27] The present participle φερόμενον probably has here an implied future force,[28] a probability made the more likely because of the reference to the return of Christ (ἐν ἀποκαλύψει)[29] with which the verse concludes. The implication is not that they presently have no grace, but that their hope is to be grounded in that fulfilled grace which comes with Christ's return,[30] when hope will become visible reality. It is that hope which will sustain them in the hard labor of remaining faithful to Christ despite the hostile opposition of the culture in which they live.

■ **14** Their metaphorical address as "children" (τέκνα) sounds the theme of newness (newly begotten, 1:3, 23; newly born, 2:2),[31] which belongs to the central thrust of the letter.[32] Because the word "obedience" that qualifies the noun is another noun in the genitive case (ὑποκοῆς), it may represent a Semiticism,[33] where such a construction is frequent, particularly with the word "sons."[34] It occurs much less frequently with the word "children," however,[35] and may here represent the genitive of quality, that is, they are children whose chief characteristic is obedience.[36] There would be precedent for this in

---

against indolence and other vices characteristic of the night (e.g., 1 Thess 5:5–6).

21 The attempt by Boismard ("Liturgie" [1], 198) to relate 1 Pet 1:4, 13 to Christ's teaching in Luke 12:33, 35–38, 42–46 is as unconvincing as his attempt to relate 1 Pet 1:14–19 and Titus 2:11–14 to a common document.

22 So, e.g., Windisch, 55 "aus rhythmischen und stilistischen Gründen" "for rhythmic and stylistic reasons." Beare (96) notes the Greek commentators attach it to νήφοντες; see also Hort, 65; cf. Michaels, 55 ("probable"); Wand, 53 ("may be taken" with "either").

23 E.g., Cranfield, 48; Moffatt, 104; Bengel, *Gnomon*, 731; Reicke, 83; Schelkle, 45; Spicq, 60. The attempt by J. Rendel Harris ("An Emendation to 1 Peter 1.13," *ExpT* 41 [1929/30] 43) to resolve the problem by finding in τελείως a scribal error for an original τὲ ἀιὲ ὡς ("keep wide awake at all times") is ingenious but probably wide of the mark.

24 Selwyn (140) and Kelly (66) note that it is unusual for an adverb to follow the verb it modifies.

25 See p. 116 n. 15 above; Beare (96) is thus correct in seeing here an ingressive force: "begin to hope." Michaels (55) finds here a "programmatic aorist," setting the course for churches to follow. Less convincing is Kelly (66): the aorist tense "adds intensity."

26 Bigg, 113.

27 Hort, 66. Michaels (55) correctly notes "probable influence of the LXX," and cites Pss 32:18; 51:10; 77:22; 146:11. One can add literally dozens of cases in the Psalms where the phrase ἐλπίσατε ἐπὶ (τὸν) κύριον (θεόν) ("set your hope upon the Lord [God]") occurs, e.g., 4:6; 5:12; 9:11; 16:7; cf. also 2 Chr 13:18; 2 Macc 7:20, 34; *Ps. Sol.* 9.11; 17.3.

28 Kelly (67) cites as examples Luke 2:34; John 17:20; cf. Michaels, 56.

29 Best, 85; Windisch, 56; Schelkle, 44, 45; Goppelt, 115; Delling, "Der Bezug," 98. Bengel (*Gnomon*, 731) argues that it refers to "both comings of Christ"; cf. Calvin (45), who thinks it refers to the parousia, even if it may also imply that "the doctrine of the gospel reveals Christ to us."

30 Kelly (67) cites *Did.* 10.6 as confirmation that it means God's redemptive action at the parousia; see also Best, 85.

31 So also Michaels, 57.

32 Such newness may reflect the new life entered into upon baptism (e.g., Reicke, 84; Goppelt, 117; Kelly, 67), but it probably also includes the conversion of the readers (e.g., v. 14b), at which time they began the course that eventuated in baptism. Deterding ("Exodus Motifs," 59) notes that in LXX Hos 11:1, τέκνα is used for Israel at the time of the exodus, indicating the beginning of their life as chosen people.

33 So, e.g., Brox, 75; Bigg, 113 (a Hebraism, designating a genitive of relationship).

34 E.g., LXX 2 Sam 7:10; 2 Chr 25:17; Ezra 6:19, 20; 10:16 1 Esdr 7:11; 1 Macc 2:47; cf. Luke 10:6.

35 E.g., Hos 10:9; 11:10; Isa 57:4, although they may also be genitive of origin, as is Hos 2:6.

36 As qualitative genitive, Hart, 48; cf. Schelkle, 45 n. 2; as more than qualitative genitive, Spicq, 62: "designant une propriété essentielle" "designating an essential property"; see also Best, 85. Beare (97) argues for an objective genitive: "Children born for obedience."

119

secular society, where the primary characteristic of children was obedience to their parents, something firmly embedded in Roman law. Obedience here, however, is not a neutral word; it stands as a virtual equivalent of "faith" (cf. 1:2, 22; cf. also Rom 1:5; 16:26)[37] and is defined in the next two verses. The metaphor thus points to their need to be as obedient to God,[38] who has newly begotten them, as children normally are to be obedient to the father who begot them.[39]

The negatived participle (μὴ συσχηματιζόμενοι), a verb used only here and in Rom 12:2 in the NT,[40] is frequently taken as an imperative[41] meaning "continue in resisting conformity," a construal supported by its coordination through the conjunction ἀλλά with the imperative γενήθητε. The force is then two separate commands: do not be conformed, (but) become holy. Yet that it is a participle modifying the main imperatival verb of the following verse,[42] and that it is in the present tense, while all imperatives in these verses are aorist, make such a construal less than certain. The further fact that the main command, "become holy," while pointing to the need for separation,[43] does not define how that

separation is to be accomplished, presents less cause for confusion if such a definition has already been given by the participle, that is, "become holy" means precisely no longer to conform to previous conduct characteristic of non-Christians. Thus while the participle carries imperatival force because of the coordinating conjunction ἀλλά, it is to be construed not so much as a further command but as the way by which becoming holy is to be accomplished: you are to be holy by not conforming to former ways.

Such prohibited conformity refers clearly to their former conduct as non-Christians. The characterization of Gentiles as those who do not know God occurs regularly in the OT.[44] Similarly, the word for the "desires" (ἐπιθυμίαις) that characterized their former time of ignorance[45] can be neutral, but here as in the rest of the NT it is used as an essentially pejorative description of non-Christian conduct.[46] It is such conduct to which Christians may no longer conform themselves.

■ 15 The adversative conjunction (ἀλλά) identifies this verse as the (positive) opposite of the (negative) preceding verse. The κατά indicates that the holiness of the God who has called them is to serve as a pattern[47] for

---

37   So also Kenneth O. Gangel, "Pictures of the Church in I Peter," *Grace Journal* 10 (1969) 32. Hort (68) sees here an echo of the covenant terminology used in 1:2; Brox (75) argues for a Pauline origin, where the word means both "hear" and "draw appropriate ethical consequences."

38   While it might here also mean obedience to Christ, Arichae ("God or Christ?" 417) argues correctly that v. 15 makes it more probable that God is intended here.

39   Gangel ("Pictures," 32) suggests that this verse may introduce 2:13—3:7. One ought not, however, confuse obedience (ὑπακοή) with subordination (ὑποτάσσω), as does Best (85), who notes as passages where obedience is emphasized 2:13, 18; 3:1. See the discussion of the relevant verses below.

40   Boismard, "Liturgie" [1], 207. Kelly (67) argues for its independence from Paul since Paul uses it in the imperative; Paul and 1 Peter "were independently appropriating a Christianized version of a Jewish apophthegm."

41   E.g., Beare, 97; Cranfield, 50; Hart, 49; Goppelt, 117.

42   Daube ("Participle," 482) similarly doubts it is imperatival, but would link it with ἐλπίσατε.

43   For the argument that this is the meaning of "holy,"

see the discussion in v. 15 below.

44   So, e.g., Schutter, *Hermeneutic*, 56 n. 102. Kelly (68) cites Ps 79:6; Jer 10:25; Wis 14:22; in the NT, Acts 17:30; Gal 4:8–9; Eph 4:18; 1 Thess 4:5; cf. also Cranfield, 50. In addition to forms of ἄγνοια, forms of οὐκ εἰδότες are also used in those passages. This traditional use for Gentiles presents a problem for those who think the readers were converted Jews; e.g., Calvin, 46; Bengel, *Gnomon*, 731.

45   The phrase ἐν τῇ ἀγνοίᾳ ὑμῶν (temporal dative: "at the time of your ignorance") coupled with the adverb πρότερον ("earlier") clearly means to describe their pre-Christian life; for a similar idea using similar language, see Eph 4:22; 1 Thess 4:5.

46   As characteristic of gentile behavior, Rom 1:24; Eph 2:3; 4:22; 1 Thess 4:5; as pejorative, Mark 4:19; Gal 5:16; 1 John 2:16–17; cf. Best, 86; Kelly, 68. Such widespread biblical use makes it unlikely that this passage depends on Eph 2:1–3, as Beare (97) argued. Such a pejorative use was also common in Stoic treatises, e.g., Epictetus *Diss.* 2.1.10; 2.16.45; 2.18.8–9; 3.9.21; 4.1.175–76; 4.4.1; 4.9.5; Dio Chrysostom *Or.* 1.13; 3.34; 4.89; 5.16, 22.

47   So, e.g., Hort, 69.

their own behavior, a point then confirmed by v. 16. The phrase can be read either with ἅγιον as substantive (τὸν ... ἅγιον: "After the pattern of the holy one who called you")[48] or with τὸν καλέσαντα as substantive ("As the one who called you is holy")[49] without significant change in the meaning of the sentence. The regular use of "the Holy One" for God in the OT,[50] reflecting God's own self-designation (Isa 43:3), supports the former; the regular use in the NT of ὁ καλέσας ("the one who called [you]") for God,[51] a use also found in 1 Pet 2:9 and 5:10, supports the latter. The use of ὁ καλέσας for God in the two later passages in 1 Peter, along with the absence of any other use of ὁ ἅγιος in this letter, probably indicates this reading here as well.

The use of "holy" to describe God is derived from such use in the OT, as the quotation in the next verse makes clear. To be appropriated by God means to be made holy;[52] thus the choice of Israel as chosen people also makes them holy, which is defined in Lev 29:26 as being set apart from all other peoples. It is such separation that our author here also means with the word "holy," a point already indicated with the prohibition in the preceding verse. Yet the word "holy" does not contain etymologically any necessary connotation of morality;[53] the moral content is, as also is apparent here, to be derived from the nature (κατά) of the God who has called and separated them from their former culture.[54] "Holiness"

is therefore not something one can "achieve" by moral effort;[55] rather it is a separation from former culture for God that entails certain behavior appropriate for this situation.[56]

Thus the command "become holy" (ἅγιοι ... γενήθητε) means to live a life worthy of God (cf. 1 Thess 2:12; 1 John 3:3; cf. also Eph 2:10). As with the other imperatives in this section, γενήθητε is aorist,[57] implying as before that a new conduct unlike the old is now required.[58] The point is not that the readers are to make themselves holy; God accomplished that when they were chosen (cf. 1:1–2 ἐκλεκτοῖς ... ἐν ἁγιασμῷ).[59] Rather, the point is that they must now conform their behavior to their new status,[60] the point already of the previous verse.

Such a transformation had to entail every aspect of their behavior (ἐν πάσῃ ἀναστροφῇ); it involved the whole of a life that continued to be led in the midst of the hostile culture.[61] Thus the holiness of the Christians was to be manifested in a life visible to all, not through a life of withdrawal into holy conventicle.[62] They had been called by the holy God, a calling that meant they were now different, but that difference had to be maintained

48 E.g., Bigg, 114; cf. Best, 86; Michaels, 51.
49 E.g., Hart, 49.
50 Pss 70:22; 77:41; 88:19; Isa 1:4; 5:16; 12:6; 14:27; 17:7; 29:23; 30:12, 15; 40:25; 45:11; 55:5; Hos 11:9; cf. 1 John 2:20; *1 Clem.* 23.5; see Best, 86; Michaels, 58.
51 E.g., Hart, 49. Beare (98) acknowledges that ὁ καλέσας is a characteristic phrase for God in Paul, but thinks that καλέσαντα in this verse modifies τὸν ἅγιον.
52 E.g., as examples of God imparting holiness to what he appropriates, Kelly (70) and Schelkle (46) cite Isa 48:2 (Jerusalem); 44:10 (Mt. Zion and temple); Num 15:40 and Deut 7:6 (Israel). Qumran assumes the same: 1QM 3.5; 16.1 (sectaries); 1QM 12.7; 1QSb 1.5 (community); cf. also Flusser, "Dead Sea Sect," 228.
53 Beare, 98; cf. 168.
54 Margot, 28. That was also true of Israel's election in the OT; they were to abandon Egyptian and Canaanite ways (Lev 18:2–4); so also Kelly, 68. Boismard ("Liturgie" [1], 192) correctly draws this parallel between Israel and the Christian community.

55 Reicke, 84.
56 Goppelt, 118; Delling, "Der Bezug," 109.
57 Bigg (116) thinks the present tense rather than the aorist would have been more usual.
58 Beare (98) finds an ingressive sense here.
59 E.g., Michaels, 59. Γενήθητε is therefore not the equivalent of ἔστε, as Hort (70) and Beare (98) correctly point out.
60 Similarly Rom 12:2; its reference to "renewal of the mind" recalls the opening of 1 Pet 1:13; cf. Best, 86.
61 Ἀναστροφή is used eleven times in the NT, where it can describe behavior either praiseworthy (i.e., Christian: 1 Tim 4:12; Heb 13:7; Jas 3:13) or reprehensible (Gal 1:13; Eph 4:22; 2 Pet 2:7). Both types appear also in 1 Peter (praiseworthy: 1:15; 2:12; 3:2, 16; reprehensible: 1:18), where the word appears more often than in any other NT writing. The word describes the totality of one's behavior in any given situation.
62 Goppelt (117) notes how different this was from Qumran, which saw "holy" as meaning total separation from the world: 1QS 3.9–11; 8.20–21;

in any and all circumstances.[63] It was precisely that aspect of the command to live by values other than those of their cultural surroundings, that is, to live "holy" lives, that created trouble for the readers, and with which they constantly needed to come to terms (e.g., 2:12; 3:9, 14–16; 4:3–4, 14–16; 5:9).

■ **16** The conjunction διότι[64] typically for 1 Peter introduces a verse from Scripture[65] as the reason for the imperative contained in the preceding verse.[66] While a sentence similar to that quoted in 1 Peter occurs in several places in Leviticus (11:44, 45; 19:2; 20:7, 26), this particular form is cited not from Lev 11:44 (LXX: ἅγιοι ἔσεσθε, ὅτι ἅγιος εἰμί), which occurs in a passage that calls upon the Passover/exodus tradition (11:45),[67] but from Lev 19:2 (LXX: ἅγιοι ἔσεσθε, ὅτι ἐγὼ ἅγιος), a verse

contained in the Holiness Code (Lev 17–26), which directs Israel in a way of life other than that of the people in whose midst they dwell,[68] a context directly appropriate to the sense of 1 Pet 1:14–15 which it is called upon to support. That direct connection is yet further evidence of the way the author of 1 Peter has appropriated for the Christian community the specific commands to, and attributes of, Israel.[69]

CD 20:2, 7; cf. 7.3.

63   For a similar emphasis, see David Schroeder, "Once you were no people . . . ," in Harry Huebner, ed., *The Church as Theological Community: Essays in Honour of David Schroeder* (Winnipeg: CMBC Publications, 1990) 46–48.

64   It is a contraction of διὰ τοῦτο ὅτι, and can give the reason for something.

65   This conjunction appears in 1 Peter only to introduce a direct citation of the OT: 1:16, 24; 2:6.

66   The close connection of vv. 15–16 is also indicated by the chiasm they form: a = 15a; b = 15b; b′ = 16a; a′ = 16b; see Brox, "Pseudepigraphischen Rahmung," 67. Michaels (59) notes that the interpretation of a Scripture passage before its citation is not unusual in 1 Peter, e.g., 2:4–6. The citation thus confirms what is said (διότι), rather than

producing it; see Best, "I Peter II 4–10," 271.

67   This citation thus cannot be used as further evidence of 1 Peter's use of the exodus tradition, as Thurston ("Interpreting First Peter," 182) does.

68   So correctly, e.g., Deterding, "Exodus Motifs," 72; Goppelt, 117.

69   So also Beare, 99. This practice was of course not unique to 1 Peter; see Jas 1:4; 1 Cor 14:20. This citation may also underlie Matt 5:48.

1

Act in Ways
Appropriate to Your Redemption

17 **And since you invoke[1] as "Father" the one who judges each person impartially on the basis of his or her own performance, you must conduct yourselves with godly fear during the time of your pilgrimage, 18/ knowing as you do that you were redeemed from your foolish ancestral way of life not with perishable things, gold or silver, 19/ but with the precious blood of Christ, as of an unblemished and spotless lamb, 20/ whose destiny was set before the creation of the world, but who was made visible at the end of the times[2] because of you 21/ who through him are faithful[3] to God who raised him from the dead and gave him glory, with the result that your trust and hope are in God.**

1 P⁷² reads καλεῖτε, "call," for ἐπικαλεῖσθε, "invoke, call upon," perhaps influenced by the καλέσαντα of v. 15.

2 Evidently the phrase ἐσχάτου τῶν χρόνων presented some difficulty, since there are a variety of attested readings. While perhaps the best witness is to ἐσχάτου τῶν χρόνων (א², A, B, C, and some others), others read ἐσχάτων τῶν χρόνων (P⁷² and many later texts), ἐσχάτου τοῦ χρόνου ("the end of time," א*, Ψ), or ἐσχάτων τῶν ἡμέρων ("the last days," 69, some few more).

3 While there is good witness to the presence of the adjective πιστούς (A, B, and a few others, along with vg), there is also a good witness to the present participle πιστεύοντας (P⁷², א, C, P, Ψ, and many minuscules). Some few minuscules have the aorist πιστεύσαντας; the change was probably influenced by the prepositional phrase εἰς θεόν more commonly used with the verb than the adjective; so also Beare, 107; Kelly, 77; Michaels, 52. The substantival adjective is more likely to mean "who are faithful to God"; the substantival participle, "who believe in God."

Analysis

Unlike the combination of participle and imperative that characterizes each of the sentences in this section (i.e., 1:13, 14–16, 17–21, 22–23; 2:1–3, 4–6),[4] these verses have the participle following rather than preceding the imperative. The sentence is long but written in balanced periods. The participle itself, εἰδότες, is frequently used in the NT to indicate the content of traditions presumed already known by the readers;[5] in this case it is also likely intended to remind the readers of traditions the author assumes they have already heard. The passage itself, in fact, reflects much of the common Christian tradition found throughout the NT: God as Father, as impartial judge, redemption through the blood of Christ, Christ as sacrificial lamb, Christ as preexistent, Christians living in the last days, resurrection and exaltation of Christ by God, God as the one in whom Christians place their trust and hope.[6] The material is used in so general a way, however, that dependence on one or more specific writings in the NT is impossible to determine.

Because of the inclusion of many of the common traditions of the Christian faith, this passage embodies the fundamental theological argument that underlies and undergirds all that follows in this letter, whether hortatory or theological. Especially clear is the intimate connection between Christian doctrine and Christian conduct: such conduct is linked to invoking God as Father (v. 17) and to the Christians' redemption by Christ's sacrifice on the cross (vv. 18–21). Also explicit in this passage is the reason why the Christians may not be conformed to the culture that surrounds them. It is expressed in the contrast between ἀναστροφὴ ἐν φόβῳ ("reverent behavior," v. 17), based on the nature of God (holy, v. 16; impartial, v. 17; Father, v. 17), and ματαία ἀναστροφή ("foolish behavior," v. 18b), based on the ways of the surrounding culture to which the readers be-

4 1:24–25 and 2:7–10 consist principally of quotations from the OT, and hence do not follow this structure.

5 It is also used to indicate things already known, e.g., Luke 8:53; John 21:12. It is characteristic of Paul to use the word to identify Christian traditions, e.g., Rom 6:9; 2 Cor 4:14; Gal 2:16; Eph 6:9; 1 Thess 1:4.

6 The suggestion that, because of such commonplaces present here, some kind of Christian hymn must

underlie this passage is rightly rejected by Brox (79); the rhythmic and stylistic elements for such an assertion to be well grounded are simply absent. See also Michaels (53), who observes correctly that the whole of vv. 13–21 presumes earlier traditions, but "the recovery of the individual units out of which the section is composed is now virtually impossible."

longed ancestrally (πατροπαραδότου; cf. 1:14).[7] Thus the Christians must now assume an entirely new way of behaving, and the whole of behavior determined by their former cultural values must be eschewed as a result.

The appropriation of OT language for Christ and for the Christian community is also clearly on display in this section. Here it is particularly the language of the sacrificial cultus that is applied to Christ (v. 19). By this appropriation, the parameters of the Christian faith become clear: based on the OT, our author sees Christ as God's new and final act to which Christians are to conform, even at the cost of abandoning former cultural involvements. All of this is set within a cosmic frame of reference, both in terms of God's decisions prior to the creation of the world and in terms of the impending conclusion of that creation (v. 20).

In that way, the readers are summoned both to understand (cf. v. 13) the importance of the events of which they are participants, events that God has planned even before he created the world, and to respond in a way appropriate to the gravity of the situation God has brought about: the impending judgment and closing of the age. It is a tribute to the author's power of thought and language that virtually the whole of what he has to say, and indeed virtually the whole of the import of the Christian faith, can be expressed in this sentence midway through the first chapter of the letter.

Comment

■ **17** The verse does not so much pose a condition ("If you summon") as draw an inference ("Since you summon");[8] there is no thought that the condition of summoning God as Father will remain unfulfilled. The emphatic position of πατέρα[9] calls attention to the contrast between God as benevolent Father and as impartial judge of the world.

The idea of God as "father," although not a commonplace, was known in both Jewish[10] and Greco-Roman traditions.[11] The origin in this verse of the practice of invoking God as Father, however, although it is expressed in the rare[12] phrase πατέρα ἐπικαλεῖσθε,[13] is almost certainly to be found in the sayings of Jesus,[14] although the language of the phrase πατέρα ἐπικαλεῖσθε is reminiscent of LXX Ps 88:27 and Jer 3:19.[15] Whether it is possible to determine more specifically the origin of the phrase used here (e.g., to derive it directly from the Lord's Prayer),[16] is questionable, however, since by the time this letter was written, such language had already passed into the liturgical vocabulary of the church.[17]

Partiality on the part of judges who varied verdicts on the basis of prestige or bribes was as much bemoaned in the ancient world[18] as it is in the modern. That the judgments of God are impartial is a commonplace in the OT[19] as it is in Jewish tradition.[20] From those sources it passed into the common tradition of the Christian

7   On this contrast, see van Unnik, "Redemption," 32–33.
8   E.g., Best, 87; Kelly, 71.
9   Spicq, 65.
10 The idea finds expression in terms of God as Father both of the king as representing Israel (e.g., 2 Sam 7:14; Ps 2:7) and of Israel itself (e.g., Jer 3:19; Mal 1:6; 2:10; Wis 2:16; 3 Macc 5:7; 1QH 9.34–36); the idea is also present when Israel is referred to as son (e.g., Hos 11:1, 3).
11 E.g., Dio Chrysostom (*Or.* 12.22, 74; 36.35–36), who notes (*Or.* 53.12) that calling God "Father" goes back to Homer; Seneca *Ep.* 107.11.
12 Goppelt (120) notes that it is found only here in early Christian literature.
13 The verb carries the connotation of "invoke" rather than simply "call" in the sense of "name"; so, e.g., Kelly, 71.
14 E.g., Matt 6:9; cf. 7:11; 11:27, 23:9; John 20:17; 1 John 1:2–3.
15 E.g., Hort, 72; Kelly, 71.
16 Michaels (61): "probably" so derived; Beare (101): "possibly"; Best (87): no direct reference; Hort (72): impossible to say confidently.
17 In addition to the Lord's Prayer, cf. Rom 8:15; Gal 4:6; cf. Goppelt, 120; Selwyn, 143; Leaney, 25.
18 E.g., Petronius *Satyr.* 14: "a case at law is nothing other than a public bribe" ("Ergo iudicium nihil est nisi publica merces").
19 E.g., Deut 10:17; 2 Chr 19:7; such partiality is thus also to be avoided in human courts, e.g., Lev 19:15; Deut 1:17; 16:19b.
20 E.g., Sir 35:12; *Jub.* 5.16; 33.18; *2 Bar.* 13.8; *Ps. Sol.* 2.18–19; cf. Shimada, *Formulary Material,* 206.

community,[21] and is also reflected here, although the adverb used to describe it (ἀπροσωπολήμπτως) is unique to this verse in 1 Peter.[22] That Christians will be judged on the basis of their works (ἔργον) is also common in the NT,[23] an idea that neither this letter nor the rest of the NT finds contradictory to the notion that the Christian lives by God's grace.[24] The point is that the Christian is not to presume on God's grace,[25] a grace that includes in itself the call to transform one's life in obedience to God (the point of 1:13–16).[26]

The consequence of being in intimate relationship ("Father") with the God who is the impartial judge of the world is to conduct one's life (ἀναστράφητε) in accordance with the will of that God, here expressed by the phrase ἐν φόβῳ. While the word φόβος can mean "fear" or "terror," that is less likely to be its meaning here. Given its present context in the midst of the discussion of conformity to God rather than to culture (1:14–16), the meaning is more likely to be "awe" or "reverence."[27] The

point is that Christians are to live in an attitude of holy reverence toward the one who through Christ has begotten (1:3) and redeemed them (1:18),[28] rather than to live in terror at the thought of divine judgment.[29]

The life that is so to be lived (ἀναστράφητε)[30] is described as one of pilgrimage or exile (τὸν τῆς παροικίας ὑμῶν χρόνον, "the time of your exile"). While the notion of Christians as exiled from their true heavenly home is found in the NT (e.g., Heb 11:13–16; cf. Phil 3:20), and has been argued as the meaning here (i.e., Christians are exiles during the time they must spend away from their true heavenly home),[31] in the present context (esp. 1:14, 18b), as well as the letter as a whole, it is more likely to refer to the Christians' present status in relation to a culture that regards any who do not conform to customs (1:14; see also 4:4) as a potential threat to social stability.[32] It is precisely their "holiness," their divine separation from secular cultural values, that renders them aliens in the eyes of that culture.[33] The use of the word

---

21 E.g., Matt 16:27; Rom 2:6, 11; 14:12; 1 Cor 3:13–14; 2 Cor 5:10; 2 Tim 4:14; Rev 2:23; 22:12; cf. Shimada, *Formulary Material*, 211. That meant it also had to disappear from dealings within the church; e.g., Gal 3:28; Col 3:11; Jas 2:1–9. The notion of Hart (49) that this passage is based on Peter's personal experience in Caesarea (Acts 10:34) is as fanciful as it is unnecessary.

22 The adverb ἀπροσωπολήμπτως occurs only here and in *1 Clem.* 1.3; the form ἀπροσωπολήπτως occurs five times: *Barn.* 4.12; Athanasius *Expositiones in Psalmes* (*PG* 27.221); Basilius *Quaestiones* (*PG* 31.1184); Clement of Alexandria *Strom.* 4.17.105.2; and John Chrysostom *Fragmenta in Job* (*PG* 64.624). Other forms of the word do appear in the NT: there is no προσωπολημψία with God: Rom 2:11; Eph 6:9; Col 3:25; God is οὐ προσωπολήμπτης: Acts 10:34.

23 See n. 21 above. Closest OT parallels are LXX Ps 61:13; Prov 24:12. Michaels (61) notes that Christian tradition (which he acknowledges) has judgment on the basis of works as a commonplace.

24 In disagreement with Goppelt (199), who finds hoping fully in grace and facing a final judgment based on one's activities contrary notions. Rather, grace means to conform one's life to God's will, which is holiness (1:16), and to live one's life in conformance to that will, not in conformity with surrounding society (1:14). Schweizer (49) notes that in this place, faith is also included in the work; Luther (203) observed that where there is no faith there can be no good works, and that, vice versa, where there are no good works there is also no faith.

Thus even though God judges us by works, it remains true that the works are totally the result of faith. It is that understanding that pervades both 1 Peter and the NT.

25 Bauer, 20; cf. Schelkle, 47.

26 See Rom 2:4–6, where the idea of judgment by works is also placed in the context of not presuming on God's grace.

27 This is clearly also the meaning in 1 Pet 2:17.

28 E.g., Kelly, 71; Selwyn, 143; Beare, 102; van Unnik, "Redemption," 31; cf. Best, 88.

29 E.g., Goppelt, 120; Brox, 70.

30 The aorist imperative again suggests doing something not done before, and has an ingressive sense.

31 E.g., Beare, 102; Schwank, "L'Epître (1 P 3,8–15)," 20; Boismard, "Liturgie" [1], 193; Cross, *Paschal Liturgy*, 50; Deterding, "Exodus Motifs," 63; Harrison, "Exegetical Studies" [97], 206–7; van Unnik, "Christianity," 82; cf. Lippert, "Leben," 241.

32 E.g., Elliott, *Home*, 52–53; Wolff, "Christ und Welt," 337; Tarrech, "Le milieu," 115. On the question of whether παροικία refers to the legal status of Christians prior to their conversion, or metaphorically to their status after such conversion, see the Introduction § III, "Readers."

33 So also Harrison, "Exegetical Studies" [97], 325; Piper, "Hope," 216; cf. Luther, 204; Calvin, 49.

125

παροικία to qualify the time span of the Christians' life[34] probably reflects more the Christians' OT heritage[35] than the secular use of the word.[36] While the word can refer to Israel's sojourn in Egypt,[37] and that image surely was part of our author's thought-world, παροικία is also used in the LXX in a metaphorical sense very similar to that found in this verse.[38] The further fact that the wording here bears striking resemblance to a phrase in 3 Macc 7:19 (τόν τῆς παροικίας αὐτῶν χρόνον), there in the context of Jews who were uprooted by Ptolemy IV Philopator, means it may as easily refer to that other time when Israel existed as political strangers—the exile. The designation of the readers as exiles in the "diaspora" (1:2) indicates this to be the more likely frame of reference.

■ **18–19** These two verses are so closely intertwined with their discussion of the contrasting means of redemption (18a, 19) that they must be treated as a unit. In addition, they present along with v. 17 a basic contrast in the way life is to be carried out: life in reverence toward God (ἀναστροφὴ ἐν φόβῳ, 1:17) that they are now to practice, and the vain and foolish way of life they formerly practiced (ἀναστροφὴ ματαία, 1:18).[39] In doing that, these two verses show how the great transformation in the lives of the readers, announced in 1:3, has in fact taken place.[40]

The participle with which v. 18 begins (εἰδότες) is probably to be understood in a causal sense.[41] In addition, this form of the participle is normally used in the Pauline correspondence to indicate the kind of elementary Christian belief in which the author can presume the readers have been instructed.[42] It is therefore not surprising that the verses so introduced reflect common Christian tradition. Some have found evidences of an underlying hymn[43] or confession,[44] but any recovery of its original form is all but eliminated by the author's appropriation of the material into the present argument.[45]

The basic thrust of the tradition the author here

---

34 Χρόνον is an accusative of duration or extent of time.

35 The word παροικία occurs some 20 times in the LXX, predominantly in the later (e.g., 1 and 2 Esdras; Judith; 3 Maccabees; Wisdom; Sirach; *Psalms of Solomon*) rather than the earlier literature, although it is used in Habakkuk, Lamentations, and the Psalms.

36 While the notion embodied in the stem παροικ- is common in Greek literature, the overwhelming majority of occurrences of the noun παροικία are in biblical and Christian authors. On the use of this word in 1 Peter, see the Introduction § III, "Readers."

37 E.g., Hart, 50; Michaels, 62; Tarrech, "Le milieu," 111. Boismard ("Liturgie" [1], 193) sees it specifically as a reference to moving toward the promised land, which for the Christians is heaven.

38 Israelites as strangers on the earth in the eyes of God: Lev 25:23; 1 Chr 29:15; Pss 38:13; 118:19 (I owe these references to Kelly, 72; and Schelkle, 47–48 n. 1). Michaels (62) notes that such metaphorical use designating people as strangers on the earth also found its way into Greek inscriptions.

39 So also van Unnik, "Redemption," 32.

40 Delling ("Der Bezug," 100) also makes this point.

41 E.g., Michaels, 63; Sieffert, "Die Heilsbedeutung," 386. Kelly (72) understands it as a participle of attendant circumstance, "knowing as you do," which in this context retains a causative flavor; Goppelt (121) argues that it is not causative, but rather provides the basis from which hope and faith are derived, a distinction without real difference.

42 It is used frequently in the Pauline literature with this sense: Rom 5:3; 6:9; 1 Cor 15:58; 2 Cor 1:7; 4:14; 5:6; Gal 2:16; Eph 6:9; Col 3:24; 1 Thess 1:4; so also Beare, 103; Best, 88; Kelly, 72. Spicq (66) thinks the content of the verses derives from an early Christian catechism and sees similarities with Heb 6:1–5. Schlier ("Adhortatio," 60) finds similarities with Titus 2:14.

43 So, e.g., Shimada (*Formulary Material*), who finds evidence in the number of hapax legomena both in the NT and in 1 Peter in these two verses (231–32), and thinks they may go back to the saying of Jesus recorded in Mark 10:45 (258–59). Given the brevity of 1 Peter, one ought not put too much weight on words used only at one point in the letter.

44 Schelkle (51) argues that vv. 19–21 come from a confession since the context of 1:17–21 needed only a statement of Jesus' salvific death, for which 1:19 would have sufficed; the remaining verses were included because they appeared in the confession. Presuming to know precisely what the author had in mind and "needed" in order to make his point verges on the speculative.

45 Nor is the author dependent on any Christian documents we have, as Kelly (75) notes in respect to a similarity to Eph 5:27. It is, however, not obvious why Kelly can conclude that, since 1 Peter does not call Christ a lamb as do, e.g., John 1:29, 36; 1 Cor 5:7, it "may be a pointer to the early date of his material."

presumes is the redemption (ἐλυτρώθητε) of Christians.[46] Such an idea of redemption, or ransom, has roots in both the Jewish and the Greco-Roman worlds. In the latter, it could refer to the ransom of prisoners of war, or, more likely in this context, to the manumission of slaves, whereby the slave deposited his or her purchase price in a temple, from which the owner would then receive the money ostensibly from the god or goddess who thereby purchased the slave from the former owner.[47] In the LXX the word is used to describe the redemption of property by paying its value to its present holder (Lev 25:26, 33, 48–49); the retribution for faults committed (Exod 21:30); the ransom of the firstborn (Exod 13:12–13; Num 3:44–51; 18:15–17); and the "atonement price" (half-shekel paid by every Israelite; Exod 30:12–16). The term is also used to describe the deliverance of Israel by God from its bondage and exile, in which case the price is normally not mentioned (Exod 6:6; Deut 7:8; cf. Isa 44:22–23; 51:11; 52:3).

Although the image of manumission of slaves is a possible derivation, the context of these two verses, as well as the general tenor of 1 Peter, makes it more probable that the origin is to be drawn from its use in the Hebrew Scriptures.[48] Such an origin is at best second-hand, however, since the author's language (εἰδότες) makes clear he intends to appeal to an already existing Christian tradition. The more direct origin is probably to be found in similar concepts of the redemptive significance of the death of Christ in the NT,[49] where it is recalled as originating with Jesus himself.[50]

The redemption to which the author refers in this context is not so much from human sin or guilt[51] as it is from a former way of life, here described as ματαία and πατροπαράδοτος. While the general meaning of ματαία is "vain" or "foolish," it is used in the LXX to describe the gods of the Gentiles (e.g., Lev 17:7; Jer 8:19; 10:15); in a similar way in the NT, it describes the pre-Christian life of converts (e.g., Acts 14:15; Rom 1:21; Eph 4:17; cf. Rom 8:20; 1 Cor 3:20). The adjective πατροπαράδοτος, which means basically traditions (Gk. παρέδοσις) handed down from the fathers (Gk. πατρές), could on the face of it refer to something valued both in the Greco-Roman world[52] and in Jewish culture (e.g., Deut 32:7; Josh 24:16–18; Isa 51:1; Jer 6:16). While some have seen its primary reference to the readers' former Jewish practices,[53] both linguistic usage[54] and its present association

46 The passive form ἐλυτρώθητε is here almost surely the "reverential passive" and assumes God as the actor: "Because you know that *God redeemed you.*"

47 On ransom, see Best, 88–89; on manumission, see Cranfield, 55; Windisch, 57; van Unnik, "Redemption," 11.

48 Michaels (65) holds that the use of the dative, instead of the genitive of price, argues for a combination of both understandings, a widely held view; cf. van Unnik, "Redemption," 24. Such a blending is of course possible, but in the larger context here, so dependent on Hebrew Scripture, I think it unlikely.

49 Rom 3:24–25; Eph 1:7; 1 Tim 2:6; Heb 9:12, 15; cf. Rom 8:23; 1 Cor 1:30; Col 1:14. Schelke (48) finds similar concepts concerning the death of Christ: ἀντίλυτρον, 1 Tim 2:6; λύτρωσις, Heb 9:12; most often ἀπολύτρωσις, Rom 3:14; 1 Cor 1:30; Eph 1:7; Col 1:14; Heb 9:15.

50 Mark 10:25//Matt 20:28; so also Michaels, 63.

51 If the notion of redemption does include God's breaking the power of sin and thus bringing one into divine fellowship, as Sieffert ("Die Heilsbedeutung," 392) argues, it is at best implicit, with the power of sin residing in the former ἀναστροφή from which one is freed.

52 In that world, the "traditions of the fathers" (Lat. *paternae traditiones*) represented something held in high regard; performing ancestral religious rites safeguarded the state, whereas renouncing such traditions was frowned on as inappropriate, e.g., Tacitus *Hist.* 5.5; cf. Willem C. van Unnik, "The Critique of Paganism in I Peter 1:28," in E. E. Ellis and M. Wilcox, eds., *Neotestamentica et Semitica: Studies in Honour of Matthew Black* (Edinburgh: Clark, 1969), esp. 140.

53 E.g., Leaney, "Passover," 246; Kamlah, cited in Brox, 81–82.

54 The word does not appear in the LXX; its earliest appearance is in an inscription, dated 135–134 BCE, recording a letter of Attalus III of Pergamum, part of the area to which 1 Peter is addressed (I owe this reference to van Unnik, "Paganism," 132); while the word occurs in secular Greek authors (e.g., Diodorus Siculus, Dionysus Halicarnassus), it is used far more frequently by Christian authors (e.g., Clement of Alexandria, Eusebius, Origen).

with ματαία argue for a reference to the pagan past of the readers.[55] It is thus precisely the gentile cultural heritage that the Christian has rejected,[56] a rejection made possible by God's act in Christ.

The contrast between former and present ways of life is paralleled by the contrast between what was not (v. 18: φθαρτοῖς ἀργυρίῳ ἢ χρυσίῳ)[57] and what was (v. 19: τιμίῳ αἵματι [Χριστοῦ]) the means of divine redemption.[58] It is difficult to find the exact contrast between the two phrases, however, since φθαρτός ("perishable") and τίμιος ("precious") are not opposites. It is perhaps best to see here an implied contrast between silver and gold, which perish[59] (see 1:7) and thus are of lesser value, and the blood of Christ, whose effects are not dimmed by time and which are therefore of greater value ("precious").[60] The ransom is thus achieved at the cost of Christ's blood; Christians were "bought with a price" (1 Cor 6:20; 7:23; cf. Rev 5:9).[61] Yet even such a parallel is far from exact, since the language (1 Cor 6:20: ἠγοράσθητε . . . τιμῆς; here: ἐλυτρώθητε . . . τιμίῳ [αἵματι]) and the grammar (1 Cor 6:20, genitive of price; here, dative of means) are quite different. The point here is not the ransom price[62] but the fact that redemption occurred not by means of[63]

anything pertaining to their former (idolatrous) way of life, but by means of God's own act through Christ (cf. vv. 20–21).[64]

The redemptive power of Christ's blood presumed here, also a commonplace in Christian tradition (e.g., Acts 20:28; Rom 3:24–25; Eph 1:7; Heb 9:12; cf. Col 1:20), is again almost surely drawn from the Hebrew Scriptures. The mention of the spotless lamb (ἀμνὸς ἄμωμος) recalls for many scholars[65] the events of Israel's exodus from Egypt. To those convinced of such an origin, the idea of the new inheritance (1:4) contrasted to the land of Canaan as the Israelites' inheritance,[66] and the covert reference to idols contained in the word φθαρτός, which recalls the golden calf in the wilderness,[67] add further weight to this idea.[68] Yet Israel was not redeemed from Egypt by the blood of the paschal lamb; rather it was by the power of God.[69] The blood of the lamb had apotropaic rather than redemptive value.[70] Since the NT references to Christ as paschal lamb leave no doubt about that context (1 Cor 5:7; John 19:36), and since the phrase ἀμνὸς ἄμωμος does not occur in the description of the original Passover lamb,[71] it seems likely that the primary reference here is not to Pass-

---

55 E.g., Selwyn, 145; Hort, 76; Bigg, 119. See 1 Pet 4:3 for another comment on their prior situation.

56 E.g., van Unnik, "Paganism," 137.

57 These two substantives are probably chosen to reinforce the polemic against the former pagan life of the readers, since they are frequently associated in the LXX with idolatry; e.g., Deut 29:17; Dan 5:23 (cf. Rev 9:20); Wis 13:10; cf. Diogn. 2.7; 1 Enoch 52.7, 9. On this point see Michaels, 65.

58 Because God is the assumed subject of the passive verb ἐλυτρώθητε these phrases cannot be considered as a dative of agent, only of instrument (against Hart, 50).

59 Φθαρτοῖς is to be seen as a substantive, modified then by ἀργυρίῳ and χρυσίῳ, rather than as an (plural) adjective modifying the two (singular) nouns.

60 Cf. Sieffert, "Die Heilsbedeutung," 393.

61 So, e.g., Schelkle, 49.

62 That inevitably raises the question of to whom, or by whom, the price was paid; yet that is no more the issue here than it was in the exodus, where it is hardly the case that God's mighty acts were somehow the price paid as compensation to the Egyptians for the loss of the Israelites (I owe the illustration to Sieffert, "Die Heilsbedeutung," 392).

63 Hence an instrumental dative of means; see n. 58 above.

64 Instructive in this regard is Heb 9:12, where, speaking within a Jewish sacrificial context, the author contrasts the blood of animals, a point drawn from the former context, with the blood of Christ, a point drawn from the new, Christian context. The same contrast is drawn here between former cultural values, in this case precious metals, and the present Christian situation.

65 E.g., Calvin, 51; Beare, 106; Moffatt, 106; Margot, 30; Spicq, 66; Deterding, "Exodus Motifs," 58; Boismard, "Liturgie" [1], 199; van Unnik, "Redemption," 19.

66 So, e.g., Selwyn, 144.

67 Hart (50) cites Exod 32:3–4; Wis 14:8 as substantiation.

68 To see in the mention of silver and gold a reflection of Ps 105:37 and Exod 12:35 and the treasures the Israelites spirited away from the Egyptians at the exodus, as does Deterding ("Exodus Motifs," 59), is somewhat fanciful.

69 So Exod 6:6: λητρώσομαι ὑμᾶς ἐν βραχίονι ὑψηλῷ; see also Deut 7:8; cf. van Unnik, "Redemption," 41.

70 Spicq, 68.

71 The phrase in Exod 12:5 is πρόβατον τέλειον ("perfect sheep").

over.[72] Our author's citation of phrases from Isaiah 53 in 2:22–25 has called attention to Isa 53:7 as a possible source of this language,[73] but the absence of any common vocabulary other than the word for lamb (ἀμνός) renders such an origin questionable.[74]

More likely as source is the general sacrificial cult practiced by Israel, in which all animals were expected to be perfect; if they were not, they were unacceptable to God.[75] The adjective ἄμωμος supports such a source.[76] It is used frequently in relation to the cultus (cf. Num 28–29) but not in the story of the exodus.[77] The addition of ἄσπιλος, although not found in the LXX,[78] reinforces the notion of cultic purity embodied in the more common ἄμωμος. The origin for the tradition embodied in this verse seems thus more likely to come from the broader cultic context[79] of the OT than specifically from the exodus account or the language of the prophet Isaiah.

The appositive phrase describing the lamb (ὡς ἀμνοῦ ἀμώμου καὶ ἀσπίλου)[80] is placed in a somewhat odd position, between αἵματι and Χριστοῦ. If the verse stood by itself, one would expect the phrase to follow the Χριστοῦ so as to allow the normal phrase αἵματι Χριστοῦ

to appear.[81] Yet its position is dictated by the author's intention to give a further description of Christ in v. 20 (προεγνωσμένον, "destined beforehand"), in addition to the description by means of the appositive ἀμνοῦ. Were the author to have allowed the phrase ἀμνοῦ ἀμώμου καὶ ἀσπίλου to follow Χριστοῦ,[82] the ensuing description in v. 20 with its participle (προεγνωσμένον) in the genitive case to modify Χριστοῦ could have been construed to describe not Christ but "lamb," which is also cast in the genitive case in order to stand in apposition to Χριστοῦ. The present word order, with Χριστοῦ placed at the end of the phrase and thus immediately preceding the further description of him in v. 20, obviates such a misunderstanding.[83]

Finally, the comparison of Christ to a lamb (ὡς ἀμνοῦ) is capable of being understood in diametrically opposite ways, since the word ὡς, used here as a relative adverb of manner, can indicate either the reality ("as")[84] or the figurative nature ("as it were")[85] of the comparison. The preponderance of the figurative uses in 1 Peter, particularly in this immediate context, argues for the latter meaning here: Christ is not so much identified as a lamb, as his sacrifice is to be compared to that of the lamb who

---

72 With Sieffert ("Die Heilsbedeutung," 395) and Schutter (*Hermeneutic*, 39 n. 69), who find no allusion here to the paschal lamb.

73 So Kelly, 72; but cf. Best (90), who nevertheless thinks the Passover lamb is the primary reference. See also Tarrech, "Le milieu," 341; Windisch, 57; Schutter, *Hermeneutic*, 39 n. 69.

74 So also Goppelt, 123; Hort, 77; Schiwy, 41; J. Dalmer, "Zu 1. Petri 1,18.19," BFCTh 2.6 (1898/99) 83.

75 E.g., Exod 29:1; Lev 22:17–25, esp. v. 23; Num 28–29; Ezek 43:22–23; cf. Heb 9:14; cf. Best, 90; Selwyn, 145–46; van Unnik, "Redemption," 37.

76 Hart (50–51) argues that the word, unintelligible to a Gentile in this use, got its meaning from its similarity to the Heb. מום, meaning "blemish," to which the α privative was added. That it is derived from the Heb. תם or תמים, meaning "perfect" or "faultless," as Michaels (65–66) suggests, is surely wrong, since the form with the α privative *negates* the root concept of the word; if such were its derivation, ἄμωμος would here have to mean "*im*perfect," hardly the author's intention.

77 See n. 71 above. Van Unnik ("Redemption," 34) remarks that it is used 86 (I count 83) times in the LXX, with the meaning that the object so described is as it should be, i.e., a morally perfect person, a

sacrificial animal without blemish, etc.

78 Van Unnik ("Redemption," 35) notes that the word has no specifically religious connotations.

79 That is also the case with the sacrificial language in Hebrews, e.g., 9:1—10:18.

80 The two adjectives point to the lamb, not Christ, as Michaels (66) rightly notes.

81 This is the only place in the NT where words intervene between αἷμα and Χριστοῦ; see 1 Cor 10:16; Eph 2:13; Heb 9:14; 1 Pet 1:2.

82 E.g., τιμίῳ αἵματι Χριστοῦ ὡς ἀμνοῦ καὶ ἀσπίλου προεγνωσμένον μὲν πρὸ καταβολῆς ("by the precious blood of Christ as of an unblemished and spotless lamb destined before the foundation").

83 The present order may add emphasis, as the authorities discussed by van Unnik ("Redemption," 21–22) suggest, but that is not the reason for it.

84 E.g., 1 Pet 2:14, 16; 4:11; 5:3; Reicke (85): "the precious blood of nothing less than the . . . lamb Christ."

85 E.g., 2:2, 5, 14, 25; 4:16; 5:8; Hort (77): the "use of ὡς excludes a distinct meaning of Christ as the Lamb."

is sacrificed for the benefit of others, as was the case in the Hebrew cultic system.

Excursus: The Jewish Proselyte Ceremonial as the Key to 1:18–19

In an attempt to answer the many perplexities arising out of an analysis of 1 Pet 1:18–19, van Unnik proposed[86] that the interpretive key is to be found in the way a Gentile became a member of the Jewish people, that is, a proselyte.

Van Unnik notes a basic problem: How is it possible that innocent blood can release us from the domination of sin (22)? Those who propose to answer the problem on the basis of understanding ἐλυτρώθητε as "ransomed" tend inevitably to interpret these verses in terms of 1 Cor 6:20; 7:23. Yet such a comparison will not stand because the language there is different (29). Another attempt to resolve the problem—seeing the reference to Israel's paschal lamb—founders on the fact that Israel was not redeemed from Egypt by the power of that blood (41).[87] A second problem also emerges: the nature of the contrast embodied in the verses. To find the antithesis to lie in the contrast between φθαρτοῖς and τιμίῳ is not successful since they are not really antithetical (27).

Observing that the major antithesis in these verses is the contrast between a former futile way of life (μάταια ἀναστροφή, v. 18b) and a present, superior way (ἀναστροφὴ ἐν φόβῳ, v. 17), van Unnik finds that the only place where sacrifice is mentioned in connection with conversion from one way of life to another is in the discussion of the conversion from paganism to Judaism, that is, the proselyte ceremonial, which includes a sacrifice (e.g., *m. Ker.* 2:1) (41–46). Further, van Unnik finds that in Lev 22:21, only a sacrificial victim that is ἄμωμος is acceptable (εἰς δεκτός) to God. Most significantly, in Lev 22:25 φθάρματα (= φθαρτά) is used to describe an unacceptable victim (38).[88] Thus the contrast in 1 Pet 1:18–19 is not between φθαρτοῖς and τιμίῳ, but rather between φθαρτοῖς, implying unacceptable, and ἀμώμου, implying acceptable, and such a contrast derives from a cultic context. This insight allows one to resolve the problem of the otherwise imperfect antithesis (φθαρτός/τιμίος).

In the proselyte ceremonial, a sacrifice was required (50),[89] and the pagan was received fully into the people of Israel once the sprinkling with the blood had occurred (57–58). Yet the blood was only one part of the larger ritual; the proselyte was received not *through* the blood of the sacrifice, but *because* the blood of the sacrifice had been sprinkled (51), thus showing that the transfer into Israel was complete. The blood was therefore precious because it could save one from Gehenna by making one a member of the covenant people (48). Thus the question about how the blood relates to the act of deliverance from one form of life to another is resolved. Van Unnik thus concludes that the figure in 1 Pet 1:19 is drawn from Jewish proselyte ritual: in the same way, Christ's sacrifice redeemed the Christian from the former futile life in paganism (52).

The proposed solution is attractive and based on impressive evidence drawn from contemporary Jewish records, but it is not without problems. For example, in order to make the cultic contrast between φθαρτοῖς and ἀμώμου work, van Unnik must accept as original a textual variant that reads φθαρτοῦ ἀργυριοῦ, so as to have a genitive form to correspond to the genitive ἀμώμου (7). Yet that variant is attested in only one manuscript, ℵ*, and is more likely to represent an attempt to find in the reference to "perishable silver" a genitive of price, rather than to attest to an original reading. The further allusions in 1 Peter to the proselyte ritual that van Unnik finds are of similarly oblique nature. While, therefore, van Unnik has provided valuable insights into these two verses, and has further demonstrated that they are to be seen against a cultic rather than paschal background, those insights can be accepted without necessary resort to a background in the proselyte ceremony.[90]

■ **20** This verse takes the form of two participial phrases that have the immediately preceding Χριστοῦ as their antecedent.[91] The formulaic nature of the language—the anaphoric use of the contrasting participles[92] set off with μέν, δέ,[93] the content clearly reflecting early Christian tradition[94]—has led to the proposal that this verse has been drawn from early liturgical/hymnic materials.[95] While this possibility surely exists, it is

86 "Redemption"; the ensuing references are to pages in that article.
87 See n. 69 above.
88 LXX Lev 22:21: ἄμωμον ἔσται εἰς δεκτόν, πᾶς μῶμος οὐκ ἔσται ἐν αὐτῷ ("it shall be without blemish to be acceptable, there shall be no blemish on it"); v. 25: ὅτι φθάρματά ἐστιν ἐν αὐτοῖς, μῶμος ἐν αὐτοῖς, οὐ δεχθήσεται ταῦτα ὑμῖν ("because there is corruption in

them, a blemish in them, they shall not be accepted for you").
89 For further information on this point see K. G. Kuhn, "προσήλυτος," *ThWNT* 6.738–39.
90 So also Brox, 82–83.
91 Robert le Déaut ("Le Targum de Gen. 22,8 et 1 Pt. 1, 20," *RechSR* 49 [1961] 104) links them to the ἀμνοῦ of v. 19, as part of his (I think unlikely)

nevertheless not beyond the linguistic capacity of the author of this letter to construct such felicitous phrases without necessary dependence on early formulations.

The primary intent of the verse, however it originated, is to link the death of Christ to God's eternal plan, thus removing it from the realm of the accidental.[96] While the question of whether events were due to accident on the one hand or to fate or the will of the gods on the other was present in the Greco-Roman philosophy of this period,[97] it is doubtful that such debate motivated the inclusion of this material here.[98] Its origin lies more probably in those Jewish traditions which maintained that the divine plan of salvation underlying world events was laid down before creation,[99] an idea whose appropriation is also evident elsewhere in early Christian tradition.[100] The passive voice of the two participles ($\pi\rho o\epsilon\gamma\nu\omega\sigma\mu\acute{\epsilon}\nu o\nu$, $\phi\alpha\nu\epsilon\rho\omega\theta\acute{\epsilon}\nu\tau o\varsigma$), indicating that all of this is God's doing, adds further assurance to the claim that the redemption brought about by the death of Jesus is

reliable precisely because it was due to the divine initiative.[101]

The existence of such a plan by which redemption was secured through the death of Christ need not, however, necessarily include the idea that Christ himself was preexistent,[102] particularly if one sees the antithesis in the verse not between the preexistence and incarnation of Christ but rather in the manifestation of a series of events designated long in advance.[103] Other references in Christian tradition may similarly be understood as having in view Christ's presence in God's plan rather than his preexistence.[104] On the other hand, the notion of the preexistence of such a savior figure is also present in Jewish tradition,[105] and the preexistence of Christ is

proposal that 1 Peter means to refer in that way to a combination of the tradition of the paschal lamb and the sacrifice of Isaac (passim).

92 See, e.g., 1 Tim 3:6 for a comparable anaphoric use of participles.

93 While the use of these two particles is limited in 1 Peter to contrasts that use phrases of similar construction (2:4; 3:18; 4:6) and that could thus be considered of similar liturgical origin, these contrasting particles are by no means an indication of liturgical language; they do not appear in 1 Tim 3:16, nor is the $\mu\acute{\epsilon}\nu$, $\delta\acute{\epsilon}$ formula with anaphoric phrases a necessary indication of liturgical/hymnic materials. See, e.g., Rom 5:16; 6:11; 7:25; 8:10, where such phrases appear but with no such indication of hymnic origin.

94 E.g., Rom 16:25–26; 1 Cor 2:7; Eph 2:9; Col 1:26; 1 Tim 1:9–10; Titus 1:2–3. While a similar content is identified as $\mu\nu\sigma\tau\acute{\eta}\rho\iota o\nu$ in 1 Cor 2:7, it is not necessary to assume with Brox (83–84) that this verse, in an earlier form of its tradition, must also have had that word as its antecedent rather than the $X\rho\iota\sigma\tau\acute{o}\varsigma$ that appears in this context.

95 Bultmann, "Bekenntnis- und Liedfragmente," 10–11. Bultmann admitted that his proposal that v. 20 originally served as the beginning of the text underlying 3:18–19, 22 was "eine blosse Vermutung" ("purely a supposition"). Shimada (Formulary Material, 264–66) thinks this material is an application of "speculation about the Son of man" in relation to Christ (281–82). That this was earlier liturgical material, see also Richard, "Christology,"

128; Beare, 106; Kelly, 75; with less certainty, Schutter (Hermeneutic, 56: "probably"). Further literature can be found in their footnotes.

96 So, e.g., Goppelt, 126.

97 E.g., Tacitus Ann. 6.22; Seneca was aware it was a problem (e.g., Ep. 88.15), but was himself convinced things happened in accordance with an immutable plan, e.g., Ep. 16.4; Oed. 980–82; cf. ad Marc. 6.21.5.

98 Nevertheless, the notion that Christianity, though new to the world, was rooted in eternity would lend it credence in a world where the romantic notion that only what is old is valid went virtually unquestioned.

99 E.g., Isa 37:26; 4 Ezra 6.1–6; 1 Enoch 48.6; 62.7; 1QS 3.15–16; so also Best, 91; Kelly, 76; Windisch, 57; Knibb, Qumran, 94.

100 E.g., Matt 13:35; 25:34; Luke 11:50; John 17:24; Heb 4:3; cf. Spicq, 69; Shimada, Formulary Material, 289–91. The suggestion by Deterding ("Exodus Motifs," 58) that the source may be traced to the fact that as at the Passover each family selected a lamb on 10th Nisan which was not sacrificed until the 14th, so Christ was selected before his sacrifice, is far-fetched at best.

101 So correctly Goppelt, 124.

102 So, e.g., Beare, 106.

103 So, e.g., Goppelt, 125; Richard, "Christology," 130.

104 E.g., Eph 1:9, 10; 3:9–11; Col 1:26, 27; 2 Tim 1:9; cf. 1 Cor 2:7; Rom 16:25; see also Hort, 80.

105 E.g., 1 Enoch 48.3, 6–7; 62.7, where the son of man, created before the existence of the world, is revealed to God's chosen ones at the end of time. Hart (51) points out that Moses' preexistence is described in

similarly maintained in early Christian tradition.[106] Since the two participles (προεγνωσμένου, φανερωθέντος) do in fact describe Christ (Χριστοῦ of v. 19) and not God's plan, it would be strange if Christ's preexistence were not also implied here.[107]

The point of the description of Christ contained in the verse is, however, not so much to provide further information about him and his relationship to God, although it does do that, as it is to emphasize that all of this occurred for the sake of the people of God. That is evident from the emphatic position of the δι᾽ ὑμᾶς.[108] It is confirmed by the fact that the first participle can be used also of Christians (1:2), and that the reference to a plan πρὸ καταβολῆς κόσμου ("before the foundation of the world") is used in reference to believers in Eph 1:4.[109] That has the effect of focusing the whole sweep of history on the readers, and sets them, exiles and aliens that they are, at center stage in the drama of salvation.[110]

The reference to the end of the ages as the time at which Christ appeared, again a familiar theme in early Christian tradition,[111] emphasizes the need to take the redemptive events seriously. The time is drawing near when that will no longer be possible. While the phrase ἐπ᾽ ἐσχάτου τῶν χρόνων ("the end of times") of itself implies not so much the last days absolutely as it does that the last of a series of ages has now begun,[112] there is enough evidence in the remainder of the letter to indicate that little time remains until the final judgment does indeed begin (1:5; 4:5, 7, 17; 5:10). Christ's appearance is therefore the sign that the final period of God's plan, which spans the whole of created time, has now begun.

■ **21** Just as the referent of v. 20 was the final word in v. 19 (Χριστοῦ), so the referent of v. 21 is the final word of v. 20 (ὑμᾶς), although the substance of v. 21 quickly becomes a description of God's redemptive actions through Christ, thus showing the true source of salvation and the object of the reader's faith and hope. The section thus ends with a discussion of the Christian's relation to God (hope and faith) as it had begun (v. 18: God as Father).

The repeated εἰς θεόν ("in God") with which the verse begins and ends makes transparent the fact that despite the necessary mediation of Christ for the faith of the Christian (τοὺς δι᾽ αὐτοῦ πιστούς, "who believe *through him*"), it is the God who was at work through Christ who remains the one in whom the Christian is to trust. The phrase πιστὸς εἰς ("trust in")[113] here probably refers to an active "trust (or believe) in" rather than to a more passive "faithful to" God.[114] The sense is that one can put one's trust in God because he has shown himself trustworthy in his redemptive action through Christ, the description of which now ensues.

The language used to describe the divine activity accomplished in Christ goes to the heart of the Christian faith, and has often been identified as part of the liturgical/confessional language of the early church.[115] While that is true of the content, the specific language in which that content is expressed in the NT urges caution in any such identification. To be sure, the confession that God raised Christ from the dead is a regular part of the

---

similar terms in *As. Mos.* 1.12–14.

106 E.g., Phil 2:6–7; Col 1:15; John 1:1–2; 17:24; cf. Best, 91; Schelkle, 50; Michaels, 67.

107 That the next verse describes believers, as this verse describes Christ, confirms that emphasis.

108 See Reicke (86), Best (91), Schelkle (51), and Michaels (67), who also find preexistence implied here. Those who find in this verse part of an earlier formulation argue that the author of 1 Peter added this phrase, e.g., Shimada (*Formulary Material*, 265, including n. 1).

109 Michaels, 66; cf. Richard, "Christology," 130; Shimada, *Formulary Material*, 29.

110 So also Selwyn, 146.

111 E.g., Acts 2:16–18; 1 Cor 10:11; Heb 1:2; 9:26; on this last passage, see Shimada, *Formulary Material*, 301–2.

112 So, e.g., Michaels 69.

113 In the NT the phrase is most characteristic of the Johannine literature; cf. Gundry ("*Verba Christi*," 339–40), who calls attention specifically to John 14:1. It is highly unlikely that that Johannine tradition is the source of the idiom here, however.

114 That it is active: Bigg (121), Michaels (68), although the latter's example in Acts 3:16 differs in both preposition (ἐπί, not εἰς) and noun (πίστις, not πιστός); that it is passive: Hort (82); that it is both: Cranfield (56).

115 E.g., Kelly, 77. Best (92) compares it in this respect to v. 20.

NT witness,[116] as is the confession of his elevation to glory. Yet the language with which this latter is expressed is different from that used here; the glorification of Christ is normally described in terms of his being elevated to God's right hand,[117] as it is in 1 Pet 3:22. It is further interesting to note that the language for Christ's glorification used here in 1 Peter (δόξαν αὐτῷ δόντα)[118] is not used in the identifiably earlier traditions.[119] If both phrases are drawn from confessional formulations, therefore, the second half of the formulation has left little trace in NT literature.[120] On that basis, given the commonness of the NT reference to God raising Christ, and the very different language used here to describe his exaltation, it is perhaps better to refrain from identifying this language as specifically drawn from an earlier stereotyped formulation.[121]

The action of God in raising and glorifying Christ leads to a final inference in this verse, introduced with the particle ὥστε. Although the particle normally introduces an actual result, and could also be so understood here,[122] it can also introduce an intended result,[123] in which case the following phrase would not be the result but the intention of the divine action.[124] While one could argue that it would be incongruous in a sentence dominated by an imperative to include a statement about the present spiritual condition of the readers,[125] such a statement does occur at the outset of this verse, where the "you" (ὑμᾶς) of v. 20 are described as those who through Christ have faith in God. The additional fact that ὥστε is used in 1 Pet 4:19 to designate result probably means it ought also to be understood here in that sense.

Thus, because the faith and hope of the readers are the direct result of God's raising and glorifying Christ, their faith and hope are also directed to and lodged in that God.[126] The nature of faith, which includes trust, and the nature of hope, which includes confidence,[127] are so closely related that we are probably correct in seeing here two aspects of the same reality.[128] While the absence of the article with ἐλπίδα has led to the suggestion that it stands in the predicate position and thus ought to be understood as meaning "your faith is also hope in God,"[129] the absent article is more likely due to style than substance, with the τήν before πίστιν understood also to apply to ἐλπίδα. As a result, the two nouns ought to be understood as coordinate, almost in the sense of a hendiadys.

The fact that the reference to "hope" concludes the verse and was also mentioned in 1:3 could suggest that it is intended as a summing up of all that is included between those two verses[130] and is thus the place where the emphasis falls in this verse.[131] Yet both grammatically (the end of the Greek sentence is the point of greatest emphasis) and stylistically (the sentence begins

---

116 E.g., Acts 2:32; 3:15; 4:10; 13:30; Rom 4:24; 8:11; 10:9; 1 Cor 6:14; 15:15; 2 Cor 4:14; Gal 1:1; Eph 1:20; Col 2:12; 1 Thess 1:10; in an identifiably early tradition, 1 Cor 15:3.

117 E.g., Acts 2:33; 5:31; Rom 8:34; Eph 1:20; Col 3:1; Heb 1:3; 8:1; 10:12; 12:2.

118 Whether one can infer from this language, as does Goppelt (127), that Christ's resurrection is at the same time his eschatological transformation, and shows he is taken into God's own being, is open to question. Equally questionable is Sieffert's assertion ("Die Heilsbedeutung," 398) that the δι' ὑμᾶς of v. 20 means v. 21 intends to present Christ only as an example of what his followers are to do.

119 See Phil 2:9; 1 Tim 3:16; reference to it is omitted from the earlier traditions sedimented in 1 Cor 15:3–8 and Col 1:15–20.

120 The closest approximations are Luke 24:26 and John 17:22, 24.

121 The phrase is from Kelly (77), who notes that it has the "ring of a stereotyped formula."

122 E.g., Kelly, 77; Hort, 85.

123 See BDF § 391.

124 Dalton, "So That Your Faith," 272; Michaels, 70.

125 So Selwyn, 147–48.

126 The theocentric nature of faith in 1 Peter is thus made evident.

127 See Hart (52), who finds "confidence" to be the primary meaning here.

128 So also Bigg, 22; Kelly, 78.

129 So, e.g., Beare, 108.

130 Dalton ("So That Your Faith," 272) notes that it also stands in 1:13 at the beginning of the section to which these verses belong.

131 Dalton, "So That Your Faith," 273.

and ends with the same phrase, εἰς θεόν),[132] the weight falls upon θεόν,[133] which could also be understood to sum up all that has been encompassed between 1:3a, with its reference to God, and this verse.[134] More probably, however, this emphasis is to serve as an *inclusio* with the reference to God in 1:17 with which this section began, thus enclosing a discussion concerned primarily with divine redemption with references to the originator of that redemption.[135]

---

132 It is tempting to see a correlation between (a) the parallel phrases in the first half of the sentence that refer to the resurrection and exaltation of Christ, and (b) the parallel concepts faith and hope in the second half, with the result that faith is based on Christ's resurrection, and hope is based on his glorification.

133 So also, e.g., Kelly, 78.

134 So Michaels, 70.

135 The similarities noted between these verses and the material in 1:3–12 point to the close connection between the *prooemium* and the subsequent development of thought in the letter. See above, "1:13—2:10 Body Opening: Analysis: 1. Structure."

1 Begotten by God's Word, You Must Love One Another

22 Now that you have sanctified your lives by your obedience to the truth,[1] the goal of which is unfeigned mutual love, you must heartily[2] and earnestly love one another, 23/ because you have been begotten anew not from perishable but from imperishable seed through the living and abiding[3] word of God;[4] 24/ wherefore, all flesh is like grass and all its glory like the grass's flower; the grass withers and the[5] flower falls; 25/ but the Lord's word remains forever. This is the word which has been proclaimed to you as the gospel.

1 A number of mss. (P, 𝔐, vg^ms) add διὰ πνεύματος ("through the Spirit"), perhaps to guard against the notion that humans can perform such obedience unaided by God.

2 Lit. "from the heart." Some mss. add καθαρᾶς ("pure"); although early (e.g., P⁷², ℵ*, C), it is, as Michaels (72) and Beare (110) suggest, probably an interpolation (cf. Rom 6:17). Michaels (72) speculates that if καθαρᾶς was the original reading it was probably dropped because of the similarity of its first two letters with those of the subsequent καρδίας.

3 Some later scribes (Ψ, a few minuscules, latt) attempted to resolve the ambiguity inherent in the word order διὰ λόγου ζῶντος θεοῦ καὶ μένοντος by placing θεοῦ ("God") immediately after λόγου ("through the word of the living and abiding God"), while a few minuscules added the definite article τοῦ to θεοῦ ("through the living and abiding word of God"). V. 25a suggests that the latter interpretation is the correct one.

4 While some few mss. add the phrase "forever" (εἰς τὸν αἰῶνα: P, 𝔐, vg^cl, sy^p; εἰς τοὺς αἰῶνας: a few minuscules), it would overload the phrase, and the overwhelming textual witness to the shorter reading is surely correct.

5 Some mss. (C, P, 𝔐) add a redundant "its" (αὐτοῦ). For other differences from the present LXX text of Isa 40:6–8, see the comments on this verse below, although, as Hort (94) suggests, "It is . . . by no means certain that St. Peter did not find all these changes already made in the text of the LXX which he used."

Analysis

This passage is the second of two units (the first is 1:13–21) that comprise the first half (1:13–25) of the body opening (1:13—2:10) of the letter; it can be divided into two thought units (vv. 22–23, 24–25) on the basis of the citation of Isaiah 40 in vv. 24–25a. Like the subunits in 1:13–21 (vv. 13, 14–16, 17–21), it is characterized by the use of participles (ἡγνικότες, ἀναγεγεννημένοι) with an imperative (ἀγαπήσατε), and like the opening unit (1:13), its imperative in v. 22 is directly modified by an adverb (τελείως ἐλπίσατε, 1:13; ἀγαπήσατε ἐκτενῶς, 1:22).[6] Typical of the careful development of thought in this letter, these verses are full of echoes of earlier discussions contained in 1:2–21, echoes that show the summarizing and even climactic nature of these verses: compare

ἡγνικότες (v. 22) with ἐν ἁγιασμῷ (v. 2), ἅγιον, ἅγιοι (v. 15); τῇ ὑπακοῇ (v. 22) with εἰς ὑπακοήν (v. 2), τέκνα ὑπακοῆς (v. 14); ἀναγεγεννημένοι (v. 23) with ἀναγεννήσας (v. 3); φθαρτῆς (v. 23) with φθαρτοῖς (v. 18) and ἄφθαρτον (v. 4); εὐαγγελισθέν (v. 25) with τῶν εὐαγγελισαμένων (v. 12).[7]

Further, the close combination in these verses of two participles that describe the present state of the readers and an imperative that points to that toward which they must strive reflects the alternation between indicative and imperative that characterizes this letter as a whole. That alternation in its turn reflects a theological conviction that sees appropriate Christian behavior as grounded in God's gracious redemption of sinful humanity in the death and resurrection of Christ.

6 See above, "1:13—2:10, Body Opening: Analysis: 1. Structure."

7 So also Kelly, 78.

Conversely, only as that theology is understood as flowing into a specific form of behavior can it be understood as a valid reflection of the new reality created by God through his act in Christ.

If the emphasis in the earlier verses of this unit dealt primarily with the conduct of the individual growing out of his or her redemption, the emphasis in these verses shifts toward the community, and the responsibility of the individuals to their fellow Christians, in anticipation of the further development of this theme at the conclusion of the body opening (2:4–10). In that way it serves as conclusion for the first half of the body opening, and as anticipatory introduction to the theme of the second half.[8]

Comment

■ **22** The close linkage of this verse with those preceding is shown by the use of the participle ἡγνικότες ("[you have] sanctified"), which is drawn from the same root as the ἅγιοι the Christians were commanded to become in v. 15. The fact that the participle is perfect, and thus describes a present state growing out of a prior action,[9] shows the author's assumption that that command has in fact been obeyed. It is the reality created by that obedience that now makes the next step in Christian life possible, namely, the wholehearted love of the other members of the Christian community.

While the verb ἁγνίζω normally refers to ritual purity in the LXX[10] and can also carry that meaning in the NT,[11] its use in the active voice here and the command it reflects in v. 15, where it concerned what the Christians were to make of their lives, mean that it probably carries more a moral than a ritual tone here.[12] The ensuing command to love gives further weight to such an interpretation. In that light, it is clear that the τάς ψυχὰς ὑμῶν is to be understood as one's whole person ("your lives"), rather than a part of it ("your souls"); it is the whole of life that comes under the realized command to be holy.

The way in which such sanctification has been achieved is by means of (ἐν) their obedience (ὑπακοή) in relation to the truth (τῆς ἀληθείας). Whether the ἐν designates means or sphere,[13] it is evident that apart from such obedience, no purification would have been achieved. The genitival form τῆς ἀληθείας attached to ὑπακοή can be understood simply to have adjectival force, and to mean no more than "true obedience,"[14] that is, genuine Christian faith, since in this letter ὑπακοή has the force virtually of "the faith" (1:2, 14). To carry such a meaning, "truth" here would have to mean "truth in general," a meaning it can have in the NT (e.g., Mark 5:33; Luke 22:59). Yet the word "truth" is often used in the NT as a synonym for "the gospel,"[15] and, as the reference to the gospel in v. 25 indicates, perhaps ought to be understood in that way here as well.[16] The genitive

---

8   While these verses round off the discussion begun in 1:13, to call them a "postscript" to 1:13–21, as does Michaels (73), is to put too little emphasis on their integral relationship to those earlier verses.

9   It means "Now that you have sanctified . . . ," thus temporal (so Bengel, *Gnomon*, 732; Hort, 87). That it gives the ground of the imperative (so Hart, 52) is less likely since that appears to be the force of the ἀναγεγεννημένοι of v. 23, which, because it is perfect, cannot have imperatival force (so Beare, 109; Hort, 87).

10   So, e.g., Beare, 109; Best, 92; but cf. LXX Jer 6:16.

11   E.g., John 11:55; Acts 21:24, 26; 24:18, but only in reference to Jewish practices.

12   Beare (109) thinks ritual and moral sense are combined in this verse.

13   Piper ("Hope," 214) assumes dative of means ("through obedience"); Selwyn (149) takes it to mean "in the sphere of" or "in the practice of." While the reluctance to see it as a dative of agency may be motivated by the desire to "save" this text from some form of "works-righteousness," it is clear that any

such sanctification brought about by means of obedience is totally dependent on the state of the Christian, which in its turn results solely from God's act of rebegetting (1:3, 23). The newly begotten person does, however, have new responsibilities, and it is within that sphere of responsibilities that the ἐν has its force as an instrumental of means.

14   E.g., Schwank et al., 29.

15   E.g., John 8:32; Rom 2:8; 3:7; 9:1; 2 Cor 6:7; Gal 2:5; Eph 1:13; Col 1:5; 1 Tim 2:4; 2 Tim 2:25; Heb 10:26; Jas 5:19; 2 Pet 2:2; 1 John 2:21.

16   So, e.g., Delling, "Der Bezug," 110. As Bauer (22) and Goppelt (131) note, the normal intention of word "truth" in the OT is to point to the faithfulness and reliability of God; in the Christian tradition it points in addition to the divine revelation by which that truth is made known (so also Schelkle, 52). All of that adds weight to this understanding.

τῆς ἀληθείας in that case could have the force of an objective genitive: "by your obedience to the truth."[17] In either case, however, whether it means "true Christian faith" or "obedience to the gospel," the force is the same: you are purified (ἡγνικότες) by your acceptance of, and your living out, the Christian faith.

Such sanctified lives have as their goal (telic εἰς)[18] "brotherly love" (φιλαδελφία).[19] This is not to be understood here as a love for humans in general; it is limited to members of the Christian community. The fact that the word employs a root indicating family relationships (ἀδελφ-) indicates the kind of love here enjoined: Christians have been incorporated into a new family by their rebegetting, and are thus to regard other Christians similarly as members of that family.[20] The multiple adverbs describing the way such familial affection is to be carried on (here, ἀνυπόκριτον; ἐκ καρδίας as adverbial phrase and ἐκτενῶς modifying ἀγαπήσατε) point to the difficulty encountered in the early communities in putting such love into practice.[21] Where such love is so greatly emphasized, there is pressure on manifesting it at all costs,[22] and the temptation arose to take advantage of such unquestioning loyalty of Christians to one another.[23]

The imperatival phrase ἀλλήλους ἀγαπήσατε calls attention to the duty of Christians to fulfill the goal of their now-sanctified lives. The reciprocal adverb limits the love to those within the Christian community,[24] a regular trait in early Christian literature[25] but with perhaps greater emphasis in this letter than elsewhere.[26] The aorist form of the imperative again carries with it an ingressive sense,[27] not because the letter addresses new converts who are now to begin a new way of acting,[28] but because the author enjoins a kind of action very different from that of their preconversion life.[29] The adverbial phrase ἐκ καρδίας (from [the] heart) means it is to originate in, and thus control, the central reality of the person involved.[30] The adverb ἐκτενῶς, upon which major emphasis falls in this sentence, probably points more to constancy and to love's unwavering character than to its fervency or intensity. Christians are to be unwavering in their familial devotion to one another, despite any pressures, whether internal or external, that may be put upon them.

The structure of the verse thus moves from an assumed reality (ἡγνικότες . . . ἀληθείας, v. 22a) to a further command (ἀλλήλους ἀγαπήσατε, v. 22b), which can be fulfilled only because of another prior, divine act (ἀναγεννημένοι, "begotten anew"). It is this second act that constitutes the import of the following verse.

---

17 So Selwyn, 149, who cites 2 Thess 2:10, 12, 13 as a similar use. This last verse shares additional vocabulary with 1 Pet 1:22 as well.

18 So also Best, 93; the following command is thus an injunction to fulfill this goal.

19 Hart (53) identifies this as the principal Christian duty on the basis of such passages as Matt 23:8; 1 Thess 4:9; to them one may add Rom 13:8; Gal 5:14; Col 3:14; 1 John 4:11.

20 E.g., Hort, 89; Goppelt, 130; cf. Bauer, 22. In Christian tradition, abandonment of human families to be incorporated into a new family began with Jesus' own disciples: Mark 10:28–30; cf. 3:31–35.

21 Cranfield (58) notes correctly that such love is understood as more than simply emotion; it involves "will and work and strenuous effort."

22 So, e.g., Goppelt, 130; hence ἀνυπόκριτον.

23 E.g., traveling "missionaries" living off the generosity of fellow Christians; see *Did.* 11.4–6; Lucian of Samosata *Pergr. mort.* 13.

24 So also 2:17; 4:8; as synonyms, φιλαδελφία in this verse, φιλάδελφοι in 3:18. On this point, see Sleeper, "Political Responsibility," 276; Best, 93; Kelly, 79.

25 E.g., John 13:34–35; 15:12, 17; Rom 12:10; 1 Thess 3:12; 4:9–10; 2 Thess 1:3; Heb 13:1; 1 John 3:23.

26 Goppelt (130) argues for this point on the basis of the sole NT use in this letter of ἀδελφότης for the Christian community (2:17; 5:9), and the sole NT use of the adjective φιλάδελφος (3:8).

27 So, e.g., Spicq, 72; Brown et al., *Peter*, 80.

28 So Beare, 100.

29 The emphasis here as in all the aorist imperatives in the section 1:13–25 is on the stark contrast between past and present ways of life. Blendinger ("Kirche als Fremdlingschaft," 131) points to the implied contrast between the kind of activity engendered by love and the kind that occurs outside the Christian community.

30 So correctly Margot, 32; it designates the seat of human will, as in Rom 10:9.

Excursus: Background and Derivation of 1:22

The language of v. 22 is rich in biblical echoes, and there have been many attempts to link such language to expressions of biblical faith either prior to or concurrent with this letter. The concepts of sanctification (or purification, ἁγνίζω, here ἡγνικότες) and obedience (ὑπακοή) are key characteristics of the covenant on Mount Sinai, for example, and hence those who find much of 1 Peter reflecting the story of the exodus from Egypt find confirmation here.[31] Van Unnik found in the reference to sanctification in this verse further evidence of the Jewish ritual of proselyte conversion that he found to underlie vv. 18–19.[32] Again, obedience and love are major characteristics of the Aqedah, as is the reference to the divine "seed" in v. 23, which recalls Isaac's wondrous birth, and hence that event has also been proposed as furnishing the background for this verse.[33]

The emphasis in Qumran on the loyalty among community members based on communal love has also been proposed as the background for the sentiment expressed in this verse.[34] It has even been suggested that a sayings schema of Essene tradition was taken up here into the Christian tradition and given a new content to adapt it to the situation of the Christian communities.[35]

Christian traditions have also been suggested as sources for the language of this verse. While the attempt to derive it directly from the sayings of Jesus recorded in John 13:34–35 and 15:12[36] has not found widespread support, derivation from liturgical material associated with Christian baptism was at one time widely accepted. The assumption that 1 Peter was based on baptismal liturgy allowed one to see in

ἡγνικότες a further allusion to it,[37] and some saw in the perfect form of that verb a reference to the immediately prior pouring of the water that happened between vv. 21 and 22.[38] Other more general references to baptism in NT literature were also called upon to support this assumption.[39]

More recently scholars have pointed to the sociological situation of the early Christian communities to find the background for this verse. Both the familial love described and the mutual love enjoined point to a community in need of internal unity to withstand deleterious pressures. While some have found this to be evidence of the need to overcome internal tensions and schisms within the community,[40] others find such injunctions necessitated by the need to maintain mutual support in the face of external pressures.[41] The lack of other evidence to indicate internal divisions with the communities to which the letter is addressed, and the indications of external pressure found elsewhere in the letter (e.g., 2:12; 3:15b-16; 4:4) argue for this latter position.

In the last analysis, however, the widespread tradition within the Christian faith that followers of Christ are to love one another renders any specific point of origin for this verse less convincing than might otherwise be the case. The language is probably best accounted for by the internal logic that drives this section as it moves from the command to be holy (1:15) to the ensuing command to act like the holy community they are (ἡγνικότες, v. 22), that is, to love one another as a reflection of the love of the holy God (1:16) who is responsible for their new life (ἀναγεγεννημένοι, v. 23).

■ **23** The perfect participle ἀναγεγεννημένοι[42] with which the verse begins serves as a causal link with the preceding

31 E.g., Boismard, "Liturgie" [1], 196.

32 "Redemption," 64; see "Excursus: The Jewish Proselyte Ceremonial as the Key to 1:18–19."

33 Hillyer, "Servant," 156.

34 Schelkle (52) cites 1QM 13.1; 15.4, 7; 1QS 6.22; CD 8.17, 19; 9.16.

35 So Goppelt (128), who cites 1QS 1.9–11; 3.4–9; 4.20–21; one may add 1QS 8.2.

36 So Gundry, "Verba Christi," 340.

37 E.g., Goppelt, 131–32; Kelly, 78; Senior, 25; Spicq, 73; Deterding, "Exodus Motifs," 62; Beare, 109–10; Best, 92.

38 See Stuhlmueller, "Baptism," 210. The reference to divine rebegetting in v. 3 cast in the aorist tense robs this grammatical point of its power; whatever happened to make the readers Christians had happened before this letter was composed.

39 E.g., Bauer (21), who cites Eph 5:26; Heb 10:22–23, as does Spicq (72); see also Kelly, 68. Gourbillon ("La Première Épître," 31) cites Jas 1:18–21 as reflecting the same liturgical pattern as that underlying 1 Pet 1:22—2:2.

40 E.g., Schelkle (53), who cites as evidence of similar schisms 1 Cor 1–4; Phil 2; 1 Clement passim.

41 E.g., Brox, 86–87; Best, 94.

42 Beare (111) finds an intended linguistic parallelism with the ἡγνικότες of v. 22, thus calling attention to a parallelism of thought.

verse,[43] explaining how it is possible for the Christians to exercise the kind of mutual love commanded in v. 22.[44] This verb, unique to this letter in the NT, here has the meaning rather of rebegetting than rebirth,[45] as is demonstrated by the ensuing discussion of the kind of "seed" that caused it, a discussion clearly more appropriate to begetting than to birth.

Because the discussion concerns such a divine rebegetting rather than rebirth, and because the rebegetting is accomplished through the hearing of God's word, allusion to baptism is rendered unlikely here.[46] Lack of baptismal allusion also renders unlikely any reference here to the rituals of rebirth allegedly practiced in the mystery religions.[47] Absence of any other clear allusion to those cults in this letter, of whose underlying theology we lack certain knowledge in any case, and the ensuing quotation from the OT in v. 24 show the frame of reference within which our author is working.

The word used for the seed ($\sigma\pi o\rho\acute{a}$)[48] by which this rebegetting occurred can also mean "sowing" or "seed-time," but here in the context of rebegetting its meaning as seed is clear enough.[49] While $\sigma\pi o\rho\acute{a}$ can be used either of plant or of human reproduction, in this context the

latter metaphor is surely in view, since it is a reference to the rebegetting of the readers; the reference to plants in the ensuing quotation from Isa 40:6–7 concerns durability, not reproduction.[50] Such rebegetting, in contrast to their original begetting, comes from imperishable seed, with the result that the ensuing life shares the characteristics of the divine and imperishable rather than the human and thus perishable world,[51] again showing how the kind of love commanded in v. 22 is now possible.[52]

The imperishable seed by which such rebegetting occurred is described in the second half of the sentence as the "word of God." Whatever difference may be implied in the use of the two prepositions $\dot{\epsilon}\kappa$ ($\sigma\pi o\rho\hat{a}s$) and $\delta\iota\acute{a}$ ($\lambda\acute{o}\gamma ov$),[53] both intend to describe the means by which the Christians' new lives were begun.[54] A certain ambiguity adheres to the phrase $\lambda\acute{o}\gamma ov$ $\zeta\hat{\omega}\nu\tau os$ $\theta\epsilon o\hat{v}$ $\kappa a\grave{\iota}$ $\mu\acute{\epsilon}\nu o\nu\tau os$. Grammatically, the adjectives ($\zeta\hat{\omega}\nu\tau os$, "living"; $\mu\acute{\epsilon}\nu o\nu\tau os$, "abiding") could modify either "word" ($\lambda\acute{o}\gamma ov$)

43 So also, e.g, Hort, 93.
44 E.g., Kelly, 80; Spicq, 75. Schelkle (53) sees the connection with v. 22 in the idea, albeit unspoken, that a new birth (sic) must express itself in new life.
45 So also, e.g., Hort, 91; cf. Eugene A. LaVerdiere, "A Grammatical Ambiguity in 1 Pet. 2:12," CBQ 36 (1974) 93. That is not to deny that the idea of rebirth is also present in this epistle, but simply to say it is not the point here.
46 As Kelly (80) indicates, such an allusion is usually tied to an understanding of $\dot{a}\nu a\gamma\epsilon\gamma\epsilon\nu\nu\eta\mu\acute{\epsilon}\nu o\iota$ as rebirth; see also Goppelt, 132; Schiwy, 4. Chevallier ("1 Pierre 1/1 à 2/10," 139) finds a similarity with the $\lambda v\tau\rho\grave{o}s$ $\pi a\lambda\lambda\iota\gamma\gamma\epsilon\nu\epsilon\sigma\acute{\iota}as$ of Titus 3:5, a (different) word that does mean rebirth. The attempt by Cross (Paschal Liturgy, 34) to rescue such an allusion in face of the begetting by word through seeing in the mention of the $\lambda\acute{o}\gamma os$ $\theta\epsilon o\hat{v}$ a reference to the baptismal formula is, as Moule ("Nature," 7) suggests, "wildly improbable."
47 As claimed by Blendinger ("Kirche als Fremdlingschaft," 128–29); with less certainty ("wahrscheinlich") Schweizer (42). Perdelwitz (Mysterienreligion, 55) saw in the contrast between corruptible and incorruptible seed the contrast between the once-for-all rebirth (sic) of the Christian and the rebirth of the mystagogue that, he claimed, had to be renewed

after a certain number of years.
48 This is also a word unique to 1 Peter in the NT. Like the more familiar $\sigma\pi\acute{\epsilon}\rho\mu a$, it too is derived from the verb "to sow" ($\sigma\pi\epsilon\acute{\iota}\rho\omega$). Hort (91) claims it is not equivalent to $\sigma\pi\acute{\epsilon}\rho\mu a$ or $\sigma\pi\acute{o}\rho os$, which could imply individual seeds, but implies rather a "quasi-collective sense," i.e., in relation to the community rather than to individual members.
49 E.g., Hort, 91.
50 Contra Michaels, 76. To argue, as does Tarrech ("Le milieu," 336), that it was chosen because the readers were from rural areas is fanciful; one suspects even urban dwellers knew something of the reproductive processes.
51 So, e.g., Minear, "House of Living Stones," 240. Spicq (75) points to Gen 1:12 to show that the seed shares the qualities of its producer; that means God's word also shares his qualities, as Windisch (58) also observes.
52 So, e.g., Kelly, 80.
53 LaVerdiere ("Grammatical Ambiguity," 92) finds $\dot{\epsilon}\kappa$ to indicate origin ($\sigma\pi o\rho\acute{a}$ is the intrinsic source of regenerated life), $\delta\iota\acute{a}$ to indicate agency ($\lambda\acute{o}\gamma os$ is the extrinsic principle or agency of regeneration). The distinction may be oversubtle.
54 So also Hort, 93; Shimada, Formulary Material, 160; cf. Selwyn, 150.

or "God" ($\theta\epsilon o\hat{v}$).[55] On the one hand, the argument that they modify "God," and hence emphasize God's qualities of life and eternity, is buttressed by a similar phrase in LXX Dan 6:27[56] and by the parallelism between $\sigma\pi o\rho\hat{a}s$ and $\lambda\acute{o}\gamma o\upsilon$, which points to a comparable parallelism between $\phi\theta a\rho\tau\hat{\eta}s$ $\dot{a}\lambda\lambda\dot{a}$ $\dot{a}\phi\theta\acute{a}\rho\tau o\upsilon$ (modifying $\sigma\pi o\rho\hat{a}s$) and $\zeta\hat{\omega}\nu\tau os$ $\theta\epsilon o\hat{v}$ $\kappa a\dot{\iota}$ $\mu\acute{\epsilon}\nu o\nu\tau os$ (modifying $\lambda\acute{o}\gamma o\upsilon$).[57] Such an understanding was incorporated, for example, into the Vulgate translation of this verse.[58]

On the other hand, that God's word is living and abiding is part of early Christian tradition,[59] and the parallelism between $\dot{a}\phi\theta\acute{a}\rho\tau o\upsilon$ and $\mu\acute{\epsilon}\nu o\nu\tau os$, each in the emphatic position in its clause, suggests that as $\dot{a}\phi\theta\acute{a}\rho\tau o\upsilon$ modifies $\sigma\pi o\rho\hat{a}s$, so $\mu\acute{\epsilon}\nu o\nu\tau os$ is to modify $\lambda\acute{o}\gamma o\upsilon$.[60] Decisive in this instance, however, is the context within which the phrase is placed. The quotation from Isaiah that follows emphasizes the abiding nature not of God but of his Word ($\dot{\rho}\hat{\eta}\mu a$ $\kappa\upsilon\rho\acute{\iota}o\upsilon$ $\mu\acute{\epsilon}\nu\epsilon\iota$), and the ensuing claim that it was just that word ($\dot{\rho}\hat{\eta}\mu a$) which they received in

the proclamation of the gospel to them make it apparent that the adjectives in this phrase are intended to modify $\lambda\acute{o}\gamma o\upsilon$, not $\theta\epsilon o\hat{v}$.[61] Such an understanding was incorporated, for example, by Luther in his translation.[62]

The use of $\lambda\acute{o}\gamma os$ in this verse, instead of the $\dot{\rho}\hat{\eta}\mu a$ found in vv. 24–25, has led to the suggestion that the "word" in v. 23 refers not to a spoken word but to God's Son, who is the incarnate $\lambda\acute{o}\gamma os$, and who by reason of his resurrection is living and by reason of his glorification is abiding.[63] On the other hand, $\lambda\acute{o}\gamma os$ can and often does refer to the gospel in the NT,[64] and the phrase $\lambda\acute{o}\gamma os$ $\theta\epsilon o\hat{v}$ meaning gospel is also pervasive in the NT.[65] On that basis, and on the basis of the context that clearly intends to identify that living and abiding word as belonging to God (v. 24) and available in the gospel (v. 25), the meaning here is probably to be understood as the gospel rather than the incarnate Son of God.

Finally, the fact that the kind of love commanded in v. 22 is possible only on the basis of the prior act of God in

---

55 E.g., LaVerdiere, "Grammatical Ambiguity," 89; Schlosser, "Ancien Testament," 68, although the latter argues a different word order would have been more appropriate if the author had intended the participles to modify $\theta\epsilon o\hat{v}$ (e.g., $\delta\iota\dot{a}$ $\lambda\acute{o}\gamma o\upsilon$ $\theta\epsilon o\hat{v}$ $\zeta\hat{\omega}\nu\tau os$ $\kappa a\dot{\iota}$ $\mu\acute{\epsilon}\nu o\nu\tau os$). With respect to a phrase found in Eusebius $History.$ $eccl.$ 3.39.4 ($\zeta\omega\acute{\eta}s$ $\phi\omega\nu\hat{\eta}s$ $\kappa a\dot{\iota}$ $\mu\epsilon\nu o\acute{\upsilon}\sigma\eta s$), the word order would argue for having $\zeta\hat{\omega}\nu\tau os$ and $\mu\acute{\epsilon}\nu o\nu\tau os$ in v. 23 modify $\theta\epsilon o\hat{v}$, the content ($\phi\omega\nu\hat{\eta}s$, "voice") for having them modify $\lambda\acute{o}\gamma o\upsilon$, and hence can provide no help. To argue with Beare (112; so apparently also Calvin, 57, although his interpretation shares the ambiguity of the phrase he is interpreting) that both refer to both is to beg the question.

56 Cf. Selwyn (151), who cites the opinion of Hort. The phrase is, however, not an exact equivalent ($a\dot{\upsilon}\tau\dot{o}s$ [$\gamma\acute{a}\rho$] $\dot{\epsilon}\sigma\tau\iota[\nu]$ $\theta\epsilon\dot{o}s$ $\zeta\hat{\omega}\nu$ $\kappa a\dot{\iota}$ $\mu\acute{\epsilon}\nu\omega\nu$). Eric F. F. Bishop argues for its modifying $\theta\epsilon\acute{o}s$ on the basis of common Semitic inheritance for both Daniel and 1 Peter, and cites as confirmation the exclusive use in the Koran of the Arabic equivalent of $\mu\acute{\epsilon}\nu o\nu\tau os$ ($qayy\bar{u}m$) for God, in each case also accompanied by $hayy$, the Arabic equivalent of $\zeta\hat{\omega}\nu\tau os$ ("The Word of a Living and Unchanging God: I Peter 1,23," $Muslim$ $World$ 43 [1953] 16).

57 LaVerdiere, "Grammatical Ambiguity," 90.

58 So also, e.g., NEB alternate translation, Goodspeed, Knox, Jerusalem (French); cf. LaVerdiere, "Grammatical Ambiguity," 91.

59 E.g., Heb 4:12; 1 John 1:1; 2:14; as pointed out by LaVerdiere ("Grammatical Ambiguity," 94).

60 So LaVerdiere, "Grammatical Ambiguity," 92.

61 That the following quotation from Isaiah is decisive, see, e.g., LaVerdiere, "Grammatical Ambiguity," 93; Schlosser, "Ancien Testament," 69; Bigg, 123; Kelly, 80; Schelkle, 53 n. 1; Walter Grundmann, "Die NHΠIOI in der urchristlichen Paränese," NTS 5 (1959) 189 n. 1; Blendinger, "Kirche als Fremdling-schaft," 128; Tarrech, "Le milieu," 335; Schutter, $Hermeneutic$, 42; Goppelt, 133. That the phrase is to be construed with $\lambda\acute{o}\gamma o\upsilon$ was also the position of the early Greek fathers (so LaVerdiere, "Grammatical Ambiguity," 89 n. 3) and remains dominant, e.g., Senior, 25; Best, 95; Moffatt, 112; Bengel, $Gnomon$, 733; Blendinger, "Kirche als Fremdlingschaft," 130; Wolff, "Christ und Welt," 335; Shimada, $Formulary$ $Material$, 160.

62 So also, e.g., RV, RSV, $NRSV$, Reicke, 82, New $American$ $Bible$; cf. LaVerdiere, "Grammatical Ambiguity," 91.

63 E.g., Schlosser, "Ancien Testament," 72; Hort, 93; Bishop, "Word," 17.

64 E.g., it is God's word, not a human word (1 Thess 2:13); it is the power of God (1 Cor 1:18), it is living and powerful (Heb 4:12), it is the word of life (Phil 2:16), it is the word that gives life (John 6:63, 68); cf. Schelkle, 53.

65 E.g., Acts 4:29; 13:44, 46; 2 Cor 2:17; Col 1:5, 25.

rebegetting Christians through the proclamation of the gospel makes apparent enough that the command in v. 22 remains a matter of divine rebirth, and hence falls outside the purview of what is normally meant by "works."[66]

■ **24–25a** The final two verses of this section (vv. 22–25) continue the discussion of the nature of the seed by which Christians have been rebegotten by God. The quotation from Isa 40:6–8 in vv. 24–25a is not so much a proof of what has been maintained in v. 23 as a comment on it, verifying as it were that what the author has said has the backing of the authoritative Scriptures of the early Christian community.[67] Scripture is used that same way in 2:6 and 3:10–12, although in the former it is accompanied by a *pesher*-like exposition.

The text that is cited is closer to the LXX than the MT. Isa 40:7, which is included in the MT, is absent from v. 24 as it is from the LXX, and both v. 24 and the LXX omit the definite article, present in the MT, in the phrase πᾶσα σάρξ ("all flesh").[68] On the other hand, in reading πᾶσα δόξα αὐτῆς ("all its glory"), 1 Peter agrees with the MT over the LXX, which reads πᾶσα δόξα ἀνθρώπου ("all human glory").[69] Of the three changes

unique to 1 Peter, the first, the addition of the ὡς ("as") between σάρξ ("flesh") and χόρτος ("grass"), simply makes explicit the metaphorical nature of the words;[70] and the second, the omission of the ἡμῶν ("our") preceding μένει ("remains") in v. 25a, does not alter the meaning of the citation. In the third change, our author has substituted κυρίου ("Lord") for θεοῦ ("God") in v. 25a against both the LXX and the MT, which read θεοῦ.[71] While there is justification for the substitution in the context—the word κύριος occurs twice in Isa 40:5,[72] where the ensuing quotation is attributed to κύριος, and the tetragrammaton normally rendered in the LXX with κύριος appears in the omitted MT Isa 40:7—it is equally likely that the substitution of κυρίου, often used for Jesus in this letter,[73] is motivated by the desire to show that already in Isaiah the coming eternal gospel was announced (so v. 25b).[74] Whether the κυρίου is to be understood as the one who speaks the ῥῆμα ("word")[75] or as its content[76] is difficult to determine. The context in Isa 40:5 argues for the former, and while either understanding would be appropriate for the application in v. 25b, its use there to describe the content of the gospel probably argues for the latter use. Such a decision is supported by the

66 Luther, 207; see n. 13 above.
67 The author clearly does not depend on the OT for the authority of what he says, nor does he wish explicitly to make the point that in the events about which he writes Scripture is fulfilled, nor do the verses serve as a type of which the Christians are the antitype (Noah is cited as type and Christians as antitype in 3:21, but it is there made explicit). What he does apparently wish to make clear to his readers is that what he is saying, and what holds true for them, is not only not counter to the OT but does in fact comport positively with it.
68 So also, e.g., Schlosser, "Ancien Testament," 69; Brox, "Pseudepigraphischen Rahmung," 67.
69 In translating כְּבֹד with the unusual δόξα 1 Peter is, however, following the LXX; cf. L. H. Brockington, "The Septuagintal Background to the New Testament Use of δόξα," in D. E. Nineham, ed., *Studies in the Gospels: Essays in Memory of R. H. Lightfoot* (Oxford: Blackwell, 1955) 1–2.
70 It is typical of 1 Peter to use it to indicate a metaphor, e.g., 1:14, 19; 2:2, 5; so also Schutter, *Hermeneutic*, 125; Brox, "Pseudepigraphischen Rahmung," 67.
71 While it is possible that the author found these changes already present in his copy of the Greek OT, as Hort (94) suggests, it is unlikely to be the case (so

Schutter, *Hermeneutic*, 125), since in at least two instances (ὡς, κύριος) the changes represent usages typical of the author of 1 Peter or are found in the immediate context of Isa 40:6–8.
72 So also Scharlemann, "Why the *Kuriou*," 353; see also n. 71 above.
73 E.g., 1:3; 2:3, 13; 3:15; cf. Schelkle (54), who affirms that "Lord" in this letter refers not to God but to Jesus.
74 Schutter (*Hermeneutic*, 130) notes that such substitution of synonyms is typical of the *pesher* tradition, a tradition 1 Peter clearly employs in 2:6–8, and that such a change would be in line with the idea enunciated in 1 Pet 1:11, namely, that the inspiring spirit of Christ was at work in the prophets (127). Less likely is the suggestion by Scharlemann ("Why the *Kuriou*," 354) that because κύριος was used in the baptismal liturgy, the change is motivated by a desire to fit this passage for such use.
75 Hence subjective genitive, as Michaels (79) affirms.
76 Hence objective genitive, as Schlosser ("Ancien Testament," 70) avers.

tendency in Christian tradition to identify the message Jesus spoke and the message spoken about Jesus,[77] and while this letter has no explicit citation of a saying of Jesus, it does refer to him in terms of the content of the Christian message (e.g., 1:3, 18–21; 2:4, 21–24; 3:18–22).

While the citation from Isaiah confirms the imperishable and abiding nature of the word of God, which is the seed by which Christians have been rebegotten (so v. 23),[78] the contrast between what is transitory and what is permanent embodied in the quotation would be highly appropriate for a beleaguered community of Christians facing what gave every appearance of being the permanent, even eternal, power and glory of the Roman Empire.[79] In such a situation, the announcement that the glitter, pomp, and power of the Roman culture was as grass when compared to God's eternal word spoken in Jesus Christ, available through the gospel preached to and accepted by the Christians of Asia Minor, would give them courage to hold fast to the latter while rejecting the former. Even the hostility of that overwhelming power becomes more bearable when its ultimately transitory nature is revealed and accepted.[80]

■ **25b** This verse abandons the imperative mode as it sums up the point both of the citation from Isa 40:6–8 and of the eternal seed by which Christians are begotten to a totally new existence. That seed, sharing the permanence of God's word, is precisely the gospel that they heard and accepted. The use of $\dot{\rho}\hat{\eta}\mu\alpha$ here instead of the $\lambda\acute{o}\gamma o\varsigma$ of v. 23 is surely influenced by its presence in the quotation given in v. 25a, yet both words refer to the same reality. It is the living and abiding word ($\lambda\acute{o}\gamma o\varsigma$) of God, by which they have been rebegotten, which is at work in the proclamation ($\dot{\rho}\hat{\eta}\mu\alpha$) of the gospel. If $\dot{\rho}\hat{\eta}\mu\alpha$ reflects Isa 40:8, quoted in v. 25a, the participle that identifies that

word as "good news" ($\tau\grave{o}$ $\epsilon\grave{v}\alpha\gamma\gamma\epsilon\lambda\iota\sigma\theta\acute{e}\nu$, "the good news that was preached") probably reflects the language of Isa 40:9, the verse that immediately follows the material cited in 1:24–25a, where participial forms of the same verb appear twice ($\dot{o}$ $\epsilon\grave{v}\alpha\gamma\gamma\epsilon\lambda\iota\zeta\acute{o}\mu\epsilon\nu o\varsigma$, "the one who announces the good news").[81]

The final phrase $\epsilon\grave{\iota}\varsigma$ $\acute{v}\mu\hat{a}\varsigma$ could mean simply that the readers were the people to whom the gospel was preached, but its emphatic position in the sentence probably means it carries a greater significance, for example, "for your benefit," perhaps even implying "for your salvation."[82] Just as Christ was at work in the prophets, who learned their work was not for themselves, but "for you" (1:11), and just as the redemption through him embodied God's plan laid down before the foundation of the world (1:20), so the announcement of that redemption that embodied the rebegetting power of God's word (1:23) was proclaimed in Asia Minor for the benefit of those who heard and accepted it (v. 25).

The reference to the gospel proclaimed to the readers echoes the language of 1:12, and shows that with this verse a transitional closure has been effected.[83] While the language of these climactic verses has concerned the rebegetting ($\dot{\alpha}\nu\alpha\gamma\epsilon\gamma\epsilon\nu\nu\eta\mu\acute{e}\nu o\iota$) of Christians, the language of the next section concerns how those so begotten and subsequently newly born ($\dot{\alpha}\rho\tau\iota\gamma\acute{e}\nu\nu\eta\tau\alpha$ $\beta\rho\acute{e}\phi\eta$) are to conduct themselves. Thus newly begotten and newly born, they are ready as the new people of God (2:9–10) to face the perils that confront them in the hostile world in which they live.[84]

---

77 So also Michaels, 79; that does, however, weaken his identification of $\kappa\upsilon\rho\acute{\iota}ο\upsilon$ as subjective genitive.

78 So also, e.g., Delling, "Der Bezug," 107; Goppelt, 133.

79 So also, e.g., Brox, 88; Isa 40:6–7 is quoted in such a context in *2 Bar.* 82.7.

80 Cf. Selwyn, 152; Michaels, 78.

81 So also, e.g., Schutter, *Hermeneutic*, 38; Schlosser, "Ancien Testament," 70.

82 So Beare (112), who compares it to the $\tau\hat{\eta}\varsigma$ $\epsilon\grave{\iota}\varsigma$ $\acute{v}\mu\hat{a}\varsigma$ $\chi\acute{a}\rho\iota\tau o\varsigma$ of 1:10.

83 E.g., Selwyn (152), who sees it, however, as bringing

a whole section to a close. The pattern of participles modifying imperatives, present since 1:13 and continuing through 2:5, argues against a major section ending with this verse. Similarly, Spicq's assertion (77) that v. 25 stands in "correspondance symétrique" with v. 12 would be more persuasive if the reference to angelic desires had not been appended at the end of the latter verse.

84 Compare the way the next two sections of the body of the letter, 2:11—4:11 and 4:12—5:11, begin.

2

Desire Appropriate Things

1 . | So after putting off every evil and every deceit, and hypocrisies[1] and envies[2] and all[3] evil speaking, 2/ as babes newly born you must yearn for the unadulterated[4] milk of God's word in order that you may grow unto salvation,[5] 3/ since[6] you have tasted[7] that the Lord is kind.[8]

1   In some texts the noun remains singular (ℵ[1], B, some others), but since that is an obvious correction, the plural is surely the preferred reading.

2   Some few late texts also change this to singular (1, t, some MSS. of Vulgate), B reads "murders" (φθόνους to φόνους), an error due to mishearing.

3   Some few MSS. (A, some others) omit "all" (πάσας), ℵ* changes the phrase to singular (πάσας καταλαλιάς to πάσαν καταλιάν), again in an attempt to bring consistency to the text.

4   Some late MSS. add καί ("and") to alleviate the sentence of the burden of two adjectives related to the same noun.

5   The phrase εἰς σωτηρίαν is omitted in the late MSS. tradition, probably to eliminate the idea of a progressive growing into something that can come alone from God, and is normally understood as an eschatological reality. It is to be retained (so also Michaels, 82).

6   A strong tradition (e.g., ℵ[2] C, P, Ψ) makes the εἰ a more emphatic εἴπερ ("since indeed"), though the meaning of the original εἰ is unchanged, and εἰ also has strong MS. witness (e.g., P[72], ℵ*, A, B).

7   P[72] adds ἐπιστεύσατε ("you believed"), which Beare ("Text," 264) thinks is a transfer of a marginal gloss, and shows the scribe here thought "tasted" meant "believed." A few other MSS. add καὶ εἴδετε ("and seen"), to conform it to LXX Ps 33:9; cf. also Quinn, "Notes," 243–44. Bornemann ("Taufrede," 147) thinks the words had already been present in 1:8: ὃν οὐκ ἰδόντες ἀγαπᾶτε.

8   P[72], K, L, and a number of minuscules change χρηστός to the phonetically identical Χριστός (ℵ, A, B, C, Ψ, some others), either due to an error of the ear, or in an attempt to make explicit the paranomasia that implies the kind Lord is Christ.

Analysis

This unit is the first half of the two units (the second is 2:4–10) that comprise the second half of the body opening[9] (1:13—2:10) of the letter. Like the other subunits of the body opening, it is characterized by a participle (ἀποθέμενοι) that modifies the main verb, again in the imperative (ἐπιποθήσατε), and like its preceding section (1:21–25), its thought is supported by a passage from Scripture.

The argument of the passage continues a line of thought already under way in the earlier verses. Just as

those who have faith and hope in God (1:21b) and have as a result sanctified their lives by such obedience (1:22a) are to move on to mutual love (1:22b), so those who have embodied such love (a love made possible by the power of God's regenerative word, 1:23–25) and have hence put off all vices contrary to it (2:1) must now once again move on to the next step, which is to make the word their consuming desire (2:2a) so that they may continue to grow toward salvation (2:2b), a salvation which they already know is based on the goodness of the Lord (2:3).

---

9   For a more detailed discussion of the body opening, see "1:13–2:10 Body Opening: Analysis," above.

Comment

■ **1** The οὖν that introduces the verse is not so much resumptive[10] as it is consecutive; it draws further inferences from the argument enunciated in 1:22–25, and indeed from the entire course of the argument that began in 1:13. While the opening participle ἀποθέμενοι has been credited with imperatival force,[11] it probably ought rather to be understood as a participle of attendant circumstances, describing an action of those who are now to make God's regenerative word their primary desire (2:2). In that sense, it shares the adverbial function of the participles that have characteristically begun each section of the body opening, and that have modified an imperative.[12] On the one hand, the verbal root of the participle (ἀποτίθημι) can refer to putting off clothing,[13] and as a result has here been seen to confirm a baptismal frame of reference for the passage.[14] On the other hand, the verb can also refer to any action of "putting away,"[15] and is regularly used in the NT for the elimination of sins, often in connection with lists of vices.[16] For that reason, it is probably better to understand it here in a more broadly traditional sense of ceasing sinful activity rather than any specific reference to a baptismal shedding of garments.[17]

The use of the word πᾶς ("all") in this list of vices[18] and the mixture of singular and plural[19] are also familiar from other such lists in early Christian literature, and further attest its background in paranetic tradition.[20] Whether or not we are to see here three groups of vices each introduced with a form of the word πᾶς that are meant to correspond to the virtues implied in 1:22,[21] it is clear that the vices mentioned are each inimical to the kind of love commanded in that verse. Thus κακία is surely a power that destroys community,[22] and is identified as directly opposed to acts motivated from love in Rom 13:10.[23] The next set of three vices—deception, hypocrisy, envy—are also inimical to a community based on mutual love, since deception and hypocrisy point to acts intended to serve the individual at the expense of the neighbor,[24] and envy means to wish better for oneself than for the other. The middle term (ὑπόκρισις, "hypocrisy") is in fact specifically identified in 1:22 as necessarily absent from community based on love. In this context, the final vice (καταλαλιά, "evil speech") probably refers to habitual disparagement of others rather than some kind of openly slanderous speech.[25] Taken

---

10 In contrast to Kelly (83), who understands it to refer to 1:22–23. Hart (54) sees it as resuming the διό of 1:13. That the οὖν here does not stand at the beginning of a major section, as did the διό in 1:13, is decisive against such an argument.

11 E.g., Thompson, "Submissive," 69; Grundmann, "Die ΝΗΠΙΟΙ," 189; Moffatt, 112; Goppelt, 133 n. 32; Hart, 54. More carefully Beare, 113; Michaels, 84: it shares the imperatival force of the governing verb. On the general question of the imperatival use of the participle, see "Excursus: Imperatival Use of Participles in 1 Peter," above.

12 1:13: ἀναζωσάμενοι—ἐλπίσατε; 1:14–16: συσχηματιζόμενοι—γενήθητε; 1:17–21: εἰδότες—ἀναστράφητε, but in reverse order; 1:22–25: ἡγνικότες—ἀγαπήσατε; see also 2:4: προσερχόμενοι—οἰκοδομεῖσθε.

13 Michaels (83) sees here a continuation of the clothing metaphor mentioned in 1:13.

14 So Kelly (84), who links it to such putting off of garments as symbolic of abandoning an unworthy past in Hippolytus *Ap. Trad.* 21; Cyril of Jerusalem *Catech.* 2.2; *Procatech.* 4. Because these writings are some two or three centuries later than our letter, they sacrifice something of their probative value.

15 So, e.g., Hort 97.

16 It is used in connection with elimination of sin (Eph 4:22; Heb 12:1), often with a list of vices (Rom

13:12–13; Eph 4:25–32; Col 3:8; Jas 1:21; cf. 1 Clem. 13.1). Best (96) notes 1QS 4:9–11 and 10:21–23 as examples of such lists in Judaism. Kelly (83) thus correctly identifies it as a technical term within early Christian paranesis.

17 Schelkle (54) notes correctly that because such a list of vices was drawn from common Christian tradition, one may not draw inferences from them regarding the particular situation of the readers. Other such lists of vices occur in Mark 7:21–22; Rom 1:29–31; 2 Cor 1:20–21; Gal 5:19–21; 1 Tim 6:4; cf. Brox, 90 n. 297; Kelly, 83.

18 Schelkle (54) notes that πᾶς occurs in lists of vices in Eph 4:31; Col 3:8; Jas 1:21; 1 Clem. 13.1.

19 Michaels (86) calls attention to the mixture of singular and plural in Gal 5:19–21, *Did.* 5.1.

20 *Did.* 5.1 also includes forms of κακία, δόλος, ὑπόκρισις, and its αἰσχρολογία is close in intent to the πάσας καταλαλιάς in this verse; their inclusion, with no reference to tie them to this verse in 1 Peter, further shows the traditional nature of these vices.

21 So Hart, 54.

22 So, e.g., Schelkle, 54; its juxtaposition to δόλος probably indicates its meaning to be malice rather than wickedness, as Hart (54) notes.

23 So also Beare, 113.

24 E.g., Schelkle, 54.

together, they represent the kind of attitudes and actions in whose presence true community based on love is impossible,[26] and that are therefore absent among those who have heeded the command to love one another.

Although the kind of vices mentioned here would surely also be avoided in interaction with those outside the Christian community,[27] the larger context of this verse makes patent that the author here has in mind the absence of such vices in the interrelationships Christians have with one another within the community of believers. The point of the verse seems to be that the kind of visible change from former behavior that characterizes actions within the community can be compared to the kind of intentional change involved in the casting off of old garments. The new behavior is then described in the following verses.

■ 2 While the emphasis to this point has been on regeneration by God (1:3) through his word (1:23–25) rather than rebirth, the result of that regeneration now becomes thematic.[28] The comparison to infants is thus motivated more by that ongoing metaphor than by the act of baptism in which clothes are put off and the person emerges as newly born.[29]

As the ὡς indicates, the verse is to be understood in a metaphorical sense:[30] because Christians have put away divisive vices (2:1) through their love of one another (1:22), they must now yearn for God's word[31] with the same single-mindedness with which an infant yearns for the milk that alone will nourish it.[32] Such metaphorical intention renders questionable the attempts to find in the mention of newborn babes a reference to the fact that the readers are recent converts to the faith.[33] Aside from the fact that such an interpretation turns the metaphor into an allegory,[34] the assumption that all the readers addressed in the vast area of northern Asia Minor would be recent converts all but defies imagination.[35] If there is an underlying significance to this metaphor, it is more likely to be the tradition that whatever their stage of spiritual development, Christians remain childlike in their faith,[36] but the reference in the second half of the verse to "growing into salvation" probably renders such a significance questionable. The use of the tautological "newborn babes," rare in non-Christian writers,[37] is

25   With Selwyn, 153.

26   So also, e.g., Margot, 35; Goppelt, 134.

27   Michaels (85) thinks the vices may intentionally refer to interaction with both fellow Christians and those outside the community.

28   The close link with the preceding context is indicated by the close link of ἀρτιγέννητα with ἀναγεγεννημένοι (1:23) and the emphasis on the λόγος/ῥῆμα θεοῦ (1:23, 25) and the λογικὸν γάλα; so also Tarrech, "Le milieu," 345; Francis, "Like Newborn Babes" 114–15.

29   So also Vanhoye, "L'Epître (I P 2,1–10)," 18; Goppelt, 135; Selwyn, 41; Best, 97. Baptismal language is here used, as in Rom 6:2–11, for wider implications of the Christian faith; see also Francis, "Like Newborn Babes," 111. That the point of reference is the Jewish proselyte ritual, where the proselyte is considered newly born (van Unnik, "Redemption," 54, 67 et passim; Spicq, 79), is attractive but probably unsustainable (so, e.g., Francis, "Like Newborn Babes," 111–12); the rabbinic sources are late (e.g., b. Yeb. 48b; 62a; 97b; cf. Str-B 2.423), and, pace van Unnik, the case for a general proselyte background for 1 Peter has not found wide acceptance. Attempts to link the verse to the exodus (Schwank et al. [32]: as Christians are children, so Israel became children before God at

Sinai; Danker ["I Peter 1:23—2:17," 95]: Israel also "grew up for her great salvation experience") seem rather contrived and hence lack persuasive power.

30   The use of ὡς in 2:5, where it obviously must be metaphorical, supports such an interpretation.

31   Λογικὸν γάλα; cf. 1:23, 25, and the discussion below.

32   So, e.g., Schelkle, 55; Bengel, Gnomon, 733; Spicq, 79; Moule, "Nature," 6; Chase ("Peter," 783) cites a similar metaphorical use of immaturity in 1 Cor 14:20 and Hermas, Sim. 9.29.

33   Such a reference is found, e.g., by Boismard ("Liturgie" [1], 196), who sees it particularly appropriate for those just baptized; see also Wand, 64; Bornemann, "Taufrede," 156; Windisch, 59; Kelly, 84; Cranfield, 61.

34   E.g., Francis ("Like Newborn Babes," 112), who argues for its allegorical intent (it is not "simply an illustrative example").

35   So also, e.g., Perdelwitz, Mysterienreligion, 25.

36   So, e.g., Michaels, 84. Bigg (126) cites as an example Matt 18:3; one could add Mark 9:42; 10:15. Less likely is the implication that new birth is to be perpetually renewed and hence always recent, as Hort (99) suggests.

37   It is used only in Lucian of Samosata Dial. mar. 318. Ἀρτιγέννητος used alone is more frequent, though still rare (e.g., Longus Daphn. 1.9.1; 1.18.1; 2.4.3,

probably used here to emphasize that early stage of the human being where the single-minded desire for nourishment is most readily apparent.

The metaphorical use of "milk" in Christian tradition is well attested,[38] and there is little justification in finding its origin in the mystery religions,[39] but it is normally used to refer to the kind of beliefs appropriate only for immature Christians who ought to be at a stage where the more solid food consumed by mature people is appropriate.[40] Such an understanding of "milk" is, however, not appropriate in this context. The point here is not that the readers are to advance beyond the stage of being immature Christians;[41] rather the point is that their desire for such milk is to be as constant and unrelenting as the infant's desire for its milk.[42]

The metaphor of the single-minded desire of the infant for its milk is qualified by the two adjectives modifying milk (λογικόν, ἄδολον), which do introduce an allegorical quality to the verse. The proper under-standing in this context of the adjective λογικός, a word derived from λόγος and hence normally pertaining either to reason or speech ("word"), is difficult to determine.[43] It occurs only one other time in the NT (Rom 12:1), where the same ambiguity inheres.

If the root λόγος is to be understood in the sense of "reason," then the meaning would be something that corresponds "reasonably," that is, appropriately to the present situation:[44] a "milk" whose content is appropriate to the Christian's situation. Since it is a "milk" that leads to growth to salvation, it points to the spiritual rather than the material dimension of reality, and hence could also perhaps be translated "spiritual."[45] Some have argued for this meaning not in terms of conforming to reason but in opposition to corporeal milk,[46] or as describing the purpose of God and his word which is true nourishment for Christians,[47] but such arguments depart from any relation to the root meanings of λογικός.[48]

If the root λόγος is to be understood in the sense of

Lucian of Samosata *Alex.* 13.7; 14.23). Use of ἀρτιγέννητα βρέφη in early Christian writers is limited to quotations of or references to 1 Pet 2:2 (Clement of Alexandria *Paed.* 1.6.44.1; Origen *Com. Joan.* 13.33.208; *Com. Matt.* 12.31; 13.26, 27; 16.25; *Frag. i ad Cor.* 12; and some few others).

38 So, e.g., Goppelt, 134.

39 As do, e.g., Windisch, 59; Beare, 115; Schelkle, 56; Perdelwitz, *Mysterienreligion*, 59; Best, 97. The usual reference is to Sallustius, *De deis* 4.10: γάλακτος τροφὴ ὥσπερ ἀναγεννωμένων ("fed on milk as those newly born"), who, however, means actual drinking as symbolic of new birth, not the point in 1 Peter. Whether such a reference from a writer of the fourth century CE can be used as "source" for the metaphor here is also open to question; see also Schelkle, 44 n. 4. Goppelt (135) and Francis ("Like Newborn Babes," 112) rightly reject such a source for this language.

40 Often cited are 1 Cor 3:1–3 and Heb 5:11–6:2. Danker ("I Peter 1:23–2:17," 95) identifies a similar tradition in the OT, e.g., Isa 28:9, where priests taunt Isaiah that his words are for children, not for them. The references to Israel as a child fed by God to which Francis ("Like Newborn Babes," 114) points (Jer 31:20; Hos 11:1; Ps 103:13) omit any reference to feeding. Frederic Manns points to such a tradition in Philo *Agric.* 9; *Migr. Abr.* 29; and at Qumran, 1QH 7.21 ("La maison où réside l'Esprit.' 1 P 2,5 et son arrière-plan juif," *SBFLA* 34 [1984] 208–9 n. 6); Goppelt (135) adds 1QH 9.35–36.

41 So, e.g., Grundmann ("Die NHΠIOI," 191; but see

contra, 196), who cites 1 Cor 13:8–13 and Phil 3:12–15 as making a similar point.

42 So also Gangel, "Pictures," 31; Calvin, 63.

43 As Danker ("I Peter 1:23—2:17" 95 n. 9), citing J. H. Moulton and G. Milligan ("Lexical Notes from the Papyri, XVI," *Expositor*, series 7, 7 [1909] 560), points out, λόγικος can also mean "metaphorical," but that is probably not its meaning here.

44 E.g., Margot, 35; Holmer and de Boor, 74.

45 Wand (65): "nourishment proper to the spiritual nature"; Peter Ketter ("Das allgemeine Priestertum: II. Das allgemeine Priestertum der Gläubigen nach dem ersten Petrusbrief," *TThZ* 56 [1947] 44): it is nourishment for the soul of a human being blessed with reason. Michaels (88) argues that the phrase λογικὸν γάλα means "holy milk," and cites several passages from Odes of Solomon, most important of which is 8.14; cf. Heinrich Schlier, "γάλα," *ThWNT* 1 (1959) 645.

46 E.g., Fransen, "Une homélie," 34.

47 So Francis, "Like Newborn Babes," 115. Best (98) argues that it means "spiritual" as it does in Rom 12:1 (he assumes dependence of 1 Pet on that verse), but there is no agreement on that as its meaning there. To call on John Chrysostom to justify the meaning "spiritual" in 1 Pet 2:2 because that is what it means for him in Rom 12:1, as does Bengel (*Gnomon* 733), is to miss Chrysostom's identification of "milk" with "the word" in his comment on this verse; Chrysos-tom's phrase (*In Illud: Collegerunt Judaei* 59.525.39) is τὸ λογικὸν γάλα τοῦ λόγου, where τοῦ λόγου is clearly an epexegetical genitive identifying γάλα. Schelkle

"word," then λογικός would express the relationship of γάλα ("milk") to the word of God as the proper nourishment for Christians.[49] This understanding is supported by the use of λόγος θεοῦ in 1:23[50] and is reinforced by the use of ῥῆμα (= "word") in 1:25a for the word of the Lord and 1:25b for the gospel.[51] Since, therefore, in this context, the word of God (λόγος θεοῦ) was the agency by which the readers were rebegotten as Christians (1:23), and since the word of the Lord (ῥῆμα κυρίου) was the good news that has been communicated to them (1:25b), some relationship between the divine word and the adjective λογικός seems most likely.[52] It would, furthermore, be appropriate for Christians who were rebegotten by the word of God to yearn for that word[53] so they may experience further growth leading to salvation.

The second adjective modifying γάλα, ἄδολον, is common enough in secular Greek but is absent from the LXX[54] and is used only here in the NT. It probably refers to the undiluted Word of God, that is, undiluted by any tendencies the later church would identify with the term "heretical."[55] Christians are thus to yearn for the undiluted word of God with the same tenacity with which an infant yearns for its milk.

The imperative ἐπιποθήσατε, typically for the body opening of the letter, is in the aorist,[56] in this case expressing a fervent desire in the religious realm, as is often the case in biblical Greek.[57] The purpose of (ἵνα), and therefore the reason for, such a desire is given in the second half of the sentence: the milk for which the readers are so heartily to yearn is the means (ἐν αὐτῷ)[58] of further growth. The antecedent of αὐτῷ in this context is most likely γάλα, although it could grammatically also have a masculine antecedent, viz., θεός ("God") or, less likely, χριστός ("Christ").[59] Given the author's keen awareness of the nearness of the parousia and the final judgment, it is more likely that σωτηρία ("salvation") refers to eschatological deliverance than to Christian maturity.[60] The point is that the purpose of yearning for and holding to God's word is a growth (αὐξηθῆτε) whose goal (εἰς is here telic) is one's deliverance at the time of the final divine judgment.

■ 3 As at the end of the previous section (1:22–25) the author uses OT language to confirm the point being

(56) derives its meaning as "spiritual" from *Corp. Herm.* 1.31: δέξαι λογικὰς θυσίας ἀγνὰς ψυχῆς καὶ καρδίας ("to receive pure lives and hearts as spiritual sacrifices").

48 Moffatt (113) argues that it is a "mistaken idea" to see in λογικός a play on λόγος in the sense of spiritual.

49 E.g., Elliott, *Elect*, 204. So also a number of others; Hart (55): "Belonging to, contained in the Word of God"; Selwyn (155): "flowing out of the Word of God"; Perdelwitz (*Mysterienreligion*, 6): "von dem Logos herstammend"; see also Bigg (126), Grundmann ("Die NHΠIOI," 189): "worthaltigen . . . Milch" (Elliott [*Elect*, 204] wrongly cites this as "worthaftig," but his citation nevertheless makes for an intriguing translation); Boismard ("Liturgie" [2], 169): "le lait de la Parole"; Reicke (89) and Kelly (85): "milk of the word."

50 E.g., Spicq, 79; Tarrech, "Le milieu," 344; Vanhoye, "L'Epître (I P 2,1–10)," 18; Hart, 55.

51 So also Schutter, *Hermeneutic*, 128.

52 So also Goppelt, 136; see also n. 47 above. Contra Beare, 115, who argues that such an idea as the "milk of the word" is "impossible."

53 The χρηστός/χριστός pun contained in 2:3 has led Hart (54) to suggest that the milk is Christ himself, a possibility also suggested by Francis ("Like Newborn Babes," 115).

54 It appears only as the adverb ἀδόλως in Wis 7:13.

55 For a similar emphasis, this time on pure and uncontaminated doctrine, see 1 Tim 6:3; 2 Tim 1:13–14; 4:3–4; Titus 1:9. That it may be intended as a positive counterpart of the δόλον of 1 Pet 2:1, see Elliott, *Elect*, 204; Kelly, 85; Schelke, 56.

56 On its force, see the comments on 1:22 and the aorist imperative verb in the phrase ἀλλήλους ἀγαπήσατε ("love one another") above.

57 E.g., LXX Pss 41:2; 118:174; Rom 1:11; 2 Cor 5:2; Phil 1:8; 2 Tim 1:4.

58 Beare (116) correctly sees it as a dative of instrument, despite the absence of ἐν.

59 Kelly (86) observes it could also be Χριστός and argues for deliberate authorial ambiguity, since δι' αὐτοῦ would have pointed unambiguously to Christ. But that is to assume the author did not want to refer to γάλα, an assumption that cannot be made.

60 So also Michaels, 89; for a contrary view, see Perdelwitz, *Mysterienreligion*, 65.

made. The language is adapted from LXX Ps 33:9,[61] from which a longer passage is cited in our letter at 3:10–12;[62] perhaps its appeal to our author lay in the fact that Psalm 33 has as its theme rescue of the faithful by God from danger.[63] The citation here functions not so much as proof from Scripture, or an indication of its fulfillment, as simply to reinforce a point able nonetheless to stand without the scriptural support. As such use shows, language from the OT seems naturally to apply to the new community of faith for our author.

The conjunctive particle εἰ is used here in the *sensum reale,* assuming the actuality of the condition,[64] and in that way furnishes a further reason for Christians to yearn for God's word. While a eucharistic reference could be found here[65]—χρηστός can mean "delicious to the taste,"[66] and Psalm 33 was considered eucharistic in the early church[67]—it was probably not intended by the author,[68] since χρηστός need not refer only to food[69] and the changes the author made in Ps 33:9 reduce the

likelihood of such a reference. A reference to a custom connected with baptism, whereby newly baptized people were given milk to drink as they came out of the water,[70] also seems unlikely, given the probability that the context does not refer to new converts.[71]

A wordplay on χρηστός/χριστός may have been intended,[72] since the continuation in the next verse makes clear that v. 3 does refer to Christ.[73] Yet the presence of κύριος ("Lord"), a normal title in early Christian tradition for Christ, would have provided sufficient clue to the meaning of this verse even if the wordplay were not intended.[74]

---

61   The objection by Perdelwitz (*Mysterienreligion*, 67) that it cannot be so derived since the καὶ ἴδετε of the psalm is omitted is unpersuasive; one cannot assume such literalism in quotation on the part of any NT author.

62   E.g., Elliott, *Elect*, 205; Selwyn (156) observes that similar language occurs at Heb 6:4–6.

63   E.g., Brox, 93; Goppelt, 37.

64   This is commonly accepted, e.g., Elliott, *Elect*, 205; Kelly, 86; Schelkle, 57 n. 2; Selwyn, 157; Wand, 65; Michaels, 90.

65   It is found, e.g., by Jonsen, "Moral Theology," 98; Beare, 116; Schiwy, 42; Bieder, *Grund und Kraft*, 15 n. 13; Ketter, "Das allgemeine Priestertum: II," 45.

66   Kelly (86) insists that must also be the meaning here, and cites Jer 24:2–5 and Luke 5:39. Tarrech ("Le milieu," 345) suggests "savoureux" because of the mention of γάλα in v. 2; a similar sense in a similar context is also found in *Odes Sol.* 19.1.

67   E.g., Kelly (87), who cites *Ap. Const.* 8.13.16; Cyril of Jerusalem *Catech.* 5.20; Jerome *Ep.* 71.6, along with the Liturgy of St. James; yet as Best (99) notes, such a hypothesis "fails for lack of evidence in this period."

68   So also Goppelt, 138; Ketter, "Das allgemeine Priestertum: II," 45.

69   Hort (103) calls such a notion "fallacious"; cf. Spicq (81), who finds the meaning here not "bon" but "excellent."

70   E.g., Reicke, 90.

71   Kelly (87), who thinks it refers to the Eucharist, notes that the change from the imperative γεύσασθε in LXX Ps 33:9 to the indicative ἐγεύσασθε here indicates the readers have already tasted such goodness, and hence rules out such a reference to a postbaptismal Eucharist. See also the discussion of ἀρτιγέννητα βρέφη ("babes newly born") in 2:2 above.

72   So, e.g., Beare, 116; the two words would have been pronounced identically when this letter was read aloud, the only way written material was read; see Achtemeier, *"Omne verbum sonat,"* 15–17, and the further literature cited there.

73   As Goppelt (137), among many others, has observed.

74   Perdelwitz (*Mysterienreligion*, 67) thus overstates when he avers that the phrase had to have meant χριστὸς ὁ κύριος or the reader would not have known that the ὅν of 2:4 referred to Christ.

2

You Are a Chosen People

4 **Because you come to him, a living stone, rejected by[1] humans but to God elect, precious, 5/ even you yourselves, as living stones, a spiritual house,[2] are being built[3] to be[4] a holy priesthood, in order to offer spiritual sacrifices acceptable to God[5] through Jesus Christ. 6/ Hence it stands written in[6] Scripture: "Behold, I am placing in Zion a cornerstone, elect, honored,[7] and the one who trusts[8] in it will surely not be put to shame." 7/ For you, therefore, who trust, there is the honor; for those who do not trust, "the very[9] stone[10] that the builders rejected has become the head of the corner," 8/ and "a stone of stumbling and a rock of offense"; they stumble over the word who disobey, for which purpose also they[11] were established. 9/ You, however, are an elect race, a royal priesthood, a holy nation, a people for God's own possession, in order that you announce the glorious deeds of the one who called you out of darkness into his marvelous light, 10/ you who once were no people but now are God's people, who once were not shown mercy but now have been shown that mercy [or: who once were not graced with mercy, but now have been so graced].**

1 Some few minuscules read ἀπό, perhaps an error of the ear provoked by the crasis inherent in ζῶντα ὑπό.

2 Since this phrase precedes the εἰς that introduces ἱεράτευμα ἅγιον and stands in the nominative case, it is to be construed as standing in apposition to the implied subject "you."

3 ℵ, A^c, C, and some minuscules read ἐποικοδομεῖσθε ("built up"); there is no compelling reason to accept this reading (with Beare, "Text," 265).

4 Although some MSS. omit the telic εἰς, the textual evidence favoring its inclusion is overwhelming.

5 The definite article τῷ before θεῷ is omitted by ℵ*, A, B, C, Ψ, and a number of minuscules, but is included by P^72, ℵ^2, P, and the majority of the minuscules; its inclusion or omission would not affect the meaning.

6 A number of minuscules read ἡ γραφή in place of ἐν γραφῇ, thus making the verb transitive: "Wherefore Scripture contains" or "says"; the later intransitive meaning with ἐν γραφῇ is found in P^72, ℵ, A, B, Ψ, and a few minuscules, and ought to be accepted on the basis of superior MS. tradition.

7 Some MSS. (B, C, a few minuscules, sa^ms, bo) rearrange the adjectives to reflect the LXX. Although there is some MS. evidence for the omission of ἐκλεκτόν ("elect") or ἀκρογωνιαῖον ("cornerstone"), it is weak and may be ignored.

8 While A, P, and some other MSS. read ἀπειθοῦντες, it is probably an attempt to harmonize the text with v. 8; ἀπιστοῦσιν is found in P^72, ℵ, B, C, Ψ, and some minuscules.

9 This renders the emphatic οὗτος found in the second half of this citation from LXX Ps 117:22.

10 The textual tradition is divided on whether "stone" is to be nominative, to agree with οὗτος, or accusative, as in LXX, to agree with ὅν, which serves as the object of the verb; the meaning remains unaffected.

11 The conjectured ἐτέθη ("it [i.e., the stone] was established") for ἐτέθησαν ("they were established") is interesting, but there is no textual evidence for such an attempt to avoid the theological difficulty contained in the verse.

Analysis

This is the final unit of the body opening (1:13—2:10) of the letter, and shares the characteristics of the units that make up that larger whole, namely, a participle (προσερχόμενοι) that modifies the main verb (οἰκοδομεῖσθε). While the other parts of the body opening have had the main verb in the imperative, the author in this final section places it in the indicative, as the final summation of the result of the discussion to this point, and as an introduction to the ensuing imperatives in the body

middle (2:11—4:10). Like two preceding sections (1:21–25; 2:1–3), this section also concludes with citations of Scripture (vv. 6–7, 9–10), but here more intentional and to a greater extent than previously, a further indication of the summarizing intent of these verses.

Because the unit is structured in such a way that vv. 4–5 announce themes that are then expanded in the following verses, such expansions occur largely in the form of a scriptural citation (v. 6) and numerous phrases also drawn from the OT (vv. 7b–8a, 9a, 10).[12]

1. Structure

Verses 4–5 set the theme and thus the basic polarity of the passage, a polarity between those who reject Christ, the divinely elect, living stone, and hence are themselves rejected, and those who accept that living stone, and are thus constituted a new people. The first half of the passage is dominated by the stone metaphor (vv. 4–8) announced in v. 4, while the second half is dominated by the idea of the people of God (vv. 9–10) announced in v. 5.[13] Similarly, the first half is dominated by the contrast between those who accept the stone (vv. 5, 6, 7a) God has chosen (v. 4c), and those who reject it (vv. 4b, 7b-8). The clear implication of the passage is that because Christians follow Christ, the elect stone (v. 4c, 6a), they themselves reflect the same divine election to become a people, a notion reinforced by the language drawn from the exodus (v. 9) and restoration (v. 10) of Israel, both examples of divine election of a people.[14] The purpose of such election is stated at the conclusion of v. 5 (offering spiritual sacrifices) and again at the conclusion of v. 9 (proclaiming the mighty deeds of God). That each comes at the end of a series of phrases describing the new people of God implies that the two are correlated.[15] Since the themes of vv. 4–5 are expanded and explained in vv. 6–10,[16] one may assume that proclamation (v. 9b) is a further explanation of offering spiritual sacrifices (v. 5b).

2. Derivation

The passage is notable as representing one of the largest collections of OT images in the NT.[17] Prominent among them are passages from Isaiah and LXX Psalm 117 that mention "stone."[18] That the stone image is common Christian tradition[19] and that these passages were closely associated in Christian apologetics[20] has led to the proposal that the author is drawing on a collection of stone testimonia already in existence,[21] or perhaps even from a prior composition in the form of a hymn or

---

12 Why the author moved from a discussion of Christians as babes to a discussion of them as living stones is not immediately apparent. For a discussion of various attempts to account for it, see below, "Excursus: The Transition from 2:1–3 to 2:4–10."

13 So also Elliott, *Elect*, 22–23; Schlosser, "Ancien Testament," 73; Selwyn, 280; cf. Goppelt (139) and Best ("I Peter II 4–10," 278), who find a similar division within the passage.

14 The implication is also present, as Boismard ("Liturgie" [1], 191) notes, that God has formed a new covenant with the Christian community, as he formed a covenant with Israel at the time of the exodus.

15 With Elliott, *Elect*, 184.

16 So also, e.g., Richard Bauckham, "James, 1 and 2 Peter, Jude," in D. A. Carson, H. G. M. Williamson, eds., *It Is Written: Scripture Citing Scripture; Essays in Honour of Barnabas Lindars, SS* (Cambridge: Cambridge University Press, 1988) 310. Whether vv. 4–5 contain a condensation and reformulation of the more original material contained in vv. 6–10 (so Elliott, *Elect*, 17, 19) or vv. 6–10 are intended to explain vv. 4–5 (so Michaels, 100–101; Best, "I Peter II 4–10" 271) is difficult to determine; whichever the case, it is clear that the ecclesiology of the second portion is based on the Christology of the first, as Schlosser ("Ancien Testament," 73) points out. See also the comments on the individual verses.

17 V. 6b = Isa 28:16; v. 7b = LXX Ps 117:22; v. 8a = Isa 8:14; vv. 9a, c-d = Isa 43:20–21; 9a, b = Exod 19:6; 10a-b = Hos 1:6, 9; 2:3, 25.

18 This is also the largest group of stone testimonia in the NT, as Klyne R. Snodgrass ("I Peter II.1–10: Its Formation and Literary Affinities," *NTS* 24 [1977] 7) and Thomas Lea ("How Peter Learned the Old Testament," *Southwestern Journal of Theology* 22 [1980] 97) note. That this may be related to the fact that the letter is attributed to "Peter," as, e.g., C. F. D. Moule ("Some Reflections on the 'Stone' Testimonia in Relation to the Name Peter," *NTS* 2 [1955/56] 57), Spicq ("La Iᵃ Petri," 56), and Lea ("How Peter Learned the OT," 101) propose, is an interesting suggestion, but it can be no more than that.

19 As several have suggested; see Elliott, *Elect*, 32. Snodgrass ("I Peter II.1–10," 106) argues that Isa 28:16 was already linked with 8:14 in Jewish tradition, and hence proved useful to the church.

20 So Moule, "Some Reflections," 57.

21 E.g., Elliott, *Elect*, 129, Pierre Sandevoir, "Un Royaume de Prêtres?" in Perrot, *Etudes*, 221. The argument of Pierre Prigent ("1 Pierre 2,4–10" *RHPhR* 72 [1992] 59) that vv. 6–10 were drawn from a document whose major point was the rejection of the gospel by nonbelievers (cf. Mark 4:10–13), a point our author then ignored in his use of that document in vv. 6–10, is in turn to ignore the importance of that question not only for 2:6–10 but also for the body middle of the letter, 2:11—4:11; see the comments on vv. 7, 8, and the analysis of the body middle, below.

rhythmic prayer.[22] While Paul does cite Hosea 2 (Rom 9:25–26) and Isaiah 8 and 28 (Rom 9:32b–33), the order is reversed from that of 1 Peter, and the two citations are separated in Romans 9 by other OT citations not found in 1 Peter (cf. Rom 9:27–29), making it unlikely that both are based on an earlier hymn, or even that such a hymn existed.[23] That the passages from LXX Psalm 117 and Isaiah 8 and 28 referring to λίθος ("stone") are nowhere else combined in the NT[24] makes even the existence of a collection of "stone testimonia" rather questionable.[25]

The similarity between this passage in 1 Peter and materials from Qumran, a similarity greater in the case of this letter than of any other NT writing,[26] has been used as a basis for seeing in the Qumran material a possible source for these verses. There are, for example, references to a new temple (e.g., 1QS 8.4–6, using Isa 28:16); to nonmaterial sacrifice (e.g., 1QS 8.4–6; 9.3–5; 4QFlor 1.6–7); to members of the community as stones

(4QpIsa[d], frag. i; cf. 1QH 6.25–27), perhaps even to the priesthood of the community as directly related to the new temple (e.g., CD 3.19—4.3).[27] Additionally, the use of the OT citations in this passage in 1 Peter also bears strong resemblance to the kind of midrashic exegesis[28] evident at Qumran, including at times *pesher*-like interpretation,[29] although such exegetical procedures are by no means limited in the NT to 1 Peter.

While these verses in 1 Peter do seem to reflect the self-understanding of the Qumran community more closely than other NT writings do,[30] direct dependence on the Qumran materials by our author is not likely.[31]

22 Especially Windisch ([2d ed.] 58), Preisker ("Anhang zum ersten Petrusbrief," in Windisch [3d ed.], 58); Selwyn, 268–77 (for a critique of Selwyn's proposal, see Elliott, *Elect,* 133–138); cf. Goppelt (139) for further references.

23 So also Elliott, *Elect,* 135–37; the argument of Selwyn (272) that 1 Pet 2:6 and Rom 9:33 make the same changes from LXX Isa 28:16 (ἐμβαλῶ becomes τίθημι; εἰς τὰ θεμέλια are omitted) loses persuasive power when it is further noted that (a) 1 Pet 2:6 has ὂν μὴ καταισχυνθῇ, Rom 9:32 οὐ καταισχυνθήσεται; and (b) Rom 9:32 expands Isa 28:16 by adding words from 8:14 ([λίθον] προσκόμματος καὶ πέτραν σκανδάλου) in a way 1 Pet 2:6 does not. Such divergences render less likely the use of the same source.

24 Ps 117: Matt 21:42//Mark 12:10//Luke 20:17; Acts 4:11; Isa 28: Rom 9:32; Isa 8: Rom 9:33. The argument of Senior (30) that LXX Ps 117:22 in Luke 20:17 is expanded by the use of Isa 8:14 in Luke 20:18 fails for lack of linguistic similarities between Isa 8:14 and Luke 20:18.

25 In agreement with, e.g., Snodgrass, "I Peter II.1–10," 105; Elliott, *Elect,* 33.

26 Best, "I Peter II 4–10," 285.

27 I owe these references to Best ("I Peter II 4–10," 285). He argues further that since the concepts were drawn from a Levitical context at Qumran, the same may be assumed for 1 Peter, a point contested by Elliott (*Elect,* e.g., 213), who sees the word ἱεράτευμα used in 1 Peter as a predicate for Israel as a whole and here designating the Christian community as the new chosen people.

28 Goppelt, 139. Selwyn (278) thinks the midrashic comments were added to an earlier hymn; but see Best ("I Peter II 4–10," 278 n. 3), who thinks no midrash is involved.

29 So, e.g., Schutter, *Hermeneutic,* 138. The suggestion of Lea ("How Peter Learned the OT," 96, 98) that our author learned such interpretation from Jesus, based on Jesus' use of Ps 118:22 in Matt 21:42 par. and Peter's use of it in Acts 4:11, has not won wide acceptance. His suggestion (99) that Jesus may also have interpreted Isa 8:14, 15 privately for his disciples is, given lack of any record of it in the Gospels, yet more speculative.

30 For 1 Pet 2:4–6, Goppelt (140) cites 1QS 8.4–11; 9.3–6; CD 3.19—4.4; on 1 Peter 2:9–10, he cites 1QM 3.13; 10.9–10; 13.7.

31 In agreement with Michaels (96), who notes that 1 Peter expected Christians to exercise their priestly calling in the midst of the world, not to withdraw from it. Elliott (*Elect,* 210–11) also finds such direct dependence unlikely, and takes issue with the suggestion of Flusser ("Dead Sea Sect," 235) that the author of 1 Peter is dependent here on a Hebrew prototype resembling 1QS 8.4–11. Conversely, rejection of any Levitical influence from Qumran on 1 Peter based on the assertion that Exod 19:6 "played absolutely no role in the Qumranic literature" (Elliott, *Elect,* 210; so also Elisabeth Schüssler Fiorenza, "Cultic Language in Qumran and in the NT," *CBQ* 38 [1976] 174) needs to be tempered in light of *Jub.* 33.20, which seems to refer to both Exod 19:6 and Isa 43:21. Parts of *Jubilees* have been found

Such dependence, if it exists at all, will have been secondary, and in all likelihood mediated through other, early Christian tradition of which our author was aware.[32]

The most probable solution is to see here elements of an early Jewish-Christian tradition subsequently taken over by the Hellenistic Christian community, as its use by Paul[33] and the authors of the Synoptic Gospels[34] indicates. It was elements of this tradition that 1 Peter used, combining them in this passage in a unique and creative way to describe the elect Christian community.[35]

3. Theological Thrust

In this final passage of the body opening, the movement from Christ as elect and precious living stone to his followers who because of their relationship to him are also as elect and precious living stones constituted into a people special to God, sums up the thought begun in 1:13 that has concerned the relationship of Christians to God through Christ (e.g., 1:18–21, 23–25) and the duties such a relationship makes incumbent upon them (e.g., 1:13–17, 22; 2:1–3). The topic of election, encountered in the opening verse of the letter, here becomes thematic,[36] but it is now clear that God's election of the Christian community (2:9) depends entirely on God's prior election of Christ (2:4, 6; cf. 1:20).[37] The twofold description of the new community (2:5; 2:9–10) shows by its language that the church has now taken over the role of Israel,[38] and that such sacrifices as God requires will now be made by this community (esp. 2:5b). This point is the basis for the idea of a "priesthood of all believers" in contrast to a class of priests,[39] and a priesthood whose chief function is to evangelize (cf. the parallelism between vv. 5b and 9b). Yet the major thrust of this passage is the elect and holy character of the eschatological covenant community,[40] and any notion of priesthood, whether as special class or the function of the whole body of believers as a special class of "priests" (e.g., for the whole of humanity), is at best secondary and derived.[41]

Finally, it is clear in this passage that if the Christian community is elect and precious to God because it is based on Christ who is elect and precious to God, then it is also true that as that elect and precious Christ was rejected by human beings (2:4b) so will be the community constituted by him (2:7b–8). This has as its point

---

32 The use of λίθος for Jesus is firmly anchored in NT tradition: Matt. 21:42 par.; Acts 4:11; Rom 9:32–33.

33 E.g., Rom 9:33; to cite Eph 2:18–22 as reflecting the same tradition-complex, as does Schüssler Fiorenza ("Cultic Language in Qumran," 173–74), remains somewhat less than compelling despite a similar context, given the lack of linguistic similarities between the two passages and the lack of any OT citations in Ephesians. To find a common tradition combining metaphors of growth and building represented in Eph 2:21 and 4:12–16, as does Michaels (93), suffers from the same lack.

34 Matt 21:42 par.

35 So also, e.g., Goppelt, 140; Michaels, 97; cf. Snodgrass, "I Peter II.1–10," 103; Brox, 94–95. The absence of βασίλειον ἱεράτευμα from Paul, but its inclusion in Rev 1:6; 5:10, may point to its currency in Asia Minor; its inclusion would be a sign of acquaintance by our author of some traditions known to his readers, though such a conclusion must remain speculative. The suggestion that Peter was influenced by Jesus and perhaps also by the way Paul and John the Baptist used λίθος, as does Lea ("How Peter Learned the OT," 100), has not met with wide acceptance.

36 A point also made by Elliott (Elect, 147).

37 This is a particular emphasis of Elliott (Elect, e.g., 145, 146, 165).

38 Typically for 1 Peter, there is no idea that the Christian community is a fulfillment of Israel, nor is there any polarity between Israel and the church; such polarity as there is exists between believers and unbelievers (2:4, 6b–8). On this point cf. Brox, "Sara zum Beispiel," 489, 491; Michaels, 95.

39 E.g., Feuillet, "Sacrifices," passim; cf. Best, "I Peter II 4–10," 286. John S. Marshall relates it to the Eucharist as a corporate priestly act, in which "the whole Church is a Priesthood" sharing in "the priestly act of our Lord's atoning work" ("'An Holy House, an Holy Priesthood' [I Peter ii.5]," ATR 28 [1946] 228). For more on this whole point, see the comments on v. 5 below.

40 The language is that of Elliott, "Rehabilitation," 11.

41 This point has been effectively made by Elliott (Elect, 225–26). See also his "Rehabilitation," 11, and the literature cited in his n. 36, as well as the comments below on v. 5 and the phrase ἱεράτευμα ἅγιον.

here the fact that such suffering does not provide evidence of rejection by God, but rather precisely of divine election.

It is such rejection by the world, here announced, that becomes thematic in the remainder of the body of the letter (2:11—5:11).

Excursus: The Transition from 2:1–3 to 2:4–10

The connection between these two passages, the one emphasizing Christians as newborn babes desiring milk, and the other pointing to Christ as the living foundation stone, is not immediately apparent. A number of suggestions have been made to account for this movement in the author's thought.

1. It is derived from rituals of the mystery religions, many of which had as an object of worship some sort of stone; the initiate would go from a ritual drink of milk to the worship of such a stone.[42]

2. It is derived from 1QH, where in 9.28 God is addressed as a rock of strength, followed in 10.24 by a description of the transitory nature of human existence contrasted with those under God's care in 9:30–32; the antidote to the transitoriness that is death (1:24) is life nourished by the Lord (2:3), who is the rock of the community (2:4).[43]

3. It is derived from Deut 32:18, which links heavenly birth and God as rock.[44]

4. It comes from Gen 16:2 and 30:3, which relate Sarah's desire to obtain children through Hagar and Rachel's through Bilhah by using a verb whose stem means "be built" (אבנה), pointing to an association of "build" (בנה), "son" (בן), and "house" (בת); this accounts for 1 Peter's juxtaposing themes of birth and building.[45]

5. It derives from Joel 3:18, which announces that the hills (= "stone" in v. 4) will run with milk (= v. 2).[46]

6. It derives from the same source as 1 Cor 10:4, where people drank from the supernatural rock which was Christ.[47]

7. The connection between Christ as the "kind Lord" (2:3b) and Christ as the living rock to whom Christians are to come (προσερχόμενοι) derives from LXX Psalm 33, since 1 Pet 2:3 is drawn from Ps 33:9a, and v. 9b calls God a "refuge," a word often associated with God as rock.[48] LXX Psalm 33 also contains a command to come to the Lord (προσέλθατε, v. 6).[49]

Of all the suggestions, the last has the merit of calling on a passage from the OT (LXX Ps 33) that is common to both passages, a point lacking in the other suggestions. Yet even it remains somewhat speculative. In the end, the reason for the connection lies in the author's theological thought, and while the movement of that thought, from the reality of Christians who depend on the word of their kind Lord to the reality of their being members of a community built upon him as a living foundation stone, is clear, the reason for the connection remains somewhat less than clear.

Comment

■ **4** The content of the verse makes clear that the κύριος ("Lord") of v. 3, to which the ὅν refers, is to be understood as Christ rather than God, despite the fact that προσέρχομαι is used in the LXX of a priest's approach to God,[50] and can be used in that way in the NT (e.g., Heb 10:1).[51] The participle προσερχόμενοι has been understood to have imperatival force,[52] although there is no general agreement on that score. Since participle and main verb (οἰκοδομεῖσθε, v. 5) will share the same force,[53] it is probably better to understand both here as indicative,[54] either informing the readers of the results of the imperatives contained in 1:13—2:3, or even giving the

42 Perdelwitz, *Mysterienreligion*, 69–70.
43 Danker, "I Peter 1:23—2:17," 94.
44 Francis, "Like Newborn Babes," 116 n. 4.
45 Norman Hillyer, "Spiritual Milk . . . Spiritual House," *TynBul* 20 (1969) 126.
46 Hart, 55.
47 Hart, 55; it is denied as a possibility by Kelly (88).
48 For more on this point, see the comments on 2:4 below.
49 Suggested as a possibility by Elliott (*Elect*, 165–66 n. 2). See also Goppelt (143), who notes in addition the appearance of the phrase καὶ ἐκ πασῶν τῶν παροικιῶν

μου ἐρρύσατό με in LXX Ps 33:5.
50 So Best, 100.
51 Ketter, "Das allgemeine Priestertum: II," 45. The other passages he proposes (Heb 4:16; 7:25; 10:22) are less germane; questionable also are the OT passages he cites (Jer 7:16; Sir 1:28).
52 Moffatt, 114; Senior, 30; Minear, "House of Living Stones," 240; Grundmann, "Die NHΠIOI," 194; Brox, 96; Goppelt, 141; Leaney, 30.
53 Beare, 119; Best, 100; Michaels, 97.
54 Grudem, 100; Elliott, *Elect*, 16, in addition to those cited in the preceding note.

means ("by coming to him") by which the building of 2:5 occurs.[55]

The appositional phrase λίθον ζῶντα ("living stone") applies a word to Christ, λίθος ("stone"), which is often applied to God in the OT,[56] continuing a christological practice already evident in v. 3, where the divine title κύριος had been similarly used.[57] The appositional phrase itself in Latin (saxum vivum, "living stone") means what it does in English (i.e., stone in its original place),[58] but in Greek it represents something of an anomaly, since λίθος means a dressed stone suitable for a building,[59] not the massive rock that could be described with the adjective "living" (ζῶντα). The phrase is used only here in biblical literature,[60] and surely refers to the fact that Christ, as risen from the dead, lives.[61]

The fate of the "living stone" is described in language borrowed from LXX Ps 117:22 and Isa 28:16. While both passages are used in the NT,[62] this combination of the two is unique. That it is the living stone that is rejected probably means the author is thinking of those contemporaries of his who reject the gospel,[63] rather than the rejection Christ suffered at the time of his crucifixion. Such a view is supported by the participle ἀποδεδοκιμασμένον ("rejected") in the perfect tense, which points to the ongoing rejection suffered by Christ.[64] The contrast embodied in these words, emphasized by the particles μέν, δέ,[65] thus suggests not the historic rejection of Jesus by the Jews but the current rejection of the Christian faith by secular Greco-Roman society. The contrast, in which the rejected stone is nevertheless elect (ἐκλεκτόν) and held precious by God (ἔντιμον),[66] points to the comfort Christians can derive from following Christ: they too, though rejected and alienated in their culture, nevertheless have God on their side and will ultimately be vindicated. That point is then implied in the next verse, where Christians are termed "living stones" and hence by implication share the fate of the "living stone."

■ 5 The grammar of this verse is complicated by the fact that the subject "you" of the passive οἰκοδομεῖσθε is overloaded with three phrases standing in relation to it: αὐτοί ("yourselves"), λίθοι ζῶντες ("living stones"), and οἶκος πνευματικός ("spiritual house"). All three may stand in apposition to the subject,[67] or the phrase οἶκος πνευματικός may be understood as a predicate nominative:[68] "You are a spiritual house who, as living stones, are being built. . . ." In this latter case, the verb stands in

---

55 E.g., Beare, 118; to place it in the context of baptism, however, as he does, is not necessary.

56 E.g., Deut 32:4; 2 Sam 23:3; Isa 26:4; 30:29; Pss 1:3; 19:15; 62:3, 7; cf. 51. As Hillyer ("'Rock-Stone' Imagery," 59 et passim) notes, this use of "rock" or "stone" as a name for God prepared the way for the messianic understanding of many such OT "stone" texts.

57 Such an understanding of λίθος as messiah is evident in Jewish tradition. As Manns ("'La maison,'" 222) notes, Targum Onkelos reads בַּר ("son") for אבן ("rock") in Ps 118:22 (the same wordplay is reproduced in Matt 3:9), and gives Isa 28:16 a messianic reading as well. The tradition that "rock" is a term for "messiah" is also mentioned in Justin Dial. 34, 36.

58 E.g., Ovid, Heroides 6.88; Metam. 5.317; 7.204; 13.810; Fas. 5.661; Virgil Aen. 1.167; 3.688.

59 It can also mean a precious stone; it is to be contrasted with πέτρος, an untreated stone, and πέτρα, the generic term for rock or stone; cf. Selwyn 148.

60 The phrase does appear in medical writings of the 6th (Aetius Amidenus Iatricorum 7.61.22) and 7th (Paulus Aeginta Epitomae medicae libri septem 7.17.75) century, where it refers to a magnet (μαγνήτης λίθος ζῶν); the phrase also appears in Christian authors.

61 So also Elliott, Elect, 34; Vanhoye, "L'Epître (I P 2,1– 10)," 20; Goppelt, 141; Bauer, 24. It has no relation to 1 Cor 10:4, as Kelly (88) rightly notes (contra, e.g., Boismard ["Liturgie" [1], 195], who links it to the baptismal theme found there and, he thinks, in 1 Peter), nor is it likely to point to the contrast between the Christian church and pagan temples (contra Selwyn, 158), or to the altar Christians are to approach to present their spiritual offerings (contra Reicke, 90). On the metaphoric nature of this phrase in relation to other, similarly metaphoric language in 1 Peter, see Achtemeier, "New-born Babes," passim.

62 Ps 117:22: Mark 12:10 and par.; Acts 4:11; Isa 28:16: Rom 9:33. The addition of "living" to this combination of passages is thus due to the author, as Vanhoye ("L'Epître [I P 2,1–10]," 19) correctly notes. Wand (66) suggests that this verse may be the source for the idea of stones being built into a tower in Herm. Sim. 9.3.3, although it is not cited there.

63 So also Michaels, 98; cf. Goppelt, 141.

64 Cf. Schelkle, 57–58.

65 The contrast is implied in LXX Ps 117:22, although the particles μέν and δέ do not appear there.

66 As Hort (108) points out, this is the normal meaning for ἔντιμον in the LXX; Beare (122) and Cranfield (64) prefer "held in honor" or "honorable" from the root meaning of τιμή. On the basis of the allusion to Isa 28:16, the meaning "held precious" is probably to be preferred here.

an absolute sense,[69] since one cannot complete the verb with the phrase "into a spiritual priesthood"; the preposition εἰς is not used in that way with this verb.[70] Perhaps the best way to resolve the meaning is to take the verb as a reverential passive,[71] with God understood as the subject, "you" as object, modified by "living stones," and "spiritual house" as object complement, thus deriving the sense: "God is constituting you, who are like living stones, a spiritual house,[72] to the end [εἰς] that a holy priesthood offer spiritual sacrifices. . . ." The comparison of chosen people to stone(s) is known both from the OT[73] and from Qumran,[74] but the status of the readers as "living stones" (λίθοι ζῶντες)[75] here clearly derives from Christ the "living stone" (λίθον ζῶντα) in v. 4; the ὡς points to their derived status since they have not yet, as has Christ, risen from the dead.[76] The ensuing description of Christ as "elect" is then also to be included as descriptive of the readers,[77] since from this point on they are described with that term, no longer in terms of stones.[78]

While the verb οἰκοδομεῖσθε could be construed as either indicative or imperative, it never bears the imperatival sense in its passive form in either the LXX or the NT[79] and hence the indicative is more likely here.[80] The phrase οἶκος πνευματικός is one of two phrases that modify the subject of the verb.[81] While the word οἶκος can describe a building—the metaphor of stones would suggest that here[82]—it can also describe the inhabitants of such a building,[83] and that is more likely the meaning here since the thought then moves to a group of people, namely, a holy priesthood.[84] The adjective πνευματικός ("spiritual") is not so much symbolic or metaphoric as it is intended to indicate its nature: it is the place where the

67 As Elliott (*Elect*, 148) and Windisch (60) note.

68 E.g., Michaels, 100; Josef Blinzler, "IEPATEYMA: Zur Exegese von 1 Petr 2,5 u. 9," in *Episcopus, Studien über das Bischofsamt: Festschrift Kardinal Michael von Faulhaber* (Regensburg: Gregorus, 1949) 51.

69 Some MSS. have solved this problem by substituting the verb ἐποικοδομεῖσθε, giving the sense of "being built up," i.e., more than they were before, as the spiritual house. See n. 3 above.

70 So also Blinzler, "IEPATEYMA" 54 n. 14.

71 Cf. Manns, "'La maison,'" 224. Vanhoye ("L'Epître [I P 2,1–10]," 22) compares it in sense to 2 Sam 7, where God will build David a house, not vice versa.

72 For a similar construction, see Mark 11:17 (quoting LXX Jer 7:11), where αὐτὸν serves as object and σπήλαιον as object complement of the verb πεποιήκατε.

73 In Isa 28:16 the stone is the new people of God who remain faithful to him; in LXX Ps 117:22, it is Israel; cf. Beare, 120–21.

74 The image of stone, particularly cornerstone, is applied to the council at Qumran in 1QS 8.7–8, not, as is often averred, to the community (e.g., Danker, "I Peter 1:23—2:17," 96; Goppelt, 142–43); in 4QpIsaᵃ the foundation of the community is the priests, the superstructure the people. The community is described as stones in 1QpHab 10.1, but it is a description of the community of the despotic priest. On this whole point, cf. Reicke, 91; Kelly, 89.

75 Comparing Christians to stones is unique here in the NT. While the metaphor of building is used in 1 Cor 3:10–15 and Eph 2:19–22, and Christ is cited as

76 foundation/cornerstone, Christians are not called stones; for that one must go to *Hermas Vis.* 3, *Sim.* 9.

76 Schweizer, 48; cf. Manns, "'La maison,'" 220.

77 Tarrech, "Le milieu," 348; Elliott, *Elect*, 147.

78 As Elliott (*Elect*, 163) notes. That they are also, like Christ, rejected by other humans is at least implied, if not stated, since such an emphasis recurs throughout the letter; see also Bauckham, "James, 1 and 2 Peter, Jude," 311.

79 Elliott, *Elect*, 163 n. 1; for the passive indicative, see 1 Cor 3:9; Col 2:7.

80 With, e.g., Bengel, *Gnomon*, 734; Hart, 55; Wand, 67; Michaels, 100; Grudem, 100; Blinzler, "IEPATEYMA," 50–51; Vanhoye, "L'Epître (I P 2,1–10)," 21; Elliott, *Elect*, 16. It is taken as imperative by, e.g., Friedrich Schröger ("'Lasst euch auferbauen zu einem geisterfüllten Haus' (1Ptr 2,4.5): Eine Überlegung zu dem Verhältnis von Ratio und Pneuma," in W. Friedberger and F. Schnider, eds., *Theologie, Gemeinde, Seelsorger* [Munich: Kösel, 1979] 139), Moffatt (114), Bigg (128), Schiwy (43), and Goppelt (144), while Schelkle (58 n. 2) finds it hard to decide.

81 The other is λίθοι ζῶντες; for their grammatical relationship to the verb, see the discussion above.

82 So Best, 101; cf. Selwyn, 159–60.

83 LSJ, 1205, s.v. "οἶκος." Spicq (84) notes such a use in Xenophon *Oecon.* 1.5.

84 With Tarrech, "Le milieu," 349; Schweizer, 47; cf. Beare, 122; Selwyn, 159–60. That the author has in mind a house church, as Wand (67) suggests, seems fanciful.

Spirit is to be found.[85] The context within which it appears—priesthood, sacrifices—suggests an intention here to describe the Christian community in terms of a new temple,[86] perhaps, in contrast to the old temple, one where God's Spirit is now truly present.[87] The idea of the community as a new temple is found in the NT[88] as it is also in some of the literature from Qumran.[89] Further support for seeing here a reference to a temple is added by the fact that when the verb οἰκοδομέω is used in the LXX of the building of the temple, the noun is regularly οἶκος.[90] Such an allusion to a new temple is, however, secondary to the description in this passage of the Christian community as the true people of God.

The phrase εἰς ἱεράτευμα ἅγιον ("[to be] a holy priesthood") is to be understood as telic,[91] giving the purpose of God's constituting Christians a spiritual house,[92] a force continued by the infinitive ἀνενέγκαι ("to offer"). Thus Christians are made a spiritual house to the end that they be a body of priests whose purpose is to offer acceptable sacrifices to God.[93] While this verse is the basis of the Reformation idea of the priesthood of all believers,[94] the point of this verse is not the priestly status of each individual Christian,[95] nor the idea that each is to function as priest for his or her fellow Christian. The priesthood in this context can be understood only as corporate[96] with a function that, as the parallel with 2:9b suggests, includes a witness to all humanity.[97] Seen within the larger context of this passage, which has as its point the fact that the community of living stones is, like the living stone from which it derives its existence,

---

85 So also Elliott, *Elect*, 154; cf. Manns, "'La maison,'" 218.

86 So Best, "I Peter II 4–10," 282; Blinzler, "IEPA-TEYMA," 54–55; Senior, 31; Michaels, 100. See also "Excursus: 1 Peter 2:5, Temple or House."

87 So Schelkle, 63; Selwyn, 291; Schlier, "Adhortatio," 73.

88 Mark 14:58; 15:29; John 2:19; 1 Cor 3:16–17; 6:19; 2 Cor 6:16; 1 Tim 3:15; Heb 3:6; 10:21; 12:18–24; Rev 3:12; 11:1; cf. Acts 7:48; 15:29. Derivation from Eph 2:19–22, suggested by some (e.g., Senior, 29), must be based more on general ideas than on specific language. While the ideas of growth and building are combined as in 1 Pet 2:2, 5, as is the notion of temple, God's Spirit, and God's household, Ephesians has a different word for "temple" (ναός), different verbs for "building" (ἐποικοδομέω, v. 20; συνοικοδομέω in v. 22), and a more specific function of Christ as cornerstone in a building whose foundation consists of apostles and prophets. If anything, Eph 2:19–22 look like a further reworking (and summarizing) of material contained in 1 Pet 2:1–11 (see also Kelly, 89; Elliott, *Elect*, 165 n. 1).

89 Best (102) cites 4QFlor 1.1–7, along with 1QS 5.5–7; 8.4–6; 9.3–5; 1QpHab 12.1–3 to show that the Qumran community came to regard itself as a new temple. That the community was a "holy house" is shown in 1QS 5.5–7; 8.4–10. On this point cf. also Schröger, "Lasst euch auferbauen," 140; Manns, "'La maison,'" 215; Knibb, *Qumran*, 128.

90 See also 2 Chr 36:23; Ps 69:9; Isa 56:7; cf. Best, "I Peter II 4–10," 280; Kelly, 89; Vanhoye, "L'Epître (I P 2,1–10)," 21.

91 The three instances in the LXX where εἰς is used with a form of οἰκοδομέω (1 Chr 22:5; 28:10; Tob 14:5), it has such a force.

92 So also Selwyn, 160; Perdelwitz, *Mysterienreligion*, 76; cf. Elliott, *Elect*, 167.

93 Similarly, e.g., Hort, 110; Cothenet, "La Première Epître de Pierre," 15.

94 It was a special emphasis of Luther, e.g., 211, 213; for a discussion of the relationship of the priesthood of all believers to this passage and to 2:9, see Elliott, *Elect*, 2, 56–57, 226; Brox, 108–10.

95 Contra Minear ("House of Living Stones," 242): each stone a priest and each priest a stone; Vanhoye ("L'Epître [I P 2,1–10]," 23): each Christian effectuates that priesthood by giving up oneself as did Christ (an idea as old as Origen, as Ketter ["Das allgemeine Priestertum: II," 47] notes); Joseph B. Wheelan ("The Priesthood of the Laity," *Doctrine and Life* 15 [1965] 545): each layperson is a priest who offers acts of virtue through the "visible sacrifice of the mass."

96 Goldstein, *Paulinische Gemeinde*, 28. As Beare (122) and Best (104) note, the emphasis is probably more on function than status; see also Elliott, *Elect*, 167.

97 With Selwyn, 292–93; Elliott, *Elect*, 185, 195, 197. Whether the author sees this in Levitical terms, with the church representing all people before God as the Levitical priests represented all Israel, as Selwyn (292) suggests (cf. also Best, "I Peter II 4–10," 286), cannot be determined from this text, as Elliott (*Elect*, 186, 213) notes.

elect and holy,[98] the corporate priesthood[99] described in this verse points to the summons to every individual to share this common priestly vocation, to the end that the community so constituted orients its life and devotion to the God to whom it owes its constitution as elect and holy people. It is in such terms, rather than in terms of the individual priesthood of each individual Christian, that the verse is to be understood.[100]

The attempt to find here a link between the priesthood of the community and Christ as high priest, whereby the community is to participate in the priestly function of Christ,[101] has no foothold in the letter itself;[102] the only participation in Christ expressly mentioned in the letter is in his suffering (2:21–25; 4:13), not in his priestly functions.[103] Similarly, the attempt to find here a link between the self-offering of Christ as priest and the sacrifice of the Eucharist[104] is based on much later evidence[105] and is probably not within the scope of the author's intention in this

passage.[106] The common priestly vocation of the community is to offer[107] "spiritual sacrifices" (πνευματικὰς θυσίας) to God, an obvious parallel to the "spiritual house" into which the community was constituted by God. The idea that such sacrifices are the ones God desires was already a commonplace in the OT,[108] was taken over into Qumran,[109] and is also found in the NT.[110] While a number of actions are identified as sacrifice(s) in the NT traditions, and a number of suggestions have been made as to the intended content of such "spiritual sacrifices" here,[111] the parallelism between 2:4b and 2:9b, where the witness to God's acts whereby the Christian community has been constituted is pointed to as a major obligation of the new

---

98 A point made convincingly by Elliott (*Elect*, 226).
99 On the priesthood of all Israel, see Isa 61:6; Best (102) notes it is also pointed to in *Jub.* 16.18; 33.20; *T. Levi* Greek Frag. 67; Philo *Sobr.* 66; *Abr.* 56. That 1 Peter shared this idea with Qumran, as Leaney, (32) suggests, is questionable, since he bases it only on the fact that lay members of the community were enjoined to keep rules of priestly purity; the differentiation between priest and lay remained in fact a central tenet of that community.
100 A point forcefully made by Elliott (*Elect*, 166–69); cf. also Goppelt, 146; Blinzler, "IEPATEYMA," 64; Spicq, 85.
101 E.g., Manns, "'La maison,'" 219–20; Vanhoye, "L'Epître (I P 2,1–10)," 23.
102 With Elliott, *Elect*, 170, 173.
103 So also Elliott, *Elect*, 172. To argue with Furnish ("Elect Sojourners," 707, 714) that imitating Christ's suffering, whose death was a sin offering, constitutes Christians as priests is labored.
104 Marshall, "Holy House," 228; Jonsen, "Moral Theology," 98; cf. Boismard, *Quatre Hymnes*, 161.
105 Elliott, *Elect*, 187.
106 So also Goppelt, 146; Best, 104; see Elliott, *Elect*, 188 n. 5.
107 The verb ἀναφέρω is used with the meaning "offer sacrifice" in Heb 7:27 (bis); 13:15; Jas 2:21.
108 E.g., Pss 40:9–10; 50:13, 14, 23; 51:16–19, 69:31–32; 141:2; Isa 1:11–17; Jer 6:20; 7:21–23; 14:12; Hos 6:6; 9:4; Amos 4:4–5; 5:21–24; Mic 6:6–8.
109 1QS 9.3–5 (wave offering of obedience to law and praise superior to animal sacrifice), 10.6 (wave

offering of praise); 4QFlor 1.6–7 (deeds of the law as burnt offering); cf. 1QS 8:2–6, where general requirements of the law are reinterpreted. Many other passages from Qumran are cited on this issue, but they bear little relation to it.
110 Rom 12:1 (bodies = entire lives); Rom 15:16 (conversion of Gentiles); Phil 2:17 (Paul's life as libation on their faith); Phil 4:18 (gift from people in Philippi); 2 Tim 4:6 (martyrdom); Heb 13:15–16 (praise, doing good, and sharing possessions); Rev 8:3, 4 (prayers of the saints); cf. Acts 10:4 (prayers and alms); Eph 5:2 (Christ's self-sacrifice).
111 E.g., prayers and praise of the assembly (Bigg, 129); offer oneself in suffering as Christ did (Feuillet, "Sacrifices," 726); Christian lives (Brox, 99). The "exact correspondence" with Rom 12:1 proposed by Feuillet ("Sacrifices," 712; cf. Boismard, "Liturgie" [1], 207) is based on a number of similar words (παραστῆσαι/ἀνενέγκαι; θυσίαν/θυσίας; ζῶσαν/ζώντες; ἅγιαν/ἅγιον; τῷ θεῷ εὐάρεστον/εὐπροσδέκτος θεῷ). Yet "living" and "holy" have very different functions in the two passages, and the forms of λογικός and συσχηματίζω are used in such different contexts as to be of little use in this argument.

people of God, suggests that such witness is to be understood here as the primary focus.[112]

The shape of the Greek text leaves ambiguous the construal of εὐπροσδέκτους ("acceptable") and διὰ Ἰησοῦ Χριστοῦ ("through Jesus Christ"). If one is to construe εὐπροσδέκτους with πνευματικὰς θυσίας ("spiritual sacrifices") (and therefore θεῷ ["to God"] with ἀνενέγκαι ["to offer"],)[113] the implication is the readers are to offer the kind of spiritual sacrifices that are acceptable to God, with the implication that there are also spiritual sacrifices that are not pleasing to God. If one construes εὐπροσδέκτους with θεῷ[114] (and therefore πνευματικὰς θυσίας with ἀνενέγκαι), the readers are to offer spiritual sacrifices, as contrasted with some other kind, because such are acceptable to God. The presence of οἶκος πνευματικός, which defines Christians in this verse, probably means Christians are to offer comparable, that is, spiritual, sacrifices that, because they are spiritual, are acceptable to God.[115]

The phrase διὰ Ἰησοῦ Χριστοῦ may be construed either with ἀνενέγκαι,[116] thus making clear that the *offering* of acceptable sacrifices is possible only through Jesus Christ, or it may be construed with εὐπροσδέκτους,[117] in which case it is only through Jesus Christ that *acceptable* sacrifices may be offered.[118] Because of the emphatic position of the phrase διὰ Ἰησοῦ Χριστοῦ at the end of the verse, it would appear most appropriate to understand that it is the entire act of offering acceptable sacrifices to God that depends on the prior enablement of Christ, probably through his resurrection (he is the "living stone" in 2:3; cf. also 1:3).

Excursus: 1 Peter 2:5, Temple or House

While many have supported the idea that our author has in mind a new temple in 2:4–10, specifically pointed to by the language of 2:5,[119] there is no universal agreement on that point. The strongest argument against such an understanding has been mounted by Elliott (*Elect*, see in addition to pages cited below his "Excursus 3: οἶκος: A Temple?" 157–59), who finds: (1) the parallelism of ἱεράτευμα ("priesthood") in v. 9 with ἱεράτευμα ἅγιον ("holy priesthood") in v. 5 demands a similar parallelism between βασίλειον in v. 9 and οἶκος πνευματικός ("spiritual house") in v. 5 (149–50); the noun βασίλειον means royal house, not temple, a meaning confirmed by its use in Philo (e.g., *Sobr.* 66; he never equates "house of God" with "temple" [153]), an interpretation, Elliott affirms, that was known to the author of 1 Peter (152). (2) If οἶκος means "temple" there is confusion, since then Christians would be both temple and priests (162). (3) Οἶκος is never used in the NT to describe Christians as God's temple, and the word clearly means "house" with no cultic connotations in 4:17 (159). (4) The anticipation of οἶκος πνευματικός in 1 Pet 1:1–2 shows the emphasis in this passage is on election, not cultic activity (177). Elliott concludes that both οἶκος πνευματικός and ἱεράτευμα ἅγιον describe the

---

112 With Elliott, *Elect*, 184; Ketter, "Das allgemeine Priestertum: II," 50; but see Best ("I Peter II 4–10," 287), who denies the force of such a parallelism since in his view a new stage of the argument is entered with v. 9. To argue against the force of the parallelism on the basis that the sacrifices in 2:5b are offered to God, not the world, as does Balch (*Wives*, 134), is to overlook the point that precisely such announcement to the world of God's deeds is to serve the God who performed them.

113 Balch (*Wives*, 134) argues that this is the normal use of the verb, with the accusative of what is offered and the dative of the one to whom it is offered, e.g., 1 Sam 18:27; 1 Chr 29:21; 2 Chr 8:12; 23:18; Isa 18:7; Heb 13:15.

114 So, e.g., Elliott, *Elect*, 161; Goppelt, 147 n. 41; Schelkle, 59; Michaels, 102; Kelly, 192. Εὐπροσδέκτους is used with a dative in the NT only at Rom 15:31; it does not appear in the LXX. A similar adjective, εὐάρεστος, is used with the dative at Rom 12:1; 14:18; 2 Cor 5:9; Eph 5:10; Phil 4:18; Heb 11:5, and in the LXX at Wis 4:10; the verbal form,

εὐαρεστέω, is used with a dative at Heb 11:5, and in the LXX at Exod 21:8; Pss 55:14; 114:9.

115 Cf. Elliott, *Elect*, 175; to see the verse with Moule ("Sanctuary," 29, 35) as a polemic against those who said Christian worship was unacceptable to God because it lacked both temple and animal sacrifice has no further support in the letter.

116 So, e.g., Elliott, *Elect*, 161; Beare, 123; Hart, 56; Calvin, 66; Bauer, 25. Michaels (102) sees offering sacrifice through Christ analogous to having faith through him (1:21).

117 So, e.g., Blinzler, "ΙΕΡΑΤΕΥΜΑ," 51; Hort, 114; Cranfield, 67 n. 1; Moffatt, 115. Boismard (*Quatre Hymnes*, 162) argues that the acceptability of sacrifices was a primary concern not only of the Jews but also of all others in the ancient world.

118 Spicq (86) avers it is impossible to tell how the author meant it to be construed.

119 E.g., Best, "I Peter II 4–10," 282; Blinzler, "ΙΕΡΑΤΕΥΜΑ," 54–55; Senior, 31; Michaels, 10.

same communal entity, namely, the followers of Christ as the elect, precious people of God (161).

Yet the clear identification of οἶκος with temple when used with the verb οἰκοδομέω in the LXX, Jesus' use of οἶκος meaning "temple" in John 2:16–17, the lack of any necessity for the kind of exact parallelism Elliott finds between vv. 5 and 9, and the capacity of the author of Hebrews to see Christ as both priest and sacrifice remove some weight from Elliott's arguments, as does the combination in this verse of references to both priests and sacrifices. While Elliott is correct that the author of 1 Peter is much more interested in the concept of Christians as a household than as a temple, one can only with great difficulty fail to find references to the temple in these phrases.

■ 6 The type of connection between vv. 5 and 6 represented by διότι—whether to give the reason or basis for v. 5[120] or simply to show the source for some of the language[121]—can only be determined after an examination of v. 6. The suggestion that ἐν γραφῇ must mean "in writing," a meaning the phrase has in the LXX,[122] rather than "in Scripture," which would require the phrase ἐν τῇ γραφῇ,[123] is unpersuasive since the latter phrase does not occur in the NT, and its absence from the LXX simply shows that the LXX translators knew no such concept as "the Scripture." The phrase περιέχει ἐν γραφῇ is thus most likely meant as an equivalent to γέγραπται ("it is written [in Scripture]").[124]

While there is no question that the language derives from Isa 28:16, the specific source is in some doubt, since the quotation reproduces neither the MT[125] nor any known text of the LXX.[126] Because the text from Isa 28:16 is also used by Paul in Rom 9:32–33 but by no one else in the NT,[127] and in both cases in a context colored by motifs of rejection and judgment,[128] and since the two quotations bear resemblances to one another,[129] some have sought the source of the language of 1 Peter in Paul.[130] Yet the differences are also significant,[131] so that while the similarities point to a common source, the differences indicate an independent use of it. The presence of Isa 28:16 in Jewish messianic and eschatological traditions[132] along with evidence for the pre-Christian character of the form of the quotation from Isaiah 28[133] point to the existence of such a common source.

The kind and position of the stone (ἀκρογωνιαῖον) to

---

120 Goppelt, 148.

121 Michaels, 102.

122 E.g., 2 Chr 2:11; 21:12; Sir 39:32; 42:7; 44:5.

123 So Selwyn, 163; Hort, 115. Moffatt (116) thought it meant reference "to some book of proof-texts from the Old Testament."

124 Michaels, 102–3; Best, 105; Kelly, 95; Bigg, 130. Hart (56) accounts for the lack of the article by identifying the phrase as a technical term.

125 E.g., Schlosser, "Ancien Testament," 76.

126 1 Peter omits ἐγώ, changes ἐμβαλῶ to τίθημι, omits εἰς τὰ θεμέλια after ἐμβαλῶ, adds ἐν before Ζιών, omits πολυτελῆ, and omits εἰς τὰ θεμέλια αὐτῆς after ἔντιμον. With the LXX, 1 Peter includes ἐπ᾽ αὐτῷ after ὁ πιστεύων.

127 Hillyer, "'Rock-Stone' Imagery," 62.

128 Elliott, Elect, 29.

129 Both begin with ἰδού contrary to the LXX, as Barnett (Literary Influence, 60) notes, but to say both add ἐπ᾽ αὐτῷ after ὁ πιστεύων as he does is to ignore the presence of that phrase in the LXX.

130 Hort (117) finds it "morally certain" that the quotation is borrowed from Paul. While Eph 2:20 also interprets Isa 28:16 christologically, as Elliott (Elect, 30) points out, the absence of the word λίθος in Ephesians makes it a most unlikely source.

131 1 Peter reproduces much more of the language of Isa 28:16 than does Paul, and, unlike Paul, uses the reference to Isa 8:14 independently (v. 8), there in association with LXX Ps 117:22, a reference absent from Rom 9:33.

132 There is a clear allusion to Isa 28:16 in 1QS 8.7–8, where the council of the eschatological community is the foundation; see Schutter, Hermeneutic, 132; Schelkle, 63; Knibb, Qumran, 128. Elliott (Elect, 27) notes that the Targum of Isa 28:16 makes the stone a king, part of a much more extensive tradition in which a variety of texts referring to "stone" were applied to the Messiah and the coming eschatological messianic age; on this point see further Elliott, Elect, 26–33, "Excursus I: A λίθος Tradition." See also Schlosser, "Ancien Testament," 78; Hillyer, "'Rock-Stone' Imagery," 72.

133 While the ἐπ᾽ αὐτῷ is omitted from B, it is present in A, and the rarity of the use of ἐπ᾽ αὐτῷ with πιστεύω in the NT (independent of quotations from Isa 28:16 [Rom 9:33; 10:11; 1 Pet 2:6], only 1 Tim 1:16) argues for its presence in the pre-Christian text; see Schlosser, "Ancien Testament," 77; Snodgrass, "I Peter II.1–10," 99.

which the text refers is not entirely clear. Since the word was unknown to secular Greek authors,[134] one must derive its meaning from this passage. While some have argued it is the keystone of an arch[135] or the highest stone in a building,[136] that its position in the foundation is emphasized and that one can stumble over it, a point underscored in 1 Pet 2:8, argues decisively that it be at ground level, and hence a cornerstone.[137] In the final analysis, however, the omission of Isaiah's reference to the foundation throws the emphasis in the quotation on the elect and precious quality of the stone rather than on its position.[138]

The quotation as a whole functions to reintroduce and expand the theme stated in 2:4. V. 6a reminds the reader of 2:4ab: Christ the living stone. In chiastic form, 2:6b–7a explicate the reference to those who acknowledge that stone's preciousness in God's eyes (2:4bb) while 2:7b-8 explicate the reference to those who reject it (2:4ba)[139] That the only unchanged part of the quotation from Isa 28:16 is the final phrase probably indicates that this was the major point of the quotation for the author.

The διότι ("hence") that introduces the quotation thus shows that it is intended to begin the explication of the themes announced in vv. 4–5.[140] The emphasis in the quotation on the adjectives (elect, precious) that were applied in 2:4bb to Christ shows the thrust is christological: it is God's own precious son upon whom build-

ing, priesthood, and new people of God are to be built. Those thus built through trust will surely be honored by God.[141]

The quotation thus serves to reinforce the point of the 2:4–12: Christ affects the fate of every person, depending on the reaction to him, whether positive or negative. For people faced with massive social rejection, such a point would make clear that their situation was due not to their abandonment or rejection by God, but precisely to the fact that it was part of God's plan that those who accepted Christ be rejected just as he himself had been rejected.[142]

■ **7a** These words are a comment on the final phrase of v. 6, specifically on the last part of the quotation, and thus bring to a close the explication, begun with v. 5, of the second half of the contrast announced in v. 4: rejected by humans but elect and honored by God.[143] The ἔντιμον ("precious") and the ὁ πιστεύων ("the one who believes") of v. 6 are picked up in the ἡ τιμή ("the honor") and the ὑμῖν . . . τοῖς πιστεύουσιν ("to you . . . who trust")[144] to make clear it is the readers who share in God's evaluation of the elect and honored cornerstone, namely, Christ. Because Christ functions in the larger passage as the key to the fate of all human beings, the τιμή cannot be the predicate, as though it represented the evaluation of Christ on the part of those who believe,[145] but rather the subject,[146] indicating that for those who

---

134 It appears, aside from Isa 28:16, only in the NT and in Christian authors; cf. Hillyer, "'Rock-Stone' Imagery," 69.

135 See Hillyer ("'Rock-Stone' Imagery," 70), although he himself does not hold that position.

136 E.g., Hillyer ("'Rock-Stone' Imagery," 65–66), drawing on Zech 4:7, where it is the top stone, although it must be noted the Hebrew words are different in Zechariah and Isaiah. Hillyer also cites evidence, primarily the reduplication of אבן in Isa 28:16 and the Egyptian *bn bn*, suggesting it means the top of a pyramid.

137 With Best, 106; Schelkle, 59 n. 2; Hort, 121. The use of this passage in 1QS 8.6–8 shows it was understood as a part of the foundation, as Hillyer ("'Rock-Stone' Imagery," 70–71) points out.

138 With Spicq, 87.

139 The same basic structure of vv. 4–5 is also repeated in vv. 6–10: the twofold reaction (v. 4b) to Christ the living stone (v. 4a), with emphasis on those who accept (v. 5), is expanded with the references to the twofold reaction (2:6b–7a, 7b–8) to Christ the elect

and precious stone (v. 6a), with emphasis on those who accept (vv. 9–10). See also Schlosser, "Ancien Testament," 75.

140 It thus does more than simply show the source for some of the language of those verses (contra Michaels, 102), but also has a broader purpose than simply to give the basis for v. 5 (contra Goppelt, 148).

141 As Beare (124) notes, the οὐ μὴ καταισχυνθῇ is a litotes meaning "shall surely be honored" or "receive honor."

142 As Schlosser ("Ancien Testament," 74) notes, the divine passive ἐτέθησαν of v. 8 forms an *inclusio* with the τίθημι of v. 6, thus showing that the whole is God's work.

143 This part of the contrast will be further explicated in vv. 9–10; so also, e.g., Goppelt, 149.

144 In addition, as Spicq (88) observes, the article with the τιμή gives it the force of a demonstrative: "that honor," making clear its reference to the ἔντιμον of v. 6. V. 7a as a whole functions as a midrashic note on v. 6b, as Selwyn (164) notes; cf. Schutter (*Hermeneutic*, 135): a "*pesher*-like hermeneutic."

believe[147] there will be honor[148] at the time of the final judgment.[149]

In contrast to those who are faithful to Christ and who therefore share in the honor God has shown to him as honored and elect cornerstone, those who do not believe in Christ, and thus reject God's cornerstone for his new people, find that cornerstone not a source of honor but of stumbling and offense.

■ **7b** The first half of this description (v. 7b) of the fate of those who reject Christ (ἀπιστοῦσιν, "who do not trust")[150] consists in a quotation from LXX Ps 117:22, with no alterations, a text that in its turn has little variation from the MT.[151] In contrast to v. 6, where a passage (Isa 28:16) rarely used in the NT was cited,[152] this verse is found in the Synoptics and Acts as well.[153]

While those who reject the stone in the other NT passages are the Jewish authorities, here those who reject Christ are not the Jews[154] but the unbelieving neighbors and authorities in the Roman provinces who are engaged in the kind of social harassment of the Christian communities that has provoked this letter.[155] Again, while the psalm is used in the other NT citations in a christological sense, namely, Jesus' divine vindication through his resurrection,[156] the point here concerns not Jesus but unbelievers.[157] In this context it is what their rejection of the stone means for them that is at issue.[158]

■ **8** This verse continues, and concludes, the exposition of the stone rejected by human beings mentioned in v. 4. The words are an allusion[159] to Isa 8:14; they differ significantly from the LXX,[160] but are virtually identical

---

145 Contra, e.g., Bigg, 135.

146 So, e.g., Hort, 117; Beare, 124.

147 The datives ὑμῖν and τοῖς πιστεύουσιν may be construed as datives of possession ("You who believe will have honor"), but in this context it is probably better to understand them as datives of advantage (e.g., Brox, 101; Hart, 56), particularly in light of the contrast in the second half of the verse; to see them as datives of reference (e.g., Hort, 118) is unnecessarily to reduce the significance of the verse.

148 While in this context τιμή is often translated "preciousness" to conform to the understanding of ἔντιμον in v. 6 as "precious," a meaning derived from the fact that τιμή can also mean "(high) price" or "value," in this eschatological context it is better to retain the sense of "honor" in both nominal and adjectival uses; so also Bigg, 131; cf. Schutter (*Hermeneutic*, 134) for further references.

149 So also, e.g., Michaels, 104. To argue that it represents honor given now, not at judgment day, as does Beare (124), is to trivialize the honor and ignore the total context of both passage and letter.

150 Unlike τοῖς πιστεύουσιν ("those who believe"; see n. 147 above), the content of the OT quotations requires that this be in fact a dative of reference, despite the apparent parallelism of the two dative forms. The point here is not that the unbelievers have, or will have, the rock, but that the rejected rock that God has elevated has become *in their case* a cause of stumbling and offense.

151 Brox, "Pseudepigraphischen Rahmung," 69.

152 Like the Isaiah passage, however, this also concerns the fate of the people of God, as Elliott (*Elect*, 25) notes correctly.

153 In Mark 12:10–11 and Matt 21:42, LXX Ps 117:23 is included; in Luke 20:17 and in Peter's paraphrase

in Acts 4:11, the quotation is limited, as in our verse, to LXX Ps 117:22.

154 Contra, e.g., Reicke, 92.

155 With Michaels, 105. For that reason Schelkle (61) is probably wrong to say, drawing on 1 Pet 2:8a, that the cornerstone is not the glorified but the crucified Jesus. That would be valid if those addressed were Jews, but since they are pagans, it is as least as likely that it was the Christian emphasis on Jesus glorified that was offensive. The divine passive ἐγενήθη, while not conclusive, points in the same direction.

156 The point is directly made in Acts 4:11, but is surely implied in the parable of the vineyard (Mark 12:1–11 par.) to which this psalm verse is attached in the Synoptics.

157 As Spicq (89) perceptively notes, the lack of the article with ἀπιστοῦσιν (in contrast to the τοῖς πιστεύουσιν) is due to the fact that they are not "un corps homogène." This is further evidence that those addressed are not the Jews.

158 So also, e.g., Calloud, "Ce que parler," 81.

159 So also Brox ("Pseudepigraphischen Rahmung," 69), who notes that one should not speak of a quotation here.

160 It is interesting to note that while the LXX changed the MT so that God is no longer the one who causes stumbling, both the author of 1 Peter and Paul apply it to God's act in Christ, thus in a sense reverting to the MT's idea of a divine cause for stumbling.

to Rom 9:33b,[161] where Paul has combined them with words he drew from Isa 28:16. Because our author cites the same two passages from Isaiah but separates them with the quotation from LXX Ps 117:22, it is less likely that he is drawing on Romans than that both he and Paul are drawing on common Christian tradition.[162] The λίθος προσκόμματος, because it causes stumbling, is again not a keystone but a foundation stone. In contrast to the πέτρα, which is native rock, λίθος is a loose stone.[163]

While the οἱ could be construed with the participle ἀπειθοῦντες, which would then form the subject of προσκόπτουσιν ("They who are disobedient stumble"), it is more likely that it functions as a relative pronoun, referring to the ἀπιστοῦσιν of v. 7, with the ἀπειθοῦντες functioning as a circumstantial participle of cause ("They, namely, the unfaithful, are the ones who stumble because they disobeyed").[164] Again, while one could construe the τῷ λόγῳ with προσκόπτουσιν ("they stumbled against the word"),[165] the use of ἀπειθέω ("disobey") with τῷ λόγῳ ("the word") in 3:1 and with τῷ τοῦ θεοῦ εὐαγγελίῳ ("the good news of God") in 4:17, both in reference to unbelievers, makes it likely it ought to be construed the same way here ("They stumble because they disobey the word").[166] Once more, the word ἀπειθέω to designate unbelievers is drawn from Christian tradition (John 3:36; Acts 14:2; 19:9; Rom 15:31), and although it refers to Jews in Acts and Romans, it is unlikely that that is the case here;[167] the hostile unbelievers with whom the letter reckons are not Jews but adherents of Greco-Roman culture.

The antecedent of the (εἰς) ὅ with which the final phrase begins is probably best understood as including the entire preceding thought, namely, that unbelievers stumble over the stone they have rejected through unbelief (vv. 7b–8a), rather than limiting it to the action implied in οἱ προσκόπτουσιν ("they stumble").[168] In either case, however, the meaning is not appreciably different. The ἐτέθησαν ("they were placed") is surely a divine passive, implying that God is the actor who has caused this, a point many have found difficult to accept.[169] Yet the idea that God is in control of all things was a commonplace in the world of 1 Peter[170] and was taken into Christian tradition,[171] as was the corollary that God also establishes the evil as well as the good,[172] a tradition also present in primitive Christian tradition.[173] It is thus difficult to avoid the obvious thrust of this last phrase,[174]

---

161 Both omit συναντήσεσθε αὐτῷ οὐδὲ ὡς between the references to the stone in Isaiah, and change πέτρας πτώματι to πέτρα(ν) σκανδάλου, this latter a word familiar in Christian tradition (e.g., Mark 6:3 // Matt 13:57; 11:6; 26:11; Luke 7:23; 1 Cor 1:23; Gal 5:11); cf. Best, "I Peter II 4–10," 281.

162 So Calloud, "Ce que parler," 80; Schelkle, 62. Kelly (95) argues for a catena of early Christian stone texts. One may also note that while Paul applies the passages to Israel, 1 Peter applies them to Gentiles.

163 E.g., Hort, 121; a play on Peter's name with πέτρα is unlikely, since Paul uses the same quotation with no reference to Peter, and it would have no point in this context, as Michaels (106) observes.

164 So also, e.g., Bigg, 33; Michaels, 106; Vanhoye, "L'Épître (I P 2,1–10)," 25.

165 E.g., Hart, 57.

166 So also, e.g., Beare, 125; Schelkle, 57. To construe it with both participle and verb, as Bigg (132) proposes, is unnecessary.

167 Contra Windisch, 61; Selwyn, 164; Calvin, 73.

168 As do, e.g., Bigg (133), Michaels (107), Schelkle (60 n. 1), and Beare (126).

169 E.g., Harris ("Emendation," 43), who conjectured an original ἐτέθη, thus referring to the stone that was set. Others (e.g., Bigg, 133) understand what was established to be disobedience as the consequence of

stumbling (or the reverse, Margot, 39), a point difficult to reconcile with the plural ἐτέθησαν. See Daniel C. Arichea and Eugene A. Nida (A Translator's Handbook on the First Letter from Peter [Helps for Translators. New York: United Bible Societies, 1980] 62), who, I think correctly, reject that interpretation.

170 E.g., Isa 40:22–24; 44:7–8; 45:1–3; Neh 9:6; 1QH 1.7–8; 19–20; 27–28; 13:1–10; 1QS 3.15–16; 11.10–11; CD 2.6–10; Seneca Oed. 980–97; Ep. 16.4. On this point, cf. Knibb, Qumran, 159, 161; Flusser, "Dead Sea Sect," 220–21; Danker, "I Peter 1:23–2:17," 96 n. 17, though with some errors in references.

171 E.g., Luke 2:34; Rom 8:29; Eph 1:4, 5, 11; 1 Thess 5:9; 1 Pet 1:2.

172 E.g., Isa 45:7; cf. Jer 18:5–11; 50:24; Prov 21:30. It was a prominent feature of the Qumran view (e.g., 1QH 2.23–25; 4.38; 15.17; CD 2.11; see also 1 Enoch 62.10), and was common among Stoics (e.g., Seneca ad Marc. 21.2–6); cf. Spicq, 91; Knibb, Qumran 26; Carmignac, "La théologie," 369; Flusser, "Dead Sea Sect," 220.

173 E.g., Rom 9:18, 22; cf. Mark 4:11–12, and the divine passives in Mark 6:52; 8:17.

174 With, e.g., Hort (123): "all attempts to explain away the statement . . . are futile"; see also Calvin (cited in

however offensive it may be to modern sensibilities.[175]

The point therefore, not only of vv. 7b–8 but of 5–7a as well, is that one's fate, in our author's view, is determined by one's relation to Christ. Either one builds on him as a precious cornerstone and thus belongs to God's people, or one stumbles over him and rejects him and is not a member of that people.[176] While this is clearly in accord with God's intention,[177] it does not exclude the responsibility of those who have rejected Christ. Because that rejection is described in terms of disobedience (ἀπειθοῦντες; cf. the positive construal of faith as obedience in 1:2), the implication of a negative decision is clear:[178] those who make it will finally have to take responsibility for it at the eschatological judgment (4:17).

■ **9** The language of this verse is drawn from Exod 19:6 and Isa 43:20–21,[179] with the passage from Isaiah interpolated into the phrases from Exodus, if the opening words (ὑμεῖς δὲ, "you, however") are taken from Exod 19:6.[180] While the emphatic ὑμεῖς δὲ that intro-

duces the verse implies a contrast to another group, namely, those who are not among God's people, the verse itself is probably to be seen more as a resumption of the description of the faithful than as a contrast specifically to the unbelievers mentioned in vv. 7b–8,[181] since that phrase was already part of a contrast beginning with v. 7a.[182] Thus, just as the first mention of a contrast in v. 4b was followed in vv. 5–6 with a further description of those who accepted Christ, so here the contrast of vv. 7–8 is followed with another such description.[183]

The first of the phrases, γένος ἐκλεκτόν ("elect race"), is drawn from Isa 43:20[184] and is placed first because it resumes the theme of Christians as elect.[185] That theme was first announced in 1:1 and continued in this passage in v. 4 with the description of Christ, to whom Christians come, as the one elect and precious to God (see also 2:6).[186] The word γένος implies common origin[187] (e.g.,

Hillyer, "'Rock-Stone' Imagery," 63); Best, 106; Bengel, *Gnomon*, 736.

175 Reicke's (93) suggestion that the thought here is comparable to the argument of Paul in Rom 11:11, 25 "in so far as the obduracy of the Jews would open the way for the conversion of the heathen" has no foundation in this text; there is no hint here that the disobedience of those who reject the word somehow creates the possibility for Christians to accept it.

176 Calvin (72): "We must either build on him, or be dashed against him."

177 Vanhoye, "L'Epître (I P 2,1–10)," 27; Cranfield, 65.

178 So also Kelly, 94. Goppelt (150) reasons that since faith is both created by God (1 Pet 1:2; Rom 8:28–30) and is something to which one responds responsibly (1 Pet 1:17; 2 Cor 5:10), so rejection must also be the responsibility both of God and of human beings; cf. Michaels, 95.

179 A point generally accepted by commentators. Goppelt's (151) assertion that the author got it from Christian tradition based on the appearance of βασιλείαν (καὶ) ἱερεῖς in Rev 1:6; 5:10 is less than convincing since neither word appears in that form in v. 9, while the language of the phrase in v. 9 (βασίλειον ἱεράτευμα) agrees directly with LXX Exod 9:16. The more likely assumption is that the author is responsible for this combination of OT passages. The relationship to passages in the Qumran literature found by Goppelt (151) is far less apparent than he asserts; on that point see also Sandevoir, "Un Royaume de Prêtres?" 227.

180 Elliott (*Elect*, 142) says they are, Best ("I Peter II 4–

10," 277) that they are not. Wolff ("Christ und Welt," 336) suggests that the material from Exodus was added to that from Isaiah.

181 Contra Best, "I Peter II 4–10," 276. As Elliott (*Elect*, 143–44 n. 418) points out, δέ does function as resumptive in 1 Pet 3:8; 4:7, and 5:10.

182 So also Elliott, *Elect*, 143.

183 Consideration of the structure of 2:4–10 as a whole thus undercuts the force of the argument of Schutter (*Hermeneutic*, 136) and Bigg (134) that the parallelism between vv. 7a and 9 shows that v. 9 explains what was meant by the τιμή of v. 7a; if anything, it explicates the content of the τοῖς πιστεύουσιν of that verse.

184 LXX: τὸ γένος μου τὸ ἐκλεκτόν, the only place in the LXX that phrase appears; that γένος ἐκλεκτόν also alludes to Exod 19:5; Deut 7:6; 14:2, as Vanhoye ("L'Epître [I P 2,1–10]," 27) suggests, is thus unlikely.

185 This idea is traced back to Jesus in the NT, e.g., Matt 22:14; Mark 13:20, 22, 27; Luke 14:7; John 13:18; 15:16. Cf. Selwyn, 165; Spicq, 90.

186 So also, e.g., Beare, 129; cf. Sandevoir, "Un Royaume de Prêtres?" 220.

187 So Goppelt, 152.

γεννάω), a point about Christians already made in 1:3, 23, and thus qualifies the significance of what follows.[188]

The second and third pair (βασίλειον ἱεράτευμα, ἔθνος ἅγιον, "a royal priesthood, a holy nation") are drawn from Exod 19:6,[189] and apply additional phrases to Christians that originally described Israel as God's elect people. The first pair, βασίλειον ἱεράτευμα, is a translation of MT ממלכ כהנים, "a kingdom of priests."[190] The difficulty here rests in that βασίλειον can be either a neuter substantive, meaning "palace" or "kingdom," or a neuter adjective, meaning "royal" and modifying "priesthood."[191] That the author of 1 Peter understood it in an adjectival sense[192] is indicated by the fact that it is one of four phrases in which each of the others has a noun that is then further modified.[193] That in this

instance the adjective precedes the noun, abnormal in Greek and not in accord with the other three instances, is accounted for by the reliance on the LXX, which in each case dictated the present order.[194] That ἱεράτευμα carried an adjective (ἅγιον) in its earlier use in v. 4 would add further confirmation.[195]

One cannot, however, rule out the possibility that it carries substantival force. In the great majority of cases where βασίλειον appears in the LXX, it has nominal force,[196] as it does in a number of versions,[197] in Philo,[198] in *Jubilees*,[199] and in the Targumim.[200] While this evidence has persuaded some to find here in v. 9 a substantive meaning "royal palace"[201] or "house of God the king,"[202] such an understanding is weakened in light of the fact that each of the other nouns in the list

---

188 This is all the more the case since the important word ἐκλεκτόν qualifies it; cf. Elliott, *Elect*, 143. Later Christians emphasized the notion of Christians as a new, or third, race, e.g., *Diogn.* 1; Tertullian *Ad Nat.* 1.8; Clement of Alexandria *Strom.* 6.5.41 (I owe these references to Michaels, 108).

189 LXX: ὑμεῖς δὲ ἔσεσθέ μοι βασίλειον ἱεράτευμα καὶ ἔθνος ἅγιον ("you shall be for me a royal priesthood and a holy nation").

190 Although a more literal Greek translation of the Hebrew would have been βασιλεία ἱερέων (as Aquila rendered it), Sandevoir ("Un Royaume de Prêtres?" 224) argues that the MT is the only possible source of the LXX rendering since, as Elliott (*Elect*, 75) also notes, the word order and sense are the same. The assumption of another Hebrew text of Exod 19:6 that read ממלבה כהנים is correctly rejected by Blinzler ("IEPATEYMA," 61); see also Elliott, *Elect*, 123. If, as Spicq (91) argues, the original meaning was "a kingdom governed by priests, a hierocracy," that may account for the present translation, which then must mean "royal priesthood" in that sense; for more on the problem of "royal priesthood," see below.

191 For summaries of the data and arguments of this much-discussed problem, see Selwyn, 165–66; Elliott, *Elect*, 120–23; Sandevoir, "Un Royaume de Prêtres?" 222.

192 A meaning accepted by the majority of commentators, e.g., Joseph Coppens, "Le sacerdoce royal des fidèles: un commentaire de I Petr. II, 4–10," in *Au Service de la Parole de Dieu: Mélanges . . . à . . . André-Marie Charue* (Gembloux: Duculot, 1969) 71; Feuillet, "Sacrifices," 704–5 n. 2; Sandevoir, "Un Royaume de Prêtres?" 228; Vanhoye, "L'Epître (I P 2,1–10)," 27; Souček, "Das Gegenüber," 5; Blinzler,

"IEPATEYMA," 62; Gangel, "Pictures," 34; Ketter, "Das allgemeine Priestertum: II," 50; Wand, 72; Beare, 129; Bigg, 134; Margot, 40; Moffatt, 118; Calvin, 75; Goppelt, 152; Schiwy, 44; Hart, 57; Schelkle, 64; Reicke, 93.

193 In addition to the two adjectives ἐκλεκτόν and ἅγιον, the phrase εἰς περιποίησιν performs an adjectival function in modifying λαός, even though, as Elliott (*Elect*, 151) notes, it is a nominal phrase.

194 Michaels, 108; Goppelt, 152–53 n. 65.

195 Hort (125) argues against two nouns in apposition, i.e., "kingdom (which is also) a priesthood," and notes further that had the author intended two nouns, he "could hardly have failed to write βασίλειον καὶ ἱεράτευμα." In a reference to Exod 19:6 in *Jub.* 33:20, both βασίλειον and ἱεράτευμα are in fact made into adjectives; cf. Elliott (*Elect*, 80–81), who also provides a good summary of the arguments for adjectival force, even though he takes it to be a substantive (72).

196 Aside from Exod 19:6; 23:22, it means kingdom: 1 Chr 28:4; 2 Macc 2:17 (with ἱεράτευμα, both nouns); Wis 1:14; 5:16; Dan 4:34, 37; 5:23,30; 7:22; crown: 2 Sam 1:10; 2 Chr 23:11; royal dignity: 1 Esdr 4:40; throne: 1 Esdr 4:44; palace: Prov 18:19; royal: 4 Macc 3:8.

197 Aquila: kingdom of priests (βασιλεία ἱερέων); Symmachus, Theodotion, Syrohexapla: "kingdom, priests"; Peshitta: "kingdom and priests"; Sahidic and Armenian: "kingdom and priesthood"; but it has adjectival force in Bohairic, Old Latin, and the Vulgate (I owe these references to Elliott, *Elect*, 78 n. 1).

198 In *Sobr.* 66 (citing "the oracles," i.e., Exod 19:6 or 23:22), he describes the twelve tribes as βασίλειον καὶ ἱεράτευμα θεοῦ, and takes βασίλειον to mean ὁ βασιλέως . . . οἶκος (one must thus qualify the assumption of Blinzler ["IEPATEYMA," 62] that in

designates a group of people,[203] a point preserved if βασίλειον is understood as an adjective.

If the status of the word βασίλειον is open to question, it is clear that the rare word ἱεράτευμα[204] is a noun, and is used in a collective sense here to refer to the Christian community, as it referred to Israel in Exodus.[205] Such priestly functions as the Christian had, therefore, were as a member of the Christian community,[206] not as a separate individual, as though each were somehow a priest.[207] It did not mean individual Christians did not have differing gifts, as 4:10–11 make clear, but one cannot determine from this text whether the Christian communities had, or were expected to have, a separate priesthood.[208] The two words together referred to the Christian community as a body of priests in the service of

God their "king" to whom they now owed their allegiance as his people.

The third couplet, also drawn from Exod 19:6,[209] points to the community as a group who shared common customs[210] that were derived from the holy God whom they served (1 Pet 1:14–16).[211] This couplet, along with the first, underlines the unity of the Christian community despite the diverse ethnic backgrounds from which they came.[212]

The fourth phrase is not found in the LXX, although similar phrases are contained in both Exod 19:5 (λαὸς περιούσιος, "a proper people") and Isa 43:21 (λαόν μου ὃν περιεποιησάμην, "my people whom I have acquired").[213]

Philo βασίλειον means "temple"); *Abr.* 56 (also citing "oracles"): βασίλειον καὶ ἱεράτευμα καὶ ἔθνος ἅγιον. For the argument that 1 Peter knew this tradition, see Elliott, *Elect*, 152; that he did not, see Best, "I Peter II 4–10," 289.

199 *Jub.* 16.18: kingdom and priests; but in *Jub.* 33.20 both βασίλειον and ἱεράτευμα are made into adjectives: "a priestly and royal nation"; cf. Elliott, *Elect*, 81.

200 Targum Onkelos: מלכין כהנין; Targum Yerushalmi I: מלכין . . . וכהנין; Targum Yerushalmi II: וכהנין מלכין; see also Codex Neofiti I (folio 150 recto, line 2: מלכין וכהנין (for the fuller texts see Elliott, *Elect*, 76–77, from whom I drew these phrases). The evidence from Rev 1:6 and 5:10 is less persuasive since the two nouns there, βασιλείαν and ἱερεῖς, are different from the forms found in v. 9 (βασίλειον, ἱεράτευμα).

201 Sandevoir, "Un Royaume de Prêtres?" 225; "royal residence": Elliott, *Elect*, 73.

202 Elliott, *Home*, 170, in parallelism to the οἶκος πνευματικός of v. 5; see also *Elect*, 196.

203 To find in βασίλειον the meaning "body of kings," as does Best (108; see also "I Peter II 4–10," 290–91), one must assume a force nowhere else evident for this word, as Best admits. That in later Jewish tradition all Israelites were regarded as sons of the kings, as Spicq (91) points out, is of reduced linguistic help because of the later date of the evidence (*m. Šabb.* 14.4; *Mekilta* on Exod 19:6).

204 It occurs three times in the LXX (Exod 19:6; 23:22; 2 Macc 2:17) and twice in Philo (*Abr.* 56; *Sobr.* 66), in every case reflecting the content of Exodus. It is used extensively by Christian writers, but was apparently unknown to secular Greek authors.

205 Cothenet, "La Première Epître de Pierre," 142;

Johannes Baptist Bauer, "Könige und Priester, ein heiliges Volk (Ex 19,6)," *BZ*, NF 2 (1958) 286.

206 E.g., Best, 108; Elliott, *Elect*, 68; Bigg, 148; Kelly, 96; Schweizer, 53.

207 Contra Wheelan ("Priesthood," 546), who says the term refers to the individual Christian layperson. Whether the author meant the church was to supplant the Levitical priesthood, as Chevallier ("Condition," 396) argues, is not clear, except to the extent that the Christian community replaced Israel *en toto*.

208 Although Beare (130) asserts that the community had no use for rites or sacrifices (see also Cranfield, 66; Schelkle, 64; Sandevoir, "Un Royaume de Prêtres?" 228), and hence no place for a priesthood, and contrariwise Ketter (228) argues that differences between priest and laity were not eliminated, this verse simply does not address that question, and hence it cannot be resolved on the basis of it, as Senior (36) notes; see also Ketter, "Das allgemeine Priestertum: II," 43. On this question, see the discussion of εἰς ἱεράτευμα ἅγιον in v. 5 above.

209 Vanhoye, "L'Epître (I P 2,1–10)," 27. The phrase also appears in Wis 17:2, but in a different context; more common in the LXX is the phrase λαὸς ἅγιος to describe Israel. 2 Macc 2:17 reduces the two words to τὸν ἁγιασμόν; Philo (*Abr.* 56) preserves them.

210 Goppelt, 152; cf. ἔθος, "custom, practice."

211 While the phrase points to the same community as the ἱεράτευμα ἅγιον of 2:5, as Elliott (*Elect*, 160) argues, its more likely derivation is the holiness command cited earlier, just as the γένος was derived from the idea of rebegetting by God in 1:3, 23.

212 See n. 188 above.

213 The phrase εἰς περιποίησιν occurs in Mal 3:17, but there is no indication the author had that verse in

That Isa 43:21 identifies the purpose of the acquiring as the announcement of his deeds (τὰς ἀρετάς μου διηγεῖσθαι), the same point made in this verse, suggests that the author had that passage in mind.[214] The εἰς that appears only here with λαός and περιποίησις may well point to a dynamic element in the author's understanding; the Christian community is under way toward being God's peculiar people,[215] although whether it also implies their salvation because the phrase εἰς σωτηρίαν (2:2; cf. 1:5) has the same preposition[216] is less sure.

The ὅπως introducing the second half of the verse gives the purpose for which the Christian community just described exists.[217] While the content of the Christians' declaration, τὰς ἀρετάς, has the basic meaning "virtues" or "praises"[218] in this context, it probably means rather "mighty deeds" or "saving acts,"[219] particularly since the one whose ἀρεταί are to be announced is defined as one who has acted to save, such salvation in its turn being based on God's act of raising Christ from the dead (e.g.,

1:3). The verb ἐξαγγέλλω is used only here in the NT; in the LXX it means "tell forth"[220] and is used primarily to mean the announcement of God's praise. While that notion may also be present in this instance, the context of 1 Peter (e.g., 3:13–16) argues against restricting it here to the context of Christian worship[221] or even to the Eucharist.[222] The telling forth of God's acts in 1 Peter is to be done both by act and by word, and the latter is surely the intention here.[223]

While the final phrase defines the one whose deeds are to be announced, it also contains within itself an indication of the content of those deeds, namely, God's salvific act in Christ,[224] described here in terms of the contrast between darkness and light. Such a contrast was familiar in the OT and in Judaism, where darkness symbolized ignorance and sin,[225] and light symbolized the presence of God[226] as well as eschatological salvation.[227]

This contrast was subsequently taken into Christian

mind here.

214 Schutter (*Hermeneutic,* 40) suggests that the author was influenced by Isa 42:12 to substitute ἐξαγγείλητε for the διηγεῖσθαι of Isa 43:21, but in fact the verb there is a form of ἀναγγέλω, not of ἐξαγγέλω.

215 This passage reflects the same structure found in 2:5, where the goal of the people was to be a priesthood (εἰς ἱεράτευμα ἅγιον) whose purpose was to offer (ἀνενέγκαι) acceptable sacrifices.

216 So, e.g., Michaels, 109; Halas, "Sens dynamique," 255, 257, 258.

217 The similarity of structure of 2:5 has led Ketter ("Das allgemeine Priestertum: II," 50) and Elliott (*Elect,* 184) to see in this verse the content of the spiritual sacrifices that Christians are to offer; Best ("I Peter II 4–10," 287) rejects such a notion. While the structures are similar, each has its unique point: 2:5 within the specific context of the temple, 2:9 within the broader context of chosen people; cf. also Best, 278.

218 E.g., Isa 42:8, where it is used as a parallel to "glory" (δόξαν).

219 So, e.g., Elliott, *Elect,* 42; Deterding, "Exodus Motifs," 62; Beare, 131; cf. Wheelan, "Priesthood," 545. Goppelt (153 n. 66), Hort (129), Bigg (135), and Schelkle (65) cite the "mighty deeds" (τὰ μεγαλεῖα) of Acts 2:11 as parallel in meaning.

220 E.g., Pss 9:15; 70:15; 72:28; 78:13; 106:22; Sir 39:10; 44:15; cf. Spicq, 192.

221 As would, e.g., Michaels (110). While Balch (*Wives,* 133) finds no reference to missionary preaching in the LXX where this verb is used, Elliott (*Elect,* 69)

argues that it there reflects the idea that Jews as a priestly community were charged with the worship of the true God and thus had a mission to fulfill in the Hellenistic world. Similarly, such announcement was the task of priests in 1QS 1.21, as Danker ("I Peter 1:23—2:17," 97) notes, but in 1QH 1.29–30 it was the task of all the people, as Knibb (*Qumran,* 161) observes. Such observations are interesting but finally not determinative for the way the word is used in 1 Peter.

222 As, e.g., Jonsen ("Moral Theology," 99) would have it. See Kelly (100–101), who cites Justin (*1 Apol.* 65.3; 67.5; *Dial.* 41.1) and Hippolytus (*Ap. Trad.* 4) to show that in the early second century, the Eucharist was understood primarily as a sacrifice of praise, which reached its climax in prayer. Best (109) rightly finds Boismard's suggestion that we see here a reference to the thanksgiving of the Eucharist "far-fetched," a judgment I would also apply to the somewhat anachronistic conclusions of Kelly.

223 So also, e.g., Best, "I Peter II 4–10," 282; Schelkle, 65; Lampe and Luz "Nachpaulinisches Christentum," 213; Elliott, *Elect,* 184; V. R. Steuernagel, "Exiled Community," 11; P. J. Robinson, "Some Missiological Perspectives from 1 Peter 2:4–10," *Missionalia* 17 (1989) 183.

224 While Christ is not mentioned here, the general tenor of 1 Peter makes clear that that is how salvation was accomplished; cf. 1:14–21, where the same phrase, "the one who called" (τὸν καλέσαντα), is used (v. 15) to identify God.

225 E.g., Selwyn (16), who cites as an example Prov 2:13.

tradition,[228] where, as in Judaism,[229] it could also be used to describe the act of conversion.[230] It was from such sources that our author drew here[231] to describe the God whose wondrous salvation was to be announced by the readers.[232] The identification of God as one who calls makes use of an almost technical term pointing to God's saving action,[233] reinforcing the salvific context of these words. The application to the Christian community in this verse of titles drawn from OT descriptions of Israel as God's elect and chosen people points again to the fact that for our author the Christian community has now become God's elect and chosen people.[234] The absence in the letter of any discussion of the relationship between Christian and Jewish communities makes it impossible to determine how the author understood that relationship,[235] whether as continuation[236] or fulfillment[237] or reenactment[238] or replacement.[239] That the author is steeped in OT language and the traditions of Israel is evident; how he understood the present status

remains unknown.

■ **10** We now learn the result of God's call from darkness to light: it is the creation of a people that before did not exist. The Christian community is thus the wondrous light that had not previously existed, but that, like creation itself, had been summoned by God's call out of darkness.[240] While the phrases that comprise this verse reflect language found in Hos 2:25,[241] they do not quote any known text and are thus allusions rather than direct quotations. Because the only other place this passage from Hosea is quoted in the NT is in Rom 9:25–26, it is possible that the author of 1 Peter drew them from that letter.[242] The differences are such, however, that dependence is not likely;[243] if there is commonality, it is

---

226 E.g., Goppelt (153 n. 67), who cites as examples Pss 36:10; 43:3; Isa 2:5.

227 Elliott, *Elect*, 43; Michaels, 11; Schelkle, 65; cf. *1 Enoch* 58.3; 1QS 1.9–11.

228 E.g., Matt 5:14–16; John 8:12; 12:35, 46; Acts 26:18; 1 Cor 4:6; Eph 5:8; Col 1:12, 13; 1 Thess 5:4–5; cf. Selwyn, 280; Best, "I Peter II 4–10," 282.

229 Goppelt (153 n. 67) cites as an example *Jos. Asen.* 8.10; 15.13.

230 E.g., Acts 16:18; 2 Cor 4:6; Eph 4:17–18; Col 1:12–13; see also *1 Clem.* 36.2; 59.2; *Barn.* 14.5–7; cf. Michaels, 11; Beare, 31. Bauer (28) and Leaney (32) note that baptism is described as illumination in Heb 6:4; 10:32.

231 The suggestion by Leaney ("Passover," 247) that the source is the exposition of Deut 26:5–8 in the haggadah is unnecessarily complex, as is the suggestion by Schwank et al. (40) that it reflects Israel's exodus from Egypt. Perdelwitz's (*Mysterienreligion*, 79) suggestion that it comes from the experience of darkness in the "Adyton" and subsequent ascent into blinding light is, as Kelly (100) affirms, "unnecessary and indeed far-fetched."

232 The description of the light as "wondrous" (θαυμαστόν) confirms its use here with salvific intent.

233 As in 1 Pet 1:15; 2:21; 3:9; 5:10; cf. Elliott, *Elect*, 44; Kelly, 100.

234 Senior (33) and Herbert McCabe ("What Is the Church?—VIII," *Life of the Spirit* 18 [1963] 162) find here language drawn from the covenant.

235 The piling up here of titles describing Israel's special status with God makes Michaels's conclusion (107)

that the titles are used with "no awareness" of Israel an overstatement. He is correct, however, in the implication that that unmistakable awareness is nowhere made explicit.

236 E.g., Danker, "I Peter 1:23—2:17," 99; Spörri, *Gemeindegedanke*, 196; Best, "I Peter II 4–10," 277.

237 E.g., Paul Wells, "Les images bibliques de l'Église dans I Pierre 2, 9–10" *Etudes Evangéliques* 33 (1973) 20; Harrington, "Church," 83; Schelkle, 64; Schwank et al., 38.

238 E.g., Deterding, "Exodus Motifs," 63; Michaels, 113; cf. also McCabe, "What Is the Church?" 163.

239 E.g., Vanhoye, "L'Epître (I P 2,1–10,)" 27; Love, "First Epistle," 85; Harrington, "Church," 82. One cannot therefore conclude with Windisch (61) that for our author Israel has been excluded from salvation.

240 On the contrast between "then" (ποτε) and now (νῦν), see below.

241 The negative names are found in Hos 1:9 (οὐ λαός [μου]) and 1:6 (οὐκ ἠλεημένη), but they are also found in 2:25, where the order is reversed; it is sufficient here to see an allusion to Hos 2:25 without adding 1:6, 9.

242 E.g., Beare, 133; Schelkle, 66; cf. Elliott, *Elect*, 45.

243 Paul quotes the second name for Israel in Hos 2:25, and then changes the first from οὐκ ἠλεημένην to οὐκ ἠγαπημένην; he then quotes Hos 2:1 in a form identical to the LXX. The author of 1 Peter limits himself to paraphrasing the two names found in Hos 2:25 in reverse order. Elliott (*Elect*, 45), Goppelt (154 n. 72), and Kelly (102) also deny dependence on Paul.

likely to rest in Christian tradition.[244] Closely tied to the point of v. 9,[245] v. 10 is carefully constructed, with first a former negative status described, then a present positive,[246] thus emphasizing a contrast between past and present.[247] Because this is a major structuring element in the author's thought, it is evident that this verse represents the climax not only of this passage but of the body opening as a whole.[248]

Taken together, vv. 9–10 are both climax[249] and transition. As climax of the passage that has addressed itself to the nature of the community and its faith,[250] it points out that those who suffer in their society as exiles and aliens are in fact the true people of God.[251] As transition it prepares the chosen community for the hostile confrontation with its antagonistic environment by assuring it that whatever happens in that confrontation, it remains God's own and chosen people. Armed with that assurance, the community can face its painful encounter with an increasingly malevolent society.

---

244 It is unlikely to reflect the desert wandering of Israel during which time a band of slaves became a people, either directly, as Brown and Meier (*Antioch and Rome,* 133) affirm, or by way of the Feast of Tabernacles, as Hillyer ("First Peter," 64) argues.

245 As Michaels (112) notes, the discussion of λαός resumes the λαὸς εἰς περιποίησιν of v. 9; and as Schiwy (44) observes, it is the existence of the Christian community as chosen people where before it did not exist that demonstrates the kind of mighty act of God to which our author referred in 2:9.

246 Elliott (*Elect,* 46) correctly rejects Selwyn's (280) conclusion that such a construction, reflecting Jewish psalmody, is distinct from the normal style of 1 Peter.

247 So also, e.g., Margot, 40; Elliott, *Elect,* 45.

248 The *inclusio* of ἔλεος (1:3) and ἠλεημένοι—ἐλεηθέντες (2:10) provides further confirmation; cf. Schutter, *Hermeneutic,* 28.

249 With, e.g., Moffatt, 118.

250 So also Hart, 58; cf. Steuernagel, "Exiled Community," 16.

251 With Elliott, "Rehabilitation," 15.

Analysis

1. Structure

The descriptive adjective with which 2:11 begins, ἀγαπητοί ("beloved"), repeated in 4:12, indicates the boundaries of this passage.[1] Further indication is provided by the benediction in 4:11b,[2] and the *inclusio* formed with the repetition of God's glorification in 2:12 (ἵνα . . . δοξάσωσιν τὸν θεον, "in order that they may glorify God") and 4:11 (ἵνα . . . δοξάζηται ὁ θεός, "in order that God may be glorified"). Unlike the body opening, however, the organization of the body middle is determined by shifts in groups addressed rather than by repeated linguistic patterns. The addressees move from the readers in general (2:11–17) to specific groups (2:18—3:7) and back to the readers in general (3:8—4:11). Within those larger groupings, the theme of subordination plays a role (2:13—3:7), due to the incorporation of portions of a household code (2:18—3:7).[3] Also characteristic of this unit as a whole are the references to the fate of Christ, especially his suffering, as the basis for the points being made (2:21–24; 3:18–20, 22; 4:1).

The abandonment of the household code with 3:8[4] points to 2:11—3:7 and 3:8—4:11 as the major subdivisions within the larger unit.[5] While the subunits within 2:11—3:7 are easily identified because of differing subjects (2:11–12: general admonition to good behavior; 2:13–17: civil obedience; 2:18–25: behavior of Christian slaves; 3:1–7: behavior of Christian wives, husbands), the subunits within 3:8—4:11 are less clear-cut since the material as a whole is addressed to all readers. Nevertheless, there are indications of such subdivisions. The author's predilection for ending units with scriptural citation (e.g., 1:24; 2:3; 2:9–10) points to 3:12 as the end of a subunit; the specific description of Christ's fate in 3:18–22 points to that as a division within the larger subunit 3:13–22; the genitive absolute used in summation points to a new subunit beginning with 4:1; and the eschatological reference in 4:7 points to the beginning of the final subunit, which ends with the benediction.

Combining these indications, one can determine the following organization in the body middle:

I. Introduction (2:11–12)
II. Call to Appropriate Subordination (2:13—3:7)
    A. All readers to civil authorities (2:13–17)
    B. Household slaves to their masters (2:18–25)
        1. Subordination by right conduct (2:18–20)
        2. Suffering Christ as basis (2:21–25)
    C. Believing wives to their unbelieving husbands (3:1–6)
    Subunit: Believing husbands to show respect for their believing wives (3:7)
III. Call to Right Conduct (3:8—4:11)
    A. All readers to nonretaliation for evil (3:8–12)
    B. All readers to right conduct facing suffering (3:13–22)
        1. Bearing undeserved suffering (3:13–17)

---

1   So also Cranfield, 69; Best, 110; Wand, 73; Goppelt, 155; Beare, 134; Moule, "Nature," 10 (as the first of two letters combined into 1 Peter; the second was 4:12—5:11). As Michaels (115) observes, the author seems here to use παρακάλω and ἀγαπητοί as Paul used the same verb with ἀδελφοί to flag the beginning of a new direction in thought (Rom 12:1; 1 Cor 1:10; 1 Thess 4:1; cf. also Heb 13:22).

2   While this benediction can form the end of a section of the letter, it is less likely to have formed the end of a document subsequently included into the letter; on this point, see the Introduction IV. A, "Literary Unity of 1 Peter."

3   It is that motif of subordination that renders 2:13—3:7 a unity, although the elements of a traditional household code are restricted to 2:18—3:7. Comparable NT household codes do not include commands about civil rulers (e.g., Eph 5:22—6:9; Col 3:18—4:1), and a comparable passage of advice about civil rulers (Rom 13:1–7) has no elements drawn from a household code. Only later (e.g., *1 Clem.* 1.2) are all these elements combined as they are

here in 1 Peter. On this matter see also Brox (117), who finds the use of imperatives in 2:13–17 and participles in 2:18–3:7 further indication of originally separate traditions.

4   The use of τὸ δὲ τέλος in v. 8 further indicates the beginning of a new unit, as Piper ("Hope," 223) and Combrini ("Structure," 42) also observe.

5   Goppelt (155) divides this section as 2:11—3:12 (duty of Christians to act responsibly within institutions of society) and 3:13—4:11 (Christians are to bear suffering such actions bring), with each section ending in paranesis on living together in the Christian community (3:8–12; 4:7–11).

2. Suffering and triumphant Christ as basis (3:18–22)
C. All readers to right conduct among unbelievers (4:1–6)
D. All readers to right conduct within the fellowship (4:7–11)

2. Theological Import

The theme of this section of the letter follows on the identification of the Christian readers as a people chosen and precious to God because they adhere to Christ (2:4–10), and is announced in the opening paragraph (2:11–12): appropriate conduct for Christians whom their contemporary culture looks upon as they do other exiles and aliens who are members of a foreign people and who follow strange and often unacceptable customs. That this fate of Christians is made inevitable by their adherence to Christ was announced in the previous section, particularly in the thematic statement in 2:4b, where Christ who for God is chosen and precious is nevertheless rejected by human beings. That affirmation that the fate of Christians is determined by the fate of Christ becomes thematic in this body middle through the strategic references to the suffering (2:21–24; 3:18–20, 22; 4:1) and triumphant (3:22) Christ as the basis for the exhortations to appropriate conduct in the midst of their hostile environment.

There is a discernible progression in the way the figure of Christ is used in this passage. One's initial impression is that the major benefit of the suffering of Christ was understood by our author to be the pattern this sets for those who follow (2:21, where the benefit "you" derive from Christ's suffering "for you" appears to be the pattern this gives "to you" for your own conduct). The chance to follow in Christ's footsteps is thus the benefit of his passion, and the ensuing description of the suffering Christ (2:22–24) describes what those footsteps entail, as they lead one back to God as wandering sheep are led back to their shepherd (2:25).[6]

That falls far short of the author's understanding of the significance of Christ's suffering, however, as was already clear from the earlier discussion of the ransoming of Christians by Christ's death (1:18–20). That broader Christology comes directly into focus in the next discussion of Christ's suffering in this passage (3:18–22), with its references to Christ the righteous one dying for the sin of the unrighteous in order to open for them the way to God (3:18).[7] The significance of Christ's suffering is then further extended by the enigmatic reference to his proclamation to imprisoned spirits (3:19), implying that there are no entities and no realms that are beyond the reach of Christ's divinely ordained activity. The concluding reference to Christ's absolute authority not only over the imprisoned spirits but also over all orders of supernatural beings (3:22) shows the final outcome of Christ's suffering, and announces Christ as the one to whom divine authority and power have been given.

The implication of such a Christology for the problem addressed in this section of 1 Peter is clear, and will later be made explicit (5:10), namely, that those who share in the suffering of Christ will also in due time share in his glory. Thus the structure of the Christology undergirds the exhortation: the hope of final vindication lends divine authority to the admonition to endure now the suffering inflicted by a hostile society. It is that connection between Christology and admonition that constitutes the primary theological thrust of this passage.

It is noteworthy, finally, that there is no idea here of withdrawing from the hostile world, and forming a kind of conventicle of the righteous in the midst of the *massa perditionis*. It is clear from the tone of this portion of the letter, as of the letter as a whole, that the author fully expects Christians to continue to participate in the life of their societies.[8] Such participation will present oppor-

---

6   While the reference to being healed by Christ's wounds in 2:24 could point beyond such an understanding of Christ's suffering, in this context the "healing" can be understood as the return described in v. 25.

7   The theological assumptions necessary to find such significance in Christ's death are the same as those made more explicit by Paul in Rom 5:8–11. That implies not so much dependence on Romans as it provides an insight into common early Christian tradition.

8   With, e.g., Senior, 40; Harrington, "Church," 85; cf.

also Schelkle, 68; Everett Falconer Harrison, "Exegetical Studies in 1 Peter," *BSac* 98 (1941) 461; Georg Schückler, "Wandel im Glauben als missionarisches Zeugnis," *ZMR* 51 (1967) 291. This was an especial emphasis of Goppelt; cf., e.g., "Der Staat" and "Mission ou Révolution?"

tunities to witness to their beliefs (3:15b) and may win some nonbelievers to the faith (e.g., 3:1–2), but whether it does or not, participation in the hostile society is to continue, even when that participation results in rejection and suffering, as it inevitably will (e.g., 2:20b; 3:17). They are, after all, exiles and aliens to the culture within which they live.

2 Thwarting False Accusations by Good Behavior

11 Beloved, I exhort you, as aliens and exiles, to abstain[1] from the desires that belong to the surrounding world, because such desires war against your very lives, 12/ by maintaining[2] your behavior among the gentiles at a high level[3], so that when they speak[4] against you as evildoers, they may, because they observe your good works,[5] glorify God in the "day of visitation."[6]

1   For the infinitive ἀπέχεσθαι (ℵ, B, Ψ, many minuscules) some texts read the imperative ἀπέχεσθε (P⁷², A, C, L, P, some minuscules and versions); the meaning is the same. Hort (131) and Bigg (135) argue that the infinitive is more likely original, since our author shows a strong preference for imperatives in the aorist; Michaels (114) argues that scribes were more likely to change imperative to infinitive, and despite predilection for imperatives in the aorist, the author does use imperatives in the present tense, e.g., 2:17. The substitution may have seemed appropriate since the infinitive presumes an ὑμᾶς that is absent. In either case, the meaning is unaffected.

2   The present participle ἔχοντες could be an adverbial participle of attendant circumstance: the readers are to abstain at the same time that they maintain good behavior, but it is more likely to be instrumental (abstention accomplished by maintaining good behavior). It is unnecessary to find here an imperatival participle.

3   One could also translate "your good behavior among the Gentiles," but the emphatic position of καλήν, and the implication that such behavior will also be acknowledged as good by non-Christians, is better rendered by the present wording.

4   Some MSS. (L, P, some minuscules) read a subjunctive καταλαλῶσιν for the future καταλαλοῦσιν, which is to be preferred with the majority of witnesses; so also Michaels, 114.

5   A, P, Ψ, and some others read aorist ἐποπτεύσαντες, perhaps because logically the observing must precede the glorifying (so Michaels, 114); the stronger witness (P⁷², ℵ, B, C, a number of minuscules) reads it as the present participle ἐποπτεύοντες.

6   Although there is no definite article, the genitive ἐπισκοπῆς renders ἡμέρα specific; it is not any day, but "the" day of visitation, a concept taken from the LXX; see the comments below.

Analysis

This opening sentence of the body middle serves to introduce the major theme that is worked out in this portion of the letter:[7] Christians who lack the legal rights and social standing as do exiles and aliens, and who are thus open to harassment on all sides, are to make sure their behavior does not give others an excuse to per-petrate such abuse. There is embodied here the conviction, also given voice in 3:13, that behavior appropriate for Christians will also be recognized as appropriate by nonbelievers, and thus will tend not only to blunt harassment and persecution but also to win over some of those who oppose them (e.g., 3:1–2).[8] Indeed, such behavior will allow the Christians to fulfill the

7   With Michaels (115), who also sees this as introducing the whole of 2:11—4:11; cf. also Best, 109; Schiwy, 45. Combrini ("Structure," 40) acknowledges

its introductory function, but limits it to the section 2:11—3:12.

8   So also Brox, 111; de Villiers, "Joy," 75; Goldstein,

mandate of 2:9, because such lives will in the end be effective "to announce the marvelous deeds of him who called you out of darkness into his marvelous light." Such a hope-filled view of the effect of the good lives of the Christians does not blind the author to the reality of Christian suffering, however; he knows Christians are open to persecution even when they do display decent and acceptable behavior (e.g., 2:20b; 3:14, 17). Yet however their good behavior may be received, Christians must persevere in it, lest they lose their promised participation in Christ's glory, a point made more explicit in the body closing.

Comment

■ **11** The vocative ἀγαπητοί, a word rare in non-Christian Greek literature, is frequently used in the NT when the readers are reminded of tradition,[9] a force it may also carry here. While it surely means "beloved (by God)," it is probably meant to speak of the author's attitude to them as well.[10] Its use with παρακαλῶ ("exhort") also conforms to Christian practice as a way of introducing detailed instructions on Christian behavior.[11] Whether the infinitive ἀπέχεσθαι is to be construed as complementary, presupposing an implied ὑμᾶς ("I exhort [you] to

abstain"),[12] or as an imperative in indirect discourse ("I exhort that exiles and aliens abstain"), is unclear.[13] The difficulty with this latter construal is the presence of ὡς with the two words that would have to function as subjects of the infinitive, forcing one still to find an implied ὑμᾶς ("I exhort [you] *as* exiles and aliens to abstain").[14] In either case, however, the meaning is unaffected: the readers, described as "aliens and exiles," are to abstain from inappropriate behavior.

The word πάροικος, originally meaning simply "neighbor,"[15] came in time, particularly in the east, to mean "resident alien,"[16] that is, one who, though not a full citizen[17] and hence having neither the obligations nor the privileges that fell to citizens,[18] nevertheless did have a recognized status and hence was not totally outside legal protection.[19] In the NT, it is most often used in the sense of "alien" (Acts 7:6, 29; 13:17) but is applied to Christians in only one place (Eph 2:19) other than here in 1 Peter.[20]

Παρεπίδημος did not come to refer to a class of people, but describes rather one who has settled in a given place on a temporary basis,[21] a sojourner, and hence without the recognized status even of a πάροικος. Rarer than

Paulinische Gemeinde, 32–33; Lippert, "Leben," 246.

9   In the form of teaching, 1 John 2:7; as exhortation, Rom 12:19; 1 Cor 10:14; 2 Cor 7:1; Jas 1:16, 19; 2:5. Cf. Selwyn, 169; Kelly, 103.

10   With Michaels, 115; Schelkle, 69; contra Wand, 74. When it means only the author's attitude, that is made explicit, as in 1 Thess 2:8, there with ὑμῖν added.

11   E.g., Rom 12:1; Eph 4:1; 1 Thess 2:8; cf. Best, 110.

12   There are only two instances in the NT where the form παρακαλῶ does not have its object given: 1 Tim 2:1, where it is followed by an accusative with infinitive, and Heb 13:19, where the accusative object (ὑμᾶς) is nevertheless presumed. In 1 Peter, the two other uses of this verb are 5:1, where the object is given, and 5:12, where it is followed by an accusative with infinitive.

13   In this latter case, παροίκους and παρεπιδήμους serve as "subjects" of the infinitive, as Beare (135) observed.

14   Goppelt (157) and Schelkle (69 n. 2) argue that the ὡς gives the basis for abstention, but it is more likely that the ὡς here points to the metaphorical character of this description of the readers.

15   Hans Schaefer, "Paroikoi," PW 18.4,1695; cf. also Wolff, "Christ und Welt," 338. Schaefer's article is a thorough discussion of the meaning of this word.

16   So Wolff, "Christ und Welt," 338; cf. also Schaefer,

"Paroikoi," 1701.

17   Normally, a πάροικος, though a resident, did not give up citizenship in his or her native country; on this point, see, e.g., William Barclay, *New Testament Words* (Philadelphia: Westminster, 1974) 284.

18   In times of peril, however, e.g., when Mithradates threatened Pergamum and Ephesus, πάροικοι could be granted full citizenship so that they could participate in military defense; see Schaefer, "Paroikoi," 1697.

19   The status was between full citizenship and total alienation and estrangement, as Schaefer ("Paroikoi," 1698) notes. The same obtained for the πάροικος (LXX) in Jewish law: less than full citizenship (e.g., Exod 12:45; Lev 22:10) but nevertheless not without provision in the law (e.g., Lev 25:6; Num 35:15).

20   The notion of the member of the people of God as a sojourner is drawn directly from the OT (e.g., Lev 25:23), as is the phrase πάροικος καὶ παρεπίδημος (LXX Gen 23:4; Ps 38:13); on this point see also n. 30 below. When Eph 2:19 uses the combination ξένοι καὶ πάροικοι, it shows it is drawing on a different tradition from that represented in 1 Peter.

21   On this point see, e.g., Barclay, *NT Words*, 282.

πάροικος,[22] it occurs in the NT only one other time outside 1 Peter (Heb 11:13).[23] Both words describe people who were foreigners in an age when foreigners, however numerous they may have been particularly in the larger cities of the empire,[24] were *eo ipso* suspect,[25] and exile from one's native land was one of the severest punishments that a city or state could impose.[26]

The application of these words to Christians is not, however, meant to indicate their political status prior to their conversion.[27] Far more common than these words to indicate aliens or exiles were the terms ἀλλότριος ("stranger")[28] and φυγάς ("exile")[29]; the combination of the two words παροίκους καὶ παρεπιδήμους occurs only in LXX Gen 23:4; Ps 38:13; 1 Pet 2:11, or writers citing one of those passages.[30] Had the author wanted to call attention to their legal status prior to their conversion, other more common terms would have been more appropriate. Rather, this combination continues our author's practice of applying to the Christians terms originally applied to Israel, in this case to Abraham,[31] and is not drawn from the secular vocabulary used to indicate classes of residents in lands other than their own.[32] That is not to say, however, that the terms did not describe the legal status under which Christians as Christians functioned.[33] It was precisely the precarious legal status of foreigners that provided the closest analogy to the kind of treatment Christians could expect from the hostile culture in which they lived.[34] Having enjoyed the legal protection and social acceptance accorded the native born prior to their conversion, it was

---

22 The stem occurs some thirty-four times in non-Christian Greek, but only four times in the adjectival form παρεπίδημος; it also appears as the verb παρεπιδημέω, less frequently as the noun παρεπιδημία.

23 As in the case of πάροικος in Eph 2:19, παρεπίδημος is linked with ξένος in Heb 11:13. As noted below, the combination πάροικος with παρεπίδημος is relatively rare in Greek literature, occurring only in Jewish or Christian authors.

24 So, e.g., Seneca *Ep., Ad. Helv.* 6.3–4; Martial *On the Spectacles* 3; cf. Juvenal *Sat.* 3.62–65. Tarrech ("Le milieu," 102) argues that in the countryside πάροικοι outnumbered natives, while in the cities the two groups were closer in number.

25 Plutarch (*Mor., Exil.* 607A) complains that ξένος ("foreigner") and μέτοικος ("immigrant") were terms of reproach, as was the word φυγάς ("exile, fugitive"). Seneca (*Benef.* 4.35.1) notes in passing that Romans were forbidden to contract marriage with a foreigner; laws generally differed for natives and foreign born (cf. Plutarch *Mor., Exil.* 601A).

26 Exile was considered a calamity in the Hellenistic world; it was illegal to help an exile even with shelter or food (cf. Plutarch *Mor., Exil.* 599F; Seneca the Elder *Cont.* 6.2), although like many other laws this one was not always observed.

27 Contra Elliott, "Peter, Silvanus and Mark," 254; Tarrech, "Le milieu," 107, 112; cf. Thurston, "Interpreting First Peter," 174, who cites Salmon (*Introduction to the New Testament*, 485) as another who holds this view.

28 Cf., e.g., Plutarch *Mor., Exil.* 602.(B).8; Dio Chrysostom *Or.* 31.84; 34.22; 41.9.

29 E.g., Plutarch *Mor., Exil.* 600B, 607B; Dio Chrysostom *Or.* 47.10; it is combined with πάροικος in 46.12.

30 The combination occurs in Philo *Conf. ling.* 79 (cf.

76–77): Gen 23:3; Clement of Alexandria *Strom.* 3.11.75: 1 Pet 2:11; *Strom.* 4.26.165: Ps 38:13; Gregory Nazianzus, *Funebris Oratio in Laudem Basilii* 49.3: Ps 38:13; Basil of Cappadocia *Homiliae super Psalmos* 29.252: Ps 38:13 and Gen 23:3.

31 It is thus less likely that this reflects "another Passover theme," as Leaney ("Passover," 247) suggests (see also n. 35 below), or that its background is the Feast of Tabernacles, as Hillyer ("First Peter," 67) has argued. Rather, as was the case in 1:1, the background is the sojourn of Abraham (παρεπίδημοι) and the later period of Jewish exile (διασπορά); on this point see also Chevallier, "Condition," 394.

32 So also Kelly, 103; Blendinger, "Kirche als Fremdlingschaft," 127–28; Michaels, 116; Talbert, "Once Again," 144. If I read Tarrech ("Le milieu," 116 n. 58) correctly, that is also the point he espouses, though in other places he more uncritically implies that it refers to their pre-Christian social situation (e.g., 107).

33 To that extent Chevallier ("Condition," 394) is correct in saying that the terms are drawn from the history of salvation, but incorrect to say they are not sociological characteristics. They are the latter, but in terms of the status Christians assume *after* conversion, not their social status *prior* to their becoming Christians.

34 Foreigners were characterized as being of another race, speaking another language, worshiping other gods, and following other customs (so Bovon, "Foi chrétienne," 40). The last two would be most apparent to non-Christians, while Christians also came to regard themselves as falling under the first category.

precisely their changed status to that of foreigner in their own homeland that precipitated the crisis our author addressed in this letter.[35]

Because the words do describe the actual social situation of Christians, it is less appropriate here to understand the terms as though they referred to exile from the true home of the Christians, which was heaven.[36] That idea is of course present in the NT[37] and becomes explicit in later Christian literature.[38] Here, however, the force seems to be not so much that Christians are exiles from heaven—the author awaits not a return to heaven but the glorious return of Christ after a final judgment[39]—as it is an acknowledgment of the kind of conditions the Christians must endure if they are to participate in that glorious future.[40]

The status the phrase describes, however, painful though it may be, is nevertheless the necessary status of those who are estranged from the values and customs of the culture within which they were formerly at home.[41] The phrase "aliens and exiles" is thus not only a description of their present reality, it is also a description of a status they are to maintain, lest by abandoning that status and reverting to their former values and customs, they estrange themselves from God. The status of exile and alien therefore describes the condition within which Christians must continue to pursue their good conduct.[42]

The phrase ἀπέχεσθαι τῶν σαρκικῶν ἐπιθυμιῶν ("to abstain from the desires that belong to the surrounding world") draws on traditional vocabulary[43] to specify how Christians as aliens and exiles are to act: they are not to

35 That changed status and its results are most clearly reflected in 1 Pet 4:3–5. It is therefore not the case that the theme of 1 Peter is God's providing to homeless aliens and exiles (πάροικοι) a home (οἶκος) in the church (contra, e.g., Elliott, *Home*, esp. 220–33), nor is it to be understood on the analogy of the exodus (contra, e.g., Leaney, "Passover," 247) and the promise of a homeland. Rather, the theme centers on the fact that God took people who *were* at home and turned them into aliens and exiles, on the analogy of God's call to Abraham, a point demonstrated by the use of the phrase πάροικοι καὶ παρεπίδημοι that otherwise occurs only in reference to him, and on the analogy of the people in the dispersion (διασπορά; 1:1) who had been exiled from their homeland. It is the change in status from people once at home in their culture to people now homeless in that same culture, and the ensuing problems, that prompted the writing of this letter.

36 This is a widespread understanding, e.g., Beare, 135; Best, 19; Schückler, "Wandel im Glauben," 290; cf. Beare, "Teaching," 293; Calvin, 78; Ketter, 234. In some instances it has been thought to have its antecedents in the idea that the soul is a stranger to the body, being exiled from another place, e.g., Plutarch *Mor., Exil.* 607D; cf. Tarrech ("Le milieu," 116 n. 58), who also cites Plato *Phaedrus* 250c.

37 E.g., Heb 13:14; cf. Cranfield, 70.

38 Probably the earliest such explicit reference is *Diogn.* 5.5–9; cf. Moffatt, 120.

39 The categories of the letter are not ontological but temporal. What the Christian awaits is not a return to heaven but a glorious future. Although that glorious future is currently guarded in heaven (1:4), it is pictured as an inheritance to come to the Christian, not a home to which the Christian is to return; the

image is one of new status, not restoration or relocation (5:10).

40 So also, e.g., Spicq, 97; Senior, "Conduct," 428; Goldstein, *Paulinische Gemeinde*, 32; Neugebauer, "Zur Deutung," 62–65; Philipps, *Kirche*, 21; P. Benedikt Schwank, "Wie Freie—aber als Sklaven Gottes (1 Petr 2,16)," *Erbe und Auftrag* 36 (1960) 10. Cf. also Bigg, 135.

41 So also, e.g., Spicq, 97; Senior, "Conduct," 428; Goldstein, *Paulinische Gemeinde*, 32; Neugebauer, "Zur Deutung," 62–65; Philipps, *Kirche*, 21; Schwank, "Wie Freie," 10.

42 So also, e.g., Goppelt, 157; van Unnik, "Redemption," 73; Wolff, "Christ und Welt," 338. Windisch (61) notes correctly that the phrase gives the theme of the exhortations that follow.

43 Similar use of ἀπέχεσθαι is found in Acts 15:20, 29; 1 Thess 4:3; 5:22; on ἐπιθυμία as bad conduct, see Rom 1:24; 6:12; 7:7; Eph 4:22; Col 3:5; 2 Tim 2:22; Jas 1:14, 15; 2 Pet 2:10; Jude 16; as characterizing the unbelieving world, see Mark 4:19; John 8:44; 1 Thess 4:5; 1 Tim 6:9; 2 Tim 2:22; Titus 2:12; 3:3; 2 Pet 1:4; 3:3; 1 John 2:17; on the necessity to resist the "desires of the flesh," see Rom 13:14; 16:1; Gal 5:24; Eph 2:3; 2 Pet 2:18; 1 John 2:16. While this language may have come in part from Greek moral philosophy (cf. Seneca *Ep.* 124.3; Dio Chrysostom *Or.* 5.16), as Beare (135) and Best (110) assert, it is unlikely that that is the source for our author.

175

adapt their conduct to that of their surrounding culture.[44] While the word ἐπιθυμίαι can be used in the NT in a good or at least neutral sense,[45] its qualification here with the adjective σαρκικός[46] indicates desires associated with the unredeemed culture within which they live[47] and in which they once participated.[48] Because they are now aliens and exiles within that society, it is no longer appropriate for them to act in accordance with its customs.[49] A further reason[50] for such avoidance is given in the final phrase, where the author again draws on traditional Christian material picturing the Christian life as spiritual warfare,[51] in this case warfare against the forces that seek to pervert the new life[52] the Christian has attained through his or her rebegetting by God.[53]

■ **12** This verse continues the thought of v. 11, now giving the positive side of living as aliens in their culture. The call to conduct[54] that is recognizably good in the eyes of nonbelievers is not unique to our author,[55] and by this time is part of Christian tradition.[56] Underlying this call is the conviction that both Christians and pagans recognize good behavior,[57] yet without the idea that the "good" is identical for both.[58] The exhortation to

44 So also, e.g., Reicke, 93. That such a call for abstention relates to a concern for the opinions of outsiders, as Balch (*Wives,* 86) avers, is to trivialize the seriousness with which 1 Peter calls for lives of holiness as the will of God, e.g., 1:2, 14–16.

45 E.g., Luke 22:15; Phil 1:23; 1 Thess 2:17; cf. 2 Tim 3:6; 4:3. There is no idea, however, that all physical appetites as such are sinful, as Kelly (104) also points out.

46 In 1 Peter the adjective refers to the human being apart from God: 1:24; 3:18; 4:1–2 (so also, e.g., Beare, 135); it is similar to the meaning it has in the DSS, as Flusser ("Dead Sea Sect," 255) points out: "humanity without the ennobling gift of divine grace." This is the only place where "flesh" carries the Pauline ethical sense, as Hort (133) notes, although the contrast here is not with "spirit" as is usual in Paul, but with "life" (ψυχή), the only place that contrast appears in the NT; cf. Schweizer, 69–70; Lippert, "Leben," 242.

47 The combination, equivalent to the ἀνθρώπων ἐπιθυμίαις in 4:2 and there opposed to God's will, indicates the way ἐπιθυμίαι σαρκικαί are to be understood here.

48 E.g., 1:14; 4:2; cf. Goppelt, 158.

49 In a sense, although the author does not dwell upon it, Christ himself was the model of the πάροικος, e.g., Matt 8:20//Luke 9:58 (I owe this insight to Blendinger, "Kirche als Fremdlingschaft," 127).

50 The αἵτινες here has almost causal force: "Because they are at war"; so also Kelly, 104; Bigg, 135; Harrison, "Exegetical Studies" [98], 460.

51 2 Cor 10:3–4; Eph 6:11–17; 1 Tim 1:18; as internal warfare, Jas 4:1–2; cf. Rom 7:23; Gal 5:16–17. The thought was not unknown in secular circles, e.g., Marcus Aurelius *Med.* 2.17: "Life is a warfare and a foreign sojourn"; Schelkle (70) also calls attention to Plato *Phaedo* 82c–83; Plutarch *Mor.* 101, 1096; Diogenes Laertius *Vitae philosophorum* 10.145; Philo *Leg. all.* 2.6, where the human being is described as being in conflict between flesh and spirit, although it

52 is doubtful that our author is drawing on that tradition. The point here is more the notion that the Christians are caught in a war of cultures, not in a war within themselves.

As in 3:20, ψυχή here refers to the whole human being, not to an inner nature (soul) as against the physical nature; so also, e.g., Kelly, 105; Hort, 134; Schweizer, 55; Cranfield, 72. Michaels (117) finds a similar use in Mark 8:35–37.

53 It is interesting to note that unlike the convenanters at Qumran, the Christians are not to withdraw from all contact with corrupt society. It is perhaps not accidental therefore that similarities to the QL are largely absent from this point on in 1 Peter; cf. also Goppelt, 156.

54 Ἀναστροφή refers to one's general conduct, public and private; cf. Lippert, "Leben," 243; Goppelt, "Mission ou Révolution?" 208.

55 Of the six times our author uses the term, four are connected to witness to the unbelievers: 2:12; 3:1–2, 16 (the other two are 1:15, 18).

56 The same expression, καλὰ ἀναστροφή, is found in Jas 3:13. The concern for the good name of Christians among nonbelievers is a regular part of the Pauline tradition: 1 Cor 10:32; Col 4:5; 1 Thess 4:12; 1 Tim 3:7; 5:14; 6:1; Titus 2:5, 8; cf. Kelly, 105.

57 E.g., Seneca (*Vit. beat.* 6.24.3): nature bids him do good to all humankind (*hominibus prodesse*) of whatever class; Dio Chrysostom (*Or.* 47.25): being roundly abused though doing kindly deeds (καλῶς ποιοῦντα) is a mark of royalty. The καλά in 2:12 is probably, as Bigg (136) suggests, the equivalent of Lat. *honestus,* meaning gracious, commanding admiration, and hence means behavior that is not only good but is seen as good by unbelievers as well, as Best (111) avers; see also Balch, "Hellenization/Acculturation," 87. Thus such good works have apologetic value, as Lampe and Luz ("Nach-paulinisches Christentum," 202–3) observe.

58 It is not, for example, a call to Christians to give up their own more radical ethic in favor of the mores of

humility, for example, found in 5:5, runs counter to Hellenistic thought,[59] and the command to be holy as God is holy[60] indicates that good conduct for Christians is conduct in accord with God's will.[61]

The participle ἔχοντες ("maintaining") is not so much imperatival[62] as it is an adverbial participle of means, that is, one is to separate oneself from the world's desires by maintaining good conduct among "Gentiles," who here, as elsewhere in 1 Peter, mean not non-Jews but nonbelievers.[63] That accusations against the Christians' conduct is a common occurrence is indicated by the temporal conjunction ἐν ᾧ, which is to be given its full temporal force here: "when" or "whenever."[64] While it is possible that the reference to accusations against Christians as "doers of evil" (κακοποιοί)[65] refers to formal legal accusations,[66] it is more likely that it refers to popular reaction against Christians because of their cultural nonconformity.[67] Whether the author also has in mind the general charges of cannibalism, incest, and

atheism commonly leveled against Christians in the second century is not certain,[68] but clearly accusations against Christians resulted from earliest times[69] because of the low reputation they earned by their unwillingness to act in full accordance with the normal customs of their respective cultures.[70]

By pointing to good works as the solution to such baseless slander, the author adopts a tactic and employs traditional language that traces its origin to Jesus recorded in Matt 5:16.[71] Doing good deeds was also a virtue acknowledged within the secular culture,[72] and the choice of καλός ("good") here links Christian ethics to the best of pagan culture to show that Christians are not a threat by reason of their standard of conduct.[73] The exhortations that follow in 2:13—3:7 are examples of the good works Christians are to do in the midst of their culture to avoid unnecessary offense to their unbelieving contemporaries.

The similarity in point to Matt 5:16 argues for taking

---

the surrounding culture, as Balch claims in his writing on 1 Peter (e.g., *Wives;* "Hellenization/Acculturation"). His argument is based on passages limited to chaps. 2–3, and is rendered impossible, for example, by such passages as 1:14, 18; 4:1–4. See also on this point Elliott's ("1 Peter") discussion of Balch's position.

59 So, e.g., Lippert, "Leben," 244.

60 That first use of ἀναστροφή in 1:15 is programmatic not only for the further use of the word but for all of the exhortations about conduct in the epistle.

61 So also, e.g., Brandt, "Wandel," 12; Elliott, *Elect,* 180.

62 Contra, e.g., Spicq, 98; Beare, 137; with, e.g., Michaels (117), who notes the imperatival force already provided by ἀπέχεσθαι. Daube ("Participle," 482) regards such a use here as "doubtful."

63 With, e.g., Beare, 127; Best, 111; contra, e.g., Wand (74–75), who thinks the word must mean some at least of the readers were Jews. This use of "Gentiles" is in accord with our author's controlling metaphor of Israel for the Christian community; for a discussion of that metaphor, see the Introduction § V.B.3, "Controlling Metaphor."

64 So also Fink, "Use and Significance," 34; contra, e.g., Kelly, 105; Hort, 135; Bigg, 136; Michaels, 117. There is no indication in the letter that a more limited sense, e.g., "in case" (*RSV*), is indicated here; such accusations are by this time common, as 3:14–17; 4:12, 14, 16; 5:9 indicate.

65 The Latin equivalent, *maleficus,* had the technical sense of "magician," but, as Beare (138) points out, nothing in the context makes that meaning likely

here.

66 So, e.g., Moffatt, 120–21, who thinks it refers to the *cognitio,* a preliminary cross-examination in which charges were considered and evidence sought.

67 So also, e.g., Reicke, 92; Beare, 137; Goppelt, 160; Brox, 114.

68 Best (111) thinks that it may but more likely that it means general slander against Christians, as does also Bigg (137). For more on that general attitude, see the Introduction § I.D.2, "Persecutions."

69 See, e.g., Matt 5:11–12; 1 Cor 4:12–15.

70 Christians were accused of being troublemakers (Acts 16:20–21; 17:6–7) and of boycotting established religion (Acts 19:24–27); see also Ignatius *Eph.* 10.2; *Trall.* 8.2; on Christianity as an evil superstition see Suetonius *Vit.* 6.16; Tacitus *Ann.* 15.44; Pliny *Ep.* 10.96.2. Cf. de Villiers, "Joy," 75; Spicq, 98; Schelkle, 70.

71 This is a widely held view; see, e.g., Goppelt, 162; Beare, 137; Best, 112; Hort, 136; Cranfield, 72; Hart, 58; Schelkle, 71; van Unnik, "Christianity," 82. In Matthew as here in 1 Peter, the point is not so much to avoid suffering as to call the attention of unbelievers to the divine origin of the Christians' activity; so also Brandt, "Wandel," 22; cf. Margot, 42. The phrase καλὰ ἔργα is also found in John 10:32–33; 1 Tim 5:10; Titus 2:7, a point also noted by, e.g., van Unnik ("Teaching," 96) and Lippert ("Leben," 243).

72 Cf., e.g., Elliott, *Elect,* 182; Goppelt, 162.

73 On the necessity, where possible, to deflect accusations of bad conduct, see Rom 12:18; 1 Cor 10:32; 1 Thess 4:12; 1 Tim 3:7; 5:14; 6:1.

177

ἐποπτεύοντες ("[because] they observe")[74] as a causal participle:[75] the nonbelievers will be led to glorify God because they observe the Christians' conduct. Grammatically the object of ἐποπτεύοντες is not ἀναστροφήν ("behavior"),[76] nor is the participle used absolutely.[77] Rather its object is the phrase ἐκ τῶν καλῶν ἔργων, which is to be understood in a partitive sense:[78] "Because they see some of your good works."[79] The result of such observation, namely, the glorification of God, occurs on the "day of visitation" (ἐν ἡμέρᾳ ἐπισκοπῆς). While it is possible that this could refer to the time of the con-

version of the nonbelievers,[80] and has been suggested to mean the trial of Christians as wrongdoers not at God's hands but at the hands of the civil authorities,[81] the use of this phrase in the Bible points rather to the time of the final judgment.[82] The thrust of the verse is therefore not that the good works Christians do will deliver them from unjust oppression when those who observe them are led to conversion, but that at the time of the final judgment nonbelievers will be brought to the realization that the Christians did what they did at God's behest and with divine approval, and thus be led to glorify God.[83]

---

74 While the term was used in the mystery religions to describe privileged glimpses of cult objects granted to the initiates who were called οἱ ἔποπται ("observers"), such a derivation here is foreign to the context, and the term has the ordinary sense of "observe"; see Kelly, 106; Bigg, 138; Hart, 59; Bieder, *Grund und Kraft*, 8.

75 Instrumental (so Michaels, 114) is also possible, but I think less likely. Its present tense probably implies observation over a longer period of time; so also Selwyn, 170; de Villiers, "Joy," 75.

76 Contra H. G. Meecham, "A Note on 1 Peter ii.12," *ExpT* 75 (1953/54) 93; ἀναστροφή is the object of the participle ἔχοντες.

77 Contra Hort (137), who calls it a "transitive absolute": "that beholding they may glorify God." In that case it is not clear how the phrase ἐκ τῶν καλῶν ἔργων is to function in the sentence.

78 For the partitive genitive as object, see John 16:17; Luke 21:16. BDF § 164 (2) notes that while it is rare in classical Greek, it is common in Semitic languages, and hence in the LXX.

79 The point is that the Christian need not attempt to make every good deed public and observable to all; nonbelievers will be impressed with the good works they do see.

80 So, e.g., Reicke, 94; Selwyn, 171; Beare, 138; Kelly, 106; Wolff, "Christ und Welt," 339; Brandt, "Wandel," 17; Harrison, "Exegetical Studies" [98], 462. Van Unnik ("Teaching," 98) thinks such an understanding "yields sheer nonsense."

81 So, e.g., Moffatt, 121; but such a possibility is denied by Lippert, "Leben," 245; Selwyn, 171; Beare, 138; Kelly, 106.

82 It bears such an eschatological meaning in Isa 10:3; Jer 6:15; Wis 3:7–8; Luke 1:68; 19:44; *1 Clem.* 1.3. A

similar meaning of "day (lit. 'time') of visitation" (מועד פקודה) is found at Qumran: 1QS 3.18; 4.6–8, 11–12, 18–19 CD ms. A 7.9; CD ms. B 19.10, as Michaels ("Eschatology," 397 n. 2) and Knibb (*Qumran*, 56, 57, 101) point out. In the LXX, God's ἐπισκοπή can mean a blessing, but when it is used with a temporal designation (ὥρα, ἡμέρα, καιρός) it refers to judgment. When Schückler ("Wandel im Glauben," 293) cites such verses as Gen 50:24–25 and Job 10:12 to show the phrase here can mean "gnädigen Kairos" ("time of mercy") (similarly Lippert, "Leben," 245: "gnädigen Heimsuchung Gottes"), he does not note that in those places, ἐπισκοπή is used without a designation of time. That the reference here is to the final judgment, see, e.g., van Unnik, "Teaching," 98–99; Best, 112; Schelkle, 72; Michaels, 119–20. Wells ("Images," 397) also notes that a variant reading in 1 Pet 5:6 adds ἐπισκοπῆς to τῷ καιρῷ, showing that that textual tradition understood ἐπισκοπή to refer to final judgment. The attempt by Danker ("I Peter 1:23— 2:17," 98) to find the background in Mal 3:13–18 rather than, e.g., Isa 10:3 is unpersuasive.

83 The conclusion of the traditional hymn in Philippians (2:10–11) points to a similar universal eschatological glorification of God. Because the reference is to the final day of judgment, the argument that the author sees here a missionary purpose to the Christians' good works (e.g., de Villiers, "Joy," 75; Bovon, "Foi chrétienne," 40; Lippert, "Leben," 246) is robbed of some of its force.

2 Subordination of Everyone to Civil Authorities

13 **Be subordinate to every human creature because of the Lord, 14/ whether to the emperor as superior or to the governors as those sent out by him to visit justice upon those who do evil but to praise those who do good, 15/ because it is the will of God that you,[1] by doing good, put to silence the ignorance[2] of foolish people; 16/ (be subordinate) as free men and women, and not as those who use their freedom as a cover for evil deeds, but as God's slaves.[3] 17/ Honor all people, love[4] your fellow Christians, fear[5] God, honor the emperor.**

1 By adding ὑμᾶς, some MSS. (C, 69, 322, 323, 1739, some Coptic versions) make explicit the "subject" of the infinitive φιμοῦν contained in the participle ἀγαθοποιοῦντας.

2 P⁷² reads the synonym ἄγνοιαν, perhaps under the influence of 1 Pet 1:14; 1241 and a few others read ἐργασίαν, shifting the focus to the deeds rather than the words of opponents. There is no reason to change the ἀγνωσίαν of the overwhelming majority of MSS..

3 A few minuscules read φίλοι for δοῦλοι, but the latter is to be preferred on the basis of over-whelming textual evidence.

4 Some MSS. (K, L, 049*, 69, 2646, many others) read the aorist (ἀγαπήσατε) rather than the present imperative, perhaps influenced by the aorist τιμήσατε that precedes it, perhaps by the ἀλλήλους ἀγαπήσατε of 1:22. On the basis of the textual evidence, and the commonness of the aorist imperative, the present tense is to be preferred as the *lectio difficilior*.

5 The δέ added by P⁷² destroys the symmetry, surely intended, of the four imperatival phrases, and is to be ignored.

Analysis

This passage, along with 2:18–25 and 3:1–7, is to be understood as an example of how Christians are to embody the exhortation contained in 2:11–13. The very general exhortation with which the passage begins ("Be subordinate to every human creature") shows that to be the case, as does the specific reference to good behavior silencing criticism based on ignorance (v. 15), which directly reflects the similar point made in v. 12. Our author is convinced that good behavior (ἀναστροφὴ καλά, v. 12; ἀγαθοποιοῦντες, v. 15) enacted in full Christian consciousness (διὰ τὸν κύριον, v. 13; cf. διὰ συνείδησιν θεοῦ, v. 19) presents the best opportunity to win approval from those who for whatever reason oppose Christians as enemies of society.[6] The presence of such advice does not presume, however, that at this point governing authorities were not hostile,[7] any more than the possibility of suffering because one was a Christian (4:14, 16) presumes full-blown official persecutions.[8] The situation was one of sporadic hostility to Christians, exhibited more by social pressure than by official policy, and these verses are a response to that situation.[9]

6 As Lampe and Luz ("Nachpaulinisches Christentum," 200) observe, this passage probably indicates that Christians were already being accused of lack of loyalty to the Roman government. The attempts at organized revolt in Asia Minor (according to Reicke [96], "during the early period of the empire") during Domitian's reign would not help groups like the Christians who even in the best of times were seen as antisocial.

7 So, e.g., Lepelley, "Le contexte," 47; Margot, 43; Kelly, 110. Chase ("Peter," 785) avers that verses like this were impossible at the time when Rev 17:6, 9

were written, or even after Nero's attack on the church.

8 Christians regularly sought to obey civil authorities and prayed for their stability even during overt persecution; e.g., *1 Clem.* 60.4—61.2; 63.1; Polycarp *Phil.* 12.3; *Mart. Pol.* 10.2; see also Tertullian *Apol.* §§ 30, 32, 33, 39; in full acknowledgment of persecutions, e.g., §§ 35, 40.

9 On this question, see the Introduction § I.D.2, "Persecutions."

The *inclusio* formed by the two imperatives that begin (ὑποτάγητε, "be subordinate") and end (τιμᾶτε, "honor") the passage, and by the opening and closing references to the emperor, shows it to be a careful literary composition. One must therefore pay attention to the deliberate limitations placed here on the status of civil government: the emperor is a "human creature" to whom subordination is due as an example of general subordination on the part of Christians within civil society.[10] That point is reinforced in the final verse, where honoring the emperor (τὸν βασιλέα τιμᾶτε) follows advice for a similar honoring of all people (πάντας τιμᾶτε). Such emphasis on the common humanity of the emperor probably reflects the growing prominence in Asia Minor of the cult of the emperor,[11] and is designed to give Christians a reason for civil obedience (loyalty will overcome false accusations, v. 15) divorced from any notion of the emperor as a deity.[12] Such advice would be as necessary for those who would see no contradiction between worshiping Christ as Lord and participating in the emperor cult as it would be for those who felt Christ's lordship precluded loyalty to the civil administration.[13]

While some have seen here a literary dependence on Rom 13:1–7,[14] the differences in meaning are so pointed that any relationship between the two probably owes more to a common tradition concerning the Christian attitude to governing authorities than to any kind of literary dependence.[15] Such a tradition of compliance with the dictates of civil rule is already found in the sayings of Jesus, who exhorted his followers to pay the necessary taxes (Mark 12:17 par.; cf. Matt 17:24–27),[16] and is further reflected is such passages as 1 Tim 2:1–3 and Titus 3:13 as well as Rom 13:1–7.[17]

Excursus: 1 Peter 2:13–17 and Romans 13:1–7

Similarities in language between 1 Pet 2:13–17 and Rom 13:1–7 have led some to conclude that the passages make a very similar point,[18] and that they may indeed stand in a direct literary relationship to one another.[19] Yet despite such similarities, 1 Peter displays a very different attitude to civil authority, and seeing it in the same light as the passage in Romans inevitably makes inaccessible the intention of the passage.[20] A careful comparison of the passages shows their very different intentions.

Comparison of language will turn up a number of

---

10 There is no notion here of God establishing civil governance, as Goppelt (180) and Kamlah ("ὑπο-τάσσεσθαι," 241) also point out. Hierocles *On Duties* 3.39.34–36 (cited in Malherbe, *Moral Exhortation,* 89–90) demonstrates the opposite: the homeland is to be regarded as a second god.

11 So also, e.g., Philipps (*Kirche,* 312) and Horst Goldstein, "Die politischen Paränese in 1 Petr und Röm 13," *BibLeb* 14 (1973) 102, both of whom speak of a "demythologizing" (*Entmythologisierung*) of the state and the emperor; Cothenet ("Le réalisme," 569) calls it a "demystifying" (*démystification*).

12 On this point, cf. Reicke, 94.

13 See on this point Goldstein, "Paränese," 103–4. That such advice was necessary because the readers were made up of the lower classes who were easily stirred to revolutionary aspirations, as Reicke (73) asserts, is to read modern presuppositions about early Christians into the text; for a discussion of the social and economic status of the readers of this letter, see the Introduction § III.B.2, "Social and Economic Status of the Intended Readers."

14 E.g., Schutter, *Hermeneutic,* 62; Kamlah, "ὑπο-τάσσεσθαι," 240 n. 14.

15 So also, e.g., Willem C. van Unnik, "A Classical Parallel to I Peter II 14 and 20," in idem, *Sparsa Collecta* 2.107–8; see the discussion in "Excursus: 1

Peter 2:13–17 and Romans 13:1–7," below.

16 E.g., Love, "First Epistle," 78; Russell, "Eschatology," 82; Leaney, 35. Michaels (123) finds a further tradition on love of enemies (Matt 5:44; Luke 6:27, 35) reflected in 1 Pet 2:13–14. By contrast, Wand (77) thinks the failure of the author to use the authority of this command of Jesus in this context shows "this code had no direct association with the gospel."

17 The attempt of Bammel ("Commands," 281) to reconstruct an original *Haustafel* which the author of 1 Peter has adapted is highly speculative, and for that reason remains unpersuasive.

18 E.g., Schutter, *Hermeneutic,* 62; Schelkle, 77.

19 E.g., Kamlah, "ὑποτάσσεσθαι," 240 n. 14. Beare (140) is more careful; while admitting some degree of literary relationship, he notes correctly that the differences are more significant than the resemblances; so also Windisch, 63.

20 As displayed by, e.g., Lohse, "Parenesis," 43. Horst Teichert notes, I think correctly, that the mistranslation of πάσῃ ἀνθρωπίνῃ as "ruling authority" is due to such an attempted conflation with Rom 13:1–7 ("1. Ptr. 2,13—eine crux interpretum?" *ThLZ* 74 [1949] 304).

similar words,[21] but they are used so differently that the similarity is all but completely overshadowed. A consideration of such words will make the point clear.

1. Both use a form of ὑποτάσσω, in Rom 13:1 referring to "superior authorities," which the rest of the passage makes clear are of divine establishment (vv. 1, 2, 4a, c). In 1 Pet 2:13 subordination is to be shown to every human creature,[22] with no word about their divine authority.[23] In a similar vein, while governing authority (ἐξουσία borne by ἄρχοντες) is established by and subordinate to God in Rom 13:1–2, governors (ἡγεμόνοι) are sent by and are hence subordinate to the emperor in 1 Pet 2:14.

2. Both use a form of ὑπερέχω ("be superior"), but in Rom 13:1 it refers to superior authorities of divine establishment, while its use in 1 Pet 2:13 refers to the "king," who has been identified as a "human creature."

3. Similarly, the phrases about punishing evildoers and praising those who do good are used in a context of divine action in Rom 13:3–4, but in a context of the purely human emperor and his governors in 1 Pet 2:14.

4. Most striking is that both passages end using forms of φόβος ("fear") and τιμάω ("to honor") in the same order. Yet their use in Rom 13:7 is very general, in 1 Pet 2:17 quite specific. More importantly, 1 Peter reserves the use of "fear" for God, while its use in Rom 13:3 refers simply to a very human fear in the presence of overwhelming governmental power directed at miscreants. The use of "honor the emperor" in 1 Pet 2:17 as a direct parallel to "honor all people" specifically divests the emperor of any and all trappings of divine authority or power.

5. Both passages use θέλημα, but in Rom 13:3 it refers to human will, in 1 Pet 2:15 to God's will.

6. The primary motive for subordination in both passages is God's will (1 Pet 2:12: διὰ τὸν κύριον, "because of the Lord"; Rom 13:5: διὰ τὴν συνείδησιν, "because of [your] conscience"), but the secondary motives are quite different: escaping fear and gaining praise in Rom 13:3; putting an end to ignorant accusations against the Christians in 1 Pet 2:15.[24]

There are other significant differences between the two passages. 1 Peter contains no reference to taxes (as in Rom 13:6–7); there is no use of abstract words for rule such as ἐξουσία or ἄρχοντες (as in Rom 13:1–3); there is no parallel in 1 Pet 2:13–17 to the idea that human rulers are God's stewards (θεοῦ διάκονος, Rom 13:4, bis) or that opposition to them is tantamount to opposition to God (Rom 13:2); and there is no reference in Romans 13 to the fact that Christians are both free and slaves of God (1 Pet 2:16). Finally, political activities, while the principal concern of 1 Pet 2:13–17, are not the exclusive concern they are for Rom 13:1–7. While Paul deals exclusively with such activity in Romans, the author of 1 Peter begins by treating emperor and governors as subsets of the class κτίσις ἀνθρωπίνη ("human creature," 2:13), and concludes with advice on the Christian's relationship to all people, to fellow Christians, and to God, in addition to the emperor (2:17).

It is therefore apparent that while there is similar vocabulary in the two passages, the use to which that vocabulary is put is quite different, and those elements in each passage for which the other has no parallel point the respective passages in different directions, the most striking of which is that the insistence in Romans 13 that rulers bear divine authority is totally absent in 1 Peter 2.[25] The passages are thus quite different,[26] and to attempt to find the same point in both because of a superficial similarity of language is to overlook the very different point each passage seeks to make.[27] The increasing importance of the emperor cult,[28] particularly in Asia Minor, by the time 1 Peter

21 E.g., Harrison, "Exegetical Studies" [98], 464.
22 Should the word "human" (ἀνθρωπωίνη) mean "created by humans" rather than simply "human," and thus refer to human institutions rather than human beings, the force remains the same: subordination is to human, not divine, authority.
23 That point is overlooked by Calvin (81) when he affirms that obedience is due to all who rule because they have been placed there by God, and that hence one is not to ask how they got that power, but to let the fact that they possess it and exercise it be sufficient.
24 Spicq ("La Iᵃ Petri," 51) sees here the same practical approach to governmental authorities that was displayed by Jesus in Matt 17:27.
25 A point made explicitly also by Goldstein ("Paränese," 97). Kelly (110) concludes from this that there can be no literary relationship between 1 Peter and Romans 13.
26 With, e.g., Philipps, Kirche, 33; Spicq, 100.
27 Lohse ("Parenesis," 43), Barnett (Literary Influence, 62), and Harrison ("Exegetical Studies" [98], 464–65) are clear examples of the kind of confusion created by attempts at harmonization against which Goldstein ("Paränese," 89) warns in his significant comparison of the two passages.
28 As Suetonius (Vit. 2.59–60) indicates, it was already beginning its rise to prominence in the lifetime of Augustus.

181

was written, and the different destinations to which Romans and 1 Peter were addressed, are probably to be understood as the reasons for the different emphases in the two letters.

Comment

■ **13** The imperative ὑποτάγητε ("be subordinate"), from a verb common in, but not exclusive to, household codes,[29] functions as a programmatic introduction to the material through 3:7.[30] Its meaning is closer to "subordinate" than to "submit" or "obey,"[31] and advocates finding one's proper place and acting accordingly,[32] rather than calling upon one to give unquestioning obedience to whatever anyone, including governing authorities, may command.[33] While its intention is as much to counter any tendency of Christians to seek to withdraw from contact with secular society as it is to calm revolutionary zeal,[34] it is nevertheless intended, as 2:16 shows, to warn the readers against assuming that as Christians they are free from normal political and moral restraints. Its point is to urge Christians to bring the same sort of responsible activity, characterized by love and humility, to secular contacts that they bring to their relationships within the Christian community.[35] The motivation for such subordination, "because of the Lord" (διὰ τὸν κύριον), confirms the basis of such subordination in Christian faith, whether "Lord" here refers to Christ,[36] or, as seems more likely, to God.[37] That phrase also qualifies subordination by placing it within the larger context of obedience to God; one is not to be subordinate in matters that go counter to God's will.[38]

Such appropriate subordination is to be given to every "human being,"[39] a translation to be preferred to "human order" or "institution,"[40] since the latter meaning is nowhere to be found in Greek literature,[41] and the examples that follow—emperor, governors[42]— are human beings, not institutions.[43] The specific qualification of the emperor[44] as a human being almost

---

29   E.g., Eph 5:21, 24; Col 3:18, 20, 22; Titus 2:9; *Did.* 4.11; *1 Clem.* 1.3; Polycarp *Phil.* 5.3; *Barn.* 19.7; but cf. Rom 13:1; Titus 3:1, not parts of a household code. The verb ὑποτάσσεσθαι is thus not so specific ("eigentümlich") to the household codes as Schelkle (73 n. 1) affirmed.

30   So also, e.g., Goppelt, 182; Balch, *Wives,* 98.

31   But see Allan Barr ("Submission Ethic in the First Epistle of Peter," *Hartford Quarterly* 2 [1962] 29), who acknowledges its primary meaning of subordination, but claims that here it nevertheless means submission; see also Selwyn, 171.

32   So also, e.g., Holmer and de Boor, 91; Margot, 43; Michaels, 124; Schlier, "Adhortatio," 77. Spicq (101) cites Luke 2:51 as an example of such accepting one's place. While it can of course mean "obey" if "obedience" is an appropriate part of such subordination, it is not a command unquestioningly to obey everything anyone says.

33   Dio Chrysostom (*Or.* 34.38), for example, advises against submitting to rulers who are insolent or greedy; cf. Luther (220–21), who says one is no longer to heed rulers who seek to lay hold of the conscience.

34   So also, e.g., Senior, 43; see in addition his "Conduct," 430.

35   So also, e.g., Schweizer (59), who cites as an example 1 Pet 5:5. A similar point is made in Rom 12:18 (cf. Brox, 125); see also Spicq, 101; Cothenet, "Les orientations," 32; Krodel, 75. The advice here is therefore against arrogance in any dealings, a point confirmed in 3:8b-9, 15b. It is therefore not moti-

vated by early Christian patriarchalism (so Windisch, 62) but rather, as Kamlah ("ὑποτάσσεσθαι," 241) rightly observes, by an attempt to realize the kind of humility Christ also displayed, a point the author makes explicit in 2:21–25.

36   So, e.g., Michaels (124), who points to this as the regular meaning in 1 Peter; Best (114), who notes it means Christ in the NT except in OT quotations or where thought demands it; and Wolff ("Christ und Welt," 339), who sees here a reference to Christ's humility that Christians are to assume. Cf. also Selwyn, 172; Hort, 140.

37   So Schelkle (73 n. 2), who rightly points in this context to 2:15a, 16b; cf. also Goldstein, "Paränese," 76.

38   With Cranfield, 76. The notion that this presumes a time of positive rapport with the state (so, e.g., Beare, 142; Schwank, "Wie Freie," 7; cf. Bovon, "Foi chrétienne," 37) is contradicted by the ensuing advice in 2:18b to slaves to be subordinate even to abusive masters (so also, e.g., Refoulé, "Bible," 465, 474).

39   With, e.g., Best, 113; Kelly, 108; Bieder, *Grund und Kraft,* 11 n. 8; Schweizer, 57; Fitzmyer, "First Peter," 365; Goldstein, "Paränese," 93; Kamlah, "ὑποτάσσεσθαι," 237 n. 1, 242; Neugebauer, "Zur Deutung," 85; Teichert, "1. Ptr. 2,13," 303–4; Holmer and de Boor 92; Krodel, 73; Spicq, 102; see also his "La Iᵃ Petri," 50; Brandt, "Wandel," 18 n. 16.

40   A popular translation; e.g., Grudem, 118; Hort, 139; Goldstein, "Paränese," 93 n. 19; Beare, 141; Hart, 59; Moffatt, 122; Wand, 77; Windisch, 63; Bauer,

surely points to an increasing tendency, particularly evident in Asia Minor, to regard the emperor as divine,[45] and thus gives a polemic edge to this verse.[46] Although one cannot speak in this context of compulsory official participation in the emperor cult,[47] pressure to participate in Asia Minor was from the beginning social rather than official, and that is probably the situation reflected here.[48] Designating the emperor as the supreme authority (ὡς ὑπερέχοντι) shows that the author is here limiting comment to human political authority since only on that level is the emperor supreme, a point underscored by the fact that the phrase διὰ τὸν κύριον is associated with subordination not to the emperor but to every human creature. The coordinating construction εἴτε . . . ὡς ("whether . . . as")[49] that links the emperor to

his subordinates further shows the limits of what the author wants to discuss, namely, human political authority, not divine authority underlying human government.

■ **14** The second instance of the coordinating εἴτε . . . ὡς indicates clearly that the one who sends the governors (ἡγεμόσι) is to be understood as the emperor, not God,[50] since the immediate antecedent for the phrase δι' αὐτοῦ ("by him") within this construction is βασιλεύς ("emperor"), not κύριον ("Lord").[51] The point is not to show God's authority underlying such governors, but that the emperor's supreme political authority is also to be respected in those he sends to represent him.[52] Since the word ἡγεμών ("governor") is a general term and could describe a number of Roman officials[53] sent by the

---

31. The closest one can come to such a meaning is to point to the regular use of κτίσις in secular Greek to mean "founding a city" (e.g., Selwyn, 172; Goppelt, 182), but that is hardly the meaning here.

41. So, e.g., Cranfield, 73–74. Even some who want it to mean "institution" or "ordinance" are forced to concede this point, e.g., Bauer, 31; Windisch, 63.

42. The case for "institution" would be strengthened if 1 Peter had used more abstract concepts, e.g., ἐξουσίαι, ἀρχαί, as is the case in Rom 13:1–2; Titus 3:1–2. Confusion of this passage with Rom 13:1–7 has led to precisely such a misinterpretation, as, e.g., Goldstein ("Paränese," 97) and Barnettt (*Literary Influence*, 62) have pointed out; see also "Excursus: 1 Peter 2:13–17 and Romans 13:1–7."

43. A similar subordination of rulers under the general rubric "human beings" is found in 1 Tim 2:1–2, where the author calls for prayers on behalf of all human beings (ὑπὲρ πάντων ἀνθρώπων) and then on behalf of rulers (ὑπὲρ βασιλέων καὶ πάντων τῶν ἐν ὑπεροχῇ ὄντων); Michaels (125) also calls attention to Titus 3:1–2, although there the order is reversed, and the word βασιλεύς is not used.

44. While βασιλεύς can mean "king," and is so used in the NT (but then its referent is clearly stated: David, Matt 1:6; Herod, Matt 2:1; cf. 14:9; Jesus as "king of the Jews," Matt 2:2, or "of Israel," Mark 15:22; John 1:49; 12:13), its normal meaning in Koine Greek is "emperor," and it is also so used in the NT (John 19:15; Acts 17:7; Rev 17:9, 12). That that is its meaning here, see also, e.g., Kelly, 109; that its original reference was to Nero, as Cranfield (75) asserts, is unlikely.

45. On this whole question, see Price, *Rituals and Power*, esp., e.g., 188, 210.

46. So also Bovon, "Foi chrétienne," 36; see Goldstein,

"Paränese," 95; Neugebauer, "Zur Deutung," 86. Tertullian (*Scorp.* 14) interpreted this to mean that the emperor is to be honored only when he keeps to his own sphere and does not assume divine honors.

47. To this extent, those who deny reference to emperor worship are correct, e.g., Lampe and Luz, "Nachpaulinisches Christentum," 198–99; cf. Balch, *Wives*, 86, 138.

48. For more on this point, see the Introduction § I.D.1.c, "Roman Policies on the Imperial Cult."

49. The ὡς may have a causal force, as Michaels (126) suggests, but it may simply be appositive, to describe further the emperor as the one who bears ultimate human political authority, and the legates as those who are sent by him.

50. With, e.g., Goppelt (185 n. 31), Michaels (126), and Kelly (110), all of whom call specific attention to its divergence from Romans 13.

51. To find the antecedent in the κύριον of v. 13 (so, e.g., Best, 114; Hart, 60) owes more to imagination than to grammar; it is a further example of the confusion of this passage with Rom 13:1–7.

52. Tacitus (*Ann.* 12.60) notes that Claudius held that judgments given by his procurators should have as much validity as his own rulings.

53. E.g., proconsul, the civil governor of a senatorial province; procurator, the official who had charge of revenues in an imperial province; praetor (cf. propraetor), who could serve as the governor of a province; see Goppelt, 185 n. 31.

emperor ($\pi\epsilon\mu\pi\acute{o}\mu\epsilon\nu o\varsigma$ = Lat. *legatus*), no specific type of authority is here intended, the point being that all legitimate political authority must be respected. The final phrase[54] describes the reason for such *legati*: to punish evil and to praise good behavior. Such a description of rulers is a commonplace in secular literature, where it is a primary characteristic of the good ruler.[55] The parallelism between punishing evil and praising good, while not a characteristic of the modern judicial system,[56] was characteristic of the ancient process,[57] but it was not limited to law courts. Governing authorities were accustomed to expressing such praise in the form of statues, inscriptions, crowns, or grants of money or special privilege to those who had in one way or another benefited the community.[58] Its meaning for the readers of this letter is less likely to refer to such public commendation than it is to the confidence that law-abiding citizens would enjoy the protection of the legal system,[59] in full knowledge, however, that Christian duty would on occasion make Christians appear to be lawless. Given that fact, Christians are not to invite additional disfavor with illegal behavior.[60]

Ἀγαθοποιέω (lit. "do good") as a description of good behavior[61] is a key word for our author.[62] Drawn from Christian tradition,[63] the word expresses, as v. 15 will show, what God desired Christians to do.[64] In this instance, therefore, we move from the purely secular plane to that of specifically Christian conduct: the Christian is to do the good that God wants, which, where it intersects with a healthy human understanding of "good," will be recognized by human civil authority. Where there is a conflict, the Christian must nevertheless do the good God wants, even if it is counter to human notions of goodness, and as a result lands the Christian in trouble with judicial authorities. That is made explicit in 3:14, 16; 4:14, 16, and is the force of the διὰ τὸν κύριον ("because of the Lord") of v. 13, and the διὰ συνείδησιν θεοῦ ("because of the consciousness of God") of 2:19.[65]

---

54 The εἰς is telic; governors are sent by the emperor for this reason, namely, to hinder evil and promote good.

55 E.g., Pliny *Pan.* 70.7; Dio Chrysostom *Or.* 39.2. Chrysostom (*Or.* 2.75) claims that an unjust ruler faces deposition by Zeus himself. See van Unnik ("Classical Parallel," 108–9), who notes the similarity between what Diodorus Siculus (*Bib. hist.* 15.1.1; 11.46.1) says is the chief task of the historian ("praise virtues and blame misdeeds") and the function of those in authority.

56 Bigg (141) calls specific attention to this difference in ancient and modern judicial procedures.

57 E.g., Dio Chrysostom *Or.* 1.17; 2.26; 32.26; cf. Pliny *Pan.* 44.6. White ("Ancient Greek Letters," 94) quotes a letter from Ptolemy II to Miletus where benefactions are promised for good acts.

58 See Goppelt, 143; Moffatt, 122; Spicq, 103. John H. Elliott ("Patronage and Clientism in Early Christian Society," *Forum* 3 [1987] 41) and Schwank ("Wie Freie," 7) note it was a practice especially common in the eastern provinces.

59 So also, e.g., Goppelt, 185; Moffatt, 122; Kelly, 109. Schelkle (74) and Best (114) see here, I think somewhat less likely, possible allusion to instances where Christians were acquitted in courts of law.

60 A point made explicit in 4:15–16.

61 As Neugebauer ("Zur Deutung," 83) notes, in Jewish thought "good deeds" meant doing more for the poor or despised than the law commanded, while in Greek thought it tended to point to acts that benefited the polis as a whole; on this point see also van Unnik, "Teaching," 92–94; Barr, "Submission Ethic," 31–32.

62 The stem ἀγαθοποι- appears six times in the letter: in 3:6 and 4:19 to describe Christian behavior generally, in 2:14, 15 to describe Christian behavior in the pagan world, and in 2:20 and 3:17 to describe Christian behavior that may cause suffering at the hands of society. On its importance, see Selwyn, 89; van Unnik, "Teaching," 84–85, 93; Elliott, *Elect,* 181.

63 E.g., Luke 6:33–35; 3 John 11 (where it specifically describes God's will for Christians). Although the word ἀγαθοποιέω is absent from Paul, the concept is present, e.g., Gal. 6:9–10; cf. Phil 4:8.

64 Its use in 1 Peter argues against the contention that, given the scorn to which Christians were subjected, it refers not simply to obeying the law but to exceptional acts of civic responsibility (e.g., van Unnik, "Teaching," 92; idem, "Classical Parallel," 107; Sleeper, "Political Responsibility," 282–83). Such a meaning is nowhere implied in the context, and would be difficult for Christians of limited means.

65 This renders nugatory Balch's contention (*Wives,* 119) that the ethic of this epistle is intended to encourage Christians "to acculturate to Roman society."

Where civic and Christian good intersect, the Christian is to perform it; where they diverge, the Christian is to follow God's will, not the emperor's decrees.[66] The former will keep the Christian from unnecessary difficulty with civil authorities; the latter virtually guarantees such difficulty.[67]

■ **15** Several points indicate that this verse gives the reason for the command to be subordinate in v. 13: (1) ὅτι in 1 Peter is regularly used to give the reason for an action or an attitude of faith;[68] (2) οὕτως is normally retrospective in the NT, and is so used in 1 Peter;[69] (3) the second half of the verse, standing in apposition to the phrase "will of God" (τὸ θέλημα τοῦ θεοῦ),[70] picks up the point in v. 13 that such submission is to be rendered "because of the Lord" (διὰ τὸν κύριον), thus tying the two verses together; (4) the unstated subject of the infinitive φιμοῦν ("silence") is to be understood as ὑμᾶς ("you"),[71] linking it with the verb of v. 13. This verse is therefore not parenthetical,[72] but indicates the reason why Christians are to be subordinated to governing authorities: because God wills the Christians to live good lives, and so give the lie to unjustified calumnies against them.[73]

The participle ἀγαθοποιοῦντας ("[by] doing good]"),

virtually a technical term for our author to describe Christians' activity within the pagan world,[74] has an instrumental function: it is by such well doing that ignorance is to be overcome.[75] While the "good" here under discussion is dictated by God's will, and hence is derived from the Christian faith rather than from any pagan ethical standards, the author assumes that such acts of political loyalty will also gain positive acknowledgment from unbelievers as well. That does not mean that the "good"[76] Christians are to do is here limited to "dutiful citizenship,"[77] nor does it imply they are to do something in the civic realm deserving special distinction.[78] To be sure it means to be useful to others and to assist in the common situations of life,[79] but because it reflects God's will the broader elements of a specifically Christian ethic (e.g., love for one's enemies) will also play a role here.[80] That is not to say our author thinks all Christian activity gains such acknowledgment; there are necessary Christian acts that will stir hostility (e.g., 3:14, 17; 4:3–4). Yet the good and decent lives of the Christians will, our author is convinced, help overcome the hostility based on ignorance[81] that they faced in their contemporary society.[82] In the end, however, failure of

---

66 So also, e.g., Michaels, 126.

67 This problem is specifically addressed in 4:12–19, but underlies the whole of the epistle.

68 In addition to this verse, it is used in 1:16; 2:21; 3:9, 12, 18; 4:1, 8, 14, 17; 5:5, 7, in each instance to give the reason for a prior statement.

69 It is also so used in 3:5; see Hort, 143; Selwyn, 172; Kelly, 110; contra Michaels, 127.

70 So also, e.g., Hort, 143; Selwyn, 172.

71 Michaels (127) thinks it was omitted to give greater emphasis to the participle ἀγαθοποιοῦντας.

72 As Michaels (127) and Hort (142), I think wrongly, assert.

73 Since the letter is addressed to Christians, one can hardly find here an appeal to the authorities to become better informed about the Christian movement, as Schiwy (47) suggests. The point is that the Christians' actions will provide them with such information.

74 The phrase is taken from Refoulé, "Bible," 469: "un 'terme technique.'" On its use in 1 Peter, see nn. 62, 63 above.

75 Michaels (127) notes correctly that the emphasis is on the instrumental participle, not on the infinitive φιμοῦν.

76 As v. 14 clearly implies; cf. also van Unnik, "Teaching," 85; Sleeper, "Political Responsibility," 274, and

the additional references cited in his n. 4.

77 As, e.g., Senior ("Conduct," 431) argues; cf. also Goppelt, 186.

78 As van Unnik ("Teaching," 92) affirms.

79 So Barr, "Submission Ethic," 32.

80 As, e.g., Michaels (lxxiv) observes, and as 2:21–25 demonstrate.

81 As Beare (143) and Best (115) point out, the word used here for "ignorance," ἀγνωσία, implies not so much lack of information (as does the word ἀγνοία in 1:14) as culpable ignorance; cf. also Hort, 144. That it was based on an optimism later to be proved wrong (so Moffatt, 123) can hardly be affirmed, since the author is well aware of suffering even when Christians do the good, as 2:20b, 3:17 specifically assert.

82 For example, Tacitus (*Ann.* 15.44) says Christians in Nero's time were hated for their vices ("per flagitia invisos") and were punished by him because of their hatred of everybody ("odium humani generis"), but even Tacitus must admit their suffering did elicit some sympathy among nonbelievers. For later imagined crimes of the Christians, see, e.g., Justin, *1 Apol.* 26.

such acknowledgment will be due not to what Christians do but to a foolish[83] unwillingness on the part of unbelievers to see in the Christians' acts what is truly good.[84]

■ 16 Like v. 15, which referred to v. 13 in giving the reason for the command that Christians should be subordinate to every human creature, v. 16 also refers to v. 13, this time to the subject (implied ὑμεῖς) of the verb ὑποτάγητε, qualifying it by means of three words (ἐλεύθεροι ["free people"], ἔχοντες ["use"], δοῦλοι ["slaves"]).[85] The position of the adversative conjunction "but" (ἀλλά) shows that the antithetical contrast is not between "free people" and "slaves of God,"[86] but between those who regard freedom as a cover for evil and those who are such slaves. That contrast, joined to "free people" by means of the consecutive conjunction "and" (καί), shows that the contrast is intended to give further information about how the Christians are to subordinate themselves to the human creatures identified in vv. 13b–14a: as free people (ἐλεύθεροι) and (καί) not as those who regard (ἔχοντες) freedom as a cover but (ἀλλ᾽) as slaves (δοῦλοι). In that structure, ἔχοντες, which is parallel to ἐλεύθεροι and δοῦλοι (each anarthrous and each introduced by ὡς),[87] is to be construed as attributive rather than predicate.

In calling Christians "free people," our author is drawing on a commonplace in NT traditions[88] which is also reflected elsewhere in this epistle.[89] Such freedom carries with it the danger of being employed in such a way that it becomes a cover (ἐπικάλυμμα)[90] for evil behavior (κακία). On the one hand, that evil could take the form of thinking it possible to regard all law and all moral customs to which they formerly were bound as overcome in Christ and therefore no longer in force.[91] That would have the effect of making the Christian community a public menace to the social order, and would have brought unnecessary suffering upon it.[92] On the other hand, such evil could also, from a Christian perspective, consist in obsequious conformity to all cultural or political demands[93] as a way to avoid persecution. That would mean in effect the dissolution of the Christian community as a distinct entity within Roman culture. It is this latter point, that the subordination to human power cannot be absolute since they have God rather than any human being as their master, that is then reinforced by the antithetic (ἀλλ᾽) phrase "as God's slaves" (ὡς θεοῦ δοῦλοι).[94] If they are God's slaves,[95] then God, and not the political powers, must be granted one's absolute subordination.

The thrust of the verse therefore is that while subordination to human creatures, including those who represent governmental power, is part of God's will, such subordination is not to be total or unquestioning, since the Christians' true master is God,[96] who through Christ

---

83 In describing the ignorant men as "foolish" (ἄφρων) the author uses a word that the LXX, especially in the Psalms, used of those who set themselves against God and hence against truth (e.g., Pss 13:1; 52:1; 73:18; 91:7; cf. Prov 1:22), and that in the NT can mean simply lacking in intelligence (1 Cor 15:36; 2 Cor 11:16 [bis], 19; 12:6, 11), but that can also describe someone who opposes God (cf. Luke 11:40; 12:20; Eph 5:17). It is in this latter sense that it is used in this verse (with, e.g., Harrison, "Exegetical Studies" [98], 465). On this whole point, see Kelly, 111; Beare, 143; Selwyn, 173.

84 Whether there are missionary overtones here, i.e., political subordination will win converts to the faith, as, e.g., Goldstein ("Paränese," 98–99) and Willem C. van Unnik ("Die Rücksicht auf die Reaktion der Nicht-Christen in der altchristlichen Paränese," in idem, *Sparsa Collecta* 2. 317) assert, is questionable, since there is nothing specific here about the conversion of unbelievers (so also, e.g., Brox 121).

85 So also, e.g., Bigg, 141; Wand, 78; Hort, 145; Michaels, 128; although the last two, mistakenly I

86 Contra, e.g., Chevallier, "Condition," 393.

87 The adverb ὡς has no causal force here, as Michaels (129) observes (contra Goppelt, 187).

88 E.g., Matt 17:26; Luke 4:18–21; John 8:32; Rom 6:18–22; 8:2; 1 Cor 7:22; 9:19; 2 Cor 3:17; Gal 5:1, 13; cf. Kelly, 111; Brox, 122; Best, 115; Schelkle, 76.

89 E.g., 3:18; cf. 1:18.

90 Lit. "a veil"; it carries here the connotation of "excuse" or "pretext"; cf. Hort, 145.

91 That Paul faced a similar problem of Christians rejecting all moral demands, see, e.g., 1 Cor 8:1–13; 10:23–11:1; cf. also Gal 5:13. On this point, see Michaels, 129; Goldstein, "Paränese," 99.

92 As, e.g., Michaels (129) points out. To say with Reicke (95) that in principle Christians are free from the bonds of society and need not have respect for the social order as such is surely to overstate the case.

93 A point made in 4:3–4.

94 So also, e.g., Philipps, *Kirche,* 32; Senior, "Conduct," 431; Neugebauer, "Zur Deutung," 85. Deterding ("Exodus Motifs," 62) sees here an echo of the

set them free from their former subjugation to futile ancestral ways (1:18; 2:9).[97] Instruction in how Christians were to carry out this program, namely, how to be free people and good citizens who nevertheless gave final obedience to God, is then provided in the following verses,[98] and indeed represents a primary intention of the letter as a whole.

■ **17** Two points clearly mark this verse as the conclusion of the section that began with 2:13. (1) The first of the four imperatival phrases that constitute this verse, "honor all people" (πάντας τιμήσατε), reflects the point of the imperatival phrase with which this section opened, "be subordinate to every human creature" (ὑποτάγητε πάσῃ ἀνθρωπίνῃ κτίσει). (2) The repetition of an imperatival form of the verb τιμάω in the first ("honor all people") and last ("honor the emperor") of the four imperatival clauses that constitute this verse rehearses the emphasis of v. 13 on the inclusion of the emperor among all human creatures.[99]

The clear intentionality thus displayed in the structure of the verse is, however, obscured by two further problems. (1) Although the verse is composed of four imperatival clauses, each following the same form (object, verb), the relationship among them is not clear. The repetition of the same verb in the first and fourth clauses hints at a chiastic arrangement (abb'a'), but to find relationships within the pairs seems forced.[100] To argue that the first and last clauses must be seen in light of the command to revere God[101] has little structural justification, and the attempt to argue that the honor paid to kings proceeds from fear of God and love of human beings[102] ignores the initial clause. Perhaps understanding the first and last to concern secular, the second and third to concern Christian, obligations would be closer to the structure of the verse. (2) The tense of the imperatives differs: a, aorist, b,b',a', present. That the first reflects the aorist of the imperative of v. 13 is clear enough;[103] why the ensuing three should be present is not. That the last three clauses represent a carrying out of the first[104] is rendered most unlikely by the third clause ("revere God"), which is hardly an example of honoring all people.[105] Yet given the author's predilection in other places for the aorist imperative, it is difficult to deny all significance here to the imperatives in the present tense.[106] Perhaps the first imperative was attracted to the aorist tense of v. 13, while the remaining

exodus, where Israel, set free by God, nevertheless remained bound to him.

95 The fact that all Christians are slaves of God is the first indication that the οἰκέται addressed in 2:18–25 are meant to be understood more broadly than just the group for whom that specific title would be appropriate; so also, e.g., Michaels, 129.

96 Cf. Selwyn (174), who notes rightly that Christian freedom rests on a change of masters; on this point see also Goldstein, "Paränese," 99.

97 With, e.g., Bauer, 34; Goppelt, 188; Senior, "Conduct," 431.

98 So also Neugebauer, "Zur Deutung," 64.

99 So also, e.g., Senior, 46; cf. his "Conduct," 431.

100 E.g., "all"/"brotherhood" "god"/"emperor" (Kelly, 112) or a/b concerning "neighbors," b'/a' concerning "overlords" (Goldstein, "Paränese," 101).

101 E.g., Combrini, "Structure," 40–41.

102 E.g., Calvin, 85.

103 Such an explanation seems preferable to the notion that it represents, as ingressive aorist, the moment of original decision to become a Christian (e.g., Selwyn, 174; Goldstein, "Paränese," 100) or, as programmatic aorist, the command to begin now and continue to practice such honor (e.g., Michaels, 131). Would that not also be true of the following three commands?

104 As, e.g., NEB. For a defense of that rendering, see Scot Snyder, "1 Peter 2:17: A Reconsideration," Filologia Neotestamentaria 4 (1991) 211–15.

105 So also, e.g., Bammel, "Commands," 279, 280. It is hard to see how the author could regard such reverence as one example among others of a Christian's duty, as Beare (144) correctly notes. To argue, as does James P. Wilson ("In the Text of 1 Peter ii.17 Is πάντας τιμήσατε a Primitive Error for πάντα ποιήσατε?" ExpT 54 [1942/43] 194), that the τιμήσατε is the corruption of an original ποιήσατε which indicates how the ensuing commands were to be carried out, i.e., as free people, lacks all textual basis and is more a product of ingenuity than of evidence.

106 As does, e.g., Schelkle (77 n. 1), who argues that both tenses of the imperative have the same force for the author, and that no deeper reason is to be sought.

three indicate the author's intention that such activity become a regular and repeated part of Christian life.

The contrast of first and last clauses indicates that the initial command to honor all implies such honor is not to be reserved for the mighty;[107] no creature of God is unworthy of it, whatever his or her station in pagan society.[108] The identification of the Christian community as ἀδελφότης, a word otherwise not used in the NT,[109] points to the new familial relationship among believers, and hence for the necessity of love to prevail (cf. 1:22; 4:8).[110] In the command to revere (φοβεῖσθε) God, the author employs a verb that, except when used in a quotation in 3:14, he uses exclusively in relation to God.[111] The repetition of the verb τιμάω rather than φοβέομαι in relation to the emperor is also based on Christian tradition[112] and reflects the order of commands in Prov 24:21, but with the specific omission of the command to "fear the king" found there.[113] The change, hardly for reasons simply of style,[114] may well reflect a rise in emperor worship in Asia Minor[115] and certainly represents a different, and devalued, understanding of imperial authority than that found in Rom 13:1–7.[116]

The concluding verse of this section thus establishes a hierarchy of values and allegiances: all people, including the emperor, are to be shown due honor and respect; fellow Christians are to be regarded as members of one's own family and shown appropriate love; God alone is to be shown reverence. It was that hierarchy of values to which the author called the readers, adherence to which made negative social pressure inevitable. The following examples of social classes who must operate in subordinate positions within secular society (i.e., slaves, wives of non-Christian husbands) illustrate the problems faced by Christians within that same society, and provide indications of how, in face of those problems, Christians are to remain faithful to the hierarchy of values given them with their faith in Christ.

107 So also, e.g., Goppelt, 188.

108 So also, e.g., Lampe and Luz, "Nachpaulinisches Christentum," 202; Krafft, "Christologie," 125.

109 It also appears in 1 Pet 5:9; it is used seven times in the LXX, but only in the later books (1 Macc 12:10, 17: a political alliance; 4 Macc 9:23; 10:3, 15; 13:19, 27: physical relationship). In post-NT times, it is used only rarely (e.g., Dio Chrysostom *Or.* 38.45) outside Christian authors. Derivation from a Mithraic term (φρατρία) is, as Kelly (113) notes, "far-fetched."

110 Found in Lev 19:18 and reflected in Qumran (e.g., CD 6.20–21), it was a prominent part of early Christian tradition (e.g., Mark 12:28–34 par.; Rom 12:9; 13:8–10; 1 John 2:9–10). The reversed order of commands concerning fellow Christians and God in Mark 12 makes it unlikely that the second and third commands in this verse derive directly from that source, as Michaels (131) avers.

111 So also, e.g., Goldstein, "Paränese," 101; Refoulé, "Bible," 470; Danker, "I Peter 1:23—2:17," 99; Senior, "Conduct," 431. In light of this verse, it is difficult to determine how Osborne ("L'utilisation," 72), in commenting on 1 Pet 3:15, can conclude that our author never used the verb with God or Christ as object ("son habitude de ne jamais employer le verbe φοβέομαι avec Dieu ou le Christ comme objet").

112 Jesus differentiated between duties to God and Caesar (Matt 22:21) and told his disciples to fear only God (Matt 10:28); so also Kelly, 113.

113 So also, e.g., Cothenet, "Le réalisme," 569; Prov 24:21 reads: φοβοῦ τὸν θεόν, υἱέ, καὶ βασιλέα. Such a subordination of the king to God is also reflected in Dio Chrysostom (*Or.* 1.45), when he argues that kings who govern in accord with the laws of Zeus are happy; those who do not are wicked.

114 As Selwyn (174) would have it. Philipps (*Kirche*, 33) sees it, correctly I think, as deliberately formulated to indicate that Christians stand in a different relationship to God than to the king.

115 So also, e.g., Margot, 45; Goldstein, "Paränese," 95; Schelkle, 77; but see Brox, 123; Hall, "For to This," 140.

116 Omission of reverence for the emperor goes against Hellenistic sentiment as well as the intention of Rom 13:1–2, 4, as Goppelt (188) notes. On this point, see "Excursus: 1 Peter 2:13–17 and Romans 13:1–7." Goldstein ("Paränese," 100) argues that it was an overreverence for the Roman state based on a misunderstanding of Romans 13 that this verse intends to combat.

2

Appropriate Conduct for Christian Household Slaves

18 You household slaves, by being sub-ordinate[1] with all godly reverence to your[2] masters, not only to those that are good and evenhanded, but also[3] to those that are unjust, 19/ because this redounds to one's favor,[4] when one, suffering unjustly, endures pain patiently because of one's consciousness of God. 20/ For what kind of glory is it if, when you do wrong and are beaten[5] for it, you endure[6] patiently? But if on the contrary, when you do good and suffer for it you endure[7] it patiently, God looks upon it with favor. 21/ Because to this very thing[8] you were called, because Christ also suffered[9] on your[10] behalf, leaving

1   The verb is here understood as an adverbial participle of means, linked to the four main verbs of v. 17. For more, see the comments on v. 18.

2   The addition of ὑμῶν (ℵ, z, the Coptic, some Latin, Syriac versions) is redundant, and simply reinforces the meaning.

3   P[72] and some minuscules omit the καί; an original omission would prompt its addition because of the normal expression οὐ μόνον . . . ἀλλὰ καί.

4   Some MSS. (C, Ψ, 33, 323, 1739, and a number of others, some Vulgate, Syriac MSS.) add παρὰ τῷ θεῷ (some other few omit the article and/or read θεοῦ), perhaps under the influence of v. 20. The same MSS. then substitute ἀγαθήν for θεοῦ ("a good conscience" instead of "a consciousness of God"—cf. 1 Pet 3:16, 21; P[72] simply adds ἀγαθήν, "a good conscience with respect to God"), thus clarifying the reading of the verse.

5   P[72], ℵ[2], P, Ψ, 322, 323, 630, 945, 1739, some others, some Syriac versions substitute the more general κολαζόμενοι ("punish") for κολαφιζόμενοι ("beat [with fists]"). The similarity of the forms makes an unintended change possible (Michaels, 134: a "careless reading").

6   Some MSS. (P[72], ℵ[2], Ψ, 69, 323, 614, 945, 1241, 1739, some others) read the present tense (ὑπο-μένετε); most (ℵ*, A, B, C, P, O49, many others) the future tense (ὑπομενεῖτε); the meaning is unchanged (see BDF § 371 [1]). Michaels (134) argues that since the future is less common in conditional sentences, it is to be preferred as the more difficult reading.

7   Again, some MSS. (P[72], Ψ, 69, 945, 1241, 1739, some others) read the present tense (ὑπομένετε); most (P[81], ℵ, A, B, P, O49, many others) the future tense (ὑπομενεῖτε).

8   Or "for this purpose."

9   Some MSS. (P[81], ℵ, Ψ, 623, 2464, some others; sy[P]) read ἀπέθανεν ("died") for ἔπαθεν ("suffered"), perhaps under the influence of traditional con-fessions, e.g., Rom 5:8; 1 Cor 15:3; 2 Cor 5:14; 1 Thess 5:10. The notion of suffering is more appropriate in this context, and should be retained (P[72], A, B, C, P, many more; some Latin, Syriac texts, the Coptic tradition), as many scholars agree, e.g., Brox, 135; Michaels, 134; Kelly, 119.

10 Some MSS. (614, 1243, 1505, some others; sy[P], bo) read "our" (ἡμῶν) and "for us" (ἡμῖν) instead of "your" (ὑμῶν) and "for you" (ὑμῖν); others (P, the later Greek MSS., some Latin, Coptic MSS.) read "our" and "for you." Such confusion of pronouns is common, and it is difficult to ascertain the original reading; here the subject ("you" understood) of the main verb would argue for second rather than first person (with P[72], ℵ, A, B, C, Ψ, 69, 1241, 1739,

you[11] a pattern so that you follow in his footsteps, 22/ [Christ,] who committed no sin, neither was any deceit found in his mouth, 23/ who although he was reviled did not revile in return, who although he suffered did not threaten, but delivered [himself] to the One who judges justly,[12] 24/ who himself bore our[13] sins in his body upon the cross, in order that we, being dead to sin, may live[14] to righteousness, by whose[15] wounds you[16] were healed; 25/ because you were straying[17] like sheep, but have now been turned to the shepherd and guardian of your[18] lives.

some Latin, Syriac, Coptic MSS.).

11   See n. 10 above.

12   A few minuscules and some Vulgate MSS. read ἀδίκως ("unjustly"), perhaps in light of πάσχων ἀδίκως in v. 19 (so Michaels, 134), but more likely in light of Christ's allowing himself to be tried and sentenced unjustly by Pilate (cf. Kelly, 122).

13   P[72], B, and a few other MSS. read ὑμῶν for ἡμῶν; lack of MSS. evidence argues against it, even though, as deviating from the text of Isa 53:4, it represents the more difficult reading.

14   C and a number of minuscules read συνζήσωμεν for the more widely attested ζήσωμεν, to emphasize Christ as the source of that life. The shorter reading is preferable here.

15   Some MSS. (א*, P, 049, the later tradition), under the influence of Isa 53:5, add αὐτοῦ, redundant in light of the οὗ with which the phrase begins.

16   A few MSS. (81, some Latin, Syriac, Coptic MSS.) change ἰάθητε to ἰάθημεν, again in accord with Isa 53:5. The paucity of evidence argues for the more difficult second person verb.

17   A number of MSS. (P[72], C, P, Ψ, the later Greek tradition) read πλανώμενα ("you were like straying sheep"); πλανώμενοι ("you were straying like sheep"), if less widely attested (א, A, B, 1505, 2495, a number of others), is preferable on grammatical grounds as completing the periphrastic imperfect ἦτε . . . πλανώμενοι, and as the more difficult reading. For different reasons, so also Bigg (149—a "needless attempt to simplify the grammar") and Michaels (134—a "bolder use of the metaphor").

18   The predictable shift in pronoun (ἡμῶν) is witnessed to by L, O49, 69*, 322, 323, 1243, and some other minuscules. Lacking any attestation that ἦμεν was read for ἦτε, one may ignore it.

Analysis

1. Form

With these verses, admonitions are given that are a regular part of NT household codes,[19] a form widely used in contemporary secular literature[20] but where advice to slaves is absent.[21] Lack of advice to slaves in such codes reflects their legal status in the Roman Empire,[22] where, according to classical theory, they were defined as chattel who, lacking citizenship, lacked the essential qualification of humanity.[23] Slave marriages had no legal force: the children produced belonged to the master; only evidence obtained from them by torture had validity in court;[24] they could not legally receive a legacy;[25] and if the master were assassinated by slaves, all

19   E.g., Col 3:18—4:1; Eph 5:22—6:9; tables of virtues also occur frequently in Christian literature, e.g., 1 Tim 2:8–15; 5:3–8; 6:1–2; Titus 2:2–10; 3:1–2; *1 Clem.* 21.6–8; Ignatius *Pol.* 4.3—5.2; Polycarp *Phil.* 4.2—6.1; *Did.* 4.9–11; *Barn.* 19.5–7.

20   For more on household codes (*Haustafeln*) see the Introduction § III.B.1 "Household Codes."

21   Best, 117; Schelkle, 80. Balch ("Household Codes," 46) finds precedent for addressing slaves in Philo *Spec. leg.* 2.67–68; 3.137, where it is contained in the framework of addressing masters (cf. Eph 6:5–8; Col 3:22–25; 1 Tim 6:1; closer to 1 Pet 2:18–25 are *Did.* 4.1; *Barn.* 19.7, where no masters are addressed), and *T. Jos.* 10.1–3; 11.1–2, which is, however, autobiographical in form and thus less relevant.

22   According to Josephus (*Ant.* 18.5.21), only at Qumran was slavery as such denied; cf. Goppelt, 191 n. 9 (where, however, the reference is wrongly given as 18.1.5).

23   Judge, *Social Pattern*, 28.

24   Cranfield, 80.

25   Pliny (*Ep.* 4.10) recounts a case where Modestus, a slave set free in his master's will, was denied that freedom since, as a legacy devised to a slave, it was

his slaves, including those manumitted, were to suffer the penalty,[26] most often crucifixion.[27] While their situation was undergoing a slow amelioration in the first century—freedom continued to be possible,[28] the slave could demand to be sold to another, kinder master,[29] Stoic thought argued that slaves were truly men and comrades[30] whom one should treat kindly and moderately[31]—they were still subject to harsh treatment.[32] For the mass of slaves, therefore, life was demeaning and often cruel, and many slaves reacted accordingly,[33] their reactions ranging from murderous assault on cruel masters[34] and the destruction of their own children by some slave women so as not to be compelled to raise them in addition to enduring slavery,[35] to flight,[36] to petty annoyance at fellow slaves who

tried to please the master.[37] Since the safety of a household depended on the obedience of its slaves, however,[38] such obedience had to be obtained.

If on the one hand the legal status of slaves was harsh, their economic status on the other hand was often better than those who were free,[39] and large numbers of freeborn sold themselves into slavery for that reason.[40] Slaves were not denied all social amenities—they could be admitted to the mystery religions,[41] and they had their own holidays[42]—and because some masters sought to obtain obedience through kindness rather than force, the bond between master and slave could be, and often was, one of genuine devotion.[43]

The Christian tradition regarding slavery finds its earliest articulation in Paul: in Christ, all distinctions of

26 Tacitus *Ann.* 13.32.

27 Despite that fact, as Seneca (*Clem.* 1.26.1) points out, such vengeance against cruel masters did take place.

28 Clifford H. Moore (*Tacitus: The Histories* [LCL 4; Cambridge: Harvard University Press, 1937] 46 n. 1) notes that complete emancipation could be effected "by the wand" (*vindicta*—a wand was laid on the slave's head during the ceremony); by having the Censor enroll the slave as citizen (*censu*); and by will (*testamento*; but see n. 25 above); informal and hence incomplete emancipation could be achieved by verbal declaration among witnesses (*inter amicos*); by written and countersigned document (*per epistulam*), and by inviting a slave to the master's table (*convivio*).

29 Plutarch *Mor.*, *De Superstitione*, 166.

30 E.g., Seneca *Ep.* 47, esp. § 10, where he argues that master and slave spring from the same stock.

31 E.g., Seneca (*Ep.* 47.12), whose advice on how to act toward slaves sounds much like the Golden Rule: "Live with those who are inferior in the way you wish superiors to live with you" ("sic cum inferiore vivas, quemadmodum tecum superiorem velis vivere"); see also *Clem.* 1.18.1.

32 Martial (*Epig.* 5.37) chides one who ought to be ashamed for bewailing the death of a paltry home-bred slave, and Seneca (*Ep.* 47.11) complains that Romans were excessively haughty, cruel, and insulting to slaves ("superbissimi, crudelissimi, contumeliosissimi sumus").

33 Philipps (*Kirche*, 39) lists five possible reactions of the slave to his or her situation: (1) accept it as divine will; (2) keep interior distance from it though outwardly conforming (so, e.g., Stoic thought); (3) conform to the role only when the master could enforce it; (4) violent revolt; (5) flight.

34 Seneca *Clem.* 26.1.

35 Dio Chrysostom *Or.* 15.8.

36 Seneca (*Ep.* 107.1) chides a friend whose total absorption in business provides his slaves with the opportunity to run away, something they apparently would do quite readily.

37 Since it is a matter of satire, it must have been rather common; see Petronius *Satyr.* 57, where such annoyance is expressed against one who tried to please a fine and dignified master ("homini maiesto et dignitoso").

38 Dio Chrysostom *Or.* 38.15; Pliny (*Pan.* 42.2) mentions as one of the virtues of Trajan's administration that obedience was restored to slaves.

39 The master was required to care for the slave, while freedom often meant lack of work and food, and hence total insecurity (cf. Schelkle, 79; Maurice Carrez, "L'esclavage dans la première épître de Pierre," in Perrot, *Etudes*, 213; Dickey, "Conditions," 402–3). Dio Chrysostom (*Or.* 31.113) noted that slaves in Phrygia, Egypt, and Libya fared better than citizens of Rhodes.

40 Dio Chrysostom, *Or.* 15.23.

41 So Philipps, *Kirche*, 38.

42 E.g., Plutarch (*Mor.*, *Quaestiones Romanae* 287E-F): the Ides of August provided one for all slaves, male and female.

43 E.g., Luke 7:2; Paul pleads for it in Phlm 15–16; cf. Judge, *Social Pattern*, 38.

race, gender, and social status have been rendered nonexistent (Gal 3:28; 1 Cor 12:13; cf. 1 Cor 7:22). The Christian slave ought to take advantage of freedom if it is offered (1 Cor 7:21), and in later times Christians bought freedom for slaves,[44] but they also sold themselves into slavery to benefit others with the proceeds.[45]

Remarkable in 1 Peter is the absence of any advice to slave owners, particularly when that was a feature of non-Christian household codes, and is included in other NT codes (Eph 6:9; Col 4:1). That this absence is due to the fact that there were no, or relatively few, slave owners in the communities addressed[46] is unlikely, since letters addressed to the same area (Ephesians, Colossians) include such advice. Nor is it likely to be due to the fact that the majority of Christians at that time were slaves,[47] or that the author hoped Christian slave owners would automatically treat their slaves justly.[48] Far more likely is the suggestion that the author chose to address his admonitions to slaves because they typify the all but defenseless vulnerability of all πάροικοι καὶ παρεπίδημοι (2:11) to the forces arrayed against them in the Roman Empire.[49] That that is the intention here is indicated by the author's earlier assertion (2:16) that all Christians are God's slaves (θεοῦ δοῦλοι), and by the fact that many of the phrases employed in this passage are elsewhere applied to all Christians.[50] That Christ's redemptive death (2:24) and his rescue of straying humanity is to be limited to household slaves are also unlikely.[51] Rather, "slaves" in this context have paradigmatic significance; they and their fate stand as exemplary both of the Christian's situation in the Roman Empire and of the Christlike reaction they must adopt to it.[52]

2. Origin

There are indications in this passage that it may have originated as a hymn: (1) the introductory ὅτι (v. 21); (2) the presence of the relative pronoun ὅς (vv. 22, 23, 24 bis); (3) the shift of pronouns from second person (v. 21) to first person (v. 24a-b) to second (vv. 24c-25); (4) the address to a wider audience than slaves, thus showing detachment from the present context.[53] Yet (1) the introductory ὅτι continues the causal particles (cf. γάρ, vv. 19, 20, 21, 25) that give structure to the entire passage; (2) the relative pronoun ὅς is common to the language of 1 Peter;[54] (3) the shift in pronouns, a shift itself based on uncertain textual traditions, is as easily accounted for by the author's own use of Isaiah 53 as his

---

44   E.g., *Hermas Sim.* 1.5: instead of fields, purchase afflicted persons (ψυχὰς θλιβομένας); cf. *Man.* 8.10, where ἐξ ἀναγκῶν λυτροῦσθαι τοὺς δούλους τοῦ θεοῦ ("to rescue slaves of God from constraints") may mean purchase freedom for Christian slaves.

45   *1 Clem.* 55.2; on this matter, cf. Goppelt, 192.

46   Often suggested, e.g., Kelly, 114–15; Spicq, 106; Hardy, *Christianity,* 38; Beare, 146; Cranfield, 80; Michaels, 138.

47   Goppelt (190) notes correctly that such an idea rests on an unhistorical construct; the evidence that allows Balch ("Hellenization/Acculturation," 92) to assert that "the educated author of this letter certainly owned slaves" is unavailable to me. For more on this topic, see the Introduction § III.B.2, "Social and Economic Status of the Intended Readers."

48   The suggestion of Best, 117.

49   So also Elliott, "Home," 206–7; Schlier, "Adhortatio," 78. As Michaels (135) points out, the same is true of the wives, who are addressed next.

50   E.g., slaves: εἰς τοῦτο γὰρ ἐκλήθητε (2:21); all: ὅτι εἰς τοῦτο ἐκλήθητε (3:9); slave: οὐκ . . . δόλος ἐν τῷ στόματι (2:22), all: χείλη τοῦ μὴ λαλῆσαι δόλον (3:10); Slave: ὃς λοιδορούμενος οὐκ ἀντελοιδόρει (2:23), all: μὴ . . . λοιδορίαν ἀντὶ λοιδορίας (3:9). Much the same point that is made in 2:21–24 is also made in 3:13–18,

where the passage is addressed to all Christians rather than just to slaves.

51   On redemption, see 1:18–20; 3:18; on rescue, see 1:18b; 2:10; 4:3; 5:10; on Christ as shepherd, see 5:4. The shift in pronoun from second to first in 2:24 may also be due to the intention to address a wider group than simply Christian slaves, as Schlosser ("Ancien Testament," 84) points out.

52   As early as Calvin, 89; see also Schelkle, 85; Schutter, *Hermeneutic,* 141; Schlosser, "Ancien Testament," 84; Goppelt, 190, 204–5; Sieffert, "Die Heilsbedeutung," 397; Goldstein, "Kirche," 41; Carrez, "L'esclavage," 209, 216; Senior, "Conduct," 434; Leaney, "Passover," 248; see also Leaney, 33; Goppelt, "Mission ou Révolution?" 210; Selwyn, 91, 104.

53   For general discussion of this problem, see Thomas P. Osborne, "Guide Lines for Christian Suffering: A Source-Critical and Theological Study of 1 Peter 2,21–25," *Bib* 64 (1983) 381–87, esp. 383–87; Schutter, *Hermeneutic,* 143–44; Kelly, 118–19. That it did originate as a hymn, see, e.g., Martin, "Composition," 31; Schlier, "Adhortatio," 60; Feuillet, "Sacrifices," 710 ("probable"); Bultmann, "Bekenntnis- und Liedfragmente," 12 (the hymn speaks in the first person, the author in the second); Lohse, "Parenesis," 58 (all but 2:21b belong to that hymn); cf. also Schelkle, 82 ("ecclesial tradition").

use of an earlier hymn;[55] (4) the wider application is part of the author's strategy and does not require another source to account for it.[56] Further, the evident use in the "hymn" of language from Isaiah 53 places it outside the OT traditions normally used in the NT,[57] particularly in reference to Jesus' passion.[58] Nor are these verses similar to the three fragments of early traditional material most widely acknowledged (1 Tim 3:16; Phil 2:6–11; Col 1:15–20): none of them reflects specific OT passages, and all include references to glory as well as suffering. If the use of an earlier hymn is unlikely,[59] the author's own use of Isaiah 53 seems probable,[60] with the adaptations intended to follow the order of Christ's passion rather than the verses of Isaiah 53, vv. 22–23 reflecting the trial, and v. 24 the crucifixion.[61] That the author had

sources other than Isaiah 53, that is, eyewitness account of the passion[62] or the notion of vicarious suffering found in later Jewish writing,[63] seems unlikely.[64]

3. Theological Thrust

The admonition to slaves in 1 Pet 2:18–25 that they subordinate themselves to their masters is based not on social convention or political custom but on the slave's obligation to God: the subordination is to be carried out with all reverence for God (v. 18), as their unjust suffering is to be borne for the same reason (v. 19).[65] Their

---

54 E.g., Michel Gourgues, O.P., "La foi chrétienne primitive face à la croix: Le témoignage des formulaires pré-pauliniens," *ScEs* 2/18 (1989) 63. Osborne ("Guide Lines," 388 n. 38) lists it as occurring in 1:6, 8 (bis), 10, 12 (tris); 2:8 (bis), 10 (bis); 3:3, 4, 6, 21(?), 22; 4:5; 5:9, 12.

55 Osborne ("Guide Lines," 388), for example, argues that v. 24a-b is a combination of Isa 53:4, 5, 12. For more on 2:24c, see below where that verse is commented on.

56 So also Osborne, "Guide Lines," 388–89.

57 References to Isaiah 53 tend to be oblique (e.g., Mark 10:45; Heb 9:28), or highly fragmentary (e.g., Rom. 4:25a): or when some portion of Isaiah is quoted, it remains unexploited in relation to the passion of Jesus (e.g., Matt 8:17; Luke 22:37). The fullest citation is in Acts 8:32–33, and while it is understood to refer to Jesus, it receives no further explication; in the passion account, Luke ignores it. The long quotation of Isaiah 53 in *1 Clem.* 16.3–14 shows its increasing popularity. See Brox, 136; Hillyer, "Servant," 159–60; Best, 120; cf. Osborne, "Guide Lines," 385. For an attempt to account for the earlier lack of its use, and its full citation in 1 Pet 2:22–24, see Achtemeier, "Suffering Servant and Suffering Christ in 1 Peter," in A. J. Malherbe and W. A. Meeks, eds., *The Future of Christology: Essays in Honor of Leander E. Keck* (Minneapolis: Fortress, 1993) 176–88.

58 The accounts in Matthew and Mark, for example, ignore Isaiah 53 in favor of Psalm 22.

59 So also, e.g., Osborne, "Guide Lines," 408; Michaels, 136.

60 So also, e.g., Osborne, "Guide Lines," 388, 395; cf. Schutter, *Hermeneutic*, 143. The chiasm to which Schlosser ("Ancien Testament," 86) calls attention (v.

21a corresponds to vv. 24–25; v. 21b corresponds to vv. 22–23) would argue that the composer of v. 21 is also the composer of the remainder of the passage.

61 V. 22 = Isa 53:9, with a change from ἀνομίαν to ἁμαρτίαν; v. 23 reflects the silent lamb of Isa 53:7; v. 24a = Isa 53:5, with the addition of αὐτός and the substitution of ἀνήνεγκεν for φέρει; v. 24c = Isa 53:5b, with the substitution of οὗ for αὐτοῦ, the deletion of ἡμεῖς, and the change from ἰάθημεν to ἰάθητε; v. 25a = Isa 53:6a, with the deletion of πάντες and the change from ἐπλανήθημεν to ἦτε . . . πλανώμενοι. Such changes are fully in line with the ancient practice of adapting quotations to fit their present context (see Achtemeier, "*Omne verbum sonat,*" 27, esp. n. 155), and probably do not represent a different Greek text of Isaiah 53, as Schutter (*Hermeneutic,* 141) also observes.

62 So Cranfield (85): partly Isaiah 53, partly eyewitness; Best (119) and Schlosser ("Ancien Testament," 87) note correctly that the dependence on the OT largely rules that out.

63 E.g., 4 Macc 6:27–29; 17:22; less clearly 2 Macc 7:37–38. 4 Macc 18.4 concerns death on behalf of the law; cf. Best, 119.

64 So also Hillyer's attempt ("Servant," 151) to link the passage with the *Aqedah* of Genesis 22 appears unnecessarily complex to explain the evidence. Similarly, Leaney's attempt ("Passover," 247) to find the background for the theme of unjust suffering in Deut 26:6 appears rather far-fetched.

65 Because the slaves are called (εἰς τοῦτο γὰρ ἐκλήθητε, v. 21) to continue to do good (ἀγαθοποιοῦντες, v. 20) as Christ did, even if such acts are displeasing to the master and hence cause suffering, the subordination advocated here can hardly mean simply docility in an unpleasant cultural situation; cf. Senior, "Conduct,"

pattern for this is the suffering Christ himself, who, characteristically for our author, is described in language drawn from the OT.[66] While there is little question that slaves are indeed addressed directly in these verses, it is also clear from the language that the address is to a broader Christian audience than simply slaves. In the midst of circumstances that provide a vulnerable life, the slave is to live in a way irreproachable either to humans or to God, in that way serving as a paradigm for the way Christians, as vulnerable in society as the slaves are in their household, are to live in the midst of hostile surroundings. The point is therefore not social conformity; the point is to live a life in accord with social custom to the extent that it is possible without compromising their faith,[67] so as not to give more offense than is necessary.[68] Yet in those events where their Christian calling collides with social custom or political expectation, they must defy that custom[69] and be ready to suffer, as was Christ,[70] rather than abandon their calling to follow God (cf. 1:14–16).

Comment

■ **18** Although οἰκέται can specify slaves attached to a household rather than, for example, those who worked in the field,[71] it can also be used generically for slaves[72] and is probably to be understood in that way here. That is not to ignore the force of this term, however; it was most likely chosen to emphasize that slaves also belong to the Christian community as members of the household of God.[73]

The participle ὑποτασσόμενοι ("being subordinated") has often been understood to have the same force as the imperative ὑποτάγητε ("be subordinated") in v. 13,[74] where the verb is applied to all Christians. Such imperatival force may not simply be assumed as a common usage, however,[75] and in this instance the participle may well be connected to the four imperatives of the preceding verse[76] and be intended to function as an adverbial participle of means. In that case, the meaning would be that slaves are to carry out the mandates of v. 17 "by being subordinate . . . to your masters."[77] The issue is not presence or absence of imperatival force; that is given in v. 17. The issue is whether in this verse ὑποτασσόμενοι represents the content of the imperative, or the means whereby the imperatival content given in v. 17 is to be carried out; the grammar suggests the latter. Such subordination in turn is to be carried out ἐν παντὶ

433.

66 For more on this point, see the Introduction § V.B.3, "Controlling Metaphor."

67 Balch ("Hellenization/Acculturation," 97) misses this point when he assumes that failure also to admonish masters reinforced Roman hierarchical society. Advice to masters simply would not furnish an appropriate analogy to the situation of Christians within hostile Roman society.

68 So also, e.g., Brox, 127.

69 As Krodel (74–75) correctly observes, Christian conduct is finally not to be determined by the whims and ill will of pagans, but by Christ.

70 The point is not to imitate Christ—that is unnecessary since he suffered for us (2:21) and died once for all for sin (3:18; cf. 2:24c). Rather, the point is to follow (ἐπακολουθήσητε) the pattern (ὑπογραμμόν) of his faithfulness to his calling, even when that does require suffering; cf. Goppelt, "Der Staat," 19.

71 E.g., Michaels (138), who sees it as referring to household servants as a particular social group. It could include house stewards, librarians, secretaries, physicians, and the like, as Moffatt (126) observes. That this means Christianity is an urban phenomenon is not necessitated, however, as Best (117) and Cranfield (79) assert.

72 Philipps, *Kirche,* 36. The word was used as a common

contrast with δεσπότης as early as Aristotle *Magna Moralia* 1.33.15–17; for Hellenistic contrast, see LXX Prov 22:7; 30:10; Dio Chrysostom *Or.* 49.13, 16; 64.7, 9–10; 65.19, 21; 75.2; Philo *Ebr.* 131; *Rer. div. her.* 6; *Fug.* 3; *Som.* 2.108; *Spec. leg.* 1.126, 127; 2.67, 84.

73 See 2:5; cf. also Schweizer, 61; Calvin, 86; Bigg, 142. That the choice of οἰκέται is dictated by the author's using a household code, as Schelkle (78 n. 2) suggests, is countered by the use of the word δοῦλοι in the household codes found in Ephesians and Colossians.

74 E.g., Bengel, *Gnomon,* 739; Kelly, 116; Hart, 60; Michaels, 138; Combrini, "Structure," 41. In light of the imperative in v. 17, Daube's ("Participle," 482) assertion that "the participle cannot be construed in the classical manner" is robbed of at least some of its force.

75 See "Excursus: Imperatival Use of Participles in 1 Peter."

76 So also, e.g., Bigg, 142; Holmer and de Boor, 92. Philipps (*Kirche,* 42) argues that, contrary to Rom 13:1 and 1 Pet 2:13, the verb in this verse has only descriptive, not imperatival, force.

77 One cannot argue for imperatival force here on the analogy of the similar material in Col 3:22 and Eph 6:5 because of the very different vocabulary used

φόβῳ ("with all [godly] reverence"), with φόβῳ ("reverence"), referring not to the slaves' attitude to their owner[78] but to God.[79] Such a meaning is dictated not only by the normal use of that word in this epistle[80] but also by the present context, where in the immediately preceding verse Christians are commanded to "fear God" (τὸν θεὸν φοβεῖσθε) and in the immediately following verse are urged to a way of acting "because of a consciousness of God" (διὰ συνείδησιν θεοῦ).[81] Such a qualification of the slaves' subordination means that they are limited to carrying out those commands of their master which do not compromise their primary allegiance to God. All other commands (e.g., the command to engage in idolatrous forms of worship, to renounce Christ, or the like) are apparently to be resisted, even when suffering is the result.[82] In this, the slave is no different from all other Christians, who must refuse such participation (e.g., 4:3–4), even though it opens them to unjust suffering by reason of their faith (e.g., 3:14–17; 4:13–14, 16).

Such limitation is to be observed regardless of what kind of master the slave serves, whether fair or perverse. The Christian slave is no more to carry out the inappropriate commands of a good master than to refuse the appropriate commands of a bad master. The word σκολιός ("curved," "bent"; in a moral sense "crooked," "perverse"),[83] the more appropriate if it was a technical term of slaves for an impossible master,[84] points here to the fact that subordination does not depend on the moral goodness of the master but on the will of God. Christians, whether slave or free, may not withdraw from their duties in the world because it is unjust.[85] While slave owners were also designated as κύριος ("lord"), even in Christian tradition,[86] our author uses δεσπότης ("master"),[87] in all likelihood because he reserves the former term for Christ (e.g., 3:15).[88]

With the first conversion of slaves, a particularly poignant problem was introduced into the Christian community. The difference between slave and master, fundamental to the self-understanding of the Greco-Roman social order, was irrelevant with relation to conduct within the Christian community (e.g., 1 Cor 12:13; Gal 3:28; Eph 6:8; Col 3:11; cf. also 1 Pet 2:16).[89] Such a different status within and without the Christian community created the particular problem for Christian slaves.[90] While there is no indication that the demand of Christian slaves for freedom was a central problem in the communities to which our letter was addressed,[91] there is no question slavery was an onerous burden for those who had to bear it. Yet any attempt to carry out a social revolution in terms of eliminating the practice of slavery would have had terrible consequences, resulting in the slaves' crucifixion and the extermination of the Christian community.[92] To live in the Roman world, slaves had to continue to subordinate themselves to their masters, however unjust the master and unfair the social institution of slavery. Yet it was precisely that situation that made slaves paradigmatic for the status of all Christians within Greco-Roman society, and led the author to address these exhortations to that particular class of Christians.

■ **19** This verse forms a unity with v. 20, the purpose of

---

there: οἱ δοῦλοι, ὑπακούετε . . . κυρίοις instead of οἱ οἰκέται, ὑποτασσόμενοι . . . δεσπόταις; the tradition those two epistles share is quite different from that found here in 1 Peter.

78 As, e.g., Wand (79) and Grudem (125) argue.
79 So also, e.g., Brandt, "Wandel," 19; van Unnik, "Die Rücksicht," 76; Thompson, "Submissive," 70; Beare, 147; Kelly, 116; Michaels, 138; Cranfield, 82; Schelkle, 80; Holmer and de Boor, 98; Goppelt, 193; Margot, 46.
80 See n. 111 on 2:17 above.
81 So also Senior, 49.
82 With Goppelt, "Prinzipien," 291; Refoulé, "Bible," 473; van Unnik, "Teaching," 93; cf. Neugebauer, "Zur Deutung," 63.
83 So also, e.g., Goppelt, "Der Staat," 16.
84 As Spicq (108) avers.

85 With Goppelt, "Der Staat," 16.
86 E.g., Eph 6:5; Col 3:22.
87 As do, e.g., 1 Tim 6:11; Titus 2:9.
88 So also, e.g., Michaels, 138; cf. Goppelt, 192.
89 So also, e.g., Bauer, 35; Philipps, *Kirche*, 23, who also observes (41) that the direct address to slaves in this letter is in itself revolutionary, and calls the entire social order into question.
90 Schelkle, 79; Philipps, *Kirche*, 40.
91 As Balch (*Wives*, 107) correctly points out.
92 Cothenet, "Le réalisme," 570. Christian masters were expected to treat their slaves equitably; see *Did.* 4.10; *Barn.* 19.7; Ignatius *Poly.* 4.3.

which is to explain why it is necessary for a slave also to be subordinate to a perverse master.[93] The two verses together present an *aba'* arrangement, with v. 19 presenting the positive statement (*a*), v. 20a the negative (*b*), and v. 20b again the positive (*a'*). The two positive statements, vv. 19 and 20b, in their turn form a chiastic parallelism: *a* = τοῦτο γὰρ χάρις ("for this redounds to one's favor"); *b* = πάσχων ἀδίκως ("suffering unjustly"); *b'* = ἀγαθοποιοῦντες καὶ πάσχοντες ("when you do good and suffer"); *a'* = τοῦτο χάρις παρὰ θεῷ ("God looks upon it with favor").[94] Finally, the repetition of the phrase τοῦτο χάρις in vv. 19a, 20b forms an *inclusio*, setting the whole off as a rhetorical unit,[95] all of which shows the care with which the author has shaped these sentences.

The τοῦτο ("this") clause functions as the apodosis of the conditional sentence whose protasis is the εἰ ("when") clause,[96] with the εἰ clause functioning therefore as the antecedent of the τοῦτο;[97] χάρις is thus defined as patiently bearing unjust suffering. The meaning of χάρις is further qualified by the parallel phrase at the end of v. 20, which adds παρὰ θεῷ ("God looks upon it"): in both cases, therefore, the discussion is carried on from the divine perspective. Nevertheless, χάρις here does not have its usual meaning of divine grace; rather, it is used in the sense of something pleasing to God.[98] The parallel κλέος ("fame," "glory") in the negative statement in v. 20a provides further indication of its meaning here.

The phrase διὰ συνείδησιν θεοῦ ("because of consciousness of God") functions here as did the phrase ἐν παντὶ φόβῳ ("with all reverence") in v. 18:[99] it qualifies the action of the verb. What is at issue here is therefore suffering caused because the slave is a Christian,[100] not simply because he or she is recalcitrant or lazy.[101] Because the word συνείδησις is modified by θεοῦ, it does not carry the normal meaning of "conscience";[102] rather, it has the meaning of "awareness" or "consciousness" of God.[103] The point is that the actions which cause the suffering are motivated by an awareness of what God's will is in the situation (cf. 2:15), not by the character of the one inflicting the unjust punishment.[104] The phrase "suffering unjustly" (πάσχων ἀδίκως) is probably to be taken as an adverbial participle of attendant circumstance ("when you suffer unjustly") rather than of means ("by suffering unjustly"); the point is that pain is to be borne patiently even in those circumstances when it is undeserved.[105] Finally, it may be noted that the author,

---

93   That is the point of the γάρ which links v. 19 to v. 18.

94   Combrini ("Structure," 41) finds a chiasm consisting of χάρις—ὑποφέρει—πάσχων (v. 19)/πάσχοντες—ὑπομενεῖτε—χάρις (v. 20b), but that omits the element of suffering unjustly, found in both halves of the chiasm.

95   So also, e.g., Michaels, 142.

96   The εἰ that introduces this clause marks it as a condition of reality, and can be rendered "when." The point is not the appropriate behavior *should* this happen, but the appropriate behavior *when* it happens, with the assurance that it will.

97   Cf. Michaels, 139.

98   An exact parallel to this use is found in Luke 6:23–25; so also, e.g., Selwyn, 89; Bigg, 143; Michaels, 135, 139. On its meaning, see Gundry, "*Verba Christi*," 341; Schutter, *Hermeneutic*, 48; Kelly, 116; Beare, 147; Best, 118; Spicq, 109.

99   So also Michaels, 140.

100   So also, e.g., Goppelt, 196; idem, "Der Staat," 16; Refoulé, "Bible," 473.

101   The definitive statement of this point is made in 4:14–16. The slaves are therefore urged to be subordinate as much as possible, since there will be enough suffering as a result of their being "insubordinate" on Christian grounds to what is required of them.

102   Its regular meaning in the NT; cf. Romans, 1 and 2 Corinthians, Hebrews. When it carries that meaning and is modified, it is with an adjective (ἀγαθή, Acts 23:1; 1 Tim 1:5, 19; 1 Pet 3:16, 21; καλή Heb 13:18) rather than a noun.

103   This is generally held; see, e.g., Brox, 127; Windisch, 64; Wand, 80; Best, 119; Moffatt, 126; Kelly, 117; Cranfield, 83; Bengel, *Gnomon*, 739; but see Schelkle, 80 n. 1. The θεοῦ is an objective genitive, as, e.g., Beare (148) and Hart (61) rightly note; Selwyn (176–77) identifies it as a genitive of "inner reference," which he differentiates from an objective genitive.

104   Cf. also Beare, 147; Holmer and de Boor, 99.

105   The notion of a slave suffering unjustly would be an anomaly for Greco-Roman culture, since the slave is chattel, and hence the categories "just" and "unjust" do not apply to a slave as they do to other human beings (Aristotle *Nicomachean Ethics* 5.6[1134b]; he also applies it to children being punished by parents; I owe this reference to Best, 118); see also Bigg, 145; Schelkle, 80. On this whole point, see also Balch, "Early Christian Criticism," 165.

by making the subject of the condition τις ("anyone"), clearly intends here to make a general statement, not one applicable to slaves alone.[106] It is further indication of the paradigmatic nature of this address to slaves.[107]

■ **20** Included within the larger chiastic arrangement of vv. 19–20,[108] this verse, intended to explain why only unjust suffering is creditworthy,[109] also displays a chiastic structure (abb'a'), with the first and last phrases providing the a and a', and the two clauses introduced by εἰ furnishing the b and b'.[110]

Taken in itself, the verse has nothing particularly Christian about it. The word κλέος, used only here in the NT, has the meaning of "fame" or "glory," and the two participles (ἀμαρτάνοντες, κολαφιζόμενοι)[111] can mean simply doing wrong[112] and being punished for it.[113] The

second conditional clause is a familiar piece of Hellenistic wisdom, namely, that suffering injustice was superior to doing it,[114] and there is nothing specifically Christian about the concept of ἀγαθοποιοῦντες;[115] it can mean simply comportment appropriate to what is good for the general welfare of one's fellow citizens.[116]

Set within the context of the closing phrase παρὰ θεῷ,[117] which parallels the phrase διὰ συνείδησιν θεοῦ of v. 19, however, the verse takes on a profoundly Christian character. The warning not to suffer because of wrongdoing is addressed specifically to Christians in 4:15,[118] doing good is identified as the will of God in 2:15,[119] and the patient endurance of unjust suffering finds its justification in the example of Christ in the immediately following verses.[120]

---

106 Cf. also Michaels, 140; Brox, 128.

107 Brox (133) is nevertheless surely wrong when he avers that the verse meant any unjust suffering, not only suffering due to one's Christian faith; that is to ignore the qualifying phrase διὰ συνείδησιν θεοῦ in this verse and τοῦτο χάρις παρὰ θεῷ in v. 20.

108 See the comments on the structure of the two verses above, under the comment on v. 19.

109 The γάρ with which it begins indicates it intends to give the reason for the preceding statement, and functions in the same way as the γάρ that introduced v. 19.

110 Goppelt (197) notes the parallelism between v. 20a and 20b, but does not call attention to their chiastic structure; he also identifies the form as that of a diatribe (196), presumably because the readers are directly addressed by means of question (v. 20a) and answer (v. 20b).

111 Because both sets of participles (ἀμαρτάνοντες καὶ κολαφιζόμενοι, ἀγαθοποιοῦντες καὶ πάσχοντες) are in the present tense, the implication is that patience (ὑπομενεῖτε) and the action of each set of them are concurrent. Because of the parallel construction between the two clauses, the causal relationship implied in the first ("because you do ill you are beaten") is probably also to be carried over into the second, as Goppelt (197) suggests, rather than seeing the latter as concessive ("even though you do good you suffer"). It was this causal relationship that gave poignancy to the predicament of Christian slaves: even when they did the good by following God's will, it might have necessarily involved disobedience to a non-Christian master, and punishment would then ensue.

112 The basic meaning of ἀμαρτάνω is to be wide of the mark, and thus, in the sphere of moral activity,

wrong.

113 One is not to find in κολαφιζόμενοι a reference to Jesus' suffering simply because the same word is used of his abuse in Mark 14:65, as Kelly (117–18) notes. That it intends to introduce the reference to Jesus' suffering, as Selwyn (178) thinks, is therefore wide of the mark: there is no indication in any Christian tradition that Jesus' abuse was the result of his having done wrong!

114 E.g., Plato *Gorgias* 509; Dio Chrysostom *Or.* 47.25; Philo *Jos.* 20 (I owe the first and third references to Wand, 80).

115 For a discussion of the difference in understanding of good acts in Judaism (basically alms to the needy) and in Greek thought (good deeds to any class of people), see van Unnik, "Teaching," 86–90. In terms of that contrast, one suspects that our author is close to the Greek understanding.

116 E.g., Refoulé, "Bible," 481; van Unnik, "Classical Parallel," 110. Even the notion of resolute endurance to suffering producing subsequent glory is familiar; cf. Seneca's reference (*Prov.* 3.9) to Regulus as a pattern of enduring torture; the greater it is, the greater will be his glory.

117 Its emphatic position at the end of the sentence shows its importance for understanding the verse.

118 As Michaels (141) notes, Christian patience is of value only in the context of doing good; in itself, suffering has no intrinsic value.

119 Michaels, 142; cf. Best, 119. To argue that this shows Christians are being advised to take over secular cultural values because the content of doing good is not defined is to overlook the fact that the readers are Christian, and are thus not ignorant of what God wants them to do.

120 Kelly (118) calls attention to the deep imprint made

The point is not, however, that such suffering is equivalent to grace.[121] While the word χάρις is used, it is paralleled by the two more general phrases τοῦτο γὰρ χάρις ("for this is grace," v. 19) and ποῖον γὰρ κλέος ("For what glory [is there]," v. 20) which define its semantic scope, and thus give to χάρις the meaning of God's favorable judgment on the activity here under discussion.[122] In its present context, therefore, the verse, particularly its second half, represents the point of this section[123] and indeed one of the major thrusts of the letter as a whole; its repetition throughout the letter[124] shows it to be paradigmatic and to represent the vocation of all Christians.[125]

■ **21** As in the case of vv. 19 and 20, the introductory conjunction γάρ[126] answers an implied question growing out of v. 20, namely, why does God look with favor on Christian slaves' suffering for doing the good?[127] The answer is that such activity conforms with their Christian call, extended to them in the gospel preached to them

(cf. 1:12, 22–25).[128] The goal of the call, identified by the telic phrase εἰς τοῦτο ("for this very thing"), looks backward to v. 20b rather than forward;[129] the ensuing ὅτι clause then gives the reason for such a call to suffering for doing good,[130] namely, the similar fate of Christ. The verb ἔπαθεν, by this time virtually a technical term for the suffering of Christ,[131] may also signify his death.[132] That meaning is a commonplace of Christian tradition, particularly with the added phrase ὑπὲρ ὑμῶν ("for you"),[133] a phrase that, in this context of exemplary suffering, seems unnecessary and thus, it is argued, shows the influence of the underlying creedal formulae.[134]

The problem with such an understanding of this phrase is presented by the presence of the word καί ("also"). Related to the verb,[135] it implies another suffering in addition to that of Christ. Since that other suffering in this context is the suffering of Christian slaves (v. 20b), the implication is that as Christ did good and suffered, so also slaves do good and suffer, and that

---

on early Christian literature by Christ's patience, e.g., Phil 2:5–8; 1 Thess 1:6; 2 Thess 3:5; Heb 13:13; *1 Clem.* 16.17; Ignatius *Eph.* 10.3. That the contrast between v. 20a and 20b is that the slave in 20a is dominated by thoughts of revenge and anger, while in 20b by thoughts of love, as Brandt ("Wandel," 20) avers, is, even given the example of Christ that follows, to psychologize the text in an unwarranted manner. That it represents the author's equivalent of Jesus' command to love one's neighbor, as Michaels (136) argues, is not immediately evident.

121 As, e.g., Goppelt (196) avers.

122 It is used the same way in Luke 1:30 of Mary, Luke 2:52 of Jesus, and Luke 6:32–35 of certain types of activity. It bears the same meaning in such passages as Exod 33:12, 16; Prov 12:2; Esth 2:15, 17; see *Hermas Man.* 5.1.5; *Sim.* 5.2.10; Philo *Gig.* 12.1; *Deus imm.* 104.1; *Abr.* 131.5. Cf. Michaels, 142; Selwyn, 89; cf. also van Unnik, "Teaching," 93.

123 The example of Christ's comportment at the time of his crucifixion, which is the burden of vv. 22–24, is intended to reinforce this point, as v. 21b makes clear.

124 E.g., 3:17; 4:15; 5:10.

125 So also, e.g., Thompson, "Submissive," 73; Goppelt, 196.

126 As a postpositive conjunction, it cannot be placed at the head of a sentence, even though it functions as the first word in its capacity as a conjunction.

127 This verse shows that there is no notion in v. 20b of some general truth such as "unjust suffering nobly endured redeems"; what is at issue is the need to

follow Christ in enduring innocent suffering.

128 Forms of καλέω function in 1 Peter as a technical term of the electing and saving call of God (e.g., 3:9; 5:10); see Goppelt, 199; cf. also Osborne, "Guide Lines," 391. As in the Jesus traditions, following him is a matter of his choosing people, not their choosing him, as Goppelt (203) points out.

129 It therefore functions in the same way as the τοῦτο of v. 20b, as Wand (81) and Michaels 142) note correctly.

130 Less likely is the explanation that it furnishes motivation for following the call, as Osborne ("Guide Lines," 390) would have it.

131 So, e.g., Goppelt, 200.

132 Cf. Luke 22:15; Acts 17:3; Heb 13:12; but it can also mean simply "suffer" as it does in Mark 8:31, where an additional reference to his death is attached.

133 Cf. Luke 22:19, 20; Rom 5:6, 8; 8:32, 34; 14:9, 15; 15:3; Eph 5:2; 1 Thess 5:10; Titus 2:14; 1 John 3:16. As 1 Cor 11:24 shows, it was also part of the eucharistic formula; cf. Kelly, 119; Schelkle, 81 n. 2; Goppelt, 199; Osborne, "Guide Lines," 390.

134 So, e.g., Schelkle (81) argues; he sees additional influence in the content of v. 24; cf. also Kelly, 119. Windisch (65) argues that the phrase ὑπὲρ ὑμῶν is included to show that Christ's suffering, while exemplary, was also representative (cf. Cranfield, 83: "vicarious") and hence unrepeatable; cf. also Best, 119.

135 Not to the phrase ὑπὲρ ὑμῶν, as Osborne ("Guide Lines," 390) notes correctly; καί functions the same way in 3:17, as Michaels (142) has observed.

as Christ suffered for them, so they are called to suffer "for him," that is, because of their devotion to him. Christ's suffering thus makes their suffering a necessary part of their Christian vocation, because, as they suffer for him, so he "also suffered for them" (καὶ Χριστὸς ἔπαθεν ὑπὲρ ὑμῶν). While this meaning may seem to lack the theological profundity of a reference to the vicarious suffering of Christ,[136] it represents a meaning attested elsewhere in the NT,[137] fits the context exactly,[138] and obviates the need to find a reference to Christ's death as well as his suffering in the verb ἔπαθεν, again something unnecessary in this context.[139] It is therefore likely that these words represent not so much the author's dependence on creedal formulae as his own composition for this particular context.[140]

In this context, the effect of Christ's suffering for us was to leave us an example to follow.[141] The word for "example" (ὑπογραμμόν) is used only here in the NT, and means literally a pattern of letters of the alphabet by means of which children, by tracing over, learned to write.[142] That pattern in turn has as its purpose (ἵνα)[143] following the example of Christ (lit. "his footsteps"),[144] the content of which is then given in vv. 22–24.[145] This has often been understood in the sense of imitating Christ. While that notion is present in the NT,[146] the verb here means not to "imitate" but to "follow" (ἐπακολουθήσητε)[147] Jesus in his willingness to endure suffering, a notion deeply rooted in early Christian tradition.[148] It is a call to discipleship rather than a call to imitation, and, as elsewhere, a call to understand slaves as paradigmatic of all Christians.[149]

■ 22 This verse begins the explication of the "pattern" (ὑπογραμμόν) provided to Christians for their behavior by

136 The author of course knows of Christ's vicarious, atoning sacrifice and refers to it where the context calls for it (e.g., 1:18–19; 2:24; cf. 1:2); that is not the case here, however.

137 Christians suffer "for" (ὑπέρ) Christ in Phil 1:29; in this context, cf. Col 1:24.

138 That a person of the obvious intelligence of our author would include an intrusive phrase such as ὑπὲρ ὑμῶν for no better reason than its traditional presence in formulae like this strains one's credulity.

139 Otherwise one needs to postulate, as does Goldstein ("Kirche," 53), the presence of two soteriological schemes in this verse, viz., Christ's representative death for the sins of all and his suffering as an example to be followed, a postulation that further strains credulity.

140 So also, e.g., Schutter, *Hermeneutic*, 64 n. 129. For more on this point, see the discussion of the origin of the material in these verses in the Analysis of this passage above ("Origin").

141 The participle ὑπολιμπάνων is probably to be construed as an adverbial participle of attendant circumstance, here displaying the result of the action of the verb ἔπαθεν.

142 Clement of Alexandria (*Strom.* 5.8.49) refers to a ὑπογραμμόν consisting of four words (μάρπτε, σφίγξ, κλωψ, ζβυχθηδόν); taken together they contain all the letters of the Greek alphabet (I was pointed to this passage by Michaels, 144). *1 Clement* also uses it in the sense of a pattern for behavior, namely, Paul as a model of patience (ὑπομονῆς), 5.7; Christ as a model of humility, 16.17; people who perform good works

as models of Christian behavior, 33.8 (cf. 30). A second meaning pointed to by Selwyn (179), namely, an architectural or artistic sketch whose details others were to fill out, is not relevant in this context.

143 To call the ἵνα clause "epexegetic," as does Beare (148), is to miss its telic force in this context; it gives the purpose of the pattern, i.e., that it be followed.

144 The word ἴχνεσιν, though never used in this sense in the LXX, is so used in Rom 4:12; cf. 2 Cor 12:18.

145 As Brox (135) rightly points out.

146 Such a notion of imitation is present in the NT, but primarily in terms of imitating other people (Paul: 1 Cor 4:16; 2 Thess 3:7, 9, churches of God: 1 Thess 2:14; faithful Christians: Heb 6:12; faith of church leaders: Heb 13:7; "the good": 3 John 11). There is one call to imitate God (Eph 5:1), but the call to imitate Jesus is indirect, i.e., to imitate Paul who imitates Jesus (1 Cor 11:1; 1 Thess 1:6).

147 Goppelt (202) correctly points to this verb as a Christian technical term for being a follower of Jesus.

148 It is based in Jesus' own words in Mark 8:34 par. and is reflected in a variety of formulations, e.g., Heb 13:13; Phil 2:5; 1 Thess 1:6, 2 Thess 3:5; *1 Clem.* 16.17 (with the word ὑπογραμμόν); Ignatius *Eph.* 10.3. Cf. Schelkle, 82; Millauer, *Leiden*, 102.

149 As shown by 3:9 with the same phrase εἰς τοῦτο ἐκλήθητε; for a similar general call to suffer, see Matt 10:38 par.; 16:24; Luke 14:27; cf. Schelkle, 81; Hiebert, "Example," 33; Calvin, 89. As Beare (149) notes, to call slaves to pattern their lives on Christ confers a considerable dignity upon them.

the behavior of Christ in a situation of unjust suffering. The emphasis is on Christ's innocence in that situation; only if the slaves, and all Christians for whom they are here paradigmatic, are similarly innocent of evil will their suffering qualify as following the pattern of Christ (cf. 3:14; 4:14).[150]

With a single exception (ἁμαρτίαν rather than ἀνομίαν), this verse corresponds exactly to the LXX of Isa 53:9b.[151] The change adapts the passage more exactly to the present context with its reference to sin in 2:19, and the subsequent reference in 2:24 to Isa 53:4, where ἁμαρτίας is used,[152] and makes it more directly related to the sinlessness of Jesus.[153] If one notes in addition that words from the νομ- stem are absent altogether from 1 Peter,[154] the likelihood increases that the change in Isa

53:9b is due directly to our author, rather than to his dependence on some source other than the text of Isaiah.[155]

■ 23 Unlike vv. 22 and 24, there is no reflection of language from Isaiah 53 in this verse; in light of the clear dependence in those verses on that passage from Isaiah, however, the silence of the sacrificial lamb described in Isa 53:7[156] could well lie behind this verse,[157] particularly if the author had in mind the silence Jesus maintained in face of the abuse he received during his trial.[158] Yet the point of the first two clauses is not specifically Jesus' silence; it is rather that in face of verbal abuse he did not retaliate in kind. Such nonretaliation in kind, while certainly true of the passion, is nevertheless also true of the whole of Jesus' career.[159] The use of the

---

150 See on this point Brox, 136; Michaels, 145. That the verse means Christ did not take part in "social and political intrigues," as Reicke (99) avers is, in this context, probably wide of the mark.

151 Osborne ("L'utilisation," 71) notes the divergence of the LXX from the MT, which has no verb to correspond with εὑρέθη. The suggestion that our verse depends on 2 Cor 5:21 (Barnettt, *Literary Influence*, 63) or that it is based on Peter's witness of the events of Jesus' trial (Moffatt, 127) is less than compelling, particularly since, according to the Gospel narratives, Peter was not present at that event, as Windisch (65) points out.

152 The two were virtually synonymous for the LXX of Isaiah, as shown by the paralleling of ἁμαρτίας with ἀνομίας in 53:5, and the use of ἁμαρτίας in 53:4.

153 A point already assumed in Christian tradition; see John 8:46; 2 Cor 5:21; Heb 4:15; 7:26; 1 John 3:5; cf. Schelkle, 84; Wand, 82.

154 So also Osborne, "Guide Lines," 394.

155 For these reasons it is unlikely, as Schelkle (83–84) would have it, that the author is dependent on an early, admittedly rarely attested (Luke 22:37 = Isa 53:12; Mark 10:45; 14:24 = Isa 53:5) Christology based on a written form of Isaiah 53 different from the LXX, or that it derives from an earlier hymn which in its turn was based on Isaiah 53, as Goldstein ("Kirche," 42) avers. It is much more likely that our author took it directly from Isa 53:9, and that he is quoting from memory, as Beare (149) argues, especially in light of ancient book technology and writing practices; see Achtemeier, *Omne verbum sonat*, 10–12 et passim.

156 Cf. the twice-repeated οὐκ ἀνοίγει τὸ στόμα, and the phrase ἀμνὸς . . . ἄφωνος.

157 Perhaps augmented, as Schlosser ("Ancien Testa-

ment," 89) suggests, by the innocent (ἄκακος) lamb of LXX Jer 11:19, which stands in a context also referring to God's righteous judgment. The suggestion of Best (121) that Isa 53:12 is reflected in this verse because both use a form of the verb παραδίδωμι (in Isaiah παρεδόθη, in our verse παρεδίδου) is less likely since the point in Isa 53:12 is related not to our verse but to the one following it, v. 24.

158 On Jesus' silence, see Mark 14:61; 15:5; Matt 26:62–63; 27:12, 14; Luke 23:9; John 19:9; cf. Selwyn, 79; Goppelt, 208. That lack of direct reference to Isaiah 53 indicates the verse is based on "eye-witness memory," as Cranfield (85) and Chase ("Peter," 787) aver, owes more to pious imagination than to the biblical or historical evidence. Even in Luke, the only account where Jesus looked at Peter (after the third denial), the look prompted Peter to leave, and only thereafter did the trial begin, a point Love ("First Epistle," 72) overlooks. More soberly, Schelkle (84) suggests the author may have known historical traditions about the trial of Jesus.

159 It is summed up in Jesus' words about loving one's enemies; cf. Matt 5:43–48 in the context of 5:38–42. It also passed into early Christian catechesis, as Kelly (121) correctly observes; cf. Rom 12:17–20; 1 Thess 5:15; 1 Pet 3:9; Polycarp *Phil.* 2.2. Patient nonretaliation was also applauded by Plutarch (*Mor.*, *De capienda ex inimicus utilitate* 90D): "in the midst of reviling (silence) is dignified" (ἡ σιγὴ . . . ἐν δὲ λοιδορίαις σεμνόν). Citing Socrates and Hercules as examples, Plutarch affirms that nothing is more dignified and noble than "to maintain silence when an enemy carries on reviling" (τοῦ λοιδοροῦντος ἐχθροῦ τὴν ἡσυχίαν ἄγειν; I was pointed to this reference by Charles H. Talbert, *Learning through Suffering: The Educational Value of Suffering in the New*

imperfect tense for the verbs in these clauses,[160] a tense that describes repeated, even habitual, action, is also more appropriate to Jesus' whole career than simply to the passion. Regular nonretaliation is further underlined by the third clause, again with its verb in the imperfect tense, where the positive aspect of non-retaliation is given, namely, leaving judgment to God. The absence of an object for the verb leaves unclear what it is that Jesus delivered over to God, whether his person,[161] in which case this could well be a rather clear reference to the passion,[162] or his cause,[163] which could have broader implications; that it refers to his enemies[164] seems less likely in a context of nonretaliation (v. 23a-b) and bearing the burden of others (v. 24).

Within its context, then, the verse stands as a com-mentary on v. 22b,[165] showing how Jesus remained sinless during his life (v. 22a)—including, to be sure, his passion[166]—in the face of unjust abuse by maintaining a stance of nonretaliation in the face of precisely the kind of verbal abuse faced by the readers.[167] The close linkage of this verse to its context[168] and its lack of reference to Isaiah 53 mark it as a composition of the author himself.[169]

■ **24** The first half of v. 24a, with its reference to Christ himself bearing our sins,[170] reflects the language of Isa 53:4, 11, and 12.[171] It is difficult to tell whether the author had one of these verses specifically in mind, since the somewhat redundant αὐτός reflects Isa 53:11, the pronoun ἡμῶν reflects 53:4,[172] and the verb form ἀνήνεγκεν reflects 53:12.[173] The second half of v. 24a

Testament and Its Milieu (Zacchaeus Studies: New Testament; Collegeville, Minn.: Liturgical Press, 1991) 47.

160 That the language is not derived directly from Isaiah 53 indicates that the choice of tenses for the verbs rests directly with the author.

161 So, e.g., Bigg, 146. Hiebert ("Example," 38) cites Gal 2:20; Eph 5:2, 25; Selwyn (179) cites Luke 23:46 (although there the verb is παρατίθημι) as examples to justify this understanding.

162 For an example of such delivering over, see Jesus' prayer in Gethsemane, Mark 14:36 par.

163 So, e.g., Kelly (121), who points to LXX Jer 11:20 (πρὸς σὲ ἀπεκάλυψα τὸ δικαίωμά μου, "I have revealed my judgment to you"), and Schlosser ("Ancien Testament," 90), who points to Josephus *Ant.* 4.33 (παραχώρησον τὴν κρίσιν τῷ θεῷ, "give way to God in the matter of judgment"); and 7.199 (περὶ πάντων ἐπιστρέψας κριτῇ τῷ θεῷ, "committing the whole matter to God as judge") as parallel formulae.

164 So, e.g., Michaels, 147. Schiwy (49) thinks it includes both Jesus and his tormentors; Osborne ("Guide Lines," 397) thinks it impossible to determine the grammatical object.

165 So also Michaels, 145; cf. Best, 120.

166 The clear reference to the passion in the following v. 24 means that event remains very much in the author's mind, although the first two phrases in this verse indicate he is here concerned more with verbal than physical abuse.

167 So also Michaels (145), who points to 2:12, 15; 3:16; 4:4 as examples; he notes that it further shows these remarks are not limited to slaves.

168 So also, e.g., Osborne, "Guide Lines," 386; cf. Schlosser, "Ancien Testament," 88.

169 Conceded even by those who see here dependence

on an earlier hymn; cf. the discussion in Osborne, "Guide Lines," 385.

170 Michel Gourgues argues that the origin of the tradition reflected here that Christ died "for our sins" lies in the anomaly that while Christians believed Christ was without sin (here, v. 22), Deut 21:22–23 says hanging from a tree meant death for sin; the solution: the sins for which Christ died were not his, but ours ("La foi chrétienne primitive," 67–68).

171 Isa 53:4, οὗτος τὰς ἁμαρτίας ἡμῶν φέρει ("this one bears our sins"); 53:11, τὰς ἁμαρτίας αὐτῶν αὐτὸς ἀνοίσει ("their sins he himself will bear"); 53:12, αὐτὸς ἁμαρτίας πολλῶν ἀνήνεγκεν ("he himself bore the sins of many"); 1 Pet 2:24aα, ὃς τὰς ἁμαρτίας ἡμῶν αὐτὸς ἀνήνεγκεν ("he who himself bore our sins").

172 The change in pronoun from second (in the verb ἐκλήθητε, v. 21) to first here is sufficiently accounted for by this dependence on the language of Isaiah 53, and need not call on an earlier confessional formulation to account for it.

173 While MT Isa 53:12 has singular (חטא) where LXX has plural, both Isaiah mss. from DSS read here the plural (חטאי); thus 1 Peter is not of necessity bound to the LXX for that plural, and may have made its own translation. On this point see Hermann Patsch, "Zum alttestamentlichen Hintergrund von Römer 4.25 und I. Petrus 2.24," *ZNW* 60 (1969) 278–79. One may also note the singular חלי in Isa 53:4.

relates that act to Christ's crucifixion with the reference to τὸ ξύλον, a word that means "wood" or anything made of it[174] and that then is used to mean the cross;[175] the author thus reflects here a strand of early Christian tradition found also in John 1:29 and Heb 9:28.[176] The allusion to Christ's death on the cross is strengthened with the phrase ἐν τῷ σώματι ("in his body").[177] The phrase ἐπὶ τὸ ξύλον ("upon the cross") used with the verb ἀνήνεγκεν ("bore") resembles a phrase customarily used in the LXX for laying a sacrifice upon the altar,[178] a fact that has led to the suggestion that we have here cultic language, with Christ playing the role of the sacrificial animal.[179] Yet the object of the verb is not Christ's body[180] but τὰς ἁμαρτίας ἡμῶν ("our sins"), and nowhere in any OT cultic language is there the notion of sins being laid upon the altar.[181] To suggest that τὰς ἁμαρτίας means "sin offering"[182] has no parallel in the LXX, and to find in τὸ ξύλον a reference to the cross as an altar has no analogy in the rest of the NT.[183] To solve that problem by finding here a reference to the scapegoat (Lev 16:20–22) upon whom the sins of the people were placed[184] overlooks that the scapegoat was not sacrificed but released in the wilderness, hardly an apt comparison

for a reference to the cross. The best solution is probably to see here the author's own adaptation of Isaiah 53 to describe the redemptive significance of Christ's death on the cross.

While v. 24b does not reflect the language of Isaiah 53, it does reflect Pauline language, particularly in the contrast "sin/righteousness" (ταῖς ἁμαρτίαις/τῇ δικαιοσύνῃ) and, if the participle ἀπογενόμενοι here refers to dying, a meaning it can bear,[185] in a second contrast between "dying/living" (ἀπογενόμενοι/ζήσωμεν).[186] Yet Paul nowhere uses ἀπογίνομαι to mean "to die,"[187] and our author, in the one other passage that has a similar contrast between death and life (3:18b), uses the verb θανατόω ("die"). Although ἀπογενόμενοι is used with a dative of reference (ταῖς ἁμαρτίαις)[188] rather than a genitive of separation, which would clearly mark its meaning as "depart from,"[189] the notion of Christ bearing one's sins away and thus one's being separated from them need not include the idea of one's dying with Christ.[190] Nor is there any hint here of the Christian's life being made possible by Christ's resurrection; rather, in light of the larger context of this verse (2:15–16, 20–21), the phrase τῇ δικαιοσύνῃ ζήσωμεν ("we may live in

174 E.g., Matt 26:47; Acts 16:24; 1 Cor 3:12; Rev 2:7.

175 Acts 5:30; 10:39; 13:29; Gal 3:13, where LXX Deut 21:23 is quoted; cf. Beare, 150; Osborne, "Guide Lines," 400. Schutter (*Hermeneutic*, 142) notes the aptness of this figure for slaves, since crucifixion was above all the death inflicted upon slaves.

176 So also, e.g., Best, 121. That the author of our verse had Deut 21:23 in mind when he added this latter phrase is thus not the necessary inference that Bigg (147) makes of it.

177 To derive the phrase from 1 Cor 11:24, as does Hart (62), is to put too fine a point on it.

178 ἀναφέρειν ἐπὶ τὸ θυσιαστήριον, e.g., Gen 8:20; Lev 14:20; 2 Chr 35:16; 1 Bar 1:10; 1 Macc 4:53; it is also found in the NT in Jas 2:21. On this matter, cf. Hiebert, "Example," 40.

179 So, e.g., Spicq, 112; Bigg, 147; Schweizer, 64; Schwank et al., 55; Selwyn, 93–94.

180 As, e.g., Schelkle (85) must maintain to avoid the notion of the sacrifice itself being our sins.

181 So Wand, 83; Beare, 149; Selwyn, 180; Bigg, 147.

182 As does, e.g., Bigg (147).

183 So Sieffert, "Die Heilsbedeutung," 402.

184 So, e.g., Goldstein, "Kirche," 43–44 n. 27; Wand, 83; Schelkle, 85. Windisch (65–66) suggests the αὐτός may be intended to stand in contrast to the high priest, who put the peoples' sins on another and did

not himself bear them.

185 See LSJ 194, s.v. "ἀπογίνομαι," 194, II.2; J. H. Moulton, G. Milligan, *The Vocabulary of the Greek Testament* (London: Hodder and Stoughton, 1914; reprinted Grand Rapids: Eerdmans, 1949) 59, and the references given in both lexicons; cf. also Windisch (66) for further instances.

186 The double contrast is typical of Paul's letter to the Romans, e.g., 5:17, 21; 6:12–13, 16–23; 8:10; see Michaels, 149; Feuillet, "Sacrifices," 710. Beare (150) thinks this means dependence on Romans 6, an idea more persuasive for those who see a baptismal tract underlying 1 Peter. Cf. Cranfield (86), who suggests that since the contrast is so prominent in that chapter where Paul discusses baptism, our author may also have had baptism in mind, although he thinks that need not imply dependence.

187 In fact, Paul never uses it; it appears only here in the NT.

188 So also, e.g., Selwyn 181.

189 A point made by Osborne, "Guide Lines," 400.

190 That is the case with the idea of Christ's death as "ransom," e.g., Mark 10:45; the same idea is present in 1 Pet 1:18–19. Kelly (123) argues that the verb means "cease from" and is unrelated to the theology of Romans 6.

righteousness") is more likely to refer to living a life in accordance with God's will.[191] The meaning of "righteousness" (δικαιοσύνη) in the one other place it is used in our letter (3:14) also points in the same direction.[192] Direct influence of Paul is thus to be discounted.

The third clause, v. 24c, is taken directly from Isa 53:5,[193] with two changes. First, our author substitutes the relative pronoun οὗ for Isaiah's αὐτοῦ ("his"), evidently for stylistic reasons; there is no change in meaning. Second, our author changes the verb from first to second person (ἡμεῖς ἰάθημεν ["we were healed"] to ἰάθητε ["you were healed"]). In doing that, he resumes the second person address contained in vv. 18–23[194] and continued in v. 25.[195] One therefore needs to account not so much for the change from first to second person in v. 24c as for the change from second to first person in v. 24a-b, since they are the only significant variations in person in this passage. The likelihood is that that change was prompted by our author's dependence in v. 24a on Isaiah 53, with its repeated reference in vv. 4, 5, 6 to τὰς ἁμαρτίας ἡμῶν ("*our* sins," cf. τὰς ἀνομίας ἡμῶν ["*our* transgressions"], v. 5), and in v. 24b because of its dependence on v. 24a. Thus, so long as the phrase "our sin" was

thematic (v. 24a, b), he used the first person, reverting immediately to the second person (24c) as soon as the discussion centering on that phrase was concluded.[196]

Whether v. 24c recalls specifically the scourging of Jesus (Mark 15:15; Matt 27:26)[197] or more generally his death[198] is probably impossible to determine. What is evident is that our author sees in Jesus' death a vicarious suffering by which a new life freed from sin is made possible,[199] a theology already nascent in the description of the suffering servant in Isaiah 53 from which this verse is largely drawn.[200] Because Christ's innocent suffering bears away the sin that separates Jesus' followers from God, they are free to endure similarly innocent suffering, because they know that such suffering, far from being evidence of their rejection by God, is in fact proof that they have been called by him (2:21). That is the reason for including in a call to suffering a statement about Christ's atoning death, not because a slavish following of an earlier tradition caused our author to include this supposedly inappropriate material at this point.

■ **25** The change in topic from being healed by Jesus' suffering to straying like sheep[201] reflects the sequence

---

191 Michaels (149) cites Titus 2:12 and 1 John 4:9 as parallels to such a meaning of ζήσωμεν; see also Goldstein, "Kirche," 46; Schweizer, 65; van Unnik, "Redemption," 56.

192 If δικαιοσύνη is, as seems likely, a dative of sphere within which something occurs or is done, such a meaning would find further support.

193 So also, e.g., Hiebert, "Example," 42; Selwyn, 181.

194 In v. 18, the ὑποτασσόμενοι, because of its dependence on the fourfold imperative verbs of v. 17, is second person; v. 20, ὑπομενεῖτε (bis); v. 21, ἐκλήθητε.

195 Ἦτε, ἐπεστράφητε, ὑμῶν.

196 That the ἰάθημεν of Isa 53:5 was changed to ἰάθητε because this final clause was particularly applicable to slaves, as, e.g., Beare (150–51) and Osborne ("Guide Lines," 388) argue, is therefore an unnecessary postulate.

197 So, e.g., Selwyn, 181.

198 E.g., Delling ("Der Bezug," 102), who denies any reference to Jesus' being whipped. It is interesting to note that there is an association of μώλωψ with οἰκέτης in Sir 23:10 with regard to an interrogation, with no reference to Isaiah 53; lack of other evidence of the use of Sirach in this passage makes unlikely any influence of that verse here, however (I owe this reference to Osborne, "Guide Lines," 405).

199 So also, e.g., Kelly, 123; Delling, "Der Bezug," 101, 109; Leaney, 39; Calvin, 92; but see Sieffert, "Die Heilsbedeutung," 402. What it does not signify is the general rule that innocent suffering nobly endured redeems, as Schiwy (49) would have it; for our author Jesus' death is hardly simply an example of a larger rule that would be true of anyone undergoing similar innocent suffering.

200 Whether or not Schelkle (86) is correct in seeing in such a theology a commonplace in early Christian tradition due to the Pauline kerygma, such a theology was also available to our author directly from the passage in Isaiah.

201 That such straying is intended to describe the life of those addressed prior to their conversion is indicated by the periphrastic imperfect ἦτε πλανώμενοι, which describes extended action in the past. On the second rather than first person of Isa 53:5–6, see the comments on v. 24c above.

of the text of Isa 53:5–6 that the author is here following.[202] The conjunction γάρ indicates that the author sees v. 25 as an explanation of the preceding clause: healing in this instance takes the form of turning to their true shepherd and overseer,[203] a combination of acts that may draw on Isa 6:10: καὶ ἐπιστρέψωσιν καὶ ἰάσομαι αὐτούς ("and they turn and I shall heal them").[204] The act of being turned[205] here suggests not so much that the readers once had been with the shepherd, had strayed, and are now being returned (e.g., Jewish Christians) as their conversion from their former status of unbelievers to that of members of the Christian community (e.g., gentile Christians),[206] the more so since this verb could be used as virtually a technical term for conversion of Gentiles.[207] While the word "shepherd" is regularly used in the OT to refer to God,[208] the absence of any reference to God as shepherd in the NT,[209] combined with its use as a description of Jesus in the NT,[210] the specific reference to Jesus as "chief shepherd" (ἀρχιποίμην) in 1 Pet 5:10, and the connection of v. 24c with v. 25 by means of the explanatory conjunction γάρ, make it more likely that it here refers to Jesus.[211] God as "overseer" (ἐπίσκοπος) is also found in the OT,[212] but

because the word ἐπίσκοπος is here closely linked to "shepherd," it too is to be understood as referring to Christ.[213] Whether it was by this time already the title of a church official[214] or simply a description[215] cannot be determined from this verse. Finally, the emphasis in this passage on the need for slaves (and all Christians) to endure unjust suffering if necessary makes it unlikely that the phrase τῶν ψυχῶν ὑμῶν has a meaning such as "souls" (in contrast to bodies). More likely is that it means here, as it did in 1:9, the total person.[216]

This verse makes explicit the contrast between "once" and "now" in respect to the lives of its readers that has been implicit in the passage as a whole, and that plays a dominant role in the theological outlook of the letter.[217] As in the case of 2:3–10, this passage closes by identifying the "now" of the readers as their current status as members of the Christian community, which they formerly were not (see 2:10). It points again to the fact that only within the Christian community do they have the assurance of the glorious future already visible in Christ's resurrection and assumption of divine authority.[218]

---

202 So also, e.g., Bigg, 151; Selwyn, 181; Goldstein, "Kirche," 45. Some (e.g., Schlosser, "Ancien Testament," 92; Kelly, 125–126) who find in this passage evidence of the author's use of earlier confessional material would not include this verse as coming from it.

203 So also Hiebert, "Example," 42; Goppelt, 211.

204 So, e.g., Michaels, 150. Such an association based on Isa 6:10 appears elsewhere in early Christian tradition, i.e., Mark 4:12; Matt 13:15; John 12:40; Acts 28:27, as Goppelt (111) notes.

205 The passive ἐπεστράφητε surely refers to divine initiative, as does the passive ἐκλήθητε in v. 21 (cf. 5:10); see also the passives of 1:3, 18, 23.

206 So also, e.g., Best, 123; Osborne, "Guide Lines," 406.

207 Acts 14:15; 15:19; 26:20; see also the adaptation in Luke 15:3–7 to reflect the gentile mission; cf. Kelly, 124; Michaels, 150; Wand, 84. The force of the aorist here as perfect (noted also by, e.g., Bigg, 149) is due more to the presence of the νῦν than to the regular use of aorist for perfect in Sanskrit, as Selwyn (181) hints.

208 E.g., Num 27:17; 1 Kings 22:17; Ps 23; Isa 40:11; Jer 23:1–4; Ezek 34:11–15; cf. Ps 119:176; Zech 11:7. Cf. Best, 123; Goppelt, 211.

209 Osborne, "Guide Lines," 403.

210 E.g., John 10:11–13; 21:15–17; Heb 13:20; Rev

7:17; cf. Mark 6:34; 14:27; Luke 12:32.

211 So also, e.g., Goppelt, 211. Windisch (66) cites in addition *Mart. Pol.* 19.2 as further evidence. But see Osborne ("Guide Lines," 404), who thinks it likely it refers to God.

212 Kelly (125) cites Job 20:29; Wis 1:6; Michaels (151) notes its presence in Philo *Leg. all.* 3.43; *Mut. nom.* 39, 216; *Som.* 1.91, to which may be added *Migr. Abr.* 82.1.

213 So also, e.g., Michaels, 151; Beare, 151; Hiebert, "Example," 43; cf. Goppelt, 211. If the two nouns form a hendiadys, it would carry a meaning something like "the shepherd who oversees your lives."

214 So, e.g., Schelkle (86), who cites Acts 20:28; Phil 1:1.

215 So, e.g., Bigg (151), who cites its virtual equivalence to "shepherd."

216 So also, e.g., Michaels, 152; Goppelt, 212.

217 See Introduction § V.B.2, "Theological Structure."

218 See also Brox, 139; it is less likely that the words are best understood in terms of the baptismal sacrament which has "now" been administered, as Beare (151) maintains (see the criticism of that point in Shimada, *Formulary Material*, 68 n. 7). Baptism has its place in the argument of this letter, but not so dominant a one as was once thought.

3
Appropriate Conduct for Christian Wives—and Husbands

1 Similarly[1] you wives, [fulfill your Christian duty] by being subordinate to your own husbands, so that even if some are disobedient to the word, they shall be gained by the behavior of their wives without a word, 2/ because they observed[2] your reverent, chaste behavior. 3/ Let your decoration not be the external sort, consisting of the braiding[3] of hair[4] and the wearing of gold or the putting on of garments, 4/ but the secret inner person, accompanied by the incorruption of a calm and quiet spirit, which is most precious before God, 5/ because in that way also holy women in former times, women who put their hope in God,[5] used to decorate themselves by being subordinate to their own husbands, 6/ as Sarah obeyed[6] Abraham when she called him "master,"[7] whose children you became when you did what is good and were free from all fear. 7/ In like manner you men, [fulfill your Christian duty] by living with the women in an enlightened way as with a weaker vessel, according her honor as also to fellow heirs[8] of the

1 Of the variations in the opening words of this text, the most significant is the omission by some MSS. (B, some Greek minuscules, some Latin, Syriac versions) of ὁμοίως; its inclusion has much stronger attestation (P⁷², ℵ, A, P, Ψ, 𝔐, some others) and is probably to be regarded as original.

2 Some MSS. (P⁷², ℵ*, 945, 1241, 1739, some other minuscules) have a present participle (ἐποπτεύοντες), where others (ℵᶜ, A, B, C, P, Ψ, 𝔐) have an aorist (ἐποπτεύσαντες); the former implies the husband will be gained as he sees the behavior, the aorist implies his gain after he sees it. Superior textual support favors the aorist, as Michaels (154) also argues.

3 Some Greek minuscules (049, 614, 1243, 1881, some others) read ἐκπλοκῆς ("letting down" [of hair]); ἐμπλοκῆς is attested in the uncials and has the stronger claim to being original.

4 The omission of τριχῶν (P⁷², C, Ψ, a few minuscules, some Coptic MSS.) would imply that gold ornaments were braided into the hair ("the braiding and wearing of gold"); less likely "the fashioning and putting on of gold ornaments," as Michaels (155) suggests. The attestation for its presence (ℵ, A, B, P, 𝔐, some Latin, Syriac, Coptic MSS.) is strong, and along with the symmetry of the threefold phrases, argues for its inclusion in the original text.

5 For the widely attested (P⁷², A, B, C, Ψ, 33, 81, 1241, 1739, other minuscules) εἰς θεόν, some MSS. (P, 𝔐) read ἐπί θεόν, some others (ℵ, 2464, a few other minuscules) read ἐπί τὸν θεόν, yet others (614, 630, 1243, 1881, some other minuscules) read εἰς τὸν θεόν. While no reading changes the meaning, the more widely attested reading is probably also the original.

6 B, Ψ, 69ᵛⁱᵈ, latt, saᵐˢˢ read the imperfect ὑπήκουεν for the aorist ὑπήκουσεν (P⁸¹, ℵ, C, P, 𝔐), thus making Sarah's obedience habitual; since the LXX has only one instance where Sarah calls Abraham κύριος (Gen 18:12), the imperfect is the more difficult reading and so has some claim on being original.

7 The Greek κύριος could of course also mean "Lord," and is used as a substitute for the sacred tetragrammaton in the LXX, but it bears no such religious significance here. As polite address to a grown man among those who spoke Greek, it could also mean "sir," but that would be too bland for this context. The implication here is one of great respect expressing itself in obedient subordination.

8 In place of συγκληρονόμοις (P⁷², P⁸¹, ℵ², B, a number of minuscules, vg), some MSS. (A, C, P, Ψ, 𝔐) read συνκληρόνομοι, making it modify "husbands." For an argument for the priority of the nominative form, see Bo Reicke, "Die Gnosis der Männer nach I. Ptr. 3:7," in W. Eltester, ed., *Neutestamentliche Studien für Rudolph Bultmann zu seinem 70. Geburtstag* (ZNW

grace of life,[9] so that your prayers are not hindered.

Beihefte 21; Berlin: Töpelmann, 1954) 297–98. Because the dative form allows the phrase to provide a reason for the apportioning of honor, and justifies neglect hindering the husband's prayers, the dative is to be preferred.

9   Some mss. (ℵ, A, C², some minuscules, syʰ, bo) add ποικίλης to the phrase χάριτος ζωῆς, probably under the influence of 4:10; the shorter reading (P⁸¹ᵛⁱᵈ, B, C*, P, Ψ, 𝔐, lat, sa) is more likely to be the original.

Analysis

While a number of traditions underlie this passage, the presence of characteristic words and phrases employed elsewhere in the letter[10] makes it apparent that these verses represent the composition of the author of the epistle. The *inclusio* formed by the phrase ὑποτασσόμεναι τοῖς ἰδίοις ἀνδράσιν ("[by] being subordinate to your own husbands") in vv. 1 and 5 is in this instance probably not intended to frame the passage, since the comment about Sarah in v. 6 is closely tied to v. 5 and cannot be regarded as an appendage to the discussion, as the *inclusio* might otherwise indicate.[11]

The subordination of wives to husbands reflected in this passage must be seen against the background of the general status of women in the Hellenistic world of that time. Dominant among the elite[12] was the notion that the woman was by nature inferior to the man.[13] Because she lacked the capacity for reason that the male had,[14] she was ruled rather by her emotions,[15] and was as a result given to poor judgment,[16] immorality,[17] intemperance,[18] wickedness,[19] avarice;[20] she was untrustworthy,[21] contentious,[22] and as a result, it was her place to obey.[23] Such a view of women was also sedimented in legal tradition: women could not vote or hold office,[24] could not take an oath or plead a case in court, could not be the legal guardian of their own minor children, and were legally dependent on either their father or a guardian.[25] To be sure, some of these measures began to be relaxed in the time of Augustus.[26] Women could petition for a change in guardian if the

10   ἀπειθοῦσιν τῷ λόγῳ (3:1), see 2:8; cf. 4:17; ἀναστροφή (3:1, 2), see 1:15, 18; 2:12; 3:16; ἐν φόβῳ (3:2), see 1:17; cf. 3:16; ἐποπτεύσαντες (3:2), see 2:12; τῷ ἀφθάρτῳ (3:4), cf. 1:4, 23; ἐλπίζουσαι εἰς θεόν (3:5), see 1:21; appeal to a biblical character, Sarah (3:6), see 3:20. I owe some of these references to Michaels, 156.

11   So also Michaels, 156.

12   "Elite" here also encompasses Jewish writers, as various references below will make apparent. Because the lower classes have left no written record, it is difficult to know whether and to what extent they may have shared the views of the literary elite.

13   E.g., Plato *Laws* 6.781; *Republic* 5.455, 457; *Ep. Arist.* 250; Philo *Ebr.* 55; Josephus *Ant.* 4.219; *Gos. Thom.* 114. There was nevertheless a certain ambiguity about such inferiority, even in the earliest sources (see the discussion of Plato and Aristotle in K. Thraede, "Frau," *RAC* 8.208–9. Such ambiguity was also voiced later on, e.g., Plutarch *Mor., Amatorius* 769B): women have prudence, intelligence, are loyal and just, have exhibited daring and courage; Seneca (*Ep., Ad Marc.* 16.1): women have just as much capacity as men for virtuous action; cf. Martial (*Epig.* 7.69), who celebrates one Theophila's judgment and intellect.

14   E.g., *Ep. Arist.* 250. When a woman did show strong intellect, she was commended for not being "womanish," e.g., Seneca *Ep., Ad Marc.* 1.1; cf. 1.5.

15   E.g., Seneca *Const.* 14.1; *Clem.* 1.5.5; Juvenal *Satire* 6.346–49; it shows itself in too-intense mourning: Seneca *De consolatione ad Polybium* 6.2; *Ep., Ad. Helv.* 16.1.

16   Juvenal *Satire* 6.362–65; Philo *Leg. Gaj.* 319; Seneca *Clem.* 2.5.1; *Ira* 3.24.3.

17   Juvenal *Satire* 6.457–60; Petronius *Satyr.* 110; Martial *Epig.* 10.69.

18   Dio Chrysostom *Or.* 30.36.

19   Seneca *Tragedies, Hippolytus* 559–62; *Octavia* 868–69. For the same notion, see *T. Reub.* 5.1–4.

20   Seneca *Contr.* 2.7.9.

21   Juvenal *Satire* 4.94–102.

22   Juvenal *Satire* 6.242–43, 268–74.

23   Pseudo-Melissa *Letter to Kleareta* 160–62 (cited in Malherbe, *Moral Exhortation*, 83); Seneca *Const.* 1.1 ("males are born to command, females to obey"); *Ira* 3.35.1; Martial *Epig.* 8.12. A man who could not control his wife was liable to be corrupted by her "depravity" (Tacitus *Ann.* 3.34), and was to be punished for her misdeeds (Tacitus *Ann.* 4.20).

24   Tacitus (*Ann.* 14.11; cf. 12.37) excoriates Agrippina, wife of Claudius and adoptive mother of Nero, for wanting political power and admission to the Senate to speak there, and rails against women in the eastern

present one proved harsh; they could inherit and hold property;[27] they could decide whom and when to marry and whether to divorce, and by decree of Augustus if a mother had three to five children, depending on her status, she acquired legal independence and full right to participate in business.[28] Despite this emancipation of women in the Augustan period, however, the idea of women remaining subordinate to men remained. The equality of women espoused in theory by the Stoic philosopher Musonius,[29] for example, in practice was denied in favor of the traditional notion that the man should rule the woman,[30] and the cults of Dionysus and Isis, which gave women a dominant role, were criticized for their excesses by Roman men.[31] The role of married women at this time was also undergoing change;[32] Plutarch, for example, urged that in the proper marriage there ought to be a mutual amalgamation of bodies, property, friends, and relations, with all material possessions held in common.[33] Yet even Plutarch held

that the wife must be subordinate to the husband, who must rule her, in a kindly way, to be sure, but he must nevertheless be the superior partner in the marriage,[34] even to the point of determining which gods the family is to worship.[35]

It is against this background that one must view the status of women reflected in the NT as a whole, and specifically in this passage in 1 Peter.[36] That the Christian faith inherently meant equal status for women in the sight of God is evident from such a passage as Gal 3:28, and from the important role played by women in the early church.[37] In that light, it has been argued that the subordination announced in this passage, reflecting an

---

provinces who arrogated to themselves military, political, and economic power (*Ann.* 3.33). In a similar vein, the Germanic Sitones were despised because they allowed women to rule, e.g., Tacitus *Ger.* 45; *Hist.* 4.61. That view made the defeat of the Romans by the Britains under Boadicea (Tacitus *Agric.* 16) all the bitterer. On the other hand, Augustus's widow, Livia, took part in the honors paid to Augustus, honors normally reserved for men; so Dio Cassius *Hist. Rom.* 56.47.1.

25 On these matters, see Lampe and Luz, "Nachpaulinisches Christentum," 191. For an excellent general summary of primary sources and secondary literature, see Thraede, "Frau."

26 Thraede ("Frau," 198: cf. 223) notes that the greatest degree of emancipation occurred in Asia Minor during the time of the emperors, i.e., the time when 1 Peter was written, and the area to which it was addressed. For a discussion of such gains, see Lampe and Luz "Nachpaulinisches Christentum," 191.

27 That was not universal, however; Dio Chrysostom (*Or.* 74.9) reports that in Athens a woman may not carry on business whose value exceeds a measure of barley.

28 On this matter, cf. Lampe and Luz, "Nachpaulinisches Christentum," 191; Balch, *Wives,* appendix IV, esp. 139–40.

29 E.g., his "That Women Too Should Study Philosophy": women as well as men have been gifted by reason, and such study will make the woman content with her lot! (Cora A. Lutz, *Musonius Rufus: "The Roman Socrates"* [Yale Classical Studies 10; New

Haven: Yale University Press, 1947], 39–43).

30 For a discussion of this point, see Balch, *Wives,* appendix V, esp. 143–44, 147.

31 See the sources given in Balch, *Wives,* 65, 71. Yet even in Greek mystery cults, e.g., the Eleusinian mystery, women had a greater degree of equality than in other areas, as Thraede ("Frau," 207–8) notes.

32 Cf., e.g., Balch, *Wives,* 145.

33 As a result, he approved a law forbidding the exchange of gifts between husband and wife because that compromised the notion that they held all things in common; see Plutarch *Mor., Con. pr.* 143A (cited in Malherbe, *Moral Exhortation,* 107).

34 *Mor., Con. pr.* 142E; cf. the discussion in Lampe and Luz, "Nachpaulinisches Christentum," 192–93.

35 Plutarch (*Mor., Con. pr.* 140D) mentions specifically that such a relationship means the wife must worship and acknowledge only the gods her husband believed in, and must exclude all "outlandish superstitions."

36 So also, e.g., Balch, *Wives,* 85; Dorothy Patterson, "Roles in Marriage; A Study in Submission: 1 Peter 3:1–7," *Theological Educator* 13 (1982) 76; Lampe and Luz, "Nachpaulinisches Christentum," 188.

37 E.g., Prisca, whose precedence over her husband in the Christian faith is probably indicated when she is mentioned ahead of him (e.g., Rom 16:3; 2 Tim 4:19); Phoebe, the only person in the NT epistles to whom the title "deacon" is applied (διάκονος, Rom 16:1); Mary, whose missionary work is acknowledged (πολλά ἐκοπίασεν, Rom 16:6), as is that of Tryphaena and Tryphosa (τὰς κοπιώσας ἐν κυρίῳ); if, as seems

extended tradition in later canonical epistles,[38] meant a lessening of, or limitation on, the emancipation Christian women had enjoyed earlier on.[39]

It must be noted, however, that this passage intends to say nothing about the subordination of women to men in general, nor even within Christian marriage,[40] but intends to be understood primarily within the context of a Christian wife married to an unbelieving husband.[41] That this was a problem very early in the Christian community is indicated not only by Paul's discussion of it in 1 Cor 7:12–16, but also by its reflection in sayings attributed to Jesus about the deleterious effect following him can have on family life (Luke 12:51–53; Mark 10:29).[42] At the root of the problem is the requirement, voiced by Plutarch, that the wife must worship and acknowledge only the gods of her husband. That obviously places the converted wife of an unconverted husband in a most difficult situation; on that critical point she may *not* be subordinated to him,[43] thus incurring his disapproval as well as that of his family and acquaintances. In such a situation, maintaining a demeanor acceptable in all other areas to her non-Christian husband and his values[44] not only lessens the tension within the household but may even contribute to the eventual conversion of the unbelieving husband.[45] Yet whether it does or not, the wife must hold fast her Christian confession and practice, whatever threats may be leveled against her.[46]

Although nothing is said in vv. 1–6 about the general status of women within the Christian community, or within Christian marriage, that status can be deduced from v. 7, addressed to Christian husbands. The fact that no parallel admonitions to masters are appended to the passage dealing with slaves indicates the author's intention to point up the differences between women in a non-Christian and in a Christian situation, and the equality they enjoy in the latter. That is done in two principal ways. First, a different word is used for the woman in a Christian household (γυναικεία) than for a wife in a non-Christian one (γυνή), almost as though the author wished here to dissociate what he had said to wives about subordination in the latter situation. Second, that impression is strengthened by the fact that the Christian man (including the husband) is to apportion honor to the women in his household (including his wife) as to equals in the eyes of God: they as much as he are

likely, Andronicus and Junia were, like Prisca and Aquila, a married couple (if the Ἰουνιᾶν of Rom 16:7 is the accusative form of the feminine Ἰουνία rather than of the masculine Ἰουνίας), there was a woman acknowledged as "noteworthy among the apostles" (ἐπίσημοι ἐν τοῖς ἀποστόλοις).

38 Eph 5:22–24; Col 3:18; 1 Tim 2:11; Titus 2:4–5; see also *1 Clem.* 1.3; 21.7; Polycarp *Phil.* 4.2; cf. Lohse, "Parenesis," 44; Goppelt, 213.

39 So, e.g., Lampe and Luz ("Nachpaulinisches Christentum," 190, 192), who suggest as possibilities a fear of looser morals, as in Rev 2:20, or a desire to separate the church from marginal Christian groups.

40 According to 1 Cor 7:4 there is equality there.

41 While husbands who are believers are not excluded (τινες), the emphasis is clearly on husbands who are not, a point made specific by the descriptive phrase "disobedient to the word" (ἀπειθοῦσιν τῷ λόγῳ; cf. 2:8; 4:17), the expressed hope of winning them to the faith (κερδηθήσονται), and the implication that Christian wives may have reason to fear (μὴ φοβούμεναι μηδεμίαν πτόησιν) for having behaved as Christians (ἀγαθοποιοῦσαι). On that score, this passage differs from the other admonitions to subordination within marriage contained in the other NT epistles; they say nothing about unbelieving husbands.

42 Cf. Bauer, 41; that it presented an ongoing difficulty is indicated in its discussion in Justin Martyr *2 Apology* 2; Tertullian *Ad ux.* 2.4, 6.

43 So also Balch, "Early Christian Criticism," 169; Senior, "Conduct," 435. Actually, on that point our author is advising *non*conformity to Hellenistic custom.

44 That is the point of the admonitions to circumspection in behavior and dress in vv. 3–6; for more on such traditions within the Hellenistic world, see the comments on the individual verses below.

45 Such a missionary element, present also in Paul's discussion of this problem (see 1 Cor 7:16), evidently provided some motivation for such advice, but it is not the main point of this admonition, as Goppelt (213) would have it.

46 That is surely the point of 3:6b; for further discussion, see the comments on the verse below. That such threats would follow is clear from the general view that if one were to upset the order of the home, the whole society would be in trouble, as Wayne A. Meeks (*The Moral World of the First Christians* [LEC 6; Philadelphia: Westminster, 1986] 113) rightly notes. See also the discussion in Dio Chrysostom *Or.* 38.14–15.

heirs of God's life-giving grace. So necessary is this second admonition that for the Christian man to ignore it is to have God ignore him: the prayers of a Christian husband and head of a household who acts otherwise will be ignored by God. The glimpse this gives of the status of a Christian woman within the Christian family, as well as in the Christian community, shows that the emancipation of women is far from diminished, and that their equality is in fact enjoined as a Christian duty (κατὰ γνῶσιν) upon Christian men.[47]

In that light, the subordination of Christian wives in a non-Christian marriage here enjoined is not a matter of theological principle so much as it is a matter of avoiding unnecessary conflict.[48] Yet it is not even an admonition to blanket conformity in every area where it would not conflict directly with her Christian faith. The illustration of submission given in vv. 3–4 does not, to be sure, conflict with certain social expectations of her unbelieving husband, but even more, they reflect activity sanctioned by Scripture and Christian tradition.[49] Even such subordination as is enjoined, therefore, is subordination authorized by the faith that above all else the Christian wife must put uppermost in her behavior. For that reason, in this instance, as in the case of Christian slaves, Christian wives here point beyond themselves to the general situation of Christians who find themselves at odds with a society within which they must remain true to their Christian confession, whatever suffering that may bring in its wake.[50]

Comment

■ 1-2 [51] The adverb ὁμοίως ("similarly") that begins this verse is intended to show not that wives like slaves must be subordinate,[52] but that, like household slaves (2:18) and Christian husbands (3:7), wives too are to obey the commands in 2:17 (honor all people, love those in the Christian community, revere God, honor the emperor), in their case by being subordinate to their husbands.[53] The participle ὑποτασσάμεναι is thus not so much imperatival[54] as it is instrumental, showing the means by which the wife is to fulfill those commands.[55] The presence of ἰδίοις ("[your] own") shows that this is not a general statement of subordination of women to men,[56] but rather of the Christian wife to her husband, whether he is Christian or not.

The purpose of such action by the wife is stated in the ἵνα clause: it is to win unbelieving husbands to the Christian faith. While the phrase καὶ εἴ τινες ("even if some") implies that not all husbands of Christian wives are nonbelievers, it is clear that the verse is directed to those Christian wives for whom that is in fact the case: the interrogative particle εἰ states a fact here, not a hypothetical possibility.[57] Whether a Christian wife with a non-Christian husband is assumed here to be unusual[58]

47   The lament about loss of such emancipation in this letter by Lampe and Luz ("Nachpaulinisches Christentum," 190) is thus shown to be without basis.
48   So also, e.g., Cranfield, 88–89; Selwyn, 106; cf. Balch, *Wives*, 105. To say the passage lacks theological justification, however, as does Refoulé ("Bible," 471), is to ignore the opening word of v. 1 (ʾΟμοίως), which links this passage to 2:18–25 with its clear christological basis for such subordination, even where it does result in suffering.
49   See the comments on v. 3 below.
50   So also, e.g., Michaels, 171. It is thus unlikely that one may conclude from this passage that there were more men than women in the churches addressed, as do, e.g., Spicq (115) and Kelly (127). They are addressed because Christian wives married to non-Christian husbands were in a difficult situation with considerable potential for suffering, as Cranfield (87) and Best (124) observe.
51   Since these two verses comprise a single sentence, they will be treated as a unit.
52   So also, e.g., Best, 124; Cranfield, 88; the presence of
ὁμοίως in 3:7 belies the assertion of Selwyn (182) that these admonitions come from a "code of subordination."
53   In agreement with Bigg, 150.
54   Such imperatival force is widely held to be present, e.g., Balch, *Wives*, 97; Kelly, 127; Bengel, *Gnomon*, 741; Michaels, 157; Selwyn, 482; Goppelt, 214. Philipps (*Kirche*, 48) is closer when he finds it more descriptive than imperative. That it can be used in the imperatival form in this context is evident in Col 3:18; that it is not used in that form here indicates a different intent with the verb.
55   See the discussion of ὑποτασσόμενοι in the comments on 2:18 above.
56   With, e.g., Selwyn, 182; contra Schweizer, 68. Even if Kelly (127) is correct that by this time ἴδιος has lost its original force, it is nevertheless included in the verse, and must therefore be taken into account.
57   So also, e.g., Beare, 153.
58   So, e.g., Grudem, 137.

or the normal case[59] is difficult to determine from this language. What is clear is that the conduct of wives with non-Christian husbands is the chief concern of the author here. The phrase ἀπειθοῦσιν τῷ λόγῳ ("disobedient to the word") may imply not only absence of belief but active opposition to the Christian faith;[60] the counsel to wives no longer to speak of it (ἄνευ λόγου ["without a word"]) would indicate further discussion to be unfruitful if not provocative. The first use of λόγος ("word") clearly means the Christian faith;[61] whether the second does so as well has been disputed,[62] but the intention is surely that the wife's Christian behavior[63] will be an effective witness even without verbal reference to the gospel, not that she is to remain dumb in the presence of her husband as she lives her Christian life.[64] It is thus to be understood as meaning "without verbal reference to the gospel." That the husband will be gained not as a compliant mate for the wife but as one converted to the Christian faith is implied in the verb κερδηθήσονται ("they shall be gained"),[65] which belongs to the language of mission.[66]

The final phrase (v. 2) supports the idea that a husband who has rejected the proclamation of the gospel can be won to it by his wife's exemplary behavior. While the participle ἐποπτεύσαντες ("[because] they observed") carries a causal force, the emphasis here is probably to be seen rather on the temporal: subsequent to the husband's seeing his wife's exemplary behavior, he will be won to her faith.[67] The description of that conduct, although it uses concepts employed in the description of the ideal wife of the Greco-Roman world,[68] is best understood in this context as pointing to Christian behavior.[69] The phrase ἐν φόβῳ refers here, as it did in 2:18, to reverence before God rather than respect for, or fear of, the husbands,[70] a point made clear in 3:6, where the author counsels against such fear of husbands.[71] Its point is as much prescriptive as descriptive, that is, it points out that the wife's subordination must be carried out within the perimeters of the faith. When such subordination would require of her an act incompatible with her faith, she is evidently not to do it. Ἁγνή probably means not simply "chaste," but "pure" in a more general sense, as in most other cases in the NT.[72]

The pronoun ὑμῶν ("your") is the first direct address to the readers in this passage and it is not repeated until v. 6 (ἐγενήθητε ["you became"]); the ὧν ("your") of v. 3

---

59 So, e.g., Beare, 153.

60 So, e.g., Balch (*Wives*, 99), citing the use of the verb ἀπειθέω in Acts 14:2; 19:9; Rom 15:31; cf. also Senior, "Conduct," 434. The other uses of the verb in 1 Pet 2:8; 3:20; 4:17 can, but need not, imply active opposition.

61 The suggestion of Beare (153–54) that it refers to the "divine principle of life and truth that inhabited all things" is wide of the mark in this context.

62 E.g., Hart (63) and Bengel (*Gnomon*, 741), who find here an example of antanaclasis (a word used in a double sense).

63 Ἀναστροφή is favored by our author, as shown by its use six times in this epistle, in contrast to only seven times in the rest of the NT. It specifies Christian behavior in 1 Peter in every instance except 1:18.

64 With, e.g., Brandt, "Wandel," 24 n. 30.

65 The use of (future) indicative rather than subjunctive with ἵνα is typical of "late, vulgar Greek" (so Bigg, 151; Beare, 154); it appears, e.g., in Mark 15:20; Luke 20:10; 1 Cor 13:3; and Rev. 3:9, but in each instance with a variant reading in the subjunctive mood; only in Gal 2:4 does it appear with no indicated alternate reading in the subjunctive. Bengel's (*Gnomon*, 741) identification of it as a "rare future subjunctive" is wide of the mark, since such a form never existed; see J. H. Moulton, *Grammar of New*

Testament Greek: Prolegomena (2d ed.; Edinburgh: Clark, 1906) 1.151: "The (future) imperative and subjunctive never existed"; so also BDF § 28, with specific reference to this verse.

66 It is so used in Matt 18:15; 1 Cor 9:22; cf. Lippert, "Leben," 250; David Daube, "Κερδαίνω as a Missionary Term," *HTR* 40 (1947) 109–20.

67 With Michaels, 158.

68 E.g., Pliny's description of his wife as incomparably discerning, chaste, full of solicitude, kindly (*Ep.* 4.19).

69 Contra Brox, 143.

70 So also, e.g., Beare, 154; Kelly, 128; Schweizer, 68; Michaels, 158; Schelkle, 88; Best, 125. But see Dennis Sylva ("Translating and Interpreting 1 Peter 3:2," *BT* 34 [1983] 147), who argues for a reference to human beings both here and in 2:18.

71 See the comments on that verse below.

72 Schelkle, 88 n. 2.

reverts to the third person γυναῖκες ("wives") of v. 1. This may indicate that the whole sentence was taken from an earlier source, and adapted to the direct address found in the admonitions to the household slaves (2:20, 21, 24, 25).[73]

The problem addressed in this verse is not simply that of a wife defying the ideal of the Hellenistic elite that women in general are to be subordinate to men,[74] but more specifically that wives in that culture were expected to assume the religion of their husbands.[75] The reason was that the household, like the republic, expressed its solidarity in a common religion, and unwillingness to share such solidarity was perceived as a threat to the state as well as to the family.[76] It was the Christian wives' necessary insubordination in the matter of sharing the unbelieving husband's religion that led to the problem addressed in these verses, with their plea that where such insubordination is not required, subordination may indeed have the effect of winning the husband to the Christian faith.[77] Such subordination is thus a matter of expediency, and is based neither on the nature of women, nor on the inequality of husband and wife in marriage; the equality of marriage partners, rooted in

the sayings of Jesus (cf. Matt 19:4–6 par.), was made explicit in early Christian tradition (cf. 1 Cor 11:11–12; Gal 3:28).[78]

In sum, the verses concern the relationship between husband and wife, with emphasis on the believing wife married to an unbelieving husband; they do not deal with the general relationship of male and female.[79] Submission in this context therefore does not mean any woman is to do anything any man may tell her.[80] Rather, in the context of this letter, the wife's ultimate submission, and thus responsibility, is to Jesus as her Lord,[81] and that ultimate submission means that the submission to her husband is secondary, and is to take the form of living out her faith so transparently that her unbelieving husband may be won to the faith.[82] The fate of such a wife, and her response, is thus exemplary for that of any Christian forced to live in unsympathetic, even threatening, surroundings.[83]

■ 3 The description of the Christian wife in vv. 3–4 follows a widespread tradition in the ancient world. Condemnation of excessive personal ornamentation can be found in Isa 3:18–24;[84] later Jewish tradition also contains references to it (e.g., *T. Reub.* 5.3; *1 Enoch*

---

73 Selwyn (183) argues for such a solution; Brox (143) thinks the whole sentence was inserted into an earlier *Haustafel*, but that would not explain the transition from third to second person.

74 Plutarch *Mor., Con. pr.* 142D: "(the wife) must speak either to her husband or through her husband"; Josephus (*Ap.* 2.201): "The woman, says (the law), is worse than the man in all things." See Philipps, *Kirche*, 48; Kamlah, "ὑποτάσσεσθαι," 239; Balch, *Wives*, 9; idem, "Household Codes," 28. Although such subordination in that context is based on the inferior nature of the female, it did not exclude mutuality in the marriage partnership; Tacitus, for example (*Agric.* 6), speaks of mutual affection and alternating self-sacrifice in a marriage.

75 Plutarch (*Mor., Con. pr.* 140D): because a husband's friends are to be a wife's friends, and because the most important of one's friends are the gods, the wife is to know only the gods her husband believes in; Balch ("Early Christian Criticism," 165) notes the same demand made by Dionysius of Halicarnassus. Michaels (157) mentions the possibility that the wife excoriated by Apuleius (*Metam.* 9.14) for taking a god other than those of the family may have been a Christian.

76 So Judge, *Social Pattern*, 35. It is that point that gives the urgency to these verses in 1 Peter.

77 For a similar solution to the problem, see 1 Cor 7:13, 16.

78 Goppelt (214) also makes a similar point.

79 With, e.g., Michaels, 157.

80 So also Schweizer, 68; Krodel, 73.

81 Shown by the participle ὑποτασσόμεναι, and the phrase ἐν φόβῳ; cf. Margot, 52. Schweizer (68) correctly points out that the verse has less to do with a takeover of traditional values than the admonition to continued faith even within a difficult situation, viz., a wife married to a nonbelieving husband; cf. also Senior, 54. It is such guidance being here provided, as Neugebauer ("Zur Deutung," 64) implies.

82 With, e.g., Moffatt, 130; Balch, *Wives,* 105; Philipps, *Kirche,* 48.

83 Cf. 2:12, 15, where similar expectations are voiced for all Christians. This point is widely recognized; see Goppelt, 214; Senior, 54; Philipps, *Kirche,* 23; Schlier, "Adhortatio," 77; cf. Beare, 153; Brox, 142.

84 God's removal of such ornamentation in the time of judgment implies dissatisfaction with it. Our author's frequent use of Isaiah in the preceding verses, esp. 2:22–25, makes knowledge of this passage likely; cf. also Love, "First Epistle," 69.

8.1),[85] as does Philo.[86] Far more widespread was the Greco-Roman tradition that the proper attire for the woman is modesty rather than expensive garments, fancy coiffures, and jewelry; among those who use, and approve of, this widespread tradition are Phintys,[87] Perictione,[88] Seneca,[89] Dio Chrysostom,[90] Juvenal,[91] Plutarch,[92] Epictetus,[93] Pliny,[94] Tacitus,[95] Lucian of Samosata,[96] and Ovid,[97] among others.[98] While the presence of this tradition in 1 Tim 2:9–11 may point to a common catechetical source,[99] its relative absence in other NT documents suggests only a limited circulation.

Whatever the source of the tradition upon which our author is drawing, it makes sense only if there were women among the readers of this letter who could afford the kind of expensive clothing and jewelry referred to.[100] Arguments against the presence of such wealth in the churches being addressed lack persuasive power;[101] early Christianity appealed to people of the widest variety of economic situations.[102]

While some of the activity described may have played a part in other cults, for example, the braiding of hair was especially important for women devotees of Isis[103] and Artemis of Ephesus,[104] there is no evidence that our author intended to counter such practices.[105] Nor does the intention seem to be to forbid all ornamentation,[106] although it was so interpreted by later Christian writers.[107] The point is rather that the attraction of the Christian wife to her pagan husband is to consist not in external adornment but in the more important internal qualities outlined in the following verse.[108] Only in that

85 Spicq (118–19) notes that jewels were often attached to charms and amulets, thus combining magic with personal adornment; it is probably for that reason that this passage in *1 Enoch* attributes such personal decoration, including cosmetics, to the demon Azazel.

86 E.g., *Virt.* 39–40; *Migr. Abr.* 97; the occasionally cited *Vit. Mos.* 2.243 (e.g., Schelkle, 89; Goppelt, 214) is irrelevant since it merely likens a daughter's inheritance to a necklace she puts on.

87 *On the Temperance of a Woman* 153.15–18. I owe this reference to Balch, *Wives*, 101; for a translation of the passage, see David Scholer, "Women's Adornment," *Daughters of Sarah* 6 (1980) 4.

88 *On the Harmony of a Woman* 143.10–14. I owe this reference as well to Balch, *Wives*, 101; Scholer ("Women's Adornment," 4) also has a translation of this text.

89 *Ep., Ad Helv.* 16.4; *Benef.* 1.10.2; 7.9.4–5.

90 *Or.* 7.117.

91 *Satire* 3.180–81; 6.457–63, 495–511.

92 *Mor., Con. pr.* 141E; see also *Mor.* 133A.

93 *Enchir.* 40.

94 *Pan.* 83.7.

95 *Ann.* 3.54.

96 *Imag.* 11.

97 *Amor.* 3.136–38; he describes what looks best on what sort of woman for seductive results.

98 The sometimes-cited passage from Quintilian *Inst.* 8 *prooem.* 20 is irrelevant since it describes the necessarily modest dress of the orator, not the woman. On the whole matter of this Greco-Roman tradition, cf. also Scholer, "Women's Adornment," passim; Goppelt, 214; Kelly, 129; Bigg, 152; Selwyn, 183; Michaels, 159; Best, 125.

99 As Selwyn (184) suggests.

100 So also, e.g., Lampe and Luz, "Nachpaulinisches Christentum," 187; Schwank et al., 58; Beare, 155; Moffatt, 130; cf. Schelkle, 89.

101 Michaels (172) argues against a reference here to wealthy Christian women, but his three arguments—(1) lack of advice to slave owners argues against wealth; (2) warnings against lavish adornment were a topos in the ancient world; (3) an author a thousand miles away could not know the economic status of the readers—the first and third cancel one another out: if the author could not know the reader's economic status, neither could he know there were no slave owners, so his lack of mention of them cannot be construed as an argument for poverty among the readers. The second (also put forward by Goppelt, 216) probably means that the author found this widespread topos appropriate for the situation of some of his readers.

102 Cf., e.g., Jas 2:1–4, and the conversion of the well-to-do Lydia (Acts 16:4). For more on this topic, see the Introduction § II.B.2, "Social and Economic Status of the Intended Readers."

103 Balch (*Wives*, 102) cites Apuleius *Metam.* 2.8–9.

104 Balch (*Wives*, 101–2) cites Xenophon of Ephesus *Anthia and Habrocomas* 1.2.2–6 as showing this. Hart (63) cites Juvenal *Sat.* 6.492–504 as describing the elaborate coiffures fashion prescribed for attendance at the "Mysteries of Adonis"; I am unable to find mention of such mysteries in the cited passage.

105 With Balch, *Wives*, 102; Michaels, 160. Nor is it persuasive to see here a description of baptismal practice, since the putting off of jewelry and clothing was only temporary and they were put back on after the baptism took place; cf. Grundmann, "Die NHΠIOI," 7.

106 So also, e.g., Calvin, 96. Grudem (140) argues against this notion by pointing out that on that logic,

way will the virtue of the Christian faith become evident, and, more importantly, will the wife act in accordance with the divine will, and so be pleasing to God.[109] That in the end is the purpose of the wife's inner adornment, as v. 4b makes clear. The wife, acting within the limits imposed on her by the social order that in this case urges a modesty in apparel also appropriate for Christians, must nevertheless have as her primary intention activity that is pleasing to God.[110]

■ 4 This verse provides the positive counterpole to the negative v. 3 regarding what is appropriate for the Christian wife who seeks to be faithful to God and to win her unbelieving husband to the faith. Grammatically the negatived contrast ("not [οὐχ] this, but [ἀλλά] this") between the external (ἔξωθεν) and secret (κρυπτός) is not, as one might expect from v. 3, between an acceptable and an unacceptable type of decoration, but rather between (negatived) external decoration (οὐχ ὁ ἔξωθεν ... κόσμος) and the (affirmed) secret person (ὁ κρυπτὸς ... ἄνθρωπος).[111] Yet the return to the idea of decoration in v. 5 (οὕτως ... ἐκόσμουν ἑαυτάς ["thus ... they used to decorate themselves"]) indicates that the contrast between unacceptable and acceptable forms of decora-

tion was nevertheless present in the author's mind. If, then, the broad intention of the verses is clear enough, it is nonetheless difficult to accommodate the apparent contrast to the actual grammatical form of the verse.[112]

The "secret person" in this context refers not so much to the general inner aspect of the human being as it does to the person who is determined by a faith that is visible directly only to God (cf. Matt 6:4, 6, 18),[113] and that is apparent to other human beings only by way of external acts (cf. v.1). The contrast is reminiscent of Paul's contrast between outer and inner person (ὁ ἔξω, ἔσω ἄνθρωπος) in 2 Cor 4:16 (cf. Rom 7:22; Eph 3:16),[114] but the use here of κρυπτός ("secret") instead of ἔσω ("inner") shows lack of dependence on Paul.[115] The genitive τῆς καρδίας is probably qualifying, defining further what the "secret person" is: the seat of thought and thus of action.[116]

The "secret person" is further defined by the phrase ἐν τῷ ἀφθάρτῳ, probably best taken as a dative of accompaniment, rendered as "together with" or "accompanied by"[117] and modifying the adjective ἄφθαρτος, here used as a neuter substantive ("incorruption").[118] The following genitival phrase (τοῦ πραέως καὶ ἡσυχίου πνεύματος

putting on clothing would also have to be prohibited.

107 E.g., Clement of Alexandria *Paed.* 3.11.66 (wrongly given as 3.66.3 in Goppelt, 216; correctly in Schelkle, 89 n. 2); Tertullian *Orat.* 20; *Cultu fem.* 1.6; 2.2, 7–13; Cyprian *De hab. virg.* 8. See Selwyn, 183; Goppelt, 216, to whom I owe some of these references.

108 So also, e.g., Schwank et al., 59; Spicq, 118. On that point, the author agrees with the criticism of excessive personal ornamentation and decoration voiced in the non-Christian world of that time, as Brox (145) also notes.

109 With Brandt, "Wandel," 24–25.

110 That was also the point of the advice to the household slave, e.g., v. 18: ἐν παντὶ φόβῳ; v. 19: διὰ συνείδησιν θεοῦ; and the call to follow Christ. Both slaves and wives can therefore serve as examples for Christian conduct within a hostile secular society.

111 The problem lies with the word ἄνθρωπος; if it read κοσμός there would be no difficulty. The actual contrast demands that one understand the relative pronoun ὧν of v. 3 as a possessive genitive, which leads to the difficult construction: "whose let be not the external ... decoration but the secret ... person."

112 This has led Kelly (129) to observe that "the whole construction is distinctly clumsy."

113 Cf. Goppelt (216), who adds Matt 6:21; 15:8, 18–19;

Rom 2:29.

114 The implied contrast between old (παλαιὸς ἄνθρωπος) and new person in Rom 6:6, to which Beare (155) calls attention, is less relevant here.

115 So also, e.g., Selwyn, 184.

116 Selwyn (184) also finds such a genitive here, although his note that it is a probable Hebraism is probably unnecessary. As Kelly (129) notes, it could also be a genitive of apposition, making "inner person" and "heart" equivalent, although this seems less likely here, as does his further suggestion of this being a possible genitive of possession, meaning "the unseen person who dwells in the heart."

117 Thornton's ("Liturgy," 184) suggested meaning "found in, expressing itself in," seems a bit remote in this context.

118 With, e.g., Beare (155), who correctly prefers this solution to seeing it as a masculine adjective modifying a presumed κοσμῷ.

["calm and quiet spirit"]) is appositional ("consisting of")[119] and further defines what the author means by the "secret person," rather than identifying the spirit as the Holy Spirit.[120] The two words that modify "spirit," "meek" and "quiet," are Christian rather than purely feminine virtues.[121] "Meek" is used by Jesus as a self-designation (Matt 11:29) and characterizes people on whom he pronounced a blessing (Matt 5:5); our author calls all people to such a virtue in 3:16.[122] Similarly, a "quiet" spirit is the ideal both for the Christian community (1 Tim 2:2) as well as for individual Christians (1 Thess 4:11; 2 Thess 3:12).[123]

The relative pronoun ὅ that introduces the final phrase may refer to "spirit,"[124] but it could also refer to the entire preceding clause[125] as indicating what is highly precious in God's sight. The latter alternative is probably the one to choose.

The thrust of the passage with its emphasis on the internal quality of the person, by implication visible only to God, is a topos in biblical thought[126] and, appropriately for this context, emphasizes the contrast between outward appearance and inner reality.[127] Because that contrast is not exclusively Christian—the Greco-Roman world also valued the inward reality of a person as opposed to an excessive outward show calculated to excite or impress—some have argued that what the author here sets forth is not a particularly Christian morality.[128] Yet the final phrase indicates clearly that the author meant it to be just that: what he has described is in fact something God values highly.

■ 5 In this verse we learn the reason (γάρ) for the advice given in vv. 3–4: This is also the way (οὕτως) holy women conducted themselves in the past (ποτε). While groups of people are identified as "holy" in the NT (e.g., holy apostles and prophets, Eph 3:5; 2 Pet 3:2; Christian believers as a class, Rom 1:7; 1 Cor 1:2; Phil 1:1), the phrase "holy women" (αἱ ἅγιαι γυναῖκες) is unique here in the Christian canon.[129] The mention of Sarah in v. 6 makes it likely that the author has in mind in the first instance the matriarchs of Jewish tradition, viz., Sarah, Rebecca, Rachel, and Leah,[130] who were holy not because of moral acts but because of their membership in God's holy people.[131] The "holy women" function therefore not so much as models of moral behavior to be imitated as examples of women who have followed the path here described.[132] That point is confirmed by the

119 Beare (155) identifies it as a "genitive of disposition," a category otherwise unidentified; cf. also Kelly, 130.

120 With Windisch, 67; Michaels, 162; contra Bigg, 152; Schelkle, 89–90; Best, 126. Goppelt (217) finds a compromise by having it refer to the human spirit shaped by the divine Spirit, a meaning also permitted by the context.

121 "Quietness" in the sense of "silence" was regarded as especially appropriate for women, e.g., Sir 26:14; Sophocles Ajax 293 ("For a woman, silence [σιγή] is a decoration [κοσμόν]"; I owe this reference to Hart, 63), a view carried over into some NT writings (e.g., 1 Tim 2:12), but its combination with πραΰς in this phrase shifts it to a more universal application here.

122 So also, e.g., Senior, 56; Philipps, Kirche, 50; Brox, 124. Balch (Wives, 102) notes the use of both words by Musonius (in that case as adverbs) to describe how a philosopher will respond to an insult ("Will the Philosopher Prosecute Anyone for Personal Injury?" [Lutz, Musonius Rufus, 78.10]).

123 Senior, 56. As Michaels (162) observes, it continued to be regarded as a significant virtue in the post-canonical church, e.g., Did. 3.8; Hermas Man. 8.10; Ps. Sol. 12.5.

124 Kelly (130) thinks that the close proximity of πνεῦμα makes it "the more natural alternative."

125 So also, e.g., Beare, 155; Best, 126. A relative pronoun is used in a similarly general way in 1:6 (ἐν ᾧ).

126 E.g., 1 Sam 16:7; Isa 61:10; Matt 6:4, 6, 18. See Philo Migr. Abr. 97, where the women who wove the material for the tabernacle exchanged decoration of the body for the (superior) decoration of piety.

127 So also, e.g., Michaels (161), who frames it in terms of what human society values and what God values.

128 So, e.g., Brox, 145. A quiet response to slander, very likely the context here addressed, was also prized in late antiquity; see the examples cited in Balch, Wives, 103.

129 A point noted also by Tarrech, "Le milieu," 377.

130 With, e.g., Michaels, 164.

131 With, e.g., Best, 126. As Schelkle (90) notes, "holy" here has its original cultic, rather than a moral, meaning.

132 So also, e.g., Goppelt, 218.

different language used to describe them from the language used to describe Christ in the preceding section, where the household slaves were in fact "called" to emulate aspects of that life. Such "calling" to follow an example is absent here. The activity most characteristic of the women for our author was their continuing hope[133] in God; the similar form of αἱ ἅγιαι ("the holy [women]") and αἱ ἐλπίζουσαι ("who hoped") makes clear that it is that aspect of holiness the author wishes to emphasize.[134]

The imperfect verb ἐκόσμουν, here designating customary or habitual action in the past ("were accustomed to decorate themselves"), shows that despite the grammatically apparent contrast in vv. 3–4 between outer decoration and inner spirit, there nevertheless was also a contrast in modes of decoration, the one external and appealing to sensual desires, the other internal and reflecting the values of the wife's faith. The repetition at the end of this verse of the phrase with which v. 1 began

(ὑποτασσόμεναι τοῖς ἰδίος ἀνδράσιν) shows a preliminary closure to the argument, with v. 6 providing an example of the holy women of the past mentioned in this verse. The participle here, as in v. 1, is not imperatival but circumstantial,[135] here either attendant circumstance ("subordinate as they were to their own husbands"), or, more likely, instrumental ("by being subordinate to their own husbands"), the same force it had in v. 1.[136]

■ 6 As a way of completing the discussion begun with v. 1, the author cites Sarah as an example (ὡς Σάρρα)[137] of a holy woman who subordinated herself to her husband. As Sarah is one example of the holy women mentioned in v. 5, so her obedience is one example of the subordination of which the author is speaking (vv. 1, 5).[138] That obedience is illustrated by her calling[139] Abraham "master,"[140] an allusion to Gen 18:12.[141] Whether the context of Abraham and Sarah resident in a foreign land also figures in this choice of Sarah as example, fitting as it would be for the context of this letter,[142] cannot be

133 Beare (156) notes correctly that the present participle used here, ἐλπίζουσαι, is durative and designates "the continuing attitude of their life."

134 Because hope in God is a major reality in this epistle (e.g., 1:21), and can characterize the Christian life (3:15), it must be understood here in its broadest sense as well. A specific reference to Jewish messianic hope is probably not meant here, as Best (126) observes correctly.

135 With, e.g., Michaels, 164.

136 Jacques Schlosser ("I Pierre 3,5b–6," Bib 64 [1983] 410) is correct that it has the same force, but incorrect in identifying that force as imperatival; but even if it were imperatival in v. 1, it is hard to see how it could have that force here.

137 So also Michaels, 164. It is unnecessary to assume with Spicq (122) that the phrase ὡς . . . τέκνα is a parenthesis, even though the argument ends formally with v. 5, since the whole of the verse explains how and why Sarah is a good example for the author.

138 Obedience (ὑπήκουσεν) is thus not a definition of the subordination (ὑποτασσόμεναι) mentioned in v. 5, but an example of it; on this point see also Elliott, Elect, 131. The imperfect ὑπήκουεν found in some mss. is an attempt to make that clear.

139 The participle καλοῦσα has an instrumental sense ("by calling"), i.e., it was this act that demonstrated her obedience to him, but it is perhaps best rendered as attendant circumstance ("when she called").

140 The rabbis also understood this text as showing Sarah's obedience to her husband, as Kelly (131) and

Schelkle (90 n. 1; he cites Str-B 3.764) note. Dorothy I. Sly ("1 Peter 3:6b in the Light of Philo and Josephus," JBL 110 [1991] 126–29) argues that our author, like Philo and Josephus, was embarrassed by Gen 16:2 where Abraham obeyed Sarah (cf. 16:2; 21:12), and so "has molded Sarah to the image of the ideal Hellenistic wife, even at the price of reversing the biblical record" (129).

141 A similar instance of husband being called "master" (κύριε) can be found in LXX 1 Kgdms 1:8, where Anna so addresses her husband (so Bengel, Gnomon, 742), but the source here is clearly from Gen 18:12, as even Mark Kiley ("Like Sara: The Tale of Terror behind 1 Pet 3:6," JBL 106 [1987] 691–92) must concede. In that light it is hard to see why Schwank et al. (61) suggest that the author was thinking of other later Jewish texts, now lost, to account for this phrase.

142 So, e.g., Kelly, 132; Moffatt, 133. Kiley ("Like Sara," 692 et passim) suggests that the context of Abraham's unjust treatment of Sarah in Genesis 12 and 20 makes her especially appropriate for this context.

determined for lack of evidence; the general high regard in which Sarah was held in both Jewish[143] and Christian[144] tradition is probably sufficient to account for her presence here.[145]

The second half of the verse describes Christian wives as children of Sarah. The aorist ἐγενήθητε ("you became") indicates a past action,[146] thus rendering it highly unlikely that the two participles (ἀγαθοποιοῦσαι, φοβού-μεναι) are to be understood as conditional, that is, "if you do good and do not fear."[147] To understand ἐγενήθητε in its usual sense means the participles are more likely to be either instrumental of means, that is, you became her children "by doing good and not fearing,"[148] or more likely as attendant circumstance, that is, you became her children "when you did what is good and did not have any fear."[149] To suggest the point at which these Christian women became "children of Sarah" as the time of their baptism[150] is to miss the point of the passage. What is at issue is not when, or how, the women ad-dressed became Christian;[151] the point is how Christian wives are to act within the potentially hostile situation of marriage to nonbelieving husbands. Sarah is thus understood not as the "mother" of the faith of these Christian women, but as an example of the way these Christian women are to act within their marriage situation. Thus they became her "children" when they emulated the respect she showed her husband Abraham, not when they were admitted to the Christian faith by baptism.[152]

Although the verb "to do good" (ἀγαθοποιέω) is not of Christian coinage,[153] in our letter it is virtually synonymous with doing God's will (see 2:15), and is so to be understood here. The second phrase (μὴ φοβούμεναι μηδεμίαν πτόησιν ["free from all fear"]), perhaps an echo of the phrase οὐ φοβηθήσῃ πτόησιν ("do not be terrorized") found in Prov 3:25,[154] means to be free from any fear[155] of other human beings.[156] Its use here, along with the reference to doing what is good, points to the

---

143 She was the mother of the Hebrew race: Gen 51:2; she was idealized as more beautiful than other women, and possessing great wisdom: 1QapGen 20.6–8; she was an example of joy in face of fear: Philo *Abr.* 205–7; *Spec. leg.* 2.54–55 (I owe these references to Selwyn, 185; Knibb, *Qumran*, 191; Balch, *Wives*, 105, respectively); cf. also Best, 127. Balch (*Wives*, 104) also calls attention to some second-century rabbinic traditions that used Gen 18:12–13 to stress the importance of peace between husband and wife. That is also a point here, provided such peace does not lead the wife to violate her Christian faith, an emphasis Balch appears to overlook.

144 She was a model of faith: Heb 11:11.

145 That Paul's use of Abraham as a type of faith also figures here, a parallelism that Schelkle (91) and Wand (91) find significant but that Brox ("Sara zum Beispiel," 490) denies, is rendered less likely by the absence of any reference to Abraham elsewhere in 1 Peter. What is apparent, as Kelly (130) also notes, is the appropriation by the Christian community of the OT traditions, with no notion of Sarah being a type of Christian wives, or Christian wives in any way representing a fulfillment of Sarah's actions.

146 To see this with Beare (156) as a gnomic aorist, and hence timeless, is rendered questionable by the absence of any kind of proverbial flavor to the phrase. It is doubtful whether our author thought it a general rule that anyone who did what is good and did not fear was a child of Sarah.

147 With, e.g., van Unnik, "Teaching," 93; Beare, 157. The apodosis of a condition implies future ful-fillment: "If A occurs [protasis], B will also occur [apodosis]."

148 So, e.g., Bigg, 153; but see Goppelt, 219.

149 The claim of Bigg (153–54) that the participles seem to be "clearly an exhortation" is wide of the mark.

150 As do, e.g., Kelly, 131: Michaels, 166.

151 That also seems to lie behind the concern expressed, e.g., by Goppelt (219), that the two participles not be the basis of the women being children of Sarah.

152 Nor can one infer anything from the status of these women prior to their baptism, e.g., that they were pagan, as Kelly (131) suggests.

153 On its use in secular culture, see the comments on 2:20 above.

154 As, e.g., Selwyn (185) suggests, although apart from the rarity of that combination of words there is no compelling contextual reason for such a derivation, as there is, for example, when the phrase is quoted by Athanasius *Morb. et val.* 6.28–30 or Origen *Frag. Luc.* 196.6–7.

155 The noun πτόησις refers to vehement emotion or excitement, and could imply someone flying into a rage, although here it is probably to be understood as a cognate accusative, and to mean "fear" or "terror."

156 Only here and in 3:14, both OT allusions and both with cognate accusative, does the word φοβέω mean "fear" with respect to human beings, rather than as normally in this letter, reverence for God; so also, e.g., Michaels, 167; Selwyn, 185.

fact that the wife is to do what is appropriate for her as a Christian even within the confines of a marriage to a non-Christian husband, a husband who may use fear and intimidation in the attempt to compel activity inappropriate for her as a Christian.[157] It is for that reason that these Christians wives are paradigmatic for the way all Christians are to live within a hostile cultural situation, and hence is the basis for their inclusion here.[158]

■ **7** Since this verse shares characteristics similar to the preceding sections dealing with household conduct—introduction with ὁμοίως ("similarly"), address, participle, advice, and then motivation—it is, despite its brevity, to be regarded as the third in the series advising household members on appropriate conduct, each of which depends on the imperatives of 2:17.[159] The participle συνοι-κοῦντες ("living with"), like the those in 2:18 and 3:1, is to be construed not as imperatival[160] but as instrumental: it indicates the way obligations are to be met.[161] While those addressed (οἱ ἄνδρες) surely include husbands, a meaning clearly intended in 3:1, the use of the adjectival substantive "female" (τῷ γυναικείῳ) instead of the noun "woman" or "wife" (τῇ γύνῃ) points to a wider meaning, and probably refers to the way males in a household deal

with its female members,[162] including of course the man's wife but not limited to her. Those female members of the household are further characterized as "the weaker vessel." The comparative adjective "weaker" (ἀσθενεστέρῳ) clearly implies that both men and women are "vessels," with the women the weaker of the two.[163] While in Hellenistic culture such weakness was taken as a description of a woman's nature, moral and intellectual as well as physical,[164] the point here is not to highlight women's spiritual or moral weakness—3:1–2 counters such an idea—but rather their physical frailty.[165] In keeping with Christian tradition, that meant that they must be given the special consideration accorded those of lesser social and physical capacity, since they too are precious in God's eyes.[166] They too must also be apportioned honor (ἀπονέμοντες τιμήν)[167] despite the lower value in which they are held in non-Christian society.[168] The use of "vessel" (σκεῦος) to describe a woman is rare in the NT,[169] where it also can be used to describe a man.[170] The intention here may be to point to human beings as creatures and hence as having no justification to take advantage of one another.[171]

The way men are to dwell with women as the weaker

157 So also, e.g., Windisch, 68; Beare, 157; Calvin, 98; Philipps, *Kirche*, 51.

158 The paradigmatic nature of this description of wives is further indicated by the inclusion of advice not to fear in 3:14, which is clearly addressed to all readers.

159 See also Goppelt, 220; Michaels, 167. Schutter (*Hermeneutic*, 64) finds it the fourth in a series illustrative of 2:12, but the dependence of the participles in 2:18, 3:1, and 3:7 on 2:17, plus the absence of ὁμοίως in 2:18, argues for it as the third in that series.

160 As, e.g., Selwyn (483) would have it; see also Goppelt, 220; Michaels, 167.

161 See also Wand (92), although he connects it to the imperative ὑποτάγητε of 2:13 rather than to the four commands of 2:17, as I would prefer to do.

162 So also Reicke, 102; idem, "Gnosis," 302. That insight renders less likely the contention of Kelly (132, 134) that συνοικοῦντες has special reference to sexual intercourse. The argument of, e.g., Schroeder ("Once you were no people," 56) and Carl D. Gross ("Are the Wives of 1 Peter 3.7 Christians?" *JSNT* 35 [1989] 89–96) that it refers to non-Christian wives of Christian husbands is also weakened if this refers to all women in the household.

163 So also Bigg, 155; Hart, 65; Wand, 93; Grudem, 144.

164 E.g., *Ep. Arist.* 250; Tacitus *Ann.* 3.34; see also n. 13

above.

165 So also, e.g., Kelly, 133; Cranfield, 91; Goppelt, 222.

166 Cf., e.g., Mark 9:33–37; 10:42–45; Matt 5:3, 5; 18:1–4, 10–14; 23:11–12; Luke 14:7–11.

167 The participle ἀπονέμεντες is circumstantial, and provides further information on how the men are to dwell with the women in the household.

168 Paul makes a similar point, using the analogy of body parts, in 1 Cor 12:22–24, as Reicke ("Gnosis," 302–3) notes.

169 The only parallel is 1 Thess 4:4, but it is questionable whether the author had that verse in mind, as Beare (157) avers.

170 Paul, in Acts 19:5, as an instrument of God. In later Christian tradition it can occasionally be used to describe a human being as container of the spirit (*Hermas Man.* 5.1.2,) or even Christ (*Barn.* 7.3; I owe these references to Goppelt, 221 n. 6).

171 For a similar use of pottery as an analogy to the human situation, see Rom 9:21–23; Jer 18:1–11.

partners is described, in addition to the circumstantial participle ἀπονέμοντες ("according"), by the prepositional phrase κατὰ γνῶσιν, also used in an adverbial sense. It probably is to be understood as playing the same role as the phrase ἐν φόβῳ ("reverent") in 3:2 and διὰ συνείδησιν θεοῦ ("because of one's consciousness of God") in 2:9, that is, enlightened by the man's knowledge of what God requires of him,[172] rather than meaning simply "considerately" or "intelligently."[173] The description of the women as coheirs of the grace of life forms a grammatical parallel to their description as weaker vessels[174] and gives further reason for men not to adopt the normal cultural attitude toward them, since in God's eyes, as heirs of grace, men and women stand on the same level.[175] The genitive ζωῆς ("life") is probably epexegetic ("grace that consists in life") rather than qualitative or adjectival ("living grace"),[176] and bears an eschatological implication: it refers to the new life awaiting the Christian subsequent to God's judgment of the world.[177]

The seriousness with which God takes the necessity of men to treat women as equal heirs to God's eschatological grace is shown in the final phrase: lack of such treatment means that men's prayers to God are hindered and so have no effect[178]—God does not listen to them.[179] While the pronoun in the phrase "your prayers" (ὑμῶν) could perhaps be understood to mean the prayers of both men and women,[180] there is nothing in the context to lead one to assume the pronoun refers to anyone but the men addressed in this verse (οἱ ἄνδρες).[181] The notion that God would ignore the prayers of women who are not treated in a Christian way would be to punish the weak who are abused, an idea hardly in accord with Christian tradition about the relation of God to the downtrodden. The point is clear: men who transfer cultural notions about the superiority of men over women into the Christian community lose their ability to communicate with God.[182]

The essential incompatibility of the Christian ethos with that of secular culture is here once more clearly on display,[183] and it is surely for that reason that this section on the Christian men and husbands is included, not because such advice was a normal part of household codes[184] or specifically to address men who had pagan wives.[185] Rather, it is included to warn men (and husbands) that the advice to wives in 3:1–6 to be sub-

---

172 So also, e.g., Senior, "Conduct," 435–36; cf. Goppelt, 221.

173 For an argument in favor of such an understanding, see Reicke, "Gnosis," passim.

174 The ὡς plays the same role in both phrases; the first is not a concessive particle, as Reicke ("Gnosis," 302) holds.

175 With, e.g., Patterson, "Roles in Marriage," 77. For a contrasting view, see *Gos. Thom.* 114: women as women cannot be saved.

176 With, e.g., Beare, 158; Spicq, 124; Kelly, 134; Windisch, 68. Χάριτος is an objective genitive: it indicates what is inherited.

177 So also, e.g., Delling, "Der Bezug," 99; Reicke, "Gnosis," 303; Michaels, 170. See 1:4 for that point in relation to the Christian's inheritance. The addition of αἰώνιον in P[72] points in the same direction.

178 The verb used here, ἐνκόπτω, means lit. "cut into." It can also mean hinder (e.g., Acts 24:4); in Paul, it means to hinder to the point of stopping something altogether (Rom 15:22; Gal 5:7; 1 Thess 2:18). The passive infinitive used here (ἐγκόπτεσθαι), if intended as divine passive, would mean that God himself is doing the hindering.

179 That liturgical acts are invalid, even useless, without proper conduct was an emphasis of the Hebrew prophets, e.g., Isa 1:10–17; Amos 5:21–24. It is also

reflected in Christian tradition, e.g., Matt 5:23–24; 1 Cor 11:20–29; Jas 4:2–3. Cf. Senior, "Conduct," 436; Spicq, 125.

180 So, e.g., Beare, 158; Michaels, 171; Selwyn, 186; Goppelt, 222; Moffatt, 134; Senior, 60; Schelkle, 91; Spicq, 125; Ketter, 249; Calvin, 100. Kelly (134) cites 1 Cor 7:5 to support this position, but the context there is quite different; it concerns acts done in mutual agreement between husband and wife.

181 So also, e.g., Reicke, 103; idem, "Gnosis," 303; Cranfield, 92; Bengel, *Gnomon*, 743; Bigg, 155; Schwank et al., 64. The assertion of Schiwy (51) that the prayers of a Christian husband for the conversion of his non-Christian wife are meant is not a necessary inference here.

182 While Hellenistic authors could argue that the husband was to treat the wife in a kindly way, it was always within the larger context of his effective rule over her; e.g., Plutarch *Mor.*, *Con. pr.* 142E (33), Callicratides *On the Happiness of Households* 106.1–10 (cited in Balch, *Wives*, 56–57).

183 With Senior, "Conduct," 436; cf. also Tarrech, "Le milieu," 125.

184 As, e.g., Senior (58) and Brox (147) claim. The absence of reference in this passage to masters or children, also normal in Christian household codes, argues against such an assumption.

ordinate to their pagan husbands did not carry with it the kind of superior status for male members of the Christian community that it did in secular society. Reciprocity is the key to such relationships within the Christian faith. The discussion of the place of men could be somewhat more succinct than that of slaves and wives, however, since (1) men and husbands do not serve as examples to the Christian community of the way Christians are to react to the oppression of secular society,[186] and (2) Christian men would also have had fewer difficulties in secular society than women, even when they lived out

their Christian convictions, given the bias against women in that culture.[187] Yet the section apparently had to be included, lest any notion of female inferiority infect the essential equality between men and women inherent within the Christian community: they are together and equally heirs of God's grace that promises life in the age to come.[188]

---

185 So Michaels, 169; John A. Hutton, "A Ruling from 'First Peter,'" *Expositor*, 8th series, 23 (1922) 426. Although analogy to 3:1–6 could suggest this, and although there surely would have been such cases, there is nothing in the verse itself to point in that direction, and the broader term "female" (γυναικεῖος) instead of the word normally used for "wife" (γύνη) argues against it.
186 So also, e.g., Balch, *Wives*, 96; Lohse, "Parenesis," 44.
187 Cf. also Schelkle, 91.
188 Goppelt, 222; idem, "Prinzipien," 292. Refoulé ("Bible," 471) notes that treating another as coheir of God's grace lies at the heart of the Christian social ethic.

3 **Appropriate Conduct
for Every Christian**

8 Finally, all of you,[1] by being of one mind,
sympathetic, loving the Christian family,
being compassionate, humble-minded,[2]
9/ not returning evil for evil or reviling for
reviling, but on the contrary blessing,[3]
because to this you have been called, in
order that you may inherit a blessing. 10/
For the one who wishes to strive after[4]
life and to see good days, let that one
restrain the[5] tongue from evil and the lips
from speaking[6] deceit. 11/ Let[7] that one
incline away from evil and do good, seek
peace and pursue it, 12/ because the
eyes of the Lord are turned to the
righteous and his ears to their prayers,
but the face of the Lord is set against
those who do evil.[8]

1 As in the case of the previous sections, the adjectives
and participles are dependent on the imperatives
contained in 2:17; understood here is something like
"Fulfill your Christian calling by. . . ."

2 A few texts read φιλόφρονες instead of the far more
widely attested, and likely original, ταπεινόφρονες,
perhaps under the influence of the preceding
φιλάδελφοι; L and a few others include both.

3 Some texts (P, some others) add εἰδότες ("Because
you know"), in that way changing the force of the
ὅτι from a causal particle to a conjunction
introducing an objective clause, and making the
subsequent phrases the content of what is known. In
light of its redundancy, and the far superior textual
witness to its absence (P72, A, B, C, K, Ψ, a number
of minuscules, the Latin, Syriac, and Coptic
versions), it is probably a later accretion to the text.

4 While the verb is ἀγαπᾶν ("love"), the meaning here
is closer to the force it bears, e.g., in Luke 11:43,
"strive for"; cf. also Wis 1:1; Luke 12:43; 2 Tim
4:10. On this point, see Kelly, 138. Reicke (105)
suggests "The one who desires to be a Christian" as
the intent.

5 Some mss. (ℵ, P, 𝔐, some Latin and Syriac mss.) add
αὐτοῦ here and after "lips" in the next phrase,
perhaps under the influence of LXX Ps 33:14,
which has σου in each of those places. The strong
witness against such additions (P72, 81, A, B, C, Ψ,
33, 81, 1739, other minuscules, some mss. of the
Vulgate) probably means they were added later.

6 There is an idiosyncratic substitution of the present
infinitive λαλεῖν for the aorist λαλῆσαι by P72; the
majority reading, also agreeing with LXX Ps 33:14,
is surely the original reading.

7 ms. evidence is about evenly divided on whether a δέ
is to be read in this verse (P72, A, B, C*, 69, 81,
614, 630, 1505, 2495, some other minuscules, lat,
syh) or not (ℵ, C2vid, P, Ψ, 𝔐, vgmss, syp, co); its
absence in LXX Ps 33:15 may argue for its later
elimination.

8 Under the influence of the conclusion of LXX Ps
33:17 (τοῦ ἐξολεθρεῦσαι ἐκ γῆς τὸ μνημόσυνον αὐτῶν;
"to eliminate their memory from the earth"), some
minuscules, along with Vulgate mss. and some Syriac
witnesses, have added τοῦ ἐξολοθρεῦσαι αὐτοὺς ἐκ γῆς
("to eliminate them from the earth").

Analysis

The structure of these verses is the same as that of the
passages beginning with 2:18–25: an address (πάντες
["all"]; see 2:18: οἰκέται ["slaves"]; 3:1: γυναῖκες ["wives"];
3:7: ἄνδρες ["men"]); a conjunctive adverb (τὸ δὲ τέλος
["finally"]; see 3:1, 7: ὁμοίως ["similarly"]); description of

how commands of 2:17 are to be fulfilled (ὁμόφρονες, κτλ.
["by [being] of one accord," et al.]; see 2:18; 3:1:
ὑποτασσόμενοι ["by being subordinate"]; 3:7: συννοι-
κοῦντες ["by dwelling with"]); basis for paranesis (3:9b,
12; see 2:21–25; 3:5–6; 3:7b).[9] The presence of such
similarities of structure to the earlier sections concerning

household slaves, wives, and men indicates it is meant to conclude (τὸ δὲ τέλος) this series beginning with 2:18, all of which have been dependent on the concluding verse of 2:13–17.[10] It therefore functions as the final section of this series, rather than as its summation.[11] To find a chiastic structure in vv. 8–11, in which the positive elements in vv. 8 and 11b have their correlation with the negative elements in vv. 9a and 10–11a,[12] is possible, but not compelling; that v. 8 refers to conduct within the Christian community, v. 9 to conduct with those outside of it, is again possible, but there is no clear indication in the text of such a shift of focus, and the citation from LXX Ps 33:13–17 is equally applicable to both situations.

While no other social code in the NT ends with such a general exhortation,[13] the content is familiar to Christian tradition (e.g., Matt 5:44; Luke 6:27–28; Eph 4:1–3, 31–32; Col 3:12–14; 1 Thess 5:13b–15; *Did.* 1.3; Polycarp *Phil.* 2.2).[14] That it more specifically reflects

portions of Rom 12:9–18 and hence shows that 1 Peter was dependent on that passage is of course possible, but the limited overlap of vocabulary, and the different order in which the elements are treated,[15] render such dependence less than certain. More likely is a common dependence on elements of early Christian tradition,[16] in each case used for the specific purpose of the author.[17] The three concluding verses reflect LXX Ps 33:13–17a,[18] a psalm also known to Christian tradition,[19] but the psalm verses are used here not so much to supply a basis for vv. 8–9 as to provide further confirmation for what has been written.[20] The passage as a whole therefore serves as a transition, linked to what has preceded it by the adverb announcing it as a concluding statement

---

9 Cf. Goppelt, 224; on its similarity to Rom 12:9–18, see below.

10 The argument of Cranfield (93) that it forms an epilogue to the section begun with 2:11 is weakened by the direct dependence of the ensuing discussion beginning with 3:13 on the content of the preceding psalm citation. In fact, 2:11–13 introduce the entire body middle, 2:11—4:11; the body closing begins with 4:12, as the repeated ἀγαπητοί ("Beloved") indicates.

11 With, e.g., Best, 128–29. If there is a summation, it probably occurs in the psalm citation in 3:10–12, which in vv. 10–11 returns to the imperatival mood that is prominent in 2:13, 17 but that is carefully avoided in the intervening 2:18—3:9. Thus 3:10–12 closes out the series of addresses dependent on the four imperatives of 2:17 by introducing a second set of four imperatives in 3:10–11, hence serving as a transition to further material begun with 3:13, addressed to the "all" introduced in 3:8.

12 Suggested by Best, 129.

13 So also, e.g., Best, 128–29; Brox, 152.

14 Cf. Goppelt, 224; Meeks, *Moral World*, 135; Schelkle, 95.

15 Φιλάδελφοι in 1 Pet 3:8 and Rom 11:10; κακὸν ἀντὶ κακοῦ in 1 Pet 3:9 and Rom 12:17a; εὐλογοῦντες in 1 Pet 3:9 and Rom 12:14; in addition, Goppelt (224) finds similarities to ὁμόφρονες in Rom 12:16, συμπαθεῖς in 12:15, εὔσπλαγχνοι and ταπεινόφρονες in 12:16. The different order of treatment in Romans is apparent.

16 So, e.g., Michaels, 174–75; Goppelt, 224.

17 The wide range of traditions reflected does show how common it was that Christians were reviled by those outside the community, as, e.g., Brox (155) also notes.

18 For the specific changes, cf. Osborne, "L'utilisation," 70–71; Schutter, *Hermeneutic*, 145. The changes will be discussed in detail in the comments on the individual verses below. Whether that means it was an independent tradition, as Brox (152) holds, or shows it to be a composition of our author, is difficult to determine.

19 These same verses are cited in *1 Clem.* 22.2–6, but in a form so close to the LXX that that must be seen as the origin of the quotation, not 1 Peter or a similar tradition. The additional absence of any LXX witness to the variations found in this passage argues for the originality of those changes, as Schutter (*Hermeneutic*, 145) also notes. Other references to LXX Ps 33 cited by Schwank ("L'Epître [1 P 3,8–15]," 19), e.g., Luke 1:53; Heb 12:14; *Barn.* 9.2, are so vague and fleeting that they cannot sustain the assumption of widespread use; only if such widespread use of the psalm is assumed can one find in those verses echoes of it. The argument of Bornemann ("Taufrede," passim) that 1 Peter in its entirety is based on this psalm has been rightly rejected, e.g., by Schutter, *Hermenentic*, 48.

20 So also, e.g., Goppelt, 226. This is 1 Peter's normal use of such citations; cf. 1:24–25a; 2:9–10. Best ("1 Peter II 4–10," 272) notes correctly that the course of the argument would not be significantly affected if the quotation had been omitted.

($\tau\grave{o}$ $\delta\grave{\epsilon}$ $\tau\acute{\epsilon}\lambda o\varsigma$) and linked to what follows by being addressed to "all" ($\pi\acute{\alpha}\nu\tau\epsilon\varsigma$).[21]

The thrust of the passage, intended to confirm that the messages addressed to slaves, wives, and men have wider application to the entire Christian community, concerns the need for Christians not to allow the hostility of secular society to creep into the community itself[22] nor to let it provoke Christians to retaliate in kind.[23] Although the verse has eschatological implications,[24] the citation of LXX Psalm 33, particularly in v. 10, indicates that it is also meant to point to current benefits for such activity.[25] Meeting hostility with kindness will prove, in our author's estimate, the only possible way to survive as a Christian community in a hostile world, yet perhaps more importantly, as the citation from LXX Psalm 33 shows, it is the only way that that community can fulfill God's will for them.

Comment

■ 8 The opening adverbial phrase ($\tau\grave{o}$ $\delta\grave{\epsilon}$ $\tau\acute{\epsilon}\lambda o\varsigma$, "finally")[26] shows this to be the final paragraph of this section (2:13—3:12), and as such brings it to a conclusion.[27] As in the case of the other passages that were addressed to various groups (2:18; 3:1; 3:7), this passage, addressed now to all readers ($\pi\acute{\alpha}\nu\tau\epsilon\varsigma$),[28] may similarly be understood as dependent on the imperatives of 2:17, and as assuming the participle $\ddot{o}\nu\tau\epsilon\varsigma$ to complete the meaning of the adjectives: "All of you, [fulfill the commands by being] of one mind."[29] However the sentence be understood, it is clear that desirable characteristics of the whole Christian community, rather than of a more limited group within it, are here described and recommended.

The adjectives describe qualities familiar in early Christian tradition, although in forms that are not widely represented. ${}^{\prime}O\mu\acute{o}\phi\rho o\nu\epsilon\varsigma$ ("similarly minded"), unique to the NT, nevertheless describes the quality of harmony within the Christian community highly prized and recommended within the tradition,[30] as it was also among secular writers of the time.[31] The word means not so much uniformity in thought as having a common goal.[32] $\Sigma\upsilon\mu\pi\alpha\theta\epsilon\hat{\iota}\varsigma$ ("sympathetic"), also unique here in the NT,[33] is similarly recognized as a desirable quality.[34] $\Phi\iota\lambda\acute{\alpha}\delta\epsilon\lambda\phi o\iota$ ("loving the family" [lit. "brothers"]), another form unique in the NT,[35] refers to mutual affection within the Christian community rather than a general love directed toward all human beings.[36] It is again a

---

21 See also the comments in n. 11 above.

22 Brox (155) finds here a reflection of the high value placed on peace within the Christian community, Reicke ("Gnosis," 304) on organic unity.

23 Lohse ("Parenesis," 44) notes that here common Christian traditions have been placed within the special purview of this letter, a purview that concerns how Christians are to act in a hostile culture. Whether these traditions were part of a baptismal catechism, as Spicq (125) suggests, remains speculative.

24 E.g., v. 9b; cf. 1:4, where such an inheritance is clearly eschatological.

25 In agreement with Neugebauer ("Zur Deutung," 78), who finds confirmation in the orientation to the present in 3:13, which immediately follows this section.

26 This is its only appearance in the NT; as Michaels (176) notes, it is similar to the Pauline $\tau\grave{o}$ $\lambda o\iota\pi\acute{o}\nu$, e.g., Phil 3:1; 4:7.

27 With, e.g., Selwyn, 188; the content indicates that it is not so much a summary, as Holmer and de Boor (116) and Wand (94) aver, as it is the concluding paragraph.

28 Schweizer (72) argues correctly that this makes clear that what was said to slaves, wives, and men was to be understood as especially, but not exclusively, valid

for them.

29 Selwyn (483) and Michaels (176) represent the more common view, which is to see these as imperative adjectives, a use otherwise extremely rare in Greek. BDF (§ 468 [2]) assumes the presence of the imperative $\dot{\epsilon}\sigma\tau\acute{\epsilon}$ for what is noted as a "peculiar use" of participles with intervening adjectives.

30 E.g., Phil 2:2, $\tau\grave{o}$ $\alpha\dot{\upsilon}\tau\grave{o}$ $\phi\rho o\nu\hat{\eta}\tau\epsilon$, $\tau\grave{o}$ $\dot{\epsilon}\nu$ $\phi\rho o\nu o\hat{\upsilon}\nu\tau\epsilon\varsigma$; 4:2, $\tau\grave{o}$ $\alpha\dot{\upsilon}\tau\grave{o}$ $\phi\rho o\nu\epsilon\hat{\iota}\nu$; cf. Rom 15:5; 1 Cor 1:10; 2 Cor 13:11; Acts 2:46; 4:32.

31 E.g., Dio Chrysostom Or. 21.15, 43 (forms of $\dot{o}\mu o\nu\phi\rho o\sigma\acute{\upsilon}\nu\eta$); 22.3, 6; 30.13 (forms of $\dot{o}\mu o\phi\rho o\nu\acute{\epsilon}\omega$); cf. also Strabo Geog. 6.3.3.34–35, a reference I owe to Kelly, 135.

32 So also, e.g., Goppelt (227), who links the common goal to a common Lord to whom allegiance is owed.

33 The verb form $\sigma\upsilon\mu\pi\alpha\theta\acute{\epsilon}\omega$ appears in Heb 4:15; 10:34; the noun $\sigma\upsilon\mu\pi\acute{\alpha}\theta\epsilon\iota\alpha$ occurs some ten times in 4 Maccabees.

34 Cf. Rom 12:15; 1 Cor 12:26, in addition to Heb 4:15; 10:34.

35 It occurs twice in the LXX, 2 Macc 15:14; 4 Macc 13:21, and in Philo Jos. 218. More common is the noun $\phi\iota\lambda\alpha\delta\epsilon\lambda\phi\acute{\iota}\alpha$; e.g., Rom 12:10; 1 Thess 4:9; Heb 13:1; 1 Pet 1:22; 2 Pet 1:7; 4 Macc 13:23, 26; 14:1; 15:10.

36 So also, e.g., Beare, 160. It is similarly used in, e.g., 2

virtue much commended in the NT, and one that became a noteworthy characteristic of the Christian community.[37] Εὔσπλαγχνοι ("compassionate"), rare in the NT,[38] describes again uniquely Christian mercy or compassion, since its derivation as a Christian virtue originates from the fact that it describes divine mercy[39] which is then enacted by Jesus.[40] Ταπεινόφρονες ("humble-minded"), once more used only here in the NT,[41] identifies nevertheless a highly commended virtue,[42] based in no small part on the conduct and teaching of Jesus himself.[43]

These adjectives thus describe in somewhat unusual vocabulary[44] esteemed qualities of conduct toward fellow Christians.[45] Further, each quality identified is in one way or another related to the general theme of subordination that has dominated the discussion since 2:18.[46] Although such subordination has to this point been pointed to as the proper attitude for slaves and wives to non-Christians, an emphasis resumed in the ensuing verse, here it is directed to the life within the Christian community.[47] Subordination is therefore, as this verse shows, not a cultural expedient, but rather something that grows out of the heart of the Christian faith. What is asked of Christians in relation to their hostile, non-Christian culture grows out of the ethic that prescribes how they are to live with one another.

■ **9** The participles in this verse (ἀποδιδόντες ["returning"], εὐλογοῦντες ["blessing"]) are the last ones to refer to the commands in 2:17, and as those others similarly placed, they are instrumental in force, that is, the commands are to be obeyed not by repaying harm and insult in like manner but rather by blessing those who so act.[48] That it is well not to respond to evil or insult in kind is known in both Hellenistic[49] and Jewish thought,[50] but the roots of

---

Macc 15:14 and Philo *Jos.* 218.

37 See the passages listed in n. 35 above. Lucian of Samosata (*Pergr. mort.* 13) claims Jesus taught that all Christians are brothers, and satirizes the extremes to which Christians went to actualize such love for fellow Christians, indicating thereby the commonness of such activity.

38 Its only other occurrence is Eph 4:32; it also appears in *T. Sim.* 4.4; *T. Benj.* 4.1; Pr Man 12:7. The more common form omits the prefix εὐ-; as the noun σπλάγχνα it is used primarily in the Epistles (but see Luke 1:78; Acts 1:18); as the verb εὐσπλαγχνίζομαι it is used exclusively in the Synoptic Gospels. Used infrequently in Hellenistic Greek, it can also describe a human feeling, e.g., courage, as in Euripides *Rhesus* 191–92.

39 E.g., Luke 1:78.

40 E.g., Matt 9:36; Mark 1:41; Luke 7:13.

41 It did become part of Christian tradition, however; see Ignatius *Eph.* 10.2; *Barn.* 19.3. Its normal form in the NT is the noun ταπεινοφροσύνη: Acts 20:19; Eph 4:2; Phil 2:3; Col 2:18, 23; 3:12; 1 Pet 5:5.

42 The stem ταπειν- is used frequently to describe good Christian conduct, e.g., Luke 18:14; Rom 12:16. Such an attitude was normally considered a vice in Hellenistic culture, e.g. Plutarch *Mor.*, *De Alexandri magni fortuna aut virtuto* 336E; *De tranquillitate animi* 475E (references I owe to Michaels, 176); Epictetus *Diss.* 1.9.10; but see Aesop *Fab. synt.* 55.13: humility of mind is more useful that empty boasting.

43 E.g., Matt 11:29; 18:4; 23:12; cf. Phil 2:7.

44 It is difficult to see any progression contained within the order in which they are mentioned. The attempt by Gundry ("*Verba Christi,*" 340) to connect φιλάδελφοι with ταπεινόφρονες on the basis of Jesus' washing the disciples' feet (humility, John 13:4–5) followed somewhat later by his command that they love one another (John 13:34) shows more the source of these virtues than their association in this list, where they are separated by another adjective.

45 Philipps (*Kirche*, 22) suggests that the unusual vocabulary shows the effort of the author to speak of widely acknowledged Christian qualities in a fresh way.

46 So also, e.g., Kamlah, "ὑποτάσσεσθαι," 243. The attempt by Krafft ("Christologie," 125) to link them all to love as the "positive side" of subordination is a bit forced, particularly since the only adjective referring to love, φιλάδελφοι, neither begins nor concludes the list.

47 So also, e.g., Best, 129; Reicke, "Gnosis," 304.

48 The argument that these are "imperatival participles" is widely employed (e.g., Daube, "Participle," 483; Kelly, 136; Michaels, 177) but unnecessary. By their instrumental nature, they carry forward the imperatival force of the verbs in 2:17, indicating how those verbs are to be fulfilled.

49 E.g., Musonius Rufus ("Will the Philosopher Prosecute Anyone for Personal Injury?"), who argues that slander (he uses words from the stem λοιδορ-) can be silently borne; see Lutz, *Musonius Rufus*, 76–80, esp. 76.17–78.16.

50 E.g., Prov 17:13; *Jos. Asen.* 28.4; cf. 23.9; 28.14 (wrongly given as 28.12 in Piper, "Hope," 220, to

this passage surely lie in the Christian paranetic tradition that belongs to the earliest strands of Christian tradition, and understands itself to be derived from the sayings[51] and conduct[52] of Jesus himself.[53] The form represented in this verse is closer in formulation to the similar paranetic tradition in Paul, however,[54] and so finds its source in the traditions upon which Paul also drew rather than in the traditions later incorporated into the Gospels.[55] That one is to bless others is also reflected in the Jesus tradition[56] and means to call God's grace upon someone, as it does in the LXX and the NT, rather than simply to speak well of someone, its common meaning in secular Greek.[57]

Since our author can use the demonstrative pronoun τοῦτο to refer either to what was previously said (2:21) or to what is subsequently to be said (4:6), it is not clear in which direction the pronoun points in this verse. If it points back to εὐλογοῦντες, it means Christians are called to bless in order to inherit a blessing for themselves; if it points forward to εὐλογίαν κληρονομήσητε, it means Christians are called to inherit a blessing of their own. On the one hand, because pointing to what precedes would make inheriting the blessing conditional on one's own conduct of blessing, a point apparently at odds with the idea that the inheritance is a hope based on Christ's resurrection (1 Pet 1:4), which assures one of God's gift of salvation (1:5, 13),[58] and because in other NT texts the phrase εἰς τοῦτο is also followed by an epexegetic ἵνα clause,[59] τοῦτο here can be understood as pointing to what follows. On the other hand, because the similar language of 2:21 clearly indicates the Christian is called to specific behavior,[60] and because in the closely preceding 3:7b prayers being heard depend on appropriate activity,[61] and in the immediately following 3:10 the one who wishes to see good days must desist from certain behavior,[62] the τοῦτο can be understood as pointing to what precedes.[63] The closer similarity of the language to 2:21 than to 4:6, and the logic of the immediate context, 3:7b and 3:10–12, probably indicate that it is to be understood as pointing to what precedes.[64] The point is not that by such acts they "earn" the inheritance, since they already stand in it, as 1:3–5 make clear. Rather, the point is that by flouting the behavior appropriate to that inheritance, they may jeopardize their eventual entrance into it.

The idea expressed in v. 9b has fewer parallels in early

---

whom I owe the preceding references); 29.3; 2 Enoch 50.1–4.

51 E.g., Matt 5:38–42, 44; Luke 6:27–28.

52 Cf. 1 Pet 2:21 with the ensuing 22–23.

53 So also, e.g., Schelkle, 94; Brox, 152; Delling, "Der Bezug," 110; Piper, "Hope," 220; Pierre Lecomte, "Aimer la vie: I Pierre 3/10 (Psaume 34/13)," EThR 56 (1981) 291.

54 E.g., 1 Cor 4:12, λοιδορούμενοι εὐλογοῦμεν ("when cursed, we bless"); Rom 12:17; 1 Thess 5:15; cf. Rom 12:14; Eph 4:1–3; Col 3:13.

55 So also, e.g., Goppelt, "Jesus," 100; Brox, 154; Piper, "Hope," 220. It may be part of an early catechetical formulation, as Michaels (177) suggests. That would explain the lack of appeal to the words of Jesus, which Beare (160) finds "most remarkable."

56 E.g., Mark 10:16 (children); Luke 24:50 (apostles); cf. Acts 3:26 (Christians).

57 So, e.g., Schelkle, 94 n. 2. That this verse reflects 1 Pet 2:5, 9a, where Christians are called "priests," since in the OT blessing was the normal function assigned to them (cf. Num 6:22–27), as Best (130) and Schelkle (94) suggest, is rightly questioned by Michaels (178).

58 So, e.g., Goppelt, 228; cf. Kelly, 137. Best (130) argues that any other understanding would seem to clash with the idea of inheritance as a gift.

59 Piper ("Hope," 224, citing A. T. Robertson) points to Acts 9:21; Rom 14:9; 2 Cor 2:9; 1 John 3:8; one may add John 18:37.

60 As Piper ("Hope," 225) also observes.

61 So also, e.g. Piper, "Hope," 220.

62 Piper ("Hope," 225–27) points out that the changes the author makes to LXX Ps 33:13 in 1 Pet 3:10, where a rhetorical question is replaced by a conditional participle (θέλων) followed by a third person imperative (παυσάτω), indicate support for understanding the ἵνα clause as the motive for the necessity of blessing one's opponents.

63 The argument of Kelly (137) that the parenthetical phrase ὅτι εἰς τοῦτο ἐκλήθητε ("because to this you were called") is awkward if the εἰς τοῦτο points backward is nullified by the fact that the phrase need not, indeed ought not, be considered parenthetical, as Piper ("Hope," 225) also points out.

64 So also, e.g., Michaels, 178. That God's grace is linked to human behavior is a commonplace of Pauline tradition, e.g., Rom 2:6–10; 14:10; 2 Cor 5:10; Eph 6:8, and goes back to the words of Jesus, e.g., Matt 18:23–35; 25:31–46; John 12:48. It is also reflected in 1 Pet 4:4–5.

Christian tradition than the content of v. 9a, but the presence of eschatological blessing and final inheritance[65] expressed here finds an echo in Heb 12:17, indicating the possible traditional origin of this material as well.[66] Similar language expressing a similar thought in the opening verses of the epistle (esp. 1:4) show that whatever its source, it represents a basic theological tenet of our author.

Because the content of this verse could describe desirable conduct either among Christians (as, e.g., 1 Cor 4:12) or between Christians and nonbelievers (as, e.g., Rom 12:14–18), it is difficult to determine whether the author here continues to address internal matters, as in the immediately preceding verse, or begins to address external matters, an address implied in 3:10–12 and made explicit in 3:13–17. That similar material in Romans 12 addresses first internal (vv. 9–13), then external (vv. 14–21) relationships,[67] along with the similar phrase (εἰς τοῦτο ἐκλήθητε ["to this you have been called"]) in 1 Pet 2:21 that describes Christ's reaction to actions of his opponents, points to this verse as the beginning of advice concerning relationships with nonbelievers.[68] Since the command of Jesus to love one's

enemies (e.g., Matt 5:44; Luke 6:27–28) belongs to the tradition that also underlies this verse, one can perhaps here see our author's appropriation of that tradition, namely, that Christian love must be extended to all, even to those who oppose the ones who exercise such love.[69]

■ 10 This verse and the following two consist in an adapted quotation of LXX Ps 33:13–17a, with v. 10 patterned after vv. 13–14 of the psalm. While there are some variations between the two texts,[70] principally in changing the address from second to third person, it is difficult to know whether they were due to a different Greek text of the psalm followed by our author,[71] were the result of quoting by memory,[72] or were made deliberately to make a point.[73] Since the changes do result in conforming the psalm verses more closely to the present context in which v. 10 repeats the logic of v. 9 and thus reinforces it,[74] and do remain minor in scope and extent,[75] they are not beyond the kind of change for

---

65 While the context here points to eschatological blessing, Christian tradition did not restrict divine blessing to the future; cf., e.g., Matt 6:11, 33. That element may also be present here, as the following verse indicates.

66 Piper, "Hope," 223; cf. van Unnik, "Redemption," 64.

67 This need not imply dependence on Romans; it probably points rather to dependence of both on common traditions, as, e.g., Kelly (136) and Piper ("Hope," 221) also point out.

68 So also, e.g., Goppelt, 228; Schlier, "Adhortatio," 78.

69 This is surely important for our author, but whether one is justified in seeing here the "centerpiece of the ethical teaching of the entire epistle" (Michaels, 178) is open to question. Michaels is surely closer to the truth than Reicke (105), however, who argues for the appropriateness of this kind of advice to the readers on the basis that most of them were poor laborers for whom revenge was in any case not possible.

70 The top line is LXX Ps 33:13–17a, the bottom 1 Pet 3:10–12; differences are underlined.

13 τίς ἐστιν ἄνθρωπος ὁ   θέλων ζωὴν ἀγαπῶν
ἡμέρας ἰδεῖν ἀγαθάς;

10a   ὁ γὰρ θέλων ζωὴν ἀγαπᾶν καὶ
ἰδεῖν ἡμέρας ἀγαθὰς

14 παῦσον   τὴν γλῶσσάν σου ἀπὸ κακοῦ καὶ χείλη σου
τοῦ μὴ λαλῆσαι δόλον

10b παυσάτω τὴν γλῶσσαν   ἀπὸ κακοῦ καὶ χείλη
τοῦ μὴ λαλῆσαι δόλον.

15a ἔκκλινον   ἀπὸ κακοῦ καὶ ποίησον ἀγαθον,

11a ἐκκλινάτω δὲ ἀπὸ κακοῦ καὶ ποιησάτω ἀγαθόν,

15b ζήτησον   εἰρήνην καὶ δίωξον αὐτήν.

11b ζητησάτω εἰρήνην καὶ διωξάτω αὐτήν.

16   ὀφθαλμοὶ κυρίου ἐπὶ δικαίους καὶ ὦτα αὐτοῦ εἰς
δέησιν αὐτῶν

12a ὅτι ὀφθαλμοὶ κυρίου ἐπὶ δικαίους καὶ ὦτα αὐτοῦ εἰς
δέησιν αὐτῶν

17a πρόσωπον δὲ κυρίου ἐπὶ ποιοῦντας κακὰ

12b πρόσωπον δὲ κυρίου ἐπὶ ποιοῦντας κακά.

71 So, e.g., Michaels, 180. Goppelt (229) suggests these verses of the psalm were already part of Christian tradition when our author quoted it, implying thereby a different version of the psalm's language.

72 So, e.g., Selwyn, 25.

73 E.g., Piper ("Hope," 226), who suggests as the reason for the change from second to third person imperative the author's intention not primarily to command in vv. 10–12 but rather to support the content and motive of v. 9.

74 In agreement with Piper, "Hope," 227.

75 Beare (161) points out correctly that the changes in 1

which memory could be held responsible, with the remembered text presenting itself as in even closer conjunction to the point being made than its "original" version.[76]

A further change in the appropriation here of the psalm text lies in the fact that while in the psalm "life" and "good days" rather clearly refer to present life,[77] in this context, particularly in light of the use of the phrase "coheirs of the grace of life" (συγκληρονόμοις χάριτος ζωῆς) in 3:7, they appear to refer to eschatological salvation.[78] Yet in that same earlier context (2:24) the reference to living does pertain to present life,[79] a meaning reinforced by the larger context in which eschatological life is already present because of the rebirth accomplished by Christ's resurrection (1:3–5, 22–24).[80] Further, verses following our passage (3:13–16) certainly have their focus on the present. As a result, one may not rule out a reference to the present in this verse as well.[81]

The psalm citation begun in this verse clearly reflects the logic of 3:8–9, with its advice to live a good life in order to achieve a desired end,[82] but its language also indicates that it is intended to conclude a larger discussion. Not only does the reference to God hearing prayers of the righteous in 3:12 echo the intent of 3:7b, but the language of 3:11a recalls the contrast between doing good and doing evil that has informed the entire paranesis which began with 2:11.[83] Indeed, the theme of the psalm as a whole is God's deliverance of the oppressed, a point transparently appropriate to the readers of this epistle.[84]

■ 11 LXX Ps 33:15 is reproduced with the addition of the conjunction δέ and the change of second person to third person imperatives.[85] The content closely parallels that of v. 9, and is evidently a further reason why this particular citation seemed appropriate to our author. The notion of pursuing peace, an idea important in Christian tradition, may also have contributed to our author finding it appropriate for inclusion here.[86] The further coupling of avoiding evil speech in Ps 33:14 and avoiding evil deeds in 33:15 also reflects the inseparability of speech and action for our author.[87]

■ 12 This verse repeats the LXX form of Ps 33:17a, with the only variant the addition of the introductory ὅτι, which with its presence gives this verse the same function in relation to vv. 10–11 that the ὅτι of v. 9b had in relation to vv. 8–9a, namely, to furnish a basis or reason for what had been said in the prior verses.[88] Because the imperatives of vv. 10–11 reflect activities expected of Christians, for example, blessing one's enemies (3:9), living righteously (2:24), and suffering for righteousness' sake (3:14, 17; 4:13–14), this verse in this context is probably to be understood as addressed principally to Christians, informing them of God's reaction to his prior

---

Peter soften the "crude barbarity" of the Alexandrian LXX; in that light it is hard to see how Michaels (179) could argue that the change from ἀγαπῶν to ἀγαπᾶν rendered the text "more awkward" than that of the LXX.

76 In addition to noting the freedom with which texts were quoted in late antiquity, one needs also to be aware that there is no guarantee that the NT author used the exact LXX text available to us. Comparisons of NT and LXX texts that assume such exact congruity need to be questioned.

77 Schelkle (95) calls attention to this as the common meaning for these phrases in the LXX; e.g., Tob 4:5; Esth 9:19, 22; Sir 14:14; 41:13; 1 Macc 10:55.

78 For this widely held view, see, e.g., Michaels, 180; idem, "Eschatology," 395; Best, 131; Piper, "Hope," 226–27; Cranfield, 96; Reicke, 105; Hart, 66.

79 It also has that meaning in the Jesus tradition, e.g., Matt 6:11, 33.

80 With Goppelt, 230.

81 So also, e.g., Neugebauer, "Zur Deutung," 79; Bigg, 157; Goppelt, 230. Schwank ("L'Epître [1 P 3,8–

15]," 20) observes correctly that both "life" and "good days" refer to one and the same life, already filled with joy now (1:6) but eventuating in eschatological joy (4:13).

82 A point emphasized by Piper ("Hope," 227).

83 Such a contrast is explicit in 2:12, 14–15, 20, and is further implied in 2:16, 21–24; 3:2, 7. On this point see also Goppelt, 228.

84 So also Wand, 95.

85 For the Greek texts, see n. 70 above.

86 Deriving from Jesus himself (e.g., Matt 5:9), it was part of the early witness, e.g., Rom 12:18; 14:19; 2 Tim 2:22; Heb 12:14. In that light, it is difficult to see how Schwank ("L'Epître [1 P 3,8–15]," 20) can affirm that 1 Peter is the only place in the NT where the image of pursuing peace occurs.

87 E.g., 2:1; 3:15b–16; the same connection is to be found in Isa 53:9, reflected in 1 Pet 2:22. On this point, see Michaels, 180.

88 Cf. Schweizer, 73.

grace.[89] Thus, the "righteous" (δικαίους) are to be understood as Christians whose acts conform to their regenerated lives in Christ;[90] although those who do evil (ποιοῦντας κακά) are surely those who oppose the Christian community from the outside, they may also include Christians who do not act in such a way.[91]

Although the Christian context can argue for understanding "Lord" (κύριος) to mean Christ rather than God,[92] the phrase "face of the Lord" (πρόσωπον κυρίου) is so firmly attached to the presence of God in the OT[93] that that is probably the way it should also be understood here.

While the verse, as the whole passage consisting of 3:8–12, is addressed primarily to Christians, the claim here that God looks with favor upon the righteous (i.e.,

those Christians who do the divine will) also provides assurance that since that is the case, nothing any evildoers can do, including those evildoers who oppose the Christian community, can ultimately harm those faithful to God's grace made reality in the risen Christ. Such implied assurance is then made thematic in the ensuing passage, with its theme stated in v. 13: No one can do ultimate harm to those who zealously follow God's will.[94]

89 So also, e.g., Goppelt, 231. That probably also accounts for the omission here of LXX Ps 33:17b, since the point here is not the destruction of the enemies of God but rather the divine disfavor also on those Christians who refuse to act appropriately to their faith.

90 Cf. also Goppelt, 231. The reference to God hearing their prayers is also reflected in 3:7b, where those who act inappropriately (i.e., the "unrighteous") will not have their prayers heard.

91 So also, e.g., Schutter, *Hermeneutic,* 147.

92 A possibility suggested, e.g., by Michaels (181), in

light of a similar change he finds in 2:3; 3:15.

93 E.g., Gen 3:8; Judg 5:5; 2 Sam 21:1, esp. in blessing, e.g., Num 6:25–26 or Zech 8:21–22, but also in disfavor, e.g., Lev 17:10; 20:3, 5, 6; 26:17 (all use πρόσωπον + ἐπί); Lam 4:16.

94 With Michaels, "Eschatology," 396.

3

Right Conduct for Every Christian: Bearing Undeserved Suffering

13 Who then is the one who is going to harm you if[1] you become zealous[2] for the good? **14/** But even if it should happen that you suffer on account of righteousness, you are blessed. You are by no means to fear them or to be distressed,[3] **15/** but sanctify Christ[4] as lord in your hearts, ready at any time to present a defense to anyone who asks[5] you for an account of the hope that exists among you, **16/** but do it with meekness and reverence, all the while maintaining a good conscience, so that when you are the victims of evil speech,[6] those who revile your good Christian behavior may be ashamed; **17/** because it is better to suffer as people who do good, should that be God's will, than as people who do evil.

1 B and some other minuscules read εἰ instead of ἐάν; B couples with that the optative γένοισθε, probably under the influence of the εἰ . . . πάσχοιτε of v. 14.

2 In place of ζηλωταί, some mss. (K, L, P, 69, 𝔐, vg^ms) substitute μιμηταί, perhaps to avoid the connotations that the word "zealot" acquired in the war of 66–70; so also Michaels, 183.

3 A few mss. (P^72, B, L) omit the phrase μηδὲ ταραχθῆτε, perhaps as redundant, or the result of the similarity of its ending to φοβηθῆτε (so Michaels, 183), but the majority retain it, and in this case the longer reading seems to have better claim on being original.

4 A later reading (P, 𝔐) substitutes θεόν for Χριστόν, in conformity with the intention of LXX Isa 8:13, perhaps also influenced by v. 12, where κύριον refers to God. Goppelt (235) argues that Χριστόν is the *lectio difficilior* and hence likely to be the correct reading.

5 ℵ^2, A, Ψ, and a few others read the more forceful ἀπαιτοῦντι ("demand"), perhaps to strengthen the impression of a challenge in a law court, but the meaning is little changed.

6 For the difficult passive καταλαλεῖσθε, a significant textual tradition (ℵ, A, C, P, 𝔐, it, vg^mss, sy, bo) reads καταλαλοῦσιν ὑμῶν ὡς κακοποιῶν ("when they speak against you as evildoers"), but in this case the more difficult reading is probably original.

Analysis

The logic of the two passages comprising 3:13–22[7] flows from the statement of the basic premise (v. 13) that nothing can bring lasting harm to the person who does what God wants.[8] An apparent exception to the premise is then presented, namely, unjust suffering (v. 14a), which in its turn leads to advice on how to react to such suffering (vv. 14b–16) since it may correspond to God's will (v. 17). The conclusion that such suffering cannot ultimately harm one is then given, demonstrated by the fact that although unjust suffering was also visited upon Christ (v. 18), it was a suffering for the benefit of those who follow him (vv. 19–21), and he emerged victorious from it (v. 22).[9] That such an understanding of the logic of this passage is on target is shown by the general similarity of this thought pattern to the thought pattern found in 2:18–25: after a statement of the premise (2:18; 3:13) there is advice on how to behave as Christians in the midst of hostility (2:19; 3:14–16), an ensuing assertion of the superiority of just (for doing good) over unjust (for doing evil) suffering (2:20; 3:17), an assertion then justified (ὅτι, 2:21; 3:18) by a discussion centering

7 For the sake of convenience I divide consideration of this passage into two parts, vv. 13–17 and 18–22; the discussion of these latter verses is so voluminous that it requires consideration as a separate unit, even though it belongs integrally with vv. 13–17. For the force of the introductory καί of v. 13, see the comment below.

8 The divine will was outlined in the preceding sections, encapsulated in the psalm quotation contained in vv. 10–12.

9 For similar discussions of the flow of thought in these verses, see, e.g., Goppelt, 232; Michaels, 184. I do not agree with Schelkle (129) that the section of which these verses are a part is dense and poorly organized, however.

on the suffering Christ (2:21–25; 3:17–22).[10] The thought pattern is thus a familiar and important one for our author.

Because the theme of this passage—Christian life in the midst of hostility—is familiar throughout the letter, one is dealing here with the core of the author's message to his readers who are facing social oppression and persecution.[11] Points touched on elsewhere are here made thematic: Christians are not to give offense (v. 13; cf. 3:9), they are to hold Christ as Lord (vv. 14–15a; cf. 1:3), they are to give the lie to accusations of evil by living a good life (v. 16; cf. 2:12, 15) because it is better to suffer for doing good than for doing evil (v. 17; cf. 1:6; 2:19–20). Indeed, ideas expressed repeatedly in this letter are concentrated in these verses: (1) Christians regularly suffer rejection and disgrace; (2) they must do what is good even if their goodness is the occasion for suffering; (3) suffering is to be due only to their doing good, not to any evil they do; (4) because they suffer for doing good they are blessed; (5) Christian lives must witness to their hope, because Christ's triumphant resurrection carries with it the promise for the Christians' future.

What is new in this section is the need for Christians to be ready to give a public defense of their faith, here, typically for our author, identified as their "hope," a defense to be given with due deference and backed by living out what they confess. One gathers the impression that our author felt it important that those who persecuted Christians should do so not in ignorance but in awareness of what it was Christians believed, perhaps in

the hope that such knowledge would ameliorate those persecutions by showing not only the harmlessness to decent society of what Christians believed and did, but also the positive force for social good that the Christians represented.[12] Such readiness on the part of Christians to bear witness to their beliefs is probably to be understood as informing the remainder of the letter's discussion of the fate of Christians in their society.

Comment

■ **13** The καί with which this verse opens functions not so much as a copulative link with the preceding sentence ("and") as it does to introduce an inference from the preceding verse,[13] and hence has the meaning "then."[14] Since the verse is therefore to be seen in light of 3:12[15]—to be zealous for the good means to walk under the benevolent gaze of God—the intention of the verse is not to make a statement about absence of social rejection or even persecution,[16] but about a far more grievous harm, one that can separate them from that God.[17] The participial phrase ὁ κακώσων ("the one who harms") derives from a verb (κακόω) that is relatively rare in the NT, occurring most often in Acts, where it states or implies persecution of Christians;[18] but the context in which it is used here indicates that more than mere social persecution is meant. The phrase "zealots for the good" (τοῦ ἀγαθοῦ ζηλωταί) employs a word (ζηλωτής) that is used in the LXX principally to describe God as "jealous,"[19] but that is fairly common in Hellenistic Greek in connection with the pursuit of various moral ideals.[20] It

---

10 On this point, see also Boismard, "Liturgie" [2], 183.

11 With, e.g., Kelly (139) and Lohse ("Parenesis," 50), both of whom see this theme continuing to the concluding paragraph; cf. also Millauer, *Leiden*, 48. I disagree on this point with Goppelt (231), who argues against 3:13—4:11 being the central portion of the letter.

12 So also, e.g., Schwank, "L'Epître (1 P 3,8–15)," 23.

13 With, e.g., Kelly, 139.

14 So BDF § 442 (7), who see its use in introducing an apodosis, with or without a protasis, as a Hebraism (as does Kelly, 140), although they acknowledge an inferential use of καί as early as Homer *Iliad* 1.478. For this use of καί in the NT, see Mark 10:26; Luke 10:29; 2 Cor 2:2; cf. John 9:36; 14:22; Rev 6:17.

15 With, e.g., Margot, 57.

16 The author assumes its existence in the immediately

following verse, as well as in 1:6; 2:19–20; 4:12–19; cf. Best, 131; Senior, 63; Schiwy, 52.

17 On this point see also, e.g., Spicq, 130; Kelly, 140; Schelkle, 11. De Villiers ("Joy," 77) further points out that enemies of Christians cannot deprive them of their final inheritance, since it is guarded by God himself (1 Pet 1:4–5). For a similar sentiment, see Pss 56:4; 118:6; Isa 50:9; Rom 8:31; cf. Luke 12:32. The universality such a notion is indicated by its reflection in Plato *Apologia* 41D; on this point see also Elliott, *Elect*, 182.

18 E.g., Acts 7:6, 19, 34; 12:1; 14:2; 18:10; cf. 9:13.

19 E.g., Exod 20:5; 34:14; Deut 4:24; 6:15; Nah 1:2.

20 Used in a general positive sense: Philo *Som.* 1.124.8; 2.39.2; *Vit. Mos.* 1.153.3; in relation to specific virtues: Philo *Abr.* 33.1, righteousness; 60.4, piety; *Spec. leg.* 1.30, piety; *Virt.* 175.3, piety, righteousness;

is in the latter sense that it is used here,[21] though the primary meaning is not to be devoted to good behavior that is correct in the eyes of civil authorities,[22] though that of course is not ruled out, but to be devoted to the good (e.g., v. 11) which keeps one under the benevolent gaze of God (v. 12a).

The thrust of the verse is therefore not to deny the presence of social persecution in the lives of Christians, something the author knows as both possibility (e.g., 1:6; 3:14) and reality (4:12–19), but rather to point out that such persecution is not capable of removing them from the divine favor shown them in Jesus Christ. Such awareness will give them courage to remain steadfast in their faith despite suffering at the hands of those who reject the gospel.[23]

■ **14a**[24] The use of the optative[25] πάσχοιτε, introduced with the phrase εἰ καί, raises the question of the reality of the suffering the author here envisions. On the one hand, if the latter phrase indicates a supposition that is more or less improbable ("even if"),[26] it would suggest a rather remote possibility of suffering, a meaning quite consonant with the optative mood.[27] In that case the verb would represent a possible qualification of the apparent statement in the preceding v. 13 that those who do God's will need fear no harm. On the other hand, a statement about the remote possibility of suffering in a letter that in other places assumes its reality[28] would seem anomalous at best. That observation, coupled with fact that the phrase εἰ καί ("even if") can describe a condition either already fulfilled or most likely to be,[29] indicates that the optative πάσχοιτε ("you suffer") has an implication here other than remote potentiality.[30] While it may reflect the author's indirect approach to the topic of suffering,[31] it seems more likely to intend to express the fact that while Christians are not undergoing continuous suffering, they do live in an environment charged with suspicion and hostility, which has erupted and can erupt into violence and persecution at any

---

Dio Chrysostom *Or.* 38.6, God; Epictetus *Diss.* 2.14.13, God; 3.24.40, truth; Plutarch *Vit., Lucull.* 38.3, honor; *Mor., Lat. viv.* 1129B, virtue; Isocrates *Ad Demonicum* 11.6, virtue. Philo also uses it in a general negative sense: *Spec. leg.* 1.333; 2.170; 4.91, 199; *Mut. nom.* 93.5; *Som.* 2.274; *Vit. Mos.* 2.55.

21 For similar use in the NT, see 1 Cor 14:12 (zealous for spiritual things); Titus 2:14 (zealous for good works). It can also be used in the sense of Jews zealous for the law (Acts 21:20); Paul zealous for God (Acts 22:3), and for the traditions of the fathers (Gal 1:14). Van Unnik ("Redemption," 65) therefore overstated the case when he observed that in the NT the word means a zealot for the law of God.

22 Contra, e.g., Goppelt, 233.

23 So also, e.g., Bovon, "Foi chrétienne," 156; Goppelt, 234.

24 Because v. 14a is a complete sentence and qualifies v. 13, while v. 14b is the beginning of a sentence completed in v. 15, they will be treated as v. 14a and vv. 14b–15.

25 The optative mood, its rarity in the NT reflecting its increasing disuse in Koine (it appears mostly in formulaic phrases, e.g., μὴ γένοιτο, εἰ τύχοι), expresses a fulfillable wish (e.g., πληθυνθείην, 1:2) or (in the NT with or without ἄν) a potential reality, often with εἰ (e.g., εἰ θέλοι, 3:17); its use in indirect discourse in the NT is limited to the Lukan literature. See Ludwig Radermacher, *Neutestamentliche Grammatik* (HNT 1; Tübingen: Mohr [Siebeck], 2d ed. 1925) 164–65; BDF §§ 384–86.

26 So, e.g., Bigg, 157. Its use in the LXX confirms such

an observation: of the eight appearances, only two seem to point to a reality (Ezek 7:1; 1 Kgdms 19:24, the latter a proverb); the remainder (Num 16:14, 29; 2 Macc 4:47; 4 Macc 5:13; Job 31:9; Ezek 21:18) designate potentiality.

27 So, e.g., Cranfield (98): suffering is somewhat remote; Michaels ("Eschatology," 396): a hypothetical discussion. Beare (163) thinks that the words on suffering may have been introduced because they belonged to Christian tradition, rather than to the reality envisioned by the author. The suggestion of F. W. Danker ("I Peter 1:23—2:17," 100 n. 38) that it describes "what is desirable," i.e., suffering for righteousness' sake, though a possible meaning of the optative, seems wide of the mark in this context.

28 See 1:6; 2:12, 19–21; 4:13–19; 5:9–10; so also Michaels, 186. On the unlikely possibility that there is a break in the historical situation between 4:11 and 4:12, thus accounting for a shift from potential to actual suffering, see the Introduction § IV.A, "Literary Unity of 1 Peter."

29 So, e.g., Hart (66): "the contingency is likely to occur." In the NT, εἰ καί only rarely indicates potentiality (1 Cor 7:21; Phil 2:17); it usually assumes the reality of what it introduces (Mark 14:29; Luke 11:8; 18:4; 2 Cor 4:16; 5:16; 7:8, 12; 11:15; 12:11; Phil 3:12; Heb 6:9).

30 That is confirmed when the author uses almost identical language in 4:19 (οἱ πάσχοντες κατὰ τὸ θέλημα τοῦ θεοῦ) to state that Christians do in fact suffer. Brox (33) finds an exact parallel to this usage in Ignatius *Rom.* 3.3, where a verb in the subjunctive

time.[32] Thus, while the author knows suffering is always a threat, he does not know whether the communities addressed in the letter will be undergoing persecution at the time he is writing, or the time they will read, the letter.[33] To express such a sporadic reality, the author has employed the optative.

The phrase διὰ δικαιοσύνην ("because of righteousness") introduces the usual qualification[34] that the suffering of which he speaks is inflicted on Christians because they do what as Christians they must, not because they do evil.[35] Those who undergo such suffering are blessed (μακάριοι), a beatitude the author repeats in slightly different form at 4:14, where the phrase ἐν ὀνόματι Χριστοῦ ("because of the name of Christ"), used in place of διὰ δικαιοσύνην ("on account of righteousness"), helps define the meaning of this latter phrase. The idea that those who suffer because of their devotion to God, already known in the OT,[36] is more likely here to reflect Matt 5:10,[37] which seems at this

point to have passed into the broader tradition.[38]

Far from contradicting v. 13, therefore,[39] v. 14 clarifies it,[40] pointing out that far from calling into question the claim of v. 13 that nothing can harm the person zealous for God's will,[41] the suffering of Christians actually confirms that claim, since those who suffer in accord with the divine will are in fact blessed rather than harmed.[42]

■ **14b-15** These verses, along with v. 16, explain how the Christians are to react to suffering imposed on them because of their faith (διὰ δικαιοσύνην ["on account of righteousness"], v. 14a). The first element in that reaction (v. 14b) is to be lack of fear, expressed here in the form of a double prohibition (μὴ φοβηθῆτε μηδὲ ταραχθῆτε ["do not fear nor be distressed"]).[43] The second element (v. 15a) is to be faithfulness to Christ as Lord, again expressed in the form of a command (ἁγιάσατε ["sanctify"]), followed by an explanation (v.

(*sic*) expresses the fact that Christians are hated by the world, a statement surely not meant to be anything other than a declaration of reality.

31   So, e.g., Richard ("Christology," 125): it may convey the writer's "delicate, indirect approach to the reality of suffering." Similarly, Dalton (*Christ's Proclamation* [2d ed.], 73) argues that the optative conveys the author's desire to spare the feeling of the readers rather than give too blunt a reference to the painful topic of persecution.

32   So also, e.g., Kelly, 141; Selwyn 191; Holmer and de Boor, 122; Roger Omanson, "Suffering for Righteousness' Sake (1 Pet 3:13—4:11)," *RevExp* 79 (1982) 439.

33   With Brox, 158.

34   E.g., 2:20; 3:9, 10–11; 4:15–16.

35   See also van Unnik ("Teaching," 94), who notes that in 2:24, δικαιοσύνη describes the status of Christians who have broken with evil. The parallelism between the position of this phrase in this sentence and the position of τοῦ ἀγαθοῦ in v. 13 further helps define it.

36   E.g., Ps 94:12; Job 5:17. Carmignac ("La théologie," 381) also cites Lev 26:41–45; Deut 30; Jer 30; Ezek 33–37, but they are of doubtful significance in this instance.

37   So also, e.g., Lecomte, "Aimer la vie," 292; van Unnik, "Teaching," 94; Kirk, "Endurance in Suffering," 49, quoting Cranfield.

38   There is no need to postulate that the author must have heard the words from Jesus himself, as Best (133) correctly observes. Nor is it necessary to question whether the author used an oral tradition of

a word of Jesus, as Schelkle (100) does. If, as seems likely, Matt 5:11–12 are a later addition to the earlier beatitudes, they must have been prompted by a situation much like the one presumed in 1 Peter, and they show the currency of the eighth beatitude. Dio Chrysostom's remark (*Or.* 47.25) that being roundly abused though doing good deeds is a mark of royalty is of doubtful significance here.

39   Contra Windisch (69), who sees here a contradiction between vv. 13 and 14, which he thinks is made endurable by the traditional nature of vv. 14–16.

40   With, e.g., Margot, 58; Schweizer, 75; Kelly, 141.

41   That God's will is for Christians to do good, see 2:15.

42   Beare (163) rightly points to the difference in meaning in these two verses between κακόω, used in an ultimate negative sense, and πάσχω. One may further note that because of the suffering of Christ, πάσχω in this letter is used without exception to refer to something positive rather than negative for the Christian.

43   Because Hellenistic Greek does not tolerate a negatived command in the aorist, the verbs are in the subjunctive mode.

15b) of how that faithfulness is to be carried out, namely, by a readiness to explain what it is that causes them to act as they do. How they are to carry out that explanation, and its intended result, is then given in v. 16.

Although the Christian traditions that one should fear none but God, and be willing openly to express one's beliefs, are anchored in words of Jesus,[44] Peter here employs Isa 8:12–13 to make his points. The relationship between LXX Isa 8:12b–13 and 1 Pet 3:14b–15a can be seen in the following comparison:

Isa 8:12b   τὸν δὲ φόβον[45] αὐτοῦ οὐ μὴ φοβηθῆτε
             οὐδὲ μὴ ταραχθῆτε
1 Pet 3:14a τὸν δὲ φόβον αὐτῶν[46] μὴ φοβηθῆτε
             μηδὲ ταραχθῆτε
Isa 8:13   κύριον αὐτὸν ἁγιάσατε καὶ αὐτὸς ἔσται
             σου φόβος.
1 Pet 3:15a κύριον δὲ τὸν Χριστὸν ἁγιάσατε ἐν ταῖς
             καρδίαις ὑμῶν.

While the word φόβος ("fear") in this context evidently means not being terrorized by those who inflict suffering on Christians, it is in line with the normal use of this concept in this letter, namely, that the only one whom the Christian is to "fear" (i.e., revere) is God.[47] If the

Christian reveres God alone, there is no need for terror in the face of any kind of danger.

Verse 15a represents the positive pole of the contrast embodied in vv. 14b–15a: do not fear them, but sanctify Christ as Lord. The substitution of τόν Χριστόν ("Christ") for αὐτόν ("him") in v. 15a, necessary for this contrast, raises the question of how it is to be construed, whether as predicative ("sanctify Christ as Lord")[48] or appositional ("sanctify the Lord, namely, Christ").[49] Important in this case is the presence of the article with "Christ," natural if it is predicative, but awkward if it is appositional, which would more normally have both words ("Lord" and "Christ") either with or without the article. The meaning in either case, however, is virtually the same: the one whom Christians must regard as holy[50] is Christ. Thus any reverence for (since Christ alone is holy), or fear of any other (since Christ is the one who determines the Christian's final fate),[51] is forbidden. The substitution of the phrase "within your hearts" (ἐν ταῖς καρδίαις ὑμῶν) for the further reference to fear in Isa 8:13b adds depth to the command, since for Peter the "heart" (καρδία) is the innermost center of the human being (3:4) and hence the source of Christian love

---

44 E.g., Matt 10:26–33, esp. v. 28; Luke 12:23–32; 21:14–15; cf. Michaels, 184; Hart, 167; Goppelt, 236. Brox (159) notes that these words of 1 Peter stand at the beginning of the tradition, evident in the martyrological literature of the early church, which praises fearlessness and calm in the face of persecution.

45 Φόβον is a cognate accusative followed by a genitive of origin or source: "the fear emanating from them." While the context of the passage in Isaiah is the threatened Assyrian invasion, in our letter it is those who inflict punishment on Christians for what they do and say as Christians.

46 While this change from LXX αὐτοῦ to the plural αὐτῶν could represents a deliberate attempt to universalize the threat (Schwank, "L'Epître [1 P 3,8–15]," 26) or to make it refer to the enemies to be mentioned in 1 Pet 3:16 (Michaels, 186), the Hebrew text of Isa 8:12 can be construed to have the antecedent of the ו of את־מוראו ("their fear") in Isa 8:12b be העם הזה ("this people") of v. 12a, in which case the plural αὐτῶν of 1 Peter may render "people" as plural in concept, and thus represent a translation (whether by our author or another is immaterial) independent of our LXX text. Any inferred reasons for the change are thus rendered questionable.

47 As in 1:17; 2:17; 3:6; so also, e.g., Cothenet, "Le

réalisme," 568; Wand, 99; Goppelt, 235; Calvin, 107. For the same double use of the concept, see 1 Enoch 96.3.

48 So, e.g., Bovon, "Foi chrétienne," 37; Selwyn, 192. Best (133) prefers predicative but concedes that it might also be taken as appositional to κύριον.

49 So, e.g., Kelly, 142; Michaels, 187 ("probably"); Schutter, Hermeneutic, 149 ("favor slightly . . . apposition"). Bigg (158) argues that the context in Isaiah 8 from which the quotation was taken demands that it be construed as appositional, but that is to put too much weight on the source.

50 The meaning of "sanctify" (ἁγιάσατε), since, as Schelkle (100) points out, Christ is already holy in his very being. The point is not to make him holy, but to acknowledge that fact, as, e.g., Beare (164) also argues, comparing it to the first petition of the Lord's Prayer.

51 A point made by Goppelt, 236.

(1:22).[52] Thus the ensuing open statement of one's hope is to be an expression of one's deepest convictions.[53]

Verse 15b is probably best understood as further definition of how such acknowledgment of Christ is to occur, namely, through being prepared[54] at all times to account for their beliefs and actions as Christians.[55] On the one hand, the forensic connotations of the word ἀπολογία ("defense")[56] coupled with the legal implications of αἰτεῖν λόγον ("to require an account") render it possible that what is described here is the Christians' legal response when hailed into court:[57] they are to undertake a defense of belief and actions rather than remain silent. On the other hand, this language can also be used to describe more private disputes.[58] While those terms could therefore describe either formal legal proceedings or informal accusations,[59] the presence of παντί ("to any one [who asks]") seems to point rather in the direction of informal demands that Christians account for why they do what they do,[60] that is, fail to

conform to accepted cultural practices. While one cannot rule out all reference to judicial proceedings,[61] the likelihood is therefore that the author has more informal social intercourse in mind as the context here. The implication would then be that Christians must take any such request as seriously as they would the requirement in a court of law to answer to formal charges.[62]

The account Christians are to give is to concern their "hope" (ἐλπίς). While one would expect here rather the word "faith" (πιστίς),[63] it is also clear that the word "hope" describes for our author the characteristic element of Christian life,[64] and is therefore the inclusive term our author uses to describe it.[65] The phrase ἐν ὑμῖν, often translated "within you," the hope each Christian holds in his or her heart, has as its more likely meaning "among you," referring to the hope common to the Christian community that binds together and upholds its

52   On this point cf. de Villiers, "Joy," 77. Osborne ("L'utilisation," 720) inexplicably accounts for the substitution by saying it is in line with the author's practice of avoiding the verb φοβέομαι with God or Christ as the object.

53   Lecomte ("Aimer la vie," 292) correctly finds here the same relationship between heart and mouth as that expressed by Paul in Rom 10:9–10.

54   While, e.g., Beare (164) argues that the adjective ἕτοιμοι has imperative force (as in his view the participles do), it is more likely that the participle ὄντες is presumed and that, as in the case of the earlier participles in 2:18—3:7, it is to be construed as an adverbial participle of means, i.e., "by being ready."

55   There is an echo here of Col 4:6, as well as an echo in the larger context of Luke 12:1–12 (do not fear, be ready to give an account), as Selwyn (193) notes. Leaney (47) finds in this advice a contradiction to Mark 13:11, where Jesus counseled his followers not to prepare a defense beforehand, but the point here is simply that one is always to be ready to do it, not that one must have prepared beforehand in detail what its content is to be.

56   It is the technical term for the defendant's rebuttal of charges in court, as, e.g., Best (134) notes, and is used in a forensic sense in Acts 25:16; Phil 1:7, 16; 2 Tim 4:16, as is the verb ἀπολογέομαι in Luke 12:11; 21:14; Acts 24:10; 25:8; 26:1, 2, 24.

57   So, e.g., Beare, 164; Margot, 10; Lampe and Luz, "Nachpaulinisches Christentum," 198.

58   Goppelt (236) notes that it is language normally used

of private disputes, and cites Plato Politicus 285E as an example (although ἀπολογία does not appear there); it is also the case with ἀπολογία in 1 Cor 9:3; 2 Cor 7:11, and with ἀπολογέομαι in 2 Cor 12:19. That this is the meaning of the language here, see, e.g., Michaels, 188; Selwyn, 193. Kelly (67) argues that "no reference is intended to formal proceedings in a court of law."

59   So, e.g., Goppelt, 236 n. 26; Best, 134; de Villiers, "Joy," 77–78.

60   So also, e.g., Omanson, "Suffering," 439; Cothenet, "Le réalisme," 567; Brox, 159; Bigg, 158.

61   So also, e.g., Kelly, 143; Tarrech, "Le milieu," 389.

62   Michaels (188) suggests that Peter sees Christians as being "on trial" every day with respect to what they do and think.

63   So, e.g., Wand, 98.

64   Wand (98) argues that it was "the special gift of the gospel to the Gentile world." While Plutarch (Mor., Quaest. Conv. 668E) mentions a philosophical school (the ἐλπίστικοι) who held hope to be the strongest bond of life, without which life is unendurable, lack of other references in Greek literature to a school of that name indicates its relative unimportance.

65   So also, e.g., Calvin, 109; Wolff, "Christ und Welt," 335; Omanson, "Suffering," 439. It is used by Peter in the same way Paul uses the word "faith," e.g., 1 Pet 1:3, 13; 3:5, as Goppelt (237), Schelkle (101), and Schweizer (64) also observe. In fact the phrase τὴν πίστιν ὑμῶν καὶ ἐλπίδα ("your faith and hope") in 1 Pet 1:21 is probably to be understood as a hendiadys, both words describing the same reality.

members.[66]

This command to be ready with an account of one's Christian life for anyone who might ask at any time is counter to the kind of attitude held by many esoteric groups in the Greco-Roman world at that time, for whom such divulgence would have been tantamount to betrayal of the community and their god(s).[67] Such open explanation of the Christian "hope," far from something to avoid, is here added to the requirements expressed by our author such as to do good, not to recompense evil or defamation in kind, and to suffer if necessary for one's faith. In this context, not even fear of further persecution is to deter the Christians from giving a full account of their "hope."[68] Cultural isolation is not to be the route taken by the Christian community. It is to live its life openly in the midst of the unbelieving world, and just as openly to be prepared to explain the reasons for it.[69]

■ **16** The ἀλλά with which this verse begins[70] has little of its adversative sense here; it serves to caution the readers not to give an account of their hope in an aggressive or arrogant manner.[71] Rather, they must meet such demands as a Christian is to meet all demands, even insults and abuse: by not retaliating in kind.[72] Such conduct must have two characteristics, πραΰτης ("meekness") and φόβος ("fear," here "reverence"). That Christian conduct is not to be abusively aggressive ("meek") formed a firm part of Christian tradition, rooted in the traditions of a saying by Jesus (Matt 11:29), and a description of him (Matt 21:5).[73] The fear is not terror of the accuser but reverence for God,[74] here understood in the sense that nothing in the defense may be contrary to, or detract from, such reverence. V. 16a thus qualifies the way the Christian's defense is to be conducted.[75]

Excursus: 1 Peter 3:16a and the Pliny-Trajan Correspondence

That the context presumed in 1 Pet 3:15–16 may be that of a formal inquiry before officials and that the conduct described thus refers to the Christians' demeanor in the presence of investigating authorities[76] led John Knox to suggest that these words were intended to counter a tendency of Christians to conduct themselves in the face of a judicial inquiry with an unseemly arrogance. Evidence for such arrogance, Knox claimed, had surfaced in Asia Minor

---

66   So also, e.g., Michaels, 189; Selwyn, 194. Kelly (143) acknowledges both possibilities, but thinks the individualist interpretation is to be preferred here. Such individualism is probably anachronistic within the thought-world of our author, however.

67   E.g., the "mystery" religions, whose very name (μυστήριον), and that of the devotees (μύστης), derived from the verb "to initiate" (μυέω), means only those initiated could share its rites and (to use modern parlance) knowledge of its belief systems. The same held true for Qumran, where secrecy was imposed from the beginning upon novices, e.g., 1QS 8.12; Josephus *Bell.* 2.141 (I owe these references to Cothenet ["Le réalisme," 570], who, however, wrongly refers to Josephus *Bell.* 2.142).

68   So also, e.g., Schwank et al., 72.

69   Whether the notion of a kind of universal missionary apologetic, as Goppelt (237) avers, is here intended is not clear, but the emphasis on open witness to the Christian faith is unavoidable; cf. also Schweizer, 74.

70   English translations attach the first phrase of v. 16 to v. 15, so that the adversative does not begin the verse. In the Greek text, however, this phrase belongs at the beginning of v. 16.

71   So also, e.g., Michaels, 189; for that reason many English translations render it "yet."

72   Our author bases that injunction on both the OT

(3:10–11, citing Psalm 34) and Jesus' own actions (2:23). It is attributed in Christian tradition to the words of Jesus himself, where the reaction of the Christian to a malevolent neighbor is nonretaliation in kind (Matt 5:39–42) based on love (Matt 5:44).

73   In those sayings, the adjectival form πραΰς appears. In the Pauline tradition, this virtue was also based on Jesus (2 Cor 10:1), and so was incumbent on all Christians (Gal 5:23; Eph 4:2; Col 3:12; 2 Tim 2:24b–25; Titus 3:2; see also Jas 1:21). On this point see also Spicq, 132.

74   So also, e.g., Lippert, "Leben," 254; Beare, 165; Senior, 65; Schelkle, 101; Michaels, 189.

75   That defenses were not always conducted in this way is indicated, for example, by 4 Maccabees (e.g., 9:1–9; 11:2–6), a book that also intends to defend a system of beliefs. On this point see also Reicke, 107–8.

76   So, e.g., Beare, 165; see also discussion of 3:15b above.

in the course of Pliny's investigation of Christians, which had led Pliny to execute some of them "not for confessing themselves Christians . . . , but for the *manner* in which they did so."[77] Such a judgment is questionable, since it presents a more benign view on the part of Pliny toward the Christian faith than he actually exhibits. It is surely true that Pliny, in the course of his letter asking advice of the emperor Trajan on how to deal with the (for Pliny) newly confronted phenomenon of Christians,[78] informed the emperor that he had questioned, and put to death, some Christians. It is also true that Pliny does not mention the content of their faith,[79] but says he had them executed because their stubborn persistence deserved such a fate.[80] Knox understands Pliny's phrase "pertinaciam certe et inflexibilem obsti-nationem" to mean they were punished for their "contumacy and inflexible obstinacy." Knox's assumption is that Pliny would not have put them to death had they not been so obnoxious in the defense of their faith.[81]

Yet it is clear from other parts of the same letter than Pliny is not so sanguine about the content of the faith. For him, it is a perverse and excessive superstition[82] that was not limited to the cities of Asia Minor but had spread even into the countryside,[83] and had caused the people to abandon their normal way of life for this perverse set of beliefs. They had deserted the temples, they no longer frequented the meat markets, and they were allowing festivals to fall into disuse.[84] In that context, one wonders whether it was really the way the Christians conducted themselves in answering

Pliny's questions that was their fatal flaw, or whether it was their persistence, in whatever way, arrogantly or not, in refusing to recant their beliefs.[85] What, in that context, would Pliny have regarded as an inoffensive persistence in refusing to recant? Given the total context of Pliny's letter, and his expressed view of the Christian faith as obnoxious superstition which threatened the Roman way of life and hence its hegemony in Asia Minor, it is not likely that a less obnoxious defense by the Christians of their per-sistence in holding the faith and refusing to recant would have spared them Pliny's death sentence. They were killed for being adherents of a detested super-stition,[86] not for their "unnecessary" obstinacy that alone Pliny supposedly found blameworthy.[87] Trajan's response confirmed Pliny's course of action: Christians who would not recant, and demonstrate that fact by sacrificing to the Roman gods, were to be punished,[88] regardless, it is clear, of their demeanor in refusing to recant.

Further qualification is provided by the participial phrase "maintaining a good conscience" (συνείδησιν ἔχοντες ἀγαθήν). The participle (ἔχοντες), rather than carrying imperative force,[89] is probably here to be understood as an adverbial participle of attendant circumstance, describing something that must also characterize those who give an account of their beliefs with appropriate meekness and reverence. The phrase "good conscience"[90] is used here in its normal Christian

77 Knox, "Pliny and I Peter," 188–89, Knox's emphasis. This would also require dating 1 Peter later than otherwise seems warranted; on that point see the Introduction § II, "Date."
78 Pliny *Ep.* 10.96.
79 He describes what he knew of them in *Ep.* 10.96.7: they bound themselves by solemn oath not to do wicked deeds, never to commit fraud, theft, or adultery, never to falsify words nor deny a trust of money when called upon to return it.
80 "Pertinaciam certe et inflexibilem obstinationem debere punire," *Ep.* 10.96.3.
81 McCaughey ("Three 'Persecution Documents,'" 39) describes what was blameworthy as "unnecessary" obstinacy.
82 "Superstitionem pravam et immodicam," *Ep.* 10.96.8.
83 *Ep.* 10.96.9.
84 *Ep.* 10.96.10.
85 Those Christians willing to recant Pliny had no problem in releasing; *Ep.* 10.96.6.
86 It is clear from the tone of Pliny's letter that any refusal to recant such a superstition would have cast them as dangerous fanatics in his eyes.
87 The word is from McCaughey, "Three 'Persecution Documents,'" 39. One wonders what Pliny would have seen as "necessary" and hence pardonable obstinacy in the Christians' refusal to recant their obnoxious superstition!
88 *Ep.* 10.97.2.
89 As, e.g., Beare (165) argues.
90 The phrase συνείδησις ἀγαθή, absent from the genuine Pauline letters but found in later NT literature (Acts 23:1; 1 Tim 1:5, 19; 1 Pet 3:16, 21), was highly prized, e.g., by Seneca (= *bona conscientia*: *Benef.* 4.12.4; *Vit. beat.* 20.5).

meaning,[91] and refers to the attitude toward God[92] that determines all other attitudes.[93] The phrase would thus give further substance to the word "reverence" (φόβου), and its intent would be that nothing in their defense should be of such nature as to compromise their Christian conscience, that is, lies or a vituperative tone. Even defense before unsympathetic inquirers must not lead one to words unworthy of one's relationship with God.

The purpose for a ready defense carried out in an appropriate way is given in the ἵνα clause that constitutes v. 16b. The prepositional phrase ἐν ᾧ has the force of a temporal conjunction, and means "when" or "whenever."[94] The passive καταλαλεῖσθε, a form of the verb καταλαλέω otherwise unknown in the NT or LXX, assumes that those who do the evil speaking are those who despise (οἱ ἐπηρεάζοντες) the Christian conduct of the readers.[95] The participial form of the verb ἐπηρεάζω, used in conjunction with καταλαλέω, indicates that Christians suffer vituperation and vilification rather than more life-threatening expressions of hostility.[96]

What incites the derision of those outside the Christian community is behavior described as "good" (ἀγαθή) and "in Christ" (ἐν Χριστῷ). While much of the behavior exhibited by Christians would also be recognized as good in the general culture,[97] the addition of the phrase ἐν Χριστῷ makes clear that "good" is here defined not by cultural norms but by the Christian faith.[98] The phrase ἐν Χριστῷ, used only in 1 Peter (3:16; 5:10, 14) outside the Pauline corpus,[99] means to conform to Christ's teaching (e.g., 1 Cor 4:17), to possess his spirit (e.g., Rom 8:1–2, 9–10; 1 Cor 6:11; 2 Cor 3:17), and to think (e.g., Phil 2:5) and act (e.g., Eph 2:10) under his influence.[100] For that reason, the phrase is probably best understood as signifying what the adjective "Christian" does in English: to think and act within the sphere of the influence of Christ.[101]

When those who vilify such action will be put to shame is difficult to determine. Its use in 1 Pet 2:12 would imply that shame in the eschatological judgment,[102] while the context here would imply shame is an immediate matter, once the truth of Christian behavior is known through the account of their action given by Christians (3:15b).[103]

The verse as a whole gives the impression not so much of formal judicial proceedings[104] as of informal vilification, or of trumped-up charges brought to the

---

91   So also, e.g., Kelly (144), who notes its different meaning in 1 Pet 2:19.
92   The point is not so much an interior psychological state, an idea far too modern to be present in this epistle, but rather how one understands one's life in relation to God; cf. also Kelly, 144.
93   So also, e.g., Best, 134.
94   So also, e.g., Fink, "Use and Significance," 34. The circumlocution "in the matter in respect of which," proposed by Hart (67), is thus unnecessary. Bigg's (159) suggestion that it be translated "the very thing where ye are spoken against," taken to refer to ἀναστροφή, is rendered unlikely by the fact that while ἀναστροφή is feminine, ᾧ cannot be.
95   Best's (134) suggestion that in this context it is preferable to render the phrase "those who revile you may be put to shame by your good behavior in Christ" departs from the grammar of the sentence: it is the good behavior that is reviled; the good behavior does not put the revilers to shame.
96   So, e.g., Beare, 166. Michaels (190) also calls attention to Luke 6:28. Such reproach by outsiders was also known to the covenanters at Qumran, e.g., 1QH 2.9b–10, 11b, 12, 16.
97   E.g., avoiding the vices listed in 4:15. See Pliny Ep. 10.96.7 for the content of his determination of Christian practice, all of which would normally be

recognized as virtues.
98   So also, e.g., Lippert, "Leben," 255; Beare, 166. The double use of "good" in this verse in specifically Christian contexts (good conscience in connection with reverence for God, good conduct in reference to Christ) shows that the author is defining that word in Christian, not cultural, terms.
99   So also, e.g., Goppelt, 238. It was probably coined by Paul, as Lippert ("Leben," 255) affirms, but is sufficiently in accord with the theological intent of this letter that its presence does not justify classifying the letter as "Pauline" on this basis, as Furnish ("Elect Sojourners," 11) argues (but see Schelkle, 101). That it is nowhere defined, as Brox (161) observes, indicates that the author assumed the readers would also be familiar with its intent, and that it was commonplace within the tradition represented by 1 Peter.
100 On this point, see Spicq, 132–33.
101 The dative case here is probably the dative of sphere, designating the context within which something occurs.
102 So, e.g., Michaels ("Eschatology," 398), who notes nevertheless the absence here of reference to the "day of visitation" (ἐν ἡμέρα ἐπισκοπῆς); cf. also Best, 134. For more on that phrase, see the comments on 2:12 above.

attention of a local magistrate[105] that can be dispelled once the true content of the Christian beliefs is known. The situation presumed is such that active but appropriately modest defense will result in lessening such vituperation, quite different from the case later in Asia Minor under Pliny and Trajan.[106] The mention of verbal defense in v. 15b and Christian activity in v. 16b shows that the words and acts of Christians are to be of a piece, emphasized by the phrase "maintaining a good conscience" (συνείδησιν ἔχοντες ἀγαθήν) in conjunction with the defense, and the description of good behavior "in Christ" (ἐν Χριστῷ): there must be no contradiction between what Christians say and what they do.

■ **17** The conjunction γάρ which introduces this verse indicates that what follows is related to the preceding argument as substantiation,[107] in this instance surely the "good Christian behavior." The point is to urge Christians to be sure that the behavior that is despised by non-Christians is good rather than evil, that is, that the

vilification they receive is due to behavior in accord with the Christian faith, not behavior that even by then-current cultural standards would be deemed evil.[108]

The idea that it is better to suffer evil or injustice rather than to inflict it was widely accepted in the Greco-Roman world,[109] and raises the question whether this verse is to be understood (1) as a kind of reflection of that common wisdom,[110] or (2) as having eschatological implications: that it is better to suffer now as a Christian at the hands of human beings than, denying that faith, to suffer at God's hands in the final judgment.[111] The validity of (1) can be argued on the basis that (a) such an idea is familiar to our author, appearing at both 2:20[112] and 4:15–16; that (b) there is no hint of a bifurcated meaning to this verse, with the first half referring to suffering now at the hands of human beings, the second half to punishment at the eschaton at the hands of God;[113] and that (c) the conjunction γάρ links it to the

103 That the point is the conversion of the those who see the good works of the Christians is argued strongly by Heinz-Jürgen Vogels, *Christi Abstieg ins Totenreich und das Läuterungsgericht an den Toten* (Freiburger Theologische Studien 102 [Freiburg: Herder, 1976], e.g., 35–36; see also 42 n. 131), who then finds in it the key to the meaning of 3:19. The point here, however, seems more to concern a lessening of persecution of Christians when the true nature of their actions is known, the point of the readiness for such an explanation in v. 15, than that such good works have as their intention the conversion of their persecutors.

104 As Pliny (*Ep.* 10.96, 97) shows, at a somewhat later time refusal to recant, regardless of whether Christian activity was accurately known, would result in death.

105 So also, e.g., Kelly, 144. While no specific accusations are mentioned here, as Brox (161) notes, an indication of such false charges can perhaps be found reflected in 4:14.

106 On this point, see "Excursus: 1 Peter 3:16a and the Pliny-Trajan Correspondence."

107 See also, e.g., Goppelt, 238.

108 For a similar point, see 4:15–16. That it also reflects 2:20, see Omanson, "Suffering," 440; Beare, 166.

109 E.g., Plato *Gorgias* 474B: οἶμαι καὶ ἐμὲ καὶ τοὺς ἄλλους ἀνθρώπους τὸ ἀδικεῖν τοῦ ἀδικεῖσθαι κάκιον ἡγεῖσθαι ("I assume that I together with other people regard it a worse thing to inflict evil than to endure it"); 474C: ἄσχιον πότερον τὸ ἀδικεῖν ἢ ἀδικεῖσθαι; ἀποκρίνου. τὸ

ἀδικεῖν ("Which is the worse, to inflict evil or to endure it; answer me. To inflict it"). See also Cicero *Tusc. disp.* 5.56: "accipere quam facere praestat iniuriam" ("It is preferable to accept rather than inflict injustice"). I owe this last reference to Brox, 162 n. 514.

110 So, e.g., Brox (163), who argues that the point here is not eschatological, but thinks that it represents a relatively inappropriate formulation, since it is hardly "better" for the Christian to suffer for doing good, since the Christian is as a matter of course always to do the good and will inevitably suffer for it. For more on the meaning of this verse, see the discussion below.

111 So, e.g., Michaels ("Eschatology," passim), who makes use of, and modifies, some arguments of Karl Gschwind, *Die Niederfahrt Christi in die Unterwelt* (NTAbh 2.3–5, Münster: Aschendorff, 1911).

112 So also, e.g., Omanson, "Suffering," 440. Beare (166) points out that it is here broadened from reference to slaves to reference to all Christians.

113 That is to overlook the fact that the suffering due to God in this verse is the suffering not of those who do evil but of those who do good, and that it occurs now, not at the eschaton.

idea of the good behavior of the preceding verse that is clearly activity in the present time.[114] The validity of (2) can be argued on the basis that (a) the verse lacks the reference to endurance found in 2:20 and hence is virtually a truism;[115] that (b) formally the saying is a *Tobspruch*, a form that, when used in the Gospels (e.g. Mark 9:43, 45, 47), clearly has an eschatological significance;[116] and that (c) the context also supports an eschatological meaning, as shown, for example, in 3:10–12, where the quotation from Psalm 34 divides human beings into doers of good and doers of evil and indicates God's reaction to them.[117] While one cannot deny an eschatological undertone running through this passage, as it does through the whole of the letter, it is probably preferable not to assume it as directly present here.

The verse appears to function as a kind of *inclusio* with 3:14a, where the suffering of those zealous for the good (τοῦ ἀγαθοῦ ζηλωταί, 3:13) makes them blessed, while in v. 17, those suffering for doing good (ἀγαθοποιοῦντες) do what is better. In both cases, "blessed" and "better," divine rather than human values are assumed.

What lifts the verse above the level of a Greco-Roman truism is the fact that the suffering of those who do what is good (as the connection with v. 16 makes clear, good in Christian, not cultural, terms)[118] is due not to the haphazard workings of human justice but rather to God's own plan (his "will").[119] The force of the optative θέλοι in this instance is not so much to assign such suffering to some hypothetical level as it is to indicate that such suffering, while not always and everywhere present, is nevertheless always possible.[120] Congruent with what our author argues in 4:15–16, he here affirms that Christians are not to provide their opponents justification for the vilification they receive. That does their cause no good at all. Their witness to the hope that animates them is helpful only when it is supported by actions consonant with that hope, actions that may bring about further suffering but that alone have the chance of causing shame to those who ignorantly revile them.

Yet more is implied here, as the ensuing verses show. Enduring God-willed unjust suffering is not simply to imitate Christ, who also suffered unjustly; to make that point v. 18 says much more than would otherwise be necessary. Rather, Christians can endure such suffering because they can look beyond it to their sure redemption achieved by Christ's self-sacrifice. Yet that sacrifice had wider implications than simply the Christians' redemption; it contained within itself implications affecting the fate of the entire cosmos. It is to that discussion that the author turns in the verses that follow.

---

114 This argument is strengthened if in fact the καταισχυνθῶσιν of v. 16 is noneschatological in tone. See the discussion there.

115 This and the following two arguments are presented by Michaels (191), who argues as persuasively as any for this view; see also his arguments in "Eschatology," esp. 398.

116 Yet as Michaels (191) himself admits, the καλός, the mark of the eschatological *Tobspruch* in the Synoptics, is absent from this verse; in its place one finds κρεῖτον, which in turn reflects more closely the form found in 1 Cor 7:9b, where there is no eschatological implication. The form thus argues against, rather than for, an eschatological background.

117 Yet again, contrary to Michaels's argument (191; see also idem, "Eschatology," 395), one need not find an eschatological tone to 3:10–12; surely God does not wait until the eschaton to turn his face away from the evil (i.e., condemn it). The divine judgment may only then be publicly revealed, but God's condemnation of evil is not limited to the end time.

118 That point is demonstrated by such words and phrases as "reverence" (φόβος), "good conscience" (συνείδησις ἀγαθή), and "Christian" (ἐν Χριστῷ).

119 As Vanhoye ("1 Pierre," 123) notes correctly, Peter invokes God's will only in those places that refer to situations of opposition to Christians: unjust criticism, insults: 2:15; 3:16–17; cf. 4:14; violent persecution: 4:12–19; ill treatment, cf. 2:19–20.

120 So also, e.g., Goppelt, 239; de Villiers, "Joy," 78; see also the comments on πάσχοιτε in v. 14, above.

3

The Suffering and Triumphant Christ

18 **Because Christ also suffered for sin[1] once for all, the righteous one for the unrighteous many, in order that he might lead you[2] to God, having been put to death by flesh,[3] but made alive by the Spirit,[4] 19/ by whom he also[5] went and made proclamation to the spirits in prison,[6] 20/ because they were disobedient back then when the patience of God waited in the days of Noah while the ark was being prepared, into which a few people,[7] that**

1   That is the text of B, P, and 𝔐. A number of texts read ἀπέθανεν ("died") rather than ἔπαθεν ("suffered"), a reading more familiar in traditional confessions (e.g., Rom 5:8; 1 Cor 15:3; 2 Cor 5:14; 1 Thess 5:10); the text was probably altered under that influence. Along with a reference to Christ's death, there are other variations, e.g., C*vid and a few other Greek mss., vgcl, syp add ἡμῶν ("for *our* sin"); ℵ(*), A, C2vid, L, 33, 945, 1739, and some other Greek mss., syh, bo add ὑπὲρ ἡμῶν ("on our behalf"), P72, A, 1241, 2495, and some others ὑπὲρ ὑμῶν ("on your behalf"), in the latter two cases perhaps added under the influence of 2:21. Here as in 2:21, ἔπαθεν is to be preferred, since the larger context concerns suffering, and the later reference to Christ's death (θανατωθεὶς μὲν σαρκί) would make such a reference here superfluous; so also, e.g., Vogels, *Christi Abstieg,* 16 n. 18; Beare, "Text," 258; Bultmann, "Bekenntnis- und Liedfragmente," 2. For an argument for the priority of ἀπέθανεν, see Best, 137; and Kazuhito Shimada, "The Christological Creedal Formula in I Peter 3:18–22—Reconsidered," *AJBI* 5 (1979) 171–72 n. 19.

2   In place of the ὑμᾶς ("you") of P72, B, P, Ψ, 𝔐, vgmss, sy, a number of mss. read ἡμᾶς ("us"), e.g., ℵ2, A, C, K, L 33, 81, 1739, some other Greek minuscules, vg, syhmg. Such confusion occurs frequently, since the pronunciation of the two pronouns was virtually identical, but the consistent second person address of 3:13–17 (cf. also 4:1) argues for the same address here; so also, e.g., Kelly, 149; Michaels, 195; van Unnik, "Redemption," 55. But see Dalton (*Christ's Proclamation* [2d ed.], 134–35), who argues for the priority of ἡμᾶς.

3   That is, mortal humans, as in 1:24. For more on this point, see the comments on this verse below.

4   The contrast of these two phrases is enhanced in the Greek by the presence of μέν in the first phrase and δέ in the second. While those two particles convey the sense of "on the one hand," "on the other hand," the addition of those phrases in the translation would make the text appear more cumbersome than it in fact is.

5   The Greek phrase ἐν ᾧ καί has led to the speculation that the letters ενωκ are either a misreading of the name Ἐνώχ (Enoch), or that by haplography the name Ἐνώχ was omitted. For more detail, see "Excursus: The Figure of Enoch in 1 Peter 3:19," below.

6   A few minuscules read τῷ ᾅδῃ ("Hades") for φυλακή, probably under the influence of the later interpretation of this verse as announcing Christ's *descensus ad inferos.*

7   A few mss. (C, P, Ψ, 𝔐, vgms, syh) change the masculine ὀλίγοι to the feminine ὀλίγαι to make clear it modifies the ensuing ψυχαί ("souls," here "people");

is to say eight, were saved through water, 21/ which[8] also now saves you[9] as baptism, its antitype, not as a putting off of the filth of the flesh but as a pledge of a good conscience to God, through the resurrection of Jesus Christ, 22/ who, having gone into heaven after angels and authorities and powers were made subordinate to him, is at the right hand of God.

the meaning of the verse remains unaltered.

8 Some minor cursives substitute ᾧ for ὅ; P[72] and ℵ* omit it entirely, an omission Tarrech ("Le milieu," 370 n. 234) thinks is the *lectio facilior*. Beare (174) thinks ᾧ is the true reading, since it is impossible to construe ὅ "in any reasonable sense," but I would agree with Kelly (160) that the majority text need not be altered to arrive at an acceptable meaning; so also Dalton, *Christ's Proclamation* (2d ed.), 196.

9 C, L, some minuscules, vg^ms read ἡμᾶς ("us"), a pronominal change extremely common in NT mss.; the textual evidence for the second person ὑμᾶς (P[72], A, B, P, Ψ, a number of minuscules, vg, sy^h) marks it as the preferred reading.

Analysis

There is little question that these verses constitute the most difficult passage in the entire letter.[10] The language in which the passage is cast is uncharacteristically rambling and its paratactic style is unusual in this letter; its internal coherence and thematic unity are not self-evident, suggesting a possible combination of earlier traditional materials; and the relationship of its content to its immediate context is not readily apparent. As a result, the intention of the passage as a whole is difficult to discern.[11]

Structure

The step or chainlike structure of the passage may be seen from the following arrangement of the text, which illustrates how ensuing clauses give further definition to preceding clauses by explicating a word that is contained in (vv. 18, 19), or more frequently that ends (vv. 20a, 20b, 21), the preceding unit.[12]

(18) ὅτι καὶ Χριστὸς ἅπαξ περὶ ἁμαρτιῶν ἀπέθανεν, δίκαιος ὑπὲρ ἀδίκων
       ἵνα ὑμᾶς προσαγάγῃ τῷ θεῷ <u>θανατωθεὶς</u> μέν σαρκὶ <u>ζωοποιηθεὶς</u> δὲ <u>πνεύματι</u>

(19)   ἐν <u>ᾧ</u> καὶ τοῖς ἐν φυλακῇ <u>πνεύμασιν</u> <u>πορευθεὶς</u>

ἐκάρυξεν

(20a) <u>ἀπειθήσασίν</u> ποτε ὅτε ἀπεξεδέχετο ἡ τοῦ θεοῦ μακροθυμία ἐν ἡμέραις Νῶε κατασκευαζομένης κιβωτοῦ

(20b) εἰς <u>ἣν</u> ὀλίγοι τοῦτ᾽ ἐστιν ὀκτὼ ψυχαί διεσώθησαν δι᾽ ὕδατος

(21)   <u>ὅ</u> καὶ ὑμᾶς ἀντίτυπον νῦν σῴζει βάπτισμα οὐ σαρκὸς ἀπόθεσις ὕπου ἀλλὰ ἀγαθῆς ἐπερώτημα εἰς θεόν δι᾽ ἀναστάσεως Ἰησοῦ Χριστοῦ

(22)   <u>ὅς</u> ἐστιν ἐν δεξιᾷ θεοῦ πορευθεὶς εἰς οὐρανόν ὑποταγέντων αὐτῷ ἀγγέλων καὶ ἐξουσιῶν καὶ δυνάμεων.

Additional structural elements provide a measure of coherence[13] to this catena of clauses, and thus provide clues to the meaning of the passage. The repetition of πορευθείς in vv. 19 and 22, in each instance used in association with deposed spiritual entities (imprisoned spirits in v. 19, subordinated spiritual powers in v. 22), forms an *inclusio*[14] in which the latter member sheds light on the former. Thus, the subordination of the spiritual powers in v. 22 suggests that the imprisoned spirits of v. 19 may refer to something other than human beings who

10 Werner Bieder ("Bo Reicke, The Disobedient Spirits and Christian Baptism," *ThZ* 2 [1946] 456) calls it a "schier unlösbare Rätsel" "nearly unsolvable puzzle"; Scharlemann ("He descended," 86) uses the phrase *locus vexatissimus*; as a result the literature on this passage is enormous, a clear indication that one cannot expect any assured results of the exegesis of it; so also Perdelwitz, *Mysterienreligion*, 82, 91; cf. Brox, 169–70.

11 In what follows, I will give an overview of problems and proposed solutions. For a more detailed discussion of the evidence and its possible resolution,

see the comments on the individual verses below.

12 For a similar though somewhat different attempt to show this structure, see C. Perrot, "La descente aux enfers et la predication aux morts," in Perrot, *Etudes*, 245.

13 While this passage may not be quite the balanced, smoothly developed hymn that Dalton ("Interpretation and Tradition," 23) finds here, neither is it so disjointed as some others imply, e.g., Shimada (*Formulary Material*, 305), Moffatt (140), and Beare (170), who see intrusions and asides as characteristic of the passage.

have died,[15] and that what Christ proclaimed to those imprisoned spirits may not have been their salvation.[16] Further, the repetition of that participle implies that Christ moved in the same direction in the former as in the latter instance, that is, heavenward, and that therefore a *descensus ad inferos* ("descent to the nether regions") may not have been envisioned here.[17]

Incorporation of Traditional Materials

Linguistic features of this passage are regularly taken to indicate the presence of earlier traditions. Among them are the following: (1) the presence (v. 18a) of ὅτι *recitativum*, used to introduce a tradition (cf. 1 Cor 11:23b; 15:3);[18] (2) the presence (v. 18b) of parallel phrases beginning with a participle and concluding with a noun in the dative case (θανατωθεὶς μὲν σαρκὶ ζῳοποιηθεὶς δὲ πνεύματι; cf. 1 Tim 3:16);[19] (3) the presence of the ἵνα phrase, often found in traditional formulations (cf. Phil 2:10; Titus 2:14; 2 *Clem.* 14.2);[20] (4) the presence of the relative pronoun ὅς, referring to

Jesus (cf. Phil 2:6; Col 1:15, 18b);[21] (5) the reference to the exaltation of Christ to God's right hand, based on Ps 110:1 (cf. Rom 8:34; Eph 1:20; Heb 1:3; Mark 16:19);[22] (6) The threefold point that Christ died, was made alive, and ascended into heaven, the content of early christological confessions;[23] (7) the threefold use of καί (vv. 18, 19, 21), which suggests a combination of traditions;[24] (8) inclusion of material (vv. 19–21) that goes beyond the needs of the immediate context;[25] (9) inclusion of linguistic hapax legomena in 1 Peter (e.g., the words ἅπαξ, μακροθυμία, the phrase περὶ ἁμαρτιῶν).[26] Some of these points are less persuasive than others: for example, (1) the ὅτι of v. 18 is not a ὅτι *recitativum*, as claimed and as present in the examples from 1 Cor 11:23 and 15:3, but serves in v. 18 as a causative conjunction; (2) the parallel phrases in v. 18b can be argued to be redactional rather than traditional;[27] (3) ἵνα is so common in the NT (used thirteen times in this letter alone) that its presence even in some traditional material

14 See also Schutter, *Hermeneutic*, 66. The *inclusio* stands even if, as, e.g., Dalton (*Christ's Proclamation* [2d ed.], 182; see also 118) argues, the repetition is due to a combination of two traditions; it was still our author who was responsible for their combination.

15 That it does refer to the dead is often simply assumed, e.g., John Henry Bennetch, "Exegetical Studies in 1 Peter," *BSac* 101 (1944) 195; Perdelwitz, *Mysterienreligion*, 86; but see Michaels, 196. For more on this point, see the comments on v. 19.

16 Cf. Dalton, *Christ's Proclamation* (2d ed.), 119.

17 Such a descent is often simply assumed, e.g., Shimada, *Formulary Material*, 318; Oscar Cullmann, *The Earliest Christian Confessions* (trans. J. K. S. Reid; London: Lutterworth, 1949) 20; Bornemann, "Taufrede," 151. To appeal to Eph 4:8–10 or Rom 10:6–7 to justify such a view as many do is of little help: both of those passages employ words to express the contrast between ascent (ἀναβαίνω) and descent (καταβαίνω) that are conspicuous here by their absence. For a more detailed discussion of this and other points, see the comments on v. 19 below.

18 E.g., Kelly, 146–47; Vogels, *Christi Abstieg*, 19.

19 E.g., Shimada, "Formula," 158; Vogels, *Christi Abstieg*, 20; Selwyn, 325–26; Schutter, *Hermeneutic*, 69; Sherman E. Johnson, "The Preaching to the Dead," *JBL* 79 (1960) 51. Michaels (197) would add the phrase προευθεὶς εἰς οὐρανόν ("went into heaven") from v. 22 to broaden the parallel.

20 Bultmann, "Bekenntnis- und Liedfragmente," 3. Vogels (*Christi Abstieg*, 20) questions whether the phrase actually derives from tradition.

21 E.g., Shimada, "Formula," 159.

22 E.g., Vogels, *Christi Abstieg*, 20. He finds the phrase referring to angels in 3:22b surprisingly close to Eph 1:21.

23 E.g., Michaels, 197; Bornemann, "Taufrede," 151–52; cf. Shimada, *Formulary Material*, 318; Bultmann, "Bekenntnis- und Liedfragmente," 9.

24 E.g., Goppelt, 240.

25 E.g., Kelly, 146–47; for more on this point, see below, "Relation to Context."

26 For a full discussion, see, e.g., Shimada, *Formulary Material*, 307–8.

27 Shimada ("Formula," 161) argues that the phrase does not harmonize with the rest of vv. 18, 19, and 22 since the participle θανατωθεὶς is redundant in light of the ἀπέθανεν (*sic*) of 3:18a, and since, given that vv. 18, 19, 22 present Christ's passion and subsequent events in sequence, the reference to the resurrection contained in the phrase ζῳοποιηθεὶς δὲ πνεύματι is out of sequence because it is followed "by a remark about the descent into Hades," it shows it cannot belong to the traditions contained in vv. 18, 19, and 22.

carries little persuasive power in this instance; (4) the presence of the relative pronoun ὅς with its antecedent as Christ is one of several relative pronouns in this passage, and is in addition a common feature of the language of 1 Peter;[28] (4) inclusion of material unnecessary in this context depends on what the context is determined to be; (5) identification of words as hapax legomena in a letter this short is of questionable value.[29] Nonetheless, inclusion of traditional materials seems evident.[30]

Less evident is the extent of their inclusion and the original form from which they were taken. Because most of the characteristics of traditional material are found in 3:18 and 22,[31] and because they appear more hymnic in form than vv. 19–21,[32] one can argue that they alone are drawn from the tradition.[33] Yet there is a strong

possibility of an allusion to traditions about Enoch in v. 19,[34] and the reference in vv. 20–21 to baptism has led to the suggestion that they originated in a baptismal catechesis, and were inserted here by the author.[35] Attempts to reconstruct the original form of a hymn from which part or all of material in this passage was drawn have led to no conclusive results. Proposals have ranged from seeing here a coherent Christ hymn[36] or a baptismal hymn[37] to a more extensive hymn from which the author has excerpted elements.[38] Lack of agreement about the reconstructed form indicates that such attempts owe at least as much to the imagination of those reconstructing them as they do to evidence in the text itself. The best conclusion remains to see traditional elements underlying these verses, traditions that were

---

28 Relative pronouns occur in addition to our passage in 1:6, 8 (bis), 10, 12 (tris); 2:4, 8, 12, 22, 23, 24; 3:3, 4, 6; 4:4; 5:9, 12.

29 While such words in v. 20 as Νῶε, κατασκευάζω, κιβωτός, and ὀκτώ are hapax legomena, it is unclear whether the author is citing a tradition or because such words would be necessary in any discussion of Noah, and a repetition of such a discussion, and hence that vocabulary, would hardly be anticipated in a letter of this length.

30 So also, e.g., C. E. B. Cranfield, "The Interpretation of I Peter iii.19 and iv.6," *ExpT* 69 (1958) 369; Omanson, "Suffering," 441; Schelkle, 102.

31 So, e.g., Vogels, *Christi Abstieg*, 17, 19; Kelly, 147.

32 So, e.g., Dalton, *Christ's Proclamation*, 97; he sees vv. 19–21 as a prose insertion.

33 So, e.g., Shimada, *Formulary Material*, 305; idem, "Formula," 158; cf. Best, 136. Because of references to the *descensus ad inferos* in v. 19 and to resurrection in v. 21c, Joachim Jeremias argued they were added to the material on Christ's death (v. 18) and *sessio ad dextram* (v. 22) that was drawn from an original confession ("Zwischen Karfreitag und Ostern: Descensus und Ascensus in der Karfreitagstheologie des Neuen Testaments," *ZNW* 41 [1942] 194).

34 Not all admit this; for example, Vogels (*Christi Abstieg*, 21–22) finds no relation of v. 19 to tradition. For more on this point, see the comments on v. 19 below.

35 For a detailed account of such an assembling of traditions, see Goppelt, 240–42; cf. also Dalton, "Interpretation and Tradition," 23–24; Claus-Hunno Hunzinger, "Zur Struktur der Christus-Hymnen in Phil 2 und 1.Petr 3," in E. Lohse with C. Burchard and B. Schaller, eds., *Der Ruf Jesu und die Antwort der Gemeinde: Exegetische Untersuchungen: Joachim Jeremias*

zum 70. Geburtstag (Göttingen: Vandenhoeck & Ruprecht, 1970) 145. Dalton (*Christ's Proclamation* [2d ed.], 117) argues that vv. 18 and 22 belonged to a creedal formula or hymn, while vv. 19–21 were a catechetical piece in prose that was inserted into it. Again, Schlier ("Adhortatio," 62) identifies vv. 20–21 as a short midrash on baptism, and finds the theological point close to that of 1:18–20, although its differing terminology points to a different origin. The unusual relation of baptism to an OT type, namely, Noah, rather than the more common relation to Christ's death (e.g., Rom 6:1–11; Col 2:12; cf. Vogels, *Christi Abstieg*, 21), may point to its origin with our author.

36 So, e.g., Hunzinger, "Zur Struktur," 143. See also Dalton ("Interpretation and Tradition" 23), who limits the hymn to 3:18, 22, however. Shimada ("Formula," 162–63) reconstructed from this passage a hymn of two strophes as follows:

Χριστὸς ἅπαξ περὶ ἁμαρτιῶν ἀπέθανεν
   ἵνα ἡμᾶς προσαγάγῃ τῷ θεῷ,
καί τοῖς ἐν φυλακῇ ἐκήρυξεν
ὅς ἐστιν ἐν δεξιᾷ τοῦ θεοῦ,
   πορευθεὶς εἰς οὐρανόν,
ὑποταγέντων αὐτῷ ἐξουσιῶν καὶ δυνάμενων.

A similar attempt, this time with three strophes and an introductory phrase, was made by Hunzinger ("Zur Struktur," 144):

   Εὐλογητὸς Ἰησοῦς Χριστός,
I   ὃς ἅπαξ περὶ ἁμαρτιῶν ἀπέθανεν,
      δίκαιος ὑπὲρ ἀδίκων,
      ἵνα ἡμᾶς προσαγάγῃ τῷ θεῷ,
II   θανατωθεὶς μὲν σαρκί,
      ζωοποιηθεὶς δὲ πνεύματι,
         ἐν ᾧ καὶ τοῖς ἐν φυλακῇ πνεύμασιν ἐκήρυξεν,
III   πορευθεὶς εἰς οὐρανόν,

probably familiar to the readers and hence needed only allusive reference (thus contributing to our difficulty in determining their precise meaning), but whose original form must necessarily elude us.[39] Whatever their origin, however, and whatever their original meaning, they now constitute part of the text of 1 Peter, and hence must be understood within the overall context and argument of that letter.

Relation to Context

The precise relationship of the content of 3:18–22 to the context within which it is found has also proved difficult to determine. One solution is to see the exhortations of 3:17 continued in 4:1, with the entire passage thus to be seen as an intrusion into an otherwise smoothly flowing argument.[40] Again, it has been argued that even if v. 18

was intended, as the ὅτι seems to indicate, to function as an explanation of 3:17, the material in vv. 19–22,[41] unrelated to that explanation, shows itself peripheral to the immediate context.[42] If, on the other hand, the passage is understood as related not simply to 3:17 but to the entire preceding passage (3:13–17),[43] then vv. 18–22 give a theological basis for the Christians' resistance to present persecution, namely, the victory of the Christ upon whom they call over the forces of evil, and their own implied victory.[44] In that case the passage is not a digression but belongs to the context,[45] and represents a line of thought important, if not indeed central, to the epistle, namely, that Christians, beset by hostile forces,

καθίσας ἐν δεξιᾷ θεοῦ
ὑποταγέντων αὐτῷ ἀγγέλων καὶ ἐξουσιῶν καὶ δυνάμεων.

37 So, e.g., Spicq, 133. Windisch (70) found here such a hymn consisting of four strophes, but he made no attempt to spell out its original form or content. For the view that it was not a baptismal hymn, see, e.g., Selwyn, 195.

38 Most notably Bultmann ("Bekenntnis- und Lied-fragmente," 14), who reconstructed the hymn by combining 1:20 (for which, e.g., Hunzinger ["Zur Struktur," 143] found no compelling reason) with 3:18–19, 22, and introduced it with a proposed introductory phrase:
(πιστεύω εἰς τὸν κύριον Ἰησοῦν Χριστόν)
τὸν προεγνωσμένον μὲν πρὸ καταβολῆς κόσμου,
    φανερωθέντα δὲ ἐπ᾽ ἐσχάτου τῶν χρόνων·
ὃς ἔπαθεν ἅπαξ περὶ ἁμαρτιῶν,
    ἵνα ἡμᾶς προσαγάγῃ τῷ θεῷ,
θανατωθεὶς μὲν σαρκί,
    ζωοποιηθεὶς δὲ πνεύματι,
ἐν ᾧ καὶ τοῖς ἐν φυλακῇ πνεύμασιν ἐκήρυξε,
πορευθεὶς (δὲ) εἰς οὐρανὸν ἐκάθισεν ἐν δεξιᾷ θεοῦ,
    ὑποταγέντων αὐτῷ ἀγγέλων καὶ ἐξουσιῶν καὶ δυνάμενων.

39 So also van Unnik ("Paganism," passim), who observes that the overlay of various traditions about atonement and the salvific contrast between Christ's death and resurrection contributes to the difficulty in regaining the form of such original tradition as may underlie these verses.

40 So, e.g., Shimada, *Formulary Material,* 310; cf. Jeremias, "Zwischen Karfreitag und Ostern," 194. D. Völter ("Bemerkungen zu I. Pt 3 und 4," *ZNW* 9 [1908] 74) included 4:1b, 6 in the interpolation as well.

41 Bultmann ("Bekenntnis- und Liedfragmente," 2) argues that the digression begins already with v. 18b, which in his view has no relation to the paranetic context.

42 So, e.g., Beare (170), Leaney (50), and Schutter (*Hermeneutic,* 67), who call it "a digression"; see also Brox, 169, 180; Hunzinger, "Zur Struktur," 144–45. For a summary of those holding this idea, see Ivan T. Blazen ("Suffering and Cessation from Sin according to 1 Peter 4:1," *Andrews University Seminary Studies* 21 [1983] 47), although he does not share that view. The attempt of Dalton (*Christ's Proclamation* [2d ed.], e.g., 19, 31 et passim) to find in 3:18–22 as a whole a justification for 3:17 seems somewhat forced. For more on that point, see below, "Point of the Passage, 3."

43 With, e.g., Kelly, 146; Holmer and de Boor, 127; Dalton, *Christ's Proclamation* (2d ed.), 127, 158.

44 That victory is made explicit, e.g., in 4:13–16; the repetition in 4:15 of the point of 3:17 shows that both belong to the same stream of thought.

45 So also, e.g., R. T. France, "Exegesis in Practice: Two Samples," in I. Howard Marshall, ed., *New Testament Interpretation: Essays on Principles and Methods* (Grand Rapids: Eerdmans, 1977) 265–66; Dalton, *Christ's Proclamation,* 85; Bo Reicke, *The Disobedient Spirits and Christian Baptism* (ASNU 13; Copenhagen: Munksgaard, 1946) 126–36. Blazen ("Suffering and Cessation," 48) sees that context continued in 4:1–6.

have in the fate of their Lord the assurance that they too will emerge from present suffering into a future victory.[46]

Point of the Passage

Because the relationship to the immediate context is not transparent, and because the meaning of the traditions that apparently constitute at least part of the passage remains ambiguous, one's understanding of the point of the passage will depend in large part on how one resolves those problems of context and meaning. One may discern four main lines of interpretation.[47]

1. Because the "spirits" to whom Christ's preaching was directed are tied to the time of Noah, and because that preaching of Christ took place "in the Spirit," one can interpret the passage to mean that Christ preached by the Holy Spirit through the lips of Noah to the wicked generation that lived before the flood.[48] Their "imprisonment" must then be interpreted to mean their imprisonment in sin which made them disobedient, and any reference to Christ's descent into hell is eliminated. Left out of account in this interpretation are the references to the rescue of Noah (v. 20b), to baptism (v. 21), and to the exaltation of Christ (v. 22); they appear simply to have been appended to vv. 18–20a, which constitute the major thrust of the passage. That the proclamation was to the living also renders problematic any relationship between this passage and the reference to Christ preaching to the dead in 4:6.

2. If the "imprisoned spirits" refer to human beings who have died[49] and are thus imprisoned by death, then those human beings belonged to the most evil generation that ever lived, that is, the one that provoked the flood, as the reference to Noah shows, thus demonstrating that if the crucified and risen Christ preached to them, evil as they were, then not even death can put the most egregious sinner beyond the reach of Christ's saving power.[50] Such preaching to Noah's generation is thus an example of a larger truth, namely, that those who died in the time before Christ, or those who died without the chance for faith in him, are not beyond the reach of his salvation.[51] Such an interpretation understands v. 19 to refer to Christ's descent to hell[52] and presumes that the content of Christ's preaching was salvation.[53] Such an interpretation can posit a unity for the passage, with Christ's ascent in heaven (v. 22) understood as the corollary to his descent to hell, thus demonstrating further Christ's power that enables him to save even the dead.[54] The difficulty with such an interpretation lies in the fact that it must assume that "spirits" here refers to human dead, something it nowhere else does,[55] and in the further fact that rather than encouraging Christians to remain faithful despite any suffering that might entail, the point of the preceding context, it would imply that even if Christians now deserted Christ, they would nevertheless be given a chance at salvation through Christ's proclamation to the sinful dead.[56]

3. If the point of v. 18 (Christ who was righteous suffered) is to provide justification for v. 17 (it is better to suffer as those who do good than those who do evil),[57] then Christ becomes the model for those who are persecuted. The purpose of following that model of unjust suffering, as v. 16 makes clear, is to shame

---

46   The argument of Dalton (*Christ's Proclamation*, 85) that 3:18—4:6 bring together some of the main themes of the letter is thus preferable to that of Brox (169), who holds that 3:19–22 are unrelated to the author's central point.

47   I have adapted the insights of Selwyn (316–17) on these lines of interpretation, principally by adding a fourth to his three. For a more detailed discussion of the content of the individual verses, see the "Comments" below.

48   So, e.g., Steuer, "1 Petr 3,17—4,6," 675; John S. Feinberg, "1 Peter 3:18–20, Ancient Mythology, and the Intermediate State," *WTJ* 48 (1986) 304. As Selwyn (316) notes, this idea is at least as old as Augustine (*Ep. Eud.* 164).

49   The reference to Christ preaching to the dead in 4:6 renders this likely, in view of those who adopt this interpretation.

50   So, e.g., Jean Galot, "La descente du Christ aux enfers," *NRTh* 83 (1961) 484. Krafft ("Christologie," 123) infers from this that even the past is altered by the event of Christ.

51   So, e.g., Cranfield, 104; cf. Hort, 276–77.

52   So, e.g., Cothenet, "Les orientations," 32; Johnson, "Preaching," 51; with many others.

53   So, e.g., Vogels, *Christi Abstieg*, 39; cf. also Goppelt, 239, again along with many others.

54   The attempt by Tarrech ("Le milieu," 370–71) to find a thematic unity here based on past (Christ's death, resurrection, proclamation, and the flood) and present (salvation by baptism/resurrection of Christ, his exaltation, and the submission to him of angelic powers) seems a bit forced.

55   On this point, see the comments on v. 19 below.

unbelievers into accepting salvation in Christ, just as Christ also rescued sinners by his unjust suffering. Such salvific results demonstrate that suffering as a good person is better than suffering as an evil one, and such results will also follow when the Christians are similarly willing to suffer.[58] Another way of seeing in this passage a call to an *imitatio Christi* is to find in vv. 18–22 a justification for the call to fearless confession enunciated in v. 15: as Christ preached the gospel even to the imprisoned spirits from the time of Noah, so Christians must have the courage to tell even the most resolute sinners what hope in Christ means.[59] Yet finding in this passage a call to imitate Christ on the basis of the similarity between 3:18–22 and 2:21–25[60] ignores the fact that such a following[61] is not invited here as it is in 2:21.[62] More importantly, lying athwart all attempts at finding the point of 3:18–22 in an *imitatio Christi* is the ἄπαξ[63] that underlines the uniqueness of Christ's suffering being described here.[64] Christians can follow the "pattern" of the suffering described in 2:22–24; they cannot follow, let alone imitate, the suffering and its consequences described in 3:18–22.

4. The resemblance between this passage and some traditions about Enoch make it possible to understand that Christ in this passage is, like Enoch, announcing to the imprisoned evil angels of the time of Noah[65] their final doom (3:19),[66] a doom assured by means of Christ's triumph over them (3:22). That triumph is similar to the triumph achieved by God (3:21) who, when he destroyed the evil world, saved his elect despite that destruction (3:20).[67] Such an interpretation severs the link between this passage and 4:6, calls into question the understanding of a "descent" in v. 19, and interprets Christ's proclamation in the same verse as an announcement not of salvation to the dead but of his own triumph, as the result of his death and resurrection, over all rebellious spiritual forces (vv. 19, 22). Because, however, such an understanding of the passage (a) respects the parallelism of the twofold πορευθείς in vv. 19 and 22, (b) accounts for the inclusion of a discussion of Noah and the flood in this passage, and (c) points to Christ as triumphant over all powers arrayed against God and thus against those who call upon him (i.e., the Christians), it gives coherence to the passage, and fits it into the context of admonition to fearless confession of one's faith despite any ensuing suffering. That point was

---

56   On this same point, see Dalton, *Christ's Proclamation* (2d ed.), 127.

57   So, e.g., Cranfield, 100–101; Vogels, *Christi Abstieg*, 19, 22, 32.

58   So, e.g., Vogels, *Christi Abstieg*, 37. He also (40) calls on 2:12; 3:1, 16 as further evidence for this interpretation, and in addition finds (25) in Col 3:13 and Eph 4:32—5:2 justification for seeing here an instance of the *imitatio Christi*; cf. also 35–36.

59   So, e.g., Reicke, *Spirits*, 130–31: one must return good for evil as Christ did, supremely in his preaching to the worst sinners. But he also died as a sin offering; therefore Christians "must be prepared if necessary to die as a sin-offering for the sake of other pagans, namely to lead them also to God" (217). For the same point, see Margot, 61. Contrariwise, Dalton (*Christ's Proclamation* [2d ed.], 187; see also 124–25) argues that the point is not to encourage such proclamation, but rather to encourage the readers simply to stand fast, a major emphasis of the author, as the summary of the letter in 5:8–9 shows.

60   As does, e.g., Vogels, *Christi Abstieg*, 28; cf. Michaels, 196.

61   Note that the verb in 2:21 is ἐπακολουθέω, not μιμέομαι, and what is to be followed is Christ's "footsteps," not Christ himself.

62   So also, e.g., Brox, 182; Dalton (*Christ's Proclamation*

[2d ed.], 123) makes the same point, although without citing any parallel to 2:21. One may also note that because such an invitation to follow is present in 2:21–25, a similar invitation implied in 3:18–22 would represent a repetition of a point already adequately made in the former passage, although too much weight may not be put on this point.

63   "Once for all" in a temporal sense; its absence from 2:21, where following is in fact invited, is significant.

64   So also, e.g., Goppelt, 240; cf. Dalton, *Christ's Proclamation* (2d ed.), 126.

65   See the interpretation of Gen 6:1–6 in *1 Enoch* 15.8–12. *1 Enoch* 10.8 affirms that the world had been corrupted by the actions and words of the evil angel Azazel.

66   Cf. *1 Enoch* 14.

67   For a more detailed consideration of the evidence, see the comments on the individual verses below.

broached in 3:13–17 and is further made explicit in the discussion immediately subsequent to this passage. For those reasons, this seems the best interpretation of 3:18–22.[68]

Theological Thrust

Placed within the particular context of Christian suffering (3:14–15; 4:1–2) and the broader context of the letter which seeks to stiffen Christian resistance in the face of increasing social pressure on Christians to conform to Greco-Roman customs even at the expense of their faith, the thrust of this passage is intended to show why the Christians will, in the end, triumph over the powers currently arrayed against them: Christ, the righteous one, can lead them, the unrighteous, to God because by his suffering and resurrection he has overcome all powers that could hinder such access.[69] That access to God in its turn is made available to Christians in baptism, a salvific event comparable only to Noah's rescue from a world similarly about to be destroyed. On that basis, Christians can face their future with confidence, despite whatever suffering that future may portend, because Christ has triumphed over the most powerful forces of the universe. The salvation

Christ promises is therefore sure, and confidence in that Lord can sustain Christians until the final judgment, whose coming is sure and whose advent will rescue Christians from their tormented lives.[70]

Comment

■ **18** The introductory ὅτι with which the verse begins is causal[71] and serves to give the reason for the preceding discussion.[72] While in this context the καί could be understood as epexegetic[73] ("indeed"), it is probably rather to be construed here as adjunctive ("also").[74] Although ἅπαξ can mean either "once" in contrast to "now" (i.e., with the same force as ποτέ) or "once for all" in contrast to something that can be repeated (i.e., with the same force as ἐφάπαξ), and has been construed both ways in this passage,[75] it is more likely in this context to mean the latter ("once for all").[76] While the καί at the beginning of the verse could, as in 2:21, imply the imitability of Christ's suffering,[77] its association with ἅπαξ, as well as the remainder of the verse (e.g., περὶ ἁμαρτιῶν, δίκαιος ὑπὲρ ἀδίκων), points clearly to the unique significance of Christ's passion,[78] and hence lends further support to its meaning here as "once for all."[79] The point of its use here may be either to underline the

68 Again, see the comments on the individual verses below for a more detailed argument of these points.

69 As Goldstein ("Kirche," 52) points out, this passage points on the one hand to the uniqueness of Christ's representative death, but on the other hand to the relationship of Christians to Christ, who is the example for Christian behavior in the face of suffering.

70 Such a thrust for this passage is widely recognized; see, e.g., Tarrech, "Le milieu," 376; Dalton, *Christ's Proclamation* (2d ed.), 121; Margot, 60; Michaels, 197; Fitzmyer, "First Peter," 366; Balch, *Wives*, 134.

71 The common construal, e.g., Spicq, 133. Vogels (*Christi Abstieg*, 19) identifies it as a ὅτι *recitativum* that also has "begründende Funktion" ("foundational function"), a solution borne out of the desire to preserve the ὅτι as a mark of tradition (as, e.g., 1 Cor 11:23; 15:3) in face of its obvious grammatical function here as a causal particle. Grammar must overcome such scholarly invention.

72 That it is related more to vv. 14–16 than solely to v. 17, see above, "Relation to Context" in the "Analysis" of this passage.

73 For this use in 1 Peter, see 4:6, 19; perhaps also 2:4; 3:14.

74 This is a common use in 1 Peter; see 1:15; 2:8, 18, 21; 3:1, 5, 7, 19, 21; 4:1, 13; 5:1.

75 For the former construal, e.g., Bieder "Reicke," 459 (reporting on the use made of it by Reicke, *Spirits*, chap. 9); for the latter, e.g., Michaels, 200; Scharlemann, "He descended," 85.

76 While it is used in the NT in addition to "once for all" (= ἐφάπαξ) in the sense of "once" in contrast to two or three times (e.g., 2 Cor 11:25; Phil 4:16; 1 Thess 2:18), it is never used to mean "once" (= ποτέ) in contrast to "now."

77 On this problem, see Goldstein ("Kirche," 47) and Schelkle (103), who admit such a meaning for καί, but nevertheless argue that the meaning of the phrase is dictated by the accompanying "once for all." Cf. also Best, 137; Cranfield, 101.

78 So also, e.g., Sieffert, "Die Heilsbedeutung," 406; Dalton, *Christ's Proclamation* (2d ed.), 130; Best, 139; Bieder, "Reicke," 461. That is a point of special importance in Hebrews (e.g., 7:27; 9:12, 26, 28; 10:2, 10) but not limited to that letter (e.g., Rom 6:10; Jude 3); on this point see Kelly, 148; Spicq, 135.

79 To attempt to argue that ἅπαξ means "once for all" but is nevertheless exemplary for all innocent sufferers, as does Schiwy (54), is an interesting attempt to combine the two meanings, but in the end fails to convince.

absolute and decisive break with sin accomplished in Christ's passion, a break that then neither can be nor needs to be repeated in the future,[80] or to point specifically to the contrast between the OT sacrifices for sin, which needed regular repetition, and Christ's unrepeatable self-sacrifice;[81] in either case, the emphasis on the uniqueness of Christ's passion is the same.[82]

While the majority of texts read that Christ died (ἀπέθανεν) rather than suffered (ἔπαθεν), the latter is more appropriate both to the immediate context (πάσχοιτε, 3:14; πάσχειν, 3:17; παθόντες, παθών, 4:1) and to the larger setting of the letter, where the emphasis is on suffering rather than dying as Christians (4:13–15; 5:1, 9–10),[83] and hence is more likely to be original.[84] The reference to Christ suffering would in any case include Christ's death,[85] a point made specific by the θανατωθείς in the latter part of the verse.[86] The phrase describing the purpose of Christ's suffering, περὶ ἁμαρτιῶν ("concerning sin"), is used in the LXX of a sin

offering (e.g., Lev 5:6–7; 6:23; Ezek 43:21; cf. Heb 5:3).[87] It is used in the same context in the NT (e.g., Rom 8:3; Heb 10:26; 1 John 2:2; 4:10) in a meaning indistinguishable from ὑπὲρ ἁμαρτιῶν ("for sin"; e.g., Gal 1:4; 1 Cor 15:3; Heb 5:1; 10:12).[88]

The ensuing phrase (δίκαιος ὑπὲρ ἀδίκων, "righteous [one] for [the] unrighteous [many]")[89] employs language familiar to NT tradition, both as a phrase[90] and, with respect to the word δίκαιος, as a description of Christ.[91] In its latter meaning it indicates why it was possible for Christ's death to be "for sin" in a unique way,[92] that is, as righteous he did not need to die for his own sin.[93] While it is clear to whom the δίκαιος refers, the ἄδικοι are not so easy to identify. There is ample evidence in the NT, particularly in Paul, that Christ's death was for the

---

80 As in Rom 6:10; so, e.g., Goppelt, 242. Dalton (*Christ's Proclamation* [2d ed.], 130) denies it can have that sense.

81 As in Heb 7:27; 9:12, 26, 28; 10:10; so, e.g., Bigg, 159; Holmer and de Boor, 128; Margot, 60. Dalton (*Christ's Proclamation* [2d ed.], 130) speculates that the contrast may be a relic of the past when Christians needed to differentiate themselves from Judaism.

82 To see here in Christ the conclusive, definitive embodiment in history of the principle of the transformation of suffering and death, as does Selwyn (195), is to make Christ subservient to a larger principle, valid apart from his passion; it seems unlikely that our author had that in mind.

83 So also Brox, 167.

84 So also, e.g., Beare, 167; Dalton, *Christ's Proclamation*, 120.

85 So also, e.g., Goppelt, 242; Selwyn, 196.

86 To attempt to resolve the problem on the basis of which would be more appropriate in the "original liturgical text" supposedly being cited here, as does Kelly (48), is to give too much credence to speculation.

87 Cf. Kelly, 148; Selwyn, 196.

88 The two phrases can be used interchangeably in the LXX as well, as Ezek 43:21 (περὶ ἁμαρτιῶν) and 43:22, 25 (ὑπὲρ ἁμαρτιῶν) show (I owe these references to Goppelt, 242). It is therefore perhaps to put too fine a point on it to argue, as does Delling ("Der Bezug," 102), that the theology reflected in 1 Pet 3:18 is pre-Pauline because of the rarity of the

phrase περὶ ἁμαρτιῶν in Paul; it does occur in Paul (Rom 8:3), and its meaning is the same as the more common Pauline ὑπὲρ ἁμαρτιῶν (which occurs only in 1 Cor 15:3; 2 Cor 5:21; and Gal 1:4).

89 As Goppelt (243) observes, in secular Greek from earliest times ἄδικος described one who broke the law (e.g., Xenophon *Mem.* 4.4.13; he can also use it in contrast to δίκαιος, e.g., 1.1.16; 1.2.19; 2.2.1–3); that such a person breaks the relationship with God derives from the OT. It is that sense that it carries in this verse, as Senior (69) also notes.

90 Matt 5:45; Acts 24:15; cf. Rev 22:11.

91 Matt 27:19; Luke 23:22; Acts 3:14; 7:52; 1 John 2:1, 29; 3:7; cf. 2 Cor 5:21; it also sums up our own author's description of Christ in 1:19 and 2:24, as Dalton (*Christ's Proclamation* [2d ed.], 133) observes. On this point see also Best, 138.

92 While there is no agreement on whether this phrase was drawn directly from tradition (so, e.g., Brox, 167) or was a redactional construction (so, e.g., Bultmann, "Bekenntnis- und Liedfragmente," 3; Shimada, *Formulary Material*, 312; Vogels, *Christi Abstieg*, 20), its function in the current text remains unaffected by its origin. It amplifies the περὶ ἁμαρτιῶν and explains why Christ by his suffering could lead us to God.

93 As Goldstein ("Kirche," 48) notes correctly, the idea that one death can be of benefit to others grows out of OT ideas of sacrifice. The notion that the death of a righteous person has atoning value goes back to Jewish martyr-theology, as exemplified explicitly in 4 Macc 6:28; 17:22, and implicitly in 2 Macc 7:37; 4

benefit of all ἄδικοι ("unrighteous," hence "sinners"),[94] but in this context[95] it is more likely the author has his readers particularly in view, describing them in their preconverted state.[96] It was for them, the formerly unrighteous,[97] that Christ the righteous one died, thus making them righteous as well.[98]

The point of Christ's innocent suffering is given in the ἵνα clause, which therefore stands as the central affirmation of this verse,[99] namely, to lead the unrighteous to God.[100] The verb προσάγω[101] from which προσαγάγῃ derives means to lead or bring someone,[102] but in its nominal form it describes access to God,[103] a meaning frequently carried by the verb in the LXX.[104] It is in this latter sense that it is used here.[105]

After explaining with the ἵνα phrase the meaning for Christians (ὑμᾶς) of the suffering of Christ, the righteous one, the author turns in the final phrase to a more detailed description of Christ's redemptive suffering.[106] The phrase itself is an antithetical[107] *parallelismus membrorum*[108] that, whether in this instance redactional[109] or drawn from a traditional formulation,[110] shares with early Christian tradition the contrast between

---

Macc 9:24; 12:17–18. Kelly (150, to whom I owe these references) also cites 1QS 5.6–7; 8.2–3, 6; 9.4; and 1QSa 1.3, but there the righteous are not so much those who suffer as those who are faithful to the rules of the community.

94 E.g., Rom 5:18–19; 1 Cor 15:22; see also Rom 1:14, 16; 3:21–25.

95 See the immediately following phrase, with its "you" (ὑμᾶς); so also Michaels (203) and Dalton (*Christ's Proclamation* [2d ed.], 134); the latter further notes that therefore it does not refer to the disobedient spirits of v. 19.

96 So also, e.g., Dalton (*Christ's Proclamation* [2d ed.], 134), who, calling on 2:12, argues that all those not yet converted are also included (but see Goldstein, "Kirche," 49). The nearer context of the following ἵνα clause takes precedence here, however.

97 See 1:18b; 2:25a; 4:2–4.

98 See 4:18; cf. 2:24.

99 On the importance of this phrase, see, e.g., Goldstein, "Kirche," 49; Goppelt, 244. It is probably too restrictive to construe it as epexegetic to περὶ ἁμαρτιῶν as Beare (168) does, although it is surely closely related to that phrase.

100 The salvation implied in such leading to God is then expanded in vv. 20–21.

101 The verb is used six times in the NT (Matt 18:24; Luke 9:41; Acts 12:6; 16:20; 27:27; 1 Pet 3:18); the nominal form προσαγωγή is used another three times, but is limited to the Pauline tradition (Rom 5:2; Eph 2:18; 3:12).

102 E.g., Matt 18:24; Luke 9:41; Acts 12:6; in a technical legal sense, Acts 16:20.

103 Rom 5:2; Eph 2:17; 3:12. Dalton (*Christ's Proclamation* [2d ed.], 135) argues for the implication of presentation at a royal court in these NT verses, and cites Exod 21:6 and Num 27:5 as further instances. While such an inference is possible, in both of these passages as in the NT verses the emphasis is on access to God, not on the trappings of a royal court. A court setting is implied in Heb 12:22–23, but without the

use of the stem προσαγ-.

104 It can be used to describe the presentation of persons to God either in a cultic setting, as, e.g., Exod 29:4, 8; 40:12; Lev 8:24; Num 8:9–10, or apart from such a setting, as, e.g., Exod 21:6; Lev 27:5. Best (138) denies, I think correctly, a cultic meaning in this verse.

105 So also, e.g., Senior, 69; Goppelt, 244. The notion of access to God can also be described without the use of the stem προσαγ-, as is evident, e.g., in Heb 10:20. To find the origin for this concept in the figure of the μυσταγωγός of the mystery religions, as does Perdelwitz (*Mysterienreligion*, 86) is, as Kelly (149) notes correctly, to leave the thought-world of our author.

106 The similarity in the point made here to that made in Rom 5:6, 8 led Foster (*Literary Relations*, 432) to argue for a high probability of literary dependence of 3:18b on them. Yet the similarity with other passages (e.g., Rom 5:2; Eph 2:18; Heb 10:19; 1 John 2:2; 4:10) argues for dependence of all such passages on a similar soteriological tradition, rather than on literary dependence on one of them, as Shimada (*Formulary Material*, 329, 342) points out.

107 Because of the contrasts between death and life, flesh and spirit.

108 Because of the identical form of aorist passive participle with dative noun.

109 So, e.g., Shimada "Formula," 161.

110 So, e.g., Beare (169: from "a liturgical stock phrase"). Shimada (*Formulary Material*, 313) thinks the phrase, while traditional, was not integral to the formulary piece he finds contained in vv. 18, 19, and 22; see also Selwyn 197. Goppelt (244) argues that it was originally a Palestinian formulation (as Rom 1:3–4) that was then developed in Hellenistic form (as 1 Tim 3:16); it is difficult to verify such speculation.

Christ dead and alive[111] as well as between Christ in relation to flesh and to spirit.[112] The contrast is of such a nature, however, as the μέν-δέ construction indicates, that the emphasis is on the second half, with the first half subordinated to it.[113] Ζωοποιηθεὶς δὲ πνεύματι ("made alive by [the] Spirit") is thus the climax of the contrast.

In the contrast between the participles[114] (θανατωθείς, ζωοποιηθείς), the point of the first one is clear and straightforward: Christ was indeed put to death upon the cross.[115] While there has been much discussion about the second participle, that is, how and in what form Christ was made alive, the verb contained in the participle (ζωοποιέω) is used in NT tradition principally to refer to the resurrection,[116] and the contrast between Christ dead and alive similarly refers to cross and resur-

rection.[117] On that basis one ought here to see in the participle ζωοποιηθείς a reference to Christ's resurrection.[118] Since, in addition, in the NT such a resurrection is understood as bodily in form, that is in all probability also the way it is to be understood in this instance.[119]

The second contrast embodied in this phrase is between two nouns, σάρξ and πνεῦμα. This contrast is frequently used in the NT,[120] and is to be understood in terms of modes of being or ways of conducting one's life, the one sinful, the other reflecting God's saving activity,[121] rather than in terms of parts of the human being, or in terms some kind of body/soul or material/spiritual dichotomy.[122] Since our author uses these terms in their

111 E.g., Rom 14:9; 2 Cor 13:4. These words referring to Christ did not pass into later Christian tradition; the only time the later fathers refer to Christ with this language, it is in relation to this verse in 1 Peter (e.g., Epiphanius *Anc.* 34.9; 44.3; 93.6; *Pan.* 25.230, 266; Origen *Com. Joan.* 6.35, 175; *Com. Rom.* frag 5); otherwise, as Goppelt (245) notes, it is used to describe Christians rather than Christ.

112 E.g., Rom 1:3–4; 1 Tim 3:16.

113 So also, e.g., Dalton, *Christ's Proclamation* (2d ed.), 137; Sieffert, "Die Heilsbedeutung," 419. Michaels (205) suggests that the μέν in this instance could be rendered "though."

114 These are to be construed as participles of attendant circumstance, explaining how the atonement took place.

115 Since both participles are in the passive voice, it is clear that in each instance something was done to Christ by others.

116 John 5:21; Rom 4:17; 8:11; 1 Cor 15:22; Eph 2:5; Col 2:13. On this point, see Kelly, 150; Best, 139; Dalton, *Christ's Proclamation* (2d ed.), 137; Schelkle, 104.

117 Cf. Rom 4:25; 8:34; 14:9; 2 Cor 4:15; 1 Thess 4:14. On this point see Vogels, *Christi Abstieg*, 20, and the further references in his n. 46; Richard, "Christology," 132; Windisch, 71; Dalton, *Christ's Proclamation* (2d ed.), 137; France, "Exegesis," 268.

118 So also, e.g., Dalton, *Christ's Proclamation* (2d ed.), 139; Sieffert, "Die Heilsbedeutung," 418; France, "Exegesis," 267. Delling ("Der Bezug," 103) speculates that the use of this word for resurrection, instead of the more usual ἐγείρω (which the author does use in 1:21), may reflect an earlier tradition of the resurrection, since in Judaism God is known as the one who makes alive, as, e.g., in the second of the

Eighteen Benedictions (it is translated in Rom 4:17).

119 With, e.g., Feinberg, "1 Peter 3:18–20," 313; Michaels, 205; cf. Margot, 61. Best (139) correctly notes that in that case, one cannot see here Christ going in bodiless fashion to preach to the "spirits" (v. 19). But see William L. Banks ("Who Are the Spirits in Prison?" *Eternity Magazine* 16 [1966] 26), who argues that "it was the disembodied human spirit of Christ that was quickened"; in that state he was able to "move about in the realm of the unseen." So also Galot ("La descente du Christ," 474, 479) finds here a glorification prior to the resurrection; he was "glorifié dans son âme" ("glorified in his spirit"); cf. Selwyn (197): Christ was quickened "in that part of his nature which belonged to the supernatural and spiritual order." If that is in fact what the author meant here, he has departed completely from traditional Christian concepts as well as use of language, something unlikely in one otherwise so embedded in, and faithful to, NT tradition.

120 E.g., Matt 26:41; Mark 14:38; Luke 24:39; John 3:6; 6:63; Rom 1:4; 8:4, 5, 6, 9, 13; Gal 3:3; 4:29; 5:16–19; 6:8; Col 2:5; 1 Tim 3:16; Heb 12:9. See also 1 Cor 5:5; 2 Cor 7:1.

121 So also, e.g., Dalton, *Christ's Proclamation* (2d ed.), 138; Kelly, 151; Scharlemann, "He descended," 87; Goppelt, 245.

122 As Dalton (*Christ's Proclamation* [2d ed.], 136) notes, such a dichotomy, familiar in Greek anthropology (see his brief discussion of Plato's *Phaedo*, 141), has nothing to do with this passage, since the categories here are not Greek but biblical, and are to be so understood. See also Omanson, "Suffering," 441.

usual NT way in this letter,[123] there is no reason to look for a different use here.[124] That lends further credence to the idea that one is not dealing here with two parts of Christ's nature, for example, his physical body and his vital principle[125] or divine nature,[126] but with Christ as a person who was put to death and was raised.[127]

How the dative case of σαρκί and πνεύματι is to be construed represents another problem with respect to this phrase. Widely represented is the construal as a dative of sphere, that is, the two spheres of existence within which Christ is described, that of human existence and that of the divine Spirit.[128] Closely related to dative of sphere is the adverbial dative, or dative of reference,[129] that is, Christ's being put to death had reference to his human flesh, his being made alive had reference either to his own spirit[130] or to the divine Spirit by whose power he was raised.[131] Yet a most natural construal of ζωοποιηθεὶς δὲ πνεύματι would be to take it as a dative of instrument: Christ was raised "by the (divine) Spirit," that is, by God, a central affirmation of the NT.[132] While such a construal has been suggested,[133] it has also been denied because the parallelism of the two phrases implies both datives (σαρκί, πνεύματι)

are to be construed the same way,[134] and that does not seem to be the case with σαρκί. It is hard to see how Christ could die "by means of the flesh" so long as "flesh" is understood either as Christ's own flesh or as a description of his human life.[135] Yet the passive form of θανατωθείς indicates something done to Christ by others,[136] and if one understands σάρξ to stand here for humanity as it does in 1:24, then it names the agency of Christ's death. In that case, it means that Christ was put to death by humans but raised by (God's) Spirit. The contrast between the human and divine attitude to Christ spelled out by our author in 2:6–8 is thus here carried forward to its final outcome: Christ put to death by unbelieving humanity, but raised by (God's) Spirit. Such a construal has the advantage of allowing us to understand Christ's resurrection in the second member of the parallel phrase in its normal form, as a bodily resurrection, since the resurrection is being described in terms of the one who brought it about (Spirit), not in terms of the sphere within which it occurred (spirit). Such a construal would therefore allow the interpretation of the phrase to remain within the normal boundaries of NT tradition. One need no longer posit here

---

123 For the idea of σάρξ see 1:24 (the fact that it is used there to mean the whole of mortal humanity will become important for the discussion below); 2:11; 3:21; 4:1, 2, 6; for πνεῦμα, see 1:2, 11, 12; 2:5; 3:4; 4:6, 14.

124 So, e.g., Dalton, "Interpretation and Tradition," 28.

125 So, e.g., Reicke, *Spirits*, 99.

126 For a summary of such views, see Sieffert, "Die Heilsbedeutung," 416.

127 So also, e.g., Kelly, 151; Schelkle, 104 n. 1; Senior, 69; Michaels, 204.

128 So, e.g., Holmer and de Boor, 101; Sieffert, "Die Heilsbedeutung," 413; Kelly, 151; Best, 139; Brox, 170; Goppelt, 246.

129 So construed by, e.g., Dalton, *Christ's Proclamation* (2d ed.), 141; Selwyn, 196; Kelly, 151; Scharlemann, "He descended," 88. Michaels (204) terms it a dative of respect, which is the same basic construal.

130 So, e.g., Scharlemann ("He descended," 88), who sees here the suggestion that Jesus was brought to life in the sense that his spirit returned to his body; such terms are used in Luke 8:55 to describe the return to life of Jairus's daughter.

131 So, e.g., Selwyn, 196; Bieder, *Höllenfahrt Jesu*, 105. A frequent explanation is to say that Christ's human flesh remained dead, whereas his spirit was revivified, so, e.g., Sieffert, "Die Heilsbedeutung," 414.

132 E.g., Acts 3:15; 4:10; Rom 10:9; 1 Cor 6:14; Gal 1:1; 1 Thess 1:10. The instrumental dative used with πνεῦμα is also common, both alone (Rom 8:13, 14; Gal 5:18) and with ἐν (Matt 12:28; Luke 4:1; Rom 15:16; 1 Cor 12:3, 9; Gal 5:18).

133 E.g., Feinberg, "1 Peter 3:18–20," 355. Bultmann ("Bekenntnis- und Liedfragmente," 4) cites as "Sachparallelen" Rom 6:4; 1 Cor 6:14. Calvin (112) implies it when he identifies "spirit" as "the divine power, *by which* Christ emerged from death a conqueror" (italics added).

134 So, e.g., Dalton, *Christ's Proclamation* (2d ed.), 141; Goppelt, 247; Bieder (*Höllenfahrt Jesu*, 105), who nevertheless affirms that it points to God as the acting agent. That is not the case, however, in the middle couplet of 1 Tim 3:16, the first couplet of which is often cited as a parallel to this participial phrase. In the second couplet, the first dative is instrumental ("seen by angels"), the second either distributive ("among the nations") or indirect object ("to the nations"). The absence of the preposition ἐν before the instrumental ἀγγέλοις in 1 Tim 3:16 adds further weight to seeing both σαρκί and πνεύματι as instrumental here in v. 18.

135 So, e.g., Best, 139; Dalton, *Christ's Proclamation*, 134.

136 So also Feinberg, "1 Peter 3:18–20," 335.

some unique affirmation about Christ's resurrection that is at odds with the remainder of such tradition.[137]

Point of the Verse

While the opening phrase (ὅτι καὶ Χριστός) of this verse reproduces the opening words of 2:21 in a context (3:17—superiority of innocent over guilty suffering) similar to that of 2:20 (superiority of undeserved over deserved punishment) and can thus lead to the assumption that a similar discussion of Christ's exemplary suffering would follow here as in 2:22–24, the additional word ἅπαξ, absent in 2:21, must also be taken into account.[138] Its presence, along with the strong emphasis on Christ's redemption of sinners through his death and resurrection, renders it unlikely that the point of v. 18 is to encourage the readers to imitate the essentially inimitable suffering of Christ.[139] Nor is the point of the verse to be limited to giving an example of the innocent suffering described in v. 17.[140] Rather, the verse serves not so much to justify the statement about the superiority

of innocent suffering in v. 17 (which itself is intended to provide further basis for the argument in v. 16) as to introduce a passage (3:18–22) that justifies the point of the whole preceding affirmation contained in the verses beginning with 3:13. The point here is not, however, that Christians must be prepared to suffer and die if necessary in order so to summon unbelievers to God in imitation of Christ who underwent death for the unrighteous.[141] The point is the objective ground and cause of salvation[142] that is the basis of the readers' confidence that despite any unjust suffering which might seem to point to the contrary, Christ by his passion and resurrection has emerged victorious over all opposing powers, a victory in which faithful Christians will also share.[143] It is the uniqueness of Christ's representative death that is emphasized in this passage,[144] and while it is true that the Christians' relationship to Christ shows them the way they must live, the ethical aspects of that relationship are not brought to the fore in this verse, nor

---

137 Even were one to take σαρκί as dative of sphere or reference, it would be possible nevertheless to retain the instrumental sense with πνεύματι, since datives in parallel phrases in the NT are not always to be construed in the same way. In addition to n. 134 above, see also 1 Cor 6:11, where the second dative is also instrumental.

138 That is the case even if, as Brox (167), Martin ("Composition," 32), and Delling ("Der Bezug," 103) argue, it is taken from the tradition. Whatever its source, it is present and must be taken into account in any discussion of the meaning of this verse.

139 As, e.g., Feuillet ("Sacrifices," 711) and Selwyn (195) would have it; cf. also Margot, 61. Reicke (Spirits, 217) qualifies the point by affirming that the reference to Christ's redemptive death means Christians "must likewise be prepared if necessary to die as a sin-offering for the sake of other pagans, namely to lead them also to God." Dalton (Christ's Proclamation, 107) observes correctly that "it is difficult to substantiate this view." So also Best (139): "This interpretation is unacceptable" because it must downplay to too large an extent the atonement language in this verse. No more convincing is the argument of Vogels (Christi Abstieg, 31) that the point is: Just as Christ did, so the Christians can bring others to God by shaming them by means of their (the Christians') suffering, because that is what God did for the Christians through Christ's suffering, namely, rescue them from sin.

140 As, e.g., Brox (168) would have it. The qualification of Steuer ("1 Petr 3,17—4,6," 676) that only v. 18a gives such an example is rendered questionable not

only by the presence in v. 18a of the phrase περὶ ἁμαρτιῶν but also by the clear linkage of the remainder of the verse to its first half with the ἵνα phrase, which has nothing to do with innocent suffering as such. On these points see de Villiers ("Joy," 78), who, citing Kelly (147), also sees the point not in Christ's innocent suffering but in his unique redemptive death, which serves as the basis of the readers' continued Christian confidence in the midst of their affliction.

141 As, e.g., Schweizer (77) wants to argue.

142 As Dalton (Christ's Proclamation [2d ed.], 122) also notes.

143 So also, e.g., France, "Exegesis in Practice," 266; de Villiers, "Joy," 78–79. Contributing to that confidence is the description in this verse of Christ's suffering as both vicarious (the righteous one for the unrighteous many) and mediatorial (to bring those unrighteous to God); so, e.g., Beare, 168; Goppelt, 243. See also Dalton (Christ's Proclamation [2d ed.], 131): Christ's death is here "both a sacrifice of expiation for sin and a covenant sacrifice," as in Matt 26:28. The attempt of Bieder (Höllenfahrt Jesu, 127) to add to such encouragement the need for suffering Christians to carry on their missionary task is to overload the verses.

144 So also, e.g., Windisch, 70.

are they in the ensuing passage.[145]

■ **19** This verse is one of the shorter, but surely the most problematic, in this letter, if not in the NT canon as a whole,[146] and eludes any agreement on its precise meaning.[147] In addition to two grammatical problems (the construal of ἐν ᾧ and the function of καί, the latter problem not always recognized), there are the questions of the identity of the spirits and the place of and reason for their imprisonment, the direction of Christ's journey (ascent or descent) and the time it occurred, and the content of his proclamation. They may be conveniently considered in that order.[148]

The most natural antecedent of ἐν ᾧ would be the immediately preceding πνεύματι of v. 18, and it has often been so construed.[149] If πνεύματι is understood to be a dative of sphere, such a construal carries with it the problem of limiting the ensuing activity of Christ to the spiritual "sphere" or mode of existence, despite the preceding reference to death and resurrection

(θανατωθεὶς μὲν σαρκὶ ζωοποιηθεὶς δὲ πνεύματι). But the other four times this prepositional phrase occurs in this letter, it can be construed as having temporal force ("when").[150] If that is the meaning it carries here, it would refer not merely to Christ's activity in the "spirit" understood as the time of his death and prior to his resurrection,[151] but to the broader preceding context with its reference to both death and resurrection.[152] It is not clear, however, that ἐν ᾧ does regularly carry temporal significance; while that is the case in 2:12 and 3:16, it is better construed as causal in 1:6 and perhaps also in 4:4.[153]

One can retain πνεύματι as the more obvious antecedent to ἐν ᾧ, as the word order indicates, however, without being obliged to explain how such activity could occur prior to the resurrection, if one construes πνεύματι not as adverbial but rather as instrumental.[154] The point, then, is not the form (spiritual) in which Christ carried on his proclamation, or the time when it

---

145 Vogels (*Christi Abstieg*, 26) is correct to affirm that the idea of following Christ is regularly bound up with the redemptive act of Christ, and he cites Phil 2:5–8 and 2 Cor 10:1 to support that affirmation; but that is not the case in this verse, nor in this passage, as also Goldstein ("Kirche," 52) would have it. Here the emphasis is on the redemptive act of Christ, not on following him.

146 Luther wrote of it: "Das ist eyn wunderlicher text und eyn finsterer spruch, als freylich eyner ym newen Testament ist, das ich noch nicht gewiss weyss, was S. Peter meynet" ("That is as strange a text and as dark a saying as any in the New Testament, so that I am not yet sure what St. Peter intended") (WA 1891, 12.367; cited in Reicke, *Spirits*, ix). Bengel (*Gnomon*) termed it a "locus mysterii plenus" ("a passage filled with mystery"; cited in Cranfield, "Interpretation," 371). Few commentators would quarrel with either judgment.

147 So Best, 150. As Brox (169–70) observes correctly, the problem lies in the fact that not all questions pertaining to the text are answerable; it is therefore impossible to claim exclusive validity for any given interpretation. For a survey of the varieties of interpretations that have been proposed, see Reicke, *Spirits*, 7–51.

148 For convenient short summaries of these problems and some proposed solutions, see Omanson, "Suffering," 442–44; Grudem, 204; Fitzmyer, "First Peter," 366–67.

149 As early as Clement of Alexandria and Origen, as Dalton (*Christ's Proclamation* [2d ed.], 145) observes.

150 Kelly (152) attributes the position to ancient commentators whose native language was Greek. See also, e.g., Feinberg, "1 Peter 3:18–20," 318; Perrot, "La descente aux enfers," 236; Dalton, *Christ's Proclamation*, 138; idem, "Interpretation and Tradition," 25; France, "Exegesis in Practice," 268–69. That it refers to Christ's divine nature, as Schelkle (103–4) avers, is unlikely, as Dalton (*Christ's Proclamation*, 140) notes.

150 1:6; 2:12; 3:16; 4:4. On this point see Selwyn, 315; Scharlemann, "He descended," 88; Reicke, *Spirits*, 103, 108; Cranfield, 103.

151 A position held, e.g., by Brooks ("1 Peter 3:21," 303; cf. also Scharlemann, "He descended," 89), but expressly denied by Bieder ("Reicke," 461). Some have attempted to obviate this difficulty by finding in ἐν ᾧ a reference to Christ's preexistence, e.g., Bieder (*Höllenfahrt Jesu*, 102), calling on 1:11 for support. Beare (170) expressly denies this as a possibility.

152 So, e.g., Michaels, 206; Fink, "Use and Significance," 37; Bieder, *Höllenfahrt Jesu*, 107. Cranfield ("Interpretation," 371) would include the whole of v. 18.

153 Spicq (137) argues, on the basis of 1:6, for a causal meaning here; I am unpersuaded.

154 See the argument for that position above, in the comments on v. 18. Such a construal also obviates the argument of Selwyn (197) that the antecedent cannot be πνεύματι because there is no example in the NT of a dative of reference serving as the antecedent to a relative pronoun, if in fact πνεύματι is not a dative of reference.

occurred, with all the difficulties attendant on either interpretation. Rather, the point is that, in addition (καί)[155] to being raised from the dead by the (power of the) Spirit, Christ went, by that same Spirit, and in risen form, to carry out the proclamation described in the remainder of the verse. Such a construal allows the language and the word order to function in their most natural form, and is for that reason the construal that most recommends itself.

A further grammatical problem is posed by the presence of καί: how is it to be construed? By its position it is clearly adjunctive ("also"), implying an additional activity,[156] rather than copulative ("and"), indicating the next in a series of steps.[157] Defining this further activity is difficult, since no activity on Christ's part is implied in the phrase ζωοποιηθεὶς δὲ πνεύματι; the passive verb makes that clear.[158] Construal of the ἐν τῷ as temporal makes the καί redundant, since nothing else that Christ does at the time of his resurrection is reported.[159] Construing the πνεύματι in v. 18 as instrumental rather than adverbial, however, alleviates the difficulty, since in that case the ἐν τῷ will also be instrumental, designating the second act in a series instigated by the Spirit, the first being Christ's resurrection, the second his proclamation. Such a solution lends further credence to the argument that the first phrase, ἐν πνεύματι, is to be understood as a dative of instrument.

Excursus: The Figure of Enoch in 1 Peter 3:19

On the basis of the fact that in the original manuscript of this epistle, the opening letters of v. 19 would have read: ΕΝΩΚΑΙΤΟΙΣΕΝΦΥΛΑΚΗ, with the first four letters (ΕΝΩΚ) looking much like the name Enoch (ΕΝΩΧ), some have conjectured that the name Enoch originally stood in the text (ΕΝΩΧΚΑΙΤΟΙΣΕΝΦΥΛΑΚΗ), with the letter Χ later omitted through haplography with the following Κ. Alternatively, since ἐν ᾧ is "characteristically Petrine," Rendel Harris suggested that the original phrase contained both ἐν ᾧ and Ἐνώχ (ΕΝΩΚΑΙΕΝΩΧΤΟΙΣΕΝΦΥΛΑΚΗ) with the entire name Ἐνώχ later omitted, again through haplography. With Enoch the subject of the verb ἐκήρυξεν in v. 19, ἐν ᾧ thus become an (awkward) introduction to the new sentence (cf. 4:4) without implying an antecedent to the relative pronoun.[160] This proposed emendation of the text may have been published as early as 1763, but it did appear in 1772, when W. Bowyer published his edition of the Greek Testament in London. In that edition, Bowyer attributed the emendation to an otherwise unidentified (and to this point unidentifiable) "S."[161] Suggested independently by the Dutch scholar Cramer in 1891,[162] the emendation has been accepted by a number of scholars,[163] including James Moffatt, who

---

155 See the comments on this word below for its problematic nature when ἐν ᾧ is construed as either adverbial or temporal.

156 To translate it as "even" and connect it with the following words, as Selwyn (198) suggests, implies an unexpected addition to Christ's normal preaching "in the spirit," namely, his preaching "even" to the imprisoned spirits. One might argue that in such a case, Christ's more normal "preaching" in his risen state was to the disciples, but there is no indication that our author has that activity in view at this point.

157 So, e.g., Dalton, *Christ's Proclamation* (2d ed.), 148–49; but then the words would have to read καὶ ἐν ᾧ. Nor can one translate with Dalton (184) "in the spirit, in which he went *and* made proclamation" (emphasis added), as though the καί connected the verbs πορευθείς and ἐκήρυξεν. To translate it that way is in fact to ignore the καί altogether, since an "and" is implied in the relationship between the two verbs.

158 The suggestion of Kelly (152) that this is another aspect of Christ's activity "in the Spirit," the first being the resurrection, is questionable for that

reason.

159 To argue that the καί places the τοῖς πνεύμασιν parallel to the ἄδικοι and the ὑμεῖς of v. 18, as does Vogels (*Christi Abstieg*, 135), finding then Christ's second act to be the bringing of salvation to the spirits as he brought salvation to the unrighteous, must assume that the ἐκήρυξεν means salvific proclamation (on this point see below), and must place in parallel the first salvific act consisting in suffering with the second act consisting in proclamation, two rather unparallel acts.

160 J. Rendel Harris, "A Further Note on the Use of Enoch in 1 Peter," *Expositor*, series 6, 4 (1901) 348–49.

161 Bieder, *Höllenfahrt Jesu*, 97; Edgar J. Goodspeed, "Some Greek Notes: IV; Enoch in I Peter 3:19," *JBL* 73 (1954) 91; cf. Dalton, *Christ's Proclamation* (2d ed.), 141.

162 Moffatt, 141.

163 See Reicke, *Spirits*, 41–42, for a list; cf. also J. Rendel Harris, "The History of a Conjectural Emendation," *Expositor*, series 6, 6 (1902) 389; Moffatt, 141.

adopted it in his translation of 1 Pet 3:19.[164]

While such a suggestion may resolve the problem of the antecedent of the ἐν ᾧ, it does so at the cost of contextual incomprehensibility: why, with no advanced warning, would the author introduce Enoch at this point in the narrative, only to omit any further reference to him, and not exploit in any way the introduction of this figure?[165] Such conjectures are useful only when the text in question is incomprehensible in its present form, and when the suggested emendation renders it comprehensible. That is manifestly not the case in this instance; while the text is difficult, it is not incomprehensible, and the suggested addition of Enoch simply serves to increase rather than decrease the problems associated with the text.[166] The conjecture regarding the mention of Enoch at the beginning of the text of v. 19 is thus to be discarded.[167]

The phrase "to the spirits in prison" (τοῖς ἐν φυλακῇ πνεύμασιν) poses the problems of (a) their identity and (b) the nature and location of their prison.

a. Their identity.[168] A traditional solution to the meaning of the "spirits" has been to identify them with the souls of human beings who have died,[169] to whose souls Christ turned when he "went" to "preach."[170] That, however, leaves unspecified to which dead persons this verse refers. There have been numerous suggestions. Some have found here a reference to the souls of all the dead,[171] or of all who died prior to the incarnation of Christ,[172] or of all those who had not accepted Christ during their lifetime for whatever reason.[173] Others would limit the reference to righteous men and women, either those of any race[174] or specifically the righteous people of the OT.[175] Alternatively, the reference to Noah and the flood in the immediate context (v. 20) could imply that the reference here is to the people of Noah's generation,[176] that is, either those who died in the flood[177] or those to whom the Spirit of Christ, present in Noah, proclaimed repentance prior to the flood;[178] more specifically, either those who refused to

---

164 "It was in the Spirit that Enoch also went"; the whole of vv. 19–22 are included within parentheses, apparently to indicate their interruption of the train of thought that moves from 3:18 to 4:1.

165 So also Scharlemann, "He descended," 88; cf. Cranfield, 102 n. 1.

166 On this point, see Dalton, *Christ's Proclamation* (2d ed.), 144.

167 Kelly (152) terms it a "brilliant but untenable guess"; so also, e.g., Beare, 171.

168 For a convenient summary of the various ways "spirits" have been identified, and some of the scholars who have made those identifications, see Shimada, *Formulary Material*, 358–62.

169 So, e.g., Perrot, "La descente aux enfers," 244; Spicq, 136. They have been interpreted in this sense both with (e.g., Holmer and de Boor, 130) and without (e.g., Brox, 171) seeing them as identical to the dead in 1 Pet 4:6. On the relationship of 3:19 to 4:6, see the comments on the latter verse below.

170 The passage most often cited to justify the identification of human souls with "spirits" (πνεύματα) is Heb 12:23, e.g., Schlier ("Adhortatio," 63) and Spicq (136), who also point to its use to refer to the souls of the dead in *1 Enoch* 22.3–13 and 103.3–4. While this last verse ("righteous dead") is a close approximation of its use in Heb 12:23, closer is the πνεύματα . . . δικαίων of the Song of the Three Holy Children, Pr Azar 64 (LXX Dan 3:86; I owe this reference to Cranfield, 102). In the NT, the word πνεῦμα is also used to refer to a mistaken identification of the risen Jesus in Luke 24:37, 39, but has there more the meaning of "ghost" or "phantom" (D reads φάντασμα in Luke 24:37). That the dead hear Christ is mentioned in John 5:25–29, as it is referred to in *Odes Sol.* 42.15–20 and the *Gospel of Peter* 41–42, but the word "spirit" is not used in these passages; on these passages, see Perrot, "La descente aux enfers," 233 n. 4, 240–41; Goppelt, 251; Smith, *Petrine Controversies,* 42. To find this verse a reflection on Luke 12:57–59, as does Vogels (*Christi Abstieg*, 86–87), reaches a bit far, as he does in citing the use of "living spirit" (πνεῦμα ζωῆς) in Gen 6:17 and 7:15 as justification for finding "spirits" to mean human "souls" (135), since those two instances include everything that lives, not just human beings. To base the meaning on the structure of the underlying hymn, as does Hunzinger ("Zur Struktur," 144), or on the meaning of "preach" as "announce salvation," as does Vogels (43–44), is to use the questionable to illumine the unclear.

171 Galot ("La descente du Christ," 481) notes this as the position of Ephraem and Cyril of Alexandria.

172 E.g., Kelly, 153; Schweizer, 78. See also Bengel (*Gnomon*, 748): "To all ages of the Old Testament, before Christ's death"; Holmer and de Boor (131–32): valid for all former generations, all the way back to Adam.

173 E.g., Holmer and de Boor, 131.

174 E.g., Johnson, "Preaching," 49; cf. also Clement of Alexandria *Strom.* 6.6.46–47.

175 So Ignatius *Magn.* 9.2; Justin *Dial.* 72.4; cf. *Hermas Sim.* 9.16.5 (I owe these references to Goppelt, 251; cf. also Dalton, "Interpretation and Tradition," 14; Schelkle, 104–5); in their context, probably also *Sib.*

listen to Christ speaking through Noah,[179] or those who repented on the basis of that proclamation prior to their death by the flood.[180]

There is strong evidence, however, against such an identification of the word "spirits" with (the souls of) human dead. In the NT the word "spirits" ($\pi\nu\epsilon\acute{\nu}\mu\alpha\tau\alpha$) is used overwhelmingly to refer not to human dead[181] but to supernatural beings,[182] primarily malevolent.[183] An absolute use of $\pi\nu\epsilon\acute{\nu}\mu\alpha\tau\alpha$ in the NT, comparable to that in v. 19, is rare, but when it occurs, it also refers to evil spirits.[184]

The inference to be drawn, therefore, would be that the "spirits" referred to in v. 19 are also supernatural,[185] and probably malevolent. There is an implication in a saying of Jesus that angelic disobedience (Satan) is responsible for evil on the earth (Luke 10:17–20), but there is no indication in the NT that Satan's followers

---

Or. 8.310–11 and *1 Enoch* 103.4. While Calvin (114) did not identify them as the righteous of the OT, his description of them as "godly souls . . . watching in hope of the salvation promised them," and whose abode ($\phi\nu\lambda\alpha\kappa\acute{\eta}$) was therefore not a prison but a watchtower, makes such an inference evident.

176 So, e.g., Perdelwitz, *Mysterienreligion*, 86; Sieffert, "Die Heilsbedeutung," 416; Galot, "La descente du Christ," 480; Goppelt, 249. As Bieder (*Höllenfahrt Jesu*, 111) points out, they had the reputation of being the most wicked of any who ever lived. See *m. Sanh.* 10.3: they have no share in the resurrection.

177 So, e.g., Cranfield, "Interpretation," 370; Beare, 172; Wand, 101.

178 So classically Augustine, who interpreted their prison as the darkness of ignorance: "Spiritus in carcere includi sunt increduli, qui vixerunt temporibus Noe, quorum spiritus, i.e. animae, erant in carne et ignorantiae tenebris velut in carcere conclusae" ("The imprisoned spirits are the unbelievers who lived at the time of Moses, whose spirits, i.e., souls, were closed up in the flesh and the darkness of ignorance as in a prison." This quotation is from Scharlemann ["He descended," 90], who cites it from Augustine *Letter* 164, *Ep. Euod.*, PL 33.709–18. While this Latin prose does not appear in the text of the letter in *PL*, it is an accurate summary of Augustine's views, esp. as stated at the opening of § 16 [*PL* 33.715]). The implication that they were in prison when Christ preached to them has been accounted for either allegorically (their imprisonment was in ignorance—so Augustine), or on a temporal basis, i.e., though from the author's perspective now in prison, they were not so when Christ preached to them (so Feinberg, "1 Peter 3:18–20," 330).

179 So, e.g., Bigg, 162.

180 So, e.g., Bengel (*Gnomon,* 748): those who repented as the flood waters rose; see also Ketter, 258. Cf. Jos. Frings ("Zu I Petr 3,19 und 4,6," *BZ* 17 [1926] 770, 778) and Steuer ("1 Petr 3,17—4,6," 676), who note, however, that it is an idea that has no scriptural

warrant, neither OT nor NT. There is in fact no biblical evidence that Noah said anything at all to his contemporaries. The closest is the identification of him as "herald of righteousness" in 2 Pet 2:5, which, in light of the regular mention of "Noah the righteous" in, e.g., Philo, is probably an epithet describing his quality, as, e.g., the "Teacher of Righteousness" at Qumran, rather than a description of anything he announced; on this point see Dalton, *Christ's Proclamation* (2d ed.), 157.

181 Its one clear use to refer to human beings in the NT, Heb 12:23, is qualified by the adjective "righteous" ($\delta\acute{\iota}\kappa\alpha\iota o\varsigma$); that is also the case in *1 Enoch* 22.3–4; 9.3, 10. Selwyn (198) concludes from this that when "spirits" occurs without a qualifying adjective, it means either persons now living on earth or supernatural beings, perhaps both, but never human dead. In the one absolute use referring to human beings (*1 Enoch* 22.13), the context makes that reference clear, as Dalton (*Christ's Proclamation* [2d ed.], 153) points out. He further suggests (164; cf. also idem, "Interpretation and Tradition," 29) that if v. 19 referred to human beings, the more likely phrase would have been $\tau o\hat{\iota}\varsigma\ \pi\nu\epsilon\acute{\nu}\mu\alpha\sigma\iota\nu\ \tau\hat{\omega}\nu\ \dot{\alpha}\pi\epsilon\iota\theta\eta\sigma\acute{\alpha}\nu\tau\omega\nu$ ("the spirits of those who disobeyed"), and that the present construction with $\dot{\alpha}\pi\epsilon\iota\theta\acute{\eta}\sigma\alpha\sigma\iota\nu$ implies that the beings were already spirits at the time they disobeyed, and hence could hardly refer to the souls of disobedient people who died.

182 E.g., Heb 1:14; 12:9 (it is unclear whether the reference here is to human or supernatural beings, or both, as Selwyn [198] notes); Rev 1:4; 3:1; 4:5; 5:6.

183 E.g., Mark 1:23, 26, 27; 3:11; 5:2, 8.

184 E.g., Matt 8:16; 12:45; Luke 10:20. That is also the case in 2 Macc 3:24; *Jub.* 15.31; *1 Enoch* 60.1–3; 1QM 12.8–9. On this point, see, e.g., Dalton, *Christ's Proclamation* (2d ed.), 153; Best, 142; Michaels, 207; Kelly, 155.

185 For the use of $\pi\nu\epsilon\acute{\nu}\mu\alpha\tau\alpha$ for angelic beings, see Heb 1:14; cf. Rev 1:4; 3:1; 4:5; 5:6; on this point, see Selwyn, 198; Knopf, 149.

are now imprisoned.[186] There is a clear Jewish tradition, however, in which the angelic beings of Gen 6:1–6, whose disobedience caused the flood,[187] were subsequently imprisoned.[188] These beings are identified as πνεύματα[189] and are clearly to be understood as non-human. Their sin was to take for themselves human wives,[190] the offspring of which union were understood to be the source of evil in the world.[191] That it is this tradition which underlies the reference to "spirits" in our verse seems therefore likely to be the case.[192]

b. The nature and location of their prison. If, as some have argued, "spirits" refers to the souls of human dead, then the prison (φυλακή) referred to must be the abode of the dead. Nowhere in the NT, however, is φυλακή used in that sense;[193] where the word is used to mean "prison," it refers either to prisons in the Greco-Roman world[194] or to the place where Satan (or demons) is imprisoned.[195] Attempts to find such a reference in the NT are either circumstantial[196] or simply ignore the context within which references to φυλακή are placed.[197] That such a prison exists for evil "spirits," however, is assumed both in the NT and in Jewish tradition, particularly the traditions concerning Enoch, although the location of the prison is unclear, that is, whether it is in the earth,[198] in the heavens,[199] or at the end of both heaven and earth.[200] Such ambiguity[201] prevents us at this point from coming to any firm conclusion about the prison's location.[202] Further considerations will be needed before such a conclusion can be drawn.

Christ's activity is described with two verbs, πορευθείς

---

186 As, e.g., Michaels (208) notes correctly; but see Rev 20:1–3, 10 in regard to Satan's future.

187 E.g., specifically *Jub.* 7.21.

188 Cf. *1 Enoch* 6–16; 18.12—19.2; 21.1–10; 54.3–6; 64–69; 106.14–15; *2 Enoch* 7.1–3; Wis 14:6; *Jub.* 5.6; *T. Naph.* 3.5; *T. Reub.* 5.6; *2 Bar.* 56.13; cf. CD 2.18. On this point, see Selwyn, 198; France, "Exegesis in Practice," 269–70. But see Perrot ("La descente aux enfers," 237), who thinks it "un détour" to appeal to disobedient angels in relation to the flood.

189 E.g., *1 Enoch* 13.6; 15.4, 6, 7; cf. *Jub.* 10.1–9; when used of people, as noted above, it carries a qualifying adjective.

190 So Gen 6:1–4. Its propinquity with Gen 6:5–6 and its description of the evil that prompted the flood caused the two to be identified as cause and effect; e.g., *1 Enoch* 10.2, 7, 22; 67.4–13; 106.14–15; Wis 14:6; *T. Naph.* 3.5; cf. 2 Pet 2:4–5; Jude 6.

191 E.g., *1 Enoch* 10.8 (where their leader is identified as Azazel); 15.1–9; *2 Enoch* 18.1–5.

192 First proposed by Spitta (so Schelkle, 106 n. 1), it has subsequently found wide acceptance; e.g., Krodel, 68; Knopf, 152; Harris, "History," 390; Omanson, "Suffering," 443–44; Tarrech, "Le milieu," 371; Kelly, 153–54; Brox, 172; Reicke, *Spirits*, 90–91; but see Bultmann ("Bekenntnis- und Liedfragmente," 4), who is unsure whether the reference is to those angels or to the souls of the rebellious people of Noah's generation, and Reicke (109), whose later uncertainty is based on the fact that he finds no sharp distinctions made between angels and human beings when speaking of persons of remote antiquity, as in Jude 6–7. Neither objection is compelling.

193 So also, e.g., Dalton (*Christ's Proclamation* [2d ed.], 160), who also argues correctly (idem, "Inter-

pretation and Tradition," 36) that the "activity of Christ's soul in the abode of the dead seems to be a non-biblical tradition."

194 E.g., Acts 5:19; 8:3; 12:4; 22:4; 2 Cor 6:5; 11:23.

195 Rev 18:2; 20:7; implied, although the word is not used, in 2 Pet 2:4.

196 E.g., Vogels (*Christi Abstieg*, 43–44), who argues that since ἐκήρυξεν must mean the proclamation of salvation, and since evil angels are not rescued (e.g., Matt 25:41), "prison" here must refer to the place of the dead rather than of angels or Satan; the questionable assumptions on which that justification is based are evident. Other attempts to find here a reference to the realm of human dead by relating it to Acts 2:27, 31, as does Davies ("Primitive Christology in I Peter," 117), or to derive it from Jesus' parable in Luke 12:58// Matt 18:30, 34, as does Vogels (136), are similarly wide of the mark.

197 E.g., Selwyn (200), who finds a prison house for the evil dead implied in Rev 18:2; 20:1–7; the context clearly indicates that it is an abode of evil spirits. *2 Bar.* 23.4 and *2 Enoch* 42.1, which he also cites, have no reference to "prison."

198 Apparently assumed by Rev 20:3 (ἄβυσσος); 2 Pet 2:4 (τάρταρος); so also in *1 Enoch* 10.4, 14.5; 15.8, 10; 18.12–14; 67.7; 103.3–7; *Jub.* 5.6; 1QH 3.17–18; on this point, see Schwank et al., 76; Reicke, *Spirits*, 116; Best, 143.

199 Eph 6:12; *2 Enoch* 7.1–3; 18.3; *T. Levi* 3.1–3; on this point, see Dalton, *Christ's Proclamation* (2d ed.), 169–70; Brox, 175–76.

200 So, e.g., *1 Enoch* 1.14; 21.1–10; cf. 18.11—19.1; on this point, see Krodel, 68–69.

201 It extends to the individual writings themselves: in *2 Enoch* 7.1–3 angels are imprisoned in the second heaven; in 18.7, Enoch tells other evil angels (the

and ἐκήρυξεν. Because of other NT evidence that speaks of Christ's descent into the netherworld,[203] πορευθείς in this verse has also traditionally been understood to refer to Christ's descent into hell, the *descensus ad inferos*.[204] Such an interpretation of the verb therefore presumes that this passage (vv. 18–22) speaks of two journeys of Christ: his descent here in v. 19, and his ascent into heaven in v. 22.[205] The difficulty with finding such a meaning here for the verb πορεύομαι, which means basically simply "proceed" or "go," is that it is nowhere used in the NT to mean "go down."[206] The verb

employed to describe such "going down" is καταβαίνω, and that is the verb which is used in those NT passages that do speak of a descent into the netherworld.[207] There is no necessity, therefore, to understand the verb πορευθείς to mean "descend"; it refers to a journey, no more.[208] On the other hand, the verb πορεύομαι is the verb used in the NT to describe Christ's ascension.[209] There is therefore no reason why πορευθείς could not also mean "ascend" here, since there is other contemporary evidence of evil spirits imprisoned in the

"Grigori") together with their prince ("Satanail") that their companions (the angels mentioned in 7.1–3) have been sentenced by God to a place "under the earth" until it and heaven end. Dalton (*Christ's Proclamation* [2d ed.], 179–80) suggests that this results from the fact that the early Jewish picture of the netherworld was in the process of giving way to a more Hellenistic idea of seven heavens, within one of which the evil were imprisoned. Jeremias ("Zwischen Karfreitag und Ostern," 200) argues that the older view that Hades was the abode of all the dead was giving way to a more Hellenistic notion that the evil souls were kept in Hades, the good souls in heaven. Both suggestions may be correct.

202 Leaney (51) notes correctly that v. 19 implies neither location. Bieder (*Höllenfahrt Jesu*, 109) suggests that the author may have had no specific location in mind. Augustine's suggestion that the prison was ignorance (see Scharlemann, "He descended," 90 n. 176), and Calvin's suggestion (114) that it meant not a prison but a watchtower, thus being the abode of the watchful souls of the OT faithful as they awaited their salvation (cf. Cranfield, "Interpretation," 369), ignore a locatable "prison," as do Galot ("La descente du Christ," 480), who finds the prison to refer not only to death but to the chains of their sin of insubordination, and Stuhlmueller ("Baptism," 211), who argues, "As the baptismal words are pronounced over the submerged or buried candidate, it can be said that Christ is preaching to the spirit of one in prison."

203 Rom 10:7; Eph 4:8–10. Further evidence of Christ's presence among the dead has been found in such passages as Matt 12:40; Acts 2:27; Rev 1:18; 5:13, but there is no reference in these latter passages to his "descent." Heb 13:20, sometimes cited, is no more significant here than any reference to Christ's being raised from the dead. On this whole point cf. Schelkle 107; Selwyn, 320–22; Holmer and de Boor, 102; Shimada, "Formula," 159.

204 Knopf (152): this passage is the first time Christ's

descent into hell is clearly portrayed; see also, e.g., Scharlemann, "He descended," 93; Galot, "La descente du Christ," 472; Beare, 172; Johnson, "Preaching," 48–51; Krafft, "Christologie," 123. That Christ descended to the realm of the dead is mentioned in Clement of Alexandria *Strom.* 6.6.45–46; Origen *Frag. Joan.* frag. 79.20–23; Athanasius *Ep. Epic.* 5.26–27 (citing Peter as his authority); Justin *Dial.* 72.4 (quoting a passage from Jeremiah that speaks of "the Lord God" [κύριος ὁ θεός] preaching salvation to the Hebrew dead; for the complete text, see n. 231 below); cf. Dalton, "Interpretation and Tradition," 17; Schelkle, 104–5. Kelly (153) also cites Ignatius *Magn.* 9.2, but it refers only to Christ raising the OT righteous. Boismard ("Liturgie" [2], 183) points out that the first creedal mention of the descent into hell is found in the acts of the Council of Sirmium in 357, under Syriac influence, and then in the synods of Nicea in 359 and Constantinople in 360. It thus came into confessions of faith fairly late, not until the fifth century in the West; on this point see also Galot, "La descente du Christ," 471. For further information, see Goppelt, 250–54 (ET 260–63), "Excurs: Die Hadespredigt Christi im religionsgeschichtlichen Zusammenhang"; Selwyn, "Early Patristic Doctrine of Christ's 'Descensus,' and Its Relation to the New Testament," 339–53; Brox, 182–89.

205 So, e.g., Vogels, *Christi Abstieg,* 136; Selwyn, 200.

206 So also, e.g., Kelly, 155–56; Dalton, *Christ's Proclamation* (2d ed.), 162. See France ("Exegesis in Practice," 271), who finds no reference here to "going down."

207 For Christ's descent, Rom 10:7; Eph 4:9–10; cf. also Matt 11:23 par. Luke 10:15. Had the author wanted to say specifically that Christ descended, he would have used καταβάς, as Bieder (*Höllenfahrt Jesu*, 107) notes; see also Dalton, *Christ's Proclamation,* 160.

208 So also, e.g., Margot, 62; cf. also Luther, 230, 231; Calvin, 113.

209 Acts 1:10–11; cf. John 14:2, 3, 28; 16:28.

heavens.[210] Further, the implication of v. 18 that this activity was undertaken by the risen Christ would make his ascent rather than his descent the more likely activity.[211] Most decisive of all is the fact that this same verb form does refer to Christ's ascension in 3:22. For that reason alone, it would seem most appropriate to understand πορευθείς in the same way here.[212] On that basis, both vv. 19 and 22 would describe the same journey, and the passage would thus describe one journey, not two, of the risen Christ.[213]

Excursus: When Did Christ "Go" and "Preach"?

A variety of solutions have been proposed concerning the time at which Christ preached to the "imprisoned spirits." Augustine[214] was evidently the first to suggest that this activity took place in the time of Noah, who, by the Spirit of Christ, preached repentance to those who subsequently, because of their refusal of that message, died in the flood. Two traditions seem combined here: the one referring to Christ's pre-incarnate activity,[215] the other holding that while the ark was being built, Noah preached repentance to his contemporaries, and that those who believed were saved, those who did not, were not.[216] While the position is most firmly associated with Augustine, other scholars have also adopted it.[217] The evident references to Christ's death and resurrection in v. 18 render questionable the notion that the events in v. 19 occurred prior to those events.

More widely held is the idea that it occurred during the interval between Christ's death on the cross and his subsequent resurrection, the *triduum mortis*,[218] during which the soul of Christ preached conversion to the souls of Noah's generation, and to all the dead.[219] On the assumption that Christ was with God during that period of time, it has been suggested that Christ went and proclaimed during his three-hour time of suffering on the cross,[220] but his living, physical presence on the cross makes this solution difficult to entertain. Again the reference to the resurrection of Christ in v. 18, which is nowhere in the NT associated with Christ's disembodied soul, weighs against this understanding.

Finally, since there is no indication in the text itself that the activity occurred between death and resurrection,[221] and because the point of ζωοποιηθεὶς δὲ πνεύματι seems to be Christ's resurrection, the activity of going and preaching would have to be subsequent to that event, that is, during Christ's ascension.[222] The context of vv. 18 and 22, and the general anthropology of the NT, which has little place for disembodied souls, seem to favor the third of the three options.[223]

210 E.g., *2 Enoch* 7.1–3; *T. Levi* 3.2; cf. Eph 6:12.
211 So also, e.g., Dalton, "Interpretation and Tradition," 19 (in agreement with Karl Gschwind); idem, *Christ's Proclamation*, 160; Bultmann, "Bekenntnis- und Liedfragmente," 5.
212 So also, e.g., Fitzmyer, "First Peter," 367; Dalton, *Christ's Proclamation* (2d ed.), 182. To argue, as do Vogels (*Christi Abstieg*, 136) and Selwyn (200), that the use of the *same* verb intends to indicate two *different* journeys is to bend the evidence to a preconceived conclusion.
213 So also, e.g., Michaels, 209; Dalton, *Christ's Proclamation* (2d ed.), 159. Whether the repeated mention of the ascension in vv. 19 and 22 is due to its importance for our author, or because of the combination of two traditions, as, e.g., Dalton (218) argues, is in the nature of the case difficult to determine, but is not decisive in arguing this position, since, pace Omanson ("Suffering," 444), in this text they are in fact combined.
214 Ep. 164.14–18, *Ep. Euod.*
215 E.g., 1 Cor 10:4; 1 Pet 1:10–11.
216 E.g., *1 Clem.* 7.6. *1 Clem.* 9.4 also makes Noah a type of Christ because Noah also announced the rebirth (παλινγενεσία) of the world.
217 E.g., Bennetch, "Exegetical Studies," 195; Grudem, 158, 239. See W. D. Morris ("1 Peter iii.19," *ExpT* 38

[1926/27] 470), who thinks Νῶε, not Ἐνώχ, was dropped from the original text.
218 E.g., Beare, 173; Reicke, *Spirits*, 118; Best, 140; Cranfield, 103; Windisch, 71.
219 So, e.g., Luther (232): "Christus . . . hat den Geistern gepredigt, das ist, Menschenseelen, unter welchen Menschenseelen Ungläubige zu Zeiten Noahs gewesen sind" ("Christ preached to the spirits, that is, to human souls, among whom were (souls of) the unbelieving from the time of Noah"); cf. also Perrot, "La descente aux enfers," 233; Cranfield, "Interpretation," 372. Best (141–42) cites as evidence Matt 12:40; Acts 2:25–27; 13:35; Rom 10:7, but only the first has a possible application here; the others simply do not imply it.
220 Fink, "Use and Significance," 38.
221 So, e.g., Dalton, *Christ's Proclamation* (2d ed.), 140.
222 So, e.g., Dalton, *Christ's Proclamation* (2d ed.), 181; France, "Exegesis in Practice," 271; Reicke, *Spirits*, 100.
223 For a general summary of the pros and cons of these various positions, see Omanson, "Suffering," 442–44.

Christ's second activity, his preaching (ἐκήρυξεν), raises the question of its content. What exactly did Christ preach to the imprisoned spirits? Taken for themselves, words from the stem κηρυγ- refer to a herald (κῆρυξ) who announced (κηρύσσω) an entrusted message (κήρυγμα). All three of those words occur in the NT, most frequently with a salvific intent, although not exclusively.[224] On the assumption that the "imprisoned spirits" refer to human beings[225] who have died and that the intent of the verb here is the same as it is in the preponderance of other NT uses,[226] a conclusion often drawn is that the content of Christ's proclamation was the gospel of salvation,[227] perhaps limited to the announcement of their need for repentance,[228] or in the form of the announcement of their salvation, either to the human dead in general,[229] to the righteous in general[230] or those of OT times,[231] to the generation of Noah,[232] to those of that generation who had repented prior to the flood,[233] or more broadly to see in them examples of the unrighteous for whom Christ suffered (3:18).[234]

Such an interpretation is not the necessary one, however. One may not ignore that εκήρυξεν, even in the

224 For more detailed discussion, see "Excursus: Use of the Stem κηρυγ- in the New Testament."

225 That Christ preached redemption to the supernatural spirits in contrast to Enoch, who announced their condemnation, has little to recommend it, as Perrot ("La descente aux enfers," 237–38) observes, calling on Heb 2:16 for support; but see Beare ("Teaching," 292), who regards redemption of fallen angels as part of the Christian idea of the universal scope of Christ's saving work. Passages such as Phil 2:10–11 may support this latter notion, but it is unlikely to be the point here.

226 Additional evidence cited for the following view is the identity of this verse with 1 Pet 4:6, where proclamation of salvation (εὐηγγελίσθη) to human dead (νεκροῖς) is clearly found, e.g., Bigg, 162; Schweizer, 77; Cranfield, "Interpretation," 371.

227 So, e.g., Beare, 172; Cranfield, 103; Schiwy, 54; Windisch, 71; Reicke, *Spirits*, 120; Best, 144.

228 So, e.g., Grudem, 160; Russell Bradley Jones, "Christian Behavior under Fire (First Epistle of Peter)," *RevExp* 46 (1949) 63 (quoting B. H. Carroll); Hart, 68 (at Christ's preaching, they repented as did the men of Nineveh); Schweizer, 77 (the same possibility of repentance included here as in 4:6); cf. Vogels, *Christi Abstieg*, 35–36 (eine positive Beschämung zum Heil: "a positive shaming with salvation as its object"). Best (150) notes, correctly I think, that there is no evidence in this passage that "there is a 'second chance' for men after death."

229 So, e.g., Holmer and de Boor, 102; Vogels, *Christi Abstieg*, 43–44; Dalton, *Christ's Proclamation* (2d ed.), 186; Galot, "La descente du Christ," 484; Senior, 70; Perrot, "La descente aux enfers," passim. Schweizer (78) would limit them to those who died before Noah, and hence before the first covenant of grace (Gen 9:9). On the other hand, Best (150) thinks one cannot deduce from this passage that all humans and all spirits will eventually be reconciled to God.

230 So, e.g., Spicq, 138; cf. Galot, "La descente du Christ," passim.

231 So, e.g., Schelkle, 104; Spicq, 138; cf. *Sib. Or.* 8.310–11: "(Christ) will come to Hades announcing hope for all the holy ones, the end of the ages and the last day." Bigg (163) also calls attention to a quotation from the OT, cited by Irenaeus (*Adv. haer.* 3.20.4, as coming from Isaiah; 4.22.1 and 5.31.1 as coming from Jeremiah), and Justin Martyr (*Dial.* 72.4, as coming from Jeremiah; he claims the Jews excised it from their Scriptures): Ἐμνήσθη δὲ κύριος ὁ θεὸς ἀπὸ Ἰσραὴλ τῶν νεκρῶν αὐτοῦ, τῶν κεκοιμημένων εἰς γῆν χώματος, καὶ κατέβη πρὸς αὐτοὺς εὐαγγελίσασθαι αὐτοῖς τὸ σωτήριον αὐτοῦ ("The Lord God remembered his dead from Israel, who were sleeping in the earth, and he went down to them and announced to them his salvation").

232 E.g., Vogels, *Christi Abstieg*, 40; Wand, 101. Schlier ("Adhortatio," 63): they were the worst of sinners; F. C. Synge ("1 Peter 3:18–21," *ExpT* 82 [1970/71] 311): their drowning was the first half of their baptism; if they now heeded Christ's good news, they could have the second half of their baptism, which consisted in being raised with Christ. Spicq (140) affirms that one can assume from the context that they gave to the preaching of Christ a better reception than they did to the announcement of Noah. Aside from the oblique reference to Noah as a "herald of righteousness" in 2 Pet 2:5 (whether it meant he was a herald who announced a message by what he said or simply by building the ark is unclear), there is no indication either here or in the OT (or in *1 Enoch*) that Noah said anything to his contemporaries either regarding their need for repentance or about the coming flood.

233 So, e.g., Ketter, 258.

234 So, e.g., Goppelt, 247. Dalton (*Christ's Proclamation* [2d ed.], 149) calls this, I think correctly, unwarranted.

NT, need not necessarily mean the proclamation of the gospel of salvation; its use in a strictly neutral sense in the NT demonstrates that.[235] There is in addition the use of πορεύομαι and κηρύσσω in Jonah 1:2 (πορεύθητι . . . καὶ κήρυξον) as part of a command to announce the destruction of Nineveh, a verbal echo of which may be found here in v. 19.[236] There exists the possibility, therefore, that even if the imprisoned spirits refers to the souls of disobedient human dead, the content of the proclamation to which v. 19 points may have been condemnation.[237]

If, however, the "imprisoned spirits" do not mean human dead but rather rebellious angels, as they are in the Enoch literature, and as seems likely to be the case here, then the notion of the announcement of the gospel of salvation seems even less likely.[238] While the influence of the figure of Enoch on the content of vv. 19–20a has not found universal acceptance—other suggested influences are the descent of Orpheus into Hades[239] or

the Latin text of Sir 24:32[240]—the confluence of similar points is so great[241] as to make such an influence extremely likely.[242] The fact that the Enoch literature was known to other NT authors adds credibility to such an influence,[243] and shows its usefulness in presenting Christ as one who recalled and transcended this OT figure.[244]

Such influence would indicate that the content of the announcement (ἐκήρυξεν) to the imprisoned spirits would be not their salvation but their condemnation.[245] In the context of Christ's resurrection (v. 18: ζωοποιηθεὶς δὲ πνεύματι), that condemnation is to be understood as the outcome of Christ's victorious rising from the dead: As the result of his resurrection, the powers of evil have been defeated,[246] and the risen Christ, on his way to the right hand of power (3:22), announces to the imprisoned angelic powers his victory[247] and hence their defeat.[248] Such an understanding takes into account the context of an activity by the risen Christ, it retains the normal

235 E.g., Luke 12:3; Rom 2:21; Rev 5:2; on this point see Dalton, "Interpretation and Tradition," 30; idem, *Christ's Proclamation* (2d ed.), 156–57. Selwyn (200) thinks the neutral meaning is more probable here.

236 So Dalton, *Christ's Proclamation,* 151. Its reflection in the use of κήρυγμα in Matt 12:41 par. Luke 11:32, to which Frings ("Zu I Petr 3,19 und 4,6," 78) points, supports such a use for it in NT tradition.

237 As, e.g., Wolff ("Christ und Welt," 553) notes, such condemnation is described in 2 Pet 2:5–9, whose author surely knew 1 Peter, as 3:1 shows. Frings ("Zu I Petr 3,19 und 4,6," 87) does conclude that Jesus announced the condemnation of the sinners of the flood generation; cf. also Bieder (*Höllenfahrt Jesu,* 114), who identifies it as the position of "the firmly confessional Lutherans." Condemnation of the unrighteous was already contained in the proclamation of the preresurrection Jesus, as is shown in such passages as Matt 13:49–50; 25:12, 41; Luke 13:27–28.

238 The evidence in the NT is that Satan and the evil angels are not to be rescued but condemned, e.g., Matt 25:41; Rev 20:10. See also Dalton (*Christ's Proclamation,* 157), who argues that while κηρύσσω nearly always means proclamation of the gospel, such a meaning "is excluded by the context of 3:19."

239 So, e.g., Perdelwitz, *Mysterienreligion,* 94. Best (144–45) notes such a descent also on the part of Odysseus, but finds *1 Enoch* a more direct influence.

240 So, e.g., Perdelwitz, *Mysterienreligion,* 88.

241 Dalton (*Christ's Proclamation* [2d ed.], 175) notes six elements: a going, a proclamation, to spirits, in

prison, who disobeyed, in the context of the flood; see also Brox, 172. In this context, it is important to note that Enoch is sent (πορεύου, *1 Enoch* 12.4; πορευθείς, 13.3; πορεύθητι, 15.2) to give the disobedient angels (in this context often referred to as πνεύματα: e.g., 10.15; 13.6; 15.4) a message of condemnation; on this point, see Bieder, *Höllenfahrt Jesu,* 101.

242 So, e.g., Bieder, *Höllenfahrt Jesu,* 117; France, "Exegesis in Practice," 270; Reicke, *Spirits,* 68; Harris, "Further Note," 347; Selwyn, 198. Dalton (*Christ's Proclamation,* 176) notes specifically the parallel between the description of Christ's activity in vv. 19–20a and *1 Enoch* 12.4; 13.3; 15.2, which he considers impossible to be accidental.

243 *1 Enoch* 1.9 is cited in Jude 14–15; the myth of Gen 6:1–6, of great importance in *1 Enoch,* is alluded to in Jude 6–7; 2 Pet 2:4. When *1 Enoch* 80.65–67 is referred to in *Barn.* 16.5, it is identified as Scripture (λέγει γὰρ γραφή). On these points, see Reicke, *Spirits,* 67; Schelkle, 106; Brox, 171.

244 So, e.g., Dalton, *Christ's Proclamation* (2d ed.), 173. As Brox (173–74) notes, one need not presume that the readers knew *1 Enoch,* simply that the author could presume they were aware of the Enoch saga in its application to Christ. Yet even that is not necessary; it need only be the case that the author found the Enoch material useful for his exposition of the activity of the risen Christ.

245 Cf. *1 Enoch* 12.4–6; 13.1; 14.3–6; 16.3.

246 In this way, the provisional defeat they suffered at the hands of the earthly Jesus (Mark 3:27; Luke

meaning of "spirits," it fits the tradition about Enoch who announced to the rebellious angels their final doom, and, given the idea of a series of heavens current in contemporary Judaism, it allows the verb πορευθείς to retain the same sense it has in 3:22, where the final step of Christ's ascension is described, the *sessio ad dextram*.[249]

Finally, this emphasis on the triumph of Jesus over the powers of evil[250] would encourage the Christian readers to remain faithful despite the pressure exerted on them by hostile forces in their contemporary world, since Christ's victory over the evil forces behind such hostility also ensured their own final victory over them,[251] and hence made resistance worthwhile. This is why they may continue to "reverence Christ as Lord" (3:14) knowing that no real harm can come to those who do remain faithful (3:13), and that any suffering they incur for it is to be preferred to caving in to the pressure and denying Christ (3:17).[252]

Such a point for the passage is to be preferred to the

notion that as Christ preached salvation even to the most evil of sinners, so Christians also must be willing to missionize even the indifferent and hostile Gentiles.[253] Nor is the notion that Christ's salvation reaches even to evil angels of the distant past likely to have encouraged the readers to continued faithfulness to Christ and resistance to hostile forces: If God relented on such evil entities, why not rely on the same treatment and deny Christ now to avoid suffering?[254]

Rather, v. 19 (along with v. 20a) reflects a tradition that adapted the legend of fallen angels as the source of evil on the earth; replaced Enoch, the man who walked with God, was taken up into heaven, and announced doom to rebellious angels, with Christ,[255] risen from the dead,[256] victorious over all evil forces, seated at God's right hand, and hence the universal Lord;[257] Christ is

10:18; 11:20; Rom 16:20; cf. Rev 12:7–12) is confirmed by the risen, victorious Lord; so also, e.g., Michaels, 208–10, cf. also lxxiii.

247 Their "imprisonment" was already accomplished by the earthly Jesus; such imprisonment was not a form of punishment in the ancient world, but the period during which those arrested awaited trial, as, e.g., Dalton (*Christ's Proclamation* [2d ed.], 159) notes; such a use of imprisonment is reflected in *1 Enoch* 22.4. These rebellious angelic powers, the source of evil on the earth (e.g., *1 Enoch* 15:9), now learn from the risen Christ of their final defeat. On this point see also Bieder, *Grund und Kraft,* 16; cf. Leaney, "Passover," 250.

248 For the same tradition, see Eph 1:21–22; 4:8; Col 2:15. A similar victory is assumed in Phil 2:9–11; cf. also Rom 8:31–39. On this point see Dalton, *Christ's Proclamation* (2d ed.), 159, 186; Margot, 63; Tarrech, "Le milieu," 372; Kelly, 156; France, "Exegesis in Practice," 271; Bieder, *Grund und Kraft,* 16–17; idem, *Höllenfahrt Jesu,* 116.

249 The genitive absolute at the end of v. 22 would then clearly be a reference to what had been already narrated here in v. 19, as Dalton (*Christ's Proclamation* [2d ed.], 118) also hints.

250 Such an emphasis is also apparent in the Pauline tradition: The rulers of this age, who crucified Christ (1 Cor 2:8) and who blind unbelievers (2 Cor 4:4), were conquered by the risen Christ (Col 2:15; Eph 4:8); that victory allows Christians to fight successfully against them (Eph 6:12) until they are finally disposed of (1 Cor 15:24–27). Dalton (*Christ's*

Proclamation [2d ed.], 185) notes correctly that this is the picture reflected here in v. 19.

251 E.g., 2:20; 4:13–19; 5:6, 10. France ("Exegesis in Practice," 272) cites a similar point in Rom 8:31–39. See also Kelly, 157; Michaels, 221; Ernest Gordon Selwyn, "Eschatology in I Peter," in W. D. Davies and D. Daube, eds., *The Background of the New Testament and Its Eschatology* (Festschrift C. H. Dodd; Cambridge: University Press, 1956) 398; Schweizer, 79.

252 See Bieder (*Höllenfahrt Jesu,* 113) and de Villiers ("Joy," 79), who also argue that the author's primary intention is focused on contemporary Christians currently undergoing suffering.

253 As affirmed by, e.g., Reicke, *Spirits,* 131; Goppelt, 250; Brooks, "1 Peter 3:21," 303; cf. Reicke, 112; Omanson, "Suffering," 443 (even though he finally rejects this option). Dalton (*Christ's Proclamation,* 190–91) argues that such a notion lacks firm foundation either in the immediate context or in Jewish or Christian tradition.

254 So also, e.g., Dalton, *Christ's Proclamation,* 108.

255 So, e.g., Dalton, *Christ's Proclamation* (2d ed.), 173; idem, "Interpretation and Tradition," 34.

256 Dalton (*Christ's Proclamation,* 171) correctly points out that the activity of the risen Christ at once recalls and transcends that of Enoch.

257 So also, e.g., Michaels, 206. Such universal Lordship is the point of his proclamation to the imprisoned spirits: not even supernatural beings can escape it. So, e.g., Schweizer (80): "kein Bereich, kein Raum, keine Zeit für die der Sieg des Christus nicht gälte" "no sphere, no place, no time for which Christ's

therefore now the one who is eminently worthy of the trust and faithfulness of those who follow him, despite the temporary depredations of evil against them.[258]

Excursus: Use of the Stem κηρυγ- in the New Testament

Of the three words derived from this stem used in the NT, the nouns (κῆρυξ, κήρυγμα) are used less frequently than the verb (κήρυσσω).

The noun κῆρυξ ("herald") occurs three times, twice referring to Paul, and used as the equivalent of ἀπόστολος ("apostle," 1 Tim 2:7; 2 Tim 1:11), and once referring to Noah (2 Pet 2:5). The verb is also used to indicate the activity of a herald another five times, identifying what John the Baptist said of Jesus (Mark 1:6) or of his own baptism (Acts 10:37), or of what others announced about Jesus (Mark 5:20//Luke 8:39; Mark 7:36).

The noun κήρυγμα ("message") is used primarily to signify the content of Christian proclamation (1 Cor 1:21, 2:4; 15:14; 2 Tim 4:17; Titus 1:3; in Rom 16:25 is it equated with "Jesus Christ") but can also designate the content of Jonah's message (Matt 12:41//Luke 11:32).

The verb κήρυσσω ("proclaim") is used principally in the NT with an object whose meaning makes it clear that Christian preaching is meant. Such objects include "gospel" (e.g., Matt 4:23; 9:35; Mark 1:14; 13:10; Gal 2:2; 1 Thess 2:9) or "word" (e.g., Rom 10:8; Tim 4:2); "kingdom of God" (e.g., Luke 8:1; 9:2; Acts 28:31) or simply "kingdom" (e.g., Acts 20:25); "Jesus" (e.g., Acts 8:5; 9:19; 19:13; 2 Cor 11:4) or "Christ" (e.g., 1 Cor 1:23; Phil 1:15); or a whole series of words (e.g., Luke 4:18). The verb can also be used absolutely, that is, without an object, in a clearly Christian sense, since the context makes its content clear (e.g., Mark 1:38, 45; 3:14; Luke 4:44; Rom 10:15; 1 Cor 9:27; 15:11). Finally, the verb can be used in a more neutral sense, simply indicating the proclamation of one who acts as a herald (e.g., Rom 2:21: the content of Jewish ethics as

they proclaim them; Gal 5:11: a hypothetical espousal of circumcision; Rev 5:2: a general angelic summons to open a scroll; perhaps also Matt 10:27//Luke 12:3, although there the context probably means the Christian message heard in secret is what is to be announced openly).

While the predominant meaning of the stem in the NT is thus Christian, it can also be used in other ways, so that its appearance does not automatically mean that the content of the proclamation is forgiveness or salvation.

■ **20** The verses preceding (18–19) and following (22) recount the salfivic and triumphant career of Christ: his suffering, death, resurrection, his announcement of triumph over supernatural forces of evil and his assumption of divine authority. They thus provide the context within which to interpret vv. 20–21, whose function appears to be to show, on the analogy of God's saving Noah and his family during the divine victory over the evil world through the flood, how the Christians through baptism share in God's victory through Christ over the supernatural powers of the evil world, a victory to be consummated with the return of Christ. Thus both content and context of vv. 20–21 show how Christians share in Christ's victorious and salvific career.

The participle ἀπειθήσασιν clearly refers to the imprisoned spirits mentioned in v. 19. Grammatically, the word stands in the predicate rather than the attributive position,[259] and so cannot rightly be rendered "who were disobedient."[260] It may well be an adverbial participle of cause ("because they were disobedient"), indicating the reason either why Christ announced his victory over them, or why they had been imprisoned. The reference to the time of Noah need not lead one to understand those "spirits" as human,[261] since the Enoch literature, with which our author appears to have been

---

victory had no validity"; cf. Schelkle, 107; Margot, 60. While the author of 1 Peter undoubtedly thought that Christ alone was the source of salvation, that is not the point he is making in this passage, as, e.g., Schwank et al. (76), Schelkle (107), and Spicq (139) want to argue; nor is it the universal reach of Christ's salvation as, e.g., Goppelt (251) and Beare ("Teaching," 292) would have it; nor is it likely to be that there is a second chance for people after death, as Best (150) notes correctly.

258 On this whole point, see Margot, 62; Dalton, *Christ's Proclamation* (2d ed.), 163; Michaels, 206.

259 That is, it tells something further about the spirits, i.e., that they were disobedient, rather than identifying them, i.e., the disobedient spirits as against, say, the obedient spirits.

260 That would require the phrase τοῖς ἀπειθήσασιν to agree with the τοῖς πνεύμασιν of v. 19.

261 As does, e.g., Krafft ("Christologie," 123). Selwyn (201) notes that in Genesis 6 the wickedness that led to the flood is ascribed to humans only; cf. also Cranfield, "Interpretation," 372; Beare, 173. Windisch (71) argues that the reference here is to humans, despite the fact that the spirits are to be understood

acquainted, clearly associates Noah and the flood with the rebellious angels and their offspring,[262] even to the point of attributing the flood to the evil angels whose taking for themselves human wives is understood as an act of disobedience,[263] the meaning this word has in its other uses in this letter.[264]

The word πoτέ means primarily any indefinite time.[265] In addition to that use in the NT,[266] it can also be used to indicate a contrast with a former condition.[267] While the word is used in both senses in our letter,[268] its combination here with ὅτε clearly indicates that it points to the general time of the flood, not the time of the flood in contrast to another time.[269] To understand πoτέ in this latter sense, as "formerly," can lead to the misunderstanding that our author meant to say that the disobedience of the spirits was not permanent.[270] Its meaning is "because they [i.e., the imprisoned spirits] were disobedient *at the time* when God's patience waited. . . ."

The reference to God's patient waiting (ἀπεξεδέχετο ἡ τοῦ θεοῦ μακροθυμία) is probably a reflection of Gen 6:3,[271] which Jewish tradition interpreted as God's longsuffering until he finally brought the flood.[272] The NT interprets God's long-suffering in terms of his delaying the final judgment, an act of mercy toward those who still oppose him.[273] In this context, the reference to God's patience is probably to be understood as the reason why God has delayed, even if not for long, his final judgment,[274] enduring for a time the evil of the contemporary society that opposes him in the form of opposing the Christian community.[275] Whether the additional idea is to be seen here that now as then God's patience met with negative reaction,[276] remains questionable, as does the assumption that the delay in the readers' time was to allow more people to be summoned to salvation through Christ.[277] Our author may hold

---

as supernatural in v. 19. It is clear in the Enoch literature, however, that the rebellious angels are the cause of human evil, e.g., *1 Enoch* 10.8; 15.1–9; *2 Enoch* 18.1–5.

262 E.g., *1 Enoch* 10.1–14; 64–67; 106.13–18; *Jub.* 5.1–5; *T. Naph.* 3.5; CD 2.18–20. 3 Macc 2:4 refers to the flood destroying the "giants." On this point, cf. Dalton, *Christ's Proclamation* (2d ed.), 168, 171–72; Fitzmyer, "First Peter," 367.

263 E.g., *1 Enoch* 106.13; *2 Enoch* 7.3; cf. CD 2.18. For a fuller discussion, see Dalton, *Christ's Proclamation* (2d ed.), 167.

264 1:2, 14, 22; 2:8; 3:1. I would argue that the use of the word here reflects the idea that those who now persecute and slander the Christians do so under the influence of the rebellious demonic powers over whom Christ has emerged victorious. On this same point, see Michaels, 211; Dalton, *Christ's Proclamation* (2d ed.), 164; see also 174 n. 45; Tarrech, "Le milieu," 376; cf. also de Villiers, "Joy," 79.

265 Dalton (*Christ's Proclamation* [2d ed.], 164), citing Selwyn, notes that classical authors use it to introduce a story; it has the equivalent function of "Once upon a time."

266 E.g., Luke 23:32; Rom 1:10; 1 Cor 9:7; Eph 5:29; Phil 4:10; 1 Thess 2:5; Heb 1:5, 13; 2 Pet 1:10, 21.

267 It is used in this way both explicitly, i.e., with "now" (Rom 11:30; Eph 2:13; 5:8; Col 1:21; 3:7; Phlm 11), and implicitly (e.g., John 9:13; Rom 7:9; Gal 1:13, 23 [perhaps 2:6]; Eph 2:2, 3, 11; Titus 3:3).

268 In sense of contrast: 2:10; with no contrast implied: 3:5.

269 As, e.g., Vogels (*Christi Abstieg*, 137) wants to do. He finds in that contrast the justification for affirming that the spirits once disobedient have since been saved by Christ's proclamation of salvation (39).

270 As does, e.g., Ketter, 257; Dalton (*Christ's Proclamation* [2d ed.], 164) warns against such a meaning as being misleading.

271 So also, e.g., Best, 146; Dalton, *Christ's Proclamation* (2d ed.), 191; Selwyn, 201.

272 E.g., *m. 'Abot* 5.2: "There were ten generations from Adam to Noah, to show how great was his long-suffering, for all the generations provoked him continually until he brought upon them the waters of the Flood" (H. Danby, *The Mishnah* [Oxford: Oxford University Press, 1933] 455). See also *1 Enoch* 60.5; 93.3. I owe these references to the scholars mentioned in the preceding note.

273 So, e.g., Rom 2:4; 3:25; see also Acts 14:16; 17:30. Cf. Selwyn, 201; Beare, 173.

274 For a similar point, see 2 Pet 3:8–9.

275 Cf., e.g., Tarrech, "Le milieu," 375.

276 As Kelly (158) affirms.

277 As, e.g., Margot (63) argues; the language used to present such an idea in 2 Pet 3:9 makes its absence here all the more obvious.

both ideas, but nothing in this context indicates that he had them in mind here. His attention is focused, as v. 21 indicates, on those inside, not those outside, the Christian community.[278]

That Noah was the one chosen by God to be saved from the evil of his contemporary world because he was righteous (Gen 6:8–9) made him a hagiographic figure in Jewish thought.[279] Nonetheless, Noah is not a major figure in the NT.[280] While his righteousness is acknowledged (Heb 11:7; 2 Pet 2:5), the typology associated with him deals rather with the suddenness of the flood than with his virtuousness.[281] If our author is using here a tradition about Noah that associated him with God's long-suffering and the eight who were saved in the ark, it is unknown to the rest of the NT.[282] Noah's appearance in this context is to provide the type (i.e., the flood) of which baptism is the antitype.[283]

While the ark served as a symbol of the church itself in early ecclesiastical tradition,[284] or its wood was taken as a reminder of the wood of the cross,[285] its fleeting mention here simply to point to the time of God's patience indicates that neither symbol is appropriate. The symbol here is salvation in relation to water ($\delta\iota'$ $\ddot{v}\delta\alpha\tau\sigma\varsigma$) rather than in relation to the ark, as is required by the typology of baptism in v. 21. The passive form of the verb in the genitive absolute phrase ($\kappa\alpha\tau\alpha\sigma\kappa\epsilon\nu\alpha\zeta\omega\mu\acute{\epsilon}\nu\eta\varsigma$ $\kappa\iota\beta\omega\tau\sigma\hat{v}$) may reflect the idea found in *1 Enoch* 67.2 that the ark was built by angels;[286] in any case, Noah's activity in its building is ignored in this phrase.

The prepositional phrase $\epsilon\dot{\iota}\varsigma$ $\ddot{\eta}\nu$, the normal meaning of which would be "into which" (viz., the ark), seems inappropriate in view of the verb $\delta\iota\epsilon\sigma\dot{\omega}\theta\eta\sigma\alpha\nu$, which presumes the meaning "in," that is, they were saved "in it," rather than presuming the action of entry "into" the ark.[287] The sense probably intended here is that they entered the ark and were saved in it, rather than being an instance of the confusion of $\epsilon\dot{\iota}\varsigma$ with $\dot{\epsilon}\nu$.[288] The use of

---

278 Note also that those led to God in 3:18 are limited to $\dot{v}\mu\hat{\alpha}\varsigma$, "you," i.e., the Christians.

279 E.g., Ezek 14:19–20; Sir 44:17; *1 Enoch* 35.1; 106.18; *Jub.* 7.20–39; Wis 10:4; cf. also Selwyn, 328; Love, "First Epistle," 84. Philo (*Leg. all.* 3.77) says the name Noah means either righteousness ($\delta\acute{\iota}\kappa\alpha\iota\sigma\varsigma$) or rest ($\dot{\alpha}\nu\acute{\alpha}\pi\alpha\nu\sigma\iota\varsigma$), hence he "rested" ($\dot{\alpha}\nu\alpha\pi\alpha\acute{v}\sigma\mu\alpha\iota$) on the good and "resisted" (i.e., ceased from, $\pi\alpha\acute{v}\sigma\mu\alpha\iota$) evil; cf. also *Migr. Abr.* 125; *Rer. div. her.* 260; *Abr.* 27, 31 (I owe these references to Goppelt, 254, although they were used there to make a different point). For an account of Noah's wondrous birth, see *1 Enoch* 106.10–11; cf. also 1QapGen 2.1–25 (I owe this last reference to Knibb, *Qumran*, 186).

280 He is mentioned neither in the Pauline nor in the Johannine tradition.

281 Matt 24:37–39 par. Luke 17:26–27.

282 Thurston ("Interpreting First Peter," 180) suggested that because 2 Pet 2:4–5, 9 and Heb 11:7 mention both the saving of Noah and the destruction of the world, our author may be drawing on a "familiar teaching in the early church" that pointed to the "paradox that the same action which saved Noah and his house condemned the world." Since those passages are the only references to Noah aside from the Gospels and our epistle, and since the Gospels know nothing of that "teaching," the basis for such a "familiar teaching" is disconcertingly small.

283 It is unlikely, as Ketter (258) would have it, that Noah is mentioned here because, as some of Noah's contemporaries repented as the flood came upon them, so the readers can hope some of their con-

temporaries will repent when the imminent end breaks in upon them.

284 E.g., Tertullian *Bapt.* 8.4; Cyprian *De cath. eccl.* 6 (the allusion in Cyprian is evanescent at best); I owe these references to Kelly (158), who further asserts that this idea is "almost certainly present here in embryo," a point with which I would not agree. Holmer and de Boor (104) simply assume an "ark typology" for this passage, again, I think, incorrectly.

285 E.g., Justin *Dial.* 138.2. Schwank et al. (78) hold this to be the intended symbolism. Lack of any mention of wood, which one does find in Justin, argues against that assumption.

286 So also, e.g., Leaney, 53; see also idem, "Passover," 250.

287 This latter act is explicit in Matt 24:38 par. Luke 17:27: $\epsilon\dot{\iota}\sigma\hat{\eta}\lambda\theta\epsilon\nu$ $N\hat{\omega}\epsilon$ $\epsilon\dot{\iota}\varsigma$ $\tau\dot{\eta}\nu$ $\kappa\iota\beta\omega\tau\acute{\sigma}\nu$ ("Noah entered into the ark").

288 So also, e.g., Dalton, *Christ's Proclamation* (2d ed.), 193–94. Kelly (158) finds in it the double sense of "going into the ark and so being saved in it." But see David Cook ("I Peter iii.20: An Unnecessary Problem," *JTS*, n.s. 31 [1980] 73, 75) and Grudem (161), who argue for the exclusive sense of "into." If one could presume the presence of the Greek participle $\epsilon\dot{\iota}\sigma\acute{\epsilon}\lambda\theta\sigma\nu\tau\epsilon\varsigma$ that would surely be the case; i.e., "into which a few, after entering, were saved" ($\epsilon\dot{\iota}\varsigma$ $\ddot{\eta}\nu$ $\dot{\sigma}\lambda\acute{\iota}\gamma\sigma\iota$ $\epsilon\dot{\iota}\sigma\acute{\epsilon}\lambda\theta\sigma\nu\tau\epsilon\varsigma$ . . . $\delta\iota\epsilon\sigma\dot{\omega}\theta\eta\sigma\alpha\nu$; cf. Matt 24:38 par. Luke 17:27: $\epsilon\dot{\iota}\sigma\hat{\eta}\lambda\theta\epsilon\nu$ $N\hat{\omega}\epsilon$ $\epsilon\dot{\iota}\varsigma$ $\tau\dot{\eta}\nu$ $\kappa\iota\beta\omega\tau\acute{\sigma}\nu$); if our author were thinking of the LXX of Gen 7:7, that would be a likely hypothesis, but it is not more than that.

ὀλίγοι to identify those saved reflects sayings of Jesus[289] but is probably chosen here rather to encourage the readers who, although they were also a small minority in the midst of the hostile Greco-Roman world, could similarly look forward to their salvation.[290] While later Christian tradition found symbolic significance in the number eight (ὀκτώ),[291] it is more likely that it reflects Gen 7:13, viz., Noah, his wife, his three sons, and their wives, and hence is to be given no symbolic significance here.[292] Ψυχαί carries the meaning "lives" or "persons"[293] rather than "souls" as a contrast to physical bodies, a contrast common in Greek philosophical thought.[294]

The final phrase of the verse is difficult to understand. The verb διασώζω is used eight times in the NT with the basic sense of "rescue" or "deliver" from some imminent danger, whether from disease, death, enemies, or the sea.[295] The passive form in this verse points to God as the one who delivers those in the ark.[296] The problem is posed by the phrase δι' ὕδατος, since the preposition διά can be understood in either an instrumental or a local sense.[297] As instrumental it would mean that the water was the instrument by means of which those in the ark were saved.[298] The difficulty with such an understanding—it was the ark, not the water, that saved them, with the water as the instrument of destruction[299]—is often resolved by appealing to the typology of the next verse, where the water of baptism is instrumental in

---

289 E.g., Matt 7:14; 22:14; for a similar idea see *4 Ezra* 7.47; 9.14–15, 20–22. The idea that only a few would be saved is unknown to Paul, as Goppelt (257) notes.

290 So also, e.g., France, "Exegesis in Practice," 272; de Villiers, "Joy," 79; Michaels, 213. Dalton (*Christ's Proclamation* [2d ed.], 194) finds a similar sentiment in Luke 12:32. But see Holmer and de Boor (132), who argue that it is meant to contrast to the large numbers now being saved through Christ.

291 Reicke (112) argues that because the sum of the first seven numbers was considered to be an eighth number, it came to be regarded as the unity and totality of the number seven, important for the OT and also for the Greco-Roman world (it was the number of the planets). Justin Martyr identified the eighth day as the one on which Christ arose (*Dial.* 138.1); in *Barn.* 15.8–9, Isa 1:13 is interpreted to mean that the seventh day is rejected and that the eighth day is now important as the beginning of a new world (I owe these references to Dalton, *Christ's Proclamation* [2d ed.], 194). Kelly (159) argues that baptism on Sunday, the eighth day, influenced the octagonal shape of ancient baptisteries; see also Hillyer, "First Peter," 69. Bieder (*Grund und Kraft*, 21) argues that it means the people of the old covenant who, having been given into the saving hand of God, already belong to the community of the final time; for this interpretation he gives no other references.

292 So also, e.g., Best, 146. Eric F. F. Bishop ("*Oligoi* in 1 Pet. 3:20," *CBQ* 13 [1951] 44–45) argues that eight is a rather large number for the Greek ὀλίγοι, and that Peter, thinking in Semitic terms, draws on an Arabic word (*bida'*) that means any number between three and ten, a reference that fits perfectly Jesus' use of

ὀλίγος in Matt 25:21, 23 (ὀλίγος = ten and four talents); knowing his Greek readers would not be aware of this, he then makes it explicit with the reference to "eight." The argument is surely learned and ingenious, but of doubtful value.

293 The plural ψυχαί is used four times in 1 Peter (1:9, 22; 2:25; 4:19) in addition to 3:20, each time meaning "selves" or "lives," as Michaels (213) also notes.

294 So also, e.g., Dalton, *Christ's Proclamation* (2d ed.), 194.

295 Matt 14:36 (its parallel in Mark 6:50 uses the verb σώζω); Luke 7:3 (its parallel in Matt 8:7 uses θεραπεύω); Acts 23:24; 27:43, 44; 28:1, 4, in addition to 1 Pet 3:20; on this point see also Spicq, 141.

296 So also, e.g., Bieder, *Grund und Kraft*, 19 n. 21.

297 Some scholars argue that our author chose it because of this ambiguity, wanting to convey both senses here; so, e.g., France, "Exegesis in Practice," 273; Cranfield, 105; Dalton, *Christ's Proclamation* (2d ed.), 195 (context shows emphasis to be on instrumental); cf. Hart, 69; Moffatt, 142. As Kelly (159) points out, however, it is unlikely the author would consciously use the preposition in both a local and an instrumental sense at the same time.

298 So, e.g., Arichea and Nida, *Translator's Handbook*, 119; Best, 147; Schelkle, 108 n. 2.

299 So, e.g., Spicq, 141. The flood serves as both divine judgment and deliverance in Jewish literature, e.g., *1 Enoch* 10.2–3; 65.10–12; 106.13–18; *Jub.* 5.3–5; Sir 44:17; Wis 10:4; 14:6; 4 Macc 15:31; as judgment only, *Sib. Or.* 1.125; *1 Enoch* 54.7–10; *2 Enoch* 34.3 (I owe these references to Michaels, 211). A flood was also posited as an instrument of judgment on human evil in Greco-Roman culture: e.g., Seneca *Ques. nat.* 3.30.4–5, 7; cf. 3.28.2.

human salvation.[300] A locative sense, viz., Noah and his family escaped "through water," is sometimes understood to mean the water through which they waded before they got into the ark.[301] In a larger, sense, however, a locative construal is more appropriate,[302] since it was in fact Noah's journey "through the waters" that led to his deliverance not only from the flood itself, but from the evil which infested the world and which the flood was intended to destroy. Thus the waters effected Noah's deliverance from his evil world as baptism effected the deliverance of the Christians from their evil, contemporary world: by passing through them, both entered a new existence.[303] Thus, as Noah was rescued through water (i.e., the flood) from an evil world and subsequently entered into a new and cleansed world, so the Christians are rescued through water (i.e., their baptism) from the evil world that surrounds them and are delivered into the new world of the Christian community. That seems to be the typology our author is here developing in vv. 20–21.[304]

■ **21** This verse is joined to its predecessor by the relative pronoun ὅ, which, together with ἀντίτυπον ("antitype") and βάπτισμα ("baptism") serve as a compound subject of the verb σῴζει. It is the interrelationship of the pronoun and the two nouns that constitutes the syntactic problem of the first phrase of the verse.[305] If, as seems likely, the relative pronoun is the subject of the verb, then the two remaining nouns stand in apposition to it.[306] There have been attempts to resolve the phrase differently: to take ἀντίτυπον as adjectival ("antitypical baptism saves you");[307] to take it as appositional to ὑμᾶς;[308] to understand βάπτισμα as a proleptic antecedent to the ὅ;[309] to include the first phrase with the end of the preceding verse, that is, ". . . saved through water which even in reference to you (is) a pattern. Baptism now saves, not . . .";[310] to substitute the dative (ᾧ) for the nominative relative pronoun, accepting the reading of a few minor texts.[311] The complexity of the sentence is, however, in all likelihood the result of the complex attempt to relate Noah and the flood as a means of deliverance to Christian baptism as a means of salvation, and ought thus to be allowed to stand.

While the introductory ὅ, as neuter singular, could be related to the entire preceding phrase,[312] it nevertheless has as its most likely antecedent the "water" (ὕδωρ) that immediately precedes it, and since the emphasis is here

300 So, e.g., Dalton, *Christ's Proclamation* (2d ed.), 195; Michaels, 213; Bieder, *Grund und Kraft*, 21 n. 27. The observation of France ("Exegesis in Practice," 273), however, that the water which destroyed the rest of humankind and from which Noah escaped was nonetheless the means of his salvation (by carrying the ark), is, as Arichea and Nida (*Translator's Handbook*, 119) note, "a little whimsical."

301 It is mentioned in *Midr. Gen. Rab.* 32 (on Gen 7:7), as, e.g., Goppelt (255) and Cook ("I Peter iii.20," 76) point out: they did not enter the ark until the water had reached their ankles. For such a locative sense, see, e.g., Bigg, 164; Selwyn, 202. As Dalton (*Christ's Proclamation* [2d ed.], 195) notes, however, it is unlikely the author of 1 Peter had that tradition in mind here.

302 So also, e.g., Cook, "I Peter iii.20," 77–78.

303 So also, e.g., Reicke, 113; idem, *Spirits*, 143; Dalton, *Christ's Proclamation*, 115, 210; Margot, 63–64; cf. Brooks, "1 Peter 3:21," 304; Schweizer, 82; Windisch, 72; Leaney, 53; Wand, 101.

304 So also, e.g., Brooks, "1 Peter 3:21," 304: "Passing through water to the appointed place was what saved them" (i.e., Noah and his family). It must be noted again, with Michaels (212), that there is no indication here of any typology involving ark and church as the means of salvation. For such an emphasis on the ark

as the means of rescue, see 4 Macc 15:31, but that is not the typology here; here the typology is restricted to flood/baptism, with water the uniting point.

305 Dalton (*Christ's Proclamation* [2d ed.], 196) finds 3:21 a very difficult verse, as does France ("Exegesis in Practice," 273); see also Tarrech, "Le milieu," 370.

306 So also, e.g., Tarrech, "Le milieu," 370; France, "Exegesis in Practice," 273. Kelly (160) finds it a clumsy construction.

307 E.g., Reicke, *Spirits*, 145; cf. Dalton, *Christ's Proclamation* (2d ed.), 198.

308 So, e.g., Cranfield, 106; Selwyn, 203. That is, however, to ignore the obvious emphasis in the text on water as the means of both Noah's and the Christians' deliverance, as Dalton (*Christ's Proclamation* [2d ed.], 198) notes.

309 So, e.g., Reicke (*Spirits*, 149–72) suggests; it is a rather artificial construct, as Dalton (*Christ's Proclamation* [2d ed.], 198) observes. It is a construction more common in Latin than in Greek.

310 So Brooks, "1 Peter 3:21," 291; such a construal rather effectively eliminates any continuity between the two verses.

311 So, e.g., Beare (174): "the antitype whereto now saves you, (even) baptism"; cf. also Calvin, 116.

312 So, e.g., Cook, "I Peter iii.20," 77; Goppelt, 256; Beare, 174; Holmer and de Boor, 133. The attempt

on baptism as another use of water for deliverance, the more obvious syntactic relationship is preferable.[313] The word ἀντίτυπον is rare in the NT; its only other occurrence is in Heb 9:24, where it refers to an inferior copy of a superior original,[314] a meaning the word is unlikely to bear in this context. Rather it is intended here to call attention to the relationship between flood (type) and baptism (antitype),[315] thus emphasizing the continuity of God's actions with both old and new Israel.[316] The appropriateness of such typology is evident when one recalls the way in which our author has appropriated the language of Israel for the Christian community. Like the word "antitype", the temporal adverb νῦν ("now") calls attention to the contrast between the time of Noah (ποτέ) and the present[317] rather than to the moment in the baptismal liturgy when the baptisands have undergone the rite.[318]

The central thrust of the verse is the affirmation that "baptism saves you"; the remainder of the verse defines what the author does not (οὐ), and does (ἀλλά), understand the word βάπτισμα ("baptism") to mean. While the verse may not be part of the actual ritual, designating the moment of baptism,[319] it surely does refer to the rite itself, not simply in a metaphorical way to Christian suffering;[320] the reference to water with which the verse begins makes that clear.[321] The power of baptism to save is drawn not from the water in some mysterious way[322] but rather from the resurrection of Christ, affirmed in the final phrase of the verse.[323] *How* one is thus saved is not explicitly stated.[324] The comparison with Paul's views is inevitable. While Paul never explicitly affirms that "baptism saves,"[325] it is clear from his discussion in Rom 6:1–11 that apart from baptism one does not share in Christ's death and resurrection. Yet in Rom 6:1–11, the benefits of baptism in this age are limited to participation in Christ's death (Rom 6:3, 6, 7); participation in his resurrection is not, as in Col 2:12; 3:1; or Eph 2:6, already realized.[326] Such participation in Christ's

---

by Synge ("1 Peter 3:18–21," 311) to relate it to the final phrase of 3:18, by arguing that 3:19–20 constitute a parenthesis, is somewhat fanciful.

313 So also, e.g., Brox, 176; Michaels, 213–14.

314 The same meaning is found for τύπος in Acts 7:44 and Heb 8:5; in most other cases in the NT, τύπος means simply "example," e.g., 1 Cor 10:6; Phil 3:17; 1 Thess 1:7; 2 Thess 3:9; 1 Tim 4:12; Titus 2:7; 1 Pet 5:3.

315 So also, e.g., Brox (177): it is a mutual clarification and interpretation. It may have the implication, as is the case with τύπος in Rom 5:14, that the antitype is superior; cf. also Dalton, *Christ's Proclamation* (2d ed.), 197; Kelly, 160.

316 On this point, see also Schelkle, 108. To suggest, as does Thurston ("Interpreting First Peter," 178), that the analogy rests in the fact that Roman accusations against Christians meant that allowing oneself to be baptized into the faith could be the equivalent of signing one's own death warrant, so that thus the water of baptism could cause death as certainly as the waters of the flood killed those of Noah's day, is somewhat far-fetched.

317 So also, e.g., Brox, 177; Bieder, *Grund und Kraft*, 20; Senior, 71.

318 As, e.g., Reicke (114) would have it; cf. also Beare, 174.

319 See the comments on νῦν above.

320 R. E. Nixon cites Mark 10:38–39 and Luke 12:49–50 as justification for such an interpretation ("The Meaning of 'Baptism' in 1 Peter 3,21," *StEv* 4 [1968] 438); see also Hillyer ("First Peter," 57), who cites

Nixon with approval.

321 On the one hand, Beare (175) argues that baptism here implies immersion, since it would be meaningless in relation to baptism by sprinkling; similarly, Wand (101): in baptism the old life is, as it were, drowned in baptismal water. On the other hand, the Qumran community apparently felt that purification could be accomplished by sprinkling; see 1QS 3.8–9 (a reference I owe to Knibb, *Qumran*, 91).

322 So also, e.g., Krafft, "Christologie," 123; Margot, 65.

323 That the phrase δι᾽ ἀναστάσεως Ἰησοῦ Χριστοῦ ("through the resurrection of Jesus Christ") is to be construed with the verb σώζει ("saves") is often argued; see, e.g., Dalton, *Christ's Proclamation* (2d ed.), 199; Bieder, *Grund und Kraft*, 19; Windisch, 73; Schweizer, 81; Bengel, *Gnomon*, 750; cf. Goldstein, "Kirche," 54. To base it as does Moffatt (143) on the fact that it "would appeal to whose who knew the contemporary representations of resurrection in cults like those of Cybele and Attis, or the aim of the Eleusinian mysteries," is surely wide of the mark.

324 In agreement with, e.g., Dalton, *Christ's Proclamation* (2d ed.), 199.

325 As Goldstein (*Paulinische Gemeinde*, 110) and Donald G. Miller ("Deliverance and Destiny: Salvation in First Peter," *Int* 9 [1955] 50) note.

326 The verb συνεγείρω, absent from the genuine letters of Paul, occurs in these verses, and in the aorist tense.

resurrection Paul understands as reserved for the future.[327] It may be that one can see in this passage a comparable development from Paul's position,[328] namely, that by baptism one already participates in the resurrection of Christ, but that is not so explicitly stated here as it is in Colossians and Ephesians. Nor does our author explicitly reserve participation in Christ's resurrection for the future, despite his awareness of the impending return of Christ. To relate baptism to the rebegetting mentioned in 1:3 may be attractive,[329] but if that were a primary emphasis, one would expect some reference to it here. The only reference is provided by the immediate context (3:18–22), namely, that Christ leads us to God because of his victory, through his death and resurrection, over the powers of evil (vv. 19, 22). It is probably in such deliverance from those powers that one ought to understand the way in which baptism saves by means of Christ's resurrection.[330] Because such deliverance from an evil world would also correspond to what water accomplished for Noah by delivering him from an evil world, it is in this direction that we ought to seek to understand what our author means by the saving power of baptism.[331]

The remainder of the verse consists in a contrast between what baptism is not, and is,[332] although it is difficult to understand clearly the content of this contrast.[333] The negative half of the contrast asserts that baptism is not σαρκὸς ἀπόθεσις ῥύπου ("putting off of the filth of the flesh").[334] The verbal noun ἀπόθεσις ("putting off") is rare in the NT; its only other occurrence is 2 Pet 1:14, where it means putting off one's physical body at the time of the parousia. The verb from which it is derived, ἀποτίθημι, is used in the NT in the middle voice in the sense of taking off one's clothes (Acts 7:58) or putting someone into prison (Matt 14:3), but more often in the sense of putting away or getting rid of one's old humanity (Eph 4:22) and its practices (Rom 13:12; Eph 4:25; Col 3:8; Heb 12:1; Jas 1:21; 1 Pet 2:1).[335] There is therefore no necessity to understand ἀπόθεσις in the sense of "washing," since that is contained neither in the verbal noun nor in the verb from which it derives.[336] Nor is there much likelihood that the readers would have thought that the mode of saving through Christ's resurrection consisted in the cleansing of the body through such lustrations.[337] To understand "filth of the flesh" not in a physical but in a moral sense, that is, as

---

327 So, e.g., Rom 6:5. See the explicit contrast in 6:8: have died, will be raised.

328 As, e.g., Goldstein (*Paulinische Gemeinde*, 110) suggests ("eine legitime Entfaltung," "a legitimate derivation"). France ("Exegesis in Practice," 275) thinks this verse is to be understood in light of Rom 6:1–11.

329 So, e.g., Elliott, "1 Peter," 540; to add 1:23 as he does overlooks the explicit reference there to the "word" (λόγος) as the agent of rebegetting.

330 See also Goppelt, 257.

331 While the intervening discussion of what baptism is not and is helps make more precise how we are to understand baptism, it is probably not correct to see in those definitions the reason why baptism saves, i.e., because the Christian at that moment makes the correct declaration, or has the right attitude to God, as do, e.g., Brooks ("1 Peter 3:21," 292, 294) and France ("Exegesis in Practice," 274). To be sure, that is close to the position of 1QS 3.8–9, where a correct attitude to God's commands precedes the ritual purification, a point also reflected in Josephus's discussion of John's baptism (*Ant.* 18.117; I owe this reference to Flusser, "Dead Sea Sect," 243), but the phrase "through the resurrection of Jesus Christ" which identifies baptism's saving power makes it unlikely that our author shared such a view.

332 The argument that the intention of this verse is to contrast Jewish and pagan lustrations through which the person becomes a new being, saved through this ritual, with baptism that is not such a magic transformation of the person (e.g., Bieder, *Grund und Kraft*, 22), has little in the context of the letter to justify it. Magical sacramentalism does not seem to have been a problem uppermost in our author's mind.

333 As Brox (178) notes, for example, the contrast to "putting off" should be "putting on," but it is difficult to justify such a meaning for ἐπερώτημα (for more on its meaning, see below). Hill ("On Suffering and Baptism," 186) is closer in defining the contrast as not between putting something off and putting something on, but between putting something off and making a commitment, even though that sacrifices any symmetry of meaning. For the expression of a true contrast between "putting off" and "putting on," see, e.g., Eph 4:22–24.

334 That both ἀπόθεσις and ἐπερώτημα are in the nominative case indicates that they also stand in apposition to βάπτισμα, and are thus to be construed as defining it.

335 On this point, see, e.g., Dalton, *Christ's Proclamation* (2d ed.), 200–201; Hill, "On Suffering and Baptism," 187.

336 The parallel with Heb 10:22 that Flusser ("Dead Sea

moral impurity,[338] is then to affirm that our author divorced such cleansing from moral impurity from the rite of baptism—that is after all what our author says baptism is *not*—a point difficult to credit.[339] An attractive alternative is to find in the putting off such filth of the flesh a reference to circumcision.[340] That the foreskin (ἀκροβυστία) is unclean is clear from such passages as Lev 19:23 and Jer 4:1–4, as from the understanding of uncircumcision as uncleanness in 1 Sam 17:26, 36 and Jer 9:26.[341] Additionally, that the foreskin can be identified as "flesh" is evident from the first definition of circumcision in the OT, Gen 17:11. Further, if, as Col 3:8–9 indicates, the verb ἀποτίθημι, from which ἀπόθεσις derives, is close in meaning to ἀπεκδύω ("to strip off"), then Col 2:11–12, which associates ἀπεκδύω with a circumcision made without hands (i.e., baptism), in which the Christian has put off τοῦ σώματος τῆς σαρκός ("the body of flesh"), would be close enough in meaning to the phrase σαρκὸς ἀπόθεσις

ῥύπου to suggest that our author similarly sees in that phrase a reference to circumcision. In that case, the negative half of the contrast points to what baptism is *not*, that is, a rite similar to Jewish circumcision that is understood here as a purely physical act.[342] Such an understanding of "putting off the filth of the flesh" is far from certain,[343] but it does make sense of the contrast, and stands in line with Peter's understanding of the Christian community as having assumed the mantle of God's people from the Jews; the difference between the former and present people of God rests on the way one is saved.

Hardly less obscure is the positive half of the contrast, συνειδήσεως ἀγαθῆς ἐπερώτημα εἰς θεόν. The difficulty centers on (1) the meaning of συνείδησις, (2) the meaning of ἐπερώτημα, and (3) the construal of the relationship between the two signified by the genitive case in which συνειδήσεως ἀγαθῆς is cast.

1. The active verbal noun συνείδησις identifies a

Sect," 245) and others see is thus obviated. Dalton (*Christ's Proclamation* [2d ed.], 203) further points out that there is no true parallel here with either Heb 10:22 or Eph 5:26. The suggestion of Vogels (*Christi Abstieg*, 39) that the contrast consists in not washing of filth of flesh but of filth of soul is thus also less than persuasive, since washing is not a necessary understanding of "putting off."

337 So also Hill, "On Suffering and Baptism," 186; Dalton, *Christ's Proclamation* (2d ed.), 200.

338 So, e.g., Michaels (215–16), who finds the closest parallel in Jas 1:21.

339 The argument of Dalton (*Christ's Proclamation* [2d ed.], 200) that "flesh" here represents a Semitic understanding of human nature as weak and prone to evil, and that putting it aside would mean a rite that purifies the whole person, does nothing to obviate this difficulty.

340 The most cogent argument for this position is to be found in Dalton, *Christ's Proclamation* (2d ed.) 199–206, in his treatment of this phrase in 3:21.

341 On the same point, see Philo (*Spec. leg.* 1.4–7), where of four reasons for circumcision, the second is the cleanliness of the whole body (1.5). Dalton (*Christ's Proclamation* [2d ed.], 205) argues that because both Philo and Jas 1:21 deal with a cleansing of an excess (James, an excess of wickedness; Philo, an excess of pleasure), this similarity may indicate that James is also thinking of circumcision, as is Philo, and the closeness between James and 1 Peter may indicate that 1 Peter also has a reference to circumcision in 3:21. That part of Dalton's argument is a bit too

convoluted to be very persuasive.

342 So Dalton, *Christ's Proclamation* (2d ed.), 201, 202; cf. also Kelly, 161–62; Reicke, *Spirits*, 188. The argument of Dalton (*Christ's Proclamation*, 233) that the contrast here is between old and new covenants, with baptism declared to have superseded the rite of the old covenant, would need to assume that "putting off the filth of the flesh" meant circumcision for such an understanding of the contrast to hold, even though he does not make that identification. Whether a discussion between the early Christian community and Jewish groups is reflected here, as Goldstein ("Kirche," 51) suggests, is difficult to determine.

343 As Dalton (*Christ's Proclamation*, 220) notes, but adds that "this hypothesis is at least worthy of serious consideration." But see Hill ("On Suffering and Baptism," 186–87): if 1 Peter is addressed to Gentiles, the attempt to define baptism by referring it to circumcision would be to interpret the obscure by the more obscure. Similarly, Traugott Holtz finds the argument "ganz unwahrscheinlich" "entirely improbable," both linguistically and contextually ("Dalton, William Joseph, S.J., Prof.: Christ's Proclamation to the Spirits. A Study of 1 Peter 3:18—4:6," *ThLZ* 92 [1967] 360).

shared or joint knowledge,[344] and is normally used in the ancient world to mean "awareness" or "consciousness."[345] Rather than a kind of subjective feeling of guilt or innocence, or the "psychological awareness of rectitude,"[346] conscience in that context refers to a good and loyal attitude of mind that eventuates in sound behavior.[347] Used two other times in this letter, it refers in one instance (2:19) primarily to consciousness, in the other (3:16) to a behavior growing out of such consciousness, but in both cases the focus is on activity pleasing to God rather than on one's inward psycho-moral state.[348] It is in that sense also that we are probably to understand "good conscience" in this phrase, namely, as a consciousness of what God wants that will lead one to do it.[349]

2. More difficult is the determination of the meaning of ἐπερώτημα.[350] A passive verbal noun derived from the verb ἐπερωτάω, it is a hapax legomenon in the NT as it is in the Greek OT.[351] In nonbiblical Greek literature, it occurs mainly in later Christian authors[352] although it is

also used by others[353] and bears the principal meaning "question" or "inquiry."[354] It appears in inscriptions in the sense of the "decree" or "decision" of some august body,[355] and in the papyri in the sense of stipulations, often of a contractual nature.[356] The verb from which it derives, ἐπερωτάω, appears more frequently in biblical Greek, normally in the sense of asking a question, more rarely in the sense of making a request (e.g., Matt 16:1).[357] Also common in that sense in nonbiblical Greek, it is used in the papyri in the aorist passive ἐπερωτηθείς ("having been asked"), in sense close to the meaning of the passive verbal noun ἐπερώτημα ("what has been asked"). The aorist passive verb is employed in a technical sense meaning the terms one has been "asked" to agree with in a contract.[358]

On the one hand, since the verb ἐπερωτάω ("ask a question, make a request") is more frequent in the NT than the verbal noun ἐπερώτημα, one can derive the meaning of the less clear noun from the clearer verb, and

---

344 As does the Latin *conscientia*, from which the English word "conscience" derives.

345 So also, e.g., Brooks, "1 Peter 3:21," 293–94.

346 The phrase is from Kelly, 163.

347 On this point see also Reicke, *Spirits*, 177; Dalton, *Christ's Proclamation* (2d ed.), 212.

348 So also, e.g., France, "Exegesis in Practice," 275; Hill, "On Suffering and Baptism," 188.

349 It has more emphasis on Christian conduct than Michaels (217) seems to allow in defining it as a correct attitude for facing God as it is the correct attitude for facing hostile interrogators in 3:16; in that verse it is precisely the Christians' *behavior* (τὴν ἀγαθὴν ἐν Χριστῷ ἀναστοφήν) that influences the interrogators.

350 While Bigg (165) argues that one cannot link εἰς θεόν to ἐπερώτημα, his objection is based on the assumption that this latter word means "petition" or "request"; since this is the less likely meaning, his objection falls, and it remains evident that the εἰς θεόν is in fact to be linked to ἐπερώτημα.

351 Dan 4:17 (Theodotion). It occurs in LXX Sir 33:3 in the form ἐρώτημα.

352 E.g., Athanasius *Ad Ant. ducem* 28.613; Basilius *Homilia in sanctum pascha et in recens illuminatos* 188; Gregory Nazianzus *In sanctum baptisma* 36.361; Chrysostom *Int. in Dan.* 56.216; Justin *Dial.* 45.1.

353 E.g., Herodotus *Hist.* 6.67; Epicurus *Gnomologium* 71; Galen *Adversus Lycum libellus* 18a.227; Thucydides *Historiae* 3.53.2; and in the *Vitae Aesopi, Vita W* 119.

354 In Herodotus *Hist.* 9.44, the active verbal noun (ἐπερώτησις) refers to addressing an oracle to the

gods; the verb (ἐπειρωτᾶν) is used in the same sense in 1.53, as Goppelt (259) observes.

355 E.g., Attica.*IG* II(2).3656: κατὰ τὸ ἐπερώτημα τῶν σεμνοτάτων ἀρεοπαγείτων; the usual formula is κατὰ τὸ ἐπερώτημα τῆς (σεμνοτάτης) βουλῆς of some city or court.

356 It is frequently used in conjunction with ἀνθωμολογημένη or ὁμολόγημα, indicating that the author agrees with certain terms; see, e.g., *P. Babatha.*20–21.r. That it concerns contractual matters, see France, "Exegesis in Practice," 275; Brooks, "1 Peter 3:21," 292–93. G. C. Richards ("I Pet. iii 21," *JTS* 32 [1931] 77) finds this meaning to be close to the Latin *stipulatio*, used regularly in contracts to identify the terms; Hill ("On Suffering and Baptism," 187) argues that it is closer to the Latin *adstipulatio* ("assent") rather than *stipulatio* ("promise, obligation").

357 In the NT, it is found primarily in the Synoptics, with two additional occurrences each in John, Acts, and the Pauline literature.

358 The usual formula is ἐπερωτηθεὶς (ὑπὸ σοῦ) ὡμολόγησα ("having been asked [by you] I have agreed"); e.g., BGU 7.1645, 1649; 11.2118; *P. Harris* 2.228; *P. Oxy.* 9.1200, 1208.

define the noun as "request" or "plea," and since it is directed to God, as a "prayer,"[359] perhaps with the further implication that the petitioner understood this as a request that bound one to shape one's behavior in light of that which one requested.[360] A Latin equivalent would be *applicatio,* a word used for the selection of a patron by a prospective client seeking to come under the former's protection and help.[361] The solemn act by which one entered in the relationship of client-patron by application[362] was termed *applicatio ad patronum,* a close verbal parallel to ἐπερώτημα εἰς θεόν,[363] a parallel that would lend support to this understanding of ἐπερώτημα.

On the other hand, since the verbal noun itself, along with the verb from which it derives, is frequently used in the papyri as part of contractual language, one can take the word to mean the pledge one takes to uphold the terms of the agreement.[364] The close association of the aorist form of the verb (ἐπερωτηθείς) with the verb meaning "acknowledge" or "confess" (ὡμολόγησα), and the fact that the baptismal liturgy of the early church included a confession of faith in response to a corresponding question,[365] would support such a view.[366] The requirement of such a pledge as part of the ritual of

admission at Qumran[367] adds further weight to such an understanding of ἐπερώτημα in this context.

3. The relationship between "conscience" and "pledge" or "request" is expressed by the genitive phrase συνειδήσεως ἀγαθῆς. On the one hand, if it is construed as a subjective genitive,[368] then the meaning is that either the prayer or the pledge arises or proceeds from a good conscience. If it is a prayer, then the baptisand addresses his or her prayer to God because of the good conscience, that is, the consciousness of God and the resulting activity, which the petitioner already possesses.[369] If it is a pledge, then it is a pledge to God of unspecified content that again arises from the good conscience the believer already possesses.[370] On the other hand, if it is construed as an objective genitive, then the good conscience is the content of the prayer or pledge made by the baptisand. If a prayer, then the baptisand addresses a prayer to God for a good conscience,[371] that is, for a consciousness of God and the ensuing appropriate activity; if a pledge, then the baptisand pledges to God that he or she will maintain a "good conscience,"[372] that is, a consciousness of God and a good and decent conduct both within and without the Christian

---

359 It is understood in that way by, e.g., Vogels, *Christi Abstieg,* 39; Holmer and de Boor, 134; Senior, 72; Grudem, 163; Beare, 175; Windisch, 73; Schiwy, 55; Michaels, 217; Schweizer, 82.

360 So, e.g., Goppelt (260), who calls it a "verpflichtende Bitte" "obligating petition."

361 E. Badian, *Foreign Clientelae (264–70 B.C.)* (Oxford: Clarendon, 1958) 8.

362 The other two ways were *deditio,* i.e., through surrender, often as a result of a military campaign, or *manumissio,* i.e., as a freed slave; on this point see A. von Premerstein, "Clientes," PW 7.26–29.

363 Ibid., 7.32.

364 It is understood in that way by, e.g., Fitzmyer, "First Peter," 367; Bieder, *Grund und Kraft,* 21; Leaney, 55; Dalton, *Christ's Proclamation* (2d ed.), 208–10; Richards, "I Pet. iii 21," 77; Kelly, 162; Spicq, 142; but see Schelkle, 109 n. 1.

365 On this point see, e.g., J. B. Souček, "Das Gegenüber," 6; Fransen, "Une homélie," 37; Selwyn, 147; Wand, 102. Acts 8:37, a later gloss, reflects this practice. Hill ("On Suffering and Baptism," 188) finds that in Cyril of Alexandria (*Hom. pasch.* 30.3; I have been unable to confirm this citation) this phrase is explained as τῆς εἰς Χριστὸν πίστεως ὁμολογία ("confession of faith in Christ"); cf. also Kelly, 162. Dalton (*Christ's Proclamation* [2d ed.], 209) notes that

366 The meaning "pledge" in the sense of a baptismal confession is accepted, e.g., by Schlier, "Adhortatio," 67; Tripp, "Eperōtēma," 269; Brox, 178; Richards, "I Pet. iii 21," 77.

367 See 1QS 1.16; 5.7–8; on this point see Knibb, *Qumran,* 82–83, 107.

368 So, e.g., Kelly, 162; Selwyn, 205; Michaels, 216.

369 So, e.g., Galot, "La descente du Christ," 483 n. 46; Michaels, 216; as a possibility, Windisch, 73.

370 So, e.g., Spicq, 141 (an oath of obedience, stated in deliberate contrast to the disobedient contemporaries of Noah); Selwyn, 205; as possibility, Cranfield, 106; Best, 148; see also Dalton, *Christ's Proclamation,* 232 ("seems less likely").

371 So, e.g., Schelkle, 109; Vogels, *Christi Abstieg,* 39; Holmer and de Boor, 134; Bauer, 50; Grudem, 163; Margot, 64; Beare, 175; Moffatt, 143; Schweizer, 82. Schiwy (55) understands it as a request to God for participation in the salvation of Christ.

372 So, e.g., Kelly, 162; Omanson, "Suffering," 444; Goppelt, 258; France, "Exegesis in Practice," 275.

according to Hippolytus (*Ap. Trad.*), Roman baptismal practice included an interrogation of the baptisand.

community.[373]

While arguments can be made for all these positions, those that hold to a subjective genitive interpretation are perhaps the weaker of them. Least persuasive is the position that the phrase is to be understood as a prayer to God arising from a good conscience, since then the content of the prayer is left unspecified, and the salvation through the resurrection of Christ provided in baptism must presume a commitment to God and its corresponding activity, in this verse identified as the way baptism saves, as being already present prior to that salvific act.[374] A similar problem is shared by understanding the phrase to mean a pledge to God arising from a good conscience, since although here the content of the pledge (good conscience) is clear, the results of the baptismal salvation must again be assumed to be present prior to baptism itself.[375]

Interpretations based on an objective genitive relationship remain the more persuasive, both structurally—the genitive σαρκός ῥύπου in the corresponding phrase clearly stands in an objective relationship to ἀπόθεσις[376]—and in relation to content. To understand the phrase as defining baptism made salvific by its relationship to the risen Christ in terms of the baptisand's prayer to God that he or she may hold fast to a sound consciousness of God and so act appropriately is attractive theologically and fits well into the larger context of the letter. The primary difficulty lies in the fact that ἐπερώτημα does not bear that meaning[377] either in inscriptions or in the papyri, where it means either "edict," often as response to a formal plea, or "pledge" as part of a contractual obligation. Semantically, therefore, the more likely meaning of the word is "pledge," and it refers to the response of the baptisand to God (εἰς θεόν) in light of the act of baptism, which is made salvific by its relationship to Christ's resurrection.

The gist of the phrase would therefore appear to be that baptism, perhaps in contrast to the initiating act of Jewish ritual, that is, circumcision,[378] which symbolized a preoccupation with physical purity, concerns the total life of the baptisand in that a part of the ritual of baptism consists in pledging to maintain the consciousness of God and the ensuing appropriate acts that are made possible through the resurrection of Christ. Because Christ's resurrection makes such activity possible, a pledge to maintain it is appropriate since maintaining such a pledge is empowered by Christ's defeat of angelic powers who represent the source and power of evil in the world. Thus baptism, as the antitype of Noah's deliverance through water from his evil contemporary world, similarly delivers the Christians from their evil contemporary world by allowing them, through their participation in the power of the risen Christ and his defeat of the powers of evil, now to live a life pleasing to God and appropriate to their redemption through Christ.[379] To accept baptism is thus to accept the responsibility, through the baptismal pledge, to maintain such a life in the midst of a hostile world,[380] a major point of the letter as a whole.[381]

■ 22 The climax of vv. 18–22 is reached with this verse, which describes Christ's exaltation at God's right hand[382] and his ascension, along with the subjugation of

---

373 So, e.g., Bieder, *Grund und Kraft*, 21–22; Brox, 178.

374 So, e.g., Michaels, 217.

375 So, e.g., Flusser ("Dead Sea Sect," 245): baptism is "the answer of a good conscience toward God." Grudem (164) objects that in that case the emphasis is "no longer on dependence on God to give salvation but . . . on one's own effort or strength of resolve."

376 In agreement with Selwyn, 204; Dalton, *Christ's Proclamation*, 233.

377 Dalton (*Christ's Proclamation* [2d ed.], 207) notes that while it can mean "question," there is "no example anywhere in . . . Greek writing where it means 'request.'"

378 Dalton (*Christ's Proclamation* [2d ed.], 214) argues that the verse represents a contrast between old and new covenants, a contrast already voiced in 1:2.

379 Cf. also Dalton, *Christ's Proclamation* (2d ed.), 190;

Reicke, 113; Calvin, 117. Contra, e.g., Brox (176), who sees no connected content among Christ's preaching to the spirits, the flood, and baptism.

380 Cf. also Brooks, "1 Peter 3:21," 305.

381 Brooks ("1 Peter 3:21," 304) finds this passage the "climax of [the author's] homily"; for a more restrained comment, see France, "Exegesis in Practice," 276.

382 Traditionally referred to as the *sessio ad dextram dei*, although the reference to sitting, in the NT normally a form of the verb καθίζω, is omitted here.

superhuman powers. The dislocation of the normal order (ascension, exaltation) is due to the author's desire to link this verse with the reference to Jesus Christ with which v. 21 concludes.[383] While early creedal material is reflected in this verse,[384] the introductory relative pronoun ὅς is probably due as much to the characteristic structure of the passage as to any direct quotation of such material.[385] The elements combined in this verse—ascension, exaltation, subjugation—occur frequently in various combinations in the NT;[386] this particular combination, however, is unique, and shows the extent to which the author was independent in his use and combination of such traditions. For that reason, although some have sought to find literary dependence here on other NT passages,[387] the similarities that exist are more likely due to common use of early tradition than to such direct borrowing.[388]

The first phrase of the verse describes Christ's *sessio ad dextram* in language that reflects Ps 110:1.[389] The psalm is quoted directly in the NT in relation to Christ's exaltation (Acts 2:34; Heb 1:13)[390] in a tradition that may well go back to a saying of Jesus (Mark 14:62 par. Luke 22:69).[391] Allusions to this tradition take two forms, the one of which retains the ἐκ δεξιῶν of the psalm,[392] the other of which employs the comparable phrase ἐν δεξιᾷ.[393] It is this latter tradition that our author follows, thus indicating his dependence on tradition rather than on the psalm directly.[394]

The second phrase describes Christ's ascension,[395] here understood as an event distinct from the resurrection.[396] The lack of any explicit connection between the ascension and the ensuing reference to the subjugation of the superhuman powers is due to the fact that the same event is envisioned here as was described in v. 19, where the same verb was used (πορευθείς) to describe Christ's journey, and the mode of subjugation there was described as his proclamation to those powers.[397]

383 So also, e.g., Dalton, *Christ's Proclamation* (2d ed.), 118; Bultmann, "Bekenntnis- und Liedfragmente," 6.

384 A common conclusion; see, e.g., Dalton, *Christ's Proclamation* (2d ed.), 117; Jeremias, "Zwischen Karfreitag und Ostern," 196.

385 The relative pronoun is used in this passage to tie some rather disparate elements together, as the use of similar relative pronouns in vv. 19, 20b, and 21 shows; it is probably for that reason also used here. For an analysis of the structure of this passage, noting the way such key words and relative pronouns link it together, see "Analysis: Structure," above.

386 Death, resurrection, exaltation: Rom 8:34; Acts 5:31; resurrection, exaltation, subjugation, Eph 1:20–21; resurrection, exaltation, Acts 2:32–33; death, exaltation, Heb 1:3b; 10:12; 12:2; exaltation, parousia, Mark 14:62; Col 3:1, 4 (cf. Heb 9:28); exaltation alone, Acts 7:55, Heb 8:1 (cf. Rev 12:5b). For a similar catalog, see Shimada, *Formulary Material*, 375 n 2.; cf. also Goppelt 261.

387 Most commonly, Rom 8:34, where the identical phrase appears; less frequently, Eph 1:20 or Col 3:1, since the language in those two passages is different, with only the phrase ἐν δεξιᾷ common to all three passages. For a thorough discussion of this problem, see Shimada, *Formulary Material*, 376.

388 With, e.g., Shimada, *Formulary Material*, 392–93, 395. There is nothing in Rom 8:34 to link the two verses other than the common phrase; otherwise language and context are quite different.

389 LXX 109:1: Εἶπεν ὁ κύριος τῷ κυρίῳ μου Κάθου ἐκ δεξιῶν μου ("The Lord said to my lord: 'Sit at my right hand'"); on this point see, e.g., France, "Exegesis in Practice," 276; Delling, "Der Bezug," 101; Vogels, *Christi Abstieg*, 20. Beare (176) holds that the imagery is from statuary found in oriental temples, especially those in Egypt, where the king is seated at the right hand of the god, but acknowledges that it entered NT tradition by way of Psalm 110.

390 Its quotation in an unrelated context in Matt 22:44 par. attests its popularity in early Christian tradition.

391 On this point see also Shimada, *Formulary Material*, 395.

392 In addition to those passages which quote it, it is found in Matt 26:64; Mark 16:19; Acts 7:55, 56. The passages in Matthew and Mark include forms of the verb καθίζω; the verses in Acts have ἑστῶτα ("standing").

393 Rom 8:34; Eph 1:20; Col 3:1; Heb 1:3; 8:1; 10:12; 12:2, of which all but Rom 8:34 also include a form of the verb καθίζω.

394 Direct quotation would have involved the phrase ἐκ δεξιῶν and the verb καθίζω; Michaels (218–19) comes to the same conclusion.

395 The phrase πορευθεὶς εἰς οὐρανόν closely resembles the description of the ascension in Acts 2:11: πορευόμενον εἰς τὸν οὐρανόν.

396 So also, e.g., Bigg, 166. As Goppelt (263) notes, in some NT traditions, exaltation occurs with the resurrection, rather than as a separate act, and with no reference to an ascension: Heb 1:3; 10:12; cf. Eph 1:20.

397 So also, e.g., Richard, "Christology," 133; Dalton, *Christ's Proclamation* (2d ed.), 118; Schiwy, 22;

The superhuman powers that have been subjugated to Christ[398] are described in terms used in the NT for powers believed to affect human life.[399] In Jewish thought such powers were believed to govern nations, and were the powers behind idolatry.[400] Lists of two or more of such powers occur, apart from this verse, only in the Pauline tradition in the NT,[401] pointing to some contact between our author and that tradition. Of the three classes named in this list, however, ἄγγελλοι and δύναμαι are combined only in Rom 8:3, 8,[402] ἐξουσίαι and δύναμαι in 1 Cor 15:24 and Eph 1:21, while the combination of ἄγγελλοι and ἐξουσίαι occurs only in this verse. That would point to broad acquaintance with such Pauline tradition, rather than dependence on any specific document for this material. The three classes in this list are probably meant as exemplary of all such powers[403] who have now found their master in the risen and exalted Christ,[404] and in this context are surely to be regarded as hostile to God and to his creation.[405] There would be no point in mentioning the subjugation of superhuman powers that already served God willingly.[406]

The readers of the letter are thus assured that the evil powers still rampant in their world, motivating the suppression of the Christian community, have been robbed of their ultimate power through Christ's resurrection and his assumption of divine authority,[407] an authority that will soon become visible with God's final judgment.[408] Therefore Christians may know that in the end, no one can truly harm them (see 3:13), since the Lord of the cosmos who rules over all supernatural powers is also the Lord whom they serve in the Christian community,[409] a Lord in whose victory over all hurtful powers they will also one day share. A beleaguered community, facing the onslaught of evil powers intent on its destruction, could find real courage in such assurance.[410]

Moffatt, 144; but see Best, 148.

398 On the one hand, Goppelt (264) argues that the idea of such subjugation was drawn from Ps 110:1b and Ps 8:7b, and cites 1 Cor 15:25, 27 and Eph 1:20, 22, where both are quoted. Michaels (220), on the other hand, finds no allusion at all in our verse to Ps 8:7. If there is any reflection of either psalm, it is by way of Christian tradition, as noted above, rather than conscious allusion to the psalms themselves. On a different tack, Bultmann ("Bekenntnis- und Liedfragmente," 7) and Windisch (73) have argued that such cosmic redemption reflects the gnostic redeemer myth, an argument I think unnecessarily speculative.

399 See Rom 8:38; 1 Cor 2:6–8; Gal 4:3; Col 2:8; Eph 1:21; 2:2; 6:12.

400 In this respect Best (148) cites *1 Enoch* 99.7; *Jub.* 1.11; 22.17. Such thought seems reflected in the NT in 1 Cor 10:19–21; Rev 9:20.

401 Lists of two or more powers are given in Rom 8:38; 1 Cor 15:24; Eph 1:21; 3:10; 6:12; Col 1:16; 2:10, 15.

402 Their combination there argues against the contention of Shimada ("Formula," 162) that the phrase ἀγγέλων καί is a secondary addition to an earlier tradition in light of the speculation about fallen angels contained in vv. 20–21.

403 With, e.g., Schelkle, 110.

404 So Schlier ("Adhortatio," 63): "Solche Ermächtigung des Erhöten ist aber auch . . . die Entmächtigung der Mächte der Welt" "Such empowerment of the exalted one is, however, also . . . the disempowerment of the powers of the world."

405 As are such powers in 1 Cor 15:24–25; Eph 1:20–22 in light of 6:12, as Dalton (*Christ's Proclamation* [2d ed.], 217) notes. But see Spicq (142–43), who finds here no distinction between good and bad powers.

406 So also, e.g., Selwyn, 208.

407 So also, e.g., Kelly, 164; Reicke, *Spirits,* 200; cf. France, "Exegesis in Practice," 266. Beare (176) observes that a similar point is reflected in 1 Cor 15:24 and Col 2:1, a fulfillment of a remembered prediction of Jesus himself (Matt 16:18; Mark 3:27; John 12:31), as Spicq (143) notes.

408 This point becomes thematic in the final portions of the letter; see 4:5, 7, 13, 17–18; 5:10.

409 A point also emphasized by Goldstein, "Kirche," 52, 53.

410 With France, "Exegesis in Practice," 276.

4

Right Conduct among Unbelievers

1 Since, then, Christ suffered[1] in the flesh, you also must arm yourselves with the same thought, namely, that the one who suffered in the flesh ceased from sin,[2] 2/ to the end that you live[3] your remaining time in the flesh not according to human desires but according to the will of God,[4] 3/ since the time past was sufficient[5] for engaging in behavior which follows the will[6] of the gentiles, carrying on in unbridled behavior, lusts, debaucheries, carousals, drinking bouts, and lawless idolatries. 4/ By this they are taken aback, namely, that you no longer go along with them in the same excess of profligacy. Because they blaspheme,[7] 5/ such people are going to have to render an account to the one who is ready to judge[8] living and dead, 6/ since it was for this purpose that the gospel was preached also to the dead, so that although they were judged by humanity according to what is appropriate to human beings,[9] they may nevertheless live by the spirit according to what is appropriate to God.

1   ὑπὲρ ἡμῶν ("for us") is added by ℵ², A, P, 𝔐, syʰ, bo, some fathers; ὑπὲρ ὑμῶν ("for you") by some minuscules, vgᵐˢ, syᵖ, ℵ* (which in addition changes the verb to ἀποθάνοντος ["died"]), perhaps in part to ward off the idea that by his death Christ ceased from his own sin. The text without the added prepositional phrase is found in P⁷², B, C, Ψ, some minuscules, and is to be accepted here as the preferred reading. So also, e.g., Kelly (165) and August Strobel ("Macht Leiden von Sünde frei? Zur Problematik von 1. Petr. 4,1f.," TZ 19 [1963] 412), who see the phrase as an interpolation of a stock formula; one may compare 2:21, which may have influenced the tradition of this verse.

2   ℵ², B, Ψ, a few others substitute dative plural ἁμαρτίαις for the genitive singular ἁμαρτίας, with little change in meaning; with the dative of reference, the meaning would be "ceased with respect to sin."

3   P⁷² reads σῶσαι ("save") for βιῶσαι ("live"), probably a misreading of its source.

4   ℵ* unaccountably substitutes ἀνθρώπου for θεοῦ.

5   A number of texts (ℵ*, 630, many minuscules, bo, Augᵖᵗ) add ὑμῖν, others (C, K, L, P, many minuscules, Hier) ἡμῖν, probably by way of clarification; the superior quality of the witness to its absence (P⁷², ℵᶜ, A, B, Ψ, 81, 945, 1739, some other minuscules, latt, sy, sa) is important here.

6   Some MSS. (P, 𝔐) read θέλημα in place of the more widely attested βούλημα; the latter word implies that this is the kind of behavior decided upon, and counseled by, non-Christians.

7   For the grammatically more difficult participle βλασφημοῦντες, some MSS. (ℵ*, C*, 81, 1739, some other minuscules) read καὶ βλασφήμουσιν ("and they slander"), thus simplifying the structure by coordinating the two verbs. The more difficult reading ought here to prevail, and probably ought to be construed with what follows; so also Michaels, 224.

8   For the idiomatic τῷ ἑτοίμως ἔχοντι κρῖναι (found in ℵ, A, C², P, 𝔐), some MSS. (B, [C*ᵛⁱᵈ], Ψ, some minuscules) read τῷ ἑτοίμως κρίνοντι ("the one who judges readily"), others (P⁷², some minuscules) τῷ ἑτοίμῳ κρῖναι ("to the one ready to judge"). There is little to choose in the meaning; the weight of MS. evidence and the idiomatic character of the longer reading indicate its originality.

9   This phrase, κατὰ ἀνθρώπους, could also be rendered "according to human standards," as the comparable phrase, κατὰ θεόν, could be rendered "according to divine standards."

Analysis

The language of vv. 1 and 6 of this passage indicates its relation to 3:18, and hence with the discussion in vv. 19–22 which grow out of that verse. Our passage begins with a reference in 4:1a to the suffering of Christ (Χριστοῦ οὖν παθόντος σαρκί) that recalls the reference to his suffering in 3:18a (Χριστὸς ἅπαξ . . . ἔπαθεν). Similarly, the outcome of that suffering, viz., the putting away of sin in 4:1b (ὁ παθὼν σαρκὶ πέπαυται ἁμαρτίας), reflects a similar point in 3:18a (περὶ ἁμαρτιῶν; cf. also 3:18aβ, ἵνα ὑμᾶς προσαγάγῃ τῷ θεῷ). Again, the contrast between flesh and spirit at the close of our passage in 4:6 recalls the same contrast in 3:18b, even to the language used to express the contrast (μέν with σαρκί, δέ with πνεύματι). The *inclusio* that in that way is formed between 3:18 and 4:6 is a clear indication that one is also to understand the paranetic material in 4:2–5 to be related to the content of this larger unit.[10] Indeed, the content of the quotation from Psalm 34 in 1 Pet 3:10–12, which introduced the discussion that began with 3:13 and includes our passage, contains the gist of the points being made here,[11] indicating both the unity of thought of the larger context and the climactic nature of 4:1–6.

The paranetic material contained in 4:2–5 applies to the lives of the readers the point made about Christ's triumph over supernatural evil powers (3:19, 22), namely, their freedom now to live in accordance with the will of God (4:2) rather than in conformity to the expectations of their contemporary culture (4:2–3), since despite the abuse that such nonconformity to contemporary cultural values brings them (4:4), God's final judgment will vindicate the way they have chosen to live (4:5–6). Strongly implied in these verses is also the contrast between past and present, between former behavior that was in conformity with "the desires of humanity" and that as a result brought no opprobrium from such humanity, and present behavior which now, because it is in conformity with the will of God, does bring such opprobrium from humans but has God's full approval (5:10).

The next set of verses, 4:7–11, points to the way Christians are to live with one another, as 4:1–6 point to the way they are to live within their contemporary culture, thus providing the conclusion to the body middle of the letter (2:11—4:11), and introducing, with the references to the impending judgment (4:5, 7a) the theme that undergirds the body closing (4:12–5:11).

The paranetic material also makes clear the basis of the abuse Christians suffer at the hands of their non-believing contemporaries (4:3–4). It does not have to do with Roman concern over foreign religions and hence with any official governmental attempt to suppress the Christian religion. It has rather to do with the fact that people who have become Christians, who once took part in the cultural activities, in the "lifestyle," of their times, no longer do so, and it is that refusal of further participation that brings abuse upon them.

Such an origin of the persecution of Christians means that it will arise wherever Christians abandon a previous mode of activity for one that denies the validity of the societal practices their contemporaries engage in. Thus such persecutions, while sporadic, depending on the mood of the populace, will nevertheless be inevitable, since there is finally nothing Christians can do to mollify those whose lifestyle the Christians have abandoned and hence indirectly, at least, condemned. Christians are necessarily nonconformists, as followers of Christ, in an age that prized social unity and conformity as one of the highest virtues, and the sufferings imposed on Christians by their nonbelieving contemporaries are therefore as unavoidable and inevitable as the sufferings visited upon Christ himself. To be a Christian meant to espouse values and a way of life that would inevitably meet cultural disapproval.

Yet Christ had triumphed over suffering and over the demonic forces that opposed him, and was elevated to the position of divine power (3:22). If Christ is thus the example of the Christians' suffering, he is also their sure

---

10 For a similar analysis, see Goppelt, 265. Johnson's attempt ("Preaching," 50) to find in 3:22—4:6 a chiastic structure is less persuasive, since the contrasting elements on occasion appear forced. Such *inclusio* indicates that 3:19–22 do not represent an interruption, or digression, in the author's train of thought, as has on occasion been argued.

11 Michaels (242) also points to this connection.

hope that despite such rejection and suffering by their contemporaries, the close of history will demonstrate that it is not they, but their persecutors, who will face the final, divine rejection.[12] It is precisely in that realization that their hope and joy were grounded, despite their inevitable conflict with a culture out of step with the will of God. The treatment of Christian groups throughout the twentieth century by social structures that espouse values similarly counter to the will of God have shown that what our author is discussing is not a problem unique to the confrontation between the Christian community and the Roman Empire. It is a problem that will recur whenever Christians are forced by their faith to oppose cultural values widely held in the secular world within which they live.

Comment

■ 1 The οὖν is resumptive[13] of 3:18,[14] as the language of the opening genitive absolute construction demonstrates,[15] but, because 3:18 and 4:1 form an *inclusio*, it is also resumptive of the intervening 3:19–22 as well.[16] The qualifying σαρκί points to Christ's human suffering,[17] and reminds the readers that Christ shared a fate both exemplary for, and, because it was human

suffering, comparable to the kind of suffering they undergo at the hands of their hostile contemporaries.[18] It is on the basis of the description of Christ in vv. 18–22, namely, that the fate of Christ who ultimately triumphed included human suffering, that the readers are now told to apply that insight to strengthen their own resolve to maintain the kind of behavior that is pleasing to God, whatever negative reaction that may ignite in their nonbelieving contemporaries.

The emphatic καὶ ὑμεῖς ("you also") underlines the applicability of Christ's human suffering to the situation of the readers. The figure of arming oneself for battle (ὁπλίσασθε)[19] uses a military metaphor familiar in the NT,[20] and implies the warlike conditions under which Christians live within the surrounding culture.[21] That the armor is an ἔννοιαν that is related to, perhaps drawn from, Christ's human suffering[22] is indicated by the αὐτήν ("same"), and is to consist in an intent or attitude.[23] Used only one other time in the NT (Heb 4:12), ἔννοια is also found in the LXX, primarily in Proverbs,[24] and refers, to be sure, to mental activity,[25] but primarily in the form of intention or disposition in the sphere of moral actions. In this verse it is clearly understood to

12 For a similar argument, see, e.g., Kelly, 165.
13 So also, e.g., Cranfield, 107.
14 With, e.g., Beare, 178. The argument that 4:1 intends to resume the discussion of 3:17, maintained, e.g., by Völter ("Bemerkungen," 75), founders on the similarity of language between 4:1a and 3:18a; the same is true of Grudem's (166) contention that 3:14, 16–18 provide the immediate context.
15 The genitive absolute here has causal force, as is commonly recognized; cf., e.g., Blazen, "Suffering and Cessation," 30.
16 With, e.g., Blazen, "Suffering and Cessation," 28; Reicke, *Spirits*, 202. But see Michaels (225) and Schelkle (114), who think vv. 19–22 are here passed over by the author.
17 In this instance σάρξ refers to the sphere within which Christ's suffering took place, as, e.g., Calvin (122) also points out; it has the same force in its later occurrence in the verse. Σαρκί here is to be construed differently from the instrumental σαρκί of 3:18, since here the issue is suffering, not death, and the verb is active, not passive.
18 The repeated σαρκί in 4:1c confirms this.
19 The aorist implies that rather than an act to be repeated, i.e., putting armor on and off, such arming is to be a permanent state, once it is undertaken.
20 E.g., Rom 6:13; 13:12; 2 Cor 6:7; 10:4; Eph 6:11–

17; 1 Thess 5:8; Jesus in Luke 11:22 used the same metaphor in reference to his battle with Satan.
21 With Brox, 191; it is less likely to have been chosen because there were soldiers stationed in the localities of the readers, as Tarrech ("Le milieu," 361) suggests.
22 As described in the genitive absolute phrase, as also, e.g., Dalton (*Christ's Proclamation* [2d ed.], 222) and Best (151) argue.
23 The reference to Christians so armed doing God's will in 4:2 may imply that such suffering in accord with God's will also characterized Christ's suffering.
24 Twelve times (1:4; 2:11; 3:21; 4:1; 5:2; 8:12; 16:22; 18:15; 19:17; 23:4, 19; 24:7); once each also in Sirach (2:14) and Susanna (28).
25 It is associated in LXX Proverbs with such terms as βουλή, γνῶσις, σοφία, and φρόνιμος, as Blazen ("Suffering and Cessation," 31) notes, which deal with human intellect directed to practical and moral ends; cf. also Dalton, *Christ's Proclamation* (2d ed.), 222. But see Goppelt (267), who argues that it means insight rather than intention, but agrees that it leads to specific behavior, in this instance the kind of behavior described in v. 2, and based on Christ's suffering.

lead to the kind of behavior described in v. 2,[26] the implication being that as Christ in his suffering acted in accordance with God's will, not human inclinations, so must the Christians.[27]

Three problems are involved in understanding the ὅτι-clause with which the verse concludes: (1) the construal of the preposition ὅτι; (2) the identification of the antecedent to ὁ παθών ("the one who suffers"); and (3) the understanding of the origin and intent of the phrase itself.

1. Ὅτι may give either the reason for a statement (ὅτι *causativum*) or its content (ὅτι *recitativum*).[28] If, on the one hand, it is understood to have causal intent, it is to be construed with the imperative, and gives further reason why, in addition to the beginning phrase of the verse, the Christians are to arm themselves to accept suffering.[29] It is used frequently in this sense in 1 Peter, in conjunction with an imperative.[30] If, on the other hand, it is understood to have explanatory force, it is to be construed with ἔννοια, and then gives the content of the thought/intent with which the Christians are to be armed.[31] It is also used in this sense in 1 Peter, with a term implying mental content.[32] While either construal is possible, the parallel use of ἔννοια with a ὅτι *recitativum* in nonbiblical Greek,[33] and the causative force already present in the genitive absolute clause with which the verse begins, throw the weight of probability in the direction of explanatory force. That is, the ὅτι clause provides further information on the content of the ἔννοια.[34]

2. The antecedent of the ὁ παθών ("the one who suffers") may be either the Χριστοῦ with which the verse begins, or a generalized form for the (plural) subject of the imperative ὁπλίσασθε, that is, the Christian. If, on the one hand, the antecedent is understood to be Christ,[35] earlier described with another participle (παθόντος) derived from the same verb (πάσχω), then the intent is to say that as Christ by his suffering conquered the power of sin, so the Christian may now similarly share in that victory.[36] The implication that in that case Christ was also a sinner if by his suffering he has ceased from sin,[37] an implication that could present a problem, is, however, negated by the author's previous statements about Christ's sinlessness.[38] If, on the other hand, the antecedent is understood to be the (baptized) Christian,[39] the implication is that the Christians who share the kind of suffering Christ underwent as a human being (σαρκί),

---

26 With, e.g., Goppelt 268.

27 The context makes clear that the author is not speaking of suffering as such, but of suffering within a Christian context, i.e., for Christian convictions firmly held, as, e.g., Blazen ("Suffering and Cessation," 46) and Michaels (225) also note.

28 "Ὅτι *explicativum*" and "expegetic ὅτι" refer to the same force for the conjunction.

29 See, e.g., Michaels, 225; Blazen, "Suffering and Cessation," 45; Dalton, *Christ's Proclamation* (2d ed.), 221.

30 1:16; 2:21; 3:9; 3:12; 4:17; 5:5; it is further used in a causal sense in 2:15; 3:18; 4:8, 14; and 5:7.

31 See, e.g., Kelly, 166; Hart, 70; Moffatt, 146; Windisch, 73; Bigg, 167; Calvin, 121. The argument of Blazen ("Suffering and Cessation," 41) and Goppelt (268) that it cannot be explanatory because then it could not refer to Christ makes an unnecessary assumption, I believe, about the antecedent of ὁ παθών; for more on this point, see the discussion of the second problem below.

32 1:12, 18; it is further used in an explanatory sense in 2:3.

33 E.g., Philo *Praem. poen.* 42; *Fug.* 99; *Spec. leg.* 4.71; Josephus *Ant.* 15.200 (I owe the first reference to Kelly, 166).

34 The basic thrust of the verse would not be materially altered if the ὅτι were to be construed as causative, however.

35 So, e.g., Michaels, 228; Strobel, "Leiden," 419.

36 So, e.g., Spicq, 143–44; Strobel, "Leiden," 420. The latter's argument that such a reference is confirmed by Ephiphanius *Pan.* 30.32.6ff (TLG 1.378.14–22), who maintains that when Lamech named his son Noah, he was issuing a prophecy of Christ, since in Christ all holy people find rest (on such a meaning for the name "Noah," see the discussion of Noah above in 3:20), lacks probative value, drawn as it is from a much later source.

37 As, e.g., Blazen ("Suffering and Cessation," 41) argues.

38 2:22; that he nevertheless bore the sins of others, see 2:24; 3:18; cf. also 1:18–19. On this point see also Strobel, "Leiden," 424; Michaels, 227–28; Kelly, 166, although the last bases his arguments on Pauline theology, itself a questionable point. For more on possible Pauline influence, see the discussion of 3 below.

39 So, e.g., Frings, "Zu I Petr 3,19 und 4,6," 76; Feuillet, "Sacrifices," 711; Combrini, "Structure," 46.

that is, because of following God's will, not human desires as v. 2 makes clear, show thereby that their behavior is no longer ruled by such sinful desires. Rather, because they follow God's will, they suffer as did Jesus, and for the same reason. Such suffering for doing God's will was in fact identified earlier by the author as the Christian's vocation (2:20–21a) based precisely on the example of Christ (2:21b–23).[40] On the basis of that context, and the fact that Christ had already been identified as the suffering one at the beginning of the verse, preference is probably to be given here to finding the antecedent of ὁ παθών to be the Christian rather than Christ.

3. The origin and intent of the ὅτι phrase may be either (a) proverbial (Jewish) thought on the value of suffering, (b) a reflection of the Pauline idea of dying with Christ in baptism and thus dying to the power of sin, or (c) a construct by which the author intended to link the Christian's suffering to that of Christ since both are in that way accomplishing God's will.

a. As a proverb, the clause would bear some such meaning as undeserved suffering rightly endured purifies from sin, and would mean that those who suffer physically (σαρκί) undergo a kind of involuntary asceticism, and are hence less susceptible to a desire to sin.[41] Such an idea is most at home within a Jewish milieu,[42] where the idea arose that the suffering of martyrs at the hands of evil people can atone for their sin.[43] Such a meaning in this letter, however, would deny that Christ's suffering and death are necessary to redeem sinners, a point the author makes explicitly in a number of passages.[44] Thus the phrase is unlikely to bear that meaning here.[45]

b. To find in this phrase the kind of thought expressed in Rom 6:7[46] would avoid such difficulties, since that thought in Romans appears in a discussion of baptism where it is clear that the Christian depends on Christ's death for his or her own release from the power of sin.[47] In that case, our author here displays an understanding of baptism directly related to that of Paul, in which the Christian's suffering would refer figuratively to sharing Christ's death in baptism.[48] Yet parallelism to Rom 6:7 would only be valid if "suffering" here referred symbolically to "dying," which it clearly does not.[49] Instead, the emphasis here is the same as at 2:21: Christians are to be willing to emulate the sufferings of Christ at the hands

---

40 On this point, see also Combrini, "Structure," 46; Dalton, *Christ's Proclamation* (2d ed.), 223; Margot, 67–68; Brox, 192; cf. Wand, 103; Schwank et al., 80.

41 So Bauer (51): "unfreiwilliger Askese" ("involuntary asceticism"); see also Moffatt, 146; Holmer and de Boor, 138–39; Arichea and Nida, *Translator's Handbook*, 128.

42 Lohse ("Parenesis," 51) claims it can be documented only in Palestinian Judaism; Seneca (*Hercules Furens* 1262) knows the sentiment "morte sandum est scelus" ("death cures sin"), but such a source is unlikely here.

43 So, e.g., Best, 151; Strobel, "Leiden," 418; Selwyn, 208. Among passages most often cited are *2 Bar.* 13.10 (cf. also 78.6); 2 Macc 6:12–16; 4 Macc. 18:3. *1 Enoch* 67.9 may also bear on this question. Lack of any evidence that the readers are in danger of undergoing martyrdom for their faith lessens the force of such an argument; so also Kelly, 167.

44 See 1:3–4, 18–20; 2:24; cf. also 5:6, 10.

45 So also, e.g., Kelly (167), who in addition thinks the claim of such a proverb extravagant, since suffering may improve character but does not remove a person from sin; cf. also Dalton, *Christ's Proclamation*, 244. That it is drawn from the experience of the initiate into a mystery religion who had to go through terror and suffering before the goal of being filled with

divinity was reached, and represents a "feststehende Sentenz eines der verschiedenen Mysterienkulte" ("traditional aphorism of one of the various mystery cults"), as Perdelwitz (*Mysterienreligion*, 85) argues, is fanciful and lacks solid evidence.

46 ὁ γὰρ ἀποθανὼν δεδικαίωται ἀπὸ τῆς ἁμαρτίας ("because the one who has died is set right from sin"); Beare (179) argues for a proverbial expression, but finds it also in that verse in Romans; see also Dalton, *Christ's Proclamation*, 102; Krodel, 70.

47 E.g., Rom 6:3, 5; see also Rom 8:3; 2 Cor 5:21; cf. Col 2:11.

48 So, e.g., Dalton (*Christ's Proclamation*, 256), who finds 1 Peter here directly dependent on Pauline baptismal theology; see also Bornemann, "Taufrede," 158; Michaels, 227–28; Leaney, 58; Kelly, 168; Cranfield, 108. But see Brox, 191–92.

49 In the discussion of baptism in Rom 6:1–11, Paul never uses a form of πάσχω to refer to dying with Christ; the verb is always ἀποθνῄσκω. When our author refers to Christ's dying, he uses the same verb, as in 3:18c.

of persecutors. Again, "sin" ($\dot{a}\mu a\rho\tau\dot{\iota}a$) in 1 Peter refers not to a power that controls human beings, but to acts that go counter to God's will, as is clear in this context in v. 2.[50] There is therefore little basis for understanding this verse in light of Pauline baptismal theology.[51]

c. The clause is best understood in light of the discussion of the emulation of the suffering Christ in 2:21–24. Because Christ suffered (2:21aβ; 4:1a), the Christians are similarly to be prepared to undergo suffering (2:21b; 4:2), a suffering that demonstrates that the one who so suffers no longer acts in a way contrary to God's will, that is, by sinning (2:22–23; 4:1c).[52] That Christ in his death bore the Christians' sins is clear in 2:24, but that is not the point in this context. Rather, the point here is that the suffering Christians undergo at the hands of their ungodly opponents demonstrates that such sufferers no longer live in ways opposed to God's will.[53] Thus one who suffers in that way has found rest from, or ceased from ($\pi\dot{\epsilon}\pi av\tau a\iota$), sin.[54] Thus the situation the readers face provides ample evidence that, precisely because they suffer as did Christ for following God's will and not the (sinful) activities of their unbelieving contemporaries, they have in fact ceased from sin, that is, activities

counter to God's will.

■ **2** The purpose[55] of being armed with that kind of understanding of the relationship between Christ-emulating suffering and sin is given in v. 2: so that Christians live their lives in accordance with God's will, not human desires. The verse as a whole, with its antithetical parallelism contrasting $\dot{a}v\theta\rho\dot{\omega}\pi\omega v\ \dot{\epsilon}\pi\iota\theta\nu\mu\dot{\iota}a\iota\varsigma$ and $\theta\epsilon\lambda\dot{\eta}\mu a\tau\iota\ \theta\epsilon o\hat{v}$ and its artful concluding phrase, shows the literary skill of the author.[56]

The adverb $\mu\eta\kappa\dot{\epsilon}\tau\iota$ points to the structural contrast of "then" and "now," embodied in the content of vv. 2–3, a contrast that informs much of the author's discussion.[57] The contrasting rules[58] of behavior are given with the phrases "human desires" and "will of God." The first phrase ($\dot{a}v\theta\rho\dot{\omega}\pi\omega v\ \dot{\epsilon}\pi\iota\theta\nu\mu\dot{\iota}a\iota\varsigma$) describes life in conformity with Hellenistic culture, as vv. 3–4 make clear.[59] The author thus chooses a word ($\dot{\epsilon}\pi\iota\theta\nu\mu\dot{\iota}a\iota$) to describe the whole non-Christian culture that was used, for example, by the Stoics to describe what is irrational and brutish in human life.[60] God's will, the rule for Christians, includes the suffering involved in opposing the dominant culture, as 3:17 and 4:19 make clear, a point reinforced in 4:4.[61] The adjective that begins the final phrase ($\dot{\epsilon}\pi\dot{\iota}\lambda o\iota\pi o\varsigma$) is

---

50 With, e.g., Omanson, "Suffering," 445; Dalton, *Christ's Proclamation* (2d ed.), 223; cf. Blazen, "Suffering and Cessation," 40. What the author means by "sin" can be seen from the list of activities in v. 3.

51 With, e.g., Lohse, "Parenesis," 52; Holtz, "Dalton," 360; see also Brox, 197.

52 With, e.g., Schweizer, 84; Blazen, "Suffering and Cessation," 41; see also Omanson, "Suffering," 445–46; Grudem, 167.

53 Taken in this sense, it is not necessary to see the phrase as parenthetical, as it is taken to be by, e.g., Goppelt, 268; Blazen, "Suffering and Cessation," 36; cf. Michaels, 228.

54 Whether $\pi\dot{\epsilon}\pi av\tau a\iota$ is middle or passive, the verb indicates a cessation from sinning, as Blazen ("Suffering and Cessation," 39) observes correctly (see his full discussion of the possibilities, 38–40); see also Brox, 192. As a perfect, it indicates action still in effect.

55 Bigg (167) finds here the result of ceasing from sin in v. 1, and calls on Rom 1:20 and 4:18 as support. But as in the case of 1 Pet 3:7, and conforming to the imperative contained in v. 1, the $\dot{\epsilon}\iota\varsigma\ \tau\dot{o}$ here is to be construed with the infinitive $\beta\iota\hat{\omega}\sigma a\iota$ to form an articular infinitive of purpose.

56 So also, e.g., Selwyn (210): a "beautifully constructed

sentence." The content bears a similarity to that of Rom 6:12–13, which describes action resulting from baptism. While the language is different enough to rule out any sort of literary dependence, both our author and Paul may be reflecting a topos of baptismal catechesis.

57 With, e.g., Brox, 193.

58 The datives here may be classified as "datives of the rule by which," found also, e.g., in Acts 15:1; on this point see Selwyn, 210.

59 It is of a piece with 1 Pet 1:14, and refers to the reason why Christians can be called exiles and aliens in 2:11.

60 E.g., Dio Chrysostom *Or.* 5.16, 22; 4.89; 9.12; 20.24; 32.79, 90; 38.17; 49.10; 78/79.38; Epictetus *Diss.* 2.1.10; 2.16.45; 2.18.9; 3.15.11; 4.9.5. It was a common Christian use; see, e.g., Mark 4:19; Rom 1:24; Eph 2:3; 1 John 2:16.

61 Similarly, in Qumran, the leaders were to follow God's will (1QS 9.13), as Knibb (*Qumran,* 141) points out.

used only here in the NT[62] but it is commonly used with χρόνος or βίος in secular Greek,[63] indicating the presence here of a common phrase. The reference to "the remaining time" probably refers rather to the short time prior to the parousia,[64] rather than to the remainder of the individual Christian's life,[65] a point sharpened by the inclusion of ἐν σαρκί ("in the flesh"), which means here, as frequently in 1 Peter, human existence,[66] rather than the sinful nature of humanity.[67] That is, Christians must live in accordance with God's will, despite the suffering that may entail, for as long as human existence in its present condition continues.[68]

■ 3 Under the rubric of the "will of the Gentiles" (τὸ βούλημα τῶν ἐθνῶν)[69] the author explicates what he meant with the phrase "human desires" (ἀνθρώπων ἐπιθυμίαις) in v. 2. The conjunction γάρ ("because") indicates that this verse justifies the command in vv. 1–2 to arm themselves with an understanding of suffering so they no longer act in a way God does not approve. The

period prior to their conversion—that is the sense of the Greek ὁ παρεληλυθὼς χρόνος—when they did act in such a way was more than sufficient (ἀρκετός) for that kind of activity.[70] The presence of ἀρκετός may also answer an implied question on the part of the readers, namely, whether they must always forego, as Christians, participation in their former culture, or whether, for special occasions, an exception could be made. The author's reply is that they participated in such culture more than enough before they became Christians.

While no "subject" is given for the infinitive κατειρ-γάσθαι, it is in all likelihood an unexpressed ὑμᾶς ("you"), derived from the second person infinitive ὁπλίσασθε in v. 1.[71] That same subject is also presumed in the accusative participle πεπορευμένους ("proceeding [in]").[72]

The list of vices, similar in content to other such lists in the NT,[73] reflects a Christian perspective,[74] even though some of the individual vices are also condemned by

62 As Davids (150) also notes.
63 E.g., Dionysius of Halicarnassus *Dem. dic.* 30.79; Pseudo-Hippocrates *Epistula ad Ptolemaeum regem de hominis fabrica* 293.9–10; Iamblichus *Protrepticus* 27.9; 30.9; Isocrates *Nicocles* 58.7; *Archidamus* 46.7–9; *Ad filios Jasonis* (*Ep.* 6.9.3–4); Lucianus *Timon* 42.8–9; Lysias *Epitaphius* 71.3; Plato *Euthydemus* 293.5–6; *Menexenus* 248b.5; *Leges* 728d.2; 899d.1; 929e.8; 944e.3–4; Plutarch *Vit., Artaxerxes* 27.4.3; *Mor., De sera numinis vindicta* 563.D.2; Polybius *Hist.* 15.10.4.
64 With, e.g., Kelly 169; Strobel, "Leiden," 420; one may compare 1 Pet 1:5b; 4:7 for the same thought. It is, however, hard to see why Strobel ("Leiden," 420) finds a not insignificant parallel in 1QpHab 7.7–8, since the point there is that the time until the end has stretched out much longer than the prophets had thought.
65 As, e.g., Michaels (229) would have it.
66 With, e.g., Davids, 150; Selwyn, 210.
67 As, e.g., Goppelt (271) argues.
68 By contrast, Filson ("Partakers," 411) finds here assurance "that the suffering will not bring death, but that such suffering will cease before the end of the age," an assurance not unambiguously present, if present at all, in this verse.
69 This categorizing of unbelieving contemporaries under the term "Gentiles" does not indicate that his readers were former Jews, as, e.g., Bigg (168) and Calvin (123) would have it. Rather, it shows again the extent to which our author has appropriated the

language of Israel for the Christian community; see also 2:12. As Schelkle (115) notes, the vices indicate a gentile past; see also Michaels, 230.
70 The Greek ἀρκετός is a meiosis, with the sense "more than sufficient" or "far too much"; so also Beare, 180; Kelly, 169; Michaels, 230.
71 So also, e.g., Strobel, "Leiden," 415.
72 A participle from the same verb (πορεύομαι) but in the present tense (πορευομένους) is used with the same meaning in 2 Pet 2:10 and 3:3 (πορευόμενοι); see also Jude 16, 18. The phrase here, πεπορευμένους ἐν, is, as Bigg (168) suggests, very likely a Hebraism. It reproduces הלך ב, a phrase used to indicate proceeding in or by, often by God's commands, e.g., LXX Lev 18:4; Deut 8:6; 4 Kgdms 10:31; and often; but also in or by some quality, such as δικαιοσύνη, e.g., Isa 33:15.
73 E.g., Mark 7:22; Rom 13:13; 1 Cor 5:10–11; 6:9–10; Gal 5:19–21; Col 3:5.
74 Such lists also appear in Jewish literature, e.g., *As. Mos.* 7.3–10; 1QS 4.9–11; on occasion to describe gentile behavior, as in Wis 13–15; cf. Rom 1:18–32; Eph 4:17–19.

secular authors.[75] The point is not that Christians participated prior to their conversion in activities considered illegal by Roman authorities;[76] the phrase with which the list reaches its climax, "abominable[77] idolatry,"[78] is not a phrase used in secular literature,[79] nor is "idolatry" a category used by secular authors to describe religions, even those of which they disapprove.[80] Rather, the point is that the readers formerly participated in activities incommensurate with the ethical standard which they are now called to share. From that perspective even activities that would have seemed normal to the secular world are now recognized as evil. One need not therefore regard the readers as having been particularly dissolute. The point is simply that they lived in a way not in accord with God's will, however acceptable or normal such conduct may have been within their culture.

The specific vices, given in the plural to indicate categories of activities rather than individual acts,[81] are typical of the NT[82] and, given the repetition of ἐπιθυμία, here as one of a number of vices instead of in the general sense found in v. 2, may indicate traditional sources for the list.[83] The word ἐπιθυμίαις, used with three words indicating consumption of alcohol—οἰνοφλυγίαις, κώμοις, πότοις[84]—may mean "sexual lust."[85] The association of three words for drinking, followed by mention of idolatry, may reflect the pervasiveness of drinking, and drink offerings, in pagan worship.[86] The first vice named, ἀσελγείαις, in classical Greek meant "brutality," but in later writers it could be used more generally of any

---

75 E.g., drunkenness, see Seneca *Ep.* 83.17; Plato (spurious) *Eryxias* 405E; Philo *Vit. Mos.* 2.185; cf. LXX Deut 21:20 (I owe the references to Plato and Philo to Selwyn, 211).

76 So, e.g., Reicke (118): "prior to their conversion the Christians had participated regularly in the activities of certain organizations in Asia Minor, where excessive drinking and unlawful worship of Oriental or Greek deities took place and hostility to the Roman state was aroused"; see also Margot, 69. The traditional Christian nature of the list of vices simply does not permit such an inference.

77 The adjective ἄθεμις means basically contrary to what has been laid down, whether by gods or humans. It has the meaning "lawless" in Acts 10:28, but probably has a broader sense of "abominable" or "detestable" here, as Best (154) also argues.

78 Its climactic nature is indicated not only by the fact that it is the last named but also that it is the only one to have an adjective attached to it, as Best (153) too points out. It is also seen as the cause of all other vices in Wis 14:27 (cf. *1 Enoch* 19.1), a point adopted by Paul in Rom 1:22–31. The list is thus unlikely to be so arbitrary and trivial as Brox (193) wants to argue.

79 To call Domitian "dominus deusque" ("Lord and God"), for example, as Martial (*Epig.* 5.8; 8.2; 9.66; cf. 4.1; 7.5; 8.6; see also Suetonius *Vit.* 8.13.2: "dominus et deus noster") does, would be scandalous idolatry to Christians but politically correct for non-Christians. Such situations where "idolatry" was practiced encompassed virtually all public festivals of Greco-Roman culture, and most private celebrations, and could not be avoided by those who took part in that culture.

80 The notion of idolatry is unique in the Hellenistic world to the Judeo-Christian tradition; the word

εἰδωλολατρία is limited to Christian literature, as Goppelt (273) also observed. While Dio Chrysostom (*Or.* 31.15) can wonder whether God may not require images or sacrifices after all, that is not a common thought, even for him.

81 With Holmer and de Boor, 140.

82 Εἰδωλολατρία: 1 Cor 10:14; Gal 5:20; Col 3:5; see also Eph 5:3–5; Rev 21:8; 22:15; cf. Acts 15:29; 21:25; ἀσελγεία: Mark 7:22; Rom 13:13; 2 Cor 12:21; Gal 5:19; Eph 4:19; 2 Pet 2:2, 7, 18; Jude 4; ἐπιθυμία: Mark 4:19; Rom 1:23; 6:12; Gal 5:16, 24; Eph 2:3; 4:22; Col 3:5; 1 Thess 4:5; 1 Tim 6:9; 2 Tim 3:6; Titus 2:12; 3:3; Jas 1:15; 2 Pet 1:4; 2:10, 18; 3:3; 1 John 2:16, 17; Jude 16, 18; κῶμος: Rom 13:13; Gal 5:21; although πότος and οἰνοφλυγία occur only here in the NT, drunkenness under the rubric μέθη is mentioned in Rom 13:13; Gal. 5:21.

83 So, e.g., Goppelt, 272; Selwyn, 211. For the traditional use of a participial form of the verb πορεύομαι to indicate following an evil way, see 2 Pet 2:10; 3:3; Jude 16, 18. Although Spicq (145) is sure ("sans doute") that the verse was framed with reference to Deut 21:20 and Isa 56:12, it seems more likely to be based on broader Christian tradition.

84 The first means general drunkenness, the second festal gatherings, whether private and domestic or public and religious, the third social drinking parties; see Selwyn, 211; Moffatt, 149. The last two were not necessarily vices in secular eyes, but were rather a part of normal social concourse. Such events could, of course, get out of hand, as Spicq (145) notes, in which case they were condemned, as they are by Seneca *Ep.* 83.17; cf. 124.3.

85 It is used in that way with similar words for alcoholic consumption, including οἰνοφλυγία, in Philo *Op. mun.* 158; *Spec. leg.* 1.192; cf. *Vit. Mos.* 2.185; *Spec. leg.*

kind of lasciviousness,[87] and may be intended here in an introductory sense, as idolatry functions as climax.

The thrust of the verse is to describe Greco-Roman life as morally out of control, and to give Christian readers further encouragement to abandon that kind of activity in which they once shared, common in secular culture but contrary to God's will.[88] Such encouragement is necessary because of their secular compatriots' negative reaction to such abandonment, as described in the following verse.

■ **4** The opening phrase ἐν ᾧ is probably to be understood in both an anticipatory and a retrospective sense; anticipatory of the genitive absolute phrase μὴ συντρεχόντων ὑμῶν . . . ("you do not go along with . . ."), understood as having a causal sense that gives the reason why the contemporaries of the Christians are put off by their activity; and retrospective of v. 2 (justified in v. 3),[89] which instructed the readers to abandon their former way of life. The relative pronoun ᾧ thus has no direct antecedent,[90] and can be translated either "therefore," "because of this,"[91] or "at," "by this." The reaction of the nonbelieving contemporaries (ξενίζονται) is not so much "amazement"[92] as it is to be "put off" or "offended" by the strangeness of the Christians' conduct, which in turn estranges (the literal meaning of χενίζονται) the Christians from their contemporaries. It was precisely this aloofness from normal cultural practices that made Christians the object of contempt and persecution.[93]

What irritated the Christians' nonbelieving contemporaries is described by the genitive absolute: they no longer participate in Greco-Roman cultural practices the way they once did. While the verb translated "participate" means literally "run with" (συντρέχω), it is less likely to be meant literally[94] than figuratively, that is, they no longer accompany their contemporaries in general participation in cultural events.[95] It was this refusal that got Christians into trouble, and made it possible for the accusation to be leveled against them that their aloofness demonstrated their hate for all other human beings.[96] The activities in which they no longer shared are described, in keeping with the similar description in v. 3, as "the same outpouring of profligacy" (τὴν αὐτὴν τῆς ἀσωτίας ἀνάχυσιν).[97] The word ἀσωτία ("prodigality"), derived from the root for "saving" (e.g., σῴζω), means lack of any salvific quality,[98] in that way describing the excesses our author thinks characterize contemporary culture.

The reaction of those who are thus surprised by the Christians' unwillingness further to participate in cultural activities is "blasphemy" (βλασφημοῦντες), a

---

1.148; 3.43.

86 Following here a suggestion by Neugebauer, "Zur Deutung," 63.

87 Bigg, 169; cf. LSJ, 255.

88 Such encouragement would certainly be appropriate in the context of baptism, but its general nature does not permit one to conclude that it demonstrates that such baptism has just taken place, as do, e.g., Beare (180) and Kelly (169); Best (153) also doubts that it presumes a context of baptism.

89 That is the function of the γάρ which introduces the verse.

90 So also, e.g., Beare, 180; it functions rather as does the same phrase in 1:6.

91 So, e.g., Michaels (233) and Fink ("Use and Significance," 35): "therefore"; Goppelt (273): "darüber" ("about which"), Selwyn (212): "wherefore." To see it functioning in an adverbial way as it did in 2:12, as does Windisch (75), is to lose its force.

92 As, e.g., Bigg (169) suggests.

93 E.g., Tacitus (*Ann.* 15.44): Nero persecuted Christians because of their "hatred of the human race"

("odium humani generis"); cf. Minucius Felix *Octavius*, esp. 12.

94 But see Lippert ("Leben," 257): "mag zunächst wörtlich gemeint sein" ("may in the first instance be meant literally"; cf. also Selwyn (213): the author has public ceremonies in mind that people ran together to see.

95 With, e.g., Goppelt 274; for this use of the word, see, e.g., Dio Chrysostom *Or.* 4.119.

96 Tacitus *Ann.* 15.44: "odium generis humani." Tacitus did not invent that phrase for Christians; it was used by other authors in other circumstances, e.g., Cicero *Tusc. disp.* 4.27; Seneca *Dialogi* 9.15.1; Pliny *Hist. nat.* 7.80.

97 Whether the genitive case is objective (so Beare, 181) or not (so Goppelt, 274 n. 47), it serves to define the character of the "outpouring" or "excess."

98 See Luke 15:13; Titus 1:6; Prov 28:7; it is associated with drunkenness in Eph 5:18. On this point see also Selwyn, 213.

reaction similar to others our author has described.[99] The word is to be construed here not so much as an interjection ("blasphemers!")[100] as a characterization of the overall reaction of unbelieving contemporaries:[101] "blasphemers that they are."[102] Alternatively it may be construed as the introduction to v. 5,[103] thus providing the immediate reason for their impending judgment ("Because they blaspheme, they will have to give an account"). This latter sense is probably to be preferred. While the verb βλασφημέω can mean "defame,"[104] the fact that the result will be divine judgment (v. 5) indicates that the author probably meant the word here in its sense of speaking ill of divine matters, that is, blaspheming God.[105] When unbelievers slander the Christians, they also, wittingly or no, slander God.

This verse describes the key problem for Christians living in a culture in which religious observances, regarded as of great importance,[106] were inextricably woven into the social fabric,[107] covering everything from domestic[108] and agricultural matters[109] to cities[110] to regional assemblies (πανηγύρεις) for religious festivals.[111] The problem for Christians consisted in the fact that their new way of life no longer allowed them the kind of full participation in the religio-cultural activities that was expected of all people living within the Roman Empire,[112] a participation they had enjoyed prior to their conversion.[113] Such participation was impossible principally because every public festival involved to one extent or another religious activities that Christians could only regard as idolatry,[114] and in avoiding that,

---

99 Καταλαλεῖν, 2:12; 3:16; ἐπηρεάζειν, 3:16; λοιδορεῖν 3:9; ταράσσειν, 3:14; ὀνειδίζειν, 4:14; cf. also 2:8. On this point see also Lippert, "Leben," 258; Michaels, 234.

100 As, e.g., Beare (181) would have it; but see Kelly (171), who specifically denies such a construal.

101 With, e.g., Kelly, 171.

102 Thus construed as a participle of attendant circumstance; cf. Bigg, 170.

103 So also, e.g., Moffatt, 149; Michaels, 234.

104 It is used as a participle with that meaning, e.g., in Luke 22:65 and 2 Pet 2:12, and in the same structure as here in Acts 13:45 and 2 Pet 2:10.

105 With, e.g., Schelkle, 115; Windisch, 75; as a possibility, Goppelt, 274. See also Senior (75): they unwittingly attack God's own people, his "living temple."

106 E.g., Dio Chrysostom, who thought honors owed to the gods as of first importance (Or. 31.7), who regularly worshiped the gods at dawn (Encomium on Hair 1), and who held that sacrilege was worse than any other error (Or. 31.36); Plutarch counted among the pleasantest things festal days, banquets at the temples, initiations and mystic rights, and prayer and adoration of the gods (Mor., De Superstitione 169D). For a list of such observances, see, e.g., Plutarch Mor., Aetia Romana et Graeca; Ovid Fasti. Although Claudius abolished many of them because there was little time left for business (Dio Cassius Hist. Rom. 60.17.1), there were still a great many left over.

107 As Price (Rituals and Power, 120–21; cf. 117) observes, religion was not so much a private as a public matter, with all residents required to participate. Individuals manifested civic virtue by serving as priests.

108 E.g., gods of the household ("lares"; cf. Juvenal Sat.

11.137–40; 12.89–92).

109 E.g., the gods of the fields (cf. Martial Epig. 10.92) and the fields' boundaries ("Terminus"; cf. Ovid Fasti 2.655–58). Even the time a graft should be inserted into a plant followed a religious rule: under a waxing moon (Pliny Hist. nat. 17.24.108).

110 Marketplaces, town halls, and city council chambers could all be regarded as holy (ἱερά; e.g., Dio Chrysostom Or. 50.1), because of the presence there of shrines and statues of the gods, as H. Lamar Crosby (LCL Dio Chrysostom 4.312 n. 1) observes.

111 Dio Chrysostom assumed everyone would participate in them (Or. 40.28) and observed that the qualities of individuals are revealed at such national festivals (Or. 27.1). The implied threat for those who did not participate is clear.

112 Price (Rituals and Power, 111–13) notes that public festivals often involved processions, and people were expected either to participate in the processions or to offer sacrifices on altars outside their houses as the procession passed by; see also Tertullian Apol. 35.

113 That need not imply that Christians once took part in "boisterous debauches" (Kelly, 8) or "Saturnalian excesses" (Reicke, 118), or that they shared the wild, orgiastic rites associated with the cults of Dionysus or Cybele-Attis (Perdelwitz, Mysterienreligion, 92). Rather, it describes a culture totally at odds with Christian values, particularly in its all-pervading idolatry.

114 The point of the climactic ἀθέμιτοι εἰδωλολατρίαι in the preceding verse.

the Christians were of necessity forced into almost total cultural nonparticipation. In addition, veneration of the emperor had spread widely,[115] particularly in Asia Minor,[116] and where it existed, participation in it was expected of all residents.[117] It was regarded as a display of loyalty to Rome,[118] and nonparticipation thus raised the specter of treason.[119] Against that background, this verse is a further description of the kind of "exiles and aliens" (2:11) Christians had become within their own society, not so much as a political threat[120] as a social threat; Christians were seen as aloof, secretive, and "socially indigestible."[121] Living in a society that put religiously impossible demands on the Christians, they could only remain apart,[122] opening themselves to the kind of social ostracism and unpopularity that devolved upon all who upset customary ways.[123] Such isolation could, and did, lead to persecution.[124]

---

115 For further discussion of the imperial cult, see the Introduction § I.D.1.c, "Roman Policies on the Imperial Cult."

116 As Price (*Rituals and Power*, 78) notes, most modern scholars share this view; see also Magie, *Roman Rule*, 452. The fact that the emperor Gaius Caligula had earlier claimed divine majesty (Suetonius *Vit.* 4.22.2; cf. Gaius's accusation against the Jews for their not recognizing him as a god in Philo *Leg. Gaj.* 353), that Vespasian had declared on his deathbed that he had become a god ("vae puto deus fio," Suetonius *Vit.* 8.23.4), and that Domitian had himself addressed as "our lord and god" ("dominus et deus noster"; Seutonius *Vit.* 8.13.2) made participation in that cult impossible for Christians.

117 E.g., the cult of Domitian at Ephesus involved the whole province (Price, *Rituals and Power*, 198; see also the discussion in chap. 5, "Festivals and Cities").

118 As early as Augustus, worship of "Rome and Augustus" was encouraged, a worship accompanied by games and public celebrations, as Selwyn ("Persecutions," 47) notes. Tacitus (*Ann.* 1.78) reports that the temple to Augustus built in Tarraco (Spain) set a precedent for all the provinces. Tiberius in the same vein identified worship of himself with veneration of the senate (Tacitus *Ann.* 4.37). Special festivals that included public vows to the emperor were held each year on January 3 (Pliny *Ep.* 10.35, 100; Tacitus *Ann.* 4.17; cf. Naphtali Lewis, ed., *Roman Civilization: Selected Readings* [New York: Columbia University Press, 1951–55] 2.555; Price, *Rituals and Power*, 214–15), the anniversary of the emperor's accession (Pliny *Ep.* 10.52), and his birthday (Letter of Claudius to Alexandrian Jews 29–32; for the text of the letter, see White, "Ancient Greek Letters," 133–36; Tiberius would not permit it, however, according to Dio Cassius *Hist. Rom.* 57.8.3). See also the inscription from Ephesus (IGR 4.1608c; cited in Price, *Rituals and Power*, 105) that describes an assembly of all Asia, gathered at Pergamum, whose purpose was to make clear "all holy, fitting intentions towards the imperial house," in this case Tiberius.

119 Trajan's advice (Pliny *Ep.* 10.82) not to construe every slight offense against himself as an act of treason implies that that had previously been the case.

120 Price (*Rituals and Power*, 125) notes that Christians were primarily a threat to traditional cults generally and only secondarily a political threat with their subversive attitude toward the emperor cult.

121 The last phrase is from Selwyn, "Persecutions," 47. See also Wolff, "Christ und Welt," 335. For a summary of the things in which Christians refused to participate, from religious festivals and the courts where oaths were required to the theaters and other amusements, see Hardy, *Christianity,* 36.

122 Pliny (*Ep.* 10.96) notes that where Christians were numerous, temples were deserted, sacred festivals were no longer observed, sacrificial animals were no longer purchased. Minucius Felix (*Octavian* 12) reports that Christians are chided for "refraining from proper pleasure," under which are included attending the theater, taking part in processions, public banquets, sacred games, and food and drink offered to the gods; Tertullian admits he does not participate in such festivals as Saturnalia and Liberalia, does not wear a garland on his head, does not attend games, and does not buy incense for sacrifice (*Apol.* 42), nor do Christians cover doorposts with laurels nor light lamps for festivals (*Apol.* 35). As Lampe and Luz ("Nachpaulinisches Christentum," 211) note, the more the Christian communities consolidated themselves, the more they will have been obvious in their "antisocial" behavior. That that process of consolidation was already under way when our letter was written is evident precisely from 4:4.

123 Seneca (*Ep.* 14.15) notes that the wise man will not upset the customs of the people, nor invite the attention of the populace with any novel ways of living, a sentiment reflected in Wis 2:12–16. See also van Unnik, "Die Rücksicht," 308.

124 So also, e.g., Moule, "Nature," 8; Selwyn, "Problem," 258. Lampe and Luz ("Nachpaulinisches Christen-

■ 5 This verse provides further description of those people described in v. 4 who are taken aback (ξενίζονται) by the Christians' new mode of conduct and who react to it with blasphemy (βλασφημοῦντες). Such blasphemy cannot go unaccounted for, and that account will have to be given at the last judgment, which in our author's view is not that far off.[125] The phrase "give an account" (ἀποδίδωμι λόγον) is forensic language, and means to answer a legal challenge in court for some activity.[126] The one to whom the account is to be given is described with the idiomatic phrase τῷ ἑτοίμως ἔχοντι κρῖναι ("the one who is ready to judge").[127] The object of the judgment—"living and dead"—makes clear that this is a reference to the final judgment, after the dead have been raised to confront the judgment together with those still alive.[128] The reference is thus to those who have died physically;[129] it does not mean those living people who are "spiritually" dead.[130] It is difficult to determine whether the one to judge is God or Christ. On the one

hand, Christ is often described as the judge in the final assize,[131] and the traditional phrase "to judge living and dead" (κρῖναι ζῶντας καὶ νεκρούς) often appears as a christological formula,[132] arguing for Christ being understood here as the one ready to judge.[133] On the other hand, God is also understood in Christian tradition to be the eschatological judge,[134] and since in this letter the other references to the final judgment assume God to be that judge (1:17; 2:23; 4:19; cf. 5:10), that is probably also the way it is to be understood here.[135] That "living and dead" are to be judged, again an early stereotypical formulation,[136] implies that the judgment is to be universal.[137] For that reason, Christians can rest assured that those who torment them now will finally be required to account for their actions before the living God.

■ 6 Despite the opening phrase, which ties the verse tightly into its context[138]—the γάρ indicates that it is meant to provide justification for the assertions in v. 5,[139] while the εἰς τοῦτο points forward to the ἵνα

---

tum," 201) note that such isolation inevitably provoked mistrust and suspicion. It was nonparticipation in public festivals that caused charges to be brought against the quindecimviral priest Thrasea (Tacitus *Ann.* 16.22) and got Clemens, a Christian convert and member of Domitian's household, into trouble (Sordi, *Christians,* 52; see Suetonius *Vit.* 8.11.1; 8.15.1).

125 The persecution implied in v. 4 is the beginning of that judgment (4:17) which will soon include non-Christians as well (5:10).

126 λόγος here means simply an account, as it does in Matt 12:36; Luke 16:2; Acts 19:40; and Heb 13:17, where the same idiom is used. It does not refer to the blasphemers being held responsible specifically for what they said, as Michaels (234) suggests, citing Matt 5:25–26 par. Luke 12:57–59, where this idiom does not appear.

127 In this idiom, the verb "to have" (ἔχειν), when used with an adverb, carries the sense of "to be"; cf. κακῶς ἔχειν ("to be ill") in Matt 4:24; 8:16; 9:12; 14:35; Mark 1:32, 34; 2:17; 6:55; Luke 5:31; 7:2. The same idiom, combined with an infinitive as it is here, is found in LXX Dan 3:15; Acts 21:13, and 2 Cor 12:14. On this matter cf. Goppelt, 275.

128 With, e.g., Schelkle, 116; cf. 1 Thess 4:16–17; 1 Cor 15:52.

129 With, e.g., Best, 155; Beare, 181.

130 So, e.g., Bieder, *Höllenfahrt Jesu,* 125; for more on this point, see the discussion of νεκροῖς in 4:6. Kelly (172–73) is correct to call this interpretation "far-fetched and unnatural."

131 E.g., Acts 17:31; Matt 25:31–33; Luke 21:34–36; cf. Mark 8:38; Luke 12:35–36.

132 E.g., Acts 10:42; Rom 14:9; 2 Tim 4:1; *2 Clem.* 1.1; *Barn.* 7.2; Polycarp *Phil.* 2.1; on this point see Goppelt, 275.

133 So, e.g., Beare, 181; Selwyn, 214, 316; Best, 154; Leaney, 60; Dalton, *Christ's Proclamation* (2d ed.), 231.

134 E.g., Matt 10:32–33; Rom 2:6; 3:6; 14:10; cf. Luke 12:8–9; Rom 2:16; 1 Cor 4:5, where Christ (= Son of Man) appears as advocate or agent in the judgment over which God presides.

135 With, e.g., Windisch, 75; Michaels, 235; Goppelt, 275. That is, of course, the Hebrew understanding as well; in addition to OT references, see *2 Bar.* 83.7; CD 1.2; 1QpHab 5.34.

136 See the passages listed in n. 132 above; on this point, cf. Kelly, 171.

137 With, e.g., Michaels, 235. In Greco-Roman tradition, no clear line about such a final judgment emerges. Seneca is a good example of the ambiguity. On the one hand, in one of his tragedies he has a character say each will suffer for what he has done (*Hercules Furens* 727–36), and quotes another to say he is ready to give a reckoning to the immortal gods should they require it (*Clem.* 1.1.4). On the other hand, in another tragedy he has a character affirm that there is nothing after death (*Troades* 397–98), and he himself apparently held that reports of ills suffered after death were mere tales (*Ep., Ad Marc.* 4), perhaps because the gods, whose nature it is to do deeds of kindness, cannot do harm (*Ep.* 95.49).

clause[140]—the verse is replete with difficulties.[141] Among them are (1) the determination of who preached what (εὐαγγελίσθη), (2) the resolution of the ἵνα clause with its parallel constructions,[142] (3) the identity of the dead (νεκροῖς),[143] and (4) the relation of this verse to 3:19.[144]

1. Although lack of an explicit subject for the passive verb εὐηγγελίσθη[145] could suggest an impersonal use of the verb ("good news was announced"), the impersonal use is very rare in the NT,[146] and since the verb is regularly used elsewhere in an active sense with Jesus as its object,[147] a personal use is more likely here as well, with the implied subject being Christ ("Christ was preached"). The similar use of the related verb κηρύσσω in the passive voice[148] lends support to such a view.[149]

2. The μέν, δέ structure of the ἵνα clause indicates that the first half (μέν) is to be understood as subordinate to the second half (δέ), and hence carries a concessive force: "although they were judged . . . nevertheless they might live."[150] The conjunction ἵνα is to be taken as final ("in order that") rather than consecutive ("so that" or "with the result that");[151] it gives the reason why the "dead" have been "evangelized," namely, not only judgment but also life. A further difficulty in understanding this verse is posed by the three sets of formal parallels that designate contrasting realities: (a) κριθῶσι/ζῶσι, (b) κατὰ ἀνθρώπους/κατὰ θεόν, (c) σαρκί/πνεύματι.

a. The verb κρίνω can mean "condemn" in the NT,[152] but it can also mean simply "judge" in the broader sense.[153] Although this latter is the meaning it carries in the other times it is used in this letter (1:17; 2:23; 4:5), one of which is in the verse immediately preceding, and thus could be the sense it carries here,[154] a negative thrust is nevertheless implied by its contrast with ζῶσι in the second half of the ἵνα clause.[155] Whether it refers to the final judgment, as it does in v. 5,[156] is rendered questionable by the remainder of the phrase; it would be peculiar to describe God's final judgment as taking place

138 So also, e.g., Dalton, *Christ's Proclamation* (2d ed.), 226.

139 With, e.g., Bigg, 170; cf. also Kelly, 175.

140 So also, e.g., Best, 155; Selwyn, 214; Kelly, 175; Michaels, 238.

141 Luther (232–33) called it "ein seltsamer und wunderlicher Text" ("a curious and strange text") and was not sure that something might not have been dropped from it. Michaels (235) argues that it was simply a footnote to v. 5, and that its omission would not affect the meaning of 3:13—4:5 to which it was appended. Brox (197–99) argues that the material was drawn from a tradition presumed but never stated, and used here in a way only partially relevant to it, thus accounting for the obscurity.

142 Spicq (147) felt this clause so obscure that no sure explanation could be proposed; cf. also Brox, 196.

143 Although νεκροῖς occurs prior to the ἵνα clause, the determination of the identity of the dead rests to some extent on the meaning of the latter, and it is thus appropriate to defer its consideration.

144 For a summary of proposed solutions, see, e.g., Dalton, *Christ's Proclamation*, 42–51.

145 This form appears only here in the NT.

146 See, e.g., Kelly (173–74), who suggests that the only real parallel would be Rom 10:10, but even that is a somewhat different construction; so also Dalton, *Christ's Proclamation* (2d ed.), 232.

147 E.g., Acts 8:35; 11:20; 17:18; Gal 1:16; it is used with Jesus as subject only rarely (Luke 4:18, 43; 8:1; 20:1), and then only during his earthly life.

148 E.g., 1 Cor 15:12; 2 Cor 1:19; 1 Tim 3:16.

149 On this whole point, see, e.g., Kelly, 174; Spicq, 146; Selwyn, 316; Bengel, *Gnomon*, 732; Dalton, *Christ's Proclamation*, 268. Brox (196) calls attention to the difference on this point between this verse, where someone other than Christ is presumed to have done the preaching, and 3:19, where Christ is specifically identified as the one proclaiming. For more on the relationship between 4:6 and 3:19, see 4 below.

150 With, e.g., Beare, 182; Dalton, *Christ's Proclamation*, 275; Hart, 72; Michaels, 238; Kelly, 172; Combrini, "Structure," 47. To find the μέν clause parenthetic, as do, e.g., Spicq (147) and Selwyn (215), amounts to the same thing.

151 With, e.g., Spicq, 147; Eduard Schweizer, "1. Petrus 4,6," *ThZ* 8 (1952) 153. The natural subordination of the μέν phrase puts the emphasis on the ζῶσι with its future connotation: they were judged but will live. But see Schelkle (116 n. 1), who finds it consecutive in force.

152 E.g., John 3:17; 5:24; Rom 3:7; Heb 13:4.

153 E.g., Acts 10:42; 17:31; 2 Tim 4:1.

154 As, e.g., Selwyn (316) affirms.

155 With, e.g., Dalton, *Christ's Proclamation* (2d ed.), 237.

156 As, e.g., Frings ("Zu I Petr 3,19 und 4,6," 85) and Reicke (*Spirits*, 206–8) argue.

"in the flesh" (σαρκί) and in some way related to human standards (κατὰ ἀνθρώπους).[157] Its contrasting parallel, ζῶσι, which by reason of the remainder of the phrase must refer to true or eternal life,[158] could imply that death itself is the judgment here referred to.[159] Yet the understanding of death as the judgment on sin, while widespread in the Bible,[160] is not entirely relevant in this context, particularly if the phrase κατὰ ἀνθρώπους is taken to refer to the opinion of non-Christian contemporaries,[161] since such an understanding of death would be foreign to them.[162] It is therefore likely that the condemnation mentioned here must be found somewhere other than in the event of death.

b. While the phrase κατὰ θεόν appears several times in the NT,[163] the phrase κατὰ ἀνθρώπους is unique to this verse.[164] Κατὰ θεόν bears the meaning "in accord with God's will" (1 Pet 5:2; Rom 8:27) or "godly" (2 Cor 7:9–11), while κατὰ ἄνθρωπον can mean "on a human level" (Rom 3:5; 1 Cor 15:32; Gal 3:15) or, closer to the apparent meaning here, "according to, or based on, human standards" (1 Cor 3:3; 9:8; Gal 1:11). Since in this case the formal parallelism between κατὰ ἀνθρώπους and κατὰ θεόν makes it virtually mandatory that they bear comparable meanings,[165] the most likely construal would be "according to human/according to divine standards,"[166] or "in the eyes of human beings/in the eyes of God."[167] Such a construal is strengthened by the

likelihood that the author has in mind the abuse described in v. 4, abuse heaped on Christians that results when they are judged by the abusers' standards.[168]

c. The datives σαρκί and πνεύματι display the same contrast between divine and human that is encountered frequently in this letter (e.g., 1:14–15; 2:4; 3:12; 4:2; 5:10). They are probably to be construed as datives of sphere within which something occurs,[169] that is, judgment occurs within the realm of human existence, while life occurs within the realm of the divine. This latter is the final result of living in accord with the will of God (4:2).

3. There is conflicting evidence on the basis of which to identify the dead to whom Christ was preached. Most compelling is the use of the same word for "dead" in v. 5 in reference to the final judgment, a use that would imply that v. 6 singles out the dead to say more about their fate. In that case the reference is to all dead who will face the final judgment.[170] That they heard the gospel would imply that at some point it had been preached in the realm of the dead,[171] and a close relationship with 3:19 then seems at hand: this verse is simply an expansion on the point that Christ made proclamation in the ream of the dead, not only to imprisoned spirits, but to all the dead who died before his incarnation.[172] That would further answer the question of the fate of those who died prior to Christ's

---

157 In general agreement with Dalton, *Christ's Proclamation* (2d ed.), 237.

158 With, e.g., Selwyn, 316; Beare, 182.

159 With, e.g., Omanson, "Suffering," 448; Holmer and de Boor, 144; Dalton, *Christ's Proclamation*, 174; Bengel, *Gnomon*, 752; Bigg, 170. That it refers to a wave of persecution ("Verfolgungswelle") in which Christians were judged, as Bieder (*Höllenfahrt Jesu*, 124–125) argues, is rendered less likely by the aorist form of κριθῶσι, which, as Dalton (*Christ's Proclamation* [2d ed.], 237) points out, indicates a specific, not a continuous, experience.

160 E.g., Gen 2:17; 3:19; Wis 2:23–24; Rom 5:12; 6:23.

161 On this matter, see below, point b.

162 But see, e.g., Dalton (*Christ's Proclamation*, 74) and Selwyn (216), who find such a biblical understanding significant at this point.

163 Rom 8:27; 2 Cor 7:9, 10, 11; Eph 4:24; 1 Pet 5:2.

164 The form normally found is κατὰ ἄνθρωπον, not κατὰ ἀνθρώπους: Rom 3:5; 1 Cor 3:3; 9:8; 15:32; Gal 1:11; 3:15.

165 With, e.g., Dalton, *Christ's Proclamation* (2d ed.), 239.

But see Best (158), who argues that the parallelism must be sacrificed by understanding the κατὰ θεόν to mean "as God lives"; so also Selwyn, 215.

166 So, e.g., Selwyn, 215.

167 So, e.g., Dalton, *Christ's Proclamation* (2d ed.), 238; cf. Krodel, 71. The parallels from 2 Macc 7:14 and 4 Macc 7.19 that Selwyn (216) cites are somewhat vague. Closer is the contrast contained in 1 Pet 2:4, as Michaels (239) notes.

168 With Dalton, *Christ's Proclamation* (2d ed.), 239.

169 So, e.g., Best, 158. The dative of respect, assumed by Goppelt (277), would carry much the same force.

170 So, e.g., Beare, 182; Hart, 172; Goppelt, 276; Omanson, "Suffering," 447; Schutter, *Hermeneutic*, 69. Bauer (52) finds here the same point as Col 1:23, as does Spicq (146).

171 So, e.g., Reicke, *Spirits*, 204; Best, 155; Schweizer, "1. Petrus 4,6," 152.

172 For more on this point, see 4 below.

incarnation,[173] and at the same time provide a justification for God's universal judgment on all creatures: all had heard the gospel, and all could thus be judged by the same standard.[174]

Such a solution is not without difficulties, however. First, there is no indication in this verse that Christ was the one doing the preaching; he is more likely to be the subject matter than the agent of the preaching mentioned in this verse.[175] Who then are we to understand did such preaching to the dead? Again, one must ask about the dead to whom the gospel was preached. If they had died prior to hearing the gospel, it would have to mean the gospel was preached to them in the realm of the dead, yet any notion of disembodied souls in Hades is a view of the afterlife quite absent from the NT.[176] Further, it would clearly imply that there is a possibility of repentance and conversion after death, again an idea quite foreign to the NT.[177] In addition, if proclamation to those who died *prior* to Christ's advent justifies a universal final judgment on both living and dead, what of those who have died *since* the advent of Christ without hearing the gospel? That would pose a problem for a universal judgment that was based on reaction to the gospel, whenever our letter may have been written.[178] Finally, if v. 6 refers to the final judgment, there will be no condemnation involved in it. The sole outcome of the judgment here is eternal life in the divine sphere; there is

no mention of any rejection of those who have rejected Christ. That is once more an idea quite foreign to the NT, where the final judgment is a time of separation of good from evil,[179] when all must give an account of their actions during their lifetime.[180] The author of 2 Peter, who knew and wished to be identified with this letter (3:1), knows of no such single outcome of final judgment. Rather, in a comparable discussion of judgment, he presents the notion of a double outcome deriving from that event,[181] an outcome that our author anticipates as well (4:18).

Many of those difficulties could be resolved if the "dead" here referred not those who have died physically but to those who were spiritually dead,[182] the state of human beings prior to their acceptance of the gospel. Such a use of the word νεκρός for those who are, or were, spiritually dead is known to NT authors,[183] and is a solution favored by some early Christian authors.[184] It would mean that while the spiritually dead who accepted the gospel were mistreated by their contemporaries, they could nevertheless already live a life empowered by God's Spirit. Such a solution has the major drawback of departing completely from the context of final judgment discussed in v. 5, to which v. 6 is closely linked (γάρ), a context that clearly indicates that νεκρούς refers to those

173 E.g., Leaney, 60; Margot, 70.

174 See, e.g., Margot, 70, 71; Leaney, 60; cf. Reicke, *Spirits*, 208–9. But see Dalton (*Christ's Proclamation* [2d ed.], 231), who denies it on the basis that it is not the main point of the passage or of the immediate context.

175 As noted above in the discussion of εὐηγγελίσθη; in fact, there is no indication of agent here at all.

176 So also, e.g., Dalton, *Christ's Proclamation* (2d ed.), 234.

177 See, e.g., Luke 16:26; Heb 9:27; cf. Bengel, *Gnomon,* 752; Omanson, "Suffering," 447. Goppelt's argument (278) that the possibility of a decision on the part of the dead for the gospel is not appropriate here is not sufficient to wish away the problem.

178 With Dalton, *Christ's Proclamation* (2d ed.), 235.

179 E.g., Matt 13:30, 40–43. For that reason Knopf (169) finds it obvious ("selbstverständlich") that our author means only those dead who come to faith as a result of the gospel preached to them will "live."

180 Cf. Matt 25:34–36, 42–43; Rom 2:6; 14:12; 2 Cor 5:10.

181 E.g., 2 Pet 3:7, 9, 10–11; cf. on this point Dalton, "Interpretation," 554–55. Interestingly enough, the closest parallel to the judgment announced here is 1 Cor 3:12–15, where regardless of the judgment on a person's work, the person will be saved. It is notable, however, that Paul is addressing *Christians* who have built on the foundation of Christ. That represents a significant clue to our author's intention as well.

182 So, e.g., Jones, "Christian Behavior," 64; Bieder, *Höllenfahrt Jesu,* 125; Karl Gschwind, *Die Niederfahrt Christi in die Unterwelt* (NTAbh 2; Münster: Aschendorff, 1911) 36–39; Senior, 76; apparently also Luther (233): "Ungläubigen 'tot'" ("unbelieving 'dead'"); and Steuer ("1 Petr 3,17—4,6," 677): "Die Toten . . . sollen von nun an ein gottgemässes Leben führen" "The dead . . . must from now on lead a divinely suitable life."

183 Luke 9:60; John 5:25; Eph 2:1, 5.

184 Cf. Clement of Alexandria *Adum. Petr.*; Augustine, *Ep. Euod.* (164) 21 (I owe these references to Goppelt, 276).

physically dead.[185] An explanation of this verse which honors that context would be preferable to one that demands such a radical change in meaning.

An attractive alternative is to understand νεκροῖς in this verse to refer to Christian dead, those who during their lifetime had heard and accepted the gospel[186] but who had died prior to the return of Christ.[187] The problem of the fate of those Christians who had died prior to the return of Christ had arisen within the community at Thessalonica, and thus one cannot rule that out here,[188] although there is no indication either in the immediate context of this verse, or in the letter as a whole, that this had been a problem for the Christians in Asia Minor.[189]

What has been the problem in this letter is the fact that Christians suffer the rejection of their non-Christian counterparts for their belief. This verse is also to be understood in terms of such a problem. Understood in that way, this verse points out that within the context of the final judgment, Christians, who had suffered not only the obloquy of their contemporaries but also the fate of death that seemed to demonstrate the fruitlessness of the life of self-denial they led (v. 4), may nevertheless look forward to vindication in the final judgment.[190] It was

for such vindication, our author says, that the gospel had been preached to Christians who have subsequently died, so that although undergoing what amounts to divine judgment on sin, they will nevertheless finally be awakened to live in the spiritual realm with God.[191] While such an interpretation must take the νεκροῖς of v. 6 to be more limited in scope than the νεκρούς of v. 5,[192] the dead of v. 6 are nevertheless included among all the dead to which v. 5 refers, and to that extent v. 6 can also be understood within the context of universal judgment.

4. The broad reference in this verse to a proclamation to the dead has led many to see here a relationship with 3:19, either in the sense that both refer to the same event,[193] with νεκροῖς here to be identified with the πνεύματα of 3:19,[194] and the ἐκήρυξεν of that verse to be identified with the εὐηγγελίσθη here,[195] or in the sense that what was limited to Noah's generation or to imprisoned spirits in 3:19 is here broadened to include the human dead as well,[196] either in the sense that they too heard the proclamation to the spirits,[197] or in the sense that Christ preached in various places in Hades, thus both to supernatural spirits and to human dead.[198] Yet the differences between 3:19 and 4:6 in language and

185 So also, e.g., Dalton, *Christ's Proclamation* (2d ed.), 232; Wand, 105; Selwyn, 316; Bigg, 170; Frings, "Zu I Petr 3,19 und 4,6," 85; Schweizer, 87; Reicke, *Spirits*, 205.

186 The agency implied by the passive εὐηγγελίσθη would thus be those who had evangelized the area in which the readers reside, as the author had stated in 1:25.

187 So, e.g., Fitzmyer, "First Peter," 367; Grudem, 159; Krodel, 70; Selwyn, 354; Dalton, *Christ's Proclamation* (2d ed.), 234. Michaels (237) would broaden this to include OT righteous as well; but see Best (155), who specifically denies such an inclusion.

188 On this point see, e.g., Dalton, *Christ's Proclamation* (2d ed.), 230. While Christians who died are described in 1 Thessalonians as "sleeping" (forms of the verb κοιμάω: 4:13, 14, 15), they are also described as "dead in Christ" (οἱ νεκροὶ ἐν Χριστῷ: 4:16).

189 An objection to such a parallelism is also raised by, e.g., Brox, 198; Margot, 71.

190 On this point see also, e.g., Dalton, *Christ's Proclamation* (2d ed.), 228–29; Scharlemann, "He descended," 93. A remarkably similar situation is described in Wis 3:2–4.

191 So also, e.g., Dalton, *Christ's Proclamation* (2d ed.), 229, 231, 236; Selwyn, 215, 338; Kelly, 174–75;

Moffatt, 150; cf. Calvin, 126. The suggestion of Spicq (147) that it could refer to Christians who, despite persecution by human tribunals, are now more alive than ever in their faithfulness to God, founders on the reference to them as "dead."

192 Schweizer (87) thinks this is a decisive argument against seeing in v. 6 a reference to Christian dead.

193 E.g., Bigg, 171; Schweizer, 77; Holmer and de Boor, 144; F. H. Chase, "Peter," 795.

194 E.g., Schweizer, "1. Petrus 4,6," 154; Vogels, *Christi Abstieg*, 44; Cranfield, 110, see also idem, "Interpretation," 371.

195 E.g., Cranfield, 110; Chase, "Peter," 795; cf. Spicq, 146.

196 E.g., Cranfield, "Interpretation," 371; Wand, 105; Goppelt, 276.

197 E.g., Arichea and Nida, *Translator's Handbook*, 135; cf. Windisch, 75; Johnson, "Preaching," 49.

198 E.g., Schelkle, 116.

intent are substantial. While Christ is clearly the one who made the proclaiming (ἐκήρυξεν) in 3:19, in this verse he is at most the subject matter of the evangelization (εὐηγγελίσθη); no agent is mentioned.[199] The two verbs are of course entirely different. Again, it is quite unlikely that the supernatural πνεύματα of 3:19 are to be equated with the clearly human νεκροῖς mentioned here,[200] nor is there any hint of any limitation to the time of Noah in this verse as there was in 3:19.[201] The emphasis on the last judgment in the context of v. 6 along with the implied vindication at that judgment of those who have accepted Christ is far from either the context or the intention of 3:19, which appears in a passage whose emphasis is the domination of Christ over all supernatural powers, with no reference at all to the last judgment. It is therefore unlikely that there is any connection between the two verses, and each ought to be understood in its own context apart from any reference to the other, lest damage be done to the author's intention in both verses.[202]

The point of v. 6 is thus not to provide justification for God's right to judge both living and dead, nor is it to give further light on the obscure event described in 3:19. The point rather is the encouragement of embattled Christians, to assure them that their faith, despite their rejection by human beings and the death that has overtaken some of their fellow believers, has not been in vain. Rather, the same judgment that will require an account from those who have blasphemously opposed the Christians (v. 5a) will also see the vindication of those Christians who had undergone what appeared to their nonbelieving contemporaries to be the judgment of death, and hence the demise of all their hopes.[203]

199 With, e.g., Bieder, *Höllenfahrt Jesu*, 127; Dalton, *Christ's Proclamation* (2d ed.), 150; Selwyn, 337; Kelly, 173; Brox, 196.
200 With, e.g., Frings, "Zu I Petr 3,19 und 4,6," 79; Selwyn, "Eschatology," 398; Fitzmyer, "First Peter," 367; Brox, 196; Dalton, *Christ's Proclamation* (2d ed.), 240; Michaels, 237.
201 With, e.g., Reicke, *Spirits*, 209; Brox, 196.
202 So also, e.g., Dalton, *Christ's Proclamation* (2d ed.), 150. Scharlemann's opinion ("He descended," 83) that linking the two requires "some beautifully executed exegetical somersaults" may be rather polemically phrased, but is nevertheless correct.
203 Cf. Dalton, *Christ's Proclamation* (2d ed.), 229, 241.

4

Right Conduct among Believers

7 | The end of all things has drawn near. Therefore maintain a sound and sober mind for the purpose of prayer, 8/ before all else holding the love for one another that is fervent, because love covers[1] a multitude of sins; 9/ being hospitable to one another without grumbling; 10/ employing for one another as good stewards of the varied grace of God the gift each one has received. If someone speaks, [let that one speak] as [announcing] oracles of God; if someone provides service, [let that one provide it] as deriving from the strength which[2] God provides[3], so that in all things God may be glorified through Jesus Christ; to whom belong the[4] glory and the power forever and ever, Amen.

1 P[72], ℵ, P, 049, 𝔐 read καλύψει, evidently pointing to the future judgment; the present tense, found in A, B, K, Ψ, and a large number of good minuscules, including 1739, and some Latin versions, is probably to be retained. Michaels (243) suggests the future could be an assimilation to Jas 5:20, but notes that *1 Clem.* 49.5 and *2 Clem.* 16.4 retain the present (probably quoting this verse), and hence make that reading "somewhat more probable."

2 P, 𝔐 substitute ὡς ("as") for ἧς ("which"), probably influenced by the preceding ὡς.

3 614, 630, 2495, and a few other minuscules substitute the noun χορηγίαν ("abundance") for the phrase ἧς χορηγεῖ ὁ θεός ("which God provides"), producing a reading "as abundance (arising) from strength," evidently placing the emphasis on the person's own wealth rather than on something more immediately supplied by God.

4 P[72] omits the articles before δόξα ("glory") and κράτος ("power"), as it omits, with some other minuscules, the final τῶν αἰώνων ("and ever"); the effect on the meaning is negligible.

Analysis

This passage serves as the conclusion of the body middle (2:11—4:11) of this letter,[5] and at the same time as a transition to the body closing (4:12—5:11). There are certain similarities to the opening paragraph of the body middle, 2:11–12, which form with these verses a kind of *inclusio* for the entire passage. There is the common presence of a reference to the end (4:7a; 2:12c), and a reference to the glorification of God (4:11b, c, 2:12b), presented in chiastic parallelism.[6] There is also a common structural form containing reference to actions to be accomplished (2:11: παρακαλῶ . . . ἀπέχεσθαι; 4:7: σωφρονήσατε, νήψατε) with appended participle(s) (2:12: ἔχοντες; 4:8: ἔχοντες; 4:10: διακονοῦντες).[7] The doxology with which 4:7–11 concludes, and the ἀγαπητοί, appearing in 4:12 as it had in 2:11, indicating the beginning of the next section, confirm the concluding function of these verses. While some have suggested that the presence of the doxology indicates the end of an original document which has been included in this letter,[8] such a doxology is used far more often within the body of a letter[9] than as its conclusion,[10] and it is so used here.

5 With, e.g., Brox, 203. Beare (183) finds here "obviously a peroration," which "suggests the conclusion of a discourse." I agree that its language suggests a conclusion, but only of a section of the letter, not of an earlier document, as Beare thinks.

6 A: The end is near (4:7a)
B: Glory to God (4:11b)
B′: God to be glorified (2:12bα)
A′: Day of visitation (2:12bβ).

7 Although Daube ("Participle," 484) is inclined to interpret these participles as having imperative value, he admits it is possible to connect them with the imperatives of v. 7. The force of the prose would be little altered either way, since in either case the author intends the actions described to be performed. The absence of compelling evidence that participles were used with imperative value in the

Hellenistic period, however, argues for retaining their participial value here, as elsewhere in the letter.

8 For a full discussion of this suggestion, see the Introduction § IV.A, "Literary Unity of 1 Peter."

9 E.g., Rom 1:25; 9:5; 11:36b; Gal 1:5; Eph 3:21; 1 Tim 1:17; Rev 1:6 (word for word = 1 Pet 4:11); cf. *1 Clem.* 20.12; 32.4; 38.4; 43.6; 45.7; 50.7; 58.2; 61.3; 64.

10 Only three times in the NT: Rom 16:26; 2 Pet 3:18; Jude 25; cf. *1 Clem.* 65.2. On the whole matter of doxologies in early Christian literature, see Brox, 202–3.

In addition to serving as the conclusion of the body middle, these verses serve also as a transition to the body closing.[11] There is the reference to the impending end in 4:11, an event that then becomes thematic in the body closing.[12] There is also the shift in emphasis from the way the community must order its life in relation to the society outside the faith to a discussion of the life of the community in itself. While the bulk of the body middle has concerned itself with the relation of Christians to hostile pagans, the key to this final section, as it is to the body closing, is the way Christians must conduct themselves toward one another, an emphasis already found in these verses with their emphasis on mutuality.[13] This passage, like the body closing, is directed specifically to a strengthening of community life, the only source of strength for those caught in a social situation of bitter prejudice against the beliefs and way of life represented by those within the community.

The Christian traditions reflected in these verses also point to their emphasis on the inner life of the community. The reference to mutual hospitality (φιλόξενοι εἰς ἀλλήλους) is echoed in the NT, both in relation to the community itself (Rom 12:13; Heb 13:2) and to its leaders (1 Tim 3:2; Titus 1:7), as is the centrality of love and the call to love one another (ἀγαπ-, 4:8; see John 13:34; 15:12; Rom 12:9; 13:8; 1 Cor 13:13; 1 John 2:10; 2 John 5), and the reference to various spiritual gifts (χαρισμ-, 4:10; see 1 Cor 12:4–6, 11) to be used for the common good (4:10; see 1 Cor 12:7).[14] Other common themes include the call to be of sound thought (σωφρον-, 4:7; see Rom 12:3; 1 Tim 3:2; 2 Tim 1:7,8; Titus 2:2, 5,

6, 12), to be sober (νηφ-, 4:7; see 1 Thess 5:6, 8, mentioned in the context of 5:1–3 and the impending end; 1 Tim 3:2, 11; 2 Tim 4:5; Titus 2:2), and the importance of ministering (or serving: διακον-, 4:11; see Mark 10:45; Rom 12:7; 1 Cor 12:5; cf. 1 Cor 16:15; 2 Cor 8:4; 9:1). There are also some linguistic parallels with James (the use of ἤγγικεν in eschatological context, 1 Pet 4:7a; Jas 5:8b; the phrase καλύπτει/καλύψει πλῆθος ἁμαρτιῶν; 1 Pet 4:8b; Jas 5:20b) that probably also reflect common dependence on earlier Christian tradition.[15] On the whole, while common Christian traditions are in evidence, it is all but impossible to locate direct literary, or even traditional, dependence.[16] Our author swims in the mainstream of Christian tradition, a situation that he shares with the other, especially the later, authors of NT letters.

Comment

■ **7** The first phrase of the verse is probably to be understood as an announcement in the light of which the remainder of the discussion in vv. 7–11 is to be understood.[17] It continues the subject matter of vv. 4–5, that is, the end, and thus displays its continuity with the preceding discussion.[18] That the end (τέλος) mentioned is the time of the final transformation of reality is indicated by the emphatic position of "all things" (πάντων)[19] at the beginning of the sentence.[20] While there are other references to that eschatological time in this letter, they are cast primarily in terms of imminent judgment (4:17–19; cf. 1:17; 4:5) or the events accompanying the end (1:4–5; 5:10), including the return of Christ (1:13; 4:13).[21] The sense of the perfect ἤγγικεν

11 With, e.g., Michaels, 244.
12 E.g., 4:13, 17–18; 5:1, 4, 6, 10.
13 Cf. the references to "each other": vv. 8, 9, 10. On this whole point, see, e.g., Goppelt (279), although he argues, I think erroneously, that these verses begin a new section of the letter.
14 Interestingly, in 1 Cor 12:8 the initial spiritual gifts have to do with speech, as is also the case in 1 Pet 4:11a. See also Rom 12:6–7a, where prophecy (speech) and service begin the list of gifts.
15 Goppelt (279) finds this passage in 1 Peter close to that of Jas 5:7–20, with a common order of discussion of the end (5:8b), of prayers (5:13–16), of the need to do things for one another (5:16), and the reference to "covering a multitude of sins" (5:20). Yet the way the similar language is used in James (patience in suffering, prayer in its relation to illness,

reclaiming wandering brothers or sisters) and the examples cited there (farmer waiting for rain, Job and suffering, Elijah and the power of prayer) are very different, and call into question any close relationship of the one text to the other.
16 Goppelt, 280.
17 So, e.g., Schweizer, 88.
18 With, e.g., Goppelt, 281.
19 While the form πάντων could also be masculine ("all men" or "all people"), it is more likely here to be neuter, "all things," as D. Edmond Hiebert also notes ("Living in the Light of Christ's Return: An Exposition of 1 Peter 4:7–11," *BSac* 139 [1982] 244).
20 With, e.g., Hiebert, "Living," 244.
21 So also, e.g., Goppelt, 281; cf. Best, 158.

("has come near") emphasizes not so much the mere approach of the end as its presence in the end-time events that are already under way (e.g., 4:17), pointing to the imminence of the consummation.[22] The announcement of the imminent end using the stem ἐγγ- is familiar to early Christian tradition, reflected in the preaching of John the Baptist (Matt 3:2) and of Jesus (Matt 4:17; 10:7; Mark 1:15; Luke 10:9, 11) and in epistolary tradition (Rom 13:12; Phil 4:5; Heb 10:25; Jas 5:8; Rev 1:3; cf. 1 Cor 7:29; Rev 22:20 for the same sense but without the stem ἐγγ-).[23] Reference to the impending end is often used, as it is here, as the basis for paranesis,[24] since knowledge that there is an end of time and a judgment gives to the present its seriousness and its meaning.[25] Although the phrase πάντων δὲ τὸ τέλος ἤγγικεν is unique to 1 Peter, therefore, the point belongs to common Christian tradition.

The two aorist[26] imperatives (σωφρονήσατε, νήψατε) may well form a hendiadys, together pointing to the disciplined life necessary not only for prayer,[27] but for the kind of mutual life with fellow Christians described in the following verses.[28] The verb underlying the first imperative (σωφρονέω) describes the ability to see things clearly for what they are, and hence to act in a way appropriate to the prevailing circumstances,[29] in this instance the imminent consummation of the age.[30] The verb from which the second imperative is formed (νήφω) means literally the opposite of drunkenness, but is probably used here, as elsewhere in the NT, in the metaphorical sense of remaining alert and in full possession of one's "sound mind," particularly in light of the imminent eschatological events.[31] The word for "prayer" (προσευχή) is, along with its verbal form (προσεύχομαι), common in the NT, and is here used in its basic meaning of calling upon God.[32] The same concern for mutuality as a condition for effective prayer, described in relation to husband and wife in 3:7, is reflected here in the emphasis on mutuality found in the succeeding verses.

■ **8** The phrase with which this verse begins (πρὸ πάντων) reflects the opening word of v. 7 (πάντων)[33] in what is probably a rhetorical play on words: since the end of *all things* is at hand (v. 6) one should, *above all* else, cultivate love within the Christian community.[34] As the εἰς ἑαυτούς[35] indicates, the author here continues his practice of limiting the scope of such love to other

---

22 On this point, see also, e.g., Spicq, 149; Michaels, 245; Calvin, 127. The origin of the perfect is probably the appearance of Jesus as the last sign before the end; since his appearance the end has come (and remains) near.

23 On this point, see also, e.g., Michaels, 245; Hiebert, "Living," 244. The perfect form ἤγγικεν is used four times in the LXX, three times to refer to time; Lam 4:18 and 1 Macc 9:10 (ὁ καιρός ἡμῶν); and Ezek 7:4 (ἡμέρα); its use in Ezek 9:1 is not in reference to time. It is also used three times in the NT without reference to time (Matt 26:45–46; Mark 14:42), in each case to refer to Jesus' imminent betrayal.

24 Closest is Mark 1:15, where the perfect ἤγγικεν is used with a double imperative; see also Rom 13:11–14; Phil 4:4–6; Heb 10:23–25; Jas 5:7–11; for such paranetic use but without the stem ἐγγ-, see Matt 24:45—25:13; Mark 13:33–37; 1 Thess 5:1–5; 1 John 2:18–19; Rev 22:12; *Barn.* 4.9; 21.3; *2 Clem.* 12.1; 16.3; Ignatius *Eph.* 11.1. On this point cf., e.g., Goppelt, 281; Kelly, 177.

25 With, e.g., Schweizer (89), who notes that eschatological hope does just the opposite of robbing the present of its meaning, as is sometimes charged; see also Brox, 203. To diminish its chronological force, as, e.g., Goppelt (282) does, is to rob it of this power.

26 Spicq (149): ingressive aorist, "begin to . . ."; Michaels

(245): "programmatic," setting a course of action for the future.

27 Michaels (246) notes rightly that both imperatives refer to prayer, not just the command to be sober; cf. also Brox, 204.

28 With Beare, 184.

29 It is used in that sense in Rom 12:3; in Mark 5:15 par. Luke 8:35, it describes the cured demoniac, who no longer acts in ways inappropriate for his ability to live with others. On this point see, e.g., Goppelt, 282; Hiebert, "Living," 246.

30 With Schelkle, 117; see also Goppelt, 283.

31 So also 1:13; 5:8; Mark 13:33–37; 1 Thess 5:1–10; it is also used metaphorically in 2 Tim 4:5, but without eschatological reference. On this point see Senior, 77; Hiebert, "Living," 246; Michaels, 246.

32 So, e.g., Goppelt, 283. For a list of the terms used to describe prayer, see 1 Tim 2:1. Goppelt's (283) contention that this word is the most inclusive term for prayer in the Christian vocabulary would be strengthened if it began the list in 1 Tim 2:1; but see Matt 21:13, where this word is used in the phrase "house of prayer."

33 So also Michaels, 246.

34 So also, e.g., Spicq, 147. As Goppelt (283) notes, the same phrase is found in Jas 5:12, which points to its traditional origin here.

members of the Christian community (1:22; 2:17; 5:14). Love for those outside the community, or for those who do evil, as enjoined by Jesus (Matt 5:43–48), falls outside the purview of this letter, perhaps because of external and internal pressures exerted by the sporadic persecutions Christians were undergoing at this time. That such love is to be fervent (ἐκτενῆ)[36] repeats a command from 1:22, indicating the importance of that kind of love within the community.[37] A love that can be quickly cooled, or that is not able to withstand the rigors of an outside persecution intent on destroying the community, is of little use.[38] The participle itself, as regularly in 1 Peter,[39] is to be construed with the two imperatives of v. 7,[40] rather than being taken as itself of imperative value.[41]

The most puzzling part of the verse consists in the final four words (ἀγάπη καλύπτει πλῆθος ἁμαρτιῶν). While the notion that love covers sin is common in the Bible and early Christian literature,[42] the closeness of this formulation to the Hebrew of Prov 10:12b[43] and its almost identical form in Jas 5:20[44] point to the proverbial status of this phrase,[45] a status probably antedating both uses in the NT.[46]

What is not clear is whose sins are covered. There are four possibilities: (1) the sins of the one who loves the other are covered by that love; (2) the sins of the one loved are covered by the one who loves; (3) the sins of both the one loving and the loved are covered; (4) the sins of the one loved, which causes that person to repent, are thereby covered. While some have argued for (3)[47] and some for (4),[48] the first two possibilities have claimed the widest support.

1. The proverb can be taken to mean that one who loves contributes to the divine forgiveness of his or her own sins.[49] Some of those who find this interpretation persuasive see a similar meaning in Luke 7:47[50] or find

---

35 That the ἑαυτούς, here replacing the more usual ἀλλήλους in similar contexts (1:22; 4:9; 5:5, 14), is due to the influence of the second half of the great command (Mark 12:32 par.: ἀγαπήσεις τὸν πλησίον σου ὡς σεαυτόν), as Hart (72) contends, is difficult to validate.

36 With, e.g., Ceslas Spicq ("L'Epître [1 P 4,7–11]," *AsSeign* 50 [1966] 18), who indicates that it means intensive rather than extensive love. The presence of the article (τὴν . . . ἀγάπην) justifies Kelly's (177) assertion that ἐκτενῆ is "clearly predicative."

37 Its repetition probably indicates that here, as in 1:22, the emphasis falls on the need to manifest such love, rather than reflecting an assumption that such love exists and urging that it be fervent, as Hiebert ("Living," 247) and Selwyn (216) suggest.

38 With, e.g., Michaels, 246; Brox, 204.

39 See "Excursus: Imperatival Use of Participles in 1 Peter," p. 117.

40 With, e.g., Hiebert, "Living," 247. It is probably an adverbial participle of attendant circumstance, indicating the kind of action that must accompany being of sober and sound mind. It could function as an adverbial participle of means ("by holding . . . love"), though that seems less likely given the introductory πρὸ πάντων.

41 As, e.g., Michaels (246) would have it.

42 See Pss 32:1; 85:2; Tob 4:10; *T. Jos.* 17.2; Luke 7:47; *1 Clem.* 50.5; Tertullian *Scorp.* 6; Origen *Hom. Lev.* 2.4.5; Clement of Alexandria *Paed.* 3.12. In Tob 12:9, Sir 3:30, and Polycarp *Phil.* 10.2 "love" is expressed in giving alms, in Matt 5:7 in mercy; on

this point, cf. Beare, 184; Brox, 205.

43 Its distance from the LXX form of Prov 10:12b (πάντας δὲ τοὺς μὴ φιλονεικοῦντας καλύπτει φιλία; "love covers all those who are not contentious") indicates that it cannot have been the source; on this point see also Best, 159; Brox, 205; Goppelt, 284.

44 The only variation is that the verb there is the future καλύψει rather than the present καλύπτει.

45 Its occurrence in *1 Clem.* 49.5 and *2 Clem.* 16.4 may be dependent on 1 Peter, and hence cannot be cited as independent evidence of its proverbial status.

46 With, e.g., Kelly, 178; Michaels, 247; Schutter, *Hermeneutic,* 125; Selwyn, 217.

47 E.g., Goppelt (285), who finds it "ambivalent"; Selwyn (217), who thinks the two views are not mutually exclusive; Reicke (122), who asserts it "undoubtedly . . . has both meanings."

48 E.g., Leaney, 62. Leslie Kline thinks this could be the meaning of Jas 5:20, but prefers a different interpretation ("Ethics for the End Time: An Exegesis of I Peter 4:7–11," *ResQ* 7 [1963] 117).

49 E.g., Krafft, "Christologie," 125; Kelly, 178; Spicq, 150; Windisch, 75. Selwyn's argument (271) that because ὅτι in 1 Peter always gives the theological ground for an injunction, sins here must mean offenses against God, founders on the fact that that is not the case with the ὅτι in 4:1, 14, and that "sin" can describe an action against another human being (2:20).

50 E.g., Kline, "Ethics," 117; Brox, 205; Bigg, 173.

here an extrapolation of Matt 6:14–15.[51] It is also the meaning assumed in *2 Clem.* 16.4, Clement of Alexandria,[52] Origen,[53] and Tertullian.[54] Such an interpretation finds in a person's love for others a kind of "secondary atonement,"[55] an interpretation rendered questionable by the assertion of our author that sins against God have been taken away by Christ (1:18–19; 2:24, 3:18).[56]

2. The proverb can be understood to mean that the one who loves another overlooks by that act that other person's offenses, whether against the one loving or against others in the community, and thus "covers" them.[57] Additional support for this interpretation is found in the fact that that is also the point of Prov 10:12,[58] and reflects the thrust of Matt 18:21–22[59] and 1 Cor 13:4–7.[60] It is also the interpretation of the proverb in *1 Clem.* 49.5.[61] The context within which this proverb appears, with its strong emphasis on mutuality both in the first part of this verse (εἰς ἑαυτούς), as well as in vv. 9 (εἰς ἀλλήλους) and 10 (εἰς ἑαυτούς), argues persuasively for this second interpretation.[62] In order to maintain a strong Christian community in the face of the pressures that the author will discuss in the passages

following these verses, there must be mutual love and forgiveness within the community itself. Only in that way will they continue to exist as the kind of community whose life can bring glory to God and to Jesus Christ (v. 11b).

■ **9** The adjective with which the verse begins (φιλόξενοι) may have imperative force,[63] but it is more likely to depend, as did the participle ἔχοντες in v. 8, on the imperatives of v. 7, thus requiring, instead of an imperatival form (e.g., ἐστέ), a participial (e.g., ὄντες) form of the verb to complete its meaning. The force is as a result not so much a command to the readers about how they are to act as it is a description of the way Christians do act. The imperatival implication is there, but in less blatant form, as though the author wished to acknowledge and urge such action at the same time. To be hospitable, widely recognized in the ancient world as a virtue,[64] lay at the basis of the earliest Christian mission[65] and was also a widely praised Christian virtue,[66] particularly for church leaders,[67] despite the potential for abuse.[68] The reference here to εἰς ἀλλήλους ("to one another"), together with the other references in this context to activity within the community, probably

51 E.g., Moffatt, 153; Best, 159. Schelkle (118) calls on both Matthew and Luke.

52 *Quis div. salv.* 38.

53 *Hom. Lev.* 2.4.5.

54 *Scorp.* 6.

55 The phrase is from Bigg, 173.

56 On this point see van Unnik, "Teaching," 102. Hiebert ("Living," 248) sees this interpretation as "a form of salvation by works."

57 So, e.g., Cranfield, 114; Bengel, *Gnomon*, 753; Schiwy, 57.

58 E.g., Goppelt, 284; Neugebauer, "Zur Deutung," 82; Wand, 14.

59 E.g., Margot, 73.

60 E.g., van Unnik, "Teaching," 102; Best, 159.

61 It is also reflected in 1QS 8.2, with its emphasis on charity toward fellow covenanters.

62 With, e.g., Omanson, "Suffering," 448; Michaels, 247; Schweizer, 89; Best, 159.

63 So, e.g., Michaels (247), who cites as a similar construction 3:8, but the participles function there, as this participle does here, in dependence on an imperative, there in relation to the imperative of 2:17, here to those in 4:7.

64 See, e.g., Aristotle *De virtutibus et vitiis* 1250b, 1251b, there joined with such virtues as ἐλεητικός, φιλόφιλος, φιλόκαλον, φιλάνθρωπος (merciful, lover of friends, of good, of people); joined to similar virtues, Epictetus *Diss.* 1.28.23; as divine characteristic, Dio Chrysostom *Or.* 1.41; 12.76; Φιλόξενος was also common as a personal name. Although the word does not occur in the LXX, its substance is there; see, e.g., Gen 18:1–8; cf. Job 31:32; Wis 19:13–14.

65 See Matt 10:11, 40; Acts 16:15; 21:7, 17; 28:14; 3 John 7–8; *Did.* 11.4; cf. 2 John 7–11. On this point, cf. Kline, "Ethics," 118; Bigg, 173; Goppelt, 285.

66 Based on some sayings of Jesus, e.g., Luke 7:44–47; 11:5–10; 14:12–14; see also Rom 12:13; 1 Tim 3:2; 5:10; Titus 1:8; Heb 13:2; *Hermas Sim.* 9.27.2; *1 Clem.* 1.2; 10.7; 11.1; 12.1, 3. On this point see Brox, 206; Selwyn, 218; Kelly, 179. Kline ("Ethics," 119) suggests (see also Omanson, "Suffering," 449) that because of the ensuing references to spiritual gifts (χάρισμα) in v. 10, hospitality may also be understood as a χάρισμα here (as in Rom 12:13), but our author has not made that point explicit.

67 E.g., 1 Tim 3:2; Titus 1:8; *Hermas Man.* 8.10; *Sim.* 9.27.2; on this point see Goppelt, 285.

68 E.g., *Did.* 4.7; see Lucian of Samosata *Pergr. mort.* 11–13, where Lucian mocks the readiness of Christians to support fellow Christians even in prison. On this point see also Lampe and Luz, "Nachpaulinisches Christentum," 194; Kline, "Ethics," 119.

intends to center attention on hospitality within specific Christian communities.[69] It may well be linked to the potential friction caused by the need for the community to meet for worship in a private house,[70] something to which the final phrase, ἄνευ γογγυσμοῦ ("without grumbling"), probably a litotes,[71] may point. Such hospitality, whether here referring to Christians traveling from other areas[72] or to those within one's community, was a necessary way to express love (v. 8)[73] and to show support for one's fellow Christians who also lived as exiles and aliens in a culture from which they could expect no support.[74]

■ **10** While it is clear from the second half of this verse that our author continues to refer to all the members of the community, as was the case in the two preceding verses, the singular ἔκαστος ("each one") with which it begins makes clear that the author understood that every individual member of the community had in fact received a gift (χάρισμα) stemming from God's abundant grace (χάριτος).[75] Like Paul, the only other author to use the term χάρισμα, our author assumes that the life of the community is constituted by such gifts of grace, without which the characteristic functions of that community would not exist.[76] Further emphasis on the communal nature and goal of such gifts of grace is provided by the phrase εἰς ἑαυτούς ("for one another"), an emphasis also found in the catalog of spiritual gifts Paul provides in 1

Cor 12:7.[77] In fact, the point of this verse in 1 Peter is the same as 1 Cor 12:4–7, with the double emphasis on (1) individual gifts for the common good, and (2) their variety, though our author presents them in reverse order, with emphasis on the first point (individual gifts for the common good) in 4:10a parallel to 1 Cor 12:7, and on the second point (variety of gifts) in 4:10b parallel to 1 Cor 12:4–6. 1 Pet 4:11 then parallels 1 Cor 12:8–11, with their specific enumeration of gifts. Such similarity could lead one to find here dependence on 1 Corinthians 12.[78] Yet Paul's understanding of χαρίσματα was not uniform; while the gifts were derived from the Spirit in 1 Cor 12:7, they were derived from God's grace in Rom 12:6.[79] Unlike that passage in 1 Cor 12:4–11, however, where the gifts are derived from the Spirit,[80] but like the passage in Rom 12:6–8, the varied gifts here have their origin in God's multifaceted grace.[81] If our author was influenced by Paul, then, such influence will have been general in nature, combining the structure of 1 Corinthians 12 with the derivation of such gifts from Romans 12,[82] rather than coming directly from the discussion in 1 Cor 12:4–11.[83] Such a reflection in this verse of the broader dimensions of Paul's discussion of divine gifts may in turn point to the passing of that element of Pauline theology into the broader stream of early tradition, from which our author then derived it, rather than having drawn it directly from Paul's letters.

---

69 With, e.g., Hiebert, "Living," 249; Cothenet, "La Première Epître de Pierre," 145.

70 As, e.g., Rom 16:3–5, 23; 1 Cor 16:19; Col 4:15; Phlm 2; on this point see also Hiebert, "Living," 249; Omanson, "Suffering," 449; Selwyn, 218.

71 That is, a negative phrase used to express a positive sentiment, here something like "with gladness," as, e.g., Beare (185) suggests.

72 Harboring strangers in times of impending persecution could be dangerous, and hence could not be taken for granted, as Schiwy (57) and Spicq (151) point out.

73 With, e.g., Brox, 206.

74 On this point see also Goppelt, 285.

75 With, e.g., Schröger, "Gemeinde," 242; Michaels, 249.

76 So also, e.g., Goppelt, 286.

77 In the (later) Pastorals, such χαρίσματα are limited to officials (1 Tim 4:14; 2 Tim 1:6); our author is obviously closer to Paul on this point.

78 As is the case, for example, with Goldstein, *Paulinische Gemeinde*, 14.

79 See also Eph 4:7, and 1 Cor 1:7 in relation to 1:4.

80 1 Cor 12:7: ἡ φανέρωσις τοῦ πνεύματος ("the manifestation of the Spirit").

81 In light of this double tradition in Paul, it is not entirely appropriate to accuse our author of having no clear understanding of Paul's doctrine of the Spirit, as does Beare (186).

82 Selwyn (219) and Kelly (181) also call attention to this relationship to Romans 12.

83 Goppelt's argument (287) that the gifts are natural talents, preempted by grace, rather than gifts of supernatural origin as was the case in 1 Corinthians 12, is difficult to substantiate on the basis of the text of this verse.

Receiving such gifts lays upon each Christian the duty to serve as a good steward of such grace. While the participle διακονοῦντες has again been understood to have imperatival force,[84] it is probably better to see it as linked to the imperatives of v. 7, describing further the characteristics of those who observe the commands given there.[85] The word "steward" (οἰκονόμος), originally designating the purely secular position of household manager (as in Luke 16:1) and then expanded to describe one who undertook broader duties (e.g., city treasurer, as in Rom 16:23), is here used figuratively[86] in the former sense,[87] perhaps influenced by the author's concept of the Christian community as a household (e.g., 2:5; 4:17).[88] Being good stewards of God's grace involves therefore employment of one's gift for the good of the household of faith, not for one's own benefit,[89] surely an appropriate reflection on the nature of the mutual love mentioned in v. 7,[90] and an equally appropriate introduction to the further description of how those gifts are to be used in the following verse.

■ **11** The enumeration of the gifts that have been given to individual Christians is here limited to two, in contrast to Paul, who names more.[91] The limitation to two here is probably due not so much to our author's inability to reach the fullness of the Pauline doctrine of divine gifts[92] as to an attempt to provide the two basic categories under which all gifts fall, speaking and actions,[93] a division of activity already arrived at in the primitive church.[94] The verb λαλεῖν ("speak") can mean "babble" in classical Greek, a meaning still found in the NT.[95] Its more normal meaning there, however, designates such Christian activities as preaching and teaching,[96] a meaning it also has here as its association with λόγια θεοῦ demonstrates.[97]

The phrase λόγια θεοῦ bears the meaning "oracles of God" in the overwhelming number of instances in the LXX [98] and that meaning of λόγια carries over to its use in the NT (Acts 7:38; Rom 3:2; Heb 5:12). What is said by those with this charismatic gift must therefore resemble (ὡς) God's own oracles. How that is to be understood, however, is ambiguous. On the one hand, λόγια θεοῦ can be construed as nominative, in which case the phrase would be the equivalent of "Scripture," and would mean the person speaking must speak as Scripture speaks.[99] On the other hand, it can be construed as accusative, in which case it means that the content of

---

84 E.g., Michaels, 249.

85 The same is the case with ἔχοντες in v. 8 and φιλόξενοι in v. 9; see the comments on them above.

86 On non-Christian religious use of this word, see John Reumann, "'Stewards of God'—Pre-Christian Religious Application of OIKONOMOS in Greek," *JBL* 77 (1958) 339–49.

87 Jesus also used it to describe a faithful follower in Luke 12:42.

88 On this point, see, e.g., Kline, "Ethics," 120; Best, 160.

89 With, e.g., Schröger, "Gemeinde," 242. Cf. Schweizer (90), who emphasizes that such service is simply the result and overflow of grace already received.

90 So also, e.g., Goppelt, 287.

91 Nine gifts in 1 Cor 12:7–11; seven in Rom 12:6–8.

92 As, e.g., Goldstein (*Paulinische Gemeinde*, 16) would have it; Brox (208) correctly disputes such a conclusion.

93 With, e.g., Goppelt, 287–88; Hart, 73; Schröger, "Gemeinde," 242; Best, 160. It is less likely that they represent simply two examples of gifts, as Goldstein (*Paulinische Gemeinde*, 14) suggests.

94 Acts 6:2–4, although there "service" was limited to the distribution of food, not likely to be the case here.

95 E.g., 1 Cor 13:11.

96 E.g., Acts 2:31; 4:20, 29; 11:14, 15; 1 Cor 2:6, 7; 2 Cor 2:17; 7:14; 12:19; Phil 1:14; Col 4:3; 1 Thess 2:2; Titus 2:15; 2 Pet 1:21; 3:16; cf. Heb 1:1–2; 5:5, where it describes God's own speech. On this point see also Kline, "Ethics," 120; Kelly, 180; Spicq, 153.

97 With, e.g., Beare, 186; Schröger, "Gemeinde," 242. John J. Kilgallen sees it as similar to 1 Cor 12:8, which mentions as charismata a word of wisdom (λόγος σοφίας) and a word of knowledge (λόγος γνώσεως) ("Reflections on Charisma[ta] in the New Testament," *Studia Missionalia* 41 [1992] 312).

98 E.g., Num 24:4, 16; LXX Ps 106:11; cf. also λόγια κυρίου: LXX Pss 11:7; 17:31; 104:19. See also the many references to τὸ λόγιον/τὰ λόγια σου = λόγια θεοῦ in LXX Ps 118; so also Deut 33:9; Isa 28:13 combines θεοῦ and κυρίου; cf. also Isa 5:24; 30:27.

99 So, e.g., Bigg, 174.

one's speech must bear the character of God's words and thus the divine intention, not the speaker's own.[100] The latter is the more likely as its parallelism to the next phrase on service indicates: as that phrase implies an imperative "let him serve," so this phrase implies an imperative "let him speak," for which then "oracles of God" would have to serve as object.[101] The point would then be the same as that of 2 Cor 2:17.[102]

Words derived from the root διακον-[103] are common in the NT[104] and can describe either the totality of Christian ministrations (e.g., Rom 11:13; 15:31; 1 Cor 12:5; 2 Cor 5:18; 6:3; Eph 4:12), or the administration of alms and attendance to physical needs (e.g., 1 Cor 16:15; 2 Cor 8:4). The contrast in this context with speaking shows that the narrower meaning is intended here,[105] describing those forms of Christian ministry other than speech which are done for the benefit of fellow Christians.[106] As the divine gift of speaking is to bear God's own seriousness and intention, so the divine gift of ministration is to be done from divine strength, and so also reflect God's intentions. The further implication would be that as those who hear Christian speech are to accept it as God's own speaking, so those who are served are to accept it as service deriving ultimately from God.[107]

The purpose of the exercise of divine gifts is expressed in the ἵνα clause: such use of gifts is to contribute to the universal (ἐν πᾶσιν)[108] glory of God.[109] That such ascription of glory to God is done διὰ Ἰησοῦ Χριστοῦ ("through Jesus Christ") means not that Christ praises God, but that Christ makes it possible for Christians to do so through the exercise of their gifts.[110]

The ensuing doxology, introduced with the dative pronoun ᾧ,[111] could, as masculine singular, have as its antecedent either Christ or God. On the one hand, the word order, with the immediately preceding "Jesus Christ," argues for him as the antecedent,[112] a point supported by the fact that doxologies ascribed to Christ do occur in the NT.[113] On the other hand, the fact that in the preceding phrase, God is the one to be glorified would argue for God as the antecedent, a point supported by a similar statement at the beginning of this section of the letter (2:12), and a similar doxology directed to God at the close of the third section (5:11), a point supported by the fact that the majority of doxologies in the NT are offered to God.[114] The context of God as the one to be glorified would argue for θεός as the antecedent.[115] The presence of the indicative verb ἐστιν makes the doxology a statement rather than allowing it the precatory force that most other NT doxologies

---

100 So, e.g., Beare, 186; Selwyn, 219; Margot, 74–75; Goppelt, 289; Hiebert, "Living," 251.

101 With, e.g., Selwyn, 219.

102 Cf. also 2 Cor 5:12; 1 Cor 2:2.

103 Διάκονος, "servant"; διακονέω, "to serve"; διακονία, "service."

104 They occur some eighty-nine times. In the LXX such words occur only seven times, and without any sense of divine ministry.

105 With, e.g., Hiebert, "Living," 251; cf. Rom 12:7.

106 So also, e.g., Spicq, 153. To limit it to caring for the sick and poor, as Schröger ("Gemeinde," 242) suggests, is to limit it unnecessarily, although such care is surely also included.

107 The structure of the descriptions of both gifts puts the emphasis on God: *God's* words, *God's* empowerment for service, as Michaels (251) correctly notes.

108 Here to be understood as neuter, as in Rom 11:36; 1 Cor 10:31. On this point see also Beare, 187; Schelkle, 120.

109 That is also to be the effect on secular society of Christian action, as the author pointed out at the beginning of this section, in 2:12. On this point see also Goppelt, 291.

110 With, e.g., Michaels, 252.

111 The following indicative ἐστιν gives to the dative here the force of possession: "whose is" or "to whom belong."

112 So, e.g., Bigg, 176; Michaels, 253; Schweizer, 91; Hart, 73.

113 2 Tim 4:18; 2 Pet 3:18; Rev 1:6; Selwyn (220) also cites *1 Clem.* 20.12 and 50.7, although they are not without ambiguity.

114 E.g., Luke 2:14; Rom 1:25; 11:36; 16:27; 2 Cor 11:31; Eph 3:21; Phil 4:20; 1 Tim 1:17; 2 Tim 4:18; Heb 13:21; Jude 25.

115 With, e.g., Best, 161; Hiebert, "Living," 252; Kelly, 181; Schelkle, 120; Windisch, 76; Goppelt, 291; Shimada, *Formulary Material*, 396. Fitzmyer ("First Peter," 368) argues, unconvincingly I think, that the doxology is addressed to God "through" Christ, but also "to" Christ, thus making the doxology, in this double aspect, unique in the NT.

appear to have.[116] The elements in the doxology, "glory" (δόξα) and "power" (κράτος), are found in only one other NT doxology (Rev 1:6), but one or the other or both also appear in combination with other elements both in the NT[117] and in the LXX.[118]

The conclusion of the doxology with the word ἀμήν[119] follows a practice attested in the OT and other Jewish literature, where the word can be used to affirm what has been said,[120] but is more commonly employed as a response, public or private, to a curse,[121] to a prayer,[122] to a blessing or praise of God, whether public[123] or private,[124] or to a doxology.[125] These uses are then carried over into the NT: affirmation,[126] praise,[127] prayer,[128] but the chief use of the word as response is, as in this verse, at the conclusion of doxologies.[129] The

presence of the doxology here does not provide conclusive evidence that a document incorporated into our epistle ended at this point.[130] While in three instances a doxology does conclude a document in the NT,[131] it is far more commonly found within the document itself.[132] It is therefore best to understand it as concluding a section of the letter here, but not as an indication of the conclusion of a formerly independent source incorporated into 1 Peter by the author.[133]

---

116 With Shimada (*Formulary Material*, 411), who cites Matt 6:13b; Rev 4:11; 5:12b as other examples of doxological statement. Goppelt's assertion (291) that the Pauline doxologies are indicative in tone, based on the two that have a form of the verb εἶναι (Rom 1:25; 2 Cor 11:31), is more ambiguous than he assumes. In their context, they could as well be precatory, as Shimada (*Formulary Material*, 411) argues.

117 E.g., 1 Tim 1:17; 6:16; Jude 25; Rev 4:9, 11; 5:13; 7:12; on this point, see, e.g., Beare, 187; Goppelt, 291. In most Pauline doxologies, δόξα alone appears, as Shimada (*Formulary Material*, 410) notes.

118 E.g., 1 Chr 19:11; Pss 28:1; 95:7–8; Job 37:22; 1 Bar 2:18.

119 Heb. אמן, from a verb meaning, in the Niphal, "reliable."

120 1 Kings 1:36; Jer 28:6; Neh 5:12.

121 Num 5:22; Deut 27:15–26.

122 Tob 8:8.

123 1 Chr 16:36; Ps 106:48; 1 Esd 9:47; 2 Esd 15:13; 18:6; 3 Macc 7:23; 1QS 1.18b–20.

124 Pss 41:13; 72:19; 89:53.

125 4 Macc 18:24.

126 The most common form of affirmation is found in the Gospels, where ἀμήν is used to introduce a solemn asseveration, e.g., Matt 5:18; Mark 3:27

Luke 4:24; John 1:51; as a response, it is found in 2 Cor 1:20; Eph 3:21; Rev 1:7; 22:20.

127 Rom 1:25; 9:5.

128 Rom 15:23; 1 Cor 14:16; Gal 6:18.

129 Rom 11:36; 16:27; Gal 1:5; Phil 4:20; 1 Tim 1:17; 6:16; 2 Tim 4:18; Heb 13:21; 1 Pet 5:11; 2 Pet 3:18; Jude 25; Rev 1:6; 5:14; 7:12; 19:4.

130 Normally thought to be a baptismal discourse, as, e.g., Beare, 187.

131 Rom 16:27; Jude 25; 2 Pet 3:18; cf. *1 Clem.* 65.2.

132 Rom 11:36; Gal 1:5; Eph 3:21; Phil 4:20; Rev 1:6; 5:13; 7:12; cf. *1 Clem.* 20.12; 32.4; 38.4; 43.6; 45.7; 50.7; 58.2; 61.3; 64; *1 Enoch* 48.10.

133 With, e.g., de Villiers, "Joy," 79; Kelly, 182; Shimada, *Formulary Material*, 415. Goppelt (291) notes that ἀμήν is not usual as the conclusion of either a letter or a sermon. For more thorough discussion of this point, see the Introduction § IV.A, "Literary Unity of 1 Peter."

300

Structure

This portion of the letter is the shortest of the three parts of the body of the letter, although it is closer in length to the body opening than to the body middle.[1] Thus there is a rough symmetry of short/long/short to the major part of the letter. The language of the body closing is somewhat more straightforward, with proportionately more indicative and imperative verbs and fewer participles, particularly adverbial participles, than the previous two parts. That imparts to this section something of the flavor of a final and summarizing admonition to the readers.[2]

Like the body opening and body middle, this section begins with a command,[3] and like the middle, begins with the vocative ἀγαπητοί ("beloved," 2:11; 4:12)[4] and ends with a doxology (4:11; 5:11). The epistolary conclusion that begins with 5:12 confirms 5:11 as the limit of the body closing. The passage is bound together by the frequent references to suffering, particularly by the threefold use of τὰ παθήματα ("the sufferings," τοῖς τοῦ Χριστοῦ παθήματα, 4:13; τῶν τοῦ χριστοῦ παθημάτων, 5:1; τὰ αὐτὰ τῶν παθημάτων, 5:9), but also by the references to οἱ πάσχοντες ("those who suffer," 4:19) and παθόντας ("after suffering," 5:10).

The body closing divides itself into three parts, with the second (5:1–5), with its emphasis on Christian behavior within the community, separating the first (4:12–19) and third (5:6–9), with their emphasis on the suffering of the Christians.[5] The structure of the passage is thus aba': a = 4:12–19, Christian suffering in eschatological context (non-Christians will also suffer); b = 5:1–6, appropriate conduct of elders, younger people, all Christians; a' = 5:7–11, appropriate conduct in eschatological suffering (God will sustain suffering Christians). a and a' are thus directed outward, to the suffering experienced outside the community, while b is directed inward, to appropriate behavior within the Christian community.

Thus the passage can be divided into three parts, each part in its turn capable of being seen in three segments, a division made more on the basis of content than linguistic structures, although the latter also play a role.

I. 4:12–19 Suffering of Christians in Present and Eschatological Context
   A. 4:12–13 Suffering of Christians and joy
      1. 4:12 Christian suffering nothing strange
      2. 4:13a Christian suffering brings joy now
      3. 4:13b Christian suffering brings joy in future
   B. 4:14–16 Suffering of Christians as Christians
      1. 4:14 As Christian, to obtain blessing
      2. 4:15 Not as outlaw
      3. 4:16 As Christian, to glorify God
   C. 4:17–19 Suffering of Christians as prelude to final judgment
      1. 4:17a Judgment begins with house of God
      2. 4:17b-18 Fate of non-Christians
      3. 4:19 Appropriate conduct for suffering Christians
II. 5:1–6 Appropriate Conduct in Community
   A. 5:1–4 Conduct of elders
      1. 5:1 Identification of elder who exhorts
      2. 5:2–3 Appropriate conduct for elders
      3. 5:4 Reward of appropriate conduct
   B. 5:5a Conduct of young people
   C. 5:5b Conduct of all
III. 5:6–9 Appropriate Conduct in Eschatological Suffering
   A. 5:6–7 Toward God
      1. 5:6 Be humble
      2. 5:7 Cast care on him
   B. 5:8–9 Toward the devil
      1. 5:8 He seeks you
      2. 4:9 Resist him as do all
   C. 5:10–11 Conclusion
      1. 5:10 Divine help in suffering
      2. 5:11 Doxology

Theological Thrust

Two themes already treated at some length in the body middle, the conduct of Christians within their community (2:18—3:7) and the suffering they must endure within a hostile society (3:8—4:11), are to be found in the body closing (suffering: 4:12–19; 5:6–11; conduct with the community, 5:1–5), with more emphasis here on Christian suffering. In addition, a number of points made in the earlier portion of the letter are picked up once more in this final part of the letter: 4:12, fire as a

---

1   The body opening has approximately 356 words, the body middle 773, the body closing 289.

2   For a discussion of the close relationship between the concluding section of the body middle (4:7–11) and the opening section of the body closing (4:12–19) see Schutter, *Hermeneutic*, 74–76.

3   1:13, ἐλπίσατε; 2:11, παρακαλῶ . . . ἀπέχεσθαι; 4:12, μὴ ξενίζεσθε.

4   A point noted also by, e.g., Goppelt, 296; Michaels, 257.

5   The first and third sections each end with a participial reference to suffering Christians: 4:19, οἱ πάσχοντες, 5:10, ὑμᾶς . . . πάθωντας.

301

metaphor for testing (1:7); 4:13a, suffering as followers of suffering Christ (2:19–23); 4:13b, joy as result of suffering (1:6; note the repetition of the words ἀγαλλιάω and πειρασμός); 4:14–16, the suffering of Christians as Christians (3:16–17; 4:4–5); 4:17, nearness of the end (4:7); 4:19, suffering a part of God's will for Christians (3:14–17; 4:1–2); 5:1–5, appropriate conduct for Christians (2:18–3:7); 5:5a, subordination (cf. humility, 5:5b, 6) within the community (2:18; 3:1); 5:8, command to be sober (4:7).

Two new considerations are introduced, however, with respect to Christian suffering. They are the announcement that Christian suffering, universal in its scope (5:9), represents the beginning of the final judgment, which will then be extended to include those outside the community (4:17–19), and the identification of the devil as the true adversary of the Christians (5:8–9). Knowing the extent of the suffering gives Christians the comfort that they have not alone been singled out for such treatment, and knowing that such suffering will, as part of God's final judgment, soon be extended to non-Christians as well, gives the further comfort that their suffering is the beginning of the end for the society that oppresses them, since it will be eliminated in God's final judgment. The identification of the devil as their true adversary informs Christians of the seriousness of their struggle, which is now to be understood as part of the warfare between God and the powers of evil, but it also gives them the comfort of knowing that Christ has already triumphed over the powers of evil (3:19, 22), and that in due time that victory will also be shared by the Christians (cf. 5:6b).

In the midst of such suffering,[6] elders of the Christian communities must exercise appropriate leadership lest the communities be crushed by events imposed from the outside. Such leadership strengthens the community and requires due subordination to the elders by those younger; yet elders are to be shepherds, not dictators, and humility on the part of all members of the community is the appropriate stance. Strengthened by such a community, Christians will be able to withstand the assaults even of Satan himself, confident that God will sustain them in these trials.

---

6   One wonders if it is mere happenstance that the section on pastoral duties (5:1–5) finds its place in the midst of the two segments that describe suffering (4:12–19; 5:6–11).

4 Christian Suffering in Eschatological Context

12 Do not be taken aback at[1] the burning that has come upon you to test you, as though something strange were happening to you; 13/ rather, as you share in the sufferings of Christ, you must rejoice, in order that you may also rejoice with great joy at the revelation of his glory. 14/ When you are reviled because of the name of Christ, you are blessed, because God's glorious Spirit[2] rests[3] upon you.[4] 15/ Now let no one of you suffer as a murderer, or a thief, or an evildoer, or as one who defrauds others,[5] 16/ but when you suffer as a Christian, do not be ashamed, but glorify God by means of that name,[6] 17/ because it is now time

1 The ἐπί that introduces the phrase τῇ ἐν ὑμῖν πυρώσει in P[72] and some other MSS. simply reinforces the burning as the reason for the reaction of the readers.

2 Some MSS. (ℵ*, A, P, 33, 81, 1241, 1739, and many other minuscules, along with some Latin versions and one Coptic version) insert an additional καὶ δυναμέως between δόξης and καὶ, making it read "the spirit of glory and power and the spirit of God." Here the shorter reading (P[72], B, K, L, Ψ, many other minuscules, Tertullian, and Clement of Alexandria) is to be preferred as less overweighted; so also, e.g., Schelkle, 124 n. 2: "kommentierende Glosse" ("commentating gloss"). Windisch (77) wonders whether καὶ τὸ τοῦ θεοῦ or καὶ τό might be an interpolation; their deletion would simplify the sentence but has no MS. evidence to support it.

3 For the present ἀναπαύεται (ℵ*, B, P, 𝔐, lat; Tert, Cl) some MSS. (A, Ψ, 81, 1243, 1505, 1852, some others) read the additionally compounded ἐπαναπαύεται, perhaps influenced by the preceding ἐφ' ὑμῖν; some other MSS. (33, 623, 1241, 1739, 2464 and others; Cyr) read the perfect ἀναπέπαυται (ἐπαναπέπαυται, P[72], ℵ[2]); the meaning remains essentially unchanged.

4 A number of later MSS. and some versions (P, Ψ, 𝔐, r, t, z, vg[ww], sy[h**], sa [bo[ms]]) read the added phrase κατὰ μὲν αὐτοὺς βλασφήμειται, κατὰ δὲ ὑμᾶς δοξάζεται ("for them it means blasphemy, but for you it means being glorified"). Michaels (265) suggests that one could retain it, (a) explaining its absence in some MSS. as perhaps due to the omission of an entire line because of the similar endings of ἀναπαύεται and δοξάζεται, and (b) pointing to its conformity with Petrine style. Peter R. Rodgers defends its integrity along similar lines, and also sees a possible incorporation of Isa 52:5 embodied in it ("The Longer Reading of 1 Peter 4:14," *CBQ* 43 [1981] 94). Its absence in earlier MSS. outweighs such considerations, however, and with Beare (192) and Kelly (188), it is to be regarded as an early gloss.

5 The variety of forms presented in the MSS. for this word indicate its obscurity: ἀλλοτριεπίσκοπος (ℵ, B, 33, 81, a few other minuscules, latt); ἀλλοτριοεπίσκοπος (P, 𝔐); ἀλλότριος ἐπίσκοπος (A, Ψ, 69, a few other minuscules); ἀλλοτρίοις ἐπίσκοπος (P[72]).

6 While the best MSS. (P[72], ℵ, A, B, Ψ, 33, 323, 1241, 1739, and a number of additional minuscules, latt, sy, bo) read ὀνόματι, most, especially the later ones (P, O49, 𝔐), substitute μέρει ("in this way" or "in this instance"; see 2 Cor 3:10; 9:3). It is difficult to see why a scribe would substitute μέρει for an original ὀνόματι, which makes μέρει a strong candidate, as the *lectio difficilior,* for the original reading, as, e.g., Michaels (257) argues. Yet the quality and extent of the textual witness to ὀνόματι make that a difficult

for judgment to begin with the house of God, but if first with us,[7] what will be the end of those who disobey God's good news? 18/ And if the righteous person is scarcely saved, where will the ungodly one and the sinner appear? 19/ Thus let those who suffer according to the will of God entrust their lives to a faithful creator by doing good.

decision to defend.

7   Some MSS. read ὑμῖν ("with you"): ℵ*, Aᶜ, 69, 1241, 2464, some other minuscules, vgᵐˢˢ.

Analysis

The limits of the passage are indicated by (1) the inclusion formed by Christian suffering, identified as sharing the suffering of Christ in v. 13 and suffering according to God's will in v. 19; (2) the change in those addressed in 5:1, namely, elders; (3) the ὥστε clause (v. 19) that draws the conclusion from the preceding discussion. The subject matter of the unit is Christian suffering both in the present (vv. 12–16) and in an eschatological perspective (vv. 17–18), followed by a summary admonition (v. 19). The present suffering divides itself into two units, the first dealing with the fact that suffering is to provoke joy among Christians (vv. 12–13), the second issuing the caveat that such suffering must be due to one's dedication to Christ rather than due to illegal behavior (vv. 14–16). The flow of thought of the first unit encompasses the fact that suffering is not to be seen as something strange for Christians (v. 12), but is rather to be understood as due to their participation in Christ's own suffering, and hence is to bring joy both now (v. 13a) and in the future at Christ's return (v. 13b). The flow of thought of the second unit begins (v. 14) and ends (v. 16) with a linking of the Christian's suffering to God's glory, with the middle (v. 15) section a disclaimer on any Christian significance of suffering inflicted as a result of illegal behavior. The flow of thought of the third unit concerns Christian suffering as the beginning of divine judgment that affects both Christians (v. 17a) and non-Christians (vv. 17b–18).[8]

The content thus reemphasizes points that the author has already made in the letter: persecution as fiery temptation that nevertheless causes joy (vv. 12–13; cf. 1:6–7); to be a Christian means to suffer (vv. 14, 16; cf. 2:21; 3:14–16; 4:4); suffering because of evil deeds is not Christian suffering (v. 15; cf. 2:20; 3:17); those who reject Christ will be judged (vv. 17b–18; cf. 2:7b–8; 4:5); one is to entrust one's life to God (v. 19; cf. 2:23b). Yet the passage is not simply a repetition; two new points are introduced. The first is that simply the name "Christian" makes the bearer liable to persecution and suffering (vv. 14, 16); the second is that Christian suffering represents the beginning of God's final judgment (v. 17).[9] The passage thus serves both as summary of past discussions and as introduction to the final section of the letter.[10]

Christian suffering constitutes the major theme of this passage, and it is treated in a variety of ways: as providing a means of testing the Christian (v. 12), as a cause for joy (v. 13b), as a way of sharing Christ's suffering (v. 13a), as a way of glorifying God (v. 16), as useless if deserved for non-Christian reasons (v. 15), and as the beginning of final judgment (v. 17), which will be harder on their tormentors than on the Christians (vv. 17b–18).[11] Many of the points made are common to Christian tradition. Persecution and suffering due to Christian identity are

8   To find here the same structure found in 3:14–17, as Michaels (257–58) suggests, is to overlook major differences between the two passages: 3:14–17 has no reference to joy (4:13), nor to final judgment (4:17), nor does it provide a reason why the one who suffers is blessed (4:14); 4:12–19 has no assurance that being zealous for the good may prevent suffering (3:13), nor any reference to explaining the faith (3:15), nor any notion that observing Christian behavior has any effect on the persecutors (3:16b). Minor differences include sanctifying Christ (3:15) and glorifying God (4:16), and the detachment of the

ἀλλά from the blessing in 4:13–14 compared to the close attachment in 3:14.

9   On these points, see also Brox, 213; Kelly, 184.

10 To identify the passage as a "digression" on the basis of these repetitions, as Michaels (257) does, is to ignore the new elements introduced, and to overlook the way this passage introduces both 5:1–5, with its emphasis on the need for strong internal leadership for the survival of a community so besieged, and 5:6–11, which resumes the theme of suffering in terms of its diabolical dimension.

11 On these points, cf. Brox, 224–25; Windisch, 77–78.

already found in the words of Jesus (Matt 5:11–12 par.; 10:17–18 par.)[12] as is the notion that such people are blessed (e.g., Matt 5:10 par.), and finding joy in that event is found both in the Jesus tradition (e.g., Luke 6:23) and in Paul (e.g., Rom 8:17). In a similar way, the roots of many of these notions lie in the OT and later Jewish tradition. The idea of joy in suffering is implied in the OT[13] and is further developed in postcanonical Jewish tradition.[14] Similarly, the idea that suffering is an anticipation of the final judgment and that it begins with God's people also finds its precursors in the OT[15] and in Jewish tradition,[16] as does the conviction that present suffering brings future joy.[17] Drawing on a variety of traditions, therefore, the author can assure his readers that despite, indeed because of, their suffering they are in God's care. Thus, relying on divine grace, they may rejoice in their trials, knowing that as they participate in this final stage of God's plan, their final destiny is a sharing in eschatological joy and glory.

Comment

■ **12** The vocative ἀγαπητοί ("beloved") represents a common NT designation for fellow Christians,[18] and its use here to begin the body closing as it also began the body middle (2:11) is a further indication of the unity of the letter. The negatived present imperative (μὴ ξενίζεσθε) shows that what is now occurring with the Christians represents not so much paralyzing shock[19] as perplexity arising from an ongoing problem,[20] a point confirmed by the present tense of the two participles (γινομένη, συμβαίνοντος).[21] By using the same verb (ξενίζω) that was used in 4:4, the author tells his readers that their reaction to the non-Christians' behavior must not be the same as non-Christians' reaction to their behavior, primarily since suffering for those who are followers of Christ in a world that rejects him is inevitable.[22] The inevitability of such suffering, a general Christian insight (e.g., 1 Thess 3:3; 2 Tim 3:12; 1 John 3:13; cf. Acts 16:22b; 20:19) based on the words of Jesus (John 15:18–21; 16:1–4, 33b; cf. Matt 10:24–25 par. Luke 6:40 par. John 13:16), is reinforced here by the genitive absolute (ὡς ξένου ὑμῖν συμβαίνοντος, "as though something strange were happening to you").[23]

The reference to the events as a πύρωσις ("burning") probably owes less to the punishment inflicted on Christians in Rome by Nero[24] than it does to the biblical metaphor of a purifying and proving fire, often with

12 Cf. also 1 Pet 4:14 with Matt 5:20 and the presence of the Spirit of God when Christians are on trial.
13 In Isaiah it takes the form of joy at the eschatological rescue of those who have suffered the exile, e.g., 52:7–12; 25:6–11; 26:7–10; 35:10 = 51:11; 61:7. See also Ps 31:7; cf. Ps 30:5. I owe several of these references to Goppelt, 299–304.
14 E.g., 4 Macc 9:29–32. Joy is also implied by the notion that righteous suffering atones for the people, e.g., 4 Macc 6:27–29; 17:21–22. Similarly, joy is implied in some Qumran traditions, where the righteous one can affirm his sufferings because of his trust in God's mercy: e.g., 1QH 9.8–10, 24–25, 34.
15 E.g., Jer 25:29; Ezek 9:6b. Michaels's argument (xxxvi) that the purpose of 4:13–17, as seen in this reference in Ezek 9:6 to suffering beginning with the "elders" of the house of Israel, is to prepare the way for the discussion of elders in 5:1–5 is somewhat fanciful.
16 E.g., 2 Macc 6:12–16.
17 E.g., 2 Bar. 48.48–50; 52.5–7; cf. 54.16: the unrighteous will suffer in the future. See also Wis 3:4–6.
18 E.g., Rom 12:19; 1 Cor 10:14; 2 Cor 6:7; Phil 2:12; Heb 6:9; Jas 1:16; 2 Pet 3:14; 1 John 3:2; Jude 20. That it is often used to introduce something already known, as, e.g., Brox (212) suggests, is not so clear from its NT usage.
19 As, e.g., Beare (189) argued.
20 With, e.g., de Villiers, "Joy," 80; Kelly, 184. See our author's earlier references to Christian suffering (1:6; 2:21; 3:14, 16b–17a; 4:1a; 4b) and rejection (2:12b).
21 So also, e.g., Kelly, 185.
22 With, e.g., Spicq, 155. The same point was made in 2:11–12, where Christians are identified as exiles and aliens; cf. also 2:7b–8.
23 Margot (76) notes that such surprise would be more likely for Christians of pagan than Jewish background, since the latter had already belonged to a group that had suffered at the hands of the Romans. On this point see also van Unnik ("Redemption," 67), who calls attention to the discussion of the persecution of Jewish proselytes in b. Yeb. 48b.
24 As argued, e.g., by Thurston ("Interpreting First Peter," 176) and Beare (190). Some Christians were burned by Nero in 64 CE as scapegoats for the fire Nero had set in Rome; see Tacitus Ann. 15.44. It is necessary to recall here that the letter is being written to Christians in Asia Minor, not to those in Rome. That the reference is due to the Christians in Asia Minor perhaps having "suffered . . . from acts of deliberate incendiarism," as Selwyn (221) speculates, is without further evidence.

eschatological overtones,[25] a metaphor already employed by our author in 1:7.[26] The purpose of the "burning" is given by the phrase πρὸς πειρασμὸν ὑμῖν ("to test you").[27] In this context, πειρασμός ("test," "temptation")[28] may well refer to the constant danger that Satan may "devour" the believer (5:8),[29] thus tempting the Christians to abandon their faith in Christ. Such testing by Satan also reveals the ultimate power that underlies those who persecute the Christian community, reinforcing the community's need to rely on God for help (cf. 4:19).

This verse thus sets the theme for the final portion of the letter. Drawing on the repeated affirmation that believers, bound to a Lord whose vocation it was to suffer, will also suffer (1:6–7; 2:18–20; 3:13–15; 4:1–3), the author reminds his readers that the suffering they now undergo[30] is nothing strange. Just as the behavior of secular society is unwelcome to Christians (1:8; 4:2–3), so Christian behavior is unwelcome to secular society.[31] In that situation, suffering is inevitable, but it comes as a test for Christians who, realizing it is the beginning of God's universal judgment, are to use it as an opportunity to glorify God and entrust their future to him.

■ **13** As the adversative conjunction ἀλλά ("but") indicates, this verse now shows the proper reaction on the part of Christians to the tempering fire that has come to test them, namely, not to regard it as something strange, but rather to rejoice[32] because of it. The second half of the verse is introduced with ἵνα, which retains its causative force here. Its meaning for the readers is that their participation in future joy depends on their present participation in suffering. If they are affronted by it, and hence seek to avoid it by denying Christ, they will not share in the glory that will accompany his return. Thus Christians are to accept such suffering with joy now, in order that (ἵνα) they may also (καί) rejoice as sharers in Christ's glory when it is revealed (cf. 5:1, 4). Unless they share Christ's sufferings (τοῖς τοῦ Χριστοῦ παθήμασιν)[33] now, they will not share his glory (τῆς δόξης αὐτοῦ) in the future.

That the one who follows God will suffer for it is known in Judaism[34] as well as in the NT,[35] as is the notion that one is also to rejoice because such suffering is undergone for God.[36] In a related Jewish tradition, the cause of the joy to be found in such suffering is the reward that will follow in the future;[37] in the NT form of

---

25 E.g., Prov 17:3; 27:21; Ps 66:10; Jer 9:6; Amos 4:9; Zech 13:9; Matt 3:3; 1 Cor 3:13; Rev 3:18; *Did.* 16.5. See also 1QM 17.8–9; 1QH 5.16. Emilie T. Sander ("ΠΥΡΩΣΙΣ and the First Epistle of Peter 4:12" [Th.D. diss., Harvard, 1966]) argues that the word צרף ("crucible") became a technical term for such a testing ordeal in Qumran, and that it furnishes the background here for πύρωσις, rather than OT tradition (the LXX has πύρωσις only at Amos 4:9 and Prov 27:21, and only in the latter place as a translation of מצרף). For a convenient summary of her ingenious if somewhat unconvincing argument, see Emilie T. Sander, "ΠΥΡΩΣΙΣ and the First Epistle of Peter 4:12," *HTR* 60 (1967) 501; for a discussion of it, see Michaels, 260.

26 In agreement with, e.g., Brox, 213; Tarrech, "Le milieu," 391; Best, 162; de Villiers, "Joy," 80.

27 With, e.g., Michaels, 261; it can be rendered "in order to test you."

28 The author used the same word in a similar context in 1:6.

29 John Strugnell calls attention to 1QS 1.17–18, which refers to a trial that comes from Belial for the purpose of testing ("Notes on 1QS 1,17–18; 8,3–4 and 1QM 17,8–9," *CBQ* 29 [1967] 580).

30 Tacitus (*Agric.* 44–45) refers to the bloodbath that Domitian unleashed in his later years. One may

speculate that some such spasm may have affected the areas in Asia Minor to which this letter is addressed, although that remains speculation.

31 With Goppelt, 296.

32 The χαίρετε is here to be understood as imperatival, in parallelism with the μὴ ξενίζεσθε of v. 12.

33 Millauer (*Leiden*, 102) correctly identifies τοῦ Χριστοῦ as subjective genitive.

34 E.g., 2 Esdr 13:16–19; *2 Bar.* 25; *Jub.* 23.13–15; cf. 1QH 2.21–22. Such suffering often means sharing in the "messianic woes," as Best (162–63) and Leaney (64) note.

35 E.g., Matt 10:24–25; Mark 8:34; 13:9–11; John 15:20; 2 Thess 2:3–10.

36 E.g., 2 Macc 6:28–30; 4 Macc 7:22; 9:29; 11:12; Jdt 8:25–27; Matt 5:11–12; Jas 1:2.

37 E.g., Dan 7:21–23; 12:1–3; Joel 2; 2 Esdr 6:18–25; *2 Bar.* 48.49–50; 52.6–7; Tob 13:14b; Wis 3:4–6; 1QpHab 8.1–3.

that tradition, the reward is most often expressed as a share in the glory of Christ.[38] Thus our author employs here a common early Christian tradition[39] that sharing in the suffering of Christ also means participation in his glory at the time of his return.[40]

The two references to rejoicing indicate on the one hand that rejoicing under suffering is entirely appropriate in the present (καθὸ κοινωνεῖτε . . . χαίρετε), but on the other hand that present joy pales in the light of the much greater joy yet to come (χαρῆτε ἀγαλλιώμενοι).[41] The idea of suffering in the midst of trials was already mentioned in 1:6, 8;[42] although the implication of future joy was also contained in the latter verse (1:8),[43] it was not made so specific as it is here. What separates present and future joy, and gives to the future its greater abundance, is the revelation of Christ's glory. While such a revelation is mentioned elsewhere in this letter (1:7, 13; cf. 1:5; 5:1), it is not clear whether our author thinks of that revelation as accomplished by the return of Christ, or simply by the revealing of the fact that he is the one who sits at the right hand of God (3:22). In either case, Christ's close relationship to the divine (τῆς δόξης αὐτοῦ)[44] is what is to be revealed.

The joy in suffering discussed here is thus unrelated to anything inherent in suffering as such: that it builds character, makes one sensitive to others, or provides an uplifting example.[45] Rather, this joy is based in specific

events (Christ's suffering and vindication) and specific expectations (a transformed future). Hence, although suffering with Christ promised eschatological vindication and joy, that joy was already a reality for those who shared his suffering. As a result that future reality has already transformed the present reality of suffering from sorrow to joy,[46] providing in that way an indication of the fact that the transformation of reality to be completed in the future has already begun for Christians.

■ **14** The εἰ with which the sentence begins, combined with a verb in the indicative mood (ὀνειδίζεσθε), emphasizes the reality of the assumption that Christians will be reproached, and hence has the force not so much of "if" as of "when."[47] The verb, used in biblical traditions to describe reproaches heaped on God (LXX) and on both God and Christ (NT), as well as those who call upon them,[48] indicates the kind of "fiery trial" (v. 12) Christians are undergoing: the emphasis is on verbal rather than physical abuse,[49] although occasional instances of the latter cannot be entirely ruled out. The description of abuse as being suffered "in the name of Christ" (ἐν ὀνόματι Χριστοῦ) employs a phrase found only here in the NT, and a preposition (ἐν) normally not used with the name of Christ in a hostile sense. Variations on the phrase ἐν τῷ ὀνόματι ['Ιησοῦ] Χριστοῦ elsewhere in the NT imply use of the name by friend or follower.[50] That means one may not assume it reflects the normal sense of

---

38 E.g., Matt 5:10–12; 10:22; Luke 6:22–23; John 16:2–3, 21–22, 33; Rom 8:17; Phil 3:10–11; 2 Tim 2:11–12; Heb 10:32–36; 11:26; 13:13–14; Jas 2:12.

39 With, e.g., Beare, 191; Kelly, 185. Its widespread use throughout the NT renders unlikely Goppelt's assertion (298) that the vocabulary here is Pauline, as it does Schelkle's judgment (123) that our author is working here specifically under the influence of Pauline theology.

40 While it is not an exclusive Judeo-Christian insight— cf. Seneca (*Prov.* 3.9): the greater Regulus's torture, the greater will be his glory ("quanto plus tormenti tanto plus erit gloriae")—it is clear that that is the tradition on which our author is drawing here.

41 Hillyer's argument ("Servant," 154), that because these two verbs also occur together in John 8:56 with respect to Abraham, this verse derives from a background in the Aqedah, is rather fanciful.

42 Michaels (262) is thus incorrect in arguing that joy in suffering is here introduced for the first time.

43 Selwyn (222) argues that 1:8 refers explicitly to the future, and should be so read. For a discussion of this

point, see the comments on 1:8 above.

44 That ἡ δόξα ("glory") belongs to divinity is shown in 4:11, where it is an attribute of God.

45 With, e.g., Schweizer, 93.

46 De Villiers ("Joy," 69) notes that such present joy distinguishes Christian suffering from that of the Jewish martyrs, whose joy was restricted to the future.

47 See BDF § 371 (1): "the condition is considered 'a real case'"; so also, e.g., Michaels, 263; Selwyn, 191.

48 E.g., Pss 43:17; 118:42; Isa 37:17; Matt 27:44; Rom 15:3; Heb 11:26.

49 Cf. 4:3–4 for the reason: social self-isolation on the part of Christians. On this point see also, e.g., Kelly, 186; Moffatt, 157.

50 Baptized in (Acts 10:48) or by (Acts 2:38) the name of Christ; healing (Acts 3:6; 4:10) or exorcisms (Mark 9:38 par.; Luke 10:17; Acts 16:18) in the name of Christ; prayer (John 14:14; Eph 5:20), confession (Phil 2:10), or ethical exhortation (2 Thess 3:6) in the name of Christ. On this point see also, e.g., Beare, 191.

suffering "for" or "because of" Christ,[51] expressions that use different prepositions, either διά[52] or ὑπέρ.[53] Rather, the weight of the phrase is on the readers' suffering as Christians (v. 16: ὡς Χριστιανός) rather than as some other kind of person (v. 15, μὴ . . . ὡς φονεύς, κλέπτης, κακοποιός, ἀλλοτριεπίσκοπος, "not . . . as murderer, thief, evildoer, defrauder"), that is, on making sure that the suffering is for the right reason, a point our author has previously emphasized (2:20; 3:17).[54] Only such suffering makes Christians blessed (μακάριοι), a point our author has also made previously (3:14). While the similarity in form (beatitude followed by ὅτι clause, Matt 5:3–10 par. Luke 6:20–21) and language (ὀνειδίσωσιν, Matt 5:11 par. Luke 6:22) to the beatitudes found in the Gospels means one cannot rule out our author's acquaintance with those traditions,[55] such similarity probably points rather to traditional formulations[56] describing the kind of abuse Christians regularly underwent at this time from their non-Christian counterparts.[57]

The ὅτι clause that follows gives the reason why suffering as Christians means blessedness: it shows that the divine Spirit rests on them. The clause is framed in uncharacteristically awkward prose, however, with repeated neuter articles[58] preceding genitival phrases tied together with a coordinating "and," thus making both phrases appear to modify "Spirit." Thus the phrase καὶ τό between τῆς δόξης and τοῦ Θεοῦ renders an otherwise simple description of the divine Spirit (τὸ τῆς δόξης τοῦ Θεοῦ πνεῦμα ["the Spirit of the glory of God"]) complex and difficult.[59] Insertion of the καὶ τό by later scribes[60] would relieve the author of responsibility for the awkward prose, but such a solution lacks clear textual evidence, and leaves open the question why a scribe would want to render a clear phrase obscure.

The reflection in the ὅτι clause of language drawn from LXX Isa 11:2[61] suggests another solution. In addition to adapting the language of Isaiah,[62] changing the verb from future (ἀναπαύσεται) to present (ἀναπαύεται), and the pronoun from "upon him" (ἐπ᾽ αὐτόν) to "upon you" (ἐφ᾽ ὑμᾶς), thus making clear that the prophecy described by Isaiah has now been fulfilled within the Christian community,[63] the author himself may have added the phrase τὸ τῆς δόξης,[64] perhaps influenced by the many genitival nouns[65] used in Isa 11:2b to describe further the divine Spirit. The additional attribution of "glory" to the Spirit may reflect a

---

51 As do, e.g., Kelly (186) and Michaels (264), who claim that this phrase represents a "technical expression" in the apostolic church for suffering for Christ; cf. also Selwyn, 222; Robinson, *Redating*, 154.

52 E.g., Matt 10:22; Mark 13:13; Luke 21:17; John 15:21; Rev 2:3.

53 E.g., Acts 5:21; 9:16; 15:26; 21:13.

54 The phrase ἐν ὀνόματι Χριστοῦ is probably to be construed as a dative of sphere, i.e., they must be sure to suffer while remaining within the "sphere" within which Christ exercises authority. A similar phrase (ἐν τῷ ὀνόματι τούτῳ) concludes this discussion in v. 16.

55 So, e.g., Kelly, 186; Windisch, 77; but see Beare (191), who thinks acquaintance with Matthew unlikely.

56 The beatitude form is not restricted to the Gospels (cf. Rom 4:7–8 [quoting LXX Ps 31:1–2]; 14:22; Jas 1:12; Rev 14:13; 16:15; 19:9).

57 With, e.g., Brox, 215; Goppelt, 305.

58 Kelly (187) identifies this repetition of articles as "cumbersome."

59 Selwyn (222) notes a similarly overloaded description in Jdt 9:8.

60 Hart (74) thinks it "not impossible" that the words were added by later scribes for the benefit of Greek readers, although how that would help them is not at all clear.

61 The LXX text reads: καὶ ἀναπαύσεται ἐπ᾽ αὐτὸν πνεῦμα τοῦ Θεοῦ, πνεῦμα σοφίας καὶ συνέσεως, πνεῦμα βουλῆς καὶ ἰσχύος, πνεῦμα γνώσεως καὶ εὐσεβείας ("And there shall rest upon him God's Spirit, the spirit of wisdom and understanding, the spirit of counsel and might, the spirit of knowledge and piety"). The phrase from 1 Pet 4:14 reads: τὸ τῆς δόξης καὶ τὸ τοῦ Θεοῦ πνεῦμα ἐφ᾽ ὑμᾶς ἀναπαύεται.

62 Some have argued for such a derivation of the phrase, e.g., Dennis E. Johnson, "Fire in God's House: Imagery from Malachi 3 in Peter's Theology of Suffering (1 Pet 4:12–19)," *JETS* 29 (1986) 289; Bigg, 177; Schutter, *Hermeneutic*, 153.

63 With, e.g., Michaels, 265.

64 So, e.g., Goppelt (305 n. 29): added to serve as antithesis to the earlier reference to abuse. Schutter (*Hermeneutic*, 154) also thinks that the phrase, "a stock-term by the NT period (cf. Rom. 9:4, ἡ δόξα)," was added to an allusion to Isa 11:2, but that it was interpolated later.

65 See the text in n. 61 above.

further linguistic usage in the LXX, namely, the translation of the word designating the visible brightness or glory (Heb כבוד) that was the sign of God's presence with the word δόξα.[66] The author will then have wanted to emphasize the actual presence of God through his Spirit with suffering Christians.

Another possibility, however, is to construe the phrase τὸ τῆς δόξης as a substantive, separate from the reference to the Spirit. Such a construction is quite possible,[67] and would then refer to the glory mentioned in the preceding verse that will be revealed in the future. The thrust would be that both the anticipation of that future glory[68] and the Spirit of God now rest upon the suffering Christians, thus making them truly blessed.[69]

The promise of the presence of the Spirit with Christians at the time of persecution is found in the Jesus tradition,[70] and knowledge of that tradition may have prompted our author to refer to that presence here in his discussion of the suffering of Christians. Since the only promise about the Spirit in the Jesus tradition is the promise that the Spirit will be present with Christians in time of persecution to instruct them in what to say to their accusers, some have concluded that our author, relying on that tradition, thinks of the presence of the Spirit not as a regular attribute of the Christian, as did Paul, but rather as an occasional presence (i.e., at the time of persecution) as implied in the Jesus tradition.[71] Yet the language here seems to reflect Isa 11:1–2 rather than the gospel traditions, and our author's discussion of gifts of grace (χάρισμα) given to each Christian (4:10–11), gifts associated in Paul with the presence of the Holy Spirit (1 Cor 12:4–11), makes such an assertion concerning our author's ideas about the sporadic presence of the Spirit with the Christian somewhat less than totally persuasive.

In sum, our author in this verse adds force to the argument that Christians are not to see their trials as something strange to their way of life (v. 12), but rather to rejoice in them (v. 13), because the presence of such suffering means they are blessed by the presence of God's Spirit, and have already a share in the eschatological glory yet to be revealed.

■ **15** The words that introduce this verse (μὴ γάρ) indicate that it serves as the basis (γάρ, "because") of the preceding verse: the divine Spirit rests upon suffering Christians provided they do not suffer (μὴ . . . πασχέτω) as something other than Christians, that is, murderers, thieves, and the like.[72] The remainder of the verse identifies four kinds of persons Christians are to avoid being, lest their suffering be for the wrong reason. Prohibition against murder (φονεύς) occurs elsewhere in list of vices in the NT, including both Gospels (Matt 19:18 par., where it is explicitly based on OT commands, e.g., Exod 20:13; cf. Matt 5:21) and epistles (Rom 13:9; Jas 2:11; cf. Rev 21:8); the same lists in the Gospels and Paul also include prohibition against thievery (κλέπτης; cf. also Rom 2:21; 1 Cor 6:10; Eph 4:28).[73]

---

66 E.g., Exod 16:7; 24:16; 29:43; 40:34; Num 14:10; 1 Kings 8:10–11; Isa 6:1–3; Ezek 1:28; Hag 2:7; cf. Luke 2:9; Rom 9:4. On this point see Cranfield, 120; Schutter, *Hermeneutic*, 42. Johnson ("Fire," 290) argues that as God's presence, his "Shekinah," rests on the temple, so God's Spirit rests on Christians, a point supported by our author's earlier reference to the church as a "spiritual house" in which spiritual sacrifices are offered by a holy priesthood (2:5).

67 For such a construction, see LXX Lev 7:7: τὸ περὶ τῆς ἁμαρτίας = the sin offering; τὸ τῆς πλαμμελείας = the trespass offering; 1 Sam 6:4: τὸ τῆς βασάνου = the offering for the plague; Matt 21:21: τὸ τῆς συκῆς = the action with respect to the fig tree; 1 Cor 10:24: τὸ τοῦ ἑτέρου = the concerns of the other; Jas 4:14: τὸ τῆς αὔριον = conditions of tomorrow; 2 Pet 2:22: τὸ τῆς ἀληθοῦς παροιμίας = the situation covered by the true proverb. In each case, as Selwyn (222) notes, the substantive to be understood (τό) is identified by the substantive in the genitive, and its precise meaning is determined by the context.

68 The significance of the τὸ τῆς δόξης, calling attention to the glory mentioned in the previous verse.

69 See also Selwyn, 223. Bieder (*Grund und Kraft*, 14 n. 10) suggests that it could mean Christ, as in Jas 2:1, but thinks it better to understand it as a genitive of quality, modifying "Spirit," a conclusion he shares with Calvin, 135.

70 Matt 10:19–20 par.; 12:11–12; Luke 21:13–15; John 14:26; 16:7–11.

71 So, e.g., Goppelt, 306; Beare, 192.

72 With Goppelt, 306.

73 Lepelley ("Le contexte," 60) argues that these two terms taken together may intend to portray rioters

The third noun (κακοποιός), unique to 1 Peter in the NT, carries the general connotation of one who does what is evil (κακοποιός, lit. "evildoer"). The verbal form (κακοποιέω) is found elsewhere in the NT, at times contrasting one who does evil with one who does what is good (Mark 3:4 par. Luke 6:9), a contrast the verbal form also expressed in our letter (2:14; 3:17). There is some evidence that the word could also be used to mean "magician,"[74] and while such a meaning could be intended here,[75] it seems better, particularly in the light of its other uses in our letter (2:12, 14), to take it in the general sense of one who does evil.[76] Like the first two, this word could also include reference to legally punishable acts,[77] but it need not be restricted to such acts,[78] and so is broader in scope that the first two words.

The fourth word (ἀλλοτριεπίσκοπος) remains a puzzle, however, since it is not used in any other NT list of vices, nor does it appear in any other place in the Greek Bible or in non-Christian Greek literature.[79] The two compo-nents of the word would mean someone who was involved in overseeing (ἐπίσκοπος) the affairs of someone else (ἀλλότριος), which in turn could mean anything from a moral or social busybody[80] to a revolutionary[81] to someone who, charged with overseeing another's goods, embezzles them.[82] Because the word is introduced with a second ὡς ("as"; the first ὡς introduced the whole series), one could deduce that the author intended to set it apart from the three legal offenses that preceded it, whether as an afterthought[83] or to indicate that it summed up the first three,[84] or perhaps to indicate that it belonged to a different (i.e., social) category.[85] Yet the fact that some early scribes did not understand ὡς to have such a function,[86] and the fact that some such device is often used in the NT to indicate the end of a list,[87] probably mean that ἀλλοτριεπίσκοπος ought here to be understood with the first three as implying illegal activity, that is, as embezzlement of the goods of another, even though the word may, like κακοποιός, have a range not limited to acts

---

who took part in subversive endeavors of the lower classes, based on the fact that such persons are regularly termed "bandits" or "brigands" in Greek and Latin literature. In this list, however, it would perhaps be better to take them in their literal and straightforward meaning, based on their use in other NT traditions.

74 A Greek papyrus (PSI I.64[21]) associates κακοποιά with φάρμακα φίλτρα ("magic charms"; Moulton and Milligan, *Vocabulary*, 317).

75 So, e.g., Johannes Baptist Bauer, "Aut maleficus aut alieni speculator (1 Petr 4,15)," *BZ*, NF 22 (1978) 110; Windisch, 77 ("vielleicht hier . . . Zauberer" ["perhaps here . . . magician"]); see also the discussion in Schutter, *Hermeneutic*, 16 n. 74. Selwyn (225) suggests that it may be used in this sense in Tertullian *Scorp.* 12; Kelly (188) notes in addition Cyprian *Testimonia* 3.37; Lactantius *Institutiones* 2.16.4; Jerome *In Danielem* 2.2; although he thinks there is no evidence that either Tertullian or Cyprian thought it meant that.

76 With, e.g., Schelkle, 124; Michaels, 267. The Latin equivalent of κακοποιός, *maleficus*, later came to be used in descriptions of Christians, e.g., Suetonius *Vit.* 6.16.2: "Christiani, genus hominum superstitionis novae ac maleficae" ("Christians, a class of people characterized by a new and evil superstition").

77 See, e.g., Matt 27:23 par.; Rom 13:4, where legal liability is implied.

78 See, e.g., Beare (193), who finds no evidence for its use in legal terminology.

79 Moffatt (158) and Goppelt (308 n. 37) suggest that

our author may have coined the word. K. Erbes speculates that it may have originated as a sarcastic comment to an overly zealous fellow Christian ("Was bedeutet ἀλλοτριοεπίσκοπος 1 Pt 4,15?" *ZNW* 19 [1919/20] 44). It was also used three times in fourth- and fifth-century Christian writings; for a detailed discussion of this terms, see "Excursus: On the Meaning of ἀλλοτριεπίσκοπος."

80 So, e.g., Chase ("Peter," 784): Christians who officiously criticize pagan morals; Selwyn (225): tactless attempts to convert neighbors; Leaney (66): someone "infringing on rights of others." For a summary of similar judgments, see Bauer, "Aut maleficus," 111.

81 So, e.g., Moffatt, 158.

82 So, e.g., Bauer, "Aut maleficus," 115.

83 Kelly, 188.

84 Bigg, 79.

85 So, e.g., Chase, "Peter," 783. Cranfield (121) thinks there may "a trace of humor in introducing the busybody into this disreputable list." Kelly (189) suggests that this may be the "only item he is really in earnest about."

86 𝔐 and bo added ὡς to the second noun (κλέπτης); P[72] added it to both the nouns that lacked it.

87 See Achtemeier ("*Omne verbum sonat*," 24–25) for examples.

punishable by law.

One could construe these four descriptions as symbolic, on the theory that no Christian could be involved in such activities, or one could understand them as catchphrases used by opponents of Christianity on the basis of which Christians were condemned. In that case, "murderer" would reflect the charge that Christians ate babies and drank human blood in the Eucharist, "thief" would reflect the suspicion that the indigent who were in fact supported by the Christian community did not need to work because they stole, "evildoer" would reflect the suspicion that Christian meetings were secret so they could plot evil, and "busybody" would reflect Christians' attempts to control the lives of others, either within the Christian community or outside it through missionary activity.[88] Yet the regular inclusion of three of these words in lists of vices, often directed specifically to the readers in the Christian community,[89] along with the presence of an imperative that clearly implies one is to avoid suffering because one does such things, indicate they are probably to be taken at face value, indicating actual deeds.[90] One ought not allow a romanticizing of the early church to blind one to the realities of those communities.

Excursus: On the Meaning of ἀλλοτριεπίσκοπος

The exact meaning of the fourth noun in 4:15 is difficult to determine, since it is a hapax legomenon in biblical and secular Greek, and appears in only three other instances in two later Christian writers. One of those authors is Epiphanius, who uses the word, either in its NT form, or as ἀλλοτριοεπίσκοπος (there are textual variants) in *Anc.* 12.5 and *Pan.* 3.128.7; the other is Dionysius the Areopagite, again with textual variants, in his 8th epistle.[91] In *Ancoratus* the word is used in a list that includes περιεργαζόμενον ("busybody") and μὴ ἰδίων ἐπιθυμοῦν ("not seeking one's own affairs"); in *Pan.* it is defined as ἐκλήπτωρ ἀλλοτρίων ("one concerned with, or contracting for, another's affairs"), understood in a pejorative sense. In Dionysius it describes someone who is to be excluded from liturgical affairs.[92] The fact that neither has obvious reference to 1 Pet 4:15,[93] and that the former is a fourth-century, the latter a fifth-century writer, means one can gain little from these uses of the word in respect to its meaning in this epistle.

Because the first of the component parts of the word, ἀλλότριος, can be used to mean the enemies of Christians or of the church (Heb 11:34; *1 Clem.* 1:1), and can be used in the *Apostolic Constitutions* to mean the devil (7.1.2; 8.6.1, 4; 8.12.20, 15.4), thus having the same force as ὁ ἐχθρός ("the enemy," Luke 10:19) and ὁ πονηρός ("the evil one," Matt 13:19, 38; John 17:15; Eph 6:16; 1 John 2:13, 14; 3:12; 5:18, 19; *Barn.* 21.3), K. Erbes[94] has argued that ἀλλοτριεπίσκοπος has a meaning equivalent to πονηρὸς ἐπίσκοπος, which he takes to mean one who is evil in the oversight of another's goods.

Others have argued for a meaning descriptive of revolutionary activity, either in the sense of actually taking part in proletarian revolt for the violent redress of grievances,[95] or in the sense of those who intervene, in more or less direct fashion and in the name of their faith, in the life of the culture, an intervention that brings on Roman suspicion of the church as a seditious organization.[96] While a number of other meanings have been suggested (those who infringe on the rights of others,[97] those who involve themselves in things

---

88 So, e.g., Brox, 217. Knox ("Pliny and I Peter," 188) thinks therefore it is not the case that Christians did such things. But see Best (164), who finds no reference to such second-century accusations.

89 In addition to lists of vices, see, e.g., Eph 4:28; 1 Cor 6:11; 1 Tim 3:3; Titus 1:7; 3:2–3; cf. also 1 Tim 5:14; 2 Pet 2:2.

90 With, e.g., Best, 164; Wand, 119; Schutter, *Hermeneutic,* 16; Schiwy, 59.

91 *Ad Demophilum monachum*; see *PG* 3.1089C.

92 John Parker, following the Latin ("qui aliena spectat"), translates "everyone who meddles with other people's business" (*The Works of Dionysius the Areopagite* [reprinted Merrick, N.Y.: Richwood, 1976] 1.156). The context, however, deals with those, particularly priests, who disregard God's law and their proper rank, a context that could give some

such meaning as "improper bishop," although there is no other confirmation for such a meaning.

93 Only if τῇ θεολογίᾳ in Dionysius means "by the word of God," and Dionysius means by that phrase to identify the NT, could this be a possible reference to 1 Peter.

94 Erbes, "Was bedeutet," 40–41.

95 So, e.g., Beare (193), who finds it the equivalent of "cupidus novarum rerum" ("one desirous of new things").

96 So, e.g., Schweizer, 19 n. 2; Moffatt, 158; see also Knox, "Pliny and I Peter," 188–90; A. Bischoff, "Ἀλλοτρι(ο)επίσκοπος," *ZNW* 7 (1906) 272. But see Cranfield (121), who denies any real evidence for such a meaning.

97 Leaney, 66.

that have nothing to do with the confession of their faith,[98] those who engage in something foreign to their character, i.e., what does not benefit them as citizens, thus repeating the advice given in another form in 2:13),[99] the two most widely held suggestions are "busybody" and "defrauder."

The former sense, "busybody," is derived from Epictetus (*Diss.* 3.22.97) where he defends the true philosopher against the charge that he occupies himself with the affairs of others rather than his own; the exact vocabulary is τὰ ἀλλότρια πολυπραγμονεῖ ("being a busybody with respect to others' affairs") and τὰ ἀνθρώπινα ἐπισκοπῇ ("he oversees things pertaining to human beings").[100] Although the word ἀλλο-τριεπίσκοπος itself does not occur in Epictetus, the two components are used in a context with words for "busybody" (i.e., περίεργος, πολυπράγμων).[101] That such busybodies were not popular in the Hellenistic world is also shown by, among others, Plutarch, who defined πολυπράγμων as one who concerned himself with strangers' business, with slanderous intent.[102] Such inappropriate interference is mentioned in the NT, but with forms of the stem περιεργ- (2 Thess 3:11: περιεργάζεσθαι; 1 Tim 5:13: περίεργος); Jesus' unwillingness to involve himself in hereditary disputes may also be noted (Luke 12:13–14). If such is the intent of this word, then it means that the author has followed three illegal acts with one that brought social oppro-brium, namely, interference in social matters,[103] whether through judgmental or tactless interference in the lives of others[104] or through overzealous attempts at conversion[105] that would have the by-product of

separating converts from their non-Christian families,[106] a point already known to the gospel tradition (Matt 10:35–37; Mark 10:28–30). The weakness in this identification of the meaning of ἀλλοτριεπίσκοπος is the fact that it would not be, like the others, a legal offense; as such it would abruptly change the direction of the list of acts to be avoided.

The sense of "defrauder" for this obscure word is based on the fact that the Latin MS. K renders the word as *curas alienas agens* ("one who takes care of others' matters"), which can mean a broker or executor who misuses that position for personal enrichment through embezzlement.[107] In that vein, it could also describe one who held in trust money in dispute (Lat. *sequester*), or, illegally, money from a candidate for public office, to be distributed to members of an association were the candidate successful.[108] Given the relatively lower social status of Christians, the former rather than the latter definition would be more likely to apply. That it means embezzling money entrusted to one for safe-keeping[109] finds interesting confirmation in the NT. That Christians did defraud one another is indicated in 1 Cor 6:7–8. The temptation for Christians in positions of authority to engage in such practices may be evidenced by the prohibition of desire for monetary gain on the part of church officials (1 Tim 3:8; Titus 1:7; 1 Pet 5:2), a desire evidently later indulged in by deacons who misused their power and robbed widows and orphans of their monies (*Hermas Sim.* 9.26.2).[110] Further hints are provided (a) by the fact that to the commands from the Decalogue cited by Jesus in Mark 10:19, there is added μὴ ἀποστερήσῃς ("do not

---

98 Bauer, "Aut maleficus," 111, citing H. von Soden.
99 Bigg, 178.
100 On this point, see, e.g., Hart, 75–76; Wand, 119. Epictetus's argument is that when a philosopher concerns himself with human affairs, he is not concerned with other people and their affairs but with himself and his own affairs.
101 A similar defense of philosophers against the charge of being busybodies may be found in Horace *Sat.* 2.3.19, who has the philosopher Damasippus claim that his concern for others' affairs ("aliena negotia curo") is aimed at their moral well-being. I owe this reference to Chase, "Peter," 783–84; see also Bauer, "Aut maleficus," 111.
102 *Mor.*, *De curiositate* 517A. I owe this reference to Michaels, 267.
103 So, e.g., Goppelt, 308; Chase, "Peter," 784. Kelly (189) argues that this is the only charge about which the author is serious, as shown by the insertion of the second ὡς; I find that insufficient evidence for such a conclusion.
104 So, e.g., Schweizer, 94.

105 So, e.g., Windisch, 77; Selwyn, 225.
106 So, e.g., de Villiers, "Joy," 86 n. 62; Best, 165.
107 So, e.g., Duplacy and Amphoux, "A propos de l'histoire du texte," 168; Brox, 220. Such a practice is described by Lucian of Samosata (*Conviv.* 32) when he has a character tell of a teacher who took, in trust, money from a foreign student, and subsequently denied by the gods he had ever received it; on this point see Bauer, "Aut maleficus," 112.
108 So Reicke, 125–26; Bauer, 57.
109 So, e.g., Bauer, "Aut maleficus," 115; Erbes, "Was bedeutet," 44; idem, "Noch etwas zum ἀλλοτριο-επίσκοπος 1 Petr 4,15," *ZNW* 20 (1921) 249; cf. Calvin, 137.
110 On these points, see Erbes, "Was bedeutet," 42–43; Bauer, "Aut maleficus," 115.

defraud"), perhaps to counter such acts; (b) by the fact that Pliny observed that Christians bound themselves by oath not to deny a deposit when demanded ("ne depositum adpellati abnegarent"; *Ep.* 10.96.7). A further hint about the meaning of the word may be provided (c) by Tertullian (*Apol.* 44.2–3), who lists four faults not characteristic of Christians: assassin (= φονεύς), cutpurse (= κλέπτης), temple robber (= κακοποιός [?]), and bribery agent (= ἀλλοτριεπίσκοπος [?]), and (d) by Aristides (*Apol.* 15.4), who says that among divine commands Christians obey is οὐκ ἐπιθυμοῦσι τὸ ἀλλότρια, which may mean not to appropriate another's deposit for oneself.[111] If this is the meaning, the word ἀλλοτριεπίσκοπος points to an act to which, as the evidence suggests, Christians were occasionally vulnerable, and against which they took pains to struggle, an act that, like the previous three, was recognized as illegal in secular society, and that could bring official as well as social opprobrium and punishment. On that basis, the meaning "one who defrauds" seems to be the preferable option, with the understanding that one so identified would be subject to rebuke whether or not the case came to the attention of the legal authorities.

■ 16 The εἰ which introduces the protasis functions here, as it did in v. 14, to indicate a condition whose reality is assumed: it is not a question of whether but of when the action will occur. In the absence of a verb, it is not clear whether one is to supply a form of "suffer," as in v. 15, or a form of "be reviled," as in v. 14. On the one hand, the similarity of structure with v. 14: (a) εἰ in the apodosis in both verses; (b) ὡς Χριστιανός in v. 16 and ἐν ὀνόματι Χριστοῦ in v. 14; (c) δοξαζέτω τὸν θεόν in v. 16 and the reference to δόξα in v. 14; (d) the advice not to be

ashamed (μὴ αἰχυνέσθω) in v. 16 and the pronouncement of Christian sufferers as μακάριοι in v. 14, could lead one to assume here a form of the verb "reproach" (ὀνειδίζειν) that is found in v. 14. On the other hand, the proximity to v. 15 and the fact that v. 16 includes a contrast "not this" (v. 15) "but this" (v. 16), could lead one to assume the same verb (πάσχειν, "suffer") in both verses. In either case, the close relationship between vv. 14 and 15 indicates that the suffering of v. 15 is related to the reproaches described in v. 14.

The identification of the reader as "Christian" (Χριστιανός), following a common practice of forming a description of followers that included the name of the leader,[112] employs a word rare in the NT[113] and apparently coined by outsiders.[114] Followers of Christ used other names for themselves in the NT, for example, "disciple" (μαθηταί, Acts 6:1; 9:19), "saints" (ἅγιοι, Rom 1:7; 1 Cor 1:2), "brothers" (ἀδελφοί, Rom 1:13; 1 Cor 1:26).[115] Yet while the word "Christian" continued to be the way outsiders characterized the followers of Christ,[116] it was soon adopted by the church as its own self-designation as well.[117] The association of this title with such sobriquets as "murderer" and "thief" can be construed to mean our author here refers to penalties imposed on Christians by courts of law simply because they were Christians.[118] It is surely true that there were occasions when Roman officials did impose the death penalty on Christians simply for being Christians, most notably under Nero and Pliny. Yet both of those instances were limited in scope and time, Nero's to Rome following the fire,[119] and Pliny's to Pontus upon his

111 So Erbes ("Was bedeutet," 43): "reissen nicht ein Depositum an sich" ("not to seize a deposit for oneself"). Aristides may have had in mind the command in Mark 10:19.

112 See, e.g., Chevallier, "Condition," 393. Premerstein ("Clientes," 37) notes that a client regularly added to his or her own name an adjective formed from the gentilic name of the patron.

113 The only other uses are Acts 11:26 and 26:28.

114 The language of Acts 11:26 implies this; in its only other occurrence in the NT (Acts 26:28) it is also used by an outsider, Agrippa. On this point see Goppelt, 309; Michaels, 268; Judge, *Social Pattern*, 44. The argument of Bauer (57) that its use in Acts 11:26 indicates legal nomenclature ("Es war zunächst eine politische Kennzeichnung" ["it was at first a political designation"]) is somewhat forced.

115 So also Beare, 193.

116 So, e.g., Tacitus (*Ann.* 15.44): "vulgus Christianos appellebat" ("commonly called Christians"); cf. also, e.g., Suetonius *Vit.* 6.16.2; Pliny *Ep.* 10.96; Lucian of Samosata *Alex.* 25; *Pergr. mort.* 11–13, 16.

117 E.g., *Did.* 12.4; Ignatius *Eph.* 11.2; *Magn.* 4; *Rom.* 3.2 (also Χριστιανισμός, "Christianity," *Rom.* 3.3); *Pol.* 7.3; *Mart. Pol.* 3.2; 10.1; 12.1–2. On this point see also, e.g., Goppelt, 309; Selwyn, 225; Michaels, 268.

118 So, e.g., Windisch, 78; Wand, 119; Schelkle, 125. Lampe and Luz ("Nachpaulinisches Christentum," 198) assume the same situation here as that outlined in Pliny *Ep.* 10.96.

119 Cf. Suetonius *Vit.* 6.16.2; Tacitus *Ann.* 15.44. Despite Tacitus's description of Christians as "detested for their crimes" ("quos per flagitia invisos") and convicted of "hatred for the human

discovery of their beliefs.[120] Those two instances do indicate that the threat of confrontation with governmental authorities constantly hung over the Christian communities,[121] not only as followers of one executed as a criminal[122] but as members of what in Roman eyes appeared to be a collegium characterized by superstition[123] in a time when all collegia were subject to investigation.[124] Yet Christianity was not declared formally illegal until 249 CE under the emperor Decius,[125] and Pliny's description of the extent of inroads made by the Christians in Pontus[126] as well as his need to consult the emperor on the correct course to be followed indicate that Christianity had not been generally considered illegal, at least in that part of Asia Minor. Such an indication is confirmed by Trajan's unwillingness to make any general rule about the punishment of Christians, and his prohibition of seeking them out.[127] Nor is there any indication in our letter that Christians faced a possible death penalty or that our author was preparing them for martyrdom.[128] What they must endure is reproach and obloquy (v. 14) for their "hostility to human society" demonstrated by their unwillingness to take part in normal social events (4:4).

Such verbal abuse and social ostracism, as our letter indicates, came more from their neighbors than as the result of any legal action taken by the authorities.[129]

The injunction that Christians not feel shame (μὴ αἰσχυνέσθω) for what they suffer as a result of their participation in the community of faith points to more than simply subjective feeling,[130] since the verb αἰσχύνω can be used in Christian tradition to mean to be ashamed of and hence to deny one's faith.[131] The contrast here to feeling shame, namely, to "glorify God" (δοξαζέτω τὸν θεόν), confirms that such a denial is meant, since glorifying God in early Christian tradition can be used, in addition to signifying praise for God's mighty acts,[132] to describe an appropriate confession of faith.[133] The thrust here therefore appears to be that suffering for being a Christian should not be met with a denial of one's faith, perhaps in the hope that one will therefore avoid such pain in the future—why that is a bad alternative is then discussed in vv. 17–19—but rather by a strong affirmation of that faith.[134]

The final phrase (ἐν τῷ ὀνόματι τούτῳ) is somewhat ambiguous. The ἐν could function as a dative of instrument, which would indicate the very bearing of the name

race" ("odio humani generis convicti sunt"), he is forced to admit that the wholesale killing of Christians evoked general sympathy for them. Such sympathy raises the suspicion that Tacitus's judgment was colored more by his own view of Christians, a view shared by other second-century writers such as Suetonius and Pliny, than by the view of the masses in the first century when the events occurred.

120 Cf. *Ep.* 10.96, where he says he punished them for their stubbornness: "pertinaciam certe et inflexibilem obstinationem debere punire" ("[such] obstinacy and inflexible stubbornness ought surely to be punished"), regardless of the content of what they believed.

121 Cf. Matt 5:10–11; 10:17–22 par.

122 Cf. Tacitus (*Ann.* 15.44), who knew that Jesus was executed in Palestine under Pontius Pilate.

123 So Suetonius *Vit.* 6.16.2: "Christiani, genus hominum supersititones novae ac maleficae" ("Christians, a race of humans given to new and evil superstitions"); Pliny *Ep.* 10.96: "superstitionem prauam et immodicam" ("depraved and unruly superstition").

124 E.g., Augustus, who dissolved all collegia that were not ancient and legitimate (Suetonius *Vit.* 2.32.1: "collegia praeter antiqua et legitima dissoluit"); Trajan, who insisted that all such societies not sanctioned by the laws of the cities where they

appeared be prohibited (Pliny *Ep.* 10.92, 93).

125 See Balch, *Wives,* 140.

126 *Ep.* 10.96; this point is emphasized by Michaels (268–69). It also points, as does Tactitus's admission that sympathy for Christians was aroused by Nero's cruelties, to the fact that hate for the Christians may not have been so widespread as some second-century Roman authors would lead one to believe.

127 Trajan's answer to Pliny is found in Pliny *Ep.* 10.97.

128 With, e.g., Bigg, 180; Price, *Rituals and Power,* 197. A comparison with Rev 2:10, 13; 6:9, where the threat of death is explicit, makes the lack of such language in our epistle all the more evident.

129 So also, e.g., Kelly, 192; Neugebauer, "Zur Deutung," 66 n. 19; Selwyn, "Persecutions," 48; Brox, 220; Goppelt, 310; Michaels, 269; Best, 165.

130 As, e.g., Michaels (269) seems to imply.

131 See Mark 8:38; 2 Tim 1:8, 12, 16; 2:15; cf. Rom 1:16. On this point see Brox, 222.

132 E.g., Gal 1:24 (Paul's conversion); Luke 2:20; often after a miracle, e.g., Mark 2:12; Luke 5:25, 26; 7:16; 13:13; 17:15; 18:43.

133 E.g., 2 Cor 9:13; Rom 15:6; cf. Rom 1:21, where failure of an appropriate acknowledgment of what God did in creation results in idolatry.

134 With, e.g., Michaels (269), who calls attention to a similar response in 3:15–16.

glorifies God,[135] but it probably ought rather be construed as a dative of sphere, indicating the "sphere" within which one is to glorify God, the sphere of the Christian faith.[136] The phrase ἐν τῷ ὀνόματι is often used in the papyri to mean "to the account of" and so "under the heading of"; in that sense it would mean here "in this capacity" (i.e., as a Christian) or "on this account" (i.e., because the person suffers as a Christian).[137] Such a meaning would support the alternate reading found in the majority of MSS., namely, ἐν τῷ μέρει τούτῳ ("in this respect").[138] Whatever the resolution may be, the general gist is clear: far from Christians being ashamed of disapproval visited upon them, they are to use that situation to glorify God.

In sum, the thrust of vv. 15–16 is that while justified suffering by a Christian for injurious activity is to be avoided (v. 15), suffering for being a Christian is to be embraced as a means of bringing glory to God (v. 16).

■ 17 The ὅτι with which this verse begins gives further reason[139] why glorifying God in suffering is both possible and necessary: such suffering represents the beginning of God's final judgment on all peoples. The word καιρός in this letter is given its meaning by its context, as is the case here; it is the "time for the beginning of judgment."[140] The judgment (τὸ κρίμα) is the final judgment,[141] of which the present suffering of the Christians is not so much a harbinger or proleptic participation as it is part of it,[142] indeed the beginning of it.[143] While the notion of final judgment is common in both OT and NT, as is the idea that such judgment will include God's own people,[144] the idea that such judgment is to come first to "God's house" is not. It is not without precedent, however; both in the OT and in subsequent Jewish literature, the notion that God begins his judgment with his own people is present,[145] at times simply to indicate how judgment will begin, at times to indicate that such suffering of the chosen purges them from sins early on, so that they are prepared for the final judgment, or have a shorter time within which to have their offenses against God multiply.[146] That it is better to suffer earlier than later is clearly implied by the question τί τὸ τέλος ("what [will be] their end?") in this verse.

Those OT passages that are closest in language and thought to the idea expressed here that judgment begins with God's own people uniformly expect that judgment

---

135 So Brox, 222. Selwyn (225) entertains it as a possibility.

136 Selwyn (225) prefers this meaning.

137 So Kelly, 191.

138 As that phrase does, e.g., in 2 Cor 3:10; 9:3. On this point see Michaels, 270; see also the note on this phrase in the translation of the passage above.

139 With, e.g., Kelly, 192; but see Goppelt (311), who does not think the verse gives the basis of v. 16, but simply provides further argument that persecution of Christians provides them an opportunity to glorify God.

140 With, e.g., Goppelt, 311; Michaels, 270. See 1:5, where καιρός is used with the adjective ἔσχατος, 1:11 where it is qualified with τίνα ἢ ποῖον, and 5:6 where it is used adverbially, ἐν καιρῷ.

141 As in 1:17; 2:23; 4:5.

142 The aorist ἄρξασθαι emphasizes that point, since it "signifies a definite event in God's dealing with the world," as Beare (194) notes correctly.

143 With, e.g., Best, 165; Schutter, *Hermeneutic*, 155, 165. For that reason it ought also not be understood as participation in the messianic woes that were to precede the judgment in apocalyptic thought, as Goppelt (311) rightly observes.

144 E.g., Jer 7:8–15; Amos 3:2; Zech 13:7–9; Matt 16:27; Rom 2:6; 1 Cor 3:12–15; cf. *1 Enoch* 1.7; 1QS

4.20–22. Schutter (*Hermeneutic*, 158–59) notes the presence of that idea even in Josephus (*Bell.* 4.386–88; 5.15–19; 6.109–10), though without identification of the specific prophecy to which reference is being made; Schutter (*Hermenentic*, 160) thinks that Josephus's summaries of the oracles "bear unmistakable affinities" with Jer 25:29 and Ezek 9:6.

145 E.g., LXX Ezek 9:6 (καὶ ἀπὸ τῶν ἁγίων μου ἄρξασθε; "and begin from my holy places [holy ones?]"); Jer 32:29 (ὅτι ἐν πόλει . . . ἐγὼ ἄρχομαι κακῶσαι; "because in the city . . . I begin to do evil"); cf. Isa 10:11–12 (first on God's own people, then on Assyria); Mal 3:1–6 (first on righteous, then on unrighteous); 2 Macc 6:12–15; *T. Benj.* 10.6–11; cf. 2 Thess 1:5–6. For its continuation in rabbinic literature, see Str-B 3.767.

146 On the former point, see Goppelt (312–13), who thinks that this element is absent from this passage; on the latter point, see, e.g., 2 Macc 6:14; Mark 13:19–20. Beare (194) finds comparable ideas in 1 Cor 11:31–32, Kelly (193) in 2 Thess 1:5–10.

to begin in the temple.[147] The further fact that in the LXX, the phrase "house of God" (οἶκος τοῦ θεοῦ or τοῦ κυρίου) refers uniformly to temple or sanctuary, not to "people of God,"[148] strongly points to the operative metaphor here being the Christians as God's temple (see 2:5)[149] (i.e., where God is present), rather than as "household of God" (i.e., God's people).[150] Yet temple imagery is so thoroughly tied in this epistle to the concept of God's people (see 2:9) that such an idea must also be present here.[151] Perhaps it would be most accurate to see here the metaphor of God's house pointing to the Christian community where, as in the sanctuary, God is present to human beings.[152]

The question with which the verse ends implies that the suffering of those who do not belong to the Christian community, the end toward which they are moving (τὸ τέλος), will be worse than that of the Christians.[153] The description of non-Christians[154] as "those who disobey God's good news" employs language and concepts common to our author in describing those who reject Christ and oppress his people.[155] As in the other NT traditions, "God's good news" refers to the Christian proclamation regarding Jesus Christ.[156] Because it is

God's good news, however, to reject that gospel is to reject God.[157]

The verse displays the continuing eschatological expectation (see also 1:13; 2:12; 4:7) that was still very much alive in Asia Minor toward the end of the first century.[158] More importantly, however, the thrust of the verse is to warn Christians facing situations where denial of their faith could appear to alleviate their suffering that such denial will in fact only guarantee that their eventual end will involve suffering far worse than any they must now endure.[159] Coupled with the statement in the previous verse that such suffering serves to glorify God, and the affirmation here that such suffering proves they belong to the community where God is present among them,[160] this warning gives added incentive to Christians to remain faithful to their Lord in any suffering on his account that they may have to endure.

■ 18 The parallelism between v. 17b and v. 18, shown by the καί ("and") that coordinates them and the conditional particle εἰ[161] with which both protases begin,[162] as well as the same general content—judgment hard on Christians;[163] judgment worse on the unrighteous[164] —makes clear that the point made by the second

147 Isa 10:11–12; Jer 25:29; Ezek 9:6; Zech 13:7–9; Mal 3:1–6. So also, e.g., de Villiers, "Joy," 81. Fransen ("Une homélie," 38) and Johnson ("Fire," 292) find the strongest influence from Ezekiel 9, although the latter argues that if Ezekiel 9 influenced the language, conceptually the passage owes more to Mal 3:1–5 and 4:1.

148 So Johnson, "Fire," 291.

149 So, e.g., Michaels, 270; Johnson, "Fire," 292–93.

150 As, e.g., Cranfield (122) and Beare (194) argue. Schlier ("Adhortatio," 73) cites as support Gal 6:10; Eph 2:19; Heb 3:6; 10:21, but the first two use a different word (οἰκεῖος) and the last refers to the temple.

151 As Johnson ("Fire," 293) correctly emphasizes.

152 Michaels (271) suggests that the use of this metaphor may reflect the recent destruction of the temple in Jerusalem, but its use earlier for the Christian community and the lack anywhere else in the letter of any reference to the existence of the Jewish people or any of their institutions make that interesting suggestion somewhat unlikely.

153 In this connection, Beare (23) calls attention to the terrors that judgment day holds for unbelievers as described in 2 Thess 1:8; Rev 6:15–17.

154 The assertion of Goppelt (314), that this refers not to non-Christians as such, but rather to those who now

persecute Christians who do obey God's gospel, goes further than the evidence permits.

155 See, e.g., 2:7–8; 3:2, where "word" = "gospel."

156 E.g., Rom 1:1; 15:16; 2 Cor 11:7; 1 Thess 2:2, 8–9; cf. Acts 20:24.

157 With, e.g., Michaels, 272.

158 So also, e.g., Delling, "Der Bezug," 99.

159 With, e.g., Cranfield, 122; Michaels, "Eschatology," 400; Goppelt, 314.

160 Brox (222) notes that this verse places the church in the center of God's plan, further incentive to remain part of that community.

161 As in vv. 16 and 17b, the condition is considered to be reality; the force is thus not so much "if" as "when."

162 With Osborne ("L'utilisation," 71), who also notes these parallels.

163 Ἡμῶν ("us," v. 17b) = ὁ δίκαιος ("the righteous one," v. 18).

164 Τῶν ἀπειθούντων τῷ τοῦ θεοῦ εὐαγγελίῳ ("those who disobey the gospel of God," v. 17b) = ὁ ἀσεβής καὶ ἁμαρτωλός ("the impious and the sinner," v. 18).

half of v. 17 is here reinforced,[165] namely, the worse fate of those who do not belong to the Christian community.[166] The verse itself is an almost exact replication of LXX Prov 11:31.[167] In its LXX form, Prov 11:31 differs considerably from the Hebrew text, most notably with "scarcely" ($\mu\acute{o}\lambda\iota\varsigma$) standing in the place of "in the land" (בארץ),[168] without which the verse would not have been useful for our author in this context.[169] The fact that there is no indication the author is quoting from the OT here does not so much cast doubt on that fact[170] as it shows again the extent to which the author has appropriated the history, Scriptures, and language of Israel for the Christian community.[171] The retention from the LXX of the verbs in the present tense underlines the present reality of the judgment that has begun with the Christian community.[172]

The word $\mu\acute{o}\lambda\iota\varsigma$, rather rare in biblical Greek,[173] has here the meaning "barely" or "with difficulty," comparable to its use in Acts,[174] rather than "scarcely," a meaning it carries in the NT only in Rom 5:7. The point is not so much the scarcity of salvation, or doubt about it, as it is the difficulty presented to God to save even a righteous person.[175] Given that fact, how sure it is that those who reject God's good news will not find salvation!

Combined with v. 13, vv. 17–18 put the entire passage (vv. 12–19) into an eschatological perspective,[176] encouraging the Christians both with the sure fate of

their opponents and with the fact that once begun, the process will also find its end, making it possible for the Christians to resist for that limited period the temptation to deny their faith and their community. Thus the contrast between the (evil) present with its suffering and the (better) future with its salvation sets the parameter of these verses, as the contrast between the (more evil) past, with its unacceptable behavior, and the (better) present, with its acceptable behavior, set the parameter in the earlier discussion in this chapter (4:3–4). If Christians remain faithful, salvation will be theirs.

■ 19 The words introducing the verse ($\ddot{\omega}\sigma\tau\epsilon$ $\kappa\alpha\acute{\iota}$) indicate a conclusion to the preceding verses is now being drawn.[177] Although the $\kappa\alpha\acute{\iota}$ could be construed with the οἱ πάσχοντες ("those who suffer"), with the implication that those who suffer should also entrust themselves to God, as would be the case also for those who do not,[178] or with the imperative παρατιθέσθωσαν ("let them entrust"), with the implication that those who suffer should in addition entrust themselves to God,[179] it is probably best to construe it with the $\ddot{\omega}\sigma\tau\epsilon$, giving it the force "so then."[180] That the kind of suffering the

---

165 With Brox, 223.

166 Osborne ("L'utilisation," 71) avers that v. 18 is the answer to the question posed in v. 17b, but the fact that both are questions (17b: τί; 18b: ποῦ) and are joined with a coordinating καί indicates that they are parallel rather than sequential.

167 The καί with which v. 18 begins does not appear in the LXX, and the μέν that in the LXX appears between ὁ and δίκαιος is absent from v. 18; with those two exceptions, the two verses are identical.

168 For a suggestion on how the LXX derived its translation, see James Barr, "בארץ-μόλις: Prov. xi. 31, I Pet. iv. 18," JSS 20 (1975).

169 With, e.g., Barr, "בארץ-μόλις," 150; Osborne, "L'utilisation," 71.

170 As, e.g., Best ("I Peter II 4–10," 272–73) suggests.

171 Only once does the author indicate a quotation (1:16); normally, he does not (e.g., 1:24–25; 2:6 [where the RSV has added a gratuitous "it stands in Scripture"]; 3:10–12).

172 With Margot, 79.

173 It occurs five other times in the NT (Acts 14:18; 27:7, 8, 16; Rom 5:7). Its only occurrence in the parts of the LXX translated from the Hebrew is Prov 11:31; in material that originated in Greek, it occurs seven times (3 Macc 1:23; 5:15; Wis 9:16; Sir 21:20; 26:29; 29:6; 32:7).

174 So also, e.g., Michaels, 272; Best, 166.

175 The idea that salvation is difficult to achieve is not unique to our author, as a saying of Jesus in Mark 10:26–27 shows; cf. also Matt 7:14; Mark 8:35; 13:13, 19–20, 22.

176 But see Brox (223), who denies such eschatological orientation. The eschatological perspective of a similar discussion in 1 Enoch 1.8–9, a writing evidently known to our author, does, however, argue strongly for such a perspective here.

177 Such language indicating a conclusion would also alert the reader to expect a change of subject matter in the subsequent discussion.

178 So, e.g., Kelly, 194.

179 So, e.g., Bigg, 181.

180 With, e.g., Michaels, 272–73; Selwyn, 226.

Christians undergo[181] is not haphazard but is in accord with God's will is shown not so much because the divine will favors suffering as because such suffering will inevitably result from following God's ways rather than those of secular society (2:15; 3:17; 4:2).[182] The verb from which the imperative παρατιθέσθωσαν is drawn bears the meaning of committing something of value to a trusted person for safekeeping;[183] it is the word Jesus used on the cross at his death[184] as well as the word used to describe the transmission of their task to those responsible for Christian proclamation and nurture.[185] The present tense indicates that the author is encouraging the readers to continue in an action they are already undertaking: entrusting their lives (τὰς ψυχὰς αὐτῶν) to God. Because of the context of suffering for their conduct that opposes the mores of secular society, ψυχάς here, as elsewhere in the letter, refers to the Christians' entire lives, not some inward or spiritual aspect of them.[186] The description of God as "faithful" (πιστῷ), employing a concept that lies at the very heart of the Christian faith,[187] makes clear why Christians can entrust something of such value to God.[188] While the noun "creator" (κτίστης) is used only here in the NT,[189]

the conviction that God is creator of all things pervades early Christian faith,[190] and its use here suggests that the God of their salvation is also the creator, and that therefore the same power at work in the very creation of the universe is now at work for their salvation.[191] That is why the readers can be encouraged to entrust their lives to the same God who brought them into existence. The concluding phrase (ἐν ἀγαθοποιΐα), which by its placement at the end of the sentence, and thus at the end of the paragraph, is strongly emphasized,[192] again employs a word unique to biblical Greek[193] but indicates a concept very important to this author. Although its use shows it can mean not only to do what is good within the Christian community[194] but also to do what is good within secular society,[195] the former sense is to be preferred here. The phrase is probably to be understood as instrumental:[196] one entrusts one's life to God precisely by doing what is good, that is, what God wills to be done, in all situations. In a culture where Christian virtues were the cause of persecution, doing what God wants is precisely to entrust oneself to him[197] even though the result of such trust will be suffering.

The verse thus indicates the conclusion to be drawn

---

181 The context makes clear that the οἱ πάσχοντες refer to Christians who suffer, not to sufferers in general.

182 On this point, cf. Vanhoye, "1 Pierre," 123.

183 Selwyn, 226; Goppelt, 316; Beare, 195; Best, 166; Bigg, 182; Bengel, *Gnomon,* 755; de Villiers, "Joy," 82.

184 Luke 23:46, a citation from LXX Ps 30:6.

185 E.g., Acts 14:23; 20:32; 1 Tim 1:18; 6:20; 2 Tim 1:12–14; 2:2.

186 With, e.g., Best, 166; Michaels, 273; Kelly, 194. One will find an exemplary case of this use in Sir 30:21, 23.

187 So also, e.g., Spicq (161), who cites as examples 2 Tim 1:12; 2:13; Heb 10:23; one may add Rom 3:3–4.

188 With, e.g., Spicq, 161; Kelly, 195.

189 It is more common in the LXX, e.g., 2 Kgdms 22:32; 2 Macc 1:24; 7:23; 13:14; Sir 24:8; cf. 4 Macc 5:25; 11:5; it then appears with increased frequency in later Christian authors, e.g., *1 Clem.* 19.2; 59.3; 62.2; Justin *Apol.* 2.6.2; Irenaeus *Adv. haer.* 1.4.1, 8.16, 13.2; and becomes still more common later on, e.g., John Chrysostom and the Cappadocian fathers, esp. Gregory of Nyssa.

190 E.g., Acts 4:24; Heb 2:10. The more common form is the substantive participle ὁ κτίσας; see Rom 1:25; Eph 3:9; Col 3:10. On this point see also de Villiers,

"Joy," 82.

191 With, e.g., Margot, 79.

192 With Beare, 196.

193 It also occurs in later Christian writers, e.g., *1 Clem.* 2.2, 7; 33.1; 34.2; Clement of Alexandria *Strom.* 4.22.137; 6.7.60; Origen *In Jer.* 1.1; Epiphanius *Pan.* 1.316, though it remains a rather rare word (it is used by the second-century CE astrologer Vettius Valens to indicate the beneficent influence of astral bodies). The verbal form ἀγαθοποιέω is more commonly used in the NT, as it is in this letter.

194 E.g., 3:6: Christian wives become Sarah's children by doing (Christian) good; 3:17: it is better to suffer for doing (Christian) good if that is God's will; cf. 3:13: who will harm you if you are zealous for what is good.

195 E.g., 2:14: the rule rewards those who do (social) good; 2:15: doing (social) good is God's will; perhaps also 2:20: for slaves to do good and suffer for it is credit with God; cf. 2:12: Christians are condemned as (social) evildoers.

196 So also, e.g., Goppelt, 317. The phrase is thus to be construed with the imperative παρατιθέσθωσαν, as Bengel (*Gnomon,* 755) also suggests. Doing good and entrusting are thus not two different acts, as, e.g., Brox (223) and Michaels (274) would have it.

197 Michaels (275) notes correctly that even though faith is not mentioned here, the admonition to entrust

from the discussion beginning with v. 12:[198] Christian suffering that occurs as part of God's plan of universal judgment is to lead Christians to continue to entrust themselves to the creator God who is faithful to his creatures who trust him and who show that trust by doing what he wants, despite the suffering that may entail.[199] It also assures the Christians that such suffering is not due to human arbitrariness, or a sign that God has abandoned them; rather it is the result of activity pleasing to God, and so is in accord with the divine will.

---

lives to God shows that faith is presupposed in the whole discussion.

198 With Goppelt, 315; Beare, 195.

199 The content of the verse is also related to other key points in the letter, e.g., 3:14–17; 4:7–11, as also Michaels ("Eschatology," 399) and Spicq (162) note, respectively.

5 Appropriate Conduct in the Community

1 So then,[1] I exhort elders among you, I who am[2] fellow elder and witness of the sufferings of Christ,[3] who am also participant in the glory that is going to be revealed: 2/ Tend the flock of God that is in your charge, exercising oversight not out of compulsion but freely, in a godly way,[4] not from desire for base gain but eagerly, 3/ not as those who lord it over their underlings but as those who become examples for the flock;[5] 4/ and when the Chief Shepherd is revealed you will obtain the unfading crown of glory. 5/ Similarly, you younger people, be subordinate to elders. All of you gird on humble-mindedness toward one another,[6] because God opposes the arrogant, but gives grace to the humble.

1 Some MSS. add τούς to the οὖν (ℵ, 623, 2464, some other minuscules, h, vg), most late MSS. substitute the article for the conjunction (P, Ψ, 𝔐), in the former case to make the group of elders specific, in the latter case perhaps because it is not apparent that 5:1 grows out of 4:19, as the οὖν implies. The οὖν is probably the original reading (P[72], A, B, 614, 630, a few other minuscules, Jerome), as Michaels (276) also argues.

2 Some MSS. (P, 1, 630, 1243, 1505, 2495, a number of other minuscules, sy[h], sa) read ὡς ("as a fellow elder") in place of the article ὁ ("the fellow elder"), the text adopted by the *NRSV*; the more difficult reading (ὁ) ought here to prevail.

3 P[72] substitutes θεοῦ ("of God"), perhaps due to christological reflection; Beare ("Some Remarks," 264) thinks that it "may reflect an unconscious Patripassianism."

4 Some MSS. (ℵ*, B, 323, sa) omit ἐπισκοποῦντες ("watching over them"), perhaps because it implied that a presbyter exercised the office of a bishop (so, e.g., Goppelt, 324 n. 17; Kelly, 200), and many later MSS., along with B, omit κατὰ θεόν ("in a godly way"). The best MS. tradition (P[72], ℵ[2], A, P, Ψ, 33, 69, 81, 1739, and a number of other minuscules, lat, syr[(p)], bo) includes both, and they should be allowed to remain (with, e.g., Michaels, 276; Best, 170; Beare, "Some Remarks," 265; but see Cranfield ["I Peter," 127] and Schelkle [127–28], who think the participle was added under influence of 2:25).

5 This entire verse is omitted in B.

6 Among many variations here, some MSS. (P[72], some others, vg[mss]) read ἐν ἀλλήλοις; others (P, 𝔐) add ὑποτασσόμενοι ("by being subordinate") after the reflexive pronoun; neither ought to be preferred to the text (ℵ, A, B, 33, 81, 1241, 1739, and a number of other minuscules, lat, sy[p], co), as Seufert ("Das Abhängigkeitsverhältnis," 277) also argues.

Analysis

Although the verse immediately following this section (5:6) also contains a form of the stem ταπειν-,[7] indicating a close relationship, it is better to understand that verse as the introduction to a new section rather than a continuation of the old,[8] in much the same way that

7 V. 5: ταπεινοῖς; v. 6: ταπεινώθητε.

8 As, e.g., Brox (225) would have it. To argue as he does that the imperative represented by the participle ἐπιρίψαντες in 5:7 shows the beginning of a new section founders on the presence of (true) imperatives throughout this material, e.g., 5:2, 5, 6, 8, 9.

words formed from the verb ὑποτάσσω are used in 2:18 and 3:1 after it was introduced in 2:13. The οὖν that begins v. 6 as it began 5:1, clearly the beginning of a new section, confirms such a division of the text.[9] The content of the passage—internal affairs of the Christian community—indicates that the author is repeating a pattern used in the immediately preceding material, where a section on matters external to the community is followed by a consideration of matters internal to it.[10] Advice addressed here to two groups (v. 1: elder, v. 5a: younger), and then to all (v. 5bα), along with the introduction of the second group in v. 5a with ὁμοίως ("similarly"), and concluding this section with a quotation from the OT in v. 5bβ, indicates that the author is again following a pattern evident earlier, where groups addressed after the first group (2:18) were also introduced with ὁμοίως (3:1, 7), followed by a section addressed to all (3:8–9), with the entire section ending with a quotation from Ps 34:13–17 (3:10–12).[11]

Since both of the words used to address groups in vv. 1 and 5 can refer simply to age groups (πρεσβύτερος = one who is older, νεώτερος = one who is younger), and since νεώτεροι does not appear in the NT as any kind of group of officials,[12] one could take the two references as simply to two general groups of people, the older and the younger. Yet the definite reference to leadership in vv. 2–3 makes clear that "elders" here does refer to a group of people acting in some kind of leadership role in the community.

The presence of advice to church leaders in other parts of the NT that is similar to that here addressed to the elders (vv. 1–4) indicates that the author is employing traditional elements.[13] In addition to such similar advice being offered in the Pastorals,[14] the general structure of the passage contains elements found also in Paul's farewell speech[15] to the elders in Ephesus (Acts 20:18b–35): statements that the speaker has carried out the service of which he speaks (1 Pet 5:1aα; Acts 20:18–22, 31), even under suffering (1 Pet 5:1aβ; Acts 20:19b, 23). Caution against overbearing leadership (1 Pet 5:3; see Mark 10:42–44), along with the additional presence of common vocabulary: ποίμνιον ποιμαίνειν, ἐπισκοπ- (5:2; Acts 20:28), αἰσχροκερδ- (5:2; 1 Tim 3:8; Titus 1:7; for the context, cf. Acts 20:33) in similar contexts gives further weight to the idea that traditional elements are here being employed. The exclusive reference to elders[16] that our passage also shares with Paul's speech in Acts (20:17; cf. Jas 5:14)[17] may indicate a less advanced community organization than that reflected, for example, in the Pastorals and in the letters of Ignatius of Antioch, where bishops, elders, and deacons are named.[18] The greetings to deacons and bishops in Phil 1:1, however, makes any conclusion about chronological sequence or development questionable.[19]

---

9   That 5:1–5 is a unit is widely accepted; cf., e.g., Goppelt, 318; Combrini, "Structure," 49.

10   Here 5:1–5 (internal) follows 4:12–19 (external); there 4:7–11 (internal) follows 4:1–6 (external).

11   On these points, see also, e.g., Michaels, 178. That it would be more appropriate for this section to appear after 3:7, as Brox (226) suggests, overlooks the need to keep internal cohesion in the face of external threats, a need that dictated the placement of this material here.

12   On the problem of how νεώτεροι is to be construed, see the comments on v. 5 below.

13   So, e.g., Goldstein, *Paulinische Gemeinde*, 17. John H. Elliott finds affinities with Mark 10:35–45 par. and John 21:15–23, which, he argues, lie at the base of the understanding of the nature of Christian leadership reflected also in this passage ("Ministry and Church Order in the NT: A Traditio-Historical Analysis [1 Pt 5,1–5 & plls.]," *CBQ* 32 [1970] 390). Brox (227) finds evidence of diverse traditions in the fact that in 4:10–11 there was no mention of elders, while in 5:1–5 there is no mention of charismata.

14   To bishops: 1 Tim 3:1–7; Titus 1:7–9; deacons: 1 Tim 3:8–13; elders: 1 Tim 5:17–19; Titus 1:5–6.

15   Michaels (278) notes the "testament-like character" of this passage, but observes correctly that if it is a farewell, it is grounded not in the author's imminent death but in an imminent parousia.

16   Michaels's (277) suggestion (based in part on the lack of an article for πρεσβυτέρους at the beginning of v. 1) that the similarity of 5:1–5 with 4:7–11 may indicate that the latter is addressed to all congregations, while the former is limited to those congregations that have elders, remains unpersuasive.

17   Goppelt (319) argues that the office originated in the Palestinian church; one may cite as evidence Acts 15:2; 16:4; 21:18. For more on this point, see the comments on v. 1 below.

18   Bishop: 1 Tim 3:1; Titus 1:7–9 elder: 1 Tim 5:17; Titus 1:5–6; deacon: 1 Tim 3:8; all three are mentioned in Ignatius *Magn.* 6.1; 13.1; *Trall.* 2; *Phld.* 10.2; *Pol.* 6.1.

19   With, e.g., Brox, 227. But see Goppelt (319–20), who finds various stages of development in this

Discussion of the necessary characteristics of leaders within the Christian community is placed here not to provide advice on how the community is to be organized, however,[20] but because in the testing situation discussed in 4:12–19, effective pastoral leadership is indispensable if the community is to survive.[21] Leaders must function pastorally, not dictatorially, if those wounded by external social pressures are to remain within the community. Conversely, there must be mutual trust within the community, especially between those with leadership responsibilities and the other members, since lack of trust within the community in the presence of severe pressure against the Christian faith in the external world would doom the community. Only with good leadership and mutual respect will the community and its individual members survive to share in the glory that is to come when the divine judgment has run its course.[22]

Comment

■ 1 Although the consecutive force of the οὖν ("so then," "therefore") is not immediately apparent,[23] it does link in a general way the discussion about the problems Christians face from external social pressure to the need for sound internal organization if the community is to survive those onslaughts.[24] The word used to identify the group addressed, πρεσβύτεροι ("elders"), can refer to age, but because of the further description of their activity in vv. 2–3, it is more likely that it refers here not specifically to older people but rather to community leaders, granted that such leaders were often picked from among the older members of a group.[25] While the word would also be understandable in that meaning to the Hellenistic culture,[26] it seems more likely that the term was borrowed from the Jewish synagogue, where it was the usual designation for a leader,[27] and may have come into Christian tradition through its use by the Jewish Christian community.[28] Although "elder," along with "bishop" and "deacon," emerged within NT times as the title of a specific church official,[29] it is not clear to what extent such organization was already present in the churches to which the letter is addressed. There is some evidence that points to the fluidity of church organization within them. For example, "elder" as a church leader is not mentioned in the letters of Paul generally assumed to be genuine, but is assumed in Acts[30] as in the Pastorals[31] to have been characteristic of his churches.[32] Again, the lack of a definite article with the word

evidence, and Kelly (197), who finds here a "relatively early stage in the evolution of church government."

20 With Philipps (Kirche, 25), who also notes that the point of the passage is not how the community should be structured, but rather the kind of mutual respect and humility necessary within a community under outside pressure, if that community is to survive.

21 With, e.g., Kelly, 196; cf. also Margot, 82–83.

22 As so often in the letter, one sees here the contrast between present suffering and future glory.

23 Spicq (163) finds the word difficult to interpret.

24 Linking the verse to the ἀγαθοποιΐα of 4:19 as an example of the specific kind of well-doing required of elders, as does Beare (197), may put too fine a point on it. That the οὖν was suggested by Ezek 9:6, a verse used by the author in 4:17a, which also speaks of suffering beginning with the elders, as Schutter (Hermeneutic, 79) maintains, is a bit imaginative.

25 With, e.g., Beare, "Some Remarks," 245; Bauer, 59; Hart, 76; Schelkle, 127; Goppelt, 321; Calvin, 143; Michl, "Die Presbyter," 60.

26 The word was so used in the Greco-Roman world; cf. Balch, "Household Codes," 44, quoting Arius Didymus: "Among these the presbyter has chief choice in counsel"; cf. also Beare, 197; Selwyn (227), citing A. Deissmann, Bible Studies, 154–55, 233–34.

27 See 1 Macc 11:23; 12:35; 1QS 6.8–9 (in these instances associated with priests). "Elder" is also used in the NT to describe a leader in the Jewish synagogue, e.g., Mark 7:3; 8:31; 11:27; 14:53; 15:1; Luke 7:3. On this point see Best, 167; Margot, 83; Schelkle, 127; Spicq, 164; Brox, 226–27.

28 So, e.g., Acts 11:30; see also Schröger, "Verfassung," 244; Leaney, "Passover," 239; Cothenet, "La Première Epître de Pierre," 147.

29 E.g., Acts 20:17; 1 Tim 5:17–19; Titus 1:5; Jas 5:14; 2 John 1; 3 John 1; cf. Rev 4:4, 10; 5:6–8; 7:11; 11:16; 14:3; 19:4. On this point see also Heinrich Greeven, "Propheten, Lehrer, Vorsteher bei Paulus," ZNW 44 (1952/53) 40; Beare, 197; Best, 167.

30 E.g., 14:23.

31 E.g., 1 Tim 5:17–19; Titus 1:5.

32 This type of leadership may thus have emerged at a later time than Paul. Schröger ("Verfassung," 251) suggests that they emerged as leaders as a result of internal stresses which arose in the churches, stresses referred to in Acts 20:29; 2 Tim 3:1; 2 Pet 3:3; 1 Clem. 44.1.

$\pi\rho\epsilon\sigma\beta\upsilon\tau\acute{\epsilon}\rho\upsilon\varsigma$ in this verse, along with the fact that in v. 5
it may refer more to age than to leadership,[33] and the
additional fact that the discussion of leadership functions
in the community in 4:10–11 assumes that all are
involved because of their spiritual gifts ($\chi\acute{\alpha}\rho\iota\sigma\mu\alpha$), with no
mention of elders, while in this discussion of leadership
there is no mention of spiritual gifts,[34] all point to the
lack of specific organization in the churches addressed.
That impression is further heightened by the inclusion in
this verse of the phrase $\dot{\epsilon}\nu$ $\dot{\upsilon}\mu\hat{\iota}\nu$ ("among you"), since that
phrase is absent, and the article is present, in the three
other specific groups our author addresses (slaves, 2:18;
wives, 3:1; husbands, 3:7).[35] The term may therefore
refer here not so much to a fixed group of leaders as to
any people who functioned in a leadership capacity, with
the assumption that such a group may well have varied in
membership from time to time.[36] While it may not be
wise to draw absolute inferences about the specific time
various types of church leadership emerged, since
various areas will have developed in different ways and at
different speeds, it is apparent that our author does not
assume a clearly defined hierarchical form of church
government.[37]

The author identifies himself in a threefold way in this
verse: (1) "fellow elder" ($\sigma\upsilon\mu\pi\rho\epsilon\sigma\beta\acute{\upsilon}\tau\epsilon\rho\upsilon\varsigma$), (2) "witness"
($\mu\acute{\alpha}\rho\tau\upsilon\varsigma$) of Christ's suffering, and (3) "participant"
($\kappa\upsilon\iota\nu\omega\nu\acute{\upsilon}\varsigma$) in future glory.

1. The author appears to have coined the Greek term
$\sigma\upsilon\mu\pi\rho\epsilon\sigma\beta\acute{\upsilon}\tau\epsilon\rho\upsilon\varsigma$, since it does not appear in Greek
literature prior to our letter, but is used frequently by
later Christian writers.[38] In this context, where the
apostle Peter is assumed to be speaking (1:1), the term
clearly implies that apostolic authority is involved in the
functioning of the elder.[39] It also serves the purpose of a
contemporary application of the traditions associated
with Peter as one of the apostolic leaders of the earliest
Christian community to the leaders of the persecuted
Christian communities of Asia Minor.[40]

2. While the phrase $\mu\acute{\alpha}\rho\tau\upsilon\varsigma$ $\tau\hat{\omega}\nu$ $\tau\upsilon\hat{\upsilon}$ $X\rho\iota\sigma\tau\upsilon\hat{\upsilon}$ $\pi\alpha\theta\eta\mu\acute{\alpha}\tau\omega\nu$
("witness of the suffering of Christ") can be construed to
mean an eyewitness to Christ's crucifixion,[41] with
support drawn from such passages as Acts 1:8, 22; 2:32;
3:15; 5:32; 10:39, 41,[42] or the frequent references to the
passion in the letter itself, at 1:11, 19; 2:21–24; 3:18—
4:1, 13,[43] or on the implied contrast in 1:8 to the
noneyewitness status of the readers,[44] the unanimous
gospel tradition that Peter was in fact not present at the
crucifixion cuts directly across any such construal.[45] A
more likely construal of "witness" in the context of
Petrine tradition is to understand it in terms of one who
bears witness to events, in this case Jesus' passion,[46] the

33 Tarrech ("Le milieu," 126) finds here further
    evidence of the term's fluidity.
34 On this point see also Brox, 227.
35 The author uses the definite article in each of those
    instances to identify them as a specific group; the
    absence of the article here seems therefore all the
    more striking.
36 With, e.g., Michaels, 279; Cranfield, 124; Johnson,
    "Asia Minor," 114.
37 It is surely not the kind of monarchial episcopate for
    which Ignatius of Antioch pleads somewhat later in
    letters addressed to many of the same churches, a
    point Cothenet ("La Première Epître de Pierre," 149)
    also makes. For further discussion of the kind of
    church governance assumed in 1 Peter, see Michl,
    "Die Presbyter"; A. Bischoff, "'Αλλοτρι(ο)επίκοπος,"
    ZNW 7 (1906) 271–74; Elliott, "Ministry."
38 E.g., Athanasius, Basil, Gregory Nazianzus, Epi-
    phanius, Eusebius; it is also used at the ecumenical
    councils of Ephesus (431) and Chalcedon (451).
39 With, e.g., Schiwy, 61; Michl, "Die Presbyter," 60; cf.
    Elliott, "Peter, Silvanus and Mark," 259. It may also

be a "polite stratagem of benevolence," as Brown et
al. (Peter, 152) suggest, but its meaning is not likely to
be exhausted with such an interpretation.
40 See also Brox, "Pseudepigraphischen Rahmung," 81.
    Meade (Pseudonymity and Canon, 176) finds in such an
    application a hermeneutical key for understanding
    the purpose of this letter: the application of the
    Petrine tradition to the new situation of persecution.
    This seems more likely than the suggestion of Selwyn
    (228) that it refers to particular memories the
    churches of northern Asia Minor had of Peter.
41 So, e.g., Reicke, 129; Selwyn, 228; Spicq, 165;
    Chase, "Peter," 787. Schiwy (60) adds the resur-
    rection.
42 So, e.g., Bigg, 186.
43 So, e.g., Schelkle, 128.
44 So, e.g., Meade, Pseudonymity and Canon, 175.
45 So also, e.g., Brox, 229; Senior, 87; Dibelius,
    "Petrusbriefe," 114; Smith, Petrine Controversies, 154;
    Delling, "Der Bezug," 101; Schweizer, 98.
46 So also, e.g., Delling, "Der Bezug," 101; Michaels,
    280–81. Best (168) notes such a use of the word in

apostolic witness to which was understood to be normative by the early church. Coupled with this may well be the idea that people bear witness to Christ's suffering by themselves participating in such suffering for the sake of Christ,[47] that is, witnessing by deed as well as word.[48] Whether or not this is intended as a reference to the martyrdom of Peter,[49] its close connection with "fellow elder"[50] indicates that the author intends to say that he, like the readers, has been called upon to suffer as part of his Christian life and witness.

3. On the one hand, the form of the verse—the author, Peter, describing himself—has led some to find here an allusion to the tradition that Peter was the first to whom the risen Jesus appeared;[51] the glory is thus the glory of the risen Lord.[52] On the other hand, the specific development in 2 Pet 1:16–18 of the tradition concerning Peter's presence on the Mount of Transfiguration[53] has led others to find in this language a similar reference to the author as a participant in the glory of that event.[54] Yet (a) the explicit futurity of the participation mentioned in this verse—it is coming glory which is yet to be revealed ($\tau\hat{\eta}s$ $\mu\epsilon\lambda\lambda o\acute{u}\sigma\eta s$ $a\pi o\kappa a\lambda\acute{u}\pi$-$\tau\epsilon\sigma\theta a\iota$ $\delta\acute{o}\xi\eta s$)—and (b) the different language employed in 2 Pet 1:16–18, calling into question any idea of further development there of our verse, along with (c) the implication here that the readers will share the glory as they share the sufferings, a sharing stated explicitly in

4:13, all argue persuasively that this cannot be a reference to a past event in Peter's life,[55] whether it be resurrection appearance or presence at the transfiguration. It refers rather to the eschatological glory in which all who remain faithful to Christ will one day share, a point our author has been at pains to make (cf. 1:5, 8–9, 21; 2:24; 3:18; 4:13, 17–18; 5:10).

The verb "exhort" ($\pi a\rho a\kappa a\lambda\hat{\omega}$) represents the purpose of the verse, if not the entire letter,[56] and hence the elaborate description of the author contained in this verse is to be understood as providing further force and persuasiveness to the ensuing exhortation to those who exercise leadership in the Christian communities. While such descriptions may well belong to the "apparatus of pseudepigraphy,"[57] their significance is not thereby exhausted. Rather, the intention appears to be to admonish and exhort the leaders of the Christian communities to whom the letter is addressed to see in their leadership an extension of the apostolic ministry and authority of Peter,[58] and thus to exercise it with all the care and devotion such an extension implies. What such leadership entails is then described in the following verses.

■ 2 This verse along with the one following gives the content of the exhortation announced in v. 1: presbyters are to tend the flock of God entrusted to them.[59] In using the imagery of tending God's flock, the author is

John 1:19; 2 Cor 1:12; Titus 1:13.

47   In this case, $\tau o\hat{u}$ $X\rho\iota\sigma\tau o\hat{u}$ is to be construed not as subjective genitive, i.e., what Christ suffered, but as objective genitive, i.e., what is suffered for Christ. Less likely but still possible would be genitive of origin, i.e., suffering whose origin for his followers is Christ.

48   With, e.g., Calvin, 144; Dibelius, "Petrusbriefe," 114; Goppelt, 322; Kelly, 198–99.

49   Leany (69) thinks such a reference "certain"; see also Meade, *Pseudonymity and Canon*, 177; Smith, *Petrine Controversies*, 154; Oscar Cullmann, *Peter, Disciple, Apostle, Martyr* (trans. F. V. Filson; 2d ed.; Philadelphia: Westminster, 1962) 89. Windisch (79) argues that if it such martyrdom is referred to as in the present, it would point to Peter now glorified in heaven, as *1 Clem.* 5.4 says. On this whole point, see Marxsen, "Der Mitälteste," passim.

50   Goppelt (324) points out that the single article with $\sigma\nu\mu\pi\rho\epsilon\sigma\beta\acute{u}\tau\epsilon\rho os$ and $\mu a\rho\tau\acute{u}s$ makes them virtually a hendiadys: to be the one is to be the other.

51   Cf. 1 Cor 15:3; Mark 16:7; Luke 24:34.

52   So, e.g., Gerald L. Borchert, "The Conduct of Christians in the Face of the 'Fiery Ordeal,'" *RevExp* 74 (1982) 456; cf. Brown et al., *Peter*, 153.

53   Brox ("Tendenz," 113) notes correctly the absence here of any attempt to relate this verse to events in Peter's life; the contrast to 2 Pet 1:16–18 underscores that point.

54   So, e.g., Meade, *Pseudonymity and Canon*, 175–76; Selwyn, 113; some qualify it by seeing the transfiguration as an anticipation of the parousia, e.g., Spicq, 165; Cothenet, "La Première Epître de Pierre," 147; Smith, *Petrine Controversies*, 155.

55   With, e.g., Kelly, 199; Michaels, 282; Best, 169.

56   So 5:12; cf. Brox, 227.

57   So Beare, 198. That the author intends to describe himself, not Peter, in these phrases, as Brox (228) and Marxsen ("Der Mitälteste," 383–84) suggest, is, in light of 1:1, highly unlikely.

58   With, e.g., Brox, 229.

59   Goppelt (324) argues that $\pi o\iota\mu\acute{a}\nu a\tau\epsilon$ is an ingressive aorist (as in 1:13, 17, 22), which calls not for continuation but for ever new beginning of the act, a

drawing on a long OT tradition, in which God is the shepherd of his people Israel,[60] a tradition that may well have taken its origin in the tradition that God led his people out of bondage like a shepherd leads his sheep.[61] Israel's leaders are then also called shepherds.[62] After evil shepherds have allowed God's flock to scatter, God will provide a true shepherd to reassemble the flock.[63] This figure of shepherd and flock was then taken into Christian tradition, beginning with Jesus as the one who was to reassemble Israel,[64] perhaps as part of his reconstitution of the chosen people through his disciples.[65] It proved an enduring tradition, and continued to be used in both NT[66] and post-NT times.[67] In the context of this letter, the immediate derivation of this command is probably to be seen in John 21:16,[68] with Peter here

understood as the mediator of that tradition.

A grammatical difficulty is presented by the phrase ἐν ὑμῖν, since its usual meaning ("among you")[69] here makes little sense.[70] It is probably to be construed as a dative of sphere, that is, the area within which something occurs, in this instance the area of the presbyter's authority, and bears some such meaning as "within your care" or "under your charge."[71]

The participle ἐπισκοποῦντες is to be construed either as an adverbial participle of attendant circumstance, indicating activity that accompanies and further defines the shepherding ("exercising oversight"), or as an adverbial participle of means, indicating how such shepherding is to occur ("by exercising oversight").[72] Since the same cluster of words is found in Acts 20:38[73]

---

contention supported by Kelly (199); cf. Spicq, 166. Since, however, the continuation is already given with the present παρακαλῶ ("I exhort") of v. 1, it is more likely that the author simply reverted here to the use of the aorist as the normal tense for the imperative, as he then does in the remaining verses of the letter (5:5, 6, 8, 14).

60 Pss 23:1–4; 28:9; 74:1; 77:20; 78:52; 79:13; 80:1; 95:7; 100:3; Isa 40:11; 63:11; Jer 13:17; 23:1–3; 50:6; Ezek 34:6, 8, 31; Mic 7:14.

61 Ps 78:52; cf. LXX Hos 13:5.

62 Isa 63:11; cf. Num 27:17.

63 Jer 23:1–4; Ezek 34:23–24; Mic 5:3–5; Zech 10:3; 11:16; *Ps. Sol.* 17.40; cf. Qumran, CD 13.7–9. On this tradition in the OT and later Jewish literature, see, e.g., Michl, "Die Presbyter," 55 n. 36; Deterding, "Exodus Motifs," 62; Goppelt, 325; Michaels, 283; Cothenet, "La Première Epître de Pierre," 148.

64 E.g., Matt 10:6; 15:24; Mark 6:34.

65 Mark 14:27–28 par. Matt 26:31–32; Matt 10:16 par. Luke 10:3; Luke 12:32; John 10:1–18; 21:16.

66 Acts 20:28; Eph 4:11.

67 *1 Clem.* 16.1; 44.3; 54.2; 57.2; Ignatius *Phld.* 2.1; *Rom.* 9.1; Polycarp *Phil.* 6.1; *Hermas,* esp. *Sim.* 9.31.5–6. On this point see, e.g., Goppelt, 324; Best, 170, Wolfgang Nauck, "Probleme des frühchristlichen Amtsverständnisses," *ZNW* 48 (1957) 201.

68 With, e.g., Hart, 76; Michaels, 282. Brown et al. (*Peter,* 153) note that if John originated, as tradition held, in Ephesus, Peter as shepherd could well have been a familiar figure to the readers of this letter.

69 Adopted, however, by the *RV.*

70 So also, e.g., Beare (199), who identifies it as a "pregnant use of the preposition."

71 With, e.g., *RSV, NRSV.* So also Cranfield ("I Peter," 127): that part of the flock committed to a particular

elder's care; less likely Selwyn (230): the flock distributed in different localities where presbyters live and work, a point supported, however, by Bigg, 188; Schiwy, 61; Windisch, 79; Reicke, 129; and Michaels, 283. Bigg (188) notes other attempts to resolve it: Erasmus, Calvin: to the best of your power; Luther: which depends upon you, is entrusted to you.

72 Calvin (145) reasoned that since oversight (ἐπισκοποῦντες, ἐπίσκοπος = "bishop") is identified as the function of an elder, the "two names, bishop and elder, are synonymous"; so too, more recently, Cothenet ("La Première Epître de Pierre," 149), who finds a similar identity in Titus 1:5, 7.

73 Ποίμνιον, ποιμαίνω, the stem ἐπισκοπ-. Nauck ("Probleme") observed that in the earliest ecclesiastical traditions words from the stems ποιμαν- and ἐπισκοπ- almost always occur together (202), and that the origin of the Christian idea of a bishop cannot be adequately accounted for from the synagogue or Greco-Roman traditions (203). Hence he argued that the similarities between the ritual prayer for the dedication of a bishop contained in Hippolytus, which mentions tending the flock (*Ap. Trad.* 3.4–5; see "Probleme," 204–6), is so close to the instruction for the overseer (מבקר) at Qumran (CD 13.7–12), which also mentions tending the flock (CD 13.9; see "Probleme," 206–7), that the latter must be the origin of the prayer in Hippolytus, thus indicating that the origin of the early Christian idea of the bishop derives from Qumran, and that our verse shares that same tradition (207).

where Paul is addressing the elders of Ephesus, his further charge to them to be guardians of orthodoxy (20:29–31) and to help the weak (20:35) may provide clues to the kind of responsibility borne generally by the elder.[74]

The ensuing three pairs of contrasting phrases (vv. 2b–3) describe how such tending and oversight are to be exercised: not under pressure but willingly, not because of any stipend but eagerly, not by harsh command but by example. While the admonitions may seem like clichés,[75] they are written within the context of v. 1, namely, the context of suffering (see also 4:12–19), and they ask here of the leaders no more than had been asked of the communities earlier (1:22; 4:8a), namely, that they act in love toward those under their charge. Because the style of these two verses—an exhortation (v. 2a) explicated by three pairs of couplets, each couplet consisting of first a negative, then a positive point—is found nowhere else in the letter except 2:22–23 and 3:18, which also appear to be traditional, it is possible that the same is true here, namely, that our author is drawing for this material on earlier tradition.[76] Yet the contrast of negative with positive (οὐ/μή with ἀλλά) is a familiar construction in 1 Peter (1:14–15, 18–19, 23; 2:18; 3:21; 4:2, 12–13), and there are no clear parallels to these three contrasts elsewhere in the NT, indicating that although tradition may underlie them, it is by no means certain that it does.

The first antithesis, employing language that is not common in biblical Greek,[77] is used nowhere else in the NT in advice on how to conduct ecclesiastical responsibility. The contrast between "not under compulsion" (μὴ ἀναγκαστῶς) and "willingly" or "freely" (ἑκουσίως) apparently exhorts elders to accept their responsibilities without undue coercion.[78] The added phrase κατὰ θεόν, qualifying ἑκουσίως, indicates the kind of willingness to be displayed, namely, a willingness to carry out their duties in accordance with what God wants, rather than simply to be enthusiastic about what they do.[79]

The second antithesis qualifies the first, in that the second term, προθύμως ("eagerly"), is virtually a synonym for ἑκουσίως,[80] and the first term, μὴ αἰσχροκερδῶς ("not in a way characterized by desire for base gain"), may be a concrete instance of the kind of compulsion to be avoided. Unlike the negated member of the first antithesis (μὴ ἀναγκαστῶς), which is not used in advice to church leaders in the NT, the warning against desire for money is a regular part of such advice,[81] as is its use to characterize untrustworthy teachers who teach for money.[82] While this may imply that by this time elders were compensated for their service,[83] a practice based on a word of Jesus (Matt 10:10) and supported by Paul,[84] and thus the intention is to urge that people not seek or accept the responsibility of elder simply for the stipend, it is as likely to be the case that since church leaders had

---

74 Some further clues may be derived from the three pairs of contrasts contained in vv. 2b–3, on which see below.

75 E.g., Brox, 230.

76 So, e.g., Nauck, "Probleme," 200; Cothenet, "La Première Epître de Pierre," 148; Eliott, "Ministry," 372–73.

77 Ἀναγκαστῶς is absent from the LXX and the NT, ἑκουσίως appears in the LXX five times (Exod 36:2; Ps 53:8; 2 Macc 14:3; 4 Macc 5:23; 8:25), in the NT one other time (Heb 10:26).

78 Whether this implies elders ere elected, as Goppelt (326) argues, citing as evidence Acts 14:23; Titus 1:5; *1 Clem.* 42.4; 44.3, is open to question, since, in each of the instances cited, the appointment rather than election of elders seems indicated.

79 With, e.g., Nauck, "Probleme," 208. Goppelt (326 n. 21) points out that words derived from the same stem as ἑκουσίως are used in LXX Judg (B) 5:2, 9; Ps 53:8; 1 Macc 2:42–44 to mean placing oneself at God's disposal, and a comparable term in the QL is virtually a description of membership (1QS 5.8, 10; cf. 1.7,

11; 5.1, 6, 21–22; 6.13), indicating how ἑκουσίως κατὰ θεόν is to be understood.

80 With, e.g., Nauck, "Probleme," 209.

81 1 Tim 3:8; Titus 1:7; *Ap. Const.* 2.6.1; 2.9.2; cf. the comparable word ἀφιλάργυρος ("no lover of money") in 1 Tim 3:3; *Did.* 15.1; Polycarp *Phil.* 5.2; see 6.1. On this point see, e.g., Nauck, "Probleme," 209; Brox, 231; Goppelt, 326; Selwyn, 231.

82 1 Tim 6:5; Titus 1:11; 2 Pet 2:3, 14; Jude 11; *Did.* 11.12. On this point see, e.g., Michl, "Die Presbyter," 56 n. 43.

83 So also, e.g., Goppelt, 326; Bigg, 188; Michaels, 285; Selwyn, 231; but see Schelkle, 129.

84 1 Cor 9:7–12a. Paul's ready acceptance of a gift from the church at Philippi (Phil 4:10) may indicate that Paul's refusal of compensation from the Christians in Corinth did not reflect his general practice.

responsibility for community funds (Acts 5:1–5; 2 Cor 8:20)[85] elders also carried that responsibility. The case of the elder Valens, accused by Polycarp of avarice (*Phil.* 11.1–4), confirms that some at least succumbed to the temptation of personal enrichment at the expense of their community,[86] and may underlie the advice in this second antithesis. The positive injunction, that they are to conduct their responsibilities eagerly (προθύμως),[87] employs a word frequently used in praise of functionaries and benefactors of a city,[88] and emphasizes the eagerness with which an elder is to assume ecclesiastical duties.

■ **3** The third antithesis belongs, according to its structure (μή [δε]-ἀλλά), with two other antitheses that described how oversight was to be exercised, but by form (participles κατακυριεύοντες, γινόμενοι) it would, like exercising oversight (ἐπισκοποῦντες, v. 2b), describe how tending the flock should be carried on. The resolution of that ambiguity, and the interpretation of the verse as a whole, depends principally on the resolution of two problems: (1) the construal of ὡς, which in its turn affects the construal of the two participles, κατακυριεύοντες and γινόμενοι; and (2) the meaning assigned to τῶν κλήρων.

1. Because the word ὡς has a variety of possible meanings, it is advisable to allow its other uses in this epistle to determine its possible meaning here.[89] While it is used in the sense of "just as" or "even as,"[90] it is used far more often either (a) in the sense of "like" or "as if" or

"as it were," indicating a metaphorical intent,[91] or (b) with the meaning "in the manner of" or "functioning as."[92] On the one hand, if sense (a) be applied here, then the ὡς indicates the use of the metaphor of oppressive secular rulers to describe a way of exercising oversight that elders are to avoid in their dealings with their flock.[93] The problem then arises, however, that one cannot construe the ὡς in that way with the second participle, which does not describe a metaphorical situation. The first participle will then be substantive, the second probably an adverbial participle of means ("by becoming examples for the flock"). On the other hand, the three other times ὡς is used to modify a participle,[94] that participle functions as a substantive, describing a class of people by their actions, and bears the meaning designated (b) above, "functioning as." If that is the meaning here, then it describes further how elders are to act in tending the flock, and can then also be understood as modifying the second participle in the verse (γινόμενοι), thus giving first the negative and then the positive manner in which elders are to tend their flock: not acting as those who lord it over others (probably secular rulers),[95] but acting as those who become examples. While both construals make good sense in this context, the ability of the second construal to allow both participles to function in the same way probably makes it the preferable construal.

85 So also Goppelt, 326; Michl, "Die Presbyter," 56 n. 43; Windisch, 79.
86 So also, e.g., Schlier, "Adhortatio," 72.
87 As noted above, it is virtually a synonym for ἑκουσίως. Goppelt's suggestion (326) that it raises the willingness of the first antithesis to passionate devotion may be a bit overstated.
88 So also Spicq, 167. It is often used in conjunction with the verb χορηγέω (lit. "supply funds for a chorus"; more generally "supply" or "provide"), thus praising such people for their readiness to provide the necessary resources for some community endeavor.
89 To dismiss it, as does Michaels (285), as having little meaning but contributing to the style and sound by echoing the -ως endings of the four preceding adverbs, is a possible but in this instance inadvisable procedure.
90 3:6; perhaps 5:12.
91 1:19, 24; 2:2, 5, 11; 2:16 (second use), 25; 4:12; 5:7.
92 1:14; 2:12, 13, 14, 16 (first use); 3:7 (bis); 4:11, 15, 16.
93 Tarrech ("Le milieu," 358–59) argues for this, on the basis of his view that the people addressed are rural, and toil as laborers on large estates. The author thus says elders are not to function as do those who rule those estates. The situation assumed is speculative, however.
94 2:12, 13, 16.
95 It has the same meaning in Mark 10:42 par. Matt 20:25 (Luke 22:25–26 is parallel in content, but uses a different verb). On this point see Hart, 76; Goppelt, 327. Its only other use, Acts 19:16, also has negative connotations. Michaels's doubt (285) that such a contrast is present, based on the author's respect for secular authority portrayed in 2:13–17, is not germane, since those verses say only to be subordinate; they say nothing of the way secular authorities rule. The same advice is give to slaves in 2:18b who do have unruly masters.

2. The precise meaning of $\tau\hat{\omega}\nu$ $\kappa\lambda\dot{\eta}\rho\omega\nu$, the object of the verb "to lord it over," is difficult to determine.[96] The word $\kappa\lambda\hat{\eta}\rho os$ can mean the lot(s) cast to determine who receives a portion or an assignment,[97] but can also mean some portion or lot that has been assigned.[98] On the basis of the meaning "ecclesiastical office" that the word later assumed,[99] some have argued that elders are here being advised not to be high-handed in assigning, and dealing with, lower ranks of clergy.[100] In a similar vein, the duty of the leader at Qumran to assign a member's place in the community[101] has led to the suggestion that a warning is here issued to the elders not to be high-handed in the way they allocate offices or functions.[102] Yet the parallelism between the phrases $\tau\dot{o}$ $\dot{\epsilon}\nu$ $\dot{\nu}\mu\hat{\iota}\nu$ $\pi o\dot{\iota}\mu\nu\iota o\nu$ in v. 2a as the object of the verb $\pi o\iota\mu\dot{a}\nu a\tau\epsilon$, and $\tau\hat{\omega}\nu$ $\kappa\lambda\dot{\eta}\rho\omega\nu$ as the object of the participle $\kappa a\tau a\kappa\nu\rho\iota\epsilon\dot{\nu}o\nu\tau\epsilon s$ in this verse, indicates that it more likely refers here to the individuals or congregations over which the various elders have responsibility.[103] On the one hand, the use of $\kappa\lambda\hat{\eta}\rho os$ here in the plural may indicate specific portions of a given community over which various elders have specific responsibility.[104] On the other hand, the plural reference to the charge may well simply reflect the plural

reference to elders, pointing to the various congregations over which the various elders have responsibility.[105] However that question be resolved, it appears more likely on the basis of the parallel with v. 2a that the reference here is to Christians in the flocks tended by the elders rather than to minor clergy assigned their roles by the elder/bishop.

The alternative to leading by high-handed authoritarianism given in v. 3b is leading by example. The idea of the leader of a Christian community functioning as an example for other Christians is limited in the NT to this reference in 1 Peter, and to the letters of Paul, where it occurs with some frequency.[106] The supreme instance of one who provided the example for Christian conduct is of course Jesus himself,[107] an example our author has used earlier.[108] The immediately following verse, where Christ is identified as the "chief shepherd," makes clear that once again he is the example to be followed, this time by the shepherd/elders. Elders are therefore to exercise their authority by showing through their conduct how Christians are to live their own lives.[109]

The thrust of these two verses, with their command and the three following pairs of antitheses, is to make

---

96   Nauck ("Probleme," 210) lists six proposals scholars have made for its meaning here: (1) the believers; (2) the land belonging to the presbyters; (3) the place of the faithful in the messianic kingdom; (4) the individual communities given to various presbyters; (5) the money received and spent for the community by the elders; (6) the eschatological portion given to each elder.

97   E.g., Matt 27:35; Acts 1:26.

98   Acts 1:17; 8:21; 26:18; Col 1:12. On this basis, Nauck ("Probleme," 212) argues that it means here the hierarchy, determined by lot, of clergy and laity in the community, a too literal interpretation of the word in this context.

99   According to Hippolytus (*Ap. Trad.* 3.5) it was the bishop's duty to assign these inferior clerical offices.

100 E.g., Schwank et al., 100; Nauck, "Probleme," 211. This meaning is also assumed by the Vulgate, which translates this phrase *neque . . . dominantes in cleris* ("not . . . lording over the clergy"). Interestingly, Hippolytus (*Ap. Trad.* 9.7) forbade elders to make such clerical assignments.

101 Assigned by priests, 1 QS 5.20–24; 6.22; 9.7; by the leader (mebaqqer), CD 13.13.

102 So, e.g., Kelly, 202. But see Tarrech ("Le milieu," 360), who argues, I think correctly, against finding anything here about the internal organization of the

community.

103 With, e.g., Beare (200): "must certainly mean the local communities"; Deterding ("Exodus Motifs," 63): "individual Christian congregations"; Goppelt (327): local community ruled by the elder. See also Moffatt, 164; Spicq, 168; Windisch, 79. Michaels (286) emphasizes the parallelism between this phrase and the phrase in v. 2a.

104 So, e.g., Cranfield, 130; Best, 170; Bigg, 188. Reicke (129) finds an analogy for this in Qumran, e.g., 1QS 6.3; CD 13.1–2. Bornemann ("Taufrede," 157) argues that it refers to newly baptized Christians assigned to the tutelage of various individual presbyters, on the assumption, no longer widely held, that this verse was part of a baptismal homily.

105 With, e.g., Moffatt, 164; Wand, 123; Windisch, 79.

106 1 Cor 4:16; Gal 4:12; Phil 3:17; 1 Thess 1:6; 2:14; 2 Thess 3:7, 9; cf. 1 Tim 4:12; Titus 2:7. Christian communities can also serve as examples, e.g., 1 Thess 1:7; 2:14.

107 E.g., John 13:15; cf. 2 Cor 8:9; Phil 2:5.

108 E.g., 2:21–23; 4:1; cf. 2:23b with 4:19.

109 With, e.g., Michl, "Die Presbyter," 57.

clear that Christian leaders are, like good shepherds, to exercise their authority for the good of those entrusted to their care, not for their own satisfaction or enrichment.[110] Christians are not the subjects of the elders, as is the case in the secular realm with leaders and subjects, but rather all Christians belong to God, and so the presbyters must carry out their duties as servants of God, not as lords of the Christians under their care.[111] Arrogance toward other Christians and arbitrary exercise of power have no place in the leadership of the church, since those leaders also stand under God's opposition to the arrogant but his graciousness to the humble (v. 5b).[112]

■ **4** The result of the elders' faithful execution of their duties, as outlined in vv. 2–3, is here announced: when Christ returns, they will receive their eschatological reward. The conjunction καί (v. 4) following the imperative of v. 2 implies a conditional sentence, with vv. 2–3 the protasis and v. 4 the apodosis: if the elders tend God's flock well (vv. 2–3) they will receive their reward (v. 4).[113] The genitive absolute phrase (φανερωθέντος τοῦ ἀρχιποίμενος) that introduces the verse is to be construed as temporal: "when the chief shepherd appears." The term "chief shepherd" (ἀρχιποίμην), although not coined by the author as once was thought, is nevertheless rare;[114] the only other comparable reference in the NT is found in the concluding doxology of Hebrews.[115]

That Christ is the chief shepherd implies that the elders who shepherd God's flock are continuing, in part at least, Christ's ministry,[116] and perhaps also implies that they will stand before Christ to be judged on how they have functioned as such shepherds of his flocks.[117] The verb in the genitive absolute phrase (φανερωθέντος) refers in the NT both to Christ's incarnation[118] and to his parousia;[119] the latter is meant here.[120] The eschatological language of the opening phrase is continued with the verb κομιεῖσθε ("you will receive"), which refers in the NT to receiving eschatological recompense, whether positive (Eph 6:8; Heb 10:36; 11:13 [some mss.], 39) or negative (Col 3:25).[121]

That a crown is the reward of the faithful shepherd/elders draws on widespread custom, since the concept of someone receiving a crown for meritorious activity was widespread in the ancient world. In Greco-Roman culture, distinguished statesmen and public benefactors received crowns in recognition of their services, and crowns were also awarded to the victors in both military activity and athletic events.[122] While not so widespread within Jewish tradition, the imagery of the crown as symbol of a special virtue or achievement is also present there, especially in the wisdom literature.[123] While the crown is emblematic of royalty,[124] it is also a regular symbol in the NT of divine eschatological recognition,[125] and the context of our verse indicates the

110 So also, e.g., Beare, 200.
111 With, e.g., Michl, "Die Presbyter," 55.
112 So also, e.g., Nauck, "Probleme," 212. The normal understanding of Christian leadership as service (διακονία, e.g., Mark 9:35; Rom 12:7; cf. 2 Cor 1:24), based on the example of Jesus (Mark 10:45), points in the same direction, as Brox (231) notes.
113 The same construction is found in Luke 10:28: "Do this and you will live" (τοῦτο ποίει καὶ ζήσῃ); cf. Gen 42:18.
114 Moulton and Milligan (*Vocabulary*, 82) report it was found on the mummy label of an Egyptian peasant; see also Beare, 201; Goppelt, 329. It does not appear elsewhere in pre-Christian Greek literature, although it is used in later Christian writings. That it originated in the Cybele cult, or was derived from the term ἀρχιβούκολος ("chief herdsman"), which was used in the Dionysius mystery and found often in inscriptions, as Perdelwitz (*Mysterienreligion*, 100) suggests, owes as much to his scholarly imagination as to any available evidence.
115 Heb 13:20: τὸν ποιμένα . . . τὸν μέγαν ("the great shepherd").

116 With, e.g., Brox, 232. That Christ was the shepherd of his people was already made clear in 2:25.
117 So, e.g., Brox, 233.
118 1 Tim 3:16; Heb 9:26; 1 Pet 1:20; *Barn.* 6.7.
119 1 John 2:28; 3:2; Col 3:4.
120 So also, e.g., Goppelt, 329; Selwyn, 231; Windisch, 79. As Michl ("Die Presbyter," 57 n. 50) observes, the reward comes at the parousia, not at the time of the death of the individual shepherd; this latter notion arose later.
121 On this point see Goppelt, 329.
122 For specific examples, see the discussion of "unfading" (ἀμαράτινον) below.
123 See Prov 4:9; 12:4; 14:24; 16:31; 17:6; Sir 1:11, 18; 6:31; 15:6; 25:6; Wis 5:16; cf. 1QH 9.25. For a discussion of the significance of "crown" in the Bible, see Spicq, 169.
124 E.g., Jer 13:18; Matt 27:29.
125 1 Cor 9:25; 2 Tim 4:8; Jas 1:12; Rev 2:10; 3:11. On this point see also Goppelt, 329; Beare, 201.

latter symbolism is the one employed here. While in some uses of the tradition, Christ himself presents the crown,[126] it is more likely here, in light of 5:10, that our author thinks of God as the one who awards it.[127]

The crown that serves as the reward of the faithful elder/shepherds is qualified by two phrases, ἀμαράντινον ("unfading"), and τῆς δόξης ("of glory"). The word ἀμαράντινον derives from the name of a dark-red flower[128] that had the reputation of resisting fading.[129] While the form of the word itself means "made of amaranths" rather than the adjective meaning "unfading" (ἀμάρατον, used in 1:4),[130] it bears the latter meaning,[131] and ought to be understood in that way here. While distinguished statesmen and public benefactors received crowns of gold from the community in recognition of services rendered,[132] the reference to an unfading crown in our verse implies a contrast with other crowns that do fade,[133] and would be more appropriate in relation to the crowns made of leaves or other vegetation received by victors whether in war[134] or in athletic contests.[135] Although the crown in this verse could be emblematic of the crown awarded at a military victory,[136] the contrast to the crown awarded to the victor in an athletic contest employed in the Pauline tradition[137] makes that the more likely candidate here.[138]

While the phrase τὸ . . . τῆς δόξης στέφανον is unique in the NT, it does appear in the LXX[139] and Jewish tradition,[140] and may originate there, an impression strengthened by the fact that the crown can symbolize eschatological reward.[141] That probably also means that the genitive τῆς δόξης is to be understood as a genitive of definition ("crown of glory")[142] rather than as epexigetic ("crown, that is, glory").[143] It is the divine, unfading crown, emblematic of God's approval and reward, that awaits those elders/shepherds who bear their responsibilities appropriately and effectively.

■ 5 The adverb ὁμοίως that begins the verse indicates that like the shepherd/elders, others also have responsibilities, in this case the younger (νεώτεροι) who are to be subordinate (ὑποτάγητε).[144] A variety of factors has led to the speculation that this material was taken from a catalog of duties (Haustafel) similar to, if not identical with, the one found in 2:11—3:7.[145] Such factors are: (1) the presence of the adverbial conjunction ὁμοίως ("similarly," 3:1, 7); (2) the use of a contrasting pair ("younger", "older") characteristic of tables of duties; (3) the apparent difference in use of πρεσβύτεροι, meaning one who exercised shepherding authority in vv. 1–4, while in this verse it apparently refers simply to age ("older persons"); (4) the use in both places of forms of ὑποτάσσω ("subordinate," 2:13, 18; 3:1); (5) the difficulty in accounting for πάντες in this verse since it does not follow a longer enumeration (as was the case in 3:8).[146]

126 2 Tim 4:8; Rev 2:10; 3:11.

127 So also, e.g., Tarrech, "Le milieu," 366 n. 222.

128 Schwank et al., 101.

129 Tarrech, "Le milieu," 365.

130 On this point see, e.g., Bigg, 189; Best 171; Michaels, 287–88. The adjective itself derives from μαραίνω with a-privative.

131 See, e.g., Philostratus Her. 741.17.

132 Moffatt, 165.

133 With, e.g., Hart, 77; Selwyn, 233; Leaney, 69; Holmer and de Boor, 168; contra Moffatt, 165; Best, 171.

134 E.g., Germanicus, who, as Martial (Epig. 2.2) reports, was given a crown of bay after his victory at Chatti; Pliny (Hist. nat. 15.5) says that cavalry squadrons were given wreaths of olive for minor triumphs.

135 Victors at the Olympic games received crowns of wild olive; at the Pythian games, bay; at the Nemean games, parsley; and at the Isthmian games, ivy; cf. Wand, 124. See also Dio Chrysostom Or. 8.15; Pliny Hist. nat. 15.5.

136 So Tarrech, "Le milieu," 364, 366.

137 1 Cor 9:25; 2 Tim 2:5.

138 With, e.g., Cranfield, 131; Michaels, 288; but see Kelly, 204. Hart's (77) suggestion that underlying this passage is the custom of crowning guests at a banquet with garlands of flowers (e.g., Wis 2:8), and the conception of the final age as a banquet at which presumably similar crownings take place, is interesting but a bit imaginative.

139 Jer 13:18: the humiliation of the king and queen includes loss of their glorious crown. The concept is also present in Isa 28:5 and Sir 47:6, although different words for "crown" are used there.

140 T. Benj. 4.1; 1QS 4.7; 1QH 9.25.

141 T. Benj. 4.1; 1QS 4.7.

142 With Selwyn, 233.

143 So Kelly, 204; Michaels, 287.

144 With, e.g., Selwyn, 107.

145 So, e.g., Boismard, "Liturgie" [2], 179, 180; Eliott, "Ministry," 389; Brox, 234; Kelly, 204.

146 Elliott ("Ministry," 389) argues that such a reconstruction would parallel Eph 5:22–6:9. Yet the latter begins with a generalization in v. 21, while this series

Such points and the conclusion are not without difficulties of their own, however, and as a result such a theory of dislocation is not entirely convincing. We may consider the points in order.

1. Since the same author is writing who wrote 2:13—3:8, it should not be surprising that he chose to link succeeding comments on responsibilities with the same adverbial conjunction, ὁμοίως. It can simply mean here that like "elders," younger people also have responsibilities within the community.

2. The use of a contrasting pair (here "younger" and "older") does occur in the previous table of duties, but only in one instance, that of wives and husbands; it is not the case with household slaves, where all reference to masters is absent. The pairing here may therefore have particular significance for our author, and may not be due simply to his taking material that reflected the formal structure of the table of duties. As in the case of the longer discussion of wives, and the brief remarks to husbands who might be tempted to take advantage of their wives on the basis of advice given to them, so here a longer discussion of the serving role of elders is followed by shorter advice to others who might be tempted to take advantage of their leaders on the basis of those remarks, perhaps ignoring the admonitions given by those with leadership responsibilities.

3. The possible difference in meaning of the word

πρεσβύτερος here ("older persons") and in v. 1 ("elder/shepherds")[147] would not be in evidence if νεώτεροι ("younger") here referred to a group based on something other than age, since then πρεσβύτεροι could continue to mean "elders" as a group exercising leadership. A number of possibilities have been suggested.

a. It could refer to the "young" in faith, that is, recent converts or neophytes within the congregation.[148] That kind of ranking did exist at Qumran,[149] and could have been carried over into the Christian communities.[150] Its appropriateness in this context is somewhat questionable,[151] however, since the πάντες in v. 5b implies that the pair includes the whole congregation.

b. Since there were organizations of young people in Greece and Asia Minor brought together for a variety of reasons and a variety of tasks,[152] it is possible that such a grouping passed into the church as well.[153] Titus 2:6–8, for example, with its exhortation that the νεώτεροι practice sound teaching, may refer to such a group of younger people.[154] Yet on the whole the existence of such a group remains problematic.[155]

c. Again, one can see in the νεώτεροι a reference to the remainder of the congregation, the equivalent of God's flock mentioned in v. 2,[156] in which the term "elder" would retain the ambiguity of the older people from whose ranks the leaders were drawn,[157] and the

---

ends with it in v. 5b; furthermore, the order in which the pairs are treated is different, as is their content. Such "parallelism" is hardly convincing.

147 Such a difference in meaning is posited by, e.g., Borchert, "Conduct of Christians," 458; Boismard, "Liturgie" [2], 179; Bengel, *Gnomon*, 756; Leaney, 70; Schweizer, 101; Calvin, 147.

148 So, e.g., Eliott, "Ministry," 379; cf 382. More specifically, Elliott thinks (385) it refers to newly baptized Christians, and cites for similar references 1:3, 21; 2:2, 4, 11–17; 4:10–11. Yet with the fading of the argument that a significant portion of this letter is taken from a baptismal homily, as he maintains in support of his position (388), most of the strength of this argument wanes.

149 See, e.g., 1QS 2.20–23; 5–6; CD 13.7–13; 14.10–12; 1QM 2.1–4; 1QSa 1.1.

150 On this point see, e.g., Eliott, "Ministry," 380–81; Ceslas Spicq, "La place ou le rôle des jeunes dans certaines communautés néotestamentaires," *RB* 76 (1969) 515.

151 With, e.g., Ketter, 273.

152 Cf. Spicq, "Place," 518–21. See also Hart (77), who refers to the σύνοδοι τῶν νεῶν ("assemblies of the young") mentioned on inscriptions from Smyrna in Asia Minor.

153 Best (171) finds that an "attractive solution"; see also Spicq, 170–71.

154 So Spicq, "Place," 521. He suggests (516–17) one duty of this group was burial of the dead, as in Acts 5:6, a suggestion Elliott ("Ministry," 378) also thinks "possible." Yet the fact that in Acts 5:10 they are called νεανίσκοι, another word meaning "young people," indicates that νεώτεροι did not function there as the title for the group. That the word designated junior clergy, as Schwank et al. (102) and Moffatt (165) suggest, lacks any convincing NT evidence, as Kelly (204) also notes; see also Beare, 201.

155 So, e.g., Schelkle, 130.

156 So, e.g., Windisch, 79; Michaels, 289; Ketter, 273; Goppelt, 331; Reicke, 130; but see Bigg, 190.

157 So also, e.g., Michaels, 288.

"younger" would have a similar ambiguity in referring to the remainder of the congregation who tended to be preponderantly younger in age than those who led it. In that case, the difficulty of using the same word "elder" in two different meanings would be avoided, since in both instances the word would refer to those who exercised leadership in the communities.[158] Such an understanding of the terms finds confirmation in a letter written to Corinth a short time after this letter was written, in which a situation was addressed where some younger members of the congregation had revolted against the elders (who were both older in years and exercised authority) and arrogated ecclesiastical authority to themselves.[159] The author calls them to exercise proper humility ($\tau\alpha\pi\epsilon\iota\nu\phi\rho\sigma\acute{\nu}\nu\eta$),[160] and to be subordinate to the presbyters ($\dot{\nu}\pi\sigma\tau\acute{\alpha}\gamma\eta\tau\epsilon$ $\tau\sigma\hat{\iota}s$ $\pi\rho\epsilon\sigma$-$\beta\nu\tau\acute{\epsilon}\rho\sigma\iota s$)[161] so the flock ($\pi\sigma\acute{\iota}\mu\nu\iota\sigma\nu$) of Christ may have peace.[162] Here the term "younger people" refers both to age and to a specific group, as does the term "elders." Whether or not the threat of such a situation underlay the churches to which our epistle was addressed, it is quite likely in this context that the same ambiguity attends the words "younger" and "elder," terms that refer here both to age and rank within the congregation.[163]

4. The verb $\dot{\nu}\pi\sigma\tau\acute{\alpha}\gamma\eta\tau\epsilon$ means here as earlier not blind obedience but subordination, finding one's proper function within a given institution, in this case the church.[164] Lack of further explication of how such subordination is to be carried out, an explication present where the verb was used earlier (2:13: all Christians; 2:18: household slaves; 3:1: wives), indicates less emphasis on the subordination as such than on the fact that even though elders/shepherds are not to be overbearing in the use of their authority, other members of the con-

gregation may not therefore ignore what they say. The use of the verb thus probably owes more to the author's intention here than to its derivation from the table of duties appearing in 2:13—3:7.

5. The argument that the $\pi\acute{\alpha}\nu\tau\epsilon s$ here should presume a longer enumeration of groups such as that found in 2:13—3:7, and that therefore this verse originally followed 3:7, founders on two points: 3:7 already has a $\pi\acute{\alpha}\nu\tau\epsilon s$ following it in 3:8, as well as an OT quotation, and the $\pi\acute{\alpha}\nu\tau\epsilon s$ refers to the entire community, and could thus be used after one pair as well as after four or more, since its referent is the whole body from which any group mentioned is drawn. In addition, here the pair "younger, older" includes the whole community, reinforcing the need on both sides, rulers and ruled, for humility.

Rather than drawing in v. 5 on a table of duties part of which was also used earlier, therefore, the author in these verses seems more likely to be following the pattern established in 2:11—3:12, more particularly evident in 3:1–12. After a lengthy series of admonitions addressed to one group (wives, 3:1–6; elders, 5:1–4) followed by a briefer admonition to those who might be tempted to take advantage of the first group (husbands, 3:7; the younger, 5:5a), the author gives admonitions for mutual humility (3:8–9; 5:4b, both including the word $\tau\alpha\pi\epsilon\iota\nu\phi\rho\sigma\acute{\nu}\nu\eta$) and concludes with an OT quotation (Ps 34:13–17 in 3:10–12; Prov 3:34 in 5:5c).[165]

The second phrase of the verse (5b) enjoins upon all readers a mutual humility toward one another. As in 1:13, the author uses a figure drawn from clothing to make his point, there the act of arranging a garment in a way more appropriate for physical labor, here apparently the act of putting on a garment appropriate for servile activity.[166] The verb itself ($\dot{\epsilon}\gamma\kappa\sigma\mu\beta\acute{\omega}\sigma\alpha\sigma\theta\epsilon$)[167] appears to

---

158 So also, e.g., Tarrech, "Le milieu," 126; cf. Eliott, "Ministry," 389.

159 *1 Clem.* 3.3; such action is characterized as sedition (57.1) growing out of jealousy and pride (3.2; 14.1).

160 56.1, the same word that occurs in v. 5b.

161 57.1, the same phrase used here.

162 54.2.

163 Somewhat later, the same ambiguity is evident when Polycarp (*Phil.* 5.3) urges the young people ($\nu\epsilon\acute{\omega}\tau\epsilon\rho\sigma\iota$) to be subordinate ($\dot{\nu}\pi\sigma\tau\alpha\sigma\sigma\sigma\mu\acute{\epsilon}\nu\sigma\nu s$) to the elders ($\tau\sigma\hat{\iota}s$ $\pi\rho\epsilon\sigma\beta\nu\tau\acute{\epsilon}\rho\sigma\iota s$) and deacons.

164 So also, e.g., Senior, 89.

165 Remarkably, the final verse of the psalm quoted in 3:12 makes the same point as the quotation from Proverbs quoted here in 5:5c, indicating the desire to make a similar point, not a borrowing from the same source, since the earlier source would hardly have included both the quotation from Psalm 34 and that from Proverbs 3.

166 This reflects a custom in Christian paranesis that often compares appropriate Christian behavior to putting on garments; see, e.g., Rom 13:12; Eph 6:11, 14; Col 3:12; 1 Thess 5:3; cf. Rev 15:6; 19:14.

167 It is a rare word; J. Rendel Harris terms it the most

derive from a word (ἐγκόμβωμα)[168] probably identifying a garment or apron a slave tied over other garments in order to perform certain menial tasks.[169] Attractive as it would be to find here a deliberate reflection of Jesus' act of self-debasement in washing the disciples' feet[170] after girding himself with a towel, such a reflection is doubtful, since the language here is very different.[171]

What is to be put on as this garment is humble-mindedness (ταπεινοφροσύνη), a word whose root in the Greek world meant an attitude expected of slaves but unworthy of free people.[172] The word itself is absent from the LXX, and is used in the NT primarily to describe the relationship of Christians to one another.[173] The mutuality of such humility is described by the reciprocal pronoun ἀλλήλοις,[174] which, despite attempts to put a full stop after it and so bring it into parallelism with the dative πρεσβυτέροις, both thus related to ὑποτάγητε ("young people, be subordinated to elders, and all to one another"),[175] is rather to be construed

with the verb ἐγκομβώσασθε ("and all of you clothe yourselves with humility toward one another").[176]

The quotation from Prov 3:34, which constitutes the third phrase in this verse (5c), is introduced with ὅτι, which typically for this letter introduces the theological ground for the ethical counsel,[177] and hence is to be translated "because."[178] The quotation itself is closer to the LXX than to the MT,[179] and because the substitution of θεός ("God") for the LXX's κύριος ("Lord") is also found in the identical quotation in Jas 4:6, where it is used in the same general context,[180] it is possible that our author and the author of James here reflect a common Christian tradition.[181] This citation from the

non-Hellenic expression in the NT ("The Religious Meaning of 1 Peter V.5.," *Expositor*, series 8, 18 [1919] 131), calls the word "quaint," and admits the meaning is elusive (133).

168 It in turn is the verbal passive noun from κομβόω, which means bind or tie. From that Bigg (191) concludes that it could refer to any article of dress that was attached by laces.

169 So, e.g., Tarrech, "Le milieu," 121. Hesychius (*Lexicon*, 3774) defines it as "an Egyptian apron"; Beare (202) cites Pollus (*Onomasticon* 4.119), who defines it as an apron a slave tied over an undergarment. With his typical combination of erudition and vivid imagination, Rendel Harris ("Religious Meaning," 139) concludes it referred not to a garment but to a rope knotted about the waist, and that the author was thus speaking not of a slave apron but of the symbolic dress of a religious person. In a similar vein, Brox (236) wonders if it refers to liturgical dress, but reaches no conclusion.

170 So, e.g., Chase, "Peter," 787; Best, 172; Kelly, 206; Moffatt, 165; Cranfield, 132; Schwank et al., 102–3; Margot, 85.

171 In John 13:4 Jesus takes a towel (λέντιον) and girds (διαζώννυμι) himself; here one girds on (ἐγκομβώσασθαι) humility (ταπεινοφροσύνη). So also Michaels (290), who thinks it possible, but "far from certain."

172 Goppelt, 333.

173 See Eph 4:2; Phil 2:3; Col 3:12; for the same idea of mutual humility but with different language, see Phil 2:3; Rom 12:10; Eph 5:21.

174 It is best construed as a dative of respect, rather than *dativus commodi* (advantage) or relationship, as Selwyn (234) would have it.

175 On this point see Bigg, 190.

176 Kelly (205) and Michaels (289) note that there is a similar sentiment in 1QS 5.23–25, where all are to obey superiors and deal with one another in humility and love.

177 See 2:21; 3:18; 4:8. Selwyn (235), Kelly (206), and Schweizer (101) also make this point.

178 With, e.g., Michaels, 290, and most other commentators.

179 As, e.g., Osborne ("L'utilisation," 71) also notes.

180 Gourbillon ("La Première Epître," 32) posits as a possible original order of the tradition the following:
God resists proud, gives grace to humble (Jas 4:6b; 1 Pet 5:5b)
Humble yourselves before God and he will elevate you (Jas 4:[7a], 10; 1 Pet 5:6)
Resist the devil and he will flee from you (Jas 4:7b; 1 Pet 5:8b–9a)
Come near to God and he will come near to you (Jas 4:8; 1 Pet 5:7? 10?).

181 So Goldstein, *Paulinische Gemeinde*, 17; Boismard, "Liturgie" [2], 177; Brox, 236. Goppelt (334) cites as further use of this tradition *1 Clem.* 30.2, and, to a less obvious extent, Ignatius *Eph.* 5.3, and notes further that arrogance is contrasted to humility in Luke 1:51 and Jas 4:6, and appears in catalogs of vices at Rom 1:30; 2 Tim 3:2; cf. Mark 7:22. That the arrogant refers to those who despise Christians

OT thus presents as the norm for the author's advice on mutual humility God's own decision to be gracious to the humble but to resist the arrogant.[182] Despite the necessary presence of authority within the Christian community, therefore, members of that community are not to carry about an arrogant attitude, but are rather to give place to fellow Christians, as God desires his people to do.

(1 Pet 2:12; 3:16; 4:4–5, 14, 16), while the humble are the Christians themselves, as Michaels (290) asserts, may be the case, but in the context it more likely refers to unacceptable and acceptable attitudes of Christians toward one another.

182 Calvin (148) comments: "We are to imagine that God has two hands; the one, which like a hammer beats down and breaks in pieces those who raise up themselves; and the other, which raises up the humble who willingly let down themselves, and is like a firm prop to sustain them."

5   Appropriate Conduct in
Eschatological Suffering

6   **Therefore accept your humble status under
God's mighty hand, in order that he may
exalt you at the proper time,[1] 7/ casting[2]
all your cares upon him, because he cares
about you.[3] 8/ Be sober, stay awake.[4]
Your adversary, the[5] devil, is prowling
about like a roaring lion, seeking someone[6] to devour.[7] 9/ Him[8] you must resist,
firm[9] in the faith, knowing as you do
that[10] the same burdens of sufferings are
being borne[11] by your fellow Christians[12]
throughout the[13] world. 10/ But the God**

1   Some MSS. (A, P, [Ψ], 33, 623, some other minuscules, vg, sy^h**, bo), probably under the influence
of 2:12, add ἐπισκοπῆς ("of visitation"), making clear
that the reference is to the parousia. But see van
Unnik ("Teaching," 97), who argues for its presence
in the original.

2   A few MSS. (0206^vid, Aug) read the imperative
ἐπιρίψατε. P^72 changes the verb to ἀπορίψαντες,
"casting your cares away"; that involves a slight
change in emphasis (from casting "upon" to "away")
but little change in meaning.

3   A few MSS. (א*, 33, a few other minuscules, vg^ms)
read ἡμᾶς, a typical substitution in NT texts. The
textual witness is not sufficient to sustain the change,
as Michaels (292) also argues.

4   A number of MSS. (P^72, א^2, L, Ψ, 049, 33, 69, 614,
1241, 1739, a number of other minuscules, latt, sy,
co) add ὅτι, to make the next phrase the reason for
the imperatives; others (א*, A, B, P, 049*, the mass
of later minuscules) omit it. In this case the omission
would be the *lectio difficilior* and should probably
prevail; see also Michaels, 293.

5   P^72 and 33 add the article ὁ; English usage requires
it, whether present in the text or not.

6   Τίνα is omitted by B, Ψ, 0206^vid, a few minuscules.
P^72, א, A, 33^vid have it without the article ("something"); the present text is represented by L and P
and the mass of minuscules. Its absence would be
the *lectio difficilior,* and if it were absent, the object of
the verb "devour" would be understood to be "you,"
the subject of the imperative verbs; see also Beare,
205; Michaels, 293.

7   P^72, A, and a great many minuscules read καταπίη
("he might devour") for καταπιεῖν ("to devour"). The
meaning of the sentence is unaffected.

8   P^72 omits the ᾧ ("him").

9   P^72 reads ἑδραῖοι for στερεοί; the meaning is not
changed.

10   Although the word ὅτι ("that") is present only in P^72
and a few minuscules, the Greek construction
(*accusativum cum infinitivo*) requires its presence in
English.

11   Some MSS. (א, A, B, K, 0206, 33, 614, 2495, a few
other minuscules) read ἐπιτελεῖσθε ("you are having
visited upon you [the same sufferings along with
your fellow Christians]"), although Michaels (293)
regards this form as a defective spelling of the
infinitive; others (B^2, P, Ψ, 𝔐, latt, sy) have the
infinitive ἐπιτελεῖσθαι. The latter is to be preferred.
Quinn ("Notes," 247–49) speculated that the text
read originally ἐπεὶ τελεῖσθαι, "because it [i.e., the
brotherhood] is being perfected"; while interesting,
it lacks any textual basis.

12   Lit. "the brotherhood" (τῇ ἀδελφότητι).

13   Although some MSS. (א^2, A, P, Ψ, 0206, 𝔐) omit the
article τῷ, the weight of evidence (P^72, א*, B, a few

**of all grace, who called you[14] into his
eternal glory in Christ,[15] will,[16] after you
have suffered a short time, himself
restore, establish, strengthen, provide
(you with) a firm foundation.[17] 11/ To
him belongs eternal dominion,[18] Amen.**

other minuscules) supports its inclusion, as Michaels
(293) also argues.

14 As in the case in v. 7, some mss. (0206, 1881, some
other minuscules, t, vg, sy^p, bo^{mss}) read ἡμᾶς ("us")
for the more widely attested ὑμᾶς ("you"). The
second person verbs argue for a second person
pronoun here.

15 A number of mss. (P^{72}, A, P, Ψ, 𝔐, latt, sy^{h**}, co)
add Ἰησοῦ ("Jesus"); it is probably a later addition,
since it is more likely that a later scribe would add it
than omit it; so also, e.g., Michaels, 293.

16 Some minuscules (614, 630, 1505, 2495, some
others) have the verbs in the optative rather than
the future, as do, e.g., 1 Thess 5:23; Heb 13:21.
Kelly (213) rightly calls it a "misguided attempt at
improvement which eliminates the vigorous
confidence of the original." Beare (207) has a similar
judgment.

17 Some mss. (P^{72}, 81, r, t, vg^{mss}) omit σθενώσει
("strengthen"), others (A, B, Ψ, 0206^{vid}, a few
others, along with vg) omit θεμελιώσει ("provide a
firm foundation"), perhaps because their similar
endings (-ωσει) caused the eye to pass over the one
or the other, i.e., a homoioteleuton; so also Goppelt,
344. Many, I think correctly, accept both as original,
however, e.g., Kelly, 213; Schelkle, 133 n. 1; Spicq,
176 n. c; Michaels, 293.

18 A number of mss. add ἡ δόξα ("glory") either before
(A, P, 𝔐, vg^{cl}, sa) or after (33, 69, 614, 1241, 1739,
some other minuscules, sy^h, bo) τὸ κράτος ("dominion"). The presence of "glory" in 4:11, and its
regular appearance in doxologies, make it more
likely that ἡ δόξα was added rather than omitted, as
Michaels (293) also argues. The same is true of the
added τῶν αἰώνιων, despite its impressive textual
witness (ℵ, A, P, Ψ, 0206^{vid}, 𝔐, latt, sy, bo^{ms}).

Analysis

Like the first segment of the body closing (4:12–19),
these verses address the behavior appropriate for
Christians in relation to the world outside the Christian
community, after the middle segment had addressed
behavior appropriate for them in relation to fellow
Christians within the Christian community.[19] The
imperative ταπεινώθητε ("humble yourselves") continues
the command in v. 5b, while the content draws inferences (οὖν, "therefore") from the quotation of Prov 3:34
in v. 5c.[20] Further explication is given in v. 7, based on

LXX Ps 54:23. As was the case in v. 2, where the
explication begun with the imperative (ποιμάνατε) was
continued with a participle (ἐπισκοποῦντες), so here the
explication introduced with the imperative (τεπεινώθητε)
in v. 6 is also continued with a participle (ἐπιρίψαντες) in
v. 7. In both cases, further exposition is then introduced
with further imperatives.[21] Thus the author is following
a similar pattern in the two segments 5:1–5 and 5:6–9.
Because this latter segment concludes the body middle, it
ends with a promise (v. 10) and a doxology (v. 11).

Because the quotation from LXX Prov 3:34 found in

19 The same alternation between external and internal
can be observed, for example, in 2:11–17 (external),
2:18—3:12 (internal), 3:13–17 (external). It con-

tinues in 4:1–6 (external) and 4:7–11 (internal).
20 With, e.g., Michaels (293), who finds v. 6 an exegesis
of the verse from Proverbs.

v. 5c is also found in Jas 4:6b, along with a reference to resisting the devil (Jas 4:7b) and to humbling oneself before God who will then exalt (4:10), it can appear that James and 1 Peter are following a common tradition.[22] Yet apart from the quotation from Proverbs, and the reference to humbling oneself in order to be exalted, the order in which the elements occur and the language used to express them are rather different.[23] The material is used to make very different points, James in a condemnation of the Christian community for its lack of Christian virtues, 1 Peter as comfort for those caught up in the suffering due to the world's opposition to the Christian community. If there was a common tradition, therefore, it was either very loose in form, or one or the other of the authors has taken great liberty with it.[24]

The remaining language of the verse reflects common Christian vocabulary and concepts, but attempts to identify the traditions more closely remain unconvincing. Finding, for example,[25] Matt 6:25 reflected in v. 7 is rendered questionable by that verse's closer similarity to LXX Ps 54:23.[26] Again, the admonition to be sober and watchful (v. 8) is echoed in 1 Thess 5:6, but in different tense, person, and order, hardly enough to justify seeing a common tradition; to find the source of both in Matt 26:41 (Jesus in Gethsemane: "watch and pray") seems yet more remote. Finally, to find the content of v. 10, which concludes the section, reflected in the concluding

material in 1 Thess 5:23–24 or Heb 13:20–21 (but also in 2 Thess 2:16–17, which does not conclude a letter), is to overlook great differences among all three in language and point. In such instances, it would perhaps be better to speak of our author's following Christian custom, rather than of his making use of specific traditions.

The eschatological language that frames this passage (vv. 6b, 10b) recalls similar language that has been increasingly evident in the latter portions of the letter,[27] indicating the author's intent here to summarize not only the body closing but in fact the letter as a whole.[28] There are also the references to present suffering and future rescue that form an *inclusio* for the section (vv. 6, 11). That such suffering of Christians is in fact in conformity to God's will is a theme that has run throughout the letter (1:6; 3:17; 4:19), and is clear here as well. Also clear is the fact that such present suffering will bring future glory (cf. 1:6–7; 4:13), and brought to the fore here is a point surely implied before: that such suffering means not being abandoned by God but remaining in his favor, because God does care about Christians who are suffering according to his will (5:7).

The summarizing nature of the material is further indicated by the fact that now at last the true nature of the Christians' opposition is made clear: it is the embodiment of supernatural evil, the devil. Christians are thus involved in more than just a conflict between competing

---

21 V. 5: ὑποτάγητε; v. 8: νήψατε, γρηγορήσατε; v. 9: ἀνίστητε.

22 So, e.g., Goppelt, 335–36; Best, 172. Boismard ("Liturgie" [2], 180) argues it comes from a baptismal homily; Kelly (207) finds considerable merit in that suggestion. See also the comments on v. 5 above concerning the quotation from Prov 3:34.

23 One may chart the material in the two letters in this way:

I Peter 5	James 4	
5c	6b	Identical quotation from Prov 3:34
6	10	Similar language (ταπεινώθητε, ὑψώσει, ὑμᾶς)
7	8a	Somewhat similar idea, no similar language (1 Peter: cast cares on God; James: draw near to God)
8b–9a	7ba	Similar idea, language: resist the devil (1 Peter: διάβολος . . . ᾧ ἀντίστητε; James: ἀντίστητε δὲ τῷ διαβόλῳ)

One can note the difference in order, even where the language is similar.

24 So also, e.g., Michaels, 293.

25 The following examples are drawn from Goppelt, 335–36.

26 The same must be said of Selwyn's contention (78) that vv. 6–7 reflect "almost exactly" Matt 25:34, where the only linguistic link is the stem μεριμν-, far less linguistic similarity than is shown with Ps 54:23.

27 E.g., 4:4–5, 13, 17; 5:4; see also the eschatological implication already embodied in 1:4b.

28 With, e.g., Goppelt, 335. This final paragraph fits in a general way Quintilian's definition of the *peroratio*: it is to be a final recapitulation, as brief as possible, which should summarize the important points (*Inst.* 6.16.2).

lifestyles or cultural understandings. They are involved in the final battle between good and evil, between God and the ultimate power of evil. It is for that reason that their remaining faithful to the Christian calling is invested with such great importance by our author. The call to resistance against the devil also shows that calls to subordination within certain social institutions have their final limitation in the need to resist any such subordination to evil. There is no question in this letter of giving in to the enemy in matters of the Christian faith. Subordination of any kind therefore has as its limit faithfulness to God; where subordination is asked that weakens that faith, Christians are to resist, and are able to resist, because God in the end will rescue them. The struggle of this culturally and economically insignificant community of followers of Christ is thus invested with more than simply cultural or social consequences. It is a matter of the final fate of the universe itself, since the one the community follows is none other than the creator and sustainer of the universe who will in the end see to the triumph of the divine will.[29] Christians who remain faithful, despite social and cultural pressure to the contrary, will themselves share in that final triumph.

Comment

■ **6** The οὖν ("Therefore") with which the verse begins, along with the repetition of the stem ταπεινο- (v. 5: ταπεινοφροσύνη, "humble-mindedness"; v. 6: ταπεινώθητε, "be humbled," or "accept your humble status"), demonstrate the close tie of this verse with the preceding material and indicate a conclusion is here to be drawn from it.[30] The focus has shifted from being

humble within the community (v. 5) to accepting the humble status forced upon Christians by the rejection and hostility of the surrounding culture (v. 6), a situation faced by all Christians of whom the author is aware (v. 9). That impression is further reinforced by the unusual use here of the aorist passive imperative (ταπεινώθητε)[31] rather than the more common active verb form with a reflexive pronoun.[32] In addition to Jas 4:10, the passive imperative occurs in the LXX in Gen 16:9 and Jer 13:18, where in the latter it means to accept a situation of humiliation, in the former it means to accept the position of being under another's will.[33] The point is not that Christians have a choice of whether they humble themselves;[34] that happens to them simply because they are Christians.[35] The point is rather that the Christians are to acknowledge that such status conforms to God's will and to accept it for that reason, since it is the path God wishes Christians to take,[36] a path that will lead finally to God's exaltation of them.[37] The author draws here on a commonplace in biblical thought, the contrast between lowliness and exaltation,[38] a contrast that, because it characterized both a number of sayings of Jesus[39] as well as his life,[40] particularly his death and subsequent resurrection,[41] became normative for Christians.[42] This is reflected throughout our epistle, where the humiliation of Christ is cited as a model for Christian behavior (2:21–24; 3:18) as his exaltation (3:22) becomes the ground for hope (1:6, 21; 4:1, 13; 5:10). That contrast is also used in this verse.

Accepting humiliation "under God's mighty hand" (ὑπὸ τὴν κραταιὰν χεῖρα τοῦ θεοῦ) is again a biblical

---

29 On this point, see also Brox, 240; Kendall, "Function," 113.

30 With, e.g., Michaels, 295.

31 The presence of the same unusual imperatival passive form in Jas 4:10 is one of the stronger arguments for seeing some kind of common source underlying James and 1 Peter in these verses, as Michaels (295) observes.

32 E.g., Matt 18:4: ὅστις . . . ταπνώσει ἑαυτόν; see also Luke 14:11; 18:14; Phil 2:8; in the LXX see Sir 18:21; 34:26.

33 The phrase is similar to our verse: ταπεινώθητι ὑπὸ τὰς χεῖρας ("accept humble status under [her] hands").

34 The implication of the active imperative with a reflexive pronoun, as, e.g., Luke 14:11; Phil 2:8.

35 E.g., 1:6–7; 2:12; 3:16; 4:14.

36 This point is also made by R. P. E. Golebiewski

("L'Epître [1 P 5,6–11]: Dieu nous console dans l'épreuve," *AsSeign* 57 [1965] 18), who points out that the passive form is more than simply a grammatical nuance. To accept humiliation and hostility is to consent to follow the path that God also caused his Son to take.

37 So here v. 6b.

38 It occurs frequently in the LXX, e.g., 1 Sam 2:7–8; Job 5:11; Ps 74:8; Isa 2:9, 11; 10:33; 40:4; Ezek 17:24; 21:31; Dan (Theodotion) 5:20; Sir 7:11.

39 E.g., Matt 23:12; Luke 14:11; 18:14; cf. Matt 18:4.

40 E.g., Luke 1:51–53; cf. 2 Cor 8:9.

41 E.g., Phil 2:8–9; 2 Cor 13:4a.

42 E.g., 2 Cor 11:7; 13:4b; Phil 2:3–4; Jas 1:9–10; cf. *1 Clem.* 59.3.

commonplace. Although the phrase "mighty hand" occurs only here in the NT, it is regularly used in the OT as a figure for God's power, particularly in relation to the exodus of Israel from Egypt,[43] but also, if less frequently, in relation to God's protection[44] as well as discipline.[45] In this context, it applies clearly to the present suffering Christians are undergoing (v. 6a), a point our author has made before in this letter (2:20; 3:17; 4:13a, 17; 5:10a),[46] but here it applies as well to Christians' eventual exaltation (6b), a point also familiar to our author (4:13b; 5:10b).

The exaltation of the suffering Christians, which is the reason[47] for their bearing the hostility and calumnies directed against them and which is the counterpart to their humiliation, lies in the future, but because it too comes from the mighty hand of God, it is nonetheless sure. The phrase $\grave{\epsilon}\nu$ $\kappa\alpha\iota\rho\hat{\omega}$ means "at the appropriate time" (e.g., Matt 24:45 par. Luke 12:42);[48] but in the context of this letter, particularly in light of the similar phrase $\grave{\epsilon}\nu$ $\kappa\alpha\iota\rho\hat{\omega}$ $\grave{\epsilon}\sigma\chi\acute{\alpha}\tau\omega$ ("in the last time") in 1:5,[49] the reference here is clearly to the parousia (4:13),[50] the eschatological period when God will restore all things (5:10). For that reason, Christians undergo suffering, namely, in order to be exalted. Our author never argues that suffering is a good thing in itself, that is, because it builds character, or is somehow inevitable in an evil world. Rather, for our author, it occurs by God's will[51] and serves the divine purpose, a purpose most clearly seen in Christ's career. That career remains determinative for our author's understanding of the fate of Christians: subordination is for the purpose of exaltation.

■ 7 The same twofold pattern—act and consequence—characterizes this verse as it characterized the preceding one. Accepting one's humble status (v. 5a) is here defined as casting one's care on God, while God's exaltation of the Christian (v. 5b) is defined as the divine care for those who do that. The participle $\grave{\epsilon}\pi\iota\rho\acute{\iota}\psi\alpha\nu\tau\epsilon\varsigma$[52] is not to be construed as itself having imperatival force, but rather it is to be taken with the imperatival $\tau\alpha\pi\epsilon\iota\nu\acute{\omega}\theta\eta\tau\epsilon$,[53] indicating concomitant action, perhaps with the implication of an instrumental force: casting one's cares on God is the means by which one accepts one's humble status. What specific cares the author has in mind are not stated, but the context of Christian persecution and suffering surely provides the clue; anxieties in the face of such hostility will have been in the forefront of Christian consciousness for these beleaguered communities.[54] Although the import of this verse, and its use of the root $\mu\epsilon\rho\iota\mu\nu\alpha$-, can suggest a reflection here of the saying of Jesus about not being anxious (Matt 6:25–34 par. Luke 12:22–31),[55] the language itself is closer to that of LXX Ps 54:23a,[56] and the latter is therefore more likely as the

---

43 E.g., LXX Exod 6:1; 13:3, 9, 14, 16; Deut 3:24; 4:34; 5:15; 6:21; 7:8, 19; 9:26; 11:2; 26:8; 34:12; Ps 135:12; Jer 32:21; Dan 9:15 (Theodotion); cf. *Barn.* 2.11.

44 LXX Ps 9:33; cf. 1 Esdr 8:60.

45 LXX Job 30:12; Ezek 20:34–35; cf. Ps 32:4. On the use of this phrase in the OT, see Goppelt, 336; Best, 173; Nauck, "Freude," 83; Schelkle, 131.

46 On this point see also Cranfield, 133.

47 The point of the $\acute{\iota}\nu\alpha$ with which the second phrase begins.

48 Selwyn (236) notes that in classical Greek it means at a propitious time, hence in relation to particular acts or events.

49 With, e.g., Beare, 204; Kelly, 209. So it was also interpreted by the scribes who added $\grave{\epsilon}\pi\iota\sigma\kappa\acute{o}\pi\eta\varsigma$ to this phrase; see the note on v. 1 above.

50 So also, e.g., Schelkle, 131; Spicq, 173; Michaels, 296; Goppelt, 337.

51 Schiwy (62) notes correctly that in this context, because God is the Lord of history, nothing occurs without his will. Even rejection is so encompassed, as

52 The verb $\grave{\epsilon}\pi\iota\rho\acute{\iota}\pi\tau\omega$ is found in the NT only one other time, to describe the disciples casting their cloaks upon the donkey Jesus is to ride into Jerusalem (Luke 19:35). The metaphorical use here presents a vivid picture of piling one's cares upon God, so they may be borne away.

53 With, e.g., Kelly, 208; Michaels, 296.

54 Best's speculation (173) that such anxiety may be what to say to one's accusers, based on the use of the same root $\mu\epsilon\rho\iota\mu\nu$- in Matt 10:19 par. Luke 12:11, seems fanciful; our author dealt with that problem in 3:15, and there is nothing in this context to give reason to think that problem is being revisited.

55 So, e.g., Cranfield, 134.

56 Ps 54:23a: $\grave{\epsilon}\pi\acute{\iota}\rho\rho\iota\psi o\nu$ $\grave{\epsilon}\pi\grave{\iota}$ $(\kappa\acute{\upsilon}\rho\iota o\nu)$ $\underline{\tau\grave{\eta}\nu}$ $\underline{\mu\acute{\epsilon}\rho\iota\mu\nu\acute{\alpha}\nu}$ $(\sigma o\upsilon)$, $\kappa\alpha\grave{\iota}$ $\alpha\grave{\upsilon}\tau\acute{o}\varsigma$ $(\sigma\epsilon)$ $\delta\iota\alpha\theta\rho\acute{\epsilon}\psi\epsilon\iota$

    1 Pet 5:7: $\pi\hat{\alpha}\sigma\alpha\nu$ $\underline{\tau\grave{\eta}\nu}$ $\underline{\mu\acute{\epsilon}\rho\iota\mu\nu\alpha\nu}$ $(\grave{\upsilon}\mu\hat{\omega}\nu)$ $\grave{\epsilon}\pi\iota\rho\acute{\iota}\psi\alpha\nu\tau\epsilon\varsigma$ $\grave{\epsilon}\pi$' $(\alpha\grave{\upsilon}\tau\acute{o}\nu)$, $\acute{o}\tau\iota$ $\alpha\grave{\upsilon}\tau\hat{\omega}$ $\mu\acute{\epsilon}\lambda\epsilon\iota$ $\pi\epsilon\rho\grave{\iota}$ $(\grave{\upsilon}\mu\hat{\omega}\nu)$

    Matt 6:25: . . . $\underline{\mu\grave{\eta}}$ $\underline{\mu\epsilon\rho\iota\mu\nu\hat{\alpha}\tau\epsilon}$ $\tau\hat{\eta}$ $\psi\upsilon\chi\hat{\eta}$ $(\grave{\upsilon}\mu\hat{\omega}\nu)$ $\tau\acute{\iota}$ $\phi\acute{\alpha}\gamma\eta\tau\epsilon$ $\hat{\eta}$ $\tau\acute{\iota}$ $\pi\acute{\iota}\eta\tau\epsilon$ $\mu\eta\delta\grave{\epsilon}$ $\tau\hat{\omega}$ $\sigma\acute{\omega}\mu\alpha\tau\iota$ $\tau\acute{\iota}$ $\grave{\epsilon}\nu\delta\acute{\upsilon}\sigma\eta\sigma\theta\epsilon$

The underlined words and parts of words indicate

source of this language.[57] Yet if the language is close to LXX Psalm 54, the intent of the saying of Jesus is surely to be found here as well, namely that because God cares for his people, mundane anxiety is pointless.[58]

This verse encapsulates the thrust of both the ethic (v. 7a) and the comfort (v. 7b) of the entire letter. One is to entrust one's life to God, even in the midst of suffering and persecution, subordinating oneself to the divine will, even when that will involves suffering at the hands of one's non-Christian contemporaries, because God's loving care is assured, and therefore the hope of vindication and exaltation at the end is sure. The fate of Christ—suffering, crucified, exalted—is thus both the pattern of activity and the ground of the Christians' faith and hope,[59] and for that reason Christians may accept their humiliation by secular forces in the sure knowledge that it represents neither their rejection by God nor their final fate at God's hands. For oppressed and suffering Christians, universally threatened by the cultural forces arrayed against them, that is the source of the strength and confidence that will enable them to survive as a community, even when their true opponent, as the next verse makes clear, is the epitome of evil itself.

■ 8 The two aorist imperatives[60] at the beginning of this verse, νήψατε ("be sober") and γρηγορήσατε ("stay awake"), are used elsewhere in the NT in an eschatological context[61] and such a context is continued here:

in light of the events now under way that lead to God's final judgment, the proper stance for Christians is not to let down their watchfulness.[62] Although the following phrase lacks a direct indication of cause, it is clear that one reason, at least, for a permanent state of watchfulness is the fact that their opponent, the devil, never lets up. Even now, he is stalking about on his mission of destruction.

Both words used to describe that opponent refer to one who levels accusations. The first, ἀντίδικος, refers to an opponent or adversary in a court of law, the only meaning it has in its other uses in the NT.[63] It has that meaning in the LXX as well,[64] but it also has there the broader meaning of those who opposed God's chosen people.[65] The reference here is probably closer to this latter meaning in the LXX than to the other NT uses. The reference here is not to one who hails Christians into the law courts but to the one who opposes God's plan and so causes suffering to be inflicted on Christians.[66] The second word, διάβολος, also has as its primary meaning "slanderer" or "accuser,"[67] but unlike ἀντίδικος, it has come in the NT to represent the devil as the rebellious prince of evil (Matt 4:1; John 13:2; Rev 12:7–9) who is the enemy of God's purposes (Matt 13:39; Acts 10:38; Eph 6:11; 1 Thess 2:18; 2 Thess 2:8–9, 26; Rev 12:9–10, 13–17) and the originator of lying and deceit (John 8:44; Acts 5:3; 2 Thess 2:10; Rev 12:9;

---

identity, words in parentheses indicate similar intention. The linguistic similarities to LXX Ps 54:23a are thus apparent.

57 With, e.g., Michaels, 296. While Wis 12:13a does contain the word μέλει in relation to God's concern for all humans, to find as does Selwyn (236) that that verse is the source of 1 Pet 5:7b is to put too fine a point on it.

58 The same general point is found in Phil 4:6–7, along with the root μεριμν-, indicating that it had already passed into Christian tradition prior to the writing of the Gospels.

59 With Schiwy, 62.

60 While the aorist tense is the normal tense for imperatives for our author (of the twenty-seven imperatives he uses, twenty are aorist), the aorists here are probably programmatic, setting a course of action to be continued from this point on; so also, e.g., Michaels, 297.

61 The two together in 1 Thess 5:6; νήψατε, 1 Thess 5:8; 1 Pet 4:7 (as participle, 1:13); γρηγορήσατε, Matt 24:42; Mark 13:35, 37; cf. 1 Cor 16:13; Col 4:2; Rev

3:2. On this point, see Best, 174; Goppelt 339.

62 The author is probably following early Christian catechetical tradition here, as, e.g., Golebiewski ("L'Epître [1 P 5,6–11]"), 20) and P. Benedikt Schwank ("Diabolus tamquam leo rugiens," *Erbe und Auftrag* 38 [1962] 15) argue, rather than specifically reflecting the scene in Gethsemane (Mark 14:34–38) where Peter was told by Jesus to stay awake (Matt 26:41), as, e.g., Cranfield ("I Peter," 135) and Moffatt (167) would have it.

63 Matt 5:25 par. Luke 12:58; 18:3.

64 E.g., Prov 18:17.

65 Isa 41:11; Jer 27:34 (50:34); 28:36 (51:36), Esth 8:11, as Schelkle (132) and Schwank ("Diabolus," 17) point out.

20:10).[68] It is in this sense that it is used here, and that in turn helps indicate what the author means with the word ἀντίδικος.

Further description of the devil is supplied by the phrase λέων ὠρυόμενος ("roaring lion"). While this is the only place in the Bible that the devil is so identified,[69] the figure of a lion does appear in the OT to describe the opponents of Israel,[70] a tradition then also continued at Qumran.[71] The word used to define the devil's desired activity, καταπιεῖν ("devour"),[72] has as its normal meaning "drink down,"[73] but it is also used of an animal swallowing its prey,[74] clearly its use here. The readers would not have had to live in an area where lions represented a threat to them[75] to understand the metaphor;[76] lions as beasts of prey were sufficiently well known that the "adversary as roaring lion" would be immediately clear.[77]

This verse continues the description of the fate of the Christian community in the time immediately before God's final judgment,[78] which includes persecution and suffering. What the verse adds is the identification of the opposition with the embodiment of supernatural evil, the devil.[79] Thus the opposition the Christians face from their non-Christian contemporaries is not something they can avoid by modifying their behavior or adapting their beliefs in such a way as to escape such opposition.[80] Only by completely abandoning the gospel and the community shaped by it, only by submitting to the satanic forces that stand in total opposition to God, can they escape the persecutions they otherwise face.[81] It is against the temptation to follow such a course of action that our author is seeking to strengthen his readers.[82] Unlike sheep, terrified by the roaring lion, who bolt in panic from the safety of their fold only to be devoured as a result,[83] the Christians are to remain watchful and sober, recognizing the situation in which they stand and holding fast to their faith and to their community, in that

66 While the opponent is supernatural (cf. Rev 12:10, where a synonym, κατηγορῶν, is used; Job 1:9–11; 2:4–5), his agents are to be thought of here as the human powers who do the bidding of the devil in persecuting Christians, as Schwank ("Diabolus," 17) observes.

67 E.g., LXX Job 1–2; Zech 3:1 (NRSV: "Satan"); cf. Schwank, "Diabolus," 17; Goppelt, 340.

68 As in the NT, the devil, Belial, is the ruler of this world in Qumran: 1QS 2.19 (cf. 1:17–18, 23–24); CD 4.12–13 (cf. 6.14; 12.23); 1QM 14.9; I owe these references to Flusser, "Dead Sea Sect," 218.

69 The closest NT parallel is, as Goppelt (339) notes, 2 Tim 4:17; see also Heb 11:33.

70 E.g., LXX Jer 27:17 (MT 50:17); 28:34–38 (MT 51:34–38); as "roaring lion," Ps 21:14; Ezek 22:25. Best (174) notes that it is continued in the Targums of Isa 35:9; Jer 4:7; 5:6; Ezek 19:6, where "lion" is translated as "king."

71 E.g., 1QH 5:5–7, 9, 13–14, 18–19; 4QpNah 1.5–6; on this point see Kelly, 210; Goppelt, 339.

72 It is an infinitive of purpose, as Selwyn (237) rightly notes.

73 Interestingly, the name Belial (Heb. בליעל), found in Qumran as God's opponent, is derived from Heb. בלע, meaning "to swallow." The choice here of this word for the activity of the satanic lion may be more than coincidental.

74 E.g., LXX Jonah 2:1; Tob 6:2; Josephus Ant. 2.246, as Kelly (210) notes. It is also so used in Jos. Asen. 12.9, along with a concatenation of words also found in this context in 1 Peter (λέων, καταδιώκει [cf.

ἀντίδικος], διάβολος, καταπιεῖν) that, were there any other indication of our author's having been influenced by that writing (there is none), would suggest it as a possible source for the language here.

75 As, e.g., Tarrech ("Le milieu," 343) avers: the readers lived in isolated villages in mountainous areas of Anatolia where they were familiar with attacks by lions.

76 Petronius (Satyr. 119.15–16) observes that lions were brought from Africa, since their teeth made them "precious" (pretiosa) for slaying people, presumably in the arena. Perdelwitz's suggestion (Mysterienreligion, 103) that the figure comes from representations of the Asian goddess Cybele being transported on a wagon pulled by roaring lions is, as Kelly (209–10) observes, too fanciful to be entertained seriously.

77 Cf. its other metaphorical uses in the NT, e.g., Rev 4:7; 9:8, 17; 13:2.

78 Cf. 4:7, 17; 5:10.

79 Our author avoids any direct identification of the devil with the power of Rome, such as is found in Rev 17:3–14; the threat remains social, not governmental. But see Bauer, 61.

80 On this point, see Refoulé, "Bible," 463.

81 On this point, see Brox, 238; Nauck, "Freude," 80; Goppelt, 341.

82 With, e.g., Cranfield, 135; Beare, 204.

83 A figure suggested by Schwank ("Diabolus," 19); it draws added strength from the earlier identification of the Christian community as a flock (5:2), as Golebiewski ("L'Epître [1 P 5,6–11]," 20) notes.

way resisting the devil (v. 9) and sharing God's triumph at the last (v. 10).

■ **9** Although the grammar of this verse is not entirely clear, there are no significant scribal corrections, and the point is clear enough. The antecedent of the relative pronoun ᾧ ("him") is the devil of the preceding verse, and it functions as the object of the imperative ἀντίστητε ("resist"). The only other places a similar command to resist the devil is found in the NT are in Jas 4:7 and, in intent, in Eph 6:11–13, not enough evidence to assume that our author drew it from early catechetical instruction,[84] although it does share with the other two passages the notion that the Christian is engaged in a spiritual warfare with the forces of evil.[85]

Whether the adjective στερεοί ("firm") functions simply as modifier of the subject of the verb ("resist him, [you who are] firm in the faith") or carries an instrumental sense ("resist him [*by being*] firm in the faith") is difficult to determine.[86] The reference to faith serves almost as an *inclusio* with the earlier references to it (1:5, 7, 9, 21),[87] and means here a personal or communal commitment of trust rather than a body of doctrine.[88] The Christians are to entrust themselves to God because God is trustworthy (4:21); only in that way can they effectively resist the forces of spiritual evil embodied in the devil.

The interpretation of the second half of the verse faces several problems: (1) the construal and meaning of

εἰδότες ("knowing"), (2) the construal and meaning of τὰ αὐτὰ τῶν παθημάτων ("the same [kinds of] suffering"), (3) the construal and meaning of ἐπιτελεῖσθαι ("be completed, paid," "complete, pay for oneself"), (4) the construal of τῇ ἀδελφότητι ("the brotherhood"), and (5) the meaning of κόσμῳ ("world").

1. The participle εἰδότες may function here as it often does in Paul to identify something already known to the readers, and may here carry a causative force ("because you know"). Its purpose is therefore not so much to announce as to remind. That it is not followed by the conjunction ὅτι ("that")[89] identifying the content of what is known has led to the assertion that it cannot mean "knowing [that] . . ." but rather "knowing [how]. . . ."[90] Yet since the accusative (τὰ αὐτά) with infinitive (ἐπιτελεῖσθαι) construction that follows the εἰδότες is used in the NT to express indirect discourse,[91] that is more likely to be the construction that is represented here.[92]

2. The phrase τὰ αὐτὰ τῶν παθημάτων[93] is unusual, and hence its meaning is not entirely clear. While it could be taken to mean simply "the same suffering," that is, the equivalent of τά αὐτὰ παθήματα,[94] it would have been simpler for the author to have written just that, had that been his intention.[95] If the genitive τῶν παθημάτων is taken in a partitive sense, it would have the force of "the same kinds of suffering,"[96] but a less forced construal would be to take it as a genitive of definition, which

---

84 With, e.g., Goppelt, 341; but see Kelly, 210. Selwyn (238) thinks the Christian community took over the tradition from the catechetical literature of Greek-speaking Jews.

85 The lists of spiritual powers in Rom 8:38; Eph 3:10; Col 1:16 belong to the same tradition of spiritual warfare against evil forces; see also Matt 4:10; Luke 10:18; Rom 16:20; Rev 20:2.

86 Michaels's (300) argument that the imperatival force of ἀντίστητε carries over to the following phrase στερεοὶ τῇ πίστει ("be firm in your faith"), which then interprets the verb, gives to the phrase a force similar to the instrumental sense.

87 Goppelt (341) notes that the noun occurs only at the beginning and end of the letter.

88 With, e.g., Michaels, 300; Golebiewski, "L'Epître (1 P 5,6–11)," 21.

89 In almost all instances when it is used in this sense in Paul, for example, it is followed by the conjunction ὅτι, as it is in our letter in 1:18, but in those instances it is followed by a finite verb, not by an infinitive.

90 So, e.g., Beare, 206; Bigg, 194; Best, 175. But this is to overlook that it is connected here to an infinitive; see the preceding note.

91 As, e.g., in Luke 4:41; see also *1 Clem.* 62.3.

92 With, e.g., Michaels (300), who notes that the former construal ("knowing how") has no explanation for the dative phrase τῇ ἀδελφότητι; see also Kelly, 211; Wand, 125.

93 While Best (175) and Moffatt (168) find in this plural a covert reference to the messianic woes, a reference they also found in 4:13; 5:1, the universal extent of suffering undergone in the communities of faith may as easily account for it.

94 So, e.g., Goppelt, 342.

95 So, e.g., Bigg, 194.

96 So, e.g., Michaels (301), who argues it would allow for the "recognition that every experience of suffering is unique"; cf. Selwyn, 238.

would allow the meaning "the same burdens that consist in suffering."[97]

3. The construal of ἐπιτελεῖσθαι depends on how one interprets the participle εἰδότες. If one takes it to mean "knowing how," then the infinitive will be taken as the middle voice: "knowing how to fulfill[98] for yourselves [the same burdens]."[99] If one takes it to mean "knowing that," the infinitive will be taken as passive: "knowing that the same burdens are being fulfilled." Because it yields to a simpler grammatical construal,[100] the passive voice of the infinitive is to be preferred here.[101]

4. The dative phrase τῇ . . . ὑμῶν ἀδελφότητι can be construed in several ways. It could be understood as a dative of disadvantage ("against your brotherhood"),[102] or alternatively as a dative of respect, or even as the indirect object of the infinitive ἐπιτελεῖσθαι, as the one upon whom the burdens are visited.[103] In light of the passive voice of the infinitive, however, the best construal is probably that of dative of agent: the same burdens are being borne *by* your fellow Christians as those which the readers are also undergoing.[104]

5. The phrase ἐν τῷ κόσμῳ admits of two interpretations: theological, the world as the place of enmity with God; or geographic, the whole world.[105] The first is the sense in which "world" is used regularly in the Johannine literature,[106] but it also bears that meaning in other places as well,[107] namely, as the place under the dominion of Satan, which is implacably at enmity with God and therefore with those who do the divine will.[108] If that is the meaning here, then the author is reminding his readers of a theological point, not commenting on the extent of the persecutions. The second is the sense that the phrase often bears in the NT, namely, the whole of the inhabited world.[109] If that is the meaning here, it would emphasize the extent and thus the universality of the suffering that the readers are also being called upon to undergo.[110] In the context of urging the readers to remain firm in the faith and to resist the devil, noting the fact that other Christians also must do the same would seem to be more to the point than simply highlighting the inevitability of suffering. The point is to put the experience of the readers within the perspective of the worldwide community of faith.[111] With all other Christians, the readers share the necessity of resisting the devil, thus sharing the suffering of Christ (4:13), know-

---

97 With, e.g., Beare, 206. This is the meaning in a closely parallel construction to be found in Xenophon (*Mem.* 4.8.8; *Apol.* 6.1): ἀναγκαῖον ἔσται τὰ τοῦ γήρως ἐπιτελεῖσθαι ("it will be necessary that the burdens of old age be borne"). I owe the reference to Hart, 178.

98 While, e.g., Best (175) and Bigg (194) see in the verb ἐπιτελέω the implication of "paying taxes," that is not the way it is used in biblical Greek. In the LXX and NT, it means "complete" or "perform"; see Rom 15:28; 2 Cor 7:1; 8:6, 11; Gal 3:3; Phil 1:6; Heb 8:5; 9:6. Nor must one assume it has the meaning "pay taxes" in Xenophon (*Mem.* 4.8.8); it can mean simply "complete" or "bear" there as well.

99 So Beare, 206.

100 If it is middle, as Beare (206) insists, the τὰ αὐτά cannot be the accusative subject of the infinitive, but must function as "cognate accusative" with the infinitive. It also fails to resolve satisfactorily the dative phrase τῇ . . . ἀδελφότατι. For more on this, see below.

101 With, e.g., Goppelt, 342; cf. Wand, 125.

102 As *dativus incommodi*; so, e.g., Selwyn, 239; Kelly, 211; Goppelt, 342.

103 So, e.g., Michaels, 300.

104 Michaels (300) admits this as a possibility.

105 It can also mean simply the sphere of human existence, e.g., 2 Cor 1:12; Eph 2:12. That may also be the sense it has in 1 Pet 1:20, but that does not seem to fit this context.

106 E.g., John 8:23; 13:1; 15:18–19; 16:33; 18:36; 1 John 5:19, among many such instances.

107 E.g., 1 Cor 3:19; Gal 6:14; 2 Pet 1:4.

108 So, e.g., Calvin, 151; Beare, 206; Borchert, "Conduct of Christians," 460.

109 E.g., Matt 4:8; 1 Cor 14:10; it occurs on occasion with an adjective meaning "entire" or "whole," e.g., Mark 14:9 (εἰς ὅλον τὸν κόσμον); Rom 1:8 (ἐν ὅλῳ τῷ κόσμῳ).

110 So, e.g., Schelkle, 132; Goppelt, 342; Kelly, 212; Michaels, 301; cf. also Robinson (*Redating*, 160), whose somewhat roundabout argument points to this understanding.

111 With, e.g., Kelly, 212.

ing that they do not stand alone with suffering arbitrarily visited only on them, but that what they must undergo is being undergone by all other Christians as well.[112] That such a universal extent of suffering implies that attacks against Christians were now being launched as an official policy of the Roman Empire, since only in that way could such universality be accounted for,[113] is not a necessary assumption. There is no evidence of such a general official persecution at the time the letter was written,[114] and such universality could be the case simply because the social reaction to Christianity assumed the same negative form wherever it came into contact with the values of Greco-Roman society.[115] The incompatibility of Roman society and Christian community is enough to account for the universality of Christian suffering.

Two points stand out in the verse. The first is the universal nature of Christian suffering. It is not a localized phenomenon; it will occur wherever the Christian community takes seriously its commitment to God. The reason is that in making that commitment of trust, they align themselves against the ultimate forces of evil, and hence can expect only unremitting hostility. Christians are enmeshed in a universal eschatological battle between good and evil, between God and the devil, and so long as this conflict rages, suffering will constitute the normal state of affairs for Christians.[116] The second point to emerge here is the fact that the origin of suffering is not God but the devil. While suffering in opposition to evil and for good has been identified as suffering in accordance with God's will (3:17; 4:17–19), it is clear here that God's will is for

Christians to resist the blandishments of evil and to suffer the inevitable consequences of their trusting relationship to God. Such suffering is thus in accord with God's will, even though its origin is with the devil, since that suffering means the Christians remain faithful to their trust in God. In the choice between suffering and apostasy, it is God's will that Christians eschew apostasy, even when that means inevitably that suffering will be inflicted upon them.[117]

■ **10** This verse, along with the next, constitutes the formal conclusion of the body closing. It presents the final outcome of the kind of life that has been described in the letter, acknowledging the suffering but pointing beyond to the final redemption of God through Jesus Christ.[118] God, the ultimate actor in the drama of salvation, is here further described with the genitival phrase πάσης χάριτος,[119] either "of all grace" or "of every grace"; the latter would denominate God as the one behind every manifestation of good the Christians have witnessed. The word χάρις is used in a variety of meanings in this letter, ranging from the current life of the Christian (1:2; 4:10; 5:12) to things that God favors (2:19, 20; 5:5) to eschatological salvation (1:10, 13; 3:7); the use of the adjective πάσης may intend to encompass all of them in this particular identification of God. Such an identification also points to grace and salvation as the ultimate outcome of the judgment God has initiated (4:17) that has brought suffering to the Christians. The subsequent phrase then identifies a further activity of this gracious God.

The additional identification of God with the phrase ὁ

---

112 With, e.g., Goppelt, 343; Brox, 239. It did not need a Christian context to be effective; Seneca (*De consolatione ad Polybium* 1.52) thought Polybius would be comforted by the knowledge that what had befallen him was suffered by all humans who preceded him, and would be by all who were yet to come.

113 So, e.g., Nauck, "Freude," 66; Foster, *Literary Relations*, 372; Windisch, 80; Schwank, "Diabolus," 16.

114 So, rightly, Lippert ("Leben," 235), who notes that the sources contain no information that the persecutions of Nero and Domitian were widespread, organized, and based on legal precepts; see also Brox, 239. For more on this point, see the Introduction § I.D.2, "Persecutions."

115 With, e.g., Goppelt, 342; Lampe and Luz, "Nach-

paulinisches Christentum," 199.

116 On this point see also Brox, 239; Refoulé, "Bible," 463; Schwank, "Diabolus," 16.

117 On this point see Windisch, 80.

118 With, e.g., Goppelt (343), who finds a similar point in 2 Cor 1:3.

119 It is probably best to take this as a genitive of quality, characterizing God as gracious.

κάλεσας ("who has called") is familiar to the readers of this epistle, since the same verb was used in 1:15 simply as a substitute for the word "God," in 2:9 to describe God as the one who brought Christians from darkness to light,[120] and in 2:21 and 3:9 to describe the kind of life God wants the Christians to lead. In the same vein, God is identified here as the one who will bring Christians to their final goal, namely, their participation in God's own glory (4:11)[121] at the final revelation of Christ (1:7; 5:1), who himself shared in such glory after his suffering and death (1:11, 21; 4:13). That such divine glory is here identified as αἰώνιον ("eternal") is meant to stand in contrast to the short period (ὀλίγον) of suffering that precedes it,[122] as the glory itself is meant to stand in contrast with the suffering.[123]

The force of the phrase ἐν Χριστῷ, in addition to emphasizing that the relationship with God is based on the career of Christ and one's relationship to it,[124] is not entirely clear.[125] If it is construed with the phrase ὁ κάλεσας ("the one who called"), it would mean God used Christ as the instrument through whom such a call was issued ("by Christ"). If it is construed with δόξαν ("glory"), it would imply that participation in God's glory comes through Christ.[126] If it is construed with the entire phrase, it would mean a Christian's entire life is in Christ.[127] While any of them is possible, the most natural in this context is to take it with ὁ κάλεσας,[128] reflecting

the role Christ plays for our author both as the instrument of God's redemption (1:18–21) and as the model for human life (2:21–23), a life that like Christ's is to include both suffering and subsequent glory.

The phrase ὀλίγον παθόντας ("after you have suffered a short time")[129] acknowledges that the reality of their life between God's call to them and their participation in eschatological glory is suffering,[130] but, as in the case of 1:6, assures them of its limited duration.[131] The ὀλίγον may refer to quality as well as quantity, that is, compared to the glory to come, any suffering, of whatever length, is minor when seen from the perspective of that glory.[132] The intensive pronoun αὐτός emphasizes that it is God "himself" who will deliver the Christians from their time of suffering,[133] serving to emphasize the reliability of such deliverance: it is finally God's work, not the Christians', and so is sure.[134] That Christian confidence is grounded not in human strength or loyalty but in the divine strength and faithfulness is reflected in this intensive pronoun αὐτός.

The four verbs with which the sentence concludes describe the actions God will take on behalf of the Christians.[135] This fourfold repetition of divine acts may be intended to reinforce the contrast between (short) suffering and (eternal) glory mentioned earlier in the verse by putting great emphasis on God's salvific acts. The future indicative form of the verbs gives them the

120 On this point see also Delling, "Der Bezug," 104.
121 For a similar use of the verb καλέω to describe God's activity resulting in the Christians' participation in glory, see Rom 8:28–30; 1 Thess 2:12; 2 Thess 2:14. While this, along with the phrase ἐν Χριστῷ, could reflect Pauline influence, it more likely reflects common use of early Christian tradition. On the question of Pauline influence, see the Introduction § I.C.5, "Pauline Letters."
122 Ὀλίγον was used in the same way in 1:6–7; for the same point see Rom 8:18; 2 Cor 4:17.
123 With, e.g., Michaels, 302; Brox, 240; Golebiewski, "L'Epître (1 P 5,6–11)," 22.
124 So also, e.g., Goppelt, 343.
125 While the phrase bears the meaning "Christian" in 3:16 and 5:14, it is clear it has further meaning here.
126 Michaels (302) notes correctly that the absence of the article τήν before ἐν Χριστῷ renders its construal with δόξαν questionable.
127 So Wand, 126. Reicke's assertion (139 n. 48) that because of the "rhythm of the clause" it ought to be construed with the following participle παθόντας,

yielding "suffer for a short time in Christ," remains unpersuasive.
128 With, e.g., Kelly, 212; Michaels, 302.
129 The ὑμᾶς ("you") functions as the antecedent of the participle here as it does as the object of the four verbs at the end of the verse.
130 So also, e.g., Goppelt, 343.
131 With, e.g., Kelly, 213.
132 So, e.g., Golebiewski ("L'Epître [1 P 5,6–11]," 22), who notes that that is the point of Rom 8:18 and 2 Cor 4:17.
133 Goppelt (344) calls attention to a similar use of the intensive pronoun in a similar context in 1 Thess 5:23 and 2 Thess 2:16, probably reflecting an early linguistic tradition.
134 On this point see Cranfield, 136.
135 As noted above, the ὑμᾶς that serves as the object of ὁ κάλεσας also serves as the object of these verbs.

character of promises, rather than of intercessions by or wishes from the author; the latter would require the optative mode.[136] The stem καταρτιδ-, from which the verb καταρτίζω derives, has the basic meaning in the NT of repair[137] or restore,[138] but is also used in the sense of equip or supply.[139] The sense here, given the kind of depredations Christians will experience as a result of their suffering, is probably "restore" in the sense of "make you whole."[140] The second verb, στηρίζω, is used in the NT in the sense of fixing or establishing something[141] but somewhat more frequently in the sense of strengthening someone or something.[142] In eschatological contexts, it tends to mean "strengthen,"[143] and that is probably the meaning here as well.[144] The verb σθενόω ("strengthen"), of which σθενώσει is the future form, appears only here in Greek literature,[145] although the form σθένω ("be strong") is quite common. Its meaning, as an *omicron* contract verb, is "render strong" or "strengthen."[146] It was probably because it was virtually synonymous with στηρίξει that it was omitted from some early Greek manuscripts.[147] The final verb, θεμελιώσει, is derived from the same root as the noun θεμέλιον, meaning the foundation of a building or a wall.[148] It is used as a verb four other times in the NT[149] with the meaning to "ground (something) firmly." The point of the future verbs here is that subsequent to the suffering, God will give the Christians an unshakable

grounding by including them in his eschatological glory. The fact that the verbs are also what is needed during the suffering, that is, strong and unshakable confidence in God, is perhaps not accidental. Christians are already to show the kind of reality that will be theirs at the time of the eschatological fulfillment.

Just as God through Christ was responsible for the new life enjoyed in the present by the readers (1:3), the mention of which began the letter, so at the letter's end the readers are reminded that their future is equally in God's hands, who will prove as reliable in the future in providing for the Christians as he has been in the past.[150] It is that knowledge that provides strength to endure whatever hardships a hostile culture may visit on the Christians.

■ **11** As was the case with the body middle (4:11), so here as well the author ends the body closing with a doxology. While most NT doxologies are precatory, the presence of the word ἔστιν in 4:11 and the indicative rather than optative mode of the verbs at the conclusion of v. 10 indicate that one ought to assume here as well the indicative ἔστιν, rather than the imperative ἔστω or the optative εἴη.[151] In addition, the construction of the dative αὐτῷ with a form of the verb εἶναι means αὐτῷ is to be construed as a dative of possession. The phrase is therefore to be translated "dominion belongs to him" rather than "to him be dominion." This is the only

---

136 For examples of similar verbs used in an intercessory form (optative mode), see 1 Thess 5:23–24; 2 Thess 2:16–17; Heb 13:20–21. If, as Goppelt (343) argues, the author is using traditional material also used by Paul and the author of Hebrews, he has nevertheless adapted it to another use.

137 Matt 4:21; Mark 1:19.

138 2 Cor 13:11; Gal 6:1; as a noun, 2 Cor 13:9.

139 1 Thess 3:10; Heb 13:21; closer to "equip" in the sense of "prepare," Rom 9:22; Eph 4:12; 2 Cor 9:5.

140 The eschatological context argues against Selwyn's (240) notion that restoration of what was lost in the persecutions is meant here, as Goppelt (344) rightly notes.

141 Luke 9:51; 16:26; 1 Thess 3:13; 2 Thess 3:3; 2 Pet 1:12; as a noun ("stability"), 2 Pet 3:17.

142 Luke 22:32; Rom 1:11; 16:25; 1 Thess 3:2; 2 Thess 2:17; Jas 5:8; Rev 3:2.

143 E.g., Luke 22:32; 1 Thess 3:2; Jas 5:8; in the compound form ἐπιστηρίζω, Acts 14:22; 15:32.

144 Schelkle (133 n. 1) observes that it belongs to the vocabulary of paranesis, but again, our author has

adapted that tradition by using it here as a promise rather than an admonition.

145 So correctly Selwyn, 240.

146 The so-called *omicron* contract verbs (ending in -οω) normally signify deliverance into the status described by the root, as verbs with an -ιζω ending mean to bring about the state the stem represents. The first two verbs are of this latter type, the last two of the former type, both types appropriate to describe actions God will undertake with Christians in the last times.

147 See the textual notes on v. 10 above.

148 E.g., Luke 6:48; 14:29; Acts 16:26; Rom 15:20; 1 Cor 3:10; Eph 2:20; Heb 6:1; Rev 21:14.

149 Three in the perfect, Matt 7:25; Eph 3:17; Col 1:23; one in the aorist, Heb 1:10.

150 On this point, see also Kendall, "Function," 113.

151 With, e.g., Selwyn, 241; Michaels, 304.

doxology in the NT in which κράτος appears alone,[152] probably because divine dominion is what allows the promises contained in the final verbs of v. 10 to be reliable.[153] Because God alone possesses eternal dominion, Christians may have confidence in their more glorious future. Additionally, with the "mighty hand" (κραταιὰ χείρ) of God mentioned in 5:6, it forms an *inclusio* for this final section.[154] This declaration, along with the promises of v. 10, forms an appropriate conclusion to the entire paranesis of the letter,[155] assuring the readers both of God's willingness and ability to uphold them in persecution and to bring them to a final, glorious restoration. Typically for a benediction, it concludes with the word ἀμήν ("amen").[156]

---

152 Κράτος appears in NT doxologies at 1 Tim 6:16 (with τιμή ["honor"]), 1 Pet 4:11 and Rev 1:6 (with δόξα ["glory"]), Jude 25 (with δόξα, μεγαλωσύνη ["majesty"], ἐξουσία ["authority"]), and Rev 5:13 (with εὐλογία ["blessings"], τιμή, δοξά).

153 So also, e.g., Goppelt, 345.

154 With Golebiewski, "L'Epître (1 P 5,6–11)," 23.

155 With Goppelt, 345.

156 For a discussion of ἀμήν, see the comments on 4:11 above.

5

Epistolary Closing

12 **By way of Silvanus, the faithful brother as I regard him, I have written to you briefly,[1] exhorting and bearing witness that this is the true grace of God; take your stand[2] in it. 13/ She who is the fellow elect one in Babylon[3] greets you, along with Mark my son. 14/ Greet one another with the kiss of love.[4] Peace to all of you who are in Christ.[5]**

1 P[72] substitutes διὰ βραχέων (see Heb 13:22) for δι' ὀλίγων ("briefly"), the reading of the overwhelming majority of mss.; the meaning remains unchanged.

2 Some mss. (P, 𝔐, h, r, vg[cl]) read ἑστήκατε ("in which you stand"), making it a declaration rather than an exhortation; along the same line a few others (1505, 2495, a few other minuscules, sy[h]) substitute ἐστέ ("you are"). The quality of the mss. (P[72], ℵ, A, B, 33, 945, 1739, a number of other minuscules, vg[st]) reading στῆτε ("take your stand") argues for it as the original, as Windisch (81) also concludes; so also, e.g., Cranfield, 138; Moffatt, 170; Michaels, 305.

3 A few minuscules read Ῥώμη ("Rome"), interpreting the author's intention. Some others (ℵ, a number of minuscules, vg[mss], sy[p]) add ἐκκλησία ("church"), again interpreting the meaning συνεκλεκτή ("fellow elect"), and changing the latter from substantival to adjectival force.

4 Some minuscules, along with vg, sy[p], read the adjective ἁγίῳ ("holy") with φιλήματι ("kiss") in place of the qualitative genitive ἀγάπης ("of love"), to bring it in line with the regular Pauline usage, as Michaels (305) also notes. The latter is preferable, since it is difficult to see why, were it in line with all other uses of φίλημα in NT epistles, anyone would change it.

5 While Ἰησοῦ ("Jesus") is added by some mss. (ℵ, P, 𝔐, vg[cl], sy[h], sa[mss], bo), its omission by others of somewhat better quality (A, B, Ψ, 33[vid] and a few other minuscules, vg[st], sy[p], sa[ms], bo[mss]) makes it likely the addition is later, particularly since it is difficult to see why any scribe who found it in his manuscript would then omit it. Roughly the same mss. also add ἀμήν, but again, its omission by a scribe is less likely than its addition, if for no other reason than out of sheer habit. But see Quinn ("Notes," 246), who, because of the omission of the entire phrase εἰρήνη ὑμῖν πᾶσιν τοῖς ἐν Χριστῷ ("peace to all of you who are in Christ") in P[72], argues that the phrase was added to the letter as a result of its being read in liturgical settings, from which this final phrase was drawn.

Analysis

The letter closing, as the epistolary opening, is closer in form to that of the NT letters, particularly those of the Pauline tradition, than to the normal Hellenistic letter. The conclusion to the normal Greek letter was the imperative ἔρρωσθε ("be strong" or "farewell") or (δι)εὐτύχει/εὐτυχεῖτε) ("be well" or "prosper"), often followed by the date;[6] that form (with ἔρρωσθε) does occur in biblical literature at 2 Macc 11:21, 33, and Acts 15:29, the latter without the date, but it is rare.[7] Our letter does share the convention of referring to the letter as "brief,"[8] a custom also reflected in Heb 13:22, but not in the Pauline letters.

Yet the similarities between these verses and the usual

6 Examples abound in the papyrus letters that have been preserved; see also Goppelt, 345.
7 It was adapted to Christian letters by Ignatius of Antioch, for example, and became his regular formula for ending his letters: *Eph.* 21.2; *Magn.* 15.1; *Trall.* 13.3; *Rom.* 10.3; *Phld.* 11.2; *Smyrn.* 13.2; *Pol.*

Pauline letter closing are numerous. (1) The conclusion of the Pauline letter often included references to those who would deliver the letter (Rom 16:1; Eph 6:21; Col 4:7, 9; cf. Acts 15:22), evidently the case with the reference to Silvanus.[9] (2) On occasion a summary of the intention of the letter would be included (Gal 6:11–17; 1 Tim 6:20–21; Phlm 21–22; Heb 13:22), as is the case here in v. 12b.[10] (3) Paul apparently was accustomed to concluding his letters with a benediction in his own hand (1 Cor 16:21; Gal 6:11; cf. Col 4:18; 2 Thess 3:17), often preceded by greetings. The greetings are present here; whether the benediction is written in the author's own hand is difficult to tell, since the author is unlikely to have been Peter himself.[11] (4) Mention of the liturgical kiss is also found elsewhere in the NT only in the Pauline letters (Rom 16:16; 1 Cor 16:20; 2 Cor 13:12; 1 Thess 5:26), although there it is called "holy kiss" rather than "kiss of love," as is the case here. (5) There is a final wish in the Pauline letters; it was for "grace" (χάρις, 1 Cor 16:23; 2 Cor 13:13; Gal 6:18; Eph 6:24; Phil 4:23; Col 4:18; 1 Thess 5:28; 2 Thess 3:18; 1 Tim 6:21; 2 Tim 4:22; Titus 3:15; Phlm 25). The final wish here, as in 3 John 15, was rather for "peace" (εἰρήνη).[12] Taken together, this evidence points to the use by our author of the NT rather than secular Hellenistic letter form, a form here strongly influenced by Paul, but without any indications of direct dependence.[13]

Comment

■ **12** The first two words of the verse contain two problems: (1) how is the preposition διά, to be understood, and (2) who is the Silvanus mentioned there?

1. The phrase διὰ Σιλουνοῦ may be understood to mean (a) Silvanus had a hand in the composition of the letter, whether as actual author, drafter, or amanuensis, or some combination of the three; or (b) Silvanus is identified by that phrase as the one who delivered the letter to its readers.[14]

a. In Eusebius's discussion of letters sent from the church at Rome he mentions a letter διὰ Κλήμεντος γραφεῖσαν (*Hist. eccl.* 4.23.11), referring to a letter (*1 Clement*) actually written "by Clement." On that analogy, one could assume that with the phrase διὰ Σιλουνοῦ the author of the letter is here being identified,[15] or at least its drafter, with the language and some at least of the thought belonging to him.[16] These final three verses would then be written in Peter's own hand, in accord with a custom also reflected in the Pauline letters (1 Cor 16:21; Gal 6:11; Col 4:18; 2 Thess 3:17).[17] If, however, Silvanus is the author, then his self-identification as "faithful brother" (τοῦ πιστοῦ ἀδελφοῦ) is a kind of self-praise one would hardly expect in this kind of letter.[18] Again, if Silvanus is the drafter, the kind of contribution to the substance of the letter assigned to him would lead one to expect Silvanus to be identified as cosender in the salutation (1:1), lack of which calls into question at least partially such a role for him.[19] An alternative is to point out that it is unlikely that Peter exercised the command of the Greek language exhibited in this letter, and to argue therefore that while the thought is from Peter, the language is from Silvanus. In that sense, while Peter is finally responsible for the content, Silvanus was the one who was responsible for its rather refined Greek.[20] Yet

---

8.3.

8 For more on this point, see the comments on v. 12.

9 That that is the probable meaning of διὰ Σιλουνοῦ, see below, "Comment," v. 12, and the Introduction § I.A.2.f, "Role of Silvanus."

10 On this point, see Brox, 241.

11 Those who argue that Peter is the author do find here evidence of a conclusion in his own hand, e.g., Cranfield, 137; Hart, 79; Wand, 128; cf. Windisch, 80; Bigg, 195.

12 Combrini ("Structure," 51) finds these verses "clearly structured as a chiasmus" consisting of A: Grace (v. 12b); B: Greetings (v. 13); B': Greetings (v. 14a); A' Peace (v. 14b). It is not clear that such was the author's intention, particularly since v. 12a must be ignored, as must the concluding exhortation in that same verse (12) which follows the first element in this

"chiasmus."

13 With, e.g., Goppelt, 346.

14 An additional possibility is suggested by Gourbillon ("La Première Epître," 17): Between missionary journeys, Silvanus requested Peter to write words of exhortation and witness in order to encourage the faithful who were undergoing calumnies and persecution; thus the letter owes its impetus to Silvanus. The suggestion owes more to imagination than to evidence.

15 So, e.g., Goppelt, 347; cf. Windisch, 80–81; Carrington, "Saint Peter's Epistle," 57; Best, 55.

16 So, e.g., Kelly, 215; Selwyn, 11; cf. Moffatt, 169.

17 So, e.g., Kelly, 214; Margot, 89.

18 So, e.g., Brox, 242.

19 So, e.g., Beare, 209; Chase, "Peter," 790; Best, 57.

20 So, e.g., Cranfield, 14; Moffatt, 86. Bigg (6) suggests

we know nothing whatever of Silvanus's linguistic training, and hence assigning the Greek to him has no basis in reality.[21] The Pauline flavor of the theology of 1 Peter can also be interpreted to point to the substantive role Silvanus played in the letter's composition,[22] but that flavor is not to be exaggerated.[23] To argue, finally, that the phrase means simply amanuensis, nothing more,[24] is to overlook the fact that in the one example we have where a scribe is acknowledged (Rom 16:22), the language is quite different.[25] To assign Silvanus a hand in the letter's composition, therefore, lacks persuasive power.

b. In early Christian literature, including the NT, the phrase γράφειν διά τινος identifies not the author of the letter, or its scribe, but its bearer, the one who delivered it to its readers.[26] Indeed, that is precisely the language used in Acts 15:23 to identify Silas as one of the group of picked men who delivered the apostolic decrees. That he could not be the bearer since one person could not have

made the trip to all the places mentioned in the opening verse[27] is countered by a glance at the kind of traveling that Acts reports of Paul on his missionary journeys. Obviously individuals could, and did, travel widely within the Roman Empire at this time.[28] Silvanus ought thus to be seen as the one who delivered the letter to its readers.[29]

To resolve this problem by affirming that Silvanus functioned as both drafter and bearer of the letter has little to commend it other than as a means preserving the obvious meaning of the phrase (sent by way of) while retaining the supposed advantage of allowing Silvanus to be responsible for the Greek employed in the letter.[30]

2. On the one hand, the name may refer to a Silvanus actually involved in some way with the letter, either to a Silvanus otherwise unknown to us from the primitive church,[31] or to the Silvanus known from the Pauline letters (2 Cor 1:19; 1 Thess 1:1; 2 Thess 1:1). If the latter is the case here, the further question arises

---

21   either Peter dictated in Aramaic and Silvanus wrote it down in Greek, or Peter dictated in Greek and Silvanus corrected it as necessary.

21   To make our total ignorance of Silvanus's linguistic ability a virtue, as do Reicke (70: simpler to assume Silvanus was "steeped in Greek culture") and Cranfield ("I Peter," 14: "there is no evidence that Silvanus was capable of writing elegant Greek, but at least there is in his case no particular reason for thinking that he was not"), is, as Beare (209) correctly noted, a "device of desperation." For more on the language in 1 Peter and its source, see the Introduction § I.A.2, "Language of 1 Peter."

22   So, e.g., Reicke, 70.

23   So, e.g., Best, 57. Spicq (178) argues that the differences between the Pauline letters and 1 Peter are too great for the coauthor of 1 and 2 Thessalonians to be the coauthor of this letter.

24   As does Beare, 209.

25   Ἀσπάζομαι ὑμᾶς ἐγὼ Τέρτιος ὁ γράψας τὴν ἐπιστολὴν ("I, Tertius who wrote [out] this letter greet you").

26   E.g., Ignatius Rom. 10.1; Phld. 11.2; Smyrn. 12.1; Pol. 8.1; Polycarp Phil. 14.1; cf. Acts 15:23. One of the later subscriptions to Romans includes the phrase ἐγράφη διὰ Φοίβης, language clearly meant to identify the bearer, not the author. On this point see, e.g., Brox, 242; idem, "Tendenz," 111; Meade, Pseudonymity and Canon, 166; Chase, "Peter," 790; Elliott, "Peter, Silvanus and Mark," 263; Michl, "Die Presbyter," 49 n. 3; Tenney, "Parallels," 86–87. Radermacher ("Der erste Petrusbrief," 292; see also Goppelt, 346) cites a document (BGU 1079) in which

the author says he sent two letters, one by way of Nedoumos, one by way of Kornious, using the identical phrase found here (διὰ νηδύμου μίαν, διὰ κρονίου . . . μίαν). Michaels (306) argues that the reference in Eusebius to Clement as author of 1 Clement by means of the phrase διὰ Κλήμεντος γραφεῖσαν (Hist. eccl. 4.23.11) is invalid here, since no one other than Clement is named in 1 Clement, and hence it must bear that meaning there. That is not the case here, however.

27   As Beare (209) argues.

28   Michaels (307) notes that Silvanus need not in fact have carried them to every place, only to the port of entry (Amisus or Amastris in Pontus), and cites Cyprian's references (Treatise 12.3.36, 37, 39) to the "Epistle of Peter to Pontus," where in fact 1 Peter is quoted. That may indicate the letter was carried from thence by several people; it may, however, simply have been Cyprian's way of summarizing the provinces named in 1 Pet 1:1 by referring simply to the first.

29   This is also the conclusion reached by E. Randolph Richards (The Secretary in the Letters of Paul [WUNT 2/42; Tübingen: Mohr [Siebeck], 1991] 73 n. 21) after a lengthy survey of the way secretaries were used in ancient letter writing (esp. pp. 15–127).

30   That it means both, see, e.g., Bigg, 5; Best, 177; Wand, 128. To base this on the presence of ἔγραψα ("I wrote") instead of ἔπεμψα ("I sent"), as do, e.g., Cranfield ("I Peter," 137) and Selwyn (241), is to overlook the regular employment of some form of the phrase γράφειν διά τινος ("to write by way of

whether that person is to be understood as identical to the Silas who is described in Acts as a leading man among the Christians (15:22), a prophet (15:32), and a companion of Paul in some of the latter's missionary journeys (Acts 15:40; 16:19, 25, 29; 17:4, 10, 14; 18:5). Although such an identity of Silas/Silvanus is possible, perhaps even probable,[32] it is finally no more than an assumption,[33] since the name was not uncommon and is also known in Hellenistic culture, appearing in Greek literature, inscriptions, and papyri.[34]

On the other hand, the name Silvanus may refer not to an actual person but represent a pseudepigraphic device intended to lend credence to the letter.[35] In that case, one must ask why that particular name was chosen. The choice may have had theological motivation. If Silas/Silvanus was a companion of Paul in Acts and a cosender of letters to the Christians in Thessalonica (1 Thess 1:1; 2 Thess 1:1),[36] and if in addition he was understood here to be a participant in a letter attributed to Peter, he would be a strong witness to the unity of the apostolic message.[37] Again, the choice may have had more practical motivation. Silas is after all identified in Acts as one who, along with some others, delivered an earlier letter containing the apostolic decrees (Acts 15:22). Furthermore, those decrees were formulated by an apostolic council at which Peter was actively involved (Acts 15:7–11).[38] Such prior associations and activity

would have made him an ideal candidate to be an apostolic delegate to deliver a letter written by Peter.[39]

What then is to be made of Silvanus? While it is possible that his inclusion belongs to the devices that normally were used in pseudepigraphic letters, and that he is thus a fictive character, his function as bearer and probably also expounder of the letter makes it more likely that an actual person is meant here. While the Silvanus/Silas of Acts and the letters of Paul could be the ones intended here, it is likely that by the time this letter was written he was, if still alive, too old to undertake such a rigorous journey. Perhaps most attractive is the suggestion that the Silvanus mentioned here is in fact the bearer but a different person from the one mentioned in other parts of the NT.[40] That remains, however, nothing more than conjecture. Whatever the solution to that problem may be, the intent of the verse is clear: the Silvanus who bears the letter does so with full apostolic approbation, and hence is to be accorded careful attention.

The identification of Silvanus as "the faithful brother" (τοῦ πιστοῦ ἀδελφοῦ)[41] in all probability belongs to the common ancient custom of commending the one who delivers a letter, a custom reflected in early Christian

someone") to identify the bearer of the letter in the Christian literature noted above.

31 So, e.g., Leaney, 72.
32 That that identity is probable: e.g., Goppelt, 348; Holmer and de Boor, 178; Reicke, 70; Chase, "Peter," 791; Windisch, 80. That the identity is certain: e.g., Cothenet, "La Première Epître de Pierre," 139. Radermacher ("Der erste Petrusbrief," 294–95) argues that Silvanus is a latinizing, Silas a graecizing of a Semitic name derived from Heb. שלח, "to send"; Spicq (177) notes that the name of the pool in John 9:7 derives from the same root.
33 So, correctly, Chase, "Peter," 791; Meecham, "First Epistle," 24.
34 On this point, see also, e.g., Bigg, 83; Best, 55.
35 So, e.g., Brox, 241; Schelkle, 133. But see Goppelt (348), who argues against mention of Silvanus as a pseudepigraphic tactic to make more likely authorship by Peter; he cites 2 Peter as an example of how that was accomplished.
36 Because of that association, Silvanus would fit better in a letter attributed to Paul, as Brox ("Tendenz,"

114) notes; but see Elliott ("Peter, Silvanus and Mark," 261), who argues such a reference in no way proves the letter to be a product of the Pauline school.
37 Paul's tirade in Gal 2:11–14 made such a reconciliation desirable.
38 So, e.g., Tenney, "Parallels," 89; Elliott, "Peter, Silvanus and Mark," 263. Aside from that one instance, however, there is no tradition that associates Peter and Silas/Silvanus, as Brox (243) notes.
39 So, e.g., Chase, "Peter," 790.
40 This is not the usual solution; see, e.g., Elliott, "Peter, Silvanus and Mark," 260. It would be helped if the Mark mentioned in 5:13 were also an unknown Christian bearing that name, a possibility to be sure, but less likely when two such familiar names are given.
41 The interjection of ὑμῖν ("to you") between "Silvanus" and his commendation as faithful brother is, as Michaels (306) notes, unusual, but its position does not impair the clarity of the author's intention.

letters.[42] Since the deliverer of a letter was also charged with providing the recipients more detailed information about the letter's contents,[43] such a commendation would make more sense if Silvanus were to be understood as the bearer of the letter rather than its drafter.[44] It assures the recipients that the one who delivers it is a reliable messenger.[45] His reliability is reinforced with the phrase ὡς λογίζομαι ("in my estimate"), here to be understood in the Pauline sense of giving an apostolic judgment[46] that therefore does not relativize but strengthens Silvanus's reliability.[47] He brings with him apostolic approbation.

The phrase δι' ὀλίγων ἔγραψα[48] ("I have written you briefly") conforms again to ancient epistolary convention: long letters were regarded as inappropriate if not indeed impolite,[49] and so authors conventionally referred to their "brief letter."[50] The phrase is thus not related to the actual length of the epistle,[51] nor to its brevity in relation to the sublimity of its content,[52] nor to the modesty of its author.[53]

The ensuing participles παρακαλῶν καὶ ἐπιμαρτυρῶν ("exhorting and bearing witness to")[54] provide an admirable summary of the entire letter,[55] which has consisted of alternating blocks of witnessing to the content of the faith[56] and exhorting to appropriate response.[57] The antecedent of ταύτην ("this") is not to be construed as χάριν, which on the contrary provides the content of that antecedent, but rather is to be construed as the epistle itself in the sense of its content,[58] that is, the exhortation to faithful endurance of rejection for the sake of faithfulness to the Christ who suffered and now rules in glory.[59] Such acceptance of and faithfulness to the suffering and glorified Christ is the "true grace of God."[60]

The εἰς that introduces the final phrase has normally the sense of "into," or "with (something) in view,"[61] but may in this instance have the force of ἐν ("in"), a substitution that occurred increasingly in the Hellenistic

---

42   E.g., Rom 16:1; Eph 6:21; Col 4:7b (perhaps also 1 Cor 16:10–11); Ignatius *Rom.* 10.1; *Smyrn.* 12.1; Polycarp *Phil.* 14.1. On this point see also Brox, 243; Grudem, 24.

43   E.g., Eph 6:22; Col 4:7a. On this point see also Hart, 79.

44   With, e.g., Grudem, 24. It also removes the unlikely possibility of self-praise on the part of the one who drafted the letter, as Goppelt (348) also points out.

45   So also, e.g., Moffatt, 169; Margot, 89. That Silvanus was unknown to the recipients and hence needed an introduction, as Michaels (309) suggests, may also have played a role.

46   As, e.g., 2 Cor 11:5; cf. Rom 3:28; 8:18; so also Goppelt, 348.

47   With, e.g., Brox, 243; Wand, 128. It is not an "odd phrase" having the effect of conveying uncertainty, as Bornemann ("Taufrede," 164) thinks.

48   The ancient letter writer wrote from the perspective of the reader; hence the act of writing would be in the past when the letter was read, and hence the regular use of the "epistolary aorist," as here. See, e.g., Beare, 209.

49   So, e.g., Demetrius *De Elocutione* 228: "The length of a letter, no less than its style, must be kept within due bounds"; if letters become too long they are no longer letters but treatises with a greeting, as in the case of letters of Plato and Thucydides (the translation is from Abraham J. Malherbe, *Ancient Epistolary Theorists* [SBLSBS 19; Atlanta: Scholars Press, 1988] 19).

50   See, e.g., Heb 13:22; Ignatius *Rom.* 8.2; *Pol.* 7.3;

Barn. 1.5; Pliny *Ep.* 3.9.27; so also Best, 171; Goppelt, 349. For further examples, see Spicq, 179.

51   As, e.g., Brox (244), Bigg (196), and Wand (129) would have it. Perdelwitz (*Mysterienreligion*, 16) is also wide of the mark with his comment: "I limit myself to the question, whether a letter of about 1675 words can truly be described as one written δι' ὀλίγων."

52   As Selwyn (242) would have it.

53   As, e.g., Schelkle, 134. To see here a relation to the ὀλίγον ("short time [of suffering]") of v. 10, as does Michaels (308), is also questionable.

54   They are to be construed as adverbial participles of attendant circumstance, giving further information on what the author intended by his writing.

55   A view widely held, e.g., Schlier, "Adhortatio," 60; Sieffert, "Die Heilsbedeutung," 372; Brox, 18; Talbert, "Once Again," 143; Goppelt, 349; Reicke, 133; Kelly, 216.

56   1:3–12, 18–21, 23–25; 2:6–10, 21–25; 3:10–12, 18–22; 4:4–6, 17–18; 5:10–11.

57   1:13–17, 22; 2:1–5, 11–20; 3:1–9, 13–17; 4:1–3, 7–16, 19; 5:1–9.

58   With, e.g., Brox, 244; Michaels, 308–9; Wand, 129; Berger, "Apostelbrief," 193.

59   To say with Schlier ("Adhortatio," 60) that "grace" here refers to the history and person of Jesus Christ is on the right track, but too broadly conceived.

60   While the author uses the word "grace" throughout the letter (1:2; 3:7; 4:10; 5:10), the closest to our passage is its use in 2:19, 20, as Vanhoye ("1 Pierre," 124) also notes; on this point see also Brox, 245.

61   Michaels (310) argues for the second meaning here.

period.[62] In either case, the exhortation[63] is to maintain one's adherence to the true grace of God about which the author has been writing.

■ **13** Continuing the formulae that characterize a number of letters in the NT, the author sends greetings to the readers (ὑμᾶς, "you") from people who are with him, giving as well, if indirectly, the location from which he writes.[64] The identity of both the persons who send greetings and the location is problematic.

The first greeter is identified as "the fellow elect one in Babylon." Because the term "fellow elect one" (ἡ συνεκλεκτή) is feminine in gender, it could refer to a woman, which, because of the later mention of "my son," could in turn refer to the author's wife. Support for such a view is drawn from the indication in Matt 8:14 that Peter was married, and from the reference in 1 Cor 9:5 to Peter's "sister-wife."[65] Later tradition reported that Peter's wife was martyred before he was.[66] Compared to the reference to Mark, however, this would be an "oddly elaborate"[67] allusion to an individual, and the addition in a number of manuscripts of the word ἐκκλησία ("church") in this text,[68] the reference to the church in 2 John 13 as the readers' "elect sister,"[69] and the greetings from

churches and then individuals in the same order in 1 Cor 16:19[70] all indicate that this is a reference to the Christian community in "Babylon."[71] As the Christians to whom the letter is addressed are the elect (1:1), so the community from which the letter is written is also elect along with them.[72]

The location of the elect community is identified as "in Babylon," which is also presumably the location from which the letter is being sent, although the location of the Babylon mentioned admits of some confusion. While one would normally assume that it referred to the Mesopotamian city of that name, contemporary records indicate that that city was at the time the letter was written little more than ruins.[73] That, added to the lack of any tradition linking Peter with this area,[74] makes it highly unlikely that it is meant as the place of origin of this letter. There was also a military stronghold on the Nile Delta during this period that bore the name "Babylon,"[75] but again, there is no indication of any Petrine contact with Egypt.[76] It is far more likely that

---

62 So also, e.g., Brox, 246; Goppelt, 350; Kelly, 217; on use of εἰς for ἐν, see James Hope Moulton, *A Grammar of New Testament Greek* (Edinburgh: Clark, 1906) 1.62–63, 234–35.

63 The verb στῆτε ("stand") is imperative.

64 For greetings to readers with an indication of location, see 1 Cor 16:19–20; Heb 13:24; cf. Phil 4:21–22; for greetings alone, see Rom 16:20–23; 2 Cor 13:12; Col 4:10, 12; 2 Tim 4:21; Titus 3:15; Phlm 23; 2 John 13; 3 John 15.

65 So, e.g., Bengel, *Gnomon*, 759. Bigg (77) speculates that she must have been "a well-known and well-loved personage in many places"; cf. Best (177), who says that if it refers to a person, it was his wife.

66 Clement of Alexandria *Strom.* 7.11.63.3.

67 The phrase is from Smothers, "Letter," 203; see also Best, 177.

68 Sinaiticus, some cursives, Vulgate, Peshitto, as Beare (210) notes; the word for "church" (ἐκκλησία) is feminine in gender.

69 Ἀσπάζεταί σε τὰ τέκνα τῆς ἀδελφῆς σου τῆς ἐκλεκτῆς ("the children of your elect sister greet you"). On this point see, e.g., Kelly, 217–18.

70 With, e.g., Best, 178.

71 With many scholars; in addition to those already mentioned, see, e.g., Margot, 90; Spicq, 180; Goppelt, 351 n. 28; Selwyn, 243; Windisch, 82;

Meecham, "First Epistle," 24. Holmer and de Boor (180) point for further support to Jer 2:2, where Israel is seen as a bride, and 2 Cor 11:2, where the Christian community is so compared. Wand (129) would trace it to the reference to the daughter of Zion in Isa 37:22.

72 With, e.g., Goppelt, 350–51; Brox, 247.

73 Josephus (*Ant.* 18.371–79) reports that Jews were forced to leave that city during the reign of Claudius (41–54 CE); Dio Cassius (*Hist. Rom.* 68.30) reports that when Trajan visited the site he found little but ruins; Diodorus Siculus (*Bib. hist.* 68.30) says only a small part of Babylon was inhabited, with most of the area within its former walls given over to agriculture; similar reports are given by Strabo (*Geog.* 16.1.5) and Pliny (*Hist. nat.* 6.121–22). Philo's comment that Jews lived in Babylon and other satrapies to the east (*Leg. Gaj.* 282) is so vague as not to provide counter-weight to the other reports. On this point see Kelly, 218; Grudem, 33; Smothers, "Letter," 204.

74 Smothers ("Letter," 207) notes that if such a contact did exist, it left no echo in the tradition.

75 It is mentioned in Strabo (*Geog.* 17.1.30) and Josephus (*Ant.* 2.315), who locate it near Old Cairo. On this point see also Kelly, 218.

76 Correctly, Schelkle, 134; Hunzinger, "Babylon als Deckname," 67. But see G. Fedalto ("Il toponimo di I

Babylon is a cryptic reference to Rome,[77] a view universally held until the period of the Reformation, at which time, because it appeared to give support to papal claims regarding Rome, that identity was disputed.[78] The equation of Rome with Babylon arose in Jewish tradition less as a result of the general persecution of the chosen people by the Babylonian Empire[79] than as a result of the conquest and destruction of Jerusalem by Roman legions in 70 CE,[80] which was seen to provide the counterpart to the similar destruction of that city by the Babylonians some centuries earlier. That identification then probably moved from Jewish tradition to the NT.[81]

The employment here of such an equation is probably not to be sought in some desire to hide from Roman authorities Christian references to Rome,[82] since there is little likelihood that such authorities had any real interest in Christian literature, and since in any case the content of this letter, particularly 2:13–17, would hardly have seemed suspicious to those authorities.[83] Rather, it is

included here to reaffirm the analogy of Christians living in conditions of diaspora (1:1) as exiles and aliens within Greco-Roman culture (1:1; 2:11).[84] In that way the author constructs an *inclusio* with the opening verse, giving to his whole letter this kind of framework,[85] and, more specifically, to identify both the author and his Christian community as sharing with the readers such exile status.[86]

It is as difficult to be certain about the identity of the Mark who sends greetings as it was of the Silvanus mentioned in v. 12. While this reference may be part of the normal practice in pseudonymous letters, where well-known figures associated with the author are mentioned,[87] in the NT the association of Mark with Paul is better attested than his relationship with Peter.[88] Later tradition associated the two in regard to the authorship of the second Gospel,[89] but one cannot be certain that such a tradition was already so widespread at the time this letter was written that the author could presume that

Petri 5, 13, . . ." *Vetera Christianorum* 20 [1983] 461–66), who argues that this is the Babylon to which the letter refers (I owe this reference to Benedetto Prete, "L'espressione *hē Babylōni syneklektē* di 1 Pt. 5,13," *Vetera Christianorum* 21 [1984] 335 n. 1).

77 So also, e.g., Hunzinger, "Babylon als Deckname," 67; Cullmann, *Peter*, 85; Wolff, "Christ und Welt" 334; Lepelley, "Le contexte," 61; Goppelt, 351; Reicke, 134; Spicq, 181; Michaels, 311. Windisch (82) suggests Jerusalem as a possibility, but thinks Rome more likely. See also the discussion of Babylon in the Introduction, "IV.C. Origin of 1 Peter."

78 On this point see Bigg, 76. So, e.g., Calvin (154): "nor do I see why it [Babylon as Rome] was approved by Eusebius and others, except that they were already led astray by that error, that Peter had been at Rome."

79 So, e.g., Blendinger, "Kirche als Fremdlingschaft," 128; Harrison, "Exegetical Studies" [97], 202; Senior, 94; Holmer and de Boor, 181; Moffatt, 170. On that basis, Assyria and Egypt would have been at least as appropriate, as Hunzinger ("Babylon als Deckname," 68) correctly notes. Even less likely as a point of origin was Vespasian's sacking of Rome, which Bigg (76) suggests would have put his name in proximity to that of Nebuchadnezzar.

80 So also, e.g., H. Millauer, *Leiden*, 195; Michl, "Die Presbyter," 49; Dibelius, "Petrusbriefe," 1114; Hunzinger, "Babylon als Deckname," 74. One must be careful of making such an equation exclusively Jewish, however, since Petronius (*Satyr.* 55) also compares Roman decadence and luxury to that of

Babylon (I owe this reference to C. P. Thiede, "Babylone, der andere Ort: Anmerkungen zu 1 Petr 5,13 und Apg 12,17," *Bib* 67 [1986] 534).

81 In Jewish tradition: *2 Bar.* 11.1–2; 67.6; *4 Ezra* 3.1–2, 28; cf. *Sib. Or.* 5.143, 159–60; in the NT: Rev 14:8; 16:19; 17:5, 18; 18:2. On this point see, e.g., Best, 178.

82 As often affirmed, e.g., Robinson, *Redating*, 151; Selwyn, 243; more tentatively, Hart, 180; Sylva, "Studies," 158, Cullmann, *Peter*, 84.

83 With, e.g., Kelly, 219; Moule, "Nature," 8–9.

84 So also, e.g., Thiede, "Babylone," 537; Selwyn, 304; Cranfield, 139; Cullmann, *Peter*, 84.

85 With Michaels, 311. One may therefore affirm its significance for an understanding of Christians living in alienation from their world without asserting, as do, e.g., Andresen ("Formular," 243) and Prete ("L'espressione," 352), that it refers to the provisional character of Christian life with no specific reference to Rome (cf. also Kelly, 219). The geographical reference need not be sacrificed for that point to be made.

86 On this point cf. Brox, 247; Cullmann, *Peter*, 84.

87 So, e.g., Bauer, 62; Spicq, 181; Tenney, "Parallels," 90. Brox ("Tendenz," 114) also notes that elements typical of pseudepigraphic letters are used very sparingly in this letter, however.

88 With Paul, Col 4:10; 2 Tim 4:11; Phlm 24; Acts 12:25; 13:5, 13; 15:37–39. With Peter, Acts 12:12, and there only indirectly (Peter appears at the home of John Mark's mother).

89 Eusebius *Hist. eccl.* 2.15.1–2; 3.39.15; 6.25.5.

the readers would have been acquainted with it.[90] While the reference may indeed be to the John Mark mentioned in Acts and in some Pauline letters,[91] it is also possible that it is a reference to a Mark otherwise unknown, since the name Μᾶρκος was a common one at this time within Greco-Roman culture.[92] The further identification of this Mark as ὁ υἱός μου ("my son") does little to add clarity to the identification. Since it is apparent that Peter was married (Matt 8:14 par.), it is possible to take the phrase literally as a description of a member of Peter's own household,[93] all the more likely if the earlier reference to the "fellow elect one" was to Peter's wife. It appears more likely, however, that the phrase is figurative,[94] pointing to one for whose entrance into the Christian faith Peter was responsible,[95] as seems, for example, also to have been the case of Paul with Timothy.[96] Yet the language in Paul is different,[97] reducing the certainty of such a conclusion. Whether therefore the reference to "Mark" is a part of the fictive apparatus of pseudonymous letters, or an actual person who stood in some intimate relationship with the Peter in whose name the letter is being written, or, less likely, with the unknown author, must remain a matter of conjecture.

The references in this verse that point to Rome as the locus of its writing[98] indicate that the letter stands as an early, perhaps the first, indication that contact in the primitive church is now moving from Rome to Asia Minor. All earlier contacts[99] had moved in the other direction.[100] With this letter the ecumenical concern of the Christian community in Rome, later confirmed by *1 Clement*, emerges, laying the foundation for its later eminence within the larger catholic church.[101] More immediately, the reference to Babylon shows the continuing appropriation of the language of Israel for the Christian community that, like Israel of old, lives as an exile in an alien culture, eagerly anticipating its restoration by its faithful Lord.

■ **14** The similarity between the conclusion of this letter and the Pauline letter form is further attested by the reference here to the Christian practice of bestowing a kiss on fellow Christians, a practice also referred to in some Pauline letters.[102] The substitution here of "kiss of love" (φίλημα ἀγάπης)[103] for the Pauline "holy kiss" (φίλημα ἅγιον) indicates that our author is more likely to be following general community practice rather than simply imitating the Pauline letter form, however. This substitution is wholly in line with the emphasis on mutual Christian love in this letter,[104] and shows the author's freedom in adapting Christian formulae to his own purposes. The employment of such a kiss, normally

90 Brox ("Tendenz," 113) thinks it quite uncertain ("völlig unsicher") that the traditions in Eusebius describing Mark as Peter's interpreter and author of the second Gospel are old enough to find an echo here.
91 Many scholars affirm this; e.g., Kelly, 220; Goppelt, 353; Selwyn, 244; Best, 179; Bigg, 80.
92 So Leaney, 72; as a possibility, Spicq, 181.
93 So R. S. T. Haselhurst, "'Mark, My Son,'" *Theology* 13 (1926) 34–35.
94 Schelkle (135) thinks it "unquestioned" ("unbestritten") that it cannot refer to Peter's physical son.
95 So, e.g., Margot, 91; Brox, 248; Goppelt, 353; Wand, 130; Bigg, 80; Michaels, 312. Kelly (220) thinks it "reflects the relationship of trust and affection between the older Christian leader and his younger disciple."
96 So, e.g., Spicq, 181.
97 Paul never refers to Timothy as υἱός ("son"), only as τέκνον ("child"): 1 Cor 4:17; 1 Tim 1:2, 18; 2 Tim 1:2; 2:1; that is also the case with Titus (1:4) and Onesimus (Phlm 10); see also 1 Cor 4:14. Haselhurst ("Mark, My Son," 34) cites this evidence as a basis for affirming the physical paternity of Peter.
98 There is no credible evidence (pace Boismard, "Liturgie" [2], 181 n. 2], who suggested Antioch) that it originated in another place, as Beare (226–27) correctly argues.
99 Paul's Epistle to the Romans, the writings of Luke, the influx of oriental religions to Rome.
100 I owe this point to Goppelt, 353.
101 Ignatius *Rom.* Intro.; 3.1 show the high esteem the Roman Christian community enjoyed in at least some eastern areas.
102 Rom 16:16; 1 Cor 16:20; 2 Cor 13:12; 1 Thess 5:26.
103 The genitive ἀγάπης is the genitive of quality, i.e., a kiss whose reality derives from Christian love.
104 See the emphasis on love within the Christian community: 1:22; 2:17; 4:8; a love also reflected in the address "beloved" (ἀγαπητοί) that the author employs at 2:11 and 4:12. On this point see also Michaels, 313.

practiced within the family,[105] but also as a gesture of greeting to friends,[106] served to emphasize the point that all Christians were to regard themselves as members of the Christian family, and hence to treat each other with kindness and consideration.[107] The fact that such a liturgical kiss later became a regular part of the eucharistic celebration[108] may indicate such was the setting that the author envisioned for the public reading of this letter.[109] Yet since worship would normally be the only time a Christian community assembled, one could suppose a context of that sort for the reading of the letter whether or not the liturgical kiss was a part of the eucharistic celebration at this time.

The wish for peace[110] as the conclusion of the letter again shows similarity to the Pauline letter form, but with characteristic independence, here substituting "peace" (εἰρήνη) for the normal Pauline wish for "grace" (χάρις),[111] although the wish for peace also occurs in the Pauline letters.[112] The wish for peace, along with grace,

was also expressed in 1:2b, thus forming, with this verse and the reference to grace in 5:12, an *inclusio*.[113] While the phrase ἐν Χριστῷ, also familiar from the Pauline letters, can carry significant theological freight, in this context it probably bears the same sense as the adjective Χριστιανός ("Christian," see 4:16), as it also does when Paul uses it in relation to persons.[114] In face of growing cultural hostility, and with official disapprobation looming on the horizon, there could be no greater boon to the Christians than the kind of peace, rooted in the Christ who suffered but now reigns in glory,[115] that will grant them the inward serenity and strength sufficient to enable them to hold fast to their faith, despite whatever opposition may confront them. It was to instill and encourage precisely that kind of peace that the letter was written.[116] The survival of the Christian community attests to the letter's success, a success repeated whenever Christians find, in threatening times, comfort and peace in its words.

---

105 So, e.g., Goppelt (354), who also claims the practice was unknown in the synagogue.

106 E.g., Luke 7:45, where Jesus chides his host for failing to practice it; see also Acts 20:37, where the community says farewell to Paul. It was this context that made Judas's betrayal of Jesus by means of a kiss so heinous (Luke 22:48).

107 The practice of kissing was also open to abuse, as can be seen from Martial's sarcastic complaint (*Epig.* 11.98) that one cannot escape determined "kissers" (*basiatores*), who will perform the act no matter what the situation. In fact Tiberius issued an edict forbidding general kissing (Suetonius *Vit.* 3.34.2) and Pliny (*Hist. nat.* 26.1–3) describes a facially disfiguring disease to which males of the noble class were subject, which could be transmitted by a kiss (I owe these references to J. C. Rolfe, *Suetonius: The Lives of the Caesars* [LCL; Cambridge: Harvard University Press, reprinted 1979] 1.342 n. c, although he wrongly cites Martial as 11.99).

108 Cf. the reference to the kiss in the context of a eucharistic discussion in Justin (*1 Apol.* 65.2), and the ordering of it in the *Ap. Const.* (8.11; see also 2.57), where clerics kiss the bishop, laymen other men, and women other women. Clement of Alexandria (*Paed.* 3.11.81.2–3) complains that some people make the church resound with the noise of their kisses (the

verb he uses, καταψοφέω, is used by Josephus [*Ant.* 6.27] of a thunderclap), and complains that such a practice has given rise to suspicion and calumny. On this point see, e.g., Moffatt, 171; Hart, 80.

109 So, e.g., Leaney, 73; Brox, 248; Spicq, 181. But see Cranfield ("I Peter," 140), who notes that its use in a eucharistic setting in NT times, while not unlikely, remains unproved. Goppelt (355) finds the later addition of ἀμήν ("amen") at the end of the verse further indication of its use in worship.

110 Unlike 5:11, which is declarative, this is to be understood with some such verb form as ἔστω ("may you all have peace") or, as in 1:2, πληθυνθείη ("may peace be multiplied to you").

111 Rom 16:20; 1 Cor 16:23; 2 Cor 13:14; Gal 6:18; Phil 4:23; 1 Thess 5:28; Phlm 25; cf. Eph 6:24; Col 4:18; 2 Thess 3:18; 1 Tim 6:21; 2 Tim 4:22b; Titus 3:15b.

112 Rom 15:33; 2 Cor 13:11; Gal 6:16; Eph 6:23; 2 Thess 3:16. It was to be granted by Jesus' disciples to those worthy of it (Matt 10:13; Luke 10:5), as Bauer (63) observes.

113 So also Michaels, 313; Schweizer, 105; Kelly, 221.

114 E.g., Rom 16:3, 7.

115 Such peace is announced by Jesus; see John 14:27; Luke 24:36.

116 See also, e.g., Spicq, 182.

Bibliography
Indices

1. Commentaries

Patristic

Clement of Alexandria
Adumbrationes in Epistola Petri Prima Catholica
(Fragment 24), GCS, *Clemens Alexandrinus* 3.203–6
(Berlin: Akademie-Verlag, 1970) (2d century).

Didymus Caecus Alexandrinus
In epistulas catholicas brevis ennaratio, PG 39.1755–
72 (4th century).

Cyrillus Alexandrinus
In epistolam I B. Petri, PG 74.1011–16 (4th
century).

Johannes Chrysostomus
Fragmenta in primam S. Petri Epistolam, PG
64.1053–58 (4th century).

Eusebius Hieronymus (Jerome)
B. Petri Apostoli Epistola prima, PL 29.877–82 (4th–
5th century).

Ammonius Alexandrinus
Fragmentum in Primam S. Petri Epistolam, PG
85.1607–10 (6th century).

Hesychius
Fragmentum in epistolam I. S. Petri, PG 93.1389–90
(6th century).

Magnus Aurelius Cassiodorus
*Complexionis canonicarum epistularum septem; epistula
Petri Apostoli ad Gentes, PL* 70.1361–68 (6th
century).

Paterius
*Liber de expositione Veteris ac Novi Testamenti: Sextus,
de Testimoniis in Epistolas catholicas, PL* 79.1097–
1100 (6th century).

Luculentius
Lectio Epistulae I beati Petri apostoli, PL 72.857–60
(7th century).

Pseudo-Euthalius
*Elenchus capitum septem Epistolarum Catholicarum,
PG* 85.679–82 (7th century).

Pseudo-Oecumenius
Comentarii in epistolas catholicas, PG 119.509–78
(7th century).

Pseudo-Hilarius Arelatensis
Expositio in epistolas catholicas, PL Suppl. III.83–106
(7th century).

Medieval

Beda Venerabilis
*Super epistolas catholicas expositio: in primum
Epistolam Petri, PL* 93.41–68 (8th century).

Isho'dad of Merv
The Commentaries of Isho'dad of Merv: vol. IV: *Acts of
the Apostles and Three Catholic Epistles* (Horae
Semiticae 10.38–39, 51–53; ed. and trans. M. D.
Gibson; Cambridge: University Press, 1913) (9th
century).

Walafridus Strabo
Glossa Ordinaria; Epistola I B. Petri, PL 114.679–88
(9th century).

Pseudo-Theophylact
Expositio in Epistolam Primam S. Petri, PG
125.1189–1252 (9th century).

Alulfus
Expositio super I. Epistolam B. Petri Apostoli, PL
79.1385–88 (10th century).

Euthymius Zigabenus
*Commentarius in XIV Epistolas S. Pauli et VII
Catholicas* (Athens: Kalogeras, 1887) (10th
century).

Dionysius bar Salîbi
In Apocalypsim, Actus et Epistulas catholicas (Corpus
scriptorum christianorum orientalium, Scriptores
Syri 2.101; ed. I. Sedlacek; Paris: 1909, 1910)
(10th century).

Martinus Legionensis
Expositio in epistolam I B. Petri apostoli, PL 209.217–
52 (10th century).

Gregorius Barhebraeus
*In Actus apostolorum et Epistulas catholicas adnota-
tiones Syricae e recognitione M. Klamroth* (Göttingen:
1878) (10th century).

Pseudo-Thomas
In septem epistolas canonicas (Paris: 1873–1882)
31.368–98 (11th century).

Renaissance and Reformation

Luther, Martin
Epistel Sanct Petri gepredigt und ausgelegt . . .
(Wittenberg: Nickel Schyrtentz, 1523); ET by E.
H. Gillett, *Martin Luther, The Epistles of St. Peter and
St. Jude Preached and Explained* (New York:
Randolph, 1859).

Bullinger, Heinrich
In D. Petri Apostoli Epistolam Utramque, in *Heinrychi
Bullingeri Commentarius* (Zurich: 1534).

Calvin, John
*Commentarius in Epistolas Catholicas Johannis Calvini
Opera quae Supersunt Omnia* (1551; reprinted
Braunschweig: 1896) 55.205–92.

Erasmus, Desiderius
Paraphrases in Novum Testamentum, in *Opera Omnia*
(Leiden: 1706) 7.1081–1100.

Coglerus, J.
In Epistolas Petri Commentarius (Wittenberg: 1564).

Alley, William
*Ptochomuseion . . . Bishop of Exceter upon the First
Epistle of Saint Peter* (London: John Day, 1565).

Hessels, J.
*In priorem B. Pauli Apostoli ad Timotheum epistolam
commentarius . . . Commentarius in priorem B. Petri
apostoli canonicam epistolam* (2 vols.; Louvain: 1568).

Hemmingius, N.
Commentaria in omnes Epistolas Apostolorum (Frankfurt am Main: 1579) 667–708.

Seventeenth Century

Aretius, B.
Commentarii in Domini nostri Jesu Christi Novum Testamentum (Bern: 1607) 487–507.

Winckelmann, J.
Commentarii in utramque Epistolam Petri (Wittenberg: 1608).

Serarius, N.
Prolegomena Bibliaca et Commentaria in omnes Epistolas Canonicas (Paris: 1612).

Byfield, Nicholas
Sermons upon the First Chapter of the First Epistle Generall of Peter (London: Nathaniel Butler and Edward Griffin, 1617).

Idem
A Commentary, or "Sermons upon the Second Chapter of the First Epistle of Saint Peter" (London: Lownes, 1623).

Idem
A Commentary ypon the Three First Chapters of the First Epistle Generall of St. Peter (London: M. Flesher and R. Young, 1637).

Laurentius, Jacobus
S. Apostoli Petri epistola catholica prior perpetuo commentario (Amsterdam: Sumptibus Henrici Laurentii, 1640).

Gerhard, Johann
Commentarius super priorem . . . D. Petri Epistolam (Jena: Gerhard, 1641).

Parëus, D.
Commentarii in epistolas canonicas Jacobi, Petri et Judae (Geneva: Ph. Parëus, 1641).

Schotanus, M.
Conciones in I. Epistolam Petri (Franeker: 1644).

Amyraut, M.
Paraphrase sur les épîtres catholiques de saint Jacques, Pierre, Jean et Jude . . . (Saumur: 1646).

Grotius, Hugo
Annotationum in Novum Testamentum pars tertia ac ultima (Paris: 1650).

Rogers, John
A Godly and Fruitful Exposition upon All the First Epistle of Peter (London: John Field, 1650).

Horneius, C.
In epistolam catholicam Sancti Apostoli Petri priorem expositio litteralis (Braunschweig: Horneius, 1654).

Carellius Francus, J.
Commentarius in I. epistolae Petri duo priora capita, in *Opera Omnia exegetica, didactica et polemica* (Freiburg: 1656) 2.269–84.

Estius, W.
In omnes beati Pauli et aliorum Apostolorum Epistolas commentaria (Paris: 1658) 2.1149–1201.

Gomarus, F.
In Priorem S. Petri Epistolam Explicatio, in Opera

Theologica Omnia (Amsterdam: 1664) 679–705.

Calov, A.
Biblia Novi Testamenti illustrata II (Dresden: 1673).

Goltzius, D.
Schriftmatige verklaringe en toepassinge tot geestelijck gebruyck, van de eerste (en tweede) algemeyne Sendbrief des apostels Petri (Amsterdam: 1689–91).

Leighton, Robert
A Practical Commentary upon the First Epistle General of St. Peter (York: J. White, 1693).

Antonides, Theodorus
Schrift-matige verklaringe over den eersten algemeinen send-brief van den H. Apostel Simeon Petrus (Leeuwarden: Gerardus Hoogslagh, 1698).

Eighteenth Century

Bibliander, Th.
Richtige Harmonie der heiligen Schrifft Alten und Neuen Testamentes (Görlitz: 1705).

Alexandre, N.
Commentarius litteralis et moralis in omnes epistolas Sancti Pauli Apostoli et in VII epistolas catholicas (Rouen: 1710)

Laurentius, Georg Michael
Kurtze Erklärung des Ersten (und anderen) Briefs St. Petri (Halle: 1716).

Streson, C.
Meditationes in I et II Epistolas Petri (Amsterdam: 1717).

Calmeth, A.
Commentaire littéral sur tous les livres de l'Ancien et du Nouveau Testament (Paris: 1726) 8.794–831.

Alphen, Hieronymus van
De eerste algemeen sendbrief van den Apostel Petrus . . . (Utrecht: Gysbert van Paddenburg en Willem Kroon, 1734).

Lange, J.
Urim ac Thummim . . . seu exegesis epistolarum Petri ac Joannis (Halle: 1734).

Wolf, J. C.
Curae philologicae et criticae in sanctorum apostolorum Jacobi, Petri, Judae et Joannis epistolas, huiusque Apocalypsin (Hamburg: 1735).

Bengel, Johann Albrecht
Gnomon Novi Testamenti (4th ed.; Tübingen: Schramm, 1742). ET: John Albert Bengel *Gnomon of the New Testament* (trans. A. R. Fausset; 5 vols.; Edinburgh: Clark, 1859).

Benson, George
A Paraphrase and Notes on the First Epistle of St. Peter (London: M. Fenner, J. Noon, and J. Hodges, 1742).

Wettstein, J. J.
Novum Testamentum Graecum editionis receptae (Amsterdam: 1752) 2.681–97.

Mathaei, C. F. Von
SS. Apostolorum septem Epistolae catholicae (Riga: 1782).

Semler, Johann Salomo
Paraphrasis in epistolam I. Petri; cum Latinae transla-tionis . . . et . . . notis (Halle: Memmerdiani, 1783).

Pott, D. J.
Epistolae catholicae graece perpetua annotatione illustratae (Göttingen: 1786).

Morus, S. F. N.
Praelectiones in Jacobi et Petri epistolas (ed. C. A. Donat; Leipzig: 1794).

Nineteenth Century

Meyer, Frederick Brotherton
Trial by Fire: Expositions of the First Epistle of Peter (New York: Revell, 1800).

Augusti, J. C. W.
Die katholischen Briefe, neu übersetzt und erklärt . . . (Lemgo: 1801–1808).

Hensler, C. G.
Der erste Brief des Apostels Petrus übersetzt und mit einem Kommentar versehen (Sulzbach: 1813).

Hottinger, J. I.
Epistolae Jacobi atque Petri cum versione germanica et commentario latino (Leipzig: 1815).

Kanter, Hubertus Philippus de
Commentatio in locum I. Petri v: 1–4 (Lugduni Batavorum [Leiden]: Luchtmans, 1823).

Eisenschmid, G. B.
Die Briefe des Apostels Petrus übersetzt, erläutert und mit erbaulichen Betrachtungen begleitet (Ronneberg: 1824).

Hahn, Johann Michael
Betrachtungen auf all Tagen des Jahrs über . . . den ersten Brief Petri . . . (Tübingen: Fues, 1824).

Steiger, Wilhelm
Der erste Brief Petri mit Berüchsichtigung des ganzen biblischen Lehrbegriffes ausgelegt (Berlin: Ludwig Oehmigke, 1832).

Mayerhoff, E. Th.
Historisch-critische Einleitung in die petrinischen Schriften (Hamburg: 1835).

Machmann, K. R.
Commentar über die Katholischen Briefe mit genauer Berücksichtigung der neuesten Auslegungen (Leipzig: 1838).

Fawcett, John
Christ Precious to Those That Believe (1 Pet 2:7) (Halifax: Millner, 1839).

Cramer, J. A.
Catenae graecorum patrum in Novum Testamentum (Oxford: 1844) 8.41–83.

Wette, W. M. L. de
Kurze Erklärung der Briefe des Petrus, Judas und Jakobus (Kurzgefasstes exegetisches Handbuch zum NT 2; Leipzig: 1847).

Brown, John
Expository Discourses on the First Epistle of the Apostle Peter (Edinburgh: Oliphant, 1848).

Alford, Henry
The Greek Testament . . . A Critical and Exegetical Commentary (London: Rivington's, 1849).

Mason, Arthur James
The First Epistle General of Peter (A Bible Commentary for English Readers; London: Cassell, 1850).

Demarest, John T.
A Translation and Exposition of the First Epistle of the Apostle Peter (New York: Moffet, 1851).

Huther, J. E.
Kritisch-exegetisches Handbuch über den 1. Brief des Petrus, den Brief des Judas und den 2. Brief des Petrus (KEK 12; Göttingen: Vandenhoeck & Ruprecht, 1851).

Wiesinger, A.
Der erste Brief des Apostels Petrus (Olshausens Commentar über sämtlichen Schriften; Königsberg: 1856).

Besser, Wilhelm Friedrich
St. Petri Brefi Bibliska Andaktsstunder forklarade for forsamlingen (Hernosand: Johansson, 1858).

Fronmüller, G. F. C.
Die Briefe Petri und der Brief Judä (Bielefeld: Velhagen und Klasing, 1859).

Schott, Theodor Friedrich
Der Erste Brief Petri erklärt (Erlangen: Deichert, 1861).

De Wette, Wilhelm Martin Leberecht
Kurze Erklärung der Briefe des Petrus, Judas und Jakobus (Leipzig: Hirzel, 1865).

Ewald, H.
Sieben Sendschreiben des Neuen Bundes übersetzt und erklärt (Göttingen: 1870).

Bisping, A.
Erklärung der sieben katholischen Briefe (Exegetisches Handbuch zum Neuen Testament 8; Münster/W: 1871).

Hofmann, J. Chr. K. von
Der Erste Brief Petri (Die heilige Schrift Neuen Testaments zusammenhängend untersucht; Nördlingen: 1875).

Camerlynck, A.
Commentarius in Epistolas catholicas (Brügge: 1876).

Witz, Ch. Alphonse
Der Erste Brief Petri (Vienna: Braumüller, 1881).

Keil, Carl Friedrich
Commentar über die Briefe des Petrus und Judas (Leipzig: Dörffling und Franke, 1883).

Huther, Johann Eduard, and Ernst Kühl
Kritisch-exegetisches Handbuch über den 1. Brief des Petrus, den Brief des Judas und den 2. Brief des Petrus (KEK 5; Göttingen: Vandenhoeck & Ruprecht, 1887).

Usteri, Johann Martin
Wissenschaftlicher und praktischer Commentar über den ersten Petrusbrief (Zurich: Hohr, 1887).

Burger, K.
Der erste Brief Petri (Nördlingen: 1888).

361

Johnstone, Robert
The First Epistle of Peter (rev. ed.; Edinburgh: Clark, 1888).

Soden, Hermann Freiherr von
Hebräerbrief, Briefe des Petrus, Jakobus, Judas (3d ed.; Hand-Kommentar zum NT; Freiburg im Breisgau: Mohr, 1890).

Goebel, S.
Die Briefe des Petrus, griechisch, mit kurzer Erklärung (Gotha: 1893).

Hartog, Arnold Hendrik de
Uitlegkundige wenken. Korte aanteekeningen op den eersten brief van den apostel Petrus (Amsterdam: Fernhout, 1895).

Beck, J. T.
Erklärung der Briefe Petri (Gütersloh: 1896).

Donner, Johannes Hendrikus
De eerste algemeene zendbrief van den apostel Petrus (Leiden: Donner, 1896).

Kühl, Ernst
Die Briefe Petri und Judae (KEK 6; Göttingen: Vandenhoeck & Ruprecht, 1897).

Weidner, Revere Franklin
Annotations on the General Epistles of James, Peter, John, and Jude (New York: Christian Literature Co., 1897).

Hort, Fenton John Anthony
The First Epistle of St. Peter: I.1—II.17: The Greek Text with Introductory Lecture, Commentary, and Additional Notes (London: Macmillan, 1898).

Twentieth Century

Jones, John Cynddylan
Studies in the First Epistle of Peter (London: Bible Christian Book Room, 1900).

Maclaren, Alexander
Ephesians, Epistles of St. Peter and St. John; 16 Expositions of Holy Scripture (New York: Doran, 1900).

Masterman, J. Howard B.
The First Epistle of St. Peter: (Greek Text) with Introduction and Notes (London: Macmillan, 1900).

Monnier, Jean
La première épître de l'apôtre Pierre (Macon: Protat frères, 1900).

Bennett, William Henry
The General Epistles: James, Peter, John, Jude (Century Bible; London: Caxton, 1901).

Bigg, Charles A.
Critical and Exegetical Commentary on the Epistles of St. Peter and St. Jude (ICC; New York: Scribner's, 1901).

Calmes, Th.
Les Epîtres catholiques, L'Apocalypse (Paris: 1905).

Eaches, Owen Philips
Hebrews, James, and I and II Peter (Clark's Peoples Commentary; Philadelphia: American Baptist Pub. Society, 1906).

Gunkel, H.
Der erste Breif des Petrus (Die Schriften des NT, vol. 2; ed. J. Weiss; Göttingen: 1906).

Weiss, Bernhard
Thessalonians-Revelation (Commentary on the NT 4; trans. G. H. Schodde and E. Wilson; New York: Funk & Wagnalls, 1906).

Van Kasteren, J. P.
Bijbellessen voor iedereen. De eerste brief van den Apostel Petrus (Utrecht: Van Rossum, 1911).

Knopf, Rudolph
Die Briefe Petri und Judä (KEK 7; Göttingen: Vandenhoeck & Ruprecht, 1912).

Blenkin, G. W.
The First Epistle General of Peter with Notes and Introduction (Cambridge Greek Testament for Schools and Colleges; Cambridge: University Press, 1914).

Vrede, W.
Der erste Petrusbrief (Die Heilige Schrift des Neuen Testaments, Bonner NT 9; Bonn: 1915).

Ross, John Murdock Ebenezer
The First Epistle of Peter: A Devotional Commentary (London: Religious Tract Society, 1918).

Schlatter, Adolph von
Die Briefe des Petrus, Judas, Jakobus, der Brief an die Hebräer, die Briefe und die Offenbarung des Johannes (Erläuterungen zum NT 3; Stuttgart: 1921).

Wohlenberg, Gustav
Der erste und zweiter Petrusbrief und der Judasbrief (3d ed.; Kommentar zum NT 15; Leipzig: Deichert, 1923).

McFadyen, Joseph Ferguson
Through Eternal Spirit: A Study of Hebrews, James, and 1 Peter (London: J. Clarke, 1924).

Holtzmann, Oscar
Die Petrus Briefe (Giessen: Töpelmann, 1926).

Plumptre, E. H.
The General Epistles of St. Peter and St. Jude, with Notes and Introduction (Cambridge Bible for Schools and Colleges; Cambridge: University Press, 1926).

Moffatt, James
The General Epistles: James, Peter, and Judas (MNTC; Garden City, N.Y.: Doubleday, Doran, 1928).

Felten, Joseph
Die Zwei Briefe des hl. Petrus und der Judasbrief (Regensburg: Manz, 1929).

Dibelius, Martin
"Petrusbriefe," *RGG* (2d ed.; ed. H. Gunkel et al.; Tübingen: Mohr [Siebeck], 1930) 4.1113–15.

Beelen, J. Th., and A. von der Heeren
De Katholeike Brieven (Brügge: 1932).

Wand, J. W. C.
The General Epistles of St. Peter and St. Jude (Westminster Commentaries; London: Methuen, 1934).

Zoellner, Wilhelm
Der Erste Petrusbrief, für die Gemeinde Ausgelegt (Potsdam: Stiftungsverlag, 1935).

Hauck, Friedrich
Die Briefe des Jakobus, Petrus, Judas und Johannes

(NTD 10; Göttingen: Vandenhoeck & Ruprecht, 1936).

Holzmeister, Urban
Commentarius in Epistolas SS. Petri et Judae Apostolorum, part I: *Epistula prima S. Petri Apostoli* (Paris: Lethielleux, 1937).

Charue, A.
Les épîtres catholiques (La Sainte Bible 12; Paris: 1938).

Lenski, R. C. H.
The Interpretation of the Epistles of St. Peter, St. John and St. Jude (Columbus, Ohio: Lutheran Book Concern, 1938).

Lilje, Hans
Die Petrusbriefe und der Judasbrief (Bibelhelfe für die Gemeinde, NT series 14; Leipzig: 1938).

Morgan, George Campbell
Peter and the Church (New York: Revell, 1938).

Braun, Herbert
Das Leiden Christi: Eine Bibelarbeit über den 1 Petrusbrief (Theologische Existenz Heute 69; Munich: Kaiser, 1940).

Selwyn, Ernest Gordon
The Epistle of Christian Courage: Studies in the First Epistle of St. Peter (London: Mowbray, 1940).

Staffelbach, G.
Die Briefe der Apostel Jakobus, Judas, Petrus und Johannes (Lucerne: 1941).

Ferrin, Howard William
Strengthen Thy Brethren: A Devotional Exposition of the First Epistle of Peter (Grand Rapids: Zondervan, 1942).

Keulers, J.
De Katholieke Brieven en het Boek der Openbaring (De boeken van het NT 7; Roermond: 1946).

Pury, Roland de
Pierres Vivantes: Commentaire de la Première Epître de Pierre (2d ed.; Neuchâtel: Delachaux et Niestlé, 1946).

Ambroggi, P. de
Le Epistole cattoliche (La Sacra Bibbia 14/1; Turin: 1947).

Cash, William Wilson
The First Epistle of St. Peter (London: Church Book Room Press, 1947).

Wuest, Kenneth Samuel
First Peter in the Greek New Testament for the English Reader (Grand Rapids: Eerdmans, 1947).

Nieboer, Joe
Practical Exposition of I Peter, Verse by Verse (Erie, Pa.: Our Daily Walk Publisher, 1948).

Brun, L.
Forste Peters-Brev (Oslo: 1949).

Cranfield, C. E. B.
The First Epistle of Peter (London: SCM, 1950).

Ketter, Peter
Hebräerbrief, Jakobusbrief, Petrusbriefe, Judasbrief (Herders Bibelkommentar; Freiburg: Herder, 1950).

Janzen, Henry H.
Glaube und Heiligung: Eine schlichte Auslegung von 1. Petrus Kapitel 1–4 Vers 7 (Karlsruhe: 1951).

Macleod, Alexander Napier
The First Epistle of Peter: A Commentary (Chinese) (Hong Kong: Christian Witness Press, 1951).

Rendtorff, Heinrich
Getrostes Wandern: Eine Einführung in den ersten Brief des Petrus (7th ed.; Die urchristliche Botschaft 20; Hamburg: Furche-Verlag, 1951).

Windisch, Hans
Die Katholischen Briefe (3d ed.; rev. and ed. H. Preisker; HNT; Tübingen: Mohr [Siebeck], 1951).

Bolkestein, Marinus Hendrik
De kerk in de Wereld: De eerste Brief van Petrus (Amsterdam: Holland uitgeversmaatschappij, 1952).

Pfendsack, Werner
Dennoch getrost: Ein Auslegung des 1. Petrus-Briefes (Basel: Reinhardt, 1952).

Reuss, Joseph
Die katholischen Briefe (Echter Bibel, Neutestamentliche Reihe; Würzburg: Echter, 1952).

Henry, Matthew
Acts to Revelation, vol. 6 of *Matthew Henry's Commentary on the Whole Bible* (New York: Revell, 1953).

Leconte, R.
Les Epîtres catholiques (La Sainte Bible de Jérusalem; Paris: 1953).

Stöger, A.
Bauleute Gottes. Der erste Petrusbrief als Grundlegung des Laienapostolats (Lebendiges Wort 3; Munich: 1954).

Selwyn, Ernest Gordon
The First Epistle of St. Peter (London: Macmillan, 1955).

Trempela, P.N.
Ὑπόμνημα εἰς τὰς ἐπίστολας τῆς καινῆς διαθήκης: vol. III: Ἡ πρὸς Ἑβραίους καὶ αἱ ἑπτα καθολικαί (Athens: 1956).

Maycock, Edward A.
A Letter of Wise Counsel: Studies in the First Epistle of Peter (World Christian Books; New York: Association, 1957).

Barclay, William
The First Letter of Peter, the Letter of Jude, and the Second Letter of Peter (Glasgow: Church of Scotland, 1958).

Diaz, R. M.
Epistoles Catòliques (Montserrat: 1958).

Vaccari, Alberto
Le Lettere cattoliche (La Sacra Bibbia 9; Rome: 1958).

Stibbs, Alan M., and A. F. Walls
The First Epistle General of Peter (Tyndale New Testament Commentaries; London: Tyndale; Grand Rapids: Eerdmans, 1959).

Cranfield, C. E. B.
I and II Peter and Jude: Introduction and Commentary (Torch Bible Commentaries; London: SCM, 1960).

Greijdanus, Seakle
De eerste brief van den apostel Petrus (Korte verklaring der Heilige Schrift; Kampen: Kok, 1960).

Margot, Jean-Claude
Les Epîtres de Pierre (Geneva: Labor et Fides, 1960).

Schneider, Johannes
Die Briefe des Jakobus, Petrus, Judas und Johannes (NTD 10; Göttingen: Vandenhoeck & Ruprecht, 1961).

Speyr, A. von
Die Katholischen Briefe (2 vols.; Einsiedeln: 1961).

Rees, Paul Stromberg
Triumphant in Trouble: Studies in I Peter (Westwood, N.J.: Revell, 1962).

Gourbillon, J. G., and F. M. Buit
La première épître de S. Pierre (Paris: 1963).

Schwank, P. Benedikt
Der erste Brief des Apostels Petrus (2d ed.; Geistliche Schriftlesung 20; Düsseldorf: Patmos, 1964).

Salguero, J.
Epistolas Católicas (Madrid: 1965).

Spicq, Ceslas
Les Epîtres de Saint Pierre (Sources Bibliques; Paris: Librairie Lecoffre, 1966).

Barth, Gerhard
Commentario a primeira epistola de Pedro (São Leopoldo: Editora Sinodal, 1967).

Clark, Gordon Haddon
Peter Speaks Today: A Devotional Commentary on First Peter (Philadelphia: Presbyterian and Reformed, 1967).

Cramer, George H.
First and Second Peter (Everyman's Bible Commentary; Chicago: Moody, 1967).

Leaney, A. R. C.
The Letters of Peter and Jude (Cambridge Bible Commentary; Cambridge: University Press, 1967).

Kenyon, Don J.
He That Will Love Life (Harrisburg, Pa.: Christian Publications, 1968).

Reinhold, Robert William
Diumvuija dia mukanda wa kumudilu a Petelo (Luluabourg: Conseil des Oeuvres Litt. en Tshiluba, 1969).

Schwank, Benedikt, Alois Stöger, and Wilhelm Thusing
The Epistles of St. Peter, St. John and St. Jude (New Testament for Spiritual Reading 11; London: Sheed and Ward, 1969).

Beare, Francis Wright
The First Epistle of Peter: The Greek Text with Introduction and Notes (3d ed.; Oxford: Blackwell, 1970).

Heijkoop, H. L.
De eerste brief van Petrus (Winschoten: Uit het Woord der Waarheid, 1970).

Schelkle, Karl Hermann
Die Petrusbriefe, der Judasbrief (3d ed.; HThKNT; Freiburg: Herder, 1970).

Bauer, Johannes Baptist
Der erste Petrusbrief (Die Welt der Bibel. Kleinkommentare zur Heiligen Schrift; Düsseldorf: Patmos, 1971).

Best, Ernest
1 Peter (New Century Bible; London: Oliphants, 1971; reprinted Grand Rapids: Eerdmans, 1982).

MacDonald, William
I Peter: Faith Tested, Future Triumphant: A Commentary (Cornerstone Commentaries; Wheaton, Ill.: Shaw, 1972).

Schweizer, Eduard
Der Erste Petrusbrief (3d ed.; Zürcher Bibelkommentare; Zurich: Theologischer Verlag, 1972).

Schiwy, Günther
Die Katholischen Briefe (Der Christ in der Welt. Eine Enzyklopädie, series VI; Das Buch der Bücher 12; Stein am Rhein: Christiana, 1973).

Schrage, Wolfgang, and Horst Robert Balz
Die katholischen Briefe (NTD 10; Göttingen: Vandenhoeck & Ruprecht, 1973).

Thevissen, G.
De eerste brief van Petrus (Het Nieuwe Testament; Roermond: Romen, 1973).

Cothenet, Edouard
"La Première Epître de Pierre, L'Epître de Jacques," in J. Delorme, ed., *Le ministère et les ministères selon le Nouveau Testament* (Parole de Dieu; Paris: Seuil, 1974) 138–54.

Brown, John
Good News for Bad Times: A Study of 1 Peter (Input Books; Wheaton, Ill.: Victor, 1975).

Brownson, William
Tried by Fire: The Message of I Peter (Grand Rapids: Baker, 1975).

Blaiklock, E. M.
First Peter: A Translation and Devotional Commentary (Waco: Word, 1977).

Köder, Sieger
Ein Hirtenbrief der Hoffnung (2d ed.; Stuttgart: Katholisches Bibelwerk, 1977).

Barbieri, L. A.
First and Second Peter (2d ed.; Chicago: Moody, 1978).

Goppelt, Leonhard
Der Erste Petrusbrief (KEK 12/1; ed. F. Hahn; Göttingen: Vandenhoeck & Ruprecht, 1978); ET by John E. Alsup, *A Commentary on 1 Peter* (Grand Rapids: Eerdmans, 1993).

Holmer, Uwe, and Werner de Boor
Die Briefe des Petrus und der Brief des Judas (Wuppertal: Brockhaus, 1978).

Adams, Jay Edward
Trust and Obey: A Practical Commentary on First Peter

(Grand Rapids: Baker, 1979).

Brox, Norbert
   Der erste Petrusbrief (EKKNT; Zurich: Benziger, 1979).

Coffman, James Burton
   Commentary on James, 1 & 2 Peter, 1, 2, & 3 John (Abilene: ACU Press, 1979).

Elliott, John H.
   1 Peter, Estrangement and Community (Chicago: Franciscan Herald, 1979).

Arichea, Daniel C., and Eugene A. Nida
   A Translator's Handbook on the First Letter from Peter (Helps for Translators; New York: United Bible Societies, 1980).

Caffin, Benjamin Charles
   1 Peter (Pulpit Commentary 22; MacLean, Va.: MacDonald, 1980).

Danker, Frederick W.
   Epistles IV (Invitation to the New Testament; Garden City, N.Y.: Doubleday, 1980).

Fabris, Rinaldo
   Lettera di Giacomo e Prima lettera di Pietro (Collana Lettura pastorale della Bibbia; Bologna: Dehoniane, 1980).

Pesch, Rudolph
   Die Echtheit eures Glaubens: Biblische Orientierungen: 1. Petrusbrief (Freiburg: Herder, 1980).

Reicke, Bo
   The Epistles of James, Peter and Jude (Anchor Bible; Garden City, N.Y.: Doubleday, 1980).

Senior, Donald
   1 and 2 Peter (NT Message 20; Wilmington, Del.: Glazier, 1980).

Mounce, R. A.
   A Living Hope: A Commentary on 1 and 2 Peter (Grand Rapids: Eerdmans, 1982).

Olsson, Birger
   Första Petrusbrevet (Kommentar till Ny testamentet 17; Stockholm: EFS-forlaget, 1982).

Patterson, Paige
   A Pilgrim Priesthood: An Exposition of the Epistle of First Peter (Nashville: Nelson, 1982).

Stronstad, Roger
   Models for Christian Living: The First Epistle of Peter (Companion Bible Commentary; Vancouver: CLM Educational Society, 1983).

Benetreau, Samuel
   La première épître de Pierre (Commentaires évangé-liques de la Bible 1/1; Vaux-sur-Seine: EDIFAC, 1984).

Stockhardt, Georg
   Lectures on the First Epistle of St. Peter (trans. E. W. Koehlinger; Fort Wayne, Ind.: Concordia Theological Seminary Press, 1984).

Grunewald, W., with K. Januck, eds.
   Die Katholischen Briefe: Das Neue Testament auf Papyrus I (Arbeiten zur Neutestamentlichen Textforschung 6; Berlin: de Gruyter, 1986).

Clowney, Edmund P.
   The Message of 1 Peter: The Way of the Cross (Downers Grove, Ill.: InterVarsity, 1988).

Grudem, Wayne A.
   The First Epistle of Peter: An Introduction and Commentary (Tyndale New Testament Commentaries 17; Grand Rapids: Eerdmans, 1988).

Michaels, J. Ramsey
   1 Peter (Word Biblical Commentary 49; Waco: Word, 1988).

Bosio, Enrico
   Epistola agli Ebrei epistole cattoliche: Giacomo, Ia e IIa Pietro, Guida, Ia, IIa, IIIa Giovanni: Apocalisse (Turin: Claudiana, 1990).

Davids, Peter H.
   The First Epistle of Peter (New International Commentary on the New Testament; Grand Rapids: Eerdmans, 1990).

Houwelingen, Pieter Harry Robert
   1 Petrus: Rondzendbrief uit Babylon (Kampen: Kok, 1991).

Marshall, I. Howard
   1 Peter (IVP New Testament Commentary Series; Downers Grove, Ill.: InterVarsity, 1991).

Harrison, Paul V.
   James, 1, 2 Peter, and Jude (Randall House Bible Commentary; Nashville: Randall House, 1992).

Hiebert, D. Edmond
   1 Peter (Chicago: Moody, 1992).

Hillyer, Norman
   1 and 2 Peter, Jude (New International Biblical Commentary; Peabody, Mass.: Hendrickson, 1992).

Briscoe, D. Stuart
   1 Peter: Holy Living in a Hostile World (Understanding the Book; Wheaton, Ill.: Shaw, 1993).

Miller, Donald G.
   On This Rock: A Commentary on First Peter (PTMS 34; Allison Park, Pa.: Pickwick, 1993).

2. Books and Articles

Aalen, S.
   "Oversettelsen av ordet ἐπερώτημα i dåpstedet 1 Pet 3,31," *Tidsskrift for Teologi og Kirke* 43 (1972) 59–117.

Achtemeier, Paul J.
   "New-Born Babes and Living Stones: Literal and Figurative in 1 Peter," in M. P. Horgan and P. J. Kobelski, eds., *To Touch the Text: Biblical and Related Studies in Honor of Joseph H. Fitzmyer* (New York: Crossroad/Continuum, 1988) 207–36.

Idem
   "1 Peter," in James L. Mays, ed., *Harper's Bible Commentary* (San Francisco: Harper & Row, 1988) 1279–85.

Idem
   "Omne verbum sonat: The New Testament and the Oral Environment of Late Western Antiquity," *JBL* 109 (1990) 3–27.

Idem

"Suffering Servant and Suffering Christ in 1 Peter" in A. J. Malherbe and W. A. Meeks, eds., *The Future of Christology: Essays in Honor of Leander E. Keck* (Minneapolis: Fortress, 1993) 176–88.

Adinolfi, Marco

La prima lettera di Pietro nel mondo greco-romano (Bibliotheca Pontificii Athenaei Antoniani 26; Rome: 1988).

Idem

"Stato civile dei cristiani 'forestieri e pelligrini' (1 Pt 2, 11)," *Anton* 42 (1967) 420–34.

Adrianopoli, L.

Il mistero di Gesù nelle lettere di San Pietro (Turin: 1935).

Agnew, Francis H. C. M.

"1 Peter 1:2—An Alternative Translation," *CBQ* 45 (1983) 68–73.

Aland, Kurt, and Barbara Aland

The Text of the New Testament (2d ed.; trans. Erroll F. Rhodes; Grand Rapids: Eerdmans, 1989).

Ambroggi, P. de

"Il sacerdozio dei fedeli secondo la prima di Pietro," *Scuola Cattolica* 75 (1947) 52–57.

Andresen, Carl

"Zum Formular frühchristlicher Gemeindebriefe," *ZNW* 56 (1965) 233–59.

Antoniotti, L.-M.

"Structure littéraire et sens de la première Epître de Pierre," *RevThom* 85 (1985) 533–60.

Arichea, Daniel C., Jr.

"God or Christ? A Study of Implicit Information," *BT* 28 (1977) 412–18.

Arnold, W. T.

The Roman System of Provincial Administration to the Accession of Constantine the Great (3d ed.; rev. E. S. Bouchier; Chicago: Ares, 1974).

Arvedson, T.

"Syneidēseōs agathēs eperōtēma (1 Petr 3, 21)," *SEÅ* 15 (1950) 55–61.

Ashcraft, M.

"Theological Themes in 1 Peter," *Theological Educator* 13 (1982) 55–62.

Aune, David E.

The New Testament in Its Literary Environment (Library of Early Christianity 8; ed. W. A. Meeks; Philadelphia: Westminster, 1987).

Badian, E.

Foreign Clientelae (264–70 B.C.) (Oxford: Clarendon, 1958).

Bagshawe, William

The Riches of Grace Displayed in . . . 2 Ephes. 7th Verse: To Which Is Added the Privilege of Passive Obedience from I Peter 4, 14 . . . (London: Parkhurst, 1674).

Balch, David H.

"Early Christian Criticism of Patriarchal Authority: I Peter 2:11—3:12," *Union Seminary Quarterly Review* 39 (1984) 161–73.

Idem

"Hellenization/Acculturation in 1 Peter," in Talbert, ed., *Perspectives on 1 Peter*, 79–102.

Idem

"Household Codes," in D. E. Aune, ed., *Greco-Roman Literature and the New Testament: Selected Forms and Genres* (SBLSBS 21; Atlanta: Scholars Press, 1988) 25–50.

Idem

Let Wives Be Submissive: The Domestic Code in 1 Peter (SBLMS 26; Chico: Scholars Press, 1981).

Bammel, Ernst

"The Commands in I Peter II.17," *NTS* 11 (1964/65) 279–81.

Banks, William L.

"Who Are the Spirits in Prison?" *Eternity Magazine* 16 (1966) 23–26.

Barnard, L. W.

"The Testimonium Concerning the Stone in the NT and in the Epistle of Barnabas," *StEv* 3 (1964) 306–13.

Barnett, Albert E.

Paul Becomes a Literary Influence (Chicago: University of Chicago Press, 1941).

Barr, Allan

"Hope (ἔλπις, ἐλπίζω) in the New Testament," *SJT* 3 (1950) 68–77.

Idem

"Submission Ethic in the First Epistle of Peter," *Hartford Quarterly* 2 (1962) 27–33.

Barr, James

"בָּארַק ־ μόλις: Prov. xi. 31, I Pet. iv.18," *JSS* 20 (1975) 149–64.

Bartensweiler, H.

Die Ehe im Neuen Testament (AThANT 52; Zurich: 1967).

Barth, Gerhard

"1 Petrus 1, 3–9 Exegese, Meditation und Predigt," *EstTeol* 6 (1966) 148–60.

Bauckham, Richard

"James, 1 and 2 Peter, Jude," in D. A. Carson and H. G. M. Williamson, eds., *It Is Written: Scripture Citing Scripture: Essays in Honour of Barnabas Lindars, SSF* (Cambridge: Cambridge University Press, 1988) 303–17.

Bauer, J. B.

"Aut maleficus aut alieni speculator (1 Petr 4,15)," *BZ*, NF 22 (1978) 109–15.

Idem

"Der erste Petrusbrief und die Verfolgung unter Domitian," in R. Schnackenburg et al., eds., *Die Kirche des Anfangs: Für Heinz Schürmann* (Freiburg: Herder, 1978) 513–27.

Idem

"Könige und Priester, ein heiliges Volk (Ex 19,6)" *BZ*, NF 2 (1958) 283–86.

Beare, Francis Wright, "Some Remarks on the Text of I Peter in the Bodmer Papyrus (P[72])," *StEv* III, part II: The New Testament Message (TU 88; ed.

F. L. Cross; Berlin: Akademie-Verlag, 1964) 263–65.

Idem

"The Teaching of First Peter," *ATR* 27 (1945) 284–96.

Idem

"The Text of 1 Peter in Papyrus 72," *JBL* 80 (1961) 253–60.

Bennetch, John Henry

"Exegetical Studies in 1 Peter," *BSac* 101 (1944) 193–98.

Benoit, P.

"Schlatter, Adolph, Première Épître de S. Pierre" (review), *RB* 47 (1938) 624–25.

Berger, Klaus

"Apostelbrief und apostolische Rede: Zum Formular frühchristlicher Briefe," *ZNW* 65 (1974) 190–231.

Bergh, Hendrik

De drangredenen tot een levendig . . . eene leerrede, over I Petr. V. vs. 7 (Te Deventer: Gerrit Brower, 1784).

Best, Ernest

"I Peter II 4–10—A Reconsideration," *NovT* 11 (1969) 270–93.

Idem

"I Peter and the Gospel Tradition," *NTS* 16 (1970) 95–113.

Idem

"The Haustafel in Ephesians (Eph. 5:22–6:9)," *Irish Biblical Studies* 16 (1994) 146–60.

Idem

"Spiritual Sacrifice: General Priesthood in the New Testament," *Int* 14 (1960) 273–99.

Betz, Otto

"The Eschatological Interpretation of the Sinai-Tradition in Qumran and in the New Testament," *RevQ* 6/21 (1967) 89–107.

Bieder, Werner

"Bo Reicke, The Disobedient Spirits and Christian Baptism" (review), *ThZ* 2 (1946) 456–62.

Idem

Grund und Kraft der Mission nach dem 1. Petrusbrief (Theologische Studien 29; Zurich: Evangelischer Verlag, 1950).

Idem

Die Vorstellung von der Höllenfahrt Jesu Christi: Beitrag zur Entstehungsgeschichte der Vorstellung vom sog. Descensus ad inferos (AThANT 19; Zurich: Zwingli, 1949).

Bischoff, A.

"Ἀλλοτρι(ο)επίκοπος," *ZNW* 7 (1906) 271–74.

Bishop, Eric F. F.

"*Oligoi* in 1 Pet. 3:20," *CBQ* 13 (1951) 44–45.

Idem

"The Word of a Living and Unchanging God: I Peter 1,23," *Muslim World* 43 (1953) 15–17.

Blanchetière, François

"Juifs et non Juifs: Essai sur la Diaspora en Asie Mineure," *RHPhR* 54 (1974) 367–82.

Blass, F., and A. Debrunner

A Greek Grammar of the New Testament and Other Early Christian Literature (trans. and rev. R. W. Funk; Chicago: University of Chicago Press, 1961).

Blazen, Ivan T.

"Suffering and Cessation from Sin according to 1 Peter 4:1," *Andrews University Seminary Studies* 21 (1983) 27–50.

Blendinger, Christian

"Kirche als Fremdlingschaft (1 Petrus 1,22–25)," *Communio Viatorum* 10 (1967) 123–34.

Blevins, J. L.

"Introduction to 1 Peter," *RevExp* 79 (1982) 401–13.

Blinzler, Josef

"IEPATEYMA: Zur Exegesis von 1 Petr 2,5 u. 9," in *Episcopus: Studien über das Bischofsamt: Festschrift Kardinal Michael von Faulhaber* (Regensburg: Gregorius, 1949) 49–65.

Boismard, Marie-Emile

"Une liturgie baptismale dans la *Prima Petri*," *RB* 63 (1956) 182–208.

Idem

"Une liturgie baptismale dans la *Prima Petri*," *RB* 64 (1957) 161–83.

Idem

"Pierre (Première épître de)," *DB Supplement* 7 (1966) 1415–55.

Idem

Quatre Hymnes baptismales dans la Première Épître de Pierre (Paris: Cerf, 1961).

Idem

"La typologie baptismale dans la première épître de Saint Pierre," *VSpir* 94 (1956) 339–52.

Bolkestein, Marinus Hendrik

"De kerk in haar vreemdelingschap volgens de eerste brief van Petrus," *Nieuwe Theologische Studiën* 25 (1942) 181–94.

Boobyer, G. H.

"The Indebtedness of 2 Peter to 1 Peter," In A. J. B. Higgins, ed., *New Testament Essays: Studies in Memory of Thomas Walter Manson* (Manchester: Manchester University Press, 1959) 34–53.

Borchert, Gerald L.

"The Conduct of Christians in the Face of the 'Fiery Ordeal,'" *RevExp* 74 (1982) 451–62.

Boring, M. Eugene

"Interpreting 1 Peter as a Letter (Not) Written to Us," *Quarterly Review* 13 (1993) 89–111.

Bornemann, W.

"Der erste Petrusbrief—eine Taufrede des Silvanus," *ZNW* 19 (1919/20) 143–65.

Bosetti, Elena

Il pastore: Christo e la chiesa nella prima lettera di Pietro (Bologna: Dehoniane Bologna, 1990).

Bousset, W.

"Zur Hadesfahrt Christi," *ZNW* 19 (1919/20) 50–66.

Bovon, François
"Foi chrétienne et religion populaire dans la première Epître de Pierre," *EThR* 53 (1978) 25–41.

Brandt, Wilhelm
"Wandel als Zeugnis nach dem 1. Petrusbrief," in W. Foerster, ed., *Verbum Dei manet in aeternum: Festschrift O. Schmitz* (Witten: Luther-Verlag, 1953) 10–25.

Brockington, L. H.
"The Presence of God (A Study in the Use of the Term 'Glory of Yahweh')," *ExpT* 57 (1945) 21–25.

Idem
"The Septuagintal Background to the New Testament Use of δόξα," in D. E. Nineham, ed., *Studies in the Gospels: Essays in Memory of R. H. Lightfoot* (Oxford: Blackwell, 1957) 1–8.

Brooks, O. S.
"1 Peter 3:21—The Clue to the Literary Structure of the Epistle," *NovT* 16 (1974) 290–305.

Brown, Raymond E., and John P. Meier
Antioch and Rome (New York: Paulist, 1983).

Brown, Raymond E., Karl P. Donfried, and John Reumann, eds.
Peter in the New Testament (Minneapolis: Augsburg, 1973).

Brox, Norbert
"Der erste Petrusbrief in der literarischen Tradition des Urchristentums," *Kairos*, NF 20 (1978) 182–92.

Idem
Falsche Verfasserangaben: Zur Erklärung der frühchristlichen Pseudepigraphia (SBS 79; Stuttgart: Katholisches Bibelwerk, 1975).

Idem
"'Sara zum Beispiel . . . ' Israel im 1. Petrusbrief," in R.-G. Müller and W. Stegner, eds., *Kontinuität und Einheit: Für Franz Mussner* (Freiburg: Herder, 1981) 484–93.

Idem
"Situation und Sprache der Minderheit im ersten Petrusbrief," *Kairos*, NF 19 (1977) 1–13.

Idem
"Tendenz und Pseudepigraphie im ersten Petrusbrief," *Kairos*, NF 20 (1978) 110–20.

Idem
"Zur pseudepigraphischen Rahmung des ersten Petrusbriefes," *BZ*, NF 19 (1975) 78–96.

Bullinger, Ethelbert William
"The Spirits in Prison": An Exposition of 1 Pet iii 17—iv 6 (London: Eyre & Spottiswoode, 1895).

Bultmann, Rudolph
"Bekenntnis- und Liedfragmente im ersten Petrusbrief," *ConNT* 11 (1947) 1–14. *Conjectanea Neotestamentica 11 in Honorem Antonii Fridrichsen* (Lund: C. W. K. Gleerup, 1947).

Burtness, James H.
"Sharing the Suffering of God in the Life of the World: From Text to Sermon in I Peter 2:21," *Int* 23 (1969) 277–88.

Calloud, Jean
"Ce que parler veut dire (1 P 1,10–12)," in Perrot, ed., *Etudes sur la Première Lettre de Pierre*, 175–206.

Calloud, J., and F. Genuyt
La première épître de Pierre: Analyse sémiotique (LD 109; Paris: Cerf, 1982).

Carmignac, Jean
"La théologie de la souffrance dans les Hymnes de Qumrân," *RevQ* 3/11 (1961) 365–86.

Carrez, Maurice
"L'esclavage dans la première épître de Pierre," in Perrot, ed., *Etudes sur la Première Lettre de Pierre*, 207–17.

Carrington, Philip
"Saint Peter's Epistle," in S. E. Johnson, ed., *The Joy of Study: Papers on New Testament and Related Subjects Presented to Honor Frederick Clifton Grant* (New York: Macmillan, 1951) 57–63.

Cerfaux, Lucien
"Regale Sacerdotium," in *Recueil Lucien Cerfaux* (BEThL 7; Gembloux: Duculot, 1954) 2.283–315.

Charles, R. H.
Appendix C, "The Gizeh Greek Fragment of Enoch," in *The Book of Enoch* (Oxford: Clarendon, 1893).

Charlesworth, James H., ed.
The Old Testament Pseudepigrapha (2 vols.; Garden City, N.Y.: Doubleday, 1985).

Chase, F. H.
"Peter, First Epistle", *Dictionary of the Bible* (ed. J. Hastings; Edinburgh: Clark, 1900) 3.779–96.

Chevallier, Max-Alain
"Comment lire aujourd'hui la première épître de Pierre," in Perrot, ed., *Etudes sur la Première Lettre de Pierre*, 129–52.

Idem
"Condition et vocation des Chrétiens en diaspora: Remarques exégétiques sur la 1ʳᵉ Epître de Pierre," *RevScRel* 48 (1974) 387–400.

Idem
"1 Pierre 1/1 à 2/10: Structure littéraire et conséquences exégétiques," *RHPhR* 51 (1972) 129–42.

Chin, Moses
"A Heavenly Home for the Homeless: Aliens and Strangers in 1 Peter," *TynBul* 42 (1991) 94–112.

Clemen, C.
"Die Einheitlichkeit des 1. Petrusbriefes," *ThStK* 78 (1905) 619–28.

Combrini, H. J. B.
"The Structure of I Peter," *Neot* 9 (1980) 34–63.

Cook, David
"I Peter iii.20: An Unnecessary Problem," *JTS*, n.s. 31 (1980) 72–78.

Coppens, Joseph
"Le sacerdoce royal des fidèles: un commentaire de I Petr. II, 4–10," in *Au Service de la Parole de Dieu: Melanges . . . à . . . André-Marie Charue* (Gembloux: Duculot, 1969) 61–75.

Cothenet, Edouard
"Les orientations actuelles de l'exégèse de la première lettre de Pierre," in Perrot, ed., *Etudes sur la Première Lettre de Pierre*, 13–42.

Idem
"Le réalisme de l'espérance chrétienne selon I Pierre," *NTS* 27 (1981) 564–72.

Idem
"Le sacerdoce des fidèles d'après la 1. Petri," *Esprit et Vie* 11 (1968) 169–73.

Coutts, J.
"Ephesians I.3–14 and I Peter I.3–13," *NTS* 3 (1956/57) 115–27.

Cranfield, C. E. B.
"The Interpretation of I Peter iii.19 and iv.6," *ExpT* 69 (1958) 369–72.

Cross, Frank L.
1 Peter: A Paschal Liturgy (London: Mowbray, 1954).

Cullmann, Oscar
The Christology of the New Testament (trans. S. C. Guthrie and C. A. M. Hall; rev. ed.; Philadelphia: Westminster, 1963).

Idem
The Earliest Christian Confessions (trans. J. K. S. Reid; London: Lutterworth, 1949).

Idem
Peter, Disciple, Apostle, Martyr (trans. F. V. Filson; 2d ed.; Philadelphia: Westminster, 1962).

Dalmer, Johannes
"Zu 1. Petri 1,18.19," BFCTh 2/6 (1898/99) 75–87.

Dalton, William Joseph
Christ's Proclamation to the Spirits: A Study of 1 Peter 3:18—4:6 (AnBib 23; Rome: Pontifical Biblical Institute, 1965).

Idem
Christ's Proclamation to the Spirits; A Study of 1 Peter 3:18—4:6 (2d ed.; AnBib 23; Rome: Pontifical Biblical Institute, 1989).

Idem
"The Church in 1 Peter," *Tantur Yearbook* (1981/82) 79–91.

Idem
"Interpretation and Tradition: An Example from 1 Peter," *Greg* 49 (1968) 11–37.

Idem
"The Interpretation of 1 Peter 3,19 and 4,6: Light from 2 Peter," *Bib* 60 (1979) 547–55.

Idem
"'So That Your Faith May Also Be Your Hope in God' (I Peter 1:21)," in R. Banks, ed., *Reconciliation and Hope: New Testament Essays on Atonement and Eschatology Presented to L. L. Morris on His 60th Birthday* (Exeter: Paternoster; Grand Rapids: Eerdmans, 1974) 262–74.

Daniel, Jerry L.
"Anti-Semitism in the Hellenistic-Roman Period," *JBL* 98 (1979) 45–65.

Danker, F. W.
"I Peter 1:23—2:17—A Consolatory Pericope," *ZNW* 58 (1967) 93–102.

Daube, David
"κερδαίνω as a Missionary Term," *HTR* 40 (1947) 109–20.

Dautzenberg, P. Gerhard
"σωτηρία ψυχῶν (1 Pt. 1:9)," *BZ* 8 (1964) 262–76.

Davies, Paul E.
"Primitive Christology in I Peter," in E. H. Barth and R. E. Cocroft, eds., *Festschrift to Honor F. Wilbur Gingrich* (Leiden: Brill, 1972) 115–22.

Déaut, Robert le
"Le Targum de Gen. 22,8 et 1 Pt. 1, 20," *RechSR* 49 (1961) 103–6.

Delling, Gerhard
"Der Bezug der christlichen Existenz auf das Heilshandeln Gottes nach dem ersten Petrusbrief," in H. D. Betz and L. Schottroff, eds., *Neues Testament und christliche Existenz: Festschrift für Herbert Braun zum 70. Geburtstag* (Tübingen: Mohr [Siebeck], 1973) 95–113.

Deterding, Paul E.
"Exodus Motifs in First Peter," *Concordia Journal* 7 (1981) 58–65.

Dickey, S.
"Some Economic and Social Conditions of Asia Minor Affecting the Expansion of Christianity," in S. J. Case, ed., *Studies in Early Christianity* (New York: Century, 1928) 393–416.

Dinkler, Erich
"Die Petrus-Rom-Frage: Ein Forschungsbericht," *ThR*, NF a) 25, b) 27 a) (1959); b) (1961) a) 189–230, 289–335; b) 33–64.

Doty, William G.
Letters in Primitive Christianity (Guides to Biblical Scholarship; Philadelphia: Fortress, 1979).

Duplacy, Jean, and Christian-Bernard Amphoux
"A propos de l'histoire du texte de la première épître de Pierre," in Perrot, ed., *Etudes sur la Première Lettre de Pierre*, 155–73.

Edelkoort, Albertus Hendrik
De rijkdom in Christus: bijbellezingen over 1 Petrus I (Rotterdam: Drukkerij Dorteweg, 1934).

Ehrman, Bart D.
"Cephas and Peter," *JBL* 109 (1990) 463–74.

Elliott, John Hall
The Elect and the Holy: An Exegetical Examination of 1 Peter 2:4–10 and the Phrase Βασίλειον ἱεράτευμα (NovTSup 12; Leiden: Brill, 1966).

Idem
"1 Peter, Its Situation and Strategy: A Discussion with David Balch," in Talbert, ed., *Perspectives on 1 Peter*, 61–78.

Idem
A Home for the Homeless: A Sociological Exegesis of I Peter, Its Situation and Strategy (Philadelphia: Fortress, 1981).

Idem

"Ministry and Church Order in the NT: A Tradition-Historical Analysis (1 Pt 5, 1–5 & plls.)," *CBQ* 32 (1970) 367–91.

Idem

"Patronage and Clientism in Early Christian Society," *Forum* 3 (1987) 39–48.

Idem

"Peter, Silvanus and Mark in 1 Peter and Acts," in W. Haubeck and M. Bachmann, eds., *Wort in der Zeit: Neutestamentlichen Studien: Festgabe für Karl Heinrich Rengstorf zum 75. Geburtstag* (Leiden: Brill, 1980) 250–67.

Idem

"The Rehabilitation of an Exegetical Step-Child: 1 Peter in Recent Research," in Talbert, ed., *Perspectives on First Peter*, 3–16. Reprinted from *JBL* 95 (1976) 243–54.

Idem

"Salutation and Exhortation to Christian Behavior on the Basis of God's Blessings (1:2—2:10)," *RevExp* 79/3 (1982) 415–25.

Epp, Eldon Jay

"New Testament Papyrus Manuscripts and Letter Carrying in Greco-Roman Times," *The Future of Early Christianity; Essays in Honor of Helmut Koester* (ed. B. A. Pearson; Minneapolis: Fortress Press, 1991) 35–56.

Erbes, K.

"Noch etwas zum ἀλλοτριοεπίσκοπος 1Petr 4,15," *ZNW* 20 (1921) 249.

Idem

"Was bedeutet ἀλλοτριοεπίσκοπος 1 Pt 4,15?" *ZNW* 19 (1919/20) 39–44.

Evang, Martin

"ἐκ καρδίας ἀλλήλους ἀγαπήσατε ἐκτενῶς: Zum Verständnis der Aufforderung und ihrer Begründungen in 1 Petr 1,22f.," *ZNW* 80 (1989) 111–23.

Fassett, Oel Ray

The Spirits in Prison (Boston: Advent Christian Publication Society, 1850).

Feinberg, John S.

"1 Peter 3:18–20, Ancient Mythology, and the Intermediate State," *WTJ* 48 (1986) 303–36.

Feldmeier, Reinhard

Die Christen als Fremde: die Metapher der Fremde in der antiken Welt, im Urchristentum und im 1. Petrusbrief (WUNT 3/2; Tübingen: Mohr [Siebeck], 1992).

Ferris, T. E. S.

"A Comparison of I. Peter and Hebrews," *CQR* 111 (1930) 123–27.

Idem

"The Epistle of James in Relation to 1 Peter," *CQR* 128 (1939) 303–8.

Feuillet, A.

"Les 'sacrifices spirituels' du sacerdoce royal des baptisés (I P 2,5) et leur préparation dans l'Ancien Testament," *NRTh* 94 (1974) 704–28.

Filson, Floyd V.

"Partakers with Christ: Suffering in First Peter," *Int* 9 (1955) 400–412.

Fink, Paul R.

"The Use and Significance of *en hōi* in I Peter," *Grace Journal* 8/2 (1967) 33–39.

Fitzmyer, Joseph A., S.J.

"The First Epistle of Peter," in R. E. Brown, J. A. Fitzmyer, and R. E. Murphy, eds., *The Jerome Biblical Commentary* (Englewood Cliffs, N.J.: Prentice-Hall, 1968) 362–68.

Idem

"Implications of the New Enoch Literature from Qumran," *TS* 38 (1977) 332–45.

Flack, Elmer E.

"The Concept of Grace in Biblical Thought," in J. M. Myers, O. Reimherr, and H. N. Bream, eds., *Biblical Studies in Memory of H. C. Allemann* (Locust Valley, N.Y.: J. J. Augustin, 1960) 137–54.

Flusser, David

"The Dead Sea Sect and Pre-Pauline Christianity," in C. Rabin and Y. Yadin, eds., *Aspects of the Dead Sea Scrolls* (Scripta Hierosolymitana 4; Jerusalem: Magnes, 1958) 215–66.

Forster, A. Haire

"The Meaning of δόξα in the Greek Bible," *ATR* 12 (1929/30) 311–16.

Foster, Ora Delmar

The Literary Relations of the "First Epistle of Peter" (Transactions of the Connecticut Academy of Arts and Sciences 17; New Haven: Yale University Press, 1913) 363–538.

France, R. T.

"Exegesis in Practice: Two Samples," in I. H. Marshall, ed., *New Testament Interpretation: Essays on Principles and Methods* (Grand Rapids: Eerdmans, 1977) 252–81.

Francis J.

"'Like Newborn Babes'—The Image of the Child in 1 Peter 2:2–3," in E. A. Livingstone, ed., *Studia Biblica 1978* (JSNTSup 3; Sheffield: JSOT Press, 1980) 3.111–17.

Fransen, Irénée

"Une homélie chrétienne: La première Epître de Pierre," *BVC* 31 (1960) 28–38.

Frederick, Stephen Carter

The Theme of Obedience in the First Epistle of Peter (Ann Arbor, Mich.: Xerox University Microfilms, 1974).

Fridrichsen, A. I.

"Till 1 Petr 3,7," *SEÅ* 12 (1947) 143–47.

Frings, Jos.

"Zu I Petr 3,19 und 4,6," *BZ* 17 (1926) 75–88.

Fritsch, C. T.

"TO ANTITYΠON," in *Studia Biblica et Semitica. Theodoro Christiano Vriezen . . . dedicata* (Wageningen: Veenman, 1966) 100–107.

Fuller, Reginald H.

"Classics and the Gospels: The Seminar," in Wm.

O. Walker, ed., *The Relationships among the Gospels: An Interdisciplinary Dialogue* (San Antonio: Trinity University Press, 1978).

Furnish, V. P.
"Elect Sojourners in Christ: An Approach to the Theology of I Peter," 28 *PSTJ* (1975) 1–11.

Gagé, Jean
Les Classes Sociales dans l'Empire Romain (Paris: Payot, 1964).

Galot, Jean
"La descente du Christ aux enfers," *NRTh* 83 (1961) 471–91.

Gamba, G. G.
"L'Evangelista Marco Segretario—'Interprete' della prima lettera di Pietro?" *Salesianum* 44 (1982) 61–70.

Gangel, Kenneth O.
"Pictures of the Church in I Peter," *Grace Journal* 10 (1969) 29–35.

Gärtner, Bertil
"The Habakkuk Commentary (DSH) and the Gospel of Matthew," *StTh* 8 (1954) 1–24.

Glaze, R. E.
"Introduction to 1 Peter," *Theological Educator* 13 (1982) 23–34.

Goldstein, Horst
"Die Kirche als Schar derer, die ihrem leidenden Herrn mit dem Ziel der Gottesgemeinschaft nachfolgen: Zum Gemeinverständnis von 1 Petr 2,21–25 und 3,18–22," *BibLeb* 15 (1974) 38–54.

Idem
Paulinische Gemeinde im Ersten Petrusbrief (SBS 80; Stuttgart: Katholisches Bibelwerk, 1975).

Idem
"Die politischen Paränese in 1 Petr und Röm 13," *BibLeb* 14 (1973) 88–104.

Golebiewski, R. P. E.
"L'Epître (1 P 5,6–11): Dieu nous console dans l'épreuve," *AsSeign* 57 (1965) 17–23.

Goodspeed, Edgar J.
"Some Greek Notes: IV: Enoch in I Peter 3:19," *JBL* 73 (1954) 91–92.

Goppelt, Leonhard
Christentum und Judentum im ersten und zweiten Jahrhundert (BFCTh 2/55; Gütersloh: Bertelsmann, 1954).

Idem
"Jesus und die 'Haustafel'-Tradition," in P. Hoffmann, ed., *Orientierung an Jesus: Zur Theologie der Synoptiker: Für Joseph Schmid* (Freiburg: Herder, 1973) 93–106.

Idem
"Mission ou Révolution? La responsabilité du chrétien dans la société d'après la Première Epître de Pierre" (trans. A. Greiner), *Positions lutheriennes* 194 (1969) 202–16.

Idem
"Prinzipien neutestamentlicher Sozialethik nach dem I Petrusbrief," in H. Baltensweiler and B.

Reicke, eds., *Neues Testament und Geschichte: Historisches Geschehen und Deutung im Neuen Testament: Oscar Cullmann zum 70. Geburtstag* (Tübingen: Mohr [Siebeck], 1972) 285–96.

Idem
"Der Staat in der Sicht des Neuen Testaments," in H. Dambois and E. Wilkens, eds., *Macht und Recht: Beiträge zur lutherischen Staatslehre der Gegenwart* (Berlin: Lutherisches Verlagshaus, 1956) 9–21.

Gourbillon, J. G.
"La Première Epître de Pierre," *Evangile* 50 (1963) 5–91.

Gourgues, Michel, O.P.
"La foi chrétienne primitive face à la croix: Le témoignage des formulaires pré-pauliniens," *Science et esprit* 2/18 (1989) 49–69.

Greeven, Heinrich
"Propheten, Lehrer, Vorsteher bei Paulus," *ZNW* 44 (1952/53) 1–43.

Grielen, Marlis
Tradition und Theologie neutestamentlicher Haustafelethik (1 Peter 2:11—3:7) (BBB 75; Frankfurt am Main: Hain, 1990).

Grillmeier, A.
"Der Gottessohn im Totenreich," in A. Grillmeier, *Mit ihm und in ihm* (Christologische Forschungen und Perspektiven; Freiburg im Breisgau: 1975) 76–174.

Grosheide, F. W.
"Kol. 3:1–4; 1 Petr. 1:3–5; 1 Joh. 3:1–2," *Gereformeerd Theologisch Tijdschrift* 54 (1954) 139–47.

Gross, Carl D.
"Are the Wives of 1 Peter 3.7 Christians?" *JSNT* 35 (1989) 89–96.

Grossouw, W.
"L'espérance dans le Nouveau Testament," *RevBib* 61 (1954) 508–32.

Groupe Orsay
"Une lecture féministe des 'codes domestiques,'" *Foi et Vie* 88 (1989) 59–67.

Grundmann, Walter
"Die ΝΗΠΙΟΙ in der urchristlichen Paränese," *NTS* 5 (1959) 188–205.

Gschwind, Karl
Die Niederfahrt Christi in die Unterwelt (NTAbh 2.3–5; Münster: Aschendorff, 1911).

Gundry, Robert H.
"Further *Verba* on *Verba Christi* in First Peter," *Bib* 55 (1974) 211–32.

Idem
"*Verba Christi* in I Peter: Their Implications Concerning the Authorship of I Peter and the Authenticity of the Gospel Tradition," *NTS* 13 (1967) 336–50.

Haenchen, Ernst
"Petrus-Probleme," *NTS* 7 (1961) 187–97.

Halas, Stanislas, SCJ
"Sens dynamique de l'expression λαὸς εἰς

περιποίησιν en 1 P 2,9," *Bib* 65 (1984) 254–58.

Hall, Randy
"For to This You Have Been Called: The Cross and Suffering in 1 Peter," *ResQ* 19 (1976) 137–47.

Hall, S. G.
"Paschal Baptism," *StEv* 6 (TU 112; ed. E. A. Livingstone; Berlin: Akademie-Verlag, 1973) 239–51.

Hanson, Anthony
"Salvation Proclaimed: I: 1 Peter 3:18–22," *ExpT* 93 (1981/82) 100–112.

Harrington, D. J.
"The Church as Minority Group," in *God's New People in Christ* (Philadelphia: Fortress, 1980) 81–94.

Harris, J. Rendel
"An Emendation to 1 Peter 1.13," *ExpT* 41 (1929/30) 43.

Idem
"A Further Note on the Use of Enoch in 1 Peter," *Expositor*, series 6, 4 (1901) 346–49.

Idem
"The History of a Conjectural Emendation," *Expositor*, series 6, 6 (1902) 378–90.

Idem
"On a Recent Emendation of the Text of St. Peter," *Expositor*, series 6, 5 (1902) 317–20.

Idem
"The Religious Meaning of 1 Peter V.5.," *Expositor*, series 8, 18 (1919) 131–39.

Harrison, Everett Falconer
"Exegetical Studies in 1 Peter," *BSac* 97 (1940) 200–209, 325–34, 448–55.

Idem
"Exegetical Studies in 1 Peter," *BSac* 98 (1941) 459–68.

Hart, J. H. A.
The First Epistle General of Peter (Expositor's Greek Testament, 5 vols.; ed. W. R. Nicoll; reprinted Grand Rapids: Eerdmans, 1974) 5.3–80.

Haselhurst, R. S. T.
"'Mark, My Son,'" *Theology* 13 (1926) 34–36.

Hemer, C. J.
"The Address of 1 Peter," *ExpT* 89 (1977/78) 239–43.

Hengel, Martin
Judentum und Hellenismus (WUNT 10; Tübingen: Mohr [Siebeck], 1969).

Herrmann, P. (84–99), J. H. Waszink (99–117), and K. Colpe (117–42)
"Genossenschaft," *RAC* 10 (1978) 83–155.

Hiebert, D. Edmond
"Designation of the Readers in 1 Peter 1:1–2," *BSac* 137 (1980) 64–75.

Idem
"Following Christ's Example: An Exposition of 1 Peter 2:21–25," *BSac* 139 (1982) 32–45.

Idem
"Living in the Light of Christ's Return: An Expo-

sition of 1 Peter 4:7–11," *BSac* 139 (1982) 243–54.

Idem
"Peter's Thanksgiving for our Salvation," *Studia Missionalia* 29 (1980) 85–103.

Hill, D.
"On Suffering and Baptism in 1 Peter," *NovT* 18 (1976) 181–89.

Idem
"'To Offer Spiritual Sacrifices . . . ' (1 Peter 2:5): Liturgical Formulations and Christian Paraenesis in 1 Peter," *JSNT* 16 (1982) 45–63.

Hillyer, Norman
"First Peter and the Feast of Tabernacles," *TynBul* 21 (1970) 39–70.

Idem
"'Rock-Stone' Imagery in I Peter," *TynBul* 22 (1971) 58–81.

Idem
"The Servant of God," *EvQ* 41 (1969) 143–60.

Idem
"Spiritual Milk . . . Spiritual House," *TynBul* 20 (1969) 126.

Holdsworth, J.
"The Sufferings in 1 Peter and 'Missionary Apocalyptic,'" in E. A. Livingstone, ed., *Studia Biblica 1978*, JSNTSup 3; Sheffield: JSOT Press, (1980) 3.225–32.

Holmer, Uwe, and Werner de Boor
Die Briefe des Petrus und der Brief des Judas (Wuppertal: Brockhaus, 1978).

Holtz, Traugott
"Dalton, William Joseph, S.J., Prof.: Christ's Proclamation to the Spirits. A Study of 1 Peter 3:18—4:6" (review), *ThLZ* 92 (1967) 359–60.

Holzmeister, Urban
"Dei . . . Spiritus super vos requiescit," *VD* 9 (1929) 129–31.

Idem
"Exordium prioris epistulae S. Petri (1 Petr. 1,1–2)," *VD* 2 (1922) 209–12.

Hunzinger, Claus-Hunno
"Babylon als Deckname für Rom und die Datierung des 1. Petrusbriefes," in H. Graf Reventlow, ed., *Gottes Wort und Gottes Land: Hans-Wilhelm Hertzberg zum 70. Geburtstag* (Göttingen: Vandenhoeck & Ruprecht, 1965) 67–77.

Idem
"Zur Struktur der Christus-Hymnen in Phil 2 und 1.Petr 3," in E. Lohse, with C. Burchard and B. Schaller, eds., *Der Ruf Jesu und die Antwort der Gemeinde Exegetische Untersuchungen: Joachim Jeremias zum 70. Geburtstag* (Göttingen: Vandenhoeck & Ruprecht, 1970) 142–56.

Hutton, John A.
"A Ruling from 'First Peter,'" *Expositor*, series 8, 23 (1922) 420–27.

Ittig, Thomas
Ob denen Todten das Evangelium soll verkundiget werden (Jena: Jo. Fridericum Ritterum, 1730).

Jeremias, Joachim
"Zwischen Karfreitag und Ostern: Descensus und Ascensus in der Karfreitagstheologie des Neuen Testamentes," *ZNW* 42 (1949) 194–201.

Johnson, Dennis E.
"Fire in God's House: Imagery from Malachi 3 in Peter's Theology of Suffering (1 Pet 4.12–19)," *JETS* 29 (1986) 285–94.

Johnson, George
"The Will of God: V: In I Peter and I John," *ExpT* 72 (1960/61) 237–40.

Johnson, Sherman E.
"Asia Minor and Early Christianity," in J. Neusner, ed., *Christianity, Judaism, and Other Greco-Roman Cults: Studies for Morton Smith at Sixty, Part Two: Early Christianity* (4 vols.; Leiden: Brill, 1975) 2.77–145.

Idem
"Early Christianity in Asia Minor," *JBL* 77 (1958) 1–17.

Idem
"The Preaching to the Dead," *JBL* 79 (1960) 48–51.

Idem
"Unresolved Questions about Early Christianity in Asia Minor," in D. E. Aune, ed., *Studies in New Testament and Early Christian Literature: Essays in Honor of Alka P. Wikgren* (NovTSup 33; Leiden: Brill, 1972) 181–93.

Johnston, G.
"The Will of God in 1 Peter and 1 John," *ExpT* 72 (1960/61) 237–40.

Jones, P. R.
"Teaching First Peter," *RevExp* 79 (1982) 463–72.

Jones, Russell Bradley
"Christian Behavior under Fire (First Epistle of Peter)," *RevExp* 46 (1949) 56–66.

Jonge, M. de
"Vreemdelingen en bijwoners: Enige opmerkingen naar aanleiding van 1 Pe 2, 11 en verwante teksten," *NedThT* 11 (1956/57) 18–36.

Jonsen, A. R.
"The Moral Theology of the First Epistle of St. Peter," *Sciences ecclésiastiques* 16 (1964) 93–105.

Judge, E. A.
The Social Pattern of the Christian Groups in the First Century (London: Tyndale, 1960).

Kamlah, Ehrhard
"ὑποτάσσεσθαι in den neutestamentlichen 'Haustafeln,'" in O. Böcher and K. Haacker, eds., *Verborum Veritas: Festschrift für Gustar Stählin zum 70. Geburtstag* (Wuppertal: Brockhaus, 1970) 237–43.

Kelly, J. N. D.
A Commentary on the Epistles of Peter and of Jude (BNTC; London: Black; HNTC; New York: Harper & Row, 1969).

Kelly, William
The Preaching to the Spirits in Prison: 1 Peter III, 18–20 (London: F. E. Race, 1903).

Kendall, David W.
"The Introductory Character of 1 Peter 1:3–12" (Ph.D. diss., Union Theological Seminary in Virginia, 1984).

Idem
"The Literary and Theological Function of 1 Peter 1:3–12," in Talbert, ed., *Perspectives on 1 Peter*, 103–20.

Kennedy, George A.
Classical Rhetoric and Its Christian and Secular Tradition from Ancient to Modern Times (Chapel Hill: University of North Carolina Press, 1980).

Idem
New Testament Interpretation through Rhetorical Criticism (Chapel Hill: University of North Carolina Press, 1984).

Ketter, Peter
"Das allgemeine Priestertum: II. Das allgemeine Priestertum der Gläubigen nach dem ersten Petrusbrief," *TThZ* 56 (1947) 43–51.

Kiley, Mark
"Like Sara: The Tale of Terror Behind 1 Peter 3:6," *JBL* 106 (1987) 689–92.

Kilgallen, John J.
"Reflections on Charisma(ta) in the New Testament," *Studia Missionalia* 41 (1992) 289–323.

Kilpatrick, G. D.
"1 Peter 1:11 τίνα ἢ ποῖον καιρόν," *NovT* 28 (1986) 91–92.

Kirk, Gorden E.
"Endurance in Suffering in I Peter," *BSac* 138 (1981) 46–56.

Kline, Leslie
"Ethics for the End Time: An Exegesis of I Peter 4:7—11," *ResQ* 7 (1963) 113–23.

Knibb, Michael A.
The Qumran Community (Cambridge Commentaries on Writings of the Jewish and Christian World, 200 BC to AD 200; Cambridge: Cambridge University Press, 1987).

Knox, John
"Pliny and I Peter: A Note on I Peter 4:14–16 and 3:15," *JBL* 72 (1953) 187–89.

Krafft, Eva
"Christologie und Anthropologie im 1. Petrusbrief," *EvTh* 10 (1950/51) 120–26.

Krodel, Gerhard
The First Letter of Peter (Proclamation Commentaries: The New Testament Witness for Preaching; Philadelphia: Fortress, 1977).

Kügler, U.-R.
"Die Paränese an die Sklaven als Modell urchristlicher Sozialethik" (Th.D. diss., Erlangen, 1976).

Kuhn, Karl Georg
"New Light on Temptation, Sin, and Flesh in the New Testament," in K. Stendahl, ed., *The Scrolls and the New Testament* (New York: Harper and Brothers, 1957) 94–113.

Idem

"προσήλυτος," *TWNT*, 6 (1959) 727–45.

Kühschelm, Roman

"'Lebendige Hoffnung' (1 Petr 1,3–12)," *BLit* 56 (1983) 202–6.

Kümmel, Werner Georg

Introduction to the New Testament (trans. H. C. Kee; Nashville: Abingdon, 1975).

Lamparter, Helmut

Lebensbewältigung oder Wiedergeburt: Eine biblische Besinnung über 1 Petrus 1, 3–9 (Metzingen: Brunnquell-Verlag, 1960).

Lampe, Peter

"Das Spiel mit dem Petrusnamen—Matt. xvi.18," *NTS* 25 (1978/79) 227–45.

Lampe, Peter, and Ulrich Luz

"Nachpaulinisches Christentum und pagane Gesellschaft," in J. Becker, ed., *Die Anfänge des Christentums* (Stuttgart: Kohlhammer, 1987) 185–216.

LaVerdiere, Eugene A.

"Covenant Theology in 1 Peter 1:1—2:10," *Bible Today* 42 (1969) 2909–16.

Idem

"A Grammatical Ambiguity in 1 Pet. 2:12," *CBQ* 36 (1974) 89–94.

Lea, Thomas

"1 Peter—Outline and Exposition," *Southwestern Journal of Theology* 25 (1982) 17–45.

Idem

"How Peter Learned the Old Testament," *Southwestern Journal of Theology* 22 (1980) 96–102.

Leaney, A. R. C.

"I Peter and the Passover: An Interpretation," *NTS* 10 (1964) 238–51.

Lecomte, Pierre

"Aimer la vie: I Pierre 3/10 (Psaume 34/13)," *EThR* 56 (1981) 288–93.

Lepelley, Claude

"Le contexte historique de la première lettre de Pierre," in Perrot, ed., *Etudes sur la Première Lettre de Pierre*, 43–64.

Lewis, N., and M. Reinhold, eds.

"The Conflict of Religions and the Triumph of Christianity," in *Roman Civilization: Sourcebook II: The Empire* (New York: Harper & Row, 1966) 552–610.

Liefeld, Theodore S.

"The Christian Hope in the New Testament," *LQ* 6 (1954) 30–41.

Lippert, Peter

"Leben als Zeugnis," *Studia Moralia* 3 (1965) 226–68.

Lohse, Eduard

"Parenesis and Kerygma in 1 Peter" (trans. John Steely), in Talbert, ed., *Perspectives on 1 Peter*, 37–60; ET of "Paränese und Kerygma im 1. Petrusbrief," *ZNW* 45 (1954) 68–89.

Love, Julian Price

"The First Epistle of Peter," *Int* 8 (1954) 63–87.

Lührmann, Dieter

"Neutestamentliche Haustafeln und antike Ökonomie," *NTS* 27 (1980) 83–97.

Lumby, J. R.

"1 Peter 3:17," *Expositor*, series 5, 1 (1890) 142–47.

Luther, Martin

D. Martin Luthers Epistel-Auslegung (ed. H. Günther and E. Volk; Göttingen: Vandenhoeck & Ruprecht, 1983).

Idem

The Epistles of St. Peter and St. Jude Preached and Explained (trans. E. H. Gillett; New York: Anson D. F. Randolph, 1859).

MacKelvey, R. J.

"Christ the Cornerstone," *NTS* 8 (1960) 352–59.

Magie, David

Roman Rule in Asia Minor to the End of the Third Century after Christ (2 vols.; Princeton: Princeton University Press, 1950; reprinted New York: Arno, 1988]).

Maier, Gerhard

"Jesustradition im 1. Petrusbrief?" in D. Wenham, ed., *Gospel Perspectives*, vol. 5: *The Jesus Tradition Outside the Gospels* (Sheffield: JSOT Press, 1985) 85–128.

Malherbe, Abraham J.

Ancient Epistolary Theorists (SBLSBS 19; Atlanta: Scholars Press, 1988).

Idem

Moral Exhortation: A Greco-Roman Sourcebook (LEC 4; Philadelphia: Westminster, 1986).

Manley, G. T.

"Babylon on the Nile," *EvQ* 16 (1944) 138–46.

Manns, Frederic

"'La maison où réside l'Esprit.' 1 P 2,5 et son arrière-plan juif," *SBFLA* 34 (1984) 207–24.

Idem

"Sara, modèle de la femme obéissante: Etude de l'arrière-plan juif de 1 Pierre 3,5–6," *BeO* 26 (1984) 65–73.

Manson, William

"Grace in the New Testament," in W. T. Whitly, ed., *The Doctrine of Grace* (New York: Macmillan, 1931) 33–60.

Marshall, John S.

"'An Holy House, an Holy Priesthood' (I Peter ii.5)," *ATR* 28 (1946) 227–28.

Martin, Ralph P.

"The Composition of I Peter in Recent Study," *Vox Evangelica* 1 (1962) 29–42.

Martin, Troy W.

Metaphor and Composition in 1 Peter (SBLDS 131; Atlanta: Scholars Press, 1992).

Idem

"The Present Indicative in the Eschatological Statements of 1 Peter 1:6, 8," *JBL* 111 (1992) 307–12.

Marxsen, Willi

"Der Mitälteste und Zeuge der Leiden Christi," in C. Andresen and G. Klein, eds., *Theologia Crucis—Signum Crucis: Festschrift für Erich Dinkler zum 70. Geburtstag* (Tübingen: Mohr [Siebeck] 1979) 377–93.

Massaux, E.

"Le texte de la Ia Petri du Papyrus Bodmer," *EThL* 39 (1963) 616–71.

May, Gerhard

"Die Zeit ist da, dass das Gericht angänge am Hause Gottes," in Franklin Clark Fry, ed., *Geschichtswirklichkeit und Glaubensbewährung* (*Festschrift* Fr. Miller; Stuttgart: Evangelisches Verlagswerk, 1967) 41–49.

McCabe, Herbert

"What Is the Church?—VIII," *Life of the Spirit* (1963) 162–74.

McCaughey, J. D.

"On Re-Reading 1 Peter," *AusBR* 31 (1983) 33–44.

Idem

"Three 'Persecution Documents' of the New Testament," *AusBR* 17 (1969) 27–40.

McNabb, V.

"Date and Influence of the First Epistle of St. Peter," *Irish Ecclesiastical Record* 45 (1935) 596–613.

Meade, David G.

Pseudonymity and Canon: An Investigation into the Relationship of Authorship and Authority in Jewish and Earliest Christian Tradition (WUNT 39; Tübingen: Mohr [Siebeck], 1986; Grand Rapids: Eerdmans, 1987).

Meecham, H. G.

"The First Epistle of St. Peter," *ExpT* 48 (1936/37) 22–24.

Idem

"A Note on 1 Peter ii.12," *ExpT* 75 (1953/54) 93.

Meeks, Wayne A.

The Moral World of the First Christians (LEC 6; Philadelphia: Westminster, 1986).

Michaels, J. Ramsey

"Eschatology in I Peter iii.17," *NTS* 13 (1967) 394–400.

Michl, Johann

"Die Presbyter des ersten Petrusbriefes," in H. Fleckenstein, ed., *Ortskirche, Weltkirche: Festgabe für Julius Kardinal Döpfner* (Würzburg: Echter, 1973) 48–62.

Millauer, Helmut

Leiden als Gnade: Eine Traditionsgeschichtliche Untersuchung zur Leidenstheologie des ersten Petrusbriefes (Europäische Hochschulschriften, 23/56; Bern: Herbert Lang, 1976).

Miller, Donald G.

"Deliverance and Destiny: Salvation in First Peter," *Int* 9 (1955) 413–25.

Minear, Paul S.

"The House of Living Stones: A Study of 1 Peter 2:4–12," *Ecumenical Review* 34 (1982) 238–48.

Mitton, C. L.

"The Relationship between I Peter and Ephesians," *JTS*, n.s. 1 (1950) 67–73.

Morris, W. D.

"1 Peter iii.19," *ExpT* 38 (1926/27) 470.

Motyer, Stephen

"The Relationship between Paul's Gospel of 'All One in Christ Jesus' (Galatians 3:28) and the Household Codes," *Vox Evangelica* 19 (1989) 33–48.

Moule, C. F. D.

"The Nature and Purpose of I Peter," *NTS* 3 (1956) 1–11.

Idem

"Sanctuary and Sacrifice in the Church of the New Testament," *JTS*, n.s. 1 (1950) 29–41.

Idem

"Some Reflections on the 'Stone' Testimonia in Relation to the Name Peter," *NTS* 2 (1955/56) 56–59.

Moulton, J. H., and G. Milligan

"Lexical Notes from the Papyri: XVI," *Expositor*, series 7, 7 (1909) 559–68.

Idem

The Vocabulary of the Greek Testament (London: Hodder and Stoughton, 1914).

Mullins, Terence Y.

"Ascription as a Literary Form," *NTS* 19 (1972/73) 194–205.

Munro, Winsome

Authority in Paul and Peter: The Identification of a Pastoral Stratum in the Pauline Corpus and 1 Peter (SNTSMS; New York: Cambridge University Press, 1983).

Nauck, Wolfgang

"Freude im Leiden: Zum Problem einer urchristlichen Verfolgungstradition," *ZNW* 46 (1955) 68–80.

Idem

"Probleme des frühchristlichen Amtsverständnisses," *ZNW* 48 (1957) 200–220.

Neugebauer, F.

"Zur Deutung und Bedeutung des 1. Petrusbriefes," *NTS* 26 (1980) 61–86.

Neumaier, Richard

Das neue Menschsein: Nach dem Zeugnis des Neuen Testaments entfaltet am 1. Petrusbrief, Kapitel 1, 1—2, 10 (Metzingen: Franz, 1978).

Neumann, Karl Johannes

"Coercitio," PW 1st series, 4.1.201–4.

Neusner, Jacob

Oral Tradition in Judaism: The Case of the Mishnah (Albert Bates Lord Studies in Oral Tradition 1; New York: Garland, 1987).

Neyrey, J.

"First Peter and Converts," *Bible Today* 22 (1984)

13–18.

Idem

"Peter, the First Letter of," in Paul J. Achtemeier, ed., *Harper's Bible Dictionary* (San Francisco: Harper & Row, 1985) 778–80.

Nixon, R. E.

"The Meaning of 'Baptism' in 1 Peter 3,21," *StEv* 4 (1968) 437–41.

Ogara, F.

"Adversarius . . . diabolus tamquam leo rugiens," *VD* 16 (1936) 166–73.

Idem

"Quis est qui vobis noceat, si boni aemulatores fueritis? (1 Pet. 3,8–15)," *VD* 17 (1937) 161–65.

Olson, Vernon S.

"The Atonement in 1 Peter" (Th.D. diss., Union Theological Seminary in Virginia, 1979).

Omanson, Roger

"Suffering for Righteousness' Sake (1 Pet 3:13—4:11)," *RevExp* 79 (1982) 439–50.

Osborne, Thomas P.

"Guide Lines for Christian Suffering: A Source-Critical and Theological Study of 1 Peter 2,21–25," *Bib* 64 (1983) 381–408.

Idem

"L'utilisation des citations de l'Ancien Testament dans la première épître de Pierre," *RThL* 12 (1981) 64–77.

Owen, E. C. E.

"δόξα and Cognate Words," *JTS* 33 (1932) 132–50.

Parsons, Samuel

We Have Been Born Anew: The New Birth of the Christian in the First Epistle of St. Peter (Rome: Pontificia Studiorum Universitas, 1978).

Patsch, Hermann

"Zum alttestamentlichen Hintergrund von Römer 4.25 und I. Petrus 2.24," *ZNW* 60 (1969) 273–79.

Patterson, Dorothy

"Roles in Marriage: A Study in Submission: 1 Peter 3:1–7," *Theological Educator* 13 (1982) 70–79.

Percy, Ernst

Die Probeleme der Kolosser- und Epheserbriefe (Skrifter utgivvne av Kungl. Humanistika Vetenskapssamfundet i Lund 39; Acta Reg. Societatis Humaniorum Litterarum Lundensis; Lund: Gleerup, 1946).

Perdelwitz, E. Richard

Die Mysterienreligion und das Problem des 1. Petrusbriefes (Religionversuche und Vorarbeiten 11/3; Giessen: Töpelmann, 1911).

Perrot, C.

"La descente aux enfers et la predication aux morts," in Perrot, ed., *Etudes sur la Première Lettre de Pierre*, 231–46.

Perrot, C., ed.

Etudes sur la Première Lettre de Pierre (LD 102; Paris: Cerf, 1980).

Philipps, Karl

Kirche in der Gesellschaft nach dem 1. Petrusbrief

(Gütersloh: Gütersloher Verlagshaus-Gerd Mohn, 1971).

Piper, John

"Hope as the Motivation of Love: I Peter 3:9–12," *NTS* 26 (1980) 212–31.

Premerstein, A. von

"Clientes," PW 7.23–55.

Prete, Benedetto

"L'espressione *hē en Babylōni syneklektē* di 1 Pt. 5,13," *Vetera Christianorum* 21 (1984) 335–52.

Price, S. R. F.

Rituals and Power: The Roman Imperial Cult in Asia Minor (Cambridge: Cambridge University Press, 1984).

Prigent, Pierre

"1 Pierre 2,4–10," *RHPhR* 72 (1992) 53–60.

Proctor, John

"Fire in God's House: Influence of Malachi 3 in the NT," *JETS* 36 (1993) 9–14.

Prostmeier, Ferdinand-Rupert

Handlungsmodelle im ersten Petrusbrief (Forschung zur Bibel 63; Würzburg: Echter, 1990).

Pryor, J. W.

"First Peter and the New Covenant," *Reformed Theological Review* 45 (1986) 44–51.

Quinn, Jerome D.

"Notes on the Text of the P[72] 1 Pt 2,3; 5,14; and 5,9," *CBQ* 27 (1965) 241–49.

Radermacher, Ludwig

"Der erste Petrusbrief und Silvanus; mit einem Nachwort in eigener Sache," *ZNW* 25 (1926) 287–99.

Ramsay, William M.

The Church in the Roman Empire before A.D. 170 (5th ed.; London: Hodder and Stoughton, 1897).

Refoulé, François

"Bible et éthique sociale: Lire aujourd'hui 1 Pierre," *Le Supplément* 131 (1979) 457–82.

Reichert, Angelika

Eine urchristliche praeparatio ad martyrium: Studien zur Komposition, Traditionsgeschichte und Theologie des 1. Petrusbriefes (BBE 22; Frankfurt am Main: Lang, 1989).

Reicke, Bo

The Disobedient Spirits and Christian Baptism (ASNU 13; Copenhagen: Munksgaard, 1946).

Idem

"Die Gnosis der Männer nach I. Ptr. 3:7," in W. Eltester, ed., *Neutestamentliche Studien für Rudolph Bultmann zu seinem 70. Geburtstag* (BZNW 21; Berlin: Töpelmann, 1954) 296–304.

Rengstorf, Karl Heinrich

"Die neutestamentlichen Mahnungen an die Frau, sich dem Manne Unterzuordnen," in W. Foerster, ed., *Verbum Dei manet in aeternum: Festschrift* O. Schmitz (Witten: Luther-Verlag, 1953) 131–45.

Reumann, John

"'Stewards of God'—Pre-Christian Religious

Application of OIKONOMOΣ in Greek," *JBL* 77 (1958) 339–49.

Reynolds, Stephen M.
  "The Zero Tense in Greek: A Critical Note," *WTJ* 32 (1969) 68–72.

Richard, Earl
  "The Functional Christology of 1 Peter," in Talbert, ed., *Perspectives on 1 Peter,* 121–40.

Richards, E. Randolph
  The Secretary in the Letters of Paul (WUNT 2/42; Tübingen: Mohr [Siebeck], 1991).

Richards, G. C.
  "I Pet. iii 21," *JTS* 32 (1931) 77.

Robertson, P. E.
  "Is 1 Peter a Sermon?" *Theological Educator* 13 (1982) 35–41.

Robinson, John A. T.
  Redating the New Testament (Philadelphia: Westminster, 1976).

Robinson, P. J.
  "Some Missiological Perspectives from 1 Peter 2:4–10," *Missionalia* 17 (1989) 176–87.

Rödding, G.
  "Descendit ad inferna," in *Kerygma und Melos* (*Festschrift* C. Marenholz; Berlin: 1970) 95–102.

Rogers, Peter R.
  "The Longer Reading of 1 Peter 4:14," *CBQ* 43 (1981) 93–95.

Rudrauf, Kilian
  Disputatio theologica inauguralis ad oraculum I. Petri III.18.19 (Giessen: Typis Henningi Mulleri, 1685).

Russell, Ronald
  "Eschatology and Ethics in 1 Peter," *EvQ* 47 (1975) 78–84.

Ryan, T. J.
  "The Word of God in First Peter: A Critical Study of 1 Peter 2:1–3" (Ph.D. diss., Catholic University of America, 1973).

Sander, Emilie T.
  "ΠΨΡΩΣΙΣ and the First Epistle of Peter," (Precis) *HTR* 60 (1967) 501.

Sandevoir, Pierre
  "Un Royaume de Prêtres?" in Perrot, ed., *Etudes sur la Première Lettre de Pierre,* 219–29.

Schaefer, Hans
  "Paroikoi," PW Halbband 36.18.4.1695–1707.

Scharfe, Ernst
  Die Petrinische Strömung der neutestamentlichen Literatur (Berlin: Reuther & Reichert, 1893).

Idem
  "Die schriftstellerische Originalität des 1. Petrusbriefes," *ThStK* 62 (1889) 633–70.

Scharlemann, Martin H.
  "An Apostolic Descant (An Exegetical Study of 1 Peter 1:3–12)," *Concordia Journal* 2 (1976) 9–17.

Idem
  "An Apostolic Salutation: An Exegetical Study of 1 Peter 1,1–2," *Concordia Journal* 1 (1975) 108–18.

Idem
  "Exodus Ethics: Part One—I Peter 1:13–16," *Concordia Journal* 2 (1976) 165–70.

Idem
  "'He descended into Hell': An Interpretation of 1 Peter 3:18–20," *CTM* 27 (1956) 81–94.

Idem
  "Why the *Kuriou* in 1 Peter 1:25?" *CTM* 30 (1959) 352–56.

Schattenmann, Johannes
  "The Little Apocalypse of the Synoptics and the First Epistle of Peter," *Theology Today* 11 (1954) 193–98.

Schelkle, Karl-Hermann
  "Das Leiden des Gottesknechtes als Form Christlichen Lebens (nach dem ersten Petrusbrief)," *BK* 16 (1961) 14–16.

Schider, J.
  "*. . . viel Gnade und Frieden!*" 1 Petr. 1,2 (Munich: Kaiser, 1939).

Schierse, Franz Joseph
  "Ein Hirtenbrief und viele Bücher," *BK* 31 (1976) 86–88.

Schlatter, Adolf von
  Petrus und Paulus nach dem Ersten Petrusbrief (Stuttgart: Calwer, 1937).

Schlier, Heinrich
  "Eine Adhortatio aus Rom: Die Botschaft des Ersten Petrusbriefes," in H. Schlier, ed., *Strukturen christlicher Existenz: Beiträge zur Erneuerung des geistlichen Lebens: Festgabe P. Friedrich Wulf* (Würzburg: Echter, 1968) 59–80.

Idem
  "γαλά," *TWNT* 1 (1933) 644–45.

Idem
  "Die Kirche nach dem 1. Petrusbrief," in J. Feiner and M. Löhrer, eds., *Mysterium Salutis* 4.1 (Einsiedeln: Benziger, 1972) 195–200.

Schlosser, Jacques
  "Ancien Testament et Christologie dans la Prima Petri," in Perrot, ed., *Etudes sur la Première Lettre de Pierre,* 65–96.

Idem
  "I Pierre 3,5b–6," *Bib* 64 (1983) 409–10.

Schmid, J.
  "Petrus der 'Fels' und die Petrusgestalt," in M. Roesle and O. Cullmann, eds., *Begegnung der Christen* (Stuttgart: Evangelisches Verlagswerk, 1959) 347–59.

Schmidt, David Henry
  The Peter Writings: Their Redactors and Their Relationships (Ann Arbor: Xerox University Microfilms, 1972).

Schmidt, P.
  "Zwei Fragen zum ersten Petrusbrief," *ZWTh* 51 (1908) 24–52.

Schnackenburg, Rudolph
  "Episkopos und Hirtenamt," in idem, *Schriften zum Neuen Testament: Exegese in Fortschritt und Wandel*

(Munich: Kösel, 1971) 246–67.

Scholer, David
"Women's Adornment: Some Historical and Hermeneutical Observations on the New Testament Passages 1 Tim 2:9–10, 1 Pet 3:3–4," *Daughters of Sarah* 6 (1980) 3–6.

Schroeder, David
"Once you were no people . . . ," in Harry Huebner, ed., *The Church as Theological Community: Essays in Honour of David Schroeder* (Winnipeg: CMBC Publications, 1990) 37–65.

Schröger, Friedrich
Gemeinde im ersten Petrusbrief: Untersuchungen zum Selbstverständnis einer christlichen Gemeinde an der Wende vom 1. zum 2. Jahrhundert (Passau: Passavia, 1981).

Idem
"'Lasst euch auferbauen zu einem geisterfüllten Haus' (1 Ptr 2,4.5): Eine Überlegung zu dem Verhältnis von Ratio und Pneuma," in W. Friedberger and F. Schnider, eds., *Theologie, Gemeinde, Seelsorger* (Munich: Kösel, 1979) 138–45.

Idem
"Die Verfassung der Gemeinde des ersten Petrusbriefes," in J. Hainz, ed., *Kirche im Werden: Studien zum Thema Amt und Gemeinde im Neuen Testament* (Munich: Schöningh, 1976) 239–52.

Schückler, Georg
"Wandel im Glauben als missionarisches Zeugnis," *ZMR* 51 (1967) 289–99.

Schüssler Fiorenza, Elisabeth
"Cultic Language in Qumran and in the NT," *CBQ* 38 (1976) 159–77.

Schutter, William L.
Hermeneutic and Composition in I Peter (WUNT 2/30; Tübingen: Mohr [Siebeck], 1989).

Schwank, P. Benedikt
"Diabolus tamquam leo rugiens," *Erbe und Auftrag* 38 (1962) 15–20.

Idem
"L'Epître (1 P 3,8–15)," *AsSeign* 59 (1966) 16–32.

Idem
"Wie Freie—aber als Sklaven Gottes (1 Petr 2,16): Das Verhältnis des Christen zur Staatsmacht nach dem Ersten Petrusbrief," *Erbe und Auftrag* 36 (1960) 5–12.

Schweizer, Eduard
"1. Petrus 4,6 . . . ," *ThZ* 8 (1952) 152–54.

Selwyn, Ernest Gordon
"Eschatology in I Peter," in W. D. Davies and D. Daube, eds., *The Background of the New Testament and Its Eschatology* (Festschrift C. H. Dodd; Cambridge: University Press, 1956) 394–401.

Idem
"The Persecutions in I Peter," *Bulletin of the Studiorum Novi Testamenti Societas* 1 (1950) 39–50.

Idem
"The Problem of the Authorship of I Peter," *ExpT* 59 (1947/48) 256–58.

Senior, Donald R.
"The Conduct of Christians in the World (2:11—3:12)," *RevExp* 79 (1982) 427–38.

Idem
"The First Letter of Peter," *Bible Today* 22 (1984) 5–12.

Seufert, W.
"Der Abfassungsort des ersten Petrusbriefes," *ZWTh* 28 (1885) 146–56.

Idem
"Das Abhängigkeitsverhältnis des I. Petrusbriefs vom Römerbrief," *ZWTh* 16 (1874) 360–88.

Idem
"Titus Silvanus (ΣΙΛΑΣ) und der Verfasser des ersten Petrusbriefes," *ZWTh* 28 (1885) 350–71.

Idem
"Das Verwandtschaftsverhältnis des 1. Petrusbriefs und Epheserbriefs," *ZWTh* 24 (1881) 178–97, 332–80.

Shimada, Kazuhito
"The Christological Credal Formula in I Peter 3:18–22—Reconsidered," *AJBI* 5 (1979) 154–76.

Idem
"A Critical Note on I Peter 1,12," *AJBI* 7 (1981) 146–50.

Idem
The Formulary Material in First Peter (Ann Arbor: Xerox University Microfilms, 1966).

Idem
"Is I Peter a Composite Writing?" *AJBI* 11 (1985) 95–114.

Idem
"Is 1 Peter Dependent on Ephesians? A Critique of C. L. Mitton," *AJBI* 17 (1991) 77–106.

Idem
"Is 1 Peter Dependent on Romans?" *AJBI* 19 (1993) 87–137.

Sieffert, E. L.
"Die Heilsbedeutung des Leidens und Sterbens Christi nach dem ersten Briefe des Petrus," *Jahrbücher für deutsche Theologie* 20 (1875) 371–440.

Sisti, A.
"Testimonianza di virtu cristiane (1 Piet 3,8–15)," *BeO* 8 (1966) 117–26.

Idem
"La vita cristiana nell'attesa della parusia (1 Piet. 4, 7–11)," *BeO* 7 (1965) 123–28.

Sleeper, C. Freeman
"Political Responsibility according to I Peter," *NovT* 10 (1968) 270–86.

Sly, Dorothy I.
"1 Peter 3:6b in the Light of Philo and Josephus," *JBL* 110 (1991) 126–29.

Smith, Terence V.
Petrine Controversies in Early Christianity (WUNT, 2/15; Tübingen: Mohr [Siebeck], 1985).

Smothers, Edgar R.
"A Letter from Babylon," *Classical Journal* 22 (1926) 202–9.

Snodgrass, Klyne R.
"I Peter II.1–10: Its Formation and Literary Affinities," *NTS* 24 (1977) 97–106.

Snyder, Scot
"1 Peter 2:17: A Reconsideration," *Filologia Neotestamentaria* 4 (1991) 211–15.

Soltau, W.
"Die Einheitlichkeit des 1. Petrusbriefes," *ThStK* 78 (1905) 302–15.

Idem
"Nochmals die Einheitlichkeit des 1. Petrusbriefes," *ThStK* 79 (1906) 456–60.

Sordi, Marta
The Christians and the Roman Empire (trans. A. Bedini; Norman: University of Oklahoma Press, 1986).

Sorg, Theo
"In Spannungen Leben," *ThBei* 4 (1973) 145–50.

Souček, J. B.
"Das Gegenüber von Gemeinde und Welt nach dem ersten Petrusbrief," *Communio Viatorum* 3 (1960) 5–13.

Spicq, C.
"L'Epître (1 P 4,7–11)," *AsSeign* 50 (1966) 15–29.

Idem
"La place ou le rôle des jeunes dans certaines communautés néotestamentaires," *RB* 76 (1969) 508–27.

Idem
"La Iᵃ Petri et le témoignage évangélique de saint Pierre," *StTh* 20 (1966) 37–61.

Spitta, Friedrich
Christi Predigt an die Geister (1 Petr. 3, 19ff.): Ein Beitrag zur neutestamentlichen Theologie (Göttingen: Vandenhoeck & Ruprecht, 1890).

Spörri, Theophil
Der Gemeindegedanke im ersten Petrusbrief (Neutestamentliche Forschung 2/2; Gütersloh: Bertelsmann, 1925).

Stambaugh, John E., and David L. Balch
The New Testament in Its Social Environment (LEC 2; Philadelphia: Westminster, 1986).

Stegmann, A.
Silvanus als Missionar und "Hagiograph" (Rottenburg: Bader, 1917).

Steuer, A.
"1 Petr 3,17—4,6," *ThGl* 30 (1938) 675–78.

Steuernagel, Valdir R.
"An Exiled Community as a Missionary Community: A Study Based on 1 Peter 2:9, 10," *Evangelical Review of Theology* 10 (1986) 8–18.

Strathmann, Hermann
"Die Stellung des Petrus in der Urkirche," *ZSTh* 20 (1943) 223–82.

Strobel, August
"Macht Leiden von Sünde frei? Zur Problematik von 1. Petr. 4,1f.," *ThZ* 19 (1963) 412–25.

Strugnell, John
"Notes on 1QS 1,17–18; 8,3–4 and 1QM 17,8–9," *CBQ* 29 (1967) 580–82.

Stuhlmueller, Carroll
"Baptism: New Life through the Blood of Jesus," *Worship* 39 (1965) 207–17.

Sylva, Dennis
"A 1 Peter Bibliography," *JETS* 25 (1982) 75–89.

Idem
"1 Peter Studies: The State of the Discipline," *BTB* 10 (1980) 155–63.

Idem
"Translating and Interpreting 1 Peter 3:2," *BT* 34 (1983) 144–47.

Synge, F. C.
"1 Peter 3:18–21," *ExpT* 82 (1970/71) 311.

Talbert, Charles H.
"The Educational Value of Suffering in 1 Peter," in idem, *Learning through Suffering: The Educational Value of Suffering in the New Testament and in Its Milieu* (Zacchaeus Studies: New Testament; Collegeville, Minn.: Liturgical Press, 1991) 42–57.

Idem
"Once Again: The Plan of 1 Peter," in Talbert, ed., *Perspectives on 1 Peter,* 141–51.

Talbert, Charles H., ed.
Perspectives on 1 Peter (NABPR Special Series 9; Macon, Ga.: Mercer University Press, 1986).

Tarrech, Armand Puig
"Le milieu de la Première Epître de Pierre," *Revista Catalana de Teología* 5 (1980) 95–129, 331–402.

Teichert, Horst
"1. Ptr. 2,13—eine crux interpretum?" *ThLZ* 74 (1949) 303–4.

Tenney, Merrill C.
"Some Possible Parallels between 1 Peter and John," in R. N. Longenecker and M. C. Tenney, eds., *New Dimensions in New Testament Study* (Grand Rapids: Zondervan, 1974) 370–77.

Thiede, C. P.
"Babylone, der andere Ort: Anmerkungen zu 1 Petr 5,13 und Apg 12,17," *Bib* 67 (1986) 532–38.

Thomas, Johannes
"Anfechtung und Vorfreude: Ein biblisches Thema nach Jakobus 1.2–18, im Zusammenhang mit Psalm 126, Röm. 5.3–5 und 1 Pet 1.5–7 . . . ," *KD* 14 (1968) 183–206.

Thompson, James W.
"'Be Submissive to Your Masters': A Study of I Peter 2:18–25," *ResQ* 9 (1966) 66–78.

Thornton, T. C. G.
"I Peter: A Paschal Liturgy?" *JTS,* n.s. 12 (1961) 14–26.

Thraede, K.
"Frau," *RAC* 8 (1972) 197–269.

Thurén, Lauri
The Rhetorical Strategy of 1 Peter: With Special Regard

to Ambiguous Expressions (Åbo: Åbo Akademis forlag, 1990).

Thurston, Robert W.
"Interpreting First Peter," *JETS* 17 (1974) 171–82.

Toit, A. B. du
"The Significance of Discourse Analysis for New Testament Interpretation and Translation: Introductory Remarks with Special Reference to I Peter 1:3–13," *Neot* 8 (1974) 54–79.

Tripp, David H.
"Eperōtēma (I Peter 3²¹): A Liturgist's Note," *ExpT* 92 (1980/81) 267–70.

van Unnik, W. C.
"Christianity according to I Peter," *ExpT* 68 (1956/57) 79–83.

Idem
"A Classical Parallel to I Peter II 14 and 20," in idem, *Sparsa Collecta* 2.106–10.

Idem
"The Critique of Paganism in I Peter 1:28," in E. E. Ellis and M. Wilcox, eds., *Neotestamentica et Semitica; Studies in Honour of Matthew Black* (Edinburgh: Clark, 1969) 129–42.

Idem
"The Redemption in 1 Peter I 18–19 and the Problem of the First Epistle of Peter," in idem, *Sparsa Collecta* 2.3–82.

Idem
"Die Rücksicht auf die Reaktion der Nicht-Christen in der altchristlichen Paränese," in idem, *Sparsa Collecta* 2.307–22.

Idem
Sparsa Collecta, vol. 2 (NovTSup 30; Leiden: Brill, 1980).

Idem
"The Teaching of Good Works in 1 Peter," in idem, *Sparsa Collecta* 2.83–105.

Vallauri, E.
"'Succincti lumbos mentis vestrae' (1 Piet 1,13): Nota per una traduzione," *BeO* 24 (1982) 19–22.

Vanhoye, Albert, S.J.
"L'Epître (I P 2,1–10): La maison spirituelle," *AsSeign* 43 (1964) 16–29.

Idem
"1 Pierre au carrefour des théologies du nouveau Testament," in Perrot, ed., *Etudes sur la Première Lettre de Pierre*, 97–128.

Villiers, J. L. de
"Joy in Suffering in I Peter," *Neot* 9 (1975) 64–86.

Vitti, A.
"Descensus Christi ad inferos ex 1 Petri 3, 19–20; 4,6," *VD* 7 (1927) 111–18.

Idem
"Eschatologia in Petri epistula prima," *VD* 11 (1931) 298–306.

Vogels, Heinz-Jürgen
Christi Abstieg ins Totenreich und das Läuterung an den Toten (Freiburger Theologische Studien 102;

Freiburg: Herder, 1976).

Völter, D.
"Bemerkungen zu I. Pt 3 und 4," *ZNW* 9 (1908) 74–77.

Idem
Der erste Petrusbrief: Seine Entstehung und Stellung in der Geschichte des Urchristentums (Strasbourg: Heitz und Mündel, 1906).

Walker, William O., ed.
The Relationships among the Gospels: An Interdisciplinary Dialogue (San Antonio: Trinity University Press, 1978).

Wand, J. W. C.
"The Lessons of First Peter: A Survey of Recent Interpretation," *Int* 9 (1955) 387–99.

Warden, Duane
"Imperial Persecution and the Dating of 1 Peter and Revelation," *JETS* 34 (1991) 203–12.

Idem
"The Prophets of 1 Peter 1:10–12," *ResQ* 31 (1989) 1–12.

Watson, G. R.
The Roman Soldier (Ithaca, N.Y.: Cornell University Press, 1969).

Weidinger, K.
Die Haustafel: Ein Stück urchristlicher Paränese (Untersuchungen zum Neuen Testament 14; Leipzig: 1928).

Weiss, Bernhard
Der Petrinische Lehrbegriff (Berlin: Schultze, 1855).

Weiss, Johannes
"Asia Minor in the Apostolic Time," in S. M. Jackson, ed., *The New Schaff-Herzog Encyclopedia of Religious Knowledge* (New York: Funk & Wagnalls, 1908) 1.316.

Wells, Paul
"Les images bibliques de l'Église dans I Pierre 2, 9–10," *Etudes Evangéliques* 33 (1973) 20–25, 53–65.

Wenschkewitz, H.
Die Spiritualisierung der Kultusbegriffe Tempel, Priester und Opfer im Neuen Testament (Angelos-Beiheft 4; Leipzig: 1932).

Wheelan, Joseph B.
"The Priesthood of the Laity," *Doctrine and Life* 15 (1965) 539–46.

White, John L.
"Ancient Greek Letters," in D. E. Aune, ed., *Greco-Roman Literature and the New Testament: Selected Forms and Genres* (SBLSBS 21; Atlanta: Scholars Press, 1988) 85–106.

Wifstrand, Albert
"Stylistic Problems in the Epistles of James and Peter," *StTh* 1 (1948) 170–82.

Wilder, Amos
Early Christian Rhetoric: The Language of the Gospel (London: SCM, 1964).

Wilson, James P.
"In the Text of 1 Peter ii.17 Is πάντας τιμήσατε a

Primitive Error for πάντα ποιήσατε?" *ExpT* 54
(1942/43) 193–94.

Winbery, C. L.
"Ethical Issues in 1 Peter," *Theological Educator* 13
(1982) 63–71.

Idem
"Introduction to the First Letter of Peter," *South-western Journal of Theology* 25 (1982) 3–16.

Wolff, Christian
"Christ und Welt im 1. Petrusbrief," *ThLZ* 100
(1975) 334–42.

Woychuck, N. A.
The Faith of Experience: Devotional Exposition of I Peter 1:3–8 (Grand Rapids: Eerdmans, 1953).

Wrede, William
"Miscellen, 3: Bemerkungen zu Harnacks Hypo-these über die Adresse des 1. Petrusbriefs," *ZNW* 1
(1900) 75–85.

Yates, Thomas
"The Message of the Epistles: The First Epistle of
Peter," *ExpT* 45 (1933/34) 391–93.

Indices

1. Passages

a / Old Testament and Apocrypha

Genesis

3:8	227
8:20	202
18:1–8	296
23:4	56, 71, 107

Exodus

6:1	339
6:6	127, 128
12:5	115, 128
12:11	115, 118
12:35	128
12:45	173
13:3, 9, 14, 16	339
13:12–13	127
15:2–4	115
15:26	115
16:3	115
16:7	309
18:10	94
19:5	163, 165
19:5–6	89, 115
19:6	12, 70, 150, 151, 163–65,
19:8	115
19:23	269
20:5	229
21:1–6	53
21:6	248
21:8	158
23:22	12, 70, 164
24:3–8	88
24:16	309
29:1	129
29:4, 8	248
29:43	309
30:12–16	127, 198
32:3–4	128
34:14	229
40:12	248
40:34	309

Leviticus

2:6	6
2:6–8	12
5:6–7	247
6:23	247
7:7	309
8:24	248
14:20	202
16:20–22	202
17:7	127
17:10	227

18:4	281
19:18	188
20:3, 5, 6	227
20:13	309
22:10	173
22:17–25	129
22:21	130
22:25	130
25:6	173
25:23	126, 173
25:26, 33, 48–49	127
26:17	227
26:41–45	231
27:5	248
36:2	326

Numbers

3:44–51	127
5:22	300
6:22–27	224
6:25–26	227
8:9–10	248
14:10	309
15:40	121
16:14, 29	230
18:15–17	127
24:4, 16	298
24:17	111
27:5	248
27:17	204, 325
28–29	115
35:15	173

Deuteronomy

3:24	339
4:24	229
4:34	339
4:37	81
5:15	339
6:15	229
6:21	339
7:6	121, 163
7:6–8	81
7:8	127, 128, 339
7:19	339
8:6	281
9:26	339
11:2	339
10:15	81
10:17	124
14:2	81
15:4	96
15:12–18	53
18:15	111
19:10	96
21:20	282
21:22–23	201

21:23	202
26:5–8	167
26:6	193
26:8	339
27:15–26	300
28:25	82
29:17	128
32:4	154
32:6, 18	86
32:7	127
32:18a	94, 153
33:9	298
34:4	96
34:12	339

Joshua

24:16–18	127

Judges

5:5	227

1 Samuel

2:7–8	338
6:4	309
16:7	214
16:13	86
17:26, 36	269
18:27	158
25:32	93, 94

2 Samuel

1:10	164
7	155
7:10	119
7:14	124
21:1	227
22:36	87
23:3	154

1 Kings

1:36	300
1:48	94
8:10–11	309
8:15	93
18:46	118
22:17	204
25:32	94

2 Kings

4:29	118
9:1	118

1 Chronicles

19:11	300
16:36	300
29:10	86, 94

2 Chronicles

2:11	159
6:4	94
19:7	124
21:12	159
22:5	156

394

7:25	153
7:26	96, 200
7:27	157, 246, 247
8:1	133, 273
8:5	267, 343
9:6	343
9:11–22	89
9:12	127, 128, 246, 247
9:14	129
9:15	127
9:24	267
9:26	132, 246, 247, 329
9:27	289
9:28	202, 246, 247
10:1	153
10:2	246
10:10	246, 247
10:12	14, 133, 247, 273
10:19	248
10:21	156, 316
10:22	153, 268
10:22–23	138
10:23	318
10:23–25	294
10:25	294
10:26	136, 247, 326
10:32	167
10:32–36	99, 101, 307
10:34	222
10:36	104, 329
10:39	104
11:5	158
11:6	101
11:7	264
11:11	216
11:13	81, 111, 174, 329
11:13–16	125
11:26	307
11:33	341
11:34	311
11:39	104, 329
12:1	144, 268
12:2	133, 273
12:9	249, 255
12:14	221, 226
12:17	20, 225
12:18–24	156
12:22–23	248
12:23	254, 255
13:1	137, 222

13:2	293, 296
13:4	96, 287
13:7	121, 199
13:12	198
13:13	197, 199
13:13–14	307
13:14	175
13:15	158
13:15–16	157
13:17	286
13:18	196
13:19	173
13:20	204, 257, 329
13:20–21	337, 346
13:21	299, 200, 336, 346
13:22	169, 348, 349, 352
13:24	353
James	
1:1	80, 82, 89
1:2	99, 101, 306
1:2–3	102
1:3	102
1:4	122
1:9–10	338
1:12	308, 329
1:14	175
1:15	175, 282
1:16	173, 305
1:19	173
1:18–21	138
1:21	144, 234, 268, 269
1:27	96
2:1	309
2:1–4	212
2:1–9	125
2:5	173
2:11	309
2:12	307
2:21	157, 202
3:13	121, 176
4:1–2	176
4:2–3	218
4:6	333, 337
4:7	333, 337, 342
4:8	333
4:10	338
4:14	309
5:7–11	294
5:7–20	293
5:8	293, 294, 346
5:12	294

5:14	321, 322
5:19	136
5:20	6, 292, 295
2 Peter	
1:2	89
1:4	175, 282, 343
1:7	222
1:10	263
1:12	346
1:14	268
1:16–18	324
1:21	110, 263, 298
2:2	136, 282, 311
2:3	326
2:4	256, 260
2:4–5	256, 264
2:5	255, 259, 264
2:5–9	260
2:7	121, 282
2:9	264
2:10	111, 175, 281, 282, 284
2:12	284
2:14	326
2:18	175, 282
2:22	309
3:2	214
3:3	175, 281, 282, 322
3:7	289
3:8–9	263
3:9	263, 289
3:10–11	289
3:11	101
3:14	305
3:15	9
3:16	298
3:18	60, 292, 299, 300
1 John	
1:2–3	124
1:7	88
2:1	247
2:2	247, 248
2:7	173
2:9–10	188
2:10	293
2:13	311
2:14	311
2:16	175, 280, 282
2:16–17	120
2:17	175, 282
2:18–19	294
2:20	121

2. Greek Words

ἀγαθός
189, 229, 231, 235,
238, 240, 269

ἀγαθοποιΐα
318

ἀγαθοποιέω
179, 184, 185, 196,
197, 216, 238

ἀγαλλιάω
11, 100, 103, 104,
302, 307

ἀγαπάω
44, 102–4, 143, 147

ἀγάπη
114, 135, 137, 144,
147, 179, 294, 348,
355

ἀγαπητός
73, 80, 169, 221,
301, 305

ἄγγελος
240, 242, 274

ἁγιάζω
232

ἁγιασμός
86, 88, 121, 135

ἅγιος
70, 80, 87, 114, 121,
122, 135, 136, 165,
214, 215, 313

ἁγνίζω
135, 136, 138, 144

ἀγοράζω
128

ἀδελφή
353

ἀδελφός
313, 349, 351

ἀδελφότης
188, 335, 342, 343

ἄδικος
240, 247, 248, 253

ἀδίκως
190, 196

ἄδολος
146, 147

αἷμα
20, 87, 88, 128, 129

αἰσχροκερδῶς
326

αἰσχύνω
314

αἰτέω
34, 233

ἀκροβυστία
269

ἀκρογωνιαῖος
159

ἀλήθεια
136–37

ἀλλήλων
137, 147, 296, 333

ἀλλοτριεπίσκοπος
308, 310, 311, 312,
313

ἀλλότριος
174, 303, 312

ἀμαράντινος
330

ἀμάραντος
96, 330

ἁμαρτάνω
197

ἁμαρτία
45, 193, 200–3, 240,
242, 247, 275, 276,
279, 280, 309

ἀμήν
300, 347, 348, 356

ἀμίαντος
96

ἀμνός
129

ἄμωμος
128–30

ἀναγγέλλω
111

ἀναγεννάω
91, 93, 94, 95, 114,
115, 135, 136, 137,
138, 139, 142, 145,
146

ἀναγκαῖος
343

ἀναγκαστῶς
326

ἀναζάω
114, 118

ἀναπαύω
308

ἀνάστασις
240, 267

ἀναστροφή
4, 121, 123, 126,
130, 178, 179

ἀναφέρω
45, 114, 125, 156,

201, 202

ἀνάχυσις
283

ἀνεκλάλητος
44

ἀνήρ
206, 217, 218, 221

ἀνθίστημι
342

ἀνθρώπινος
187, 312

ἄνθρωπος
141, 176, 213, 237,
275, 287, 280, 281,
288

ἀνομία
45, 193, 200, 203

ἀντίδικος
341

ἀντίτυπος
240, 266

ἀνυπόκριτος
16, 137

ἅπαξ
20, 240–42, 245,
246, 251, 276

ἀπειθέω
162, 163, 210, 240,
255, 262, 316

ἀπεκδέχομαι
240, 263

ἀπεκδύω
269

ἀπέχω
172, 175

ἀπιστέω
114, 161, 162

ἀπογίνομαι
202

ἀποδίδωμι
223, 286

ἀποδοκιμάζω
154

ἀπόθεσις
240, 268, 269

ἀποθνήσκω
189, 239, 241, 242

αποκαλύπτω
17, 92, 98, 106, 111,
119, 324

ἀπολογία
233

ἀπονέμω
217, 218

ἀποστερέω
312

ἀποστέλλω
111

ἀπόστολος
17, 80, 259

ἀποτίθημι
20, 22, 114, 144

ἀπροσωπολήμπτως
125

ἀργύριον
128, 130

ἀρετή
166

ἀρκετός
281

ἀρτιγέννητος
114, 115, 142, 145,
148

ἀρχιποίμην
204, 329

ἄρχων
181

ἀσθενής
217

ἄσπιλος
129

•

βάπτισμα
240, 266, 267

βασίλειον
38, 70, 152, 158,
163–65

βασιλεύς
180, 183, 188

βίος
281

βλασφημέω
283, 284, 286

βούλημα
275, 281

βρέφος
56, 142, 145, 148

•

γάλα
145–48

γένος
70, 163, 165

γίνομαι
216, 305, 327

γογγυσμός
297

γραφή
6, 12, 149, 159

γράφω
159, 349, 350, 352

γρηγορέω
11, 340

γυναικεῖος
208, 211, 217

γυνή
208, 217, 218

•

δεκτός
130, 157

δεξιός
240, 242, 273

δέον
99, 101

δεσπότης
195

δηλόω
105, 109, 111

διάβολος
17, 20

διακονέω
18, 292, 298

διάκονος
181

διασπορά
82

διασώζω
240, 264, 265

δίδωμι
45, 133

διηγέομαι
166

δίκαιος
202, 203, 225, 231,
240, 242, 246, 247,
255, 264, 281, 316,
317

δικαιοσύνη
202–3, 231

δοκίμιον
20

δόξα
44, 45, 90, 103, 105,
109, 111, 112, 133,
141, 166, 169, 292,
300, 303, 306–9,
313, 314, 324, 330,
336, 345, 347

δοξάζω
44, 103, 169, 313,
314

δοῦλος
56, 179, 186, 192,
194

κύριος
140–42, 147, 225,
227, 298, 316
κῶμος
282

•

λαλέω
220, 284, 298
λαός
70, 92, 165, 168
λέων
182, 341
λίθος
56, 151, 152, 154,
155, 159, 162
λογία
20, 34, 224, 233,
271, 298, 347
λογίζομαι
352
λογικός
146
λόγος
135, 139, 140, 142,
145, 146, 210, 268,
286, 298
λυπέω
101
λυτρόω
127, 128, 130

•

μαθητής
313
μακάριος
231, 308, 313
μακροθυμία
240, 241, 263
Μάρκος
355
μάρτυς
323, 324
μάταιος
123, 126–28, 130
μέλλω
324
μένω
139–40, 141
μόλις
317

•

νεκρός
259, 286, 287, 289,
290, 291
νεώτερος
14, 321, 331

νήφω
114, 118, 292, 294,
336, 340
Νῶε
240, 242, 258, 264

•

ξενίζω
283, 286, 305
ξένος
305
ξύλον
14, 45, 202

•

οἰκέτης
56, 57, 186, 194, 221
οἰκοδομέω
114, 149, 153, 154,
155, 156
οἶκος
154–56, 158, 159,
164, 175, 316
οἰνοφλυγία
282
ὀκτώ
242, 265
ὀλίγος
58, 101, 239, 240,
264, 265, 345, 348,
352
ὁμοίως
205, 209, 217, 221,
321, 330, 331
ὁμολογέω
270
ὁμόφρων
221
ὀνειδίζω
284, 307, 308, 313
ὄνομα
231, 303, 307, 308,
313–15
ὁπλίζω
277, 278, 281
ὁράω
44, 99, 102, 103,
114, 120, 123, 126,
127, 143, 144, 220,
342, 343
οὐρανός
67, 97, 111, 240–42,
273

•

πάθημα
70, 108, 110, 111,
301, 306, 323, 342

παλιγγενσία
93
πανήγυρις
284
παράδοσις
127
παρακαλέω
173, 324, 352
παρατίθημι
317, 318
παρεπίδημος
20, 56, 71, 80, 81,
82, 173, 174, 192
παρέρχομαι
281
παροικία
125, 126
πάροικος
71, 174
πάσχω
23, 28, 189, 190,
196, 198, 199, 230,
239, 242, 247, 276,
301, 309, 313, 317
πατήρ
86, 124, 127
πατροπαράδοτος
127
παύω
276, 303
πειρασμός
106, 306
πέμπω
184
περιεργάζομαι
311, 312
περίεργος
312
περιέχω
12, 159
περιποιέω
165
περιούσιος
165
πέτρα
151, 154, 162
πέτρος
41, 80, 154
πιστεύω
103, 114, 160
πίστις
16, 20, 87, 97, 101,
104, 132, 149, 161,
162, 233, 271

πιστός
80, 114, 123, 132,
318, 349, 351
πλῆθος
45, 293, 295
πληθύνω
89, 230, 356
πνεῦμα
86, 88, 112, 135,
154, 155, 157–59,
164, 214, 240–42,
249–56, 258, 260,
262, 287, 288, 290,
291, 297
πνευματικός
154, 157, 158, 164
ποιέω
225, 227
ποιμαίνω
321, 324, 328, 336
ποίμνιον
321
ποῖος
109, 198, 315
πολυπραγμονέω
312
πολύς
93, 102, 127, 159,
312
πολύτιμος
102
πονηρός
311
πορεύομαι
240, 242, 257, 260,
273, 281, 282
ποτέ
109, 167, 214, 237,
240, 246, 263, 267
πότος
282
πραΰς
213
πραΰτης
234
πρεσβύτερος
321, 322, 323, 330,
331, 332, 333
προγινώσκω
129, 131, 132, 242
πρόγνωσις
86
προμαρτύρομαι
109

προσάγω
240, 242, 248
προσέρχομαι
114, 149, 153
προσευχή
294
προσεύχομαι
294
πρόσκομμα
162
προσκόπτω
162
πρόσωπον
225, 227
προφήτης
111
πτόησις
208, 216
πύρωσις
305, 306

•

ῥαντισμός
20, 87
ῥῆμα
140–42, 145, 147
ῥύπος
268, 269, 272
ῥώννυμι
348

•

σαρκικός
175, 176
σάρξ
18, 45, 141, 175,
176, 239, 240, 241,
242, 249, 250, 251,
252, 268, 269, 276–
79, 281, 287, 288
Σάρρα
215
σθενόω
336, 346
σθένω
336, 346
Σιλουανός
7–8, 349
σκεῦος
217
σκολιός
195
σπορά
20, 80–82, 83, 94,
139, 140, 174, 175
στερεός
335, 342

411

415

417

In the design of the visual aspects of *Hermeneia*, consideration has been given to relating the form to the content by symbolic means.

The letters of the logotype *Hermeneia* are a fusion of forms alluding simultaneously to Hebrew (dotted vowel markings) and Greek (geometric round shapes) letter forms. In their modern treatment they remind us of the electronic age as well, the vantage point from which this investigation of the past begins.

The Lion of Judah used as visual identification for the series is based on the Seal of Shema. The version for *Hermeneia* is again a fusion of Hebrew calligraphic forms, especially the legs of the lion, and Greek elements characterized by the geometric. In the sequence of arcs, which can be understood as scroll-like images, the first is the lion's mouth. It is reasserted and accelerated in the whorl and returns in the aggressively arched tail: tradition is passed from one age to the next, rediscovered and re-formed.

"Who is worthy to open the scroll and break its seals. . . ."
Then one of the elders said to me
"weep not; lo, the Lion of the tribe of David,
the Root of David, has conquered,
so that he can open the scroll and
its seven seals."
Rev. 5:2, 5

To celebrate the signal achievement in biblical scholarship which *Hermeneia* represents, the entire series will by its color constitute a signal on the theologian's bookshelf: the Old Testament will be bound in yellow and the New Testament in red, traceable to a commonly used color coding for synagogue and church in medieval painting; in pure color terms, varying degrees of intensity of the warm segment of the color spectrum. The colors interpenetrate when the binding color for the Old Testament is used to imprint volumes from the New and vice versa.

Wherever possible, a photograph of the oldest extant manuscript, or a historically significant document pertaining to the biblical sources, will be displayed on the end papers of each volume to give a feel for the tangible reality and beauty of the source material.

The title-page motifs are expressive derivations from the *Hermeneia* logotype, repeated seven times to form a matrix and debossed on the cover of each volume. These sifted-out elements will be seen to be in their exact positions within the parent matrix. These motifs and their expressional character are noted on the following page.

Half-titles to introduce the volume in question are further derivations from the main title and may include other expressive or pictorial elements. In *First Peter* the swath of dots forms a dominant stream against which two dots are in dynamic tension. "Appropriate conduct" is a weighing and balancing of two directions.

Horizontal markings at gradated levels on the spine will assist in grouping the volumes according to these conventional categories.

The type has been set with unjustified right margins so as to preserve the internal consistency of word spacing. This is a major factor in both legibility and aesthetic quality; the resultant uneven line endings are only slight impairments to legibility by comparison. In this respect the type resembles the handwritten manuscripts where the quality of the calligraphic writing is dependent on establishing and holding to integral spacing patterns.

All of the type faces in common use today have been designed between A.D. 1500 and the present. For the biblical text a face was chosen which does not arbitrarily date the text, but rather one which is uncompromisingly modern and unembellished so that its feel is of the universal. The type style is Univers 65 by Adrian Frutiger.

The expository texts and footnotes are set in Baskerville, chosen for its compatibility with the many brief Greek and Hebrew insertions. The double-column format and the shorter line length facilitate reading and the wide margins to the left of footnotes provide for the scholar's own notations.

Kenneth Hiebert

Category of biblical writing,
key symbolic characteristic,
and volumes so identified.

1
Law
(boundaries described)
   Genesis
   Exodus
   Leviticus
   Numbers
   Deuteronomy

2
History
(trek through time and space)
   Joshua
   Judges
   Ruth
   1 Samuel
   2 Samuel
   1 Kings
   2 Kings
   1 Chronicles
   2 Chronicles
   Ezra
   Nehemiah
   Esther

3
Poetry
(lyric emotional expression)
   Job
   Psalms
   Proverbs
   Ecclesiastes
   Song of Songs

4
Prophets
(inspired seers)
   Isaiah
   Jeremiah
   Lamentations
   Ezekiel
   Daniel
   Hosea
   Joel
   Amos
   Obadiah
   Jonah
   Micah
   Nahum
   Habakkuk
   Zephaniah
   Haggai
   Zechariah
   Malachi

5
New Testament Narrative
(focus on One)
   Matthew
   Mark
   Luke
   John
   Acts

6
Epistles
(directed instruction)
   Romans
   1 Corinthians
   2 Corinthians
   Galatians
   Ephesians
   Philippians
   Colossians
   1 Thessalonians
   2 Thessalonians
   1 Timothy
   2 Timothy
   Titus
   Philemon
   Hebrews
   James
   1 Peter
   2 Peter
   1 John
   2 John
   3 John
   Jude

7
Apocalypse
(vision of the future)
   Revelation

8
Extracanonical Writings
(peripheral records)

ΔΙΑΤΗCΤΩΝΓΥΝΕΚΩΝΑΝΑCΤΡΟΦΚ

ΑΝΕΠΟΓΟΥΚΕΡΔΗΘΗCΟΝΤΑΙ ΕΠΟΠΤΕΥCΑ

ΝΤΕCΤΗΝΕΝΦΟΒΩ ΑΓΝΗΝΑΝΑCΤΡΟΦ

ΥΜΩΝ ΩΝΕCΤΩΟΥΚΟ ΕΞΩΘΕΝ

ΕΜΠΛΟΚΗCΚΑΙΠΕΡΙΘΕCΕΩCΧΡΥCΙ

ΩΝΗΕΝΔΥCΕΩCΙΜΑΤΙΩΝΚΟCΜΟC

ΑΛΛΟΚΡΥΠΤΟCΤΗCΚΑΡΔΙΑCΑΝΘΡΩΠΟC

ΕΝΤΩΑΦΘΑΡΤΩΤΟΥΠΡΔΕΩCΚΑΙΗCΥ

ΧΙΟΥ ΠΝC Ο ΕCΤΙΝ ΕΝΩΠΙΟΝΤΟΥ

ΘΥ ΠΟΛΥΤΕΛΕC ΟΥΤΩCΓΑΡΠΟΤΕ

ΚΑΙΑΙΑΓΙΑΙΓΥΝΕΚΕC ΔΙΕΠΕΙΧΟΝ

ΟΝΕΙCΘΗ ΕΧΟCΝΟΥΠΕΘΝΤΑC

ΥΠΟΤΑCCΟΜΕΝΕΤΟΙCΙΔΙΟΙCΑΝΔΡΑCΙΝ

ΩC CΑΡΡΑ ΤΑΙCΑΔΡΑCΑΝ ΥΠΕΤΕΙΚΟΝ

CΕΝ ΚΝ ΑΥΤΟΝΚΑΛΟΥCΑ ΗC ΕΓΕΝΗ

ΘΗΜΕΝΤΕ ΤΕΚΝΑ ΑΓΑΘΟΠΟΙΟΥCΑI